LONGMAN

Study Dictionary

of American English

PEARSON
Longman

NEW

Pearson Education Limited
Edinburgh Gate
Harlow
Essex
CM20 2JE, England, UK
and Associated Companies throughout the world

www.longman.com/dictionaries

First edition published 2006
Fourth impression 2008

ISBN 1405 831650 (Paperback edition)
ISBN 13: 978-1-4058-3165-9
ISBN 1405 831669 (Cased edition)
ISBN 13: 978-1-4058-3166-6

Set in Helvetica by Letterpart, UK

Printed and bound in the United States of America

Acknowledgements

Director
Della Summers

Projects Director
Michael Mayor

Senior Publisher
Laurence Delacroix

Managing Editor
Stephen Bullon

Editorial Manager
Cait Hawkins

Editors
Karen Cleveland-Marwick
Chris Fox
Stephen Handorf
Karen Stern

Lexicographers
Evadne Adrian-Vallance
Lucy Hollingworth
Elizabeth Manning
Michael Murphy
Martin Stark
Laura Wedgeworth

Project Manager
Alan Savill

Production Manager
Clive McKeough
David Gilmour

Corpus Development
Steve Crowdy

Computational Linguist
Allan Ørsnes

Production Editor
Alexandra Jaton
Jane Townsend

Project and Database Administrator
Denise McKeough

Technical Support Manager
Trevor Satchell

Pronunciation Editor
Dinah Jackson

Proofreaders
Philip Hillyer
Jane Horwood
Wendy Lee
Sue Lightfoot
Adèle Linderholm
Ruth Noble
Daphne Trotter
Carol Osborne

Workbook Section
Linda Butler

Design Project Manager
Linda Ward

Picture Researcher
Karen Jones
Sandra Hilsdon

Design
Mick Harris

Marketing
Jillian Elston

Keyboarder
Pauline Savill
Tracey Garrick

Administrative Assistance
Janine Trainor

Artwork
Chris Pavely (Pavely Arts),
Jo Blake (Beehive Illustration),
Kevin Jones Associates,
Ray and Corinne Burrows (Beehive Illustration),
Mark Turner (Beehive Illustration),
Peter Wilks (Simon Girling Associates)

The publishers would like to express their gratitude to their special adviser **Dr Kate Kinsella**, Teacher Trainer and School Consultant, San Francisco State University, Department of Secondary Education, for her keen interest, highly informed and focused guidance, and continued support throughout the development of this new dictionary.

The publishers would also like to thank all the dedicated teachers who have attended focus groups and given their informed feedback on sample text, in particular:

J. J. Lee Gilbert, Cuba Munsey, Karen Ball, Veronica Fern-McElarney, Margaret K. Lee, Dolores T. Andrews, Adriana Bo, Claire Trepanier, Nancy Rodriguez, Pilar Meija, Wayne Miller, Lorie Johnson, Trudie Heney, Susanna Cawley, Ms Barlow, Kelly Taggart, Sue Bolender, Jane Ardell, Cathy Personius, Steven Kirk, Marlene Churgel, David Roberts, Patricia Armendariz, Ann Ly, Kristien Evans, Donna Minick, Janet Ennis, Sarah Windes, Christina Park, Joyce Gordon, Doris Noriega, Lauri Buehler, Lisa Barnes, Shelly De Simone, Catherine Bunch, Devra Miller, Kim Shults, Ann Pappas, Ann Sokolovskaya, Marty Roberts, Adele Alvarez, Ross Russell, Jim Ybarra, Vanessa Henson, Ryan Coy, Courtney Gonzalez, Xavier Haase, Toni Costantino, Dorothea Jordan, Liane Cismowski, Laura Hill, Corinne Christiansen, Kevin Feldman, Cyndi Stauffer, John F. Fox, Lisa Visendi.

TABLE OF CONTENTS

Introduction	v
Guide to the Dictionary	vi–vii
The Dictionary A–Z	**1–782**
Picture Dictionary	A1
Workbook	A33
Irregular Verbs	783
School Content Vocabulary	786
Weights and Measures	801
Geographical Names	802
Workbook Answer Key	805
Pronunciation Table	inside back cover

Photography credits

We are grateful to the following for permission to reproduce photographs:
Dartboard – Corbis (Royalty Free); Well – Corbis (Chris Lisle); Rush hour – Corbis (Bob Krist); Aquarium – Alamy (Bill Bachman); Exhaust – Alamy (INSADCO Photography); Exhibition – Alamy (Janine Wiedel Photography); Fingerprint – Alamy – PHOTOTAKE Inc; Bruise – John Birdsall; Straighten – Royalty Free (Business Hands); Chimpanze – NHPA (Michael Leach). All other pictures Hemera Techologies Inc "Copyright ©2006 (Pearson Education) and its licensors. All rights reserved"

Alamy Images: (A26–27) (truck) (Peter Horree), (train/railway line) (Thomas J. Preston), (subway station) (PCL), (cab/taxi) (Joe Fox), (bus/bus stop) (David R Frazier/Photolibrary), (crosswalk) (Culliganphoto), (cycle) (TNT Magazine), (motor home) (Allan Ivy), (ship) (Andre Jenny), (motorcycle) (Guillen photo), (plane/runway) (EK Aviation), (A24–25) (rollerblading) (Swerve); Corbis: (A26–27) (police car) (Alan Schein Photography), (rowboat) (Ariel Skelley); Getty Images: (A26–27) (pickup truck) (Photographers Choice), (A24–25) (running) (Iconica)

All other images:
Dorling Kindersley
Hemera Photo Objects (Royalty Free)
iStockphoto.com (Royalty Free)
PhotoDisc (Musical Instruments/Royalty Free)
PhotoDisc (Sports and Recreation/Royalty)
www.comstock.com (Food Icons/Royalty Free)

Every effort has been made to trace the copyright holders and we apologise in advance for any unintentional omissions. We would be pleased to insert the appropriate acknowledgement in any subsequent edition of this publication.

Picture Research by Sandra Hilsdon

INTRODUCTION

by **Kate Kinsella**,
Ed.D., San Francisco State University,
Department of Secondary Education

A dictionary can be an invaluable resource for young language learners as they tackle the vocabulary demands of challenging reading curricula and academic writing tasks.

Unfortunately, the curricular mainstay of U.S. upper-elementary and secondary classrooms is a collegiate desk dictionary, and as the root word "college" suggests, this lexical tool was designed for a mature adult reader with a highly literate command of English. As a consequence, definitions are overly precise and concise at the expense of clarity, and often include another form of the target word or even more sophisticated words.

Standard desk dictionaries also fail to provide familiar synonyms within a school-aged youth's "personal thesaurus" and illustrative examples drawn from commonplace experiential realms. Students in grades 4–9 are generally too mature for the junior picture dictionary that served them well in the primary grades but far too immature for the comprehensive dictionary that they will need in advanced high school and collegiate coursework. When students find themselves more confused and frustrated than illuminated by a vocabulary resource, they are bound to rely upon unproductive coping strategies like rote copying or abandoning any independent study efforts in hopes of an eventual teacher explanation. Repeated unsuccessful forays into a dictionary have a long-lasting negative impact on struggling learners who internalize their disappointing endeavors as a personal failure rather than a glaring curricular mismatch.

I teach and coach instruction throughout the U.S. in highly diverse 4–12 classrooms, including striving readers and English learners who are woefully under-prepared for the language demands of their grade level curricula. The teachers need a potent lesson-planning tool that will aid them in effectively and efficiently preparing to teach the most critical terms to a linguistically vulnerable class. Likewise, the learners need a non-intimidating resource that won't leave them utterly bewildered and paralyzed with confusion when they are assigned independent vocabulary work.

I am elated to finally be able to wholeheartedly recommend an appropriate dictionary for the mixed-ability intermediate or secondary classroom. The **Longman Study Dictionary** meets all of my criteria for a "considerate" vocabulary development resource for younger learners. The visual impact of the page spread is appealing, and the judicious use of color and graphics all make page navigation more manageable.

Furthermore, the meticulously crafted definitions are conscientious explanations written using familiar language within a school-aged youth's daily register rather than the arguably precise yet elusive synonyms and syntax characteristic of the academic lexicon. These accessible explanations are complemented by evocative, familiar contexts that help a less experienced young learner build a powerful mental anchor, increasing the odds of word comprehension and successful application.

Equally valuably, the **Longman Study Dictionary** highlights high-incidence academic vocabulary in striking Word Family Boxes, drawing students' attention to critical words for academic endeavors. Knowledge of the most commonly used academic words across grade levels and subject areas can significantly boost a student's comprehension level of school-based reading material and performance on high stakes writing assignments. These academic "tool kit" words are given lexical status in this learners' dictionary, which should facilitate lesson planning for teachers and independent word study for developing English language users.

A considerate, developmentally appropriate dictionary should be an educational civil right at every grade level. I sincerely hope the **Longman Study Dictionary** makes its way into as many school libraries, classrooms and backpacks as possible to support young aspiring learners in making the academic language and literacy strides that underlie educational success.

GUIDE TO THE DICTIONARY

Different meanings are shown clearly, with the most common meaning first.

Definitions explaining the meaning of a word are written in clear simple language, using the 2000-word Longman Defining Vocabulary.

Words with the same or opposite meaning are shown after the definition.

Pictures help you to understand the meaning of a word.

Irregular forms of verbs are shown at the beginning of an entry.

Simple examples show you how to use a word and help to explain its meaning.

Phrasal Verbs are shown in alphabetical order at the end of an entry.

The dictionary contains words that are often used in science lessons and course books.

A label before a definition shows that a word is formal or informal.

Derived words are shown at the end of an entry. These words can be easily understood from the meaning of the main word.

con·clude /kən'klud/ Ac *verb, formal*
1 to decide that something is true from the information you have: *He concluded that Tina had not taken the money.*
2 to end a meeting, speech, event, etc.: *She concluded the meeting by thanking everyone.* | *The fair concluded with* (=ended with) *a fireworks display.* SYNONYM **finish, end**; ANTONYM **begin, start**

diameter

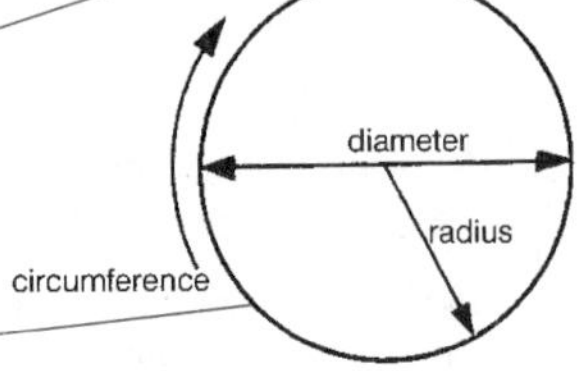

di·am·e·ter /daɪ'æmətɚ/ *noun*
a line or measurement from one side of a circle to the other, through the center: *The table is five feet in diameter* (=it measures five feet across).

eat /it/ *verb* **ate** /eɪt/ **eaten** /'itn/
1 to put food in your mouth and swallow it: *She was eating an apple.* | *I'm still eating my dinner.* | *Do you want something to eat* (=some food to eat)?
2 to have a meal: *We usually eat at about 6.*

PHRASAL VERBS

eat out
to eat in a restaurant: *They usually eat out once a week.*

eat something up
1 to finish eating all of something: *Eat up your breakfast! We're late!*
2 to use too much of something: *This class is eating up all of my time. I don't have time to study anything else.*
3 eat it up *informal* = to enjoy something very much: *If you give the kids a computer game, they'll just eat it up.*

en·zyme /'enzaɪm/ *noun*
a chemical that is produced in plants and animals and that causes a chemical process to start: *Enzymes in the stomach change food so that it can be digested.*

e·rupt /ɪ'rʌpt/ *verb*
1 *formal* if violence erupts, it suddenly happens: *Fighting could erupt again at any time.*
2 if a VOLCANO erupts, it sends out smoke, fire, and rock into the sky: *More than 800 people died when the volcano erupted.*
—**eruption** /ɪ'rʌpʃən/ *noun* an occasion when a VOLCANO erupts

globe /gloʊb/ Ac *noun*
1 **the globe** = the world: *Our company has offices all over the globe.*
2 a round object that has a map of the Earth on it: *The teacher used a globe to show how the ships sailed from England to America.*

WORD FAMILY look at the words:
→ globe *noun*
→ global *adjective*
→ globally *adverb*

The dictionary contains words that are often used in academic writing.

Common phrases have their own definition, and the meaning of the whole phrase is explained.

Word Family boxes have lists of words that are from the same family.

hap·py /ˈhæpi/ *adjective* **happier**, **happiest**
1 feeling pleased, for example because your life is good, or something good has happened: *Pete is very happy at his new school.* | *I was really happy to hear your good news!* ANTONYM **sad**

THESAURUS:
cheerful someone who is cheerful seems happy and smiles a lot: *Tom's a very cheerful little boy.*
pleased happy because someone has done something good, or something good has happened: *Her parents were pleased that she had done so well in college.*
glad happy because something good has happened. You use glad especially when you are telling other people that you are happy about something: *I'm really glad you can come to the party.*
delighted *formal* very happy because something good has happened: *She will be delighted when she hears the news.*

Comparative and superlative forms of adjectives are shown at the beginning of an entry.

Part of speech

Thesaurus boxes explain words with similar meanings to the word you are looking up, helping to increase your vocabulary.

in·for·ma·tion /ˌɪnfɚˈmeɪʃən/ *noun*
facts that you get from someone or give someone: *Can you give me some information about where to buy this book?* | *Before you start on the project, I have one more important piece of information for you.*

GRAMMAR:
Do not say "an information" or "informations." Say, for example, some/any information, a lot of information, or a piece of information: *Where can I find some information about your company?* | *All of this information is in the book.* | *I need a couple more pieces of information before I can finish my report.*

Pronunciation

Grammar and Usage Notes give you help to choose the correct word and not make mistakes.

judg·ment *also* **judgement** /ˈdʒʌdʒmənt/ *noun*

Different spellings are shown at the beginning of an entry.

jump¹ /dʒʌmp/ *verb*
jump² *noun*

Words that are spelt the same but have different parts of speech have separate entries.

Aa

a /ə; *strong* eɪ/ *also* **an** *indefinite article*
1 used when you are mentioning someone or something new, or describing one person, thing, etc.: *He wants to buy a car.* | *Her mother's a teacher.*
2 used with "hundred," "thousand," etc. to mean "one": *a thousand dollars* (=$1,000)
3 for each, or in each: *The candy cost 75 cents a bag, so two bags cost $1.50.* | *She calls me twice a week – on Tuesday and on Thursday.* SYNONYM **per**

> **GRAMMAR: a**
>
> **a, an**
>
> Use **a** if the word that is after it starts with a consonant sound: *a car* | *a white egg* | *a house* | *I bought a CD today.*
>
> Use **an** if the word that is after it starts with a vowel sound (the sounds shown by the letters a, e, i, o, or u): *an apple* | *an orange sweater* | *I waited an hour.*

A /eɪ/ *noun*
1 the best GRADE that you can get on a test or in a class: *I did a really good job on my book report, and I got an A.*
2 the sixth note in the musical SCALE of C, or the musical KEY based on this note

a•ban•don /əˈbændən/ Ac *verb, formal*
1 to leave a person, place, or vehicle and not go back: *He abandoned his family and moved to another state.*
2 to stop doing something because of problems: *They abandoned the search when it became too dark to see.*
—**abandonment** *noun* the action of abandoning someone or something

ab•bre•vi•a•tion /əˌbriviˈeɪʃən/ *noun*
the short form of a word: *"Mr." is the abbreviation for "Mister."*

ABC's /ˌeɪbiˈsiz/ *noun*
the letters of the English alphabet: *She's learning her ABC's and can recognize most of the letters.*

ab•do•men /ˈæbdəmən/ *noun, formal*
the front part of your body between your chest and your legs
—**abdominal** /æbˈdɑmənəl/ *adjective, formal* relating to your abdomen

ab•duct /əbˈdʌkt/ *verb, formal*
to take someone away by force in order to keep him or her as your prisoner: *Terrorists abducted the reporters and kept them as prisoners.* SYNONYM **kidnap**
—**abduction** /əbˈdʌkʃən/ *noun* when someone is abducted: *the abduction of a child*

a•bil•i•ty /əˈbɪləti/ *noun* plural **abilities**
if you have the ability to do something, you can do it: *Her ability to speak Spanish was very useful when she was in Mexico.* | *He has a lot of athletic ability and does well in sports.*

> **THESAURUS: ability**
>
> **skill** something that you do very well because you have learned and practiced it: *This class will help you improve your writing skills.*
>
> **talent** a natural ability to do something well: *He plays the trumpet really well – he has a lot of talent.*
>
> **knack** *informal* a natural ability to do something well: *Kate seems to have a knack for learning languages.*

a•ble /ˈeɪbəl/ *adjective*
able to do something = if you are able to do something, you can do it: *I'd like to be able to play a musical instrument.*

> **WORD FAMILY look at the words:**
>
> → **able** *adjective*
> → **unable** *adjective*
> → **ability** *noun*

ab•nor•mal /æbˈnɔrməl/ Ac *adjective, formal*
different from usual in a way that is strange or dangerous: *If the boy's abnormal behavior continues, you should take him to a doctor.* ANTONYM **normal**
—**abnormally** *adverb, formal*: *The strange weather conditions and extra traffic are causing abnormally high pollution levels.*
—**abnormality** /ˌæbnɔrˈmæləti/ *noun, formal* something that is abnormal

A

a•board /ə'bɔrd/ *adverb, preposition*
on or onto a ship, airplane, or train: *Everyone aboard the plane survived.*

a•bol•ish /ə'bɑlɪʃ/ *verb, formal*
to officially end a law, system, etc.: *The country recently abolished the death penalty.*
—**abolition** /ˌæbə'lɪʃən/ *noun* the act of abolishing something: *the abolition of slavery*

a•bor•tion /ə'bɔrʃən/ *noun*
the act of ending a PREGNANCY: *She decided not to have an abortion and keep the baby.*

a•bout /ə'baʊt/ *adverb, preposition*
1 used to say what the subject of a book, conversation, thought, etc. is: *She was reading a book about horses.* | *He was worried about the family's money problems.*
2 a little more or less than a particular number or amount: *The sun sets at about six o'clock.* | *There were about 50 students at the meeting.* SYNONYM **approximately**

THESAURUS: about

approximately a little more or a little less than a number, amount, distance, or time: *A kilo is approximately two pounds.*
around used when guessing a number, amount, time, etc., without being exact: *"What time will you get home?" "Around nine, I think."*
roughly a little more or a little less than a number, used when you are saying a number you know is not exact: *Roughly 7,000 cars cross the border every day.*
or so *informal* used when you cannot be exact about a number, amount, or period of time: *I saw him a week or so ago.*

3 be about to do something = if you are about to do something, you will do it very soon: *They have their coats on. I think they're about to leave.*
4 *informal* almost: *He could fix just about anything, so we never had to throw things away.*
5 what about/how about a) used to make a suggestion: *How about looking under the bed for the ball?* **b)** used to ask a question relating to another person or thing involved in a situation: *What about the food? Was it good?*
6 used to say that someone or something has a particular quality or feature: *There's something weird about that guy – he never looks at me when he's talking to me.*

a•bove /ə'bʌv/ *adverb, preposition*
1 in or to a higher position than something else: *Raise your arm above your head.* | *He heard a noise in the room above.* ANTONYM **below**
2 more than a number, amount, or level: *Temperatures rose above freezing today to 35 degrees.* | *The program is for kids age 8 and above.* ANTONYM **below**
3 above all *formal* = most importantly, or more than anything else: *Above all, children want to feel safe and loved.*
4 *formal* before, in the same piece of writing: *The drugs mentioned in the paragraph above are not being sold yet.* ANTONYM **below**

a•bridged /ə'brɪdʒd/ *adjective, formal*
an abridged book, play, etc. has been made shorter: *I read an abridged version of the book, so it didn't take as long.*

a•broad /ə'brɔd/ *adverb*
in or to a foreign country: *I want to go abroad after college – maybe to Russia.*

a•brupt /ə'brʌpt/ *adjective*
1 sudden and unexpected: *There was an abrupt knock at the door.*
2 using few words in a conversation so that you appear unfriendly or impolite: *She was very abrupt on the phone, and I thought she must be angry.*
—**abruptly** *adverb*: *The train stopped abruptly and I almost fell over.*

ab•sence /'æbsəns/ *noun, formal*
a time when you are not in a place where you are expected to be: *My assistant will deal with any problems in my absence* (=while I am away).

ab•sent /'æbsənt/ *adjective, formal*
not at work, school, a meeting, etc. when other people expect you to be there: *Ten children were absent from class today because of colds.* ANTONYM **present**
—**absentee** /ˌæbsən'ti/ *noun* someone who is absent: *Ten people were at the meeting, but there were three absentees.*

ab•so•lute /'æbsəlut/ *adjective*
complete or total: *I have absolute confidence in you – I'm sure you'll do well in this job.*

ab·so·lute·ly /ˌæbsəˈlutli/ *adverb*
1 completely or totally: *Are you absolutely sure? If you're not certain, we'll try something else.*
2 used to emphasize what you are saying: *There's absolutely nothing you can do to stop me – I'm going to do it no matter what you do.*
3 used to say yes in a strong way when you completely agree: *"Would you like to come along?" "Absolutely."*

ab·sorb /əbˈsɔrb/ *verb, formal*
1 if something absorbs liquid, gas, or energy, it takes it in and holds it: *The towel absorbed most of the water.*
2 to learn and completely understand new information: *There was too much information in the article – I couldn't absorb it all.*
3 be absorbed in something = to be so interested in something you are doing or watching that you do not pay attention to other things: *I pretended to be absorbed in my work.*
—**absorbent** *adjective* able to absorb liquid: *Which brand of diaper is most absorbent?*

ab·sorb·ing /əbˈsɔrbɪŋ/ *adjective, formal*
an absorbing book, movie, etc. is so interesting that you continue reading or watching it with great attention

ab·stract /æbˈstrækt/ Ac *adjective*
1 relating to ideas rather than specific real things or events: *Are animals capable of abstract thought? For example, do they feel love?*
2 abstract art consists of shapes and patterns that do not look like real things or people

ab·surd /əbˈsɚd/ *adjective*
completely silly: *That's an absurd idea! We could never do that.*
—**absurdly** *adverb*

a·bun·dance /əˈbʌndəns/ *noun, formal*
a lot of something: *There is an abundance of information about this on the Internet. It would take months to read it all.*

a·bun·dant /əˈbʌndənt/ *adjective, formal*
more than enough: *We have an abundant supply of fuel, so we don't need to worry about not having enough.* SYNONYM **plentiful**

a·buse¹ /əˈbyus/ *noun*
1 cruel or violent treatment of someone: *He was accused of child abuse when he broke his daughter's arm.*
2 the use of something in a way it should not be used: *He has a history of drug abuse* (=he has taken illegal drugs in the past).
3 *formal* rude things that are said to someone: *People were shouting abuse at the soldiers.*

a·buse² /əˈbyuz/ *verb*
1 to do cruel or violent things to someone: *He admitted that he abused his wife by hitting her.*
2 to use something in a way it should not be used: *Did the senator abuse his power by giving jobs to his friends?*
—**abusive** /əˈbyusɪv/ *adjective* using very unkind words or violence: *Her abusive husband had seriously hurt her several times.*

AC *noun*
1 alternating current the type of electric current used in buildings for electrical equipment
2 *informal* another word for AIR CONDITIONING

ac·a·dem·ic /ˌækəˈdemɪk/ Ac *adjective*
relating to education, especially in a college or university: *The school has very high academic standards – you have to be very smart to go there.*

a·cad·e·my /əˈkædəmi/ Ac *noun* plural **academies**
1 a school or college where students are taught a particular subject or skill: *a military academy*
2 an organization whose aim is to encourage art, science, literature, etc.: *the National Academy of Sciences*

ac·cel·er·ate /əkˈseləˌreɪt/ *verb*
if a vehicle or its driver accelerates, it moves faster: *The car accelerated down the hill.*

ac·cent /ˈæksent/ *noun*
1 a way of pronouncing words that shows that you come from a particular place: *He had a strong Russian accent.*
2 a mark above a letter that shows how to pronounce that letter: *There is an accent over the second "e" in "René."*
➔ See Thesaurus box at **language**

A

ac•cept /əkˈsept/ *verb*
1 to take something that someone offers you: *Are you going to accept their offer?* | *He wouldn't accept any money from us.* ANTONYM **refuse**
2 accept an invitation = to say yes when you have been invited somewhere: *She asked me to come for a visit, and I accepted her invitation gladly.*
3 to admit or agree that something is true or cannot be changed: *She refused to accept that he was dead.*
4 to let someone join a university, organization, etc.: *I've been accepted to Harvard.* ANTONYM **reject**

ac•cept•a•ble /əkˈseptəbəl/ *adjective*
satisfactory: *They tried to make a deal that would be acceptable to both groups so that everyone would be happy.*
➔ See Thesaurus box at **satisfactory**

ac•cept•ance /əkˈseptəns/ *noun*
1 the act of taking something that is offered to you: *His acceptance of the job offer meant the family had to move.*
2 the act of agreeing that something is true or cannot be changed: *There is little acceptance of the theory among scientists. Only a few scientists believe it is true.*

ac•cept•ed /əkˈseptɪd/ *adjective*
accepted ideas are considered true or right by most people: *It is generally accepted that being very fat is dangerous to your health.*

ac•cess[1] /ˈækses/ Ac *noun*
1 the ability to have or use something: *The library allows anyone to have access to the Internet.*
2 a way of getting into a place: *Stores must improve access for customers in wheelchairs.*

access[2] *verb*
to look at information that is available, especially on a computer: *I couldn't access the file.*

ac•ci•dent /ˈæksədənt/ *noun*
1 a situation in which someone is hurt or something is damaged without anyone intending for it to happen: *Her parents were killed in a car accident.* | *He had an accident and broke his leg.*
2 by accident = if something happens by accident, it is not intended or planned: *I found the information by accident – I wasn't even looking for it.* SYNONYM **accidentally**; ANTONYM **on purpose**
3 be an accident = if something bad that happens is an accident, it is not intended or planned: *The explosion was an accident – no one meant for it to happen.*

ac•ci•den•tal /ˌæksəˈdentəl/ *adjective*
happening without being intended or planned: *It was an accidental shooting, so he will not have to go to jail.* ANTONYM **deliberate**

ac•ci•den•tal•ly /ˌæksəˈdentəli/ *adverb*
if you do something accidentally, you do it without intending to: *I accidentally left my keys in the car.* ANTONYM **deliberately**

ac•com•mo•date /əˈkɑməˌdeɪt/ Ac *verb, formal*
to have enough space for a particular number of people or things: *The room can accommodate 300 people.*

ac•com•mo•da•tions /əˌkɑməˈdeɪʃənz/ *plural noun*
a place to live or stay: *The cost of the vacation includes hotel accommodations.*

ac•com•pa•ny /əˈkʌmpəni/ Ac *verb*
accompanied
1 *formal* to go somewhere with someone: *He accompanied her to the hospital so she would not feel alone.*
2 to play music while someone is playing or singing the main tune: *My sister sang, and I accompanied her on the piano.*

ac•com•plish /əˈkɑmplɪʃ/ *verb*
to succeed in doing something: *We've accomplished our goal of raising $45,000.*
—**accomplishment** *noun* something that you have succeeded in doing: *His biggest accomplishment was winning the New York Marathon.*

ac•cord /əˈkɔrd/ *noun*
of your own accord *formal* = if you do something of your own accord, you do it without being asked or forced to do it: *I didn't tell him to go – he left of his own accord.*

ac•cord•ing•ly /əˈkɔrdɪŋli/ *adverb, formal*
1 in a way that is appropriate because of the situation or because of what has been done or said: *We listened to students' ideas and made changes accordingly.*

A

2 as a result of something: *The cost of health care continues to rise. Accordingly, the senator is introducing a bill that would help poor families pay for health care.* SYNONYM **therefore**

ac'cording to *preposition*
1 used to say where your information comes from: *According to our records, you owe us $520.* | *It's the best movie Spielberg has ever made, according to Melissa* (=Melissa said this).
2 in a way that obeys a rule or follows a plan: *You will be paid according to the amount of work you do.* | *Everything went according to plan* (=happened in the way that had been planned)*, and there were no real problems.*

ac•cor•di•on /ə'kɔrdiən/ *noun*
a musical instrument that you play by moving the sides apart and together and pressing buttons
➔ See picture on page A21

ac•count[1] /ə'kaʊnt/ *noun*
1 *also* **bank account** an arrangement with a bank to keep your money for you: *I don't have much money in my account* (=there is not much of my money in the bank). | *a checking account* (=one that you can use to write checks from) | *a savings account* (=one in which you save money so that the amount increases)
2 *formal* a written or spoken description of an event or situation: *Can you give us an account of what happened?*
3 take something into account = to consider a particular fact when judging or deciding something: *We take the patient's age into account when we decide which medicine is best for him or her.*
4 on account of something = because of something: *He couldn't lift anything heavy on account of his bad back.*
5 accounts = a record of the money that a company has received and spent

account[2] *verb*
PHRASAL VERB
account for something
1 to explain something that has happened: *How do you account for her success? Was it talent, hard work, or something else?*
2 to be a particular part of an amount: *In California, Asian Americans account for over 12 percent of the population.*

ac•count•a•ble /ə'kaʊntəbəl/ *adjective*
responsible for what you do or make happen, and having a duty to explain it: *Teachers should be held accountable for their decisions* (=they should have to explain their decisions and be punished if their decisions are bad).

ac•count•ant /ə'kaʊntənt/ *noun*
someone whose job is to keep records of how much money a business has received and spent

ac•count•ing /ə'kaʊntɪŋ/ *noun*
the job of being an accountant

ac•cu•mu•late /ə'kyumyəˌleɪt/ Ac *verb, formal*
1 to gradually get more and more of something: *During his life he accumulated a huge amount of money.*
2 if something accumulates, it gradually increases in amount: *Dust had accumulated in the corners of the room because he never cleaned anything.*
—**accumulation** /əˌkyumyə'leɪʃən/ *noun, formal* a large amount of something that has increased gradually

ac•cu•ra•cy /'ækyərəsi/ Ac *noun*
1 the quality of being correct or true: *Check the accuracy of your answers before you give the teacher your test.*
2 the ability to hit the thing that you are trying to hit: *The bombs can be aimed with amazing accuracy.*

ac•cu•rate /'ækyərɪt/ Ac *adjective*
1 correct in every detail: *I checked the figures with a calculator to see if they were accurate.* ANTONYM **inaccurate**
2 an accurate shot, throw, etc. succeeds in hitting the thing that you are trying to hit: *He made an accurate throw to first base.*
—**accurately** *adverb*

WORD FAMILY look at the words:
➔ **accurate** *adjective*
➔ **inaccurate** *adjective*
➔ **accurately** *adverb*
➔ **accuracy** *noun*

➔ See Thesaurus box at **right**[1]

A

ac•cu•sa•tion /ˌækyəˈzeɪʃən/ *noun*
an occasion when someone says that another person has done something wrong: *She made accusations of violence against him, and the police arrested him.*

ac•cuse /əˈkyuz/ *verb*
to say that someone has done something wrong: *Terry accused her of cheating.* | *He was accused of murder.*
WORD FAMILY → **accusation** *noun*

ac•cus•tomed /əˈkʌstəmd/ *adjective, formal*
be accustomed to (doing) something = if you are accustomed to something, it is not strange or unusual for you: *We were accustomed to working together after sharing an office for five years.* SYNONYM **be used to (doing) something**

ace /eɪs/ *noun*
a PLAYING CARD with one symbol on it. It has the highest or lowest value in a game: *the ace of hearts*

ache[1] /eɪk/ *verb*
if part of your body aches, it hurts for a long time: *My legs were aching after walking so far.*
→ See Thesaurus box at **hurt**[1]

ache[2] *noun*
a continuous pain: *She felt an ache in her chest where she had been hit.*

a•chieve /əˈtʃiv/ Ac *verb*
to succeed in doing or getting something you want: *She achieved her goal of becoming a lawyer.*
—**achievable** *adjective* able to be achieved: *an achievable goal*

WORD FAMILY look at the words:
- → **achieve** *verb*
- → **achievable** *adjective*
- → **achievement** *noun*

a•chieve•ment /əˈtʃivmənt/ Ac *noun*
something important or difficult that you do successfully: *One of his greatest achievements was to win a gold medal at the Olympic Games.*

ac•id /ˈæsɪd/ *noun*
a liquid chemical substance that can burn things: *The acid had burned a hole in the metal.*
—**acidic** /əˈsɪdɪk/ *adjective* relating to or containing acid: *acidic soil*
—**acidity** /əˈsɪdəti/ *noun* the fact of containing or being acid

ˌacid ˈrain *noun*
rain that contains acid and that damages plants, trees, and rivers

ac•knowl•edge /əkˈnɑlɪdʒ/ Ac *verb*
1 to accept or admit that something is true or correct: *Angie acknowledged (that) she had made a mistake and apologized.*
2 to show someone that you have seen or heard him or her: *She didn't even acknowledge me when I said "hi."*
3 to let someone know that you have received something from him or her: *She never acknowledged my letter, so I don't know if she got it.*
—**acknowledgement** *noun* the act of acknowledging someone or something

ac•ne /ˈækni/ *noun*
a skin problem that makes a lot of red spots appear on your face, and is common among young people: *She had terrible acne when she was a teenager and she tried to cover her face with her hair.*

a•corn /ˈeɪkɔrn/ *noun*
the nut of an OAK tree

acoustic

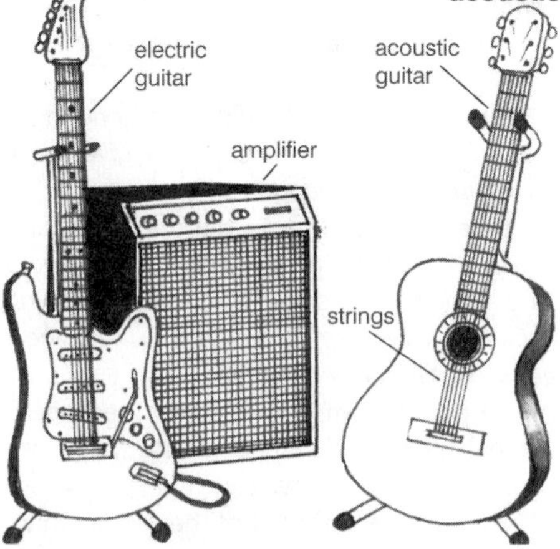

a•cous•tic /əˈkustɪk/ *adjective*
1 an acoustic musical instrument or performance is not electric or does not use electric instruments: *I have an acoustic guitar. I've never played an electric guitar.*
2 *formal* relating to sound and the way people hear things: *You need good acoustic skills to understand spoken language.*

A

ac•quaint•ance /ə'kweɪntəns/ *noun, formal*
someone you have met, but do not know well: *He's an acquaintance of mine from church, but we have never spent much time together.*

ac•quaint•ed /ə'kweɪntɪd/ *adjective, formal*
if you are acquainted with someone, you know him or her, but not very well: *Are you acquainted with Professor Green?* | *Why don't you two get acquainted* (=start to learn more about each other)?

ac•quire /ə'kwaɪɚ/ Ac *verb, formal*
to get or buy something: *The museum acquired the painting for $5.6 million.*
—**acquisition** /ˌækwə'zɪʃən/ *noun, formal* something that you have acquired: *The painting is a new acquisition.*
➔ See Thesaurus box at **buy**

a•cre /'eɪkɚ/ *noun*
a unit for measuring an area of land, equal to 4,840 square yards or about 4,047 square meters: *a 40-acre farm*

ac•ro•bat /'ækrəˌbæt/ *noun*
someone who entertains people by doing difficult physical actions such as walking on his or her hands or balancing on a high rope in a CIRCUS

a•cross /ə'krɔs/ *adverb, preposition*
1 from one side of something to the other: *A boy suddenly ran across the road.* | *They are building a bridge across the river.* | *At its widest point, the river is 2 miles across.*
2 on the opposite side of something: *Ben lives across the street from us.*

act¹ /ækt/ *verb*
1 to do something: *When someone has a heart attack, you need to act quickly.* | *We're acting on the advice of our lawyer* (=doing what he or she says).
2 to behave in a particular way: *Nick's been acting strange recently.* | *Pam's acting like a child.*
3 to perform in a play or movie: *She's acted in several Hollywood movies.*
4 to have an effect or use: *The honey acts as a kind of glue, holding the pieces of bread together.*

WORD FAMILY look at the words:
➔ act *noun*
➔ act *verb*
➔ action *noun*
➔ activity *noun*
➔ active *adjective*

act² *noun*
1 something that you do: *He carried the old lady's bags as an act of kindness.*
2 *also* **Act** a law that the government has made: *the Civil Rights Act*
3 *also* **Act** one of the main parts of a play: *In Act II, Ross and Diane get married.*
4 a short piece of entertainment that is part of a television or theater show: *The two men performed a short comedy act.*
5 behavior that is not sincere: *He never loved me. It was just an act* (=he was just pretending).

act•ing /'æktɪŋ/ *noun*
the activity of performing in plays or movies: *She's beautiful, but she's not very good at acting.*

ac•tion /'ækʃən/ *noun*
1 the process of doing something, especially in order to achieve something: *The government needs to take action* (=start doing something) *to stop the rise in crime.* | *The best course of action* (=way of dealing with the situation) *is to tell her the truth.*
2 something that you do: *Alan's quick actions saved Sarah's life after the car accident.*
3 the effect that a substance has on something: *The rocks are worn away by the action of the waves.*

ac•ti•vate /'æktəˌveɪt/ *verb, formal*
to make something start working: *This button activates the alarm.*

ac•tive /'æktɪv/ *adjective*
1 someone who is active can move and do things easily: *Although Bob is over 70, he's still very active and goes for a long walk every day.* ANTONYM **inactive**
2 in grammar, if a verb or sentence is active, the person or thing doing the action is the SUBJECT of the verb: *In the sentence "The boy kicked the ball," the verb "kick" is active.* ANTONYM **passive**

A

ac·tiv·i·ty /æk'tɪvəti/ *noun* plural **activities**
1 something that you do for enjoyment in a regular organized way: *She enjoys outdoor activities such as hiking and riding bikes.*
2 things that people do because they want to achieve a particular aim: *It's impossible for the government to stop all terrorist activities.*
3 a situation in which a lot of things are happening or a lot of things are being done: *Sally loved the noise and activity of the city.*

ac·tor /'æktɚ/ *noun*
someone who performs in plays or movies or in television shows: *He wanted to go to Hollywood and become a movie actor.*
➔ See Thesaurus box at **movie**

ac·tress /'æktrɪs/ *noun*
a woman who performs in plays or movies or in television shows
➔ See Thesaurus box at **movie**

ac·tu·al /'æktʃuəl/ *adjective*
used for emphasizing that something is real or exact: *Were those his actual words or are you changing it a little?* | *I know the White Sox won the game, but I don't remember the actual score.*

ac·tu·al·ly /'æktʃuəli/ *adverb*
1 used to emphasize the truth of a situation, rather than what people may think: *They were never actually married.* | *What actually happened?* SYNONYM **really**
2 used to add new information to what you have just said, to give your opinion, or to start saying something new: *I've known Barbara for a long time, since we were babies, actually.* | *Actually, I think I'll stay home tonight instead of going out.*

a·cute /ə'kyut/ *adjective, formal*
1 very serious or severe: *There is an acute shortage of food in some parts of the country and people are starving.* | *She had to take medication for her acute back pain.* SYNONYM **extreme**
2 an acute sense is able to notice small differences in things: *Dogs have an acute sense of smell that they can use to find people.*

a·cute·ly /ə'kyutli/ *adverb*
used to emphasize how strongly you feel about a serious situation: *We are acutely aware of the problem and are trying very hard to fix it.* SYNONYM **extremely**

ad /æd/ *noun, informal*
another word for an ADVERTISEMENT: *She put an ad in the newspaper to sell her bike.*

A.D.
used to show that a year came after the birth of Jesus Christ: *He became emperor of Rome in 161 A.D.*

a·dapt /ə'dæpt/ Ac *verb*
1 to change the way you do things because you are in a new situation: *The fox is good at adapting to changes in its surroundings.*
2 to change something so that you can use it in a different way: *He adapted the car to run on a battery.*
WORD FAMILY ➔ **adaptable** *adjective*
➔ See Thesaurus box at **change**[1]

a·dapt·a·ble /ə'dæptəbəl/ Ac *adjective*
someone who is adaptable is good at changing the way he or she does things in a new situation: *For this job you need to be adaptable and able to deal with unexpected situations.*

add /æd/ *verb*
1 to put something with another thing: *Add more garlic to the sauce.*
2 to put numbers together to get the total: *If you add 5 and 3, you get 8.* ANTONYM **subtract**
3 to say more about something: *He told me about the mistake, and added that it wasn't his fault.*
4 to increase the amount or cost of something: *Sales tax adds 5% to the bill* (=because of sales tax, the bill has increased by 5%).

PHRASAL VERB
add up
1 add something up = to put numbers together to get the total: *If you add up these numbers, you can calculate the total profit.*
2 to seem true or reasonable: *Her explanation of what happened doesn't add up.*

WORD FAMILY look at the words:
➔ **add** *verb*
➔ **addition** *noun*
➔ **additional** *adjective*

ad•dict /'ædɪkt/ *noun*
someone who cannot stop taking harmful drugs: *She was a drug addict and had lost her job, home, and friends.*
—**addicted** /ə'dɪktɪd/ *adjective* not able to stop taking a harmful drug: *He was addicted to heroin and couldn't stop, even though he was very sick.*
—**addiction** /ə'dɪkʃən/ *noun* the problem someone has when they need to take a harmful drug regularly: *Her addiction to alcohol ruined her life.*

ad•di•tion /ə'dɪʃən/ *noun*
1 in addition = used in order to add another piece of information to what you have just said: *In addition to repairing cars, he also sells them.*
2 the process of adding numbers together to get a total: *Most children learn addition in first grade.* ANTONYM **subtraction**
3 something that is added to something else, especially in order to improve it: *This product is a new addition to the company's range of software.*

ad•di•tion•al /ə'dɪʃənəl/ *adjective*
more than you already have: *Additional information is available on our website.* SYNONYM **extra**
➔ See Thesaurus box at **more**[2]

ad•dress[1] /'ædres/ *noun*
1 the details of where someone lives or works, including the number of the building and the name of the street and town, etc.: *Write your name and address at the top of the form.*
2 a series of letters or numbers used to send an email to someone, or to reach a page of information on the Internet: *Give me your email address and I'll send you the pictures.*
3 /ə'dres/ a formal speech: *The president's address was broadcast live on TV.*

ad•dress[2] /ə'dres/ *verb*
1 to write a name and address on an envelope, package, etc.: *There's a letter here addressed to you* (=the letter has your name and address written on it).
2 *formal* to speak directly to a group of people: *The senator addressed a large crowd of people.*
3 address a problem/question/issue, etc. *formal* = to try to solve a problem: *There are serious problems that we need to address and find a solution for.*

ad•e•quate /'ædɪkwət/ Ac *adjective, formal*
enough for a particular purpose: *Her income is not adequate to pay the bills.* ANTONYM **inadequate**
—**adequately** *adverb, formal* in a way that is enough for a particular purpose: *You must be adequately prepared for the test.*
➔ See Thesaurus boxes at **satisfactory** and **enough**

ad•ja•cent /ə'dʒeɪsənt/ Ac *adjective, formal*
next to something: *Their yard is adjacent to the river, so they go fishing whenever they want.*

ad•jec•tive /'ædʒɪktɪv/ *noun*
in grammar, a word that describes a noun. In the sentence "I bought a new car," "new" is an adjective.

ad•just /ə'dʒʌst/ Ac *verb*
1 to change or move something slightly to make it better: *How do you adjust the color on the TV? It's too green.*
2 to gradually become more familiar with a situation: *The kids are slowly adjusting to their new school – they're making more friends and their grades are improving.*
➔ See Thesaurus box at **change**[1]

ad•just•a•ble /ə'dʒʌstəbəl/ *adjective*
something that is adjustable can be changed or moved slightly to make it better for a particular purpose: *an adjustable desk lamp*

ad•just•ment /ə'dʒʌstmənt/ Ac *noun*
1 a small change made to a machine, system, or calculation: *We made some adjustments to our plan because Carol couldn't come on May 15.*
2 a change in the way you behave or think: *Moving to the city was a difficult adjustment for us.*

ad•min•is•tra•tion /əd,mɪnə'streɪʃən/ Ac *noun*
1 the U.S. president and the people who work for him or her after he or she is elected: *the Bush Administration*
2 the work of organizing or managing the work in a company or organization: *We're*

A

looking for someone with experience in administration.

WORD FAMILY look at the words:
→ **administration** *noun*
→ **administrator** *noun*
→ **administrative** *adjective*

ad•min•is•tra•tive /əd'mɪnə,streɪtɪv/ Ac *adjective*
connected with organizing or managing the work in a company or organization: *The company has cut its administrative staff* (=the people who do jobs organizing or managing work) *in half.*

ad•min•is•tra•tor /əd'mɪnə,streɪtɚ/ Ac *noun*
someone whose job is to help organize a particular area of work in a company or organization: *She is a college administrator and professor.*

ad•mi•ra•ble /'ædmərəbəl/ *adjective*
someone or something that is admirable has many good qualities that you respect: *He had many admirable qualities, especially honesty.*

ad•mi•ral /'ædmərəl/ *noun*
an officer who has a very high rank in the Navy

ad•mi•ra•tion /,ædmə'reɪʃən/ *noun*
a feeling of great respect and liking for someone or something: *I have great admiration for his work – it's the best I've seen.*

ad•mire /əd'maɪɚ/ *verb*
to feel great respect and liking for someone or something: *I really admire the way she's raising her kids.* | *I admire Tanya for always telling the truth.*

THESAURUS: admire
respect to admire someone because of his or her knowledge, skill, personal qualities, etc.: *She's a good teacher, and the students respect her.*
look up to someone to admire and respect someone: *He was a good player, and the other kids looked up to him.*

WORD FAMILY look at the words:
→ **admire** *verb*
→ **admiration** *noun*
→ **admirable** *adjective*

ad•mis•sion /əd'mɪʃən/ *noun*
1 the price you pay to go to a movie, museum, sports event, etc.: *Admission to the museum is $8.* | *an admission fee*
2 the right to become a student at a college or school: *Tom has applied for admission to City College.*
3 *formal* a statement or action that shows that something bad about yourself is true: *If he runs away from the police, people will consider it an admission of guilt.*

ad•mit /əd'mɪt/ *verb* **admitted, admitting**
1 to say that something is true, although you would prefer not to say it: *Okay, I admit (that) I was wrong – I shouldn't have lied.*
2 to allow someone to enter a place: *No one will be admitted to the game without a ticket.*

ad•o•les•cent /,ædl'esənt/ *noun*
a young person between 12 and 17 years old who is becoming an adult: *At fifteen, Bill was a shy adolescent.*
—**adolescence** *noun* the time of your life when you are an adolescent: *Adolescence can be a difficult time because your body is changing and so are your responsibilities.*
→ See Thesaurus box at **child**

a•dopt /ə'dɑpt/ *verb*
1 to become the legal parents of a child that is not your own child: *The Bakers wanted to adopt a child because Christine could not become pregnant.*
2 *formal* to begin to use a new way of doing something: *The city has adopted a new method for reducing crime.*
—**adoption** /ə'dɑpʃən/ *noun* the act of adopting a child

a•dor•a•ble /ə'dɔrəbəl/ *adjective*
very pretty or easy to love: *Amber was an adorable little girl with big brown eyes and curly hair.*

a•dore /ə'dɔr/ *verb*
to love someone or something very much: *She adored her sons and was willing to do anything for them.*

a•dult /ə'dʌlt/ Ac *noun*
a person who is not a child: *The tickets are $8 for adults and $5 for children.*
—**adulthood** *noun* the time of your life when you are an adult

A

ad•vance¹ /əd'væns/ *noun*
1 in advance = before something happens or before you do something: *It's a good idea to get tickets in advance. They're selling quickly.*
2 progress, or a change that brings progress: *Advances in medicine mean that we will all live longer.*

advance² *verb*
1 if medicine, computers, etc. advance, they improve: *Technology has advanced greatly in the past few years. Computers, for example, are faster, more powerful, and cheaper.*
2 *formal* to move forward to a new position: *The soldiers advanced steadily across the valley.* ANTONYM **retreat**

ad•vanced /əd'vænst/ *adjective*
1 using very modern ideas or equipment: *Our company uses the most advanced computer systems, so we are confident we can do the best job.*
2 working at a difficult level in a subject: *This class is for advanced students who have taken at least three years of English.*

ad•van•tage /əd'væntɪdʒ/ *noun*
1 a skill or quality that helps you to be successful: *If you speak Spanish, it's an advantage, because we do a lot of work in Latin America.* ANTONYM **disadvantage**
2 something that is good about a place, situation, etc.: *We live close to the kids' school, which is an advantage.* ANTONYM **disadvantage**
3 take advantage of something = to use an opportunity: *If you get the opportunity to go to Japan, you should take advantage of it.*
4 take advantage of someone = to use a person in a way that is not fair: *I sometimes feel that they take advantage of me at work, asking me to work extra hours without pay.*

ad•ven•ture /əd'ventʃɚ/ *noun*
an exciting thing that you do, when new things happen to you: *Our trip to Africa was a real adventure.*

ad•verb /'ædvɚb/ *noun*
in grammar, a word that tells you more about a verb, an adjective, another adverb, or the whole sentence: *In the sentence "He walked slowly," "slowly" is an adverb.*

ad•ver•tise /'ædvɚˌtaɪz/ *verb*
1 if a business advertises, it tries to make people buy its products or use its services, using pictures, short movies, etc.: *The company advertises on TV and the Internet.*
2 to put a notice in a newspaper, magazine, etc. to try and find someone to do a job, share an apartment, etc.: *The school is advertising for a new principal.*
—**advertising** *noun* the business of advertising things on television, in newspapers, etc.: *I'd really like to work in advertising.*

WORD FAMILY look at the words:
→ **advertise** *verb*
→ **advertisement** *noun*
→ **advertising** *noun*

ad•ver•tise•ment /ˌædvɚ'taɪzmənt/ *noun*
1 a picture, short movie, etc. which tries to make people buy a product or use a service: *I like that new advertisement for shampoo on TV.* SYNONYM **ad**

THESAURUS: advertisement

commercial an advertisement on TV or radio: *a funny commercial for cat food*
billboard a very large sign at the side of a road or on a building, used as an advertisement: *Billboards lined the streets, advertising cars and movies.*
poster an advertisement printed on a large piece of paper, often with a picture on it: *a movie poster outside the theater*
flier a piece of paper with an advertisement on it, often given to you in the street: *They were handing out fliers for the restaurant.*
junk mail letters that companies send to your house in order to advertise something, that you get even though you do not want them: *We seem to get so much junk mail!*
spam emails that are advertising something, that you get even though you do not want them: *Is there a way to stop spam arriving in my inbox?*

2 a notice in a newspaper, magazine, etc. that is trying to find someone to do a job, share an apartment, etc.: *There are lots of advertisements for computer programmers in the paper.*

ad•vice /əd'vaɪs/ *noun*
ideas that help someone to decide what he or she should do: *I need some good advice*

A

on how to cut my hair. | Can you give me some advice?

WORD FAMILY look at the words:
→ **advice** *noun*
→ **advise** *verb*
→ **adviser** also **advisor** *noun*

ad•vise /əd'vaɪz/ *verb*
to tell someone what you think he or she should do: *His doctor advised him to stop smoking.*
—**adviser** *also* **advisor** *noun* someone whose job is to advise people, for example about money, the law, etc.: *I went to see a career adviser about what jobs were available.*

ae•ro•bics /e'roʊbɪks/ *noun*
exercise that you do with music: *I do aerobics in a class at the gym once a week.*
→ See Thesaurus box at **exercise²**

aer•o•sol /'erəˌsɔl/ *noun*
a container with liquid inside. You press a button on the container to force out the liquid at high pressure

af•fair /ə'fer/ *noun*
1 a sexual relationship between two people who are not married to each other: *He was having an affair with another man's wife.*
2 a special event such as a party or wedding: *Thanksgiving is usually a family affair* (=only for members of the family).
3 affairs = events and activities relating to a particular subject: *In tonight's speech, the president will speak about foreign affairs* (=situations in countries around the world and relationships between governments).
→ **love affair**

af•fect /ə'fekt/ Ac *verb*
to make someone or something change, especially in a bad way: *The medicine may affect your ability to stay awake, so do not drive after you take it.*
WORD FAMILY → **effect** *noun*

af•fec•tion /ə'fekʃən/ *noun*
a feeling that you like or love someone you know well: *Bart had a great affection for her – they'd been friends for years.*
—**affectionate** *adjective* showing that you like or love someone: *My father was never very affectionate and we did not have a close relationship.*
—**affectionately** *adverb* in an affectionate way: *She smiled at him affectionately.*

af•flu•ent /'æfluənt/ *adjective, formal*
having a lot of money: *The kids are from affluent families, so they never worry about money.* SYNONYM **rich, wealthy**
—**affluence** *noun* the state of being rich

af•ford /ə'fɔrd/ *verb*
to have enough money to buy or do something: *I can't afford to buy a new car – I only have $600.*

af•ford•a•ble /ə'fɔrdəbəl/ *adjective*
affordable prices, rents, etc. are not too expensive: *The restaurant serves fresh food at affordable prices, so it's always very busy.*

a•fraid /ə'freɪd/ *adjective*
1 frightened of something that may hurt you or be dangerous: *A lot of people are afraid of spiders. | Mary's afraid to walk home alone at night, so I drove her home.* SYNONYM **scared, frightened**
2 worried about something that may happen in the future: *She loved him and she was afraid of losing him. | Joey was afraid (that) the other kids would laugh at him.*
3 I'm afraid = used in order to politely tell someone something that may annoy or upset them: *I'm afraid (that) there are no more tickets left.*
→ See Thesaurus box at **frightened**
→ See picture on page A23

Af•ri•can /'æfrɪkən/ *noun*
someone from Africa
—**African** *adjective* relating to Africa: *African art*

ˌAfrican A'merican *noun*
an American with dark skin, whose family first came to the U.S. from Africa
—**African-American** *adjective* being or relating to an African American

af•ter /'æftɚ/ *preposition, conjunction, adverb*
1 later than something else: *Let's go have dinner after the movie. | I went straight home after I left the party. | I can come tomorrow or the day after* (=the day after tomorrow).

THESAURUS: after
afterward after an event or time that has been mentioned: *He said afterward that it had been the scariest experience of his life.*

A

next after now, or after you have done something else: *What should we do next?*

later after the time now, or after the time you are talking about: *We can clean up later.*

subsequently *formal* after an event in the past: *I met her subsequently at a meeting in Seattle.*

2 moving behind and toward someone or something: *"Stop!" he shouted, running after the man.*

3 five/ten/a quarter, etc. after = used to say how many minutes past the hour it is: *"What time is it?" "It's twenty after two* (=2:20)*."* SYNONYM **past**; ANTONYM **to**

4 after all = used in order to say that something you expected to happen did not happen: *We brought our umbrellas, but it didn't rain after all.*

af•ter•noon /ˌæftɚˈnun/ *noun*
the time between 12 noon and the evening: *I have two classes in the afternoon, but I'm free until noon.* | *We went to the park on Friday afternoon.* | *Would you like to come to my house this afternoon* (=today in the afternoon)*?*

af•ter•shave /ˈæftɚˌʃeɪv/ *noun*
a liquid with a nice smell that a man puts on his face after he SHAVEs

af•ter•ward /ˈæftɚwɚd/ *also* **afterwards** *adverb*
after an event or time: *They met in 1983 and got married soon afterward.*
➔ See Thesaurus box at **after**

a•gain /əˈgen/ *adverb*
if you do something again, you repeat what you have done: *Could you say that again? I didn't hear you.* | *I've tried calling her again and again* (=repeating it many times) *but she's never there.* | *My computer crashed, so I had to start my paper all over again* (=from the beginning).

a•gainst /əˈgenst/ *preposition*
1 next to the surface of something, or touching it: *Let's put the couch against that wall.*
2 if you are against an idea, plan, etc., you do not agree with it and you do not want it to happen: *John was against the idea of selling the house – he wanted to keep it.* ANTONYM **for**
3 if you are playing against a team, you are competing with that team in a game: *The team will play against the Cowboys on Saturday.*
4 if you fight against a country or against a bad situation, you try to defeat that country or stop that situation: *They fought against the Russians during the war.* | *the war against crime*
5 against the law/the rules = not allowed by the law or the rules: *It's against the law to smoke in here.*

age /eɪdʒ/ *noun*
1 the number of years that you have lived: *Children usually start school at the age of 5* (=when they are 5 years old). | *Paul's younger than I am, but Patrick is my age* (=the same age as I am).
2 a time in someone's life: *Everyone should save some money for their old age* (=the time when they are old).
3 a period of time in history: *We are living in the computer age.*
4 ages *informal* = a long time: *I've lived in this town for ages.*
5 the state of being old: *The photograph was brown with age.*

a•gen•cy /ˈeɪdʒənsi/ *noun* plural **agencies**
1 a business that helps people to arrange something or find something they need: *We got the flights and hotel through a travel agency* (=a business that helps people arrange their travel).
2 a part of a government that does a special job: *NASA is the name of the U.S. space agency.*

a•gen•da /əˈdʒendə/ *noun*
1 a list of the subjects that the people at a meeting will discuss: *Money for the new hospital is the first thing on the agenda, so that is what we will discuss first.*
2 a list of things that an organization is planning to do: *More training for teachers is high on the agenda* (=it is an important thing on the list).

a•gent /ˈeɪdʒənt/ *noun*
1 a person or company that arranges things or does work for other people: *A travel agent found the hotel for us.*

A

2 someone whose job is to get secret information about another country, organization, or person: *an FBI agent*
→ **real estate agent**

ag•gra•vate /ˈægrəˌveɪt/ *verb*
1 *formal* to make an illness, injury, or bad situation worse: *Exercise may aggravate your injury, so wait until it is healed before exercising.*
2 to annoy someone: *Sometimes my sister really aggravates me. She talks too much.* SYNONYM **irritate**

ag•gres•sive /əˈgresɪv/ *adjective*
1 a person or animal that is aggressive gets angry or violent easily: *Girls are usually less aggressive than boys.*
2 an aggressive way of doing something is forceful and shows that you are determined to succeed: *Their plan for raising money is very aggressive: they plan to call and email every one in the neighborhood.*
—**aggression** /əˈgreʃən/ *noun* the quality of being aggressive: *His voice was loud and full of aggression.*

ag•ile /ˈædʒəl/ *adjective, formal*
able to move quickly and easily: *He was young and agile, and climbed the fence easily.*

ag•i•tat•ed /ˈædʒəˌteɪtɪd/ *adjective*
very worried or upset: *I saw that the boy was becoming agitated and tried to calm him down.*

a•go /əˈgoʊ/ *adverb*
5 minutes/1 hour/2 years, etc. ago = five minutes, one hour, etc. before now: *The show started 10 minutes ago.* | *We went there a long time ago* (=a long time before now).

GRAMMAR: ago

ago, for, since

Ago, **for**, and **since** are all used to talk about time.

Ago is used to say how far back in the past something happened. It comes after a length of time: *My grandfather died two years ago.*

For is used to say how long something has lasted. It comes before a length of time: *My aunt has been here for three days.* | *The meeting continued for five hours.*

Since is used to say when something started. The exact day, date, or time comes after it: *He's been here since Sunday.* | *I've been going to school here since 2006.*

ag•o•ny /ˈægəni/ *noun* plural **agonies** *formal*
very bad pain: *He was screaming in agony.*
—**agonizing** /ˈægəˌnaɪzɪŋ/ *adjective, formal* very painful: *She had an agonizing pain in her chest.*

a•gree /əˈgri/ *verb*
1 if you agree with someone, you think that what they say is right: *I agree with you. It's too expensive.* | *Most people agree (that) this is a serious problem.* | *We don't agree on how to deal with money. He says I spend too much.* ANTONYM **disagree**
2 to say that you will do something: *Dad agreed to give us a ride into town.* ANTONYM **refuse**
3 to decide something: *Can we all agree on a date for the next meeting?*

PHRASAL VERB

agree with something
to think that something is right: *I don't agree with their decision – I don't think it's fair.*

a•gree•a•ble /əˈgriəbəl/ *adjective, formal*
1 pleasant and nice to be with: *He was an agreeable old man, and people enjoyed talking with him.*
2 if someone is agreeable to an idea, they agree to it: *He was agreeable to trying a different restaurant, so we went to the new Thai place.*

a•gree•ment /əˈgrimənt/ *noun*
1 an arrangement or promise between organizations, countries, people, etc.: *The company has reached an agreement* (=made an agreement) *with the bank to borrow money.* | *Both countries wanted a peace agreement* (=agreement not to fight each other anymore).
2 a situation in which people agree about an idea: *All of us were in agreement about what we should do next.* ANTONYM **disagreement**

ag•ri•cul•ture /ˈægrɪˌkʌltʃɚ/ *noun*
the activity of growing crops and raising animals for people to eat: *Most of the people outside the cities and towns work in agriculture.* SYNONYM **farming**

—**agricultural** /ˌægrɪˈkʌltʃərəl/ *adjective* relating to agriculture

a·head /əˈhed/ *adverb*

1 in front of someone or something: *Mom was walking ahead of us, so she didn't see what happened.* | *He looked straight ahead* (=directly in front of him).

2 go ahead *informal* = if you tell someone to go ahead, you are saying that he or she can do something: *"Can I make some coffee?" "Go ahead."*

3 in the future: *The problem will become worse in the years ahead.* | *Try to plan ahead* (=plan for the future).

4 if you get ahead, you are successful in your work or life: *You need to work hard if you want to get ahead.*

5 ahead of schedule/time = earlier than people had planned: *Everything was ready ahead of schedule. Even the food arrived early.*

aid[1] /eɪd/ Ac *noun*

help, such as money, food, or equipment, for people who need it: *The U.S. is sending aid to the refugees.*

aid[2] *verb*

formal to help someone: *Murphy had aided the prisoner to escape.*

AIDS /eɪdz/ *noun*

Acquired Immune Deficiency Syndrome a very bad disease that makes your body unable to fight other diseases

aim[1] /eɪm/ *noun*

1 the thing that you are trying to achieve: *What is the main aim of your research?* SYNONYM **goal**

→ See Thesaurus box at **purpose**

2 take aim = to point a gun in the direction of someone or something and get ready to shoot: *He took aim and fired the gun.*

aim

aim[2] *verb*

1 to plan or intend to do something: *We aim to finish by Friday.*

2 to point something in the direction of someone or something and get ready to fire it or throw it at them: *The man aimed his gun at the target.*

3 be aimed at someone = to be made or intended for a particular person or group: *The magazine is aimed at teenagers.*

air[1] /er/ *noun*

1 the gases around the Earth, which we breathe: *There wasn't a lot of air in the room and it was hard to breathe.* | *fresh air*

2 the air = the space above you: *The balloon went up into the air.*

3 by air = using an airplane: *The quickest way to get there is by air.*

4 be on the air = to be broadcasting on television or radio: *Quiet everyone! We'll be on the air in a few seconds.*

air[2] *verb*

1 to broadcast a program on television or radio: *The show will air at 9 tomorrow night.*

2 air your views/opinions = to tell people what you think about something: *Everyone will have a chance to air his or her views and ask questions.*

ˈair conˌditioner *noun*

a machine that makes the air in a room, car or building stay cool

ˈair conˌditioning *noun*, *abbreviation* **AC**

a system of machines that makes the air in a room, car or building stay cool: *It's very hot here in the summer, so it's good to have a car with air conditioning.*

—**air-conditioned** *adjective*: *an air-conditioned office*

air·craft /ˈerkræft/ *noun* plural **aircraft**

an airplane or other vehicle that can fly: *The aircraft can carry 600 passengers.*

air·fare /ˈerfer/ *noun*

the price of an airplane ticket

ˈair force *noun*

the part of a country's military that uses airplanes to fight: *He learned to fly planes while he was in the air force.*

air·line /ˈerlaɪn/ *noun*

a company that takes passengers and goods to different places by airplane: *The major airlines have raised their prices for flights this summer.* | *an airline pilot*

A

air•mail /ˈermeɪl/ *noun*
the system of sending letters, packages, etc. to another country by airplane
—**airmail** *adjective*, *adverb* using or relating to airmail: *She sent the book airmail.*

airplane

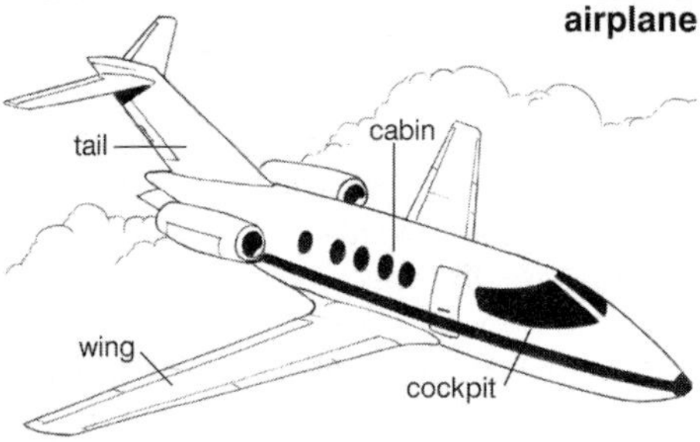

air•plane /ˈerpleɪn/ *noun*
a vehicle that flies through the air: *We flew on a small airplane between Detroit and Chicago.* SYNONYM **plane**

air•port /ˈerpɔrt/ *noun*
a place where airplanes take off and land, that has buildings for passengers to wait in: *The plane landed at Los Angeles airport.*

ˈair raid *noun*
an attack in which bombs are dropped from airplanes

air•y /ˈeri/ *adjective*
an airy room or building has a lot of space and fresh air: *The house was bright and airy with lots of windows.*

aisle

aisle /aɪl/ *noun*
a long passage between rows of seats in a theater, airplane, church, etc.: *The bride and her father walked down the aisle to the front of the church.*

a•jar /əˈdʒɑr/ *adjective*
a door or window that is ajar is not completely closed: *He left the door ajar so that he could hear the phone.*

ajar

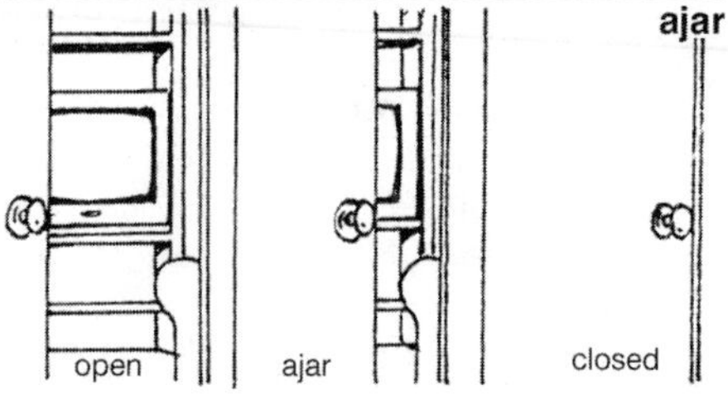

a•larm¹ /əˈlɑrm/ *noun*
1 a piece of equipment that makes a noise to warn people of danger: *a fire alarm* | *Someone accidentally set off the car alarm* (=made it start making a noise).
2 the part of an ALARM CLOCK that makes a noise to wake you up: *The alarm went off at 6 and woke me up.*

alarm² *verb*, *formal*
to make someone feel very worried or frightened: *I don't want to alarm you, but there's some smoke coming from the hall.*
—**alarmed** *adjective* worried or frightened about something: *She seemed alarmed by the news that her daughter had not called.*

aˈlarm clock *noun*
a clock that will make a noise at a particular time to wake you up: *I set the alarm clock for 7:00.*
→ See picture on page A10

al•bum /ˈælbəm/ *noun*
1 a group of songs or pieces of music on a CD, record, etc.: *Have you heard the band's new album?*
2 a book in which you put photographs, stamps, etc. that you want to keep: *a photo album*

al•co•hol /ˈælkəˌhɔl/ *noun*
drinks such as beer or wine that can make you drunk: *You're not allowed to drink alcohol unless you're over 21.*

al•co•hol•ic¹ /ˌælkəˈhɔlɪk/ *adjective*
1 containing alcohol or relating to alcohol: *an alcoholic beverage* (=a drink that contains alcohol)
2 used for describing someone who is an alcoholic: *Her alcoholic husband could not keep a job.*

alcoholic² *noun*
someone who cannot control how much alcohol he or she drinks
—**alcoholism** /ˈælkəhɔlˌɪzəm/ *noun* a serious medical problem in which someone cannot control how much alcohol he or she drinks

a•lert /ə'lɚt/ *adjective*
always watching and ready to notice anything unusual, dangerous, etc.: *It's important to stay alert when you're driving.*

al•gae /'ældʒi/ *noun*
a very simple plant without stems or leaves that lives in or near water

al•ge•bra /'ældʒəbrə/ *noun*
a type of mathematics that uses letters and symbols to represent numbers and amounts

al•i•bi /'æləbaɪ/ *noun*
something that proves that someone was not where a crime happened and is therefore not guilty of the crime: *The man had an alibi for where he was during the crime, and the police had to release him.*

a•li•en /'eɪliən/ *noun*
1 *formal* a foreigner who is visiting or living in a country: *Every year thousands of illegal aliens* (=a foreigner who is in a country illegally) *cross the border.*
2 a creature from another world: *In the movie, the aliens try to take over the Earth.*

a•li•en•ate /'eɪliəˌneɪt/ *verb, formal*
to do something that makes someone unfriendly or unwilling to support you: *High ticket prices for football games have alienated many fans.*

a•like /ə'laɪk/ *adjective, adverb*
very similar: *Sarah and her sister look very much alike.*
➔ See Thesaurus box at **similar**

al•i•mo•ny /'æləˌmoʊni/ *noun*
money that someone has to pay regularly to his or her former wife or husband after a DIVORCE

a•live /ə'laɪv/ *adjective*
living and not dead: *He was lost in the mountains for days, but he stayed alive by eating berries and leaves.*

all[1] /ɔl/ *adjective, pronoun*
1 the whole amount of something: *Have you done all your homework so that you're ready for school tomorrow? | I've spent all of the money, and I don't have any left.*
2 every one of a group of things or people: *Someone ate all the cookies, so I didn't get one. | He's 90 and older than all of us.*

USAGE: all

All, **each**, and **every** are all used to talk about every person or thing in a group.

When you are thinking about the whole group together, use **all**: *All the children were given balloons.*

When you are thinking about the people or things in the group separately, use **every** or **each**: *Every child at the party was given a balloon. | Each child at the party was given a balloon.*

3 not ... at all = used when you want to emphasize a negative sentence: *He's not like you at all* (=he's very different from you).
4 all kinds/sorts = very many different types of things or people: *She has acted in all kinds of movies: action, mystery, romance, etc.*

all[2] *adverb*
1 completely or entirely: *The house is all clean and neat so don't make it messy. | I'm glad it's all over* (=completely finished).
2 all over = everywhere: *I've been looking all over for you. Where were you?*
➔ **after all** at **after**, **all of a sudden** at **sudden**

al•lege /ə'ledʒ/ *verb, formal*
to say that something is true or someone has done something wrong, although it has not been proved: *He alleged that police officers punched and beat him.*

al•ler•gy /'ælɚdʒi/ *noun* plural **allergies**
a condition that makes you sick when you eat, touch, or breathe a particular thing: *He has an allergy to cats, so he can't be around them.*
—**allergic** /ə'lɚdʒɪk/ *adjective* having an allergy: *I'm allergic to nuts, so I have to be careful not to eat them.*

al•ley /'æli/ *also* **al•ley•way** /'æliˌweɪ/ *noun*
a narrow street between buildings

al•li•ance /ə'laɪəns/ *noun*
an agreement between countries, groups, etc. to work together or fight together: *The alliance between the United States and Britain is strong and has lasted through several wars.*

A

al•li•ga•tor /ˈælə,geɪtɚ/ *noun*
a large animal with a long body and a big mouth with sharp teeth: *Alligators live in hot wet places like Florida.*

al•lo•cate /ˈælə,keɪt/ Ac *verb, formal*
to decide to use money, time, etc. for a particular purpose: *The money was allocated for the construction of a new swimming pool.*
—**allocation** /,æləˈkeɪʃən/ *noun* the action or result of allocating money, time, etc.

al•low /əˈlaʊ/ *verb*
to say that someone can do something: *Smoking is not allowed in public buildings.* | *Her parents don't allow her to stay out late – she has to be home by 8:00.* ANTONYM **forbid**

THESAURUS: allow

Allow is used in both formal and informal English: *You're not allowed to use a calculator during the test.*

Let is informal and is used a lot in spoken English: *Will your mom let you come to the party?*

Permit is formal and is mainly used in written English: *Smoking is not permitted in this building.*

al•low•ance /əˈlaʊəns/ *noun*
money that you are given regularly or for a special reason: *The kids get an allowance of two dollars every week.*

all ˈright *adjective, adverb*
1 used to say "yes", when someone asks or suggests something: *"Can I borrow your pen?" "All right."* SYNONYM **OK**
2 good enough, but not excellent: *"How was the movie?" "It was all right."* SYNONYM **OK**
3 not sick, in pain, or upset: *"Do you feel all right?" "I'm fine, thanks."* SYNONYM **OK**
4 it's all right = used when telling someone not to be afraid or worried: *It's all right now. Mommy's here.*
5 is it all right ... ? = used when asking if you can do something: *Is it all right if I close the window?*
6 that's all right = used in order to tell someone that you are not angry when they say they are sorry to you: *"Sorry, I'm late!" "That's all right."*
7 used in order to say you are happy about something: *"I got the job!" "All right!"*

al•ly /əˈlaɪ/ *noun* plural **allies**
a person or country that helps another, especially in war: *The U.S. and Canada were allies in World War II.*

al•mond /ˈɑmənd/ *noun*
a flat white nut with pale brown skin and a slightly sweet taste
➔ See picture on page A13

al•most /ˈɔlmoʊst/ *adverb*
nearly but not quite: *The house is almost finished. We just have to paint it.* | *He ate almost all the cake – there was only a little piece left.* | *We see each other almost every day.*

a•lone /əˈloʊn/ *adjective, adverb*
1 without any other people: *The old man lived alone and had no one to talk to.* | *They leave the dog alone in the house all day.*

THESAURUS: alone

on your own without anyone helping you: *Did you make this on your own?*

(all) by yourself without anyone helping you: *She raised four children by herself.*

solo done alone, without anyone else helping you: *Charles Lindbergh made the first solo flight across the Atlantic Ocean.*

2 *formal* only that person or thing: *She alone knows the truth.*
➔ **leave someone alone, leave something alone** at **leave**[1]

a•long /əˈlɔŋ/ *adverb, preposition*
1 moving forward on a road, path, line, etc. toward one end of it: *We took a walk along the river.* SYNONYM **down**
2 next to something: *An old stone wall runs along* (=is in a position next to) *the road for more than a mile.* SYNONYM **beside**
3 with someone: *Can I bring a friend along* (=with me)?

a•long•side /ə,lɔŋˈsaɪd/ *adverb, preposition*
next to the side of something: *A big ship came alongside our boat.*

a•loud /əˈlaʊd/ *adverb*
in a voice that you can hear: *His mother read the story aloud to him.*

al•pha•bet /ˈælfə,bet/ *noun*
the letters of a language: *The last letter of the English alphabet is "Z."*
—**alphabetical** /,ælfəˈbetɪkəl/ *adjective* in

the order of the letters of the alphabet: *The books are arranged in alphabetical order.*

al·read·y /ɔl'redi/ *adverb*

1 before now: *I've seen that movie twice already.*

2 before the time when something happens: *By the time we arrived, the plane had already left.*

3 used when you are surprised because something happens sooner than you expected: *Is it 5:30 already? I thought it was only about 4.*

USAGE: already

Already is used in order to talk about something that has happened: *I've already read the book we're studying in my English class.*

All ready is used in order to say that someone is ready to do something, or that something is completely prepared: *Are you all ready to go? | Dinner is all ready.*

al·so /'ɔlsoʊ/ *adverb*

used when you want to say that another thing is true about someone or something: *Mike speaks French. He can also speak a little Spanish. | The food is not only delicious, but also inexpensive.* SYNONYM **too**

USAGE: also

Also, **too**, and **as well** mean the same thing, but you use them in different ways.

Also is more formal than **too**, and is used more often in writing than in speech: *Tom was very tired, and he was also hungry.*

Too and **as well** are less formal and you use them more often in spoken English: *Tom's hungry, and I am too. | Oh, are you coming as well?*

In sentences with "not" or "nothing," use **either** rather than **also** or **too**. Do not say "Tom was also not hungry." or "Tom was not hungry too." Say "Tom was not hungry either."

GRAMMAR: also

Use **also** before a verb, unless the verb is "be": *Dave also plays baseball.*

Use **also** after the verb "be": *His sister is also tall.*

If there are two or more verbs together, **also** comes after the first one: *Gina can also play the piano.*

al·tar /'ɔltɚ/ *noun*

a table or other flat surface, used by the priest in religious ceremonies

al·ter /'ɔltɚ/ Ac *verb, formal*

to change something: *We had to alter our plans because of the rain.*

→ See Thesaurus box at **change**[1]

al·ter·nate[1] /'ɔltɚˌneɪt/ Ac *verb*

if you alternate between two things, you do one thing first, then you do the second thing, then you do the first thing again, etc.: *She alternated between feeling happy and feeling sad.*

al·ter·nate[2] /'ɔltɚnɪt/ Ac *adjective*

used instead of someone or something else: *The road was closed and so we had to take an alternate route.* SYNONYM **alternative**

al·ter·na·tive[1] /ɔl'tɚnətɪv/ Ac *adjective*

1 an alternative plan, way of doing something, etc. can be used instead of another one: *There may be an alternative way of dealing with the problem.*

2 different from the usual way of doing something: *She believes in alternative medicine, and takes herbs instead of regular medicine.*

—**alternatively** *adverb* used when you are mentioning a different possibility: *You could visit one of the city's museums. Alternatively, you could spend the day in Central Park.*

alternative[2] *noun*

something you can choose to do or use instead of something else: *There are a lot of alternatives to using your car: you can take the bus or ride a bicycle.*

al·though /ɔl'ðoʊ/ *conjunction*

used when something seems surprising, considering something else you are saying: *Although he's over 60, he still goes running every day.*

al·ti·tude /'æltəˌtud/ *noun*

the height of something above sea level: *They were flying at an altitude of 30,000 feet.*

al·to·geth·er /ˌɔltə'geðɚ/ *adverb*

1 including everyone or everything: *The trip cost $2,000 altogether.*

2 completely – used when you want to emphasize what you are saying: *She wants*

A

to stop working altogether and just stay at home.

a•lu•mi•num /ə'lumənəm/ *noun*
a very light silver-gray metal, used to make cans

al•ways /'ɔlweɪz/ *adverb*
1 every time, or at all times: *He always goes to bed before midnight.* | *It's always very cold in the Arctic.*

THESAURUS: always

permanently forever or for a very long time: *His eyesight may be permanently damaged.*

forever for all time in the future: *It's so nice here that I'd like to stay forever.*

for good used to say that a change is permanent: *I've given up smoking for good.*

USAGE: always

Always means "all the time" or "every time": *Her clothes are always so nice.* | *I always see him on Tuesdays.*

Still is used to say that a situation that began in the past has not changed and is continuing: *He still lives with his parents.*

Yet is used in sentences with "not" in them and in questions to talk about something that you expect to happen, but which has not happened: *I haven't finished the book yet.* | *Is Mark back from lunch yet?*

2 for a very long time: *I've always wanted to go to New York – ever since I was a little kid.*
3 you can/could always... = used when suggesting that someone should do something: *You could always drive instead of flying.*

GRAMMAR: always

Use **always** before a verb, unless the verb is "be": *We always eat dinner together.*

Use **always** after the verb "be": *Jeff is always late for school.*

If there are two or more verbs together, **always** comes after the first one: *I have always lived in this town.*

am /əm; *strong* æm/ *verb*
the form of the verb BE that is used with "I". "I am" is often shortened to "I'm": *I am so happy that she won.*

a.m. /ˌeɪ 'em/
used to show that a time is in the morning: *I start work at 9:00 a.m.*

am•a•teur /'æmətʃə/ *adjective*
doing something for enjoyment, not for money and not as a job: *The competition is for amateur athletes, not professionals.* ANTONYM **professional**

a•maze /ə'meɪz/ *verb*
to surprise or impress someone very much: *It amazes me that they're still married – they argue so much.*
—**amazed** *adjective* very surprised or impressed: *I was amazed at how much it all cost.*
—**amazing** *adjective* very surprising or impressive: *The movie was amazing – I've never seen anything like it.*

WORD FAMILY look at the words:

→ **amazed** *adjective*
→ **amazing** *adjective*
→ **amaze** *verb*
→ **amazement** *noun*

a•maze•ment /ə'meɪzmənt/ *noun*
the feeling you have when you are very surprised or impressed: *They all looked at the boy in amazement as he stood up and began to sing.*

am•bas•sa•dor /æm'bæsədə/ *noun*
an important official who represents his or her country in another country: *the U.S. ambassador to France*

am•big•u•ous /æm'bɪgyuəs/ Ac *adjective*
something that is ambiguous is not clear because it can be understood in more than one way: *The question was ambiguous, and I wasn't sure how to answer.*

am•bi•tion /æm'bɪʃən/ *noun*
1 something that you want very much to do: *My ambition is to become a writer someday.*
2 the feeling that you want to try to be successful, rich, etc.: *Craig has a lot of ambition, and I'm sure he'll be very successful in his career.*

A

am•bi•tious /æm'bɪʃəs/ *adjective*
wanting very much to be successful: *She was very ambitious and decided to start her own company.*

am•bu•lance /'æmbyələns/ *noun*
a special vehicle for taking sick or injured people to the hospital: *Can someone call an ambulance? I think this man is really sick.*
➔ See picture on page A26

am•bush /'æmbʊʃ/ *noun*
a sudden attack by someone who has been secretly waiting in a hidden place: *Three U.S. soldiers were killed in an ambush.*
—**ambush** *verb* to suddenly attack someone after secretly waiting in a hidden place

a•mend /ə'mend/ Ac *verb, formal*
to make small changes or improvements to the words of a law: *The law needs to be amended so that it helps more people.*
—**amendment** *noun* a change to the words of a law: *an amendment to the Constitution*

A•mer•i•can /ə'merɪkən/ *adjective*
from the U.S.: *My wife is American.* | *an American company*
—**American** *noun* someone from the U.S.

A,merican 'dream *noun*
the American Dream = the idea that everyone in the U.S. has the opportunity to become successful if he or she works hard

am•mu•ni•tion /,æmyə'nɪʃən/ *noun*
things such as bullets, bombs, etc. that are fired from guns

am•nes•ty /'æmnəsti/ *noun* plural **amnesties** *formal*
an official order that allows prisoners to be free, or that allows people not to be punished for a crime

a•moe•ba /ə'mibə/ *noun*
a very small creature that has only one cell

a•mong /ə'mʌŋ/ *also* **a•mongst** /ə'mʌŋst/ *preposition*
1 included in a larger group of people or things: *Brad was among the ten students who received the award.*
2 in the middle of a lot of people or things: *The rabbit disappeared among some trees.*

> **USAGE: among**
>
> **Among** and **between** are both used to talk about where someone or something is.
>
> Use **among** when there are two or more people or things on each side or all sides of someone or something: *Denise was among a group of her friends.*
>
> Use **between** when there is one other person or thing on each side of someone or something: *I sat between Alex and Sarah.*

3 happening to or relating to a group of people: *Heart disease is common among men over the age of 50.*

a•mount /ə'maʊnt/ *noun*
a quantity of something: *$80,000 is a very large amount of money.*

> **USAGE: amount**
>
> Use **amount** with nouns that are things you cannot count: *a large amount of water*
>
> Use **number** with nouns that are things you can count: *a large number of cars*

amp /æmp/ *also* **am•pere** /'æmpɪr/ *noun*
a unit for measuring an electric current

am•phib•i•an /æm'fɪbiən/ *noun*
an animal such as a FROG that can live on land and in water

am•ple /'æmpəl/ *adjective*
more than enough: *The car has ample room for five people, so four people will not be a problem.*

am•pu•tate /'æmpyə,teɪt/ *verb, formal*
to cut off a part of someone's body for medical reasons: *He was wounded in the left leg, and the doctors had to amputate it.*
—**amputation** /,æmpyə'teɪʃən/ *noun, formal* the act of cutting off part of someone's body

a•muse /ə'myuz/ *verb*
to make someone laugh or smile: *My joke seemed to amuse him.*
—**amused** *adjective* if you are amused, you think that something is funny: *She listened to his speech, looking amused.*

amuse

a•muse•ment /ə'myuzmənt/ *noun*
the feeling you have when you think something is funny: *They looked at each other and smiled in amusement.*

a'musement ,park *noun*
a place where people go to enjoy themselves by riding on large machines

a•mus•ing /ə'myuzɪŋ/ *adjective*
funny and entertaining: *an amusing story* | *I didn't find his remarks very amusing although some other people laughed.*
→ See Thesaurus box at **funny**[1]

an /ən; *strong* æn/ *indefinite article*
used instead of "a" when the following word begins with a vowel sound: *an animal* | *an X-ray* | *an hour*

GRAMMAR: an

an, a

Use **an** if the word that is after it starts with a vowel sound (the sounds shown by the letters a, e, i, o, or u): *an apple* | *an orange sweater* | *I waited an hour.*

Use **a** if the word that is after it starts with a consonant sound: *a car* | *a white egg* | *a house* | *I bought a CD today.*

a•nal•o•gy /ə'nælədʒi/ Ac *noun, formal*
make/draw an analogy = if you make an analogy between two situations, you say that they are similar in some ways: *We can make an analogy between a brain and a computer – both take in information and process it.*

a•nal•y•sis /ə'næləsɪs/ Ac *noun*
careful examination of something in order to understand it or to find out what it contains: *Scientists have made a detailed analysis of the problem.*

an•a•lyst /'ænl-ɪst/ Ac *noun*
1 someone whose job is to analyze things: *a financial analyst*
2 another word for a PSYCHOANALYST

an•al•yze /'ænl,aɪz/ Ac *verb*
to examine something carefully in order to understand it or to find out what it contains: *We did the experiment in class and then analyzed the results for homework.*

WORD FAMILY look at the words:

→ **analyze** *verb*
→ **analysis** *noun*
→ **analyst** *noun*

a•nat•o•my /ə'nætəmi/ *noun*
1 the scientific study of the structure of the body: *The biology course contains a section on anatomy.*
2 the structure of the body of a person or animal: *The human anatomy is very complex.*
—**anatomical** /,ænə'tɑmɪkəl/ *adjective* relating to anatomy

an•ces•tor /'æn,sestə/ *noun*
a member of your family who lived a long time before you were born: *His ancestors came to the U.S. from Germany over a hundred years ago.*

an•chor /'æŋkə/ *noun*
1 someone who reads the news on television or radio and introduces news reports: *the evening news anchor on CNN*
2 a heavy metal object that is lowered into the water to prevent a ship or boat from moving

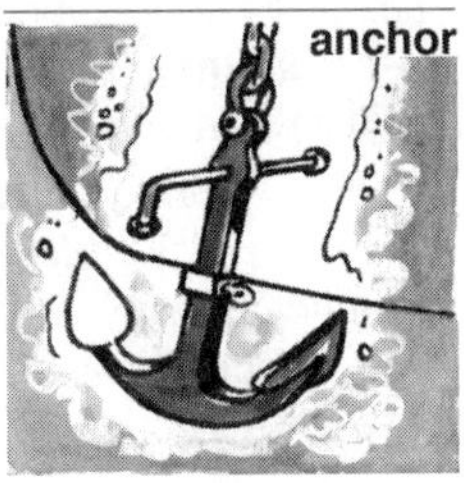

an•cient /'eɪnʃənt/ *adjective*
thousands of years old: *an ancient city* | *People have been living on the Nile since ancient times.*
→ See Thesaurus box at **old**

and /ən, ənd; *strong* ænd/ *conjunction*
a word used for joining two words or parts of a sentence: *They have a cat and a dog.* | *We saw a movie, and then we went to a restaurant.*

an•ec•dote /'ænɪk,doʊt/ *noun, formal*
a short story that you tell people about something interesting or funny that happened to you: *The book is full of anecdotes about his life in Paris.*

a•ne•mi•a /ə'nimiə/ *noun*
a medical condition in which there are not enough red cells in your blood: *Sometimes teenagers get anemia because they don't eat enough healthy food.*
—**anemic** *adjective* having anemia

an•es•thet•ic /ˌænəsˈθetɪk/ *noun*
a drug that stops you from feeling pain during a medical operation: *The doctor gave her a general anesthetic* (=affecting all of her body) *for the surgery.*
—**anesthesia** /ˌænəsˈθiʒə/ *noun* the use of drugs to stop someone from feeling pain during a medical operation: *He was under anesthesia* (=he had been given a drug to stop him feeling any pain).

an•gel /ˈeɪndʒəl/ *noun*
a spirit who lives with God in heaven, usually shown in pictures as a person with wings
—**angelic** /ænˈdʒelɪk/ *adjective* like an angel, or relating to angels

an•ger[1] /ˈæŋgɚ/ *noun*
a strong feeling that you have when you think someone has behaved very badly or a situation is very unfair: *Her voice was full of anger.*

anger[2] *verb, formal*
to make someone angry: *His rude behavior angered me.*

an•gle /ˈæŋgəl/ *noun*
the shape that is formed when two straight lines meet each other: *A square has four angles of 90 degrees.*

angle

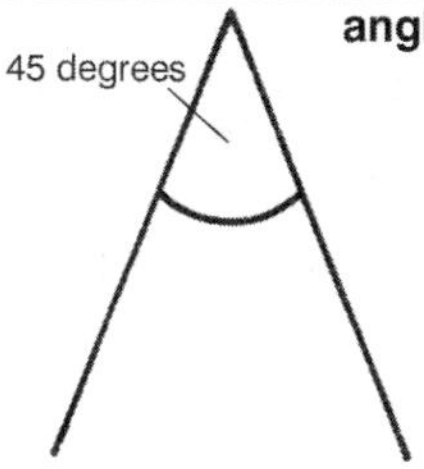

an•gry /ˈæŋgri/ *adjective* **angrier**, **angriest**
feeling a strong emotion because you think someone has behaved very badly or a situation is very unfair: *I was angry at him for treating me like a child.* | *She still feels angry about the lies he told her.* | *The man suddenly got angry and started yelling.*
→ See picture on page A23
—**angrily** *adverb*: *"I don't need any more advice from you," he said angrily.*

THESAURUS: angry

annoyed a little angry: *I get annoyed with the kids when they don't help around the house.*

irritated feeling annoyed and not patient with people or things: *Everyone was talking at once, and I started to feel irritated.*

furious very angry: *I was furious with my sister for not telling me something so important.*

mad *informal* angry: *She got really mad when he wouldn't listen.*

WORD FAMILY look at the words:

→ **angry** *adjective*
→ **angrily** *adverb*
→ **anger** *noun*
→ **anger** *verb*

an•guish /ˈæŋgwɪʃ/ *noun, formal*
a feeling of great unhappiness because something very bad has happened to you or because you feel very worried: *"Don't hurt my daughter," she cried in anguish.*

an•i•mal /ˈænəməl/ *noun*
a living moving creature that is not a human: *The zoo has many large animals, such as elephants and lions.*

an•i•ma•tion /ˌænəˈmeɪʃən/ *noun*
the process of making movies that use drawings: *They use a lot of computer animation in the movie to make it look like the house is flying.*
→ See Thesaurus box at **movie**

an•kle /ˈæŋkəl/ *noun*
the joint between your foot and your leg: *My foot twisted to one side and I hurt my ankle.*
→ See picture on page A2

an•ni•ver•sa•ry /ˌænəˈvɚsəri/ *noun*
plural **anniversaries**
the date when you celebrate something important that happened on the same day in a previous year: *Our wedding anniversary is in June.*

an•nounce /əˈnaʊns/ *verb*
to tell people about an important plan or decision: *The coach announced (that) he was leaving the team.*

an•nounce•ment /əˈnaʊnsmənt/ *noun*
an official public statement that tells people some important news: *The principal will make an important announcement this afternoon.*

an•noy /əˈnɔɪ/ *verb*
to make someone feel a little angry: *His bad singing was starting to annoy me.* SYNONYM **irritate**
—**annoying** *adjective* something that is

A

annoying makes you feel a little angry: *The woman had an annoying high voice.*

an•noy•ance /ə'nɔɪəns/ *noun, formal*
the feeling of being slightly angry: *Her annoyance at his stupid jokes was obvious.* SYNONYM **irritation**

an•noyed /ə'nɔɪd/ *adjective*
slightly angry: *I was annoyed that no one had told me about the change.* | *I was getting annoyed with her because she wasn't listening.* SYNONYM **irritated**
➔ See Thesaurus box at **angry**

an•nu•al /'ænyuəl/ Ac *adjective*
happening once a year: *the annual meeting*
—**annually** *adverb*

a•non•y•mous /ə'nɑnəməs/ *adjective*
someone who is anonymous does not tell you his or her name: *an anonymous letter* (=from someone who does not give his or her name)
—**anonymously** *adverb*

a•no•rex•i•a /ˌænə'reksiə/ *noun*
a mental illness that makes people stop eating because they think they are fat
—**anorexic** *adjective* having anorexia

an•oth•er /ə'nʌðɚ/ *adjective, pronoun*
1 one more person or thing of the same kind: *Do you want another cup of coffee?* | *Do you like it? I can buy another one for you.*
2 a different person or thing: *Is there another room we could use? This one is too small.*
3 more of something, for example time or money: *Let's wait another ten minutes – I'm sure he'll be here soon.*
➔ See Thesaurus box at **more**[2]

an•swer[1] /'ænsɚ/ *verb*
1 to say or write something after you have been asked a question: *"Did you see anyone else?" "No," she answered.* | *I couldn't answer all the questions on the test.*

> **THESAURUS: answer**
>
> **reply** to answer someone – used especially in written English: *"Are you coming?" "Yes," she replied.*
>
> **respond** *formal* to answer someone, especially in a way that gives a lot of details: *The speaker will respond to questions at the end of his talk.*

2 answer the phone/door = to pick up the telephone when it rings, or go to the door when someone knocks or rings a bell: *Let me answer the phone if it rings.*

answer[2] *noun*
1 something that you say or write when someone asks you a question: *His answer to my question was "no."* | *Can you give me an answer as soon as possible?* | *What was the answer* (=the correct answer on a test) *to question number 3?*
2 something that solves a problem: *There are no easy answers to the problem of crime* (=it is difficult to find a solution). SYNONYM **solution**

'answering maˌchine *noun*
a machine that records messages from people calling you when you cannot answer your telephone: *I left a message on his answering machine asking him to call me.*

ant /ænt/ *noun*
a common small black or red insect that lives in groups

an•tac•id /ˌænt'æsɪd/ *noun*
a drug that stops the burning feeling in your stomach when you have eaten too much, drunk too much alcohol, etc.

Ant•arc•tic /æn'tɑrktɪk/ *noun*
the Antarctic *also* **Antarctica** = the very cold, most southern part of the world
—**Antarctic** *adjective*: *Antarctic explorers*

an•te•lope /'æntəlˌoʊp/ *noun*
an animal that has long horns, can run very fast, and is very graceful: *A herd of antelope ran quickly across the field.*

an•ten•na /æn'tenə/ *noun*
1 a piece of equipment on a television, car, roof, etc. for receiving radio or television signals
2 plural **antennae** /-ni/ one of two long thin things on an insect's head that it uses to feel things
➔ See picture on page A28

an•ti•bi•ot•ic /ˌæntɪbaɪ'ɑtɪk/ *noun*
a medicine that kills BACTERIA and cures infections

an•tic•i•pate /æn'tɪsəˌpeɪt/ Ac *verb, formal*
to expect that something will happen: *The team has practiced hard for the game tomorrow, so I do not anticipate any problems.*
—**anticipation** /ænˌtɪsə'peɪʃən/ *noun* the idea or feeling you have when you expect

something to happen: *The audience waited for the singer with great anticipation.*

an·ti·freeze /ˈæntɪˌfriz/ *noun*
a substance that is put in the water in car engines to stop it from freezing

an·ti·his·ta·mine /ˌæntɪˈhɪstəˌmin/ *noun*
a medicine that is used to treat an ALLERGY (=a bad physical reaction to a substance): *I take antihistamines to help me stop sneezing.*

an·ti·per·spi·rant /ˌæntɪˈpɚspərənt/ *noun*
a substance that you put under your arms to stop you from SWEATing

an·tique /ˌænˈtik/ *noun*
an old piece of furniture or other object that is usually valuable: *His house was full of beautiful antiques and old paintings.*
—**antique** *adjective*: *antique furniture*
➔ See Thesaurus box at **old**

antique

an·ti·sep·tic /ˌæntɪˈseptɪk/ *noun*
a chemical substance that is put on a wound to prevent it from becoming infected: *The hospital smelled like antiseptic.*
—**antiseptic** *adjective* helping to prevent infection: *an antiseptic cream*

ant·ler /ˈæntlɚ/ *noun*
one of the horns that look like tree branches which animals such as DEER have

an·to·nym /ˈæntəˌnɪm/ *noun*, *formal*
a word that means the opposite of another word: *"Long" is an antonym of "short."* ANTONYM **synonym**

anx·i·e·ty /æŋˈzaɪəti/ *noun*, *formal*
a strong feeling of worry about something: *There is a lot of anxiety about final exams, which start next week.* SYNONYM **worry**

anx·ious /ˈæŋkʃəs/ *adjective*, *formal*
1 very worried about something: *She was anxious about her baby being sick.* SYNONYM **worried**
2 feeling strongly that you want to do something or want something to happen: *I was anxious to know if she had won the race.* SYNONYM **eager**
—**anxiously** *adverb*: *They waited anxiously for news.*
➔ See Thesaurus box at **worried**

an·y¹ /ˈeni/ *adjective*, *pronoun*
1 some – used in questions and negative statements: *Is there any ice cream left?* | *I don't have any friends at school. No one talks to me.* | *I haven't read any of his books.*

> **GRAMMAR: any**
>
> **any, a**
>
> Use **any** with nouns that you cannot count or nouns that show that there is more than one thing: *Do you have any money?* | *There weren't any books that I wanted to read.*
>
> Use **a** when there is only one thing: *Do you have a car?*
> ➔ **a**

2 used when something is true about every thing or person in a group: *You can buy it at any book store.* | *Any of these women could do the job – just pick one.*

any² *adverb*
even a small amount – used in questions and negative statements: *Are you feeling any better?* | *She couldn't walk any farther.*

an·y·bod·y /ˈeniˌbɑdi/ *pronoun*, *informal*
another word for ANYONE

an·y·how /ˈeniˌhaʊ/ *adverb*, *informal*
another word for ANYWAY

an·y·more *also* **any more** /ˌeniˈmɔr/ *adverb*
not anymore = used to say that something that happened or was true does not happen now or is not true now: *He doesn't work here anymore. He quit last month.*

an·y·one /ˈeniˌwʌn/ *pronoun*
1 someone or a person – used in questions and negative statements: *I didn't know anyone was in here.* | *Is anyone else* (=any other person) *coming?*

A

GRAMMAR: anyone

someone, anyone

In questions and sentences with "not" in them, we usually use **anyone** and not **someone**: *Have you told anyone about this?* | *I didn't see anyone there.*

In other sentences, we use **someone**: *There's someone here to see you.*

2 any person, it does not matter who: *The game is so simple that anyone can play it.*

an•y•place /ˈeniˌpleɪs/ *adverb*, *informal*
another word for ANYWHERE

an•y•thing /ˈeniˌθɪŋ/ *pronoun*
1 something or a thing – used in questions and negative statements: *We don't know anything about her.* | *Do you need anything else* (=any other thing)*?*

GRAMMAR: anything

something, anything

In questions and sentences with "not" in them, we usually use **anything** and not **something**: *Did you see anything you liked?* | *I didn't have anything to eat.*

If you are offering someone some food, a drink, etc., it sounds more polite to use **something**: *Would you like something to eat?*

2 used when you are saying that someone does not care which thing they choose, use, etc.: *My dog will eat anything, so I have to keep him away from harmful things.*
3 or anything *informal* = or something else of the same kind: *I hope it isn't cancer or anything.*

an•y•time *also* **any time** /ˈeniˌtaɪm/ *adverb*
at any time: *You can call me anytime. Don't worry if it's too late or too early.*

an•y•way /ˈeniˌweɪ/ *adverb*
1 in spite of something: *It's probably not serious, but you should see a doctor anyway.*
2 used to change the subject of a conversation, or return to the main subject or story: *Anyway, where do you want to go for lunch?*
3 used when you are mentioning a more important fact: *I haven't been invited to the party, but I didn't want to go anyway.*
4 used when you are adding something that limits what you have said: *I can't help you. Not right now, anyway.*

an•y•where /ˈeniˌwer/ *adverb*
1 in or to any place: *I can't find my keys anywhere – I've looked all over the house.* | *Have you been anywhere else* (=to any other place)*?* | *You can go anywhere you want in the building.*

GRAMMAR: anywhere

somewhere, anywhere

In questions and sentences with "not" in them, we usually use **anywhere** and not **somewhere**: *I haven't seen it anywhere.*

In other sentences, we use **somewhere**: *He lives somewhere near here.*

2 anywhere from one to ten, etc. = between one and ten, etc.: *These trips lasted anywhere from one to three days.*

a•part /əˈpɑrt/ *adverb*
1 separated by distance or time: *The two cities are six miles apart.* | *Our birthdays are only two days apart.*
2 separated into many pieces: *He had to take the camera apart to fix it.* | *The plane's left engine began to come apart.*
→ **fall apart** at **fall**[1]
3 apart from someone or something = besides or except for something: *Apart from one terrible singer, the concert was excellent.*

a•part•ment /əˈpɑrtmənt/ *noun*
a place to live that consists of a set of rooms in a large building: *She lives in a one-bedroom apartment.* | *a large apartment building* (=building containing apartments)

ap•a•thy /ˈæpəθi/ *noun*, *formal*
the feeling of not being interested in something or not caring enough about something to take action: *There is a lot of apathy among young people about the election – no one really cares.*
—**apathetic** /ˌæpəˈθətɪk/ *adjective*, *formal*
not interested in something or not caring about something

ape /eɪp/ *noun*
a large animal like a monkey but with no tail or a very short tail: *Gorillas and chimpanzees are apes.*

a•piece /əˈpis/ *adverb*
for each: *The apples are 25 cents apiece.* SYNONYM **each**

A

a•pol•o•gize /ə'pɑlə,dʒaɪz/ *verb*
to say that you are sorry about something that you have done: *He apologized for being late.* | *She was very upset. I think you should apologize to her.*
—**apologetic** /ə,pɑlə'dʒetɪk/ *adjective, formal* saying or showing that you are sorry about something: *When I showed them the mistake, they were very apologetic.*

a•pol•o•gy /ə'pɑlədʒi/ *noun* plural **apologies**
something that you say or write to show that you are sorry about something that you have done: *The senator made a public apology for his mistakes.* | *She lied to me. I think she owes me an apology.*

WORD FAMILY look at the words:
→ **apology** *noun*
→ **apologize** *verb*
→ **apologetic** *adjective*

a•pos•tro•phe /ə'pɑstrəfi/ *noun*
the mark ', which is used to show that letters or figures have been left out, or used with "s" to show that something belongs to or is connected with someone: *don't* (=do not) | *'96* (=1896/1996, etc.) | *Sarah's book* (=the book that belongs to Sarah)

ap•palled /ə'pɔld/ *adjective*
very shocked and upset: *The boy's mother was appalled at the violence he was watching on TV.*

ap•pa•rat•us /,æpə'rætəs/ *noun* plural **apparatus** or **apparatuses** *formal*
tools or equipment used for a particular purpose, especially for something scientific or technical: *The divers are using a new apparatus for breathing under water.*

ap•par•ent /ə'pærənt/ Ac *adjective*
1 easily seen or understood: *He was having trouble breathing, and it was apparent that he needed medical help.* SYNONYM **clear, obvious**
2 seeming to be true or real: *She was upset by his apparent lack of sympathy.*

ap•par•ent•ly /ə'pærəntli/ Ac *adverb*
used when mentioning something that you have heard is true, although you are not completely sure about it: *He was late for school today. Apparently, he overslept.*

ap•peal[1] /ə'pil/ *verb*
1 *formal* to ask someone, especially the public, for money, help, information, etc.: *The organization is appealing for money to help the earthquake victims.* | *City officials appealed to everyone to use less water because supplies were low.*
2 to formally ask a more important court to change a decision that a less important court made: *His lawyers appealed the court's decision.*

PHRASAL VERB
appeal to someone
to seem attractive or interesting to someone: *The idea of going to college did not appeal to him. He wanted to get a job instead.*

appeal[2] *noun*
1 *formal* a strong request for money, help, information, etc. to the public or other group of people: *The teachers made an appeal to parents for money and help.*
2 the act of asking a more important court to change a decision that a less important court has made: *His appeal of the court's decision was unsuccessful.*
3 the quality that makes you like something: *The band's music has a lot of appeal for young people.*

ap•peal•ing /ə'pilɪŋ/ *adjective*
attractive or interesting: *They try to make their products appealing to kids by using cartoon characters and bright colors.*

ap•pear /ə'pɪr/ *verb*
1 to seem: *The man appeared to be asleep.* | *She appeared nervous.*
2 to begin to be seen: *A face appeared at the window.*
3 to take part in a movie, television program, play, etc.: *He appeared in several horror movies.*

WORD FAMILY look at the words:
→ **appear** *verb*
→ **disappear** *verb*
→ **appearance** *noun*
→ **disappearance** *noun*

→ See Thesaurus box at **seem**

ap•pear•ance /ə'pɪrəns/ *noun*
1 the way someone or something looks to other people: *Don't try and change your appearance – you look great.*
2 a time when someone or something

arrives somewhere or when you can see someone or something in a place: *This was his first appearance in court.*

ap•pen•di•ci•tis /əˌpendəˈsaɪtɪs/ *noun*
an illness in which your appendix gets bigger, becomes painful, and often has to be taken out

ap•pen•dix /əˈpendɪks/ Ac *noun*
1 a small closed tube that is part of your BOWEL which can become swollen and painful: *He had an operation to take out his appendix.*
2 plural **appendixes** or **appendices** /-dɪsiz/ a part at the end of a book that has additional information: *There is an appendix at the back of the book with a list of other books on this subject.*

ap•pe•tite /ˈæpəˌtaɪt/ *noun*
the feeling that you want to eat something: *When I was sick, I lost my appetite and hardly ate anything.*

ap•plaud /əˈplɔd/ *verb, formal*
to hit your hands together many times, for example to show that you enjoyed a play, concert, speech, etc.: *When she finished the song, the audience applauded for a long time.*
SYNONYM **clap**

ap•plause /əˈplɔz/ *noun*
the sound of people hitting their hands together many times to show that they enjoyed something or think someone is good: *The team gave Ted a round of applause* (=they applauded for a short time).

ap•ple /ˈæpəl/ *noun*
a hard round red or green fruit that is white inside: *apple pie* | *an apple tree*
➔ See picture on page A13

ap•ple•sauce /ˈæpəlˌsɔs/ *noun*
a thick smooth food made from cooked apples

ap•pli•ance /əˈplaɪəns/ *noun*
a piece of electrical equipment such as a REFRIGERATOR or a DISHWASHER that is used in someone's home: *kitchen appliances*
➔ See Thesaurus box at **machine**[1]

ap•pli•ca•tion /ˌæplɪˈkeɪʃən/ *noun*
1 a formal written request for a job, a place at a college, etc.: *a job application* | *Please fill out an application if you are interested in the class.* | *The club president gave me an application for membership.* | *I sent in my application form for the M.A. program.*
2 a piece of SOFTWARE: *My computer can run almost any application.*

ap•ply /əˈplaɪ/ *verb* **applied**, third person singular **applies**
1 to formally ask for something in writing, such as a job or a chance to go to a college: *Fifteen people applied for the job.* | *He applied to law school.*
2 to affect or be true for a particular person or thing: *The rules apply to every student at this school.*
3 *formal* to spread something such as paint on a surface: *She applied her lipstick.*
—**applicant** /ˈæplɪkənt/ *noun* someone who is applying for a job, the chance to go to a college, etc.

WORD FAMILY look at the words:
➔ **apply** *verb*
➔ **application** *noun*
➔ **applicant** *noun*

ap•point /əˈpɔɪnt/ *verb*
to choose someone for a job or position: *She was appointed to the position by the president.* | *He appointed John Mason as chairman.*

ap•point•ment /əˈpɔɪntmənt/ *noun*
1 a meeting that has been arranged for a particular time and place: *I'd like to make an appointment with Dr. Hanson on Tuesday.* | *I have an appointment at six.*
2 the act of choosing someone for a job or position: *the appointment of a new Supreme Court Justice*

ap•pre•ci•ate /əˈpriʃiˌeɪt/ Ac *verb*
1 to be grateful for something: *We really appreciate your help.* | *Thanks for meeting with me. I appreciate it.*
2 *formal* to understand a situation or problem: *I appreciate that learning a new language quickly is very difficult.*
WORD FAMILY ➔ **appreciation** *noun*

A

ap•pre•ci•a•tion /əˌpriʃiˈeɪʃən/ Ac *noun*
the feeling of being grateful for something: *They showed their appreciation for her support by giving her a gift.*

ap•pren•tice /əˈprentɪs/ *noun*
someone who is learning how to do a job such as being a MECHANIC or a PLUMBER, by doing the job with someone who teaches him or her how to do it: *He started as an apprentice and in time became a skilled mechanic.*

ap•proach[1] /əˈproʊtʃ/ Ac *verb*
1 to move closer to someone or something: *A woman approached me in the street to ask me a question.*
2 if something is approaching, it will happen soon: *Winter was approaching and the weather was getting colder.*

approach[2] *noun*
a way of dealing with a problem or a difficult situation: *We need a new approach to the way we teach math. Our old ways of teaching it aren't working.*

ap•pro•pri•ate /əˈproʊpriɪt/ Ac *adjective*
correct or good for a particular person, situation, time, etc.: *Is the movie appropriate for young children?* | *It is not appropriate to call someone just after a funeral.* ANTONYM **inappropriate**
—**appropriately** *adverb*

ap•prov•al /əˈpruvəl/ *noun*
1 official permission: *The teacher gave his approval to the students' plans for their science project and told them to get started.*
2 the belief that someone or something is good or is doing something right: *She tried very hard to win her parents' approval* (=make her parents like her and praise her).

ap•prove /əˈpruv/ *verb*
1 to think that something or someone is good or right: *Do her parents approve of her new boyfriend?* ANTONYM **disapprove**
2 to give official permission for something: *The plan was approved by California voters.*

ap•prox•i•mate•ly /əˈprɑksəmətli/ Ac *adverb*
used when saying that a number or amount is not exact: *The plane will land in approximately 20 minutes.*
—**approximate** *adjective* not exact
➔ See Thesaurus box at **about**

ap•ri•cot /ˈeɪprɪˌkɑt/ *noun*
a small soft yellow-orange fruit with a single large seed
➔ See picture on page A13

A•pril /ˈeɪprəl/ *noun, written abbreviation* **Apr.**
the fourth month of the year, between March and May: *Lucy's birthday is on April 5th.* | *The flowers start to bloom in April.* | *We went to California last April.* | *We're going to see my aunt next April.*

a•pron /ˈeɪprən/ *noun*
a piece of clothing that you wear over your other clothes in order to keep them clean, especially when you are cooking

ap•ti•tude /ˈæptəˌtud/ *noun, formal*
a natural ability that makes you good at learning how to do something: *I didn't play football in high school, because I never had much aptitude for sports.*

aquarium

a•quar•i•um /əˈkweriəm/ *noun*
1 a glass container for keeping fish in
2 a building where people go to look at fish or other water animals

A•quar•i•us /əˈkweriəs/ *noun*
1 the 11th sign of the ZODIAC, represented by someone carrying water
2 someone born between January 20 and February 18

Ar•ab /ˈærəb/ *adjective*
from the Middle East or North Africa: *a group of Arab women*
—**Arab** *noun* someone from the Middle East or North Africa

Ar•a•bic /ˈærəbɪk/ *noun*
the language spoken in the Middle East and North Africa

A

ar•bi•trar•y /ˈɑrbəˌtreri/ Ac *adjective*
decided without any reason or planning, in a way that seems unfair or wrong: *The principal should not make arbitrary decisions. We expect him to have good reasons for his actions.*

arc /ɑrk/ *noun*
a curved line, especially one that forms part of a circle: *The sun moves across the sky in a big arc.*

ar•cade /ɑrˈkeɪd/ *noun*
a special room or small building where people go to play VIDEO GAMEs

arch /ɑrtʃ/ *noun* plural **arches**
a curved shape at the top of a door, window, bridge, etc.: *The roof of the church was supported by huge arches.*

ar•chae•ol•o•gy *also* **archeology** /ˌɑrkiˈɑlədʒi/ *noun*
the study of ancient societies, by looking at bones, tools, and other objects that have been buried in the ground for a long time
—**archaeologist** *noun* someone who studies ancient societies, by looking at the remains of bones, tools, and other objects: *Archaeologists are still digging in parts of the old city.*
—**archaeological** /ˌɑrkiəˈlɑdʒɪkəl/ *adjective* relating to archaeology

ar•chi•tect /ˈɑrkəˌtekt/ *noun*
someone whose job is to design buildings: *My brother wants to be an architect – he's always loved to draw buildings.*

ar•chi•tec•ture /ˈɑrkəˌtektʃɚ/ *noun*
the style and design of a building or buildings: *The city is famous for its architecture. Many of its buildings are well-known around the world.*

Arc•tic /ˈɑrktɪk/ *noun*
the Arctic = the most northern part of the Earth, including parts of Alaska and Greenland, and the Arctic Ocean

are /ɚ; *strong* ɑr/ *verb*
the present tense plural of BE

ar•e•a /ˈeriə/ Ac *noun*
1 a particular part of a place, city, country, building, etc.: *There are many computer companies in the Seattle area* (=in the part of the U.S. near Seattle). | *This is the dining area* (=the part of a building where people eat).

THESAURUS: area

region a large area of a country or the world: *the northwest region of Russia*
zone an area that is different in a particular way from the areas around it: *a no-parking zone*
district a particular area of a city or the country: *San Francisco's Mission District*
neighborhood an area of a town where people live: *a friendly neighborhood*
suburb an area outside the center of a city where people live: *a suburb of Boston*

2 a subject or part of a subject: *The two scientists were involved in very different areas of research.*
3 the size of a flat surface or shape: *You measure the area of a room by multiplying the length by the width.*

ˈarea ˌcode *noun*
in the U.S. and Canada, the three numbers before a telephone number that you use to call someone who lives outside your local area

a•re•na /əˈrinə/ *noun*
a large building used for watching sports games, listening to concerts, or other events: *Hundreds of people were waiting to enter the sports arena for the game.*

aren't /ˈɑrənt/ *verb*
1 the short form of "are not": *They aren't coming to the party.*
2 the short form of "am not", used in questions: *I'm next, aren't I?*

ar•gue /ˈɑrgyu/ *verb*
to disagree with someone, usually by talking or shouting in an angry way: *My parents were always arguing with each other.* | *We used to stay up late arguing about politics.*

THESAURUS: argue

argue or **have an argument**: *My parents were arguing about money.* | *We've had arguments before, but they've never been very serious.*
fight or **have a fight** *informal* to argue with someone: *My brothers are always fighting.* | *The neighbors had a huge fight.*

A

WORD FAMILY look at the words:
→ **argue** *verb*
→ **argument** *noun*
→ **argumentative** *adjective*

ar•gu•ment /ˈɑrgyəmənt/ *noun*
1 a disagreement, especially one in which people are angry and shout: *I had an argument with my mom last night about getting home late.*
2 a reason or set of reasons that you give to support an opinion: *We had to write a paper about the arguments for and against the death penalty* (=the reasons why you think it is a good or a bad system).

ar•gu•men•ta•tive /ˌɑrgyəˈmentətɪv/ *adjective, formal*
someone who is argumentative often argues with people: *He is very argumentative in class and it makes the other students uncomfortable.*

ar•id /ˈærɪd/ *adjective, formal*
getting very little rain, and therefore very dry: *the hot, arid regions of Central Africa*

Ar•ies /ˈeriz/ *noun*
1 the first sign of the ZODIAC, represented by a RAM
2 someone born between March 21 and April 19

a•rise /əˈraɪz/ *verb* **arose** /əˈroʊz/ **arisen** /əˈrɪzən/ **arising** *formal*
to happen or appear: *Some difficult questions arose during the meeting.*

a•rith•me•tic /əˈrɪθmətɪk/ *noun*
the science of numbers involving adding, dividing, multiplying, etc.

arm¹ /ɑrm/ *noun*
1 the part of your body between your shoulder and your hand: *The nurse stuck the needle into his arm. | She held the baby in her arms.*
2 the part of a chair, SOFA, etc. that you rest your arms on: *I put my drink on the arm of the chair.*
→ **arms**
→ See picture on page A2

arm² *verb*
to provide someone with weapons: *The money is being used to arm terrorist groups.*

ar•ma•dil•lo /ˌɑrməˈdɪloʊ/ *noun*
a small animal with a pointed nose and a hard shell that lives in hot dry parts of North and South America

arm•chair /ˈɑrmtʃer/ *noun*
a chair with sides that you can rest your arms on
→ See picture at **seat**

armed /ɑrmd/ *adjective*
having a weapon: *An armed policeman guarded the door.*

armed ˈforces *plural noun*
a country's army, navy, air force, etc.: *the Canadian armed forces*

ar•mor /ˈɑrmɚ/ *noun*
a cover that protects a person or a vehicle from attack: *The soldiers were wearing body armor to protect themselves from bullets.*
—**armored** *adjective* having armor: *an armored truck*

arm•pit /ˈɑrmˌpɪt/ *noun*
the hollow place under your arm where it joins your body

arms /ɑrmz/ *plural noun*
weapons such as guns and bombs: *He ordered the men to put down their arms.*

ar•my /ˈɑrmi/ *noun* plural **armies**
a military force that fights wars on land: *My father was in the army. | After high school she joined the army* (=became a member of the army).

a•ro•ma /əˈroʊmə/ *noun, formal*
a strong pleasant smell: *I could smell the delicious aroma of fresh coffee.*
—**aromatic** /ˌærəˈmætɪk/ *adjective, formal* having a strong pleasant smell
→ See Thesaurus box at **smell¹**

a•rose /əˈroʊz/ *verb*
the past tense of ARISE

a•round /əˈraʊnd/ *adverb, preposition*
1 surrounding something or someone: *He put his arms around her. | There is a high fence all around the prison.*
2 in or to many parts of a place: *They walked around the old part of the city.*
3 in or near a particular place: *Is there a bank around here?*
4 in a circular movement: *The earth goes around the sun.*
5 used when saying that a number, amount,

A

or time is not exact: *We got back home around 10 o'clock.* SYNONYM **about**

6 in the opposite direction: *I need to turn the car around and go back the other way.*

➔ See Thesaurus box at **about**

a·rouse /ə'raʊz/ *verb, formal*

to make someone have a particular feeling: *Her strange behavior aroused the suspicions of the police* (=made them think something was wrong).

ar·range /ə'reɪndʒ/ *verb*

1 to put a group of things or people in a particular order or position: *She arranged the flowers in the vase.*

2 *formal* to make plans to do something: *We arranged to meet outside the restaurant.*

ar·range·ment /ə'reɪndʒmənt/ *noun*

the things that you do in order to prepare for something to happen: *We have to make all the arrangements for the party – I'll buy the food and drinks, and you reserve the room and get the decorations.*

ar·rest /ə'rest/ *verb*

if the police arrest someone, they take the person away because the police think that he or she has done something illegal: *The police arrested him and charged him with murder.*

—**arrest** *noun* a situation in which the police stop someone and take him or her away: *After his arrest, the officers took him to the police station.*

ar·riv·al /ə'raɪvəl/ *noun*

1 the act of arriving somewhere: *Soon after his arrival in New York he got a job on a newspaper.* ANTONYM **departure**

2 a person or thing that has arrived recently: *The principal welcomed the new arrivals to the school.*

ar·rive /ə'raɪv/ *verb*

to get to a place: *What time does the plane arrive in Chicago?* | *The letter arrived yesterday and I read it immediately.*

THESAURUS: arrive

get to *informal* to arrive at a particular place: *What time will you get to Atlanta?*

reach to arrive at a particular place: *The climbers reached the top of Mt. Everest.*

come if someone comes, he or she arrives at the place where you are: *She came home yesterday.*

turn up also **show up** to arrive somewhere – used when someone is waiting for you: *Lee turned up an hour late for the meeting.*

land to arrive somewhere in an airplane or boat: *Marie's flight landed at 10:15.*

ar·ro·gance /'ærəgəns/ *noun*

a rude and unfriendly attitude that shows that a person thinks that he or she is better than other people: *She hated his arrogance and the disrespect he showed for other people.*

ar·ro·gant /'ærəgənt/ *adjective*

behaving in a rude and unfriendly way because you think that you are more important than other people: *He was an arrogant young man who never listened to other people's advice.*

—**arrogantly** *adverb*

➔ See Thesaurus box at **proud**

ar·row /'æroʊ/ *noun*

a long thin piece of wood or metal, with a point at one end and feathers at the other end, that you shoot from a BOW

ar·son /'ɑrsən/ *noun*

the crime of deliberately making a building start burning

art /ɑrt/ *noun*

1 things such as paintings, drawings, or photographs, that are created for people to look at and enjoy: *Several famous works of art were stolen from the museum.* | *Do you like modern art?*

THESAURUS: art

Types of Art

painting a picture that you make using paint

drawing a picture that you make using a pen or pencil

photograph a picture that you take using a camera

sculpture an object that you make out of stone, wood, or clay

2 the activity of creating paintings, drawings, etc. for people to look at and enjoy: *She's studied art in college.*

3 the arts = painting, music, literature, etc., all considered together

A

WORD FAMILY look at the words:

➔ **art** *noun*
➔ **artist** *noun*
➔ **artistic** *adjective*

ar•ter•y /'ɑrtəri/ *noun* plural **arteries**
one of the tubes that carries blood from your heart to the rest of your body: *Your arteries will become blocked if you eat too much fatty food.*

ar•thri•tis /ɑr'θraɪtɪs/ *noun*
a disease that causes pain and swelling in the joints of your body: *My grandmother has arthritis in her knees, and she finds it hard to walk.*

ar•ti•choke /'ɑrtɪˌtʃoʊk/ *noun*
a round green vegetable with short thick pointed leaves
➔ See picture on page A12

ar•ti•cle /'ɑrtɪkəl/ *noun*
1 a piece of writing in a newspaper, magazine, etc.: *I read an article on him in "Time Magazine."*
2 a thing, especially one of a group of things: *The police found several articles of clothing in the bushes.*
3 in grammar, the word "the" is called "the definite article," and "a" or "an" is called "the indefinite article"
➔ See Thesaurus box at **thing**

ar•ti•fi•cial /ˌɑrtə'fɪʃəl/ *adjective*
not real or natural, but made by people: *Many foods contain artificial coloring.* | *She has an artificial leg.*
—**artificially** *adverb*

art•ist /'ɑrtɪst/ *noun*
someone who produces art: *Picasso was an amazing painter and one of the world's greatest artists.*
➔ See picture on page A16

ar•tis•tic /ɑr'tɪstɪk/ *adjective*
1 good at making art: *My sister's very artistic – she is especially good at drawing.*
2 relating to art: *The country has a long cultural and artistic history.*

as /əz; *strong* æz/ *adverb, preposition, conjunction*
1 as... as = used to compare people or things: *I'm not as old as you.* | *This one is just as good as the other one.*
2 used to say what someone's job is, or what something is used for: *She works as a teacher.* | *We can use this box as a table.*
3 while something is happening: *The phone rang just as I was leaving.*
4 as if/as though = used when you are saying how someone or something seems: *Her eyes were red and she looked as if she had been crying.*
5 *formal* because: *He decided not to go out, as it was already late.* SYNONYM **since**

ASAP *also* **a.s.a.p.** *adverb, informal*
as soon as possible: *Finish your classwork ASAP.*

as•cend /ə'send/ *verb, formal*
to go up higher: *The plane ascended into the clouds.* SYNONYM **rise**; ANTONYM **descend**
—**ascent** *noun, formal* the act of going up higher: *The ascent of the mountain took six hours.*

ash /æʃ/ *noun*
the gray powder that is left after something has burned: *A cloud of smoke and ash rose up from the burning building.*

a•shamed /ə'ʃeɪmd/ *adjective*
if you are ashamed, you feel guilty about something you have done: *I felt ashamed that I had been so mean.* | *Ben had lied to her, and he was ashamed of himself* (=ashamed of his behavior).

a•shore /ə'ʃɔr/ *adverb, formal*
onto the land beside the ocean or a lake: *The ship stopped in Miami, and we all went ashore.*

ash•tray /'æʃtreɪ/ *noun*
a small dish that you use for cigarette ASHes, when you are smoking

A•sia /'eɪʒə/ *noun*
one of the seven CONTINENTs, with countries such as China, Russia, India, Pakistan, and Saudi Arabia in it

A•sian /'eɪʒən/ *adjective*
from Asia, especially East Asia: *an Asian woman*
—**Asian** *noun* someone from Asia

a•side /ə'saɪd/ *adverb*
to one side: *Jack stepped aside so I could pass.* | *Remove the meat from the pan and set it aside.*

ask /æsk/ *verb*
1 to say something that is a question, in order to get information, help, etc.: *"What's*

A

your name?" she asked. | *Can I ask a question?* | *Why don't you ask your teacher for help?* | *If you need anything, just ask.*

THESAURUS: ask

order to ask for food or drinks in a restaurant: *Dave ordered a hamburger.*

demand to ask for something in a strong or angry way: *He demanded to be paid for the hours he had worked.*

request *formal* to ask for something officially or in a polite way: *Visitors are requested not to smoke in the hospital.*

beg to ask for something that you want very much, often when you ask many times: *"Please can I have one?" she begged.*

question if the police question someone, they ask them a lot of questions in order to get information: *The police questioned two men about the robbery.*

2 to invite someone to go somewhere: *If I ask Tracy to the party, do you think she'll go with me?*

a•sleep /ə'slip/ *adjective*
sleeping: *The kids are already asleep, so don't make a lot of noise.* | *I was so tired that I fell asleep* (=started sleeping) *after dinner.* ANTONYM **awake**

as•par•a•gus /ə'spærəgəs/ *noun*
a long thin green vegetable with a pointed top
→ See picture on page A12

as•pect /'æspekt/ Ac *noun, formal*
one of the parts of a situation or problem: *Learning to write clearly is an important aspect of the class.*

as•phalt /'æsˌfɔlt/ *noun*
a hard black substance used for covering roads

as•pirin /'æsprɪn/ *noun* plural **aspirins** or **aspirin**
a medicine that makes you feel less pain: *If you have a headache, take an aspirin.*

ass /æs/ *noun*
a type of DONKEY

as•sas•sin /ə'sæsən/ *noun*
someone who kills an important person

as•sas•si•nate /ə'sæsəˌneɪt/ *verb*
to kill an important person: *President Lincoln was assassinated by a man who was angry that the South had lost the Civil War.*
—**assassination** /əˌsæsə'neɪʃən/ *noun* the act of killing an important person: *the assassination of Martin Luther King Jr.*
→ See Thesaurus box at **kill**

as•sault /ə'sɔlt/ *verb, formal*
to attack and hurt someone: *He was arrested for assaulting a police officer.* SYNONYM **attack**
—**assault** *noun, formal* an act of assaulting someone: *She had to go to the hospital after she was injured in an assault downtown.*
→ See Thesaurus box at **crime**

as•sem•ble /ə'sembəl/ Ac *verb*
1 to put the different parts of something together: *This picture shows you how to assemble the bed.* SYNONYM **put together**
2 if people assemble, they come together in a group: *All the students assembled in front of the school.*

as•sem•bly /ə'sembli/ Ac *noun* plural **assemblies**
1 a meeting of a large group of people: *I had to give a talk during a school assembly.*
2 *formal* the process of putting something together: *The instructions make assembly of the table easy.*

as•ser•tive /ə'sɚtɪv/ *adjective, formal*
if you are assertive, you act in a confident way and say what you think: *We try to teach our students to be assertive in a group and state their opinions openly.*
—**assertively** *adverb*
—**assertiveness** *noun*

as•sess /ə'ses/ Ac *verb, formal*
to make a judgment about a person or situation: *The teacher must assess each child's progress and write a report for the parents.*
—**assessment** *noun* the judgment that you make about a person or situation: *What's your assessment of the problem?*

as•set /'æset/ *noun*
someone or something that helps you to be successful: *Craig is an asset to the company, and I think we should be paying him more.*

A

as•sign /ə'saɪn/ Ac *verb*
to give someone a job to do: *The soldiers were assigned to guard the bank.*

as•sign•ment /ə'saɪnmənt/ Ac *noun*
a piece of work that someone has told you to do: *Did the teacher give you a homework assignment* (=school work to do at home)? | *The reporter was on assignment in China* (=doing some work there).

as•sist /ə'sɪst/ Ac *verb, formal*
to help someone do something: *You can take extra classes to assist you in improving your English.* SYNONYM **help**

as•sist•ance /ə'sɪstəns/ Ac *noun, formal*
help for someone: *The government gives financial assistance* (=help with money) *to students who do not have enough money for college.* | *Can I be of any assistance* (=can I help you)? SYNONYM **help**

as•sist•ant /ə'sɪstənt/ Ac *noun*
someone whose job is to help a more important person with their work: *The managers have assistants to make appointments for them.*

as•so•ci•ate¹ /ə'soʊʃiˌeɪt/ *verb, formal*
1 to make a connection between two things or ideas in your mind: *My grandfather died when I was away in California, so I'll always associate California with feeling sad.*
2 to spend time with someone, either because you work in the same place or because you are friends with him or her: *When he went to New York, he began associating with artists and writers.*

as•so•ci•ate² /ə'soʊʃiɪt/ *noun, formal*
someone that you work with: *The research was done by Professor Gray and his associates.* | *a business associate* (=someone you do business with)

asˌsociate de'gree *noun*
a DEGREE that you can get after two years of study at a college in the U.S.

as•so•ci•a•tion /əˌsoʊsi'eɪʃən/ *noun*
an organization of people who do the same type of work or are similar in another way: *the International Association of Firefighters*

as•sort•ed /ə'sɔrtɪd/ *adjective*
of various different types: *I got a bag of assorted candy because I wanted to have a variety.*

as•sume /ə'sum/ Ac *verb*
to think that something is probably true: *I assumed that they were sisters because they look so much alike.*
—**assumption** /ə'sʌmpʃən/ *noun, formal* the act of assuming that something is true

as•sure /ə'ʃʊr/ Ac *verb, formal*
to tell someone something in order to take away any doubts he or she has: *The doctor assured me that I was fine and that I didn't need to worry.*
—**assurance** *noun* something that someone tells you to take away any doubts that you have

as•ter•isk /'æstərɪsk/ *noun*
a mark like a star (*), used in writing. It usually shows that there is more information at the bottom of the page or in another place.

asth•ma /'æzmə/ *noun*
a medical problem that sometimes makes it difficult to breathe normally
—**asthmatic** /æz'mætɪk/ *adjective* having asthma or relating to asthma: *My son is asthmatic so he has trouble running long distances.*

as•ton•ish /ə'stɑnɪʃ/ *verb*
to surprise someone very much: *The team's win astonished everyone – no one expected it.*
—**astonished** *adjective* very surprised: *We were astonished by the mean things he said.*
—**astonishing** *adjective* very surprising

as•ton•ish•ment /ə'stɑnɪʃmənt/ *noun, formal*
great surprise: *Ken looked at her in astonishment when she took off her wig.*

as•trol•o•gy /ə'strɑlədʒi/ *noun*
the study of how the position of the stars and PLANETs may affect people's lives
—**astrologer** *noun* someone who tells people how astrology might affect their lives

as•tro•naut /'æstrəˌnɔt/ *noun*
someone who travels in space: *There were three astronauts living on the space station.*

as•tron•o•my /ə'strɑnəmi/ *noun*
the science that studies stars, PLANETs, space, etc.: *Nick always liked stars, so he decided to study astronomy.*
—**astronomer** *noun* a scientist who studies astronomy

A

as·tute /ə'stut/ *adjective, formal*
able to understand things quickly: *Brandon was an astute politician and able to deal with difficult situations quickly.*
—**astutely** *adverb*

at /ət; *strong* æt/ *preposition*
1 in a particular place: *Meet me at my house.* | *John's at school but he'll be home in an hour.* | *Write your name at the top of the page.*
2 used for saying when something happens: *The movie starts at 8:00.* | *At night, the streets are empty.*
3 toward someone or something: *All the children were looking at the teacher.* | *Jake smiled at me.*
4 used for talking about the age, price, speed, etc. where something happens: *I started school at age five.* | *You shouldn't be driving at this speed* (=so fast). | *I bought these jeans at half price* (=half the normal price).
5 good/bad, etc. at something = able or not able to do something well: *Debbie is good at math, so she can figure it out for you.*
6 at lunch/dinner = not working because you are eating lunch or dinner: *I didn't answer the phone because I was at lunch when you called.*
7 used to say @, the symbol in email addresses

ate /eɪt/ *verb*
the past tense of EAT

a·the·ist /'eɪθiɪst/ *noun*
someone who does not believe that there is a god
—**atheism** *noun* the belief that there is no god

ath·lete /'æθlit/ *noun*
someone who is good at sports and often plays sports: *You can earn a lot of money as a professional athlete* (=someone who is paid to play a sport).

ath·let·ic /æθ'letɪk/ *adjective*
1 relating to sports: *Basketball is part of the school's athletic program.*
2 able to play sports very well: *Bobby was very athletic and played football, basketball, and baseball.*

At·lan·tic /ət'læntɪk/ *noun*
the Atlantic = the ocean that is between America and Europe: *The ship was sailing across the Atlantic from England to America.*

at·las /'ætləs/ *noun*
a book with maps in it: *a world atlas* (=with maps of every country in the world)

ATM *noun*
Automated Teller Machine a machine, usually in a wall, that you can use to get money from your bank

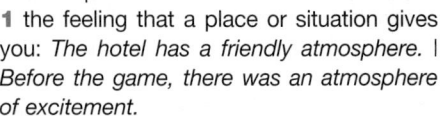

ATM

at·mos·phere /'ætməsˌfɪr/ *noun*
1 the feeling that a place or situation gives you: *The hotel has a friendly atmosphere.* | *Before the game, there was an atmosphere of excitement.*
2 the air around the Earth or another PLANET: *Most of the Earth's atmosphere is nitrogen and oxygen.*
—**atmospheric** /ˌætməs'ferɪk/ *adjective* relating to an atmosphere

at·om /'ætəm/ *noun*
the smallest part of a chemical substance that can exist alone: *Water is made of two atoms of hydrogen and one atom of oxygen.*

a·tom·ic /ə'tɑmɪk/ *adjective*
relating to atoms: *atomic particles* (=the small things that make up atoms) | *the atomic bomb* (=a very powerful bomb made by dividing atoms)

aˌtomic 'energy *also* **atomic power** *noun*
the power that comes from dividing atoms, and is used for making electricity

at·tach /ə'tætʃ/ Ac *verb*
1 to fasten one thing to another: *Please attach a photograph to your application form.*
2 be attached to someone/something = to feel that you like or love a person, animal, home, etc. that you have

attach

known for a long time: *People often get very attached to their pets.*

3 to connect a document to an email in order to send them together: *I've attached a report of the meeting.*

WORD FAMILY look at the words:

→ **attach** *verb*
→ **attachment** *noun*
→ **detach** *verb*

→ See Thesaurus box at **fasten**

at•tach•ment /ə'tætʃmənt/ Ac *noun*

1 a strong feeling that you like or love someone or something: *She felt a strong attachment to her youngest sister and was very protective of her.*

2 a document, picture, etc. that you connect to an email and send with it: *I sent the pictures as an attachment.*

at•tack¹ /ə'tæk/ *noun*

an action using violence to try and hurt someone or something: *There were two attacks on policemen in the neighborhood.*

→ **heart attack**

—**attacker** *noun* someone who attacks another person

attack² *verb*

1 to try to hurt someone: *The man attacked him with a knife.*

2 if a group such as an army attacks a place, it fights the people in it and damages buildings: *The army attacked the city from the south.*

3 to say bad things about someone or something: *All the newspapers attacked the President.* SYNONYM **criticize**

at•tain /ə'teɪn/ Ac *verb, formal*

to achieve something you want: *He finally attained his dream of becoming a U.S. citizen.*

—**attainment** *noun, formal* the act of attaining something

at•tempt¹ /ə'tempt/ *noun*

the act of trying to do something difficult or new: *Several people had made an attempt to climb the mountain and failed.* | *My first attempt at skiing did not go very well.*

attempt² *verb*

to try to do something difficult or new: *A prisoner had attempted to escape by climbing the wall.*

→ See Thesaurus box at **try¹**

at•tend /ə'tend/ *verb, formal*

1 to be at a meeting, special event, etc.: *I am not able to attend the meeting next week.*

2 attend school/college = to be a student at a school or college: *My daughter plans to attend college next Fall.*

at•tend•ance /ə'tendəns/ *noun, formal*

the act of going regularly to school, a class, a meeting, etc.: *She has a very good attendance record in this class* (=she goes to class regularly).

at•tend•ant /ə'tendənt/ *noun*

someone whose job is to take care of customers on an airplane, at a gas station, etc.: *A friendly flight attendant brought us our drinks.*

at•ten•tion /ə'tenʃən/ *noun*

1 the act of listening or looking carefully: *Now, class, I want you all to pay attention* (=listen and look). | *I was too far away, and I couldn't get the kids' attention* (=make them listen and look).

2 care or treatment that you give to someone or something: *Some of the people needed medical attention* (=treatment from a doctor).

at•ten•tive /ə'tentɪv/ *adjective*

an attentive person listens and looks carefully: *Students who are attentive have higher test scores.*

at•tic /'ætɪk/ *noun*

a space or room under the roof of a house: *There are a lot of old toys up in the attic.*

at•ti•tude /'ætəˌtud/ Ac *noun*

the way you think or feel about someone or something: *Later, my attitude toward him changed, and I began to like him more.* | *You'll work better if you have a positive attitude* (=good feeling about your work).

at•tor•ney /ə'tɚni/ *noun* plural **attorneys**

another word for a LAWYER: *My attorney advised me not to sign the contract.*

at•tract /ə'trækt/ *verb*

1 to make someone like or feel interested in something: *The TV networks are trying to*

A

attract more viewers to the show. | *I didn't want to attract attention, so I stayed very quiet.*

2 if a place or thing attracts people or animals, they go to it because it is interesting, good, etc.: *Disneyland attracts many visitors every year.*

3 be attracted to someone = to like someone in a sexual way

WORD FAMILY look at the words:

→ **attract** *verb*
→ **attraction** *noun*
→ **attractive** *adjective*
→ **unattractive** *adjective*

at•trac•tion /ə'trækʃən/ *noun*

1 the feeling of liking someone or something very much: *She felt a strong attraction to the handsome young man who had helped her.*

2 something that is interesting or fun to see or do: *The statue is one of the city's main tourist attractions* (=places that many tourists visit).

3 a quality or feature that makes you like something: *The main attraction of sailing is the feeling of freedom.*

at•trac•tive /ə'træktɪv/ *adjective*

1 pretty or nice to look at: *She's a very attractive woman, and men are always trying to meet her.* | *They live in a neat, attractive house.* ANTONYM **unattractive**

2 something that is attractive is interesting or is something that you want: *It's a very attractive offer, and I think I will probably accept it.* | *Advertising makes alcohol seem attractive to young people.* ANTONYM **unattractive**

→ See Thesaurus box at **beautiful**

a•typ•i•cal /eɪ'tɪpɪkəl/ *adjective, formal*

not typical or usual: *He was an atypical teenager who loved listening to classical music.* SYNONYM **unusual**; ANTONYM **typical**

auc•tion /'ɔkʃən/ *noun*

an event at which things are sold to the person who offers the most money: *He bid $500 for the painting at an auction.*

—**auction** *verb* to sell something at an auction

—**auctioneer** /ˌɔkʃə'nɪr/ *noun* a person whose job is to sell things at auctions

au•di•ence /'ɔdiəns/ *noun*

the people watching or listening to a play, concert, speech, etc.: *The audience stood up and clapped after she sang.* | *Several members of the audience left the theater in the middle of the play.*

au•di•o /'ɔdiou/ *adjective*

relating to recording and broadcasting sound: *The audio equipment wasn't working and we couldn't hear anything.*

au•di•o•vis•u•al /ˌɔdiou'vɪʒuəl/ *adjective*

showing and playing recorded pictures and sound: *We sell audiovisual products such as CD-ROMs.*

au•dit /'ɔdɪt/ *verb*

to officially examine a company's financial records to check that they are correct: *The company's accounts were audited last year and no problems were found.*

—**audit** *noun* an act of auditing something

—**auditor** *noun* someone who audits companies

au•di•tion /ɔ'dɪʃən/ *verb*

if a performer auditions, he or she does a short performance so that someone can decide if the performer is good enough to be in a play, show, etc.: *He auditioned for a part in the Broadway show, "Oklahoma!," but he didn't get the part.*

—**audition** *noun* an action of auditioning for something: *She had an audition for a soap commercial.*

au•di•to•ri•um /ˌɔdɪ'tɔriəm/ *noun*

a large building or room used for concerts or public meetings

Au•gust /'ɔgəst/ *noun, written abbreviation* **Aug.**

the eighth month of the year, between July and September: *My birthday is on August 19th.* | *They sold their house in August.* | *It was very hot here last August.* | *Next August, we're going to Mexico.*

aunt /ænt/ *noun*

the sister of your mother or father, or the wife of your uncle: *My favorite aunt is my Aunt Jean.*

au•then•tic /ɔ'θentɪk/ *adjective*

real: *The restaurant is owned by Mexicans and serves authentic Mexican food.* | *The painting looks like it was done by Picasso,*

A

but is it authentic?
—**authenticity** /ˌɔθən'tɪsəti/ *noun* the quality of being authentic

au·thor /'ɔθɚ/ Ac *noun*
someone who has written a book: *He is the author of three books about American history.*

au·thor·i·tar·i·an /ɔrˌθɔrə'teriən/ *adjective*
forcing people to obey strict rules: *The authoritarian government did not allow anyone to criticize the president.*

au·thor·i·ta·tive /ə'θɔrəˌteɪtɪv/ Ac *adjective*
an authoritative piece of writing is respected because the person who wrote it knows a lot about the subject: *She has written an authoritative book on China. Anyone who is truly interested in China should read it.*

au·thor·i·ty /ə'θɔrəti/ Ac *noun*
1 the power that someone has because of his or her official position: *You're not my boss – you have no authority over me.* | *He does not have the authority to fire people.*
2 the authorities = the people who are in charge of a particular place: *If you know anything about the accident, please report it to the authorities* (=tell them about it).
3 someone who knows a lot about a subject: *Dr. Ballard is an authority on politics in Russia.*

au·thor·ize /'ɔθəˌraɪz/ *verb*
to give official permission for something: *I have not been authorized to give you any information. You'll have to talk to my supervisor.*
—**authorization** /ˌɔθərə'zeɪʃən/ *noun* official permission to do something: *You'll need authorization from the principal to do that.*

au·to /'ɔtoʊ/ *adjective*
relating to cars: *the auto industry* (=all the companies that make cars)

au·to·bi·og·ra·phy /ˌɔtəbaɪ'ɑgrəfi/ *noun* plural **autobiographies**
a book that someone writes about his or her own life: *She has described her unhappy childhood in her autobiography.*
—**autobiographical** /ˌɔtəbaɪə'græfɪkəl/ *adjective* relating to autobiographies

au·to·graph /'ɔtəˌgræf/ *noun*
a famous person's name, written by him or her: *A fan came up and asked for the singer's autograph.*
—**autograph** *verb* to write your autograph on something

au·to·mat·ed /'ɔtəˌmeɪtɪd/ Ac *adjective*
using machines to do a job, rather than people: *The factory is almost completely automated, and there are not many people working there now.*
—**automation** /ˌɔtə'meɪʃən/ *noun* the use of machines to do a job, rather than people

au·to·mat·ic /ˌɔtə'mætɪk/ Ac *adjective*
1 an automatic machine works by itself after being started: *When the fire started, an automatic alarm system made the train stop.*
2 done without thinking: *Her scream was an automatic response to the shocking picture.*

au·to·mat·i·cally /ˌɔtə'mætɪkli/ *adverb*
1 without thinking: *She automatically assumed that he was poor because his clothes were old and dirty.*
2 if a machine does something automatically, it does it without being operated by someone: *The doors opened automatically as we walked into the building.*

au·to·mo·bile /ˌɔtəmə'bil/ *noun*, *formal*
a car

au·top·sy /'ɔˌtɑpsi/ *noun* plural **autopsies**
an official examination of a dead body to discover the cause of death: *An autopsy showed that she had died of a heart attack.*

au·tumn /'ɔtəm/ *noun*, *formal*
the season before winter, when the leaves fall off the trees: *The tree's leaves turn red in the autumn.* SYNONYM **fall**

a·vail·a·ble /ə'veɪləbəl/ Ac *adjective*
if something is available, you can have it, buy it, or use it: *There is little food available to people in the region because there has been no rain.* | *There is a lot of money available for research.* | *The tools you need are readily available* (=easy to get or find) *at any hardware store.*
—**availability** /əˌveɪlə'bɪləti/ *noun* the state of being available: *The availability of guns in the U.S. is surprising to many foreigners.*

A

av•a•lanche /ˈævəˌlæntʃ/ *noun*
a large amount of snow or rocks that falls down a mountain

av•e•nue *also* **Avenue** /ˈævənu/ *noun*
written abbreviation **Ave.** used in the names of streets in a town or city: *He lives on Melrose Avenue.*
➔ See Thesaurus box at **road**

av•erage¹ /ˈævrɪdʒ/ *adjective*
1 calculated by adding several numbers together and dividing the total by the number of numbers you added together: *The average age of the students is 20.*
2 typical or ordinary: *How will these changes affect the average American worker?*
➔ See Thesaurus box at **normal**

average² *noun*
1 the amount that you get by adding several numbers together and then dividing the total by the number of numbers you added together: *The average of 2, 9, and 10 is 7* (=because 2+9+10=21, divided by 3=7).
2 on average = usually: *On average, women live longer than men.*
3 above/below average = higher or lower than the usual number or level: *Her test scores were well above average* (=much higher than the usual level).
—**average** *verb* to be or have a particular number as an average: *He is averaging 17 points a game.*

a•vi•a•tion /ˌeɪviˈeɪʃən/ *noun, formal*
the activity of flying or making aircraft: *The plane crash was one of the worst accidents in the history of aviation.*

av•id /ˈævɪd/ *adjective*
doing something a lot, because you like doing it: *She is an avid reader – she always has a book with her.*

av•o•ca•do /ˌævəˈkɑdoʊ/ *noun* plural **avocados**
a fruit with a green or dark purple skin and a large seed, eaten as a vegetable

a•void /əˈvɔɪd/ *verb*
1 to stay away from someone or something: *Paul's been avoiding me all day – I think he's mad at me.*
2 to not do or be involved in something, usually something bad: *He had to stop the car suddenly to avoid hitting a child on a bike.*
—**avoidable** *adjective* able to be avoided: *an avoidable mistake*
—**avoidance** *noun* the act of avoiding something

a•wait /əˈweɪt/ *verb, formal*
to wait for something: *The soldiers made a camp and awaited their orders.*

a•wake¹ /əˈweɪk/ *adjective*
not asleep: *I have trouble staying awake in class if I go to bed too late the night before.* | *The kids were still wide awake* (=completely awake) *at midnight.*

awake² *verb* **awoke** /əˈwoʊk/ **awoken** /əˈwoʊkən/ *formal*
to wake up: *I awoke as usual at 6 a.m.*

a•ward¹ /əˈwɔrd/ *noun*
a prize given to someone for doing something good: *Sam won an award for the best poem.* SYNONYM **prize**

award² *verb*
to give someone an award: *He was awarded the Nobel Prize for physics.*

a•ware /əˈwer/ Ac *adjective*
if you are aware of a fact or situation, you know about it: *Are you aware of the dangers of smoking?* | *He was aware (that) someone was following him, and he started to walk faster.* ANTONYM **unaware**
—**awareness** *noun*: *They want to raise public awareness about the disease through advertisements and TV programs.*

a•way /əˈweɪ/ *adverb*
1 if you go away, you move further from a person, place, or thing: *Go away!* | *He quickly moved away from the window.*
2 3 miles/40 feet, etc. away = used to say how far it is to a place, person, or thing: *The nearest city is five miles away.* | *I was standing about 10 feet away from him.*
3 not at home, at work, or in school: *I'm sorry, Ms. Parker is away this week.*
4 2 weeks/5 years, etc. away = used to say how much time will pass before something happens: *Christmas is only a month away. Are you ready?*
5 into a safe place: *It's time to clean up. Put all your toys away now, please.*

awe /ɔ/ *noun*
a feeling of great respect or admiration: *We were in awe of our father* (=had great respect for him).

awe•some /ˈɔsəm/ *adjective*
1 *informal* extremely good: *This pie's awesome! Can I have some more?*
2 very great or impressive: *the awesome power of the huge waterfall*

aw•ful /ˈɔfəl/ *adjective*
1 very bad: *an awful movie* | *The weather was awful and we had to stay inside the whole week.* | *I'm going home because I feel awful* (=I feel sick).
2 an awful lot *informal* = very much or a very great amount: *The shoes cost an awful lot of money, and I couldn't afford them.*
→ See Thesaurus box at **bad**

aw•fully /ˈɔfli/ *adverb, informal*
very: *She looked awfully tired.*

a•while /əˈwaɪl/ *adverb*
for a short time: *I waited awhile, then rang the bell again.*

awk•ward /ˈɔkwɚd/ *adjective*
1 moving or behaving in a way that does not seem relaxed or comfortable: *I felt awkward and shy, and didn't want to talk to anyone.*
2 embarrassing or difficult: *You're asking me to criticize my teacher, and that puts me in a very awkward position* (=difficult situation).
3 difficult to use or handle: *The camera is so small that it is awkward to use.*
—**awkwardly** *adverb*: *They hugged awkwardly, as if they had never met before.*
—**awkwardness** *noun*

awn•ing /ˈɔnɪŋ/ *noun*
a sheet of material, especially outside a store, that keeps the sun or the rain off

a•woke /əˈwoʊk/ *verb*
the past tense of AWAKE

ax *also* **axe** /æks/ *noun*
a tool with a metal blade on a long handle, used for cutting wood: *He was chopping up logs with an ax.*

ax•is /ˈæksɪs/ *noun* plural **axes** /ˈæksiz/
1 a line at the side or bottom of a GRAPH, where you put a series of numbers. The line that goes from top to bottom is the vertical or "y" axis, and the line that goes across from side to side is the horizontal or "x" axis.
2 an imaginary line through the middle of something that is turning, for example the Earth

ax•le /ˈæksəl/ *noun*
the bar that connects two wheels on a vehicle

Bb

B

B /bi/ *noun*
1 a GRADE that you get on a test or in a class for doing work that is good, but not excellent: *I got a B on the quiz, but I know I can get an A next time.*
2 the seventh note in the musical SCALE of C, or the musical KEY based on this note

B.A. *noun*
Bachelor of Arts a university degree in a subject such as History or Art: *He has a B.A. in English Literature.*

ba•boon /bæ'bun/ *noun*
a large monkey that lives in Africa and south Asia

ba•by /'beɪbi/ *noun* plural **babies**
a very young child: *The baby's crying.* | *She had a baby* (=gave birth to a baby) *last year.* | *a baby girl*
➔ See Thesaurus box at **child**

'baby ˌcarriage *also* **'baby ˌbuggy** *noun*
a thing with wheels, in which a baby can lie and be pushed along

ba•by•sit /'beɪbiˌsɪt/ *verb* **babysat** /'beɪbiˌsæt/ **babysitting**
to take care of a child while his or her parents are not at home: *Will you babysit for me tonight* (=take care of my child tonight)*?*
—**babysitting** *noun* the activity of taking care of a child while his or her parents are not at home: *Babysitting is a good way for teenagers to earn money.*

ba•by•sit•ter /'beɪbiˌsɪtɚ/ *noun*
someone who is paid to babysit a child: *The babysitter is coming at 6:00 because we need to leave by 6:15.*

bach•e•lor /'bætʃəlɚ/ *noun*
a man who has never been married: *He was 42, and still a bachelor.*

'bachelor's deˌgree *noun*
a degree you get from a college or university after successfully completing four years of study: *I got my bachelor's degree from Hunter College.*

back¹ /bæk/ *noun*
1 the part of your body between your neck and your waist which is the other side from your chest and stomach: *His back was hurting from lifting boxes all morning.* | *I lay on my back, looking up at the clouds.*
2 the part of something that is farthest from the front: *The answers to the questions are in the back of the book.* | *The pool's in back of* (=behind) *the house.* ANTONYM **front**
3 behind someone's back = if you do something bad or unkind behind someone's back, you do it without him or her knowing: *You shouldn't say mean things about her behind her back.*
4 in the back of your mind = a thought or feeling in the back of your mind is one that affects you, even though you are not thinking about it all the time: *There was always a slight fear that something bad was going to happen in the back of his mind.*
5 get off someone's back *informal* = to stop annoying someone after telling them to do something again and again: *I'll do it in a minute. Just get off my back!*

back² *adverb*
1 to or in the place where someone or something was before: *Put the milk back in the refrigerator when you're done with it.* | *I'll be back home in an hour.*
2 into or in the condition that someone or something was in before: *I woke up at 5 a.m. and couldn't get back to sleep.*
3 in the direction that is behind you: *I looked back over my shoulder.*
4 doing the same thing to someone that he or she has done to you: *Sarah smiled, and the boy smiled back.*
5 away from someone or something: *She pulled back the curtains to let the sun in.*
6 back and forth = in one direction and then in the opposite direction several times: *He walked back and forth across the floor.*

back³ *verb*
1 *also* **back up** to move backward, or to make a vehicle move backward: *We slowly backed away from the snake.* | *She backed the car into the garage.*
2 to support someone or something: *Several environmental groups backed the new law.*

B

PHRASAL VERBS

back down
to admit that you are wrong or to not continue with what you intended to do, when people oppose you: *She was yelling at me, but she backed down when she realized she was wrong.*

back off
informal to stop telling someone what to do: *Back off! I don't need your advice.*

back out
to decide not to do something you promised to do: *They backed out of the deal at the last minute.*

back someone or something up
to say or show that what someone is saying is true: *There is no evidence to back up what he says.*

back⁴ *adjective*
1 in or on the back of something: *The back door was open.* SYNONYM **rear**; ANTONYM **front**
2 a back street/road = a street or road that is not a main one

back•ache /ˈbækeɪk/ *noun*
a pain in your back: *She had a backache from moving furniture.*

back•bone /ˈbækboʊn/ *noun*
1 the line of bones down the middle of your back SYNONYM **spine**
2 courage and determination: *Peter doesn't have the backbone to be a good manager and make difficult decisions.*
➔ See picture on page A2

back•break•ing /ˈbækˌbreɪkɪŋ/ *adjective*
backbreaking work is very difficult physical work

back•ground /ˈbækgraʊnd/ *noun*
1 someone's education, family, and experience: *We come from very different backgrounds; his family was wealthy and mine was poor.* | *He has a background in accounting, so I'm sure he can do the job.*
2 the area that is behind the main things or people in a picture: *Here's a picture of Mary with our house in the background.*
3 the conditions or past events relating to something: *I'll tell you a little more about the background of the problem so you'll understand it better.*

back•log /ˈbæklɔg/ *noun*
an amount of things that you have not yet been able to deal with: *The company has a huge backlog of orders, and customers have to wait months to receive their goods.*

back•pack /ˈbækpæk/ *noun*
a bag that you carry on your back
➔ See picture at **bag**

back•pack•ing /ˈbækˌpækɪŋ/ *noun*
the activity of walking or traveling carrying a backpack: *We went backpacking in the Rockies.*
—**backpacker** *noun* a walker or traveler with a backpack

back•stage /ˌbækˈsteɪdʒ/ *adverb*
behind the stage in a theater: *He was allowed to go backstage after the concert to meet the band.*

back•stroke /ˈbækstroʊk/ *noun*
a way of swimming on your back, in which you move one arm up and then the other

back•up /ˈbækʌp/ *noun*
a copy or another thing that you can use if necessary: *Make a backup of any work you do on the computer in case the computer crashes.* | *I always have a backup plan for when something goes wrong.*

back•ward¹ /ˈbækwɚd/ *also* **backwards** *adverb*
1 in the direction that is behind you: *She took a step backward away from me.* ANTONYM **forward**
2 toward the beginning: *Count backward from 10 to 1.* ANTONYM **forward**
3 with the back part in front: *You have your T-shirt on backward – turn it around.*

backward² *adjective*
1 toward the direction that is behind you: *She left without a backward glance.* ANTONYM **forward**
2 developing more slowly than others: *It was a backward area with no running water or telephones.*

back•yard *also* **back yard** /ˈbækˌyɑrd/ *noun*
the area of land behind a house: *He was sitting under a tree in the backyard.*

ba•con /ˈbeɪkən/ *noun*
meat from the back or sides of a pig which

has been put in salt or smoke: *bacon and eggs*
➔ See Thesaurus box at **meat**

B

bac•te•ri•a /bæk'tɪriə/ *plural noun*
singular **bacterium** /-riəm/ *formal*
very small living things that sometimes cause disease: *Cook meat well to kill any bacteria.*

bad /bæd/ *adjective* **worse** /wɚs/ **worst** /wɚst/
1 not nice or enjoyable: *I'm sorry, but I have some bad news.* | *There was a bad smell coming from his gym shoes.* ANTONYM **good**

THESAURUS: bad

awful very bad: *The weather was awful.*
terrible very bad or serious: *The food was terrible.* | *a terrible accident*
horrible very bad or upsetting: *I had a horrible weekend. Everything went wrong.*
lousy *informal* very bad in quality: *It was a lousy movie.*

2 not able to do something well: *a bad driver* | *Brian is really bad at sports – he can't even catch a ball.* ANTONYM **good**
3 of low quality: *Her handwriting is so bad I can't read it.* ANTONYM **good**
4 damaging or harmful: *Smoking is bad for you.* ANTONYM **good**
5 serious or severe: *He couldn't go out because he had a bad cold.* | *The problem is getting worse.*
6 morally wrong or evil: *I'm not a bad person, but I have made some mistakes.* ANTONYM **good**
7 too bad *informal* = used to say that you are sorry about a sad or unpleasant situation: *It's too bad you can't stay any longer.*
8 feel bad = to feel ashamed or sorry about something: *I felt bad about lying to him.*
9 not bad *informal* = acceptable or fairly good: *The pay isn't bad and I enjoy the work.*
10 a bad time = a time that is not appropriate or convenient: *Is this a bad time to call?*
11 food that is bad is not safe to eat because it is not fresh: *The milk has gone bad.*

badge /bædʒ/ *noun*
a small piece of metal or plastic that you wear or carry to show people that you work for a particular organization: *a police badge*

bad•ly /'bædli/ *adverb* **worse** /wɚs/ **worst** /wɚst/
1 in a way that is not good or satisfactory: *The book is badly written and difficult to understand.* | *The team played very badly and lost the game.* ANTONYM **well**
2 very severely: *Our house was badly damaged during the storm.*

baf•fled /'bæfəld/ *adjective, formal*
if you are baffled by something, you cannot understand it: *She was baffled by his strange reaction.*

bag

bag /bæg/ *noun*
a container made of paper, plastic, cloth, or leather: *a bag of potatoes* | *She was carrying two grocery bags full of food.*

ba•gel /'beɪgəl/ *noun*
a type of bread that is shaped like a ring
➔ See picture at **bread**

bag•gage /'bægɪdʒ/ *noun*
the bags that you take with you when you travel on an airplane, train, or bus: *We saw the baggage being taken off the plane.*

bag•gy /'bægi/ *adjective*
baggy clothes are big and loose ANTONYM **tight**

bail[1] /beɪl/ *noun*
money left with a court of law so that someone does not have to stay in prison until his or her TRIAL: *He was released on bail* (=let out of prison when bail was paid).

bail[2] *verb*
PHRASAL VERB
bail someone out
to help a person or organization get out of trouble: *Young people often expect their parents to bail them out by paying the money they owe.*

bait /beɪt/ *noun*
food that you use to attract fish or animals so that you can catch them: *We used worms for bait, but we didn't catch any fish.*

bake /beɪk/ *verb*
to cook something such as bread or cakes in an OVEN: *Bake the rolls for 15 minutes.*
➔ See Thesaurus box at **cook**[1]

bak•er•y /'beɪkəri/ *noun* plural **bakeries**
a place where bread, cakes, etc. are made or sold
—**baker** *noun* someone whose job is making bread, cakes, etc.

bal•ance[1] /'bæləns/ *noun*
1 the ability to stand or walk steadily, without falling: *When the bus stopped suddenly, she almost lost her balance* (=was unable to stay standing). | *He hit me again when I was still off balance* (=not standing steadily) *and I fell down.*
2 a situation in which different things are in the right amounts or have the right amount of importance: *He was finding it difficult to strike a balance between family and work* (=make sure that they had equal importance in his life).
3 on balance = used when telling someone your opinion after considering all the facts: *On balance, I'd say it was a fair decision.*

balance[2] *verb*
1 to put or have something in a steady position, or to be in a steady position: *She was balancing a plate of food on her knees and trying not to spill anything.* | *He turned slowly, trying to balance on one foot.*
2 to make sure that different things are in the right amounts or have the right amount of importance: *My mother was trying to balance her children's needs with the needs of her parents.*

bal•anced /'bælənst/ *adjective*
including different things in the right amounts: *You should eat a healthy balanced diet with plenty of protein, fruits, and vegetables.*

bal•co•ny /'bælkəni/ *noun* plural **balconies**
1 a structure on the outside of a building, above ground level, where people can stand or sit: *She stood on the balcony looking up at the mountains.*
2 the seats upstairs in a theater

bald /bɔld/ *adjective*
if you are bald, you have little or no hair on your head: *He was going bald* (=becoming bald) *and decided to shave off all of his hair.*

'bald ˌeagle *noun*
a large North American bird with a white head and neck: *The bald eagle is a symbol of the United States.*

bale /beɪl/ *noun*
a large amount of something such as paper or HAY that is tied tightly together: *a bale of hay*

ball /bɔl/ *noun*
1 a round object that you throw, hit, or kick in some games: *tennis balls* | *He threw the ball to Michael.*
2 something made into a round shape: *a ball of string*
3 in baseball, a time when a ball is thrown and the hitter does not try to hit it because it is not in the correct area
4 be on the ball *informal* = to be able to think or act quickly: *We need an assistant who's really on the ball.*
5 a large important party at which people dance

bal•le•ri•na /ˌbælə'rinə/ *noun*
a woman who dances in ballets: *She stood on her toes like a ballerina.*

bal•let /bæ'leɪ/ *noun*
a performance in which a story is told using dancing and music, without words: *We went to see the ballet "Swan Lake."* | *a ballet dancer*

bal•loon /bə'lun/ *noun*
a small colored rubber bag that can be filled with air or gas: *Before my birthday party, we blew up lots of balloons* (=blew air into them).

bal•lot /'bælət/ *noun*
a piece of paper that is used for voting: *Today voters will be casting their ballots* (=voting) *for a new representative.*

ball•park /'bɔlˌpɑrk/ *noun*, *informal*
a place for playing baseball

ball•point pen /ˌbɔlpɔɪnt 'pen/ *noun*
a pen with a small ball at the end that rolls ink onto the paper

ball•room /'bɔlrum/ *noun*
a large room for formal dances: *A band was playing in the ballroom.*

ba•lo•ney /bə'loʊni/ *noun*, *informal*
1 something that is said that is silly or not true: *"Things are getting better." "That's*

B

baloney!" (=said when you think something is silly or not true) SYNONYM **nonsense**
2 another spelling of BOLOGNA: *a baloney sandwich*

bam•boo /ˌbæmˈbu/ *noun*
a tall plant with hard hollow stems, often used for making things such as furniture, especially in Asia

ban[1] /bæn/ *noun*
an official order saying that something is not allowed: *Should Congress lift the ban on* (=end it) *some illegal drugs?*
➔ See Thesaurus box at **forbid**

ban[2] *verb* **banned, banning**
to say officially that something is not allowed: *They want to ban chemical weapons.* | *He was banned from the club after the fight.*

ba•nan•a /bəˈnænə/ *noun*
a long curved fruit with a yellow skin
➔ See picture on page A13

band /bænd/ *noun*
1 a group of musicians that plays popular music: *He used to play in a rock band.*
2 *formal* a small group of people who do something together: *They were attacked by a band of armed men.* SYNONYM **group**
3 a narrow piece of something which goes around something else to hold it or decorate it: *She ties her hair back with a rubber band.*

ban•dage /ˈbændɪdʒ/ *noun*
a long piece of cloth that you put around a wound: *Her head was wrapped in a bloody bandage.*
—**bandage** *verb* to put a bandage around a wound: *A nurse bandaged my injured leg.*

ˈBand-Aid *noun, trademark*
a small piece of material that you stick over a small cut on your skin

ban•dan•na *also* **bandana** /bænˈdænə/ *noun*
a square piece of colored cloth that you wear around your head or neck

ban•dit /ˈbændɪt/ *noun*
someone who robs people who are traveling: *The train was attacked by bandits.*

bang[1] /bæŋ/ *verb*
1 to make a loud noise by hitting something: *He banged on the door with his hands.*
2 to hit a part of your body on something by accident: *I banged my knee on the corner of the bed.*
➔ See Thesaurus box at **hit**[1]

bang[2] *noun*
a sudden loud noise like the noise made by a gun: *The door slammed shut with a bang.*

bangs /bæŋz/ *plural noun*
hair that is cut short across your FOREHEAD

ban•is•ter /ˈbænəstɚ/ *noun*
a row of wooden posts with a BAR along the top that you hold onto when you use stairs

ban•jo /ˈbændʒoʊ/ *noun* plural **banjos**
a musical instrument like a GUITAR, but with a circular main part
➔ See picture on page A21

bank[1] /bæŋk/ *noun*
1 the company or place where you can keep your money or borrow money: *I went to the bank to get some money.* | *I don't have much money in the bank.*
2 the land along the side of a river or lake: *The city is on the banks of the Hudson River.*
➔ See Thesaurus box at **shore**

bank[2] *verb*
to use a particular bank: *She banks with First National.*

ˈbank acˌcount *noun*
an agreement with a bank that allows you to keep money there and take money out: *How much money do you have in your bank account?* SYNONYM **account**

bank•er /ˈbæŋkɚ/ *noun*
someone who has an important job in a bank

bank•ing /ˈbæŋkɪŋ/ *noun*
the business of banks, which involves lending and borrowing money

bank•rupt /ˈbæŋkrʌpt/ *adjective*
unable to pay your debts, so that you have to close your business: *Many small stores have gone bankrupt because they cannot compete with the big supermarkets.*
—**bankruptcy** *noun* a situation in which a person or company is bankrupt

ban•ner /ˈbænɚ/ *noun*
a long piece of cloth with writing on it: *The protesters were carrying banners that said "Peace Now."*

ban•quet /ˈbæŋkwɪt/ *noun*
a formal meal for many people: *There was a formal banquet at the conference with all kinds of food.*

bap•tism /ˈbæptɪzəm/ *noun*
a Christian ceremony in which someone is touched or covered with water, in order to become a member of a Christian church
—**baptize** /ˈbæptaɪz/ *verb* to put water on someone in a religious ceremony, to make that person a member of a Christian church. When babies are baptized, they are also officially given their name

bar[1] /bɑr/ *noun*
1 a place that sells alcoholic drinks and where you can stay to drink them: *We went out for a drink at a bar.*
2 a COUNTER where alcoholic drinks are served: *He was standing at the bar getting beer.*
3 a small block of something: *a bar of soap* | *a candy bar*
4 a long narrow piece of metal or wood: *an iron bar*
5 behind bars = in prison
➔ **snack bar**

bar[2] *verb* **barred, barring**
1 to officially stop someone from doing something: *Photographers are barred from taking pictures inside the courtroom.*
2 to put a piece of wood or metal across a door or window to stop people from going in or out: *She barred the door and called the police.*
➔ See Thesaurus box at **forbid**

bar•be•cue /ˈbɑrbɪˌkyu/ *noun*
a meal or party where you cook food outside: *We're having a barbecue on Saturday and making hotdogs and hamburgers.*
SYNONYM **cookout**
➔ See Thesaurus box at **meal**

ˌbarbed ˈwire *noun*
wire with short sharp points on it, used for making fences: *The prison was surrounded by high barbed wire fences.*

bar•ber /ˈbɑrbɚ/ *noun*
a man whose job is to cut men's hair
—**barbershop** *noun* a store where men's hair is cut

bare /ber/ *adjective*
1 if part of someone's body is bare, it is not covered by clothes: *The children were running around in bare feet.*
2 if a room or cupboard is bare, it has nothing in it: *The cupboard was bare and she had nothing to feed her children.*
SYNONYM **empty**
3 without any decoration: *bare white walls*
SYNONYM **plain**
4 basic and with nothing extra: *We only had enough money for the bare necessities* (=the most basic things that you need to live).

bare•foot /ˈberfʊt/ *adjective, adverb*
not wearing any shoes or socks: *We walked barefoot in the sand.*

bare•ly /ˈberli/ *adverb*
only just: *She was very sick and barely able to walk.*

bar•gain[1] /ˈbɑrgən/ *noun*
something that is surprisingly cheap and is much less than its usual price: *I got the car for $2,000, which was a real bargain.*

bargain[2] *verb*
to try to persuade someone to lower the price of something: *I had to bargain with him to get a good price.*

barge /bɑrdʒ/ *noun*
a boat with a flat bottom, used for carrying goods on a CANAL or river: *The coal was taken up the river by barge.*

bark[1] /bɑrk/ *verb*
if a dog barks, it makes a short loud sound: *The dog barked at us as we walked past.*

bark[2] *noun*
1 the sound a dog makes
2 the outer covering of a tree

bar•ley /ˈbɑrli/ *noun*
a grain used for making food and alcohol

barn /bɑrn/ *noun*
a large building on a farm for storing crops or keeping animals in

bar•rel /ˈbærəl/ *noun*
1 a large container with curved sides and a flat top and bottom: *a barrel of beer*
2 the part of a gun that the bullets are shot through

bar•ren /ˈbærən/ *adjective, formal*
land that is barren cannot grow plants: *a barren desert*

B

bar•ri•cade /ˈbærəˌkeɪd/ *noun*
something that is put across a road to prevent people from going past: *Police set up barricades on all the roads out of the city to try to catch the men.*

bar•ri•er /ˈbæriɚ/ *noun*
1 a problem that stops people from doing something: *A lack of education is a barrier to many good jobs.*
2 a fence or wall that stops people from entering a place: *The police put up barriers to hold back the crowds.*

bar•ri•o /ˈbæriˌoʊ/ *noun* plural **barrios**
an area in a city where many poor Spanish-speaking people live: *He grew up in the barrio and didn't learn English until he went to school.*

bar•tend•er /ˈbɑrˌtendɚ/ *noun*
someone whose job is to make and serve drinks in a bar

base¹ /beɪs/ *noun*
1 the lowest part or surface of something: *The maker's name is written on the base of the clock.*
2 the main place where someone works or lives: *The company's base is in Atlanta.*
3 a place where people in the army, navy, etc. live and work: *an army base*
4 one of the four places that a player must touch in order to score a point in baseball: *He ran to second base.*

base² *verb*
to have your main office, home, etc. in a particular place: *The company is based in New York.*

PHRASAL VERB
base something on something
1 to use something as the model for developing something else: *They based the movie on the book by Dan Brown.*
2 to use something as a reason for doing something: *She based her decision on her experience as a teacher.*

base•ball /ˈbeɪsbɔl/ *noun*
1 a game in which two teams try to score points by hitting a ball and running around four bases: *I used to play baseball when I was in high school.*
2 the ball used in this game
➔ See picture on page A24

base•ment /ˈbeɪsmənt/ *noun*
the part of a building that is below the level of the ground: *We keep our bikes in the basement during the winter.*

bas•es /ˈbeɪsiz/ *noun*
the plural of BASIS

bash /bæʃ/ *noun*
informal a party: *We're having a big bash for his birthday.*
➔ See Thesaurus box at **party**

bash•ful /ˈbæʃfəl/ *adjective*
shy and embarrassed, and not wanting to talk to other people: *When she asked him to dance, he gave her a bashful smile.* SYNONYM **shy**
➔ See Thesaurus box at **shy**

ba•sic /ˈbeɪsɪk/ *adjective*
1 relating to the simplest and most important parts of something: *The basic problem is that we don't have enough money.* | *He doesn't understand the basic principles of mathematics.*
2 very simple and not advanced: *The equipment in the hospital was very basic.*
➔ **basics**

WORD FAMILY look at the words:
➔ **basic** *adjective*
➔ **base** *verb*
➔ **base** *noun*
➔ **basis** *noun*
➔ **basically** *adverb*
➔ **the basics** *noun*

ba•si•cally /ˈbeɪsɪkli/ *adverb*
1 *informal* used when you are giving a simple explanation of a situation: *Basically, he needs to lose weight.*
2 in the most important ways, without considering small details: *The two pictures are basically the same; I had to look carefully to see any differences.*

basics /ˈbeɪsɪks/ *noun*
the basics = the most important facts or things that you need to know: *My mom taught me the basics of cooking.*

ba•sil /ˈbeɪzəl/ *noun*
a plant with sweet-smelling green leaves, used in Italian cooking

ba•sin /ˈbeɪsən/ *noun*
1 a large area of land that is lower in the middle than at the edges: *the Amazon basin*

2 a large bowl, especially one for water: *She poured the water into a basin and used it to wash her face.*

ba•sis /ˈbeɪsəs/ *noun* plural **bases** /ˈbeɪsiz/

1 **on a daily/weekly/monthly, etc. basis** *formal* = every day, week, month, etc.: *We meet here on a daily basis, usually at 10.*

2 **on the basis of something** = because of a particular fact or situation: *People are sometimes rejected for jobs on the basis of their age* (=because they are too young or too old).

3 the information or ideas from which something develops: *The idea of "less government" was the basis of his campaign for president.*

bas•ket /ˈbæskɪt/ *noun*

1 a container made of thin pieces of wood, plastic, or wire, used for carrying or holding things: *They took the food to the park in a picnic basket.* | *a shopping basket*

2 a round metal ring with a net hanging off it, used when playing basketball: *Try to shoot the ball through the basket.*

bas•ket•ball /ˈbæskɪtˌbɔl/ *noun*

1 a game between two teams, in which each team tries to throw a ball through a net

2 the ball used in this game

→ See picture on page A24

bass /beɪs/ *noun*

1 *also* **bass guitar** a GUITAR that plays low notes

2 another word for a DOUBLE BASS

→ See picture on page A21

bas•soon /bəˈsun/ *noun*

a very long wooden musical instrument with a low sound that you play by blowing into it

→ See picture on page A21

bat[1] /bæt/ *noun*

1 a long wooden stick used for hitting the ball in baseball

2 an animal with wings that flies at night

bat[2] *verb* **batted, batting**

to hit a ball with a bat: *The crowd was silent as he came up to bat.*

batch /bætʃ/ *noun*

a group of things or people that are made, arrive, or are dealt with at the same time: *I baked another batch of cookies.*

bath /bæθ/ *noun* plural **baths** /bæðz/

if you take a bath, you wash your body while sitting in a BATHTUB: *The kids take a bath almost every day.*

bathe /beɪð/ *verb, formal*

to wash yourself or someone else in a bath

bathing suit /ˈbeɪðɪŋ ˌsut/ *noun*

a piece of clothing that you wear for swimming: *She was wearing a blue one-piece bathing suit.*

bath•robe /ˈbæθroʊb/ *noun*

a loose piece of clothing that ties around your waist that you wear after you take a bath or SHOWER

bath•room /ˈbæθrum/ *noun*

a room where there is a toilet and usually a bathtub or a SHOWER: *Mommy, I have to go to the bathroom!* (=I want to use the toilet)

bath•tub /ˈbæθtʌb/ *noun*

a long container that you fill with water and wash yourself in

→ See picture on page A11

bat•ter[1] /ˈbætɚ/ *noun*

1 a mixture of flour, eggs, milk, etc. that is used for making cakes and similar things: *pancake batter*

2 the person who is trying to hit the ball in baseball

batter[2] *verb*

to hit someone or something very hard many times: *The waves battered against the rocks.*

bat•tered /ˈbætɚd/ *adjective*

old and not in good condition: *a battered old guitar*

bat•ter•y /ˈbætəri/ *noun* plural **batteries**

an object that provides electricity for a radio, camera, toy, etc.: *The battery in the camera is dead* (=it has no power left).

→ See picture on page A28

bat•tle[1] /ˈbætl/ *noun*

1 a fight between two armies or groups, especially during a war: *Hundreds of soldiers were killed in the battle.*

2 a situation in which people are arguing or struggling to win or achieve something: *He finally won his case after a long legal battle.* | *She died last year after a long battle with cancer.*

B

battle² *verb*
to try hard to achieve something or deal with something: *Doctors battled for six hours to save his life.*

bat•tle•ship /ˈbætl̩ˌʃɪp/ *noun*
a very large ship used in wars

bawl /bɔl/ *verb, informal*
to cry loudly: *The baby was bawling in the back of the car.*

bay /beɪ/ *noun*
an area of an ocean or lake that is partly enclosed by a curve in the land: *She swam across the bay in 30 minutes.* | *the San Francisco Bay*

B.C.
Before Christ used when a year came before the birth of Jesus Christ: *He was killed in 44 B.C.*

be /bi/ *verb* **was, were, been**
1 used to describe and give information about people or things: *The room was blue and white.* | *My mother is a teacher.*
2 used with the -ing form of another verb when saying that something is happening now: *I am painting a picture.* | *It's raining.*
3 used with the -ing form of another verb when saying that you have made plans to do something in the future: *We are going to Hawaii on vacation next month.*
4 used with the past participle of verbs when saying that something happens to someone or something: *The house was built 50 years ago.*
5 there is/are/were, etc. = used when saying that something exists or happens: *There was a beautiful view from the top of the mountain.* | *There are three apples in the kitchen.*
6 be good/be careful, etc. = used when telling someone to behave in a particular way: *Be careful! The knife's very sharp.*
7 someone is to do something *formal* = used when saying strongly that someone must do something: *You are to be home by 10 o'clock.*

beach /bitʃ/ *noun*
an area of sand or small stones at the edge of an ocean or a lake: *Do you want to go to the beach?* | *We spent the day at the beach swimming and lying in the sun.*
➔ See Thesaurus box at **shore**

beach

bea•con /ˈbikən/ *noun*
a light or electronic signal used to guide boats, airplanes, etc.

bead /bid/ *noun*
a small ball of plastic, wood, glass, etc. used for making jewelry: *The necklace was made of colored glass beads.*

beak /bik/ *noun*
the hard pointed mouth of a bird: *The bird held a worm in its beak.*

beak•er /ˈbikɚ/ *noun*
a glass cup with straight sides used in chemistry for measuring liquids

beam¹ /bim/ *noun*
1 a line of light or energy: *A beam of light from his flashlight shone through the window.*
2 a long piece of wood or metal used when building houses, bridges, etc.: *The roof was supported by thick wooden beams.*
➔ See Thesaurus box at **smile**¹

beam² *verb*
1 to smile in a happy way: *He beamed proudly after his son scored the goal.*
2 to send out light, radio signals, or television signals: *The TV shows are beamed across the world by satellite.*

bean /bin/ *noun*
1 a seed or a seed container of a plant that you cook and eat as a vegetable: *green beans*
2 a dried seed that is made into a powder in order to make drinks such as coffee and some foods: *coffee beans*
➔ See picture on page A12

bear¹ /ber/ *noun*
a large strong animal with thick fur and sharp CLAWS: *Bears live in the woods near our*

house.
➔ **polar bear, teddy bear**

bear² *verb* **bore** /bɔr/ **borne** /bɔrn/
1 *formal* to accept something that is very painful or very difficult: *She didn't think she could bear the pain any longer.* SYNONYM **stand**
2 bear the responsibility/blame for something *formal* = to be responsible for something bad that has happened: *The company must bear responsibility for the accident.*
3 bear left/right = to turn toward the left or right
4 *formal* **bear in mind** = to consider a fact when you are deciding what to do or when making a judgment: *Bear in mind that he is only 8 years old, so he will not understand everything.* SYNONYM **remember**
5 bear the weight of something = to support the weight of something: *The ice wasn't thick enough to bear his weight.* SYNONYM **hold**
6 *formal* to bring or carry something: *They came bearing gifts.*

bear·a·ble /ˈberəbəl/ *adjective*
if a situation is bearable, it is difficult but you can accept it: *His friendship was the only thing that made my life bearable.*

beard

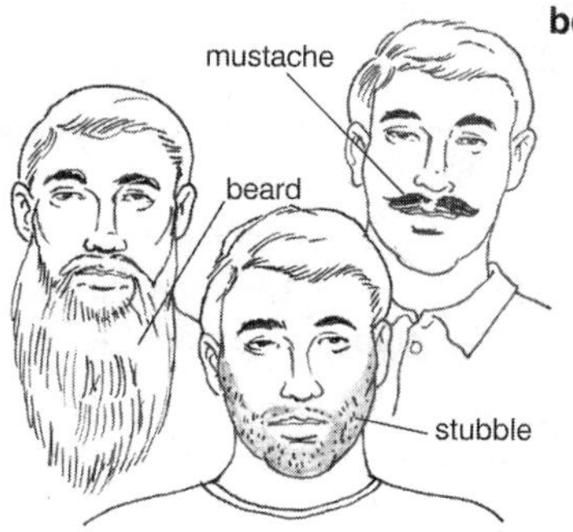

beard /bɪrd/ *noun*
the hair that grows on a man's chin: *The old man had a long white beard.*

beast /bist/ *noun, formal*
an animal, especially one that is dangerous or strange: *The jungle was full of all kinds of wild beasts.*

beat¹ /bit/ *verb* **beat, beaten** /ˈbitn/
1 to get more points, votes, etc. than other people in a game or competition: *New York beat Boston 4–1.* | *She often beats me at tennis.*
2 to hit someone or something many times: *My father used to beat me with a big stick.* | *The waves were beating against the rocks.*
3 to make a regular sound: *She could feel her heart beating.*
4 to mix foods together quickly using a fork or a kitchen tool: *Beat the eggs.*
5 beat it! *informal* = an impolite way to tell someone to leave immediately
➔ See Thesaurus boxes at **hit¹**, **mix¹**, and **win¹**
➔ See picture on page A14

beat² *noun*
1 the pattern of sounds in a piece of music: *I could hear the beat of the music from the party downstairs.*
2 one of a series of regular movements or sounds: *His heart rate went up to 120 beats a minute.*

beau·ti·ful /ˈbyutəfəl/ *adjective*
1 very nice to look at. You use beautiful especially about a woman, a place, or an object: *She is a very beautiful woman.* | *The views from the top of the mountain were beautiful.* | *a beautiful Chinese vase*

THESAURUS: beautiful

attractive used about a man or woman who is nice to look at: *She's a very attractive woman.*
good-looking used about anyone who is nice to look at: *a tall good-looking man*
beautiful used about a woman, girl, or baby who is very nice to look at: *Elena looked beautiful in her blue dress.*
pretty used about a girl or woman who is nice to look at: *a pretty girl with long brown hair*
handsome used about a man or boy who is nice to look at: *Dad looked really handsome in his suit.*
cute used about a baby, child, or young person who is nice to look at: *I think Todd's really cute.* | *What a cute baby!*

2 a beautiful song, book, poem, etc. gives you a lot of pleasure: *The music was beautiful.*
—**beautifully** *adverb* in a way that looks or sounds very good: *He plays the piano beautifully.*

B

beau·ty /ˈbyuti/ *noun* plural **beauties**
1 the quality of being beautiful to look at: *The mountains in Yosemite are famous for their beauty.* | *She was a woman of great beauty.*
2 the quality that a very good poem, painting, piece of music, etc. has when it gives you a lot of pleasure: *the beauty of his music*

bea·ver /ˈbivɚ/ *noun*
a North American animal that has thick fur and a wide flat tail and lives in houses made of sticks in the water: *The beavers are building a dam in the stream.*

be·came /bɪˈkeɪm/ *verb*
the past tense of BECOME

be·cause /bɪˈkɔz/ *conjunction*
used when you are giving the reason for something: *She was tired because she had been standing up all day.* | *The game was canceled because of the rain.*

be·come /bɪˈkʌm/ *verb* **became** /bɪˈkeɪm/, **become**
1 to begin to be something: *The weather is becoming cooler as fall begins.* | *It became clear that she was lying.*

USAGE: become

Become, **get**, and **go** can all mean "to begin to be something," but they are used in different ways.

Become is used in both written and spoken English: *He's becoming a very good tennis player.* | *The area has become popular with mountain bikers.*

Get and **go** are less formal than **become**, and are used more often in spoken English: *I got very hungry.* | *Have you gone crazy?*

Become can be used in front of an adjective (=word that describes something) or a noun: *It became clear that Scott was not doing his work.* | *The noise from the airport is becoming a problem.*

Get and **go** are used only in front of an adjective: *It's getting dark.* | *Beethoven went deaf when he was 40 years old.*

2 to start to have a job or position: *She wants to become a doctor.* | *Bush became president in 2000.*

bed /bed/ *noun*
1 a piece of furniture for sleeping on: *I usually go to bed around ten o'clock.* | *She was lying in bed reading.* | *Go upstairs, it's time for bed* (=it is time to go to sleep). | *He never makes his bed* (=he never puts the sheets neatly back on his bed). | *a double bed* (=a bed for two people)
2 the ground at the bottom of the ocean, a river, or a lake: *The river bed is sandy.*
3 an area of ground that has been prepared for plants to grow in: *The flower beds are full of roses.*
➔ See picture on page A10

ˌbed and ˈbreakfast *also* **B&B** /ˌbi: ənd ˈbi: / *noun*
a house or a small hotel where you pay to sleep and have breakfast

bed·room /ˈbedrum/ *noun*
a room for sleeping in: *This is Mark's bedroom.* | *a three-bedroom house*

bed·spread /ˈbedspred/ *noun*
a large cover that goes on top of a bed
➔ See picture on page A10

bed·time /ˈbedtaɪm/ *noun*
the time when you usually go to bed: *It's past your bedtime! Get upstairs now.*

bee /bi/ *noun*
a yellow and black insect that flies, makes HONEY, and can sting you: *The bees were buzzing around from flower to flower.*

beech /bitʃ/ *noun*
a large tree with smooth gray branches and small nuts

beef /bif/ *noun*
meat from a cow: *a slice of roast beef*
➔ See Thesaurus box at **meat**

bee·hive /ˈbihaɪv/ *noun*
a place where bees live SYNONYM **hive**

been /bɪn/ *verb*
1 the past participle of BE
2 have been to = to have gone to a place and come back: *Have you ever been to Mexico?*

GRAMMAR: been

been and gone

Been and **gone** are past participles of **go**. A past participle is a form of a verb that shows an action happening in the past.

Has been is the way you say that someone has visited a place in the past: *George has been to Denver* (=George has visited Denver before, but is not there now).

Has gone is the usual way to say that someone has traveled to a place in the past: *George has gone to Denver* (=George has traveled to Denver and is there now).

beep /bip/ *verb*
if an electronic machine or a car horn beeps, it makes a sound: *The computer beeps when you press the wrong key.* | *Some guy beeped his horn at me.*
—**beep** *noun* the sound that an electronic machine or a car horn makes

beer /bɪr/ *noun*
a yellow or brown alcoholic drink: *a glass of beer* | *Would you like a beer?*

beet /bit/ *noun*
a round dark red vegetable that grows under the ground

bee•tle /ˈbitl/ *noun*
an insect with a hard round back

be•fore¹ /bɪˈfɔr/ *preposition, conjunction*
1 earlier than something or someone: *I usually take a shower before breakfast.* | *The other students finished the test before me.* | *She started school before I did.* | *He arrived the day before yesterday* (=two days ago). ANTONYM **after**

THESAURUS: before

prior to something *formal* before: *Please be at the gate at least 30 minutes prior to the plane's departure.*

earlier near the beginning of a period of time, an event, or a process: *I saw Kim earlier today.*

previously before now, or before a particular time: *We had passed the building about ten minutes previously.*

2 in front of someone or something else in a list or order: *S comes before T in the alphabet.* ANTONYM **after**
3 if one place is before another as you go toward it, you will reach it first: *Turn right just before the stop light.* ANTONYM **after**
4 *formal* in a place that is in front of someone or something: *The speaker stood before the crowd.*

before² *adverb*
at an earlier time: *Have you two met each other before?* | *I had seen the same man the day before* (=the previous day).

be•fore•hand /bɪˈfɔrˌhænd/ *adverb*
before something happens: *The teacher had warned us beforehand that the test was going to be difficult.*

beg /bɛg/ *verb* **begged, begging**
1 to ask someone for food or money because you are very poor: *People had to beg for food.*
2 to ask for something in a way which shows you want it very much: *She begged them to help her.*
3 I beg your pardon *formal* **a)** you use this to ask someone politely to say something again: *"It's 5 dollars." "I beg your pardon?" "I said it's 5 dollars."* SYNONYM **excuse me** **b)** you use this to say you are sorry: *Oh, I beg your pardon, did I hurt you?* SYNONYM **sorry**
➔ See Thesaurus box at **ask**

be•gan /bɪˈgæn/ *verb*
the past tense of BEGIN

beg•gar /ˈbɛgɚ/ *noun*
someone who asks people for food and money in order to live: *A beggar asked him if he had a dollar.*

be•gin /bɪˈgɪn/ *verb* **began** /bɪˈgæn/ **begun** /bɪˈgʌn/ **beginning**
1 to start: *The concert will begin at 8:00.* | *The musicians began playing.* | *It's beginning to rain.* | *Let's begin with exercise 5.* | *The word "psychology" begins with a "p."* (="p" is the first letter) ANTONYM **end, stop, finish**
2 to begin with = used when talking about the first part of something: *She wasn't very good at the game to begin with.*

be•gin•ner /bɪˈgɪnɚ/ *noun*
someone who is starting to do something or learn something: *a guitar class for beginners*

be•gin•ning /bɪˈgɪnɪŋ/ *noun*
the start or first part of something: *The beginning of the movie is really exciting, but it gets boring later.* | *Everyone has to take a test at the beginning of the year. Then at the end of the year, we can see if we improved.* | *In the beginning I didn't like him very much, but now I think he's great.* SYNONYM **start**; ANTONYM **end**

B

be•gun /bɪˈgʌn/ *verb*
the past participle of BEGIN

be•half /bɪˈhæf/ Ac *noun, formal*
on behalf of someone/on someone's behalf = speaking or doing something instead of someone because that person has asked you to speak or do something: *Her lawyer spoke on her behalf.* SYNONYM **for**

be•have /bɪˈheɪv/ *verb*
1 to do or say things in a particular way: *Lions in a zoo do not behave like lions in the wild.*
2 behave (yourself) to be polite and do things in a way other people think is good: *His mother told him to behave. | If you behave yourself, you can stay up late.* ANTONYM **misbehave**

WORD FAMILY look at the words:
→ **behave** *verb*
→ **behaviour** *noun*
→ **well-behaved** *adjective*

be•hav•ior /bɪˈheɪvyɚ/ *noun*
the things that a person or animal does: *Did you notice anything unusual about his behavior? | It's important to reward children for good behavior.*
WORD FAMILY → **behave** *verb*

be•hind /bɪˈhaɪnd/ *preposition, adverb*
1 at the back of someone or something: *The drugstore is behind the supermarket. | She was sitting behind me and throwing things at the back of my head.*
2 not as successful as someone or something: *Our team was behind the other team at half time, but we beat them in the second half.*
3 supporting a person, idea, etc.: *All of his friends were behind him so he felt very confident.*
4 late in doing the things that you have to do: *I'm sorry to keep you waiting. I'm running behind today* (=I'm late and I have not done everything that I have to do).
5 responsible for causing something: *The police believe a local gang is behind the killings.*

beige /beɪʒ/ *noun*
a pale brown color
—**beige** *adjective*: *a beige sweater*

be•ing[1] /ˈbi-ɪŋ/ *verb*
the present participle of BE

being[2] *noun*
1 a living thing: *The movie is about strange beings from outer space.*
2 come into being *formal* = to start to exist: *The country came into being at the beginning of the last century.*

be•lief /bəˈlif/ *noun*
a strong feeling that something is definitely true or right: *It is important to respect other people's religious beliefs. | He has a strong belief in God.*
→ See Thesaurus box at **religion**

be•lieve /bəˈliv/ *verb*
1 to be sure that something is true or that someone is telling the truth: *Don't believe everything that you read in the newspapers. | Do you believe in God?* (=Do you believe that God exists?)
2 to think that something is true, although you are not completely sure: *I believe she will be back on Monday, but I could be wrong.*
→ See Thesaurus box at **think**

bell /bel/ *noun*

1 a metal object that makes a ringing sound when you hit it or shake it: *The church bells were ringing.*
2 a piece of electrical equipment that makes a ringing sound: *She rang the door bell.*

bel•ly /ˈbeli/ *noun* plural **bellies** *informal*
your stomach: *He had a big belly from drinking too much beer.*

ˈbelly ˌbutton *noun, informal*
the small hollow place in the middle of your stomach SYNONYM **navel**

be•long /bɪˈlɔŋ/ *verb*
if something belongs somewhere, that is where it is usually kept: *The plates don't belong in this cupboard. They should be over there.*
PHRASAL VERB
belong to
1 belong to someone = if something belongs to you, you own it: *The land belongs*

to me and my family, and we can use it for whatever we want. | Who does this book belong to?
2 belong to something = to be a member of a group or organization: *He belongs to a private golf club.*

be•long•ings /bɪˈlɔŋɪŋz/ *plural noun*
the things that you own, for example clothes, pens, or books: *Remember to take all your personal belongings with you when you leave the plane.*
➔ See Thesaurus box at **property**

be•loved /bɪˈlʌvɪd/ *adjective, formal*
used about someone who you love very much: *His beloved wife had died many years earlier.*

be•low /bɪˈloʊ/ *adverb, preposition*
1 in a lower place or position than someone or something else: *Her apartment is below mine, so she can hear me walking around.* | *Read the story and then answer the questions below.* SYNONYM **under**; ANTONYM **above**
2 less than a particular number or amount: *It's 10 degrees below zero outside!* ANTONYM **above**
3 lower in rank: *She never talks to people below her in the company.* ANTONYM **above**

belt /belt/ *noun*
1 a band of leather or cloth that you wear around your waist and that holds up your pants: *a brown leather belt* | *He buckled his belt* (=fastened it).
2 a circular band of material such as rubber that moves parts of a machine: *The belt makes the wheels in the machine turn around.*
➔ **conveyor belt**, **seat belt**
➔ See picture on page A6

bench /bentʃ/ *noun*
a long seat for two or more people, often one that does not have a back: *They sat together on a bench in the park and watched the pigeons.*
➔ See picture at **seat**

bend¹ /bend/ *verb* **bent** /bent/
1 to move a part of your body so that it is not straight or so that you are not standing upright: *Bend your knees, but keep your back straight.* | *He bent down to tie his shoelace.*
2 to push or press something so that it is no longer flat or straight: *He bent the stick with his hands.*
➔ See picture on page A4

bend² *noun*
a curve in something such as a road or river: *There was a sharp bend in the road and we had to slow down.*

be•neath /bɪˈniθ/ *adverb, preposition, formal*
under or below something: *She could feel the warm sand beneath her feet.* SYNONYM **under**

ben•e•fi•cial /ˌbenəˈfɪʃəl/ Ac *adjective*
if something is beneficial, it has a good or helpful effect: *More exercise will be beneficial for your health.*

ben•e•fit¹ /ˈbenəfɪt/ Ac *noun*
1 an advantage or other useful thing that you get from something: *Now we have the benefits of modern science to help us do things quickly.*
2 money or other things that you get because you work for a company, belong to a government system, etc.: *The company provides medical benefits for all its workers.*

WORD FAMILY look at the words:
➔ **benefit** *noun*
➔ **benefit** *verb*
➔ **beneficial** *adjective*

benefit² *verb* **benefitted** or **benefited, benefitting** or **benefiting**
if you benefit from something or if it benefits you, it helps you: *Most people will benefit from the changes to the tax system.*

bent

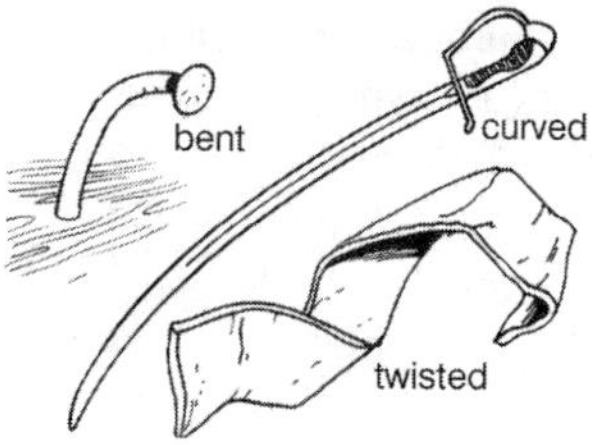

bent¹ /bent/ *verb*
the past tense and past participle of BEND

bent² *adjective*
not straight – use this about things that are usually straight: *a bent nail*

B

ber•ry /'beri/ *noun* plural **berries**
a type of small soft fruit with very small seeds: *We picked some wild berries in the woods.*

ber•serk /bɚ'sɚk/ *adjective*
go berserk *informal* = to suddenly become very angry or violent: *The man went berserk and started hitting her.*

be•side /bɪ'saɪd/ *preposition*
1 next to or very close to someone or something: *He sat down beside her and started talking to her.*
2 used when you are comparing two people or things: *So many bad things had happened to her that my problems seemed small beside hers.*
3 be beside the point = to not be important compared to something else: *"He's very good-looking." "That's beside the point – we need a good actor!"*

be•sides /bɪ'saɪdz/ *preposition, adverb*
1 in addition to something or someone: *Besides going to college, she works 15 hours a week.* | *Who's going to be there besides David and me?*
2 *informal* used when giving another reason: *It doesn't take long to walk to my house. Besides, I need some exercise.*

best¹ /best/ *adjective*
better than anyone or anything else: *He's the best player on the team – no one can play as well as he can.* | *This is the best ice cream I've ever eaten.* | *She's my best friend* (=the friend that you like better than anyone else). ANTONYM **worst**

best² *adverb*
1 in a way that is better than any other: *They are trying to find out which drug works best.*
2 like someone or something best = to like someone or something more than anyone else or anything else: *Which song do you like best?*

best³ *noun*
1 the best = someone or something that is better than all the others: *There are a lot of good players on the team, but he is the best.* | *She always wants her children to have the best of everything* (=the best things).
2 do your best = to try as hard as you can to do something: *I did my best on the test, but I don't know if I passed.*
3 at best = the most that you can expect: *At best he will get an 85 on the exam.*

ˌbest 'man *noun*
a male friend who helps a man who is getting married and stands next to him during the wedding. The best man usually gives a speech at the meal after the wedding

bet¹ /bet/ *verb* **bet, betting**
1 to try to win money by guessing the result of a race, game, competition, etc.: *She bet all her money on a horse race.* SYNONYM **gamble**
2 I bet... *informal* = used when saying that you think something is true or likely to happen: *I bet he'll be late.*
3 you bet! *informal* = used in order to emphasize that you really mean "yes" when someone asks you a question: *"Is the prize really $20,000?" "You bet it is!"*

bet² *noun*
an agreement to risk money on the result of a race, game, competition, etc.: *He placed a bet on a horse* (=he tried to win money by saying that the horse would win the race).

be•tray /bɪ'treɪ/ *verb*
1 to do something that will harm your country or group: *He was put in prison for betraying his country by giving secret information to the enemy.*
2 to behave dishonestly toward someone who trusts you or loves you: *Her husband betrayed her and went to live with another woman.*

bet•ter¹ /'betɚ/ *adjective*
1 of a higher skill, quality, or standard than someone or something else: *His car is much better than mine, but it cost a lot more too.* | *She's better at video games than I am so she always wins when we play.* | *Your English is getting better* (=improving). ANTONYM **worse**
2 if you feel better, you feel less sick than before: *He had a sore throat yesterday, but he says that he's feeling better today.* ANTONYM **worse**
→ See Thesaurus box at **healthy**

bet•ter² *adverb*
1 in a way that is more skillful than someone or something else: *My sister can sing much better than me.*
2 like someone or something better = to

like someone or something more than someone or something else: *I like the blue shirt better, but the green one's okay too.*
3 had better do something = used when saying that someone should do something: *You'd* (=you had) *better go home now – your mom is probably worried.*
4 be better off = to have more money, or a better position or job, than you had before: *Most people are better off than they were 10 years ago.*

be•tween /bɪˈtwin/ *preposition, adverb*
1 in the space in the middle of two things, people, etc.: *I was sitting between two people I didn't know and felt uncomfortable.*

> **USAGE: between**
>
> **Between** and **among** are both used to talk about where someone or something is.
>
> Use **between** when there is one other person or thing on each side of someone or something: *I sat between Alex and Sarah.*
>
> Use **among** when there are two or more people or things on each side or all sides of someone or something: *Denise was among a group of her friends.*

2 in the period after one time, age, or event and before another: *The library is open between 9 and 5 o'clock.*

bev•er•age /ˈbevərɪdʒ/ *noun, formal*
a drink: *The restaurant sells alcoholic beverages.*

be•ware /bɪˈwer/ *verb*
used when you are warning someone to be careful about something: *The sign on the gate said "Beware of the dog!"*

be•wil•dered /bɪˈwɪldɚd/ *adjective*
very confused and not sure what to do or think: *She was bewildered by all their questions.*
—**bewildering** *adjective* making you feel confused and not sure what to do or think

be•yond /bɪˈyɑnd/ *preposition, adverb, formal*
1 on the other side of something: *Beyond the river, I could see the woods.*
2 later than a particular time, date, etc.: *We need to plan beyond the end of this year.*
3 more than a particular amount, level, or limit: *The price was beyond the amount that they could afford.*
4 be beyond someone = to be too difficult for someone to understand: *The science was all beyond him and he couldn't understand any of the discussion.*

bicycle

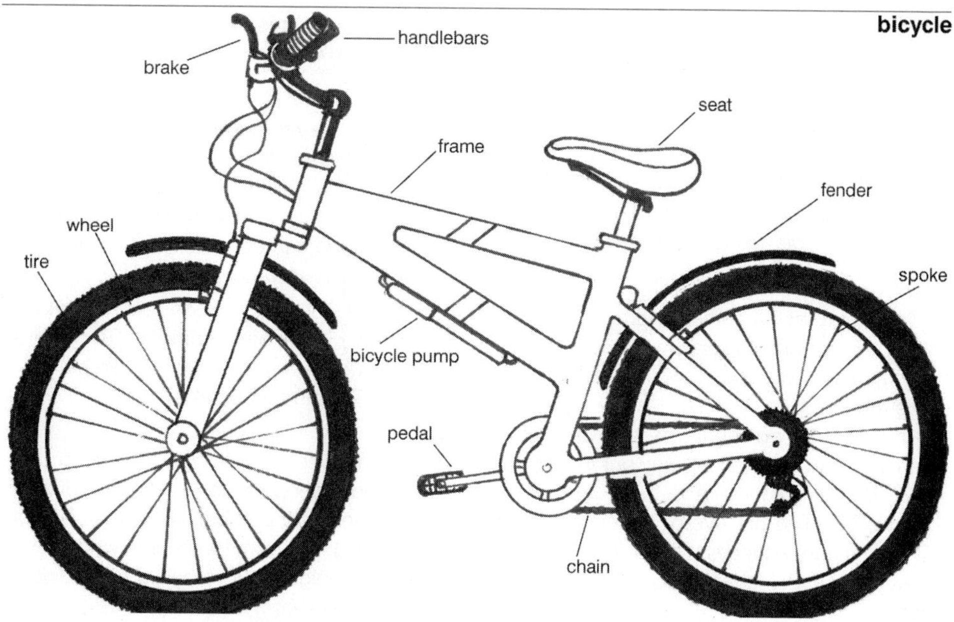

B

bi•as /ˈbaɪəs/ *noun*
an opinion about a person, group, or idea that makes you treat them unfairly or differently: *Some employers have a bias against women* (=treat women unfairly).
—**bias** *verb* to influence someone or something in an unfair way: *I don't want to bias you by telling you my opinion of his work.*
—**biased** *adjective* unfairly preferring one person, group, or idea over another: *I thought the article was very biased toward Democrats* (=unfairly in favor of Democrats).

WORD FAMILY look at the words:

→ **bias** *noun*
→ **bias** *verb*
→ **biased** *adjective*
→ **unbiased** *adjective*

bib /bɪb/ *noun*
a piece of cloth or plastic that you tie under a baby's chin to stop food from falling on his or her clothes

Bi•ble /ˈbaɪbəl/ *noun*
the Bible = the Holy book of the Jewish or Christian religions: *He believes everything that's in the Bible.*
—**biblical** /ˈbɪblɪkəl/ *adjective* relating to the Bible

bib•li•og•ra•phy /ˌbɪbliˈɑgrəfi/ *noun*
plural **bibliographies**
a list of books on a particular subject: *Remember to include a bibliography with all your sources at the end of your report.*

bi•cy•cle /ˈbaɪsɪkəl/ *noun*
a vehicle with two wheels that you ride by pushing the PEDALs with your feet: *She usually rides her bicycle to work.* SYNONYM **bike**

bid[1] /bɪd/ *noun*
1 an offer to pay a particular price for something that several people want to buy: *I tried to buy a painting at the auction, but my bid was too low.*
2 an offer to do work for someone at a particular price: *The company put in a bid to build the city's new library.*
3 an attempt to achieve or gain something: *Clinton made a successful bid for the presidency in 1992* (=attempt to become president).

bid[2] *verb* **bid, bidding**
1 to offer to pay a particular price for something that several people want to buy: *He bid $150,000 for the painting, but someone bid even higher.*
2 to offer to do work for someone at a particular price: *Companies were invited to bid for the contract to clean the offices.*
—**bidder** *noun* someone who makes a bid: *The property will go to the highest bidder.*

big /bɪg/ *adjective* **bigger, biggest**
1 large: *She lives in a big house with six bedrooms.* ANTONYM **small**

THESAURUS: big

large big or bigger than usual in size or amount: *New York is the largest city in America.* | *Large numbers of people watched the game.*
huge very big: *He ate a huge amount of food.* | *a huge television set*
enormous very big: *Their cat is enormous!* | *a park full of enormous trees*
gigantic extremely big or tall: *The airport is gigantic.* | *a gigantic wave*
Big and **large** mean the same thing, but **large** is slightly more formal: *That's a big piece of cake!* | *It's the largest building in Chicago.*
Use **large**, not **big**, to describe amounts: *Kelly gets large amounts of homework.*
Use **big**, not **large**, to describe something that is important: *This is a big opportunity for me.*

2 important or serious: *We have some big problems we need to deal with.* | *It was the biggest mistake of my life and I wish I could go back and change it.* ANTONYM **small**
3 successful or popular: *His last movie was a big hit and earned millions of dollars.*

ˌbig-ˈheaded *adjective, informal*
someone who is big-headed thinks that they are better than other people: *Don't be so big-headed – you've only won two games.*
→ See Thesaurus box at **proud**

big•ot /ˈbɪgət/ *noun*
someone who has strong and unkind opinions about people who belong to a different race, religion, or political group: *a racist bigot*
—**bigoted** *adjective* someone who is bigoted is a bigot: *My father is very bigoted about people from other countries.*

—**bigotry** *noun* behavior that is typical of a bigot

bike /baɪk/ *noun, informal*
1 a bicycle: *The kids were riding their bikes around the neighborhood.*
2 a MOTORCYCLE
—**biker** *noun* someone who rides a bike or a MOTORCYCLE

bi•ki•ni /bɪˈkini/ *noun*
a piece of clothing in two parts that women wear on the beach when it is hot

bi•lin•gual /baɪˈlɪŋgwəl/ *adjective*
1 able to speak two languages: *Their kids are bilingual – they speak both Spanish and English.*
2 written or spoken in two languages: *a bilingual dictionary*

bill[1] /bɪl/ *noun*
1 a list of things that you have bought or that someone has done for you, showing how much you have to pay for them: *Have you paid the electric bill?* | *The bill for the repairs was $600.*
2 a piece of paper money: *a ten-dollar bill*
3 a plan for a new law: *The House of Representatives passed a new gun-control bill* (=made it a law).
4 a bird's beak: *a duck's bill*
➔ See Thesaurus box at **money**

bill[2] *verb*
to send a bill to someone to tell them how much money they must pay: *They've billed me for things I didn't order.*

bill•board /ˈbɪlbɔrd/ *noun*
a big sign, next to a road, used for advertising something
➔ See Thesaurus box at **advertisement**

bil•lion /ˈbɪlyən/ *number* plural **billion** or **billions**
1 1,000,000,000: *$7 billion*
2 *also* **billions** *informal* a very large number of people or things: *There were billions of people at the baseball game last night.*
—**billionth** *number* 1,000,000,000th or 1/1,000,000,000

ˌBill of ˈRights, the *noun*
a written statement of the most important rights of the citizens of the U.S. It is part of the U.S. Constitution: *The Bill of Rights gives people the freedom to follow whatever religion they choose.*

bin /bɪn/ *noun*
a large container for storing things: *a flour bin*

bind /baɪnd/ *verb* **bound** /baʊnd/
to tie someone or something with rope or string: *They bound his arms and legs with a rope so that he wouldn't escape.*

binge /bɪndʒ/ *noun, informal*
an occasion when you eat too much or drink too much alcohol in a very short time: *He went on a drinking binge last Saturday and was sick all day Sunday.*
—**binge** *verb* to eat or drink a lot in a very short time: *Whenever she feels sad, she binges on chocolate.*

bin•go /ˈbɪŋgoʊ/ *noun*
a game played for money or prizes in which someone picks numbers from a box and says what they are. If you have the right numbers in a line on your card, you win

bin•oc•u•lars /bɪˈnɑkyələ˞z/ *plural noun*
an object like a large pair of special glasses that you hold up and look through to see things that are far away: *He watched the football game through a pair of binoculars.*

bi•o•de•grad•a•ble /ˌbaɪoʊdɪˈgreɪdəbəl/ *adjective*
something that is biodegradable is able to be destroyed by natural processes in a way that does not harm the environment: *Most types of plastic are not biodegradable and will remain solid for thousands of years.*

bi•og•ra•phy /baɪˈɑgrəfi/ *noun* plural **biographies**
a book about a person's life: *He wrote a biography of Nelson Mandela.*
—**biographer** *noun* someone who writes a book about a person's life

bi•ol•o•gy /baɪˈɑlədʒi/ *noun*
the scientific study of living things: *Biology was my favorite subject at school because I liked learning about other living things.*
—**biologist** *noun* someone whose job involves studying biology
—**biological** /ˌbaɪəˈlɑdʒɪkəl/ *adjective* relating to biology or living things

birch /bə˞tʃ/ *noun*
a tree with smooth BARK like paper, or the wood of this tree

B

B

bird /bɚd/ *noun*
an animal with wings and feathers that can usually fly. Female birds produce eggs

birth /bɚθ/ *noun*
1 give birth = if a woman gives birth, she produces a baby from her body: *Sue gave birth to a healthy baby girl on Tuesday.*
2 the time when a baby comes out of its mother's body: *The baby weighed seven pounds at birth* (=when she was born).
3 the character, language, social position, etc. that you have because of the family or country you come from: *Her father was Mexican by birth* (=he was born in Mexico), *but later became a U.S. citizen.*
4 the birth of something = the time when something new starts: *the birth of television in 1927*

ˈbirth cerˌtificate *noun*
an official document that shows when and where you were born

ˈbirth conˌtrol *noun*
ways of stopping a woman from becoming PREGNANT (=having a baby growing inside her body) SYNONYM **contraception**

birth·day /ˈbɚθdeɪ/ *noun*
the date of the day when you were born: *My birthday is April 10.* | *I got ten birthday cards.* | *Happy Birthday!* (=you say this to someone on his or her birthday)

birth·place /ˈbɚθpleɪs/ *noun*
the place where someone was born: *Westmoreland County, Virginia, is the birthplace of George Washington.*

bis·cuit /ˈbɪskɪt/ *noun*
a type of bread that you bake in small round shapes

bi·sect /ˈbaɪsekt/ *verb, formal*
to divide something into two equal parts: *The city is bisected by a freeway.*

bish·op /ˈbɪʃəp/ *noun*
a priest with a high rank who is in control of the churches and priests in a large area

bi·son /ˈbaɪsən/ *noun* plural **bison** or **bisons**
a North American wild animal that looks like a large cow with thick hair on its neck and shoulders

bit¹ /bɪt/ *noun*
1 a (little) bit = slightly: *I felt a little bit tired, so I took a break.*
2 a small piece or amount of something: *The floor was covered with bits of broken glass.*
3 quite a bit = a large amount: *He got quite a bit of help from his brother on the project.*
4 the smallest unit of information that a computer uses

bit² *verb*
the past tense of BITE

bite¹ /baɪt/ *verb* **bit** /bɪt/ **bitten** /ˈbɪtn/ **biting**
1 to cut or crush something with your teeth: *The dog bit him when he tried to pet it.* | *Jim bit into the apple.*
2 if an insect bites you, it puts a small amount of poison into your body so that you have a lump or red mark on your skin: *Ouch! A mosquito bit me.*

bite² *noun*
1 the act of cutting or crushing something with your teeth: *He took a bite of the cake.*
2 a wound made when an animal or insect bites you: *a mosquito bite*
3 a bite (to eat) *informal* = a quick meal: *We can grab a bite before we leave.*

bit·ten /ˈbɪtn/ *verb*
the past participle of BITE

bit·ter /ˈbɪtɚ/ *adjective*
1 angry for a long time because you feel something bad or unfair has happened to you: *She felt very bitter about losing her job.*
2 having a strong taste that is not sweet, like coffee without sugar: *The fruit tasted bitter, so I threw it out.*
3 making you feel very unhappy and upset: *Losing the game was a bitter disappointment*
4 bitter weather is extremely cold: *a bitter wind*
—**bitterly** *adverb* in a way that shows you are very angry, upset, or unhappy: *Fans were bitterly disappointed by the team's loss.*
—**bitterness** *noun*

bi·week·ly /baɪˈwikli/ *adjective, adverb*
happening or done every two weeks: *a biweekly meeting* | *The magazine is published biweekly.*

bi·zarre /bɪˈzɑr/ *adjective*
very unusual and strange: *His bizarre behavior was caused by his illness.*
➔ See Thesaurus box at **strange¹**

black¹ /blæk/ *adjective*
1 having a color that is darker than every other color, like the sky at night: *a black horse*
2 *also* **Black** someone with dark-colored skin whose family originally came from Africa: *Black kids and white kids worked together to plan the event.*
—**blackness** *noun* the quality of being black or very dark

black² *noun*
1 the darkest color, like the color of the sky at night: *She was wearing black.*
2 **blacks** *also* **Blacks** = people with dark-colored skin whose families originally came from Africa

black•ber•ry /ˈblækˌberi/ *noun* plural **blackberries**
a small sweet dark purple fruit that grows on a bush
➔ See picture on page A13

black•bird /ˈblækbɚd/ *noun*
a common American and European bird. The male blackbird is completely black

black•board /ˈblækˌbɔrd/ *noun*
a dark smooth board, usually in a school, that you write on with CHALK: *The teacher wrote the date on the blackboard.*

black•mail /ˈblækmeɪl/ *noun*
the practice of making someone do what you want by saying that you will tell secrets about them: *"Give me the money, or I'll tell your wife." "This is blackmail!"*
—**blackmail** *verb* to use blackmail: *He tried to blackmail her by threatening to tell the police about the stolen money.*
—**blackmailer** *noun* someone who uses blackmail

ˌblack ˈmarket *noun*
the system in which people buy and sell things illegally: *During the war some types of food could only be bought on the black market.*

black•out /ˈblækaʊt/ *noun*
1 a period of darkness in an area of buildings or houses, when the electricity stops working: *Our neighborhood had a blackout last night so we couldn't watch TV.*
2 if you have a blackout, you cannot see, hear, or feel anything because you are ill or have hit your head: *Since the accident, Sam has suffered from blackouts and he can't remember later what happened.*

blad•der /ˈblædɚ/ *noun*
the part of your body where URINE (=liquid waste) stays before it leaves your body
➔ See picture on page A2

blade /bleɪd/ *noun*
1 the flat cutting part of a knife, tool, or weapon: *The blade on this knife is very sharp.*
2 a single piece of grass: *a blade of grass*

blame¹ /bleɪm/ *verb*
1 if you blame someone, you say or think that he or she is responsible for something bad that has happened: *The fans blamed the coach for the team's defeat.* | *He's blaming all his problems on me.*
2 **I don't blame you/her/them, etc.** = you say this when you think that what someone is doing or thinking is reasonable: *"She got really mad at him for being so late." "I don't blame her!"*

blame² *noun*
responsibility for a mistake or for something bad: *I always get the blame when things go wrong.* | *He tried to put the blame for the broken window on his brother* (=say his brother broke the window).

bland /blænd/ *adjective*
1 without any excitement, strong opinions, or special qualities: *The group's latest CD is pretty bland; all the songs sound the same.*
2 bland food has very little taste: *The food was bland – it had no flavor.*
➔ See Thesaurus box at **taste¹**

blank¹ /blæŋk/ *adjective*
1 a blank sheet of paper, tape, etc. has nothing written or recorded on it: *She started writing on a blank page.* | *Do we have any blank CDs? I want to download some music.*
2 **go blank** = if your mind goes blank, you suddenly cannot remember something: *I was so nervous that my mind went blank when I stood up to speak.*
3 a blank expression or look shows no emotion, understanding, or interest: *I said hello, but she just gave me a blank look as if she did not know me.*
—**blankly** *adverb* if you look at someone or something blankly, you do not show any emotion, understanding, or interest: *I asked*

B

the boy where his mother was, but he just stared at me blankly.

blank² *noun*
an empty space on a piece of paper where you are supposed to write a word or letter: *Answer the test questions by filling in the blanks* (=writing in the spaces).

blan•ket /ˈblæŋkɪt/ *noun*
1 a thick cover that keeps you warm in bed: *I put another blanket on the bed because I was cold.*
2 a blanket of fog/cloud/snow, etc. = a thick layer of something that covers something: *The ground was covered in a thick blanket of snow.*
→ See picture on page A10

blare /bler/ *verb*
to make a very loud unpleasant noise: *Music was blaring from the car radio and everyone nearby could hear it.*

blast¹ /blæst/ *noun*
an explosion: *Three soldiers died in the blast that destroyed the building.*

blast² *verb*
1 to break something into pieces by making it explode: *The buildings had been blasted by terrorist bombs.*
2 if music or another sound blasts, it makes a very loud noise: *Music was blasting from two huge speakers, and it hurt my ears.*

bla•tant /ˈbleɪtənt/ *adjective*
very noticeable and shocking: *She told a blatant lie that we all knew wasn't true.* SYNONYM **obvious**

blaze¹ /bleɪz/ *verb*
to burn or shine very brightly and strongly: *A fire was blazing in the room.*

blaze² *noun*
1 the strong bright flames of a fire: *The blaze burned several buildings and caused thousands of dollars of damage.*
2 a very bright light or color: *They walked out of the house into a blaze of sunshine.*
→ See Thesaurus box at **fire¹**

bleach /blitʃ/ *noun*
a strong chemical used to make clothes white, or to kill GERMs
—**bleach** *verb* to make something whiter or lighter in color: *Her hair isn't naturally blond – she bleaches it.*

bleach•ers /ˈblitʃɚz/ *plural noun*
rows of seats where people sit to watch sports

bleak /blik/ *adjective*
1 without anything to make you feel happy or hopeful: *She had no job, and her future seemed bleak.* ANTONYM **bright**
2 a bleak day is cold, gray, and often cold: *a bleak day in the middle of winter* ANTONYM **bright**

blear•y /ˈblɪri/ *adjective*
unable to see clearly because you are tired or have been crying: *My eyes were bleary from lack of sleep.*

bleed /blid/ *verb*
bled /bled/
1 if part of your body bleeds, blood comes out of it: *His knee was bleeding after he fell off his bike.*
2 if colors bleed when they get wet, they mix together: *Wash brightly colored clothes separately, in case the colors bleed.*
WORD FAMILY → **blood** *noun*

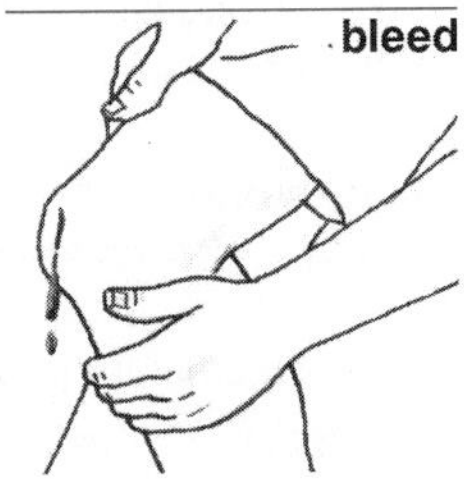

blem•ish /ˈblemɪʃ/ *noun*
a small mark that spoils the appearance of something or someone: *The makeup is good for covering up blemishes on your skin.*
→ See Thesaurus box at **mark²**

blend¹ /blend/ *verb*
to mix things together, especially foods: *Blend the milk and the eggs until the mixture is smooth.*
→ See Thesaurus box at **mix¹**

blend² *noun*
a mixture of two or more things or people: *The city has an interesting blend of old and new buildings.*

blend•er /ˈblendɚ/ *noun*
a small electric machine that you use to mix liquids together

bless /bles/ *verb*
1 Bless you! = said when someone SNEEZEs
2 if God blesses someone, he helps and protects that person: *May God bless you and keep you safe.*
3 to make something holy: *The priest blessed the bread and the wine.*

B

bless•ing /ˈblesɪŋ/ *noun*
1 something good that improves a situation and makes you happy: *The cool breeze was a blessing on such a hot day.*
2 if you give someone your blessing, you say that you agree with what that person is doing and want him or her to be successful: *She got married with her parents' blessing – they were very happy for her.*
3 protection and help from God, or a prayer asking for this: *They asked for God's blessing on their journey.*

blew /blu/ *verb*
the past tense of BLOW

blimp /blɪmp/ *noun*
an aircraft without wings that is filled with gas and looks like a very large BALLOON

blind[1] /blaɪnd/ *adjective*
unable to see: *A dog was leading a blind man across the street.* | *When she was two, she went blind* (=became blind).
—**blindness** *noun*

blind[2] *verb*
to make someone unable to see: *He was blinded by the explosion, and could not see anything for a few hours.*

blind[3] *noun*
a piece of cloth or other material that you pull down to cover a window: *Is it OK if I close the blinds? The sun is so bright.*
➔ See picture on page A9

blind•fold /ˈblaɪndfoʊld/ *noun*
a piece of cloth that you use to cover someone's eyes so that she or he cannot see
—**blindfold** *verb* to cover someone's eyes with a blindfold

blink /blɪŋk/ *verb*
1 to open and close your eyes very quickly: *The boy blinked and rubbed his eyes.*
2 if a light blinks, it quickly goes on and off: *A light on her computer kept blinking.*

blink•er /ˈblɪŋkɚ/ *noun*
a light that goes on and off to show that a car is turning left or right
➔ See picture on page A28

bliss /blɪs/ *noun, formal*
perfect happiness: *When they first married, they lived a life of complete bliss.*
—**blissful** *adjective* very happy
—**blissfully** *adverb*

blis•ter /ˈblɪstɚ/ *noun*
a raised area of skin that is filled with liquid and is usually caused by rubbing or burning: *New shoes always give me blisters.*
➔ See Thesaurus box at **mark**[2]

bliz•zard /ˈblɪzɚd/ *noun*
a very bad storm with a lot of snow and wind
➔ See Thesaurus box at **snow**[1]

bloat•ed /ˈbloʊtɪd/ *adjective*
if you feel bloated, your stomach feels too full and too big: *I felt bloated after eating so much meat.*

blob /blɑb/ *noun*
a small drop of a thick liquid such as paint or ice cream: *There was a blob of paint on the end of his nose.*

block[1] /blɑk/ *noun*
1 an area or distance in a city from the place where two streets cross to the next place where two streets cross: *We walked for two or three blocks until we saw the park.*
2 a solid piece of wood, stone, etc.: *Before electricity, people kept food cold using blocks of ice.*
3 one of a set of solid wooden shapes that children build things with: *My little sister was building a tower with her blocks.*
4 a group of things of the same kind or an amount of something, considered as a single unit: *I bought a block of tickets for the concert so that we could all sit together.*

block[2] *verb*
1 to stop people or things from moving through or along something: *A big truck was blocking the road.*
2 **block someone's view** = if something blocks your view, it stops you from being able to see in front of you: *A tall man in front of me was blocking my view.*
3 to stop something from happening, developing, or succeeding: *Congress blocked the president's plan.*

block•age /ˈblɑkɪdʒ/ *noun*
something that stops other things from moving through a pipe, tube, etc.: *I think there's a blockage in the pipe under the sink – the water's not going down.*

blond *also* **blonde** /blɑnd/ *adjective*
blond hair is light yellow in color: *She had long blond hair.*

—**blonde** *noun* a woman who has pale yellow hair

B

blood /blʌd/ *noun*
the red liquid that your heart pumps through your body: *After the accident her face was covered in blood.*

ˈblood ˌpressure *noun*
the force with which blood moves around your body. If your blood pressure is high, it can make you more likely to have a heart attack: *My father has high blood pressure, so he has to be careful not too eat too much salt.*

blood•shed /ˈblʌdʃed/ *noun*
the killing of people in fighting or a war

blood•stream /ˈblʌdstrim/ *noun*
blood as it flows around the body: *It takes a few minutes for the drug to enter the bloodstream* (=go into your blood).

blood•thirst•y /ˈblʌdˌθɚsti/ *adjective*
enjoying killing and violence: *The man was attacked and beaten by a bloodthirsty crowd.*

ˈblood ˌvessel *noun*
one of the tubes through which blood flows in your body

blood•y /ˈblʌdi/ *adjective*
1 covered in blood: *He had a bloody nose.*
2 with a lot of killing and violence: *Hundreds were killed in the bloody battle.*

bloom¹ /bluːm/ *verb*
if a plant blooms, its flowers are open: *The spring flowers were blooming in the fields.*

bloom² *noun*
1 be in bloom = if a plant is in bloom, its flowers are open: *The sunflowers are in bloom at this time of year.*
2 a flower: *The rose has beautiful pink blooms.* SYNONYM **blossom**

blos•som¹ /ˈblɑsəm/ *noun*
a flower on a tree or bush: *In April the cherry trees are covered in blossoms.*

blossom² *verb*
if a tree or a bush blossoms, it produces flowers: *The apple trees are already starting to blossom.*

blot¹ /blɑt/ *verb* **blotted, blotting**
to press soft paper or cloth onto a wet surface in order to dry it: *I used a tissue to blot the coffee that spilled on the desk.*

blot² *noun*
a mark or spot that spoils something or makes it dirty

blouse /blaʊs/ *noun*
a shirt for a woman or girl: *She is wearing a white blouse and a blue skirt.*
➔ See picture on page A6

blow¹ /bloʊ/ *verb* **blew** /blu/ **blown** /bloʊn/
1 if the wind blows, it makes the air move: *A cold wind was blowing from the east.* | *The wind blew the leaves off the trees* (=it made the leaves fall off the trees).
2 to send out air or smoke through your mouth: *She blew on her soup to cool it.*
3 to cause a whistle, car horn, etc. to make a sound: *The man in the car behind me started blowing his horn to get me to move.*
4 blow your nose = to clear your nose by blowing air through it into a piece of cloth or TISSUE
5 blow it *informal* = to be unsuccessful when you are doing something, because you make a mistake: *I should have gotten an A on the test, but I blew it and got a D.*

PHRASAL VERBS

blow something out
to blow air on a flame and make it stop burning: *She blew out all the candles on her birthday cake.*

blow up
1 blow (something) up = if something blows up, it is destroyed in an explosion: *The soldiers blew up the bridge using dynamite.*
2 blow something up = to fill something with air or gas, especially a BALLOON: *We blew up the balloons for the party.*

blow² *noun*
1 something very sad and shocking that happens to you: *Her father's death was a terrible blow to her.*
2 a hard hit with a hand, tool, or weapon: *He was killed by a blow to the side of his head.*

ˈblow dry *verb* third person singular **blow-dries, blow-dried**
to dry hair using a machine that blows hot air

ˈblow ˌdryer *noun*
a piece of equipment that you hold in your hand and use to dry your wet hair

blown /bloʊn/ *verb*
the past participle of BLOW

blue¹ /blu/ *adjective*
1 having the same color as a clear sky during the day: *She has beautiful blue eyes.*
2 *informal* sad: *Why are you feeling blue? Did something bad happen?*

blue² *noun*
the color of the sky on a clear day: *She was dressed in blue* (=she was wearing blue clothes).

blue•ber•ry /ˈbluˌberi/ *noun* plural **blueberries**
a small dark blue round BERRY that has a sweet taste: *blueberry muffins*

blue•bird /ˈbluˌbɚd/ *noun*
a small North American wild bird that sings and has a blue back and wings

ˌblue-ˈcollar *adjective*
blue-collar workers do physical work, rather than working in offices

blues /bluz/ *noun*
the blues = a style of music that came from the African-American culture in the southern U.S. Blues songs often tell about the sad or difficult things in someone's life

bluff¹ /blʌf/ *verb*
to pretend that something is true, in order to get an advantage for yourself: *He told me that someone else had offered him more money for the car, but I knew he was bluffing. He was just trying to get me to pay more.*

bluff² *noun*
an attempt to make someone believe that you will do something, even though this is not true: *She's threatening to leave her job, but I'm sure it's a bluff. She'll never quit.*

blunt /blʌnt/ *adjective*
1 speaking in a very direct and honest way which may upset people: *I didn't expect such a blunt answer – she didn't even give an explanation.*
2 **a blunt object/instrument** = an object that is not sharp and is used to hit someone: *Police say the man was hit on the head with a blunt instrument.*
—**bluntly** *adverb*: *"He's not coming with us because I don't like him," she replied bluntly.*

blur /blɚ/ *noun*
if something is a blur, you cannot see or remember it clearly: *So much has happened this past year, it's all a blur when I try to remember it.*

blurred /blɚd/ *adjective*
1 *also* **blurry** having a shape that is not clear: *a blurry old photograph of his grandmother*
2 if your EYESIGHT is blurred, you cannot see clearly

blurt /blɚt/ *verb*
also **blurt out** to say something suddenly and without thinking, usually because you are nervous or excited: *Another student blurted out the answer before I could say anything.*

blush /blʌʃ/ *verb*
if you blush, your face becomes red, usually because you are embarrassed: *She blushed when he told her she was beautiful.*

Blvd.
the written abbreviation of **boulevard**

board¹ /bɔrd/ *noun*
1 a large wide piece of wood, plastic, etc., that you use for writing or doing things on: *The new teacher wrote her name on the board.* | *a chess board* | *a cutting board* (=for cutting food on)
2 a long thin flat piece of wood used for making floors, walls, fences, etc.: *He cut two six-foot boards in half with a saw.*
3 a group of people in a school, company, etc. who make the rules and important decisions: *The school board decided to build a new gym at the high school.*
4 **on board** = on an airplane, ship, etc.: *There were over 500 passengers on board when the boat sank.*
5 the meals that are provided for you when you pay to stay somewhere: *College students have to pay tuition as well as room and board* (=a place to live and eat food).

board² *verb, formal*
to get on an airplane, ship, train, etc. in order to travel somewhere: *The passengers were waiting to board the plane.* SYNONYM **get on**

PHRASAL VERB

board something up
to cover a window or door with wooden

B

boards: *They boarded up all the doors to stop people from getting into the building.*

boast /boʊst/ *verb*
to talk too proudly about what you have done, what you own, etc.: *Scott kept boasting about winning the game, and it was starting to annoy us.* SYNONYM **brag**
—**boastful** *adjective* talking too proudly about what you have done, what you own, etc.

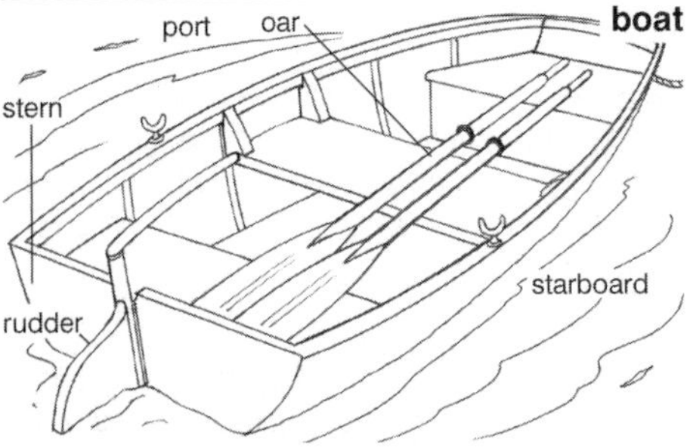

boat /boʊt/ *noun*
a small ship: *You can only get to the island by boat.* | *a fishing boat* (=for fishing on the ocean)

bob /bɑb/ *verb* **bobbed, bobbing**
to move up and down quickly on water: *Boats were bobbing up and down on the waves.*

bob•cat /ˈbɑbkæt/ *noun*
a wild cat that has no tail and lives in North America

bod•y /ˈbɑdi/ *noun* plural **bodies**
1 the physical structure of a person or animal: *Exercise is good for your body.* | *He made a drawing of the human body and wrote the names of all the parts on it.*
2 the main part of a person or animal, not the head, arms, or legs: *She has a short body and long legs.*
3 a dead person: *They found a body in the woods and called the police.* SYNONYM **corpse**
4 the main part of something: *The body of the airplane was not damaged in the crash.*

ˈbody ˌbuilding *noun*
hard exercise that some people do to get big muscles
—**body builder** *noun* someone who does body building

bod•y•guard /ˈbɑdiˌgɑrd/ *noun*
someone whose job is to stop another person getting attacked or hurt: *The president's bodyguards go with him wherever he goes.*

bo•gus /ˈboʊgəs/ *adjective*
not real or honest: *These results are based on a bogus study, so we cannot accept them.* SYNONYM **fake**

boil /bɔɪl/ *verb*
1 if a liquid boils, it gets very hot and produces BUBBLEs and steam: *Water boils at 100 degrees centigrade.* | *I boiled some water and added the spaghetti.*
2 to cook food in very hot water: *Boil the potatoes for 25 minutes.*
—**boiling point** *noun* the temperature of a liquid when it begins to boil
➔ See Thesaurus box at **cook**[1]
➔ See picture on page A14

boil•er /ˈbɔɪlɚ/ *noun*
a big container that heats the water for a building

bois•ter•ous /ˈbɔɪstərəs/ *adjective, formal*
noisy and full of energy: *A boisterous crowd was yelling and throwing things as they watched the game.*

bold /boʊld/ *adjective*
1 a bold action, plan, etc. shows that you are not afraid to do something dangerous or new: *It was a bold move for the coach to hire so many new players.*
2 bold colors, flavors, letters, etc. are very strong and clear: *She painted her bedroom in bright bold colors.*

bo•lo•gna *also* **baloney** /bəˈloʊni/ *noun*
a type of SAUSAGE used for making sandwiches

bolt[1] /boʊlt/ *noun*
1 a piece of metal that slides across to lock a door
2 a type of screw that goes inside a NUT (=round circle of metal) and is used for holding two things together
3 a bolt of lightning/a lightning bolt = a sudden flash of bright light in the sky during a storm

bolt[2] *verb*
to lock a door with a bolt: *She closed the door and bolted it so no one could get in.*

B

bolt[3] *adverb*
sit/stand bolt upright = to sit or stand with your back very straight because you are frightened: *She heard a noise and sat bolt upright in bed.*

bomb[1] /bɑm/ *noun*
a weapon that explodes and causes damage: *The bomb went off* (=exploded) *near the airport and damaged some small buildings.*

bomb[2] *verb*
1 to attack a place with bombs: *Enemy aircraft bombed the city, destroying many homes.*
2 *informal* if a play, movie, etc. bombs, it is not successful: *His second movie bombed – almost no one went to see it.*

bom•bard /bɑmˈbɑrd/ *verb, formal*
to attack a place for a long time with guns and bombs: *For three days, the army bombarded the city until much of it was destroyed.*
—**bombardment** *noun* the act of bombarding a place

bomb•er /ˈbɑmɚ/ *noun*
1 an airplane that drops bombs on a place
2 someone who puts a bomb somewhere

bond /bɑnd/ Ac *noun, formal*
a strong feeling of love or trust that people have for each other: *There was a special bond between Carlos and his younger brother.*

bone /boʊn/ *noun*
one of the hard parts that form the frame of the body: *Sam fell and broke a bone in his arm.*

bon•fire /ˈbɑnˌfaɪɚ/ *noun*
a large outdoor fire: *The kids wanted to make a bonfire with the branches to cook hotdogs.*

bo•nus /ˈboʊnəs/ *noun*
1 some money that you get from your employer that is more than your regular pay: *If employees work hard, they get a bonus at the end of the year.*
2 something good that is more than you expected: *He's very nice, and he's good-looking, which is a bonus!*

bon•y /ˈboʊni/ *adjective*
1 very thin: *He had long bony fingers.*
2 bony fish has a lot of small bones in it

boo[1] /bu/ *verb*
to shout "BOO" to show that you do not like a play, performer, etc.: *The crowd booed when he announced that the game had been canceled.*

boo[2] *noun*
1 a word people shout to show that they do not like a play, performer, etc.: *There were boos from the audience when the singer forgot the words to the song.*
2 a word you shout as a joke, to surprise someone who does not know you are there: *Tammy hid behind the door, ready to yell "Boo!"*

boo•by trap /ˈbubi træp/ *noun*
a bomb that is hidden and that explodes when you touch something connected to it

book[1] /bʊk/ *noun*
1 something that you read that has a lot of pages inside a cover: *I'm reading a good book.* | *Do you like books by William Faulkner* (=written by him)? | *The book is about hip hop music.*

THESAURUS: book

Types of book

nonfiction books which talk about real things, people, or events: *I like reading nonfiction, especially history and biography.*

fiction books which describe people and events that have not really happened: *It's fiction, but it gives you an idea about what life as a slave was like.*

literature fiction that people think is important: *My class on American Literature is reading "Huckleberry Finn."*

reference book a book such as a dictionary or encyclopedia that you look at to find information: *I checked a reference book to see when the Civil War ended.*

textbook a book that is used in the classroom: *a science textbook*

novel a book about people and events that have not really happened: *All three novels are about the same characters.*

2 pieces of paper fastened together in a cover for writing on: *an address book* (=for writing down people's addresses)
3 a book of stamps/tickets = a number of stamps or tickets inside a cover

B

book² *verb*
1 if someone is booked for a crime, the police write a formal statement saying that he or she may be guilty of the crime: *Newton was arrested and booked for robbery.*
2 if you book a seat on an airplane, a hotel room, etc. it is kept for you until you use it: *I booked a flight to Houston.*

book·case /ˈbʊk-keɪs/ *noun*
a piece of furniture with shelves for books
→ See picture on page A8

book·keep·er /ˈbʊkˌkipɚ/ *noun*
someone whose job is keeping a record of the money that a business receives and spends SYNONYM **accountant**

book·keep·ing /ˈbʊkˌkipɪŋ/ *noun*
the job of keeping a record of the money that a business receives and spends SYNONYM **accounting**

book·let /ˈbʊklət/ *noun*
a very short book that has information about something: *The eight-page booklet is full of advice for travelers.*

book·shelf /ˈbʊkʃelf/ *noun* plural **bookshelves** /ˈbʊkʃelvz/
a shelf that you keep books on
→ See picture on page A10

book·store /ˈbʊkstɔr/ *noun*
a store that sells books

boom¹ /bum/ *noun, formal*
1 a deep loud sound, like the sound of guns or drums: *At night we could hear the boom of the big guns.*
2 a time when businesses suddenly make a lot more money: *Recently, there has been a boom in tourism as more and more people travel.* ANTONYM **slump**

boom² *verb*
to make a deep loud sound, like the sound of guns or drums: *Guns boomed in the distance, and we were all scared.*

boost /bust/ *verb*
to increase or improve something: *If we practice hard, we boost our chances of winning.*
—**boost** *noun* an act of increasing or improving something: *The movie's success gave his career a boost* (=improved his career).

boot¹ /but/ *noun*
a shoe that covers your foot and sometimes part of your leg: *If it's snowing outside, you'll have to wear your boots.*
→ See picture at **shoe**

boot² *also* **boot up** *verb*
to start the program that makes a computer ready to use: *I made coffee while my computer was booting up.*

booth /buθ/ *noun*
a small place where one person goes to do something: *You can go into a booth in the store to listen to the music.* | *a phone booth*

bor·der /ˈbɔrdɚ/ *noun*
1 the line between two states or countries: *We crossed the border between the U.S. and Mexico.*

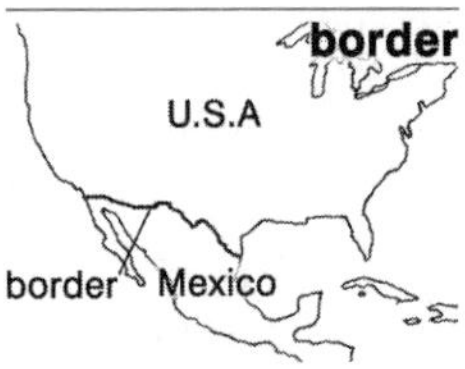

2 a narrow area of a different color around the edge of something: *She was wearing a black skirt with a red border.*

bore¹ /bɔr/ *verb*
the past tense of BEAR

bore² *verb*
if something bores you, you are not interested in it: *The movie really bored me, so I left.*

WORD FAMILY look at the words:
→ **bore** *noun*
→ **bore** *verb*
→ **bored** *adjective*
→ **boring** *adjective*
→ **boredom** *noun*

bore³ *noun*
someone or something that is not interesting: *This homework is a bore!*

bored /bɔrd/ *adjective*
if you are bored, you feel that what you are doing is not interesting: *Lisa felt bored with her life and wanted to do something new and exciting.*
—**boredom** *noun* the state of feeling bored
→ See picture on page A23

bor·ing /ˈbɔrɪŋ/ *adjective*
not interesting: *We watched a boring show on TV and I almost fell asleep.*

B

THESAURUS: boring

dull not interesting or exciting: *The book was really dull.*

tedious *formal* boring, and continuing for a long time: *Typing the lists was tedious work.*

not interesting: *The movie wasn't very interesting.*

born /bɔrn/ *adjective*

1 be born = to begin life when you come out of your mother's body: *I was born in Guatemala in 1999.*

2 a born leader/athlete, etc. = someone who is naturally good at being a leader, good at sports, etc.: *Michelle was a born actress – she's been acting since she was a little girl.*

borne /bɔrn/ *verb*

the past participle of BEAR

bor•ough /ˈbɚoʊ/ *noun*

an area of a large city with its own government that is responsible for the schools, hospitals, roads, etc. in the area: *There are five boroughs in New York City.*

bor•row /ˈbɑroʊ/ *verb*

1 to use something that belongs to another person and give it back later: *Can I borrow your bike? I need to go to the library.*

USAGE: borrow

If you **borrow** something from someone, you take something that someone gives you for a short time, and then you give it back: *Can I borrow your pen?*

You cannot say "Can I lend your pen?"

If you **lend** something to someone, you give it to him or her so that she or he can use it for a short time: *I lent that DVD to Rick.* | *Mom, could you lend me some money?*

You cannot say "Could you borrow me some money?"

2 if you borrow money from a bank, the bank gives you the money and you promise to pay it back: *Ellen borrowed $5,000 from the bank to pay for the car.*

bor•row•er /ˈbɑroʊɚ/ *noun, formal*

someone who borrows money from a bank

boss¹ /bɔs/ *noun*

a person at work who has a higher position than you and who directs your work: *Danny asked his boss if he could leave work early.*

boss² *verb*

boss someone around = to tell someone what to do in an annoying way: *My brother's always bossing me around and I don't like it.*

boss•y /ˈbɔsi/ *adjective*

someone who is bossy often tells other people what to do in an annoying way: *I don't like Marcia. She's so bossy and always thinks she's right.*

bot•a•ny /ˈbɑtn-i/ *noun*

the study of plants: *If you like plants, maybe you should study botany.*

—**botanist** *noun* a scientist who studies plants

both /boʊθ/ *adjective, pronoun*

used for talking about two people or things: *John and Reggie are both very tall.* | *"Which of these two dresses do you like?" "I like both."* | *Hold the bowl in both hands.*

GRAMMAR: both

both, both of

Do not say "The both men were from Los Angeles." Say: *Both of the men were from Los Angeles*, *both men were from Los Angeles*, or *both the men were from Los Angeles.*

Do not say "his both sisters." Say: *both of his sisters* or *both his sisters.*

both•er¹ /ˈbɑðɚ/ *verb*

1 to annoy someone by wanting attention when he or she is busy: *Don't bother your dad; he's working.*

2 to make someone feel worried or upset: *When I get bad grades, it really bothers me.*

3 to make an effort to do something: *Pete didn't bother to answer her – he just kept talking.* | *I'll never get the job, so why bother to apply?*

4 if a part of your body bothers you, it hurts a little: *My ankle's bothering me – maybe I should go to the doctor.*

bother² *noun*

something or someone that annoys or upsets you: *I don't want to be a bother, but could I ask for some help?*

B

bot·tle /ˈbɑtl/ *noun*
something that you buy or keep liquids in, usually made of glass or plastic: *I bought a bottle of soda.*
—**bottled** *adjective* bottled water, beer, etc. is water or beer that you buy in a bottle

bot·tom¹ /ˈbɑtəm/ *noun*
1 the lowest part or side of something: *Look at the picture at the bottom of the screen.* | *There's some mud on the bottom of your shoes.* ANTONYM **top**
2 the ground under an ocean or river: *The bottom of the river is rocky.* | *The ship sank and it's now at the bottom of the ocean.*
3 *informal* the part of your body that you sit on
4 the lowest position in a class, company, etc.: *His grades are bad, and he's always at the bottom of the class.* ANTONYM **top**

bottom² *adjective*
the bottom shelf, drawer, etc. is the lowest one: *We keep the toys on the bottom shelf so the kids can reach them.*

bought /bɔt/ *verb*
the past tense and past participle of BUY

boul·der /ˈboʊldɚ/ *noun*
a large rock: *A huge boulder rolled off the mountain onto the beach.*

bou·le·vard /ˈbʊləvɑrd/ *noun*
a wide road in a city: *We drove down Sunset Boulevard.*
→ See Thesaurus box at **road**

bounce¹ /baʊns/ *verb*
1 if a ball bounces, it hits the ground, a wall, etc. and moves up or away again: *He waited on the street, bouncing his basketball.* | *The ball bounced off the wall and hit me in the head.*
2 to move up and down because you are walking or jumping on something soft: *Stop bouncing on the bed!*
→ See picture at **jump**

bounce² *noun*
an act of bouncing: *Catch the ball on its first bounce.*

bounc·er /ˈbaʊnsɚ/ *noun*
someone whose job is making people leave clubs and bars if they are too noisy or violent

bounc·y /ˈbaʊnsi/ *adjective*
1 a bouncy ball moves quickly up and away after it hits something
2 full of energy: *His walk was quick and bouncy.*

bound¹ /baʊnd/ *verb*
the past tense and past participle of BIND

bound² *adjective*
1 be bound to do something = to be sure to do something: *Our team is bound to win – we have the best players.*
2 *formal* going toward a place: *The plane was bound for Miami.*
3 *formal* having a duty to do something: *We are all bound by the law* (=must do what the law says).

bound³ *verb, formal*
1 be bounded by something = if a place is bounded by a wall, river, road, etc., the wall, etc. goes around it: *The city is bounded by the river on two sides.*
2 to move or jump with a lot of energy: *George bounded down the stairs and ran out the door.*

bound⁴ *noun, formal*
a big jump into or over something: *With one bound he was over the gate.*

bound·a·ry /ˈbaʊndəri/ *noun* plural **boundaries**
1 the line that divides two areas of land: *Lake Ontario is on the boundary between New York State and Canada.*
2 the limit of what is possible or normal: *His behavior was outside the boundaries of what the school says is acceptable* (=his behavior was not acceptable at school).

bound·less /ˈbaʊndləs/ *adjective, formal*
something that is boundless seems to have no limit: *He's a writer with a boundless imagination – his books are all different but very interesting.*

boun·ti·ful /ˈbaʊntəfəl/ *adjective, formal*
if something is bountiful, there is a lot of it: *There was a bountiful crop of rice that year and everyone had enough to eat.*

bou·quet /boʊˈkeɪ/ *noun*
some flowers that are tied together to give as a present or to carry: *a bouquet of roses*

bout /baʊt/ *noun*
1 a short period of illness or activity: *I had a bout of the flu.* | *A bout of very cold weather killed many plants.*
2 a BOXING or WRESTLING match

bou•tique /buˈtik/ *noun*
a small store that sells fashionable clothes

bow¹ /baʊ/ *verb*
to bend your head or the top part of your body forward, in order to show respect or thank an AUDIENCE: *The conductor bowed as the audience applauded.* | *David bowed his head in prayer.*

bow² /baʊ/ *noun*
1 an act of bowing: *The actors took a bow* (=bowed) *and the curtain came down.*
2 the front part of a ship or boat: *He sat in the bow of the boat.*

bow

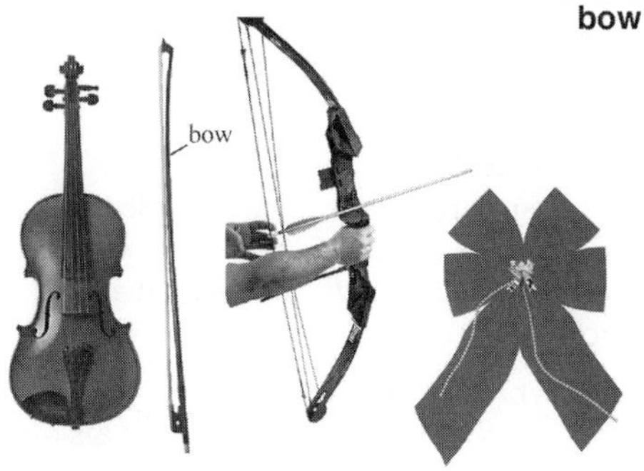

bow³ /boʊ/ *noun*
1 a piece of cloth, string, etc. tied in a knot with two LOOPs and two free ends: *The girl had a pretty pink bow in her hair.*
2 a long thin piece of wood held in a curve by a tight string, used for shooting ARROWs: *Native Americans hunted with bows and arrows.*
3 a long thin piece of wood with hair stretched from one end to the other, used for playing string instruments such as the VIOLIN

bow•el /ˈbaʊəl/ *noun*
the long tube inside your body through which food goes after it leaves your stomach
SYNONYM **intestine**

bowl /boʊl/ *noun*
a deep round dish or container: *He ate a bowl of cereal.*

bowl•ing /ˈboʊlɪŋ/ *noun*
an indoor game in which you try to knock down a group of objects by rolling a heavy ball at them: *The kids and I went bowling yesterday.*

bow tie /ˈboʊ taɪ/ *noun*
a man's tie which has a knot with two LOOPs and two free ends

box¹ /bɑks/ *noun*
1 a container with four sides, usually made of CARDBOARD (=stiff thick paper) or wood: *I put all her clothes in a box and sent them to her.* | *a box of chocolates*
2 a small area on an official form for people to write information in: *Write your name in the box at the top of the form.*

box² *verb*
to fight someone as a sport while wearing big leather GLOVEs

box•er /ˈbɑksɚ/ *noun*
someone who boxes as a job

box•ing /ˈbɑksɪŋ/ *noun*
the sport of fighting while wearing big leather GLOVEs: *He performed well today in the boxing ring* (=the area where boxers fight).
➔ See picture on page A24

ˈbox ˌoffice *noun*
a place in a theater, concert hall, etc. where you can buy tickets: *Tickets are on sale now at the box office.*

boy /bɔɪ/ *noun*
a male child or a young man: *He likes most of the boys in his class.* | *How old is your little boy* (=your young son)*?*
—**boyish** *adjective* looking or behaving like a boy: *He's 30 but still has a boyish face.*
—**boyhood** *noun*, *formal* the time when someone is a boy: *a boyhood friend* (=a friend he had when he was a boy)

boy•cott /ˈbɔɪkɑt/ *verb*
to refuse to buy something, use something, or do something, as a way of protesting: *Several countries will boycott the competition because they believe it is unfair.*
—**boycott** *noun*: *The group organized a boycott of the company's products to try to improve conditions for the company's workers.*

boy•friend /ˈbɔɪfrend/ *noun*
a boy or man that someone has a romantic relationship with: *Carol and her boyfriend went to a movie on Friday.*

ˈBoy Scouts *plural noun*
an organization for boys that teaches them practical skills
—**Boy Scout** *noun*

bra /brɑ/ *noun*
a piece of underwear that a woman wears to support her breasts

B

brace•let /ˈbreɪslət/ *noun*
a piece of jewelry that you wear around your wrist
→ See picture at **jewelry**

brac•es /ˈbreɪsɪz/ *plural noun*
wires which some people have on their teeth to make them straight

brack•et /ˈbrækɪt/ *noun*
1 one of the pair of marks [ ] put around extra information: *What do the numbers in brackets mean?*
2 age/income, etc. bracket *formal* = a particular range of ages, incomes, etc.: *people in the 18–24 age bracket* (=people who are between 18 and 24 years old)

brag /bræg/ *verb* **bragged, bragging**
to talk too proudly about what you have done, what you own, etc.: *He was bragging about the cool things he got for his birthday and trying to make us jealous.* SYNONYM **boast**

braid[1] /breɪd/ *verb*
to twist together three amounts of hair, pieces of rope, etc. so that they form one piece: *Her mother was braiding her long hair.*

braid[2] *noun*
three amounts of hair twisted together into a shape like a rope: *She wore her hair in braids.*

braille /breɪl/ *noun*
raised round marks that blind people can read by touching them: *The labels on the chemicals are in braille so blind people can read them.*

brain /breɪn/ *noun*
the part inside your head that controls how you think, feel, and move: *Which part of the brain controls how we move?* | *The drug can cause brain damage.*
→ See picture on page A2

brains /breɪnz/ *plural noun, informal*
the ability to think well: *The kid's definitely got brains – he always gets perfect scores on his tests.*

brain•storm /ˈbreɪnˌstɔrm/ *verb*
if a group of people brainstorms, they try to think of many different ways of doing something in order to solve a problem: *We were brainstorming about new ways to get children to read.*

brain•wash /ˈbreɪnwɑʃ/ *verb*
to make someone believe something that is not true, by repeating it many times and making him or her unable to think clearly: *They claim that the group brainwashes its members to get money from them.*

brain•y /ˈbreɪni/ *adjective, informal*
able to think well and learn quickly: *He's a brainy little boy who always knows the right answer.*

brake[1] /breɪk/ *noun*
the part of a bicycle, car, etc. that you use to make it go more slowly or stop: *When I saw the child in the road, I slammed on the brakes* (=made the car stop quickly).
→ See picture at **bicycle**

brake[2] *verb*
to make a bicycle, car, etc. go more slowly or stop by using its brakes: *She braked suddenly when a dog ran into the road in front of her.*

bran /bræn/ *noun*
the crushed outer part of wheat or a similar grain

branch[1] /bræntʃ/ *noun*
1 a part of a tree that grows out from the main part: *He climbed up into the lowest branches of the tree.*
2 a store, bank, group, etc. that is part of a large organization: *The bank has branches all over the country.*
3 one part of a large subject of study or knowledge: *Geometry is a branch of mathematics.*

branch[2] *verb*
PHRASAL VERB
branch out
to do something new in addition to what you usually do: *She designs clothes for women, but she has recently branched out into men's clothing.*

brand /brænd/ *noun*
a type of product made by a particular company: *What brand of soap do you use?*
→ See Thesaurus box at **type**[1]

bran•dish /ˈbrændɪʃ/ *verb, formal*
to wave something around in a threatening way: *He ran into the store brandishing a knife and demanding money.*

ˌbrand-ˈnew *adjective*
new and never used before: *I've never had a brand-new car – I always buy used cars.*

bran•dy /ˈbrændi/ *noun* plural **brandies**
a strong alcoholic drink made from wine

brash /bræʃ/ *adjective*
behaving and talking too confidently: *He was a brash young salesman who sometimes offended customers.*

brass /bræs/ *noun*
1 a very hard bright yellow metal that is a mixture of COPPER and ZINC: *a brass doorknob*
2 the brass (section) = the people in an ORCHESTRA or band who play musical instruments such as the TRUMPET or horn

brat /bræt/ *noun, informal*
a child who behaves badly: *Stop acting like a spoiled brat and help me.*

brave /breɪv/ *adjective*
not afraid or not showing fear: *brave soldiers*
—**bravely** *adverb*

brav•er•y /ˈbreɪvəri/ *noun, formal*
brave behavior, or the quality of being brave: *He showed great bravery in the battle and saved many other men.* SYNONYM **courage**; ANTONYM **cowardice**

bread /bred/ *noun*
a food made by mixing flour, water, and YEAST, and then baking it: *white bread* | *She cut me a slice of bread* (=one thin piece). | *a loaf of bread* (=an amount of bread that you can cut slices from)

breadth /bredθ/ *noun, formal*
1 the distance from one side of something to the other: *The wall is one foot in breadth.* SYNONYM **width**
2 the fact that something includes a large number of different things: *They were impressed by his breadth of knowledge* (=the fact that he knew many different things).

break[1] /breɪk/ *verb* **broke** /broʊk/ **broken** /ˈbroʊkən/
1 if something breaks, or if you break it, it separates into pieces, especially when it is hit or dropped: *The plate fell on the floor and broke.* | *Who broke that window?* | *I broke my leg* (=broke the bone in my leg). | *Break up the ice with a hammer* (=break it into many pieces).

THESAURUS: break

smash used when a plate, glass, or window breaks because it has been hit with a lot of force: *The baseball hit the window and smashed it.*

shatter used when a plate or glass breaks into a lot of small pieces: *I dropped a glass, and it shattered everywhere.*

crack used when a plate, glass, window, etc. is broken so that there is a line between two parts of it: *This cup is cracked.*

tear used about paper or cloth: *I tore my jeans when I fell down.*

snap used about something that breaks into two pieces, making a loud noise: *The stick snapped in two.*

burst used when something with liquid inside it breaks: *Our pipes had burst in the freezing weather.*

pop used when a bubble or balloon breaks: *The game is to pop the balloons by sitting on them.*

2 to damage a machine so that it does not work: *Jimmy broke the DVD player.*
3 to do something that a law or rule says you must not do: *Students who break the rules will have to stay after school.*
4 break a promise = to not do what you promised to do: *I said I wouldn't tell anyone her secret, but I broke my promise.*
5 break a record = to do something faster or better than it has ever been done before:

B

He broke the world record in the 400 meters.

6 break the news to someone = to tell someone about something bad that has happened: *She began to cry as the police broke the news to her.*

7 break for lunch/coffee, etc. = to stop working in order to eat or drink something

8 break free = to escape from a person who is holding you or from a situation: *She managed to break free from the man and run away.*

9 break even = to neither make a profit nor lose money: *We broke even in our first year of business.*

PHRASAL VERBS

break down

1 if a car or a large machine breaks down, it stops working: *My car broke down on the highway.*

2 to be unable to stop yourself from crying: *She broke down during the funeral.*

break in/break into something

to use force to get into a building, usually in order to steal things: *They broke into the house through the back window.*

break something off

to end a relationship or discussion: *They've broken off their engagement.*

break out

1 if something bad such as a fire, war, or disease breaks out, it begins to happen: *The fire broke out at two o'clock in the morning.*

2 to begin to have red spots on your skin either from ACNE or because of an illness: *The girl had broken out in a rash* (=started to have red spots from an illness). | *Chocolate makes me break out.*

break up

to end a relationship with a boyfriend or girlfriend: *She'd just broken up with Joe.*

break² *noun*

1 a period of time when you stop working, studying, etc.: *I'm tired. Let's take a break.* | *She's on her lunch break* (=not working because she is eating lunch). | *Spring break* (=spring vacation from college) *is at the end of March.*

2 a period of time when something stops for a while and then starts again: *She waited for a break in the conversation.*

3 give someone a break *informal* = to stop annoying or criticizing someone: *Give me a break! I've heard enough jokes about me today.*

4 a chance to become successful: *The band's big break came when they sang on a national TV show.*

5 a space between two parts of something: *a break in the clouds*

break·down /ˈbreɪkdaʊn/ *noun*

1 another word for a NERVOUS BREAKDOWN: *My father had a breakdown when I was eleven and had to quit his job and spend time in a hospital.*

2 the failure of a relationship or system: *There was a breakdown in the peace talks and the fighting began again.*

3 an occasion when a car or a piece of machinery stops working

break·fast /ˈbrekfəst/ *noun*

the first meal of the day: *I had bacon and eggs for breakfast.*

→ See Thesaurus box at **meal**

ˈbreak-in *noun*

an occasion when someone uses force to get into a building in order to steal things: *There was a break-in at the office and several computers were stolen.*

break·through /ˈbreɪkθru/ *noun*

an important achievement by someone who is trying to make, find, or do something new: *Scientists have made an important breakthrough in the treatment of heart disease that will save many lives.*

break·up /ˈbreɪkʌp/ *noun*

the act of ending a marriage or other relationship: *He was very unhappy after the breakup of his marriage.*

breast /brest/ *noun*

1 one of the two round parts on a woman's chest that can produce milk

2 the part of a bird's or person's body between the neck and the stomach: *a chicken breast*

breast·stroke /ˈbrestˌstroʊk/ *noun*

a way of swimming in which you push your arms forward and then move them around to your sides

breath /breθ/ *noun*

1 the air that you take in and let out when you breathe: *Take a deep breath* (=breathe in a lot of air once). | *He had bad breath* (=his breath smelled bad).

2 hold your breath = to deliberately not breathe for a while, after breathing in: *I stayed under water until I couldn't hold my breath anymore.*

3 be out of breath = to be having difficulty breathing because you have been running or exercising: *I was out of breath from climbing so many stairs.*

4 catch your breath = to begin breathing normally again after you have been running or exercising: *I had to sit down to catch my breath.*

5 under your breath *formal* = in a quiet voice: *He swore under his breath.*

breathe /brið/ *verb*
to take air into your body through your nose or mouth and let it out again: *He's not dead – he's still breathing.* | *I don't want to breathe your cigarette smoke.* | *OK, now breathe out slowly* (=let the air come out of your body slowly).
—**breathing** *noun*: *His breathing was very loud.*

THESAURUS: breathe

pant to breathe quickly with short breaths, especially after exercising: *The boys were panting after the race.*

be out of breath if you are out of breath, it is hard to breathe normally because you have been exercising or you are sick: *She has a disease that makes her feel out of breath.*

gasp to breathe quickly and loudly, because it is hard to breathe because you have been exercising or you are sick: *She rode the bike as fast as she could, until she was gasping for breath.*

wheeze to breathe with a noise in your throat and chest, because you are sick: *He has the flu and is wheezing and coughing.*

WORD FAMILY look at the words:

➔ **breathe** *verb*
➔ **breath** *noun*
➔ **breathing** *noun*

breath·less /ˈbreθləs/ *adjective*
if you are breathless, you are having trouble breathing: *I was breathless from running.*

breath·tak·ing /ˈbreθˌteɪkɪŋ/ *adjective, formal*
extremely beautiful, impressive, or surprising: *Our hotel room had a breathtaking view of the mountains.*

breed[1] /brid/ *noun*
one type of an animal that is kept as a pet or on a farm: *What is your favorite breed of dog? I like poodles.*

breed[2] *verb* **bred** /bred/
1 if animals breed, they have babies
2 to keep animals in order to produce young ones: *He breeds horses.*

breeze /briz/ *noun*
a light gentle wind: *There was a nice cool breeze blowing through the window.*
—**breezy** *adjective* with the wind blowing: *a breezy day*
➔ See Thesaurus box at **wind**[1]

brew /bru/ *verb*
1 to make a drink by leaving tea leaves or crushed coffee beans in boiling water: *She brewed a pot of coffee.*
2 to make beer
3 be brewing = if something bad is brewing, it will happen soon: *Trouble was brewing, and I knew something bad was going to happen.*
—**brewery** *noun* a place where beer is made

bribe /braɪb/ *verb*
to give money or a gift to someone so that they will do something illegal or dishonest for you: *He bribed the guard to leave the door unlocked so he could escape.*
—**bribe** *noun* money or a gift that is used to bribe someone: *Three police officers have been accused of taking bribes* (=accepting money to do something dishonest).
—**bribery** *noun* the action of bribing someone

brick /brɪk/ *noun*
a hard block of baked clay, used for building

bride /braɪd/ *noun*
a woman who is getting married or who has just gotten married: *The bride and groom were just leaving the church.*
—**bridal** *adjective* relating to a bride or a wedding: *a bridal gown*

bride·groom /ˈbraɪdgrum/ *noun*
another word for GROOM

B

brides•maid /ˈbraɪdzmeɪd/ *noun*
a girl or woman who helps a bride at her wedding

bridge

bridge /brɪdʒ/ *noun*
1 a structure built over a river, road, etc. so that people or vehicles can go from one side to the other: *We looked down at the water as we drove across the Golden Gate Bridge.*
2 a card game for four people

brief /brif/ Ac *adjective, formal*
1 continuing for a short time: *After a brief period without work, he found another job.* ANTONYM **long**
2 using only a few words: *He gave a brief description of the man, but he couldn't describe him exactly.*
—**briefly** *adverb*: *She spoke briefly to reporters this morning but did not say anything new.*

brief•case /ˈbrifkeɪs/ *noun*
a flat box or bag with a handle, used for carrying papers
➔ See picture on page A6

brief•ing /ˈbrifɪŋ/ Ac *noun*
an occasion when someone gives you all the information you need about a situation: *A White House spokesman explained the situation at a press briefing* (=an occasion when information is given to reporters).

bright /braɪt/ *adjective*
1 having or producing a lot of light: *a bright sunny day* | *the bright lights in the football stadium*
2 bright colors are strong and easy to see: *a bright red sweater*
3 quick at learning things: *Susan is a very bright child.* SYNONYM **intelligent**
—**brightly** *adverb*: *The sun shone brightly.* | *brightly colored ribbons*
—**brightness** *noun*
➔ See Thesaurus box at **intelligent**

bright•en /ˈbraɪtn/ *also* **brighten up** *verb*
1 to become brighter or lighter: *The sky was brightening.*
2 to make something look more colorful and attractive: *Flowers would brighten up this room.*
3 *formal* to become or look happier: *His face brightened when he heard the good news.*

bril•liant /ˈbrɪlyənt/ *adjective*
1 extremely intelligent or good at your work: *a brilliant scientist*
2 a brilliant light or color is very bright: *The sky was a brilliant blue.*
—**brilliantly** *adverb*
—**brilliance** *noun*
➔ See Thesaurus box at **intelligent**

brim[1] /brɪm/ *noun*
1 the part of a hat that sticks out around your head: *a hat with a wide brim*
2 the brim = the top of a container, such as a glass: *The glass was filled to the brim* (=completely full).

brim[2] *verb*
be brimming with something = to be full of something: *She was brimming with confidence after her win.*

bring /brɪŋ/ *verb* **brought** /brɔt/
1 to take someone or something with you to a place or person: *Will you bring me a glass of water?* | *Can I bring a friend to the party?* | *My father brought this doll back from Japan.* | *She brought her daughter along* (=with her).

THESAURUS: bring

bring to take something or someone to a place: *You should bring her some flowers.* | *Elise brought her friend with her to the party.*

take to move something from one place to another, or help someone go from one place to another: *You'd better take your jacket – it's getting cold.* | *I can take you home after the concert.*

get to go to another place and come back with something or someone: *Just a minute while I get my jacket.*

2 to make something happen or come: *Every change brings new problems.* | *Her* *songs have brought pleasure to millions of people.*

3 to cause something to be in a particular position or state: *The injury brought his career in baseball to an end* (=ended his career). | *We want to bring down* (=reduce) *our costs.*

4 cannot bring yourself to do something = to not be able to make yourself do something: *I couldn't bring myself to talk about my mother's death for a long time.*

PHRASAL VERBS

bring something about

formal to make something happen: *How can we bring about these changes?*

bring someone in

to ask someone to help or become involved in a situation: *The local police brought in the FBI to help with the case.*

bring something on

to make something bad begin, for example an illness: *Stress can bring on a heart attack.*

bring something out

1 to make something easier to notice, see, taste, etc.: *The color of the shirt brings out the blue in your eyes.*

2 bring out the best/worst in someone = to make someone behave in the best or worst way that he or she can: *Becoming a father has brought out the best in Dan.*

bring up

1 bring someone up = to care for and educate a child: *She brought up three children by herself.* SYNONYM **raise**

2 bring something up = to mention a particular subject in a conversation or discussion: *That's a good idea. I'll bring it up at the meeting.* SYNONYM **raise**

brink /brɪŋk/ *noun*

the brink (of something) *formal* = a situation in which something, usually something bad, will soon happen, if it is not prevented: *The country is on the brink of war, but leaders are trying to avoid it.*

brisk /brɪsk/ *adjective*

quick and full of energy: *We took a brisk walk to get our hearts pumping.*

—**briskly** *adverb*

bris•tle /ˈbrɪsəl/ *noun*

a short stiff hair, wire, etc.: *a brush with short bristles*

Brit•ish[1] /ˈbrɪtɪʃ/ *adjective*

from Great Britain: *the British government*

British[2] *noun*

the British = people from Great Britain: *The British love soccer.*

brit•tle /ˈbrɪtl/ *adjective*

hard but easily broken: *Her bones are very brittle, so her hip broke easily when she fell.*

broad /brɔd/ *adjective*

1 wide: *He has very broad shoulders and looks very strong.* | *a broad smile* ANTONYM **narrow**

2 including many different kinds of things or people: *The college offers a broad range of classes, from carpentry to literature.* ANTONYM **narrow**

3 in broad daylight = during the day when it is light: *He was attacked in broad daylight.*

broad•cast /ˈbrɔdˌkæst/ *verb* **broadcast**

to send out a radio or television program: *The music awards will be broadcast on national television.*

—**broadcast** *noun* a program on the radio or television: *a news broadcast*

—**broadcaster** *noun* someone who speaks on radio or television programs

broad•ly /ˈbrɔdli/ *adverb, formal*

1 in a general way: *I know broadly what to expect, but I would like to know more specific details.* SYNONYM **generally**

2 smile/grin broadly = to have a big smile on your face

Broad•way /ˈbrɔdweɪ/ *noun*

an area of New York City where there are many theaters: *The show opens on Broadway next month.*

broc•co•li /ˈbrɑkəli/ *noun*

a vegetable with groups of small green flower BUDs on thick stems

➔ See picture on page A12

bro•chure /broʊˈʃʊr/ *noun*

a thin book that gives information or advertises something: *a travel brochure* (=a brochure giving information about places for vacations)

broil /brɔɪl/ *verb*

to cook something under or over direct heat: *She broiled the chicken in the oven.*

broke[1] /broʊk/ *verb*

the past tense of BREAK

B

broke² *adjective*
1 if you are broke, you have no money at all: *I'd like to lend you the money, but I'm broke.*
2 go broke *informal* = if a business goes broke, it can no longer continue because it has no money
→ See Thesaurus box at **poor**

bro•ken¹ /'broʊkən/ *verb*
the past participle of BREAK

broken² *adjective*
1 something that is broken is damaged or in pieces because it has been hit, dropped, etc.: *Don't move him – I think his leg is broken.* | *There was broken glass on the floor from the window.*
2 not working correctly: *What time is it? My watch is broken.*

bronze /brɑnz/ *noun*
a brownish metal made by mixing COPPER and TIN: *a bronze statue*

brook /brʊk/ *noun*
a small stream

broom /brum/ *noun*
a brush with a long handle, used for sweeping floors

broth /brɔθ/ *noun*
a clear soup: *chicken broth*

broth•er /'brʌðɚ/ *noun*
a boy or man who has the same parents as you: *This is my little brother* (=younger brother) *Charlie.*
—**brotherly** *adjective* kind, loyal, etc., like the behavior of a brother should be: *brotherly love*

'brother-in-law *noun*
1 the brother of your husband or wife
2 the husband of your sister

brought /brɔt/ *verb*
the past tense and past participle of BRING

brown /braʊn/ *adjective, noun*
the color of coffee, wood, or soil: *dark brown hair*

browse /braʊz/ *verb*
1 to look at things in a store, or at pages of a magazine, when you do not have a particular purpose: *She likes browsing through fashion magazines.*
2 to search for information on the Internet: *People can now browse the Internet even faster.*

bruise /bruz/ *noun*
a dark mark on your skin where it has been hit: *She had a big bruise on her arm where she had bumped into the door.*
—**bruised** *adjective* having one or more bruises: *She cried when she saw his bruised and bloody face.*
—**bruise** *verb* to get a bruise: *He bruised his knee in this afternoon's game.*
→ See Thesaurus boxes at **injury** and **mark²**

bruise

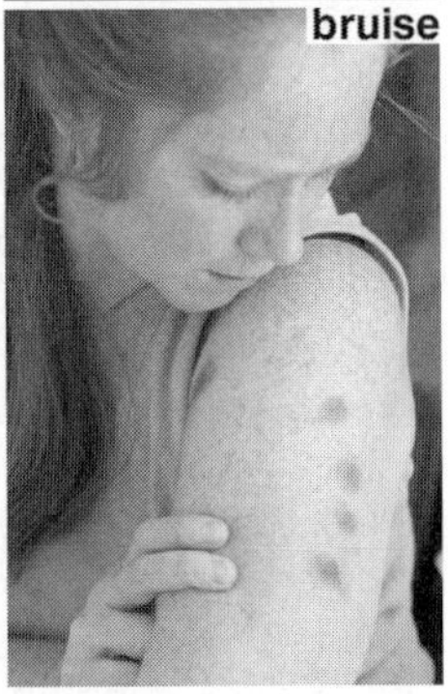

brunch /brʌntʃ/ *noun*
a meal that you eat in the late morning, as a combination of breakfast and LUNCH: *Let's meet at the restaurant and have brunch at about 11:30.*
→ See Thesaurus box at **meal**

bru•nette /bru'net/ *noun*
a woman with dark brown hair

brunt /brʌnt/ *noun*
bear/take the brunt of something = to be affected most severely by something: *The front part of the truck bore the brunt of the collision.*

brush

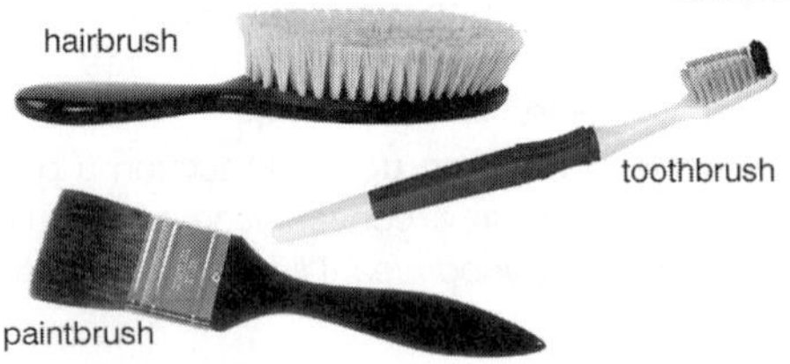

brush¹ /brʌʃ/ *noun*
an object consisting of strong hairs fastened to a handle, used for cleaning, painting, etc.
→ **hairbrush, paintbrush, toothbrush**

brush² *verb*
1 to clean your teeth or make something such as hair look neat using a brush: *Have you brushed your teeth today?* | *She was brushing her hair in front of the mirror.*
2 to remove something from a surface by moving a brush or your hand across the surface: *She brushed the crumbs off her lap.*
3 to touch someone or something lightly as

you go past: *Her sleeve brushed my arm as she walked past.*
➔ See Thesaurus box at **touch**[1]

bru•tal /ˈbrutl/ *adjective*
very cruel or violent: *a brutal attack*
—**brutally** *adverb*: *He was brutally murdered.*
—**brutality** /bruˈtæləti/ *noun* the quality of being brutal

B.S. *noun*
Bachelor of Science a university degree in a science subject

bub•ble[1] /ˈbʌbəl/ *noun*
a ball of air in a liquid: *soap bubbles* | *the bubbles in a glass of soda*

bubble[2] *verb*
if a liquid bubbles, it produces bubbles, usually because it is boiling: *Heat the sauce until it starts to bubble.*

buck /bʌk/ *noun*
1 *informal* a dollar: *It costs 75 bucks.*
2 a male DEER or rabbit
➔ See Thesaurus box at **money**

buck•et /ˈbʌkɪt/ *noun*
an open container with a handle, used for carrying and holding liquids: *He put the fire out with a bucket of water.*

buck•le /ˈbʌkəl/ *noun*
a metal object used to fasten a belt, shoe, bag, etc.
—**buckle** *verb* to fasten something using a buckle: *He got into the car and buckled his seat belt.*
➔ See picture at **watch**[2]

bud /bʌd/ *noun*
a young flower or leaf that has not yet opened: *The buds on the rose bushes were just starting to open.*

Bud•dhis•m /ˈbudɪzəm/ *noun*
a religion based on the teachings of Buddha. It includes the belief that if people stop wanting things, they will no longer suffer.
—**Buddhist** *noun* someone whose religion is Buddhism

bud•dy /ˈbʌdi/ *noun* plural **buddies** *informal*
a friend: *He's one of Mike's buddies from school.*

budge /bʌdʒ/ *verb*
not budge = if people or things do not budge, they do not move at all when someone wants them to move: *I pulled, but the dog wouldn't budge.*

budg•et[1] /ˈbʌdʒɪt/ *noun, formal*
an amount of money that a person or organization can spend: *The company has a budget of $35 million this year.*

budget[2] *verb, formal*
to plan how much money you can spend: *We budgeted $1,500 for our vacation.*

buf•fa•lo /ˈbʌfəˌloʊ/ *noun* plural **buffaloes** or **buffalo**
a North American wild animal that looks like a large cow with thick hair on its neck and shoulders SYNONYM **bison**

buf•fet /bəˈfeɪ/ *noun*
a meal when people go to get the food they want from a table with lots of different kinds of food on it: *There was a lunch buffet with lots of salads, pasta, and sandwiches.*

bug[1] /bʌg/ *noun*
1 *informal* an insect
2 *informal* an illness that passes from one person to another easily: *Three kids in my class had a stomach bug and stayed home from school.*
3 a small problem in a computer program that stops it from working well: *There must be a bug in the software – it's not working right.*

bug[2] *verb* **bugged, bugging** *informal*
to annoy someone: *That music is really bugging me. Can you turn it off?*

build /bɪld/ *verb* **built** /bɪlt/
1 to make a building, a bridge, etc.: *My grandfather built this house himself.* | *The church was built of wood* (=made from wood).
2 *also* **build up** to make something develop and get stronger: *Exercise will help to build up your muscles.*

WORD FAMILY look at the words:
➔ **build** *verb*
➔ **builder** *noun*
➔ **building** *noun*

B

build•er /ˈbɪldɚ/ *noun*
a company or person whose job is building things: *The company is the nation's largest home builder.*

build•ing /ˈbɪldɪŋ/ *noun*
1 a house, school, or anything with a roof and walls: *a twenty-story building* (=one with twenty levels) | *We have a pool at our apartment building* (=building in which there are many places to live). | *The office was in a tall building on Main Street.*
2 the process of making a house, school, road, etc.: *The building of the railroad took years.* SYNONYM **construction**

build•up /ˈbɪldʌp/ *noun*
a gradual increase: *There was a buildup of troops along the border.*

built /bɪlt/ *verb*
the past tense and past participle of BUILD

bulb /bʌlb/ *noun*
the glass part of an electric light: *We need a new bulb in the bedroom.* SYNONYM **light bulb**

bulb

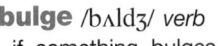

bulge /bʌldʒ/ *verb*
if something bulges, it curves out because there is something inside or under it: *His pockets were bulging with money.*
—**bulge** *noun* the curved shape something makes when it bulges

bulk /bʌlk/ Ac *noun*
1 the bulk (of something) = most of something: *The bulk of the work has been done.*
2 the large size of something or someone: *The dinosaurs moved slowly because of their bulk.*

bulk•y /ˈbʌlki/ Ac *adjective*
big and heavy: *He was wearing a bulky black sweater over his shirt.*

bull /bʊl/ *noun*
a male cow, or the male of some other big animals

bull•dog /ˈbʊldɔg/ *noun*
a type of dog with a strong body and chest and short fur

bull•doz•er /ˈbʊlˌdoʊzɚ/ *noun*
a powerful vehicle used for moving dirt and rocks

bulldozer

bul•let /ˈbʊlɪt/ *noun*
a small piece of metal that comes out of a gun when you fire it: *Who fired the bullet that killed him?*

bul•le•tin /ˈbʊlətɪn/ *noun*
information given in a short report or letter: *The church sends out a weekly bulletin to all its members.*

ˈ**bulletin** ˌ**board** *noun*
1 a board on a wall where people put information: *There's more information on the bulletin board in the cafeteria.*
2 a place on a system of computers where you can leave messages for other people to read: *I posted a message on the bulletin board on the company's website.*
➔ See picture on page A18

bul•let•proof /ˈbʊlɪtˌpruf/ *adjective*
something that is bulletproof is made of material that stops bullets passing through it: *The windows in the bank were made of bulletproof glass.*

ˈ**bull's-eye** *noun*
the center of a TARGET, that you aim at when you shoot

bul•ly /ˈbʊli/ *noun* plural **bullies**
someone who frightens or hurts people in order to make them do things
—**bully** *verb* to frighten or hurt people in order to make them do things: *He bullied me into giving him my money.*

bum /bʌm/ *noun, informal*
someone who is very lazy or does no work: *Get up, you lazy bum!*

bum•ble /ˈbʌmbəl/ *also* **bumble around** *verb*
to move around in a way that is not steady: *Josh was bumbling around in the dark, trying to find the light switch.*

bum•ble•bee /ˈbʌmbəlˌbi/ *noun*
a large BEE

bump¹ /bʌmp/ *verb*
to hit something by accident: *Joey fell and bumped his head on the table.* | *I hurt my arm when I bumped into the door.*
PHRASAL VERB
bump into someone *informal*
to meet someone you know when you are not expecting it: *I bumped into a friend who I hadn't seen in five years.*

bump² *noun*
1 a raised area on your skin where you hit it on something: *How did you get that bump on your head?*
2 a raised area on the ground: *There were a lot of bumps in the road, so we drove slowly.*
➔ See Thesaurus box at **injury**

bump•er /ˈbʌmpɚ/ *noun*
the part at the front and back of a car that protects it if it hits anything
➔ See picture on page A28

bump•y /ˈbʌmpi/ *adjective*
a bumpy road is not smooth to drive on: *Their ranch was at the end of a bumpy dirt road.*

bun /bʌn/ *noun*
a small round type of bread for one person: *a hamburger bun*

bunch /bʌntʃ/ *noun*
1 a bunch of bananas/flowers/grapes, etc. = a group of bananas, flowers, etc.: *He gave me a bunch of roses.*
2 *informal* a lot of something: *I went to the mall with a bunch of my friends.* | *The doctor asked me a whole bunch of questions.*
➔ See Thesaurus box at **group¹**

bun•dle /ˈbʌndl/ *noun*
a bundle of papers/letters/clothes/sticks = a group of papers, etc. that are usually tied together: *She went to her desk and took out a bundle of old letters.*
➔ See Thesaurus box at **group¹**

bun•gle /ˈbʌŋgəl/ *verb*
to do something badly: *He bungled a kick early in the game, and they lost by one point.*

bunk /bʌŋk/ *noun*
1 one of two beds that are attached together, one on top of the other: *At camp, I slept on the top bunk.*
2 a narrow bed on a ship or train, joined to the wall

ˈbunk beds *noun*
two beds that are built one on top of the other

bun•ny /ˈbʌni/ *also* **ˈbunny ˌrabbit** *noun*
plural **bunnies**
a word used by children to mean "rabbit"

buoy /ˈbui/ *noun*
an object that floats on water, used for showing which parts of an area of water are safe or dangerous: *The buoys mark the areas where boats can go.*

bur•den /ˈbɚdn/ *noun, formal*
something you are responsible for that is difficult or that worries you: *My father's long illness was a burden on my mother.*
—**burdensome** *adjective, formal* difficult or worrying to deal with: *burdensome debts*

bu•reau /ˈbyʊroʊ/ *noun*
1 a government department: *the Federal Bureau of Investigation*
2 an organization that collects or provides information: *I worked as a reporter for the Chicago City News Bureau.*

bu•reauc•ra•cy /byʊˈrɑkrəsi/ *noun, formal*
official systems that are annoying because there are a lot of rules and it takes a long time to do things: *It took three months to get a visa because of all the bureaucracy.*
—**bureaucratic** /ˌbyʊrəˈkrætɪk/ *adjective* relating to bureaucracy: *a bureaucratic government department*

bur•glar /ˈbɚglɚ/ *noun*
someone who goes into houses, cars, etc. to steal things: *Burglars broke into the house and stole the TV.*
—**burglary** *noun* an occasion when someone steals things from a house, car, etc.: *There have been several burglaries in our neighborhood recently.*
—**burglarize** *verb* to go into a house, car, etc. and steal things

B

bur·i·al /ˈberiəl/ *noun, formal*
the act of putting a dead person into the ground: *The tombs were used for burial of important people.*

burn¹ /bɚn/ *verb* **burned** or **burnt** /bɚnt/
1 to destroy or damage something with fire: *We burned all the trash.* | *Many buildings are still burning in the city.*
2 to hurt your body with fire or something hot: *Ricky burned his hand on the stove.*
3 if a fire is burning, it is producing flames and heat: *A fire was burning in the fireplace.*
PHRASAL VERBS
burn something down
if a building burns down, fire destroys it: *The old hotel burned down a few years ago.* | *The police say that the two men burned the building down.*
burn up
to be destroyed by great heat: *The satellite will burn up as it falls back to Earth.*

burn² *noun*
an injury or mark caused by fire or heat: *She was taken to the hospital and treated for burns.*

burn·out /ˈbɚnaʊt/ *noun*
the state of being extremely tired and unable to work any longer: *He stopped coaching in 2003 because of burnout.*

burnt /bɚnt/ *verb*
a past tense and past participle of BURN

burp /bɚp/ *verb*
if you burp, gas comes up from your stomach through your mouth and makes a noise: *Ross finished his dinner and burped loudly.*
—**burp** *noun* the noise you make when you burp

bur·row /ˈbɚoʊ/ *noun*
a hole in the ground that a rabbit or another small animal digs and lives in
—**burrow** *verb* if an animal burrows, it digs a hole in the ground

burst¹ /bɚst/ *verb* **burst**
1 to break open suddenly because of pressure from air, water, etc. inside: *The balloon burst with a loud bang.* | *Don't burst the balloon – you'll scare the kids.*
2 burst into tears = to start crying suddenly: *"I hate you!" she shouted, and burst into tears.*
3 burst out laughing = to start laughing suddenly: *"Look at his big ears," she said, and burst out laughing.*
→ See Thesaurus box at **break¹**

burst² *noun*
a burst of something = a short period when there is suddenly more activity, noise, strong feelings, etc.: *He won the race in a final burst of speed.* | *The concert finished, and there was a loud burst of applause.*

bur·y /ˈberi/ *verb* **buried**, third person singular **buries**
1 to put a dead person into the ground: *My grandfather was buried in the city graveyard.*
2 to hide something by putting it in the ground or covering it with something: *The pirates buried their treasure on this island.*

bus /bʌs/ *noun* plural **buses**
a large vehicle that people pay to travel on: *Are you going to drive or go by bus?* | *Five people got on the bus.*
→ See picture on page A26

bush /bʊʃ/ *noun*
a plant like a small tree: *a rose bush*

bush·el /ˈbʊʃəl/ *noun*
a unit for measuring dry food, equal to 8 gallons or 36.4 liters

bush·y /ˈbʊʃi/ *adjective*
bushy hair or fur is thick and strong: *The man had a large nose and bushy eyebrows.*

bus·i·ly /ˈbɪzəli/ *adverb*
in a busy way: *Dad was in the kitchen, busily cooking breakfast.*

busi·ness /ˈbɪznɪs/ *noun*
1 the work of buying and selling goods or providing services: *These days, we can do business over the Internet.* | *I'd love to have a job in the music business* (=work relating to music). | *He travels all over the world on business* (=doing his work).
2 a company that earns money by selling things or providing services: *My brother started his own business, repairing computers.*
3 mind your own business *informal* = used when telling someone in a rude way that they should not ask you about something because it is private: *"Do you love Craig?" "Mind your own business!"*
4 none of your business *informal* = if something is none of your business, you should not expect to know about it: *It's none*

of his business, how much money I earn.
➔ See Thesaurus box at **company**

busi•ness•man /ˈbɪznɪsˌmæn/ *noun* plural **businessmen** /ˈbɪznɪsˌmen/
someone who works in business or who owns a business: *Perry was a very successful businessman and owned his own company.*

busi•ness•wom•an /ˈbɪznɪsˌwʊmən/ *noun* plural **businesswomen** /ˈbɪznɪsˌwɪmɪn/
a woman who works in business or who owns a business

ˈbus ˌstation *noun*
a place where buses start and finish their trips

ˈbus stop *noun*
a place where buses stop so people can get on and off: *I'm getting off at the next bus stop.* SYNONYM **stop**
➔ See picture on page A26

bust[1] /bʌst/ *noun*
1 a model of someone's head, shoulders, and upper chest: *a bust of Beethoven*
2 the size of a woman's chest area: *This shirt is good for women with a large bust.*

bust[2] *adjective, informal*
go bust = a business that goes bust stops working because it does not have enough money: *During that time, a lot of small businesses went bust.*

bus•tle /ˈbʌsəl/ *verb, formal*
1 if a place bustles with activity, life, etc., it is full of people and activity: *The streets of the city were bustling with people shopping.*
2 to move around in a busy way: *I could hear Mom bustling around downstairs, making breakfast.*

bus•y /ˈbɪzi/ *adjective* **busier**, **busiest**
1 someone who is busy is working or has a lot to do: *Can we talk later? I'm busy right now.*
2 if a telephone line is busy, someone is talking on it when you try to call them: *I called her earlier, but her line was busy.*
3 a busy place or time is full of things happening and people working hard: *There are 900 students at the school, so it's a pretty busy place. | The summer is always a busy time of year because of the tourists.*
ANTONYM **quiet**

bus•y•bod•y /ˈbɪziˌbɑdi/ *noun* plural **busybodies**
someone who wants to know about other people's private lives, in a way that is annoying: *She's such a busybody – she's always watching me.*

B

but[1] /bət; *strong* bʌt/ *conjunction*
1 used before you say something that is a little unexpected: *We all felt tired but happy. | Dan's young, but he's not stupid.*
2 used before you give the reason why you cannot do something: *I'd love to come to your house, but I have homework to do.*
3 except for: *This weekend we did nothing but watch movies and eat!*
4 used after "excuse me" and "I'm sorry": *Excuse me, but I didn't hear what you said.*

but[2] *preposition*
except for someone or something: *There's nobody here but me.*

butch•er[1] /ˈbʊtʃɚ/ *noun*
a person or store that sells meat
➔ See picture on page A16

butcher[2] *verb*
to kill animals in order to use or sell the meat

butt[1] /bʌt/ *noun*
1 *informal* the part of your body that you sit on SYNONYM **buttocks**
2 the end of a cigarette after most of it has been smoked: *The ashtray was full of cigarette butts.*

butt[2] *verb*
PHRASAL VERB
butt in
to interrupt someone when he or she is speaking, or try to get involved in what someone is doing: *Julie kept butting in as I was trying to tell my story.*

but•ter /ˈbʌtɚ/ *noun*
a yellow substance made from milk that you spread on bread or use in cooking: *Do you want some butter on your bread?*

but•ter•fly /ˈbʌtɚˌflaɪ/ *noun* plural **butterflies**
an insect with large and usually colored wings

B

but•ter•milk /ˈbʌtɚˌmɪlk/ *noun*
the liquid that is left after butter has been made, which you can drink or use in cooking

but•ter•scotch /ˈbʌtɚˌskɑtʃ/ *noun*
a type of candy made from butter and sugar boiled together

but•tocks /ˈbʌtəks/ *plural noun, formal*
the part of your body that you sit on SYNONYM **butt**

but•ton /ˈbʌtn/ *noun*
1 a small round object on your shirt, coat, etc. that you push through a hole to fasten it: *He sewed the button back on his shirt.*
2 a small part of a machine that you press to make it work: *She pushed the pause button on the DVD player.*
3 a small metal or plastic pin with a message or picture on it: *Should teachers wear buttons with political messages on them to class?*
—**button** *verb* to fasten clothing using buttons: *She buttoned her jacket and went outside.*
➔ See Thesaurus box at **fasten**
➔ See picture on page A6

buy /baɪ/ *verb* **bought** /bɔt/
to get something by paying money for it: *Her parents bought her a new car.* | *I bought a nice sweater from that store.* | *They're buying new computers for the school.*

> **THESAURUS: buy**
>
> **purchase** *formal* to buy something: *You can purchase tickets by phone.*
>
> **acquire** *formal* to buy a company or property: *The group acquires land to protect the plants and animals on it.*
>
> **get** to buy or obtain something: *I never know what to get Dad for his birthday.*

—**buyer** *noun* someone who wants to buy something from another person: *He has found a buyer for his boat.*

buzz¹ /bʌz/ *verb*
1 to make a continuous noise like the sound of a BEE: *Insects buzzed around my face.*
2 if a group of people or a place is buzzing, there is a lot of excitement, talk, or activity: *The crowd was buzzing with excitement before the band came in.*

buzz² *noun*
a noise like the sound of a BEE: *I could hear the buzz of voices in the next room.*

buz•zard /ˈbʌzɚd/ *noun*
a large wild bird that eats dead animals SYNONYM **vulture**

buzz•er /ˈbʌzɚ/ *noun*
a button that makes a buzzing sound when you press it: *Press the buzzer to let them know you're here.*

by¹ /baɪ/ *preposition*
1 near or beside: *He was standing by the window and looking out.*
2 past: *She walked by me without saying hello.*
3 used for showing who or what does something: *Her cat was hit by a truck.* | *a play by Shakespeare*
4 used for saying what someone uses to do something, or how someone achieves something: *Your tickets will be delivered by mail.* | *We came back by bus.* | *You can save money by eating more meals at home.*
5 not later than a particular time: *I have to be back by 6:00.*
6 used for saying which part of something someone holds: *She grabbed him by the arm.*
7 used when giving the two parts of a measurement: *The room is 24 feet by 36 feet.*
8 **(all) by yourself** = alone or without help: *I was scared to go there by myself.*
➔ **by the way** at **way**

by² *adverb*
1 past: *We watched the cars go by.*
2 **by and large** *formal* = used when talking generally about something: *By and large, the new system is working well, but there are a few small problems.*

bye /baɪ/ *also* **bye-ˈbye** *informal*
another word for GOODBYE

by•pass /ˈbaɪpæs/ *noun*
a medical operation that is done so that blood can flow through different tubes when tubes in the heart are blocked: *a heart bypass operation*

by•stand•er /ˈbaɪˌstændɚ/ *noun*
someone who is present when something happens: *The men also shot two innocent bystanders* (=people who they did not intend to shoot and who were not part of the trouble).

byte /baɪt/ *noun*
a unit for measuring the amount of information a computer can use, equal to 8 BITs: *There are one million bytes in a megabyte.*

Cc

C[1]
the written abbreviation of **Celsius** or **Centigrade**: *Water boils at 100° C.*

C[2] /si/ *noun*
1 a GRADE that you get on a test or in a class for doing average work: *Carol got a C in math.*
2 the first note in the musical SCALE of C, or the musical KEY based on this note

cab /kæb/ *noun*
1 a car driven by someone who people pay to take them to places: *I took a cab to the airport.* SYNONYM **taxi**
2 the part of a truck or train where the driver sits
➔ See picture on page A26

cab•bage /ˈkæbɪdʒ/ *noun*
a large round vegetable with thick green or purple leaves
➔ See picture on page A12

cab•driv•er /ˈkæbˌdraɪvɚ/ *noun*
someone who drives a taxi

cab•in /ˈkæbɪn/ *noun*
1 a small house made of wood, usually in a forest or the mountains: *He lived in a log cabin in the woods.*
2 a small room in which you sleep on a ship
3 the area inside an airplane where the passengers sit
➔ See picture at **airplane**

cab•i•net /ˈkæbənɪt/ *noun*
1 a piece of furniture with doors and shelves, or drawers: *He looked in the kitchen cabinets for something to eat.*
➔ **file cabinet**
➔ See picture on page A9 and A11
2 an important group of politicians who help the leader of a government: *The cabinet members discussed the problem with the president.*

ca•ble /ˈkeɪbəl/ *noun*
1 several wires carrying electricity, telephone signals, etc., covered with rubber or plastic: *I connected my computer to my printer with a cable.*
2 television that is broadcast using cables and is paid for by the person watching it: *a football game on one of the cable channels*
3 a thick strong metal rope: *The bridge is supported by steel cables.*

cac•tus /ˈkæktəs/ *noun* plural **cacti** /ˈkæktaɪ/ or **cactuses**
a desert plant that has thick stems covered with sharp points

ca•fe *also* **café** /kæˈfeɪ/ *noun*
a restaurant where you can buy drinks and simple meals: *We stopped at a cafe for coffee.*

caf•e•te•ri•a /ˌkæfəˈtɪriə/ *noun*
a restaurant in a factory, school, etc., where people take food from a COUNTER: *All the employees eat in the same cafeteria.*

caf•feine /kæˈfin/ *noun*
a substance in coffee, tea, and some other drinks that makes people feel more active

cage /keɪdʒ/ *noun*
a structure made of wires or bars in which birds or animals can be kept: *Go clean out the rabbit cage.*

cake /keɪk/ *noun*
1 a sweet food made by baking a mixture of flour, fat, sugar, and eggs: *Do you want a piece of cake? | She made him a birthday cake with 11 candles on it.*
2 a salmon/rice/potato, etc. cake = fish, rice, etc. that has been formed into a flat round shape and cooked
3 be a piece of cake *informal* = to be very easy: *This job should be a piece of cake.*

cal•ci•um /ˈkælsiəm/ *noun*
an ELEMENT that helps form teeth, bones, and CHALK: *Calcium makes bones strong.*

cal•cu•late /ˈkælkyəˌleɪt/ *verb*
to find out something by adding numbers together, multiplying them, etc.: *Calculate how much money you will need to spend.*

WORD FAMILY look at the words:
➔ **calculate** *verb*
➔ **calculation** *noun*
➔ **calculator** *noun*

cal•cu•la•tion /ˌkælkyəˈleɪʃən/ *noun*
the act of adding numbers together, multiplying them, etc.: *The teacher did a few*

C

calculations to find the answer to the math problem.

cal•cu•la•tor /ˈkælkyəˌleɪtɚ/ *noun*
a small machine that can add numbers together, multiply them, etc.
→ See picture on page A18

cal•en•dar /ˈkæləndɚ/ *noun*
a set of pages that show the days in a year: *Mark the day of the party on your calendar.*
→ See picture on page A18

calf /kæf/ *noun* plural **calves** /kævz/
1 a young cow or BULL
2 the back of your leg between your knee and your foot
→ See picture on page A2

call[1] /kɔl/ *verb*
1 to telephone someone: *I'll call you tomorrow.* | *I called them up and explained the problem.*
2 to give someone or something a name or description: *She was from a small town called Irondale* (=whose name was Irondale). | *Are you calling me a liar* (=saying that I lied)?
3 to ask or order someone to come to you: *The doctor called her into his office.* | *Call an ambulance!*
4 to say or shout something so that someone can hear you: *"I'm coming!" Paula called.* | *I called out his name.*
5 *formal* to ask publicly for something to be done: *The group is calling for tougher laws to protect the environment.* | *Some people are calling on him to resign* (=strongly asking him to resign).
6 call the shots *informal* = to be the person who decides what will be done in a situation

PHRASAL VERBS

call (someone) back
to telephone someone again, or to telephone someone who tried to telephone you earlier: *Can I call you back later?*

call someone in
to ask or order someone to come and help you with a difficult situation: *the Governor called in the army to stop the violence.*

call something off
to decide that a planned event will not happen or will not continue: *The game was called off because of the rain.*
→ See Thesaurus box at **shout**[1]

call[2] *noun*
1 an action of talking to someone by telephone: *I got a call yesterday from Teresa.* | *Ask her to give me a call.* | *I'll make a few phone calls.*
2 be on call = to be ready to go to work if you are needed: *The doctors are on call 24 hours a day.*
3 a request or demand for someone to do something: *There have been calls for him to resign.*
4 *informal* a decision: *It's a tough call.*
5 the high sound that a bird or animal makes

call•er /ˈkɔlɚ/ *noun, formal*
someone who is making a telephone call: *Several callers said they really liked the new radio show.*

calm[1] /kɑm/ *adjective*
1 not angry or upset: *Try to stay calm, even if other people are getting angry.*
2 if an area of water is calm, it is still or is not moving very much: *The wind had stopped, and the lake was calm again.*
—**calmly** *adverb*
—**calmness** *noun*

calm[2] *verb*

PHRASAL VERB

calm down
to become calmer, or to make someone calmer: *Calm down. We have plenty of time left.*

cal•o•rie /ˈkæləri/ *noun*
a unit for measuring the amount of energy a particular food can produce: *A potato has about 90 calories.*

calves /kævz/ *noun*
the plural of CALF

cam•cord•er /ˈkæmˌkɔrdɚ/ *noun*
a small piece of equipment that you can use to record moving pictures and sound

came /keɪm/ *verb*
the past tense of COME

cam•el /ˈkæməl/ *noun*
a large animal with one or two HUMPs (=large raised parts) on its back that lives in the desert and carries goods or people: *Camels can survive without water for many days.*

cam•er•a /ˈkæmərə/ *noun*
a piece of equipment used for taking photographs, or for making movies or television

programs: *a digital camera | I used my father's camera to take the picture.*

cam•er•a•man /ˈkæmərəmæn/ *noun*
someone whose job is to use a movie or television camera

ˈcamera phone *noun*
a CELL PHONE with a camera: *Sally took a picture at the concert with her camera phone.*

cam•ou•flage /ˈkæməˌflɑːʒ/ *noun*
clothes, colors, etc. that hide people, animals, or things by making them look like the things around them: *The soldiers were dressed in camouflage and they were difficult to see in the field.*
—**camouflage** *verb* to hide people, animals, or things by making them look like the things around them

camp¹ /kæmp/ *noun*
1 a place where people stay in tents for a short time: *We hiked back to camp and started a fire for dinner.*
2 a place where children stay and do special activities during their vacation: *The kids are going to a summer camp on the lake.*

camp² *verb*
to set up a tent and stay in it for a short time: *We camped on the shore of the lake.*

cam•paign¹ /kæmˈpeɪn/ *noun*
a series of actions in business, politics, etc. that are intended to achieve something: *She began a campaign against drug use in schools. | the senator's 2008 presidential campaign* (=campaign to become president)

campaign² *verb*
to try to persuade politicians or the public to do something: *The governor is campaigning for re-election.*

camp•er /ˈkæmpɚ/ *noun*
1 a vehicle which you can live in while you are on vacation
2 someone who is staying in a tent on vacation: *Yellowstone National Park is popular with hikers and campers.*

camp•ing /ˈkæmpɪŋ/ *noun*
the activity of living in a tent for a short time: *Do you want to go camping in the mountains this weekend?*

camp•site /ˈkæmpsaɪt/ *noun*
a place where people can camp: *The park has about 300 campsites.*

cam•pus /ˈkæmpəs/ *noun*
the land or buildings of a college: *Many students live on campus, but some live in nearby apartment buildings.*

can¹ /kən; *strong* kæn/ *verb*
1 to be able to do something: *She can speak French because she lived in France for five years.*
2 to be allowed to do something: *You can leave when you finish your work.*
3 Can you...? = used for asking someone to do something for you: *Can you pass me the salt?*

can² /kæn/ *noun*
a metal container in which food or a liquid is sold: *I opened up a can of soup.*

Ca•na•di•an /kəˈneɪdiən/ *adjective*
from Canada
—**Canadian** *noun* someone from Canada

ca•nal /kəˈnæl/ *noun*
a long narrow hole full of water that has been dug so that boats or water can go from one place to another: *The Panama Canal connects the Atlantic and Pacific Oceans.*

ca•nar•y /kəˈneri/ *noun* plural **canaries**
a small yellow bird that sings and is often kept as a pet

can•cel /ˈkænsəl/ *verb*
to stop something that you had planned or arranged: *We had to cancel our trip, because Jen got sick.*
—**cancellation** /ˌkænsəˈleɪʃən/ *noun* the act of canceling something: *The snow forced the cancellation of many flights.*

can•cer /ˈkænsɚ/ *noun*
a serious illness in which cells in one part of the body grow in a way that is not normal: *She used to smoke a lot, and now she has lung cancer.*

Can•cer /ˈkænsɚ/ *noun*
1 the fourth sign of the ZODIAC, represented by a CRAB
2 someone born between June 22 and July 22

can•di•date /ˈkændəˌdeɪt/ *noun*
someone who wants to be chosen for a job: *Who was the Democratic candidate for president in 2000?*

can•dle /ˈkændl/ *noun*
a piece of WAX with a piece of string through the middle that you burn to produce light: *I lit some candles when the lights went out.*
→ See picture at **light**[1]

can•dy /ˈkændi/ *noun* plural **candies**
one or more pieces of sweet food made of sugar or chocolate: *I gave her a piece of candy.*

ˈcandy bar *noun*
a long narrow piece of candy, usually covered with chocolate

cane /keɪn/ *noun*
a thin stick that you can lean on when you walk: *He injured his leg and now walks with a cane.*

canned /kænd/ *adjective*
canned food is sold in a can: *canned tomatoes*

can•non /ˈkænən/ *noun*
a large gun, usually on wheels, used in past times: *They attacked the fort with cannons.*

can•not /ˈkænɑt/ *verb*
can not: *Thank you for the offer, but I cannot accept it.* SYNONYM **can't**

canoe

ca•noe /kəˈnu/ *noun*
a light narrow boat which you move by using a PADDLE (=piece of wood with a wide flat end): *They paddled up the river in their canoe.*
—**canoeing** *noun* the activity of traveling in a canoe

can't /kænt/ *verb*
the short form of "cannot": *I know you told me his name, but I can't remember it*

can•ta•loupe /ˈkæntəlˌoʊp/ *noun*
a sweet MELON (=large fruit) that is orange inside
→ See picture on page A13

can•vas /ˈkænvəs/ *noun*
1 a type of strong cloth that is used to make tents, sails, bags, etc.: *The tent was made out of canvas.*
2 a piece of canvas on which a picture is painted

canyon

can•yon /ˈkænjən/ *noun*
a deep valley with very steep sides: *The Colorado River flows through the Grand Canyon.*

cap /kæp/ *noun*
1 a cloth hat with a curved part sticking out at the front: *a baseball cap*
2 a cover that closes a bottle, tube, etc. or goes on the end of a pen: *She took the cap off the bottle of aspirin.*
→ **kneecap**
→ See picture on page A6

ca•pa•ble /ˈkeɪpəbəl/ Ac *adjective*
1 **be capable of (doing) something** = to have the abilities or qualities that are needed to do something: *He's very fast – I think he's capable of winning a gold medal.* ANTONYM **incapable**
2 able to do a job well: *She's a very capable lawyer. She's won every one of her cases in the last three years.*
—**capability** /ˌkeɪpəˈbɪləti/ *noun* the ability to do something: *With its strong military, the country has the capability to protect itself.*

WORD FAMILY look at the words:
→ **capable** *adjective*
→ **incapable** *adjective*
→ **capability** *noun*

ca•pac•i•ty /kəˈpæsəti/ Ac *noun* plural **capacities** *formal*
1 the amount that something can contain: *The tank has a capacity of 20 gallons* (=it can hold 20 gallons of liquid).
2 the ability to do or produce something: *Young children have a great capacity for learning.*

cape /keɪp/ *noun*
1 a long loose piece of clothing without SLEEVEs that fastens around your neck: *Batman wears a black cape.*
2 an area of land surrounded on three sides by the sea: *She lives on Cape Cod on the coast of Massachusetts.*

cap·i·tal /ˈkæpətl/ *noun*
1 the city where a country's or state's main government is: *Rome is the capital of Italy.*
2 *also* **capital letter** the large form of a letter, used for example to begin a name or sentence: *"T" is a capital letter.* | *Please write your name in capitals.*
3 *formal* money that you use to start a business or to make more money: *He needed capital to buy a factory and equipment.*

cap·i·tal·ism /ˈkæpətlˌɪzəm/ *noun*
a system in which businesses belong mostly to private owners, not to the government: *Under capitalism, companies compete with each other.*
—**capitalist** *adjective* relating to capitalism: *a capitalist economy*

ˌcapital ˈpunishment *noun, formal*
the punishment of legally killing someone for a crime: *The state doesn't have capital punishment, so he won't be executed.* SYNONYM **death penalty**

cap·puc·ci·no /ˌkæpəˈtʃinoʊ/ *noun*
plural **cappuccinos**
coffee made with hot milk with bubbles

Cap·ri·corn /ˈkæprɪˌkɔrn/ *noun*
1 the tenth sign of the ZODIAC, represented by a GOAT
2 someone born between December 22 and January 19

capsize

cap·size /ˈkæpsaɪz/ *verb, formal*
if a boat capsizes, it turns over in the water: *Fourteen people died when the boat capsized in freezing water.*

cap·sule /ˈkæpsəl/ *noun*
a very small object with medicine inside that you swallow whole
➔ See Thesaurus box at **medicine**

cap·tain /ˈkæptən/ *noun, written abbreviation* **Capt.**
1 someone who is in charge of a ship or airplane: *The captain ordered the men to leave his ship.*
2 an officer in the army, air force, etc.: *Captain Smith was flying the plane.*
3 someone who leads a sports team: *Troy was chosen to be the captain of the football team.*

cap·tion /ˈkæpʃən/ *noun*
words above or below a picture in a newspaper, book, etc. that give information about it: *The caption said that the man in the picture was a tourist.*

cap·tive /ˈkæptɪv/ *noun, formal*
someone who is kept as a prisoner, especially in a war: *The men refused to free their captives.*

cap·tiv·i·ty /kæpˈtɪvəti/ *noun, formal*
the state of being kept somewhere so that you are not free: *The elephants were born in captivity* (=in a zoo) *and have never been free.*

cap·ture /ˈkæptʃɚ/ *verb*
1 to catch a person or animal in order to keep him, her, or it somewhere: *Police have captured the gang leader.* SYNONYM **catch**
2 to get control of a place during a war: *The town was captured by enemy soldiers.*
—**capture** *noun* the act of capturing someone or something: *We heard about the capture of the terrorists on the radio.*

car /kɑr/ *noun*
1 a vehicle with four wheels and an engine that carries a small number of people: *She got into the car and drove away.* | *You can't park your car in front of the driveway.*
2 a part of a train for passengers or goods: *The train had several freight cars* (=carrying goods).
➔ See picture on page A28

car·a·mel /ˈkærəməl/ *noun*
candy made of cooked sugar, butter, and milk

C

car·bo·hy·drate /ˌkɑrboʊˈhaɪdreɪt/ *noun*
a substance in foods such as sugar, rice, bread, or potatoes that gives your body energy: *Bread is a good source of carbohydrates.*

car·bon /ˈkɑrbən/ *noun*
a chemical ELEMENT that DIAMONDS are made of, and that is contained in coal

carbon di·ox·ide /ˌkɑrbən daɪˈɑksaɪd/ *noun*
the gas that people breathe out

carbon mo·nox·ide /ˌkɑrbən məˈnɑksaɪd/ *noun*
a poisonous gas that is produced when engines burn gasoline

card /kɑrd/ *noun*
1 a folded piece of stiff paper with a picture on the front that you send to people at special times: *I have to buy a birthday card for my sister.*
2 a small piece of plastic or stiff paper that has information about someone or something: *My phone number and email address are on my business card.*
3 one of a set of 52 pieces of stiff paper that are used for playing games: *a deck of cards* (=set of cards)
4 cards = a game in which people use a set of cards: *Let's play cards.*
➔ **credit card, postcard**

card·board /ˈkɑrdbɔrd/ *noun*
very thick stiff paper: *She packed her things in cardboard boxes.*

car·di·nal /ˈkɑrdənəl/ *noun*
1 a priest of very high rank in the Roman Catholic Church
2 a bright red bird

care¹ /ker/ *verb*
1 if you care about someone or something, that person or thing is important to you: *He cares deeply about his children.* | *I don't care what you do.*
2 who cares? = used for saying that you do not think something is important: *"It's pretty expensive." "Who cares? It'll be fun!"*

PHRASAL VERB

care for someone or something
1 to do things for someone who is old or sick, or for a young child: *She took time off to care for her sick mother.*
2 not care for someone or something *formal* = to not like someone or something: *I don't really care for yogurt.*

care² *noun*
1 the activity of doing things for someone who is old or sick, or for a young child: *Your father is very sick. He will need constant medical care.* | *Who's taking care of* (=caring for) *the baby?*
2 take care of something a) to keep something in good condition: *Karl will take care of the house while we're on vacation.* **b)** to deal with something and do what needs to be done: *Her husband took care of all the bills* (=paid them).
3 the quality of being very careful: *They checked the measurements with great care to make sure there were no mistakes.*
4 take care *informal* used when saying "goodbye" to someone you know: *"OK, I'll talk to you soon." "Yeah, take care."*

WORD FAMILY look at the words:

➔ **care** *noun*
➔ **careful** *adjective*
➔ **carefully** *adverb*
➔ **careless** *adjective*
➔ **carelessly** *adverb*
➔ **carelessness** *noun*
➔ **carefree** *adjective*

ca·reer /kəˈrɪr/ *noun*
a job that you know a lot about and that you do for a long time: *During her career as an actress, she appeared in 42 movies.* | *I enjoyed my career in journalism.*
➔ See Thesaurus box at **job**

care·free /ˈkerfri/ *adjective, formal*
without any problems or worries: *He remembered the carefree days of his childhood.*

care·ful /ˈkerfəl/ *adjective*
thinking about what you are doing, so that you do not cause something bad to happen: *a careful driver* | *Be careful with that hot pan!* | *She was careful not to wake him up.*
ANTONYM **careless**
—**carefully** *adverb*: *Please listen carefully.*

care·less /ˈkerləs/ *adjective*
not thinking about what you are doing so that something bad may happen: *Careless driving causes accidents.* | *I got three questions wrong on the test because of careless mistakes* (=mistakes made because you are

not thinking carefully). ANTONYM **careful**
—**carelessly** *adverb*
—**carelessness** *noun*

ca•ress /kə'res/ *verb, formal*
to gently touch or kiss someone in a way that shows love: *She caressed the baby's face.*
—**caress** *noun* an act of caressing someone
➔ See Thesaurus box at **touch**[1]

car•go /'kɑrgoʊ/ *noun* plural **cargoes**
the things that a ship, plane, etc. is carrying: *The ship was carrying a cargo of oil.*

Car•ib•be•an /ˌkærə'biən/ *adjective*
from the islands in the Caribbean Sea, such as the Bahamas and Jamaica

car•ni•val /'kɑrnəvəl/ *noun*
1 an outdoor event where people can ride on special machines and play games for prizes: *The kids had fun on the rides at the carnival.* SYNONYM **fair**
2 a public event at which people play music, wear special clothes, and dance in the streets: *It was carnival time in Rio.*

car•ni•vore /'kɑrnəˌvɔr/ *noun, formal*
an animal that eats meat: *Dogs are carnivores.*
—**carnivorous** /kɑr'nɪvərəs/ *adjective* carnivorous animals eat meat

car•ol /'kærəl/ *noun*
a Christmas song: *A choir sang Christmas carols at the concert.*

car•pen•ter /'kɑrpəntɚ/ *noun*
someone whose job is making things out of wood: *The carpenter was making some shelves.*
—**carpentry** *noun* the activity of making things out of wood

car•pet /'kɑrpɪt/ *noun*
a heavy material for covering a floor or stairs, or a piece of this material: *The carpet felt thick and warm under my feet.*
➔ See picture on page A10

'car pool *noun*
a group of people who ride together in a car to work or school
—**carpool** *verb* if people carpool, they ride together in a car to go to work or school

car•riage /'kærɪdʒ/ *noun*
a vehicle for people to ride in that is pulled by horses

car•rot /'kærət/ *noun*
a long orange vegetable that grows under the ground
➔ See picture on page A12

car•ry /'kæri/ *verb* **carried**, third person singular **carries**
1 to have something in your hands, arms, pocket, etc. as you go somewhere: *They carried the boxes out of the house.* | *She was carrying a grocery bag.* | *He always carries a gun.*
2 if a vehicle, pipe, wire, etc. carries something, it takes it from one place to another: *The bus was carrying 25 passengers.*
3 if you carry a disease, you can pass it to others: *Many diseases are carried by insects.*
4 be/get carried away = to be so excited that you do something that is not sensible: *Don't get carried away – we're not sure that we've won.*
5 *formal* to have or involve something: *Any job in a hospital carries certain risks.*

PHRASAL VERB
carry out something
to do something in a planned and organized way: *Who carried out this attack?*
➔ See picture on page A4

cart /kɑrt/ *noun*
1 a metal basket or table on wheels: *I pushed the shopping cart to the checkout counter.*
2 a vehicle pulled by a horse, used for carrying heavy things: *The farmer loaded the hay into the cart.*

car•ton /'kɑrtn/ *noun*
a small CARDBOARD box that contains liquid food or a drink: *a carton of milk*

car•toon /kɑr'tun/ *noun*
1 a movie or television program with characters that are drawn and not real: *Who is your favorite cartoon character? I like Mickey Mouse.*
2 a funny drawing in a newspaper
—**cartoonist** *noun* someone who draws cartoons
➔ See Thesaurus boxes at **movie**, **picture**[1], and **television**

car•tridge /'kɑrtrɪdʒ/ *noun*
a small container that you put inside a machine or gun to make it work: *The printer needs a new ink cartridge.*

C

C

carve /kɑrv/ *verb*
1 to cut a piece of wood or stone into a particular shape, or to cut lines into the surface: *He carved a little statue out of wood.*
2 to cut pieces from a large piece of cooked meat: *Dad always carves the turkey.*
—**carving** *noun* an object or decoration made by carving wood or stone: *a carving of an owl*
→ See Thesaurus box at **cut**[1]
→ See picture on page A14

'car wash *noun*
a place where you can take your car to be washed

case /keɪs/ *noun*
1 an example of a particular event or thing: *Parents are supposed to sign report cards, but in some cases students never show them to their parents.* | *It wasn't my fault – it was a case of being in the wrong place at the wrong time.*
2 the situation that exists: *We live far apart now, but that won't always be the case.* | *"I'll be home late tonight." "Well, in that case* (=since that is the situation), *I won't cook dinner."*
3 (just) in case = in order to be prepared for something that might happen: *I'll take an umbrella in case it rains.*
4 a crime that the police are trying to find out the truth about: *The police are trying to solve a murder case.*
5 something that a court of law deals with: *He thought he would win the court case, but the judge ruled against him.*
6 in any case = used when mentioning a more important fact: *He wouldn't listen to us. In any case, it's too late now.* SYNONYM **anyway**
7 an argument that someone or something is good or bad: *There is a good case for changing the rule, so I think we should do it.*
8 a container for storing something: *a violin case*
→ **upper case**, **lower case**

cash[1] /kæʃ/ *noun*
the coins and paper money that you use for buying things: *I don't have any cash – I'll have to use my credit card.*
→ See Thesaurus box at **money**

cash[2] *verb*
cash a check = to get paper money by giving the bank, a hotel, etc. a check for the same amount: *I need to cash this check at the bank.*

cash•ier /kæ'ʃɪr/ *noun*
someone whose job is taking the money that customers pay: *Bill worked as a cashier at the gas station.*

'cash ˌregister *noun*
a machine in a store that shows how much customers have to pay and where money is kept

ca•si•no /kə'sinoʊ/ *noun* plural **casinos**
a place where people try to win money by playing games: *the casinos of Las Vegas*

cas•ket /'kæskɪt/ *noun*
a box in which a dead body is buried SYNONYM **coffin**

cas•se•role /'kæsəˌroʊl/ *noun*
a meal made of a combination of different foods that are cooked slowly together in an OVEN: *The recipe is for a fish casserole made with potatoes and other vegetables.*

cas•sette /kə'set/ *noun*
a small plastic case with tape inside, used for playing or recording music, movies, etc.: *I need a blank video cassette to record the show on.* SYNONYM **tape**

cast[1] /kæst/ *verb* **cast**
1 to choose an actor for a part in a movie, play, etc.: *They cast a famous actor in the leading role.*
2 cast your ballot/vote = to vote in an election: *You can cast your ballot at 12 places across the city.*

cast[2] *noun*
1 a hard cover that doctors put around a broken bone until it gets better: *His left arm was in a cast for six weeks after he broke it.*
2 all the actors in a play or movie: *There was a party after the play was over for all the cast members.*

cas•tle /'kæsəl/ *noun*
a large building with high walls that was built to protect the people inside from attack: *The castle was built on a hill above the city.*

C

cas•u•al /ˈkæʒuəl/ *adjective*
1 casual clothes are not formal, and you usually wear them when you are not working: *The new store sells casual clothes like jeans and sweatshirts.*
2 relaxed and not worried about things: *She has a very casual attitude about everything and doesn't take anything very seriously.*
—**casually** *adverb*: *Jon was casually dressed in a T-shirt and jeans.*

cas•u•al•ty /ˈkæʒuəlti/ *noun* plural **casualties** *formal*
someone who is hurt or killed in an accident or war: *The fighting lasted for 12 hours, and there were heavy casualties* (=a lot of people hurt or killed).

cat /kæt/ *noun*
1 a small animal that people often keep as a pet: *At home we have two cats and a dog.*
2 any large wild animal that is related to cats: *Big cats such as lions often live in groups.*
➔ See picture at **pet**

cat•a•log *also* **catalogue** /ˈkætlˌɔg/ *noun*
a book with pictures and information about things you can buy from a company: *I looked through a catalog to find some clothes to order.*

ca•tas•tro•phe /kəˈtæstrəfi/ *noun*, *formal*
something terrible that happens and causes very serious problems or damage: *The earthquake was the worst catastrophe in the history of the country.* SYNONYM **disaster**
—**catastrophic** /ˌkætəˈstrɑfɪk/ *adjective*, *formal* causing very serious problems or damage: *The whole area was hit by catastrophic floods, and much of the city was destroyed.*

catch¹ /kætʃ/ *verb* **caught** /kɔt/
1 to stop something that is moving through the air, using your hands: *Sammy caught the ball and threw it to me.* ANTONYM **drop**
2 to stop a person or animal that wants to escape from you: *A police officer ran after the thief and caught him.*
3 to get a fish or animal by using a net, hook, or trap: *How many fish did you catch?*
4 **catch a train/plane/bus** = to get on a train, etc. to go somewhere: *I catch the 7:30 train to work.*
5 to get an illness: *If you catch a cold, you should stay at home.*
6 to get stuck on something by mistake: *His shirt caught on the fence and tore.*
7 **catch your breath** = to begin to breathe normally again after you have been breathing faster than usual: *It was a steep climb, so we stopped to catch our breath.*

PHRASAL VERBS

catch on
1 to understand something: *Some of the kids in the class catch on fast, but others have more trouble learning.*
2 if a new idea, thing, etc., catches on, it becomes popular: *I don't think electric cars will ever catch on.*

catch up
to reach the same place as a person, car, etc. that was in front of you: *I had to run to catch up with her.*
➔ See picture on page A4

catch² *noun*
1 the act of catching a ball: *That was a great catch! Did you see how high he jumped?*
2 a hook for fastening something: *The catch on my necklace broke.*
3 a hidden problem in a situation that seems to be very good: *The shows are on TV every day without advertising. But there's a catch – they are only shown between 1 and 3 a.m.*
4 **play catch** = to play a game of throwing a ball between people: *The kids were in the yard playing catch.*

catch•y /ˈkætʃi/ *adjective*
a catchy tune is nice and easy to remember: *That song's really catchy – I've been singing it all day.*

cat•e•go•ry /ˈkætəˌgɔri/ Ac *noun* plural **categories**
a group of people or things that are like each other in some way: *Guns, knives, and swords all belong in the category of weapons.*
—**categorize** /ˈkætəgəˌraɪz/ *verb* to put people or things into groups by deciding that they are like each other in some way: *The students are categorized according to their ability.*
➔ See Thesaurus box at **type¹**

ca•ter•ing /ˈkeɪtərɪŋ/ *noun*
the job of providing and serving food and drinks at parties, meetings, etc.: *Who is*

C

doing the catering for the wedding? What kind of food are they serving?

cat•er•pil•lar /ˈkætəˌpɪlə/ *noun*
the young form of some insects, with a small round body and many legs: *Soon the caterpillar will turn into a butterfly.*

cat•fish /ˈkætfɪʃ/ *noun*
a fish with long hairs around its mouth, that lives mainly in rivers and lakes

ca•the•dral /kəˈθidrəl/ *noun*
a big important church: *We visited some beautiful old cathedrals in Europe.*

Cath•olic /ˈkæθlɪk/ *adjective*
belonging to the part of the Christian religion that has the Pope as its leader: *the Catholic church* (=the Catholic religion) SYNONYM **Roman Catholic**
—**Catholic** *noun* someone who believes in the Catholic religion
—**Catholicism** /kəˈθɑləˌsɪzəm/ *noun* the Catholic religion

cat•sup /ˈketʃəp/ *noun*
another spelling of KETCHUP

cat•tle /ˈkætl/ *plural noun*
cows and BULLs that are kept on a farm: *In the field, there was a herd of cattle* (=a large group of cows).

Cau•ca•sian /kɔˈkeɪʒən/ *noun, formal*
a person who has pale skin SYNONYM **white**
—**Caucasian** *adjective* having pale skin: *a Caucasian man with blond hair and blue eyes*

caught /kɔt/ *verb*
the past tense and past participle of CATCH

cau•li•flow•er /ˈkɔlɪˌflaʊə/ *noun*
a white vegetable with green leaves around the outside

cause¹ /kɔz/ *noun*
1 a person or thing that makes something happen: *It seems likely that a bomb was the cause of the plane crash.*
2 something good that a group of people believe should happen: *The men were prepared to fight for a good cause.*

cause² *verb*
to make something happen, especially something bad: *Heavy traffic is causing long delays.*

cau•tion /ˈkɔʃən/ *noun*
if you do something with caution, you are careful because it could be dangerous: *You should always approach big animals with caution.*

cau•tious /ˈkɔʃəs/ *adjective*
careful about something that could be dangerous, unpleasant, etc.: *Young children are often cautious about trying new food.*
—**cautiously** *adverb*: *Lizzy cautiously put one foot in the water.*
—**cautiousness** *noun*

WORD FAMILY look at the words:
→ **cautious** *adjective*
→ **cautiously** *adverb*
→ **cautiousness** *noun*
→ **caution** *noun*

cav•al•ry /ˈkævəlri/ *noun*
soldiers in the past who fought while they were on horses

cave /keɪv/ *noun*
a big hole in the side of a cliff or under the ground: *The cave goes 500 feet into the side of the mountain.*

cav•i•ty /ˈkævəti/ *noun* plural **cavities**
a hole inside something: *The dentist told me that I have a cavity in my tooth that needs to be filled.*

cc *abbreviation*
1 cubic centimeter: *a 2,000 cc engine*
2 used for showing that you are sending a copy of an email or business letter to someone else

CD *noun*
compact disc a small round piece of plastic that records and plays music or computer information: *Do you want to listen to my new CD? The music is really good.*

CˈD ˌplayer *noun*
a piece of equipment used for playing music on CDs
→ See picture on page A28

CD-ROM /ˌsi di ˈrɑm/ *noun*
a CD that stores a large amount of computer information: *You can buy the dictionary as a book, or you can buy it on CD-ROM.*

cease /sis/ Ac *verb, formal*
to stop: *By noon, the rain had ceased.*
—**ceaseless** *adjective, formal* happening without stopping: *He listened to the ceaseless noise of the wind.*

cease•fire /ˈsisˌfaɪɚ/ *noun*
a time during a war when the enemies agree to stop fighting: *Both sides agreed to a ceasefire during the peace talks.*

ce•dar /ˈsidɚ/ *noun*
a tall tree with thin leaves like needles, or the wood from this tree: *She kept extra blankets in a cedar chest.*

ceil•ing /ˈsilɪŋ/ *noun*
the top part of a room above your head: *It's a big old house with high ceilings.*
➔ See picture on page A8

cel•e•brate /ˈseləˌbreɪt/ *verb*
to do something special because it is a special occasion: *All our tests are over, so let's have a party to celebrate!*
WORD FAMILY ➔ celebration *noun*

cel•e•brat•ed /ˈseləˌbreɪtɪd/ *adjective, formal*
famous: *His father was a celebrated pianist.*

cel•e•bra•tion /ˌseləˈbreɪʃən/ *noun*
something special you do on a special occasion, especially a party: *You are all invited to my son's 21st birthday celebration!*
➔ See Thesaurus box at party

ce•leb•ri•ty /səˈlebrəti/ *noun* plural **celebrities**
a famous person: *Everyone likes reading about the lives of actors, athletes, and other celebrities.*

cel•er•y /ˈseləri/ *noun*
a vegetable with long green stems that you can eat uncooked
➔ See picture on page A12

cell /sel/ *noun*
1 the smallest part that forms an animal or plant: *Billions of cells make up the human body.* | *brain cells* (=that form the brain)
2 a small room where a prisoner is kept: *The prisoners spend most of the day in their cells.*

cel•lar /ˈselɚ/ *noun*
a room under a house where things are stored: *There are some old chairs down in the cellar.* | *a wine cellar*

cel•lo /ˈtʃeloʊ/ *noun*
a big musical instrument that you hold between your knees and play with a BOW (=type of stick)
—**cellist** *noun* someone who plays the cello
➔ See picture on page A21

ˈcell phone *also* **cell•u•lar phone** /ˌselyəlɚ ˈfoʊn/ *noun*
a small telephone that you carry with you: *The man next to me was talking on his cell phone.*

cell phone

Cel•si•us /ˈselsiəs/ *noun written abbreviation* **C**
a temperature scale in which water freezes at 0° and boils at 100°: *In summer, temperatures reach 40 degrees Celsius.* SYNONYM **Centigrade**

ce•ment /sɪˈment/ *noun*
a material used for building made of a powder mixed with water and sand, that becomes hard when it is dry: *The floors of the building were made of cement.*

cem•e•ter•y /ˈseməˌteri/ *noun* plural **cemeteries**
an area of land where dead people are buried: *My father's grave was in the middle of the cemetery.*

cen•sor /ˈsensɚ/ *verb*
if people in authority censor newspapers, books, movies, etc. they take out any parts that they do not want people to see: *In some countries, newspapers are censored, and no criticism of the government is allowed.*
—**censorship** *noun* the act of censoring books, movies, etc.: *Do you agree with the censorship of books?*

cen•sus /ˈsensəs/ *noun* plural **censuses**
an official act of counting all the people in a country and collecting information about them: *According to the census, 97% of all homes have telephones.*

cent /sent/ *noun*
an amount of money that is worth 1/100 of a dollar: *I gave the kids 75 cents for candy.*

cen•ten•ni•al /senˈteniəl/ *also* **cen•ten•a•ry** /senˈtenəri/ *noun*
a special day or year that is 100 years after something happened or began: *In 2001 the university celebrated its centennial – it was founded in 1901.*

cen•ter /ˈsentɚ/ *noun*
1 the middle of something: *There was an old table in the center of the room with chairs around it.*

C

2 a shopping/sports, etc. center = a big building where people shop, play sports, etc.: *Why don't we look for some new clothes for you at the shopping center?*
3 a business/banking/research, etc. center = a place that is important for a particular activity: *Montreal is an important business center.*
4 the player in basketball who plays near the BASKET: *Sophie was tall and usually played center on the basketball team.*

WORD FAMILY look at the words:

→ center *noun*
→ central *adjective*
→ centrally *adverb*

ˈcenter field *noun*
the area in baseball in the center of the OUTFIELD

Cen·ti·grade /ˈsentəˌgreɪd/ *noun*
another word for CELSIUS

cen·ti·me·ter /ˈsentəˌmitɚ/ *noun, written abbreviation* **cm**
a unit for measuring length, equal to 1/100 of a meter or 0.39 inches: *He was 182 centimeters tall.*

cen·ti·pede /ˈsentəˌpid/ *noun*
a creature like a long insect with many legs

cen·tral /ˈsentrəl/ *adjective*
in the center of an area: *Our apartment is in a central location and it's easy to get anywhere in the city.* | *Kazakhstan and other countries of Central Asia*
—**centrally** *adverb*: *The hotel is centrally located near the government buildings.*

cen·tu·ry /ˈsentʃəri/ *noun plural* **centuries**
a period of 100 years: *There were huge changes in technology during the last century* (=1900–2000). | *the 21st century*

ce·ram·ics /səˈræmɪks/ *plural noun*
pots, plates, etc. made from clay
—**ceramic** *adjective* made of clay: *We used ceramic tiles for the kitchen floor.*

ce·re·al /ˈsɪriəl/ *noun*
food made from grain that people eat for breakfast with milk: *We had a breakfast of cereal and fruit.*

cer·e·mo·ny /ˈserəˌmoʊni/ *noun plural* **ceremonies**
an important public or religious event that involves special words and actions: *It was a beautiful wedding ceremony* (=when people get married).
—**ceremonial** /ˌserəˈmoʊniəl/ *adjective* relating to a ceremony: *the ceremonial opening of Congress*

cer·tain /ˈsɚtn/ *adjective*
1 if you are certain, you are sure about something: *I'm certain (that) I've seen that man before.* | *He was born in 1984 – I'm certain about that.* SYNONYM **sure**
2 make certain = to do what is necessary in order to be sure about something: *Just make certain that you don't miss your flight.*
3 *formal* if something is certain to happen, it is definitely going to happen: *It's almost certain to rain again tomorrow.*
—**certainty** *noun* the quality of being certain

WORD FAMILY look at the words:

→ certain *adjective*
→ uncertain *adjective*
→ certainly *adverb*
→ uncertainly *adverb*
→ certainty *noun*
→ uncertainty *noun*

cer·tain·ly /ˈsɚtnli/ *adverb*
1 used when saying that something is definitely true: *The kids in this class are certainly smart. Their test scores are very high.* SYNONYM **definitely**
2 *formal* of course: *"Could you get us some water, please?" "Certainly."*

cer·tif·i·cate /sɚˈtɪfəkət/ *noun*
a birth/marriage/death, etc. certificate = an important piece of paper that shows when you were born, married, etc.: *You may need your birth certificate in order to get a visa.*

cer·ti·fy /ˈsɚtəˌfaɪ/ *verb* **certified**, third person singular **certifies**
to officially say that something is true: *Two doctors certified that the patient was dead.*

ce·sar·e·an /sɪˈzeriən/ *also* **ceˌsarean ˈsection** *noun*
an operation in which doctors cut open a woman's body to take a baby out: *When her first baby was born, she had a cesarean.*

chain¹ /tʃeɪn/ *noun*
1 a line of metal rings joined together: *Maria wore a silver chain around her neck.*
2 a number of stores, hotels, etc. owned by the same person or company: *The company owns a chain of stores around the world.*
➔ See picture at **bicycle**

chain² *verb*
to tie people or things together, using a metal chain: *The prisoners were chained together at the ankles.*

chain•saw /ˈtʃeɪnsɔ/ *noun*
a tool used for cutting wood, that works using a motor

ˈchain store *noun*
a store that belongs to a large group that a big company owns: *I try not to shop at chain stores if I can use a small local business instead.*

chair /tʃer/ *noun*
1 a piece of furniture for one person to sit on: *There were six chairs around the kitchen table.*
2 another word for a CHAIRPERSON
➔ See picture at **seat**

chair•man /ˈtʃermən/ plural **chairmen** /ˈtʃermən/ *noun*
someone who controls a meeting, organization, or university department: *Randall became the new chairman of the committee.*
—**chairmanship** *noun* the position of being a chairman: *He took over the chairmanship in May.*

chair•per•son /ˈtʃerˌpɚsən/ *noun* plural **chairpersons**
someone who controls a meeting, organization, or university department: *Ann Wright is chairperson of the technology committee.*
SYNONYM **chair**

chair•wom•an /ˈtʃerˌwʊmən/ *noun* plural **chairwomen** /ˈtʃerˌwɪmɪn/
a woman who controls a meeting, organization, or university department

chalk /tʃɔk/ *noun*
a white stick that you use for writing or drawing: *Nick did a drawing on black paper using chalk.*

chal•lenge¹ /ˈtʃæləndʒ/ Ac *noun*
1 something difficult that you need skill to do well: *I'm not looking for an easy job – I want something that will be a challenge for me.*
2 *formal* the act of asking questions about whether something is right, fair, or legal: *There will be legal challenges to the new law by groups who believe it is unfair to poor families.*

WORD FAMILY look at the words:
➔ **challenge** *noun*
➔ **challenge** *verb*
➔ **challenging** *adjective*

challenge² *verb*
1 to ask someone to play a game or to fight against you: *They challenged us to a game of basketball.*
2 to question whether something is right: *I encourage my students to challenge what I say.*

chal•leng•er /ˈtʃæləndʒɚ/ Ac *noun*
someone who is competing against another person to win a game, election, etc.: *There was only one real challenger for the presidency.*

chal•leng•ing /ˈtʃæləndʒɪŋ/ Ac *adjective*
difficult in an interesting way: *Sometimes kids should read books that are challenging for them instead of just reading easy fun ones.*

champ /tʃæmp/ *noun, informal*
another word for a CHAMPION: *Ten years ago, he was an Olympic champ.*

cham•pagne /ʃæmˈpeɪn/ *noun*
a type of wine with a lot of BUBBLEs in it: *It was a special occasion, so we had champagne.*

cham•pi•on /ˈtʃæmpiən/ *noun*
a person or team that has won a sports competition or game: *She was a world champion in gymnastics and rarely lost a competition.*

cham•pi•on•ship /ˈtʃæmpiənˌʃɪp/ *noun, also* **championships** *plural noun*
a competition to find the best player or team in a sport: *the National basketball championships*
➔ See Thesaurus box at **competition**

C

C

chance /tʃæns/ *noun*
1 an opportunity to do something: *I hope I get the chance to travel after I finish college.* SYNONYM **opportunity**
2 a possibility that something will happen: *Do you think there's a chance that I'll get on the team?*
3 take a chance = to do something that is a risk: *Don't take any chances when you are driving. Drive safely at all times.*
4 the way that something surprising happens without anyone planning it: *By chance, we met again two years later when we were both staying at the same hotel.*

chan•cel•lor /ˈtʃænsələ˞/ *noun*
1 the most important person in some universities
2 the leader of the government in some countries: *the Chancellor of Germany*

chan•de•lier /ˌʃændəˈlɪr/ *noun*
a frame decorated with pieces of glass that holds lights and hangs from the ceiling: *A heavy chandelier hung over the dining table.*

change¹ /tʃeɪndʒ/ *verb*
1 to become different: *My father changed after Ricky died.* | *The leaves change color in Fall.*

> **THESAURUS: change**
>
> **alter** *formal* to change something or to make something change: *I altered my schedule so that I could take the advanced Spanish class.*
>
> **adapt** *formal* to change something to make it work better in a new situation: *The room has been adapted so that people in wheelchairs can use it.*
>
> **adjust** *formal* to change something a little bit to make it better: *She adjusted the volume on the TV, to make it a little bit louder.*
>
> **reform** *formal* to change a system or organization and make it better: *plans to reform the tax system*
>
> **transform** *formal* to change the way something looks or does things completely: *They've completely transformed the downtown area.*

2 to start having something different or new: *Do you think I should change my hairstyle?* | *The company changed its name to Cortland Capital.*
3 to put on different clothes: *Remember to change your shirt before you go out.* | *I got changed for soccer practice.*
4 change your mind = to change your ideas about something: *I thought I liked Brandon, but I've changed my mind.*
5 change a $10/$20, etc. bill = to give a ten, twenty, etc. dollar bill to someone and get the same amount back in smaller bills or coins: *I'm going to change this $50 bill at the bank.*
6 change dollars/pounds, etc. = to give dollars, pounds, etc. to someone and get the same amount back in money from a different country: *Where can I change my dollars into pesos?* SYNONYM **exchange**

change² *noun*
1 something that is different: *I noticed a change in his behavior. He was more confident.* | *How about eating out for a change* (=something different that is enjoyable)*?*
2 the money you get back in a store, when you pay more than something costs: *Here's your change, ma'am.*
3 coins, not bills: *Do you have any change on you?*
➔ See Thesaurus box at **money**

chan•nel /ˈtʃænl/ Ac *noun*
1 a television station: *There's a good show on channel 2.*
2 a long area of water that flows between two areas of land: *We crossed the English Channel and landed in France.*

chant /tʃænt/ *verb*
to say the same word or phrase many times: *People marched through the city chanting "Victory!"*
—**chant** *noun* something people say or sing many times: *The whole audience stood and joined in the chant.*

cha•os /ˈkeɪɑs/ *noun, formal*
a very confused situation: *Five bombs exploded, and the city was in chaos.*
—**chaotic** /keɪˈɑtɪk/ *adjective, formal* without any order: *We have six children, so the house is pretty chaotic.*

chap•el /ˈtʃæpəl/ *noun*
a small church, or part of a church

chap·e·rone /ˈʃæpəˌroʊn/ *noun, formal*
someone who goes somewhere with a young person to make sure they behave well: *Sara went to the dance with the kids as a chaperone.*
—**chaperone** *verb* to go with someone as a chaperone

chap·ter /ˈtʃæptɚ/ Ac *noun*
a part of a book: *There are ten chapters in the book, and I'm reading Chapter 5 now.*
➔ See Thesaurus box at **part**[1]

char·ac·ter /ˈkærɪktɚ/ *noun*
1 what a person, place, etc. is like: *"How would you describe Lilly's character?" "She's very quiet but very funny."*
2 a person in a book, play, movie, etc.: *Esther is the main character* (=the most important person) *in the book.*
3 good or interesting qualities that people have: *I liked him a lot – he had a lot of character.*

WORD FAMILY look at the words:
➔ **character** *noun*
➔ **characteristic** *noun*
➔ **characteristic** *adjective*

char·ac·ter·is·tic /ˌkærɪktəˈrɪstɪk/ *noun*
a quality that is typical of someone or something: *"What are the characteristics of a good leader?" "He or she should be honest, intelligent, and strong."*
—**characteristic** *adjective* typical of someone or something: *This angry behavior is characteristic of many teenagers.*

char·coal /ˈtʃɑrkoʊl/ *noun*
a black substance used as FUEL, or for drawing: *Charcoal is the best fuel for barbecues.*

charge[1] /tʃɑrdʒ/ *noun*
1 the amount of money you pay to do something: *There's no charge for entry to the museum* (=it is free).
2 be in charge of something = to be the person who organizes or controls something: *Mr. Taylor is in charge of all school sports, so if you have a question, ask him.*
3 a formal statement made by the police that someone has done something wrong: *The theft charges against him turned out to be true.*
4 the amount of electricity there is in something: *There's no charge left in the battery – you'll have to buy a new one.*
➔ See Thesaurus box at **cost**[1]

charge[2] *verb*
1 if you charge an amount of money for something, people must pay you that amount for it: *The swimming pool charges $4 for adults.*
2 to buy something with a CREDIT CARD: *"How would you like to pay?" "I'll charge it."*
3 if the police charge someone, they say formally that he or she has done something wrong: *Police charged the boy with burglary when they found him with a stolen stereo.*
4 to move forward very fast in an angry way: *The bull turned and charged toward us.*
5 if a BATTERY charges, it takes in and stores electricity: *It takes three hours to charge the battery in the cell phone.*

ˈcharge card *noun*
a CREDIT CARD that you use to buy things in a particular store

cha·ris·ma /kəˈrɪzmə/ *noun, formal*
a special quality that makes a lot of people like you: *He had a lot of charisma and was a natural leader.*
—**charismatic** /ˌkærɪzˈmætɪk/ *adjective* a charismatic person has charisma

char·i·ta·ble /ˈtʃærətəbəl/ *adjective*
relating to charities: *Many young people volunteer to do charitable work to help people in their communities.*

char·i·ty /ˈtʃærəti/ *noun* plural **charities**
an organization that gives money or help to people who need it: *The school collected $1,000 and gave it to a charity.*

charm[1] /tʃɑrm/ *noun*
1 an attractive quality or way of acting with other people: *She had a lot of charm and many friends.*
2 something that may bring you good luck: *Ruby wore the silver bracelet as a charm.*

charm[2] *verb, formal*
to make people like you a lot, by the way you act: *José was good-looking and charmed all the girls.*

charm•ing /ˈtʃɑrmɪŋ/ *adjective, formal*
very pleasing or attractive: *Everyone liked her and said she was a charming woman.*

chart /tʃɑrt/ Ac *noun*
1 a drawing, series of numbers, etc. that shows information about something: *In class today, we measured our heights, and made a chart to show it.*
2 the charts = a list of the most popular songs, produced each week: *The song reached number 2 on the charts.*
3 a map, especially of oceans or stars: *Long ago, sailors used these charts to find their way across the oceans.*

C

chase /tʃeɪs/ *verb*
to follow someone or something quickly, because you want to catch him, her, or it: *A police officer chased after the man, but he escaped.*
—**chase** *noun* an act of chasing: *The best part of the movie is the car chase through New York.*

chat /tʃæt/ *verb* **chatted, chatting**
1 to talk with friends or in a friendly way: *All the girls were chatting about the party on Saturday night.*
2 to send and receive messages in a chatroom on the Internet
—**chat** *noun* a friendly talk
→ See Thesaurus box at **talk**[1]

ˈ**chat room** *noun*
a place on the Internet where you talk to people by writing messages to them, and they can reply immediately

chat•ter /ˈtʃætɚ/ *verb*
to talk a lot about unimportant things: *She chattered about the weather and her clothes.*
—**chatter** *noun* a lot of talk about unimportant things

cheap /tʃip/ *adjective*
1 something that is cheap does not cost a lot of money: *I bought two pairs of jeans because they were really cheap.* ANTONYM **expensive**
2 cheap material, furniture, wine, etc. is not good quality: *Don't buy cheap furniture – it doesn't last long.*
3 someone who is cheap does not like to spend money: *He was too cheap to get her a birthday gift.* ANTONYM **generous**

cheap•ly /ˈtʃipli/ *also* **cheap** *informal adverb*
for a low price: *I know where you can get a computer really cheaply if you don't have a lot of money.*

cheat[1] /tʃit/ *verb*
1 to do something that is not honest because you think it will help you succeed: *Molly cheated on the history test, and the teacher caught her.*
2 to deceive someone, especially by taking too much money from them: *The salesman cheated me out of $200 and I want to complain to someone.*

cheat[2] *also* **cheat•er** /ˈtʃitɚ/ *noun*
someone who does things that are not honest: *Gus was a liar and a cheat.*

check[1] /tʃek/ *verb*
1 to look carefully at something to see if it is correct, good, etc.: *When you finish the test, don't forget to check your answers.*
2 to ask someone about something: *If you're worried, why don't you check with your doctor?*

PHRASAL VERBS

check in
to go to the desk at a hotel, airport, etc. to say that you have arrived: *We got to the hotel, checked in, and went out to eat.*

check something off
to put a mark (✓) next to something on a list: *Check the kids' names off as they get on the bus.*

check out
1 to pay the bill and leave a hotel: *You must check out before 12 o'clock.*
2 check something out to find out whether something is good or correct: *We wanted to check out the new sushi restaurant downtown.*
3 check something out to borrow a book from a library: *I went to the library and checked out a book on Japan.*

check[2] *noun*
1 a piece of printed paper that you write an amount of money on and use to pay for things: *Can I pay by check?* | *I wrote a check for $300.*
2 a careful look at something to see if it is correct, good, etc.: *I did a quick check to make sure all the doors were locked.*

check

sign a check

3 a piece of paper you get in a restaurant, hotel, etc. that shows how much you must pay: *Can I have the check, please?* SYNONYM **bill**
4 a mark (✔) that you put next to an answer to show that it is correct, or next to something on a list: *My teacher put a check by each right answer.*
5 a pattern of squares on something: *He wore a shirt with blue and white checks.*

check·book /ˈtʃekbʊk/ *noun*
a book of checks that you use to pay for things

check·er /ˈtʃekɚ/ *noun*
something you can use on a computer to check something: *The software includes a spell checker and a grammar checker.*

check·ered /ˈtʃekɚd/ *adjective*
having a pattern of squares in two different colors: *It was a little Italian restaurant with red and white checkered tablecloths.*

check·ers /ˈtʃekɚz/ *noun*
a game for two people, who use 12 round pieces each on a board with a pattern of squares: *Let's play a game of checkers.*

ˈcheck-in *noun*
1 the process of telling someone at a hotel, airport, etc. that you have arrived: *Please allow at least an hour for check-in before your flight.*
2 a place at a hotel, airport, etc. where you go to say that you have arrived: *When I got to the check-in counter, I couldn't find my plane ticket.*
➔ See picture on page A30

ˈchecking acˌcount *noun*
a bank account that you can use to write checks

check·list /ˈtʃekˌlɪst/ *noun*
a list of things you have to do or remember: *I made a checklist of things I need to do before the trip.*

check·out /ˈtʃek-aʊt/ *noun*
1 *also* **checkout counter** a place in a store where you pay for goods: *The store was busy and there was a long line at the checkout.*
2 the time by which you must leave a hotel room: *Checkout is at noon.*

check·up *also* **check-up** /ˈtʃek-ʌp/ *noun*
an examination by a doctor or DENTIST to see if you are healthy: *You should have regular medical checkups.*

ched·dar /ˈtʃedɚ/ *also* **ˈcheddar cheese** *noun*
a smooth yellow cheese

cheek /tʃik/ *noun*
the soft round part of your face under your eyes: *She had bright blue eyes and pink cheeks.*
—**cheekbone** *noun* the bone in your cheek
➔ See picture on page A2

cheer[1] /tʃɪr/ *verb*
to shout as a way of showing that you support or like someone or something: *The fans in the football stadium cheered loudly.*

cheer

PHRASAL VERB
cheer up
1 to feel happier: *Cheer up – it's not so bad.*
2 **cheer someone up** = to make someone feel happier: *I bought Mom some flowers to cheer her up.*
➔ See Thesaurus box at **shout**[1]

cheer[2] *noun*
a shout that shows that you support or like someone or something: *Everyone gave a loud cheer when the band came on stage.*

cheer·ful /ˈtʃɪrfəl/ *adjective*
happy or seeming happy: *I like Sandra – she's always cheerful.*
—**cheerfully** *adverb*: *"Hi guys," Joey said cheerfully.*
—**cheerfulness** *noun*
➔ See Thesaurus box at **happy**

cheer·lead·er /ˈtʃɪrˌlidɚ/ *noun*
someone who encourages a crowd to cheer at sports events

C

cheese /tʃiz/ *noun*
a solid food made from milk: *Do you want cheese on your hamburger?*

cheese•cake /'tʃizkeɪk/ *noun*
a sweet cake made with soft white cheese

chees•y /'tʃizi/ *adjective, informal*
a cheesy movie, show, etc. is silly and has been made in a way that is not new or interesting: *Dad was watching a really cheesy game show on TV so I went to my room.*

chee•tah /'tʃitə/ *noun*
a wild cat with black spots in Africa that can run very fast

chef /ʃef/ *noun*
someone whose job is cooking in a restaurant: *He works as a chef in a big restaurant.*
➔ See picture on page A16

chem•i•cal[1] /'kemɪkəl/ Ac *noun*
a substance used in chemistry or produced by a chemical process: *The river was full of dangerous chemicals from the factory.*

WORD FAMILY look at the words:
➔ **chemical** *noun*
➔ **chemical** *adjective*
➔ **chemistry** *noun*

chemical[2] *adjective*
relating to substances that are made or used in chemistry: *The substances change in a chemical reaction when they are put together.*

chem•ist /'kemɪst/ *noun*
a scientist who does work related to chemistry

chem•is•try /'keməstri/ *noun*
the science of studying substances and the way that they change or combine with each other: *I want to study chemistry in college and then work for a drug company.*

che•mo•ther•a•py /ˌkimoʊ'θerəpi/ *noun also* **che•mo** /'kimoʊ/ *informal*
the treatment of CANCER using special drugs

cher•ish /'tʃerɪʃ/ *verb, formal*
if you cherish something, it is very important to you: *I cherish the memories of when my children were little.*

cher•ry /'tʃeri/ *noun* plural **cherries**
a small round fruit with dark red skin and a long stem: *a cherry tree*
➔ See picture on page A13

chess /tʃes/ *noun*
a game for two players, which you play on a board that has black and white squares. The aim of the game is to trap the opposing player's king: *Do you want to play another game of chess?*

chest /tʃest/ *noun*
1 the front part of your body between your neck and stomach: *She felt a sudden pain in her chest and was afraid she was having a heart attack.*
2 a large strong box that you use to keep things in: *Many of her possessions were in a large wooden chest.*
➔ See picture on page A2

chest•nut /'tʃesnʌt/ *noun*
a type of nut that is red-brown on the outside and pale yellow on the inside, which you can cook and eat: *a chestnut tree*

ˌchest of 'drawers *noun* plural **chests of drawers**
a piece of furniture with drawers that clothes can be kept in SYNONYM **dresser**
➔ See picture on page A10

chew /tʃu/ *verb*
1 to bite food several times with your teeth, in order to break it up so that you can swallow it: *The dog was chewing a piece of meat.*
2 to bite something several times without eating it: *Students are not allowed to chew gum in the classroom.*
—**chewy** *adjective* food that is chewy has to be chewed a lot before it is soft enough to eat: *The meat was very chewy and hard to eat.*

'chewing gum *noun*
another word for GUM: *Do you want a piece of chewing gum?*

chic /ʃik/ *adjective*
fashionable and attractive to look at: *They stayed at a chic hotel in Manhattan.*

Chi•ca•no /tʃɪ'kɑnoʊ/ *noun*
someone living in the U.S. who was born in Mexico or whose family came from Mexico
—**Chicana** *noun* a woman living in the U.S. who was born in Mexico or whose family came from Mexico

chick /tʃɪk/ *noun*
a baby bird: *a hen and her chicks*

chick·en¹ /ˈtʃɪkən/ *noun*
1 a farm bird that is kept for its eggs and meat
2 the meat from this bird: *His favorite food is fried chicken.*
3 *informal* someone who does not have any courage: *Don't be such a chicken! You can do it.*
—**chicken** *adjective, informal* afraid to do something: *He was so chicken, he wouldn't even get in the water.*

chicken² *verb*
PHRASAL VERB
chicken out
to decide not to do something that you have said you will do because you are too afraid: *He said he wanted to go skiing with us, but then he chickened out at the last minute.*

ˈchicken pox *also* **chick·en·pox** /ˈtʃɪkənˌpɑks/ *noun*
a disease that children often get, which causes ITCHY red spots on the skin and a fever

chief¹ /tʃif/ *noun*
1 the leader of a group or organization: *the chief of police*
2 the leader of a tribe: *an American Indian chief*

chief² *adjective*
most important: *Coffee is one of the country's chief exports.* SYNONYM **main**

ˌchief ˈjustice *noun*
the most important judge in a court of law, especially in the U.S. Supreme Court

chief·ly /ˈtʃifli/ *adverb*
mainly: *The disease chiefly affects women, but some men also get it.*

child /tʃaɪld/ *noun* plural **children** /ˈtʃɪldrən/
1 a young person who is not yet fully grown: *Children love computer games.* | *We went there when I was a child, but that was many years ago.* SYNONYM **kid**

THESAURUS: child

Child is a word that you can use to talk about **young children** and **teenagers**. You do not normally use child to mean a **baby**.

Kid is an informal word for a **child**.

You are a **baby** when you are first born.

A very young baby who cannot walk or talk yet is called an **infant**.

You are a **teenager** between 13 and 19.

An **adolescent** is a child between about 11 and 17, when he or she is developing into an adult.

2 a son or daughter: *They have three children: a daughter and two sons.* SYNONYM **kid**

child·care /ˈtʃaɪldˌker/ *noun*
an arrangement in which someone takes care of children while their parents are at work: *Both of her children are in childcare since she works full time.*

child·hood /ˈtʃaɪldhʊd/ *noun*
the time when you are a child: *We've been friends since childhood – we went to elementary school together.*

child·ish /ˈtʃaɪldɪʃ/ *adjective*
1 behaving in a silly way that makes you seem younger than you really are: *"I don't want to eat my vegetables." "Don't be so childish!"* SYNONYM **immature**
2 suitable for a child, but not for an adult: *I'm an adult – I'm not interested in childish games.*
—**childishness** *noun*

child·less /ˈtʃaɪldləs/ *adjective*
having no children: *a childless couple*

chil·dren /ˈtʃɪldrən/ *noun*
the plural of CHILD

chil·i /ˈtʃɪli/ *noun* plural **chilies**
1 *also* **ˈchili ˌpepper** a small thin type of red or green pepper with a very hot taste
2 a dish made with beans, chilis, and usually meat

chill¹ /tʃɪl/ *verb*
1 to make something cold: *Chill the dessert before you serve it.*
2 *also* **chill out** *informal* to relax: *We were just chilling in front of the TV.*

chill² *noun*
1 a feeling of being frightened: *He was the meanest person I'd ever met, and every time I saw him a chill ran down my spine* (=I felt very frightened).
2 a feeling of coldness: *Take a sweater – there's a chill in the air.*
3 **chills** = a feeling of being cold, caused by being sick: *First I had chills and then a fever.*

C

chill•y /ˈtʃɪli/ *adjective*
chilly weather or places are cold and make you uncomfortable: *a chilly day in March*
➔ See Thesaurus box at **cold**[1]

chime /tʃaɪm/ *verb*
if a clock or bell chimes, it makes a ringing sound: *The clock chimes every hour.*
—**chime** *noun* the ringing sound of a clock or bell

chim•ney /ˈtʃɪmni/ *noun*
a pipe that takes smoke from a fire out through the roof of a building

chim•pan•zee /ˌtʃɪmpænˈzi/ *noun* also **chimp** /tʃɪmp/ *informal*
an African animal that is like a monkey without a tail: *Chimpanzees are very intelligent animals and can make simple tools.*

chimpanzee

chin /tʃɪn/ *noun*
the front part of your face below your mouth: *She rested her chin on her hands.*
➔ See picture on page A2

chi•na /ˈtʃaɪnə/ *noun*
plates, cups, etc. that are made from white clay of good quality: *a beautiful china teacup*

Chi•nese[1] /ˌtʃaɪˈniz/ *adjective*
from China: *a Chinese vase*

Chinese[2] *noun*
1 any of the languages that come from China, such as Mandarin or Cantonese
2 **the Chinese** = people from China

chip[1] /tʃɪp/ *noun*
1 a thin dry flat piece of potato or TORTILLA that has been fried in oil: *a bag of potato chips*
2 a small piece of metal or plastic that a computer uses to store information or to work: *The new computer chip is ten times more powerful than the old one.*
3 a small piece of something, such as wood, stone, or chocolate: *You can use the wood chips to make a fire.*
4 a small hole, crack, or mark on a plate, cup, etc. where a piece has broken off: *This plate has a chip in it.*
5 a small flat colored piece of plastic used in games instead of money: *a gambling chip*

chip[2] *verb* **chipped, chipping**
to break a small piece off something: *I chipped one of my fingernails opening the can.*
—**chipped** *adjective* with a piece broken off: *a chipped tooth*

chip•munk /ˈtʃɪpmʌŋk/ *noun*
a small brown animal that has black and white lines on its fur: *Chipmunks eat mainly nuts and seeds, and live in holes in the ground.*

chi•ro•prac•tor /ˈkaɪrəˌpræktɚ/ *noun*
someone who treats medical problems such as back pain by moving and pressing the muscles and bones

chirp /tʃɚp/ *verb*
if a bird or insect chirps, it makes short high sounds: *The birds were chirping in the trees.*

chis•el /ˈtʃɪzəl/ *noun*
a metal tool with a sharp edge that you use to cut wood or stone

chlo•rine /ˈklɔrin/ *noun*
a strong-smelling gas that is used to keep swimming pools clean

choco•late /ˈtʃɑklɪt/ *noun*
1 a sweet brown food that is eaten as candy or is used in cooking: *a chocolate cake | Most candy bars have chocolate in them.*
2 a small candy that is made of or covered with chocolate: *a box of chocolates*

ˌchocolate ˈchip *noun*
a small piece of chocolate put in foods such as cookies and cakes: *chocolate chip cookies*

choice /tʃɔɪs/ *noun*
1 the chance to choose between two or more things or people: *Voters have a choice between three people for mayor. | The restaurant offers a good choice of food.*
2 the person or thing that someone has chosen: *I'm not sure if I made the right choice of career.*

choir /kwaɪɚ/ *noun*
a group of people who sing together: *She sings in the church choir.*

choke /tʃoʊk/ *verb*
1 to have difficulty breathing because your throat is blocked or there is not enough air: *He choked on a piece of bread.*

2 to press your hands around someone's throat so that he or she cannot breathe: *Let go of her throat! You're choking her!*

chol•er•a /ˈkɑlərə/ *noun*
a very serious disease of the stomach, which people usually catch by drinking dirty water, especially in tropical countries

cho•les•ter•ol /kəˈlestəˌrɔl/ *noun*
a substance in your blood that may cause heart disease: *Foods such as steak and eggs are high in cholesterol* (=they contain a lot of cholesterol).

choose /tʃuz/ *verb* **chose** /tʃoʊz/ **chosen** /ˈtʃoʊzən/ **choosing**
1 to decide which one of a group of things or people that you want: *She chose the black dress instead of the red one.* | *There are so many books to choose from.*

THESAURUS: choose

pick to choose something or someone from a group of people or things: *Danielle picked the green dress.*

select *formal* to choose something or someone by thinking carefully about which is the best: *John selected the music for our wedding.*

decide on something to choose one thing from many possible choices: *Have you decided on a name for the baby?*

opt for something *formal* to choose one thing instead of another: *Students in this area can opt for one of three different schools.*

2 to decide to do something: *Many students are choosing to stay longer at college rather than graduating and looking for a job.*
➔ See Thesaurus box at **decide**

chop[1] /tʃɑp/ *also* **chop up** *verb* **chopped, chopping**
to cut food, wood, etc. into smaller pieces: *Chop the onions into thin slices.*

PHRASAL VERBS

chop something down
to make a tree fall down by cutting it with a heavy sharp tool

chop something off
to remove something by cutting it with a sharp tool: *We chopped off the branches that were too close to the house.*
➔ See Thesaurus box at **cut**[1]
➔ See picture on page A14

chop[2] *noun*
a small flat piece of meat on a bone: *a pork chop*

chop•sticks /ˈtʃɑpstɪks/ *plural noun*
a pair of thin sticks that people in parts of Asia use for eating food

chord /kɔrd/ *noun*
a combination of three or more musical notes played at the same time: *I can play a few chords on the guitar.*

chore /tʃɔr/ *noun*
a job that you have to do: *I need to do some chores around the house like cleaning the bathroom.*

cho•re•og•ra•phy /ˌkɔriˈɑgrəfi/ *noun*
the art of arranging how dancers should move during a performance

cho•rus /ˈkɔrəs/ *noun*
1 the part of a song that is repeated after each VERSE: *I don't know all the words of the song. I only know the chorus.*
2 a large group of people who sing together: *She used to sing in the school chorus.*
SYNONYM **choir**

chose /tʃoʊz/ *verb*
the past tense of CHOOSE

chos•en /ˈtʃoʊzən/ *verb*
the past participle of CHOOSE

chow•der /ˈtʃaʊdɚ/ *noun*
a thick soup made with milk, potatoes, and often fish: *clam chowder*

chris•ten /ˈkrɪsən/ *verb*
to officially give a child its name at a Christian religious ceremony: *She was christened Mary Louise.*
—**christening** *noun* a Christian ceremony at which a child is given its name

Chris•tian /ˈkrɪstʃən/ *adjective*
relating to the religion that is based on the teaching of Jesus Christ: *Christian beliefs*
—**Christian** *noun* someone who believes in the religion that is based on the teaching of Jesus Christ: *His parents are both Christians and go to church every Sunday.*

Chris•ti•an•i•ty /ˌkrɪstiˈænəti/ *noun*
the religion that is based on the teaching of Jesus Christ

Christ•mas /ˈkrɪsməs/ *noun*
1 December 25, the day when Christians celebrate the birth of Jesus Christ: *I still have to buy Christmas presents for my family.*

C

2 the period of time before and after this day: *My grandparents are coming to stay with us for Christmas.*

ˌChristmas ˈDay *noun*
December 25, the day when Christians celebrate the birth of Jesus Christ

ˌChristmas ˈEve *noun*
December 24, the day before Christmas

chrome /kroʊm/ *also* **chro·mi·um** /ˈkroʊmiəm/ *noun*
a shiny metal that is used as a covering for other metals on cars and furniture: *The table was made of chrome and glass.*

chro·mo·some /ˈkroʊməˌsoʊm/ *noun*
a part of every living cell that contains the GENEs that control the size, shape, color, etc. of a plant or animal: *Only males have Y chromosomes.*

chron·ic /ˈkrɑnɪk/ *adjective*
a chronic illness, condition, or problem is one that continues for a long time and cannot be cured: *She has chronic back pain and is never comfortable.*

chron·o·log·i·cal /ˌkrɑnlˈɑdʒɪkəl/ *adjective, formal*
arranged according to the order in which something happened: *The dates are listed in in chronological order starting in 1950 and continuing to the present.*

chry·san·the·mum /krɪˈsænθəməm/ *noun*
a garden plant with large brightly colored flowers

chub·by /ˈtʃʌbi/ *adjective*
slightly fat: *He was a chubby little boy, but now he's very thin.*
➔ See Thesaurus box at **fat**[1]

chuck·le /ˈtʃʌkəl/ *verb*
to laugh quietly: *She chuckled to herself when she read his funny letter.*
—**chuckle** *noun* a quiet laugh
➔ See Thesaurus box at **laugh**[1]

chunk /tʃʌŋk/ *noun*
a large thick piece of something that does not have an even shape: *He broke a chunk off the chocolate bar.*
—**chunky** *adjective* thick and heavy
➔ See Thesaurus box at **piece**

church /tʃɚtʃ/ *noun*
1 a building where Christians go to have religious services: *She goes to church every Sunday.*
2 *also* **Church** one of the separate groups within the Christian religion: *the Catholic Church*

chute /ʃut/ *noun*
a tube or sloping surface that things or people can slide down: *The old laundry chute leads to the basement.*

ci·der /ˈsaɪdɚ/ *also* **ˈapple ˌcider** *noun*
a drink made from apples

ci·gar /sɪˈgɑr/ *noun*
a thick tube of rolled tobacco leaves that people smoke: *He was smoking a smelly cigar.*

cig·a·rette /ˈsɪgəˌret/ *noun*
a thin tube of tobacco rolled in white paper that people smoke: *a pack of cigarettes*

cin·e·ma /ˈsɪnəmə/ *noun, formal*
movies in general: *We studied French cinema and learned about all the famous directors.*

cin·na·mon /ˈsɪnəmən/ *noun*
a sweet-smelling brown SPICE used in baking: *Sprinkle cinnamon on top of the cookies.*

cir·cle[1] /ˈsɚkəl/ *noun*
1 a round shape like the letter O: *They sat in a circle around the fire.*
2 a group of people who know each other and like the same things: *She has a large circle of friends.*

WORD FAMILY look at the words:
➔ **circle** *noun*
➔ **circle** *verb*
➔ **circular** *adjective*
➔ **semicircle** *noun*

➔ See picture at **shape**[1]

circle[2] *verb*
1 to draw a circle around something: *Circle the correct answer.*
2 to move in a circle around something: *The plane circled the airport before landing.*

cir•cuit /ˈsɚkɪt/ *noun*
the complete path that an electric current travels around: *an electrical circuit*

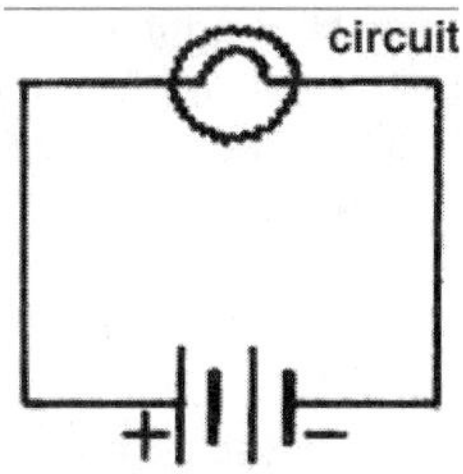

cir•cu•lar /ˈsɚkjələ/ *adjective*
shaped like a circle: *They sat around a circular table.*

cir•cu•late /ˈsɚkjəˌleɪt/ *verb, formal*
1 to go around inside something: *Blood circulates around the body.*
2 to send information to a group of people: *The report was circulated to everyone in the department.*

cir•cu•la•tion /ˌsɚkjəˈleɪʃən/ *noun, formal*
1 the movement of blood around your body: *Exercise can improve your circulation.*
2 the number of copies of a newspaper or magazine that are sold each time it is printed: *The newspaper has a daily circulation of 400,000.*

cir•cum•ference /sɚˈkʌmfrəns/ *noun, formal*
the distance around the outside of a circle or a round object: *Measure the circumference of your head by wrapping a string around it.*
➔ See picture at diameter

cir•cum•stan•ces /ˈsɚkəmˌstænsɪz/ Ac *plural noun*
1 the conditions or facts that are involved in an event or situation: *She had not been told about the circumstances of his death and she wanted to know what had happened.* | *I'm not surprised that he was upset, under the circumstances* (=because of the situation).
2 under no circumstances = used for saying that something will or should never happen: *Under no circumstances should you lend him money. He'll never pay you back.*

cir•cus /ˈsɚkəs/ *noun*
a show, often in a large tent, that is given by a group of performers and sometimes animals that has come to a town: *We saw clowns and elephants at the circus.*

cite /saɪt/ Ac *verb, formal*
to mention something as an example, as proof of something else, etc.: *His bad attitude was cited as a reason for firing him from the job.*

cit•i•zen /ˈsɪtəzən/ *noun*
someone who lives in a particular town, state, or country and has legal rights there: *I have the same rights as any other American citizen.* | *She is a citizen of Canada.*
—**citizenship** *noun* the state of legally belonging to a particular country, and having rights and duties there: *She has applied for U.S. citizenship.*

cit•rus /ˈsɪtrəs/ *also* **ˈcitrus ˌfruit** *noun, formal*
fruits such as oranges or LEMONS, or the trees they grow on: *The drink had a citrus flavor.*

cit•y /ˈsɪti/ *noun* plural **cities**
a very large town: *I've always lived in big cities like New York and Los Angeles.*

ˌcity ˈhall *also* **City Hall** *noun*
the local government of a city, or the building it uses as its offices: *The mayor held a news conference at City Hall yesterday.*

civ•ic /ˈsɪvɪk/ *adjective, formal*
relating to a city or the people who live in it: *The plan is supported by local civic leaders including the mayor and city council members.*

civ•il /ˈsɪvəl/ Ac *adjective, formal*
1 relating to laws about business, property, etc. rather than crimes: *The company is facing three civil lawsuits.*
2 not military or religious: *We were married in a civil ceremony, not in church.*
3 polite but not very friendly: *Please try to at least be civil, even if you can't be friendly.*
—**civility** /səˈvɪləti/ *noun, formal* behavior that is polite but not very friendly

ˌcivil engiˈneering *noun*
the activity of building roads, bridges, large buildings, etc.

ci•vil•ian /səˈvɪlyən/ *noun*
anyone who is not in the army, navy, etc.: *Many innocent civilians were killed in the attack.*
—**civilian** *adjective*

C

civ·i·li·za·tion /ˌsɪvələˈzeɪʃən/ *noun*
a society that is well organized and developed: *the ancient civilizations of Greece and Rome*

civ·i·lized /ˈsɪvəˌlaɪzd/ *adjective*
1 a civilized society is well organized, and has good laws and ways of living: *All civilized societies have some form of government.*
2 behaving in a polite and sensible way: *Let's discuss this in a civilized way, without yelling at each other.*

ˌcivil ˈliberties *plural noun*
the right of citizens to do whatever they want if it does not harm the rights of other people

ˌcivil ˈrights *plural noun*
the legal rights that every citizen of a country has: *The civil rights movement of the 1960s worked for an end to unfair treatment for people of different races.*

ˌcivil ˈwar *noun*
a war between groups of people who live in the same country: *Four hundred thousand people were killed in the civil war between the two regions of the country.*

claim[1] /kleɪm/ *verb*
1 to say that something is true, even though it might not be: *He claims (that) he's 19, but he only looks about 16 to me.*
2 to ask for something that belongs to you or that you have a right to have: *Lost items can be claimed between 10 a.m. and 4 p.m.*

claim[2] *noun*
1 a statement that something is true, even though it might not be: *The company made false claims about the safety of its products. It actually knew they were dangerous.*
2 an official request for something that you think you have a right to have: *He made an insurance claim after his house was destroyed in the storm.*

clam /klæm/ *noun*
a small ocean animal that has two rounded shells, or the meat from this animal: *We dug in the mud for clams.*

clamp[1] /klæmp/ *verb*
to hold or put something firmly in a particular position: *He clamped his hand over her mouth so she couldn't scream.*

PHRASAL VERB
clamp down *informal*
to become very strict in order to stop people from doing something: *The courts are clamping down on drunk drivers and giving very severe punishments.*

clamp[2] *noun*
a tool used for holding things together tightly

clan·des·tine /klænˈdestɪn/ *adjective, formal*
secret: *Only a few people knew about the clandestine meeting.*

clang /klæŋ/ *verb*
to make a loud sound like metal being hit: *The gate clanged shut behind him.*
—**clang** *noun* a loud sound like metal being hit

clap /klæp/ *verb* **clapped, clapping**
to hit your hands together loudly to show that you like something: *The audience was clapping and cheering for the band.*
➔ See picture on page A3

clar·i·fy /ˈklærəˌfaɪ/ Ac *verb* **clarified**, third person singular **clarifies** *formal*
to make something easier to understand: *Can you clarify these ideas in your paper? I'm not sure exactly what you mean.*
—**clarification** /ˌklærəfəˈkeɪʃən/ *noun* the action of clarifying something

clar·i·net /ˌklærəˈnet/ *noun*
a wooden musical instrument like a long black tube that you play by blowing into it
➔ See picture on page A21

clar·i·ty /ˈklærəti/ Ac *noun, formal*
the quality of being clear and easy to understand: *Try to improve the clarity of your writing by using simple language and giving more details and examples.*

clash[1] /klæʃ/ *verb*
1 *formal* to fight or argue with someone: *The police clashed with the angry crowd.*
2 if colors or patterns clash, they look bad together: *The orange curtains clashed with the purple carpet.*

clash[2] *noun, formal*
a fight or argument: *The deaths were the result of a clash between two gangs.*

clasp[1] /klæsp/ *verb, formal*
to hold something tightly: *She clasped her hands tightly together as if she was praying.*

clasp² *noun*
a small metal object used for fastening a bag, piece of jewelry, etc.: *She undid the clasp of her necklace.*

class /klæs/ *noun*
1 a group of students who are taught together: *How many students are in your class?* | *He graduated in the class of '05* (=the group of students who finished in 2005).
2 a period of time during which students are taught: *I loved all my science classes in high school.* | *Bob wasn't in class today.*
3 a group of people in a society that earn a similar amount of money, have similar types of jobs, etc.: *Rich people pay higher taxes than the middle class.*
4 *formal* a group of things that are similar in some way: *These four classes of weapons are illegal.*

clas•sic¹ /ˈklæsɪk/ Ac *adjective*
very typical or good: *a classic rock song* | *This is a classic example of how hard work can bring success.*
➔ See Thesaurus box at **old**

classic² *noun*
a book, movie, or song which is very good and which people have liked for a long time: *"Moby Dick" is a classic of American literature.*

clas•si•cal /ˈklæsɪkəl/ Ac *adjective*
1 relating to classical music: *a classical pianist*
2 relating to ancient Greece and Rome: *stories from classical mythology*

ˌclassical ˈmusic *noun*
music by people such as Mozart and Beethoven that is considered to be serious and important

ˌclassified ˈad *noun*
a small advertisement that you put in a newspaper, for example offering to sell something or offering a job: *I looked in the classified ads every day to find an apartment.*

clas•si•fy /ˈklæsəˌfaɪ/ *verb* **classified**, third person singular **classifies** *formal*
to decide which group something belongs to: *Whales are classified as mammals, not fish, because the babies are born alive and drink their mothers' milk.*
—**classification** /ˌklæsəfəˈkeɪʃən/ *noun* the process or result of classifying things

class•mate /ˈklæsmeɪt/ *noun*
someone who is in the same class as you at school or college: *I'm younger than most of my classmates.*

class•room /ˈklæsrum/ *noun*
a room in a school where students are taught

class•y /ˈklæsi/ *adjective* **classier**, **classiest** *informal*
extremely good in quality or behavior: *It's a classy restaurant and the prices are pretty high.*

clat•ter /ˈklætɚ/ *verb*
if things clatter, they make several loud noises by hitting something: *The pans clattered to the floor.*
—**clatter** *noun* loud noises made by things hitting together

clause /klɔz/ Ac *noun*
1 in grammar, a group of words that contains a subject and a verb: *The sentence "I'll do it if I can" contains two clauses: "I'll do it" and "if I can."*
2 a part of a legal document: *I read every clause in the contract very carefully.*

claus•tro•pho•bi•a /ˌklɔstrəˈfoubiə/ *noun*
a strong fear of being in a small enclosed place
—**claustrophobic** *adjective* having a feeling of claustrophobia: *I get claustrophobic in elevators.*

claw /klɔ/ *noun*
a sharp curved nail on the foot of an animal or bird: *The cat dug its claws into the carpet.*
—**claw** *verb* if an animal claws something, it tears it with its claws

clay /kleɪ/ *noun*
sticky soil that is used for making pots or bricks: *a clay pot*

clean¹ /klin/ *adjective*
1 not dirty: *Are your hands clean?* | *He put on a clean shirt.* ANTONYM **dirty**
2 not involving sex, drugs, or anything illegal: *He was known for his clean and healthy lifestyle.*
3 come clean *informal* = to tell the truth about something after keeping it a secret: *I*

C

finally came clean with my parents, and told them I had cheated on the test.
—**cleanliness** /ˈklenlinɪs/ *noun* the state of being clean and not dirty

C

clean² *also* **clean up** *verb*
to make something clean or neat: *I need to clean the bathtub.* | *She's cleaning up her room.*

THESAURUS: clean

do the dishes/wash the dishes to wash plates and pans after a meal: *It's Becky's turn to wash the dishes!*
scrub to clean something by rubbing it very hard: *The floor was so dirty I had to scrub it with a brush.*
dry to dry plates, dishes, etc. that have been washed: *If you wash the dishes, I'll dry them.*
do the housework to clean the house: *My mom and dad work all week, so we all help do the housework on Saturday.*
dust to clean small, light pieces of dirt off of furniture: *Even small children can help you dust.*
vacuum to clean carpets with a special machine: *Irma was vacuuming the living room.*
sweep to clean the dirt from the floor using a broom (=brush with a long handle): *I swept the kitchen floor.*
mop to clean the floor with water and a mop (=soft brush on a long handle): *Kenny spilled some juice, so I had to mop the floor.*
do the laundry to wash clothes: *I do a load of laundry every day.*

—**cleaning** *noun*: *I do all the cleaning.*
PHRASAL VERB
clean something out
to make the inside of a room, cupboard, etc. clean or neat, especially by taking things out of it: *We cleaned out the garage last Sunday.*

clean•er /ˈklinɚ/ *noun*
1 a machine or substance that is used to clean things: *a vacuum cleaner* | *a bottle of glass cleaner*
2 someone whose job is to clean houses or other buildings
3 the cleaners = a DRY CLEANERS: *Could you pick up my suit from the cleaners?*

cleanse /klenz/ *verb, formal*
to make something completely clean: *Cleanse the cut with soap and water.* SYNONYM **clean**

cleans•er /ˈklenzɚ/ *noun*
1 a substance used for cleaning your skin
2 a substance used for cleaning surfaces in a house, office, etc.

clear¹ /klɪr/ *adjective*
1 easy to understand, hear, or read: *I gave him clear instructions on what to do.* | *She spoke in a clear voice.*
2 impossible to doubt or make a mistake about: *It was clear (that) he was angry.* | *He made it clear (that) he wasn't interested.*

THESAURUS: clear

noticeable very easy to notice: *There was a noticeable difference in her behavior.*
obvious easy to notice: *It was obvious that Sally wanted to win.*
conspicuous very easy to notice, especially because something is different from other things: *I felt conspicuous in my red coat.*
striking unusual or interesting enough to be noticed: *The stories are a striking example of how well children can write.*

3 be clear about something = if you are clear about something, you understand it completely: *Are you clear about what I expect you to do?*
4 if a substance is clear, you can see through it: *clear glass bottles* SYNONYM **transparent**
5 having edges, shapes, and details that are easy to see: *The TV has a very clear picture.*
6 a clear sky has no clouds: *The sky was clear and the sun was shining.* ANTONYM **cloudy**
7 not blocked by anything: *Standing by the window, I had a clear view of everything that happened.*

clear² *verb*
1 to move things from a place, especially a large space, so that it is neat or empty: *They cleared the land so that they could grow crops.* | *Patty helped clear the table* (=take away the dirty dishes, forks, etc.).
2 to prove or say officially that someone has

not done something wrong: *The jury cleared Johnson of the murder charge.*

3 to give or get official permission to do something: *It sounds like a good idea, but let me clear it with my boss.*

4 clear the air = to talk about a problem or disagreement, so that bad feeling does not continue: *I'm glad we've cleared the air.*

PHRASAL VERB

clear up

1 clear something up = to explain something or make it clearer: *There's a misunderstanding that I want to clear up.*

2 if the sky clears up, the cloud goes away

clear•ance /ˈklɪrəns/ *noun*
official permission to do something: *The pilot was given clearance to land the plane.* SYNONYM **permission**

clear•ing /ˈklɪrɪŋ/ *noun*
a small area in a forest where there are no trees

clear•ly /ˈklɪrli/ *adverb*
1 without any doubt: *Clearly, we have a problem here.* SYNONYM **obviously**
2 in a way that is easy to hear, see, or understand: *Please speak more clearly. I can't understand you.*
3 if you cannot think clearly, you are confused

clench /klentʃ/ *verb, formal*
if you clench your hand or teeth, you close your hand or mouth tightly: *He clenched his fist like he wanted to hit me.*

cler•gy /ˈklɚdʒi/ *plural noun, formal*
official religious leaders, such as priests: *Priests and other members of the clergy attended the meeting.*

cler•i•cal /ˈklerɪkəl/ *adjective*
relating to office work: *A clerical worker typed the report.*

clerk /klɚk/ *noun*
1 someone whose job is to keep records, accounts, etc. in an office
2 someone who deals with people arriving at a hotel: *Please return your keys to the clerk at the front desk.*
→ **sales clerk**

clev•er /ˈklevɚ/ *adjective*
intelligent and good at thinking of ideas: *She's a clever lawyer and very good at defending her clients.*
—**cleverly** *adverb*
—**cleverness** *noun*
→ See Thesaurus box at **intelligent**

cli•ché /kliˈʃeɪ/ *noun*
a phrase or idea that has been used many times before, and so is now boring: *I didn't want to hear clichés like "Time heals all wounds."*
→ See Thesaurus box at **phrase**

click /klɪk/ *verb*
1 to make a short hard sound: *The door clicked shut.*
2 if you click on something on a computer screen, you press a button on the MOUSE to make the computer do something: *Click on the button at the bottom of the screen to open a new page.*
—**click** *noun* a clicking sound: *I heard the click of a light switch.*
→ See picture on page A22

cli•ent /ˈklaɪənt/ *noun*
someone who pays to use the services of a business, a lawyer, etc.: *Mr. Johnson is one of the law firm's most important clients.*

cli•en•tele /ˌklaɪənˈtel/ *noun, formal*
the people who go to a particular store, restaurant, etc.: *It's a fashionable bar with a young clientele* (=the people who go are young).

cliff /klɪf/ *noun*
an area of high rock with steep sides that often go down to the ocean: *We walked along the cliff above the beach.*

cli•mate /ˈklaɪmət/ *noun*
the type of weather that a place has: *In the south of the country, the climate is hot and dry.*
—**climatic** /klaɪˈmætɪk/ *adjective, formal* relating to a climate: *A lot of climatic change is caused by humans.*

cli•max /ˈklaɪmæks/ *noun*
the most important or exciting thing that happens: *Winning the gold medal was the climax of his sports career.*

climb[1] /klaɪm/ *verb*
1 if you climb a tree, a mountain, some stairs, etc., you go up toward the top: *It was a beautiful day, so we decided to climb the mountain.*

2 to increase in amount or level: *During the day, the temperature climbed to 90 degrees.*

climb² *noun*
an act of going up a tree, a mountain, etc., toward the top: *It was a steep climb to the top of the hill.*
➔ See picture on page A4

climb·er /ˈklaɪmɚ/ *noun*
someone who climbs mountains or rocks as a sport: *a rock climber*

climb·ing /ˈklaɪmɪŋ/ *noun*
the sport of climbing mountains or rocks: *We love to go climbing in the mountains on vacation.*
➔ See picture on page A24

cling /klɪŋ/ *verb* **clung** /klʌŋ/
to hold onto someone or something tightly: *The boy was frightened, and clung to his mother.*

clin·ic /ˈklɪnɪk/ *noun*
a place where people can get medical treatment or advice: *I work at the health clinic at the university and we see a lot of sick students this time of year.*

clin·i·cal /ˈklɪnɪkəl/ *adjective, formal*
relating to treating people who are sick: *The health department is now starting some clinical research.*

clip¹ /klɪp/ *noun*
a small object used for holding pieces of paper, hair, etc. together: *He fastened the pages together with a paper clip.*

clip² *verb*
1 to hold pieces of paper, hair, etc. together with a clip: *Please clip your photo to the front of the form.*
2 to cut small pieces off something to make it look neater: *He was sitting in the bathroom clipping his toenails.*
➔ See Thesaurus box at **fasten**

clip·board /ˈklɪpbɔrd/ *noun*
a flat board with a clip that holds paper onto it: *The men were carrying clipboards so that they could take notes.*

clip·pers /ˈklɪpɚz/ *plural noun*
a tool for cutting small pieces off something: *Do you have any nail clippers? My fingernails are too long.*

clock /klɑk/ *noun*
1 an instrument on a wall, table, etc. that shows the time: *She looked at the clock on the wall: It was 11:15.* | *an alarm clock* (=that rings a bell to wake you up)

clock

2 around the clock = all day and all night: *I had to work around the clock to finish my paper.*

clock·wise /ˈklɑk-waɪz/ *adverb*
moving in the same direction as the HANDs (=parts that point to the time) of a clock: *We were told to run clockwise around the track.* ANTONYM **counterclockwise**

clog /klɑg/ *noun*
a shoe that covers your toes but is open in the back
➔ See picture at **shoe**

clone /kloʊn/ *noun*
an exact copy of a plant or animal that scientists produce from one of its cells: *By taking just one cell, they could create a perfect clone.*
—**clone** *verb* to produce a clone from a plant or animal: *Scientists have managed to clone several different animals.*

close¹ /kloʊz/ *verb*
1 to shut something: *Don't forget to close the door.* SYNONYM **shut**; ANTONYM **open**
2 if a business closes, it stops doing business until the next day: *"What time does the mall close tonight?" "9:00 p.m."* ANTONYM **open**
3 *also* **close down** if a business closes, it stops existing: *The factory closed down six months ago.* ANTONYM **open**
4 to end a speech, movie, book, etc. in a particular way: *The book opens before the war and closes 30 years later.* ANTONYM **open**

WORD FAMILY look at the words:

➔ **close** *verb*
➔ **closed** *adjective*
➔ **closure** *noun*

close² /kloʊs/ *adjective*
1 near someone or something: *Our house is close to the beach.* SYNONYM **near**

2 likely to experience something soon: *We haven't found the answer yet, but we're getting closer.* SYNONYM **near**

3 **close to** = near a particular time or number: *It was close to midnight.* | *The canyon has close to one million visitors each year.*

4 close friends or families like or love each other a lot: *We were close friends in high school.*

5 giving careful attention to something: *Use the microscope, if you want to take a closer look.*

6 **a close call** = a situation you are in that is dangerous, but that you escape from: *I had a close call yesterday in the car. A guy in a van almost hit me.*

—**closeness** *noun*

➔ See Thesaurus box at **near**[1]

close[3] /klouz/ *noun, formal*
the end of an activity or time: *The 20th century was coming to a close* (=was ending).

closed /klouzd/ *adjective*
1 not open: *Make sure all the windows are closed so the rain doesn't get in.* SYNONYM **shut**
2 not doing business: *The store's closed on Sundays, so we'll have to go shopping on Saturday.*
➔ See picture at **ajar**

ˌclosed ˌcircuit ˈtelevision *noun*
cameras which are used in public places to help prevent crime: *The burglars were caught on closed circuit television.*

close-knit /ˌklous ˈnɪt/ *adjective, formal*
a close-knit family or group of people know each other well and live near each other: *It's a small town and a very close-knit community.*

close·ly /ˈklousli/ *adverb, formal*
if you look at someone or something closely, you look very carefully: *She was watching him closely because she didn't trust him.*

clos·et /ˈklɑzɪt/ *noun*
an area where you keep your clothes, built into the wall of a room: *Let me hang your coat up in the closet.*

close-up /ˈklous ʌp/ *noun*
a photograph that is taken very near to someone or something: *I wanted to get a close-up of her face so that you could see her beautiful eyes in the picture.*

clo·sure /ˈklouʒɚ/ *noun, formal*
the act of closing a building, factory, school, etc. permanently: *The school's closure upset many parents.*

clot /klɑt/ *noun*
some blood that has become solid: *The blood clot had cut off the flow of blood to his brain.*
—**clot** *verb* if blood clots, it becomes solid

cloth /klɔθ/ *noun*
1 material used for making clothes and other things: *Mom was making a shirt from a piece of cotton cloth.*
2 a piece of material that you use for doing something: *Wipe the kitchen counters with a damp cloth.*

clothe /klouð/ *verb, formal*
to provide clothes for someone: *They were poor, and it was hard for them to feed and clothe their children.*

clothes /klouðz/ *plural noun*
the things that you wear on your body: *I need some new winter clothes.*

> **GRAMMAR: clothes**
>
> **Clothes** means all the things people can wear: *His clothes are always so nice.*
>
> If you want to talk about one thing that you can wear, you have to say **a piece of clothing**, **an article of clothing** *formal*, or **an item of clothing** *formal*: *She picked up each piece of clothing and folded it carefully.*
>
> You can also just say the name of the piece of clothing, such as **pants**, **a shirt**, or **a dress**.

➔ See picture on page A6

clothes·line /ˈklouðzˌlaɪn/ *noun*
a rope that you hang wet clothes on so they will dry

clothes·pin /ˈklouðzpɪn/ *noun*
something you use to fasten wet clothes to a line so they will dry

cloth·ing /ˈklouðɪŋ/ *noun, formal*
clothes: *If you're going skiing, you'll need warm clothing.*

cloud[1] /klaud/ *noun*
1 a white or gray shape in the sky, that rain sometimes falls from: *At that moment, the sun went behind a cloud.*

C

2 a mass of smoke, dust, steam, etc.: *The fire sent up a huge cloud of smoke.*

cloud² *verb*

PHRASAL VERB

cloud up/over

to become cloudy: *It started to cloud up and get colder.*

cloud·y /ˈklaʊdi/ *adjective*

if it is cloudy, there are a lot of clouds in the sky: *Tomorrow will be cloudy with some rain.*

clo·ver /ˈkloʊvɚ/ *noun*

a small green plant with three round leaves

clown /klaʊn/ *noun*

a person who entertains people by wearing funny clothes and a big red nose, and doing silly things: *He earned some money as a clown at children's birthday parties.*

club /klʌb/ *noun*

1 a group of people who meet because they share an interest: *Kim joined the jazz club at school.* | *Are you a member of the drama club?*

2 a place where people go to meet each other in the evenings: *Let's go to a dance club tonight.* | *a comedy club*

3 a card used in card games, with symbols that look like black leaves with three round parts on it: *the king of clubs*

4 a heavy stick used as a weapon

club·bing /ˈklʌbɪŋ/ *noun*

the activity of going to clubs to dance and meet people: *A lot of young people go clubbing on the weekend.*

ˌclub ˈsoda *noun*

water with a lot of BUBBLEs in it that you can mix with other drinks

clue /klu/ *noun*

some information that helps you find the truth or the right answer: *Police are still searching for clues to why she disappeared.*

clump /klʌmp/ *noun*

a clump of grass/trees/bushes, etc. = some grass, trees, etc. growing close together: *She sat down in a clump of long grass.*

clum·sy /ˈklʌmzi/ *adjective*

someone who is clumsy moves in an awkward way, and drops or breaks things: *He was a clumsy man, with big rough hands.*

—**clumsily** *adverb* in a clumsy way: *Mina stood up, clumsily knocking over a glass of water.*

—**clumsiness** *noun* the quality of being clumsy

clung /klʌŋ/ *verb*

the past tense and past participle of CLING

clus·ter /ˈklʌstɚ/ *noun, formal*

a group of things that are close together: *There was a small cluster of houses near the river, but the rest of the land was empty.*

clutch /klʌtʃ/ *verb, formal*

to hold something tightly: *"Don't go," she said, clutching his arm.*

➔ See Thesaurus box at **hold¹**

clut·tered /ˈklʌtɚd/ *adjective*

if a surface or room is cluttered, it is covered or filled with a lot of things in a way that is not organized: *His desk is always cluttered with lots of paper and books.*

—**clutter** *verb* to cover a surface, fill a room, etc., with a lot of things in a way that is not organized

cm.

the written abbreviation of **centimeter**: *The plant's leaves are around 5 cm. long.*

c/o /ˌsi ˈoʊ/ *abbreviation*

in care of used on letters to give the address where someone is staying when it is not the place that they usually live: *Send the letter to me c/o Anne Miller, 8 Brown St., Peoria, IL.*

coach¹ /koʊtʃ/ *noun*

1 someone who trains people in a sport, or in singing, acting, etc.: *The football coach worked with the players after school.*

2 the cheapest type of seats on an airplane or a train: *We flew coach to Atlanta because it was the cheapest way to go.* SYNONYM **economy**

coach² *verb*

to train people in a sport, in singing, in acting, etc.: *Mr. Davis coaches our soccer team.*

coal /koʊl/ *noun*
a hard black substance that forms below the ground and that people burn to produce heat: *The process of digging coal out of holes deep in the ground can be very dangerous.*

coarse /kɔrs/ *adjective, formal*
rough and thick, not smooth or fine: *Farm workers' clothes were made of coarse cloth that felt rough against the skin.* ANTONYM **fine**

coast /koʊst/ *noun*
the land next to the ocean: *The beaches on the southeastern coast of the U.S. are usually sandy.*
—**coastal** *adjective* near the coast: *Many coastal areas were flooded after the hurricane.*
➔ See Thesaurus box at **shore**

ˈcoast guard *noun*
the Coast Guard = the military organization whose job is watching ships and activity in the ocean

coast·line /ˈkoʊstlaɪn/ *noun*
the land at the edge of the ocean: *From the ship, we could see the rocky coastline.*

coat /koʊt/ *noun*
1 something that you wear over other clothes to keep you warm outdoors: *It was a snowy day, so I put on my big winter coat.*
2 a coat of paint = a layer of paint that you put on a surface: *The walls really need another coat of paint.*
➔ See picture on page A6

ˈcoat ˌhanger *noun*
another word for a HANGER

coax /koʊks/ *verb*
to try to get someone to do something by talking to them gently and kindly: *With great difficulty, I coaxed him into eating something.*
➔ See Thesaurus box at **persuade**

co·bra /ˈkoʊbrə/ *noun*
a poisonous snake of Africa and Asia

cob·web /ˈkɑbweb/ *noun*
a net of fine threads which a SPIDER makes. This word is used when the spider is not using it anymore: *The old house was dirty and full of cobwebs.*

cock·pit /ˈkɑkˌpɪt/ *noun*
the part of an airplane or race car where the pilot or driver sits
➔ See picture at **airplane**

cock·roach /ˈkɑk-roʊtʃ/ *noun*
a large brown insect that lives in dark or dirty places

cock·tail /ˈkɑkteɪl/ *noun*
a drink made from mixing alcohol with other types of drinks: *We decided to order cocktails instead of beer.*

C

co·coa /ˈkoʊkoʊ/ *noun*
1 a hot chocolate drink: *Would you like a cup of cocoa?*
2 a brown powder that tastes like chocolate and is used in cooking: *Add one tablespoon of cocoa to the cake mix.*

co·co·nut /ˈkoʊkəˌnʌt/ *noun*
a very large brown nut which has liquid inside and white flesh that people eat: *Coconuts grow on palm trees.*
➔ See picture on page A13

cod /kɑd/ *noun* plural **cod**
an ocean fish that people eat

code /koʊd/ Ac *noun*
1 a set of rules or laws that tells people how they must behave: *There's a strict code of conduct for all police officers.*
2 a special way of using words, numbers, etc. to send messages that are secret: *During the war, reports were sent in code.*
➔ **area code**, **zip code**

co·erce /koʊˈɚs/ *verb, formal*
to make someone do something by using threats: *She said he coerced her into signing the agreement.* SYNONYM **force**
➔ See Thesaurus box at **force**[1]

cof·fee /ˈkɔfi/ *noun*
1 a hot brown drink that you make from special beans: *Let's have a cup of coffee!*
2 brown beans or the powder from them used to make a hot drink: *I bought a jar of coffee.*

ˈcoffee shop *noun*
a small restaurant that serves coffee and cheap meals: *He sometimes takes his computer to the coffee shop to work.* SYNONYM **cafe**

cof·fin /ˈkɔfɪn/ *noun*
the box in which a dead person is buried SYNONYM **casket**

co·her·ent /koʊˈhɪrənt/ Ac *adjective, formal*
clear and easy to understand: *The newspaper gave a coherent explanation of events*

that helped me understand what had happened. ANTONYM **incoherent**
—**coherently** *adverb*: *She was shocked and unable to speak coherently.*

C

coil[1] /kɔɪl/ *also* **coil up** *verb*
to wind something around and around in circles: *She coiled some hair around her finger.*

coil[2] *noun*
a piece of rope, wire, or hair that is wound around in a circle: *There was a big coil of rope in the bottom of the boat.*

coin /kɔɪn/ *noun*
a piece of money made of metal: *Andy took a few coins from his pocket to pay for the candy.*
➔ See Thesaurus box at **money**

co•in•ci•dence /koʊˈɪnsədəns/ Ac *noun*
a situation in which things that you had not planned happen together in a surprising way: *It was a strange coincidence that we saw each other again in the same place exactly five years later.*
—**coincide** /ˌkoʊɪnˈsaɪd/ *verb, formal* if two things coincide, they happen at the same time: *The movie's release coincided with the start of the summer vacation.*

co•la /ˈkoʊlə/ *noun*
a sweet brown drink with a lot of BUBBLEs in it: *a can of cola*

cold[1] /koʊld/ *adjective*
1 having a low temperature: *It's cold outside today* (=the weather is cold). | *Drink your coffee before it gets cold.* ANTONYM **hot, warm**

THESAURUS: cold

cool cold in a pleasant way, especially after it has been hot: *It's very hot during the day, but cooler at night.*

chilly cold, but not very cold: *The water in the pool felt chilly.*

frosty very cold, with the ground covered in frost (=ice that is white and powdery and covers things when the temperature is very cold): *It was a bright, frosty morning.*

freezing very cold, so that water outside becomes ice: *It was freezing cold last night.*

icy very cold: *An icy wind cut through his jacket.*

2 if you are cold, you feel uncomfortable, because it is not warm enough: *Shut the window if you feel cold.* ANTONYM **hot**
3 cold food has been cooked, but is not warm when you eat it: *For lunch, we had cold chicken and salad.* ANTONYM **hot**
4 not friendly to people: *I met him once, and he seemed cold and formal.*

cold[2] *noun*
1 a common illness that blocks your nose, makes your throat painful, etc.: *I had a cold and stayed at home.* | *If your clothes are wet, you'll catch a cold* (=get this illness).
2 the cold = cold weather: *Don't stand out there in the cold!*

ˌcold-ˈblooded *adjective*
a cold-blooded animal, such as a snake, has a body temperature that changes with the air or ground around it

ˈcold cuts *plural noun*
thin pieces of different kinds of cooked meat that you eat cold

cold•ly /ˈkoʊldli/ *adverb*
in an unfriendly way: *"I'm busy. Don't bother me," Sarah said coldly.*

cold•ness /ˈkoʊldnɪs/ *noun*
1 unfriendliness: *He was surprised by her coldness and didn't know how to react.*
2 low temperature

col•lapse[1] /kəˈlæps/ Ac *verb*
1 if a building, wall, bridge, etc. collapses, it suddenly falls down and is destroyed: *The building collapsed during the fire.*
2 to suddenly fall down or become unconscious because you are sick or very weak: *He collapsed at the end of the race and he was taken to the hospital.*
3 if a system collapses, it suddenly fails and cannot continue: *The economy collapsed after the war and it took years to recover.*

collapse[2] *noun, formal*
1 a sudden failure in the way a system works, so that it cannot continue: *the collapse of Communism in the former Soviet Union*

2 a situation in which a building, wall, bridge, etc. falls down

3 a situation in which a person falls down because he or she is sick or very weak

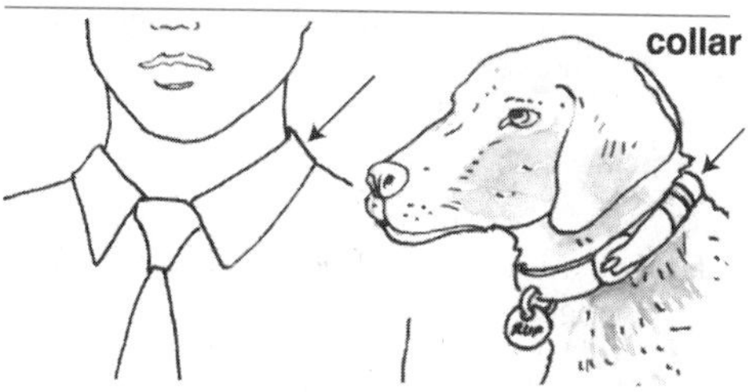

col•lar /ˈkɑlɚ/ *noun*

1 the part of a shirt, coat, dress, etc. that fits around your neck: *Put the tie around your neck and fold your collar down over it.*

2 a narrow band of leather or plastic put around the neck of a dog or cat: *The leash attaches to the dog's collar.*

col•lar•bone /ˈkɑlɚˌboʊn/ *noun*

one of a pair of bones that go from the base of your neck to your shoulders

➔ See picture on page A2

col•league /ˈkɑlig/ Ac *noun*

someone who works with you in the same office or organization: *She showed the letter to one of her colleagues.*

col•lect¹ /kəˈlekt/ *verb*

1 to get things and bring them together: *The teacher collected all the test papers from the students.*

2 to get and keep objects of the same type because you think they are attractive, interesting, or valuable: *She collects old coins.*

3 *formal* to come together and form a large group or amount: *Dust had collected under the sofa.* SYNONYM **gather**

WORD FAMILY ➔ **collector** *noun*

collect² *adverb*

call collect = if you call collect, the person who receives the phone call pays for the call

col•lec•tion /kəˈlekʃən/ *noun*

a group of similar things that have been gathered together: *The museum has a fine collection of modern art.*

col•lege /ˈkɑlɪdʒ/ *noun*

1 a large school where you can study after high school: *I'm planning to go to college in the fall to study biology.*

2 the part of a university that teaches a particular subject: *the College of Medicine* SYNONYM **school**

—**collegiate** /kəˈlidʒɪt/ *adjective* relating to college: *collegiate sports*

col•lide /kəˈlaɪd/ *verb*

to crash violently into something or someone: *His car collided with a bus, but luckily no one was killed.* SYNONYM **crash**

col•li•sion /kəˈlɪʒən/ *noun*

a violent crash, especially between two cars, planes, etc.: *The plane was involved in a collision with a military aircraft.* SYNONYM **crash**

co•logne /kəˈloʊn/ *noun*

a liquid with a pleasant smell that you put on your skin

co•lon /ˈkoʊlən/ *noun*

1 the mark (:) used in writing to introduce a list, examples, etc.

2 the lower part of the INTESTINEs, in which food is changed into waste matter

colo•nel /ˈkɚnl/ *noun, written abbreviation* **Col.**

an officer who has a high rank in the Army, Air Force, or Marines

col•o•nize /ˈkɑləˌnaɪz/ *verb*

to control another country or area, and send people from your own country to live there: *Argentina was colonized by Spain.*

—**colonization** /ˌkɑlənəˈzeɪʃən/ *noun* the process of colonizing a place

col•o•ny /ˈkɑləni/ *noun* plural **colonies**

a country or area that is ruled by a more powerful country, usually one that is far away: *The island used to be a French colony but it is now independent.*

col•or¹ /ˈkʌlɚ/ *noun*

1 red, blue, yellow, green, orange, etc.: *"What color is your new car?" "Blue." | My favorite color is orange. | The room was decorated in bright colors.*

C

2 people/men/women, etc. of color = people who are not white: *There were many people of color at the meeting, but most people were white.*

color² *verb*
1 to add colors to a picture on a piece of paper using colored pencils, pens, or CRAYONS: *The little girl sat at the table coloring.*
2 if you color your hair, you make it a different color from its natural color SYNONYM **dye**

col•or•blind /ˈkʌlɚˌblaɪnd/ *adjective*
1 unable to see the difference between particular colors: *My brother's colorblind. He can't tell the difference between red and green.*
2 treating all races of people fairly and equally: *We want a colorblind society, where everyone is treated equally.*

col•or•ful /ˈkʌlɚfəl/ *adjective*
having a lot of bright colors: *The dancers wore colorful clothes.*

col•or•ing /ˈkʌlərɪŋ/ *noun*
1 the color of something, especially someone's hair, skin, eyes, etc.: *The birds have the same yellow and green coloring.*
2 a substance used for giving a particular color to something, especially food: *artificial food coloring*

col•or•less /ˈkʌlɚləs/ *adjective*
not having any color: *Water is a colorless liquid.*

col•umn /ˈkɑləm/ *noun*
1 a tall stone post used to support a building: *There were two big columns on either side of the entrance to the temple.*
2 an article by a particular writer that appears regularly in a newspaper or magazine: *He writes a sports column for the Los Angeles Times.*
3 a row of words or numbers that goes down a page: *What is the last number at the bottom of the column?*

co•ma /ˈkoʊmə/ *noun*
a serious medical condition in which someone is not conscious for a long time, usually after an accident or illness: *After the accident he was in a coma for six days.*

comb /koʊm/ *noun*
a flat piece of plastic or metal with a row of thin parts like teeth on one side, which you use to make your hair neat
—**comb** *verb* to make your hair neat with a comb: *He was combing his hair and getting ready to go out.*
➔ See picture on page A11

com•bat /ˈkɑmbæt/ *noun*
fighting during a war: *Her husband was killed in combat.*
➔ See Thesaurus box at **war**

com•bi•na•tion /ˌkɑmbəˈneɪʃən/ *noun*
two or more different things that are used together or that happen together: *The sauce had an interesting combination of flavors.*

com•bine /kəmˈbaɪn/ *verb*
to join together: *The two chemicals combine to form a powerful explosive.* | *The movie combines comedy and excitement.*
➔ See Thesaurus box at **mix¹**

come /kʌm/ *verb* **came** /keɪm/ **come**
1 to move toward or arrive at the place where you are: *There was a big truck coming straight toward us so we jumped to one side.* | *The letter came yesterday.* | *What time did she come home last night?*
2 to go with someone somewhere: *We're going to see a movie tonight. Do you want to come?*
3 to be in a particular position in a group of people or things: *P comes before Q in the alphabet.*
4 to reach a point: *The water came up to my knees.*
5 to be available to buy in a particular size, with particular features, etc.: *The shoes come in all sizes.*
6 come open/loose/undone, etc. = to become open, loose, etc.: *The door had come open in the wind.*
7 come as a surprise/a shock/a relief, etc. = to make someone feel surprised, shocked, etc.: *The news came as a surprise to everyone.*
8 how come? *informal* = used in order to ask someone why something happened or is true: *How come it always rains when we go for a bike ride?* SYNONYM **why**
9 for years to come/in the days to come = for many years after this time, or in the days

after this time: *People will remember this day for years to come.*

PHRASAL VERBS

come about *formal*

to happen: *This problem came about because someone was not doing his or her job correctly.*

come along

to go somewhere with someone: *You're welcome to come along to the meeting.*

come apart

to split into pieces: *The book was wet, and it came apart in my hands.*

come around

if someone comes around, they decide to agree with you after disagreeing with you: *I know she's mad at you right now, but she'll come around.*

come back

to return from a place: *When is your sister coming back from Europe?*

come down

to become lower in price, level, etc.: *The price of computers keeps coming down, so you'll be able to find something affordable.*

come down with something

to get an illness: *I think I'm coming down with the flu.*

come from

1 come from somewhere = to have been born in a particular place: *"Where do you come from?" "Cincinnati."*

2 come from something = used when saying what the origin of something is: *The word "etc." comes from Latin.*

come in *also* **come into something**

to enter the room or house where you are speaking from: *Come in and sit down.*

come off

to become separated from the main part of something: *The door handle came off in my hand.*

come on

1 if a light or machine comes on, it starts working: *She pressed the button, and the lights came on.*

2 used when telling someone to hurry or try something: *Come on! We're late!*

come out

1 if a book, movie, record, etc. comes out, it becomes available for people to buy or see: *Her new movie comes out early next year.*

2 if information about something comes out, people find out about it: *It was several months before the truth came out.*

come over

to visit someone at his or her house: *Do you want to come over on Friday night?*

come through something

to get to the end of a dangerous or difficult situation without being harmed or damaged: *She came through all her problems and is now happily married.* SYNONYM **survive**

come to

1 come to $20/$3, etc. = used when saying what the total cost of something is: *The meal came to $50, which was more than I had expected to pay.*

2 when it comes to something = relating to a particular subject: *I'm terrible when it comes to money. I spend too much.*

come up

1 to come close to you, especially in order to speak to you: *A man came up to me and asked me what time it was.*

2 if a problem comes up, it happens: *Please let me know if any problems come up.*

3 to be mentioned in a conversation: *The subject of money is sure to come up, so be prepared.*

4 be coming up = to be happening soon: *My mom's birthday is coming up – I need to get her a present.*

come up with something

to think of an idea, name, plan, etc.: *They still haven't come up with a name for the baby.*

come•back /'kʌmbæk/ *noun*

if someone or something makes a comeback, they become popular or successful again: *The singer is hoping to make a comeback with her first CD in eight years.*

co•me•di•an /kə'midiən/ *noun*

someone whose job is to tell jokes and make people laugh SYNONYM **comic**

com•e•dy /'kɑmədi/ *noun* plural **comedies**

a funny movie, play, television program, etc. that makes people laugh: *The movie is a very funny comedy about two boys growing up in Texas.*

→ See Thesaurus box at **movie**

com•et /ˈkɑmɪt/ *noun*
an object in the sky that looks like a very bright ball with a tail moving through SPACE

C

com•fort¹ /ˈkʌmfət/ *noun*
1 a feeling of being relaxed and of not having any unpleasant feelings: *I just wanted to be in the comfort of my own home after being away for so long.* ANTONYM **discomfort**
2 something that makes you feel less upset or worried: *It was a comfort to know that my parents understood how I felt.*

WORD FAMILY look at the words:

→ **comfort** *noun*
→ **comfort** *verb*
→ **comfortable** *adjective*
→ **uncomfortable** *adjective*
→ **discomfort** *noun*

comfort² *verb*
to make someone feel less worried or unhappy: *He tried to comfort her and tell her that everything would be OK.*

com•fort•a•ble /ˈkʌmftəbəl/ *adjective*
1 comfortable chairs, beds, clothes, etc. make you feel physically relaxed: *The bed was very comfortable, and I slept well.*
2 if you are comfortable, you feel physically relaxed: *Are you comfortable? Would you like another pillow?*
—**comfortably** *adverb*

com•ic¹ /ˈkɑmɪk/ *adjective*
funny or amusing: *a comic actress*

comic² *noun*
1 a magazine that tells a story using a series of drawings SYNONYM **comic book**
2 someone whose job is to tell jokes and make people laugh SYNONYM **comedian**

com•i•cal /ˈkɑmɪkəl/ *adjective*
funny, especially in a strange or unexpected way: *The team played so badly, it was almost comical.*

ˈcomic book *noun*
a magazine that tells a story using a series of drawings: *I used to love reading comic books about Spider-Man and Superman.*

com•ics /ˈkɑmɪks/ *plural noun*
the comics = the part of a newspaper that has COMIC STRIPs

ˈcomic strip *noun*
a series of pictures that are drawn inside boxes and tell a story

com•ma /ˈkɑmə/ *noun*
the mark (,) used in writing to show a short pause

com•mand¹ /kəˈmænd/ *noun*
1 an order from someone in authority to do something: *The general gave the command to attack.* SYNONYM **order**
2 control of a large group of soldiers, a ship, etc.: *The general was in command of over a thousand soldiers.*
3 knowledge of something, especially a language: *She has a good command of English.*

command² *verb*
1 to tell someone who has less authority than you that he or she must do something: *The police officer commanded him to stop.*
2 to be the leader of a group of soldiers: *General Eisenhower commanded the U.S. forces in Europe during World War II.*

com•mand•er *also* **Commander** /kəˈmændə/ *noun*
an officer in charge of a military organization or group

com•mem•o•rate /kəˈmeməˌreɪt/ *verb, formal*
to show that you remember an important person or event: *The statue commemorates the soldiers who died during the war.*

com•mence /kəˈmens/ Ac *verb, formal*
to begin: *The work will commence in January and end in July.* SYNONYM **start**

com•ment¹ /ˈkɑment/ Ac *noun*
a short phrase or sentence, in which you give your opinion about someone or something: *Does anyone want to make any other comments about the book before we move on to a new topic?*

comment² *verb*
to give an opinion about someone or something: *The police have refused to comment on the case.*

com•men•tar•y /ˈkɑmənˌteri/ Ac *noun*
plural **commentaries**
a spoken description of an event, given while the event is happening

com•men•ta•tor /ˈkɑmənˌteɪtɚ/ Ac *noun*
someone on television or radio who describes an event as it is happening, or who gives their opinions about a subject: *a sports commentator*

com•merce /ˈkɑmɚs/ *noun, formal*
the activity of buying and selling goods and services: *The agency is trying to create jobs and increase commerce.* SYNONYM **trade**

com•mer•cial¹ /kəˈmɚʃəl/ *noun*
an advertisement on television or radio: *Don't believe everything you see in commercials on TV. They just want to sell you something.* SYNONYM **ad, advertisement**
➔ See Thesaurus box at **advertisement**

commercial² *adjective, formal*
1 relating to business and the buying and selling of things: *There is a lot of commercial activity near the port.*
2 relating to making money or a profit: *The CD was a commercial success. The band sold millions of copies.*
—**commercially** *adverb*

com•mis•sion /kəˈmɪʃən/ Ac *noun*
1 a group of people who have the official job of learning about something or controlling something: *The president set up a commission to look at the causes of the disaster.*
2 an amount of money that is paid to a person each time they sell a product as part of his or her job: *Employees can earn a 30% commission on each car they sell.*

com•mit /kəˈmɪt/ Ac *verb* **committed, committing**
1 to do something wrong or illegal: *Are the police sure that Rogers committed the crime?*
2 commit suicide = to kill yourself deliberately
3 commit yourself (to doing something) = to say that you will definitely do something: *He won't commit himself to paying any money until he knows how much the work will cost.*
WORD FAMILY ➔ **commitment** *noun*

com•mit•ment /kəˈmɪtmənt/ Ac *noun*
1 a promise to do something or behave in a particular way: *When you marry someone, you make a commitment to stay with that person for the rest of your lives.*
2 the hard work and loyalty that someone gives to an organization, activity, etc.: *She shows a lot of commitment to her job. She always comes in early and works late.*

com•mit•tee /kəˈmɪti/ *noun*
a group of people who have been chosen to do a particular job, for example to make decisions about something: *I'm on the finance committee – we make decisions about the company's money.*

com•mon /ˈkɑmən/ *adjective*
something that is common is often seen or often happens: *"Smith" is a very common last name in the U.S.* ANTONYM **rare**
—**commonly** *adverb* often or usually: *Aspirin is a very commonly used drug. People take it for many health problems.*

ˌcommon ˈsense *noun*
the ability to behave in a sensible way and make practical decisions: *It's not hard to figure out the answer – you just have to use your common sense.*

com•mu•ni•cate /kəˈmyunəˌkeɪt/ Ac *verb*
to exchange information, ideas, or opinions with someone: *We communicate with each other mostly by email and by phone.*
WORD FAMILY ➔ **communication** *noun*

com•mu•ni•ca•tion /kəˌmyunəˈkeɪʃən/ Ac *noun*
1 the act of speaking or writing to someone and being understood by him or her: *We are trying improve communication between doctors and patients so that patients know exactly what their choices are.*
2 communications = ways of sending information between places using computers, telephones, radios, etc.: *Modern communications such as email make it possible for people to work from their homes.*

com•mu•nism /ˈkɑmyəˌnɪzəm/ *noun*
a political system in which the government controls the production of all goods, and there is no privately owned property
—**communist** *noun* someone who believes in and supports communism
—**communist** *adjective* relating to communism: *a communist country*

C

com·mu·ni·ty /kə'myunəti/ Ac *noun* plural **communities**
1 all of the people who live in the same town or area: *All the children in our community go to the same school.*
2 a group of people in an area who belong to the same race, religion, etc. or do the same activity: *Miami has a large Cuban community.*

com'munity ,college *noun*
a college that people can go to, usually for two years, in order to learn a skill or to prepare to go to another college or university

com·mute /kə'myut/ *verb*
to travel regularly in order to get to work: *He commutes to work by train.*
—**commute** *noun* the regular journey that someone makes to get to work: *My commute to the office takes a half hour if I go by car.*
—**commuter** *noun* someone who travels to work each day: *The roads are full of commuters in the mornings and the late afternoons.*

com·pact[1] /'kɑmpækt/ *adjective*
small compared with other things of the same type: *This compact camera can fit in your pocket.*

compact[2] *noun*
1 *also* **compact car** a small car: *The parking space was small, only big enough for a compact.*
2 a small flat container with a mirror and powder for a woman's face

,compact 'disc *noun*
another word for a CD

com·pan·ion /kəm'pænyən/ *noun*
someone you spend a lot of time with: *My dog was my companion. He went everywhere with me.*

com·pa·ny /'kʌmpəni/ *noun* plural **companies**
1 a business that makes or sells things or provides a service: *I work for a computer company.*

THESAURUS: company

firm a company that usually does something for you rather than making things: *She works for a law firm.*

business a company that makes or sells things or that does something for you, and that often only a small number of people work for: *She started her own business making food for weddings.*

corporation a large company that often includes several smaller companies: *Different parts of the corporation make everything from breakfast cereal to ice cream.*

2 if you have company, there are other people with you or talking to you: *There's a new car in their driveway. It looks like they have company.* | *I'll stay here to keep you company* (=I will stay with you so that you are not alone).
3 a group of soldiers, usually with 100 to 200 people in it: *Our company was attacked by enemy planes.*

com·par·a·tive /kəm'pærətɪv/ *noun*
the comparative = the form of an adjective or adverb that is used when comparing something with other things. The comparative of "good" is "better."

com·pare /kəm'per/ *verb*
to think about how two or more things, people, etc. are different or the same: *We compared the prices of all the hotels, and this one was the cheapest.* | *The teacher asked us to compare and contrast the two stories* (=show how they were the same and how they were different).

WORD FAMILY look at the words:

→ **compare** *verb*
→ **comparison** *noun*
→ **comparative** *noun*

com·par·i·son /kəm'pærəsən/ *noun*
1 in comparison/by comparison = used when you are comparing two people or things: *Our house is small in comparison with theirs. Ours has one floor, and theirs has three.*
2 an act of saying how you think two things are the same or different: *A comparison of the two paintings showed that they were by different artists.*

com·part·ment /kəm'pɑrtmənt/ *noun*
a separate part of a large container: *He put his bag in the compartment above his seat on the plane.*

com·pass /ˈkʌmpəs/ *noun*
an instrument with a needle that shows you if you are facing north, south, east, or west

compass

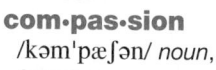

com·pas·sion /kəmˈpæʃən/ *noun, formal*
sympathy for someone who is suffering: *He had great compassion for the poor people of the city and often brought food to them.*
—**compassionate** *adjective, formal* showing compassion

com·pat·i·ble /kəmˈpætəbəl/ Ac *adjective, formal*
1 if two things are compatible, they can exist or be used together without problems: *You won't have any trouble using the software – it's compatible with your computer.*
2 if two people are compatible, they can have a good relationship because they like the same things or think in the same ways: *My parents are very compatible – they never argue.*
—**compatibility** /kəmˌpætəˈbɪləti/ *noun, formal* the quality of being compatible

WORD FAMILY look at the words:
→ **compatible** *adjective*
→ **incompatible** *adjective*
→ **compatibility** *noun*
→ **incompatibility** *noun*

com·pel /kəmˈpel/ *verb* **compelled, compelling** *formal*
to force someone to do something: *He was compelled to give up his job because he had to take care of his son.*
→ See Thesaurus box at **force**[1]

com·pen·sate /ˈkɑmpənˌseɪt/ Ac *verb, formal*
1 to pay someone money because something bad has happened to them or something they own: *He had to compensate the woman for damaging her car.*
2 to make something bad have a smaller effect on a situation: *He is very smart, and that compensates for his lack of experience.*

com·pen·sa·tion /ˌkɑmpənˈseɪʃən/ Ac *noun, formal*
money that is paid to someone because something bad has happened to them or to something they own: *He received over $1 million in compensation* (=as payment) *for his injuries.*

com·pete /kəmˈpit/ *verb*
to take part in a race or competition: *How many runners will be competing in the race?*

WORD FAMILY look at the words:
→ **compete** *verb*
→ **competition** *noun*
→ **competitor** *noun*
→ **competitive** *adjective*

com·pe·tent /ˈkɑmpətənt/ *adjective*
having enough skill or knowledge to do something to a satisfactory standard: *The car has some problems, but a competent mechanic can fix them easily.*
—**competently** *adverb*
—**competence** *noun* the ability to do something to a satisfactory standard

com·pe·ti·tion /ˌkɑmpəˈtɪʃən/ *noun*
1 an organized event in which people or teams try to be the best at doing something: *He decided to enter the competition and see if he could win.*

THESAURUS: competition
championship a competition to find the best player or team in a sport: *the Iowa State Girls' Basketball Championships*
tournament a competition in which many players or teams play against each other until there is one winner: *We're playing in a volleyball tournament at the beach this weekend.*
contest a competition in which a judge or group of judges decides the winner: *The school held a contest for the best poster about healthy eating.*

2 a situation in which people are all trying to get the same thing, although not everyone will be able to succeed: *There is a lot of competition for jobs now, so you really have to make an effort.*

com·pet·i·tive /kəmˈpetətɪv/ *adjective*
1 wanting to be more successful than other people or companies: *Steve is very competitive. He hates to lose.*

C

2 a competitive activity is done by people or companies who are all trying hard to win or be successful: *We work in a very competitive industry. You have to work hard to succeed.*

C

com•pet•i•tor /kəm'petətə/ *noun*
a person, team, company, etc. that is competing with another one: *Their main competitor is a large company that sells cheaper computers.*

com•plain /kəm'pleɪn/ *verb*
to say that you are annoyed, not satisfied, or not happy about something or someone: *She decided to complain about the food to the manager because it was cold and tasted bad.*

com•plaint /kəm'pleɪnt/ *noun*
a statement in which someone complains about something: *There have been a lot of complaints about the noise.*

com•plete[1] /kəm'plit/ *adjective*
1 including everything or everyone: *This is a complete list of all the people in the class.* ANTONYM **incomplete**
2 in every way: *That class was a complete waste of time. I already knew about all that.*
3 finished: *Our research is almost complete. We will be finished this week.*
—**completeness** *noun*
➔ See Thesaurus box at **done**[2]

complete[2] *verb*
to finish doing or making something: *The book took five years to complete.*

com•plete•ly /kəm'plitli/ *adverb*
in every way: *It's a completely new idea. Nobody's ever done this before.*

com•plex[1] /kəm'pleks/ Ac *adjective*
something that is complex has a lot of different parts and is difficult to understand or deal with: *The human brain is very complex. Scientists don't fully understand it yet.* SYNONYM **complicated**
—**complexity** /kəm'pleksəti/ *noun* the quality of being complex

com•plex[2] /'kɑmpleks/ Ac *noun*
a group of buildings or one large building used for a particular purpose: *My grandmother lives in an apartment complex for older people.*

com•plex•ion /kəm'plekʃən/ *noun*
the color and appearance of the skin on your face: *She has blond hair and a pale complexion.*

com•pli•cate /'kɑmplə,keɪt/ *verb*
to make a problem or situation more difficult: *If you try to explain all the details, you'll just complicate the situation.*

com•pli•cat•ed /'kɑmplə,keɪtɪd/ *adjective*
difficult to understand or deal with: *The instructions were too complicated for a child to understand.* SYNONYM **complex**; ANTONYM **simple**

com•pli•ca•tion /,kɑmplə'keɪʃən/ *noun*
something that makes a situation more difficult: *There's just one complication with your plan: we don't have enough money.*

com•pli•ment[1] /'kɑmpləmənt/ *noun*
something you say that shows you like someone or something: *Paula got a lot of compliments on her new dress. She looked great in it.*

com•pli•ment[2] /'kɑmplə,ment/ *verb*
to say that you like what someone has done, what someone is wearing, etc.: *They complimented him on his excellent French.*

com•ply /kəm'plaɪ/ *verb* **complied**, third person singular **complies** *formal*
to follow a law or rule: *If you do not comply with the law, you will have to pay a fine.*

com•po•nent /kəm'poʊnənt/ Ac *noun, formal*
a part of a machine or system: *The factory produces components that are used in cars.*

com•pose /kəm'poʊz/ *verb*
1 be composed of something *formal* = to be made of two or more things: *Water is composed of hydrogen and oxygen.*
2 to write a piece of music: *Who composed the music for the movie?*
—**composer** *noun* someone who writes music

com•po•si•tion /,kɑmpə'zɪʃən/ *noun*
a piece of music or poetry that someone writes: *The song is one of her early compositions.*
➔ See Thesaurus box at **music**

com•pound /ˈkɑmpaʊnd/ Ac *noun*
1 a substance that is made of two or more different substances: *The chemical compound is made of two elements.*
2 an area that contains a group of buildings and is surrounded by a fence or wall: *a prison compound*
3 *also* **compound noun** two or more words that are used together as a noun. For example, the noun "ice cream" is a compound

com•pre•hend /ˌkɑmprɪˈhend/ *verb, formal*
to understand or imagine something: *It is difficult to comprehend what it is like to be in a war zone if you've never experienced it.* SYNONYM **understand**

com•pre•hen•sive /ˌkɑmprɪˈhensɪv/ Ac *adjective, formal*
including everything that is necessary: *The city has a comprehensive plan for dealing with an earthquake. It includes rules and advice for everyone living and working here.*

com•prise /kəmˈpraɪz/ Ac *verb, formal*
to be made up of something: *The World Trade Organization comprises more than 100 countries.*

com•pro•mise¹ /ˈkɑmprəˌmaɪz/ *noun*
an agreement in which both people or groups accept something different from what they wanted at the beginning: *The company and its employees finally reached a compromise. Employees agreed to work more hours, and the company will pay them more.*

compromise² *verb*
to make an agreement by accepting something that is different from what you wanted at the beginning: *Neither side wanted to compromise, so they never made a deal.*

com•pul•so•ry /kəmˈpʌlsəri/ *adjective, formal*
if something is compulsory, it must be done because of a rule or law: *In some countries, the law says that all 18-year-olds have to do compulsory service in the military.* SYNONYM **mandatory**; ANTONYM **voluntary**

com•put•er /kəmˈpyutɚ/ Ac *noun*
an electronic machine that stores information and uses programs to help you find, organize, or change the information: *I do most of my school work on my computer.*
➔ See picture on page A20

con¹ /kɑn/ *noun*
1 a disadvantage of something: *List pros and cons* (=advantages and disadvantages) *of each plan to help you decide what to do.* ANTONYM **pro**
2 *informal* a trick to get someone's money or make someone do something: *The whole deal turned out to be a con to trick me out of my money.*

con² *verb* **conned, conning** *informal*
to trick someone, especially in order to take his or her money: *That guy just conned me out of $20* (=tricked me so that I gave him $20)*!*

con•ceal /kənˈsil/ *verb, formal*
to hide something: *He concealed the gun under his coat.*
—**concealment** *noun, formal* the act of hiding something

con•ceit•ed /kənˈsitɪd/ *adjective*
too proud of what you can do, how you look, etc.: *I don't want to seem conceited, but I think I was the most attractive person there.*
➔ See Thesaurus box at **proud**

con•ceive /kənˈsiv/ Ac *verb, formal*
1 to imagine what something is like: *It is impossible to conceive of the size of the universe.*
2 to become PREGNANT: *She may be too old to conceive.*
—**conceivable** *adjective, formal* possible, or able to be imagined: *The book covers every conceivable aspect of the game.*

WORD FAMILY look at the words:
➔ **conceive** *verb*
➔ **conception** *noun*
➔ **conceivable** *adjective*

con•cen•trate /ˈkɑnsənˌtreɪt/ Ac *verb*
to think very carefully about what you are doing: *It's difficult to concentrate with all this noise.* | *Quiet! I'm trying to concentrate on my homework.*

con•cen•tra•tion /ˌkɑnsənˈtreɪʃən/ Ac *noun*
the act of thinking very carefully about what you are doing: *The children got tired and lost concentration* (=stopped thinking carefully about what they were doing).

C

con·cept /'kɑnsept/ Ac *noun, formal*
a general idea about how something is or should be: *The book teaches you about some of the basic concepts of biology.* | *It is sometimes difficult for young children to understand the concepts of right and wrong.*
—**conceptual** /kən'septʃuəl/ *adjective* relating to concepts

con·cep·tion /kən'sepʃən/ Ac *noun, formal*
1 the idea that one person has about something in his or her mind: *Different people have different conceptions of beauty* (=have different ideas about what is beautiful).
2 the act of becoming PREGNANT, so that a baby starts to develop: *A baby is born about 40 weeks after conception.*

con·cern¹ /kən'sɚn/ *noun*
1 a feeling of worry about something important, or the fact of caring about it: *There is growing concern about the amount of traffic in the city.* | *We understand your concern for your children's safety.*
2 something that you feel worried about or care about: *His main concern was the cost of fixing the car.*

concern² *verb*
1 to be about something or someone: *The story concerns a man who lives in Russia.*
2 to involve someone or be important to someone: *What we're planning doesn't concern you.*
3 *formal* to make someone feel worried: *Her daughter's problems at school concerned her greatly.*

con·cerned /kən'sɚnd/ *adjective*
1 worried about something important: *We're all concerned about her health – she's been so sick lately.*
2 thinking that something is important: *He seems more concerned about his business than about his family.*
3 involved in something: *Everyone concerned with the project should come to the meeting.*
4 as far as I'm concerned = in my opinion: *As far as I'm concerned, the whole idea is crazy.*
➔ See Thesaurus box at **worried**

con·cern·ing /kən'sɚnɪŋ/ *preposition, formal*
about: *I have a question concerning tomorrow's meeting.*

con·cert /'kɑnsɚt/ *noun*
a performance given by musicians or singers: *We went to a concert last night.* | *a rock concert*

con·cise /kən'saɪs/ *adjective, formal*
short and not containing too many words: *His answers were clear and concise.*

con·clude /kən'klud/ Ac *verb, formal*
1 to decide that something is true from the information you have: *He concluded that Tina had not taken the money.*
2 to end a meeting, speech, event, etc.: *She concluded the meeting by thanking everyone.* | *The fair concluded with* (=ended with) *a fireworks display.* SYNONYM **finish, end**; ANTONYM **begin, start**
WORD FAMILY ➔ **conclusion** *noun*

con·clu·sion /kən'kluʒən/ Ac *noun*
1 *formal* a decision that something is true, which you make after thinking about it a lot: *His conclusion was that both students had cheated on the test.* | *We've come to the conclusion that the book is too difficult for our students.*
2 the end or final part of a book, movie, etc.: *Every essay should have a clear conclusion that restates the main ideas.*

con·clu·sive /kən'klusɪv/ Ac *adjective, formal*
proving that something is true: *There is no conclusive evidence that he is guilty, but many people think that he is.*

con·crete /'kɑŋkrit/ *noun*
a substance that is used for making buildings. It is a mixture of a gray powder with sand and water, which becomes hard when it dries: *The bridge is made of concrete and steel.*

con·cus·sion /kən'kʌʃən/ *noun*
a small amount of damage to the brain, caused by hitting your head: *One player had a concussion after he fell.*

con·demn /kən'dem/ *verb, formal*
1 to say very strongly that you do not approve of someone or something: *Politicians from all parties condemned the bombings.*

2 to give someone a severe punishment for a crime: *The murderer was condemned to death by the court.*
—**condemnation** /ˌkɑndəmˈneɪʃən/ *noun* the act of condemning something

con•den•sa•tion /ˌkɑndənˈseɪʃən/ *noun*
small drops of water that appear on a cold surface when warm air touches it: *There was a lot of condensation on the window, which made it difficult to see out.*

con•dense /kənˈdens/ *verb*
1 to make a speech or piece of writing shorter: *Try to condense your essay onto just one page.*
2 to make a liquid thicker by removing some of the water from it: *condensed soup*
3 if gas or warm air condenses, it becomes a liquid as it becomes cooler

con•de•scend•ing /ˌkɑndɪˈsendɪŋ/ *adjective*
showing that you think you are better than someone else: *I didn't like his condescending tone of voice. It made me feel stupid.*

con•di•tion /kənˈdɪʃən/ *noun*
1 the state of something, or of someone's body or mind: *The car is in very good condition* (=it is not damaged and works well). | *His physical condition has improved.*
2 conditions = the situation in which someone lives, or in which something happens: *Their living conditions are terrible – there is not enough light, and everything is very dirty.* | *Bad weather conditions are making driving dangerous.*
3 a medical problem, especially one that affects someone for a long time: *My father has a heart condition.*
4 something that must happen before something else can happen: *One of the conditions of getting the job was that I had to improve my English.*

con•di•tion•er /kənˈdɪʃənɚ/ *noun*
a liquid that you put on your hair when you wash it in order to make it less dry and easier to comb: *shampoo and conditioner*

con•do•min•i•um /ˌkɑndəˈmɪniəm/ *also* **con•do** /ˈkɑndoʊ/ *noun, informal*
a building that consists of a number of apartments with different owners, or one of these apartments

con•done /kənˈdoʊn/ *verb, formal*
to say that it is acceptable to do something that other people think is wrong: *He does not condone any kind of drug use, and reports anyone he sees using drugs.*

con•duct¹ /kənˈdʌkt/ [Ac] *verb*
1 *formal* to do something in an organized way: *The police are conducting an investigation into the murder.*
2 if something conducts electricity, it allows electricity to go through it: *Gold conducts electricity better than most other metals.*
3 to stand in front of the musicians in an ORCHESTRA and direct their playing: *The Boston Pops Orchestra was conducted by John Williams.*

con•duct² /ˈkɑndʌkt/ [Ac] *noun, formal*
the way someone behaves: *He was fired because of his unprofessional conduct.*
SYNONYM **behavior**

con•duc•tor /kənˈdʌktɚ/ *noun*
1 someone who conducts the musicians in an ORCHESTRA
2 a person who sells and checks tickets on a train

cone /koʊn/ *noun*
1 an object with sloping sides which is round at one end and pointed at the other: *an ice cream cone* (=a cone that has ice cream in it)
2 the hard brown fruit of a PINE or FIR tree

con•fer /kənˈfɚ/ [Ac] *verb* **conferred, conferring** *formal*
to discuss something with other people, in order to get their opinion: *You should confer with the other team members before you decide.*

con•fer•ence /ˈkɑnfrəns/ [Ac] *noun*
1 a large formal meeting, usually on several days, where people who are interested in a subject can listen to talks and discuss ideas: *She has been asked to speak at an international conference* (=one with people from many countries). | *The scientific reports were presented at a conference on climate change.*
2 a meeting at which a small number of people discuss something: *There was a parent-teacher conference at the school to talk about Andy's behavior.*

C

con•fess /kən'fes/ *verb*
to tell someone that you have done something wrong: *He has confessed to the crime and will have to go to prison.*

con•fes•sion /kən'feʃən/ *noun*
a statement that you have done something wrong: *He made a full confession at the police station.*

con•fide /kən'faɪd/ *verb, formal*
to tell someone about something personal and private: *He had confided to friends that he was unhappy.* | *I'm glad she felt she could confide in me.*

WORD FAMILY look at the words:
→ confide *verb*
→ confidential *adjective*
→ confidentially *adverb*

con•fi•dence /'kɑnfədəns/ *noun*
1 the feeling that you are able to do things well: *She's a smart girl who has a lot of confidence.* | *He was shy, and lacked confidence* (=did not have much confidence).
2 the feeling that you can trust someone or something to be good or successful: *The coach has confidence in me. He knows I can hit the ball.*
3 in confidence *formal* = if you tell someone something in confidence, you do not want him or her to tell anyone else

con•fi•dent /'kɑnfədənt/ *adjective*
1 someone who is confident believes that they can do things well and does not feel nervous: *Are you feeling confident about your exam or do you need to study more?*
2 sure that something will happen: *I'm confident (that) the problem can be solved if we try hard.*
—**confidently** *adverb*

con•fi•den•tial /ˌkɑnfə'denʃəl/ *adjective*
if information is confidential, you must not show it or talk about it to other people: *a confidential report* | *Doctors must keep patients' records confidential* (=they must not show the records to other people).
—**confidentially** *adverb*

con•fined /kən'faɪnd/ Ac *adjective*
1 be confined to someone or something *formal* = to affect only one group of people, or to happen only in one place: *Luckily the fire was confined to one floor of the building.*
2 a confined space or area is very small: *He disliked confined spaces like elevators.*

con•firm /kən'fɚm/ Ac *verb*
1 to say or show that something is definitely true: *The doctors confirmed that she had cancer.*
2 to tell someone that an arrangement is now definite: *Confirm your flight reservation at least two days before you leave.*
WORD FAMILY → confirmation *noun*

con•fir•ma•tion /ˌkɑnfɚ'meɪʃən/ Ac *noun*
a statement or letter saying that something is definitely true or will definitely happen: *The school sent a confirmation of the test scores to each student.*

con•fis•cate /'kɑnfəˌskeɪt/ *verb*
if people in authority confiscate something that belongs to you, they take it away from you: *The police confiscated his camera for taking pictures where he wasn't supposed to.*
—**confiscation** /ˌkɑnfə'skeɪʃən/ *noun* the act of confiscating something

con•flict¹ /'kɑnˌflɪkt/ Ac *noun*
a fight or argument between people, groups, or countries: *There was often conflict between the two brothers and they did not like spending time together.* | *The organization has helped to resolve the conflict* (=end the conflict).
→ See Thesaurus box at war

con•flict² /kən'flɪkt/ Ac *verb*
if two ideas, statements, etc. conflict with each other, they are completely different: *Some of the teachers' opinions conflicted with the principal's, so they had a meeting to discuss their disagreements.*

con•form /kən'fɔrm/ Ac *verb*
to behave in the way that most people behave: *There's always pressure on kids to conform.*

con•front /kən'frʌnt/ *verb*
1 to deal directly with a difficult problem or situation: *We try to help people to confront their problems and find solutions for them.*
2 to speak to someone strongly about a serious matter that he or she will probably

not want to discuss: *Her mother confronted her about her smoking.*
3 *formal* if you are confronted with a problem, you need to deal with it: *The new government has been confronted with numerous problems.*

con·fron·ta·tion /ˌkɑnfrənˈteɪʃən/ *noun*
an angry argument or fight: *There have been confrontations between police and protesters.*

con·fuse /kənˈfyuz/ *verb*
1 to make someone feel that he or she does not understand something: *His directions to the house really confused me, and I took a long time to find it.*
2 to think wrongly that a person or thing is someone or something else: *It's easy to confuse Sue with her sister – they look so similar.*
—**confusing** *adjective* something that is confusing is difficult to understand because it is complicated and not clear: *The instructions in the book were really confusing, and none of the students understood what to do.*

WORD FAMILY look at the words:
→ **confuse** *verb*
→ **confusion** *noun*
→ **confusing** *adjective*
→ **confused** *adjective*

con·fused /kənˈfyuzd/ *adjective*
someone who is confused does not understand something clearly: *We're a little confused about what we're supposed to be doing.*
→ See picture on page A23

con·fu·sion /kənˈfyuʒən/ *noun*
the feeling that you do not understand something or do not know what to do: *There was a lot of confusion about the new rules at first.*

con·ges·tion /kənˈdʒestʃən/ *noun*
1 a situation in which the roads are too full of cars, trucks, etc.: *How can we reduce traffic congestion in our cities?*
2 a situation in which your nose or another part of your body is full of too much liquid: *It was hard to breathe because of my congestion.*
—**congested** *adjective* experiencing congestion: *a congested street*

con·grat·u·late /kənˈgrætʃəˌleɪt/ *verb*
to tell someone that you are pleased because something good has happened to him or her, or because he or she has done something well: *I congratulated them on the birth of their daughter.*

con·grat·u·la·tions /kənˌgrætʃəˈleɪʃənz/
used when congratulating someone: *You won? Congratulations!* | *Congratulations on your graduation from high school.*

con·gre·ga·tion /ˌkɑŋgrəˈgeɪʃən/ *noun*
the people who are in a church during a service: *The minister asked the congregation to stand.*

Con·gress /ˈkɑŋgrɪs/ *noun*
the group of people who have been chosen to make the laws in some countries. In the U.S., Congress is divided into the Senate and the House of Representatives: *The bill has been approved by both houses of Congress.*

con·gress·man /ˈkɑŋgrɪsmən/ *noun*
plural **congressmen** /ˈkɑŋgrɪsmən/
a man who is a member of the House of Representatives

con·gress·wom·an /ˈkɑŋgrɪsˌwʊmən/ *noun* plural **congresswomen** /ˈkɑŋgrɪsˌwɪmɪn/
a woman who is a member of the House of Representatives

con·ju·gate /ˈkɑndʒəˌgeɪt/ *verb, formal*
to give the different forms of a verb, for example the present tense, past tense, and past participle: *We learned to conjugate verbs in Spanish.*

con·junc·tion /kənˈdʒʌŋkʃən/ *noun, formal*
1 a word such as "but," "and," or "while" that connects parts of sentences or phrases
2 **in conjunction with someone or something** = with someone or something else: *The worksheets should be used in conjunction with the video.*

con·nect /kəˈnekt/ *verb*
1 to join one thing to another: *Connect the speakers to the stereo.* | *Has the phone been connected yet* (=been joined to the telephone network)? | *Click here to connect to*

the Internet (=join your computer to the Internet). ANTONYM **disconnect**
2 to show or think that a thing or person is related to or involved in something: *There is no evidence to connect him with the crime.*

C

con·nect·ed /kə'nektɪd/ *adjective*
1 if two things or events are connected, there is some kind of relationship between them: *The police think that the two murders may be connected with each other.* SYNONYM **related**
2 if two things are connected to each other, they are joined together: *The speakers aren't even connected to the stereo – of course you can't hear anything.*

con·nec·tion /kə'nekʃən/ *noun*
1 a relationship between things, people, ideas, etc.: *There is a direct connection between smoking and lung disease.* | *He said he had no connection with the organization.*
2 the process of joining two or more things together, especially using wires: *You get free Internet connection at the hotel.*
3 an airplane, bus, or train that leaves soon after another one arrives, so that people can change from one to the other and continue their trip quickly: *I missed my connection at the airport* (=I failed to catch my next plane).

con·nois·seur /ˌkɑnə'sɚ/ *noun, formal*
someone who knows a lot about something such as art or food: *a connoisseur of fine wines*

con·quer /'kɑŋkɚ/ *verb, formal*
to defeat a country or group of people in a war and take their land: *The Romans conquered much of Europe.*
—**conqueror** *noun* a leader or nation that conquers a country or group of people

con·quest /'kɑŋkwest/ *noun, formal*
the defeat and control of a country or group of people: *The Spanish conquest of Central America took place in the 16th century.*

con·science /'kɑnʃəns/ *noun*
the feeling inside you that tells you whether it is right or wrong to do something: *I had a guilty conscience about lying to my mother* (=I felt guilty about it).

con·sci·en·tious /ˌkɑnʃi'enʃəs/ *adjective, formal*
taking care to do things very well: *He was a conscientious student who spent a lot of time on his homework.*
—**conscientiously** *adverb, formal*

con·scious /'kɑnʃəs/ *adjective*
1 knowing about a situation or realizing something: *I was conscious of people staring at me.* | *fashion-conscious teenagers* (=young people who know and care about fashion) SYNONYM **aware**
2 awake and able to understand what is happening: *He was still conscious when he arrived at the hospital.* ANTONYM **unconscious**

WORD FAMILY look at the words:

→ **conscious** *adjective*
→ **unconscious** *adjective*
→ **consciously** *adverb*
→ **unconsciously** *adverb*
→ **consciousness** *noun*
→ **unconsciousness** *noun*

con·scious·ly /'kɑnʃəsli/ *adverb*
if you do something consciously, you know that you are doing it and you deliberately make an effort to do it: *She consciously chose to wear her best skirt for the date.* ANTONYM **unconsciously**

con·scious·ness /'kɑnʃəsnɪs/ *noun*
the state of being awake and able to understand what is happening: *Charlie hit his head and lost consciousness.*

con·sec·u·tive /kən'sekyətɪv/ *adjective, formal*
consecutive periods of time, events, etc. happen one after the other: *It rained for three consecutive days and we really wanted to see the sun again.*

con·sen·sus /kən'sensəs/ Ac *noun, formal*
agreement between everyone in a group: *The committee failed to reach a consensus on what should be done.*

con·sent /kən'sent/ Ac *noun, formal*
permission to do something: *We need your parents' written consent before you can go on the school trip.* | *Her father gave his consent to the marriage* (=said that he would allow it).

—**consent** *verb*, *formal* to say that you will allow something to be done: *He had not consented to medical treatment, so doctors did not perform the operation.*

con·se·quence /ˈkɑnsəˌkwens/ Ac *noun*, *formal*
something that happens as a result of an action: *She never thinks about the consequences of her actions.* | *He broke the law, and now he must face the consequences* (=accept the bad results of his actions).
WORD FAMILY ➔ **consequently** *adverb*

con·se·quent·ly /ˈkɑnsəˌkwentli/ Ac *adverb*, *formal*
as a result of something: *The winter was very cold, and consequently many animals died.*

con·ser·va·tion /ˌkɑnsəˈveɪʃən/ *noun*
1 the activity of protecting plants and types of animals: *There are new laws to encourage the conservation of wildlife.*
2 the activity of using energy, water, etc. carefully and not wasting any: *The city has organized a program of water conservation since water supplies are low.*

con·ser·va·tion·ist /ˌkɒnsəˈveɪʃənɪst/ *noun*
someone whose work is about the activity of protecting plants and types of animals

con·serv·a·tive /kənˈsəvətɪv/ *adjective*
1 supporting political ideas that include less government involvement in people's lives and little social change: *Republicans are more conservative than Democrats.* SYNONYM **right-wing**
2 believing that the old ways of doing things are best: *Most old people who live in farm country are very conservative.*

con·serve /kənˈsəv/ *verb*, *formal*
1 to use energy, water, etc. carefully and not waste it: *We must teach young people to conserve energy by turning off lights and computers.*
2 to stop plants and types of animals from being destroyed: *If we do not conserve the rainforests, they will disappear from the Earth.*

con·sid·er /kənˈsɪdə/ *verb*, *formal*
1 to think about something: *She's considering studying engineering at college.*
2 to have an opinion about something or someone: *I considered her to be an excellent teacher.*
➔ See Thesaurus box at **think**

con·sid·er·a·ble /kənˈsɪdərəbəl/ Ac *adjective*, *formal*
a considerable amount is a lot: *He earns a considerable amount of money, so he buys a lot of expensive things.*

con·sid·er·a·bly /kənˈsɪdərəbli/ Ac *adverb*, *formal*
if something is considerably bigger, higher, etc., it is a lot bigger, higher, etc.: *That store is considerably more expensive than the others.*

con·sid·er·ate /kənˈsɪdərət/ *adjective*, *formal*
a considerate person thinks about what other people feel or need: *Alex is such a kind and considerate boy. He's always doing nice things for other people.*
—**considerately** *adjective*, *formal*
➔ See Thesaurus box at **kind**[2]

con·sid·e·ra·tion /kənˌsɪdəˈreɪʃən/ *noun*
careful thought about something: *It's a new idea, and it needs careful consideration.*

con·sid·er·ing /kənˈsɪdərɪŋ/ *preposition*, *conjunction*
used when you give your opinion, for saying that it is important to remember a particular fact: *She did well on her exams, considering that she'd been sick.*

con·sist /kənˈsɪst/ Ac *verb*, *formal*
PHRASAL VERB
consist of something
to be formed of something: *The audience consisted largely of teenagers.*

con·sist·ent /kənˈsɪstənt/ Ac *adjective*
1 always doing something in the same way: *Ben is the team's most consistent player* (=he's always good). ANTONYM **inconsistent**
2 if one description, report, etc. is consistent with another, they contain the same facts or ideas: *The man's explanation was consistent with the evidence, so it is probably true.*
—**consistently** *adverb*: *Zoe has achieved consistently good grades this semester – she's gotten A's and B's on everything.*
—**consistency** *noun*, *formal* the quality of always doing something in the same way:

C

C

He has some athletic skills, but he lacks consistency.

con•sole /kən'soʊl/ *verb, formal*
to help someone to feel less sad: *No one could console her when her dog died.*
—**consolation** /ˌkɑnsə'leɪʃən/ *noun, formal* something that makes you feel less sad

con•sol•i•date /kən'sɑləˌdeɪt/ *verb, formal*
to combine two or more things to form a single thing that is more effective or easier to deal with: *We consolidate information from a wide range of sources.*
—**consolidation** /kənˌsɑlə'deɪʃən/ *noun, formal* the act of consolidating something

con•so•nant /'kɑnsənənt/ *noun*
any letter of the alphabet except a, e, i, o, and u: *The word "bird" begins and ends with a consonant.*

con•spic•u•ous /kən'spɪkyuəs/ *adjective, formal*
very easy to notice: *Put the sign in a conspicuous place so that lots of people see it.*
—**conspicuously** *adverb, formal*: *Dave was conspicuously absent from the meeting* (=his absence was very noticeable).
➔ See Thesaurus box at **clear**[1]

con•spir•a•cy /kən'spɪrəsi/ *noun* plural **conspiracies**
a secret plan that people make together to do something bad: *There was a conspiracy to assassinate the president that involved many people.*
—**conspirator** *noun, formal* someone who is part of a group that is planning a conspiracy

con•stant /'kɑnstənt/ Ac *adjective*
1 happening all the time: *Tiny babies need constant attention.*
2 staying at the same level: *While she's sick, keep her room at a constant temperature.*
—**constantly** *adverb*: *Technology is constantly changing.*

con•stel•la•tion /ˌkɑnstə'leɪʃən/ *noun*
a group of stars that has a name: *You can see the major constellations in the night sky.*

con•sti•pa•tion /ˌkɑnstə'peɪʃən/ *noun*
difficulty in moving solid waste out of the body: *Plenty of fruit and vegetables help to prevent constipation.*
—**constipated** /'kɑnstəˌpeɪtɪd/ *adjective* having constipation

con•sti•tute /'kɑnstəˌtut/ Ac *verb, formal*
to form a part of something: *Women constitute 51% of the population.*
—**constituent** /kən'stɪtʃuənt/ *noun, formal* one of the parts that form something

con•sti•tu•tion *also* **Constitution** /ˌkɑnstə'tuʃən/ Ac *noun*
a set of laws and ideas that govern a country, state, or organization: *The Constitution says what kind of laws the government can make.*
—**constitutional** *adjective* relating to a constitution: *the constitutional rights of the people*

con•struct /kən'strʌkt/ Ac *verb, formal*
to build something: *The college is planning to construct a new library.*

WORD FAMILY look at the words:
➔ **construct** *verb*
➔ **construction** *noun*
➔ **reconstruction** *noun*

con•struc•tion /kən'strʌkʃən/ Ac *noun*
the process of building something: *A new airport is now under construction* (=people are in the process of building it).

con•sul /'kɑnsəl/ *noun*
a person who lives in a foreign city and whose job is to help other people from the same country who live there: *He was the U.S. consul in Tunis for several years.*

con•sult /kən'sʌlt/ Ac *verb, formal*
to ask a doctor, lawyer, etc. for advice or information: *Before you sign any contract, consult your lawyer.*
—**consultation** /ˌkɑnsəl'teɪʃən/ *noun, formal* a meeting or discussion that you have to get advice or information: *The decision was reached after consultation with parents and teachers.*

WORD FAMILY look at the words:
➔ **consult** *verb*
➔ **consultation** *noun*
➔ **consultant** *noun*

con•sult•ant /kən'sʌltənt/ Ac *noun*
someone whose job is to give advice about something: *He's a successful business consultant and works with many different companies.*

con•sume /kən'sum/ Ac *verb, formal*
1 to use fuel, time, etc.: *Small cars consume less fuel.*
2 to eat or drink something: *You should try to reduce the amount of salt you consume.*
→ **time-consuming**

con•sum•er /kən'sumə/ Ac *noun, formal*
anyone who buys goods or uses services: *Consumers will buy more if the prices are lower.*

con•sump•tion /kən'sʌmpʃən/ Ac *noun, formal*
energy/fuel, etc. consumption = the amount of electricity, gas, etc. that something uses: *Driving more slowly reduces the car's fuel consumption.*

con•tact[1] /'kantækt/ Ac *noun*
1 the act of talking or writing to someone: *I don't have much contact with John since he moved away.*
2 be/keep/stay in contact with someone = to talk or write to someone who you do not see often: *Jane lives in Canada now, but I keep in contact with her by email.*
3 the state of two people or things touching each other: *These two wires should not come into contact* (=touch).

contact[2] *verb*
to telephone or write to someone: *I think you should contact the police.*

'contact ˌlens *noun*
a small round piece of plastic you put in your eye to help you see clearly

con•ta•gious /kən'teɪdʒəs/ *adjective*
a contagious disease can pass from one person to another: *Children's diseases are highly contagious, so if one child gets sick, they all get sick.* SYNONYM **infectious**

con•tain /kən'teɪn/ *verb*
1 to have something inside: *His wallet contained $50.*
2 to include something in a letter, report, etc.: *Your essay must contain your own ideas.*

con•tain•er /kən'teɪnə/ *noun*
something you buy or keep things in: *She put the cookies in a plastic container with a tight lid.*

con•tam•i•nate /kən'tæməˌneɪt/ *verb, formal*
to make water, food, etc. dirty or dangerous: *Some of these chemicals contaminate our rivers.*
—**contamination** /kənˌtæmə'neɪʃən/ *noun* the act of contaminating water, food, etc.: *the contamination of the city's water supply*

con•tem•plate /'kantəmˌpleɪt/ *verb, formal*
to think about doing something important: *I could not contemplate getting married yet – I'm too young.*
—**contemplation** /ˌkantəm'pleɪʃən/ *noun, formal* the act of thinking about something important

con•tem•po•ra•ry /kən'tempəˌreri/ Ac *adjective, formal*
contemporary art, music, etc. is modern: *I like contemporary art better than 19th century art.*

con•tempt /kən'tempt/ *noun, formal*
a complete lack of respect for someone or something: *"You'll never be able to do it," he said with contempt.*
—**contemptuous** *adjective, formal* without any respect: *She gave him a contemptuous look when he made the mistake.*

con•tend /kən'tend/ *verb, formal*
to compete to get something: *Their team is contending for the national championship.*
—**contender** *noun* someone who is competing to get something: *He's a top contender for the gold medal.*

con•tent[1] /kən'tent/ *adjective*
happy and satisfied: *Are you content with your life or are there changes you want to make?*

con•tent[2] /'kantent/ *noun, formal*
1 contents = the things that are inside a box, bag, etc.: *The guard looked through the contents of her purse.*
2 the ideas that are contained in a book, speech, etc.: *The content of the book is not appropriate for children.*

C

C

con·tent·ed /kən'tentɪd/ *adjective*
happy and satisfied: *They seem like a very contented family. They don't argue much.*

con·test /'kantest/ *noun*
a competition: *At the fair there was a contest to see who could eat the most hot dogs.*
➔ See Thesaurus box at **competition**

con·test·ant /kən'testənt/ *noun*
someone who competes in a contest: *There will be only three contestants in the game.*

con·text /'kantekst/ Ac *noun*
the situation that is related to something, and that helps you to understand it: *We have to think about the law in its historical context. What was society like then?*

con·ti·nent /'kantənənt/ *noun*
one of the large areas of land on the Earth, such as Africa, Europe, and Asia: *the African continent*
—**continental** /ˌkantə'nentl/ *adjective* relating to a continent, but not its islands: *a map of the continental United States*

con·tin·u·al /kən'tɪnyuəl/ *adjective, formal*
happening a lot or all the time: *Their continual arguing upset me.*

con·tin·u·a·tion /kənˌtɪnyu'eɪʃən/ *noun, formal*
a situation in which something continues to happen: *The college offers graduating high school students a continuation of their education.*

con·tin·ue /kən'tɪnyu/ *verb*
1 if something continues, it is happening and it does not stop: *Maya has continued to study hard at school this year. | He plans to continue his work with the university.*
2 to start again after a pause: *An hour later the fighting continued.*
—**continuity** /ˌkantə'nuəti/ *noun, formal* the state of continuing: *Our traditions give us a sense of continuity.*

WORD FAMILY look at the words:
- ➔ **continue** *verb*
- ➔ **continuity** *noun*
- ➔ **continual** *adjective*
- ➔ **continuous** *adjective*
- ➔ **continuously** *adverb*
- ➔ **discontinue** *verb*

conˌtinuing eduˈcation *noun*
classes for adults who want to study something

con·tin·u·ous /kən'tɪnyuəs/ *adjective, formal*
happening without stopping: *Learning is a continuous process that happens until we die.*
—**continuously** *adverb, formal*: *It rained continuously for two days.*

con·tour /'kantʊr/ *noun*
the curved shape or edge of something: *This model shows the contours of the Earth's surface.*

con·tra·cep·tion /ˌkantrə'sepʃən/ *noun*
ways of stopping a woman from becoming PREGNANT SYNONYM **birth control**

con·tra·cep·tive /ˌkantrə'septɪv/ *noun*
something people use to stop a woman from becoming PREGNANT: *She didn't want to have a baby, so she wanted information about contraceptives.*
—**contraceptive** *adjective*: *the contraceptive pill*

con·tract[1] /'kantrækt/ Ac *noun*
a written agreement to work for someone, buy something, etc.: *Dave signed a three-year contract with an oil company.*

con·tract[2] /kən'trækt/ Ac *verb, formal*
1 to get a serious disease: *Thousands of people contracted the disease and died.*
2 to become smaller: *Metal contracts as it cools.* ANTONYM **expand**

con·trac·tion /kən'trækʃən/ *noun*
a short form of a word or words: *"Don't" is a contraction of "do not."*

con·trac·tor /'kanˌtræktɚ/ Ac *noun*
a company or person that does work for other companies, especially building work: *Her father was a building contractor.*

con·tra·dict /ˌkantrə'dɪkt/ Ac *verb*
if one statement, fact, etc. contradicts another one, they are different and both cannot be true: *The two boys' stories about the fight contradicted each other.*
—**contradiction** /ˌkantrə'dɪkʃən/ *noun* a difference between two statements, facts, etc. that cannot both be true
—**contradictory** /ˌkantrə'dɪktəri/ *adjective, formal* contradictory statements or facts

are different, and both cannot be true: *The two witnesses gave contradictory statements in court, and it was not clear who was telling the truth.*

con·tra·ry[1] /'kɑnˌtreri/ Ac *adverb, formal*

contrary to something = different from something that people think or say: *Contrary to what most people think, a little fat is good for you.*

contrary[2] *noun, formal*

on the contrary = used when saying that the opposite is true: *"Is the population decreasing?" "On the contrary, it is increasing."*

—**contrary** *adjective, formal* different from or not agreeing with something: *contrary opinions*

con·trast[1] /'kɑntræst/ Ac *noun*

a big difference between people or things: *There is a big contrast between the rich and the poor in the United States.*

con·trast[2] /kən'træst/ Ac *verb*

1 if two things contrast, they are or look very different: *I like the way the red walls contrast with the wood floors.*

2 to compare two people or things and show that they are different: *The teacher told us to compare and contrast these two poems* (=show how they are the same and how they are different).

con·trib·ute /kən'trɪbyut/ Ac *verb, formal*

1 to give money or help for something: *My parents contribute to my college fees.*

2 to take part in something: *All the students contributed to the discussion.*

—**contributor** *noun, formal* someone who gives money or help for something: *He was a major contributor to the Republican party.*

WORD FAMILY look at the words:

→ **contribute** *verb*
→ **contribution** *noun*
→ **contributor** *noun*

con·tri·bu·tion /ˌkɑntrə'byuʃən/ Ac *noun, formal*

1 some money that you give to help pay for something: *Everyone made a contribution of $3 to buy Elsa a present.*

2 something you do that helps something be successful: *Her work here made a great contribution to the school.*

con·trol[1] /kən'troʊl/ *noun*

1 the ability to make someone or something do what you want: *Some parents don't have any control over their kids.*

2 under control = if a situation is under control, it is happening the way you want: *Don't worry, everything is under control.*

3 out of control = if something is out of control, you cannot make it do what you want: *The car went out of control and hit a tree.*

4 the power to decide what happens in a country, organization, etc.: *At the moment, the Republicans are in control of Congress* (=have this power).

5 the ability to stay calm when you are angry or upset: *I just lost control and punched him!*

6 controls = the things that you press or turn to make a vehicle work: *The pilot was already at the plane's controls.*

control[2] *verb* **controlled, controlling**

1 to make someone or something do what you want: *I couldn't control the horse, and it began to run.*

2 to have the power in a country, organization, etc.: *Nicholls was the man who controlled the company.*

con·tro·ver·sy /'kɑntrəˌvəsi/ Ac *noun*

plural **controversies**

a lot of disagreement among people: *There was a lot of controversy over who should pay to fix the bridge.*

—**controversial** /ˌkɑntrə'vəʃəl/ *adjective* causing a lot of disagreement among people: *Using animals for scientific experiments is a controversial issue – many people oppose it, but others say it is necessary.*

con·ven·ience /kən'vinyəns/ *noun*

the quality of being useful and easy to use: *Most people like the convenience of a credit card.* ANTONYM **inconvenience**

con'venience ˌstore *noun*

a store where you buy food, newspapers, etc. and that is often open 24 hours each day

con·ven·ient /kən'vinyənt/ *adjective*

1 useful and easy to use or get to: *The Internet is a convenient way to shop.* ANTONYM **inconvenient**

C

2 a convenient time is good for you to do something, because you are not busy then: *Is 2 o'clock convenient for you?* ANTONYM **inconvenient**

C

con•vent /ˈkɑnvent/ *noun*
a place where women who follow a religious life live together

con•ven•tion /kənˈvenʃən/ Ac *noun*
a large meeting of people who belong to the same organization, do the same work, etc.: *the Democratic Convention*

con•ven•tion•al /kənˈvenʃənəl/ Ac *adjective*
of the type that has been used for a long time: *Microwave ovens are much faster than conventional ovens.*
➔ See Thesaurus box at **normal**

con•ver•sa•tion /ˌkɑnvəˈseɪʃən/ *noun*
1 a talk between two or more people: *I had an interesting conversation with your teacher.* | *My sister and I had a conversation about love and marriage.*
2 make conversation = to talk to someone to be polite: *Everyone stood around, making conversation.*

con•verse[1] /kənˈvəs/ Ac *verb, formal*
to have a conversation with someone: *He stood in the middle of the room conversing with his guests.* SYNONYM **talk**
➔ See Thesaurus box at **talk**[1]

con•verse[2] /ˈkɑnvəs/ Ac *noun*
the converse *formal* = the opposite of something: *Clearly, if x = y, the converse is also true: y = x.*
—**conversely** *adverb, formal*: *What do you like most about your job, and conversely what do you like least?*

con•ver•sion /kənˈvəʒən/ Ac *noun*
the act of changing from one form, religion, etc. to another one: *Our conversion to the new digital system will soon be complete.*

con•vert /kənˈvət/ Ac *verb*
1 to change something into something else: *The old barn was converted into a house.*
2 to change your religion: *When she married, she converted to Islam.*

con•ver•ti•ble /kənˈvətəbəl/ Ac *noun*
a car with a roof that you can fold back or remove

con•vey /kənˈveɪ/ *verb, formal*
to express feelings or ideas to someone: *The poem conveys strong emotions to the reader.*

conˈveyor belt *noun*
a long moving band of rubber or metal, used for moving things from one place to another: *The bags move through the airport on a conveyor belt.*

con•vict[1] /kənˈvɪkt/ *verb*
to decide that someone is guilty of a crime in a court of law: *The man was convicted of murder and sent to prison.*

con•vict[2] /ˈkɑnvɪkt/ *noun, formal*
someone who is guilty of a crime and is sent to prison: *In the past, all the convicts were sent to an island.*

con•vic•tion /kənˈvɪkʃən/ *noun*
1 *formal* a strong belief: *Her mother has strong religious convictions and doesn't believe in smoking or drinking at all.*
2 a decision made in a court of law that someone is guilty of a crime: *The young man had two previous criminal convictions, so the judge gave him a strict punishment.*

con•vince /kənˈvɪns/ Ac *verb*
1 to make someone believe something: *He convinced me that he was telling the truth.*
2 to persuade someone to do something: *I convinced Kate to stay at the party with me.*
—**convincing** *adjective* making you believe that something is true: *The reason she gave for being late was very convincing.*
➔ See Thesaurus box at **persuade**

con•vinced /kənˈvɪnst/ Ac *adjective*
certain that something is true: *I'm convinced (that) I saw him at the party.* SYNONYM **sure**

con•voy /ˈkɑnvɔɪ/ *noun*
a group of vehicles traveling together: *A convoy of military trucks drove into town.*

cook[1] /kʊk/ *verb*
to make food ready to eat, by cutting, mixing, heating, etc. it: *I'll cook dinner tonight.*

THESAURUS: cook

bake to cook food such as bread in the oven: *Jeanie baked some cookies.*

fry to cook food in oil on the top part of the stove: *I fried an egg for breakfast.*

roast to cook meat or vegetables in an oven: *The beef needs to roast for three hours.*

boil to cook food in very hot water on the top part of the stove: *Boil the potatoes until they are tender.*

grill to cook food over strong heat, especially over a fire: *Dad grilled a steak on the barbecue.*

steam to cook vegetables by placing them in a container over very hot water, so that the steam from the hot water cooks them: *Steaming the broccoli keeps in more of the vitamins.*

➔ See picture on page A14

cook² *noun*
someone who makes food ready to eat: *Kevin works as a cook at the college.*
➔ See picture on page A16

cook·book /ˈkʊkbʊk/ *noun*
a book that tells you how to make different foods: *There is a good recipe for making apple pie in the cookbook.*

cook·ie /ˈkʊki/ *noun*
a small flat sweet cake: *She's making chocolate chip cookies.*

cook·ing /ˈkʊkɪŋ/ *noun*
the activity of preparing and cooking food: *I do most of the cooking at our house.*

cook·out /ˈkʊkaʊt/ *noun*
an occasion when a meal is cooked outdoors: *We're going to have hamburgers and hot dogs at the cookout.*

cool¹ /kul/ *adjective*
1 *informal* used to show that you like or admire someone or something: *He's a really cool guy.*
2 *informal* used in order to say "yes" to something: *"Do you mind if I bring my sister?" "No, that's cool."* SYNONYM **OK, fine**
3 a little cold: *A cool breeze came from the ocean.*
4 calm: *Stay cool – don't let him make you mad.*
—**coolly** /ˈkul-li/ *adverb* in a calm or unfriendly way: *"Can I come with you?" "I don't care what you do," she said coolly.*
➔ See Thesaurus box at **cold¹**

cool² *also* **cool down** *verb*
to become colder: *When you take the cake out of the oven, let it cool for a while.* | *A soda will cool you down on a hot day.*
PHRASAL VERB
cool off *also* **cool down**
1 if you cool off, you do something to make yourself less hot: *It was hot, so we went swimming to cool off.*
2 to stop being angry: *Don't talk to him until he cools off.*

cool³ *noun*
1 keep your cool = to stay calm in a difficult situation: *The players kept their cool and started scoring.*
2 lose your cool = to become angry or upset in a difficult situation: *Be polite, and try not to lose your cool.*

cool·er /ˈkulɚ/ *noun*
a box in which you can keep food or drinks cool

cooped up /ˌkupt ˈʌp/ *adjective, informal*
if you are cooped up in a small place, you have to stay there for a long period of time, and you feel very uncomfortable: *Let's go out. I've been cooped up in this apartment all day.*

co·op·er·ate /koʊˈɑpəˌreɪt/ Ac *verb*
to work together with someone else, or do what someone asks you to do: *If we all cooperate, we can get this done faster.* | *He may cooperate with the police and tell them where the stolen money is.*

WORD FAMILY look at the words:
➔ **cooperate** *verb*
➔ **cooperation** *noun*
➔ **cooperative** *adjective*

co·op·er·a·tion /koʊˌɑpəˈreɪʃən/ Ac *noun*
the act of working together with someone else or doing what someone asks you to do: *Cooperation between teachers and parents helps students get the same messages at school and at home.*

co·op·er·a·tive /koʊˈɑpərətɪv/ Ac *adjective*
someone who is cooperative does what he or she is asked to do: *When I asked him to help us, he was very cooperative. He started helping that day.*

co·or·di·nate /koʊˈɔrdnˌeɪt/ Ac *verb, formal*
to organize something complicated, so that everyone does the right thing at the right time: *Sam is coordinating the campaign, so if*

you have questions about what to do, ask him.

—**coordinator** *noun* someone who coordinates an activity

WORD FAMILY look at the words:

→ coordinate *verb*
→ coordination *noun*
→ coordinator *noun*

C

co•or•di•na•tion /koʊˌɔrdnˈeɪʃən/ Ac *noun*

1 someone's ability to use his or her body parts together effectively: *It takes good eye-hand coordination to catch a ball.*

2 *formal* the act of coordinating an activity

cop /kɑp/ *noun, informal*

a police officer: *The cops came into the bar and stopped the fight.*

cope /koʊp/ *verb*

to be able to deal with a difficult situation without becoming too upset, worried, or angry: *When my parents got divorced, my mother didn't cope with the situation very well. She just yelled at us all the time.*

cop•i•er /ˈkɑpiɚ/ *noun*

a machine that quickly copies documents onto paper by photographing them SYNONYM **photocopier**

co-pi•lot /ˈkoʊˌpaɪlət/ *noun*

a pilot who helps the main pilot fly an airplane

cop•per /ˈkɑpɚ/ *noun*

an orange-brown metal: *Electrical wires are often made of copper.*

cop•y[1] /ˈkɑpi/ *verb* **copied**, third person singular **copies**

1 to make or write something that is the same as something else: *To copy a file, press F3.* | *He copied his friend's answers on the test.*

2 to deliberately do what someone else has done: *Other bands have copied our music.*

PHRASAL VERB

copy something down

to write down the exact words that are said by someone or written somewhere: *She copied down the homework assignment.*

copy[2] *noun* plural **copies**

1 something that is made to look exactly the same as something else: *She made a copy of the letter to send to her lawyer.*

2 one of many books, magazines, or newspapers that are exactly the same: *Do you have another copy of this book?*

cop•y•right /ˈkɑpiˌraɪt/ *noun*

the legal right to produce and sell a book, play, movie, or recording: *The university owns the copyright on the book, and it cannot be reproduced without the university's permission.*

cor•al /ˈkɔrəl/ *noun*

a hard substance under the ocean made from the bones of very small sea creatures: *Many fish live around the coral reef* (=large line of coral under the ocean).

cord /kɔrd/ *noun*

1 a piece of wire covered with plastic, used for connecting electrical or electronic equipment: *She unplugged the phone cord.*

2 a piece of thin rope: *a thin piece of nylon cord*

cor•du•roy /ˈkɔrdəˌrɔɪ/ *noun*

thick strong cotton cloth with raised lines: *brown corduroy pants*

core[1] /kɔr/ Ac *noun*

1 the central or most important part of something: *These four players are the core of the team. We would not win without them.*

2 the hard central part of a fruit such as an apple: *He ate the apple and threw the core away.*

3 the central part of the Earth or any PLANET: *The Earth's core is very hot.*

core[2] *adjective*

core things are the most important and basic ones: *All the students take four core classes. They must take these classes to graduate.*

cork /kɔrk/ *noun*

1 the light outer part of a type of tree, which is used for making things: *The bulletin board was covered in cork.*

2 a piece of this material that is put in the top of a wine bottle to close it

cork•screw /ˈkɔrkˌskru/ *noun*

a tool used for pulling corks out of bottles

corn /kɔrn/ *noun*

a tall plant with yellow seeds that you can cook and eat: *an ear of corn* (=the part on which the yellow seeds grow) | *We had corn on the cob* (=a cooked ear of corn).

→ See picture on page A12

corn·bread /ˈkɔrnbred/ *noun*
bread made from small pieces of dried corn

corned beef /ˌkɔrnd ˈbif/ *noun*
BEEF that has been put in salt water and SPICEs to preserve it

cor·ner /ˈkɔrnɚ/ *noun*
1 the point at which two roads, walls, edges, etc. meet: *Meet me on the corner of Main Street and Elm Street.* | *There was a TV in the corner of the room.* | *She lives around the corner from my house* (=in a street that joins the street where my house is).
2 see/watch something out of the corner of your eye = to see or watch something that is to the side, without turning your head: *Suddenly, out of the corner of my eye, I saw something coming toward me.*

corn·flakes /ˈkɔrnfleɪks/ *plural noun*
a breakfast food consisting of flat pieces made from corn which is eaten with milk

corn·y /ˈkɔrni/ *adjective, informal*
corny jokes, songs, movies, etc. are silly and very familiar: *Why do you keep playing those corny old love songs?*
→ See Thesaurus box at **funny**[1]

cor·po·ral /ˈkɔrpərəl/ *noun, written abbreviation* **Cpl.**
an officer with a low rank in the Army or Marines

cor·po·rate /ˈkɔrpərɪt/ Ac *adjective*
belonging to or relating to a corporation: *The company has moved its corporate headquarters* (=main office) *to Houston.*

cor·po·ra·tion /ˌkɔrpəˈreɪʃən/ Ac *noun*
a large business: *Large corporations can sell their products at lower prices than small businesses.*
→ See Thesaurus box at **company**

corpse /kɔrps/ *noun*
a dead human body: *The police found a corpse in the park and are now looking for the killer.* SYNONYM **body**

cor·rect[1] /kəˈrekt/ *adjective*
right or without any mistakes: *If you give the correct answer, you get one point.* | *He showed me the correct way to hold the baseball bat.* | *"Your name is Ives?" "Yes, that's correct."* SYNONYM **right**; ANTONYM **incorrect, wrong**
—**correctly** *adverb*: *Did I say your name correctly?*
→ See Thesaurus box at **right**[1]

WORD FAMILY look at the words:
→ **correct** *adjective*
→ **correct** *verb*
→ **correction** *noun*

C

correct[2] *verb*
1 to make something right or better: *Your eyesight can be corrected with glasses.*
2 to mark or fix the mistakes in something: *Our teacher was correcting the tests.*
3 to tell someone that what he or she has said or done is not right and tell them what is right: *Some of the things he said weren't true, but I didn't want to correct him.*

cor·rec·tion /kəˈrekʃən/ *noun*
a change that makes something right or better: *He made a few corrections to his test before he turned it in.*

cor·re·spond /ˌkɔrəˈspɑnd/ Ac *verb, formal*
1 if two people correspond, they write letters to each other: *They've been corresponding since they met on vacation last year.* SYNONYM **write**
2 to be like something else or be related to something else: *These numbers correspond to different computer files. Each file has its own number.*

cor·re·spond·ence /ˌkɔrəˈspɑndəns/ Ac *noun, formal*
1 a relationship or connection between two things: *There is a correspondence between each letter of the alphabet and the sounds it represents.*
2 letters that people send and receive: *These letters are my grandfather's correspondence with his family in Italy.*

cor·re·spond·ent /ˌkɔrəˈspɑndənt/ *noun, formal*
someone whose job is to report news for a newspaper or a television company: *She was a foreign correspondent for the Washington Post* (=she reported foreign news).

C

cor•re•spond•ing /ˌkɔrəˈspɑndɪŋ/ Ac *adjective, formal*
relating to or similar to something: *They gave her a more important job and a corresponding increase in pay.*
—**correspondingly** *adverb*

cor•ri•dor /ˈkɔrədɚ/ *noun, formal*
a passage between two rows of rooms in a large or important building: *He walked down the corridors of the old hospital.* SYNONYM **hall**

cor•rupt¹ /kəˈrʌpt/ *adjective*
a corrupt official is dishonest and uses his or her position wrongly, for money: *A corrupt police officer was protecting the drug dealer.*
—**corruption** /kəˈrʌpʃən/ *noun* the situation that exists when officials are corrupt: *There was a lot of government corruption. Many of the leaders received money from criminal groups.*

corrupt² *verb, formal*
to make someone dishonest or bad: *Power often corrupts people.*

cos•met•ics /kɑzˈmetɪks/ *plural noun*
substances that people use to make their faces more attractive: *She bought some lipstick and other cosmetics.*

cosˌmetic ˈsurgery *noun*
medical operations that some people have to make themselves look better: *She had cosmetic surgery to try to make herself look younger.*

cost¹ /kɔst/ *noun*
1 the amount of money you have to pay for something: *The high cost of health care is a problem for many families.* | *The MP3 player is now available at a cost of about $85.*

THESAURUS: cost

expense an amount of money that you spend on something: *Food was our main expense, because the camping place only cost a couple of dollars a night.*

price the amount of money you must pay for something: *House prices keep going up.*

charge the amount of money that you have to pay for someone to do something for you or to use something: *The books cost $49.50, and there's a mailing charge of $6.75.*

fee the amount of money you have to pay to go into a place or join something, or that you pay to a lawyer, doctor, etc.: *The membership fee is $325 a year.* | *Tuition fees* (=the money you pay to be taught at a college) *have gone up again.*

fare the amount of money you have to pay to travel somewhere by bus, airplane, train, etc.: *We got a good deal on the air fare.*

rent the amount of money you have to pay to live in or use a place that you do not own: *My rent is $1,200 a month.*

2 what is lost in order to get something else: *The costs of the war, measured in human life, were very high.*
3 at all costs/at any cost = used to emphasize that something must be done, even if it takes a lot of effort: *He likes to win at all costs, even if he has to cheat to do it.*

cost² *verb*
1 to have a particular price: *The book costs $15.* | *How much did that bag cost?*
2 to make someone lose something important: *His mistake cost him his life* (=he died because of his mistake).

co-star /ˈkoʊ stɑr/ *noun*
an actor's co-star in a movie, play, or television program is another actor who also has an important part in it: *She said she loved working with her co-star, Brad Pitt.*
—**co-star** *verb* to be one of the main actors that work in a movie, play, or television program

cost•ly /ˈkɔstli/ *adjective, formal*
1 costing a lot of money: *The medical treatment is very costly, and few people can afford it.* SYNONYM **expensive**
2 causing a lot of problems: *The team made some costly mistakes, and they lost by three runs.*

ˌcost of ˈliving *noun*
the amount of money you need to spend in order to buy the food, clothes, etc. that you need to live: *The cost of living is much higher in California than in Iowa.*

cos•tume /ˈkɑstum/ *noun*
special clothes that someone wears in order to look like someone or something else: *He wore a clown costume to the Halloween party.*

cot /kɑt/ *noun*
a narrow bed that folds up and can be stored in a small space

cot·tage /ˈkɑtɪdʒ/ *noun*
a small house in the country

ˈcottage ˌcheese *noun*
a soft wet white cheese

cot·ton /ˈkɑtn/ *noun*
1 cloth made from the cotton plant: *a cotton shirt* | *The dress was made of cotton.*
2 a plant with white threads around its seeds that are used for making cloth: *Cotton was an important crop in the southern part of the country.*

ˈcotton ball *noun*
a small soft ball made from cotton, used for cleaning skin

ˈcotton ˌcandy *noun*
sticky candy that looks like cotton threads: *The kids bought cotton candy at the fair.*

couch /kaʊtʃ/ *noun*
a long, comfortable seat that at least two or three people can sit on: *She was lying on the couch, watching TV.* SYNONYM **sofa**
➔ See picture at **seat**

ˈcouch poˌtato *noun, informal*
someone who spends a lot of time sitting and watching television

cou·gar /ˈkugɚ/ *noun*
a large brown wild cat from the mountains of western North and South America SYNONYM **mountain lion**

cough¹ /kɔf/ *verb*
if you cough, air suddenly comes out of your throat with a short rough sound: *The smoke made him cough.*

cough² *noun*
1 an illness that makes you cough a lot: *He had a bad cough and a runny nose.*
2 the sound made when you cough: *She gave a nervous cough before she spoke.*

could /kəd; *strong* kʊd/ *verb*
1 used when saying what someone was able to do or was allowed to do: *I could hear children laughing.* | *He said I could borrow his car.*
2 used when saying that something is possible or might happen: *He could be a great singer if he tried harder.* | *It could be difficult to find a good chef to replace him.*
3 could have = used when saying that something was possible, but did not actually happen: *She could have been killed.*
4 used when making a polite request: *Could I ask you a couple of questions?* | *Could you bring me back a cup of coffee?*
5 used when suggesting something: *We could have a barbecue.*

could·n't /ˈkʊdnt/ *verb*
the short form of "could not": *It was so funny. We couldn't stop laughing.*

could've /ˈkʊdəv/ *verb*
the short form of "could have": *He could've called and told me he was going to be late.*

coun·cil /ˈkaʊnsəl/ *noun*
a group of people who have been chosen to make laws or decisions: *The city council has approved plans for the new football stadium.*

coun·sel /ˈkaʊnsəl/ *verb, formal*
to help someone who has a problem by listening to him or her and giving advice: *He counsels students with personal problems.*
—**counseling** *noun* the activity of listening to someone and giving advice: *The center offers free counseling to anyone who is having problems with drugs.*

coun·sel·or /ˈkaʊnsəlɚ/ *noun*
1 someone whose job is to help people who have a problem, by listening to him or her and giving advice: *He discussed his future plans with a career counselor* (=someone who advises people about their careers).
2 someone, usually a young person, who takes care of a group of children at a camp

count¹ /kaʊnt/ *verb*
1 to find out how many things there are in a group: *We counted all the votes, and Maria is the new class president.*
2 to say numbers in the right order: *He's only three, but he can count to 50.*
3 to be important: *We won, and that's all that counts* (=nothing else is important). | *I felt my opinion didn't count for anything* (=wasn't important).
4 count me in/out *informal* = used for saying that you want to do something with other people, or that you do not want to do something with them: *Count me out – I'm too tired to go out tonight.*

PHRASAL VERB

count on someone or something
to depend on someone or something: *He's*

C

very nice. You can always count on him to help.

count² *noun*
1 the process of counting: *The teachers made a count of* (=counted) *all the children as they got on the bus.*
2 an amount that has been counted: *At last count, he's seen the movie six times.*
3 lose count = to forget a total when it keeps changing: *I've lost count of how many boyfriends she's had. There have been a lot.*
4 one of the crimes that the police say someone has done: *He was guilty on two counts of robbery.*

count·down /ˈkaʊntdaʊn/ *noun*
the period of time just before something happens, especially when someone counts backward until it happens: *The countdown to the launch of the space shuttle has begun.*

coun·ter /ˈkaʊntɚ/ *noun*
1 a flat surface in a kitchen where you can prepare food: *She washed the dishes and cleaned the kitchen counters.*
2 a flat surface where you pay or are served in a store, bank, restaurant, etc.: *The girl behind the counter took my order.*
➔ See picture on page A9

coun·ter·act /ˌkaʊntɚˈækt/ *verb, formal*
to reduce the bad effect of something, by having the opposite effect: *The drug can counteract memory problems in some people. They can get some of their memory back.*

coun·ter·at·tack /ˈkaʊntɚəˌtæk/ *noun, formal*
an attack that you make against someone who has attacked you
—**counterattack** *verb* to attack someone who has attacked you

coun·ter·clock·wise
/ˌkaʊntɚˈklɑk-waɪz/ *adjective, adverb*
in the opposite direction to the way the hands of a clock move: *Turn the lid counterclockwise.* ANTONYM **clockwise**

coun·ter·feit /ˈkaʊntɚfɪt/ *adjective*
made to look exactly like something else in order to trick people: *I called the police because the woman gave me a counterfeit 50-dollar bill.*
➔ See Thesaurus box at fake

count·less /ˈkaʊntləs/ *adjective, formal*
very many: *I had seen the movie countless times before, and I didn't need to see it again.*

coun·try /ˈkʌntri/ *noun* plural **countries**
1 a large area of land with its own government or ruler: *China is a huge country.* | *She has traveled to many foreign countries in her job.*

THESAURUS: country

nation a country, its people, and its government: *Rich nations should do more to help poor nations.*

state *formal* a country and its government – used to talk about a country as a political organization: *All the farms were owned by the state, rather than by the people who worked on them.*

land *formal* a country or place – used mostly in poetry and stories: *The people of America came from many lands.*

2 the country = areas that are not near towns and cities: *He had a house in the country.*

ˈcountry ˌmusic *also* **ˌcountry and ˈwestern** *noun*
popular music from the southern and western U.S.: *country singers such as Garth Brooks and LeAnn Rimes*

coun·try·side /ˈkʌntriˌsaɪd/ *noun*
land that is not near towns and cities: *We went for a drive through the Virginia countryside.*

coun·ty /ˈkaʊnti/ *noun* plural **counties**
a part of a state: *Orange County is one of the 58 counties in the state of California.*

coup /ku/ *noun, formal*
1 *also* **coup d'état** /ˌku deɪˈtɑ/ an occasion when a group of people suddenly take control of their country by force: *The president was forced out of office in a military coup* (=one done by soldiers).
2 an impressive achievement: *Winning the scholarship to Yale was quite a coup.*

cou·ple /ˈkʌpəl/ Ac *noun*
1 a couple *informal* = two, or a small number: *I waited for a couple of hours and then tried calling again.*
2 two people who are married or have a romantic relationship: *There was a young couple with a baby standing next to me.*

cou•pon /ˈkupɑn/ *noun*
a piece of paper that allows you to pay less money for something: *The coupon gives you 50 cents off a box of cereal.*

cour•age /ˈkɚɪdʒ/ *noun*
the quality of being brave: *He didn't have the courage to tell her she was wrong.* SYNONYM **bravery**
—**courageous** /kəˈreɪdʒəs/ *adjective* brave: *a courageous decision*
—**courageously** *adverb*

cou•ri•er /ˈkʊriɚ/ *noun*
someone whose job is to take documents and packages directly to people

course /kɔrs/ *noun*
1 of course a) used when something is not surprising: *Of course, she was really upset when she found out he'd been hurt.* **b)** used in order to say "yes" strongly: *"Are you going to watch the game?" "Of course!"*
2 of course not = used in order to say "no" strongly: *"Do you mind if I'm a little late?" "Of course not."*
3 a class in a particular subject: *He took a computer course.* | *a course in English literature*
4 one of the parts of a meal: *We had soup before the main course.*
5 an area where golf is played or races are held: *He spends too much time on the golf course.*
6 the planned direction taken by a boat or airplane to reach a place: *During the flight we had to change course to fly around a big storm.* | *The ship was blown off course* (=in the wrong direction).
7 a course of action *formal* = something you can do to deal with a situation: *The best course of action would be to tell the police.*
8 in/during/over the course of something *formal* = during a period of time or while something happens: *I learned a lot in the course of the interview.*

court /kɔrt/ *noun*
1 a place where legal judgments are made, or the people there: *a court of law* | *He had to appear in court as a witness.* | *She told the court that she was sorry for lying.* | *They refused to pay him, so he took them to court* (=made them be judged in a court).
2 an area made for playing a game such as tennis or basketball: *The players were practicing on the court.*
3 the place where a king or queen lives and works, or the people there

cour•te•ous /ˈkɚtiəs/ *adjective, formal*
polite: *People should show respect and be courteous to each other.*
—**courteously** *adverb*

cour•te•sy /ˈkɚtəsi/ *noun* plural **courtesies**
polite behavior: *She didn't have the courtesy to apologize, even though it was her fault.*

court•house /ˈkɔrthaʊs/ *noun*
a building containing courts of law and government offices

ˌcourt-ˈmartial *noun*
an occasion when a soldier is judged by a military court: *The soldier is facing a court-martial for being drunk while on duty.*
—**court-martial** *verb* if a soldier is court-martialed, he or she is judged by a military court

court•room /ˈkɔrtrum/ *noun*
a room where judgments are made by a court of law: *Everyone in the courtroom waited to hear what the jury would decide.*

court•yard /ˈkɔrtyɑrd/ *noun*
an open space surrounded by walls or buildings: *There are four houses built around a courtyard.*

cous•in /ˈkʌzən/ *noun*
a child of your aunt or uncle: *I usually see my cousins when we all go to my grandmother's house.*
→ See Thesaurus box at **family**

cov•er[1] /ˈkʌvɚ/ *verb*
1 *also* **cover up** to put something over something else: *She covered the child with a blanket.*
2 to be over the whole of a surface or thing: *The ground was covered with snow.*
3 to include or deal with something: *My literature class covered all the major writers.*
4 to report an event for a newspaper or a television or radio program: *A team of reporters will be covering the event.*

PHRASAL VERBS

cover for someone
1 to do someone's work because he or she is sick or is somewhere else: *I'll be covering for Sandra next week.*

C

2 to protect someone by lying: *Can you cover for me? Just say I had an appointment.*

cover something up
to prevent people from discovering something bad: *She tried to cover up her mistake.*

cover² *noun*
1 the outside of a book or magazine: *Her picture was on the cover of Vogue.*
2 protection from attack or bad weather: *The soldiers ran for cover when the shooting started.* | *As the rain started, we took cover* (=found protection) *under a tree.*
3 something that is used to cover something else: *a mattress cover*

THESAURUS: cover

lid a cover for a box, pot, or other container: *The water will boil faster if you put the lid on the pan.*

top the cover for a container or a pen: *He keeps leaving the top off the Coke bottle and putting it back in the fridge.*

wrapper paper or plastic that is around something you buy: *Don't throw the candy wrapper on the ground! Put it in the trash can.*

cov•er•age /ˈkʌvərɪdʒ/ *noun*
1 the way a news event is reported: *He criticized the media coverage of the trial – he didn't think reporters were telling the whole story.*
2 the protection your insurance gives you, so that you get money if you are injured, if something is stolen, etc.: *Some families have no health coverage* (=insurance which pays for medical care).

cov•er•ing /ˈkʌvərɪŋ/ *noun*
something that covers something else: *carpet and types of floor covering*

cov•ers /ˈkʌvɚz/ *plural noun*
sheets, BLANKETs, etc. that cover you when you are in bed: *She lay in bed and pulled the covers up to her chin.*

ˈcover-up *noun*
an attempt to prevent the public from discovering the truth about something: *There was a cover-up of the governor's illegal actions by his staff.*

cow /kaʊ/ *noun*
a large female animal that is kept on farms for its milk or meat: *There were cows eating grass in the field.*

cow•ard /ˈkaʊɚd/ *noun*
someone who is not brave at all: *The boys called him a coward because he wouldn't fight.*
—**cowardly** *adjective, formal* not brave: *He was too cowardly to complain.*
—**cowardice** /ˈkaʊɚdɪs/ *noun, formal* behavior that is not brave

cow•boy /ˈkaʊbɔɪ/ *noun*
a man whose job is to take care of cattle: *Two cowboys rode up to the ranch on their horses.*

cow•girl /ˈkaʊgɚl/ *noun*
a woman whose job is to take care of cattle

coy•o•te /kaɪˈoʊti/ *noun*
a small wild dog that lives in North America and Mexico: *We heard the howl of a coyote.*

co•zy /ˈkoʊzi/ *adjective*
a cozy place is small, warm, and comfortable: *a cozy little house*
—**cozily** *adverb*
—**coziness** *noun*

crab /kræb/ *noun*
a sea animal with ten legs and a flat shell: *Crabs usually have large front claws.*

crack¹ /kræk/ *verb*
to break something so that it gets a line on its surface: *I just cracked my favorite coffee mug.* | *The plaster on the walls had cracked.*
—**cracked** *adjective*: *a cracked mirror*
➔ See Thesaurus box at **break¹**

PHRASAL VERBS

crack down
to become more strict in dealing with a type of crime: *Police are cracking down on drunk drivers and making lots of arrests.*

crack someone up *informal*
to make someone laugh a lot: *She tells the funniest stories. She cracks me up.*

crack² *noun*
1 a thin line where something is broken: *There were cracks in the walls.*
2 a very narrow space between two things or two parts of something: *The letter had fallen through a crack between the floorboards.* SYNONYM **gap**

3 a sudden short loud noise: *I heard the crack of a rifle.*

4 **take a crack at (doing) something** *informal* = to try to do something: *I thought I'd take a crack at writing some songs to see if I was any good.*

➔ See Thesaurus box at **hole**

crack·down /ˈkrækdaʊn/ *noun*
an attempt to stop a type of crime by being more strict: *Most people support the police crackdown on drug dealing.*

crack·er /ˈkrækɚ/ *noun*
a thin hard piece of baked bread: *Do you want some cheese and crackers?*

crack·le /ˈkrækəl/ *verb*
to make a lot of short sharp noises: *There was a fire crackling in the fireplace.*
—**crackle** *noun* a series of short sharp noises: *the crackle of gunfire*

cra·dle /ˈkreɪdl/ *noun*
a bed for a baby, which can move from side to side: *She rocked the cradle* (=made it move from side to side), *until the baby was asleep.*

craft /kræft/ *noun*
a skilled activity in which you make something using your hands: *You can learn crafts such as sewing and woodworking.*

crafts·man /ˈkræftsmən/ *noun* plural **craftsmen** /ˈkræftsmən/
someone who is very skilled at making things with his or her hands: *The furniture was made by craftsmen from this area.*
—**craftsmanship** *noun* the skill of a craftsman

craft·y /ˈkræfti/ *adjective*
good at getting what you want using good plans or tricks: *I could tell from his crafty expression that he was planning something.*
—**craftily** *adverb*

cram /kræm/ *verb* **crammed, cramming**
1 to force a lot of things or people into a small space: *I managed to cram all my stuff into the tiny closet.*
2 **be crammed with something** = to be very full of things or people: *The garage was crammed with junk.*

cramp /kræmp/ *noun*
a bad pain that you get when a muscle becomes tight: *One runner got leg cramps and had to leave the race.*

cramped /kræmpt/ *adjective*
a cramped room or building is too small: *She wanted to move out of her cramped apartment to a bigger place.*

cran·ber·ry /ˈkrænˌberi/ *noun* plural **cranberries**
a small sour red fruit that grows on a bush: *We always have cranberry sauce with the turkey on Thanksgiving.*
➔ See picture on page A13

crane /kreɪn/ *noun*
1 a tall machine with a long metal arm for lifting heavy things: *There were two cranes at the construction site moving heavy metal beams.*
2 a water bird with very long legs

crash[1] /kræʃ/ *verb*
1 if a car or airplane crashes, it has an accident and hits something hard: *The plane crashed in the mountains.* | *He crashed his car into a tree.*
2 to hit something hard, making a loud noise: *A baseball crashed through our living room window.*
3 if a computer crashes, it suddenly stops working: *My computer crashed and I lost all of my homework.*
4 *informal* to sleep at someone's house instead of going to your own home: *It's late – can I crash here tonight?*
5 *informal* if you crash, you go to sleep very quickly: *I was so tired, I came home at 8:30 and crashed.*

crash[2] *noun*
1 an accident in which a car or airplane hits something hard: *He was killed in a plane crash.*
2 a sudden loud noise made by something falling or breaking: *The plate fell to the ground with a crash.*
3 an occasion when the value of STOCKs suddenly falls by a large amount: *a stock market crash*

crate /kreɪt/ *noun*
a large box used for carrying fruit, bottles, etc.: *a crate of wine bottles*

C

cra·ter /ˈkreɪtɚ/ *noun*

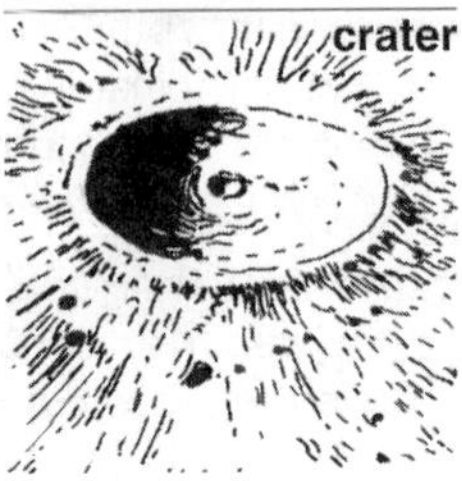

1 a large round hole in the ground made by a bomb or a falling rock: *There are large round craters on the moon that you can see from earth.*
2 the round hole at the top of a VOLCANO

crawl¹ /krɔl/ *verb*
1 to move along on your hands and knees: *The baby crawled toward his father.*
2 if an insect crawls somewhere, it moves there: *There were ants crawling all over the food.*
→ See picture on page A4

crawl² *noun*
the crawl = a way of swimming with your face down in which you move one arm up beside your head, and then the other

cray·on /ˈkreɪɑn/ *noun*
a stick of colored WAX that children use to draw pictures

craze /kreɪz/ *noun*
something that is very popular for a short time: *It's the latest fitness craze* (=popular way of exercising).

cra·zy /ˈkreɪzi/ *adjective* **crazier**, **craziest**
informal
1 not thinking or behaving in a sensible way: *He took all my money. I was crazy to trust him.* | *Whose crazy idea was it to go hiking in a snow storm?*
2 be crazy about someone or something = to like or love someone or something very much: *He's crazy about his new girlfriend.*
3 like crazy = very much or very quickly: *We've been working like crazy to get the job done.*
4 *informal* mentally ill: *She went crazy and started hearing voices that weren't really there.*

THESAURUS: crazy

mentally ill having an illness of the mind that affects the way you behave: *a hospital for people who are mentally ill*

insane *formal* seriously mentally ill: *A doctor said that Smith was insane at the time of the crime.*

nuts *informal* crazy: *Are you nuts? That will never work.*

—**craziness** *noun*

creak /krik/ *verb*
if something such as a door or wooden floor creaks, it makes a long high noise when it is moved or pressed: *The old door creaked as it opened.*
—**creak** *noun* a long high noise that something makes when it is moved or pressed
—**creaky** *adjective* a creaky door, floor, etc. creaks: *the creaky wooden stairs*
→ See picture on page A22

cream /krim/ *noun*
1 the thick part of milk, which is often used separately: *Do you take cream in your coffee?*
2 a yellowish-white color
3 a thick smooth substance that you put on your skin: *a jar of face cream*
—**cream** *adjective* having a yellowish-white color

ˈcream cheese *noun*
a type of soft white cheese: *I'll have a bagel with cream cheese, please.*

creamy /ˈkrimi/ *adjective*
1 having a yellowish-white color: *a creamy shirt*
2 thick and smooth like cream, or containing cream: *a creamy sauce*

crease /kris/ *noun*
a deep line on a piece of paper where it has been folded, on your skin, etc.: *There were deep creases in the old woman's face.*
—**creased** *adjective* having creases

cre·ate /kriˈeɪt/ Ac *verb*
to make something new: *How do I create a new file on my computer?* | *The changes to the system created a lot of problems.*
—**creator** *noun* the person who created something: *the creator of the TV series*

WORD FAMILY look at the words:

→ **create** *verb*
→ **creator** *noun*
→ **creative** *adjective*
→ **creation** *noun*
→ **creativity** *noun*
→ **creatively** *adverb*

→ See Thesaurus box at **invent**

cre·a·tion /kri'eɪʃən/ Ac *noun, formal*
1 the act of creating something: *This project will lead to the creation of 300 new jobs.*
2 something that has been created: *This dish is my own creation – I didn't have a recipe.*

cre·a·tive /kri'eɪtɪv/ Ac *adjective*
good at thinking of new ideas or making new things: *She's very creative. She designs all her own clothes.*
—**creatively** *adverb*
—**creativity** /ˌkrieɪ'tɪvəti/ *noun* the quality of being creative

crea·ture /'kritʃɚ/ *noun*
an animal, fish, or insect: *I try not to hurt any living creature.*

cre·den·tials /krə'denʃəlz/ *plural noun, formal*
someone's achievements, which prove that he or she has the ability to do something: *Only students with excellent academic credentials are accepted.*

cred·it[1] /'kredɪt/ Ac *noun*
1 praise given to someone for doing something: *You have to give her credit for trying.* | *I can't take all the credit – Nick helped a lot too.*
2 a way of buying things in which you pay for them later: *We bought the furniture on credit because we didn't have enough cash.*
3 a unit used to measure the amount of work completed at a college or university: *She needs 30 more credits to graduate.*
4 an amount of money that is put into someone's bank or other account: *A credit of $65 has been added to your account.* ANTONYM **debit**

credit[2] *verb*
1 to add money to a bank or other account: *The refund will be credited to your account by the end of the month.* ANTONYM **debit**
2 credit someone with (doing) something *formal* = to say that someone achieved something or has an ability: *James Watt is credited with inventing the steam engine.*

'credit card *noun*
a small plastic card that you use to buy things and pay for them later: *Can I pay with a credit card?*

cred·i·tor /'kredɪtɚ/ Ac *noun, formal*
a person or organization that you owe money to

cred·its /'kredɪts/ Ac *plural noun*
the credits = a list of all the people involved in making a television program or movie

creek /krik/ *noun*
a small river: *The boys went fishing in the creek.*

creep /krip/ *verb* **crept** /krept/
to move slowly and quietly: *I got up during the night and crept downstairs, trying not to wake anyone up.*

creep·y /'kripi/ *adjective, informal*
making you feel a little frightened: *"Dracula" is a really creepy movie.*

cre·ma·to·ri·um /ˌkrimə'tɔriəm/ *noun*
plural **crematoriums** or **crematoria** /ˌkrimə'tɔriə/
a building where the bodies of dead people are burned
—**cremate** /'krimeɪt/ *verb* to burn the dead body of a person
—**cremation** /krɪ'meɪʃən/ *noun* the act or ceremony of burning a dead body

cre·ole /'krioʊl/ *noun*
a language that is a mixture of a European language and another language: *The language that they speak is a creole. It's a mixture of French and African languages.*

crept /krept/ *verb*
the past tense and past participle of CREEP

cres·cent /'kresənt/ *noun, formal*
a curved shape like a thin moon, that is pointed on the ends: *The beach was a crescent of white sand.*
➔ See picture at **shape**[1]

crest /krest/ *noun, formal*
the top of a hill or a wave: *The crests of the waves were bright white in the sun.*

crev·ice /'krevɪs/ *noun, formal*
a deep crack in rock, the ground, etc.: *His foot got stuck in a crevice as he was climbing the mountain.*

crew /kru/ *noun*
1 the people who work on a ship or airplane: *The flight crew welcomed us onto the plane.*
2 a film/camera/TV, etc. crew = a group of people who work together making movies, programs, etc.: *A television camera crew*

C

was waiting outside the courthouse.
➔ See Thesaurus box at **group**[1]

crib /krɪb/ *noun*
a baby's bed with high sides: *Timmy slept in a crib until he was two.*

C

crick /krɪk/ *noun*
a sharp pain in your neck or back: *I have a crick in my neck and it hurts when I turn my head.*

crick•et /ˈkrɪkɪt/ *noun*
1 a small brown insect that jumps and makes a short high noise: *Outside at night, I could hear the crickets chirping* (=making this noise).
2 a game in which you hit a ball and run between two sets of sticks

cried /kraɪd/ *verb*
the past tense and past participle of CRY

cries /kraɪz/
the plural of CRY

crime /kraɪm/ *noun*
1 a bad act, that is not allowed by law: *Stealing is a crime.* | *You may go to jail if you commit a crime* (=do something that is not allowed by law).

THESAURUS: crime

Crimes that involve stealing things

theft the crime of stealing things: *Car theft is a serious problem in this area.*

robbery the crime of stealing something from a person, bank, store, etc.: *He went to prison for a bank robbery.*

burglary the crime of going into someone's home or a building in order to steal money or valuable things: *They stole all my grandmother's jewelry in the burglary.*

shoplifting the crime of taking things from a store without paying for them: *She was caught shoplifting in the grocery store.*

Crimes that involve attacking people

assault a crime in which someone uses violence against another person and hurts him or her: *After the fight, he was arrested for assault.*

mugging a crime in which someone is attacked and robbed in a public place: *Muggings are common, so you shouldn't walk by yourself.*

murder a crime in which someone is deliberately killed: *Lawyers are trying to prove that he committed the murder.*

2 things that people do that are not allowed by law: *There's no crime in this neighborhood. We don't even lock our doors at night.*
3 it's a crime *informal* = used when saying that something that happens is not good: *It's a crime to throw away all that good food.*

crim•i•nal[1] /ˈkrɪmənəl/ *adjective*
relating to crime: *Her son went to jail because he had been involved in some criminal activity.* | *the criminal justice system* (=the system of police, courts, etc. that catches and punishes criminals)

criminal[2] *noun*
someone who does something that is not allowed by law: *These dangerous criminals should stay in jail.*

crim•son /ˈkrɪmzən/ *noun, formal*
a dark red color
—**crimson** *adjective, formal* having a crimson color: *The plant has crimson flowers.*

cringe /krɪndʒ/ *verb*
1 to feel embarrassed by something or someone: *Sometimes Mom and Dad are so embarrassing that they make me cringe.*
2 to move away from someone or something because you are frightened: *He raised his hand to hit the dog, and the dog cringed.*

crip•ple /ˈkrɪpəl/ *verb*
if an accident or disease cripples someone, he or she cannot walk anymore: *He fell off a horse, and it crippled him for life.*

cri•sis /ˈkraɪsɪs/ *noun* plural **crises** /ˈkraɪsiz/
a time when a situation is very bad or dangerous and someone must deal with important problems: *The country is in an economic crisis: prices are rising and there are few jobs.*

crisp /krɪsp/ *adjective*
1 crisp food feels firm when you bite it: *I like crisp green apples.*
2 crisp air or weather is cold and dry: *In the mountains, the air was fresh and crisp.*
—**crispness** *noun* the quality of being crisp

crisp•y /ˈkrɪspi/ *adjective*
crispy food is pleasantly hard because it has been cooked or dried: *The chicken was crispy on the outside.*

cri·te·ri·a /kraɪˈtɪriə/ Ac *plural noun*
singular **criterion** /kraɪˈtɪriən/
a rule or standard that you use to make a decision or judgment: *The criteria for being able to vote are that you must be 18 years old and a citizen of the U.S.*

crit·ic /ˈkrɪtɪk/ *noun*
1 someone whose job is writing about music, movies, books, etc., and saying whether they are good or bad: *The critics loved the CD, and so did the public.*
2 someone who criticizes someone or something: *He was unable to satisfy all of his critics.*

crit·i·cal /ˈkrɪtɪkəl/ *adjective*
1 if you are critical, you think or say that something is bad: *Mrs. Watts is always really critical of my work – she finds every mistake.*
2 having an important effect on whether a situation goes well or badly: *The last year of high school is a critical time because students are preparing for college or work.*
3 in critical condition = very sick or very badly hurt, and likely to die: *She was taken to the hospital in critical condition.*

crit·i·cally /ˈkrɪtɪkli/ *adverb*
1 in a way that shows you think something is bad: *Mom looked at my new hair cut critically. "It's not the best cut," she said.*
2 critically injured/wounded = very badly injured and likely to die: *Two men were critically injured in the attack.*
3 *formal* used when emphasizing that something will have an important effect on whether a situation goes well or badly: *People are dying here, so food and medicine are critically important.*

criticism /ˈkrɪtəˌsɪzəm/ *noun*
1 things that you say are bad about someone or something: *Her criticism of my singing really hurt my feelings.*
2 things that someone writes about art, music, etc. to say whether it is good or bad: *a book of literary criticism*

crit·i·cize /ˈkrɪtəˌsaɪz/ *verb*
to say that someone or something is bad: *Everyone criticized the movie because it was not like the book.* ANTONYM **praise**

WORD FAMILY look at the words:
→ criticize *verb*
→ criticism *noun*
→ critical *adjective*
→ critic *noun*

croak /kroʊk/ *verb*
when a FROG croaks, it makes a low sound

croc·o·dile /ˈkrɑkəˌdaɪl/ *noun*
a REPTILE with a long body, thick skin, and a long mouth with many sharp teeth, that eats meat and lives in or near water

cro·cus /ˈkroʊkəs/ *noun*
a small purple, yellow, or white flower that appears in early spring

crois·sant /krwɑˈsɑnt/ *noun*
a type of small soft bread in a curved shape, that people eat for breakfast: *I'll have coffee and a croissant.*
→ See picture at bread

crook /krʊk/ *noun, informal*
a person who takes people's money in a dishonest way: *The car salesman was a crook. He told me the car was worth $5,000, but it was only worth $1,500.*

crook·ed /ˈkrʊkɪd/ *adjective*
1 not straight: *Do you think the picture over there looks crooked* (=is hanging in a way that is crooked)*?*
2 *informal* not honest in a way that involves taking other people's money: *Two crooked businessmen were put in jail for stealing money from their own company.*

crop /krɑp/ *noun*
1 a plant such as corn, wheat, etc. that farmers grow: *Most of the land is used for growing crops.*
2 a good/big/bumper, etc. crop = a large amount of corn, wheat, fruit, etc. that is produced in one year: *There was a bumper crop of apples last year and there were plenty of apples in the stores.*

cross[1] /krɔs/ *verb*
1 to go from one side of a road, river, etc. to the other: *Be careful when you cross the street.*
2 cross your legs/arms = to put one leg or arm over the other one: *Jack sat down and crossed his legs.*
3 cross your mind = if something crosses your mind, you think about it: *It suddenly*

C

crossed my mind that she might be sick or hurt, and I started to worry.
4 cross the line = to behave in a way that is beyond the limits of acceptable behavior: *The police crossed the line when they started hitting the prisoner.*

PHRASAL VERBS

cross something off (something)
to draw a line through something on a list because you have bought it, done it, etc.: *I bought bananas yesterday, so cross them off the list.*

cross something out
to draw a line through something you have written because it is not correct: *If you make a mistake, cross it out.*

cross² *noun*
1 an object that is used as a symbol of the Christian religion, with one part going across the other in the shape of a "t": *There was a gold cross on her necklace.*
2 a cross between something and something = something that is a mixture of one thing and another: *Her expression was a cross between pain and anger.*

ˌcross-exˈamine *verb*
to ask someone a lot of questions in a court of law after someone else has already asked questions: *Next, his lawyer cross-examined the first witness.*

cross•ing /ˈkrɔsɪŋ/ *noun*
1 a place where a railroad crosses a road: *Every railroad crossing is marked by lights and a warning bell.*
2 an act of crossing a border: *They built a wall on the border where the most illegal crossings happen.*
3 a place where you can cross a road, river, border, etc. safely or legally: *a pedestrian crossing* (=where people can walk across a road)

cross-leg•ged /ˈkrɔs ˌlegɪd/ *adjective, adverb*
if you sit cross-legged, you sit with each foot resting on the opposite leg: *We sat cross-legged on the floor.*

ˌcross-ˈreference *noun*
a note in a book telling you to look on another page for more information

cross•roads /ˈkrɔsroʊdz/ *noun* plural **crossroads**
a place where one road goes across another: *Stop at the crossroads, and look left and right.*

ˌcross ˈsection *also* **cross-section** *noun*
a group of people or things that includes a variety of different types: *Our research was based on a cross section of people of all ages.*

cross•walk /ˈkrɔswɔk/ *noun*
a place on a street that is marked with lines, so cars stop to let people cross: *Stay in the crosswalk when you cross the street.*
➔ See picture on page A26

cross•word puz•zle /ˈkrɔswɚd ˌpʌzəl/ *also* **crossword** *noun*
a game in which you write the correct words into a pattern of squares: *I always do the crossword puzzle in the newspaper.*

crossword puzzle

crouch /kraʊtʃ/ *also* **crouch down** *verb*
to bend your knees and lean forward, so your body is close to the ground: *Tom quickly crouched down, so that they would not see him.*
➔ See picture on page A4

crow /kroʊ/ *noun*
a large black bird with a loud cry

crowd /kraʊd/ *noun*
1 a large group of people: *A crowd gathered to watch the parade.*
2 *informal* a group of friends or people who are similar: *I went to the party with Brian and the rest of our crowd.*
—**crowd** *verb* to come together in a large group: *Thousands of baseball fans crowded into the stadium.*
➔ See Thesaurus box at **group¹**

crowd•ed /ˈkraʊdɪd/ *adjective*
full of people, cars, etc.: *In the summer, the streets are crowded with tourists.*

crown /kraʊn/ *noun*
a circle of gold and jewels that a king or queen wears on his or her head: *The king wore a gold crown on his head.*
—**crown** *verb* to put a crown on the head of a new king or queen in a special ceremony: *Louis was crowned king of France.*

cru•cial /ˈkruʃəl/ Ac *adjective, formal*
very important: *Eating fruits and vegetables is crucial to staying healthy.*
—**crucially** *adverb, formal*
➔ See Thesaurus box at **important**

cru•ci•fix /ˈkrusəˌfɪks/ *noun*
an object that shows Jesus Christ hanging on a CROSS: *There was a large crucifix at the front of the church.*

crude /krud/ *adjective*
1 offensive or rude, especially because of talking about sex: *crude sexual language*
2 *formal* not good or not of a high standard: *Thirty-five years ago, computer technology was crude.* ANTONYM **sophisticated**
3 *also* **ˈcrude oil** oil that is in its natural condition, as it comes out of the ground: *Saudi Arabia exports a lot of crude oil.*
—**crudely** *adverb, formal* if something is crudely drawn, built, etc., it is done without much skill and is not of a high standard: *Their houses were simple and crudely built.*

cru•el /ˈkruəl/ *adjective*
1 a cruel person is very unkind, or hurts people or animals: *I hate people who are cruel to animals.*
2 a cruel disease, punishment, etc. makes people suffer a lot: *The punishment seemed too cruel for the crime.*
—**cruelly** *adverb*: *The dog had been cruelly treated and was now afraid of people.*
—**cruelty** *noun* the act of hurting people or animals: *The military ruler was well-known for his cruelty.*

cruise[1] /kruz/ *noun*
a vacation on a large boat traveling on the ocean: *Have you ever been on a cruise in the Caribbean?*

cruise[2] *verb*
to move at a steady speed in a car, airplane, or boat: *We cruised along at 65 miles per hour.*

crumb /krʌm/ *noun*
a very small piece of bread, cake, etc.: *She finished the cake and brushed the crumbs off her skirt.*
➔ See Thesaurus box at **piece**

crum•ble /ˈkrʌmbəl/ *verb*
if something very old or dry crumbles, it breaks into pieces: *Many of the old stone walls are crumbling.*
—**crumbly** *adjective* breaking into small pieces easily: *Add a little water to stop the dough from becoming crumbly.*

crum•ple /ˈkrʌmpəl/ *also* **crumple up** *verb*
to crush paper or cloth and make it smaller: *Charlie crumpled the paper into a ball and threw it away.*

crunch[1] /krʌntʃ/ *noun*
1 a noise that sounds like teeth biting something hard, or feet on snow: *She bit into the carrot with a loud crunch.*
2 the time when a situation is so bad that you must do something to fix it or fail completely: *We're coming to the crunch at the end of the semester when we have to start studying really hard to pass our final exams.*

crunch[2] *verb*
1 to bite food that is hard so that it makes a noise: *Rob crunched an apple.*
2 to make a noise like someone walking on snow or rocks: *I heard boots crunching on the snow.*
—**crunchy** *adjective* crunchy food is firm and makes a noise when you bite it: *Vegetables should be fresh and crunchy.*
➔ See picture on page A22

crush /krʌʃ/ *verb*
to push down hard on something and break or damage it: *The tree fell and crushed the car.*
➔ See Thesaurus box at **press**[1]
➔ See picture on page A14

crust /krʌst/ *noun*
1 the outer part of bread, a PIE, etc.: *Cut the crust off the bread if it's burnt.* | *thick pizza crust*
2 **the earth's crust** = the hard layer on the surface of the Earth

C

crutch /krʌtʃ/ *noun*
a special stick that you can put under your arm to help you walk: *He was on crutches* (=using crutches) *after he broke his leg.*

cry¹ /kraɪ/ *verb* **cried**, third person singular **cries**
1 if you cry, tears come out of your eyes: *Sad movies always make me cry.*

> **THESAURUS: cry**
>
> **sob** to cry a lot in a noisy way: *When my mother died, my dad just sobbed.*
>
> **be in tears** to be crying: *We were all in tears as we said goodbye.*
>
> **weep** *formal* to cry a lot because you feel very sad: *My mother wept quietly as we drove away.*

2 *also* **cry out** to shout something loudly: *"Wait for me!" she cried.* | *The boy cried out for help.*
3 to make a loud sound because you are uncomfortable, frightened, etc.: *The baby's crying again.*

cry² *noun* plural **cries**
1 a loud sound you make when you are frightened, hurt, happy, etc.: *She gave a sudden cry of pain.*
2 a loud shout: *There was a cry of "Stop, thief!"*
3 a sound that some animals or birds make: *Outside, I could hear the cry of seagulls.*

cryp•tic /ˈkrɪptɪk/ *adjective, formal*
hard to understand: *The textbook was full of cryptic diagrams that the teacher didn't explain.*

crys•tal /ˈkrɪstl/ *noun*
1 high-quality glass: *The best wine glasses are made of crystal.*
2 a small shape that forms when a liquid becomes solid: *It was so cold that there were ice crystals on the window.*

cub /kʌb/ *noun*
the baby of some wild animals, for example a lion: *The mother tiger had four cubs.*

cube /kyub/ *noun*
1 a square object with six equal sides: *He put an ice cube in each glass.*
2 **the cube of something** = the number you get when you multiply a number by itself twice: *The cube of 3 is 27.*
—**cube** *verb* if you cube a number, you multiply it by itself twice: *2 cubed is 8* (=2 x 2 x 2 = 8).
➔ See picture at **shape¹**

cu•bic /ˈkyubɪk/ *adjective*
a cubic inch/centimeter/yard, etc. = a measurement of the amount of space inside something, which you get by multiplying its length by its height by its width: *The box is two feet high by three feet long by four feet wide, so it measures 24 cubic feet.*

cu•bi•cle /ˈkyubɪkəl/ *noun*
a small separate area in a room: *The office was divided into small cubicles, with a desk in each one.*

cu•cum•ber /ˈkyuˌkʌmbɚ/ *noun*
a long thin green vegetable, that you usually eat uncooked: *a tomato and cucumber salad*
➔ See picture on page A12

cud•dle /ˈkʌdl/ *verb*
to hold someone close to you, because you love them: *Robbie's mom cuddled him on the couch.*
—**cuddly** *adjective* soft, warm, and nice to hold: *a cuddly puppy*

cuddle

cue /kyu/ *noun*
a signal that it is time for someone to do something: *The actors were waiting for their cue to come on stage.*

cuff¹ /kʌf/ *noun*
1 the end of a sleeve on a shirt, dress, etc., where it fastens: *The button on my cuff has fallen off.*
2 a narrow piece of cloth that is turned up at the bottom of your pants
3 **cuffs** *informal* = another word for HANDCUFFS

cuff² *verb, informal*
to put HANDCUFFS on someone's hands: *Police cuffed the man's hands behind his back and put him in the police car.*

cul•prit /ˈkʌlprɪt/ *noun, formal*
someone who has done something wrong: *There was a burglary last night, and police are still looking for the culprit.*

cup

cult[1] /kʌlt/ *noun*
a small religious group with strange or extreme ideas and a strong leader who controls the group: *The members of the cult always dressed in red.*

cult[2] *adjective*
a cult movie, person, etc. is very popular among a small group of people: *The strange movie quickly became a cult favorite.*

cul•ti•vate /ˈkʌltəˌveɪt/ *verb, formal*
1 to grow crops and plants by preparing the land for them: *Most of the farmers cultivate rice.*
2 cultivate a skill/relationship/reputation, etc. = to work hard to develop a skill, relationship, etc.: *He tries to cultivate relationships with professors who can help him in his career.*
—**cultivation** /ˌkʌltəˈveɪʃən/ *noun* the act of growing crops by preparing the land for them: *The wet black soil is perfect for cultivation of many crops.*

cul•tur•al /ˈkʌltʃərəl/ Ac *adjective*
1 relating to a society and its way of life: *There are big cultural differences between the U.S. and Japan.*
2 relating to art, literature, music, etc.: *New York is the cultural center of the eastern U.S.*

cul•ture /ˈkʌltʃə/ Ac *noun*
1 the ideas and way of life of a society: *I love traveling and meeting people from different cultures.*
2 art, literature, music, etc.: *If you like culture, you should live in the city.*
WORD FAMILY → **cultural** *adjective*

ˈculture ˌshock *noun*
a feeling you sometimes get when you visit a foreign country and everything seems strange and confusing: *American travelers to Asia sometimes suffer from culture shock because there are so many differences.*

cup /kʌp/ *noun*
1 a small, round container with a handle, that you use for drinking tea, coffee, etc.: *Would you like a cup of coffee* (=some coffee in a cup)?
2 a measure of eight FLUID OUNCEs, used in cooking: *Stir in a cup of flour.*
3 *also* **Cup** a prize for winning in a competition, shaped like a bowl: *The Americans were expected to win the Gold Cup.*

cup•board /ˈkʌbəd/ *noun*
a piece of furniture with doors and shelves: *There wasn't much food in the kitchen cupboard.* SYNONYM **cabinet**
→ See picture on page A9

cup•cake /ˈkʌpkeɪk/ *noun*
a small cake for one person

curb /kəb/ *noun*
the edge of a SIDEWALK, where it joins the road: *A big black car was parked at the curb.*

cure /kyʊr/ *verb*
1 to make an illness better: *Many types of cancer can be cured.*
2 to find a way to stop something bad from happening: *It is impossible to cure the traffic problems in the downtown area.*
—**cure** *noun* a way of making an illness go away: *Scientists have still not found a cure for the disease.*
—**curable** *adjective* if an illness is curable, it is possible to make it go away: *The infection is curable.*

cur•few /ˈkəfyu/ *noun*
1 the time by which parents tell their children they must be home at night: *My curfew is 9:00 on school nights.*
2 the time after which the government makes people stay indoors: *There was more fighting, and the army imposed a curfew from 10 p.m. to 5 a.m.*

cu•ri•ous /ˈkyʊriəs/ *adjective*
wanting to know or learn about something: *Young kids are naturally curious about the world and eager to learn.*
—**curiously** *adverb*: *"What do you mean?" she asked, looking at him curiously.*
—**curiosity** /ˌkyʊriˈɑsəti/ *noun* the feeling of being curious: *Jack's eyes were wide with curiosity.*

WORD FAMILY look at the words:

→ curious *adjective*
→ curiously *adverb*
→ curiosity *noun*

C

curl[1] /kɚl/ *noun*
a piece of hair that grows in the shape of a circle: *The little girl had long blond curls.*
—**curly** *adjective* curly hair has many pieces that grow in the shape of circles: *My hair's straight, but Rosa's is curly.*

curl[2] *verb*
to make straight hair hang in the shape of a circle: *Do you think I should curl my hair?*
PHRASAL VERB
curl up
to lie or sit with your arms and legs close to your body: *She curled up under a blanket to watch TV.*

curl•er /'kɚlɚ/ *noun*
a small metal or plastic tube for making hair curl

cur•ren•cy /'kɚənsi/ Ac *noun* plural **currencies** *formal*
the type of money that a country uses: *The U.S. currency is the dollar.*
→ See Thesaurus box at **money**

cur•rent[1] /'kɚənt/ *adjective, formal*
the current situation, year, president, etc. is the one that there is now: *Who is the current president of the United States* (=who is president now)*?*

current[2] *noun*
a flow of electricity, water, or air: *A strong current pulled the swimmers out into the ocean.* | *The electric current flows along these wires.*

cur•rent•ly /'kɚəntli/ *adverb, formal*
at this time: *The school currently has about 2,000 students, an increase from last year.* SYNONYM **now**
→ See Thesaurus box at **now**[1]

cur•ric•u•lum /kə'rɪkyələm/ *noun* plural **curricula** /kə'rɪkyələ/ or **curriculums** *formal*
all of the subjects that are taught at a school, college, etc.: *Science is an important part of the school's curriculum.*

curse[1] /kɚs/ *verb*
1 to say or think bad and angry things about someone or something: *The car stopped working, and Mark cursed the man who had sold it to him.*
2 to say bad words that show you are angry: *The computer crashed again, and Kate cursed.* SYNONYM **swear**

curse[2] *noun*
1 magic words that are used to bring someone bad luck: *In the story, the witch puts a curse on the girl and says she will always be poor.*
2 a bad word or words that you say when you are angry: *Tom dropped his glass and whispered a curse.*

cur•sor /'kɚsɚ/ *noun*
a shape you can move on a computer screen that shows where you are writing: *Place the cursor at the place on the screen where you want to type.*
→ See picture on page A20

cur•tain /'kɚtn/ *noun*
a piece of cloth that you can pull across a window, stage, etc.: *The sun was shining in my eyes, so I closed the curtains.*
→ See picture on page A10

curve[1] /kɚv/ *noun*
a line that bends like part of circle: *The driver was going too fast when he came to a curve in the road, and the car rolled over.*

curve[2] *verb*
to bend or move in a curve: *The road curves around to the right.* SYNONYM **bend**
—**curved** *adjective* bending in a curve: *I drew a curved line on the page.*

cush•ion /'kʊʃən/ *noun*
a bag filled with soft material that you sit on or rest against: *Dad lay back against the sofa cushions.*
→ See picture on page A8

cus•to•di•an /kə'stoʊdiən/ *noun*
someone whose job is taking care of a public building: *The school's custodian often has to clean up the children's messes.* SYNONYM **janitor**

cus•to•dy /'kʌstədi/ *noun, formal*
1 the legal right to take care of a child: *They divorced, and Janet got custody of the kids.*
2 in/into custody = if someone is in custody, they are in prison until they go to court: *The police took two men into custody after the shooting.*

cus•tom /ˈkʌstəm/ *noun*
something traditional that people in a society do: *The custom of drinking tea was brought from China to Japan.*

cus•tom•er /ˈkʌstəmɚ/ *noun*
someone who buys things from a store or company: *Every day, the store serves about 800 customers.*
➔ See picture on page A15

cus•tom•ize /ˈkʌstəˌmaɪz/ *verb*
to change something to make it more useful for a particular person or purpose: *You can customize the T-shirt by adding your own picture.*

cus•toms /ˈkʌstəmz/ *plural noun*
a place where your bags can be searched when you leave or enter a country: *All travelers' baggage must go through customs.*
➔ See picture on page A30

cut¹ /kʌt/ *verb* **cut, cutting**
1 to divide something into pieces using a knife or scissors: *Do you want me to cut the cake?* | *First, cut the paper in half* (=into two pieces).

THESAURUS: cut

Cutting food

chop to cut meat or vegetables into pieces: *Chop the onion and add it to the pan.*

slice to cut bread, meat, or vegetables into thin pieces: *She sliced tomatoes for the salad.*

peel to cut the outside part off an apple, potato, etc.: *Peel the potatoes and boil them.*

carve to cut pieces from a large piece of cooked meat: *Dad started carving the turkey.*

grate to cut cheese, vegetables, etc. into very small pieces using a special tool with holes in it, that you rub the food against: *Grate the cheese over the macaroni.*

Cutting other things

saw to cut wood, using a saw (=a tool with a row of sharp points): *I sawed the board in half.*

chop to cut something such as a tree into pieces, using an ax: *Joe was chopping wood for the fire.*

mow to cut grass using a special machine: *I need to mow the lawn.*

trim to cut off a small amount of something to make it look neater, for example hair or a bush: *I got my hair trimmed on Saturday.*

2 to hurt yourself with a knife or something else that is sharp: *I cut my finger on some broken glass.*
3 to make hair, grass, etc. shorter: *I'm going to get my hair cut* (=by a hairdresser).
4 *also* **cut back/down (on) something** to reduce the amount of something: *You need to cut the amount of fat you eat.* | *Try to cut back on the hours you work, and get some rest.*
5 to remove writing or a picture from a computer document: *Now cut and paste the picture into the other document* (=cut it and move it into the other document).

PHRASAL VERBS

cut something down
to cut a tree and make it fall to the ground: *Too many trees are being cut down.*

cut something off
1 to stop the supply of electricity, water, etc. to a building: *For three days our electricity was cut off.*
2 to remove something from the main part with a knife or scissors: *Cut off all the dead flowers.*
3 if you are cut off when you are on the telephone, the telephone stops working: *I was talking to Mom on the phone, and I got cut off.*

cut something out
1 to remove something from inside something with a knife or scissors: *The kids were cutting pictures out of the magazine.*
2 to stop doing or eating something: *I'm trying to cut out chocolate.*
3 cut it/that out! *informal* = used for telling someone to stop doing something that is annoying you: *You're making too much noise. Cut it out!*

cut something up
to cut something into smaller pieces: *Can you cut up some onions?* SYNONYM **chop up**

cut² *noun*
1 an injury you get if something sharp cuts your skin: *She had a deep cut on her arm.*

C

2 a hole in something that you make with scissors, a knife, etc.: *Make a cut in the paper.*
3 *formal* the act of reducing the amount or number of something: *Everyone had to take a cut in pay, because the company was losing money.*
➔ See Thesaurus box at **injury**

cute /kyut/ *adjective*
1 if a baby, small child, or animal is cute, they are attractive to look at: *That little boy is so cute!*
2 sexually attractive: *That girl is really cute. Are you going to talk to her?*
—**cuteness** *noun*
➔ See Thesaurus box at **beautiful**

cut•ler•y /ˈkʌtləri/ *noun, formal*
knives, forks, and spoons SYNONYM **silverware**

cy•ber•space /ˈsaɪbɚˌspeɪs/ *noun*
the imaginary place that computer messages go to when they travel between computers: *The email invitation must be lost in cyberspace.*

cy•cle /ˈsaɪkəl/ Ac *noun*
a set of events that happen again and again in a pattern: *Life is a cycle of birth and death.* | *This class is studying the life cycle of butterflies.*
—**cyclic** /ˈsɪklɪk/ *also* **cyclical** *adjective, formal* happening again and again in a pattern: *the cyclical nature of the seasons*

cy•cling /ˈsaɪklɪŋ/ *noun*
the activity or sport of riding a bicycle: *My brother likes cycling better than baseball.*
➔ See picture on page A24

cy•clist /ˈsaɪklɪst/ *noun*
someone who rides a bicycle, especially in races: *More than 800 cyclists will compete in the 100 mile race.*

cyl•in•der /ˈsɪləndɚ/ *noun*
1 a long round shape or object, like a tube: *Cans are cylinders.*
➔ See picture at **shape**[1]
2 a part in an engine or machine, shaped like a tube: *The engine has six cylinders.*
➔ See picture on page A28
—**cylindrical** /səˈlɪndrɪkəl/ *adjective, formal* having a long round shape, like a tube: *The castle has four cylindrical towers.*

cym•bal /ˈsɪmbəl/ *noun*
a musical instrument made of thin metal, that you hit to make a sound
➔ See picture on page A21

cyn•ic /ˈsɪnɪk/ *noun, formal*
someone who never believes that people are good or that good things will happen: *Some cynics say that people only care about money.*
—**cynical** *adjective, formal* a cynical person is a cynic: *Since her divorce she's been very cynical about men.*

Dd

D /di/ *noun*
1 a GRADE that you get on a test or in a class for doing work that is not very good: *You got a D on the test – you'll have to study harder next time.*
2 the second note in the musical SCALE of C, or the musical KEY based on this note

'd /d/ *verb*
1 the short form of "had": *He'd eaten all the cake before anyone else had a piece.*
2 the short form of "would": *I'd love to come to the party.*

dab[1] /dæb/ *noun*
a small amount of something: *I like pasta with a dab of butter.*

dab[2] *verb*
1 *also* **dab at** to lightly touch something several times, especially with a cloth: *She started to cry and dabbed at her eyes with a tissue.*
2 to put a small amount of something on something else: *She dabbed some sun-screen on her cheeks.*

dachs•hund /ˈdɑkshʊnt/ *noun*
a small dog with short legs and a long body

dad /dæd/ *noun, informal*
another word for FATHER: *Mom and dad bought me a new computer.* | *Dad, can I borrow $20?*

dad•dy /ˈdædi/ *noun* plural **daddies**
a word for FATHER used by small children: *Where's Daddy?*

daf•fo•dil /ˈdæfəˌdɪl/ *noun*
a yellow flower that opens in the spring

dag•ger /ˈdægɚ/ *noun*
a short knife used as a weapon SYNONYM **knife**

dai•ly /ˈdeɪli/ *adverb, adjective*
every day: *Try to exercise daily.* | *Do you get a daily newspaper?*

dair•y /ˈderi/ *noun* plural **dairies**
1 a building where milk is kept and butter and cheese are made: *The dairy produces several types of cheese.*
2 *also* **dairy products** foods made from milk, such as butter, cheese, and yoghurt: *She doesn't eat butter or other dairy products.*

dai•sy /ˈdeɪzi/ *noun* plural **daisies**
a small white flower with a yellow circle in the middle: *The field was covered with daisies.*

dal•ma•tian /dælˈmeɪʃən/ *noun*
a white dog with black spots

dam

dam /dæm/ *noun*
a wall that is built to keep back the water in a river or the ocean: *The dam broke and water from the river flooded the town.*
—**dam** *verb* to stop a river from flowing by building a dam

dam•age[1] /ˈdæmɪdʒ/ *noun*
harm that breaks or destroys something: *The floods caused a lot of damage.*

damage[2] *verb*
to harm something, so that it is broken or destroyed: *Her car was badly damaged in the accident.*
—**damaging** *adjective* causing harm to something: *These chemicals are damaging to the environment.*

damp /dæmp/ *adjective*
a little wet: *His hair was still damp from the shower.*
—**dampness** *noun*

damp•en /ˈdæmpən/ *verb, formal*
to make something a little wet: *She went to the sink to dampen the cloth.*

dance[1] /dæns/ *verb*
to move your body to music: *Tom was dancing with a pretty girl.* | *People at the party were dancing to Brazilian music.*

—**dancer** *noun* someone who dances: *She's a really good dancer.*

dance² *noun*
1 an act of dancing: *He did a little dance to the music.*
2 a party where people dance: *Are you going to the school dance?*

D

dan•de•li•on /ˈdændəˌlaɪən/ *noun*
a small yellow flower that grows wild: *He used weed killer on the lawn to get rid of all the dandelions.*

dan•druff /ˈdændrəf/ *noun*
dry skin that comes off your head in very small white pieces: *She bought a new shampoo to stop her dandruff.*

dan•ger /ˈdeɪndʒɚ/ *noun*
a possibility that something bad will happen or you will be hurt: *The sign said "Danger of falling rocks." | Claire was scared – she knew she was in danger.*

THESAURUS: danger

risk the chance that something bad may happen: *Smoking increases the risk of lung cancer.*
hazard *formal* something that may be dangerous or cause accidents, problems, etc.: *The sidewalks were so broken up that they had become a safety hazard.*

WORD FAMILY look at the words:

→ **danger** *noun*
→ **dangerous** *adjective*
→ **dangerously** *adverb*
→ **endanger** *verb*

dan•ger•ous /ˈdeɪndʒərəs/ *adjective*
likely to harm someone: *Police say that the man has a gun and is dangerous.*
—**dangerously** *adverb*: *She was driving dangerously fast.*

dan•gle /ˈdæŋgəl/ *verb*
to hang down and swing from side to side: *A bunch of keys dangled from his belt.*

Dan•ish¹ /ˈdeɪnɪʃ/ *adjective*
from Denmark: *a Danish scientist*
—**Dane** *noun* someone from Denmark

Danish² *noun*
the language spoken in Denmark

dare /der/ *verb*
1 dare someone to do something = to say that someone must do something to show they are not afraid: *I dare you to jump!*
2 not dare (to) do something *formal* = to not be brave enough to do something: *Craig didn't dare tell his father what had happened.*
3 don't you dare (do something) *informal* = said when telling someone that they must not do something: *Don't you dare be late!*

dar•ing /ˈderɪŋ/ *adjective, formal*
if something you do is daring, it is brave or dangerous: *They made a daring escape over the mountains.*

dark¹ /dɑrk/ *adjective*
1 without light: *No one was home and the house was dark.* ANTONYM **light**
2 not light in color: *My favorite color is dark blue. | She has dark hair.*

WORD FAMILY look at the words:

→ **dark** *adjective*
→ **dark** *noun*
→ **darken** *verb*
→ **darkness** *noun*

dark² *noun*
a place or time with no light: *A lot of kids are scared of the dark. | I try to get home before dark* (=before night begins).

dark•en /ˈdɑrkən/ *verb, formal*
to become dark: *The sky darkened and rain began to fall.*

dark•ness /ˈdɑrknəs/ *noun*
the state of having no light: *He couldn't see his own hand in the darkness of the cave.*

dar•ling /ˈdɑrlɪŋ/ *adjective*
loved a lot, or easy to love: *He was a darling little boy.*
—**darling** *noun* used when speaking to someone you love: *Welcome home, darling.*

darn /dɑrn/ *verb*
to repair a hole in socks or other clothes by sewing: *I darned that hole in your sock.*

dart /dɑrt/ *verb*
to move suddenly and quickly: *A cat darted across the road.*

darts /dɑrts/ *noun*
a game in which you throw pointed objects at a board with numbers on it: *They played a game of darts in the basement.*

darts

dash¹ /dæʃ/ *verb*
to go somewhere very quickly: *She dashed into the bank just before it closed.*
➔ See Thesaurus box at **run¹**

dash² *noun*
1 a short fast run somewhere: *I made a dash for the house to get my umbrella when it started to rain.*
2 a dash of lemon/sugar/oil, etc. = a small amount of lemon, etc.: *Add just a dash of vinegar.*
3 a mark (–) used in writing to show a pause
4 a short running race: *He ran the 50-yard dash for the track team.*

dash•board /ˈdæʃbɔrd/ *noun*
the part of a car in front of the driver that has the instruments and controls on it
➔ See picture on page A28

da•ta /ˈdeɪtə/ Ac *noun*
information or facts: *The scientists are collecting data for their report.*

da•ta•base /ˈdeɪtəˌbeɪs/ *noun*
a large amount of information stored in a computer system: *The college has a database of students' names and addresses.*

date¹ /deɪt/ *noun*
1 a particular day of the month or year, shown by a number: *"What's today's date?" "It's August 11."* | *What's the date of the next meeting?* | *I need your full name and your date of birth* (=the day, month, and year you were born). | *Have you set a date* (=chosen a day) *for the wedding?*
2 to date = until now: *The movie has made $16.8 million to date.*
3 at a later date = at a time in the future: *You will be given more details at a later date.*
4 an arrangement to go to a restaurant, movie, etc. with someone you like in a romantic way: *Alison went out on a date with Mark on Saturday night.*
5 a small sweet brown fruit
➔ **out-of-date, up-to-date**
➔ See picture on page A13

date² *verb*
1 to write today's date on something: *He dated the letter May 14, 2006.*
2 to have a romantic relationship with someone: *How long have you been dating Mary?*
PHRASAL VERB
date from something *also* **date back to something**
to have existed since a particular time: *The law dates back to the 17th century.*

dat•ed /ˈdeɪtɪd/ *adjective*
no longer fashionable or modern: *That dress looks a little dated now.* SYNONYM **old-fashioned**

daugh•ter /ˈdɔtɚ/ *noun*
someone's female child: *She has two daughters and one son.* | *She was the daughter of a local farmer.*

ˈdaughter-in-law *noun* plural **daughters-in-law**
the wife of someone's son: *This is my daughter-in-law, Kim – she's my son Peter's wife.*

daunt•ed /ˈdɔntɪd/ *adjective, formal*
afraid or worried about something you have to do: *He felt daunted by all the work he had to do.*

daunt•ing /ˈdɔntɪŋ/ *adjective, formal*
frightening or worrying: *Being captain of the team can be daunting. There's a lot of responsibility.*

dawn /dɔn/ *noun*
the time of day when light first appears: *The sun woke me up at dawn.* SYNONYM **daybreak, sunrise**; ANTONYM **dusk**

day /deɪ/ *noun*
1 a period of time equal to 24 hours. There are seven days in a week: *We spent three days in Paris.* | *The letter arrived two days ago.* | *"What day is it today?" "Tuesday."* | *I saw her the day before yesterday.* | *We're leaving for Arizona the day after tomorrow.* | *The next day he went swimming.* | *I saw Tim the other day* (=a few days before now).
2 the time when it is light, between morning and night: *It was a sunny day.* ANTONYM **night**

WORD FAMILY look at the words:

→ day *noun*
→ daily *adjective*
→ daily *adverb*
→ midday *noun*

day·break /ˈdeɪbreɪk/ *noun, formal*
the time of day when light first appears: *They got ready in the dark and left at daybreak.* SYNONYM **dawn, sunrise**; ANTONYM **dusk**

day·care /ˈdeɪker/ *noun*
a place that takes care of young children during the day when their parents are at work: *My kids are in daycare three days a week while I work.*

day·dream /ˈdeɪdrim/ *verb*
to think about nice things so that you forget what you should be doing: *She was daydreaming about her boyfriend when the teacher called her name.*
—**daydream** *noun* thoughts about nice things that make you forget what you should be doing
—**daydreamer** *noun* someone who daydreams when he or she should be working

day·light /ˈdeɪlaɪt/ *noun*
the light that comes from the sun during the day: *He opened the curtains to let the daylight into the room.*

day·time /ˈdeɪtaɪm/ *noun*
the part of the day when it is light: *I can't sleep in the daytime – the sun and noise outside keep me awake.* ANTONYM **nighttime**

daze /deɪz/ *noun*
in a daze = unable to think clearly, for example because you are hurt or very surprised: *When I heard I'd won the $100,000 prize, I just sat there in a daze.*

dazed /deɪzd/ *adjective*
unable to think clearly, for example because you are hurt or very surprised: *He had fallen off his bike, and he looked a little dazed.*

daz·zle /ˈdæzəl/ *verb*
to make someone admire someone or something a lot: *We were dazzled by her talent and charm.*

daz·zling /ˈdæzlɪŋ/ *adjective*
1 very impressive and attractive: *The dancers gave a dazzling performance.*
2 a dazzling light is so bright that you cannot see clearly for a short time: *the dazzling sun*

DC *noun*
direct current the type of electric current that comes from batteries (BATTERY)

D.C. *abbreviation*
District of Colombia the area containing the city of Washington, the CAPITAL of the U.S.

dead[1] /ded/ *adjective*
1 no longer alive: *Her mother is dead.* | *She found a dead body* (=a dead person) *in the woods.*
2 a machine or piece of equipment that is dead is not working because there is no power: *The car engine is completely dead.* | *a dead battery*
3 complete or exact: *There was dead silence. Even the baby was quiet.* | *Hit the nail dead center* (=exactly in the center) *so it doesn't bend.*

dead[2] *adverb*
1 *informal* very: *I'm dead tired.*
2 exactly: *Do you see it now? It's dead ahead* (=exactly in front of you).

dead[3] *noun, formal*
1 the dead = people who are dead: *Today is a day when we remember the dead.* ANTONYM **the living**
2 in the dead of winter/night = in the middle of winter or in the middle of the night

dead end

ˌdead end *noun*
1 a street with no way out at one end: *We live on a dead end, so there's not much traffic.*
2 a situation from which no progress is possible: *The discussions reached a dead end because the two groups couldn't agree.*

dead·line /ˈdedlaɪn/ *noun*
a date or time by which you must finish something: *The deadline is Wednesday, but I'm going to finish before then.*

dead·ly /ˈdedli/ *adjective*
something that is deadly can kill you: *Hundreds of thousands of people have been killed by the deadly virus.*

deaf /def/ *adjective*
not able to hear: *He was born deaf and learned sign language as a child.* | *a school for the deaf* (=deaf people)
—**deafness** *noun*

deaf•en /ˈdefən/ *verb, formal*
to be so loud that it becomes difficult for people to hear: *The noise of the explosion deafened us.*
—**deafening** *adjective, formal*: *a deafening bang*

deal¹ /dil/ *noun*
1 an agreement, especially in business or politics: *They made a deal to sell the land to the city.*
2 a great deal/a good deal = a large quantity or amount: *The students have learned a great deal.*
3 the way someone is treated: *All we want is a fair deal* (=to be treated fairly).
4 the process of giving out cards to players in a card game: *It's your deal.*
5 (no) big deal *informal* = used to show that you do not think something is very important: *So you lost one game. That's no big deal.*
6 make a big deal out of something *informal* = to make something seem more important than it really is: *He had a tiny cut on his arm, and he was making a big deal out of it.*

deal² *also* **deal out** *verb* **dealt** /delt/
to give cards to each player in a card game: *I began dealing out the cards.*
PHRASAL VERBS
deal in something
to buy and sell a particular product: *The store deals in jewelry.*
deal with someone/something
1 if you deal with a problem, you do something to make sure the problem no longer exists: *We have to find new ways to deal with the problem of pollution.*
2 if a book, movie, play, etc. deals with a particular subject, it is about that subject: *This book deals with the subjects of love and family.*
3 to do business with someone: *We've been dealing with their company for ten years.*

deal•er /ˈdilɚ/ *noun*
1 someone who buys and sells a particular kind of thing: *An experienced car dealer sold us the van.* | *an art dealer*
2 the person who gives out the cards in a card game
—**dealership** *noun* a business that sells a particular company's product, especially cars: *We bought our car at a local car dealership.*

dealt /delt/ *verb*
the past tense and past participle of DEAL

dean /din/ *noun*
a university or college official with a high rank: *Ms. Thompson is the Dean of the Business School.*

dear¹ /dɪr/
oh dear = said when something bad has happened: *Oh dear! We're going to be late.*

dear² *noun*
used when speaking to someone you like or love: *Thank you, dear.*

dear³ *adjective*
1 Dear = used before someone's name or title to begin a letter: *Dear Sue, Thank you for the present.* | *Dear Dr. Ward: I'm writing to ask you for some advice.*
2 *formal* a dear friend or relative is very important to you and you love them very much: *Mark became a dear friend.*

death /deθ/ *noun*
1 the end of someone's life: *The sudden death of his mother was a terrible shock.* | *Heart disease is the most common cause of death in the U.S.* ANTONYM **birth**
2 scared to death/bored to death *informal* = very scared or bored: *She was scared to death when she saw the snake.*

ˈdeath ˌpenalty *noun*
the legal punishment of being killed for a serious crime: *He got the death penalty for killing a police officer.*

de•bat•a•ble /dɪˈbeɪtəbəl/ Ac *adjective, formal*
something that is debatable is not certain because people have different opinions about it: *It's debatable whether this book is as good as the last one she wrote.*

de•bate¹ /dɪˈbeɪt/ Ac *noun, formal*
1 discussion of a subject that often continues for a long time and in which people express different opinions: *There has been a lot of debate in the newspapers about the new law – a lot of people support it, but many oppose it.*

2 a formal discussion of a subject in which people take turns expressing different opinions: *He took part in a college debate on gun control.*

debate² *verb, formal*
1 to think about something carefully before making a decision: *I'm still debating what to do. I just can't decide.*
2 to discuss a subject formally so that you can make a decision or solve a problem: *The Senate will debate the bill Monday before taking a vote.*

deb•it /ˈdebɪt/ *noun, formal*
an amount of money that is taken out of your bank account: *Your bank statement shows all your debits and credits.* ANTONYM **credit**
—**debit** *verb* to take money out of your bank account: *$25 has been debited from your account.*

de•bris /dɪˈbri/ *noun, formal*
the pieces of something that are left after it has been destroyed in an accident, explosion, etc.: *The street was full of debris after the explosion.*

debt /det/ *noun*
money that a person or organization owes: *Because of my student loans, I am $20,000 in debt* (=I owe $20,000). | *He has paid back all his debts.*

debt•or /ˈdetɚ/ *noun, formal*
someone who owes money

de•but /deɪˈbyu/ *noun, formal*
the first time that an actor, sports player, etc. performs in public: *He made his debut as a movie actor in 1995, and he has appeared in many movies since then.*

dec•ade /ˈdekeɪd/ Ac *noun*
a period of ten years: *The building is now four decades old* (=40 years old).

de•caf•fein•at•ed /diˈkæfəˌneɪtəd/ *also* **de•caf** /ˈdikæf/ *adjective, informal*
decaffeinated drinks do not contain CAFFEINE: *I drink decaffeinated coffee because caffeine makes me nervous.*

de•cay¹ /dɪˈkeɪ/ *verb*
1 if something decays, natural chemical processes slowly destroy it: *The dead animal had started to decay.*
2 *formal* if buildings, structures, or areas decay, their condition slowly becomes worse: *The old hospital has been empty for years and is starting to decay.*

decay² *noun, formal*
the process of decaying: *Sugar causes tooth decay.*

de•ceased /dɪˈsist/ *adjective, formal*
dead: *She still spoke often about her deceased husband.*

de•ceit /dɪˈsit/ *noun, formal*
behavior that makes someone believe something that is not true: *I will never forgive her for her deceit and lies.*
—**deceitful** *adjective* someone who is deceitful tells lies
—**deceitfully** *adverb*: *She acted deceitfully by lying about her age.*

de•ceive /dɪˈsiv/ *verb, formal*
to make someone believe something that is not true: *He deceived her by saying he was a millionaire, even though he had no money at all.*

WORD FAMILY look at the words:

→ **deceive** *verb*
→ **deception** *noun*
→ **deceit** *noun*
→ **deceitful** *adjective*
→ **deceptive** *adjective*

→ See Thesaurus box at **lie²**

De•cem•ber /dɪˈsembɚ/ *noun, written abbreviation* **Dec.**
the 12th month of the year, between November and January: *Her birthday is on December 6.* | *They got married in December.* | *We went to Mexico last December.* | *We're going to Tucson next December.*

de•cen•cy /ˈdisənsi/ *noun*
polite and morally good behavior that shows respect for other people: *I try to treat all my students with respect and decency.*

de•cent /ˈdisənt/ *adjective*
1 acceptable and good enough: *Everyone should have a decent education.*
2 decent people are good and honest: *He is a decent, caring man.*

de•cent•ly /ˈdisəntli/ *adverb*
1 in a way that is acceptable and good enough: *I don't need a lot of money, just a decently paid job.*
2 in a way that treats people fairly and kindly: *He's always treated me decently, so I can't complain.*

de•cep•tion /dɪ'sepʃən/ *noun*
the act of deliberately making someone believe something that is not true: *His lies and deception hurt his family deeply.*

de•cep•tive /dɪ'septɪv/ *adjective, formal*
1 something that is deceptive seems to be one thing, but is in fact very different: *Some snakes move with deceptive speed* (=move faster than you think or expect).
2 something that is deceptive makes people believe something that is not true: *Don't believe the ads you see on TV. They can be very deceptive.*
—**deceptively** *adjective*

de•cide /dɪ'saɪd/ *verb*
1 to choose what you are going to do after thinking about it: *I decided to stay home instead of going to the movie.* | *Ted decided (that) the car would cost too much.* | *He can't decide what to do.*

THESAURUS: decide

make up your mind *informal* to decide something, after thinking about it for a long time: *Have you made up your mind about which college you want to go to?*

choose to decide which things you want out of a number of them: *I let the kids choose their own clothes.*

resolve *formal* to decide to do something in a determined way: *She had resolved to work hard and not disappoint her parents.*

2 to be the reason why something has a particular result: *One goal decided the game, and we won by a point.*

PHRASAL VERB
decide on something
to choose one thing from many possible choices: *Have you decided on a name for the baby?*

WORD FAMILY look at the words:

→ **decide** *verb*
→ **decision** *noun*
→ **decisive** *adjective*
→ **indecisive** *adjective*

dec•i•mal[1] /'desəməl/ *noun*
the part of a number which comes after the mark (.) and is less than one: *The numbers 0.5 and 0.178 are decimals.*

decimal[2] *adjective, formal*
based on the number ten: *We count using a decimal counting system: 10, 20, 30, etc.*

ˌdecimal 'point *noun*
the mark (.) before a decimal

de•ci•sion /dɪ'sɪʒən/ *noun*
a choice that you make: *He chose to be a doctor instead of a businessman. I think he made the right decision.*

de•ci•sive /dɪ'saɪsɪv/ *adjective, formal*
1 good at making decisions quickly: *A manager needs to be a decisive leader.* ANTONYM **indecisive**
2 an action, event, etc. that is decisive has a big effect on the way that something develops: *It was the decisive battle in the war. Two months later, the war ended.*
—**decisively** *adverb*

deck /dek/ *noun*
1 a set of playing cards: *a deck of cards*
2 a wooden floor built out from the back of a house: *We had a picnic on the deck behind the house.*
3 one of the levels on a ship, especially the one where you can walk or sit outside: *Let's go up on deck and look at the ocean.*

dec•la•ra•tion /ˌdekləˈreɪʃən/ *noun, formal*
an official or serious statement about something: *Congress has the power to make a declaration of war.* | *a declaration of love*

de•clare /dɪ'kler/ *verb, formal*
to say officially what will happen or what you have decided: *The U.S. declared war on England in 1812.* | *Doctors declared that he died of natural causes.*

de•cline[1] /dɪ'klaɪn/ Ac *verb, formal*
1 to become weaker, smaller, or less good: *Her health declined rapidly, and she died two weeks later.*
2 to say no to an invitation, offer, or request, usually politely: *Mary declined Jay's invitation to dinner.*
→ See Thesaurus boxes at **decrease**[1] and **reject**

decline[2] *noun, formal*
a situation in which something becomes weaker, smaller, or less good: *There has been a decline in the company's profits since last year, and the company is going to lay off workers.*

de·com·pose /ˌdikəm'poʊz/ *verb, formal*
to be slowly destroyed by a natural process: *The meat had started to decompose.*
—**decomposition** /ˌdikɑmpə'zɪʃən/ *noun, formal* the process of decomposing

de·con·tam·i·nate /ˌdikən'tæməˌneɪt/ *verb, formal*
to remove a dangerous substance from somewhere: *The company is working to decontaminate the polluted river.*
—**decontamination** /ˌdikənˌtæmə'neɪʃən/ *noun, formal* the process of decontaminating something

dec·o·rate /'dekəˌreɪt/ *verb*
1 to make something look more attractive by adding pretty things to it: *We decorated the Christmas tree.*
2 *formal* to give someone an official sign of honor, such as a MEDAL: *The soldiers were decorated for their bravery.*
—**decorative** /'dekərətɪv/ *adjective, formal* pretty and used to make something look more attractive: *a decorative vase*

dec·o·ra·tion /ˌdekə'reɪʃən/ *noun*
a pretty thing that you use to make something look more attractive: *We put Halloween decorations like pumpkins and ghosts in the yard.*

de·crease¹ /dɪ'kris/ *verb*
to become smaller in number, amount, size, etc., or to make something do this: *Computer prices decreased last year, so I decided to buy a new one.* ANTONYM **increase**

THESAURUS: decrease

go down to become lower or less in level, amount, size, quality, etc.: *The price of computers has gone down.*
drop to become lower in level or amount: *Sales have dropped 15% this year.*
fall to decrease to a lower level or amount: *Temperatures fell below zero last night.*
plummet to suddenly and quickly become lower: *Sales of the car have plummeted.*
diminish *formal* to become smaller or less important: *The country's financial problems have increased rather than diminished.*
decline *formal* to become smaller or weaker: *The number of babies born in Western countries has declined.*

➔ See Thesaurus box at **reduce**

de·crease² /'dikris/ *noun*
the process of becoming less, or the amount by which something becomes less: *There has been a recent decrease in crime.* ANTONYM **increase**

de·crep·it /dɪ'krepɪt/ *adjective, formal*
old and in bad condition: *The buildings were old and decrepit.*

ded·i·cate /'dedəˌkeɪt/ *verb*
1 if you dedicate a book, movie, song, etc. to someone, you say publicly that you wrote it to show how much you love and respect him or her: *The book was dedicated to her husband.*
2 dedicate your life/yourself, etc. to something = to give all your attention and effort to one thing: *He dedicated his life to helping other people.*

ded·i·cat·ed /'dedəˌkeɪtɪd/ *adjective, formal*
someone who is dedicated works very hard at something because it is important to them: *Our teacher is very dedicated. She always stays after school to help us.*

ded·i·ca·tion /ˌdedə'keɪʃən/ *noun, formal*
a situation in which you work very hard because you believe that what you are doing is important: *I admire his dedication to the job. He never quits until the work is finished.*

de·duct /dɪ'dʌkt/ [Ac] *verb, formal*
to take an amount away from a larger amount: *Taxes are deducted from your pay.*
—**deductible** *adjective* a deductible amount of money is one that you can take away from the amount of money you must pay taxes on
—**deduction** /dɪ'dʌkʃən/ *noun* the process of taking an amount away from a larger amount, or the amount that is taken away: *I earn about $2,000 a month, after deductions.*

deed /did/ *noun, formal*
1 an action, especially if it is very good or very bad: *She was well known for her good deeds, such as giving money to the poor.*
2 an official agreement that says who owns property: *She had the deed to the land, so no one could take it from her.*

deep¹ /dip/ *adjective*

1 if something is deep, there is a long distance between the top and the bottom: *The path was covered in deep snow.* | *a deep lake* ANTONYM **shallow**

2 used for talking about the distance from the top to the bottom of something: *The pool is three feet deep.*

3 going far in from the outside or from the front edge of something: *Terry had a deep cut in his forehead.*

4 a deep feeling or belief is very strong: *It was clear that he felt a deep love for his children.*

5 a deep sound is very low: *The old man had a deep voice.*

6 a deep color is dark and strong: *The bush has red berries and deep green leaves.* ANTONYM **light, pale**

7 serious and often difficult to understand: *The two professors were having a deep conversation about philosophy.*

8 deep sleep = if someone is in a deep sleep, it is difficult to wake him or her

9 be in deep trouble *informal* = to be in serious trouble or in an extremely difficult situation: *You're going to be in deep trouble when I tell Mom what you did.*

10 deep in thought/conversation, etc. = thinking or talking so much that you do not notice anything else: *I was deep in thought and didn't hear her when she said "hello."*

deep² *adverb*

a long way into or below the surface of something: *Some bones were hidden deep beneath the ground.* | *These fish live deep in the ocean.*

deep·en /ˈdipən/ *verb, formal*

if a serious situation deepens, it becomes worse: *Over the next few months, Carla's problems deepened, and she became more and more unhappy.*

ˈdeep freeze *noun*

a large metal box in which food can be stored at very low temperatures for a long time SYNONYM **freezer**

ˈdeep-fry *also* **deep fry** *verb*

to cook food in a lot of hot oil: *Add the oil and deep-fry the potatoes.*
—**deep-fried** *adjective*: *deep-fried chicken*

deep·ly /ˈdipli/ *adverb, formal*

extremely or very much: *I was deeply sorry to hear that your sister had died.*

deer /dɪr/ *noun* plural **deer**

a large wild animal that lives in the forest, eats plants, can run fast, and has long thin legs and a short tail: *Male deer have large horns called antlers.*

de·fault¹ /dɪˈfɔlt/ *noun*

1 by default = if you win a game, competition, etc. by default, you win because your opponent did not play or there were no other competitors: *The other team didn't show up, so we won by default.*

2 the thing or things your computer will use unless you tell it to use something else: *Green is the default, but you can change the color if you want.*

3 *formal* the action of defaulting on a legal agreement: *The default of a loan can lead to legal problems.*

default² *verb, formal*

to fail to pay back money that you owe or to do something you are legally supposed to do: *He defaulted on his loan payments, and the bank took his car.*

de·feat¹ /dɪˈfit/ *verb, formal*

to beat someone in a game, war, election, etc.: *She has already defeated some very good players.*
→ See Thesaurus box at **win¹**

defeat² *noun, formal*

a time when you do not win or succeed: *Our football team has only had one defeat in the last ten games.* SYNONYM **loss**; ANTONYM **victory**

D

de•fect[1] /ˈdifekt/ *noun, formal*
a problem in the way something is made, so that it does not work correctly: *There was a defect in the car's engine that caused the fire.* | *The chemical can cause birth defects* (=physical problems that babies are born with).

de•fect[2] /dɪˈfekt/ *verb*
to leave your own country or group and go to an opposing one: *His parents defected to the U.S. from Russia.*
—**defector** *noun* someone who defects
—**defection** /dɪˈfekʃən/ *noun* the act of defecting

de•fec•tive /dɪˈfektɪv/ *adjective, formal*
a defective machine, product, etc. has a problem, so that it does not work correctly: *The microwave was defective, so I took it back to the store.*

de•fend /dɪˈfend/ *verb*
1 to protect someone or something from attack: *We have the right to defend ourselves from people who try to hurt us.*
2 to say something to show you support someone or something that has been criticized: *The mayor defended his plan to raise taxes.*
—**defender** *noun* someone who defends someone or something

WORD FAMILY look at the words:
→ **defend** *verb*
→ **defense** *noun*
→ **defender** *noun*
→ **defensive** *noun*
→ **defensive** *adjective*

de•fend•ant /dɪˈfendənt/ *noun, formal*
the person in a court of law who, according to someone else, did something illegal: *This evidence proves that the defendant is guilty.*

de•fense /dɪˈfens/ *noun*
1 something that you do to protect someone or something from attack or criticism: *She wrote to the newspaper in defense of our plan.*
2 the weapons, people, and systems that a country uses to protect itself from attack: *The country needs a strong defense to protect itself from its enemies.*
3 /ˈdifens/ the players on a sports team whose job is to try to prevent the other team from scoring points: *Our defense did a good job – the other team only scored 12 points.*
4 the defense = the people in a court of law who are trying to show that someone is not guilty of a crime: *It will be hard for the defense to prove that he is not guilty.*

de•fense•less /dɪˈfensləs/ *adjective, formal*
unable to protect yourself from being hurt or criticized: *How could she hit a defenseless child?*

de•fen•sive[1] /dɪˈfensɪv/ *adjective*
1 behaving in a way that shows you think you are being criticized: *She got really defensive when I asked her why she was late.*
2 used for or relating to the defense of something: *Defensive weapons are used only if we are attacked.*
—**defensively** *adverb*
—**defensiveness** *noun*

defensive[2] *noun*
on the defensive = ready to defend yourself, because you have been criticized or attacked: *The teacher's criticism put me on the defensive* (=made me want to defend myself).

de•fer /dɪˈfɚ/ *verb* **deferred, deferring** *formal*
to delay something until a later date: *You can defer payment of your student loan for six months.*

de•fi•ant /dɪˈfaɪənt/ *adjective, formal*
refusing to obey someone: *The police told him to stop, but he was defiant.*
—**defiantly** *adverb*
—**defiance** *noun* behavior in which you refuse to obey someone: *The students were told to leave the school because of their defiance of the rules.*

de•fi•cient /dɪˈfɪʃənt/ *adjective, formal*
not having or containing enough of something: *The food they eat is deficient in iron, so they need to get iron some other way.*
—**deficiency** *noun* the state of not having enough of something: *Vitamin deficiencies can cause serious illness.*

def•i•cit /ˈdefəsɪt/ *noun, formal*
the difference between the amount of money that you have and the higher amount that you need: *The country's budget deficit is*

over 2.5 billion dollars, and it has to borrow money or raise taxes. ANTONYM **surplus**

de•fine /dɪˈfaɪn/ Ac *verb*
to explain the exact meaning of a word: *A "lie" can be defined as "something that you say that is not true."*

def•i•nite /ˈdefɪnət/ Ac *adjective*
1 certain and not likely to change: *I asked her if she wanted to see him, and her answer was a definite "no."*
2 clear and noticeable: *There are definite signs of improvement.*

ˌdefinite ˈarticle *noun*
the word "the"

def•i•nite•ly /ˈdefɪnətli/ Ac *adverb*
1 without any doubt: *Your arm's definitely broken. I can tell from the way it's hanging.*
2 used to emphasize that you are saying "yes": *"Are you going to be there?" "Definitely."*

def•i•ni•tion /ˌdefəˈnɪʃən/ Ac *noun*
an explanation of what a word means, especially one in a dictionary: *Look up the definition of "insect" in the dictionary.*

de•fin•i•tive /dɪˈfɪnətɪv/ Ac *adjective, formal*
a definitive book, description, etc. is so good that there cannot be a better one: *He wrote the definitive book on the Civil War. All other researchers rely on his work.*

de•formed /dɪˈfɔrmd/ *adjective*
if part of someone's body is deformed, it has the wrong shape: *He was born with a deformed foot and had to wear a special shoe.*
—**deformity** *noun, formal* a condition in which part of your body is deformed: *people with physical deformities*

de•fraud /dɪˈfrɔd/ *verb, formal*
to trick someone in order to get money from them: *He defrauded his clients of over $5 million before he was arrested.*

de•frost /diˈfrɔst/ *verb*
if frozen food defrosts, it gets warmer until it is not frozen anymore: *Defrost the chicken in the refrigerator.*

de•fy /dɪˈfaɪ/ *verb* third person singular **defies, defied** *formal*
to refuse to obey someone or something: *Her parents wanted him to be a doctor, but he defied them and became an actor.*
➔ See Thesaurus box at **disobey**

de•grade /dɪˈgreɪd/ *verb, formal*
to make someone lose people's respect or feel bad about themselves, for example because they are treated badly: *Treating prisoners like animals degrades them.*

de•grad•ing /dɪˈgreɪdɪŋ/ *adjective, formal*
something that is degrading makes you lose respect for yourself: *It was degrading to have to ask strangers for money.*

de•gree /dɪˈgri/ *noun*
1 a unit for measuring temperature: *It's very cold today. The temperature is only about 20 degrees.*
2 a unit for measuring the size of an angle: *The angles of a triangle add up to 180 degrees.*
3 an official statement that you have successfully completed all your studies at a university or college: *Ryan has a degree in chemistry.* | *He got his law degree from Columbia University.*
4 the level or amount of something: *The two art students showed a high degree of talent.* | *I felt responsible to some degree* (=partly) *for what happened.*

de•hy•drat•ed /diˈhaɪˌdreɪtɪd/ *adjective*
if you are dehydrated, you do not have enough water in your body: *It was hot, and I was getting dehydrated. I needed some water.*
—**dehydration** /ˌdihaɪˈdreɪʃən/ *noun* the state of being dehydrated

de•lay[1] /dɪˈleɪ/ *verb* **delayed**, third person singular **delays**
1 to make someone or something late: *Our flight was delayed by bad weather.*
2 to wait until a later time to do something: *We've decided to delay the trip until next month.*

delay[2] *noun* plural **delays**
a time when people have to wait before something happens: *The bus will arrive in ten minutes. We are sorry for the delay.*

del•e•gate[1] /ˈdeləgət/ *noun*
someone who is chosen to speak, vote, and make decisions for a group: *She is a delegate to the United Nations from Angola.*

del•e•gate² /ˈdeləˌgeɪt/ *verb*
to give part of your work to someone who has a lower position than you: *He is not very good at delegating work to people who work for him. He tries to do everything himself.*

del•e•ga•tion /ˌdeləˈgeɪʃən/ *noun*
a group of people that represents an organization and goes somewhere to take part in discussions: *A delegation of American business leaders is visiting China to try to increase trade between the two countries.*

D

de•lete /dɪˈlit/ *verb*
to remove parts of a piece of writing, or to remove a whole computer document: *Some files had been deleted from my computer, and I lost some of my work.*
—**deletion** /dɪˈliʃən/ *noun* the act of deleting something

del•i /ˈdeli/ *noun*
a small store that sells cheese, cooked meat, bread, etc. SYNONYM **delicatessen**

de•lib•er•ate¹ /dɪˈlɪbərət/ *adjective*
planned and intended: *This was not a mistake. It was a deliberate act of stealing money from the organization.*

de•lib•e•rate² /dɪˈlɪbəˌreɪt/ *verb, formal*
to think about something very carefully or talk about it carefully with other people: *The jury has been deliberating for two days about whether she is guilty.*

de•lib•er•ate•ly /dɪˈlɪbərətli/ *adverb*
if you do something deliberately, you intended to do it, and it is not an accident: *He deliberately tripped the other runner, so that he could win.* SYNONYM **on purpose**

del•i•ca•cy /ˈdelɪkəsi/ *noun* plural **delicacies** *formal*
something good to eat that is expensive or rare: *In France, snails are considered a delicacy, and they are served in the best restaurants.*

del•i•cate /ˈdelɪkət/ *adjective*
1 easily damaged or broken: *Grandma's china cups are very delicate. Be careful with them.*
2 needing to be dealt with very carefully in order to avoid problems: *It was a very delicate situation. We were worried we might say something to offend them.*
3 small and beautiful: *Babies have such tiny delicate fingers.*

del•i•ca•tes•sen /ˌdelɪkəˈtesən/ *noun*
a small store that sells cheese, cooked meat, bread, etc. SYNONYM **deli**

de•li•cious /dɪˈlɪʃəs/ *adjective*
delicious food tastes very good: *This pie is delicious! Can I have another slice?*
➔ See Thesaurus box at **taste¹**

de•light¹ /dɪˈlaɪt/ *noun, formal*
1 great pleasure: *She laughed with delight.*
2 something that is very enjoyable: *The CD is a delight to listen to. I've been listening to it almost every day.*

delight² *verb, formal*
to give someone great pleasure: *Her books delight readers all over the world.*

de•light•ed /dɪˈlaɪtɪd/ *adjective, formal*
very happy or pleased: *I'm delighted to meet you.* | *His parents are delighted with his progress at school.*
➔ See Thesaurus box at **happy**

de•light•ful /dɪˈlaɪtfəl/ *adjective, formal*
very nice: *It was a delightful evening. Everyone left with a smile.*
—**delightfully** *adverb, formal*

de•lin•quent /dɪˈlɪŋkwənt/ *adjective, formal*
a delinquent child or young person behaves very badly or does illegal things
—**delinquent** *noun* a delinquent child or young person: *a school for juvenile delinquents*

de•lir•i•ous /dɪˈlɪriəs/ *adjective, formal*
confused and having strange ideas because you are very sick: *He was delirious with fever and did not recognize me.*

de•liv•er /dɪˈlɪvɚ/ *verb*
1 to take a letter, package, etc. to a particular place: *They delivered the letter to the wrong house.*
2 deliver a speech/lecture, etc. = to make a speech to a group of people: *The president will deliver the speech on television tomorrow evening.*
3 deliver a baby = to help a baby come out of its mother's body
4 to do what you have promised to do: *Will he deliver on his promise to help us?*

de•liv•er•y /dɪˈlɪvəri/ *noun* plural **deliveries**
1 the act of bringing something to a particular place, or something that is brought: *Delivery of a package usually takes two days.* | *I'm expecting a delivery.*
2 the process of a baby being born: *She was taken straight to the delivery room* (=hospital room where babies are born).

del•ta /ˈdeltə/ *noun*
a place where a large river divides into smaller rivers near the ocean: *The Mississippi River Delta is on the Gulf of Mexico.*

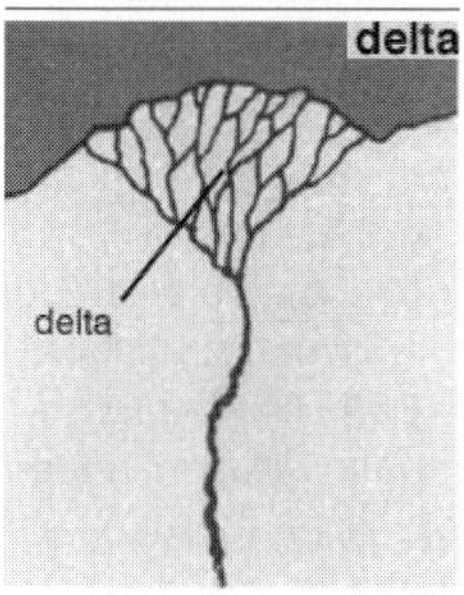

del•uge¹ /ˈdelyudʒ/ *noun, formal*
a large amount of things that someone gets at the same time: *We've received a deluge of applications – about 5,000 emails and letters.*

deluge² *verb, formal*
if people deluge someone with things, they send a large number at the same time: *The radio station was deluged with complaints.*

de•luxe /dɪˈlʌks/ *adjective*
better and more expensive than other things of the same type: *The winner will get two nights in a deluxe hotel in Los Angeles.*

delve /delv/ *verb*
PHRASAL VERB
delve into something *formal*
to search for more information about someone or something: *I didn't believe him, so I delved into his college records.*

de•mand¹ /dɪˈmænd/ *noun*
1 if there is a demand for something, people want to buy it: *Demand for computers is increasing.* | *Tickets for the concert are in great demand* (=wanted by a lot of people).
2 a strong request: *School officials met with the student protesters to find out what their demands were.*

demand² *verb, formal*
to ask for something in a strong way: *The man pulled out a gun and demanded money.* | *My father demanded that I finish college.*
➔ See Thesaurus box at **ask**

de•mand•ing /dɪˈmændɪŋ/ *adjective*
1 a demanding job is difficult or takes up a lot of your time: *She has a demanding job as a TV producer.*
2 wanting good work or a lot of attention: *The coach was very demanding. We started practice every day at 7:00 a.m.*

de•mands /dɪˈmændz/ *plural noun*
the things that you need to do that are difficult or take up your time: *He could not deal with the demands of his job and quit after a year.*

de•mer•it /dɪˈmerɪt/ *noun*
a warning that is given to a student or a soldier when he or she does something wrong

de•moc•ra•cy /dɪˈmɑkrəsi/ *noun* plural **democracies**
1 a system in which the people of a country can choose the government by voting: *They wanted to bring democracy to the country.*
2 a country which has democracy: *We live in a democracy.*

WORD FAMILY look at the words:
➔ **democracy** *noun*
➔ **democrat** *noun*
➔ **democratic** *adjective*
➔ **democratically** *adverb*

➔ See Thesaurus box at **government**

Dem•o•crat /ˈdeməˌkræt/ *noun*
a member of the Democratic Party: *Most Democrats support the bill.*

dem•o•crat•ic /ˌdeməˈkrætɪk/ *adjective*
1 a democratic country or system is one in which everyone has the right to vote in order to choose the government or make decisions: *Education is important in a democratic society. People need to be informed to vote.*
2 Democratic relating or belonging to the Democratic Party: *the Democratic presidential candidate*
—**democratically** *adverb*: *a democratically elected government*

Demoˈcratic ˌParty *noun*
the Democratic Party = one of the two main political parties of the U.S.

D

D

de•mol•ish /dɪˈmɑlɪʃ/ *verb*
to completely destroy a building or other structure: *Ten houses were demolished to make space for a new park.*
—**demolition** /ˌdeməˈlɪʃən/ *noun* the act of demolishing something: *The group is opposed to the demolition of the old building. The group wants the building to stay.*

de•mon /ˈdimən/ *noun*
an evil creature or spirit

dem•on•strate /ˈdemənˌstreɪt/ Ac *verb*
1 to show something: *He demonstrated how to use the machine. | We have demonstrated that this method works better than the old methods.*
2 to protest or show support for something in public with a lot of other people: *A crowd of people were demonstrating against the war.*
—**demonstrator** *noun* someone who is protesting or showing support for something: *Demonstrators marched through the streets holding "NO WAR" signs.*
→ See Thesaurus box at **explain**

dem•on•stra•tion /ˌdemənˈstreɪʃən/ Ac *noun*
1 the act of showing something: *Could you give me a demonstration of the software? I'm not sure I understand how it works.*
2 an event at which a lot of people protest or show support for something in public: *Students at the university held a peaceful demonstration to protest the new rules.*

de•mor•al•ized /dɪˈmɔrəˌlaɪzd/ *adjective*
unhappier, less confident, and less willing to make an effort than before: *We lost three games in a row, and we were feeling demoralized.*
—**demoralizing** *adjective* making someone feel demoralized: *Failing a test is demoralizing.*

de•mote /dɪˈmoʊt/ *verb*
to change someone's rank or position to a lower one: *He was demoted from sergeant to private.* ANTONYM **promote**
—**demotion** /dɪˈmoʊʃən/ *noun* when someone is demoted

den /den/ *noun*
1 a room in a house where people relax, watch television, etc.
2 the home of a lion, FOX, etc.

de•ni•al /dɪˈnaɪəl/ Ac *noun*
1 a statement saying that something is not true: *He repeated his denial, saying, "I did not take the money!"* ANTONYM **admission**
2 the situation of refusing to believe something bad: *She's in denial about her illness. She won't even say the word "cancer."*

den•im /ˈdenəm/ *noun*
a strong cotton cloth, usually blue, which is used to make JEANS: *a denim jacket*

de•nom•i•na•tion /dɪˌnɑməˈneɪʃən/ *noun, formal*
one of many groups who have the same religion, but slightly different beliefs: *The Catholic Church is the largest Christian denomination in the U.S.*

de•nom•i•na•tor /dɪˈnɑməˌneɪtɚ/ *noun*
the number below the line in a FRACTION

de•note /dɪˈnoʊt/ Ac *verb, formal*
to represent or mean something: *The symbol $ denotes "dollars."*

dense /dens/ *adjective*
1 made of or containing things that are very close together: *The island is covered by a dense forest, and it is difficult to travel from one side to the other.*
2 *informal* not intelligent: *Don't be so dense – the answer is obvious.*
—**densely** *adverb*: *a densely populated city* (=with people living very close together)

den•si•ty /ˈdensəti/ *noun*
how heavy something is in comparison to its size: *The rock has a high density and is heavier than you might expect.*

dent /dent/ *noun*
a bent part of a surface made when something hits the surface: *There was a big dent in the car door where the baseball hit it.*
—**dent** *verb* to make a dent in something: *I'm sorry I dented the car.*

den•tal /ˈdentl/ *adjective*
relating to your teeth: *I'm having some dental work done* (=I'm having my teeth fixed).

den•tist /ˈdentɪst/ *noun*
someone whose job is to do work on people's teeth: *I went to the dentist to have my teeth cleaned and checked.*
→ See Thesaurus box at **doctor**
→ See picture on page A16

den•tures /ˈdentʃɚz/ *plural noun*
false teeth worn by people who have lost their real teeth: *He took his dentures out of his mouth at night.*

de•ny /dɪˈnaɪ/ Ac *verb* **denies, denied**
1 to say that something is not true: *She denied that there was a problem.* | *He denied cheating on the test.* ANTONYM **admit**
2 *formal* to not let someone have or do something: *In the past, women were denied the right to vote.*

WORD FAMILY look at the words:
→ **deny** *verb*
→ **denial** *noun*
→ **undeniable** *adjective*
→ **undeniably** *adverb*

de•o•dor•ant /diˈoʊdərənt/ *noun*
a substance that you put under your arms so that you do not smell bad

de•part /dɪˈpɑrt/ *verb, formal*
to leave: *The train will depart from track 9.* ANTONYM **arrive**

de•part•ment /dɪˈpɑrtmənt/ *noun*
a part of a business, college, government, etc.: *The company is divided into six departments, and I work in the finance department.* | *the U.S. Department of Education*
→ See Thesaurus box at **part**[1]

deˈpartment ˌstore *noun*
a large store that sells many different kinds of things including clothes

de•par•ture /dɪˈpɑrtʃɚ/ *noun, formal*
the action of leaving a place: *The flight's departure was delayed because of the snow storm.* ANTONYM **arrival**

de•pend /dɪˈpend/ *verb*
it/that depends = said when you are not sure about something because you do not know what will happen: *"Are you coming to my house later?" "It depends. I might have to work."*
PHRASAL VERB
depend on someone/something
1 to need the help or support of someone or something else: *I didn't like depending on my parents for money.*
2 to be affected by something that is not fixed or certain: *The amount of money you spend depends on how much you buy.*

de•pend•a•ble /dɪˈpendəbəl/ *adjective*
someone or something that is dependable will always do what you need that person or thing to do: *He is a dependable worker. He comes to work on time, and he doesn't leave until he's done.* | *a dependable car*

de•pend•ent[1] /dɪˈpendənt/ *adjective*
needing someone or something in order to live or continue: *Jan's children are still dependent on her for money.* ANTONYM **independent**
—**dependence** *noun* the state of being dependent on someone or something

dependent[2] *noun, formal*
a child or other person who someone must buy everything for: *He is not married and has no dependents.*

de•port /dɪˈpɔrt/ *verb*
to make someone from a foreign country return to that country: *The illegal immigrants will be deported back to their home country.*
—**deportation** /ˌdipɔrˈteɪʃən/ *noun* when someone is deported
—**deportee** /ˌdipɔrˈti/ *noun* someone who is deported

de•pos•it[1] /dɪˈpɑzɪt/ *noun*
1 the first part of a large cost that you pay, when you are going to pay the rest later: *We put down a deposit of $1,000 on the car; we'll pay the rest when we bring it home.*
2 an amount of money that is put into someone's bank account: *I'd like to make a deposit of $250* (=put $250 into my bank account). ANTONYM **withdrawal**

deposit[2] *verb*
to put money into a bank account: *She immediately deposited the money in her savings account.* ANTONYM **withdraw**

de•pot /ˈdipoʊ/ *noun*
1 a place where a large quantity of things are stored: *Soldiers found a small weapons depot containing guns and bombs.*
2 a small train station or bus station

de•pre•ci•ate /dɪˈpriʃiˌeɪt/ *verb, formal*
to go down in value: *The car will depreciate more than $2,000 during the first year that you own it, from $18,000 to $15,800.*
—**depreciation** /dɪˌpriʃiˈeɪʃən/ *noun* the process of losing value

D

de•press /dɪ'pres/ Ac *verb*
to make someone feel very sad: *Funerals depress me.*

de•pressed /dɪ'prest/ Ac *adjective*
very sad: *She felt depressed about losing her job.*
➔ See Thesaurus box at **sad**

D

WORD FAMILY look at the words:
➔ **depressed** *adjective*
➔ **depressing** *adjective*
➔ **depress** *verb*
➔ **depression** *noun*

de•press•ing /dɪ'presɪŋ/ Ac *adjective*
making you feel sad: *The news about the war is so depressing.*

de•pres•sion /dɪ'preʃən/ Ac *noun*
1 a feeling of great sadness that sometimes makes you unable to live normally: *After her youngest child left home, she suffered from depression.*
2 a long period when the economy is bad and many people do not have jobs: *During the Great Depression of the 1930s my great-grandfather could not find work for many years.*

de•prive /dɪ'praɪv/ *verb*
PHRASAL VERB
deprive someone of something
to stop someone from having something that he or she needs or should have: *They deprived the prisoners of food and sleep to punish them.*

de•prived /dɪ'praɪvd/ *adjective*
not having the things that you need for a comfortable or happy life: *He had a deprived childhood; his family was very poor and often did not have enough to eat.*
—**deprivation** /ˌdeprə'veɪʃən/ *noun, formal*
the state of being deprived
➔ See Thesaurus box at **poor**

depth /depθ/ *noun*
1 the distance from the top of something to the bottom: *The depth of the river is about 30 feet.*
2 the distance from the front of an object to the back: *Do the shelves have enough depth to hold these wide books?*
3 how strong, great, or serious something is: *I understand the depth of your feelings for this city, because I love living here too.*

dep•u•ty /'depyəti/ *noun* plural **deputies**
1 a deputy director/superintendent/chief, etc. = someone who is directly below someone in an important position: *She is the deputy editor of the magazine; her boss is the editor.*
2 someone whose job is to help a SHERIFF

der•e•lict /'derəˌlɪkt/ *adjective, formal*
a derelict building or vehicle is in bad condition because no one has used it in a long time: *They built a new prison to replace the derelict old one.*

de•rive /dɪ'raɪv/ Ac *verb*
PHRASAL VERB
derive from something *also* **be derived from something**
to develop or come from something else: *Our word "science" derives from the Latin word "scientia," meaning "knowledge."*

de•scend /dɪ'send/ *verb*
1 *formal* to go down: *We got in the elevator on the fifth floor and descended to the first floor.* ANTONYM **ascend**
2 be descended from someone = to be related to a person who lived a long time ago: *He is descended from a Native American chief.*

de•scend•ant /dɪ'sendənt/ *noun*
someone who is related to a person who lived a long time ago: *Queen Elizabeth II is a direct descendant of Queen Victoria.*

de•scent /dɪ'sent/ *noun, formal*
1 the action of going down: *The plane began its descent to the airport.*
2 the state of being related to people from another country who lived a long time ago: *He is of Italian descent* (=his family came from Italy a long time ago).

de•scribe /dɪ'skraɪb/ *verb*
to say what someone or something is like: *Can you describe the man who took your purse?* | *I'm so confused. It's hard to describe how I feel.*
WORD FAMILY ➔ **description** *noun*

de•scrip•tion /dɪ'skrɪpʃən/ *noun*
a written or spoken statement that tells what someone or something is like: *Kate gave us a description of her new house: it is a brick house with three bedrooms and a big yard.*

des•ert¹ /ˈdezɚt/ *noun*
a large area of hot dry land where few plants grow: *The Sahara desert in northern Africa is the largest desert in the world.*

de•sert² /dɪˈzɚt/ *verb*
to leave your family, home, etc. and not go back: *He deserted his wife and children and moved to a different state.*
—**desertion** /dɪˈzɚʃən/ *noun* the action of deserting someone

de•sert•ed /dɪˈzɚtɪd/ *adjective*
if a place which usually has people in it is deserted, there are no people there: *Everyone stays home at night, and the streets are deserted.* SYNONYM **empty**

de•sert•er /dɪˈzɚtɚ/ *noun*
a soldier who has left the army without permission

de•serve /dɪˈzɚv/ *verb*
if you deserve something, you should get it because of what you have done: *After working so hard, you deserve a rest.* | *The team played well – they deserved to win.*

de•sign¹ /dɪˈzaɪn/ Ac *noun*
1 the form or structure of something that is made: *I like the design of the car; it's beautiful.*
2 a drawing of something new that will be made: *Have you seen the designs for the new house?*
3 a pattern used for decorating something: *The vase is decorated with a simple design of flowers.*
4 the process of making a drawing of something new that will be made: *He studied design in college.*

design² *verb*
to draw or plan something that is going to be made or built: *Did you design your dress yourself?*
—**designer** *noun* someone who designs new things: *a fashion designer*

de•signed /dɪˈzaɪnd/ Ac *adjective*
made or planned for a particular purpose or type of person: *The exercise program is designed to improve your general fitness.* | *The game is designed for younger children.*

de•sir•a•ble /dɪˈzaɪrəbəl/ *adjective, formal*
if something is desirable, people want it because it is good or useful: *The most desirable homes are in this beautiful neighborhood.*
—**desirability** /dɪˌzaɪrəˈbɪləti/ *noun* the quality of being desirable

de•sire¹ /dɪˈzaɪɚ/ *noun, formal*
a strong feeling of wanting something: *She has a strong desire for independence. She will not take money from anyone.*

desire² *verb, formal*
to want something: *The witch said to the girl, "I will give you what you desire most, but you must help me first."*

desk /desk/ *noun*
a table that you can sit at to write and work: *Marie sat down at her desk and turned on her computer.*
➔ See picture on pages A10 and A18

desk•top com•put•er /ˌdesktɑp kəmˈpyutɚ/ *also* **desktop** *noun*
a computer that is small enough to be used on a desk
➔ See picture on page A20

des•o•late /ˈdesəlɪt/ *adjective, formal*
a place that is desolate is empty and makes you feel sad and lonely: *We drove along a desolate stretch of road without trees, grass, or buildings.*

de•spair /dɪˈsper/ *noun, formal*
a very sad feeling, when you have no hope at all: *When I realized I could not move, I was in despair.*
—**despair** *verb, formal* to feel despair

des•per•ate /ˈdespərət/ *adjective*
wanting something very much, and willing to do anything to get it or do it: *I had almost no money, and I was desperate for a job.*
—**desperately** *adverb*: *The doctors tried desperately to save her life.*
—**desperation** /ˌdespəˈreɪʃən/ *noun, formal* the state of feeling desperate: *Finally, in*

desperation, she asked her parents for the money.

de•spise /dɪ'spaɪz/ *verb, formal*
to hate someone or something and have no respect for them: *She despised him for hitting her.* SYNONYM **hate**
➔ See Thesaurus box at **hate**[1]

de•spite /dɪ'spaɪt/ Ac *preposition*
although something happens or exists: *Despite the bad weather, we enjoyed our trip* (=the weather was bad, but we enjoyed our trip anyway).

D

des•sert /dɪ'zɚt/ *noun*
sweet food that you eat after the main part of a meal: *Would you like some dessert?*

des•ti•na•tion /ˌdestə'neɪʃən/ *noun, formal*
the place that you are traveling to: *At about 10:00, we reached our destination* (=arrived at the place we were traveling to).

des•tined /'destənd/ *adjective*
if you are destined to do something, you will definitely do it in the future: *My mother said she knew when I was a little girl that I was destined to become famous.*

des•ti•ny /'destəni/ *noun* plural **destinies**
the things that will definitely happen to someone in the future: *It was his destiny to become a leader.* SYNONYM **fate**

de•stroy /dɪ'strɔɪ/ *verb* **destroyed**, third person singular **destroys**
to damage something so badly that there is not much of it left: *The building was destroyed by fire.*

WORD FAMILY look at the words:
➔ **destroy** *verb*
➔ **destruction** *noun*
➔ **destructive** *adjective*

de•stroy•er /dɪ'strɔɪɚ/ *noun*
a small fast military ship with guns

de•struc•tion /dɪ'strʌkʃən/ *noun*
the act of destroying something: *The environmental group wants to stop the destruction of the forests.*

de•struc•tive /dɪ'strʌktɪv/ *adjective*
causing a lot of damage: *The computer virus is very destructive; it can make you lose all your files.*

de•tach /dɪ'tætʃ/ *verb, formal*
to remove something from the thing that it is attached to: *You can detach the hood from the jacket.*

de•tached /dɪ'tætʃt/ *adjective, formal*
not having an emotional feeling about something: *During the funeral, he seemed detached; he did not cry at all.*
—**detachment** *noun* the state of being detached

de•tail /'diteɪl/ *noun*
1 one small fact or piece of information about something: *She wanted to know every detail of the trip, including where we ate dinner, the people we met, and how much everything cost.*
2 in detail = in a way that includes a lot of details: *She described the dress in detail; she said it was green with short sleeves and yellow and white flowers.*

de•tailed /dɪ'teɪld/ *adjective*
including a lot of details: *He gave a long and detailed explanation of his idea, including exactly how much each item would cost.* | *It is a detailed map, showing every house on the street.*

de•tain /dɪ'teɪn/ *verb, formal*
to officially stop someone from leaving a place: *Police detained one of the men for two nights.* SYNONYM **hold**

de•tect /dɪ'tekt/ Ac *verb, formal*
to find or notice something that is not easy to see, hear, etc.: *They had detected cracks in the plane's wings.* SYNONYM **notice**
—**detector** *noun* a piece of equipment that detects something: *We had to walk through a metal detector at the airport.*
—**detection** /dɪ'tekʃən/ *noun, formal* the act of detecting something

WORD FAMILY look at the words:
➔ **detect** *verb*
➔ **detection** *noun*
➔ **detector** *noun*

de•tec•tive /dɪ'tektɪv/ Ac *noun*
a police officer whose job is to find out who has committed a crime

de•ten•tion /dɪ'tenʃən/ *noun*
a punishment by which a student has to stay at school after the other students have left: *I got detention for talking too much in class.*

de•ter /dɪˈtɚ/ *verb* **deterred, deterring** *formal*
to stop someone from doing something by making it difficult: *Do you think higher cigarette prices would deter people from smoking?*

de•ter•gent /dɪˈtɚdʒənt/ *noun*
a liquid or powder like soap that is used for washing clothes, dishes, etc.: *He poured laundry detergent into the washing machine.*

de•te•ri•o•rate /dɪˈtɪriəˌreɪt/ *verb, formal*
to become worse: *Her health deteriorated until she could not take care of herself anymore.*
—**deterioration** /dɪˌtɪriəˈreɪʃən/ *noun, formal* the process of deteriorating

de•ter•mi•na•tion /dɪˌtɚməˈneɪʃən/ *noun*
a strong desire to do something, even when it will be difficult: *He has been practicing very hard; his determination to win is very clear.*

de•ter•mine /dɪˈtɚmɪn/ *verb, formal*
1 to find out the facts about something: *Police are trying to determine if his death was an accident.*
2 to control what size, level, type, etc. something is: *Grades are determined by how good a student's work is.*

de•ter•mined /dɪˈtɚmɪnd/ *adjective*
having a strong desire to do something, even when it will be difficult: *She was determined to become a doctor, so she worked hard to earn the money to go to medical school.*

de•test /dɪˈtest/ *verb, formal*
to hate someone or something very much: *I detest cigarettes; I will not go into a room when someone is smoking.* SYNONYM **despise, hate**
➔ See Thesaurus box at **hate**[1]

det•o•nate /ˈdetnˌeɪt/ *verb, formal*
if someone detonates a bomb, it explodes: *The terrorist tried to detonate the bomb.*

de•tour /ˈditʊr/ *noun*
a way of going from one place to another that is longer than the usual way: *We had to take a detour because they were fixing the road.*

dev•as•tate /ˈdevəˌsteɪt/ *verb, formal*
to damage something very badly: *The city was devastated by an earthquake.*
—**devastation** /ˌdevəˈsteɪʃən/ *noun, formal* great damage

devastated /ˈdevəˌsteɪtɪd/ *adjective, formal*
extremely upset: *She was devastated when her parents got divorced.*

dev•as•tat•ing /ˈdevəˌsteɪtɪŋ/ *adjective, formal*
1 making someone feel extremely upset: *The news of her sister's sudden death was devastating.*
2 causing a lot of damage: *The storm was devastating to the Florida coast.*

de•vel•op /dɪˈveləp/ *verb*
1 to become bigger, better, more important, etc.: *Caterpillars develop into butterflies.* | *I want to develop my career as a singer.*
2 to begin to have an illness, problem, or quality: *Her baby developed a fever during the night.* | *Then a problem developed* (=began).
3 to design and produce something new: *The company is developing a new type of plane.*
4 to make pictures out of film from a camera

de•vel•oped /dɪˈveləpt/ *adjective*
1 developed countries/nations = rich countries that have a lot of industry
2 fully/highly/well developed = if something is fully, highly, etc. developed, it has become big or effective: *He has big well-developed muscles.*

de•vel•op•ing /dɪˈveləpɪŋ/ *adjective*
developing countries/nations = poor countries that are trying to increase their industry and trade

de•vel•op•ment /dɪˈveləpmənt/ *noun*
1 the process of growing: *When a woman is three months pregnant, the baby's brain is still at an early stage of development.*
2 a new event or piece of work that changes a situation: *The magazine tells you about the latest developments in science* (=the newest things that are happening in science). | *There's been a new development in the peace talks.*
3 a group of new buildings, or the process of building them: *They have started building a new housing development where the farm used to be.*

D

D

de•vi•ate /ˈdiviˌeɪt/ Ac *verb, formal*
to do something different from what has been planned or what is normal: *You must not deviate from these instructions, or the plan will fail.*
—**deviation** /ˌdiviˈeɪʃən/ *noun* the act of deviating

de•vice /dɪˈvaɪs/ Ac *noun*
a machine or small object that is used to do a particular thing: *A corkscrew is a device for opening wine bottles.*
➔ See Thesaurus box at **machine**[1]

dev•il /ˈdevəl/ *noun*
the devil = the most powerful evil spirit in some religions, such as Christianity

de•vi•ous /ˈdiviəs/ *adjective, formal*
using tricks or lies to get what you want: *He had thought of a devious plan to steal the money.*

de•vise /dɪˈvaɪz/ *verb, formal*
to think of a way of doing something: *The teacher devised a game to make math more fun.*
➔ See Thesaurus box at **invent**

de•vote /dɪˈvoʊt/ Ac *verb*
devote yourself/your time/your life to something = to spend all your time doing something: *I devoted myself to finishing my project.* SYNONYM **dedicate**

WORD FAMILY look at the words:
➔ **devote** *verb*
➔ **devotion** *noun*
➔ **devoted** *adjective*

de•vot•ed /dɪˈvoʊtɪd/ Ac *adjective*
1 loving and caring about someone a lot: *His girlfriend was completely devoted to him, and spent all her time with him.*
2 be devoted to something = to deal with only one thing: *This chapter of the book is devoted to poetry.*

de•vo•tion /dɪˈvoʊʃən/ Ac *noun*
the condition of loving or caring about someone or something a lot: *His devotion to his family is easy to see; he loves to be with his wife and kids whenever he can.*

de•vour /dɪˈvaʊɚ/ *verb, formal*
to eat something quickly because you are very hungry: *The children devoured the candy immediately.*

de•vout /dɪˈvaʊt/ *adjective*
very religious: *a devout Hindu*

dew /du/ *noun*
the small drops of water that form on things outdoors during the night: *The grass was wet with dew* (=covered with dew).

di•a•be•tes /ˌdaɪəˈbitiz/ *noun*
a disease in which you have too much sugar in your blood
—**diabetic** /ˌdaɪəˈbetɪk/ *adjective* someone who is diabetic has diabetes
—**diabetic** *noun* someone with diabetes

di•ag•nose /ˌdaɪəgˈnoʊs/ *verb, formal*
to find out and say what illness someone has: *In March, he was diagnosed with cancer* (=a doctor said he had cancer).

di•ag•no•sis /ˌdaɪəgˈnoʊsəs/ *noun* plural **diagnoses** /ˌdaɪəgˈnoʊsiz/ *formal*
the process or result of diagnosing an illness: *The doctor made a diagnosis of heart disease.*

di•ag•o•nal /daɪˈægənəl/ *adjective*
a diagonal line joins two opposite corners of a square: *Draw a diagonal line from one corner to the other.*
—**diagonal** *noun* a diagonal line
—**diagonally** *adverb*: *Fold the piece of paper diagonally* (=in a diagonal line).

diagonal
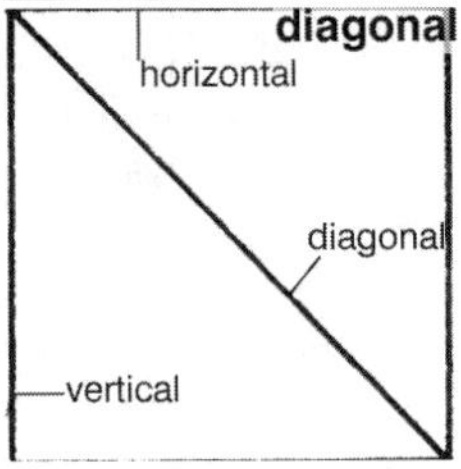

di•a•gram /ˈdaɪəˌgræm/ *noun*
a drawing that you make to show what shape or arrangement something has, or how it works: *There is a diagram of the engine on the next page.*

di•al[1] /ˈdaɪəl/ *verb*
to press the buttons or turn the dial on a telephone in order to make a call: *I dialled her number, but nobody answered the phone.* SYNONYM **call**

dial

dial[2] *noun*
a round flat part of a clock, telephone, or other machine that has numbers on it, or

that can be turned in order to choose numbers: *If you want to listen to a different station, turn the dial on the radio.*

di·a·lect /ˈdaɪəˌlekt/ *noun*
a form of a language that is spoken in one area: *There are many dialects of German.*
→ See Thesaurus box at **language**

di·a·logue *also* **dialog** /ˈdaɪəˌlɔg/ *noun*
conversation in a book, play, or movie: *The dialogue didn't sound real – people don't talk like that.*

ˈdial tone *noun*
the sound you hear when you pick up a telephone before making a call

diameter

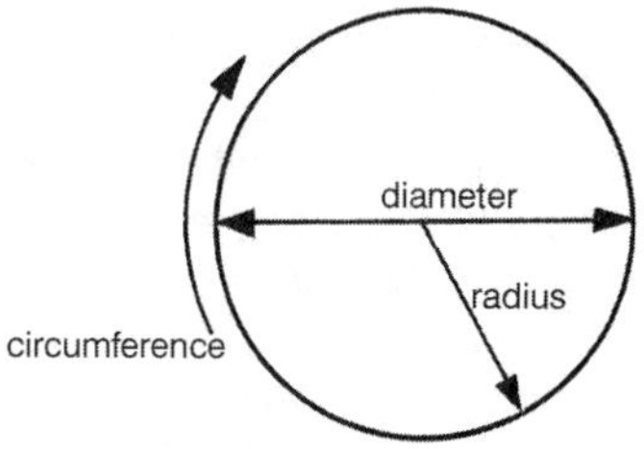

di·am·e·ter /daɪˈæmətɚ/ *noun*
a line or measurement from one side of a circle to the other, through the center: *The table is five feet in diameter* (=it measures five feet across).

di·amond /ˈdaɪmənd/ *noun*
1 a very hard, clear, expensive stone, used in jewelry: *He bought her a diamond engagement ring.*
2 a shape with four equal sloping sides, with its points at the top, bottom, and sides
3 a card used in card games, with red diamond shapes on it: *the three of diamonds* (=a card with three diamond shapes)
4 the area in a baseball field that is inside the four BASEs

di·aper /ˈdaɪpɚ/ *noun*
a piece of cloth or paper that is put around a baby's bottom to hold its waste: *I think we need to change the baby's diaper* (=put on a new one).

di·ar·rhe·a /ˌdaɪəˈriə/ *noun*
an illness in which your body waste is liquid and comes out often: *I had diarrhea after eating some meat that was not fresh.*

di·a·ry /ˈdaɪəri/ *noun* plural **diaries**
a book in which you write about the things that happen to you each day: *Do you keep a diary* (=write in a diary regularly)?

dice /daɪs/ *plural noun* singular **die** /daɪ/
two small blocks of wood or plastic with a different number of spots on each side, used in games: *She rolled the dice* (=threw them onto a surface).

dic·tate /ˈdɪkteɪt/ *verb*
1 to say words for someone else to write down: *She dictated a letter to her secretary.*
2 to tell people exactly what they must do: *You can't dictate how I should live my life!*

dic·ta·tion /dɪkˈteɪʃən/ *noun*
the act of saying words so that someone can write them down exactly as you say them

dic·ta·tor /ˈdɪkteɪtɚ/ *noun*
a leader of a country who has complete power: *Dictators often put people who oppose them in prison.*
—**dictatorship** /dɪkˈteɪtɚˌʃɪp/ *noun* a country that is ruled by a dictator

dic·tion·ar·y /ˈdɪkʃəˌneri/ *noun* plural **dictionaries**
a book that shows words in ALPHABETICAL order and says what they mean: *If you don't know what a word means, look it up in a dictionary* (=find the meaning in a dictionary).

did /dɪd/ *verb*
the past tense of DO

did·n't /ˈdɪdnt/ *verb*
the short form of "did not": *She didn't have enough money to buy a new car.*

die¹ /daɪ/ *verb* **died, dying**
1 to stop living: *My grandmother died last year.* | *He died of cancer* (=died because he had cancer).
2 **be dying to do something** *informal* = to want to do something very much: *I'm dying to know what happened, but my parents won't tell me.*

PHRASAL VERBS

die down
if something dies down, it becomes less strong: *The wind died down, and the rain stopped.*

die out
if a type of animal or thing dies out, it disappears completely: *Scientists have different ideas about why dinosaurs died out.*

die² *noun*
the singular of DICE

die•sel /ˈdizəl/ *also* ˌ**diesel** ˈ**fuel** *noun*
a type of FUEL used in some engines, for example in big trucks

di•et /ˈdaɪət/ *noun*
1 the type of food that you eat each day: *Fruit and vegetables are part of a healthy diet.*
2 a plan to eat less food or eat a particular type of food: *No dessert for me – I'm on a diet* (=trying to eat less food).
—**diet** *verb* to try to eat less food or eat a particular type of food: *You look thinner. Have you been dieting?*
—**dietician** /ˌdaɪəˈtɪʃən/ *noun* someone who studies food and advises people on what to eat

D

dif•fer /ˈdɪfɚ/ *verb, formal*
to be different: *How does the movie differ from the book?*

dif•ference /ˈdɪfərəns/ *noun*
1 a way in which one thing is not the same as another: *There are several differences between baseball and softball – one is that the ball in softball is bigger and softer.* | *What's the difference in price between the two cars?* | *I can't tell the difference between the two dogs* (=I can't see how they are different from each other). ANTONYM **similarity**
2 make a difference = to have a good effect on a situation: *Exercise can make a big difference in how you feel* (=change the way you feel in an important way).
3 make no difference = to be unimportant or to have no effect: *It makes no difference to me whether your hair is long or short – I like it both ways.*

dif•ferent /ˈdɪfrənt/ *adjective*
not the same: *My sister and I like different kinds of music.* | *Ben feels different from most kids at his school, because he doesn't like sports.* ANTONYM **the same**
—**differently** *adverb*

WORD FAMILY look at the words:
→ **different** *adjective*
→ **differently** *adverb*
→ **differ** *verb*
→ **difference** *noun*

dif•fer•en•ti•ate /ˌdɪfəˈrenʃiˌeɪt/ Ac *verb, formal*
to know that two things are different from each other: *I can't differentiate between the colors red and green; the two colors look the same to me.*

dif•fi•cult /ˈdɪfɪˌkəlt/ *adjective*
not easy to do, understand, or deal with: *The first question on the test was difficult, and I got it wrong.* | *It's difficult for us to guess what will happen.* SYNONYM **hard**; ANTONYM **easy**

dif•fi•cul•ty /ˈdɪfɪˌkəlti/ *noun*
1 a problem or something that causes trouble: *I have difficulty* (=have problems) *getting to sleep.* | *She walks with difficulty, because she hurt her knees.*
2 the quality of being difficult: *The worksheets have different levels of difficulty.*

dig /dɪg/ *verb* **dug** /dʌg/ **digging**
to make a hole in the ground by moving earth: *The kids had fun digging in the sand.* | *I dug a hole and put the plant in it.*

PHRASAL VERBS

dig something into something
to push something hard into something else: *She dug her fingernails into my arm.*

dig something up
to take something out of the ground: *The dog dug up a bone in the backyard.*

di•gest /daɪˈdʒest/ *verb*
when you digest food, it changes in your stomach into a form your body can use: *Some babies can't drink cow's milk because they can't digest it easily.*
—**digestible** *adjective* easy to digest

di•ges•tion /daɪˈdʒestʃən/ *noun*
the process of digesting food
—**digestive** /daɪˈdʒestɪv/ *adjective* relating to digestion

dig•it /ˈdɪdʒɪt/ *noun, formal*
any of the numbers from 0 to 9: *a four-digit number such as 9723*

dig•i•tal /ˈdɪdʒɪtl/ *adjective*
1 using a system in which information is represented in the form of ones and zeros: *It's a digital camera, so it doesn't have film.*
2 giving information in the form of numbers: *It is easy for children to read digital clocks.*

dig•ni•fied /ˈdɪgnəˌfaɪd/ *adjective*
calm, serious, and making people feel respect: *The professor was a tall, dignified old man.*

dig•ni•ty /ˈdɪgnəti/ *noun*
calm, serious behavior that makes people respect you: *Everyone respected her because she always behaved with great dignity.*

dike /daɪk/ *noun*
a wall or bank built to keep back water and prevent flooding

di•lem•ma /dəˈlemə/ *noun*
a situation in which you have to make a difficult choice between two actions: *This is my dilemma: should I ask him to the party, or should I wait and hope he asks me?*

dil•i•gent /ˈdɪlədʒənt/ *adjective, formal*
someone who is diligent works hard and carefully: *Connie is a diligent student and always does extra work.*
—**diligently** *adverb*
—**diligence** *noun* the quality of being diligent

di•lute /daɪˈlut/ *verb*
to make a liquid weaker by adding water or another liquid: *You can dilute the drink with water.*
—**dilution** /daɪˈluʃən/ *noun* the act of diluting something

dim /dɪm/ *adjective* **dimmer, dimmest**
not bright: *I couldn't read the sign because the light was too dim.*
—**dimness** *noun*

dime /daɪm/ *noun*
a coin that is worth 10 cents
➔ See Thesaurus box at **money**

di•men•sion /dɪˈmenʃən/ Ac *noun*
the length, height, or width of something: *The dimensions of the room are 10 feet by 12 feet* (=10 feet wide and 12 feet long).

di•min•ish /dɪˈmɪnɪʃ/ Ac *verb, formal*
to become smaller or weaker: *The noise had diminished, so we could talk without shouting.*
➔ See Thesaurus box at **decrease**[1]

din /dɪn/ *noun, formal*
a loud, continuous, and annoying noise: *I could not hear him because of the din of the crowd.*

dine /daɪn/ *verb, formal*
to have dinner: *He had been invited to dine with the president.*

din•er /ˈdaɪnɚ/ *noun*
1 a small restaurant that serves cheap meals
2 *formal* someone who is eating in a restaurant: *The other diners did not look up when we came in.*

ˈdining room *noun*
a room in a house where you sit down at a table to eat meals

ˈdining ˌtable *also* **ˈdining room ˌtable, dinner table** *noun*
a table at which you eat meals at home

D

din•ner /ˈdɪnɚ/ *noun*
the main meal of the day, usually eaten in the evening: *We usually have dinner around 6:30.* | *We had fish for dinner.*

di•no•saur /ˈdaɪnəˌsɔr/ *noun*
a large animal that lived millions of years ago and no longer exists: *Dinosaurs were reptiles.*

dip[1] /dɪp/ *verb*
dipped, dipping
to put something into a liquid and quickly take it out again: *I dipped my toe into the water to feel if it was cold.*

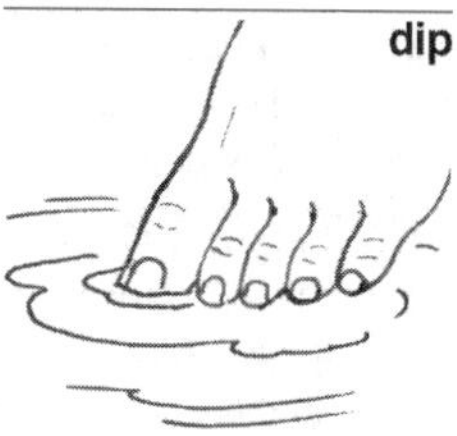

dip[2] *noun*
a thick mixture that you can dip CHIPs, vegetables, etc. into before you eat them: *There was a cheese dip for the potato chips.*

di•plo•ma /dɪˈploʊmə/ *noun*
a document that you get when you have successfully completed high school, college, etc.: *He earned his high school diploma in 2001.*

dip•lo•mat /ˈdɪpləˌmæt/ *noun*
someone who officially represents his or her government in a foreign country and helps to solve problems between the countries

dip•lo•mat•ic /ˌdɪpləˈmætɪk/ *adjective*
1 relating to the work of diplomats: *We must use diplomatic efforts to end the war.*
2 if you are diplomatic, you deal with people without upsetting them: *I tried to be diplomatic when I told her she had made a mistake.*
—**diplomacy** /dɪˈploʊməsi/ *noun* the work of diplomats: *In this case, diplomacy has failed.*
—**diplomatically** /ˌdɪpləˈmætɪkli/ *adverb* in a way that does not upset people: *"You're both right in a way," she said diplomatically.*

di•rect¹ /də'rekt/ *adjective*

1 going straight from one place to another: *What's the most direct route to the airport?*

2 with no other person, thing, or event involved: *The case was solved as a direct result of her phone call to police.* ANTONYM **indirect**

3 saying exactly what you mean in an honest and clear way: *She's always very direct, so you don't have to guess what she's thinking.* ANTONYM **indirect**

—**directness** *noun* the quality that a direct person has

direct² *verb*

1 the person who directs a movie or play tells the actors what to do: *The movie was directed by Joel Coen.*

2 *formal* to tell someone the way to a place: *He directed me to the airport.*

3 *formal* to aim something at a particular person, place, etc.: *A lot of advertising is directed at children.*

di•rec•tion /də'rekʃən/ *noun*

the way that someone or something is moving or pointing: *I think we're going in the wrong direction – we should be heading north.* | *He walked in the direction of the house* (=toward the house).

di•rec•tions /də'rekʃənz/ *plural noun*

information about how to get to a place, or about how to do something: *Could you give me directions to the airport?* | *Follow the directions on the bottle* (=do what they tell you to do).

di•rect•ly /də'rektli/ *adverb*

1 with no other person, thing, or event involved: *He was driving the car that hit the boys; he is directly responsible for their deaths.*

2 exactly in a particular position or direction: *Lucas sat directly behind us.*

di•rec•tor /də'rektɚ/ *noun*

1 the person who tells the actors what to do in a movie or play

2 someone who controls an organization or one of its activities: *The director of the museum is in charge of all the employees.*

→ See Thesaurus box at **movie**

di•rec•to•ry /daɪ'rektəri/ *noun* plural **directories**

1 a book containing a list of people, businesses, etc.: *Is his phone number in the telephone directory?*

2 a sign in a building that tells you where to find someone or something: *Check the directory for the doctor's office number.*

3 a list of FILEs on part of a computer: *How do I create a new directory on the C drive?*

dirt /dɚt/ *noun*

soil from the ground: *He was digging a hole and had dirt all over his clothes.* SYNONYM **soil**

dirt•y /'dɚti/ *adjective* **dirtier, dirtiest**

1 not clean: *My hands were dirty because I'd been working outside.*

> **THESAURUS: dirty**
>
> **filthy** very dirty: *The carpet was filthy.*
>
> **dusty** covered with dust: *piles of dusty books*
>
> **muddy** covered in mud: *My boots were all muddy.*
>
> **greasy** covered with a lot of oil or grease (=an oily substance): *His hair was greasy; it looked like it hadn't been washed in a week.*

2 relating to sex and thought to be bad: *The teacher heard him telling dirty jokes to the other kids.*

dis•a•bil•i•ty /ˌdɪsə'bɪləti/ *noun* plural **disabilities**

a physical or mental condition that makes it difficult for someone to do things: *Buildings should be changed so that people with disabilities can use them.*

dis•a•bled /dɪs'eɪbəld/ *adjective*

someone who is disabled cannot use a part of his or her body in the way that most people can: *The building was built to make it easy for the disabled* (=disabled people) *to move around.*

→ See Thesaurus box at **handicapped**

dis•ad•van•tage /ˌdɪsəd'væntɪdʒ/ *noun*

1 something that may make someone less successful than other people: *Because I didn't speak Spanish and everyone else did, I was at a disadvantage* (=had problems).

2 a bad feature of something: *One disadvantage of this treatment is that it is expensive.*

dis•ad•van•taged /ˌdɪsəd'væntɪdʒd/ *adjective, formal*

someone who is disadvantaged has social problems that make it difficult for him or her

to succeed: *The government provides money to help disadvantaged students.*
➔ See Thesaurus box at **poor**

dis•a•gree /ˌdɪsəˈgri/ *verb*
to have a different opinion from someone else: *He thought it was a good idea to ask the college for more money, but I disagreed with him.* | *We disagree about how to run the business.* ANTONYM **agree**

dis•a•gree•a•ble /ˌdɪsəˈgriəbəl/ *adjective, formal*
not pleasant or nice: *He's a disagreeable man, and I don't enjoy spending time with him.*

dis•a•gree•ment /ˌdɪsəˈgrimənt/ *noun*
a situation in which people disagree or argue: *We had a disagreement with our neighbors, and we haven't spoken to them for weeks.*

dis•ap•pear /ˌdɪsəˈpɪr/ *verb*
1 to become impossible to see or find: *My watch has disappeared – someone must have taken it.*
2 to stop existing: *The snow had disappeared.*
—**disappearance** *noun* the act of disappearing: *They were very worried about their son's disappearance.*

dis•ap•point /ˌdɪsəˈpɔɪnt/ *verb*
to make someone sad because something does not happen or is not as good as expected: *I'm sorry to disappoint you, but the trip has been canceled.*
—**disappointed** *adjective* sad because something does not happen or is not as good as expected: *I'm disappointed that I didn't win.*
—**disappointing** *adjective* making you feel disappointed: *The team has had a disappointing season.*

WORD FAMILY look at the words:

➔ **disappoint** *verb*
➔ **disappointed** *adjective*
➔ **disappointing** *adjective*
➔ **disappointment** *noun*

dis•ap•point•ment /ˌdɪsəˈpɔɪntmənt/ *noun*
1 a feeling of sadness because something has not happened or is not as good as expected: *She tried to hide her disappointment at not winning.*
2 someone or something that is not as good as you hoped or expected: *Their second album was a disappointment.*

dis•ap•prov•al /ˌdɪsəˈpruvəl/ *noun*
the opinion that someone or something is bad or wrong: *My sister's disapproval of my behavior made me mad.* ANTONYM **approval**

dis•ap•prove /ˌdɪsəˈpruv/ *verb*
to think that someone or something is bad or wrong: *Her parents disapproved of her boyfriend.* ANTONYM **approve**

dis•arm /dɪsˈɑrm/ *verb*
if a country or group disarms, it reduces the number of weapons and soldiers it has: *Both sides must disarm before they can discuss peace.*
—**disarmament** *noun* the process of disarming

dis•as•ter /dɪˈzæstɚ/ *noun*
1 a sudden event such as an accident or flood that causes great harm or damage: *Over the past two years the country has been hit by three natural disasters* (=floods, earthquakes, storms, etc.).
2 a complete failure: *The party was a total disaster; everyone went home early.*
—**disastrous** *adjective, formal* very bad: *It was a disastrous decision.*

dis•be•lief /ˌdɪsbəˈlif/ *noun, formal*
a feeling that something is not true: *When they told him he had won the money, he shook his head in disbelief.*

disc /dɪsk/ *noun*
another spelling of DISK

dis•card /dɪˈskɑrd/ *verb, formal*
to get rid of something because you do not need it: *Take the magazines you want and discard the rest.* SYNONYM **get rid of, throw out**

dis•cern /dɪˈsɚn/ *verb, formal*
to see or understand something that is not easy to see or understand: *It was difficult to discern a difference between the twin sisters.*
—**discernible** *adjective, formal* able to be seen

dis•charge /dɪsˈtʃɑrdʒ/ *verb*
1 to officially allow or tell someone to leave a place or organization: *He was discharged from the hospital last night.*

D

2 *formal* to send out or let out a substance: *The factory was discharging chemicals into the river.*

—**discharge** /ˈdɪstʃɑrdʒ/ *noun*, *formal* the action of discharging someone or something, or something that is discharged

dis•ci•ple /dɪˈsaɪpəl/ *noun*
a follower of a teacher or thinker: *Peter was one of Jesus's twelve disciples.*

D

dis•ci•pline[1] /ˈdɪsəplɪn/ *noun*
a situation in which you obey rules and orders, or control your own behavior: *There was no discipline in the classroom. Students were talking and nobody was working.* | *You need self-discipline to go to college.*

discipline[2] *verb*
to punish someone who has not obeyed a rule or order: *How should parents discipline their children?*

dis•close /dɪsˈkloʊz/ *verb*, *formal*
to let people know a fact that was a secret: *She refused to disclose her age.* SYNONYM **reveal**

—**disclosure** /dɪsˈkloʊʒɚ/ *noun* the act of letting people know something that was a secret

dis•com•fort /dɪsˈkʌmfɚt/ *noun*, *formal*
slight pain or a feeling of not being relaxed: *If your bed is causing you discomfort, get rid of it.*

dis•con•nect /ˌdɪskəˈnekt/ *verb*
to separate something from the thing it is connected to: *Disconnect the computer from the power supply.*

dis•con•tin•ue /ˌdɪskənˈtɪnyu/ *verb*, *formal*
to stop doing or providing something: *That product has been discontinued; we will not be selling it anymore.*

dis•count /ˈdɪskaʊnt/ *noun*
a reduction in the usual price of something: *I get a 10% discount on everything I buy from the store because I'm a student.*

dis•cour•age /dɪˈskɚɪdʒ/ *verb*
1 to make someone not want to do something: *Her parents tried to discourage her from becoming a singer, because they thought she wasn't good enough.* ANTONYM **encourage**
2 to make someone feel less confident: *I only got a C on the first test, but I tried not to let that discourage me.*

—**discouraged** *adjective* feeling less confident because of something that has happened: *Don't be discouraged. You'll do better next time!*

—**discouraging** *adjective* making you feel less confident: *The beginning of the game was discouraging, because the other team scored 15 points in the first six minutes.*

dis•cov•er /dɪˈskʌvɚ/ *verb*
1 to find something hidden or unknown: *A new insect has been discovered.* | *One day they will discover the cure for cancer.*
2 to find out a fact: *She discovered that her boyfriend was dating another girl.* | *I finally discovered what my mother was hiding in the closet.*

➔ See Thesaurus box at **find**

dis•cov•er•y /dɪˈskʌvəri/ *noun* plural **discoveries**
1 the act of finding out a fact: *Scientists made an important discovery about the way the disease begins.*
2 the act of finding something hidden or unknown: *The discovery of a new planet caused great excitement.*

dis•creet /dɪˈskrit/ *adjective*
careful not to let too many people know something: *He asked me to be discreet because he didn't want people to know where he was.*

—**discreetly** *adverb*

dis•cre•tion /dɪˈskreʃən/ Ac *noun*, *formal*
1 the right to decide what should be done in a particular situation: *You can spend the money at your discretion* (=in the way that you choose).
2 the quality of being discreet: *Discretion is important when you work here, because there are a lot of secrets that we don't want other companies to know.*

dis•crim•i•nate /dɪˈskrɪməˌneɪt/ Ac *verb*
1 to unfairly treat one person or group differently from another: *We do not discriminate against people because of their race.*
2 *formal* to know that two things are different from each other: *Babies can discriminate between a man's voice and a woman's voice.* SYNONYM **differentiate**

—**discrimination** /dɪˌskrɪməˈneɪʃən/ *noun* the act of discriminating against someone:

They accused the company of racial discrimination for hiring a white man who had less experience than a black man who wanted the job.
—**discriminatory** /dɪˈskrɪmənəˌtɔri/ *adjective, formal* discriminating against someone: *These discriminatory laws stop women from getting paid as well as men.*

dis•cuss /dɪˈskʌs/ *verb*
to talk about something in a serious way: *You should discuss your problems with your teacher.*
➔ See Thesaurus box at **talk**[1]

dis•cus•sion /dɪˈskʌʃən/ *noun*
a talk in which people give their ideas about something: *We all read the book and then had a class discussion about it.*

dis•ease /dɪˈziz/ *noun, formal*
a serious illness: *There is no cure for this disease yet.*

dis•fig•ure /dɪsˈfɪgyɚ/ *verb, formal*
if a part of a person's body is disfigured, it has been damaged and looks bad: *The woman's face had been disfigured in the attack.*

dis•grace /dɪsˈgreɪs/ *noun, formal*
1 something or someone that makes people feel ashamed: *After he was caught stealing, his father told him that he was a disgrace to the family.*
2 in disgrace = if you are in disgrace, you have done something bad and people are ashamed of you: *He left the school in disgrace after hitting a teacher.*

dis•grace•ful /dɪsˈgreɪsfəl/ *adjective, formal*
very bad and wrong: *The students' behavior was disgraceful; they didn't even care that they had damaged school property.*
—**disgracefully** *adverb*

dis•guise[1] /dɪsˈgaɪz/ *verb*
1 to make yourself look different, because you want to hide who you are: *She disguised herself as a man.*
2 to hide your feelings or the truth about something: *Dan tried to disguise his feelings for Katie because he didn't want her to know he liked her.*

disguise[2] *noun*
unusual clothes that you wear to hide who you are: *The movie star went out in disguise to avoid reporters.*

dis•gust /dɪsˈgʌst/ *verb*
if something bad disgusts you, you feel strongly that it is very bad or unpleasant: *His cruel behavior disgusted me.*
—**disgusted** *adjective* feeling strongly that something is very bad or unpleasant: *I knew that she was lying, and I was disgusted with her.*
—**disgust** *noun* a strong feeling that something is very bad or unpleasant: *She looked around the dirty little room in disgust.*

dis•gust•ing /dɪsˈgʌstɪŋ/ *adjective*
very bad or unpleasant: *This medicine tastes disgusting!*

dish /dɪʃ/ *noun*
1 a container used for cooking or holding food: *Mom came in with a dish of spaghetti.*
2 the dishes = all the plates, cups, bowls, etc. that you use for a meal: *It's your turn to wash the dishes.*
3 food that you prepare in a particular way: *The restaurant serves some great seafood dishes.*

dish•cloth /ˈdɪʃklɔθ/ *noun*
a cloth used for washing dishes

dis•hon•est /dɪsˈɑnɪst/ *adjective*
not honest: *She says she has never tried cigarettes, but I think she's being dishonest.*
—**dishonesty** *noun* the quality of not being honest

dis•hon•or /dɪsˈɑnɚ/ *noun, formal*
when people do not respect you, because you have done something bad: *Now he faced the dishonor of going to prison.*
—**dishonor** *verb* to do something that shows you do not respect someone or something: *If men refused to fight in a war, they dishonored their country.*

dish•tow•el /ˈdɪʃˌtaʊəl/ *noun*
a cloth used for drying dishes
➔ See picture on page A9

dish•wash•er /ˈdɪʃˌwɑʃɚ/ *noun*
1 a machine that washes dishes: *It only took a minute to load the dishwasher* (=put the dirty dishes in it).

D

D

2 someone whose job is washing dishes in a restaurant
➔ See picture on page A9

dis•il•lu•sioned /ˌdɪsəˈluʒənd/ *adjective, formal*
no longer believing that someone or something is good, interesting, etc.: *He was studying at the business school, but he became disillusioned with it and quit.*
—**disillusionment** *noun* the state of being disillusioned

dis•in•fect /ˌdɪsɪnˈfekt/ *verb*
to clean something with a chemical that kills BACTERIA: *Hospital rooms are regularly cleaned and disinfected.*

dis•in•fect•ant /ˌdɪsɪnˈfektənt/ *noun*
a chemical that kills BACTERIA, used for cleaning something

dis•in•te•grate /dɪsˈɪntəˌgreɪt/ *verb, formal*
to break up into small pieces: *The paper got wet and disintegrated in my hands.*
—**disintegration** /dɪsˌɪntəˈgreɪʃən/ *noun* the process of disintegrating

disk /dɪsk/ *noun*
1 a flat piece of plastic or metal used for storing computer information: *Store the document on disk.*
2 a flat round object: *People used to think that the Earth was a disk.*

ˈdisk drive *noun*
the part of a computer that you put a disk into

dis•like[1] /dɪsˈlaɪk/ *verb, formal*
to not like someone or something: *A lot of kids dislike vegetables.*
➔ See Thesaurus box at **hate**[1]

dislike[2] *noun, formal*
a feeling of not liking someone or something: *Maria couldn't hide her dislike for Hank; she wouldn't even talk to him.* ANTONYM **liking**

dis•lo•cate /dɪsˈloʊkeɪt/ *verb*
to make a bone move out of its normal place: *Pete dislocated his shoulder playing football.*

dis•loy•al /dɪsˈlɔɪəl/ *adjective, formal*
doing things that do not support your friends, your country, etc.: *If a friend asks you to keep a secret, it would be disloyal to tell people.* ANTONYM **loyal**
—**disloyalty** /dɪsˈlɔɪəlti/ *noun* the act of being disloyal

dis•mal /ˈdɪzməl/ *adjective, formal*
making you feel unhappy and without hope: *It was a gray, rainy, dismal day.*
—**dismally** *adverb*

dis•may /dɪsˈmeɪ/ *noun, formal*
a feeling of being worried or upset: *I realized with dismay that I'd missed my bus.*
—**dismayed** *adjective, formal* feeling worried or upset: *We were dismayed to find that the car had been stolen.*

dis•miss /dɪsˈmɪs/ *verb, formal*
1 to refuse to think about an idea: *Think about it for a few days – don't just dismiss the idea.*
2 to tell someone that they can leave: *Mrs. Burrows dismissed the class, and they went outside.*
3 if your employer dismisses you, you are told to leave your job: *The man had been dismissed from his job for stealing.* SYNONYM **fire**
—**dismissal** *noun* the act of dismissing someone

dis•o•be•di•ent /ˌdɪsəˈbidiənt/ *adjective, formal*
refusing to obey someone: *My dog is very disobedient. He never comes when I call him.* ANTONYM **obedient**
—**disobedience** *noun* an act of refusing to obey someone: *The soldier was punished for disobedience.*
—**disobediently** *adverb*

dis•o•bey /ˌdɪsəˈbeɪ/ *verb*
to not obey a person or a rule: *You must not disobey the school rules.*

THESAURUS: disobey

break a rule/law to disobey a rule or law: *If you drink and drive, you're breaking the law.*

rebel to disobey or fight against someone who has power over you: *Hannah rebelled against her parents' strict rules.*

defy *formal* to refuse to obey someone or something: *Mark had never defied his father before.*

violate *formal* to do something that does not obey a law, rule, agreement, etc.: *The sale may violate international trade laws.*

dis•or•der /dɪs'ɔrdɚ/ *noun, formal*
1 a situation in which things are not organized or neat: *The room was in complete disorder; there were clothes and books all over the floor.* ANTONYM **order**
2 an illness: *The doctor said her strange behavior was caused by a mental disorder* (=illness of the mind).

dis•or•der•ly /dɪs'ɔrdɚli/ *adjective, formal*
1 not organized or neat: *Disorderly piles of clothes lay on the floor.* ANTONYM **orderly**
2 showing bad or violent behavior: *The class was loud and disorderly, and the teacher could not control them.*

dis•or•ga•nized /dɪs'ɔrgəˌnaɪzd/ *adjective*
without enough order or organization: *The meeting was completely disorganized; we didn't finish anything.* ANTONYM **organized**

dis•o•ri•ent•ed /dɪs'ɔriˌentɪd/ *adjective, formal*
confused about what is happening or where you are: *I fell and hit my head, and when I stood up I felt a little disoriented.*

dis•patch /dɪ'spætʃ/ *verb, formal*
to send a person or thing somewhere: *A new spacecraft will soon be dispatched to Mars.*

dis•pense /dɪ'spens/ *verb, formal*
to give advice or help to people: *The organization dispenses legal advice to the public.*

dis•pens•er /dɪ'spensɚ/ *noun*
a machine or piece of equipment that gives you something when you push a button: *There was a soap dispenser next to the sink.*

dis•place /dɪs'pleɪs/ Ac *verb, formal*
to take the place of someone or something by forcing them to leave: *In Europe, the Euro has displaced other currencies.*
—**displacement** *noun* the act of displacing someone or something

dis•play[1] /dɪ'spleɪ/ Ac *noun* plural **displays**
1 an interesting way of showing things that is organized for people to come and see: *There is a display of all the students' work in the hall.* | *a fireworks display*
2 on display = in a public place for people to see: *The princess's dresses are now on display.*

display[2] *verb, formal*
1 to put things in a place where people can see them: *Your answers to the test questions will be displayed on the board.*
2 to show a feeling or quality: *Her face clearly displayed her anger.*

dis•pos•a•ble /dɪ'spoʊzəbəl/ Ac *adjective*
disposable things are for you to use once or a few times, and then throw away: *I bought a cheap disposable camera.*

dis•pose /dɪ'spoʊz/ Ac *verb, formal*
PHRASAL VERB
dispose of something
to throw away or destroy something: *We need better ways to dispose of waste.* SYNONYM **get rid of something**
—**disposal** *noun, formal* the act of disposing of something: *a garbage disposal site*

WORD FAMILY look at the words:
→ **dispose** *verb*
→ **disposal** *noun*
→ **disposable** *adjective*

dis•prove /dɪs'pruv/ *verb, formal*
to show that an idea, statement, etc. is not true: *Recent research has disproved some of the old ideas.* ANTONYM **prove**

dis•pute /dɪ'spyut/ *noun, formal*
a serious argument: *The two men got into a dispute over money.*
—**dispute** *verb, formal* to say that you think something is not true: *He claims that he won, but I dispute that.*

dis•qual•i•fy /dɪs'kwɑləˌfaɪ/ *verb* **disqualified**, third person singular **disqualifies**
to stop someone from taking part in a race, game, etc., because he or she has done something wrong: *He was disqualified for pushing another player.*
—**disqualification** /dɪsˌkwɑləfə'keɪʃən/ *noun* the act of disqualifying someone

dis•re•spect•ful /ˌdɪsrɪ'spektfəl/ *adjective*
showing no respect for someone or something: *Don't be disrespectful to your mother – listen when she's talking to you.* ANTONYM **respectful**

D

dis•rupt /dɪs'rʌpt/ *verb, formal*
to stop something from happening in a normal way by causing problems: *Bad weather disrupted flights into the airport.*
—**disruption** /dɪs'rʌpʃən/ *noun, formal* the action of disrupting something: *Please be quiet – I don't want any more disruptions during class.*
—**disruptive** /dɪs'rʌptɪv/ *adjective* causing problems by acting badly: *The boy was very disruptive in class, making funny noises when the teacher wasn't looking.*

dis•sat•is•fied /dɪ'sætɪsˌfaɪd/ *adjective*
unhappy about something because you do not think it is good enough: *A lot of teenage girls are dissatisfied with the way they look* (=they think they do not look good enough). ANTONYM **satisfied**
—**dissatisfaction** /dɪˌsætɪs'fækʃən/ *noun* the feeling of being dissatisfied: *Some of our customers have expressed dissatisfaction, so we're working hard to improve our service.*

dis•si•dent /'dɪsədənt/ *noun, formal*
someone who criticizes the government in a country where this is a crime: *Several dissidents have been put in jail.*

dis•sim•i•lar /dɪ'sɪmələ˞/ Ac *adjective, formal*
not the same: *The twins look alike, but they are dissimilar in other ways.* ANTONYM **similar**

dis•solve /dɪ'zɑlv/ *verb*
if sugar, salt, etc. dissolves in a liquid, it becomes part of the liquid and you cannot see it anymore: *Stir the mixture until the sugar dissolves.* | *Dissolve the tablets in warm water.*

dis•tance /'dɪstəns/ *noun*
1 the amount of space between two places: *Measure the distance between the two points on the line.* | *My house is just a short distance from here.*
2 in the distance *formal* = far away from you, but near enough to see: *We could see the ocean in the distance.*
3 keep your distance = to stay away from someone or something: *The dogs looked mean, so I kept my distance.*

dis•tant /'dɪstənt/ *adjective, formal*
1 far away: *From the road we could see distant mountains.*
2 not friendly or not caring: *He listened to me, but he seemed distant.*

dis•tilled /dɪ'stɪld/ *adjective*
distilled water/alcohol, etc. = water, etc. that has been heated until it is gas and then left to cool into a liquid again, in order to make it more pure
—**distill** *verb*
—**distillation** /ˌdɪstə'leɪʃən/ *noun* the process of making distilled water, etc.

dis•tinct /dɪ'stɪŋkt/ Ac *adjective*
1 a distinct feeling, possibility, etc. is clear and definite: *I had the distinct feeling that he didn't like me.*
2 if two things are distinct, they are different from each other: *There are two distinct types of elephants – Asian and African.*

dis•tinc•tion /dɪ'stɪŋkʃən/ Ac *noun*
1 a clear difference: *The law makes a distinction between children and adults* (=it says that there is a difference between them).
2 *formal* the quality of doing something very well: *In college, she performed with great distinction.*
3 have the distinction of doing something = to do something special that everyone admires: *Who will have the distinction of speaking at the ceremony?*

dis•tinc•tive /dɪ'stɪŋktɪv/ Ac *adjective, formal*
different from others and easy to recognize: *This cheese has a very distinctive flavor.*

dis•tinct•ly /dɪ'stɪŋktli/ Ac *adverb*
very clearly: *I distinctly remember what he said to me before he left.*

dis•tin•guish /dɪ'stɪŋgwɪʃ/ *verb, formal*
1 to see the difference between things: *Young children do not distinguish between TV shows and advertising.*
2 to show that someone or something is different: *The male bird's bright feathers distinguish it from the female.*

dis•tin•guished /dɪ'stɪŋgwɪʃt/ *adjective, formal*
very good and admired by a lot of people: *He had a distinguished career as a scientist.*

dis•tort /dɪ'stɔrt/ Ac *verb, formal*
to change something and make it look or sound different from normal: *The funny mirrors distorted our reflections.*

—**distortion** /dɪˈstɔrʃən/ *noun* the act of distorting something

dis•tract /dɪˈstrækt/ *verb*
to make someone stop paying attention to something: *Her music was distracting me from my homework.*
—**distraction** /dɪˈstrækʃən/ *noun* something that makes you stop paying attention: *I can't work at home – there are too many distractions.*

dis•tress¹ /dɪˈstres/ *noun, formal*
1 a feeling of great sadness or worry: *You could see the distress in the child's eyes as she said goodbye to her parents.*
2 in distress = in a very difficult situation and needing help: *Our organization tries to help children in distress in the poorest areas of the world.*
—**distressed** *adjective, formal* feeling very sad or worried: *She was crying and very distressed about her missing sister.*

distress² *verb, formal*
to make someone sad or worried: *The awful news distressed us all.*
—**distressing** *adjective, formal* making you feel very sad or worried: *It was distressing to see her so sick.*

dis•trib•ute /dɪˈstrɪbyət/ Ac *verb, formal*
1 to give something to people: *The money was distributed among the poorest people.*
2 to take goods to stores and companies for them to sell: *The company makes and distributes building materials.*

WORD FAMILY look at the words:
→ **distribute** *verb*
→ **distribution** *noun*
→ **distributor** *noun*

→ See Thesaurus box at **give¹**

dis•tri•bu•tion /ˌdɪstrəˈbyuʃən/ Ac *noun*
1 the act of giving things to people: *Students helped with the distribution of the newspaper.*
2 the act of taking goods to stores and companies for them to sell: *the distribution of goods by trains and trucks*
—**distributor** /dɪˈstrɪbyətɚ/ *noun* a company that supplies goods to shops or other companies: *The company is a distributor of cellular phones.*

dis•trict /ˈdɪstrɪkt/ *noun*
an area of a city, country, etc.: *She works in the financial district of the city.*
→ See Thesaurus box at **area**

ˌdistrict atˈtorney *also* **D.A.** *noun*
a lawyer for the government of an area in the U.S.: *He's the D.A. for Harris County.*

dis•trust /dɪsˈtrʌst/ *noun, formal*
a feeling that you cannot trust someone: *He had a distrust of politicians; he thought they were all liars.*
—**distrust** *verb, formal* to not trust someone or something
—**distrustful** *adjective, formal* not trusting someone or something: *Kim was distrustful of strangers.*

dis•turb /dɪˈstɚb/ *verb*
1 to interrupt what someone is doing: *Don't disturb Dad – he's working.*
2 *formal* to make someone feel worried or upset: *The strange way she acted had disturbed him.*
—**disturbing** *adjective, formal* making you feel worried or upset: *The news about Marta's accident was very disturbing.*

dis•turb•ance /dɪˈstɚbəns/ *noun, formal*
1 something that interrupts what you are doing: *I really need to work without any disturbance.*
2 a situation in which people fight or cause trouble in public: *Three men were arrested for causing a disturbance.*

ditch /dɪtʃ/ *noun*
a long narrow hole in the ground where water collects at the side of a road: *I jumped across the ditch and into the field.*

dit•to /ˈdɪtoʊ/ *informal*
used when saying that you think the same as someone else: *"I hate school." "Ditto."*

dive /daɪv/ *verb* **dived** or **dove** /doʊv/ **dived**
1 to jump into water with your head and arms going in first: *Jack dived into the swimming pool.*
2 to go down suddenly: *The plane began to dive.*
→ See Thesaurus box at **jump¹**
→ See picture at **jump²**

D

div·er /ˈdaɪvɚ/ *noun*
1 someone who swims under water using equipment for breathing: *The island is very popular with divers.*
2 someone who dives into water as a sport

di·verse /dəˈvɚs/ Ac *adjective, formal*
full of many different types of people or things: *We are a very diverse group. We have students from over 50 countries.*
WORD FAMILY → **diversity** *noun*

di·ver·si·ty /dəˈvɚsəti/ Ac *noun, formal*
a range of many different people or things: *I love the diversity of wildlife in this country.*
SYNONYM **variety**

di·vert /dəˈvɚt/ *verb, formal*
if cars, airplanes, etc. are diverted, they have to change their direction: *The plane going to Atlanta was diverted to Memphis.*

di·vide /dɪˈvaɪd/ *verb*
1 *also* **divide up** to separate something into parts or groups: *The teacher divided the class into groups.*
2 *also* **divide up** to share money, time, etc. between people or activities: *Most students divide their time between school, family, and friends.*
3 to find how many times a number will go into a bigger number: *15 divided by 3 is 5.*
ANTONYM **multiply**
4 *formal* to make people disagree: *The war divided the nation.*
WORD FAMILY → **division** *noun*

di·vine /dɪˈvaɪn/ *adjective, formal*
relating to a god: *the divine power of God*

ˈdiving board *noun*
a board that you can stand on before jumping into water: *He jumped off the diving board, and dived into the pool.*

di·vi·sion /dɪˈvɪʒən/ *noun*
1 the act of finding how many times a number will go into a larger number: *The kids are learning to do division and multiplication.*
2 a part of a company, army, or organization: *"Which part of the company do you work for?" "The sales division."*

di·vorce¹ /dɪˈvɔrs/ *noun*
the end of a marriage by law: *His wife wants to get a divorce.*

divorce² *verb*
to end a marriage by law: *My parents got divorced when I was six.*

THESAURUS: divorce

separate to start to live apart from your husband or wife: *We've been separated for a year, and now we're getting a divorce.*

split up/break up to end a marriage or a long romantic relationship: *When Andy was nine, his parents split up. | Lisa has broken up with her boyfriend.*

leave someone to stop living with your husband, wife, or partner: *Her husband left her after 27 years of marriage.*

di·vulge /dəˈvʌldʒ/ *verb, formal*
to give information about something secret: *He always refused to divulge how much money he earned.* SYNONYM **disclose, reveal**

diz·zy /ˈdɪzi/ *adjective*
feeling unable to stand up steadily because you are sick, or you have been turning around in circles: *I feel a little dizzy, so I think I'll lie down.*
—**dizziness** *noun*

DJ *noun*
disk jockey someone whose job is to play the music on the radio or in a club where you can dance

DNA *noun*
a substance in the cells of your body that carries GENETIC information

do¹ /du/ *auxiliary verb* **did** /dɪd/ third person singular **does** /dʌz/
1 used with "not" before another verb to make a negative sentence: *She does not have a car. | I didn't understand him.*
2 used with another verb to ask a question: *Do you know where he lives?*
3 used with "not" to tell someone not to do something: *Do not tell anyone. | Don't hit me!*
4 used to make the meaning of another verb stronger: *I did clean the bathroom – I just forgot to tell you.*

do² *verb* **did** /dɪd/ **done** /dʌn/ third person singular **does** /dʌz/
1 to deal with some work, a job, etc.: *Don't forget to do your homework. | "What are you doing?" "I'm just making lunch." | I'll do the ironing.*
2 **What do you do (for a living)?** = used when asking someone what their job is: *"What do you do for a living?" "I'm a computer programmer."*

3 What is someone or something doing? = used when asking for an explanation of someone's actions: *What is the dog doing on my desk?* | *What are you doing with my wallet?*
4 do well/badly = to be successful or unsuccessful: *He's doing very well in his new job.* | *William did badly on the test.*
5 do someone good = to make someone feel better or more healthy: *The vacation did us all good.*
6 something will do = used when saying that something is good enough: *This shirt's a little small, but it will do.*
7 to act in a particular way: *I expect the kids in my class to do as I say* (=do what I tell them to do).
8 do your hair/nails/makeup, etc. = to make your hair, etc. look nice: *Wait a second while I do my hair.*
9 do 90 miles/100 km, etc. *informal* = to travel at 90 miles an hour, or to cover a distance of 90 miles: *He was doing 60 miles per hour when he hit the other car.*
10 do your own thing *informal* = to do what you enjoy doing: *On the weekend, I like to do my own thing.*

PHRASAL VERBS

do something over
to do something again, especially because you did it badly: *If you mess up on the test, you can do it over.*

do with something
1 what did you do with something? = used when asking where someone has put something: *What did you do with those pictures?*
2 I could do with something *informal* = used when saying that you need or want something: *I could do with some help.*
3 have something to do with something = to be about something: *The book has something to do with the Civil War.*

do without something
to live or continue without something: *It's difficult to do without a car in Los Angeles.*

do·a·ble /ˈduəbəl/ *adjective, informal*
possible to do: *It's a difficult project, but I think it's doable.*

dock¹ /dɑk/ *noun*
a place where a ship or boat stops, so that people or things can get on or off: *The ship was sitting at the dock.*

dock² *verb*
if a ship docks, it sails into a dock: *The ship docked in Brooklyn.*

doc·tor /ˈdɑktɚ/ *noun*
1 someone whose job is treating people who are sick: *If you're still sick tomorrow, you should go to the doctor.*

> **THESAURUS: doctor**
>
> **physician** *formal* a doctor: *Dr. Meadows is our family physician.*
>
> **surgeon** a doctor who cuts open someone's body to fix or replace something: *Surgeons operated on his knee.*
>
> **specialist** a doctor who knows a lot about a particular type of medicine: *He's one of the world's leading heart specialists.*
>
> **psychiatrist** a doctor who treats mental illness: *The psychiatrist gave her some pills to help her depression.*
>
> **dentist** a doctor who takes care of people's teeth: *You should see a dentist every six months.*
>
> **pediatrician** a doctor who treats children who are sick: *I took my son to a pediatrician because he seemed to be losing weight.*

2 someone who has the highest type of university degree: *He's a Doctor of Philosophy.* SYNONYM **Ph.D.**
➔ See picture on page A16

doc·tor·ate /ˈdɑktərɪt/ *noun*
the highest type of university degree: *She earned a doctorate in biology.* SYNONYM **Ph.D**

doc·u·ment /ˈdɑkyəmənt/ Ac *noun*
1 a formal letter, written report, etc. that has facts or information in it: *Keep all your financial documents in a safe place.*
2 a piece of work that you write and keep on a computer: *Don't forget to save your document before you close the program.*

doc·u·men·ta·ry /ˌdɑkyəˈmentri/ *noun*
plural **documentaries**
a movie or television program that gives facts and information on something: *Did you see that documentary on insects?*
➔ See Thesaurus box at **television**

D

D

doc•u•men•ta•tion /ˌdɑkyəmən'teɪʃən/ Ac *noun, formal*
documents that show that something is true: *Keep careful documentation of how much everything costs.* SYNONYM **records**

dodge /dɑdʒ/ *verb*
1 to move quickly in order to avoid someone or something: *I dodged past him and kicked the ball.*
2 to avoid talking about something or doing something: *Answer me – don't try to dodge the question!*

doe /doʊ/ *noun*
a female DEER

do•er /'duɚ/ *noun, informal*
someone who does things, and does not only talk about doing them: *Are you a doer or a talker?*

does /dəz; *strong* dʌz/ *verb*
the third person singular of the present tense of DO

does•n't /'dʌzənt/ *verb*
the short form of "does not": *The baby doesn't have any teeth yet.*

dog /dɔg/ *noun*
an animal that people often keep as a pet or use for guarding buildings: *My dog barks when he hears a strange noise.*
➔ See picture at **pet**

doll /dɑl/ *noun*
a toy that looks like a baby or small person: *Katy loves playing with her dolls.*

dol•lar /'dɑlɚ/ *noun*
the money used in the U.S. and some other countries, shown by the sign $: *These pants cost 40 dollars.* | *The book cost $15* (=fifteen dollars).

'dollar sign *noun*
the sign $, used to mean a dollar

dolphin

dol•phin /'dɑlfɪn/ *noun*
a very intelligent gray ocean animal with a long pointed nose: *We saw a group of dolphins playing in the waves.*

do•main /doʊ'meɪn/ Ac *noun, formal*
1 a particular area of work or knowledge: *I work mainly in Europe, but Jan's domain is China.*
2 an area of land that is controlled by one person, group, government, etc.

dome /doʊm/ *noun*
a round curved roof: *If you look across the city, you can see the dome of the cathedral.*

do•mes•tic /də'mestɪk/ Ac *adjective, formal*
1 relating to things that happen inside a country, rather than things that happen in other countries: *The president's speech is about taxes and other domestic policies.*
2 relating to life at home: *Bob and I share the domestic chores* (=jobs around the home).
—**domestically** *adverb* inside one country: *Most of these goods are made domestically.*

dom•i•nant /'dɑmənənt/ Ac *adjective, formal*
very important or powerful: *Japan has a dominant position in the electronics market.*
—**dominance** *noun* the state of being dominant

dom•i•nate /'dɑməˌneɪt/ Ac *verb*
to have the most influence or the most important position: *Men still dominate the field of movie directing, but more and more women are making movies.*
—**domination** /ˌdɑmə'neɪʃən/ *noun, formal* the position of dominating something

WORD FAMILY look at the words:
➔ **dominate** *verb*
➔ **domination** *noun*
➔ **dominant** *adjective*
➔ **dominance** *noun*

dom•i•no /'dɑməˌnoʊ/ *noun* plural **dominoes**
a small piece of wood or plastic with spots on one side, used in playing a game: *The kids are playing dominoes* (=playing a game using these).

do•nate /'doʊneɪt/ *verb*
1 to give money to an organization that needs help: *Our school donated $500 to the Red Cross.*
2 donate blood/an organ, etc. = to give some of your blood or a part of your body to

help someone who is sick: *Hospitals are asking more people to donate blood.*
—**donation** /doʊˈneɪʃən/ *noun* money that you give to help an organization: *Do you want to make a donation to charity?*

done[1] /dʌn/ *verb*
the past participle of DO

done[2] *adjective*
1 finished: *"Are you finished?" "Not yet, I'll be done in a minute."*

THESAURUS: done

finished done, or having come to the end of doing something: *Are you finished with your homework?*

complete finished, and having all the parts you need: *My history report is almost complete.*

over if an event, activity, or period of time is over, it has ended: *The game was over by 10 o'clock.*

through if you are through with something, you have finished using it or doing it: *Are you through with those scissors?*

2 cooked enough to be eaten: *Is the chicken done yet?*

don•key /ˈdɑŋki/ *noun*
an animal like a small horse with long ears: *The donkey was carrying a heavy load on its back.*

do•nor /ˈdoʊnɚ/ *noun*
1 a blood/organ donor = someone who gives blood or a part of his or her body to help someone who is sick: *The hospital needs more blood donors.*
2 someone who gives something, especially money, to an organization: *He is a generous donor to the Democratic Party.*

don't /doʊnt/ *verb*
the short form of "do not": *I don't know.*

do•nut /ˈdoʊnʌt/ *noun*
another spelling of DOUGHNUT

doom /dum/ *noun*
something bad that is certain to happen: *As usual, the news was full of doom and gloom* (=news about bad things that will happen).

doomed /dumd/ *adjective*
certain to fail, be disappointing, etc.: *The idea was doomed from the beginning – we knew it was not going to work.*

door /dɔr/ *noun*
1 the thing that you open to get into a house, room, or car: *I opened the door and went inside.* | *Go out the door and turn right.*
2 get/answer the door = to open the door when someone knocks or rings the bell: *Can you get the door, Jody? I'm on the phone.*
3 next door = in the room, house, etc. next to where you are: *A very nice family lives next door.*
4 at the door = waiting outside the door of a house or apartment: *There's someone at the door who wants to talk to you.*
➔ See picture on page A8

door•bell /ˈdɔrbel/ *noun*
a button by a door that you push to make a sound inside a building: *I went up to the door and rang the doorbell* (=pushed it).

door•knob /ˈdɔrnɑb/ *noun*
a round handle that you turn to open a door: *There was no sound inside, so I turned the doorknob.*

door•mat /ˈdɔrmæt/ *noun*
a thick piece of material beside a door for you to clean your shoes on: *Ted wiped his boots on the doormat before he went inside.*

door•step /ˈdɔrstep/ *noun*
a step in front of the door of a house: *The dog was standing on the doorstep, wanting to come inside.*

door•way /ˈdɔrweɪ/ *noun*
an opening into a room or building, where there is a door: *Cindy stood in the doorway and watched the people in the street.*

dor•mi•to•ry /ˈdɔrməˌtɔri/ *noun, formal*
plural **dormitories**, *also* **dorm** *informal*
a large building at a college where students live: *She lived in my dorm freshman year.*

dos•age /ˈdoʊsɪdʒ/ *noun, formal*
the amount of medicine that you should take: *The correct dosage is one pill per day.*

dose /doʊs/ *noun*
an amount of medicine: *Take a small dose of the liquid at bedtime.*

dot /dɑt/ *noun*
1 a small round mark or spot: *She was wearing a black skirt with white dots.*
2 on the dot *informal* = exactly at the right time: *Mark arrived at 6:00 on the dot.*

D

D

doub•le[1] /ˈdʌbəl/ *adjective*
1 having two parts: *A double door opens onto the porch.*
2 twice the usual amount or size: *I'll have a double cheeseburger with fries.*
3 a double bed = a bed for two people: *The room had a double bed.*
4 double digits = the numbers from 10 to 99: *The best three players scored in double digits.*

double[2] *verb*
to become twice as big: *In 30 years, San Francisco doubled in size.*
➔ See Thesaurus box at **increase**[1]

double[3] *noun*
1 something that is twice as big as something else: *"He offered me $200." "OK, I'll give you double."*
2 someone who looks like someone else: *He earned a lot of money working as a double for Tom Cruise.*

ˌdouble ˈbass *noun*
a very big musical instrument like a VIOLIN, that you play while you are standing up SYNONYM **bass**
➔ See picture on page A21

ˌdouble-ˈcheck *verb*
to check something again, so you are sure about it: *I think I locked the door, but I'll double-check.*

ˌdouble ˈnegative *noun*
the use of two negative words when it is correct to use only one: *The sentence "I don't want nobody to help me" has a double negative. You should say "I don't want anybody to help me".*

doubt[1] /daʊt/ *verb*
to think that something may not happen or be true: *Kate might come, but I doubt it. She said she was tired.* | *I doubted that she was telling the truth.*

WORD FAMILY look at the words:
➔ **doubt** *noun*
➔ **doubt** *verb*
➔ **doubtful** *adjective*
➔ **doubtless** *adverb*

doubt[2] *noun*
1 a feeling that something is not right or true: *Don't get married if you have any doubts.*
2 there's no doubt about it *also* **without (a) doubt** = used when saying that something is definitely true: *Without a doubt, this is their best CD yet.*
3 beyond (a) doubt = if information is beyond doubt, it is definitely correct: *All the evidence proved beyond a doubt that he was guilty.*

doubt•ful /ˈdaʊtfəl/ *adjective, formal*
1 probably not likely to happen or not true: *He injured his leg and it's doubtful that he'll be able to play in the game.*
2 not sure about something: *I'm still doubtful about whether I should trust him.*

doubt•less /ˈdaʊtləs/ *adverb, formal*
used when saying that something is very likely: *The hotel will doubtless be very expensive, because it's right in the middle of the city.* SYNONYM **definitely, undoubtedly**

dough /doʊ/ *noun*
a soft mixture of flour and water that you use to bake bread, cookies, etc.
—**doughy** *adjective* soft and white, like dough: *The bread was a little doughy inside, because it hadn't been baked long enough.*

dough•nut /ˈdoʊnʌt/ *noun*
a small round cake that is shaped like a ring

dove[1] /dʌv/ *noun*
a small white bird often used as a sign of peace

dove[2] /doʊv/ *verb*
a past tense of DIVE

down[1] /daʊn/ *adverb, preposition*
1 toward a lower place: *A tree fell down during the night.* | *We began to climb down the mountain.* ANTONYM **up**
2 toward a place that is further along a street, path, etc.: *I saw George walking down the street.*
3 toward a lower level: *Can you turn the TV down?* ANTONYM **up**
4 write/note/take, etc. something down = to write something on paper: *He wrote down my phone number.*
5 toward the south of a country: *First, we drove down to Texas.* ANTONYM **up**
➔ **come down with** at **come**

down[2] *adjective*
1 sad: *You look down. Are you okay?*
2 lower in amount than before: *The number of students at the school is down this year.* ANTONYM **up**

3 a computer system that is down is not working: *All the computers in the office are down.*

down³ *noun*
the soft feathers of a bird: *The pillow was filled with down.*

down·fall /ˈdaʊnfɔl/ *noun, formal*
a situation when someone or something stops being successful: *He wanted more and more power, and that led to his downfall.*

down·heart·ed /ˌdaʊnˈhɑrtɪd/ *adjective, formal*
sad or without hope: *Don't look so down-hearted – everything will be fine.*

down·hill /ˌdaʊnˈhɪl/ *adverb, adjective*
toward a lower level of land: *The land slopes downhill to the river.* ANTONYM **uphill**

down·load /ˈdaʊnloʊd/ *verb*
to move information, programs, etc. to your computer from the Internet or another piece of equipment: *The software can be down-loaded from the Internet.*

ˌdown ˈpayment *noun*
a payment for something that is the first part of the larger amount you will pay over a long period: *My parents put a down payment on a house in Oakland.*

down·pour /ˈdaʊnpɔr/ *noun*
a lot of rain that falls in a short time: *We got very wet in a sudden downpour on the way home.*
➔ See Thesaurus box at **rain¹**

down·right /ˈdaʊnraɪt/ *adverb*
downright dangerous/silly/ugly, etc. *informal* = used to emphasize that someone or something is very dangerous, silly, etc.: *He's downright lazy – he never helps me do anything at home.*

down·size /ˈdaʊnsaɪz/ *verb*
to reduce the number of people who work for a company: *A lot of big companies are downsizing.*

down·stairs /ˌdaʊnˈsterz/ *adverb, adjective*
down the steps in a building to or on a lower floor: *I went downstairs and opened the front door.* | *my downstairs neighbor* ANTONYM **upstairs**

down·town /ˌdaʊnˈtaʊn/ *adverb, adjective*
to or in the middle of a city, where there are a lot of stores and businesses: *Let's go down-town after work and go shopping.* | *The hotel's in downtown Austin.*

down·ward /ˈdaʊnwɚd/ *also* **downwards** *adverb*
toward a lower place or level: *The path led downward to the edge of the lake.* ANTONYM **upward**
—**downward** *adjective* moving toward a lower place or level: *a downward movement in prices*

doze /doʊz/ *verb*
to sleep for a short time: *I was dozing on the couch.*
PHRASAL VERB
doze off
to start sleeping when you do not intend to: *Grandpa dozed off watching TV.*
➔ See Thesaurus box at **sleep¹**

doz·en /ˈdʌzən/ *number*
1 a group of 12 things: *You can either buy six eggs or a dozen.*
2 *informal* a lot: *I've heard this story dozens of times – he tells it at every party.*

Dr. /ˈdɑktɚ/
the written abbreviation of **Doctor**

drab /dræb/ *adjective*
not colorful or interesting: *The room was drab, with gray walls and a brown carpet.*

draft¹ /dræft/ Ac *noun*
1 a piece of writing, a drawing, etc. that you intend to change until it is the way you want: *Can I show you the first draft of my history paper?*
2 cold air blowing into a room: *There's a draft in here. Is the window open?*
3 **the draft** = a system that makes people join the military: *Men who were sick avoided the draft.*
4 a system in which football players, basket-ball players, etc. are chosen to play on professional teams: *the NBA draft of college players*

draft² *verb*
1 to write or draw something that you intend to make changes to later, until it is the way you want it to be: *I drafted a letter to my*

congressman, and asked other students to add anything they thought was important.
2 to tell someone that he or she must join the military for a period of time: *He was drafted during the Vietnam War, and fought there for several years.*
—**draft** *adjective* relating to a draft of a piece of writing or a drawing: *I gave the draft report to my teacher for comments.*

D

draft•y /ˈdræfti/ *adjective*
a drafty room or building has cold air blowing through it: *Old houses are often drafty.*

drag /dræg/ *verb* **dragged, dragging**
1 to pull something heavy along the ground: *The boys dragged the boat onto the beach.*
2 to pull someone in a strong or violent way: *Two men dragged him out of his car.*
➔ See Thesaurus box at **pull**[1]
➔ See picture on page A4

drag•on /ˈdrægən/ *noun*
a fierce animal in stories that can fly and breathe out fire

drag•on•fly /ˈdrægənˌflaɪ/ *noun* plural **dragonflies**
a large flying insect, with a long body

drain[1] /dreɪn/ *noun*
1 a pipe or hole that carries away dirty water: *Leaves had blocked the drains in the streets.*
2 down the drain *informal* = if something goes down the drain, it is unsuccessful or it is wasted: *Since then, his career has gone down the drain; he hasn't made a single movie.*
3 a drain on something = something that uses a lot of time, money, energy, etc.: *Filling out all these forms is a drain on our time.*

drain[2] *verb*
1 if a liquid drains, it flows away: *The bath water slowly drained away.*
2 to make the liquid flow away from something: *When the pasta is cooked, drain it.*

dra•ma /ˈdrɑmə/ Ac *noun*
1 a play for the theater, television, radio, etc.: *Is the play a drama or a comedy?*
2 acting and plays in general: *Ben loves music and drama.*
3 exciting things that happen: *It was an exciting game, with plenty of drama.*
—**dramatist** /ˈdræmətɪst/ *noun, formal* someone who writes plays

WORD FAMILY look at the words:

➔ **drama** *noun*
➔ **dramatic** *adjective*
➔ **dramatically** *adverb*
➔ **dramatize** *verb*
➔ **dramatist** *noun*
➔ **dramatization** *noun*

➔ See Thesaurus box at **movie**

dra•mat•ic /drəˈmætɪk/ Ac *adjective*
1 very sudden, exciting, or noticeable: *There has been a dramatic improvement in his work; he was getting C's and D's, and now he's getting A's.*
2 showing a lot of emotion in a noticeable way: *Stop being so dramatic – you're embarrassing me.*
3 related to plays and the theater: *Arthur Miller's dramatic works* (=plays written for the theater)
—**dramatically** *adverb* in a very sudden, exciting, or noticeable way: *The company's profits have increased dramatically.*

dram•a•tize /ˈdræməˌtaɪz/ Ac *verb*
to use a real event or story from a book to write a play, movie, or television program: *They are dramatizing her life story for TV* (=making a television movie about her life).
—**dramatization** /ˌdræmətəˈzeɪʃən/ *noun* the action of dramatizing something

drank /dræŋk/ *verb*
the past tense of DRINK

drape /dreɪp/ *verb, formal*
to put cloth or clothing over or around something: *He draped his coat over a chair.*

drapes /dreɪps/ *also* **drap•e•ries** /ˈdreɪpəriz/ *plural noun*
heavy curtains

dras•tic /ˈdræstɪk/ *adjective*
drastic actions or changes have a big effect: *The new school principal is planning to make drastic changes; the first one will be to fire several teachers.*
—**drastically** *adverb*: *The cost of oil has increased drastically in the past few months.*

draw[1] /drɔ/ *verb* **drew** /dru/ **drawn** /drɔn/
1 if you draw something, you use a pen or pencil to make a picture of it: *She was drawing a picture of a tree.* | *I'll draw you a map of how to get there.*
2 *formal* to pull something from a container

or across something: *He drew a piece of paper from his pocket.*
3 to move someone or something by pulling him, her, or it gently: *She drew the curtains* (=closed the curtains by pulling them gently).
4 draw near/closer *formal* = to become closer in time or space: *Christmas is drawing near.*
5 to attract or interest someone: *The movie drew large crowds* (=many people came to see it).
6 draw the line (at something) = to refuse to do something because you do not approve of it, although you are willing to do other things: *I will help you, but I draw the line at telling lies* (=I will not tell lies).
7 draw blood *formal* = to make someone bleed: *The dog bit her so hard that it drew blood.*

PHRASAL VERBS

draw back
to move back from something: *The crowd drew back to let the police get to the injured man.*

draw something up
1 to think of and write a list, plan, etc.: *The teachers drew up a list of equipment they needed.*
2 if a car draws up somewhere, it stops there: *A car drew up outside the house.*

draw² *noun*
1 something that attracts people to see it: *The town's new museum will be a big draw for visitors.*
2 one player's turn to take a card in a game of cards: *It was my draw, and I picked the ten of hearts.*

draw•back /ˈdrɔbæk/ *noun, formal*
something that might be a problem or disadvantage: *The main drawback to living in New York is that the cost of apartments is so high.*

drawer /drɔr/ *noun*
a part of a piece of furniture that is shaped like a long thin box and which slides in and out: *The pens are in the top drawer of my desk.*
➔ See picture on page A18

draw•ing /ˈdrɔɪŋ/ *noun*
1 a picture you make with a pen or pencil: *a drawing of a cat*
2 the art or skill of making pictures with a pen or pencil: *I am not good at drawing.*
3 an event in which someone's name is picked by chance from many names, and he or she wins a prize: *There will be a drawing today, and some lucky person will win a new car.*
➔ See Thesaurus box at **art**

drawn /drɔn/ *verb*
the past participle of DRAW

dread¹ /dred/ *verb, formal*
to feel very worried about something that is going to happen: *I have a test tomorrow, and I'm dreading it.*

dread² *noun, formal*
a strong fear of something that is going to happen or may happen: *Flying always fills her with dread.*

dread•ful /ˈdredfəl/ *adjective, formal*
very bad or unpleasant: *The performance was dreadful – I just wanted it to end.*
—**dreadfully** *adverb*

dream¹ /drim/ *noun*
1 the images that you see in your mind when you are asleep: *I had a dream about my dog last night.*
2 something that you hope will happen: *Her dream was to become a drummer in a band.*

dream² *verb* **dreamed** or **dreamt** /dremt/
1 to see images in your mind while you are asleep: *I dreamed that I was flying.*
2 to think about something that you hope will happen: *She dreamed of becoming a pilot.*

dream•er /ˈdrimɚ/ *noun*
someone who has dreams or ideas that are not likely to happen: *The inventor was often accused of being a dreamer.*

dreamt /dremt/ *verb*
a past tense and past participle of DREAM

dream•y /ˈdrimi/ *adjective*
1 a dreamy look, smile, etc. shows that you are thinking about something pleasant rather than about what is happening around you: *Whenever he talks about his girlfriend he gets a dreamy look on his face.*
2 pleasant, peaceful, and relaxing: *They play dreamy music in my dentist's office to try to make people relax.*
—**dreamily** *adverb* thinking about pleasant things rather than what is happening around you: *She looked dreamily at the sky.*

D

D

drear·y /ˈdrɪri/ *adjective, formal*
not exciting and making you feel sad or bored: *I was sick of the dreary rainy weather and wanted some sunshine.*

drench /drentʃ/ *verb, formal*
to make something completely wet: *The rain drenched us.*
—**drenched** *adjective*: *I forgot my umbrella and got drenched.*

dress¹ /dres/ *verb*
to put clothes on someone or on yourself: *Can you dress the kids while I make breakfast?* | *He got dressed* (=put on his clothes) *quickly.*
PHRASAL VERB
dress up
1 to wear your best clothes for a special occasion: *Everybody dressed up for the party.*
2 to wear special clothes that make you look like someone or something else: *I dressed up as a robot for Halloween.*
➔ See picture on page A6

dress² *noun*
1 a piece of clothing that a woman or girl wears, which covers the top of her body and part of her legs: *She was wearing a red dress.*
2 *formal* clothes for men or women of a particular type or for a particular occasion: *Everyone at the event was in formal dress* (=wearing formal clothes).
3 a dress shirt/dress shoes, etc. = a shirt, shoes, etc. that you wear with formal clothes such as a SUIT

ˈdress code *noun*
a standard of what you should wear for a particular situation: *The restaurant has a strict dress code. Men have to wear a suit and tie.*

dress·er /ˈdresɚ/ *noun*
a piece of furniture with drawers, used for keeping clothes in: *All my T-shirts are in the top drawer of that dresser.*

dress·ing /ˈdresɪŋ/ *noun*
1 a mixture of oil and other things that you pour over SALAD: *What kind of salad dressing would you like?*
2 another word for STUFFING: *I'm making dressing for the turkey.*

ˈdressing room *noun*
a room where an actor gets ready before going on stage or television

dress·mak·er /ˈdresˌmeɪkɚ/ *noun*
a person whose job is to make clothes for women

dress·y /ˈdresi/ *adjective*
dressy clothes are ones you wear for special or formal occasions: *I bought some dressy shoes for the wedding.*

drew /dru/ *verb*
the past tense of DRAW

drib·ble /ˈdrɪbəl/ *verb*
1 if a liquid dribbles somewhere, it flows in a slow thin stream: *Blood from a cut dribbled down the side of his face.*
2 to move a ball forward by bouncing (BOUNCE) it again and again in basketball, or kicking it again and again in SOCCER

dried /draɪd/ *verb*
the past tense and past participle of DRY

dri·er /ˈdraɪɚ/ *noun*
another spelling of DRYER

drift /drɪft/ *verb*
to move along slowly in the air or water: *The leaves drifted slowly down from the trees.*
PHRASAL VERB
drift apart
if people drift apart, they gradually stop having a close relationship: *Over the years, my college friends and I have drifted apart.*

drill

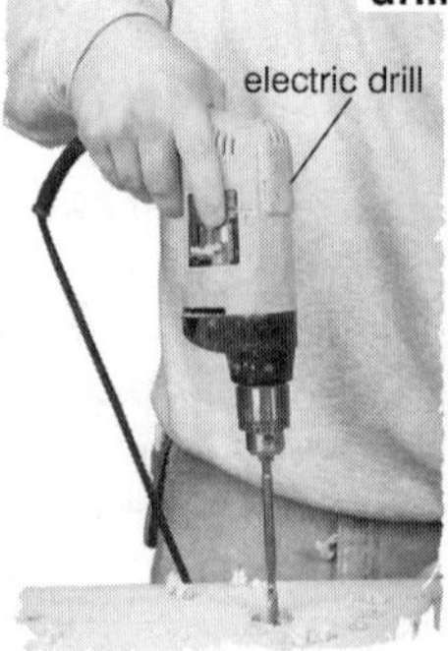

drill¹ /drɪl/ *noun*
1 a tool or machine used for making holes in something hard: *He used an electric drill to make a hole in the wall.*
2 a method of teaching something by making people repeat the same thing many times: *The teacher was doing a pronunciation drill with his class.*

drill² *verb*
1 to make a hole with a drill: *The dentist drilled a hole in my tooth.*
2 to teach people something by making them repeat the same thing many times: *The*

teacher was drilling the students in pronunciation.
➔ See Thesaurus box at **practice**[2]

drink[1] /drɪŋk/ *noun*
1 an amount of something such as water, juice, etc. that you can drink: *Are you thirsty? Would you like a drink of water?*
2 an alcoholic drink: *We had a couple of drinks at the bar before we went to bed.*

drink[2] *verb* **drank** /dræŋk/ **drunk** /drʌŋk/
1 to take liquid into your mouth and swallow it: *Ray was drinking Coke.* | *Do you want something to drink* (=a glass of a drink)?
2 to drink alcohol, especially regularly: *Don't drink and drive.*

drink•a•ble /ˈdrɪŋkəbəl/ *adjective*
water that is drinkable is safe to drink

drink•er /ˈdrɪŋkɚ/ *noun*
someone who often drinks alcohol: *Greg's a heavy drinker* (=he drinks a lot of alcohol).

ˈdrinking ˌfountain *noun*
a piece of equipment in a public place that gives you water to drink when you push a button or turn a handle: *Is there a drinking fountain in the building? I'm really thirsty.*

drip /drɪp/
verb **dripped, dripping**
1 if a liquid drips from something, it falls in drops: *Water was dripping from the ceiling, and I knew something was wrong.*

drip
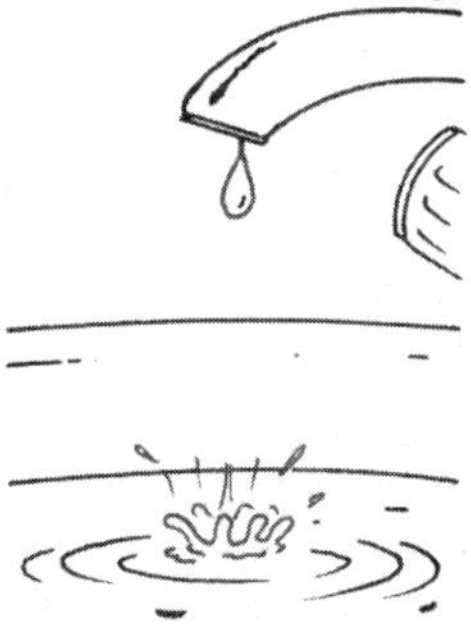

2 if something is dripping, drops of a liquid are falling from it: *My nose is dripping – do you have a tissue?*
—**drip** *noun* a small amount of liquid that falls from something
➔ See Thesaurus box at **pour**

drive[1] /draɪv/ *verb* **drove** /droʊv/ **driven** /ˈdrɪvən/ **driving**
1 to make a car, bus, etc. move in the direction you want: *She's learning to drive.* | *He was driving a red car.*
2 if you drive someone somewhere, you take him or her there in a car: *Many parents drive their children to school.* | *I drove her home after the party.*
3 drive someone crazy/nuts/insane *informal* = to make someone feel very annoyed or angry: *Stop making that noise! You're driving me crazy!*

drive[2] *noun*
1 a trip in a car: *Let's go for a drive.* | *It's a three-hour drive to the lake.*
2 a part of a computer that can read or store information: *the C drive*
3 a strong natural need: *the male sex drive*
4 a planned effort to achieve a particular result, especially by an organization: *The government is continuing its drive to reduce crime.*
5 determination and energy to succeed: *He has a lot of drive.*
6 used in the names of roads: *We live at the end of Maple Drive.*

driv•en /ˈdrɪvən/ *verb*
the past participle of DRIVE

driv•er /ˈdraɪvɚ/ *noun*
someone who drives: *A truck driver stopped and asked us if we needed help with the car.*
➔ See picture on page A26

ˈdriver's ˌlicense *noun*
an official card with your name, picture, etc. on it that says you are legally allowed to drive: *You need to show a driver's license or other form of ID to enter the club.*

ˈdrive-through *adjective*
a drive-through restaurant, bank, etc. is one that you can use without getting out of your car

drive•way /ˈdraɪvweɪ/ *noun*
the road or area for cars between a house and the street: *Park your car in the driveway.*

driz•zle /ˈdrɪzəl/ *verb*
if it is drizzling, it is raining very lightly: *The rain isn't too bad. It's just drizzling.*
—**drizzle** *noun* a light rain
➔ See Thesaurus box at **rain**[1]

drool /drul/ *verb*
if you drool, liquid flows out of your mouth: *The dog began to drool when it saw the food.*
—**drool** *noun* a flow of liquid that comes out of your mouth: *He wiped the drool from the baby's mouth.*

droop /drup/ *verb*
if something droops, it hangs down because it is old or weak: *The flowers had started to droop because there had been no rain.*

drop¹ /drɑp/ *verb* **dropped, dropping**
1 if you drop something you are holding, you let it fall, often by accident: *She dropped a glass when she was drying the dishes.*
2 to fall: *Several apples had dropped from the tree.*
3 to become lower in level or amount: *The price of gas has dropped again.* SYNONYM **fall, go down**
4 to let someone out of your car when you are driving somewhere: *You can just drop me at the corner.*
5 to stop doing something or continuing with something: *I wasn't doing very well, so I dropped French* (=stopped studying French).
PHRASAL VERBS
drop by *also* **drop in**
to visit someone who does not know you are coming: *Ed dropped by yesterday.*
drop off
1 drop someone off = to take someone to a place in a car, before going to another place: *Can you drop the kids off at my sister's house on your way to work?*
2 to begin to sleep: *The baby dropped off to sleep.*
3 to become less in level or amount: *The number of kids playing hockey has dropped off recently* (=there are fewer kids playing).
drop out
to stop going to school or college before you have finished your studies, or to stop an activity before you have finished it: *She dropped out of high school two months before graduation.* | *The injury forced him to drop out of the race.*
→ See Thesaurus box at **decrease¹**
→ See picture on page A4

drop² *noun*
1 a very small amount of liquid: *Put a drop of oil on the wheel.*
2 a situation in which the amount or level of something becomes lower: *There has been a drop in the price of computers – you can get a good one now for 400 dollars less than last year.*
3 lemon/fruit/chocolate, etc. drop = a candy that tastes like LEMON, fruit, etc.

ˈdrop-in *adjective*
if a place offers a drop-in service, you can go and get service, advice, etc. without telling them that you are coming first: *The patients can come to a drop-in medical clinic at the end of the month.*

drop•out /ˈdrɑp-aʊt/ *noun*
someone who leaves school or college without finishing it: *Many high-school dropouts have trouble finding jobs.*

drought /draʊt/ *noun*
a long period of dry weather when there is not enough rain: *The country has had two years of severe drought; farmers cannot grow anything.*

drove /droʊv/ *verb*
the past tense of DRIVE

drown /draʊn/ *verb*
if someone drowns, they die from being under water for too long: *Many people drowned when the ship sank.*

drows•y /ˈdraʊzi/ *adjective*
tired and almost asleep: *The room was so hot that I began to feel drowsy.* SYNONYM **sleepy**
—**drowsiness** *noun*: *This medicine can cause drowsiness, so take it before you go to bed.*

drug¹ /drʌg/ *noun*
1 an illegal substance that people smoke, swallow, etc. to give themselves a pleasant feeling, for example MARIJUANA or COCAINE: *He has never taken drugs* (=used drugs).
2 a medicine: *A new drug is being used to treat cancer.*
→ See Thesaurus box at **medicine**

drug² *verb*
to give someone drugs, usually to make him or her sleep: *The thieves drugged him and stole his money.*

ˈdrug ˌdealer *noun*
someone who sells illegal drugs SYNONYM **dealer**

drug•store /ˈdrʌgstɔr/ *noun*
a store where you can buy medicine, soap, TOOTHPASTE, etc.

drum¹ /drʌm/ *noun*
1 a round musical instrument which you hit with your hand or a stick: *Johnny plays the drums in a band.*
2 a large round container for storing liquids such as oil or chemicals: *an oil drum*
➔ See picture on page A21

drum² *verb* **drummed, drumming**
1 to hit something many times in a way that sounds like drums: *He drummed his fingers on the table.*
2 to play a drum

drunk¹ /drʌŋk/ *adjective*
if someone is drunk, he or she has drunk too much alcohol and cannot think or act normally: *He got drunk and ran his car into a tree.*

drunk² *verb*
the past participle of DRINK

drunk³ *noun*
someone who is drunk or who often gets drunk

drunk·en /ˈdrʌŋkən/ *adjective, formal*
behaving in a way that shows you are drunk: *A drunken crowd of people came out of the bar.*
—**drunkenness** *noun*

dry¹ /draɪ/ *adjective* **drier** or **dryer**, **driest** or **dryest**
1 something that is dry has no water in it or on it: *I got wet in the rain, so I went home to put on dry clothes.* | *The soil in the pot was dry, and the plant was dying.* ANTONYM **wet**
2 if the weather is dry, there is no rain: *It's been a very dry summer. We haven't had rain for a month.* ANTONYM **wet**
3 if your mouth, throat, or skin is dry, it does not have enough of the natural liquid that is usually in it: *My skin gets so dry in the winter.*
4 dry wine/champagne, etc. = wine, etc. that is not sweet: *a glass of dry white wine*

dry² *verb* **dried**, third person singular **dries**
if something dries, it no longer has any water in it or on it: *She was drying her hair with a towel.* | *Julia hung the wet clothes outside to dry.*

ˈdry-clean *verb*
to take clothes to a business that cleans them with chemicals, not water and soap: *It's a wool suit, so it has to be dry-cleaned.*

ˌdry ˈcleaners *noun*
a business that dry-cleans clothes

dry·er *also* **drier** /ˈdraɪɚ/ *noun*
a machine that dries things, especially clothes or hair: *Can you put the wet clothes in the dryer?*

du·al /ˈduəl/ *adjective*
having two of something, or two parts: *She plays a dual role in the movie – the main character and her mother.*

du·bi·ous /ˈdubiəs/ *adjective, formal*
1 if you are dubious about something, you are not sure whether it is good or true: *Anna's parents felt dubious about her new boyfriend. They thought he was too old for her.* SYNONYM **doubtful**
2 not real or honest: *He's a dubious businessman who cannot be trusted.*

duck¹ /dʌk/ *noun*
1 a common bird that floats on water and has short legs and a wide beak: *We went to the pond to feed the ducks.*
2 the meat from a duck

duck² *verb*
to lower your body or head very quickly to avoid something: *He threw a book at me, and I ducked.*

duck·ling /ˈdʌklɪŋ/ *noun*
a young duck

duct /dʌkt/ *noun*
1 a tube in a building for carrying air or electric wires: *There was no warm air coming from the heating duct.*
2 a thin narrow tube inside your body, a plant, etc. that liquid or air goes through: *If your tear duct is blocked, your eye becomes too dry.*

dude /dud/ *noun, informal*
a man or boy. This is often used to talk to someone instead of using his name: *Hey dude, what are you doing?*

due /du/ *adjective*
1 expected to happen or arrive at a particular time: *The flight from Chicago is due to arrive at 7 p.m.* | *The baby is due in March.*
2 if something is due on a particular date, it should be given to someone on or before that date: *Your English papers are due on Friday.*
3 due to something = if one thing is due to another, the first thing happens as a result of

the second thing: *Her success was due to hard work.*

du•el /ˈduəl/ *noun*
a fight in past times between two people with guns or swords: *He was killed in a duel.*
—**duel** *verb* to fight with guns or swords

dues /duz/ *plural noun*
money that you pay regularly to be a member of an organization: *Do you have to pay dues to be a member of the club?*

du•et /duˈet/ *noun*
a piece of music for two performers: *He wrote a duet for flute and violin.*

dug /dʌg/ *verb*
the past tense and past participle of DIG

dull[1] /dʌl/ *adjective*
1 not interesting or exciting: *The book was so dull that I fell asleep reading it.* SYNONYM **boring**
2 a dull pain is not strong: *I had a dull ache in my shoulder.*
3 not bright or shiny: *The wall was painted a dull gray color.*
4 not sharp: *The knife was too dull to cut the string.*
5 a dull sound is not clear or loud, like something heavy falling on the floor: *I heard a dull thud, and I realized that my sister had fallen out of bed.*
→ See Thesaurus box at **boring**

dull[2] *verb, formal*
to make a pain or feeling less noticeable: *The drug dulled the pain, so that she was able to sleep.*

du•ly /ˈduli/ *adverb, formal*
done in a way that is correct, expected, or that follows the rules: *An employee noticed the problem and duly reported it to her boss.*

dumb /dʌm/ *adjective, informal*
stupid: *I felt really dumb when I couldn't get the box open.* ANTONYM **smart**

dum•my /ˈdʌmi/ *noun* plural **dummies**
1 *informal* someone who is stupid: *Don't be such a dummy!* SYNONYM **idiot**
2 a plastic figure of a person: *They crash the cars with dummies inside to see how badly they are damaged.*

dump[1] /dʌmp/ *verb*
1 to drop or put something somewhere in a careless way: *She dumped her suitcase in the middle of the room and left it there.*
2 to leave something somewhere because you do not want it: *It is illegal to dump garbage here.*
3 *informal* to end a relationship with someone: *Tammy dumped her boyfriend because she likes someone else.*

dump[2] *noun*
1 a place where you can take things you do not want and leave them there: *We took two bags of garbage and a broken chair to the dump.*
2 *informal* a place that is unpleasant because it is dirty and ugly: *Your apartment's a dump. Do you ever clean it?*

dune /dun/ *noun*
a hill made of sand: *We walked over the sand dunes to the beach.*

dun•geon /ˈdʌndʒən/ *noun*
a dark prison under the ground, used in past times: *He was kept in the dungeon of the castle for two years.*

dunk /dʌŋk/ *verb*
1 to quickly put something into a liquid and then take it out again: *He dunked his cookie in his coffee.*
2 to jump up by the basket and throw the ball down through it in BASKETBALL

du•o /ˈduoʊ/ *noun*
two people who do something together: *The story is about a singing duo who fall in love with each other.*

du•plex /ˈdupleks/ *noun*
a house that is divided into two separate places for people to live

du•pli•cate[1] /ˈdupləkɪt/ *noun, formal*
an exact copy of something that you can use in the same way: *He made a duplicate of the house key to give to his sister.* SYNONYM **copy**
—**duplicate** *adjective* made as an exact copy of something: *a duplicate key*

du•pli•cate[2] /ˈdupləˌkeɪt/ *verb, formal*
1 to do the same thing as someone else: *We don't want our employees to duplicate each other's work because it wastes time.*
2 to copy something exactly: *It is illegal to duplicate the DVD.*

du·pli·ca·tion /ˌdupləˈkeɪʃən/ *noun, formal*
1 the act or process of copying something exactly: *The duplication of this software is a crime.*
2 the act or process of repeating something in exactly the same way: *Make sure you know what everyone else in your group is doing so that there is no duplication of effort* (=two people doing the same thing).

dur·a·ble /ˈdʊrəbəl/ *adjective, formal*
staying in good condition for a long time: *Plastic window frames are more durable than wood.*
—**durability** /ˌdʊrəˈbɪləti/ *noun* the state or quality of being durable: *Steel is used in large buildings because of its strength and durability.*

dur·ing /ˈdʊrɪŋ/ *preposition*
1 all through a period of time: *During the day when my mom is at work, my little sister stays at my grandmother's house.*
2 at some point in a period of time: *Henry died during the night.*

dusk /dʌsk/ *noun*
the time when it starts to become dark at the end of the day: *The street lights go on at dusk.* SYNONYM **twilight**; ANTONYM **dawn**

dust[1] /dʌst/ *noun*
very small pieces of dirt that look like a powder: *She never cleans her house; there is dust on all the furniture.*

dust[2] *verb*
to clean the dust from something with a cloth: *I dusted the shelves in my bedroom.*
➔ See Thesaurus box at **clean[2]**

dust·pan /ˈdʌstpæn/ *noun*
a flat container with a handle that you use with a brush to remove dust and waste from the floor

dust·y /ˈdʌsti/ *adjective*
covered with dust: *I found some dusty old books that nobody had touched for years.*
➔ See Thesaurus box at **dirty**

Dutch[1] /dʌtʃ/ *adjective*
from the Netherlands: *She's Dutch, and she lives in Amsterdam.* | *a Dutch company*

Dutch[2] *noun*
1 the language used in the Netherlands
2 the Dutch = the people of the Netherlands

du·ti·ful /ˈdutɪfəl/ *adjective, formal*
a dutiful person does what other people expect them to do: *He was a dutiful son who always obeyed his parents.*
—**dutifully** *adverb, formal*: *Every Sunday she dutifully went to church.*

du·ty /ˈduti/ *noun* plural **duties**
something that you should do because it is right or it is part of your job: *Parents have a duty to protect their children.*

DVD *noun*
digital video disc a flat round object like a CD that you use on a computer or on a piece of equipment called a DVD player to play movies: *I was watching a DVD on my laptop.*

dwarf /dwɔrf/ *noun*
1 an imaginary creature that looks like a small man
2 a person who is much shorter than usual. Many people think this use is offensive

dwell /dwel/ *verb* **dwelled** or **dwelt** /dwelt/ *formal*
to live in a particular place: *The story is about some tiny creatures that dwell in the forest.*

PHRASAL VERB
dwell on/upon something
to think or talk for too long about something unpleasant: *I tried not to dwell on my mistake; I tried to think about how to fix it instead.*

dwell·ing /ˈdwelɪŋ/ *noun, formal*
a house, apartment, etc. where people live

dye[1] /daɪ/ *noun*
a substance you use to change the color of your hair, cloth, etc.: *She bought some black hair dye.*

dye[2] *verb*
to change the color of something using a dye: *She dyes her hair. Sometimes it's red, and sometimes it's blond.*

dy·nam·ic /daɪˈnæmɪk/ Ac *adjective*
full of energy and ideas: *Our teacher is very dynamic. She's always thinking of new ways to make the class interesting.*

dy·na·mite /ˈdaɪnəˌmaɪt/ *noun*
a substance that can cause powerful explosions: *They blew up the building with dynamite.*

D

Ee

E /i/ *noun*
the third note in the musical SCALE of C, or the musical KEY based on this note

E

each /itʃ/ *adjective, pronoun, adverb*
every person or thing separately: *She had a bag in each hand.* | *The kids were given $5 each.* | *Each of her friends gave her a different present.* | *Twelve guests came to the party, and they each brought something to eat.*

USAGE: each

Each, **every**, and **all** are all used to talk about every person or thing in a group.

When you are thinking about the people or things in the group separately, use **each** or **every**: *Each child at the party was given a balloon.* | *Every child at the party was given a balloon.*

When you are thinking about the whole group together, use **all**: *All the children were given balloons.*

ˌeach ˈother *pronoun*
1 used for showing that each of two or more people does something to the other or others: *Sarah and Rob love each other and want to get married.*
2 used for talking about the positions and situations that two or more people or things are in: *Our houses are next to each other, so we're neighbors.*

ea·ger /ˈigɚ/ *adjective*
wanting to do something very much: *He was eager to meet his new teacher.*
—**eagerly** *adverb*: *She opened the letter eagerly and ripped it by mistake.*
—**eagerness** *noun*: *We were surprised by his eagerness to do the work; he seemed really excited.*

ea·gle /ˈigəl/ *noun*
a big wild bird with a beak like a hook that eats small animals

ear /ɪr/ *noun*
the two parts of your body that you hear with: *Mark whispered something in her ear.*
➔ See picture on page A2

ear·ache /ˈɪreɪk/ *noun*
a pain inside your ear: *I had an earache and couldn't sleep.*

ear·ly[1] /ˈɚli/ *adjective* **earlier**, **earliest**
1 before the usual or expected time: *I was early for my appointment, so I had to wait.* | *We can have an early dinner at about 5:00.* ANTONYM **late**
2 near the beginning of the day: *It was early in the morning, about 5:00 a.m.* ANTONYM **late**
3 near the beginning of a period of time: *We're leaving in the early afternoon, around 1:00.* ANTONYM **late**

early[2] *adverb*
1 before the usual or expected time: *She came to the party early to help me get ready.* ANTONYM **late**
2 near the beginning of the day: *He got up very early, at about 5:30 in the morning.* ANTONYM **late**
3 near the beginning of a period of time: *He'll be back early in January, probably on the 3rd.* ANTONYM **late**

earn /ɚn/ *verb*
1 to get money for the work you do: *Alan earns $40,000 a year.* | *I'd like to earn some extra money. Do you have any work I could do for you?*

THESAURUS: earn

make to earn or get money: *Debbie makes a little money by babysitting.*

get *informal* to receive money for doing work or selling something: *How much did you get for mowing their lawns?*

be paid/get paid to be given money for doing a job: *I get paid $7.50 an hour.*

2 to get something good because you have worked hard or done something well: *You've earned a rest after all that hard work!*

ear•nest /ˈɚnɪst/ *adjective, formal*
serious about what you are saying or doing: *He made an earnest effort to do better in school.*

earn•ings /ˈɚnɪŋz/ *plural noun, formal*
money that you get from working: *I try not to spend all of my earnings.*
➔ See Thesaurus box at **pay**[2]

ear•phones /ˈɪrfoʊnz/ *plural noun*
a small piece of equipment connected by a wire to a radio, MP3 PLAYER, etc., which you put in or over your ears so that only you can listen to it

ear•ring /ˈɪrɪŋ/ *noun*
a piece of jewelry that you fasten to your ear: *She was wearing a pair of gold earrings.*
➔ See picture at **jewelry**

earth *also* **Earth** /ɚθ/ *noun*
the PLANET that we live on: *The Earth moves around the sun.*

THESAURUS: earth

earth the planet we live on: *The earth moves around the sun.*

world the planet we live on – used when you are thinking of the earth as a place where there are people and countries, mountains, and oceans, etc.: *This has to be one of the most beautiful places in the world.*

You can use **earth** to mean "the world": *It's the highest mountain on earth.* | *It's the highest mountain in the world.*

When you compare the earth's surface to the ocean, use **land**: *Five weeks after sailing from Ireland, they saw land.*

When you compare the earth's surface to the sky, use **earth**: *The space shuttle returned to earth safely.*

earth•quake /ˈɚθkweɪk/ *noun*
a sudden shaking of the earth that often causes a lot of damage: *The earthquake damaged thousands of buildings and killed several people.*

earth•worm /ˈɚθwɚm/ *noun*
a thin brown WORM that lives in soil

ease[1] /iz/ *noun, formal*
1 with ease = if you do something with ease, it is very easy: *He won the race with ease.*
2 at ease = feeling comfortable and confident: *The teacher used games to make the new students feel at ease.*

ease[2] *verb*
to become less bad or unpleasant: *The doctor gave me drugs to ease the pain.*
➔ See Thesaurus box at **reduce**

ea•sel /ˈizəl/ *noun*
a frame that you put a drawing or painting on while you are making it

easel

eas•i•ly /ˈizəli/ *adverb*
1 without difficulty: *You can find information easily on the Internet.*
2 easily the best/easily the biggest, etc. *informal* = much better, bigger, etc. than the others: *She is easily the most intelligent girl in the class.*

east[1] *also* **East** /ist/ *noun*
1 the direction from which the sun rises: *Which way is east?*
2 the east = the eastern part of a country or area: *We live in the east of the city.*
3 the East a) the part of the U.S. on the east coast of the U.S., especially the states north of Washington D.C.: *She was born in the East.* **b)** the countries in Asia, especially China and Japan: *I would love to travel in the East.*
➔ See picture at **north**[1]

east[2] *adjective*
1 in, to, or facing the east: *Our hotel was on the east coast of the island.*
2 east wind = a wind that comes from the east

east[3] *adverb*
toward the east: *We drove east along Brooklyn Avenue.* | *The window faces east.*

Eas•ter /ˈistɚ/ *noun*
a religious holiday in March or April, when Christians remember Jesus Christ's return to life after dying on the cross

ˈEaster egg *noun*
an egg that has been colored and decorated for Easter: *At Easter we look for Easter eggs that are hidden around the house.*

east•ern /ˈistɚn/ *adjective*
in or from the east: *Several eastern states, such as New York and Massachusetts, have passed the law.*

ˌEastern ˈDaylight Time *also* **EDT**
the time that is used in the eastern U.S. for almost half the year, including the summer. Eastern Daylight Time is one hour ahead of Eastern Standard Time

easterner /ˈistɚnɚ/ *noun*
someone who comes from the eastern part of a country

ˌEastern ˈStandard Time *also* **EST**
the time that is used in the eastern U.S. for almost half the year, including the winter

east•ward /ˈistwɚd/ *adverb, adjective*
toward the east: *The plane was traveling eastward, from Chicago to New York.*

eas•y¹ /ˈizi/ *adjective* **easier**, **easiest**
1 not difficult: *The first question was easy.* | *The book is easy to read.* ANTONYM **hard**
2 relaxing because you have no problems or worries: *She has an easy life, with a big house and lots of money.*

WORD FAMILY look at the words:
→ **easy** *adjective*
→ **easily** *adverb*
→ **ease** *noun*
→ **ease** *verb*

easy² *adverb*
1 take it easy a) to relax and not do very much: *I've been working so hard lately, I need to take it easy for a while.* **b)** used for telling someone to become less angry or upset: *OK, you don't need to yell – just take it easy.*
2 go easy on someone *informal* = to not punish someone too severely or not become too angry with them: *He's very upset about his mistake, so go easy on him.*
3 go easy on something *informal* = to not use or eat too much of something: *I have to go easy on the desserts because I'm getting fat.*
4 that's easier said than done = you say this when someone has suggested something that sounds simple but is not: *I know I should just ask her to be quiet, but that's easier said than done.*

eas•y•go•ing /ˌiziˈgoʊɪŋ/ *adjective*
an easygoing person is not easily worried or annoyed: *Her parents are really easygoing; they never yell at her.*

eat /it/ *verb* **ate** /eɪt/ **eaten** /ˈitn/
1 to put food in your mouth and swallow it: *She was eating an apple.* | *I'm still eating my dinner.* | *Do you want something to eat* (=some food to eat)?
2 to have a meal: *We usually eat at about 6.*

PHRASAL VERBS

eat out
to eat in a restaurant: *They usually eat out once a week.*

eat something up
1 to finish eating all of something: *Eat up your breakfast! We're late!*
2 to use too much of something: *This class is eating up all of my time. I don't have time to study anything else.*
3 eat it up *informal* = to enjoy something very much: *If you give the kids a computer game, they'll just eat it up.*

eat•en /ˈitn/ *verb*
the past participle of EAT

eaves•drop /ˈivzdrɑp/ *verb* **eavesdropped**, **eavesdropping** to listen secretly to other people's conversation: *She stood outside the door so that she could eavesdrop on their conversation.*

ec•cen•tric /ɪkˈsentrɪk/ *adjective*
behaving in a way that is unusual and different from most people: *He dressed in an eccentric way, often wearing two different shoes.*
—**eccentric** *noun* an eccentric person
→ See Thesaurus box at **strange¹**

ech•o¹ /ˈekoʊ/ *noun* plural **echoes**
a sound that you hear again because it comes back off the surface of a wall, hill,

etc.: *I could hear the echo of my voice from the other side of the cave.*

echo² *verb*
echoed if a sound echoes, you hear it again because it comes back off a wall, hill, etc.: *When he shouted, his voice echoed around the valley.*

e•clipse /ɪˈklɪps/ *noun*
an occasion when you cannot see the sun because the moon is in front of it, or when you cannot see the moon because it is covered by the Earth's shadow: *an eclipse of the moon*

e•col•o•gy /ɪˈkɑlədʒi/ *noun*
the study of the environment and the relationship between it and all the plants, animals, and humans who live there
—**ecologist** *noun* someone who studies ecology
—**ecological** /ˌikəˈlɑdʒɪkəl/ *adjective*

ec•o•nom•ic /ˌekəˈnɑmɪk/ Ac *adjective*
relating to business, industry, and trade in a country or area: *The economic situation in the U.S. is improving; there are more jobs, and people are spending more.*
—**economically** *adverb*

ec•o•nom•i•cal /ˌekəˈnɑmɪkəl/ Ac *adjective*
not costing a lot of money to buy or use: *It's more economical to buy one large package of pasta than two or three small ones.* | *an economical car that gets 39 miles per gallon*

ec•o•nom•ics /ˌekəˈnɑmɪks/ Ac *noun*
the study of how countries' financial systems work, and how money, goods, and services are produced and used
—**economist** /ɪˈkɑnəmɪst/ *noun* someone who knows a lot about economics and advises people about this: *Some economists say that we need higher taxes.*

e•con•o•mize /ɪˈkɑnəˌmaɪz/ *verb*
to reduce the amount of money, goods, etc. that you use: *I'm trying to economize by taking my lunch to school, instead of buying it.*

e•con•o•my /ɪˈkɑnəmi/ Ac *noun*
the system of trade and industry in a country or area: *China's economy is growing rapidly.*

WORD FAMILY look at the words:
→ **economy** *noun*
→ **economist** *noun*
→ **economic** *adjective*
→ **economics** *noun*

ec•stat•ic /ɪkˈstætɪk/ *adjective, formal*
feeling extremely happy and excited: *I was ecstatic when I found out that I got an A on my English test!*

edge /edʒ/ *noun*

1 the part of something that is farthest from the center: *She was sitting on the edge of the bed.*
2 the area beside a steep slope: *We looked over the edge of the cliff, down to the ocean.*
3 the thin sharp part of a tool used for cutting: *You will need a knife with a sharp edge.*
4 on edge = nervous and worried: *Everyone was on edge, because we were worried about our final exams.*

edg•y /ˈedʒi/ *adjective*
nervous and easily upset: *I was feeling edgy because my brother and I had been arguing.*

ed•i•ble /ˈedəbəl/ *adjective*
something that is edible is safe to eat or good enough to eat: *I didn't pick the berries because I wasn't sure if they were edible.*
ANTONYM **inedible**

ed•it /ˈedɪt/ Ac *verb*
to make a book, movie, etc. ready for people to read or see, by removing mistakes, deciding what to include, etc.: *When the author is finished writing, I will edit the book.*

e•di•tion /ɪˈdɪʃən/ Ac *noun*
a set of copies of a book, newspaper, etc., that is produced at a particular time: *There are two editions of the newspaper – one in the morning and one in the evening.*

ed•i•tor /ˈedətɚ/ Ac *noun*
1 the person who is in charge of a newspaper or magazine: *the editor of the Los Angeles Times newspaper*
2 someone whose job is to decide what

should be included in a newspaper, magazine, book, etc.: *a children's book editor*

ed•i•to•ri•al[1] /ˌedəˈtɔriəl/ Ac *noun*
a piece of writing in a newspaper that gives an opinion rather than reporting facts: *There was an editorial on the president's new energy policy in yesterday's paper.*

editorial[2] *adjective*
relating to editing: *the editorial staff of the newspaper*

E

ed•u•cate /ˈedʒəˌkeɪt/ *verb, formal*
to teach someone: *He was educated at Stanford University.*
—**educator** *noun, formal* a teacher at a school, college, or university

ed•u•cat•ed /ˈedʒəˌkeɪtɪd/ *adjective*
an educated person has had a good education and has read a lot of books: *The magazine is read mostly by educated people.*

ed•u•ca•tion /ˌedʒəˈkeɪʃən/ *noun*
the activities of teaching and learning: *They want their children to get a good education.*

eel /il/ *noun*
a long thin fish that looks like a snake

ef•fect /ɪˈfekt/ *noun*
1 the way in which something that happens changes someone or something, or the result that something has: *Smoking has a very bad effect on your health.* SYNONYM **influence**
2 take effect = to start to influence someone or something, or to start to work: *The drug should take effect in about ten minutes.*
3 in effect = used when you are describing what the real situation is, instead of what it seems to be: *In effect, she's now my boss.*
➔ **side effect**
➔ See Thesaurus box at **result**[1]

ef•fec•tive /ɪˈfektɪv/ *adjective*
producing the result that you want to happen: *We need a more effective way to teach reading because the one we use now is not working.* ANTONYM **ineffective**
—**effectively** *adverb*: *The new heating system is not working effectively; the rooms are still too cold.*
—**effectiveness** *noun*

ef•fi•cient /ɪˈfɪʃənt/ *adjective*
1 working well and getting things done quickly: *The waiter wasn't very efficient; he was so slow that the food got cold.* ANTONYM **inefficient**
2 doing something in a way that does not waste time, money, energy, effort, etc.: *Try to organize your study time in an efficient way, so that you have time to do other things.* ANTONYM **inefficient**
—**efficiency** *noun* the way in which you do something, so that you do not waste time, energy, and effort: *The company needs to improve the efficiency of its factories because they waste too much energy.*
—**efficiently** *adverb*

ef•fort /ˈefɚt/ *noun*
1 the physical or mental energy that you use to do something: *Moving a piano takes a lot of effort.* | *You need to put more effort into your homework* (=work harder at it).
2 an attempt to do something: *She started riding her bicycle to school, in an effort to* (=to try to) *lose weight.*

ef•fort•less /ˈefɚtləs/ *adjective, formal*
if someone does something in an effortless way, it seems to be easy for them: *It's a very hard song to sing, but she makes it look effortless.*
—**effortlessly** *adverb, formal*

EFL *noun*
English as a Foreign Language the activity of teaching English to people whose first language is not English, and who do not live in an English-speaking country

e.g. /ˌi ˈdʒi/ *abbreviation, formal*
an abbreviation that means "for example": *He enjoys studying science subjects, e.g. chemistry and physics.*

egg /eg/ *noun*
1 a round object with a hard surface that contains a baby bird, insect, snake, etc.: *The bird lays its eggs in the spring.*
2 an egg from a chicken, used as food: *I had a fried egg for breakfast.*

egg•plant /ˈegplænt/ *noun*
a large vegetable with a shiny dark purple skin
➔ See picture on page A12

egg•shell /ˈegʃel/ *noun*
the hard outside part of an egg

e•go /ˈiɡoʊ/ *noun*
the opinion that you have about yourself: *He has a very big ego* (=he thinks he is very important).

eight /eɪt/ *number*
1 8: *This pasta dish will serve eight people.*
2 eight O'CLOCK: *Dinner will be at eight.*
3 eight years old: *Annie's brother is eight.*

eight•een /ˌeɪˈtin/ *number*
1 18: *I've been awake for eighteen hours.*
2 eighteen years old: *I'm planning on having a big party when I'm eighteen.*
—**eighteenth** /ˌeɪˈtinθ/ *number* 18th or 1/18

eighth /eɪtθ/ *number*
1 8th
2 1/8

eight•y /ˈeɪti/ *number*
1 80
2 the eighties a) *also* **the '80s** the years between 1980 and 1989: *My dad graduated from high school in the eighties.* **b)** *also* **the '80s** temperatures between 80 and 89 degrees Fahrenheit or Celsius: *The temperature was in the eighties all week.*
3 be in your eighties = to be between 80 and 89 years old: *My grandfather is in his eighties.*
—**eightieth** /ˈeɪtiɪθ/ *number* 80th or 1/80

ei•ther[1] /ˈiðɚ/ *conjunction*
either ... or = used when saying that there are two or more possibilities: *We can either take the bus, or we can fly.*

either[2] *pronoun, adjective*
1 one or the other of two people or things: *"Do you want chocolate or strawberry ice cream?" "Either is fine!"* | *Either team could win.*
2 used in negative sentences, when saying that something is true about both of two things or people: *"Which one of these dresses do you like best?" "I don't like either of them."*
3 either side/end/hand, etc. = both sides, ends, etc.: *He stood in the door with a policeman on either side of him.*

either[3] *adverb*
used in negative sentences to mean "also": *"I can't swim." "I can't either."*

e•lab•o•rate /ɪˈlæbərət/ *adjective, formal*
having a lot of small details or parts that are connected together in a complicated way: *The carpet had a very elaborate design.*
—**elaborately** *adverb*

e•las•tic /ɪˈlæstɪk/ *noun*
a type of rubber material that can stretch and then return to its usual size
—**elastic** *adjective* made of elastic: *The pants have an elastic waist, so that they are easy to put on.*

el•bow /ˈelboʊ/ *noun*
the joint where your arm bends
→ See picture on page A2

el•der /ˈeldɚ/ *adjective, formal*
elder sister/brother/daughter, etc. = the sister, brother, etc. who was born first: *My elder sister is a nurse.*

el•der•ly /ˈeldɚli/ *adjective*
old: *an elderly woman with white hair*

el•ders /ˈeldɚz/ *plural noun, formal*
your elders are people who are older than you are: *Young people should have more respect for their elders.*

el•dest /ˈeldɪst/ *adjective, formal*
the eldest son or daughter was born first: *My eldest daughter is 17.*

e•lect /ɪˈlekt/ *verb*
to choose someone for an official position by voting: *She was elected to Congress in 2000.*

e•lec•tion /ɪˈlekʃən/ *noun*
an event in which people vote to choose someone for an official position: *Who do you think will win the next presidential election?*
—**electoral** /ɪˈlektərəl/ *adjective* relating to elections

e•lec•tric /ɪˈlektrɪk/ *adjective*
needing electricity in order to work: *an electric guitar*

WORD FAMILY look at the words:
→ **electric** *adjective*
→ **electricity** *noun*
→ **electrical** *adjective*
→ **electrician** *noun*

e•lec•tri•cal /ɪˈlektrɪkəl/ *adjective*
1 relating to electricity: *The machine uses electrical power.*
2 using electricity: *The store sells electrical goods like televisions and kitchen appliances.*

E

e•lec•tri•cian /ɪˌlekˈtrɪʃən/ *noun*
someone whose job is to put in and repair electrical equipment: *We need an electrician to fix the light switch.*
→ See picture on page A16

e•lec•tric•i•ty /ɪˌlekˈtrɪsəti/ *noun*
a type of energy that is used to make lights, televisions, etc. work, and is carried through wires: *The new light bulbs use less electricity than the old ones.*

e•lec•tron /ɪˈlektrɑn/ *noun*
a very small piece of matter that moves around the NUCLEUS (=central part) of an atom

e•lec•tron•ic /ɪˌlekˈtrɑnɪk/ *adjective*
1 electronic equipment uses electricity and very small parts such as computer CHIPs and TRANSISTORs: *Computers and other electronic equipment can be easily damaged by water.*
2 made or done using electronic equipment: *The band plays electronic music.*
—**electronically** *adverb*

e•lec•tron•ics /ɪˌlekˈtrɑnɪks/ *noun*
the technology used for making equipment that uses electricity, for example radios and televisions

el•e•gant /ˈeləgənt/ *adjective, formal*
very beautiful and graceful: *She was a tall elegant woman who always dressed in beautiful clothes.*
—**elegance** *noun, formal* the quality of being elegant: *I love the elegance of the city's old buildings.*

el•e•ment /ˈeləmənt/ Ac *noun*
1 *formal* one part of something: *The most important element in any movie is the story, and the characters are second.*
2 *formal* a small amount of something, for example danger, truth, risk, etc.: *There is always an element of risk when you're climbing a big mountain.*
3 a basic chemical substance, for example OXYGEN or HYDROGEN, that consists of only one type of atom

el•e•men•tary /ˌeləˈmentri/ *adjective*
basic and simple: *The youngest students are learning elementary mathematics.*

eleˈmentary ˌschool *noun*
a school in the U.S. for the first five or seven years of a child's education: *Our elementary school has kindergarten through sixth grade.*
SYNONYM **grade school**

el•e•phant /ˈeləfənt/ *noun*
a very large gray animal with big ears, a TRUNK (=a long nose that it can use to pick things up), and TUSKS (=long teeth): *Elephants live in parts of Africa and Asia.*

el•e•va•tion /ˌeləˈveɪʃən/ *noun, formal*
the height of a place, measured from the level of the ocean: *The city is in the mountains at an elevation of 7,000 feet.*

el•e•va•tor /ˈeləˌveɪt̬ɚ/ *noun*
a machine like a small room that takes people from one level to another in a building: *I took the elevator to the 26th floor.*

e•lev•en /ɪˈlevən/ *number*
1 11: *There are eleven players on a soccer team.*
2 eleven O'CLOCK
3 eleven years old: *I was eleven when my sister was born.*

e•lev•enth /ɪˈlevənθ/ *number*
1 11th
2 1/11

elf /elf/ *noun* plural **elves** /elvz/
a small imaginary person with pointed ears, who appears in stories

el•i•gi•ble /ˈelədʒəbəl/ *adjective, formal*
allowed to do something: *People are eligible to vote at the age of 18.*
—**eligibility** /ˌelədʒəˈbɪləti/ *noun, formal* the right to do something

e•lim•i•nate /ɪˈlɪməˌneɪt/ Ac *verb, formal*
1 to get rid of something completely: *Credit cards almost eliminate the need for cash.*
2 be eliminated = to be defeated in a sports competition, so that you can no longer take part in it: *Our team was eliminated in the first part of the competition, so we went home.*

e•lite[1] /eɪˈlit/ *adjective*
an elite group has the best people or things and therefore is highly respected: *She was one of an elite group of very popular girls at school.*

elite[2] *noun*
a small group of people who are powerful or important because they have money, knowledge, special skills, etc.: *He was a member of the powerful political elite in Washington, D.C.*

elm /elm/ *noun*
a large tall tree with broad leaves

e•lope /ɪˈloʊp/ *verb, formal*
if two people elope, they go away secretly to get married

el•o•quent /ˈeləkwənt/ *adjective, formal*
able to express your ideas and opinions in a way that is clear and beautiful: *He gave a short but eloquent answer to a difficult question.*
—**eloquently** *adverb*
—**eloquence** *noun* the quality of being eloquent

else /els/ *adverb*
1 another thing or person: *"Thanks for the cookies." "You're welcome. Do you want anything else to eat?"* | *Someone else must have taken the money – I didn't take it.* | *We have tried everything to make it work; there's nothing else we can do.*
2 or else = used when saying that there will be a bad result if someone does not do something: *Hurry up, or else you'll be late for school!*

else•where /ˈelswer/ *adverb, formal*
in or to another place: *She didn't know anyone at college; her friends from high school had gone elsewhere.*

ELT *noun*
English Language Teaching the activity of teaching English to people whose first language is not English

elves /elvz/ *noun*
the plural of ELF

e•mail *also* **e-mail** /ˈi meɪl/ *noun*
1 an electronic message that is sent from one computer to another: *I got an email from her yesterday.*
2 a system that allows you to send and receive messages by computer: *I'll send the pictures by email.* | *What's your email address?*
—**email** *also* **e-mail** *verb* to send a message to someone's computer using email: *He emailed them to tell them when he was arriving.*
➔ See picture on page A20

e•man•ci•pate /ɪˈmænsəˌpeɪt/ *verb, formal*
to make someone free and able to have the same rights as other people in society: *American slaves were emancipated after the Civil War.*
—**emancipation** /ɪˌmænsəˈpeɪʃən/ *noun, formal* the act of emancipating someone: *the emancipation of women*

em•bark /ɪmˈbɑrk/ *verb, formal*
to go onto a large ship or airplane
PHRASAL VERB
embark on something
to start something new and exciting: *He embarked on a new career as a teacher.*

em•bar•rass /ɪmˈbærəs/ *verb*
to make someone feel embarrassed: *I didn't want to embarrass her by talking about her problems in front of her friends.*

em•bar•rassed /ɪmˈbærəst/ *adjective*
feeling worried and upset about what other people will think of you: *I was embarrassed because I had made such a stupid mistake.*

WORD FAMILY look at the words:
➔ **embarrassed** *adjective*
➔ **embarrassing** *adjective*
➔ **embarrassment** *noun*

em•bar•rass•ment /ɪmˈbærəsmənt/ *noun*
the feeling of being embarrassed: *She tried to hide her embarrassment, but her face was all red.*

em•bas•sy /ˈembəsi/ *noun* plural **embassies**
the office used by officials who work for their country's government in a foreign country: *He works at the Mexican Embassy in Washington, D.C.*

emblem

national emblem of Canada   Olympic emblem

em•blem /ˈembləm/ *noun*
a picture, shape, or object is a sign or symbol for a country, company, idea, etc.: *The national emblem of Canada is the maple leaf.*

E

em•brace /ɪm'breɪs/ *verb, formal*
to put your arms around someone and hold him or her in a caring way: *They embraced each other and said goodbye.* SYNONYM **hug**
—**embrace** *noun, formal* the action of embracing someone

em•broi•der•y /ɪm'brɔɪdəri/ *noun*
1 patterns or pictures that you sew on cloth as a decoration: *The dress had beautiful silk embroidery.*
2 the skill of sewing patterns on to cloth as a decoration
—**embroider** *verb* to sew patterns on cloth as a decoration

em•bry•o /'embri,oʊ/ *noun*
an animal or human that has not yet been born and has just begun to develop

em•er•ald /'emərəld/ *noun*
a valuable bright green jewel: *an emerald ring*

e•merge /ɪ'mɚdʒ/ Ac *verb, formal*
to appear after being covered or hidden: *The sun emerged from behind the clouds.*

e•mer•gen•cy /ɪ'mɚdʒənsi/ *noun* plural **emergencies**
a very serious and dangerous situation that you must deal with immediately: *Call an ambulance! This is an emergency!*
—**emergency** *adjective* relating to or used for emergencies: *If there is a fire, please use the emergency exit.*

e'mergency ,room *noun*
the part of a hospital that treats people who have been hurt in a serious accident and need immediate attention: *They took him to the emergency room after he was hit by a car.*

em•i•grate /'emə,greɪt/ *verb, formal*
to leave your own country in order to live in another: *His family had emigrated from France to Canada.*
—**emigration** /,emə'greɪʃən/ *noun, formal* the action of emigrating

WORD FAMILY look at the words:

→ **emigrate** *verb*
→ **emigration** *noun*
→ **immigrate** *verb*
→ **immigration** *noun*
→ **immigrant** *noun*

e•mis•sions /ɪ'mɪʃənz/ *plural noun, formal*
smoke and chemicals that are produced by cars, factories, etc.: *Emissions from cars are causing a lot of damage to the environment.*

Em•my /'emi/ *noun* plural **Emmies**
a prize given every year to the best program, actor, etc. on U.S. television

e•mo•tion /ɪ'moʊʃən/ *noun*
a strong feeling such as love or hate: *Men often don't like to show their emotions.* | *Her voice was full of emotion.*

e•mo•tion•al /ɪ'moʊʃənəl/ *adjective*
1 showing strong feelings to other people, especially by crying or shouting: *Everyone was very emotional, because it was sad to say goodbye.*
2 relating to your feelings generally: *The first five years are an important time in a child's emotional development.*
—**emotionally** *adverb*

em•pa•thize /'empə,θaɪz/ *verb, formal*
to understand someone else's feelings and problems, because you have been in the same situation yourself: *I empathized with the book's main character because he was exactly my age.*
—**empathy** *noun, formal* the ability to empathize: *I felt a lot of empathy for him because his family was very similar to mine.*
—**empathetic** /,empə'θetɪk/ *adjective, formal* able to empathize

em•per•or /'empərɚ/ *noun*
the ruler of an EMPIRE: *a Roman emperor*

em•pha•sis /'emfəsɪs/ Ac *noun* plural **emphases** /'emfəsiz/
1 special importance: *Schools put too much emphasis on passing tests and exams* (=they give it too much importance).
2 special importance that is given to part of a word or phrase by saying it louder or higher, or by printing it in a special way: *In "hotel," the emphasis is on the second syllable.* SYNONYM **stress**
WORD FAMILY → **emphasize** *verb*

em•pha•size /'emfə,saɪz/ Ac *verb*
to say or show that something is important: *He emphasized the need for students to learn grammar when they study a foreign language.*

em•pire /'empaɪɚ/ *noun*
1 a group of countries that are all controlled by one ruler or government: *the Roman Empire*
2 a big group of companies, people, or activities that are all controlled by one person: *He runs a huge media empire, including newspaper and magazine publishers and television companies.*

em•ploy /ɪm'plɔɪ/ *verb*
1 to pay someone to work for you: *The company employs over 5,000 people.*
2 *formal* to use something: *The police employed new technology to find the people who broke into the computer system.*
—**employable** *adjective* having the skills that you need to get a job with a company: *He had no experience, so he wasn't very employable.*

WORD FAMILY look at the words:
→ **employ** *verb*
→ **employer** *noun*
→ **employee** *noun*
→ **employment** *noun*
→ **unemployed** *adjective*
→ **unemployment** *noun*

em•ploy•ee /ɪm'plɔɪ-i/ *noun*
someone who is paid to work for a person, organization, or company: *a government employee* | *How many employees are there in your company?* SYNONYM **worker**

em•ploy•er /ɪm'plɔɪɚ/ *noun*
a person, company, or organization that pays people to work for them: *Employers are looking for people who have experience doing the job.*

em•ploy•ment /ɪm'plɔɪmənt/ *noun, formal*
work that you do to earn money: *He's still looking for employment, but there are not many jobs right now.* SYNONYM **work**

em•pow•er /ɪm'paʊɚ/ *verb, formal*
to give someone the confidence, power, or right to do something: *She empowers her students to succeed by taking them into real work situations to learn.*

em•press /'emprɪs/ *noun*
the female ruler of an EMPIRE, or the wife of an EMPEROR

empty

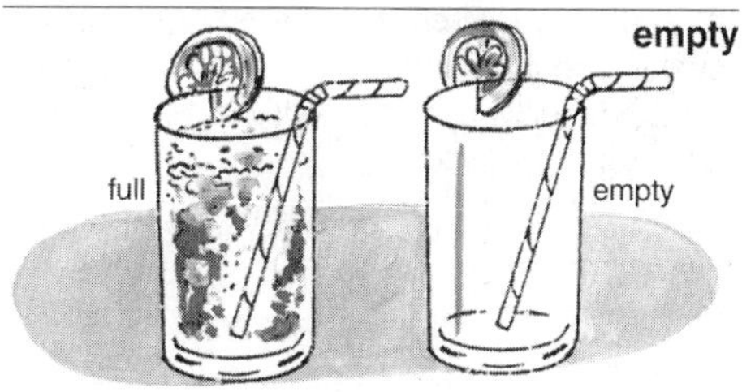

emp•ty[1] /'empti/ *adjective* **emptier, emptiest**
1 having nothing inside: *an empty box* | *Your glass is empty.* ANTONYM **full**
2 having no one inside: *an empty restaurant* ANTONYM **full**
3 if your life feels empty, it seems to have no purpose and you feel unhappy because nothing interesting is happening: *After the divorce, my life felt empty.*

empty[2] *verb* **emptied**, third person singular **empties**
1 to remove everything that is inside of something else: *Can you empty the dishwasher?*
2 if a place empties, the people inside it leave: *The theater began to empty.*

en•a•ble /ɪ'neɪbəl/ Ac *verb, formal*
to make it possible for someone or something to do something: *The Internet enables you to find out information about almost anything.*

en•act /ɪ'nækt/ *verb, formal*
to make a new law: *Congress enacted a new law to cut taxes.*

en•close /ɪn'kloʊz/ *verb, formal*
1 to put something inside an envelope with a letter: *I enclosed a picture of our house with the letter.*
2 be enclosed by something = to be surrounded by something, for example a fence or wall: *The yard was enclosed by a high wall.*

en•clo•sure /ɪn'kloʊʒɚ/ *noun, formal*
an area that is surrounded by something such as a wall or fence: *The animals are kept in a large enclosure.*

en•coun•ter[1] /ɪn'kaʊntɚ/ Ac *noun, formal*
1 a situation when you have to deal with something: *My first encounter with racism was at school when a white boy would not sit next to me.*

E

2 a situation when you meet someone: *He wrote about his encounter with the singer, who he met at a party.*

encounter² *verb, formal*
to have something happen to you: *Did you encounter any problems?*

en·cour·age /ɪn'kɚɪdʒ/ *verb*
1 to try to persuade someone to do something: *My parents encouraged me to study law, saying that they would pay for college if I did.* ANTONYM **discourage**
2 to make someone feel more hopeful and more confident: *The good news encouraged everyone to keep working.* ANTONYM **discourage**
—**encouraging** *adjective* making you feel more hopeful and more confident: *The latest test scores are encouraging because they mean that students are getting better at math.*
—**encouragement** *noun* things that you say in order to try to persuade someone to do something or make him or her feel more confident: *The coach said a few words of encouragement to the team.*
→ See Thesaurus box at **persuade**

E

en·cy·clo·pe·di·a /ɪn,saɪklə'pidiə/ *noun*
a large book, set of books, or CD-ROM that contains a lot of facts about many subjects or about one particular subject: *My encyclopedia gives the population and the capital city of every country in the world.*

end¹ /end/ *noun*
1 the last part of something: *I didn't see the end of the movie.* | *My birthday is at the end of July.* | *The meeting came to an end* (=it finished) *and we all got ready to leave.* ANTONYM **beginning**
2 the part of a place or long object that is farthest from its beginning or center: *We live at the far end of the street.*

> **THESAURUS: end**
>
> **point** the sharp end of something: *the point of a pencil*
>
> **tip** the end of something, often something long or that sticks out: *the tip of your nose*

3 in the end = after thinking about something for a long time, or after a lot of other things have happened: *We couldn't decide between going to Florida or Mexico, but in the end, we chose Mexico.* SYNONYM **finally**
4 make ends meet = to have just enough money to buy what you need: *My father had to do two jobs in order to make ends meet.*
→ **dead end**

end² *verb*
to finish, or to make something finish: *World War II ended in 1945.* | *I tried to end the conversation.* ANTONYM **begin**

PHRASAL VERBS

end in something
to have a particular result, or to finish in a particular way: *Their marriage ended in divorce.*

end up
to arrive somewhere after many other things have happened, when you did not plan to arrive in that place: *We went out to eat and then to a movie, and ended up at Joe's house.*

en·dan·ger /ɪn'deɪndʒɚ/ *verb, formal*
to put someone or something in a dangerous or harmful situation: *Smoking seriously endangers your health.*

en,dangered 'species *noun*
a type of animal or plant that soon might not exist anymore because there are very few left: *The Siberian tiger is now an endangered species.*

end·ing /'endɪŋ/ *noun*
the end of a story, movie, play, etc.: *The movie has a happy ending, and they get married.*

end·less /'endləs/ *adjective*
continuing for a very long time, so that you become tired or annoyed: *The meeting was endless, lasting for more than four hours.*

en·dorse /ɪn'dɔrs/ *verb*
1 to officially say that you support or approve of someone or something: *The mayor endorsed the plan today, saying, "I believe it will be a very good thing for our city."*
2 to sign your name on the back of a check: *You need to endorse the check to get cash for it.*
—**endorsement** *noun* a statement in which you officially say that you support or approve of someone or something

en•dur•ance /ɪnˈdʊrəns/ *noun, formal*
the ability to continue doing something difficult or painful for a long time: *The 26 mile race is a test of the runners' endurance.*

en•dure /ɪnˈdʊr/ *verb, formal*
1 to suffer pain or deal with a very difficult situation for a long time: *People have endured months of fighting.*
2 *formal* to continue for a long time: *Their marriage has endured for over 50 years.*

en•e•my /ˈenəmi/ *noun* plural **enemies**
1 someone who hates you and wants to harm you or prevent you from being successful: *She has made a lot of enemies during her career.* ANTONYM **friend**
2 the people that you are fighting in a war: *The enemy started firing rockets at us.* | *enemy soldiers* ANTONYM **ally**

en•er•get•ic /ˌenɚˈdʒetɪk/ Ac *adjective*
very active and doing things with a lot of energy: *He was an energetic coach, who often ran up and down the court with the players.*
—**energetically** *adverb*

en•er•gize /ˈenɚˌdʒaɪz/ *verb*
to make someone feel more determined and full of energy: *The president's speech energized us, and made us want to work hard for our country.*

en•er•gy /ˈenɚdʒi/ Ac *noun* plural **energies**
1 the physical and mental strength that makes you able to do things: *She was young and full of energy.*
2 power that is used to produce heat, make machines work, etc.: *The U.S. gets most of its energy from oil, coal, and natural gas.*

WORD FAMILY look at the words:
→ **energy** *noun*
→ **energetic** *adjective*
→ **energetically** *adverb*
→ **energize** *verb*

en•force /ɪnˈfɔrs/ Ac *verb, formal*
to make people obey a rule or law: *The police have the job of enforcing the law.*
—**enforcement** *noun* the process of making people obey a rule or law: *law enforcement*

en•gage /ɪnˈgeɪdʒ/ *verb, formal*
engage someone in conversation = to begin talking to someone: *A woman sat down next to me and engaged me in conversation.*

PHRASAL VERB
engage in something
to do an activity: *Only 10% of Americans engage in regular exercise.*

en•gaged /ɪnˈgeɪdʒd/ *adjective*
two people who are engaged have agreed to marry each other: *They got engaged in May, and they got married a year later.*
→ See Thesaurus box at **married**

en•gage•ment /ɪnˈgeɪdʒmənt/ *noun*
an agreement to marry someone: *The couple announced their engagement in March.*

en•gine /ˈendʒɪn/ *noun*
1 the part of a vehicle or machine that produces power to make it move: *The car's engine made a funny sound when it started.*
2 the part of a train that pulls the other CARs along a railroad SYNONYM **locomotive**
→ See picture on page A28

en•gi•neer /ˌendʒəˈnɪr/ *noun*
1 someone whose job is to design, build, and repair machines, electrical or electronic equipment, roads and bridges, etc.: *The engineers are trying to fix the problem with the plane's engines.* | *a civil engineer* (=someone who designs and builds roads or bridges)
2 someone who controls the engines on a train or ship

en•gi•neer•ing /ˌendʒəˈnɪrɪŋ/ *noun*
the profession or activity of designing, building, and repairing machines, electrical or electronic equipment, roads and bridges, etc.

En•glish[1] /ˈɪŋglɪʃ/ *noun*
1 the language used in places such as the U.S., Canada, and the U.K.: *My sister speaks very good English.*
2 the English = the people of England: *The English love soccer.*

English[2] *adjective*
from England: *Her husband is English.* | *the English language*
—**Englishman** *noun* a man from England
—**Englishwoman** *noun* a woman from England

E

en•grossed /ɪn'groʊst/ *adjective, formal*
so interested in something that you do not notice anything else: *He was engrossed in his book and didn't see me leave the room.*

en•joy /ɪn'dʒɔɪ/ *verb*
1 if you enjoy something, you like doing it, watching it, etc.: *Did you enjoy the movie?* | *I enjoyed watching the game.*

THESAURUS: enjoy

like to enjoy something, or think that it is nice or good: *I liked the movie a lot; it was really good.*

love to like something very much, or enjoy doing something very much: *My daughter loves to read.*

have a good/great time to enjoy doing something or going somewhere, usually with other people: *Did you have a good time at the party?*

have fun to enjoy doing something: *The kids were having fun in the pool.*

2 enjoy yourself = to be happy and have fun in a particular situation: *I enjoyed myself at the party.*
—**enjoyment** *noun* pleasure that you get from doing something

en•joy•a•ble /ɪn'dʒɔɪəbəl/ *adjective, formal*
giving you pleasure: *We had an enjoyable afternoon playing in the water at the beach.*
SYNONYM **fun**
➔ See Thesaurus box at **nice**

en•large /ɪn'lɑrdʒ/ *verb*
to make something become bigger, for example a picture or a photograph: *I'm going to enlarge these two pictures on my computer.*

en•light•en•ing /ɪn'laɪtnɪŋ/ *adjective, formal*
making someone learn or understand something better: *The experience of traveling alone was enlightening; I saw and learned so many new things.*

en•list /ɪn'lɪst/ *verb*
to join the army, navy, etc.: *Her son has enlisted in the army.*
—**enlistment** *noun* the action of enlisting

e•nor•mous /ɪ'nɔrməs/ Ac *adjective*
extremely large in size or amount: *You should see their house – it's enormous!*
SYNONYM **huge**
—**enormously** *adverb*
➔ See Thesaurus box at **big**

e•nough /ɪ'nʌf/ *adverb, adjective, pronoun*
1 as much, as many, as big, etc. as is needed: *We don't have enough money to buy a new car.* | *Is this room big enough for both of you?*

THESAURUS: enough

plenty a large amount that is enough or more than enough: *Try to eat plenty of fruits and vegetables.*

sufficient *formal* as much as you need for a particular purpose: *We weren't given sufficient time to finish the test.*

adequate *formal* enough for a particular purpose: *The light was not adequate for reading.*

2 *spoken* if you have had enough of someone or something, you are tired and annoyed because of him, her, or it: *I have had enough of the kids today; they just fight all the time.*

en•roll /ɪn'roʊl/ *verb*
to officially join a school, university, etc.: *He enrolled at the local community college.*

en•sure /ɪn'ʃʊr/ Ac *verb, formal*
to make certain that something happens: *Please ensure that you have all your luggage with you when you get off the plane.*

en•ter /'entɚ/ *verb*
1 to go or come into a place: *He entered the room quietly and sat down.*

THESAURUS: enter

go in to move into a particular place: *Frank opened the door, and we went in.*

come in if someone comes in, he or she enters the room where you are: *Jim came in to the classroom, carrying his books.*

sneak in to go somewhere quietly and secretly: *He snuck in through the back door of the house.*

get in to move into a place: *"How did the burglars get in?" "Through the window."*

trespass *formal* to go onto someone's land without permission: *The sign said "No Trespassing."*

2 to start studying or working somewhere:

Many older students are now entering college.

3 to take part in a competition, race, or election: *Over 100 athletes entered the race.*

4 to put information into a computer by pressing the keys, or to write information on a form, document, etc.: *Enter your name and address.*

5 enter into an agreement/a contract, etc. *formal* = to officially make an agreement

WORD FAMILY look at the words:

→ enter *verb*
→ entry *noun*
→ entrance *noun*

en•ter•prise /ˈentɚˌpraɪz/ *noun*
1 a company or business: *a successful business enterprise*
2 the ability to think of and try new things, especially in business: *She showed enterprise by making bracelets and selling them to her friends.*

en•ter•tain /ˌentɚˈteɪn/ *verb*
1 to do something that interests people or makes them laugh: *He entertained them with funny stories about his life in Hong Kong.*
2 to treat someone as a guest by providing food and drink for him or her: *The company spends a lot of money on entertaining business clients.*
—**entertaining** *adjective* interesting and enjoyable: *an entertaining movie*

en•ter•tain•er /ˌentɚˈteɪnɚ/ *noun*
someone whose job is to tell jokes, sing, etc.: *a popular TV entertainer*

en•ter•tain•ment /ˌentɚˈteɪnmənt/ *noun*
things for people to watch and do in order to enjoy themselves: *At the party there were singers and other live entertainment* (=people who perform). | *the entertainment industry* (=businesses that are involved in making movies, television programs, popular music, etc.)

en•thrall•ing /ɪnˈθrɔlɪŋ/ *adjective, formal*
someone or something that is enthralling is so interesting, exciting, or enjoyable that you give all your attention to him, her, or it: *The audience was completely still and silent through the whole enthralling performance.*
—**enthralled** *adjective* if you are enthralled by something, you enjoy it so much that you give it all your attention

en•thu•si•as•m /ɪnˈθuziˌæzəm/ *noun*
a strong feeling of interest and excitement: *The students were full of enthusiasm and were ready to work hard.*

en•thu•si•ast /ɪnˈθuziˌæst/ *noun, formal*
someone who likes and is very interested in something: *My father is a baseball enthusiast; he watches every game he can.* SYNONYM **fan**

en•thu•si•as•tic /ɪnˌθuziˈæstɪk/ *adjective*
showing a lot of interest and excitement about something: *The kids are very enthusiastic about the idea of a party.*
—**enthusiastically** *adverb*

en•tire /ɪnˈtaɪɚ/ *adjective*
all of something: *I spent the entire day cooking for the party.*

en•ti•tle /ɪnˈtaɪtl/ *verb, formal*
1 to give someone the right to have or do something: *Membership at the YMCA entitles you to use all of its sports equipment.*
2 be entitled = to have a particular title: *The book was entitled "The Lion, the Witch, and the Wardrobe."*
—**entitlement** *noun, formal* the amount of something that you are allowed to have according to the rules

en•trance /ˈentrəns/ *noun*
1 a door, gate, or other opening that you go through to enter a place: *He went into the building through the main entrance.* ANTONYM **exit**
2 the right or ability to go into a place: *Entrance to the park costs $10.00.*

en•trée /ˈɑntreɪ/ *noun*
the main food that you eat at a meal: *The entrée was a chicken dish, served with potatoes and vegetables.*

en•tre•pre•neur /ˌɑntrəprəˈnɚ/ *noun*
someone who starts a company, arranges business deals, and takes risks in order to make a profit: *The company was started by a couple of young entrepreneurs in 2005.*

en•try /ˈentri/ *noun*
1 the right or ability to go into a place: *He was refused entry into* (=not allowed to enter) *the United States.*

E

2 the act of becoming involved in doing something: *the United States' entry into the war*
3 a person or thing that takes part in a competition, race, etc.: *This painting is the winning entry of the competition.*
4 *also* **entryway** a door, gate, or opening that you go through to go into a place: *The entry is in the back of the building.* SYNONYM **entrance**
5 a word and its definition in a dictionary: *The dictionary has over 100,000 entries.*

E

ˈentry-ˌlevel *adjective*
an entry-level job is at the lowest position in a company, and is intended for people who have little or no experience: *After college, she found an entry-level job in a software company.*

en•vel•op /ɪnˈveləp/ *verb, formal*
to cover something completely: *The building was quickly enveloped in smoke from the fire.*

en•ve•lope /ˈenvəˌloʊp/ *noun*
a paper cover that you put a letter in: *She wrote the address on the envelope.*

en•vi•ous /ˈenviəs/ *adjective*
wishing that you had something that someone else has: *Jackie was envious of her sister's success.*
—**enviously** *adverb*: *He looked enviously at John's new car.*

en•vi•ron•ment /ɪnˈvaɪrənmənt/ Ac *noun*
1 the environment = the natural world, including water, air, land, plants, and sometimes animals, that can be harmed by the way humans live: *We are trying to protect the environment by making companies stop polluting the air and water.*
2 the people and things around you that affect your life: *A police officer's work environment* (=where he or she works) *is sometimes very dangerous.*
—**environmental** /ɪnˌvaɪrənˈmentl/ *adjective* related to the environment: *environmental pollution*
—**environmentally** *adverb* in a way that relates to the environment: *The bicycle is an environmentally friendly form of transport* (=it does not harm the environment).

en•vy[1] /ˈenvi/ *noun*
the feeling of wanting something which someone else has: *She looked with envy at Ben's new computer.*

envy[2] *verb* **envied**, third person singular **envies**
if you envy someone, you wish you had something that he or she has: *I envy Meg – her parents buy her anything she wants.*

en•zyme /ˈenzaɪm/ *noun*
a chemical that is produced in plants and animals and that causes a chemical process to start: *Enzymes in the stomach change food so that it can be digested.*

ep•ic[1] /ˈepɪk/ *adjective, formal*
an epic story or trip is very long, exciting, or impressive: *an epic novel*

epic[2] *noun*
a book, poem, or movie that tells a long story about brave actions and exciting events: *"The Odyssey" is an epic written by Homer.*

ep•i•dem•ic /ˌepəˈdemɪk/ *noun*
a large number of cases of a disease that happen at the same time: *the AIDS epidemic*

ep•i•lep•sy /ˈepəˌlepsi/ *noun*
a medical condition in the brain that can make someone suddenly become unconscious or unable to control his or her movements for a short time
—**epileptic** /ˌepəˈleptɪk/ *noun* someone who has epilepsy: *Her son is an epileptic.*
—**epileptic** *adjective* related to epilepsy: *She had an epileptic fit* (=a short time when she became unconscious or couldn't control her movements).

ep•i•sode /ˈepəˌsoʊd/ *noun*
1 a television or radio program that is one of a series of programs that tell a story: *I watched an old episode of "The Simpsons" last night.*
2 an event or a short period of time during which something specific happened: *The death of his wife was a sad episode in his life.*

e•qual[1] /ˈikwəl/ *adjective*
1 the same in size, value, amount, etc.: *She cut the cake into eight equal parts.* | *Both teams scored an equal number of points in the basketball game.* | *The two towns are*

equal in size. | *A dime is equal to ten pennies.*
2 having the same rights, opportunities, etc. as everyone else: *Women fought for equal rights, such as the right to be paid as well as men.*

equal[2] *verb* **equaled** or **equalled, equaling** or **equalling**
1 to be as large as something else: *Four plus four equals eight.*
2 *formal* to be as good as someone or something else: *He equalled the world record in the 200 meter race at the Olympic Games.*

equal[3] *noun*
someone with the same abilities or rights as someone else: *Young people want adults to treat them as equals.*

e•qual•i•ty /ɪˈkwɑləti/ *noun, formal*
a situation in which people from different groups have the same rights and opportunities: *Women haven't yet achieved equality with men in the workplace.* ANTONYM **inequality**

e•qual•ly /ˈikwəli/ *adverb*
1 just as much: *Jim and his sister are equally intelligent* (=they have the same level of intelligence).
2 in equal parts or amounts: *We divided the work equally* (=everyone had the same amount of work).

ˈequal sign *noun*
the sign (=) that you use in mathematics to show that two things are the same size, number, or amount

e•qua•tion /ɪˈkweɪʒən/ Ac *noun*
a statement in mathematics showing that two quantities are equal, for example 2 x 3 = 6: *The teacher gave the class a mathematical equation with one of the numbers missing.*

e•qua•tor *also* **Equator** /ɪˈkweɪtɚ/ *noun*
the equator = an imaginary line around the Earth that divides it equally into its northern and southern halves: *The island is 80 miles north of the equator.*
—**equatorial** /ˌekwəˈtɔriəl◂/ *adjective, formal* near the equator, or relating to the equator
→ See picture at **globe**

e•qui•lat•er•al tri•an•gle /ˌikwəˌlætərəl ˈtraɪˌæŋgəl/ *noun*
a TRIANGLE whose three sides are all the same length

e•qui•nox /ˈikwəˌnɑks/ *noun*
one of the two times each year when day and night are equal in length everywhere on earth: *The spring equinox is on March 20.*

e•quip /ɪˈkwɪp/ Ac *verb* **equipped, equipping**
to provide the tools or equipment that someone needs to do something: *The city has equipped all the schools with new computers.*

e•quip•ment /ɪˈkwɪpmənt/ Ac *noun*
the tools, machines, clothes, etc. that you need for a particular activity: *I didn't have the right equipment to change the tire.* | *We bought several new pieces of equipment for the chemistry lab.* | *sports equipment*

eq•ui•ty /ˈekwəti/ *noun, formal*
the amount of money that you would have left if you sold something you own, such as a house, and paid off the money you borrowed to buy it: *He has $100,000 of equity in his home.*

e•quiv•a•lent[1] /ɪˈkwɪvələnt/ Ac *adjective*
equal in amount, value, rank, etc. to something or someone else: *The certificate is equivalent to a high school diploma.*

equivalent[2] *noun*
something that is equal in amount, value, rank, etc. to something else: *The car cost the equivalent of six months' pay.*

e•ra /ˈɪrə/ *noun, formal*
a period of time in history: *the Cold War era of the mid-20th century*

e•rad•i•cate /ɪˈrædəˌkeɪt/ *verb, formal*
to destroy or remove something completely: *We have eradicated the disease, smallpox, from the world.*
—**eradication** /ɪˌrædəˈkeɪʃən/ *noun, formal*: *One of the group's goals is the eradication of poverty.*

E

e•rase /ɪˈreɪs/ *verb*
to completely remove written or recorded information: *Make sure that you erase any incorrect answers on your test paper.* | *I erased the file from the computer.*

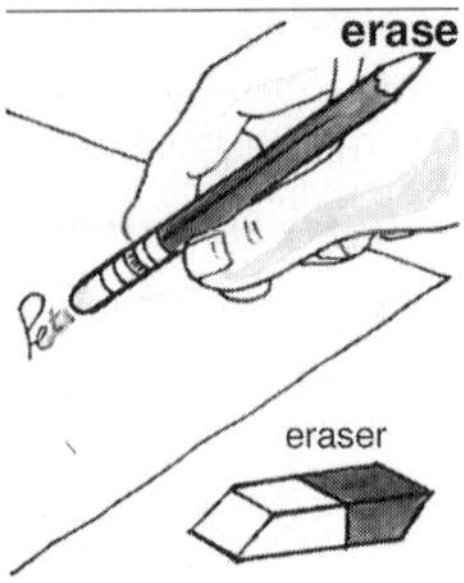

e•ras•er /ɪˈreɪsɚ/ *noun*
1 a piece of rubber that you use to remove pencil or pen marks from paper
2 an object that you use to clean marks from a BLACKBOARD or WHITEBOARD
➔ See picture at **erase**

e•rect¹ /ɪˈrekt/ *adjective*
in a straight upright position: *The rabbit stopped to listen, with its ears erect.*

erect² *verb, formal*
to build something: *The town hall was erected in 1892.*

e•rode /ɪˈroʊd/ Ac *verb, formal*
if land erodes, it is gradually destroyed by the weather or by water: *The ocean is eroding the beaches.* | *The river bank has started to erode.*
—**erosion** /ɪˈroʊʒən/ *noun, formal* the gradual destruction of land by the weather or by water: *Planting trees will help to prevent soil erosion.*

e•rot•ic /ɪˈrɑtɪk/ *adjective*
involving or producing sexual feelings: *an erotic painting*
—**erotically** *adverb*: *She was dancing erotically.*

er•rand /ˈerənd/ *noun*
a short trip away from home or work in order to do something, for example to buy something: *I have some errands to do downtown.*

er•rat•ic /ɪˈrætɪk/ *adjective, formal*
not following a regular pattern: *Her behavior became more and more erratic – she was always losing things and forgetting people's names.*
—**erratically** *adverb, formal*: *He was driving erratically before the accident.*

er•ror /ˈerɚ/ Ac *noun*
a mistake: *I made one error on the math test, so I got a 95.*

e•rupt /ɪˈrʌpt/ *verb*
1 *formal* if violence erupts, it suddenly happens: *Fighting could erupt again at any time.*
2 if a VOLCANO erupts, it sends out smoke, fire, and rock into the sky: *More than 800 people died when the volcano erupted.*
—**eruption** /ɪˈrʌpʃən/ *noun* an occasion when a VOLCANO erupts

es•ca•late /ˈeskəˌleɪt/ *verb, formal*
1 if an argument or fight escalates, it quickly becomes worse: *The argument escalated into a violent fight.*
2 to become higher or increase: *The price of gas continues to escalate.*
—**escalation** /ˌeskəˈleɪʃən/ *noun, formal* the action of escalating: *an escalation of fighting*

es•ca•la•tor /ˈeskəˌleɪtɚ/ *noun*
moving stairs that carry people from one level of a building to another: *We took the escalator to the first floor of the store.*

es·cape¹ /ɪ'skeɪp/ *verb*

1 to avoid something bad that could have happened to you: *The girl climbed through a window to escape the fire.* | *The two boys escaped punishment by blaming another child.*

2 to get away from a place when someone is trying to stop you: *He escaped from prison by making a tunnel.*

—**escaped** *adjective*: *escaped prisoners*

escape² *noun*

1 the act of getting away from a place or a bad situation: *They made their escape from the jail while the guards were not looking.*

2 a way of forgetting about a bad or boring situation for a short time: *Movies are a good form of escape, because you can forget about your problems for a while.*

es·cort¹ /ɪ'skɔrt/ *verb*

to go somewhere with someone, in order to protect or guard him or her: *The policemen escorted the prisoners to the courthouse.*

es·cort² /'eskɔrt/ *noun*

the person or group of people that goes somewhere with someone in order to protect or guard him or her: *The governor always travels with a police escort.*

ESL *noun*

English as a Second Language the activity of teaching English to students whose first language is not English, but who live in an English-speaking country: *an ESL student*

es·pe·cial·ly /ɪ'speʃəli/ *adverb*

1 used to say that something is more true of one person or thing than of other people or things: *He is especially good at math.*

2 for a particular person or reason: *She bought new clothes especially for the trip.*

es·pres·so /e'spresoʊ/ *noun*

very strong coffee that you drink in small cups

es·say /'eseɪ/ *noun*

a short piece of writing about a particular subject: *I had to write an essay about Abraham Lincoln for history class.* SYNONYM **paper**

es·sence /'esəns/ *noun, formal*

the most basic and important quality of something: *The essence of the problem is that many poor people cannot afford to buy computers.*

es·sen·tial /ɪ'senʃəl/ *adjective*

important and necessary: *If you live in the country, a car is essential because there are not many buses.*

➔ See Thesaurus box at **important**

es·sen·tial·ly /ɪ'senʃəli/ *adverb*

used to talk about the most basic facts about something: *The story is essentially true, although the writer changed the names of some of the people in it.*

es·tab·lish /ɪ'stæblɪʃ/ Ac *verb, formal*

1 to start a company, organization, etc. that will exist for a long time: *The school was established in 1922.*

2 to start having regular communication or a relationship with another person, group, country, etc.: *We established a relationship with a school in Guatemala, so that the students can write to each other.*

es·tab·lish·ment /ɪ'stæblɪʃmənt/ Ac *noun, formal*

a company or any public or private organization: *Harvard is a famous educational establishment.*

es·tate /ɪ'steɪt/ Ac *noun*

1 all of someone's property and money, especially everything that is left after he or she dies: *She left her estate to her three children when she died.*

2 a large area of land with a large house on it, that is owned by one person, family, or organization

➔ **real estate**

es·teem /ɪ'stim/ *noun, formal*

respect and admiration for someone: *The teacher was held in high esteem* (=admired and respected) *by all her students.*

➔ **self-esteem**

es·ti·mate¹ /'estə,meɪt/ Ac *verb*

to make a reasonable guess at the size, amount, or time of something: *I estimate that the job will be finished by Friday.*

es·ti·mate² /'estəmɪt/ Ac *noun*

1 the size, amount, or time that someone guesses something to be: *The manager wants an estimate of how much time we'll*

E

need to finish the job. | *The camera should cost you less than $300, but that's a rough estimate* (=not a very exact guess).
2 a statement of how much it will probably cost to build or repair something: *The painting company sent me an estimate for painting the house.*

etc. /et 'setrə/ *adverb*
etcetera used at the end of a list to show that you could add similar things: *He's been to many European countries: France, Germany, Spain, etc.*

E

e·ter·nal /ɪ'tɚnl/ *adjective*
continuing forever: *The possibility of eternal life is an important idea in some religions.*
—**eternally** *adverb*: *We believe that the soul lives eternally.*

e·ter·ni·ty /ɪ'tɚnəti/ *noun*
1 time that does not end: *Although Shakespeare is dead, his works will live on for eternity.*
2 an eternity *formal* = a period of time that seems long because you are annoyed, worried, etc.: *We waited for an eternity, and the bus still didn't come.*

eth·ic /'eθɪk/ Ac *noun*
1 ethics = rules that people use to decide what is right and wrong: *He wrote a book about medical ethics* (=rules that doctors use to decide what is right and wrong).
2 an idea or belief that influences people's behavior and attitudes: *The college has a strong ethic of fairness* (=they believe strongly that things should be fair).

eth·i·cal /'eθɪkəl/ Ac *adjective, formal*
1 involving beliefs about what is right and wrong: *Whether to use animals in scientific tests is a difficult ethical question.*
2 morally good or correct: *Is it ethical for doctors to use drugs to control people's behavior?*
—**ethically** *adverb*

eth·nic /'eθnɪk/ Ac *adjective*
relating to a particular race or nationality: *The college has students from a wide variety of ethnic backgrounds.*
—**ethnicity** /eθ'nɪsəti/ *noun, formal* the race or nationality that someone belongs to: *It is wrong that people are treated unfairly because of their ethnicity.*

et·i·quette /'etɪkət/ *noun, formal*
the rules of polite behavior: *Etiquette is important at occasions such as weddings and funerals.*

Eu·rope /'yʊrəp/ *noun*
the CONTINENT that is north of the Mediterranean Sea and west of the Ural mountains: *He visited Poland and other countries in Eastern Europe.*

Eu·ro·pe·an /ˌyʊrə'piən/ *adjective*
from Europe: *He speaks several European languages including French and Italian.*
—**European** *noun* someone from Europe: *The Portuguese may have been the first Europeans to visit Australia.*

e·vac·u·ate /ɪ'vækyuˌeɪt/ *verb, formal*
to move people from a dangerous place to a safe place: *The police evacuated the library after someone called to say that there was a bomb in the building.*
—**evacuation** /ɪˌvækyu'eɪʃən/ *noun* the action of moving people from a dangerous place to a safe place: *As the storm came closer, the mayor ordered the evacuation of the city.*

e·vade /ɪ'veɪd/ *verb, formal*
1 to avoid doing something you should do, or avoid talking about something: *The senator evaded the question because he did not know the answer.*
2 to avoid being caught by someone who is trying to catch you: *The prisoner, who escaped last night, has evaded capture.*

e·val·u·ate /ɪ'vælyuˌeɪt/ Ac *verb, formal*
to judge how good, useful, or successful someone or something is: *Scientists are evaluating the new drug to decide if it works well.*
—**evaluation** /ɪˌvælyu'eɪʃən/ *noun, formal* a judgment about how good, useful, or successful someone or something is: *The evaluation of the new computer system found that there were many problems.*

e·vap·o·rate /ɪ'væpəˌreɪt/ *verb, formal*
if a liquid evaporates, it changes into steam or a gas: *Sea water evaporates and leaves salt behind.*
—**evaporation** /ɪˌvæpə'reɪʃən/ *noun, formal* the process of evaporating: *In warm weather, evaporation causes the water level of the lake to drop.*

e•va•sion /ɪˈveɪʒən/ *noun, formal*
1 the act of avoiding doing something that you should do: *He was in prison for tax evasion* (=not paying taxes).
2 the act of deliberately avoiding talking about something or answering a question: *The politician's speech was full of lies and evasions.*

e•va•sive /ɪˈveɪsɪv/ *adjective, formal*
not willing to answer questions directly: *He was very evasive when I asked him where he had been.*

eve /iv/ *noun*
the night or day before a religious day or a holiday: *We're going to a big party on New Year's Eve.* | *Christmas Eve*

e•ven[1] /ˈivən/ *adverb*
1 used when adding something surprising: *He keeps everything, even old bus tickets.* | *The mountains always have snow on them, even in summer.*
2 used when making a comparison stronger: *Then he bought an even bigger car.*
3 **even if** = used when emphasizing that something will still be true if another thing happens: *I'll finish the job even if I have to work all night.*

even[2] *adjective*
1 flat, level, or smooth: *You need a large even surface to work on.*
2 an even rate, temperature, etc. does not change much: *Store the chemicals at an even temperature.*
3 divided equally, so that there is the same amount of something in each place, for each person, etc.: *Divide the dough into three even amounts.* SYNONYM **equal**
4 an even number can be divided exactly by two: *2, 4, 6, and 8 are even numbers.* ANTONYM **odd**
5 **be even** *informal* = to no longer owe someone something, especially money: *I paid five dollars more, so if you give me five dollars, we'll be even.*
6 a game or competition that is even is one where the teams are equal and as good as each other: *The first half of the game was very even – neither team scored.*
—**evenness** *noun*
—**evenly** *adverb* divided or spread equally: *Spread the frosting evenly over the cake.*
➔ See Thesaurus box at **flat**[1]

even[3] *verb*
PHRASAL VERBS
even (something) out
if things even out, the differences between them become smaller: *The company is trying to even out the difference between the numbers of men and women* (=make the numbers of men and women almost the same).
even something up
to make something become equal or the same: *O'Malley hit a home run to even up the score.*

E

eve•ning /ˈivnɪŋ/ *noun*
1 the end of the day and the early part of the night: *We usually eat at around 6 in the evening.* | *Do you want to come to my house tomorrow evening?*
2 **(good) evening** = said in order to greet someone in the evening: *Good evening ladies and gentlemen, and welcome to our performance.*

e•vent /ɪˈvent/ *noun*
1 something that happens, especially something important, interesting, or unusual: *He described the events that occurred before the fight.*
2 something that has been organized, such as a party, sports game, or show: *The Super Bowl is one of the most important sporting events of the year.*

e•vent•ful /ɪˈventfəl/ *adjective*
full of interesting or important events: *The trip was very eventful – we saw and did a lot of exciting things.*

e•ven•tu•al /ɪˈventʃuəl/ Ac *adjective, formal*
happening at the end of a long period of time or after a lot of other things have happened: *Roger was the eventual winner of the tennis match, after playing for more than three hours.*
—**eventually** *adverb*: *We eventually arrived at my sister's house, over three hours late.*

ev•er /ˈevɚ/ *adverb*
1 at any time: *Have you ever been to New York?* | *Nothing ever makes Paul angry.* | *That was one of the best meals I've ever had.*
2 **ever since** = all the time since something happened: *He went to college in Colorado and has lived there ever since.*

GRAMMAR: ever

You use **ever** when you ask a question, but not when you answer a question: *"Have you ever been to San Francisco?" "Yes, I have been there."*

➔ **forever**

ever- /evɚ/
always: *I looked out at the ever-changing view from the bus window.*

E

ev·er·green /ˈevɚˌgrin/ *adjective*
an evergreen tree or plant does not lose its leaves in winter
—**evergreen** *noun* an evergreen tree or plant

evergreen

ev·ery /ˈevri/ *adjective*
1 used to talk about each of the people or things in a particular group: *Every student will receive a certificate.* | *They cut down every single tree in the yard; there is not one tree left.*

USAGE: every

Every, **each**, and **all** are all used to talk about every person or thing in a group.

When you are thinking about the people or things in the group separately, use **every** or **each**: *Every child at the party was given a balloon.* | *Each child at the party was given a balloon.*

When you are thinking about the whole group together, use **all**: *All the children were given balloons.*

2 used in order to show how often something happens: *He calls his girlfriend every day.* | *He came to see us every other day* (=every two days). | *I still see her every now and then* (=sometimes but not often). | *We visit them every so often* (=sometimes but not often).

ev·ery·bod·y /ˈevriˌbɑdi/ *pronoun*
another word for EVERYONE

ev·ery·day /ˈevriˌdeɪ/ *adjective*
ordinary, usual, or happening every day: *Going to school is part of everyday life for most children.*

ev·ery·one /ˈevriˌwʌn/ *pronoun*
every person: *She knew everyone at the party.* SYNONYM **everybody**; ANTONYM **no one, nobody**

GRAMMAR: everyone

every one, everyone

Every one is used to emphasize that you mean each person or thing in a group: *I've read every one of his books.*

Everyone means all the people in a group: *Everyone had a book to read.*

ev·ery·thing /ˈevriˌθɪŋ/ *pronoun*
1 each thing or all things: *I think everything we need is in the car.* | *There's only bread left – my brothers ate everything else* (=all other things). ANTONYM **nothing**
2 used when you are talking in general about your life or about a situation: *Everything's going wrong today: I was late for school, and now I've lost my keys.* ANTONYM **nothing**
3 be everything = to be more important than anything else: *Money isn't everything; your family, friends, and your health are more important.*

ev·ery·where /ˈevriˌwer/ *adverb*
in every place or to every place: *I've looked everywhere, but I still can't find the map.* | *People here are the same as people everywhere else* (=in all other places).

e·vict /ɪˈvɪkt/ *verb*
to legally force someone to leave the house he or she is living in: *Frank was evicted from his apartment because he did not pay the rent.*
—**eviction** /ɪˈvɪkʃən/ *noun* the act of evicting someone: *The family's eviction from their home left them with nowhere to live.*

ev·i·dence /ˈevədəns/ Ac *noun*
1 things that you see, hear, or learn that make you believe that something exists or is true: *There is clear evidence that eating too much fat can lead to heart disease.*
2 in a court of law, the facts and objects that a lawyer shows the court in order to prove that something is true: *The gun was an important piece of evidence in the murder trial.*

ev•i•dent /ˈevədənt/ Ac *adjective, formal*
clear and easily seen: *It was evident that she was unhappy because she was crying.*
—**evidently** *adverb*: *He was evidently in pain because he kept screaming.*

e•vil /ˈivəl/ *adjective*
very cruel or bad: *He was an evil killer.*
—**evil** *noun* something that is very cruel or bad: *Poverty is one of the greatest evils of our time.*

ev•o•lu•tion /ˌevəˈluʃən/ Ac *noun, formal*
the scientific idea that plants, animals, and humans have developed from very simple forms over millions of years
—**evolutionary** /ˌevəˈluʃəˌneri/ *adjective, formal* related to evolution: *She is studying the evolutionary development of birds.*

e•volve /ɪˈvɑlv/ Ac *verb, formal*
to develop gradually: *The sun is a star that has evolved over billions of years.*

ex /eks/ *noun, informal*
your ex is someone who used to be your wife, husband, GIRLFRIEND, or BOYFRIEND

ex- /eks/
used at the beginning of words to show that someone used to be something: *Jake is my ex-boyfriend – I was going out with him last year.* SYNONYM **former**

ex•act /ɪgˈzækt/ *adjective*
1 completely correct: *The exact time is 11:27 a.m.* | *I can't remember the exact date that we moved here, but it was in early July.*
2 the exact opposite = something that is as different as possible from another thing: *I thought I would hate my new school, but I actually felt the exact opposite – I loved it.*

ex•act•ly /ɪgˈzæktli/ *adverb*
1 used when saying that something is completely correct, the same, etc.: *We got home at exactly six o'clock.* | *The twins look exactly alike to me.*
2 said when you agree with someone: *"So you think we should tell him 'no'?" "Exactly!"*
3 not exactly = used when saying that something is not at all true: *It's not exactly cheap* (=it's expensive).

ex•ag•ger•ate /ɪgˈzædʒəˌreɪt/ *verb*
to make something seem bigger, better, worse, etc. than it really is: *You're exaggerating a little when you say their house is huge – it only has three bedrooms.*
—**exaggeration** /ɪgˌzædʒəˈreɪʃən/ *noun* a statement in which you exaggerate: *He said it will cost a million dollars, but that may be an exaggeration.*

ex•am /ɪgˈzæm/ *noun*
1 an important test at the end of a course in school or college: *When do you take your history exam?*
2 a set of medical tests: *I had an eye exam yesterday.*

ex•am•i•na•tion /ɪgˌzæməˈneɪʃən/ *noun*
1 the process of looking at something carefully: *The police made a careful examination of the room where the murder happened.*
2 *formal* an exam

ex•am•ine /ɪgˈzæmɪn/ *verb*
to look at something carefully in order to find out or decide something: *The doctor examined me, but he couldn't find anything wrong.*

ex•am•ple /ɪgˈzæmpəl/ *noun*
1 something of a particular kind that you mention or show in order to make something clear: *Can anyone give me an example of a verb?* | *The car is a good example of an invention that changed people's lives.*
2 for example = used when giving an example: *Many countries, for example Mexico and Japan, have a lot of earthquakes.*
3 set an example = if you set an example, you do something good that should be copied by other people: *Try to share your toys and set a good example for your brother.*

ex•as•per•at•ed /ɪgˈzæspəˌreɪtɪd/ *adjective*
feeling very annoyed: *He never listens to me, and I get so exasperated with him.*
—**exasperating** *adjective* something that is exasperating makes you feel very annoyed
—**exasperation** /ɪgˌzæspəˈreɪʃən/ *noun* a very annoyed feeling

ex•ceed /ɪkˈsid/ Ac *verb, formal*
to be more than a particular amount: *The total cost exceeded $100.*

ex•cel /ɪkˈsel/ *verb* **excelled, excelling** *formal*
to do something very well: *He excelled in baseball.*

E

ex·cel·lent /ˈeksələnt/ *adjective*
extremely good: *You should definitely go to the restaurant – the food was excellent.*
—**excellence** *noun, formal* the quality of being excellent: *The university is famous for the excellence of its teachers.*
→ See Thesaurus box at **good**[1]

WORD FAMILY look at the words:
→ **excellent** *adjective*
→ **excellence** *noun*
→ **excel** *verb*

E

ex·cept[1] /ɪkˈsept/ *preposition*
not including someone or something: *We're open every day except Monday* (=but not Monday). | *Everyone went to the show, except for Scott and Danny.*

except[2] *conjunction*
used when adding something that shows why your statement is not completely true or exact: *I have earrings like those, except they're silver not gold.*

ex·cep·tion /ɪkˈsepʃən/ *noun*
someone or something that is not included in a statement, rule, group, etc.: *Most history books are boring, but this one is an exception* (=this one is not boring). | *Everyone has improved, with the exception of Matt* (=except Matt).

ex·cep·tion·al /ɪkˈsepʃənəl/ *adjective, formal*
1 very good in a way that is unusual: *She is an exceptional student who always has the best grades in the class.*
2 unusual and not happening often: *The roads had melted in the exceptional heat.*
—**exceptionally** *adverb, formal*: *an exceptionally cold winter*
→ See Thesaurus box at **good**[1]

ex·cess[1] /ˈekses/ *adjective, formal*
more than is needed or allowed: *Cut the excess fat off the meat.*

ex·cess[2] /ɪkˈses/ *noun*
in excess of something *formal* = more than something: *He earns in excess of $200,000 a year.*

ex·ces·sive /ɪkˈsesɪv/ *adjective*
too large or too much: *Paying $80 for a T-shirt seems excessive.*
—**excessively** *adverb*

ex·change[1] /ɪksˈtʃeɪndʒ/ *noun*
the act of giving someone something and getting something similar from him or her: *I gave him the book in exchange for a CD* (=I gave him the book and he gave me a CD). | *an exchange of ideas* (=when people tell their ideas to each other)

exchange[2] *verb*
to give someone something and get something similar from him or her: *This skirt is too small; can I exchange it for a larger one?*

exˈchange rate *noun*
the value of the money of one country compared to the money of another country: *The exchange rate was 120 yen to the dollar.*

ex·cite /ɪkˈsaɪt/ *verb*
to make someone feel happy and eager or interested: *There is no new music that really excites me right now.*
—**excitable** *adjective* someone who is excitable becomes excited easily

ex·cit·ed /ɪkˈsaɪtɪd/ *adjective*
happy and eager or interested: *I'm really excited about going to camp – I think it will be a lot of fun.*

WORD FAMILY look at the words:
→ **excited** *adjective*
→ **exciting** *adjective*
→ **excitement** *noun*

→ See picture on page A23

ex·cite·ment /ɪkˈsaɪtmənt/ *noun*
the feeling you have when you are excited: *There was a lot of excitement in the town about the festival.*

ex·ci·ting /ɪkˈsaɪtɪŋ/ *adjective*
something that is exciting makes you feel excited: *an exciting movie about pirates and battles at sea*

ex·claim /ɪkˈskleɪm/ *verb, formal*
to say something loudly and suddenly because you are surprised, excited, or angry: *"I didn't expect to see you here!" exclaimed Laura.*
—**exclamation** /ˌekskləˈmeɪʃən/ *noun* something that someone exclaims

exclaˈmation ˌpoint *noun*
the sign (!), which is used after something that someone says when they feel a strong feeling such as anger, surprise, excitement, etc.: *Come here!* | *I don't believe it!*

ex•clude /ɪk'sklud/ [Ac] *verb*
1 to not allow someone or something to enter a place or to do an activity: *The club is very old-fashioned and excludes women.* ANTONYM **include**
2 to deliberately not include something: *The author excluded some important information from the book because she did not want readers to know about it.*
—**excluding** *preposition* not including: *The store is open every day excluding Sundays* (=but not Sundays).
—**exclusion** /ɪk'skluʒən/ *noun, formal* when someone or something is excluded

ex•clu•sive /ɪk'sklusɪv/ [Ac] *adjective, formal*
1 exclusive places are for people who have a lot of money or belong to a high social class: *They bought an expensive house in an exclusive neighborhood.*
2 used by only one person or group, and not shared: *The pool is for the exclusive use of the hotel's guests* (=only guests can use it).

ex•clu•sive•ly /ɪk'sklusɪvli/ [Ac] *adverb*
only: *This class is exclusively about Algebra; we will not be doing any Geometry.*

ex•cur•sion /ɪk'skɚʒən/ *noun, formal*
a short trip made for pleasure: *We went on an excursion to the city on Saturday to go shopping.*

ex•cuse¹ /ɪk'skyuz/ *verb*
1 excuse me = said when you want to politely ask someone to listen to you, leave a group of people, or say sorry for doing something rude: *Excuse me, is this the way to the train station?* | *Oh, excuse me, I didn't mean to bother you.*
2 excuse me? = said when you want someone to say something again: *"What time is it?" "Excuse me?" "I asked what time it is."*
3 to forgive someone for something that is not very bad: *Please excuse my bad handwriting.*
4 to allow someone to leave a place or not to do something: *The teacher excused her from class so that she could go to the nurse's office.*

ex•cuse² /ɪk'skyus/ *noun*
a reason that you give for doing something that you should not do: *What was his excuse for being late?* | *Stop making excuses.* | *I was trying to think of an excuse to leave because I was bored.*
➔ See Thesaurus box at **reason**

ex•e•cute /'eksəˌkyut/ *verb*
to kill someone as an official punishment: *He was found guilty of murder and executed.*
—**execution** /ˌeksə'kyuʃən/ *noun* when someone is executed: *His execution will happen on November 14.*
➔ See Thesaurus box at **kill**

ex•ec•u•tive¹ /ɪg'zekyətɪv/ *noun*
an important manager in an organization or company: *He became a successful business executive leading a large company.*

executive² *adjective*
1 relating to making decisions in a company or organization: *She's on the executive committee that makes decisions for the organization.*
2 the executive branch *formal* = the part of a government, led by an official such as a president, that is in charge of making sure that laws are used and followed correctly

ex•empt /ɪg'zempt/ *verb, formal*
to give someone special permission not to do something: *One student was exempted from the exam because he was in the hospital.*
—**exempt** *adjective, formal* not having to do something: *Private schools are exempt from this rule, but public schools have to follow it.*
—**exemption** /ɪg'zempʃən/ *noun, formal* the state of being exempt

ex•er•cise¹ /'eksɚˌsaɪz/ *noun*
1 physical activity that you do in order to stay strong and healthy: *I don't get much exercise.* | *Have you done your leg exercises yet?*
2 a set of questions that you do in order to learn or practice something: *For homework, do exercises 1 and 2.*

exercise² *verb*
to do physical activity so that you stay strong and healthy: *I exercise in the gym, and I swim twice a week.*

THESAURUS: exercise

run/go running to move quickly using your legs: *He runs about three miles every other day.* | *I try to go running three times a week.*

E

jog/go jogging to run at a slow steady speed: *She was jogging in the park.* | *Sam and I go jogging together.*

swim/go swimming to move through water using your legs and arms: *Kate swam 30 laps of the pool.* | *Older people often go swimming for exercise, because it is not as hard on your joints.*

aerobics exercises with music: *She goes to an aerobics class twice a week.*

lift weights to lift heavy pieces of metal to make your muscles stronger: *Members of the football team were lifting weights.*

work out to do exercises to make your body stronger: *I always feel a lot better after I've worked out.*

in shape/out of shape if you are in shape, you are healthy and strong because you exercise; if you are out of shape, you are not healthy and strong: *I'm taking a dancing class, and it's helping me get in shape.* | *You can't run the length of the block? You're so out of shape!*

warm up to prepare for an activity or sport by doing gentle exercises: *Always warm up before playing any sport.*

workout a time when you do exercises to keep your body strong and healthy: *Rock climbing is a great workout!*

gym a building or room that has equipment for exercising: *I go to the gym in the morning before work.*

ex•er•tion /ɪg'zɚʃən/ *noun, formal*
a lot of physical effort: *The doctor said that too much exertion could lead to another heart attack.*

ex•hale /eks'heɪl/ *verb, formal*
to breathe air out of your nose or mouth: *Take a deep breath, then exhale slowly.* ANTONYM **inhale**

ex•haust[1] /ɪg'zɔst/ *verb*
to make someone very tired: *The long walk exhausted her.*
—**exhausting** *adjective* making you feel extremely tired: *It was a long and exhausting trip.*

exhaust[2] *noun*
1 the gas that is produced when a machine such as a car is working
2 *also* **exhaust pipe** a pipe at the back of a car that exhaust comes out of

exhaust

ex•haust•ed /ɪg'zɔstɪd/ *adjective*
extremely tired: *They were exhausted from the tough game.*
—**exhaustion** /ɪg'zɔstʃən/ *noun* the state of being exhausted: *Two runners were taken to the hospital suffering from exhaustion.*

exhibit

ex•hib•it[1] /ɪg'zɪbɪt/ Ac *verb*
to show something such as art in a public place: *Her paintings have been exhibited at several galleries.*
—**exhibitor** *noun* someone who is exhibiting his or her work or products

WORD FAMILY look at the words:
- → **exhibit** *verb*
- → **exhibit** *noun*
- → **exhibition** *noun*
- → **exhibitor** *noun*

exhibit[2] *also* **ex•hi•bi•tion** /ˌeksə'bɪʃən/ Ac *noun*
a public show of something such as art: *an exhibition of photographs*

ex•ile[1] /'egzaɪl/ *verb, formal*
if the people who control your country exile you, they force you to leave the country for political reasons: *The new leader exiled many of his enemies.*

exile[2] *noun*
1 someone who is in exile has been forced to leave his or her own country for political reasons: *He spent many years living in exile in Europe.*
2 someone who has been exiled: *Her parents were Russian exiles* (=they were forced to leave Russia).

ex•ist /ɪɡˈzɪst/ *verb*
to be in the world: *The building no longer exists – it was destroyed in a fire.*

ex•ist•ence /ɪɡˈzɪstəns/ *noun*
the state of existing: *She believed in the existence of ghosts.* | *The elephant is the largest land animal in existence* (=the largest one that exists).

ex•ist•ing /ɪɡˈzɪstɪŋ/ *adjective*
an existing thing is one that exists now or that you have now: *The company is working hard to keep its existing customers happy, but we also need more new customers.*

ex•it /ˈeɡzɪt/ *noun*
1 a door through which you can leave a room, building, or airplane: *There are two exits at the back of the plane.* ANTONYM **entrance**
2 a place where vehicles can leave a HIGHWAY (=large road): *Take the next exit* (=use the next exit).

ex•ot•ic /ɪɡˈzɑtɪk/ *adjective*
something that is exotic is unusual and exciting because it is foreign: *They went on vacations to exotic islands.*

ex•pand /ɪkˈspænd/ Ac *verb*
to become larger: *When you blow air into a balloon, it expands.* | *We've decided to expand our business by opening a new store.* ANTONYM **contract**

ex•pan•sion /ɪkˈspænʃən/ Ac *noun*
the process of expanding: *The city is making plans for the expansion of the airport, which will be twice as big when it is finished.*

ex•pect /ɪkˈspekt/ *verb*
1 to think that something will happen: *Nobody expected her to win the election.* | *The movie was better than I expected.*
2 be expecting someone or something = to be waiting for someone or something to arrive: *I'm expecting a package in the mail.*
3 to demand or feel strongly that someone should do something: *Students are expected to return their homework on Friday.*
4 be expecting (a baby) = if a woman is expecting, she is going to have a baby
—**expectation** /ˌekspekˈteɪʃən/ *noun* a belief or strong hope that something will happen: *She has high expectations for her daughter* (=she believes her daughter will do well).

ex•pe•di•tion /ˌekspəˈdɪʃən/ *noun, formal*
a long and carefully organized trip, especially to a dangerous place: *They are planning an expedition to the North Pole.*

ex•pel /ɪkˈspel/ *verb* **expelled, expelling**
to officially make someone leave a school, organization, or country: *He was expelled from school for selling drugs.*

ex•pend•i•ture /ɪkˈspendətʃɚ/ *noun, formal*
the total amount of money that a person or organization spends: *The state's expenditure on education needs to increase.*

ex•pense /ɪkˈspens/ *noun*
money that you have to spend on something: *I need money for my medical expenses* (=money spent on medical treatment). | *He took computer classes at his own expense* (=he paid for the classes himself).
→ See Thesaurus box at **cost**[1]

ex•pen•sive /ɪkˈspensɪv/ *adjective*
something that is expensive costs a lot of money: *expensive jewelry* | *The other jackets were too expensive.* ANTONYM **cheap, inexpensive**
—**expensively** *adverb*

WORD FAMILY look at the words:
→ **expensive** *adjective*
→ **inexpensive** *adjective*
→ **expensively** *adverb*
→ **expense** *noun*

ex•pe•ri•ence[1] /ɪkˈspɪriəns/ *noun*
1 something that happens to you: *Seeing the whales in the ocean was an amazing experience.* | *I got sick after eating at that restaurant, and my friend had a similar experience.*
2 knowledge or skill that you get from doing a job or activity: *Our new English teacher has 20 years of teaching experience.*

experience² *verb*
if you experience something, it happens to you: *Have you ever experienced an earthquake?*

ex•pe•ri•enced /ɪk'spɪriənst/ *adjective*
good at doing something because you have been doing it for a long time: *We felt safer flying with such an experienced pilot.*
ANTONYM **inexperienced**

E

ex•per•i•ment¹ /ɪk'sperəmənt/ *noun*
a scientific test that you do to learn about something or show something: *We did an experiment in class to find out which metals rust.*

ex•per•i•ment² /ɪk'sperə͵ment/ *verb*
1 to try using things in order to find out what the results are: *Experiment with different types of grilled fish, and decide which ones you like most.*
2 to do a scientific test in order to find out or show something: *The company does not test its products by experimenting on animals.*
—**experimentation** /ɪk͵sperəmən'teɪʃən/ *noun* the act of experimenting

ex•pert /'ekspɚt/ Ac *noun*
someone with special skills or knowledge of a subject: *He is an expert on art from the 20th century.* | *a computer expert*
—**expert** *adjective* having the skills of an expert: *an expert swimmer*
—**expertly** *adverb*

ex•per•tise /͵ekspɚ'tiz/ Ac *noun, formal*
special skills or knowledge: *We need someone with expertise in teaching young children.*

ex•pire /ɪk'spaɪɚ/ *verb*
if a document expires, it is then no longer legal: *My driver's license expires in September* (=it is not legal after September).
—**expiration** /͵ekspə'reɪʃən/ *noun* the act of expiring: *Check the expiration date on your credit card* (=the date after which you cannot use it anymore).

ex•plain /ɪk'spleɪn/ *verb*
1 to tell someone about something so that he or she can understand it: *Don explained the rules of the game to me.* | *Could you explain how the camera works?*

> **THESAURUS: explain**
>
> **tell** to give someone facts or information in speech or writing: *Can you tell me how to get to the Empire State Building?*
>
> **show** to tell someone how to do something or where something is: *Ellen showed me how to work the coffee maker.*
>
> **demonstrate** *formal* to show or describe how to use or do something: *The coach demonstrated the correct way to shoot the ball toward the basket.*
>
> **go through something** to explain something carefully, especially one step at a time: *Mrs. Riddell went through the homework assignment.*

2 to give or be the reason for something: *I explained why my sister was not with me.* | *He explained that he was late because he had left his wallet at home.*
WORD FAMILY → **explanation** *noun*

ex•pla•na•tion /͵eksplə'neɪʃən/ *noun*
1 a reason why something happened: *He gave no explanation for his strange actions.*
2 a statement in which you tell someone about something so that he or she can understand it: *I didn't understand her explanation of what the word means in English.*
→ See Thesaurus box at **reason**

explicit /ɪk'splɪsɪt/ Ac *adjective*
said or written in a way that is very clear: *The teacher gave her class explicit instructions not to leave their seats or talk while she was out of the room.*
—**explicitly** *adverb*

ex•plode /ɪk'sploʊd/ *verb*
to burst into small pieces with a loud noise and a lot of force: *The bomb exploded at 6:16.*

> **WORD FAMILY look at the words:**
>
> → **explode** *verb*
> → **explosion** *noun*
> → **explosive** *adjective*
> → **explosive** *noun*

ex•ploit /ɪk'splɔɪt/ Ac *verb, formal*
to use someone or something in an unfair way: *The company exploited its workers, making them work extra hours with no extra pay.*
—**exploitative** *adjective, formal* someone

who is exploitative exploits people or things —**exploitation** /ˌeksplɔɪˈteɪʃən/ *noun, formal* the act of exploiting someone or something

ex•plore /ɪkˈsplɔr/ *verb*
1 to travel around an area in order to find out what it is like: *They wanted to explore the island.*
2 to think carefully about all the parts or results of something: *He was exploring the possibility of going to graduate school.*
—**explorer** *noun* someone who explores unknown places: *a famous Antarctic explorer*
—**exploration** /ˌekspləˈreɪʃən/ *noun* the activity of traveling around an area to find out what it is like: *the exploration of North America in the 1700s*

ex•plo•sion /ɪkˈsploʊʒən/ *noun*
an occasion when something such as a bomb explodes: *The explosion damaged three houses.*

ex•plo•sive[1] /ɪkˈsploʊsɪv/ *adjective*
1 able or likely to explode: *The chemical is highly explosive, so we have to handle it carefully.*
2 an explosive situation is likely to become violent very quickly: *We knew the situation was explosive, and that fighting could begin any time.*

explosive[2] *noun*
a substance that can cause an explosion: *Dynamite is a type of explosive.*

ex•port[1] /ekˈspɔrt/ Ac *verb*
to sell things to another country: *The company exports machines to Russia.* ANTONYM **import**
—**exporter** *noun* a person, company, or country that exports things

ex•port[2] /ˈekspɔrt/ Ac *noun*
1 something that is sold to another country: *The country's main export is coffee.* ANTONYM **import**
2 the business of selling and sending things to another country: *The export of these animals is illegal.* ANTONYM **import**

WORD FAMILY look at the words:

➔ **export** *verb*
➔ **export** *noun*
➔ **exporter** *noun*

ex•pose /ɪkˈspoʊz/ Ac *verb, formal*
1 to show something that has been covered or hidden: *He pulled up his shirt, exposing his belly.*
2 to put someone in a situation or place where something bad could affect them: *They did not want to expose their child to the disease.*

ex•po•sure /ɪkˈspoʊʒɚ/ Ac *noun, formal*
the state of being in a bad or harmful situation with nothing to protect you: *His illness was caused by exposure to dangerous chemicals.*

ex•press[1] /ɪkˈspres/ *verb*
to say, write, or show what you think or feel: *We want the kids to talk to us and to express their feelings.* | *He's shy, and he has trouble expressing himself* (=expressing his thoughts and feelings).
➔ See Thesaurus box at **say**[1]

express[2] *adjective*
1 an express train/bus = a train or bus that travels very quickly: *I took the express train to Baltimore.*
2 express mail = mail that arrives more quickly than normal: *The package was sent by express mail.*

ex•pres•sion /ɪkˈspreʃən/ *noun*
1 the look on someone's face: *He had a sad expression on his face as we said goodbye.*
2 a word or words with a particular meaning: *Do you know what the expression "what's up?" means?*
3 an expression of thanks/love, etc. *formal* = an action that shows what you think or feel: *I wrote him a note as an expression of my thanks.*
➔ See Thesaurus box at **phrase**

ex•pres•sive /ɪkˈspresɪv/ *adjective*
showing your thoughts or feelings: *I always know what she is thinking, because she has very expressive eyes.*
—**expressively** *adverb*: *Poets use words expressively.*

ex•press•ly /ɪkˈspresli/ *adverb, formal*
with a very clear purpose or reason: *The school was started expressly to give poor children a better education.*

E

ex·press·way /ɪk'spres,weɪ/ *noun*
a wide road that lets cars travel quickly through a city: *The truck was traveling north on the expressway.*

ex·pul·sion /ɪk'spʌlʃən/ *noun, formal*
an act of ordering someone to leave a school, an organization, or a country forever: *Expulsion from school is a very severe punishment.*

ex·quis·ite /ɪk'skwɪzɪt/ *adjective, formal*
very beautiful: *She wore an exquisite diamond necklace.*

E

ex·tend /ɪk'stend/ *verb*
1 to make something longer: *We decided to extend our visit to Mexico for another week.*
2 to cover a particular area: *The fire extended for 15 miles across the plain.*

ex,tended 'family *noun*
a family group that includes parents, children, grandparents, and other family members: *In the summer, we had a big party for our extended family and friends.*

ex·ten·sion /ɪk'stenʃən/ *noun*
1 more time that you are allowed to do something: *If students are sick, they can ask for an extension to finish their work.*
2 one of many telephones in a building that are connected to a central system: *Call the office and ask for extension 358.*
3 *formal* the process of making something longer or bigger: *The extension of the railroad to the West Coast took many years.*

ex·ten·sive /ɪk'stensɪv/ *adjective, formal*
large in amount or area: *The storm caused extensive damage to the town, destroying most of the houses.*
—**extensively** *adverb, formal: Police searched the area extensively, looking in every house.*

ex·tent /ɪk'stent/ *noun*
1 how big or important something is: *At first, we did not realize the extent of the problem, until hundreds of people complained.*
2 to some extent = partly: *I agree with him, to some extent, but not completely.*

ex·te·ri·or¹ /ɪk'stɪriə˞/ *noun, formal*
the outside of something: *The exterior of the house was painted blue.* ANTONYM **interior**

exterior² *adjective, formal*
on the outside of something: *We turned on the exterior lights of the house, so we could see who was in the backyard.* ANTONYM **interior**

ex·ter·mi·nate /ɪk'stə˞mə,neɪt/ *verb, formal*
to kill all of a particular group of living things: *They use chemicals to exterminate the insects that get into buildings.*
—**exterminator** *noun* someone whose job is to kill insects and small animals in people's houses
—**extermination** /ɪk,stə˞mə'neɪʃən/ *noun, formal* the act of exterminating living things: *The pollution has caused the extermination of some types of fish.*

ex·ter·nal /ɪk'stə˞nl/ Ac *adjective, formal*
outside something: *The man had no sign of external injuries* (=injuries on the outside of his body). ANTONYM **internal**
—**externally** *adverb*

ex·tinct /ɪk'stɪŋkt/ *adjective*
an extinct type of plant or animal does not exist now: *Why did the dinosaurs become extinct* (=stop existing)?
—**extinction** /ɪk'stɪŋkʃən/ *noun, formal* the state of being extinct: *Several species of plants are near extinction* (=are almost extinct).

ex·tin·guish /ɪk'stɪŋgwɪʃ/ *verb, formal*
to make a fire stop burning: *Finally, the forest fires were extinguished.* SYNONYM **put out**

ex·tin·guish·er /ɪk'stɪŋgwɪʃə˞/ *noun*
another word for a FIRE EXTINGUISHER

ex·tra¹ /'ekstrə/ *adjective, adverb*
1 more than you usually get, pay, etc.: *Can I have a hamburger with extra cheese? | If you want a bigger room, you have to pay extra.*
2 in addition to what you need or are using: *We have an extra room for guests.*
→ See Thesaurus box at **more²**

extra² *noun*
something that is added to a product or service and that costs more: *The price of the trip does not include extras such as taxes and the price of food.*

ex·tract /ɪk'strækt/ Ac *verb*
formal to remove something from a place: *The dentist extracted one of my teeth.*

ex·tra·cur·ric·u·lar /,ekstrəkə'rɪkyələ˞/ *adjective, formal*
extracurricular activities are activities, such as sports or music, that students choose to

do, and that are not part of the work they have to do

ex•traor•di•nar•y /ɪkˈstrɔrdnˌeri/ *adjective*
very unusual or surprising: *Gerry had extraordinary talent – he was performing on stage when he was four years old.*

ex•trav•a•gant /ɪkˈstrævəgənt/ *adjective, formal*
spending or costing too much money: *They had extravagant parties with live music and champagne.*
—**extravagance** *noun, formal* the act of spending too much money: *Her extravagance resulted in serious money problems.*

ex•treme /ɪkˈstrim/ *adjective*
1 very large in degree: *Martha was now in extreme pain.*
2 an extreme case/example = a situation that is unusually bad: *In extreme cases, the spider's bite can kill a person.*
3 extreme opinions are very unusual and often not sensible: *Some members of the party have extreme views.*
4 extreme sports are more dangerous than usual: *extreme skiing*

ex•treme•ly /ɪkˈstrimli/ *adverb*
very: *The test was extremely difficult.*

ex•tro•vert•ed /ˈekstrəˌvɚtɪd/ *adjective, formal*
an extroverted person is confident and likes being with people ANTONYM **introverted**
—**extrovert** *noun, formal* someone who is confident and likes being with people.
➔ See Thesaurus box at **shy**

eye /aɪ/ *noun*
1 the part of your face that you see with: *Gina has big blue eyes.*
2 keep an eye on someone or something = to watch someone or something to make sure they are safe: *Can you keep an eye on the baby while I go to the store?*
3 in someone's eyes = in someone's opinion: *In Joey's eyes, she's perfect.*

eye

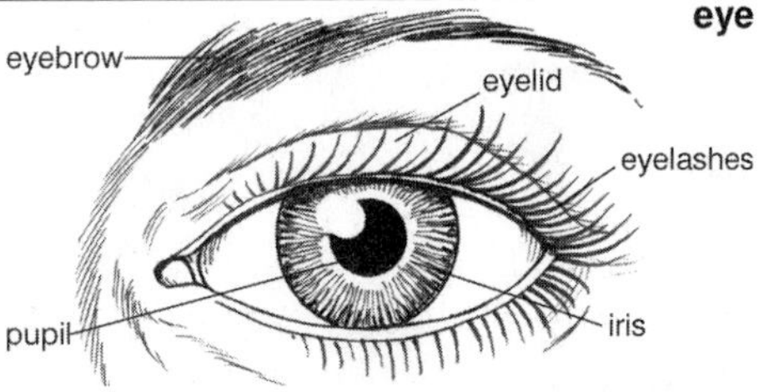

4 catch someone's eye = to get someone's attention: *A beautiful red dress caught my eye, so I went into the store to look at it.*
5 see eye to eye = to agree with someone: *I don't always see eye to eye with my parents.*
6 the hole in a needle that you put thread through
7 the eye of a storm/hurricane/tornado = the center of a big storm

eye•ball /ˈaɪbɔl/ *noun*
the whole of your eye, including the part inside your head

eye•brow /ˈaɪbraʊ/ *noun*
the line of short hairs above your eye: *He had thick black eyebrows.*
➔ See picture at **eye**

ˈeye ˌcontact *noun*
the action of looking directly at someone's eyes: *She was shy, and she usually did not like to make eye contact with other people.*

eye•glass•es /ˈaɪˌglæsɪz/ *plural noun*
another word for GLASSES

eye•lash /ˈaɪlæʃ/ *noun*
one of the small hairs that grow on your eyelids
➔ See picture at **eye**

eye•lid /ˈaɪlɪd/ *noun*
the piece of skin that covers your eye when it is closed
➔ See picture at **eye**

eye•shad•ow /ˈaɪˌʃædoʊ/ *noun*
color that women put on their eyelids to make them look attractive

eye•sight /ˈaɪsaɪt/ *noun*
the ability to see: *My eyesight is good.*

Ff

F¹ /ef/ *noun*
1 a GRADE that you get when you fail a test or a class: *Jill got an F in biology.*
2 the fourth note in the musical SCALE of C, or the musical KEY based on this note

F²
the written abbreviation of **Fahrenheit**: *It's 32°F.*

fa·ble /ˈfeɪbəl/ *noun*
a story, especially one with animals, that teaches us something: *The fable teaches that it is important to work slowly and carefully.*
➔ See Thesaurus box at **story**

fab·ric /ˈfæbrɪk/ *noun*
cloth: *She made the curtains out of a thick cotton fabric.* SYNONYM **material**

fab·u·lous /ˈfæbyələs/ *adjective*
very good or attractive: *We had a fabulous time in New York City.*

face¹ /feɪs/ *noun*
1 the front of your head, with your eyes, nose, and mouth: *She has a very pretty face.*
2 the part of a clock or watch that you look at to see the time: *The watch face has the numbers 12, 3, 6, and 9 on it.*
3 the expression on someone's face: *the children's happy faces* | *"What's that terrible smell?" she said, and she made a face* (=changed her expression to show she did not like something).
4 the front side or surface of something: *They climbed the north face of the mountain.*
➔ See picture at **watch**²

face² *verb*
1 to be looking or pointing toward someone or something: *Mom turned to face me.* | *Our house faces the park, so we just walk across the street to play.*
2 to deal with a difficult situation, or with someone who is upset or angry: *I knew Dad would be mad, and I couldn't face him.*
3 to accept that something bad is true: *She couldn't face the fact that her son was dying.*

ˈface-lift *noun*
an operation on your face to make you look younger: *Do you think she's had a face-lift?*

fa·cial¹ /ˈfeɪʃəl/ *adjective, formal*
relating to the face: *a man with a lot of facial hair*

facial² *noun*
a treatment to clean the skin on your face and make it softer: *How much does it cost to have a facial?*

fa·cil·i·tate /fəˈsɪləˌteɪt/ Ac *verb, formal*
to make something happen more easily: *Computers can facilitate learning.*

fa·cil·i·ties /fəˈsɪlətiz/ Ac *plural noun, formal*
rooms, equipment etc. for a particular purpose: *The university has very good sports facilities, including a new gym.*

fact /fækt/ *noun*
1 something that is true: *The book has lots of interesting facts about plants.*
2 in fact = used when you are saying that something is true, especially something a little surprising: *It looks difficult, but in fact it's fairly easy.*
3 a fact of life = something difficult or unpleasant that everyone has to accept: *For kids, tests at school are just a fact of life.*
—**factual** /ˈfæktʃuəl/ *adjective* relating to facts: *You can find more factual information about the subject on our website.*

fac·tion /ˈfækʃən/ *noun, formal*
a small group of people who have different ideas from other people in a group: *Political parties often split into factions.*

fac·tor /ˈfæktɚ/ Ac *noun*
1 *formal* one of many things that affects a situation: *The weather could be an important factor in tomorrow's game – if it snows our team will have the advantage.*
2 a number that you can divide into another number exactly: *3 is a factor of 15, because 3 × 5 = 15.*

fac·to·ry /ˈfæktəri/ *noun* plural **factories**
a building where goods are made: *My grandfather worked in a shoe factory.*

fac•ul•ty /ˈfækəlti/ *noun* plural **faculties**
formal
the teachers in a school, college, or department: *The college faculty wants to increase the number of students.*

fad /fæd/ *noun*
something popular that people do or like for a short time: *This new diet is just another fad.*

fade /feɪd/ *verb*
to become less bright in color: *If you wash these jeans a lot, they will fade.*

Fahr•en•heit /ˈfærən,haɪt/ *noun*
written abbreviation **F** a system of measuring temperature in which water freezes at 32° and boils at 212°

fail /feɪl/ *verb*
1 to not succeed at something: *The doctors tried everything, but they failed to save the little girl's life.* ANTONYM **succeed**
2 *formal* to not do something that you should do, or not succeed at something: *We were an hour late, because our flight failed to arrive on time.*
3 if you fail a test, you do not pass it: *I failed my math test.* ANTONYM **pass**
4 if a business fails, it cannot continue working because it has no money: *The business failed last year.*
WORD FAMILY → **failure** *noun*

fail•ing /ˈfeɪlɪŋ/ *noun*
a problem or weakness in a person, system, or idea: *One of the mayor's failings is that he only hires his friends.*

fail•ure /ˈfeɪlyɚ/ *noun*
1 someone or something that is not successful: *The movie was a total failure – no one went to see it.* ANTONYM **success**
2 a situation when something stops working correctly: *He died from heart failure.* | *There was a mechanical failure, so the plane had to go back to the airport.*
3 a situation when someone does not do what he or she should do or does not succeed in doing something: *Mike's teacher called his parents about his failure to do his homework.*

faint¹ /feɪnt/ *adjective*
1 a faint sound, smell, light, etc. is not strong or clear: *I heard a faint sound downstairs.*
2 feeling weak and unsteady: *He was faint with hunger.*

faint² *verb*
to become unconscious for a short time: *When they told her the bad news, she fainted.*

fair¹ /fer/ *adjective*
1 dealing with people or situations in an equal way: *Why can Danny go, but not me? It's not fair!* | *All prisoners have the right to a fair trial.* ANTONYM **unfair**
2 fair hair/skin = hair or skin that is light in color: *Both the sisters have fair hair.* ANTONYM **dark**
3 a fair price = a price that is not too much: *$1,000 seems like a fair price for a computer.*
4 good enough, but not very good: *Her test scores in science were fair but not great.* SYNONYM **average**
5 fair weather is sunny
—**fairness** *noun* the quality of dealing with people in an equal way: *The students respected their teacher for her fairness.*

fair² *noun*
1 an outdoor event where you can ride on exciting machines, and play games to win prizes. Sometimes farmers show their animals and crops at a fair: *the Ohio state fair*
2 an event at which businesses or other organizations show or sell things: *the school science fair*

fair•ly /ˈferli/ *adverb*
1 fairly good/large, etc. = good, large, etc., but not very good, large, etc.: *The apartment is fairly large.* | *He speaks Spanish fairly well.*
2 in an equal way: *Divide the candy fairly, so that everyone gets the same amount.*

fair•y /ˈferi/ *noun* plural **fairies**
a very small imaginary person who can do magic

F

'fairy tale *noun*
a story for children in which magic things happen

faith /feɪθ/ *noun*
1 a strong belief that someone or something is good or will succeed: *I didn't do well at school, but my parents always had faith in me.*
2 belief in God: *My faith in God helped me through the bad times.*
3 a religion: *We have people of all faiths at our school.* | *the Christian faith*
➔ See Thesaurus box at **religion**

F

faith•ful /'feɪθfəl/ *adjective*
1 loyal to someone or something: *Jack's been a very faithful friend.*
2 if you are faithful to your wife, husband, etc., you do not have a relationship with anyone else: *Lisa had always been faithful to Greg.* ANTONYM **unfaithful**
3 describing or showing something exactly, without changing it: *The movie is faithful to the book – the director has not changed the story at all.*

faith•ful•ly /'feɪθfəli/ *adverb*
1 in a loyal way: *He served the king faithfully for 20 years.*
2 in an exact way: *The book faithfully records their trip, giving details about every town they went to.*

fake *adjective* /feɪk/
not real, but looking like something real: *He was arrested for making fake passports.*

THESAURUS: fake

false not real, but made to look real – used about teeth, hair, nails, etc.: *Grandpa has false teeth.*

imitation made to look like something real – used about materials that look expensive, but are made of something cheaper: *an imitation leather jacket*

counterfeit *formal* counterfeit money or a counterfeit product is made to look real in order to trick people: *counterfeit lottery tickets* | *a million dollars in counterfeit bills*

phony *informal* not real and intended to trick people: *The photographs showing him in London were all phony – he's never been to England.* | *a phony address*

forged illegally copied in order to trick people – used about writing, documents, paintings, etc.: *The two men used forged passports to try to enter the U.S.*

fall¹ /fɔl/ *verb* **fell** /fel/ **fallen** /'fɔlən/
1 *also* **fall down** to drop down onto the ground by mistake: *Be careful you don't fall!* | *Chris fell down and hurt his knee.*

THESAURUS: fall

trip to hit your foot against something, so that you fall or almost fall: *I'm always tripping over that cat!*

slip to slide on something that is wet or icy, so that you fall or almost fall: *She slipped on the ice and broke her leg.*

stumble to put your foot down in a bad way or hit your foot against something, so that you almost fall: *Megan started for her room and stumbled over the rug.*

lose your balance to fall or almost fall, for example, when you are climbing a ladder or riding a bicycle: *Eddie bumped into me and I lost my balance.*

2 if snow, rain, etc. falls, it moves down toward the ground: *The leaves on the trees were beginning to fall.*
3 if a price, amount, etc. falls, it becomes less: *The price of computers has fallen.* ANTONYM **rise**
4 fall asleep = to start to sleep: *Tommy fell asleep on the couch.*
5 fall in love *also* **fall for someone** = to begin to love someone: *As soon as I saw her, I fell in love with her.*
6 fall ill/silent = to become ill or silent: *Suddenly, everyone in the room fell silent.*

PHRASAL VERBS

fall apart
1 to break into pieces: *My old shoes are falling apart – both of them have holes in them.*
2 to stop working well or stop dealing with situations well: *When I got divorced, I was so unhappy that I just fell apart.* | *The economy is falling apart; prices are rising and there are no jobs.*

fall back on something
to use something if it becomes necessary: *Make sure you keep some extra money to fall back on.*

fall behind
to be slower than other people, or late in doing something: *Going up the hill, Anna had fallen behind the other runners.* | *Don't fall behind in your school work.*

fall for something
to believe that something you are told is true, when it is not: *I told him a complete lie, and he fell for it.*

fall through
if a deal, plan, etc. falls through, it fails to happen: *The business deal fell through at the last minute.*

➔ See Thesaurus box at **decrease**[1]
➔ See picture on page A4

fall[2] *noun*
1 the season before winter, when the leaves fall off the trees in cool countries: *My brother's starting college in the fall.*
2 the act of dropping down onto the ground by mistake: *He had a bad fall from a ladder.*
3 a situation when a price, amount, etc. suddenly becomes less: *There's been a fall in the number of students who want to study nursing.* SYNONYM **drop**; ANTONYM **rise**

fall•en /ˈfɔlən/ *verb*
the past participle of FALL

false /fɔls/ *adjective*
1 not true or correct: *false statements* | *Read the paragraph and say whether these statements are true or false.*
2 not real, but made to look real: *Grandpa has false teeth.*
➔ See Thesaurus boxes at **fake** and **wrong**

ˌfalse aˈlarm *noun*
a situation when people think that something bad is happening, but it is not: *Everyone thought the building was on fire, but it was a false alarm.*

fal•si•fy /ˈfɔlsəˌfaɪ/ *verb* **falsified**, third person singular **falsifies** *formal*
to change information so that it is not true: *He went to jail for falsifying the company's financial records.*
—**falsification** /ˌfɔlsəfəˈkeɪʃən/ *noun, formal* the act of falsifying something

fame /feɪm/ *noun*
the state of being known and admired by a lot of people: *The band rose to fame* (=became famous) *in the 1990s.*

fa•mil•iar /fəˈmɪlyɚ/ *adjective*
1 be familiar with something = to know something well: *I'm familiar with New Haven because I went to college there.*
2 a familiar person or thing is one that you recognize: *Her face is familiar, but I can't remember her name.*
—**familiarity** /fəˌmɪliˈærəti/ *noun, formal* when you know something well: *You will need a familiarity with this software to do the job.*
—**familiarize** /fəˈmɪlyəˌraɪz/ *verb* to get to know something well: *Read the story so that you familiarize yourself with the characters.*

F

fam•i•ly /ˈfæməli/ *noun* plural **families**
1 a group of people who are related to each other, especially parents and their children: *My family and I are going skiing in Colorado.* | *My family has lived in this neighborhood for a long time; my grandparents grew up here.*

THESAURUS: family

relative a member of your family: *Most of my relatives are in California.*

relation a member of your family – used about people such as aunts, cousins, etc., not your parents, brothers, or sisters: *There are some relations in Montana that I've never met.*

folks *informal* your parents or family: *Did you tell your folks about it?*

immediate family *formal* your parents, children, brothers, and sisters: *Only members of the immediate family went to the funeral.*

grandparents also **grandfather/grandpa** and **grandmother/grandma** your parents' father and mother: *My grandparents live on a farm.* | *Grandma taught me how to make bread.*

aunt/uncle the sister or brother of your mother or father, or the person who is married to your aunt or uncle: *Uncle Carl isn't married, so I don't have an aunt.*

cousin a child of your aunt or uncle: *I played a lot with my cousins because they lived close to us.*

stepfather/stepmother the person your mother or father has married, but who is not your father or mother: *My stepfather is really nice.*

stepbrother/stepsister the son or daughter of the person who has married one of your parents: *I have two stepbrothers, but they don't live with us; they live with their own mother.*

2 the children you have: *I always wanted to have a big family* (=a lot of children).

ˈfamily ˌname *noun*
your last name, that you share with the other people in your family: *Todd's family name is Dyson.* SYNONYM **last name**

ˌfamily ˈtree *noun*
a drawing that shows how all the people in a family are related to each other

F

fam•ine /ˈfæmɪn/ *noun*
a very bad situation when a lot of people do not have enough food to eat: *Thousands of people died in the famine.*

fa•mous /ˈfeɪməs/ *adjective*
known and admired by a lot of people: *She's a famous writer.* | *San Francisco is famous for its great food.*

WORD FAMILY look at the words:

➔ **famous** *adjective*
➔ **infamous** *adjective*
➔ **fame** *noun*

fan¹ /fæn/ *noun*
1 someone who likes a particular person or thing very much: *She's a big fan of the band.* | *Gary's a sports fan.*
2 a machine or object you can use to make the air move and cool you: *It was hot, so I turned on the fan.*

fan² *verb* **fanned, fanning**
to make yourself feel cool by waving something that makes the air move: *She fanned her face with a newspaper.*

fa•nat•ic /fəˈnætɪk/ *noun*
someone who has extreme and dangerous ideas: *Some of the terrorists are religious fanatics* (=having very strong ideas about religion).
—**fanatical** *adjective, formal* having extreme ideas that may be dangerous: *The men belonged to a fanatical group that wanted to end democracy.*
—**fanaticism** /fəˈnætəˌsɪzəm/ *noun, formal* the state of having extreme ideas

fan•cy /ˈfænsi/ *adjective* **fancier, fanciest**
1 special and expensive: *We had a big dinner in a fancy restaurant.*
2 not plain or simple: *I don't like fancy wallpaper; I want something with just a simple pattern.*

fang /fæŋ/ *noun*
a long sharp tooth of a dog, snake, etc.: *The big dog growled, and I saw its fangs.*

fan•ny pack /ˈfæni pæk/ *noun*
a small bag for carrying money, keys, etc., that you wear around your waist

fan•ta•size /ˈfæntəˌsaɪz/ *verb*
to think about doing, having, etc. something exciting even though it is very unlikely to happen: *I sometimes fantasize about winning millions of dollars.*

fan•tas•tic /fænˈtæstɪk/ *adjective*
1 very good or attractive: *You look fantastic in that dress!* | *That's a fantastic idea.*
2 strange or imaginary: *The movie is about fantastic creatures from another world.*
➔ See Thesaurus box at **good¹**

fan•ta•sy /ˈfæntəsi/ *noun* plural **fantasies**
1 something that you imagine happening, but that is not real: *I used to have fantasies about becoming a movie star.*
2 a story, movie, etc. that is about imaginary events, creatures, etc., and not about the real world: *I like to read science fiction and fantasies.*

far¹ /fɑr/ *adverb* **farther** /ˈfɑrðɚ/ or **further** /ˈfɚðɚ/, **farthest** /ˈfɑrðɪst/ or **furthest** /ˈfɚðɪst/
1 a long distance: *Did you have to walk far to get to the subway?* | *Which of you guys can swim the farthest* (=the longest distance)*?*

GRAMMAR: far

When you are talking about distances, you can use **far** in questions and sentences with "not" or "nothing": *How far is it to the stadium?* | *It's not very far.*

You can also use **far** after "too," "as," and "so": *It's too far to walk.* | *I ran as far as I could.* | *I wish he didn't live so far away.*

But do not use **far** in other kinds of sentence. For example, do not say "It's far to Boston from here." Say: *"It's a long way to Boston from here."*

2 How far ...? = used when asking what the

distance is to get somewhere: *"How far is it to the ocean?" "Only about ten miles."*
3 as far as something = to a particular place or point: *We walked as far as the river.*
4 so far = until now: *There haven't been any problems so far.*
5 by far the largest/the best, etc. = much larger, better, etc. than any others: *I think they are by far the best new band.*
6 far bigger/better/smarter, etc. *formal* = a lot bigger, better, etc. than someone or something else: *She did a far better job than I could have.*
7 go too far = to do something bad that people cannot accept: *He's always been mean, but this time he went too far.*
8 far off/away = a long way from where you are: *Far off, we could hear the sound of guns.*
9 so far, so good *informal* = used when saying that things have been good until now: *"How's your new school?" "So far, so good."*
10 as far as I know ... = used when saying that you think something is true, but you are not sure: *As far as I know, they still live in Washington, but I could be wrong.*
➔ **as far as someone's concerned** at **concerned**
➔ See picture at **near**[1]

far[2] *adjective* **farther**, **farthest**
a long distance away: *My apartment isn't far.* | *They live at the far end of the street* (=the most distant end). ANTONYM **near**
➔ **furthest**

farce /fɑrs/ *noun*
1 a funny play or movie in which a lot of silly things happen
2 a situation in which things seem too silly to be true: *The class was a farce – we didn't learn anything.*

fare /fer/ *noun*
the price you pay to travel by bus, train, airplane, etc.: *How much is the bus fare to get downtown?*
➔ See Thesaurus box at **cost**[1]

ˌFar ˈEast *noun*
the Far East = the countries of east Asia, such as China and Japan: *He's traveled a lot in the Far East.*

fare•well /ferˈwel/ *noun*, *formal*
goodbye: *We said farewell to our friends.*
—**farewell** *adjective* relating to the time when someone leaves a place: *Everyone came to his farewell party.*

farm /fɑrm/ *noun*
an area of land used for growing food or raising animals: *We drove past lots of farms with corn growing in the fields.*
—**farmer** *noun* a person who works on a farm
—**farming** *noun* the work of growing food or raising animals

farm•house /ˈfɑrmhaʊs/ *noun*
the house on a farm where the farmer lives

farm•land /ˈfɑrmlænd/ *noun*
land used for farming: *The farmer had to sell most of his farmland.*

farm•yard /ˈfɑrmyɑrd/ *noun*
an area with farm buildings around it: *There were goats and chickens in the farmyard.*

far•sight•ed /ˈfɑrˌsaɪtɪd/ *adjective*
a farsighted person cannot see things that are near to them clearly: *I can't read without glasses, because I'm farsighted.* ANTONYM **nearsighted**

far•ther /ˈfɑrðɚ/ *adjective*, *adverb*
the comparative of FAR: *The downtown area was farther away* (=more distant) *than I thought.*

> **USAGE: farther**
>
> Use **farther** to talk about distance: *Room 211 is just a little farther down the hall.*
>
> Use **further** to talk about time, amounts, or the level of something: *Your grades cannot drop further, or you won't be able to play on the soccer team.* | *I don't want to discuss this any further.*
>
> Many people use **further** in spoken English to talk about distance, but many teachers think that this is not correct.

far•thest /ˈfɑrðɪst/ *adjective*, *adverb*
the superlative of FAR: *Which planet is farthest from* (=most distant from) *the sun?*

fas•ci•nate /ˈfæsəˌneɪt/ *verb*
to interest someone very much: *Stories about magic fascinate children.*
—**fascinated** *adjective* very interested: *The audience was fascinated as the dancers performed.*
—**fascinating** *adjective* very interesting: *History is a fascinating subject.*

F

fas•ci•na•tion /ˌfæsəˈneɪʃən/ *noun, formal*
a very strong interest in something or someone: *She has a fascination with famous movie stars.*

fash•ion /ˈfæʃən/ *noun*
1 a style of clothes, hair, or doing something that is popular at a particular time: *Teenage clothing fashions change every year.*
2 in fashion = liked or worn by a lot of people now: *Long skirts are in fashion again.*
3 out of fashion = not liked or worn by people now: *My old coat is completely out of fashion now.*

F

fash•ion•a•ble /ˈfæʃənəbəl/ *adjective*
1 in the style that is popular now: *Short jackets are fashionable this year.*
2 a fashionable restaurant, area, etc. is expensive, and a lot of rich people go there: *She lived in a fashionable area of Manhattan.*

fast¹ /fæst/ *adjective*
1 moving or doing something quickly: *Jake's a really fast runner.* | *Some kids are fast learners.* ANTONYM **slow**
2 if a clock or watch is fast, it shows a time that is later than the real time: *My watch is fast – it says it's 5:30, but it's only 5:15.* ANTONYM **slow**

fast² *adverb*
1 quickly: *Don't drive so fast!*

THESAURUS: fast

quickly used about people or things that move very fast, or that do not take a lot of time: *I ran quickly down the stairs.* | *She undressed quickly and got into bed.*

rapidly used especially about things that happen very fast: *Unemployment rose rapidly.*

swiftly *formal* used about people or things that happen or move fast: *Harris got up and walked swiftly to the window.*

2 fast asleep = sleeping very well: *By 10 o'clock, he was already fast asleep.*

fast³ *verb*
to eat little or no food, especially for religious reasons: *During this month, Muslim people fast during the daytime.*

fas•ten /ˈfæsən/ *verb*

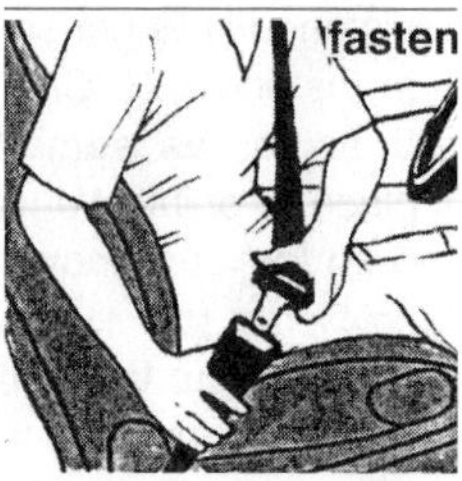

1 to join together the two sides of something: *Fasten your seat belts.* | *The bag fastens with a zipper at the top.*
2 to attach something to another thing: *We can fasten the cloth to the paper with a staple.*

THESAURUS: fasten

attach to fasten something firmly to another object or surface: *Please attach a check to your order form.*

glue to fasten things together using glue: *The children glued shapes onto the paper to make pictures.*

tape to fasten something using tape: *Michelle taped a card to the present.*

staple to fasten something using staples (=small pieces of bent wire that go through paper): *The paper was stapled together in the left corner.*

clip to fasten things together using a clip (=a small object that goes over paper to hold it together): *The pages were clipped together.*

tie to fasten a tie or shoes, etc. by making a knot: *Tie your shoelaces; you'll trip!*

button to fasten the buttons on a shirt, coat, etc.: *Craig buttoned up his jacket.*

zip to fasten clothes, bags, etc. with a zipper: *I can't zip up these jeans; they're too tight.*

fas•ten•er /ˈfæsənɚ/ *noun*
a button, pin, etc. that you use to attach things to each other: *There was a small fastener, like a hook, at the top of the zipper.*

ˈfast food *noun*
food that comes from a restaurant where they make and serve food quickly: *We bought hamburgers and fries at a fast food restaurant.*

fat¹ /fæt/ *adjective*
having too much flesh on your body: *You'll get fat if you eat all that chocolate!* ANTONYM **thin**

THESAURUS: fat

You can call yourself **fat**, but it is not polite to tell someone else that they are fat: *I'm getting really fat.*

overweight used as a more polite way of describing someone who is fat: *He's a little overweight.*

heavy used for describing someone who is big or fat: *a heavy woman in her fifties*

obese *formal* used about someone who is very fat in a way that is dangerous to their health: *Obese people often have heart disease and other health problems.*

chubby used about someone, especially a baby or a child, who is slightly fat: *a chubby little boy*

plump used to say that someone, especially a woman or a child, is slightly fat in a pleasant way: *Mrs. Wilson was a plump, kind-looking woman.*

➔ **thin**

fat[2] *noun*

1 an oily substance in food such as milk, cheese, or butter: *I try to eat food that is low in fat* (=does not have a lot of fat).

2 the soft substance under the skin of people and animals: *Women have more fat on their bodies than men.*

fa•tal /ˈfeɪtl/ *adjective*

a fatal accident, disease, etc. causes someone to die: *Several people have died in fatal accidents on this road.*

—**fatally** *adverb*: *He was fatally wounded in the attack and died two days later.*

fa•tal•i•ty /fəˈtæləti/ *noun* plural **fatalities** *formal*

a death in an accident or an attack: *Several people were hurt, but there were no fatalities.*

fate /feɪt/ *noun*

1 a power that some people think controls what happens to you in your life: *I knew it was fate that I met her, and I knew I wanted to marry her.* SYNONYM **destiny**

2 *formal* the things that will happen to someone or something: *The jury will now decide the man's fate; they must decide how many years he will stay in prison.*

fa•ther /ˈfɑðɚ/ *noun*

1 your male parent: *My father was a doctor.* SYNONYM **dad**

2 *also* **Father** a priest in some Christian churches: *Do you know Father Vernon?*

—**fatherhood** /ˈfɑðɚhʊd/ *noun* the state of being a male parent

—**fatherly** *adjective* typical of a good father: *He gave me some fatherly advice before I left for college.*

ˈfather-in-law *noun* plural **fathers-in-law**

the father of your husband or wife

ˈFather's Day *noun*

a day when people give cards and gifts to their fathers, on the third Sunday in June

fa•tigue /fəˈtig/ *noun, formal*

the state of being very tired: *Some of the men were sick from fatigue.*

—**fatigued** *adjective, formal* very tired

fat•ten /ˈfætn/ *also* **fatten up** *verb*

to make a person or animal fatter: *My mom thinks I'm too thin, and she's always trying to fatten me up.*

fat•ty /ˈfæti/ *adjective*

containing a lot of fat: *Too much fatty food is bad for you.*

fau•cet /ˈfɔsɪt/ *noun*

the thing that you turn on and off to control the water coming from a pipe: *I filled my glass with water and turned off the faucet.*

➔ See picture on page A9

fault /fɔlt/ *noun*

1 be someone's fault = if something bad is your fault, you caused it to happen: *It's my fault we're late – I thought the meeting started at 3:00.*

2 something a little bad in someone's character: *I've always been lazy – it's one of my faults.*

3 be at fault = to have caused something bad that has happened: *The report on the accident said the pilot was at fault.*

4 a large crack in the rocks that form the Earth: *the San Andreas fault*

5 find fault with someone or something = to criticize someone or something: *My English teacher is always finding fault with my work.*

—**faultless** *adjective* having no mistakes

fault•y /ˈfɔlti/ *adjective*

not working correctly: *The accident happened because the truck had faulty brakes.*

F

fa•vor¹ /ˈfeɪvɚ/ *noun*
1 something helpful you do for someone: *Can you do me a favor and give me your notes from history class?*
2 be in favor of something = to support or agree with something: *Most of the people at the meeting were in favor of the plan.*

favor² *verb*
to like someone or something better than other things, or to treat someone better than other people: *Mrs. Adams clearly favors her daughter and ignores her son.*

F

fa•vor•able /ˈfeɪvərəbəl/ *adjective, formal*
1 a favorable opinion, report, etc. shows that people think someone or something is good: *I've heard favorable reports about his work; all of his teachers say he does very well in school.*
2 likely to make someone or something succeed: *The plants grow quickly in the favorable climate.*
—**favorably** *adverb, formal* in a way that shows you think someone or something is good: *Everyone reacted favorably to the plan, saying that they would be happy to help.*

fa•vor•ite¹ /ˈfeɪvərɪt/ *adjective*
your favorite person or thing is the one you like most: *My favorite sport is baseball.*

favorite² *noun*
someone's favorite = something that someone likes more than any others: *I like all her books, but this one is my favorite.*

fawn /fɔn/ *noun*
a young DEER

fax /fæks/ *noun*
1 a copy of a document that is sent through a telephone line and then printed on paper: *I'll send you a fax with all the information that you need.*

2 *also* **ˈfax maˌchine** a machine used for sending and receiving faxes: *Do you have a fax?*
—**fax** *verb* to send a fax: *Please fax me your report.*

fear¹ /fɪr/ *noun*
1 the feeling you get when you are afraid: *His voice was full of fear.* | *She has a fear of heights* (=she is afraid of being in high places).
2 something bad that you are worried could happen: *There are fears that hundreds of people may have been killed.*

fear² *verb, formal*
1 to feel afraid or worried that something bad could happen: *His mother feared that something terrible must have happened to him.*
2 to be afraid of someone or something: *Everyone feared her.*

fear•ful /ˈfɪrfəl/ *adjective, formal*
afraid: *Doctors are fearful of getting the disease because it passes so easily from person to person.*
—**fearfully** *adverb*

fear•less /ˈfɪrləs/ *adjective*
not afraid of anything: *a fearless soldier*
—**fearlessly** *adverb*
—**fearlessness** *noun*

feast¹ /fist/ *noun*
a large meal for many people: *a wedding feast*

feast² *verb*
PHRASAL VERB
feast on something *formal*
to eat a lot of food with great enjoyment: *We feasted on chicken, green beans, and potatoes.*

feat /fit/ *noun, formal*
an impressive achievement needing a lot of skill, effort, or strength: *The bridge took years to plan and build, and is an amazing feat of engineering.*

feath•er /ˈfeðɚ/ *noun*
one of the light soft things that cover a bird's body: *a bird with beautiful green feathers*

fea•ture¹ /ˈfitʃɚ/ Ac *noun*
1 an important, interesting, or typical part of something: *The cell phone has a lot of useful features, such as a camera and calendar.*
2 a part of someone's face, for example his or her mouth and nose: *She loved his strong handsome features.*
3 a piece of writing about a subject in a newspaper or a magazine, or a special report on television or on the radio: *There is*

a big feature on Tom Cruise in this week's magazine.

feature[2] *verb*
if something features a person or thing, that person or thing has an important part in it: *The movie features Julia Roberts* (=she is the star in the movie).

Feb·ru·ar·y /ˈfebyuˌeri/ *noun, written abbreviation* **Feb.**
the second month of the year: *My birthday is in February.*

fed /fed/ *verb*
the past tense and past participle of FEED

fed·er·al /ˈfedərəl/ Ac *adjective*
relating to the central government of a country which consists of several states: *federal law*
—**federally** *adverb*

fed·er·a·tion /ˌfedəˈreɪʃən/ *noun*
an official group of organizations or states: *the U.S. Gymnastics Federation*

ˌfed ˈup *adjective, informal*
annoyed or bored, and wanting change: *I'm fed up with the way he treats me.*

fee /fi/ Ac *noun*
an amount of money that you pay to do something: *The trip to New York costs $200 for food, transportation, and entrance fees to museums.* | *legal fees* (=money paid to a lawyer)
➔ See Thesaurus box at **cost**[1]

fee·ble /ˈfibəl/ *adjective, formal*
1 extremely weak: *"I don't feel very good," she said in a feeble voice.*
2 not good or effective: *I made a feeble attempt to apologize, but I don't think she believed I meant it.*
—**feebly** *adverb*
—**feebleness** *noun*

feed /fid/ *verb* **fed** /fed/
1 to give food to a person or animal: *Did you feed the dog?*
2 if animals feed on something, they eat it: *Cows feed on grass.*
3 to continuously put small amounts of something into another thing: *The numbers are fed into a computer and the computer calculates the answer.*

feed·back /ˈfidbæk/ *noun*
things people say about how good something is or how well someone has done something: *People in the program have given us a lot of positive feedback* (=feedback that shows they like it).

feel[1] /fil/ *verb* **felt** /felt/
1 to experience a physical feeling such as coldness or tiredness, or an emotion such as sadness or happiness: *She was feeling tired, and she wanted to go to bed.* | *I sometimes feel slight pain in my teeth.* | *"How do you feel?" "I feel a lot better today."*
2 if something feels hot, cold, etc., it seems hot, cold, etc. when you touch it or are in it: *It feels very hot in here.*
3 to touch something with your fingers in order to find out about it: *Feel my forehead. Does it seem hot to you?* | *He felt around for the light switch.*
4 to notice something that is touching you: *She felt a bug crawling up her leg.*
5 if you feel that something is true, you think that it is probably true: *He feels that the teacher treated him unfairly.*
6 feel like (doing) something = to want to do something or have something: *I feel like going out tonight – do you want to go to a movie?*
7 feel free = used when offering something to someone or when giving someone permission to do something: *Feel free to use my car.*

PHRASAL VERB
feel for someone
to feel sympathy for someone: *I really felt for her when she said she had been crying all night.*
➔ See Thesaurus box at **touch**[1]

feel[2] *noun*
1 the feeling you have when you touch something: *The coat has a nice soft feel.*
2 the ability to do something well, because you have a natural skill or because you have done it many times before: *He seems to have a real feel for baseball – he can hit and throw easily.*
3 get a feel for something = to become used to doing something or using something: *It's an easy camera to use, and you quickly get a feel for it.*

feel·ing /ˈfilɪŋ/ *noun*
1 an emotion that you feel in your mind, such as happiness, excitement, or love:

F

There's always a great feeling of excitement before the race starts.
2 something you feel in your body, such as pain or cold, or the ability to feel things in your body: *He has no feeling in his legs.*
3 a belief or opinion about something: *My feeling is that he did not steal the money.* SYNONYM **opinion**
4 someone's feelings = the way someone feels at a particular time, for example whether he or she feels sad, happy, etc.: *She says mean things to me, because she doesn't care about my feelings.* | *I didn't want to hurt her feelings* (=make her feel upset or sad).

F

feet /fit/ *noun*
the plural of FOOT

fe•line /ˈfilaɪn/ *adjective, formal*
relating to cats

fell¹ /fel/ *verb*
the past tense of FALL

fell² *verb, formal*
to cut down a tree

fel•low¹ /ˈfeloʊ/ *adjective*
fellow workers/students/citizens, etc. = the people you work with, study with, live with, etc.

fellow² *noun*
an old-fashioned word for a man

fel•o•ny /ˈfeləni/ *noun* plural **felonies** *formal*
a serious crime such as murder: *They charged him with two felonies, murder and arson* (=deliberately burning a building).

felt¹ /felt/ *verb*
the past tense and past participle of FEEL

felt² *noun*
a thick soft material made of wool, hair, or fur that has been pressed flat: *A piece of felt inside the hat makes it feel softer.*

ˌfelt tip ˈpen *noun*
a pen that has a hard piece of felt at the end that the ink comes through

fe•male¹ /ˈfimeɪl/ *noun*
a girl or woman, or an animal that belongs to the sex that can have babies or produce eggs: *The female is brown in color, but the male is red.* ANTONYM **male**

female² *adjective*
belonging to the sex that can have babies or produce eggs: *A female horse carries her baby for about 340 days before it is born.* ANTONYM **male**

fem•i•nine /ˈfemənɪn/ *adjective*
having qualities that are considered to be typical of women: *Most people think of pink as a feminine color.* ANTONYM **masculine**
—**femininity** /ˌfeməˈnɪnəti/ *noun* the quality of being feminine

fem•i•nism /ˈfeməˌnɪzəm/ *noun*
the belief that women should have the same rights and opportunities as men
—**feminist** *noun* someone who believes strongly that women should have the same rights and opportunities as men
—**feminist** *adjective* relating to feminism

fence /fens/ *noun*
1 a structure made of wood, metal, etc. that surrounds a piece of land and keeps people or animals in or out: *There is a high fence all around the prison.*
2 on the fence *informal* = trying to avoid saying which side of an argument you agree with: *I wish she'd stop sitting on the fence and tell me what she really thinks!*

fencing

fenc•ing /ˈfensɪŋ/ *noun*
a sport in which two people fight each other with light thin swords

fend•er /ˈfendɚ/ *noun*
the side part of a car that covers the wheels: *There was a scratch on the rear left fender of the car.*
➔ See picture at **bicycle**

fern /fɚn/ *noun*
a plant with green leaves shaped like large feathers and no flowers

fe•ro•cious /fəˈroʊʃəs/ *adjective, formal*
extremely violent or severe: *Tigers are ferocious hunters, but they do not usually kill humans.* | *A ferocious storm damaged the roads in the area.*
—**ferociously** *adverb*

—**ferocity** /fəˈrɑsəti/ *noun* the quality of being ferocious

Fer•ris wheel /ˈferɪs wil/ *noun*
a big wheel with chairs that go up into the air for people to ride on at an AMUSEMENT PARK

fer•ry /ˈferi/ *noun* plural **ferries**
a boat that carries people and cars across an area of water: *When we were in New York, we took the ferry from Manhattan to Staten Island.*
➔ See picture on page A26

fer•tile /ˈfɚtl/ *adjective*
1 able to produce good crops: *The land next to the river is very fertile.*
2 able to produce children: *The test showed that she was still fertile, so they decided to try to have a baby.*
—**fertility** /fɚˈtɪləti/ *noun* the state of being fertile

fer•til•iz•er /ˈfɚtlˌaɪzɚ/ *noun*
a substance that is put on the soil to help plants grow: *Waste from farm animals is often used as fertilizer.*
—**fertilize** *verb* to add substances to the soil to make plants grow: *Fertilize the seeds after you plant them.*

fes•ti•val /ˈfestəvəl/ *noun*
1 a special occasion when people celebrate something: *There will be food, music, and dancing at the festival.*
2 an event at which many films, plays, pieces of music, etc. are shown or performed: *the Cannes film festival*

fes•tive /ˈfestɪv/ *adjective, formal*
happy or relating to celebrations: *We usually drink wine on festive occasions.*

fetch /fetʃ/ *verb*
to go and get something and bring it back: *The dog fetched the stick from behind the bushes.*

fe•tus /ˈfitəs/ *noun*
a baby before it is born: *Smoking can cause damage to the fetus.*

feud /fyud/ *noun*
an angry argument between two people or groups that continues for a long time: *There was a violent feud between the two families, and two of the brothers killed each other.*
—**feud** *verb* to have a feud with someone

fe•ver /ˈfivɚ/ *noun*
an illness in which you have a very high temperature: *She feels very hot – I think she has a fever.*
—**feverish** *adjective* having a fever
➔ **hay fever**

few /fyu/ *pronoun, adjective*
1 a few = a small number of things or people: *I only had a few coins in my pocket.* | *"How many people know about this?" "Only a few."*
2 not many: *There are few things as exciting as traveling to a new place on vacation.*

GRAMMAR: few

fewer, less
Use **fewer** before nouns whose form shows that there is more than one: *There were fewer cars on the roads in the 1950s.* | *Fewer people were in the class than I expected.*
Use **less** before nouns that are things you cannot count: *There is less water in this cup than in that one.* | *This book has less information than the other one.*

3 quite a few = a fairly large number of people or things: *Quite a few people came to the meeting.*
4 be few and far between = to be rare: *Good jobs are few and far between these days.*

fi•an•cé /ˌfiɑnˈseɪ/ *noun*
a man who has agreed to marry a particular woman: *This is my fiancé, Ted.*

fi•an•cée /ˌfiɑnˈseɪ/ *noun*
a woman who has agreed to marry a particular man: *Ron and his fiancée were at the party.*

fi•as•co /fiˈæskoʊ/ *noun* plural **fiascoes** or **fiascos**
an event that is not successful at all, in a way that is very embarrassing or disappointing: *The food was burnt, the ice cream had all melted, so the whole dinner was a complete fiasco.*

fib /fɪb/ *noun, informal*
a small, unimportant lie: *You shouldn't tell fibs because then people won't believe you when you tell the truth.* ANTONYM **the truth**

F

—**fib** *verb, informal* to tell a small lie to someone SYNONYM **lie**
➔ See Thesaurus box at **lie**[2]

fi•ber /ˈfaɪbɚ/ *noun*
1 parts of plants that you eat but do not DIGEST, that help food to move through your body: *My doctor says that I need to eat more fiber.*
2 a mass of threads used to make rope, cloth, etc.: *The dress is made from some kind of artificial fiber.*

fic•tion /ˈfɪkʃən/ *noun*
1 books and stories about imaginary people and things: *He wrote fiction for children.* ANTONYM **nonfiction**
2 *formal* something that is not true: *The singer says that the newspaper stories about her are complete fiction.*
➔ See Thesaurus box at **book**[1]

F

fid•dle[1] /ˈfɪdl/ *noun, informal*
a VIOLIN

fiddle[2] *verb*
to keep moving and touching something because you are bored or nervous: *She stopped listening and started fiddling with her hair.*

fidg•et /ˈfɪdʒɪt/ *verb*
to keep moving your hands or feet because you are bored or nervous: *The children started fidgeting in their seats because they were bored.*

field /fild/ *noun*
1 an area of land in the country where crops are grown or animals feed on grass: *There were fields of wheat for mile after mile.*
2 an area of ground where sports are played: *a baseball field | The team ran out on the field.*
3 a subject that people study or a type of work that they are involved in: *Professor Kramer is an expert in the field of biology.*
4 **oil/gas/coal field** = an area where there is a lot of oil, gas, or coal under the ground

ˈ**field trip** *noun*
an occasion when students go somewhere to learn about a particular subject

fierce /fɪrs/ *adjective*
1 a fierce person or animal looks very violent or angry and ready to attack: *The house was guarded by a fierce dog.*
2 involving a lot of energy and strong feelings: *The two football teams are in a fierce battle for first place.*
3 fierce heat, cold, weather, etc. is very extreme or severe: *The heat was fierce, so we stayed inside where it was cool.*
—**fiercely** *adverb*
—**fierceness** *noun*

fi•er•y /ˈfaɪəri/ *adjective*
1 full of strong or angry emotion: *She had a fiery way of speaking that got our attention.*
2 very bright and with a lot of red or yellow colors, like a fire: *a fiery sunset*
3 burning with a lot of flames: *The plane was destroyed in a fiery crash.*

fi•es•ta /fiˈestə/ *noun*
a party or religious holiday with dancing, music, etc., in places where people who speak Spanish live: *At fiesta time the streets are full of people singing and dancing.*

fif•teen /ˌfɪfˈtin/ *number*
1 15: *There are fifteen steps up to the second floor.*
2 fifteen years old: *Her brother's fifteen.*
—**fifteenth** /ˌfɪfˈtinθ/ *number* 15th or 1/15

fifth /fɪfθ/ *number*
1 5th
2 1/5

fif•ty /ˈfɪfti/ *number*
1 50
2 **the fifties a)** *also* **the '50s** the years between 1950 and 1959: *The city was built in the fifties.* **b)** *also* **the 50s** the numbers between 50 and 59 especially when used for measuring temperature: *The temperature was in the fifties and it was raining.*
3 **be in your fifties** = to be between 50 and 59 years old: *My mother is in her fifties.*
—**fiftieth** /ˈfɪftiɪθ/ *number* 50th or 1/50

fig /fɪg/ *noun*
a small soft sweet fruit with red-brown flesh that is often eaten dried
➔ See picture on page A13

fig.
the written abbreviation of **figure** (=a numbered drawing in a book): *See fig. 3.1 on page 45.*

fight[1] /faɪt/ *verb* **fought** /fɔt/
1 to use physical force or weapons to try to hurt someone: *The men were fighting*

outside the bar, and one of them pulled out a knife. | My father fought in the Vietnam war.

2 to argue: *My parents were always fighting with each other.*

3 to try hard to do or get something: *Parents and teachers are fighting to keep the school open.*

4 to try hard to stop something: *Martin Luther King spent his whole life fighting against racism.*

PHRASAL VERB

fight back

1 to try hard to win when you are losing: *Lewis fought back to win the match.*

2 to begin arguing or fighting with someone who attacks or insults you, instead of doing nothing: *If they say mean things to you, don't just stand there – fight back!*

3 to try hard not to have or show a feeling: *She fought back her tears.*

➔ See Thesaurus box at **argue**

fight² *noun*

1 a situation in which two people or groups attack each other and try to hurt each other using physical force: *I got into a fight with another boy, and he hit me in the face.*

2 an argument: *My family often has fights about money.*

3 the process of trying very hard to achieve something or prevent something: *The country had a long fight for independence.*

fight•er /ˈfaɪtɚ/ *noun*

1 someone who continues to try to do something although it is difficult: *She has cancer, but she's a fighter and I know she'll get better.*

2 someone who fights as a sport SYNONYM **boxer**

3 *also* **fighter plane** a small fast military airplane that can destroy other airplanes

fig•u•ra•tive /ˈfɪgyərətɪv/ *adjective*

a figurative word or expression is used in a different way from its usual meaning, to give you a picture or idea in your mind: *"A mountain of debt" is a figurative way of saying "a large amount of debt."*

—**figuratively** *adverb*

fig•ure¹ /ˈfɪgyɚ/ *noun*

1 a number or amount: *the company's sales figures* (=the numbers that tell how much of a product they sold)

2 an important or famous person: *Thomas Jefferson was one of the most important figures in American history.*

3 the shape of a woman's body: *My sister has a great figure.*

4 the shape of a person that is difficult to see: *I could see a dark figure in the distance, but I couldn't see who it was.*

5 a shape in mathematics: *a six-sided figure*

6 *written abbreviation* **fig.** a numbered drawing in a book: *See also Figure 2.1, page 20.*

figure² *verb*

1 to think that something is likely to be true after thinking about a situation: *We figured that you might need some help, so we came.*

2 that figures/it figures *informal* = used when you are not surprised or disappointed, because a situation is the way you expected it to be: *"He says that he needs more money to pay for college." "That figures!"*

PHRASAL VERBS

figure on something *informal*

to expect something or include it in your plans: *"How much do you want to pay for the car?" "We figured on paying about $5,000."*

figure out

1 figure someone or something out = to understand someone or something: *I still can't figure out why she lied to me.*

2 figure something out = to find an answer to a problem: *Let's figure out a way to help her.*

➔ See Thesaurus box at **think**

ˈfigure ˌskating *noun*

a type of skating (SKATE) in which you move in patterns on the ice

—**figure skater** *noun* someone who does this type of skating

file¹ /faɪl/ Ac *noun*

1 a set of papers, records, etc. that contain information about a particular person or subject: *The school keeps files on each student.*

2 a box or folded piece of heavy paper in which you keep loose papers: *She took a paper from a file that was marked "2006 Taxes."*

3 information on a computer that is stored under a particular name: *I pushed the wrong button and accidentally deleted the file.*

4 a metal tool with a rough surface that you rub on something to make it smooth: *Use a nail file to make your nails less rough.*

5 in single file = moving in a line, with one person behind another: *They walked into the room in single file.*
→ See picture on page A18

file[2] *verb*
1 to store papers or information in a particular order or a particular place: *The papers are filed in alphabetical order.*
2 to ask for something to be dealt with by a court of law or other official organization: *They have filed a complaint with the company, saying that the company charged them too much money.*
3 to walk in a line of people, one behind another: *The students filed out of the classroom.*
4 to make something smooth by rubbing it with a special tool: *She was busy filing her nails.*

ˈfile ˌcabinet *noun*
a tall piece of furniture with drawers in which you store pieces of paper
→ See picture on page A18

fil•et /fɪˈleɪ/ *noun*
another spelling of FILLET

fill /fɪl/ *verb*
1 *also* **fill up** to put something in a container or space so that it becomes full: *She filled the bowls with soup.*
2 *also* **fill up** to become full of something: *Smoke filled the room.* | *Her eyes filled with tears.*

PHRASAL VERBS

fill in
1 fill something in = to write something in a space on a piece of paper: *Fill in the blanks in these sentences.*
2 fill someone in = to tell someone about things that have happened recently: *I'll fill you in on all the news later.*
3 to do someone's job because he or she is not there: *Could you fill in for Bob while he's sick?*

fill something out
to write the necessary information on an official piece of paper: *You have to fill out this form.* SYNONYM **complete**

fil•let *also* **filet** /fɪˈleɪ/ *noun*
a piece of meat or fish without bones: *a salmon fillet*

fill•ing /ˈfɪlɪŋ/ *noun*
1 a small amount of metal that a DENTIST puts into a hole in your tooth: *He had a gold filling.*
2 the food that you put in a PIE, SANDWICH, etc.

film[1] /fɪlm/ *noun*
1 the material that you put in a camera: *I used six rolls of film while I was on vacation.*
2 a movie: *"Brokeback Mountain" is a great film.*
3 *formal* a very thin layer of liquid or powder: *A thin film of grease covered everything in the kitchen.*
→ See Thesaurus box at **movie**

film[2] *verb*
to use a camera to make a movie or a television program: *He is currently filming an action movie.*
—**filmmaker** *noun* someone who makes movies

fil•ter[1] /ˈfɪltɚ/ *noun*
something that you put a gas or liquid through in order to remove unwanted substances: *The water filter cleans chemicals and other dangerous things out of the water you drink.*

filter[2] *verb*
1 to clean a liquid or gas using a filter: *Filter the water until it is clear.*
2 *formal* if light filters into a place, only some of it comes in: *Sunshine filtered through the curtains.*

filth /fɪlθ/ *noun, formal*
a lot of dirt: *Look at the filth in this place – it's disgusting!*

filth•y /ˈfɪlθi/ *adjective* **filthier**, **filthiest**
very dirty: *I didn't want to go into the bathroom because it was filthy.*
→ See Thesaurus box at **dirty**

fin /fɪn/ *noun*
one of the flat parts of a fish's body that it uses to swim

fin

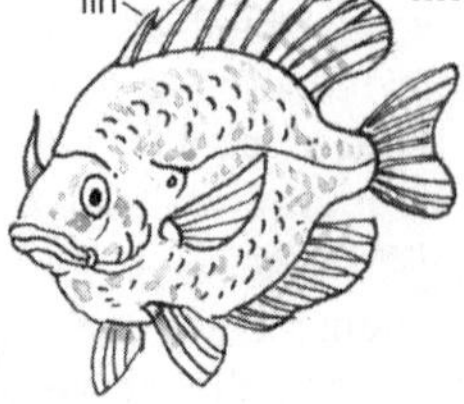

fi•nal[1] /ˈfaɪnl/ Ac *adjective*
1 last: *The final page of the book was missing.*
2 if a decision or offer is final, it cannot be

changed: *You don't have to make a final decision yet.*

WORD FAMILY look at the words:

→ **final** *adjective*
→ **final** *noun*
→ **finally** *adverb*
→ **finalist** *noun*
→ **semifinal** *noun*

final² *noun*
1 the last and most important game, race, or stage in a competition: *The team is very excited to have reached the finals.*
2 an important test that students take at the end of a SEMESTER: *How did your finals go?*
—**finalist** *noun* someone who is in the final of a competition

fi·nal·ly /ˈfaɪnl-i/ Ac *adverb*
1 after a long time: *I finally read that book you gave me last year.*
2 used before saying the last of a series of things: *And finally, I'd like to thank my teachers for all the help they gave me.*

fi·nance¹ /fəˈnæns/ Ac *noun*
the control of money, especially for a company or a government: *She's an accountant in the Finance Department.*

WORD FAMILY look at the words:

→ **finance** *noun*
→ **finance** *verb*
→ **financial** *adjective*
→ **financially** *adverb*

finance² *verb*
to provide a lot of money to pay for something: *Who will finance the project?*

fi·nanc·es /fəˈnænsɪz/ Ac *plural noun*
the money that a person or organization has, and how it is organized: *The company's finances were a mess, so they hired an accountant.*

fi·nan·cial /fəˈnænʃəl/ Ac *adjective*
relating to money: *He has financial problems and is looking for a second job.*
—**financially** *adverb*: *My parents support me financially* (=give me the money I need to live).

find /faɪnd/ *verb* **found** /faʊnd/
1 to see or get something that you have been looking for, or that someone has lost: *I can't find my keys.* | *Have you found a job yet?* | *He found a dollar bill on the street.*

THESAURUS: find

discover to find something that was hidden or that people did not know about before: *Scientists have discovered a new type of dinosaur.*

trace *formal* to find someone or something that has disappeared: *The police are trying to trace a man who was seen near the house that night.*

locate *formal* to find the place where something is: *We couldn't locate the source of the radio signal* (=we couldn't find where the radio signal was coming from).

track someone/something down to find someone or something after searching in different places: *Detectives finally tracked her down in California.*

2 to learn new information as a result of tests or experience: *Researchers have found that people who have pets stay healthier.*
3 to have an opinion about someone or something: *Do you find him attractive* (=do you think he is attractive)? | *I found it difficult to understand her* (=it was difficult for me to understand her).
4 **be found somewhere** = to live or exist somewhere: *This type of bear is found only in China.*
5 **find your way (somewhere)** = to arrive at a place without being told how to get there: *I found my way home using a map.*
6 **find someone guilty/not guilty** *formal* = to officially decide that someone is guilty or not guilty of a crime: *He was found guilty of murder.*

PHRASAL VERB
find out something
to get knowledge of a fact: *I'll find out what time the movie starts.* | *If Dad ever finds out about this, he'll be really mad.*

fine¹ /faɪn/ *adjective*
1 good enough or acceptable: *Your work is fine.* | *"I'll give the book back to you tomorrow." "That's fine."* SYNONYM **okay, all right**
2 healthy and happy: *"How are you?" "Fine, thanks."*
3 very thin, or made of very small pieces: *a fine layer of dust*

4 *formal* very good: *It's a fine school.*
—**fine** *adverb* in an acceptable way: *The equipment is working fine.*
—**finely** *adverb* into very small pieces: *finely chopped onion*
➔ See Thesaurus box at **healthy**

fine² *noun*
money that you have to pay as a punishment for breaking a law or rule: *The company had to pay a fine of $500,000 for polluting the river.*

fine³ *verb*
to make someone pay money as a punishment: *He was fined $50 for driving too fast.*

F

fin•ger /ˈfɪŋɡɚ/ *noun*
1 one of the long parts at the end of your hand: *He pointed his finger at the house.*
➔ **index finger**
2 keep/have your fingers crossed = to hope that something will happen the way you want: *We get our grades today, so I'm keeping my fingers crossed that I get an "A."*
➔ See picture at **hand¹**

fin•ger•nail /ˈfɪŋɡɚˌneɪl/ *noun*
the hard flat part at the end of your finger: *She bit her fingernails.*
➔ See picture at **hand¹**

fin•ger•print /ˈfɪŋɡɚˌprɪnt/ *noun*
a mark that a finger makes which shows a pattern of lines: *Did the person who stole the money leave any fingerprints?*

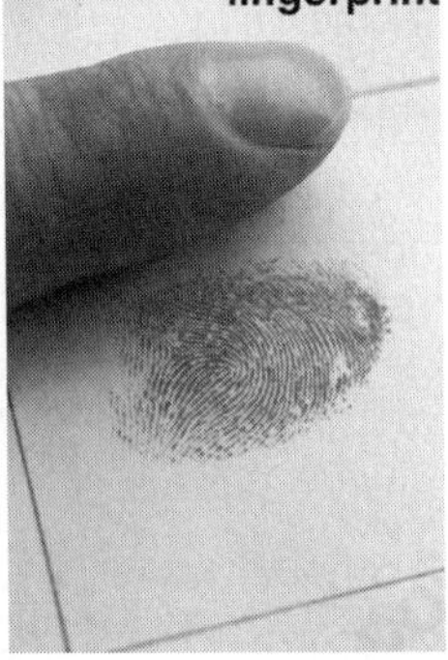
fingerprint

fin•ger•tip /ˈfɪŋɡɚˌtɪp/ *noun*
the end of a finger: *She touched the flower with her fingertips.*

fin•ish¹ /ˈfɪnɪʃ/ *verb*
1 to come to the end of doing or making something: *Have you finished your homework?* | *Everyone applauded when she finished speaking.* | *She finished second* (=came second) *in the race.* ANTONYM **start, begin**
2 *also* **finish off** to eat or drink the rest of something: *Who finished off the cake?*

finish² *noun*
1 the end of an event: *The race had an exciting finish.* | *I enjoyed the show from start to finish.*
2 the way that the surface of an object looks: *The table had a shiny finish.*

fin•ished /ˈfɪnɪʃt/ *adjective*
1 if you are finished, you have come to the end of doing something: *I waited until he was finished talking, and then I spoke.* SYNONYM **done**
2 be finished with something = to no longer need to use something: *Are you finished with the scissors?* SYNONYM **done**
➔ See Thesaurus box at **done²**

ˈfinish line *noun*
the line that you cross at the end of a race: *The winner is the first person who crosses the finish line.*

fi•nite /ˈfaɪnaɪt/ Ac *adjective, formal*
something that is finite is a particular size or will not last forever: *There is a finite amount of oil in the ground.* ANTONYM **infinite**

fir /fɚ/ *noun*
a tree with leaves shaped like needles that do not fall off in winter: *Our Christmas tree is a fir.*

fire¹ /faɪɚ/ *noun*
1 flames and heat that burn things: *a forest fire* | *The fence caught fire* (=started to burn). | *The house is on fire* (=burning)*!* | *They put out the fire* (=stopped it from burning) *with buckets of water.* | *He set fire to his ex-wife's house* (=made it burn).

THESAURUS: fire

flame the bright part of a fire that you see burning in the air: *a candle flame*

in flames burning very strongly: *The whole house was in flames.*

blaze the flames from a fire, or a large and dangerous fire: *Firemen fought to keep the blaze under control.*

2 a pile of burning wood or coal that provides heat: *She lit the fire.*
3 shooting with guns: *The soldiers opened fire on the crowd* (=started shooting at the crowd).

fire² *verb*
1 to make someone leave his or her job: *She was fired from her job for being late.*

2 to use a gun: *Someone fired a shot.* | *He fired at the car.*

ˈfire aˌlarm *noun*
a piece of equipment that makes a loud noise to warn people of a fire in a building: *We all left the building when the fire alarm went off* (=made a noise).

fire·crack·er /ˈfaɪɚˌkrækɚ/ *noun*
a small FIREWORK that explodes loudly

ˈfire deˌpartment *noun*
an organization whose job is to stop fires: *The person who noticed the fire called the fire department.*

ˈfire drill *noun*
an occasion when people practice how to leave a building safely if there is a fire

ˈfire ˌengine *noun*
a large vehicle that carries people and equipment to stop fires
➔ See picture on page A26

ˈfire esˌcape *noun*
metal stairs on the outside of a building that people can use to escape from a fire

ˈfire exˌtinguisher *noun*
a metal container with water or chemicals in it, used for stopping small fires

fire·fight·er /ˈfaɪɚˌfaɪtɚ/ *noun*
someone whose job is to stop fires
➔ See picture on page A16

fire·house /ˈfaɪɚˌhaʊs/ *noun*
a small FIRE STATION

fire hydrant /ˈfaɪɚ ˌhaɪdrənt/ *noun*
a metal object in the street, from which FIREFIGHTERs can get water to stop fires

fire·man /ˈfaɪɚmən/ *noun* plural **firemen** /ˈfaɪɚmən/
a man whose job is to stop fires

fireplace

fire·place /ˈfaɪɚˌpleɪs/ *noun*
an open place in the wall of a room where you can have a fire: *A fire was burning in the fireplace.*

fire·proof /ˈfaɪɚˌpruf/ *adjective*
something that is fireproof cannot be damaged by fire: *They keep their records in a fireproof file cabinet.*

ˈfire ˌstation *noun*
a building where FIREFIGHTERs and their vehicles stay until they are needed

fire·wood /ˈfaɪɚwʊd/ *noun*
wood for burning on a fire: *We gathered firewood and then made a fire.*

fire·works /ˈfaɪɚˌwɚks/ *plural noun*
objects that explode and make bright lights in the sky, which people use to celebrate special days: *People were watching the 4th of July fireworks display* (=show of fireworks exploding).

firm[1] /fɚm/ *adjective*
1 something that is firm does not bend much when you press it: *I need a firm bed to sleep on – mine is too soft.* ANTONYM **soft**
2 definite, strong, and not likely to change: *a firm decision* | *I'm a firm believer in getting lots of exercise* (=I believe strongly that exercise is important).
3 strong and in control: *You need to be firm with children or they won't behave.*
4 holding something strongly: *I kept a firm grip on my purse so that nobody would steal it.*
—**firmly** *adverb*: *She told him firmly that he must wait.*
➔ See Thesaurus box at **hard**[1]

firm[2] *noun*
a business or small company: *a law firm*
➔ See Thesaurus box at **company**

first[1] /fɚst/ *number, pronoun*
1 coming before the other things or people: *I've only read the first chapter of the book.* | *The first time I flew on a plane, I was really nervous.* | *The second week of our vacation was better than the first.*
2 **at first** = in the beginning, before there is a change: *At first I thought he was weird, but now I really like him.*
3 **in the first place** = at the beginning of something that happened: *Don't blame me – it was your idea in the first place.*
4 **first thing** = as soon as you get out of bed: *I'll call him first thing in the morning when I wake up.*
5 **at first glance** = the first time you look at

F

something, when you do not notice details: *At first glance, it looked like there was no damage to the car, but then I saw a small dent in the door.*

first² *adverb*
1 before the other things or people: *Andy arrived at the house first.* | *First of all, choose a subject to write about* (=do this first).
2 before doing something: *I'd like to come over, but I have to finish my homework first.*
3 for the first time: *I first heard this story when I was a child.*

first³ *noun*
a first = something that has never happened before: *"Dad actually washed the dishes tonight." "That's a first."*

ˌfirst ˈaid *noun*
simple medical treatment that you give quickly to someone who is injured or sick: *a first aid kit* (=a container with medicine and other things you can use for giving first aid)

ˌfirst-ˈclass *adjective*
of the best kind: *It's a first-class hotel with beautiful rooms and a great restaurant.*
—**first class** *adverb* if you travel first class, you travel in one of the best seats: *He always flies first class.*

ˌfirst ˈfloor *noun*
the part of a building that is on the same level as the ground: *Her office is on the first floor of the building.* SYNONYM **ground floor**

ˌfirst-geneˈration *adjective*
first-generation American/Canadian, etc. = an American, Canadian, etc. whose parents came to live in America, Canada, etc. from another country

ˌfirst ˈlady *noun*
the wife of the president of the U.S.: *The first lady will give a speech about education.*

first·ly /ˈfɚstli/ *adverb, formal*
used before saying the first of several things: *Firstly, I would like to thank everyone for coming.*

ˈfirst name *noun*
the first of your names that your parents choose for you: *Mrs. Green's first name is Caroline.*
➔ See Thesaurus box at **name¹**

ˌfirst ˈperson *noun*
the first person = "I" and "we", and the verb forms you use with them: *Tell a story in the first person* (=using "I" or "we").

ˌfirst-ˈrate *adjective, formal*
extremely good: *She is a first-rate writer whose books have won many awards.*

fish¹ /fɪʃ/ *noun* plural **fish** or **fishes**
an animal without legs that lives in water, or the meat of this animal: *How many fish did you catch?* | *We had fish for dinner.*

fish² *verb*
to try to catch fish: *Dad's fishing for trout.*
—**fishing** *noun* the activity of trying to catch fish: *Let's go fishing this weekend.*

ˌfish and ˈchips *noun*
fish cooked in oil, and FRIES

fish·bowl /ˈfɪʃboʊl/ *noun*
a round glass container that you keep pet fish in

fish·er·man /ˈfɪʃɚmən/ *noun* plural **fishermen** /fɪʃɚmən/
a man who catches fish as a job or a sport

ˈfishing ˌrod *noun*
a long stick with a long string at the end, used for catching fish

ˈfish stick *noun*
a long piece of fish covered in little pieces of bread

fish·y /ˈfɪʃi/ *adjective*
1 *informal* seeming bad or dishonest: *There was something fishy about his story, and I didn't trust him.*
2 tasting or smelling like fish

fist /fɪst/ *noun*
a hand with the fingers closed tightly together: *He hit me with his fist.*

fit¹ /fɪt/ *verb* **fit, fitting**
1 to be the right size and shape for someone or something: *My old jeans still fit me.* | *This lid doesn't fit very well on the container.*
2 if something fits into a place or container, there is enough space for it: *Her clothes wouldn't fit in her suitcase.* | *We can't fit any more people into the car.*
3 to be what someone has described or needs: *He fits the description of the man who broke into the house.*

PHRASAL VERB
fit in
to be accepted by the other people in a

group: *She hoped she would fit in at her new school.*

fit² *adjective*

1 healthy and strong: *I run because I want to be physically fit.* ANTONYM **unfit**

2 good enough for someone or something: *He is not fit to be a teacher.* ANTONYM **unfit**

fit³ *noun*

1 have/throw a fit *informal* = to become very angry and shout a lot: *Mom's going to have a fit when she sees that you broke this.*

2 a short period of time when you are sick, angry, crazy, etc. and cannot control yourself: *a coughing fit | In a fit of rage, he kicked the TV.*

3 be a good/perfect fit = to fit well or be suitable: *The skirt was a perfect fit, so I bought it.*

fit•ness /ˈfɪtnəs/ *noun*

the condition of being healthy and strong: *You should try running to improve your fitness.*

five¹ /faɪv/ *number*

1 5: *There are five apples left in the bag.*

2 five O'CLOCK

3 five years old: *You can't start kindergarten till you're five.*

five² *noun*

a piece of paper money worth $5: *I paid with a five.*

fix /fɪks/ *verb*

1 to repair something: *I fixed your bike.*

2 to prepare a meal or drink: *Mom was fixing dinner in the kitchen.* SYNONYM **make**

3 to decide on an exact time, place, etc.: *Have you fixed a date for the wedding?*

PHRASAL VERB

fix something up

to decorate or repair a room or building: *We fixed up the guest bedroom, so now it's blue and has new curtains.*

➔ See Thesaurus box at **repair²**

fix•ture /ˈfɪkstʃɚ/ *noun*

a piece of equipment that is attached inside a house, such as an electric light or a FAUCET: *There are new fixtures in the bathroom.*

fizz /fɪz/ *noun*

the BUBBLEs of gas in some types of drinks: *The soda has lost its fizz.*

—**fizz** *verb* if a liquid fizzes, the gas in it comes out

—**fizzy** *adjective* a fizzy drink has bubbles of gas in it

➔ See picture on page A22

flab•by /ˈflæbi/ *adjective, informal*

if a part of your body is flabby, it has soft loose fat: *a fat woman with flabby arms*

—**flab** *noun, informal* soft loose fat on a person's body

flag /flæg/ *noun*

a piece of cloth with a picture or pattern on it that is used as a symbol or a signal: *The American flag is red, white, and blue.*

flag•pole /ˈflægpoʊl/ *noun*

a tall pole for a flag

flair /fler/ *noun, formal*

a natural ability to do something very well: *He has a flair for learning foreign languages – he can speak six of them well.*

flake /fleɪk/ *noun*

1 a flat thin piece that has broken off something: *The paint was coming off the door in flakes.*

2 *informal* someone who does not do what he or she says he will do: *Carla is such a flake, she'll probably forget that the party's tonight.*

flak•y /ˈfleɪki/ *adjective*

1 easily breaking into flat thin pieces: *flaky pastry*

2 *informal* someone who is flaky easily forgets things or does strange things

flame /fleɪm/ *noun*

1 hot bright gas that you see when something is burning: *a candle flame*

2 in flames = burning strongly: *The house was in flames and the firefighters were still not there.*

➔ See Thesaurus box at **fire¹**

fla•min•go /fləˈmɪŋgoʊ/ *noun* plural **flamingos** or **flamingoes**

a tall pink water bird with long thin legs and a long curved neck

flam•ma•ble /ˈflæməbəl/ *adjective, formal*

something that is flammable burns very easily: *Gasoline is a flammable liquid.*

flan•nel /ˈflænl/ *noun*

soft cotton or wool cloth used for making warm clothes: *It was cold, so he put on a flannel shirt.*

flap[1] /flæp/ *verb* **flapped, flapping**
1 if a bird flaps its wings, it moves them up and down: *The bird flapped its wings and flew away.*
2 if a piece of cloth, paper, etc. flaps, it moves in one direction and then the other: *The ship's sails flapped in the wind.*

flap[2] *noun*
a thin flat piece of cloth, paper, etc. that is attached at one side to something: *He licked the flap of the envelope and closed it.*

flare[1] /fler/ *also* **flare up** *verb*
to suddenly begin to burn very brightly: *The fire flared up, and we could see the people around us for a minute.*

F

flare[2] *noun*
an object that burns with a very bright light that you use as a signal: *Police had lit warning flares along the highway near the accident.*

flared /flerd/ *adjective*
flared pants or skirts are wider toward the bottom

flash[1] /flæʃ/ *verb*
1 to shine brightly for a short time: *Lightning flashed in the sky.* | *an ambulance with flashing lights* (=lights that flash again and again)
2 to move very quickly: *A car flashed past.*
→ See Thesaurus box at **shine**[1]

flash[2] *noun*
1 a sudden quick bright light: *We saw a flash of lightning.*
2 a bright light on a camera that you use when taking photographs inside a building: *The flash always makes me blink.*
3 in a flash = very quickly or suddenly: *The day went by in a flash, and suddenly it was time to go home.*

'flash card *noun*
a card with a word or picture on it that you use for practicing things you are learning

flash•light /ˈflæʃlaɪt/ *noun*
a small electric light that you carry in your hand: *He was shining his flashlight on my face.*
→ See picture at **light**[1]

flash•y /ˈflæʃi/ *adjective, informal*
flashy clothes, cars, etc. are very noticeable or look expensive and show that you want people to notice you: *She wears flashy jewelry and tight clothes.*

flat[1] /flæt/ *adjective* **flatter, flattest**
1 smooth and level, with no slopes or raised parts: *There are no hills in this road; it's flat for the next 50 miles.*

> **THESAURUS: flat**
>
> **level** a surface or area that is level goes across something and does not go up or down, so that every part of it is at the same height: *Make sure the shelves are level.*
>
> **smooth** having an even surface, without any holes or raised areas: *a smooth round stone* | *a baby's smooth skin*
>
> **even** flat, level, and smooth: *The surface should be even and clean before you put any paint on it.*
>
> **horizontal** a horizontal line, position, or surface is straight and flat and goes across something without going up or down: *The room had a horizontal stripe painted halfway up the wall.*

2 a flat tire does not have enough air inside it
3 E flat/B flat, etc. = a musical note that is slightly lower than E, B, etc.
4 a drink that is flat has no bubbles in it when it should have bubbles: *The ginger ale is flat.*
—**flatness** *noun*: *the flatness of the farm land*

flat[2] *adverb*
1 with every part touching a surface, and no parts raised: *He was lying flat on his back looking at the ceiling.*
2 in 10 seconds/two minutes, etc. flat *informal* = very quickly, in 10 seconds, two minutes, etc.: *I was out of the house in 10 minutes flat.*
3 if you sing or play music flat, you sing or play slightly lower than the correct note
ANTONYM **sharp**

flat•ly /ˈflætli/ *adverb, formal*
in a firm way: *She flatly denied the rumors* (=said firmly that they were not true).

flat•ten /ˈflætn/ *verb*
to make something flat: *The heavy rain flattened the plants.*

flat•ter /ˈflætɚ/ *verb*
1 be/feel flattered = to feel happy because someone shows that he or she likes or admires you: *When they asked me to join their club, I felt flattered.*

2 to say nice things to someone, sometimes when you do not really mean it: *I flattered her by saying her performance was wonderful.*
—**flattery** *noun* nice things that you say to someone, sometimes when you do not really mean it: *She tried using flattery to get me to do her work.*
—**flatterer** *noun* someone who flatters someone else

fla•vor¹ /ˈfleɪvɚ/ *noun*
the taste of a food or drink: *The Mexican soup has a spicy flavor.* | *My favorite flavor of ice cream is chocolate.*
—**flavorful** /ˈfleɪvɚfʊl/ *adjective* having a strong, good taste: *a flavorful stew*

flavor² *verb*
to give food or drink a particular taste: *He flavored the sauce with lemon and herbs.*

fla•vor•ing /ˈfleɪvərɪŋ/ *noun*
a substance used to give food or drink a particular taste: *This yogurt contains no artificial flavorings.*

flaw /flɔ/ *noun*
a mark, weakness, or bad part that makes something not perfect: *There was a flaw in our lawyer's argument, and the other lawyers used it to win the case.* SYNONYM **weakness**
—**flawed** *adjective* having one or more flaws

flea /fli/ *noun*
a very small jumping insect that bites animals to drink their blood: *Their dog has fleas.*

ˈflea ˌmarket *noun*
a market, usually in the street, where old or used things are sold

flee /fli/ *verb* **fled** /fled/ *formal*
to leave a place very quickly in order to escape from danger: *Many people have fled the country since the war started.*

fleet /flit/ *noun*
1 a group of vehicles that are controlled by one company: *The company owns a fleet of trucks.*
2 a group of ships: *The navy attacked the enemy fleet.*

flesh /fleʃ/ *noun*
1 the soft part of a person's or animal's body: *The lion bit into the zebra's flesh.*
2 the soft part inside a fruit or vegetable: *the sweet yellow flesh of a mango*
3 in the flesh = if you see someone in the flesh, you see someone who you had only seen in pictures, in movies, etc. before: *I saw Brad Pitt in the flesh, on the street in New York!*
—**fleshy** *adjective* having a lot of flesh: *fleshy arms*

flew /flu/ *verb*
the past tense of FLY

flex•i•ble /ˈfleksəbəl/ Ac *adjective*
1 able to change easily: *My schedule is flexible; I can travel any day this week.*
2 easy to bend: *a flexible rubber tube*
—**flexibility** /ˌfleksəˈbɪləti/ *noun* the quality of being flexible

flick /flɪk/ *verb*
to move something with a quick movement of your finger: *He flicked the switch from "off" to "on."*
—**flick** *noun* a quick movement of your finger or wrist
→ See Thesaurus box at **movie**
→ See picture on page A3

flick•er /ˈflɪkɚ/ *verb*
to burn or shine with a light that is not steady: *The candles flickered in the wind.*
→ See Thesaurus box at **shine¹**

fli•er /ˈflaɪɚ/ *noun*
1 a sheet of paper advertising something: *They gave fliers advertising the restaurant to people on the street.*
2 someone who flies an airplane or travels in an airplane
→ See Thesaurus box at **advertisement**

flight /flaɪt/ *noun*
1 a trip on an airplane, or the airplane making a particular trip: *She was tired after the long flight.* | *When is the next flight to Miami?*
2 the act of flying through the air: *a picture of a bird in flight* (=flying)
3 a flight of stairs = a set of stairs between one floor and the next: *I had to walk up six flights of stairs.*

ˈflight atˌtendant *noun*
someone whose job is to take care of the passengers on a plane

flim•sy /ˈflɪmzi/ *adjective*
1 a flimsy object is not strong or thick: *I was sitting in a flimsy plastic chair, and it broke.*
2 a flimsy argument, excuse, etc. is difficult to believe: *She said she couldn't go, and*

F

gave me a flimsy excuse about her dog being sick.

fling[1] /flɪŋ/ *verb* **flung** /flʌŋ/
to throw or move something quickly with a lot of force: *He flung the rope to the man in the water.*
→ See Thesaurus box at **throw**[1]

fling[2] *noun, informal*
a short romantic relationship that is not serious: *We went out for a few months, but it was just a fling.*

flip /flɪp/ *verb* **flipped, flipping**

flip

1 *also* **flip over** to turn over quickly: *The car went off the road and flipped over.* | *Flip the hamburger over to cook the other side.*
2 if you flip a SWITCH, you quickly change its position: *I flipped the switch, and the music came on.*
3 *also* **flip out** *informal* to suddenly become very angry or upset: *He flipped out when he found out she was going out with someone else.*
PHRASAL VERB
flip through something
to look quickly at the pages of a book or magazine

flip·per /ˈflɪpɚ/ *noun*
1 a flat part that some large sea animals have, which they use to swim: *Seals and turtles have flippers.*
2 a large flat rubber shoe that you wear in order to swim faster

flirt /flɚt/ *verb*
to behave as if you are sexually attracted to someone, but not in a serious way: *You were flirting with her at the dance!*
—**flirtatious** /flɚˈteɪʃəs/ *adjective* someone who is flirtatious likes to flirt or flirts a lot

float /floʊt/ *verb*
1 to stay on the surface of a liquid: *The tiny boat floated on the pond.* | *The ball fell into the water and floated away* (=moved away on the surface of the water). ANTONYM **sink**
2 to stay in the air or move slowly through the air: *The balloon floated up into the sky.*

float

flock /flɑk/ *noun*
a group of sheep, goats, or birds: *a flock of geese*
→ See Thesaurus box at **group**[1]

flood[1] /flʌd/ *noun*
a very large amount of water that covers land that is usually dry: *The floods destroyed many homes.*

flood[2] *verb*
1 to cover an area with water: *The river flooded the fields.* | *The basement flooded, and all our books and clothes got wet.*
2 be flooded with something = to receive so many letters or calls that you cannot deal with them all: *The radio station was flooded with complaints when they changed the type of music they played.*
—**flooding** *noun* a situation in which a place is flooded: *The heavy rain could cause flooding.*

flood·light /ˈflʌdlaɪt/ *noun*
a very bright light, used at night to light the outside of buildings, sports fields, etc.

floor /flɔr/ *noun*
1 the surface that you stand on in a building: *He cleaned the kitchen floor.* | *Don't leave your clothes on the floor.*
2 one of the levels in a building: *We live on the third floor of our apartment building.*

floor·board /ˈflɔrbɔrd/ *noun*
a long flat piece of wood that is part of a floor: *The old floorboards made a noise when I stepped on them.*

flop /flɑp/ *verb* **flopped, flopping**
1 to sit down or fall in a loose, heavy way: *I was so tired that I went home, flopped on the bed, and fell asleep.*
2 *informal* to be unsuccessful: *The movie*

flopped, and the producers lost a lot of money.

—**flop** *noun, informal* something that is not successful: *The play was a flop; audiences hated it.*

flop·py /ˈflɑpi/ *adjective*
soft and hanging loosely down: *The dog had long floppy ears.*

ˌfloppy ˈdisk *also* **floppy** *noun*
a flat piece of plastic, used for storing information from a computer
➔ See picture on page A20

flo·ral /ˈflɔrəl/ *adjective, formal*
made of flowers or decorated with pictures of flowers: *The dress had a pretty floral pattern.*

flo·rist /ˈflɔrɪst/ *noun*
someone who works in a store that sells flowers
➔ See picture on page A16

floss /flɔs/ *verb*
to clean between your teeth with special string: *I floss regularly.*
—**floss** *also* **dental floss** *noun* special string that you use to clean between your teeth

floun·der /ˈflaʊndɚ/ *noun*
a flat ocean fish, or the meat from this fish

flour /flaʊɚ/ *noun*
a powder made from wheat that is used for making bread, cakes, etc.

flour·ish /ˈflɚrɪʃ/ *verb*
to grow well or develop well: *His business is flourishing, so he just hired three new employees.*

flow¹ /floʊ/ *verb*
if a liquid flows, it moves along steadily: *The river flows through a wide valley to the ocean.*
➔ See Thesaurus box at **pour**

flow² *noun*
a steady movement of liquid: *They tried to stop the flow of blood.*

flow·er /ˈflaʊɚ/ *noun*
1 a pretty colored part on a plant: *This plant has yellow flowers in the spring.* | *He brought her a bouquet of flowers* (=bunch of flowers).
2 a small plant that produces flowers: *I planted those flowers myself.*
—**flower** *verb, formal* if a plant flowers, it produces flowers: *The plant flowers in early summer.*
—**flowered** *adjective* decorated with pictures of flowers: *flowered wallpaper*

flow·er·bed /ˈflaʊɚˌbed/ *noun*
an area of earth in which flowers are grown

flow·er·pot /ˈflaʊɚˌpɑt/ *noun*
a pot in which you grow plants

flown /floʊn/ *verb*
the past participle of FLY

flu /flu/ *noun*
the flu = a disease that is like a bad cold but is more serious, usually with a fever: *I had the flu last week.*

fluc·tu·ate /ˈflʌktʃuˌeɪt/ Ac *verb, formal*
if an amount or number fluctuates, it goes up and down more than once: *Her weight fluctuated between 120 and 150 pounds.*
—**fluctuation** /ˌflʌktʃuˈeɪʃən/ *noun* a change up and down: *Fluctuations in temperature will harm the plant.*

flu·ent /ˈfluənt/ *adjective*
able to speak a language very well: *She is fluent in French.* | *He spoke fluent English.*
—**fluently** *adverb*: *She speaks Spanish fluently.*
—**fluency** *noun* the quality of being fluent in a language

fluff /flʌf/ *noun*
soft light pieces that come off wool, fur, etc.: *There's a piece of fluff on your skirt.*

fluff·y /ˈflʌfi/ *adjective*
soft and light, or with soft fur: *a fluffy baby rabbit*

flu·id /ˈfluɪd/ *noun, formal*
a liquid: *My doctor told me to drink lots of fluids to help me get better.*
—**fluid** *adjective* able to flow or move like a liquid

flung /flʌŋ/ *verb*
the past tense and past participle of FLING

flunk /flʌŋk/ *verb, informal*
to fail a test or class: *I flunked my history exam because I didn't study at all.*

PHRASAL VERB
flunk out *informal*
to have to leave a college because your work is not good enough: *He flunked out of college and had to find a job.*

F

flur•ry /ˈflɚi/ *noun* plural **flurries** *formal*
1 a sudden increase in activity for a short time: *There was a flurry of activity as we got ready for the party to start.*
2 a small amount of snow that falls and blows around: *We had flurries, but the snow didn't even stick to the ground.*

flush /flʌʃ/ *verb*
1 if you flush a toilet, you make water go through it to clean it
2 *formal* if you flush, your face becomes red because you are embarrassed or angry

flushed /flʌʃt/ *adjective*
if someone's face is flushed, it is red: *His face was flushed because he had been running.*

F

flus•tered /ˈflʌstɚd/ *adjective*
feeling nervous and confused: *She got flustered and forgot what she wanted to say.*

flute /flut/ *noun*
a musical instrument like a pipe that you hold across your lips and blow
—**flutist** *noun* someone who plays the flute
➔ See picture on page A21

flut•ter /ˈflʌtɚ/ *verb*
1 to make small movements in the air: *The flags fluttered in the wind.*
2 if a small bird or an insect flutters somewhere, it flies there: *Butterflies fluttered over the fields.*

fly¹ /flaɪ/ *verb* **flew** /flu/ **flown** /floʊn/ third person singular **flies**
1 to move through the air: *The bird flew away.*
2 to travel by airplane: *We flew to Phoenix Arizona to visit my family.*
3 to control an airplane: *Kathy is learning to fly a plane.*
4 if a flag is flying, it is being shown on a pole
5 *formal* to suddenly move very quickly: *I flew down the stairs to see what was making the noise.*
WORD FAMILY ➔ **flight** *noun*

fly² *noun* plural **flies**
1 a common small flying insect: *There were flies all over the food.*
2 the part at the front of a pair of pants that you can open: *Your fly is unzipped.*

fly•er /ˈflaɪɚ/ *noun*
another spelling of FLIER

ˌflying ˈsaucer *noun*
a space vehicle from another PLANET, which some people believe they have seen SYNONYM **UFO**

foal /foʊl/ *noun*
a very young horse

foam /foʊm/ *noun*
1 a lot of very small BUBBLEs on the top of a liquid: *The soap bubbles made a white foam in the sink.*
2 a very light but solid substance that changes shape easily when it is pressed: *a foam mattress* | *The box has foam inside to keep the glasses from breaking.*

fo•cus¹ /ˈfoʊkəs/ Ac *verb*
1 to give your attention to a particular thing: *I have to focus on school now because I have final exams soon.*
2 to move part of a camera, TELESCOPE, etc. so that you can see something clearly: *The camera focuses automatically.*
—**focused** *adjective* giving your attention to a particular thing: *Stay focused, or you won't finish your work on time.*

focus² *noun*
1 the thing that is given most attention: *The main focus of this book is the history of the city.*
2 attention that you give to a particular thing: *At the kids' club, the focus is on fun.*
3 in focus/out of focus = if a photograph or something seen through a TELESCOPE is in focus, it is clear and easy to see. If it is out of focus, it is not clear.

foe /foʊ/ *noun, formal*
an enemy: *Are they friends or foes?* ANTONYM **ally, friend**

fog /fɑg/ *noun*
cloudy air near the ground that is difficult to see through: *There was thick fog, so he drove slowly.*
—**foggy** *adjective* if it is foggy, there is fog in the air: *a foggy morning*

foil /fɔɪl/ *noun*
very thin metal, used for covering food: *Cover the pan with aluminum foil, and put it in the oven.*

fold¹ /foʊld/ *verb*

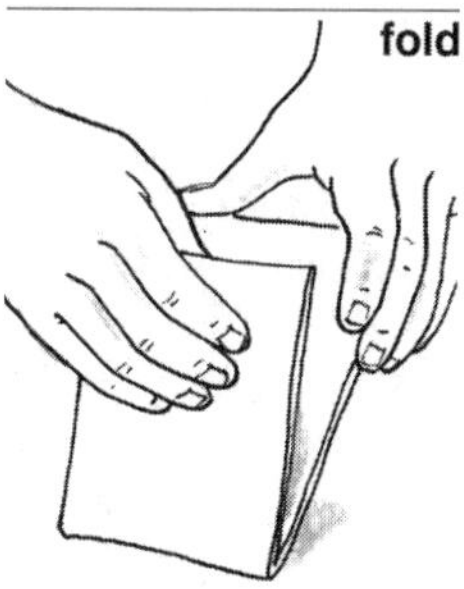

1 to bend a piece of paper or cloth so that one part covers another part: *Could you fold those towels for me?* | *Fold the piece of paper in half* (=fold it so that one half covers the other).

2 *also* **fold up** to make something such as a table smaller by bending parts of it: *Fold up the ironing board when you are done.* | *a folding chair* (=a chair that can be folded)

3 fold your arms = to bend your arms so that they are resting across your chest

fold² *noun*

a line or part where paper, cloth, etc. is bent: *Fold the paper, and cut along the fold.*

fold•er /ˈfoʊldɚ/ *noun*

1 a large folded piece of strong paper, in which you keep documents: *Put all your homework in this folder and put it in your backpack.*

2 a group of FILEs that are stored together on a computer: *You can move files from one folder to another.*

fo•li•age /ˈfoʊli-ɪdʒ/ *noun, formal*

the leaves of a plant or tree: *This bush has dark green foliage.*

folk /foʊk/ *adjective*

folk music, dancing, etc. is traditional and typical of the ordinary people of a particular country: *They sang an old folk song from the Civil War.* | *a book of folk tales* (=traditional stories)

folks /foʊks/ *plural noun, informal*

1 people in general: *Some folks might not like the idea.*

2 your parents: *Have you told your folks that you're getting married?*

→ See Thesaurus box at **family**

fol•low /ˈfɑloʊ/ *verb*

1 to move along behind someone else: *I followed him up the steps.* | *I think we're being followed* (=someone is trying to follow us secretly).

2 to happen or come immediately after something else: *I heard a yell, followed by a loud crash.* | *The rules of the game are as follows* (=they will be explained next).

3 to continue on a road, or go in the same direction as a river: *Follow the road to the coast.*

4 follow instructions/rules/advice, etc. = to do what someone tells you to do or suggests that you do: *If you follow the instructions written on the box, you can build a little toy car.* | *I followed my dad's advice, and put my money in a savings account.*

5 to understand something such as an explanation or story: *The movie was hard to follow, because there were so many characters.*

6 to deliberately do what someone else has done: *The younger kids followed his lead* (=did what he did). | *He followed in his father's footsteps and became a doctor.*

PHRASAL VERBS

follow through

to do what you have promised to do or started doing: *Will he follow through on his promise?*

follow up (something)

to find out more about something, or to do more about something: *We always follow up on complaints by calling people again to talk to them about the problem.*

fol•low•er /ˈfɑloʊɚ/ *noun*

someone who believes in someone's ideas or supports them: *Buddha told his followers to help others.*

fol•low•ing¹ /ˈfɑloʊɪŋ/ *adjective*

the following day/year/chapter, etc. = the next day, year, etc.: *I was born in 1992, and my sister was born the following year* (=1993).

following² *preposition*

after: *He died following an accident.*

fond /fɑnd/ *adjective, formal*

be fond of someone or something = to like someone or something: *She was very fond of her aunt.*

—**fondly** *adverb*

—**fondness** *noun He has a fondness for video games and plays them all the time.*

F

food /fud/ *noun*
things that people, animals, and plants eat: *We went to the grocery store to buy food.* | *I love Chinese food.* | *dog food*

ˈfood ˌprocessor *noun*
a piece of electrical equipment that cuts or mixes food very quickly

ˈfood stamps *plural noun*
special pieces of paper that the U.S. government gives to poor people to buy food with

fool¹ /ful/ *noun*
1 a stupid person: *Don't be a fool – it's a great job, so take it.* SYNONYM **idiot**
2 make a fool of yourself = to do something silly or embarrassing, which other people can see: *I don't dance at parties because I don't want to make a fool of myself.*

F

fool² *verb*
to make someone believe something that is not true: *She fooled her parents into thinking she was sick.*
PHRASAL VERB
fool around
1 to behave in a silly way or have fun: *Stop fooling around and start studying!*
2 to have a sexual relationship that is not serious: *He was fooling around with some girl he didn't even know.*

fool·ish /ˈfulɪʃ/ *adjective*
silly or not sensible: *Don't do anything foolish.* SYNONYM **stupid**
—**foolishly** *adverb*: *I foolishly agreed to help them take the money.*
—**foolishness** *noun*

WORD FAMILY look at the words:
→ **foolish** *adjective*
→ **foolishly** *adverb*
→ **foolishness** *noun*
→ **fool** *noun*
→ **fool** *verb*

fool·proof /ˈfulpruf/ *adjective*
a foolproof idea is sure to be successful: *This plan is foolproof – there's no way we can fail.*

foot /fʊt/ *noun*
1 plural **feet** /fit/ the part of your body at the end of your leg, which you stand on: *My brother has big feet.* | *I've been on my feet* (=standing up) *all day.*
2 plural **feet** or **foot**, *written abbreviation* **ft.** a length equal to 12 inches or 30.5 centimeters, used for measuring things: *Craig is six feet tall.*
3 on foot = if you go somewhere on foot, you walk there: *We went across the bridge on foot.*
4 the foot of something = the bottom of something tall or high such as a mountain, tree, or set of stairs: *They stopped at the foot of the mountain.*
5 put your foot down = to say very firmly what someone must do or must not do: *My mother put her foot down and said I could not go.*
6 get/rise/jump, etc. to your feet *formal* = to stand up after you have been sitting
7 set foot in something *formal* = to go into a place: *I left home to go to college, and I never set foot in that town again.*
→ See picture on page A2

foot·ball /ˈfʊtbɔl/ *noun*
1 a game in which two teams carry, kick, or throw a ball into an area at the end of a field to win points: *I'm going to a football game tonight.*
2 the ball with points at both ends that you use in this game
→ See picture on page A24

foot·print /ˈfʊtˌprɪnt/ *noun*
a mark made by a foot or shoe: *There were footprints in the snow.*

foot·step /ˈfʊtstep/ *noun*
the sound of each step when someone is walking: *I heard footsteps behind me.*

foot·wear /ˈfʊtwer/ *noun, formal*
shoes, boots, etc.: *Choose comfortable footwear for hiking.*

for¹ /fɚ; *strong* fɔr/ *preposition*
1 intended to be given to someone or used by someone: *I have a present for you.* | *It's a movie for kids, not adults.*
2 with a particular purpose: *a knife for cutting bread* | *They are fighting for freedom* (=in order to have freedom). | *What did you do that for* (=why did you do it?)?
3 used when saying how long: *I've known her for five years.*

GRAMMAR: for

for, since, ago

For, **since**, and **ago** are all used to talk about time.

For is used to say how long something has lasted. It comes before a length of time: *My aunt has been here for three days.* | *The meeting continued for five hours.*

Since is used to say when something started. The exact day, date, or time comes after it: *He's been here since Sunday.* | *I've been going to school here since 2006.*

Ago is used to say how far back in the past something happened. It comes after a length of time: *My grandfather died two years ago.*

4 if you do something for someone, you do it because it will be helpful or useful to him or her: *Let me lift that box for you.* | *He plays for the Boston Red Sox.*

5 because of or as a result of something: *What did you get for your birthday?*

6 intending or meant to go to a place: *She just left for school.*

7 used when saying how far: *We walked for about 6 miles.*

8 used when mentioning a price: *I got this jacket for $70.*

9 if you have something for breakfast, dinner, etc., you eat it at that meal: *We had steak for dinner last night.* | *"What's for lunch?" "Pasta."*

10 if you are happy, sad, etc. for someone, you are happy, sad, etc. because something has happened to him or her: *I'm really happy for you – you deserved to win.*

11 in support of or in agreement with someone or something: *Who did you vote for?* ANTONYM **against**

12 with a particular meaning: *What's the Spanish word for oil?*

for² *conjunction, formal*
because: *We left quickly, for we knew we were in great danger.*

for•bid /fɚˈbɪd/ *verb* **forbade** /fɚˈbæd/ **forbidden** /fɚˈbɪdn/ *formal*
to order someone not to do something: *I forbid you to see him again.* ANTONYM **permit**

THESAURUS: forbid

not allow/permit/let to say that someone must not do something, and stop him/her doing it: *His parents don't allow him to go out on school nights.* | *Smoking is not permitted inside the hospital.*

ban to officially say that people must not do something or that something is not allowed: *Fires are banned in the campground.*

prohibit *formal* to say officially that someone cannot do something because of a rule or law: *The law prohibits people from owning these rare birds as pets.*

bar *formal* to officially prevent someone from doing something: *Reporters were barred from the courtroom.*

—**forbidden** *adjective* not allowed: *Alcohol is forbidden for Muslims.*

force¹ /fɔrs/ *verb*
1 to make someone do something that he or she does not want to do: *You can't force me to be a doctor if I don't want to be one.*

THESAURUS: force

make to force someone to do something: *You can't make a kid eat something he doesn't like.*

coerce *formal* to make someone do something by using threats: *Young children were coerced into becoming soldiers.*

compel *formal* to force someone to do something: *I felt compelled to succeed, as my parents had helped me so much.*

pressure to try to make someone feel they should do something that he or she does not really want to do: *Don't let your friends pressure you into trying alcohol.*

2 to use your strength to move something: *The police had to force open the door.*

force² *noun*
1 a group of people who do military or police work: *The U.S. is withdrawing its military forces.*
2 violent physical action that someone uses to make someone do something or to get something: *The government says it will use force to stop the protesters.*
3 physical power: *The force of the explosion*

F

threw me to the ground. | *Waves were hitting the rocks with great force.*

4 something that moves things or has an effect on them: *The force of gravity pulls everything downward.*

5 join forces = if people join forces, they start working together: *Several groups have joined forces to raise money for the charity.*

6 in force = if a law or rule is in force, it exists and must be obeyed

forced /fɔrst/ *adjective*
a forced action is one that someone makes you do or that you make yourself do: *a forced marriage* (=one that the two people do not choose or want)

F

force•ful /ˈfɔrsfəl/ *adjective*
powerful and strong: *She had a forceful way of speaking that convinced people to do things.*
—**forcefully** *adverb*: *He argued forcefully against the plan.*

fore•arm /ˈfɔrɑrm/ *noun*
the part of your arm between your hand and your elbow
➔ See picture on page A2

fore•cast /ˈfɔrkæst/ *noun*
a description of what is likely to happen: *I was watching the weather forecast* (=a description telling if it will be rainy, sunny, etc.)
—**forecast** *verb* to say what is likely to happen: *They are forecasting that the summer will be very dry.*

fore•fa•thers /ˈfɔrˌfɑðɚz/ *plural noun, formal*
1 someone from the past who helped to start a country, organization, or way of thinking that still exists: *Our nation's forefathers wrote the constitution that we use today.*
2 another word for ANCESTORs: *Our forefathers fished in these lakes five hundred years ago.*

fore•front /ˈfɔrfrʌnt/ *noun*
in/at the forefront of something *formal* = doing important things first that many other people will also do: *The company was at the forefront of change when the Internet started to become used.*

fore•head /ˈfɔrhed/ *noun*
the part of your face above your eyes: *He wiped the sweat from his forehead.*
➔ See picture on page A2

for•eign /ˈfɑrɪn/ *adjective*
from or relating to a country that is not your own: *Can you speak a foreign language?* | *I watch a lot of foreign films.*

for•eign•er /ˈfɑrənɚ/ *noun*
someone who comes from a country that is not your country

fore•man /ˈfɔrmən/ *noun* plural **foremen** /ˈfɔrmən/
1 someone who is in charge of a group of workers: *a factory foreman*
2 the leader of a JURY

fore•most /ˈfɔrmoʊst/ *adjective, formal*
the best or most important: *The country's foremost writers came to the White House for a special dinner.*

fore•see /fɔrˈsi/ *verb* **foresaw** /fɔrˈsɔ/ **foreseen** /fɔrˈsin/ *formal*
to know that something will happen in the future: *He foresaw the war that began two years later.* SYNONYM **predict**

for•est /ˈfɔrɪst/ *noun*
a large area of land covered with trees: *The animal lives high up in trees in the forest.* SYNONYM **woods**
➔ See Thesaurus box at **tree**

for•ev•er /fəˈrevɚ/ *adverb*
1 for all of the future: *You can't live forever.* | *I wanted the vacation to last forever.* SYNONYM **always**
2 *informal* for a very long time: *Greg will probably be a student forever.* | *It'll take forever to walk to Amy's house.*
3 go on forever *informal* = to be extremely long or large: *Their yard seemed to go on forever.*
➔ See Thesaurus box at **always**

fore•word /ˈfɔrwɚd/ *noun*
a short piece of writing at the beginning of a book that gives information relating to the book

for•gave /fɚˈgeɪv/ *verb*
the past tense of FORGIVE

forge /fɔrdʒ/ *verb*
to illegally copy a document, a painting, money, etc. in order to make people think it is real: *He forged his wife's signature on the*

check. | *a forged passport* SYNONYM **fake**
—**forger** *noun* someone who illegally copies documents, paintings, etc.

for·ger·y /ˈfɔrdʒəri/ *noun* plural **forgeries**
1 a document, painting, or piece of paper money that someone has illegally copied: *The police discovered that her passport was a forgery and arrested her.* SYNONYM **fake**
2 the crime of illegally copying something

for·get /fɚˈget/ *verb* **forgot** /fɚˈgɑt/ **forgotten** /fɚˈgɑtn/ **forgetting**
1 to be unable to remember facts, information, or something that happened: *I've forgotten her name – do you know it?* | *I know you told me what this means, but I forgot.* | *He forgot all about our anniversary.*
2 to not remember to do something that you should do: *I forgot to lock the door.*
3 to not remember to bring something that you should have taken with you: *I forgot my sunglasses.*

USAGE: forget

You can say "I forgot my homework."
You cannot say "I forgot my homework at home."
When you want to talk about the place where you left something by mistake, you must use "leave": *I left my homework at home.*

4 to stop thinking or worrying about someone or something: *I'll never forget how I felt when my grandmother died.*
5 forget it *informal* **a)** used in order to tell someone that something is not important: *"I'm sorry, I shouldn't have yelled at you." "Forget it."* **b)** used in order to tell someone to stop asking or talking about something because it is annoying you: *I'm not buying you that bike, so just forget it.*

for·get·ful /fɚˈgetfəl/ *adjective*
if you are forgetful, you often forget things that you should remember: *Many old people become forgetful.*
—**forgetfulness** *noun*

for·give /fɚˈgɪv/ *verb* **forgave** /fɚˈgeɪv/ **forgiven** /fɚˈgɪvən/
to stop being angry with someone who has done something wrong: *I can't forgive him for the terrible things he said.* | *If anything bad happened to the kids, I'd never forgive myself.* | *"I'm sorry." "That's OK – you're forgiven* (=I forgive you)*."*
—**forgiveness** *noun*: *He was really sorry for what he'd done and asked for forgiveness.*

fork¹ /fɔrk/ *noun*
1 a small tool that you use for picking up food when you eat: *He washed his knife and fork, and put them away.*
2 a place where a road or river divides into two parts: *Go left when you come to the fork in the road.*
➔ See picture on page A9

fork² *verb*
if a road or river forks, it divides into two parts

form¹ /fɔrm/ *noun*
1 one type of something: *You'll need two forms of ID, like a passport and a driver's license.* SYNONYM **kind**
2 the way in which something exists or appears: *The data on a computer is stored in digital form.*
3 an official document with spaces where you have to write information: *Please fill out the form in black ink.* | *a job application form*
4 *formal* a shape: *The dark form in the trees was a bear.*

form² *verb*
1 to start to exist: *Winter is coming, and ice is forming on the lake.* SYNONYM **develop**
2 to make a particular shape: *He formed a circle with his thumb and finger.*
3 to start a new organization or group: *We formed the company back in 1990.* SYNONYM **create**
4 to make something by combining two or more parts: *You can often form an adverb by adding the letters "ly" to the end of an adjective.*
5 to be part of something: *Rice forms a basic part of Chinese meals.*

for·mal /ˈfɔrməl/ *adjective*
1 formal language, clothes, or behavior are used in very important or official situations: *men's formal wear* (=clothes for important events, parties, etc.) ANTONYM **informal**
2 a formal occasion is an important event, such as a wedding or important dinner or party: *Jack won't wear a tie, even on formal occasions.*
3 official and public: *The president made a formal announcement.* ANTONYM **informal**

4 formal education/training/qualifications = education in a subject or skill that you receive in school, not from experience
—**formally** *adverb*: *The winner will be formally announced this afternoon.*

WORD FAMILY look at the words:

→ **formal** *adjective*
→ **informal** *adjective*
→ **formally** *adverb*
→ **informally** *adverb*
→ **formality** *noun*
→ **informality** *noun*

F

for•mal•i•ty /fɔr'mæləti/ *noun* plural **formalities** *formal*
something that you must do as part of an official activity: *We had to sign the contract and deal with a few other formalities.*

for•mat /'fɔrmæt/ Ac *noun*
1 the way in which something such as computer document, television show, or meeting is organized or arranged: *The talk-show format is popular on daytime TV.*
2 the size, shape, design, etc. of a book or magazine

for•ma•tion /fɔr'meɪʃən/ *noun*
1 *formal* the act of making something new: *The formation of a new government will take a long time.*
2 something that has been formed into a particular shape, or the shape into which it has been formed: *The rock formations in the desert were beautiful.*

for•mer[1] /'fɔrmɚ/ *adjective*
1 having a particular job or position in the past, but not now: *Two former U.S. presidents, Bill Clinton and George Bush, were at the ceremony.*
2 existing in the past, but not now: *the former Soviet Union*

former[2] *noun*
the former *formal* = the first of two people or things that are mentioned: *She had to decide between the red dress and the blue one. The former cost $125 and the latter $85.* ANTONYM **latter**

for•mer•ly /'fɔrmɚli/ *adverb*
in the past, not now: *New York was formerly called New Amsterdam* (=New Amsterdam was the name it had before).

for•mu•la /'fɔrmyələ/ Ac *noun*
1 a series of numbers or letters that represent a mathematical or scientific rule: *a mathematical formula*
2 a liquid food for babies that is similar to a mother's milk: *She fed the baby formula.*

fort /fɔrt/ *noun*
1 a strong building used by soldiers for defending an important place: *The soldiers were in a fort on the hill.*
2 a place where an army lives and trains

forth /fɔrθ/ *adverb, formal*
toward a place that is in front of you: *The soldiers went forth into battle.*
→ **back and forth** at **back[1]**

for•tress /'fɔrtrɪs/ *noun*
a large strong building that soldiers use for defending an important place

for•tu•nate /'fɔrtʃənət/ *adjective, formal*
if you are fortunate, something good has happened to you or you are in a good situation: *We were fortunate to arrive before it started snowing.* | *You're fortunate that you have such wonderful parents.* SYNONYM **lucky**; ANTONYM **unfortunate**

WORD FAMILY look at the words:

→ **fortunate** *adjective*
→ **unfortunate** *adjective*
→ **fortunately** *adverb*
→ **unfortunately** *adverb*
→ **fortune** *noun*
→ **misfortune** *noun*

for•tu•nate•ly /'fɔrtʃənətli/ *adverb*
happening because of good luck: *We arrived at the airport late, but fortunately our flight was late too.* ANTONYM **unfortunately**

for•tune /'fɔrtʃən/ *noun*
1 a very large amount of money: *She could make a fortune* (=earn a lot of money) *as a fashion model.*
2 luck and the influence it has on your life: *I had the good fortune to find a job as soon as I got to St. Louis.*
3 the good or bad things that happen to you: *A year later his fortune changed when he met Karen.*
4 tell someone's fortune = to tell someone what will happen to them in the future, for example by using special cards

'fortune ˌteller *noun*
someone who uses special cards or looks at your hands in order to tell you what is going to happen to you in the future

for•ty /ˈfɔrti/ *number*
1 40
2 the forties a) *also* **the '40s** the years between 1940 and 1949 **b)** the temperatures between 40 and 49 degrees Fahrenheit or Celsius
3 be in your forties = to be aged between 40 and 49
—**fortieth** *number* 40th or 1/40

for•ward[1] /ˈfɔrwɚd/ *adverb*
1 *also* **forwards** toward a place that is in front of you: *The crowd moved forward into the park.* | *He leaned forward and kissed her.* ANTONYM **backward**
2 toward a situation that develops and becomes better: *You have to forget about the mistakes you made and move forward.*
→ **look forward to something** at **look**[1]

forward[2] *adjective*
1 toward a place that is in front of you: *the forward movement of the car*
2 *formal* very friendly and open with someone you do not know well: *She was very forward and told us all about her personal problems.*
3 forward thinking/planning = plans or ideas that help you to prepare for the future: *If we do some forward planning now, we should be ready if an emergency happens.*

forward[3] *verb*
to send a letter, email etc. that has been sent to you, to another person: *I'll forward the email I got from Kristin to you right now.*

fos•sil /ˈfɑsəl/ *noun*
part of an animal or plant that lived a very long time ago, which has been preserved in rock: *Scientists found fossils of dinosaurs in the rocks.*

fossil
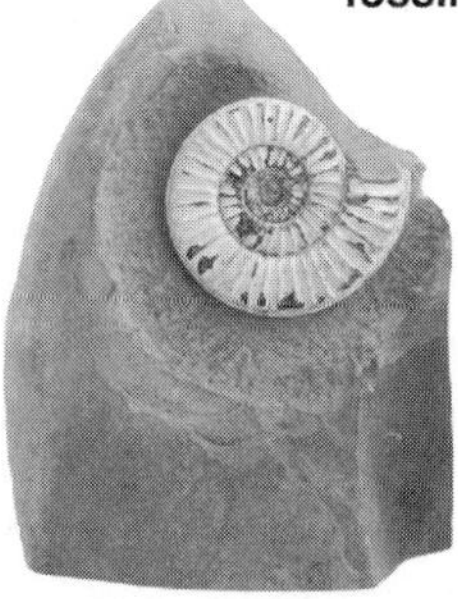

foster /ˈfɑstɚ/ *adjective*
relating to an arrangement in which a child has been taken into someone's home without those people becoming the child's legal parents: *He lived with foster parents for three years before our family adopted him.* | *a foster home*

fought /fɔt/ *verb*
the past tense and past participle of FIGHT

foul[1] /faʊl/ *adjective, formal*
1 a foul smell is very unpleasant: *A foul smell was coming from the garbage.*
2 foul language = rude and offensive words: *I don't allow foul language like that in my house.*
3 foul weather = bad weather, with strong winds, rain, or snow: *We canceled the trip because of the foul weather.*
4 in a foul mood = in a very bad mood and likely to get angry: *I was in a foul mood and didn't want to talk to anyone.*

foul[2] *noun*
an action in a sport that is not allowed by the rules: *In basketball, when you have five fouls you have to leave the game.*

foul[3] *verb*
to do something that is not allowed by the rules of a sport: *He turned to shoot the ball, and Bailey fouled him.*

found[1] /faʊnd/ Ac *verb*
the past tense and past participle of FIND

found[2] *verb*
to start an organization, town, or institution: *The college was founded in 1701.*

foun•da•tion /faʊnˈdeɪʃən/ Ac *noun*
1 a solid base built below the ground to support the building which is on top of it: *The men were laying the foundation* (=building it) *for a new office building.*
2 an idea, fact, or system from which a religion, way of life, etc. develops: *The Constitution is the foundation of the U.S. government.*
3 an organization that gives or collects money to be used for special purposes: *the National Science Foundation*

found•er /ˈfaʊndɚ/ Ac *noun*
someone who starts a business, organization, school, etc.

F

foun•tain /ˈfaʊntən/ *noun*
an object that sends water up into the air: *There was a big fountain in the middle of the park.*

four /fɔr/ *number*
1 4: *Our house has four bedrooms.* | *She met four of her friends in the coffee shop.*
2 four O'CLOCK: *I'll meet you at four.*
3 four years old: *She'll be four next week.*

four•teen /ˌfɔrˈtin/ *number*
1 14: *I found fourteen dollars in my jeans pocket.*
2 fourteen years old: *My Mom wouldn't let me have a TV in my room till I was fourteen.*
—**fourteenth** *number* 14th or 1/14

F

fourth /fɔrθ/ *number, noun*
1 4th
2 1/4 SYNONYM **quarter**

ˌFourth of Juˈly *noun*
a national holiday in the U.S. to celebrate the time when the U.S. first became an independent nation SYNONYM **Independence Day**

fowl /faʊl/ *noun*
a bird such as a chicken that is kept for its meat and eggs

fox /fɑks/ *noun*
a wild animal like a small dog with dark red fur and a thick tail

foy•er /ˈfɔɪɚ/ *noun*
a room at the entrance of a house or large public building such as a hotel or theater

frac•tion /ˈfrækʃən/ *noun*
1 a number that is smaller than 1, such as 3/4 or 1/2: *We're learning how to add fractions at school.*
2 a very small amount of something: *For a fraction of a second it was quiet, and then someone laughed.*
—**fractional** *adjective* very small
—**fractionally** *adverb* by a very small amount

frac•ture¹ /ˈfræktʃɚ/ *noun*
a crack or break in something such as a bone or rock

fracture² *verb*
to crack or break something such as a bone or rock: *He fractured his arm when he fell.*

frag•ile /ˈfrædʒəl/ *adjective*
easily broken or damaged: *The old wine glass was fragile and it broke.*
—**fragility** /frəˈdʒɪləti/ *noun* the quality of being fragile

frag•ment /ˈfrægmənt/ *noun*
a small piece that has broken off a larger object: *The nurse removed fragments of glass from his hand.*
→ See Thesaurus box at **piece**

fra•grance /ˈfreɪgrəns/ *noun*
1 a nice smell: *the sweet fragrance of roses* SYNONYM **smell**
2 *formal* another word for PERFUME

fra•grant /ˈfreɪgrənt/ *adjective*
having a nice smell: *I could smell the fragrant flowers as I walked by the garden.*
—**fragrantly** *adverb*

frail /freɪl/ *adjective*
someone who is frail is thin and weak: *Grandpa looked small and frail in the hospital bed.*
—**frailty** *noun* the condition of being frail

frame¹ /freɪm/ *noun*
1 a structure made of wood or metal that surrounds a picture, door, or window: *a picture frame* | *a door frame*
2 the structure that supports a house, piece of furniture, or vehicle: *a bicycle frame*
3 frames = the part of a pair of glasses that holds the glass LENSes
4 frame of mind = the way you are feeling at a particular time: *Melissa was in a good frame of mind; she talked about the future in a very positive, happy way.*

frame² *verb*
1 to put a picture in a frame: *I'll get the photograph framed and give it Mom for her birthday.*
2 to try to make someone seem guilty of a crime by deliberately giving false information: *He claims that he didn't do anything wrong and that the police framed him.*

frame•work /ˈfreɪmwɚk/ Ac *noun*
1 the basic structure of a building or vehicle, which supports the rest of the building or vehicle: *They have just built the steel framework of the city's tallest building.*
2 the basic structure of a system: *The idea of quality is an important part of the framework of our educational system.*

frank /fræŋk/ *adjective*
someone who is frank says things in an honest and direct way: *To be completely frank with you, Mr. Lee, you don't have enough experience for the job.*
—**frankly** *adverb*: *He always speaks frankly and honestly.*
—**frankness** *noun*

fran•tic /ˈfræntɪk/ *adjective*
1 extremely hurried and not organized: *We realized we were late, and there was a frantic rush to get to the airport.*
2 very worried, anxious, and upset: *He didn't come home, and his mother is frantic with worry.*
—**frantically** *adverb*

fraud /frɔd/ *noun*
1 the crime of deceiving people in order to get money or goods: *The police arrested him for tax fraud* (=deceiving the government so you do not pay taxes).
2 someone who pretends to be someone else in order to deceive people: *He wasn't a real doctor – he was a fraud.*

fraud•u•lent /ˈfrɔdʒələnt/ *adjective, formal*
intended to trick people: *He tried to buy the TV with a fraudulent check, but the bank called the police.*
—**fraudulently** *adverb*

fray /freɪ/ *verb*
if a cloth or rope frays, its threads become loose at the edge because it is old or torn: *The blanket was old and fraying around the edges.*
—**frayed** *adjective*

freak[1] /frik/ *noun, informal*
1 someone who people think is strange or frightening because of the way he or she looks or behaves: *Some freak thought it would be funny to scare the kids.*
2 someone who is very interested in a particular subject or activity, so that other people think he or she is strange: *He is a 14-year-old computer freak who can make a computer do anything.*

freak[2] *adjective*
a freak accident, storm, etc. is very unusual and strange: *A wall fell down in a freak accident and injured two people.*

freck•le /ˈfrekəl/ *noun*
one of many small brown spots on someone's skin: *a little girl with red hair and freckles*
—**freckled** *adjective* having freckles: *She has freckled skin that burns easily in the sun.*
→ See Thesaurus box at **mark**[2]

free[1] /fri/ *adjective*
1 able to do what you want, and not controlled by someone else: *You're free to leave at any time.*
2 not costing any money: *I won free tickets to the concert.*
3 if food, water, etc. is free of something, it does not have that thing in it: *sugar-free bubble gum*
4 not busy doing other things: *Are you free for lunch* (=use this to ask someone if he or she is not too busy to come to lunch with you)? | *What do you enjoy doing in your free time* (=the time when you are not working or studying)?
5 not being used: *Excuse me, is this seat free?*
→ **feel free** at **feel**[1]
WORD FAMILY → **freedom** *noun*

free[2] *adverb*
1 *also* **for free** without having to pay any money: *Students can visit the museum for free* (=paying no money).
2 moving without being controlled or held: *The horses were running free in the field.*

free[3] *verb*
to let someone leave a place where he or she has been forced to stay: *President Lincoln freed the slaves during the Civil War.*

free•bie /ˈfribi/ *noun, informal*
something that a store or business gives you, that you do not have to pay for: *The bank was giving away a radio as a freebie to new customers.*

free•dom /ˈfridəm/ *noun*
1 the state of being free and allowed to do what you want: *Kids had more freedom 30 years ago, when parents did not worry about letting them play outside.*

2 the legal right to do something, without the government stopping you: *The First Amendment says that all Americans have freedom of speech* (=the legal right to say what you want).

free•ly /ˈfrili/ *adverb*
without anyone or anything controlling or stopping something: *People can now travel freely across the border.*

free•way /ˈfriweɪ/ *noun*
a very wide road on which cars can go very fast: *We took the freeway down to Los Angeles.*

F

freeze /friz/ *verb* **froze** /froʊz/ **frozen** /ˈfroʊzən/
1 if water freezes, it becomes solid and hard because it is so cold: *The water in the bucket froze during the night.* ANTONYM **thaw**
2 if you freeze food, you put it in a FREEZER so that you can keep it longer: *Buy two packs of chicken and freeze one.* ANTONYM **thaw**
3 be freezing *informal* = to feel very cold: *It's freezing in here; can we turn up the heat?* | *I'm freezing – I guess I need a warmer coat.*
4 to suddenly stop moving and stay very still: *Officer Greer shouted, "Freeze!"*
➔ **frozen**

freez•er /ˈfrizɚ/ *noun*
a large piece of electrical equipment that freezes food so that you can keep it for a long time: *Put the ice cream in the freezer.*
➔ See picture on page A9

freez•ing /ˈfrizɪŋ/ *noun*
above/below freezing = if the weather is above freezing or below freezing, the temperature is above or below the point at which water freezes (32°F or 0°C): *It was below freezing all day, so we stayed inside.*
➔ See Thesaurus box at **cold**[1]

freight /freɪt/ *noun, formal*
things that trucks, airplanes, or ships take from one place to another: *Trucks take freight from the warehouse to the stores.* | *a freight train* (=one that carries freight)

French[1] /frentʃ/ *adjective*
from France
—**Frenchman** *noun* a man from France
—**Frenchwoman** *noun* a woman from France

French[2] *noun*
1 the language spoken in France and some parts of Switzerland and Canada
2 the people of France

French fries /ˌfrentʃ ˈfraɪz/ *plural noun*
potatoes cut into thin long pieces and cooked in hot oil: *I ordered a hamburger and French fries.*

French toast /ˌfrentʃ ˈtoʊst/ *noun*
bread that you put into a mixture of eggs and milk and then cook in a pan: *Do you want French toast for breakfast?*

fren•zy /ˈfrenzi/ *noun*
a person or animal that is in a frenzy is very worried and excited, and cannot control his, her, or its behavior: *The dogs go into a frenzy of barking and jumping when someone comes to the door.*
—**frenzied** *adjective* feeling very worried and excited

fre•quen•cy /ˈfrikwənsi/ *noun, formal*
1 the number of times that something happens: *The new traffic lights should lower the frequency of accidents.*
2 the rate at which a sound or light WAVE pattern is repeated: *Dogs can hear higher frequencies than humans can.*

fre•quent /ˈfrikwənt/ *adjective, formal*
happening very often: *They make frequent trips to New York.* ANTONYM **infrequent**
—**frequently** *adverb*: *He's frequently late for school – at least once a week.*

WORD FAMILY look at the words:
➔ **frequent** *adjective*
➔ **infrequent** *adjective*
➔ **frequently** *adverb*
➔ **infrequently** *adverb*
➔ **frequency** *noun*

fresh /freʃ/ *adjective*
1 fresh food or flowers have been picked or made only a short time ago: *Eat lots of fresh fruit and vegetables to stay healthy.*
2 adding to or replacing what was there before: *Do you want a fresh cup of coffee?*
3 new and different from what has been done before: *She has some fresh ideas about teaching science.* ANTONYM **old**
4 fresh air = air from outside, especially clean air: *I'm going for a walk to get some fresh air.*

5 fresh water has no salt and comes from rivers and lakes

—**freshly** *adverb*: *freshly baked bread*

—**freshness** *noun*: *The flowers began to lose their freshness.*

→ See Thesaurus box at **new**

fresh·en /ˈfreʃən/ *also* **freshen up** *verb, formal*

to change or clean something so that it seems newer: *Abby freshened up her makeup.*

fresh·man /ˈfreʃmən/ *noun*

a student in the first year of high school or college: *He'll be a freshman in high school this fall; he's going into the ninth grade.*

fret /fret/ *verb*

to worry about things that are not very important: *Keisha was fretting about being late for the party.*

fric·tion /ˈfrɪkʃən/ *noun, formal*

1 if there is friction between people, they disagree and argue with each other a lot: *There was friction between Dad and me for several years before I left home.*

2 the action of one surface rubbing against another: *The brakes on the bike work by the friction of the brake pad against the tire.*

Fri·day /ˈfraɪdi/ *noun, written abbreviation* **Fri.**

the sixth day of the week: *Diane won't be here Friday.* | *I have class on Friday.* | *Next Friday is my birthday.* | *I talked to Jim last Friday.* | *Do you have plans for Friday night?*

fridge /frɪdʒ/ *noun, informal*

a short word for a REFRIGERATOR: *Put the milk back in the fridge.*

fried[1] /fraɪd/ *verb*

the past tense and past participle of the verb FRY

fried[2] *adjective*

cooked in hot oil: *Jim ate a fried egg on toast.*

friend /frend/ *noun*

1 someone whom you like very much and enjoy spending time with: *I'm meeting a friend for lunch.* | *Tom, this is Martha; she's a friend of mine.* | *Tony has been my best friend since second grade.* ANTONYM **enemy**

2 make friends = to start having someone as a friend: *It can be hard to make friends at a new school.*

3 be friends = to be someone's friend: *I've been friends with her for a long time.*

—**friendship** *noun* the state of being friends with someone: *The two girls have formed a close friendship.*

friend·ly /ˈfrendli/ *adjective* **friendlier, friendliest**

someone who is friendly talks to people and behaves in a nice way: *The neighbors seem very friendly.*

—**friendliness** *noun*

fries /fraɪz/ *plural noun*

a short word for FRENCH FRIES: *He ordered a hamburger and fries.*

fright /fraɪt/ *noun*

a feeling of fear: *The boy saw the gun and started shaking with fright.*

> **WORD FAMILY look at the words:**
>
> → **fright** *noun*
> → **frighten** *verb*
> → **frightening** *adjective*
> → **frightened** *adjective*

fright·en /ˈfraɪtn/ *verb*

to make someone feel afraid: *The loud noise frightened her.* SYNONYM **scare**

fright·ened /ˈfraɪtnd/ *adjective*

feeling afraid: *I was always a little frightened of my father.*

> **THESAURUS: frightened**
>
> **afraid** frightened because you think that you may get hurt or that something bad may happen: *She was afraid to go by herself, so she asked her friend to go with her.*
>
> **scared** afraid and nervous about something: *I've always been scared of dogs.*
>
> **terrified** very frightened: *I'm terrified of heights.*
>
> **petrified** very frightened: *He's petrified of snakes.*

fright·en·ing /ˈfraɪtn-ɪŋ/ *adjective*

making you feel afraid: *It was frightening to realize that we were lost in the woods.* SYNONYM **scary**

—**frighteningly** *adverb*

frill /frɪl/ *noun*

1 a piece of cloth with many small folds in it, that you use to decorate clothes or other

things made of cloth: *a dress with lots of frills*
2 something that is nice but not really needed, that can be added to something you buy: *The car has no frills – no air conditioning, no sunroof, no electric windows.*
—**frilly** *adjective* having a lot of frills as decoration: *a frilly blouse*

fringe /frɪndʒ/ *noun*
1 a decoration made of hanging threads, which is sewn to the edge of something such as a curtain or piece of clothing: *a cowboy jacket with leather fringe*
2 *formal* the area that is furthest from the center of something: *New homes are being built on the fringes of the city.* SYNONYM **outskirts**

F

frisk•y /ˈfrɪski/ *adjective*
full of energy, happiness, and fun: *a frisky kitten*

frog /frɔg/ *noun*
a small green or brown animal that lives in or near water and has long legs for jumping: *A frog jumped out of the pond.*

from /frəm; *strong* frʌm/ *preposition*
1 used to say where something starts: *He drove all the way from Colorado to Florida. | Mike brought his report card home from school.*
2 used to say when something starts: *The morning class is from 9:00 to 11:00. | Twenty years from now you'll probably be married and have kids yourself. | You have to go to bed by nine o'clock from now on* (=starting now and going on into the future).
3 used to say how far away something is: *I live about a mile from the school.*
4 used to say where someone was born, lives, or works: *My grandfather came from Mexico. | I'm from Minneapolis. | Someone from the library is going to talk to the class.*
5 used to say who has given or sent something: *Who is the present from?*
6 used to say where something was originally: *Will you get me a chair from the kitchen? | This box is from China.*
7 used to say what something is made of: *Ice cream is made from milk and sugar.*
8 used to say where you are when you see or do something: *From the top of the mountain, you can see the ocean.*

front[1] /frʌnt/ *noun*
1 the part of something that is furthest forward: *The front of the store is painted blue. | Good students usually sit near the front of the room.* ANTONYM **back**
2 the most important side of something, that you look at first: *The book had a picture of a lion on the front. | The front of your T-shirt has ketchup on it.* ANTONYM **back**
3 in front of someone or something a) ahead of someone or something: *There's a big tree in front of their house. | Two girls were standing in front of me in line.* **b)** facing someone or something: *They ate dinner in front of the TV.* ANTONYM **behind**
4 in front of someone = when someone is there: *Her parents never argue in front of their kids.*
5 out front = in the area near the entrance to the building that you are in: *The boys were playing out front.*

front[2] *adjective*
at, on, or in the front of something: *The front door was locked. | He got in the front seat of the car.* ANTONYM **back**

fron•tier /frʌnˈtɪr/ *noun*
1 the frontier = the edge of an area of land where people have not lived before and where they are just beginning to live: *In the 1880s, the land that is now Colorado and Utah was still the frontier.*
2 *formal* the place where two countries meet: *There has been fighting along the frontier.* SYNONYM **border**

frost /frɔst/ *noun*
a white powder of ice that covers things that are outside when it is very cold: *The trees were white with frost.*
—**frosty** *adjective* very cold and with frost
→ See Thesaurus box at **snow**[1]

frost•bite /ˈfrɔstbaɪt/ *noun*
if you get frostbite, parts of your body freeze and are badly damaged: *His hands had frostbite after he got lost and spent the night in the snow.*

frost•ing /ˈfrɔstɪŋ/ *noun*
a mixture made with sugar, that you put on a cake: *a cake with chocolate frosting* SYNONYM **icing**

frown /fraʊn/ *verb*
to look angry or unhappy by moving your EYEBROWS and the edges of your mouth

downward: *The coach frowned as Steve missed the shot.*
—**frown** *noun* an angry or unhappy expression you make when you frown

froze /froʊz/ *verb*
the past tense of FREEZE

fro•zen[1] /ˈfroʊzən/ *verb*
the past participle of FREEZE

frozen[2] *adjective*
1 food that is frozen has been kept very cold: *a bag of frozen peas*
2 made into ice because of the cold: *People were skating on the frozen lake.*
➔ See picture at **melt**

fruit /frut/ *noun*
something such as an apple or orange that grows on a plant or tree, can be eaten as food, contains seeds, and is usually sweet: *Bananas are my favorite fruit.* | *I always have a piece of fruit in my lunch box.*

fruit•ful /ˈfrutfəl/ *adjective, formal*
producing something that is good or useful: *Spielberg has had a fruitful career as a movie director.*

frus•trate /ˈfrʌstreɪt/ *verb*
1 if something frustrates you, it makes you feel annoyed or angry because you cannot do or have what you want: *It really frustrates me when my parents don't listen to me.*
2 *formal* to stop someone from being able to do something: *Computer problems frustrated their effort to finish the work on time.*
—**frustrated** *adjective* annoyed and angry because you cannot do or have what you want: *David got really frustrated because he couldn't understand the math homework.*
—**frustrating** *adjective* making you feel frustrated: *It's so frustrating when the team plays really well, but we still lose.*
—**frustration** /frʌˈstreɪʃən/ *noun* the feeling of being frustrated: *He couldn't do the puzzle, and started crying in frustration.*

fry /fraɪ/ *verb* **fried**
to cook something in hot oil, butter, etc.: *I fried some bacon for breakfast.*
➔ See Thesaurus box at **cook[1]**
➔ See picture on page A14

ˈfrying ˌpan *noun*
a round flat pan with a handle that you use to fry food
➔ See picture on page A9

ft.
the written abbreviation of **foot**

fudge /fʌdʒ/ *noun*
a kind of soft candy, made with butter, sugar, milk, and usually chocolate: *He ate a piece of fudge.*

fu•el /ˈfyuəl/ *noun*
a substance such as coal, gas, or oil that you can burn to make heat or power: *The plane has enough fuel to fly from Chicago to Los Angeles.*
—**fuel** *verb* to put fuel in a car, airplane, etc.

fu•gi•tive /ˈfyudʒətɪv/ *noun, formal*
someone who is trying to avoid being caught by the police: *He is a fugitive who the police have been looking for for months.*

ful•fill /fʊlˈfɪl/ *verb, formal*
to do something you wanted or promised to do: *Mr. Jackson fulfilled his promise and gave Robert a job.*
—**fulfillment** *noun* the act of doing something you wanted or promised to do

full /fʊl/ *adjective*
1 something that is full has as many things or people as possible in it: *This suitcase is full; I can't fit any more clothes into it.* | *a full carton of milk* ANTONYM **empty**

THESAURUS: full

filled with something full of something: *The bucket was filled with water.*

packed extremely full of people or things: *The stadium was packed with fans.*

crammed full of people or things: *The book is crammed with information.*

2 be full of something = to contain many things of the same kind: *Eric's essay is full of mistakes.* | *The room was full of people.*
3 if you are full, you have eaten a lot and cannot eat any more: *"Would you like some more soup?" "No thanks. I'm full."*
4 complete and including everything: *What is your full name and address?* | *It was a full year before she was able to get a job.*
5 the highest level or biggest amount of something that is possible: *The ship was going at full speed.* | *I bought this dress on sale; I didn't pay full price for it.*
➔ See picture at **empty[1]**

F

ˌfull-ˈlength *adjective*
1 not shorter than the usual length: *"Snow White" was the first full-length cartoon movie.*
2 showing all of a person: *a full-length mirror*
3 a full-length skirt or dress reaches the ground

ˌfull ˈmoon *noun*
the moon when it looks completely round

ˌfull-ˈtime *adverb*
if you work or study full-time, you work or study for the usual number of hours that people are expected to: *Angela works full-time and takes an evening class.*
—**ˈfull-time** *adjective* working or studying full-time: *a full-time student*

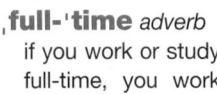

ful·ly /ˈfʊli/ *adverb*
completely: *The snake can be six feet long when it is fully grown.*

fum·ble /ˈfʌmbəl/ *verb*
1 to try to hold, move, or find something with your hands in an awkward way: *Gary fumbled for the light switch in the dark.*
2 to drop a football after catching it: *He caught the pass, but then fumbled the ball as he fell.*
—**fumble** *noun* the act of dropping a football

fumes /fyumz/ *plural noun*
gas or smoke that has an unpleasant smell: *Exhaust fumes from cars, buses, trucks, and planes pollute the air.*

fun¹ /fʌn/ *noun*
1 enjoyment or pleasure that you get from an activity: *Swimming is a lot of fun.* | *All the kids were having fun at the party.* | *He began running in college for fun, and now he's on the track team.*

USAGE: fun

Use **fun** to talk about situations or activities that you enjoy: *Swimming is a lot of fun.*

Use **funny** to describe someone or something that makes you laugh: *The movie was so funny we couldn't stop laughing.*

2 make fun of someone or something = to make unkind jokes about someone or something: *Some children made fun of him because he liked to dance.*

fun² *adjective*
an activity that is fun is enjoyable: *There are lots of fun things to do at the beach.*

func·tion¹ /ˈfʌŋkʃən/ Ac *noun*
1 the purpose that something has, or the job that something or someone does: *The function of the kidneys is to remove waste from your body.*
2 a large party or social event: *The room is available for weddings and other social functions.*
—**functional** *adjective* designed to be useful or do a particular job, rather than to look attractive

WORD FAMILY look at the words:

→ **function** *noun*
→ **function** *verb*
→ **functional** *adjective*

function² *verb, formal*
to work in a particular way: *The air conditioning isn't functioning properly.* SYNONYM **work**

PHRASAL VERB
function as something
to be used in a particular way: *The building still functions as an office.*

fund¹ /fʌnd/ Ac *noun*
1 an amount of money that is collected for a particular purpose: *the congressman's campaign fund*
2 funds = the money that an organization needs or has: *The organization helps raise funds for the school.*

fund² *verb*
to pay money for an activity, organization, or person: *The government is funding the project.* SYNONYM **pay for**

fun·da·men·tal /ˌfʌndəˈmentl/ Ac *adjective, formal*
1 relating to the most basic and important parts of something: *When my dad lost his job, there was a fundamental change in the way we lived.* SYNONYM **basic**
2 necessary for something to exist or develop: *Water is fundamental to life.* SYNONYM **necessary**
—**fundamentally** *adverb, formal*: *The band's*

music is fundamentally different now; they used to play rock, but now they play hip-hop.

fu·ner·al /ˈfyunərəl/ *noun*
a ceremony at which a dead person's body is buried or CREMATED (=burned): *There will be a funeral service in the Baptist church.*

fun·gus /ˈfʌŋgəs/ *noun* plural **fungi** /ˈfʌndʒaɪ/ or **funguses**
a growing thing like a plant without leaves that grows in wet places: *Mushrooms are a type of fungus.*
—**fungal** *adjective* caused by a fungus: *fungal infections*

funk·y /ˈfʌŋki/ *adjective, informal*
1 fashionable and interesting in an unusual way: *She was wearing some really funky pants.*
2 funky music has a strong RHYTHM that is easy to dance to

fun·nel /ˈfʌnl/ *noun*
a tube that is wide at the top and narrow at the bottom, used for pouring liquids or powders into a container

funnel

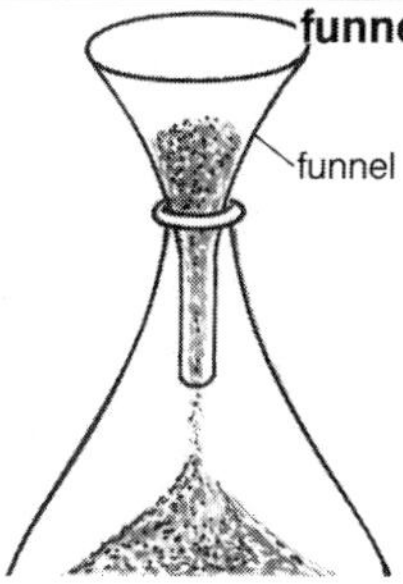

funny /ˈfʌni/ *adjective* **funnier**, **funniest**
1 if something is funny, it makes you laugh: *She told a funny story about forgetting to bring her shoes to the wedding.* | *I thought the show was very funny.*

THESAURUS: funny

hilarious very funny: *This book is hilarious; it's all about this guy's trip through Europe and the stupid things that happen.*
witty using words in a funny and intelligent way: *She's a smart, witty woman who always has something interesting to say.*
corny *informal* corny jokes, stories, movies, etc. are like ones you have heard or seen before and are so silly that they are not funny: *Dad told us a few corny jokes he'd heard at work.*
amusing *formal* funny and entertaining: *The movie is full of amusing surprises.*
humorous *formal* funny: *There's a humorous story in the newspaper about a dog that flies kites.*

2 strange and difficult to understand or explain: *We heard a funny noise.* | *Your voice sounds funny. Do you have a cold?*
3 feel funny = to feel slightly sick
➔ See Thesaurus box at **strange**[1]

fur /fɚ/ *noun*
the thick soft hair that covers the bodies of some animals, such as dogs and cats: *The dog's fur was thick and soft.*
—**fur** *adjective* made of fur: *a fur coat*

fu·ri·ous /ˈfyʊriəs/ *adjective*
1 very angry: *Dad was furious that I had taken the car without asking.*
2 happening very quickly or done with a lot of energy or anger: *New businesses started opening at a furious pace* (=very quickly).
—**furiously** *adverb*
➔ See Thesaurus box at **angry**

fur·nace /ˈfɚnɪs/ *noun*
a large container with a fire inside it, used to produce heat in a building or to melt metal

fur·nish /ˈfɚnɪʃ/ *verb*
1 to put furniture and other things into a room, house, etc.: *We furnished the room with two beds and a dresser.*
2 *formal* to give or provide something: *The U.S. embassy can furnish you with a visa application form.*
—**furnished** *adjective* a furnished room, building, etc. already has furniture in it: *a furnished apartment*

fur·nish·ings /ˈfɚnɪʃɪŋz/ *plural noun, formal*
the furniture and other things in a room, such as curtains, lights, etc.

fur·ni·ture /ˈfɚnɪtʃɚ/ *noun*
objects such as chairs, tables, and beds that you use in a room, office, etc.: *The only piece of furniture in the room was an old sofa.* | *office furniture*

GRAMMAR: furniture

Do not say "furnitures." You can say **some furniture**, **any furniture**, or **pieces of furniture**: *When we first got married, we didn't have any furniture at all.*

F

fur•ry /ˈfəi/ *adjective*
1 a furry animal has a body that is covered in fur
2 covered with fur or in a material that looks like fur: *furry slippers*

fur•ther¹ /ˈfəðə/ *adverb*
1 more, or to a greater degree: *I have nothing further to say because I don't have any new information.*
2 take something further = to continue doing something at higher or more serious levels: *The lawyers decided not to take the case further because they knew they couldn't win.*
3 used to say that a place is a greater distance away than another place: *We sailed further down the coast toward North Carolina.* SYNONYM **farther**
4 used to say that a time is longer away than another time: *We have to plan for the future and look further ahead, beyond the next ten years.* SYNONYM **farther**

> **USAGE: further**
>
> Use **further** to talk about time, amounts, or the level of something: *Your grades cannot drop further, or you won't be able to play on the soccer team.* | *I don't want to discuss this any further.*
>
> Use **farther** to talk about distance: *Room 211 is just a little farther down the hall.*
>
> Many people use **further** in spoken English to talk about distance, but many teachers think that this is not correct.

➔ See Thesaurus box at **more²**

further² *adjective, formal*
additional or more: *Further information is available on the website.* SYNONYM **more**

fur•ther•more /ˈfəðəˌmɔr/ [Ac] *adverb, formal*
in addition to what has already been written or said: *Mary had no family. Furthermore, she had few friends to help her.*

fur•thest /ˈfəðɪst/ *adjective, adverb*
1 at the greatest distance from a place or person: *The houses furthest away from the center of town are the most expensive.* SYNONYM **farthest**
2 to the greatest degree or amount: *Smith's book has probably gone furthest* (=done the most) *in explaining these events.*

fu•ry /ˈfyʊri/ *noun*
a feeling of very strong anger: *She was shaking with fury and yelling at the man who hit her car.*

fuse /fyuz/ *noun*
1 a thin wire inside a piece of electrical equipment that breaks and prevents damage to the equipment if too much electricity passes through it: *The lights went out when a fuse blew* (=broke).
2 a part that is connected to a bomb, used for making a bomb explode: *He lit the fuse and ran.*
3 have a short fuse = used for saying that someone becomes angry: *Mom has a short fuse* (=gets angry easily) *when she's tired.*

fu•sion /ˈfyuʒən/ *noun, formal*
1 a combination of separate things: *a fusion of Japanese and Californian cooking*
2 a process in which different substances are combined together, using heat: *The Sun produces energy by nuclear fusion.*

fuss¹ /fʌs/ *noun*
1 attention, excitement, or activity that is given to something unimportant: *They wanted a quiet wedding without any fuss.*
2 make a fuss/kick up a fuss = to complain or become angry about something, especially something unimportant: *Don't be afraid to make a fuss if they don't give you what you asked for.*
3 make a fuss over someone = to give too much attention to someone: *Don't make a fuss over him; he's just crying because he wants attention.*

fuss² *verb*
PHRASAL VERBS
fuss over someone
to give a lot of attention to someone, especially a child: *The women started fussing over Kate's baby.*
fuss with something
to continuously move or touch something in a way that shows you are nervous: *Stop fussing with your clothes; you look great!*

fuss•y /ˈfʌsi/ *adjective* **fussier, fussiest**
1 someone who is fussy about something is not satisfied until every detail is exactly right, which makes them difficult to please: *He's*

very fussy about his clothes – he won't wear anything that he thinks isn't cool. SYNONYM **picky**

2 a fussy baby cries a lot

—**fussily** *adverb*

—**fussiness** *noun*

fu·tile /ˈfyutl/ *adjective, formal*

actions that are futile have no chance of being successful, and are not worth doing: *I made a futile attempt to calm her down, but she just kept crying.*

—**futility** /fyuˈtɪləti/ *noun, formal* the fact that something you do is futile: *We realized the futility of our efforts to put out such a huge fire.*

fu·ture¹ /ˈfyutʃɚ/ *noun*

1 the future = the time after the present: *He talked about his plans for the future.* | *We plan to open a new library in the near future* (=soon). ANTONYM **past**

2 the things that will happen to someone or something in the future: *The president said he had great plans for the country's future, with better jobs and health care for everyone.* | *the future of the human race*

3 the future = the FUTURE TENSE

future² *adjective, formal*

relating to or happening in the future: *What are your future plans?* | *A good degree will help you in your future career.* ANTONYM **past**

ˈfuture ˌtense *noun*

the form of a verb that you use when you are talking about the future. In English "I will go" is in the future tense.

fuzz·y /ˈfʌzi/ *adjective, informal*

1 covered with short soft hair or fur: *fuzzy slippers*

2 unclear and confusing: *It happened a long time ago and my memory is fuzzy now.*

3 if a sound or picture is fuzzy, it is not clear: *Unfortunately, a lot of the photographs are fuzzy.*

Gg

g.
the written abbreviation of **gram**

G /dʒi/ *noun*
the fifth note in the musical SCALE of C, or the musical KEY based on this note

gadg•et /ˈgædʒɪt/ *noun*
a small tool or machine, especially a new one: *He has a new gadget for opening jars.*
➔ See Thesaurus box at **machine**[1]

G

gag /gæg/ *noun*
1 *informal* a joke: *The show had some good gags in it.*
2 a piece of cloth that someone ties over your mouth so that you cannot speak
—**gag** *verb* to tie a piece of cloth over someone's mouth: *They tied him up and gagged him.*

gain /geɪn/ *verb*
1 to get something important or useful: *It was four hours before firefighters gained control of the fire.* | *I've gained a lot from taking the writing class; I feel much more confident.* ANTONYM **lose**
2 gain weight/speed/popularity, etc. = to become heavier, faster, more popular, etc.: *If you eat a lot of fried food, you will gain weight.* ANTONYM **lose**
—**gain** *noun* the act of gaining something: *What is the reason for his weight gain?*

gait /geɪt/ *noun, formal*
the way that someone walks: *He walked with an unsteady gait.*

gal•ax•y /ˈgæləksi/ *noun* plural **galaxies**
a very large group of stars: *There are billions of stars in the galaxy.*
—**galactic** /gəˈlæktɪk/ *adjective, formal* relating to a galaxy

gale /geɪl/ *noun*
a very strong wind: *Several trees blew down in the gale.*
➔ See Thesaurus box at **wind**[1]

gal•ler•y /ˈgæləri/ *noun* plural **galleries**
a room or building where people can look at or buy art: *We went to an exhibit at the National Gallery of Art.*

gal•lon /ˈgælən/ *noun*
a unit for measuring liquid, equal to eight PINTS: *I put five gallons of gas in the car.*

gallop

gal•lop /ˈgæləp/ *verb*
if a horse gallops, it runs very fast
—**gallop** *noun* the fastest speed that a horse can run: *He was riding at a gallop.*

gam•ble[1] /ˈgæmbəl/ *verb*
to try to win money by playing cards, guessing the result of a race or game, etc.: *He couldn't stop gambling and lost all his money.*
—**gambler** *noun* someone who gambles
—**gambling** *noun* the activity of gambling

gamble[2] *noun*
an action that might not have a successful result: *I took a gamble, and quit my job to become an actor.* SYNONYM **risk**

game /geɪm/ *noun*
1 a sport or enjoyable activity in which you try to win: *My favorite game is basketball.* | *My brother spends a lot of time playing computer games.* | *The kids were outside playing games.*

THESAURUS: game

sport a physical activity in which people or teams play against each other and try to win: *Her favorite sport is basketball.*
recreation activities that you do for fun: *Kids need safe places for recreation.*
hobby an activity that you do in your free time: *Her hobbies are reading and music.*

2 a particular occasion when people play a

type of game: *We won the basketball game last night.* | *Let's play a game of chess.*

3 play games (with someone) = to behave dishonestly toward someone: *Don't play games with me – I know you're not telling me the truth.*

4 wild animals and birds that people hunt: *He hunts deer and other game.*

'game show *noun*

a television program in which people play games in order to win prizes

➔ See Thesaurus box at **television**

gang¹ /gæŋ/ *noun*

1 a group of people who do something together: *A gang of kids were hanging out on the basketball court.*

2 an organized group of young people living in a city who may cause trouble and be involved in violent activities: *A teenage gang member was shot in his car last night.*

➔ See Thesaurus box at **group¹**

gang² *verb*

PHRASAL VERB

gang up on someone

if a group of people gangs up on someone, they all criticize, attack, or make jokes about him or her: *My brothers used to gang up on me and tease me.*

gang·ster /'gæŋstɚ/ *noun*

a member of a group of violent criminals

gap /gæp/ *noun*

1 an empty space between two things or two parts of something: *I squeezed through a gap in the fence.* | *She has a big gap between her two front teeth.*

2 a difference between two people, things, or groups: *We should be trying to bridge the gap between rich and poor* (=make the difference between rich people and poor people smaller).

3 something that is missing, so that something else is not good or complete: *The new information fills a gap in our knowledge of biology* (=makes our knowledge more complete).

➔ See Thesaurus box at **hole**

gap·ing /'geɪpɪŋ/ *adjective*

a gaping hole is very wide: *There were gaping holes in his pants.*

ga·rage /gə'rɑʒ/ *noun*

1 a building connected to your house where you keep your car: *Did you close the garage door?*

2 a place where cars are repaired: *The guy at the garage said he could fix my car today.*

3 another word for a PARKING GARAGE

ga'rage ˌsale *noun*

a sale of things that you no longer want, inside or outside your garage: *My parents bought a lot of our toys at garage sales.*

gar·bage /'gɑrbɪdʒ/ *noun*

1 waste food, paper, etc., or the container you put it in: *Throw the wrapper in the garbage.* | *Can somebody take out the garbage* (=put it outside so that a garbage truck can take it away)?

THESAURUS: garbage

trash things that you throw away, such as old food and dirty paper: *Six bags were full of trash.*

refuse *formal* things that you throw away, such as old food and dirty paper: *The city buries the refuse it collects.*

litter garbage, especially pieces of paper, food containers, etc., that people leave on the ground in public places: *The Scouts picked up litter in the park.*

waste *formal* things that are left after you have used something: *Is there a way to safely get rid of waste from nuclear power stations?*

2 *informal* something someone says that is very bad or silly: *I'm not going to listen to this garbage – nothing you are saying is true.*

'garbage ˌcan *noun*

a large container outside your home in which you put waste SYNONYM **trash can**

➔ See picture on page A9

'garbage colˌlector *also* **'garbage ˌman** *noun*

someone whose job is to take away the things inside garbage cans

'garbage ˌtruck *noun*

a large vehicle that carries away things from garbage cans

gar·den /'gɑrdn/ *noun*

a piece of land where you grow flowers or vegetables, next to your house or in a public place: *She's outside working in the vegetable garden.*

G

gar•den•ing /ˈgɑrdnɪŋ/ *noun*
the work of growing plants in a garden: *My Dad does all the gardening.*
—**gardener** *noun* someone who works in a garden, especially as a job

gar•gle /ˈgɑrgəl/ *verb*
to clean your throat by breathing out while you have a liquid in the back of your mouth: *If you have a sore throat, try gargling with salt water.*

gar•lic /ˈgɑrlɪk/ *noun*
a small plant like an onion that is used to give a strong taste to food
—**garlicky** *adjective* tasting or smelling of garlic
➔ See picture on page A12

G

gar•ment /ˈgɑrmənt/ *noun, formal*
a piece of clothing: *The women wore simple black garments.*

gas /gæs/ *noun* plural **gases**
1 a liquid that you put in a car to make it go: *I had to stop for gas.* SYNONYM **gasoline**
2 a substance like air. People burn some kinds of gas to heat their houses or cook food: *Oxygen is a gas.* | *a gas stove*
3 the gas = the PEDAL that you use to make a car go faster: *He started the car and stepped on the gas* (=pushed down on the pedal).

gas•e•ous /ˈgæsiəs/ *adjective, formal*
in a form like air: *gaseous fuels*

gash /gæʃ/ *noun*
a deep cut: *She had a gash in her leg that was bleeding.*
—**gash** *verb* to make a deep cut in something

gas•o•line /ˌgæsəˈlin/ *noun*
a liquid that you put in a car to make it go SYNONYM **gas**

gasp /gæsp/ *verb*
to breathe in quickly and loudly, once or several times: *The audience gasped with surprise.* | *She put her head above the water and gasped for air.*
—**gasp** *noun* a quick breath in: *a gasp of astonishment*
➔ See Thesaurus box at **breathe**

ˈgas ˌstation *noun*
a place where you can buy gas for your car

gate /geɪt/ *noun*
1 a door in a fence or outside wall: *Who left the gate open?*
2 a place where you leave an airport building to get on a plane: *Passengers for Flight 186 should go to Gate 7.*
➔ See picture on page A30

gate•way /ˈgeɪtweɪ/ *noun*
the gateway to something = a place from which you can reach another place: *St. Louis was once the gateway to the western part of the U.S.*

gath•er /ˈgæðɚ/ *verb*
1 to come together in a group: *A crowd gathered to watch the fight.* | *Children gathered around him.*
2 *also* **gather up** to bring things from different places together: *She gathered up her clothes and put them in a suitcase.*
3 to think something because of what you have heard: *I heard her talking to her friend, and I gather (that) they are moving to Chicago.*

gath•er•ing /ˈgæðərɪŋ/ *noun*
a meeting of a group of people: *We have a family gathering every summer when all my cousins, aunts, and uncles come to our house.*

gauge¹ /geɪdʒ/ *noun*
an instrument that measures something: *The gas gauge showed that the car needed more gas.*

gauge² *verb*
to find out or measure how good, big, etc. something is: *How do teachers gauge the amount of progress a student has made?* | *I wanted to ask him to help me, so I talked to him for a minute to gauge his mood* (=find out if he was in a good mood or bad mood). SYNONYM **find out, measure**

gauze /gɔz/ *noun*
a type of very thin cloth used for covering wounds and making clothes

gave /geɪv/ *verb*
the past tense of GIVE

gay /geɪ/ *adjective*
1 sexually attracted to people of the same sex: *Do you think he's gay?* SYNONYM **homosexual**; ANTONYM **straight**
2 an old-fashioned word meaning bright or happy: *The room was painted in gay colors.*

gaze /geɪz/ *verb*
to look at someone or something for a long time: *He gazed at his reflection in the mirror.*
—**gaze** *noun, formal* a long, steady look: *She turned her gaze back to the TV* (=looked back at the TV).
→ See Thesaurus box at **look**[1]

gear /gɪr/ *noun*
1 part of a car, bicycle, etc. that makes it move well at different speeds: *She shifted into first gear, and the car moved forward slowly.*
2 special equipment or clothes that you need for an activity: *camping gear*

gear•shift /ˈgɪrˌʃɪft/ *noun*
a stick that you move to change gears when driving a car
→ See picture on page A28

GED *noun*
General Equivalency Diploma an official piece of paper that people who did not finish HIGH SCHOOL can get by taking a test

gee /dʒi/
something you say when you are surprised, excited, etc.: *Gee, that pie smells good!*

geese /gis/ *noun*
the plural of GOOSE

gel /dʒel/ *noun*
a thick clear wet substance: *He uses hair gel to make his hair stick up.*

gel•a•tin /ˈdʒelətən/ *noun*
a clear substance that is used to make foods such as Jell-O more solid

gem /dʒem/ *noun*
1 a valuable stone that has been cut into a particular shape: *diamonds and other gems* SYNONYM **jewel**
2 *informal* something that is very good or special: *This book is a gem that every teenager should read.*

Gem•i•ni /ˈdʒeməˌnaɪ/ *noun*
1 the third sign of the ZODIAC, represented by TWINS
2 someone born between May 21 and June 21

gem•stone /ˈdʒemˌstoʊn/ *noun*
a valuable stone

gen•der /ˈdʒendɚ/ Ac *noun, formal*
1 the fact of being male or female: *You cannot choose the gender of a baby.*
2 in grammar, the fact of being MASCULINE, FEMININE, or NEUTER: *In some languages, like Spanish, nouns have different genders.*

gene /dʒin/ *noun*
a part of a cell in a living thing that controls what the living thing is like, for example what color someone's eyes are, how tall a plant is, etc.

gen•er•al[1] /ˈdʒenərəl/ *adjective*
1 relating to the whole of something or to the main parts: *Except for one cold, my general health has been good.* | *The class is a general introduction to computers.*
2 in general a) usually or mostly: *In general, I am happier than I used to be.* SYNONYM **overall b)** used when talking about all things or people of one type: *I like animals in general, and dogs in particular.*
3 including or relating to most people, things, etc.: *The drug is not yet available for general use* (=use by most people).

WORD FAMILY look at the words:
→ **general** *adjective*
→ **generally** *adverb*
→ **generalize** *verb*
→ **generalization** *noun*

general[2] *noun*
an officer with a very high rank in the Army, Air Force, or Marines

gen•er•al•ize /ˈdʒenərəˌlaɪz/ *verb*
to say something about people or things of a particular kind which may not be true about all of them: *You shouldn't generalize about women by saying that they are all bad drivers.*
—**generalization** /ˌdʒenərələˈzeɪʃən/ *noun* a statement in which someone generalizes: *Don't make generalizations because they are almost never true.*

gen•er•al•ly /ˈdʒenərəli/ *adverb*
1 usually or mostly: *I generally go to bed at about 11, but sometimes it's later.* | *Her school work is generally very good.*
2 by most people: *She is generally thought to be* (=most people think she is) *one of the best singers in the world.*

gen•er•ate /ˈdʒenəˌreɪt/ Ac *verb*
to produce something: *We burn coal to generate electricity.* | *The program will generate a lot of new jobs.*
WORD FAMILY → **generator** *noun*

G

gen·er·a·tion /ˌdʒenəˈreɪʃən/ Ac *noun*
1 the people in a society or family who are about the same age: *Three generations of my family have lived in this house – first my grandparents, then my parents, and now me.*
2 a period of about 25 years, which is the time between two generations of a family: *A generation ago, video games were pretty simple.*

gen·er·a·tor /ˈdʒenəˌreɪtɚ/ *noun*
a machine that makes electricity

gen·er·os·i·ty /ˌdʒenəˈrɑsəti/ *noun*
generous behavior: *Thank you for your generosity; the money you have given us has been very helpful to our work.*

G

gen·er·ous /ˈdʒenərəs/ *adjective*
someone who is generous gives a lot of help, money, things, etc.: *She's always been generous to the kids.* | *He is generous with his time* (=is willing to spend time helping people). | *generous gifts*
—**generously** *adverb*

ge·net·ics /dʒəˈnetɪks/ *noun*
the study of GENEs
—**genetic** *adjective* relating to or caused by genes: *He was born with a genetic disease that caused problems with his heart.*

ge·nius /ˈdʒiniəs/ *noun*
someone who has much more intelligence, ability, or skill than is usual: *Mozart was a musical genius who was writing music when he was five years old.*

gen·o·cide /ˈdʒenəˌsaɪd/ *noun, formal*
an attempt to kill a whole race of people

gen·re /ˈʒɑnrə/ *noun, formal*
a particular type of art, music, writing, etc.: *Science fiction is my favorite genre of literature.*

gen·tle /ˈdʒentl/ *adjective*
1 kind, and careful not to hurt anyone or anything: *Be gentle with the baby – don't hurt her.*
2 not strong, loud, or extreme: *She sang in a gentle voice, and I fell asleep.* | *The gentle breeze was just enough to keep us cool.*
—**gently** *adverb*: *His mother gently wiped away his tears.*
—**gentleness** *noun*

gen·tle·man /ˈdʒentlmən/ *noun* plural **gentlemen** /ˈdʒentlmən/
1 a polite word for a man you do not know: *Can you show this gentleman to his seat?* | *Thank you, ladies and gentlemen.*
2 a man who is polite and behaves well: *He was always a gentleman around my parents, so they liked him.*

gen·u·ine /ˈdʒenyuɪn/ *adjective*
real, not pretended or false: *Her surprise was genuine – she really didn't know about the party.* | *Is the stone a genuine diamond?*
—**genuinely** *adverb*: *He seemed genuinely sad; I don't think he was trying to make us feel sorry for him.*

ge·og·ra·phy /dʒiˈɑgrəfi/ *noun*
the study of the Earth's surface and the countries of the world: *We're studying the geography of South America in science class.*
—**geographical** /ˌdʒiəˈgræfɪkəl/ *also* **geographic** *adjective* relating to the Earth's surface and the countries of the world: *The map shows geographical features such as mountains and rivers.*

ge·ol·o·gy /dʒiˈɑlədʒi/ *noun*
the study of rocks and soil
—**geologist** *noun* someone who studies rocks and soil
—**geological** /ˌdʒiəˈlɑdʒɪkəl/ *adjective* relating to rocks and soil: *the geological processes that form rocks*

ge·om·e·try /dʒiˈɑmətri/ *noun*
the study of shapes, lines, etc. and the mathematics relating to them
—**geometric** /ˌdʒiəˈmetrɪk/ *adjective* relating to or made of shapes, lines, etc.: *a geometric pattern*

germ /dʒɚm/ *noun*
a living thing that can make you sick, which is too small to see: *Sneezing spreads germs.*

Ger·man /ˈdʒɚmən/ *noun*
1 someone from Germany
2 the language spoken in Germany, Austria and parts of Switzerland
—**German** *adjective* from Germany

ˌGerman ˈshepherd *noun*
a large strong dog that is used by the police and for guarding property, and has black, gray, or brown fur

ges·ture[1] /ˈdʒestʃɚ/ *noun*
a movement of your hand, arms, or head, that shows what you mean or how you feel: *He made a gesture with his hands to show that he didn't understand what I was saying.*

gesture[2] *verb*
to move your hand, arms, or head, in order to tell someone something: *I gestured for the waiter to come over to our table.*

get /get/ *verb* **got** /gɑt/ **gotten** /ˈgɑtn/ **getting**
1 to receive or be given something: *Did you get my email? | I got an A in Spanish. | She got lots of presents for her birthday from her friends. | I got a shock when I saw how high the price was.*
2 to obtain or buy something: *Where did you get those shoes* (=what store did you buy them in)?
3 have got = to have something. "Have got" is used in spoken English. We usually shorten it to "I've/you've/they've got", and "she's/he's got": *I've got a lot of work to do.*
4 to become: *It gets very hot here in the summer.*

USAGE: get

Get, **become**, and **go** can all mean "to begin to be something," but they are used in different ways.

Get and **go** are less formal than **become**, and are used more often in spoken English: *I got very hungry. | Have you gone crazy?*

Become is used in both written and spoken English: *He's becoming a very good tennis player. | The area has become popular with mountain bikers.*

Get and **go** are used only in front of an adjective (=word that describes something): *It's getting dark. | Beethoven went deaf when he was 40 years old.*

Become can be used in front of an adjective or a noun: *It became clear that Scott was not doing his work. | The noise from the airport is becoming a problem.*

5 to move somewhere: *Get down on the floor! | They couldn't get out of the building.*
6 to arrive or reach somewhere: *We got home very late.* SYNONYM **arrive**
7 to catch an illness or disease: *I think I'm getting a cold. | I got sick, and couldn't go to the restaurant.*
8 to go onto a bus, plane, train, etc.: *He got the next plane to New York.* SYNONYM **catch**
9 to bring someone or something back from somewhere: *She's gone to get the kids from school.* SYNONYM **pick up**

USAGE: get

get to go to another place and come back with something or someone: *Just a minute while I get my jacket.*

bring to take something or someone to a place: *You should bring her some flowers. | Elise brought her friend with her to the party.*

take to move something from one place to another, or help someone go from one place to another: *You'd better take your jacket – it's getting cold. | I can take you home after the concert.*

10 to arrange for something to be done: *I need to get my car fixed.*
11 get to do something = if you get to do something, you are able to do it: *We got to see a lot of famous places.*
12 get someone to do something = to persuade someone to do something: *I'll see if I can get them to change the dates.* SYNONYM **persuade**
13 to reach a particular stage in a process: *I started reading the book, but I never got to the end.*
14 to understand something: *I didn't get the joke.*

PHRASAL VERBS

get ahead
to become more successful in your work: *She wants to get ahead and run her own company.*

get along (with someone)
to have a friendly relationship with someone: *The two boys seem to get along well with each other.*

get around something
to avoid something that will cause problems: *I'm sure there is a way of getting around the problem.*

get around to doing something
to do something you have been intending to do for a long time: *I still haven't gotten around to calling her – I've been too busy.*

get away
to escape: *The police tried to stop the man, but he got away.*

get back
1 to return: *When do you get back from your vacation?*
2 to reply to someone at a later time: *Thanks for your call. I'll get back to you soon.*

get behind
to be late with your work, your payments for something, etc.: *I'm getting behind with my homework.*

get in
1 to arrive somewhere: *What time does your flight get in?*
2 get something in = to give something to someone, especially written work: *Make sure that you get your assignment in on time.* SYNONYM **turn in**

get into something
1 to be allowed to go to a school, college, or university: *She is hoping to get into Harvard.*
2 to start to be in a situation, especially one that involves trouble or problems: *When he was young he was always getting into trouble with the police.*

get off (something)
1 to leave a bus, train, airplane, etc.: *She got off at the next bus stop.* | *We had to get off the plane, because of problems with the engine.*
2 to finish work: *What time do you get off work?*

get on
1 to go onto a bus, train, airplane, etc.: *I couldn't get on because the bus was full.* | *We had to run to get on the train.*
2 get on with something = to continue or to make progress with a job, work, etc.: *I need to get on with my work, or I won't finish it on time.*

get out
1 to leave: *The professor kept talking, and we finally got out of class at 5 o'clock.*
2 get something out = to remove something, especially a mark on cloth: *I spilled wine on my shirt, and the stain was hard to get out.*

get out of (doing) something
to avoid doing something that you should do: *He's lazy, and he always tries to get out of doing any work.*

get over
1 to feel better after a bad experience or an illness: *She never got over the death of her son.*
2 can't get over something = used when you feel very surprised by something: *I can't get over how tall you are – you've grown about three inches since I last saw you!*

get through
1 to succeed in calling someone on the telephone: *I finally got through to him, after trying four times.*
2 get through something = to succeed in dealing with a bad experience: *It was hard work, but I got through it.*
3 get through something = to finish doing something: *I have so much work to get through.*

get up
1 to get out of your bed after you have been sleeping: *She usually gets up at 6.*
2 to stand up: *He got up and started walking toward the door.*

get·a·way /ˈgetəˌweɪ/ *noun*
make your getaway *informal* = to escape from somewhere: *The robbers made their getaway in a car parked outside the jewelry store.*

ˈget-toˌgether *noun*
a small informal meeting or party: *We're having a little get-together with some friends. Do you want to come?*
➔ See Thesaurus box at **party**

ghet·to /ˈgetoʊ/ *noun* plural **ghettos** or **ghettoes**
a part of a city where poor people live in bad conditions, especially people of one particular race or social class: *He grew up in the ghetto, in one of the poorest areas of Chicago.*

ghost /goʊst/ *noun*
the spirit of a dead person that some people think they can see: *The owner says she saw the ghost of a young girl in the old house.*
—**ghostly** *adjective* frightening and making you think of ghosts: *We heard a ghostly sound that we couldn't explain.*

gi·ant¹ /ˈdʒaɪənt/ *adjective*
very big, and much bigger than other things of the same type: *There was a giant screen in the baseball stadium.*

giant² *noun*
a very tall strong man, who appears in children's stories

gift /gɪft/ *noun*
1 something that you give to someone as a present: *The scarf was a birthday gift from her daughter.* SYNONYM **present**
2 a natural ability to do something well: *He has many gifts – he can sing, he can dance, and he is also very funny.* SYNONYM **talent**

gift·ed /ˈgɪftɪd/ *adjective*
having the natural ability to do something very well: *She is a gifted dancer.* SYNONYM **talented**
➔ See Thesaurus box at **intelligent**

gig·a·byte /ˈgɪgəˌbaɪt/ *noun*
a unit for measuring computer information, equal to 1,024 MEGABYTEs

gi·gan·tic /dʒaɪˈgæntɪk/ *adjective*
extremely large: *The gigantic tree was as tall as the house.*
➔ See Thesaurus box at **big**

gig·gle /ˈgɪgəl/ *verb*
to laugh quickly and in a silly way, in a high voice: *The girl giggled at her boyfriend's joke.*
—**giggle** *noun* the sound of someone giggling
➔ See Thesaurus box at **laugh¹**

gill /gɪl/ *noun*
one of the parts at the sides of a fish's head with which it breathes

gim·mick /ˈgɪmɪk/ *noun, informal*
something unusual but not really useful, that a company uses to make you want to buy something: *Although the software is free, it's just a gimmick to make you buy more of the company's products.*
—**gimmicky** *adjective*

gin /dʒɪn/ *noun*
a strong clear alcoholic drink made from grain and berries: *She ordered a gin and tonic.*

gin·ger /ˈdʒɪndʒɚ/ *noun*
a light brown root with a strong taste, which is often used, for example, in Chinese cooking

ˈginger ˌale *noun*
a sweet, gold-colored drink with bubbles

gin·ger·bread /ˈdʒɪndʒɚˌbred/ *noun*
a type of cookie or cake with ginger in it: *a gingerbread man* (=a cookie in the shape of a person)

gi·raffe /dʒəˈræf/ *noun*
a very tall African animal with a very long neck and long legs, and dark spots on its yellow-brown fur: *Giraffes have long necks so that they can eat the leaves off trees.*

girl /gɚl/ *noun*
1 a female child: *She is a pretty little girl.*
2 a daughter: *They have two boys and a girl.*
—**girlish** *adjective* like a little girl: *She has a girlish laugh.*

girl·friend /ˈgɚlfrend/ *noun*
1 a girl or woman with whom you have a romantic relationship: *He's had lots of girlfriends.*
2 a woman or girl's female friend: *My sister is always talking to her girlfriends on the phone.*

G

ˈGirl ˌScouts *noun*
an organization for girls that teaches them practical skills and helps them do outdoor activities such as camping and HIKING
—**Girl Scout** *noun* a girl who is a member of this organization

give /gɪv/ *verb* **gave** /geɪv/ **given** /ˈgɪvən/
1 to let someone have something as a present: *She gave him a watch for his birthday.*
2 to put something in someone's hand: *I gave my coat to the waiter.*
3 to provide something for someone: *Can I give you some help?* | *Sugar gives you energy quickly.*
4 to tell someone information or details about something: *I gave her my phone number.*
5 to let someone do something: *The teacher gave me permission to miss the class.*
6 to do an action: *She gave a big smile as she read the email.* | *Give me a call* (=call me on the telephone) *tonight.*
7 to do a performance or talk: *The singer is giving a concert in New York.* | *I have to give a speech at the wedding.*
8 to cause someone to have something: *I don't want to give you my cold.* | *My computer has been giving me problems.*

9 to make someone have a punishment: *The judge gave him 5 years in prison.*

10 give way = to break or fall down suddenly under pressure: *The branch gave way because he was too heavy for it.*

11 give or take = used when saying that a number or amount is not exact: *The show lasts about an hour, give or take five minutes* (=it may be five minutes longer or shorter).

PHRASAL VERBS

give something away

to give someone something without asking for money: *I gave my old clothes away.*

give something back

to return something to its owner: *I'll give the money back to you next week.*

G

give in

to finally agree to do something that you did not want to do: *The kids kept asking for candy, and finally she gave in and bought them some.*

give off something

to produce a smell, light, heat, sound, etc.: *The old meat gave off a terrible smell.*

give something out

to give something to each person in a group: *The teacher gave out the exam to the students.*

THESAURUS: give

pass to take something and put it in someone's hand: *Could you pass me the salt?*

hand to pass something to someone: *He handed me a card with his phone number on it.*

hand out/pass around to give something to each of the people in a group: *Mr. Goodman handed out the tests.* | *Pass those cookies around, please.*

distribute *formal* to give things to a large number of people: *The money will be distributed to a number of schools in the area.*

give up

1 to stop trying to do something because it is too difficult: *I couldn't find the keys anywhere, so I gave up.*

2 give up something = to stop doing something that you have done a lot: *My dad gave up smoking about 10 years ago.* SYNONYM **stop**

3 give yourself up = to allow yourself or someone else to be caught by the police or enemy soldiers: *The man threw down his weapon and gave himself up to the police.*

giv•en[1] /ˈgɪvən/

the past participle of GIVE

given[2] *adjective*

any given/a given ... = any particular time, period, or situation that is being used as an example: *In any given year, over half of all accidents happen in the home.*

given[3] *preposition*

taking something into account: *Given his age, my grandfather is still very healthy and strong.*

gla•cier /ˈgleɪʃɚ/ *noun*

a large area of ice that moves very slowly over an area of land: *Much of Alaska is covered in glaciers and snow.*

glad /glæd/ *adjective*

1 happy because something has happened: *I'm so glad that you're feeling better.* | *She was glad to be home again.*

2 be glad to do something = to be willing and happy to do something: *I would be glad to help you.*

→ See Thesaurus box at **happy**

glad•ly /ˈglædli/ *adverb*

in a way that shows you are happy or eager: *I gladly accepted his offer.*

glam•or•ous /ˈglæmərəs/ *adjective*

attractive and exciting because of being rich and successful: *the glamorous lives of Hollywood actors* | *a glamorous super model*

glam•our *also* **glamor** /ˈglæmɚ/ *noun*

the attractive and exciting quality of being connected with wealth and success: *the glamour of Hollywood*

glance[1] /glæns/ *verb*

1 to look at someone or something quickly and then look away: *He glanced at his watch while he was talking.*

2 glance through something = to read something very quickly: *She glanced through a magazine in the doctor's office.*

→ See Thesaurus box at **look**[1]

glance[2] *noun*
1 a quick look: *She cast a glance* (=looked quickly) *around the room to see who was there.*
2 at a glance = immediately and by looking very quickly: *I knew at a glance that something was wrong.*
➔ **at first glance** at **first**[1]

gland /glænd/ *noun*
a part of your body that produces a substance such as SWEAT or SALIVA: *Sweat glands help to keep your body cool when it is very hot.*

glare[1] /gler/ *verb*
1 to look angrily at someone or something for a long time: *She glared at me, then asked me why I had lied to her.*
2 to shine with a strong bright light that hurts your eyes: *The sun glared down on us all afternoon on the beach.*

glare[2] *noun*
1 a strong bright light that hurts your eyes: *He wore dark glasses to protect his eyes from the glare of the sun.*
2 a long angry look: *She gave him an angry glare.*

glass /glæs/ *noun*
1 a hard clear material that is used for making windows, bottles, etc.: *The windows of the car are made of very strong glass.* | *a glass bottle*
2 a glass container used for drinking: *a wine glass* | *a glass of milk*
➔ See picture on page A9

glass·es /ˈglæsɪz/ *plural noun*
two round pieces of glass that you wear in front of your eyes in order to see better: *I have to wear glasses for reading.* | *You need a new pair of glasses.*

glaze /gleɪz/ *also* **glaze over** *verb*
if your eyes glaze, they show no expression because you are bored or tired: *Her eyes glazed over as soon as I started talking about my work.*

gleam /glim/ *verb*
1 to shine because of being very clean: *He washed the windows until they gleamed.*
2 if your eyes or face gleam, they show that you are excited: *Her eyes gleamed with excitement as she stepped onto the beach.*
—**gleam** *noun*: *There was an excited gleam in his eyes.*

glee /gli/ *noun*
a feeling of excitement and satisfaction, especially because something bad happens to someone: *He watched with glee as the other player hit the ball out of the tennis court.*
—**gleefully** *adverb* with a lot of excitement

glide /glaɪd/ *verb*
to move smoothly and quietly: *We watched the sailboats glide across the lake.*

glid·er /ˈglaɪdɚ/ *noun*
a light airplane that flies without an engine

glim·mer[1] /ˈglɪmɚ/ *noun*
1 a slight feeling or look: *There is still a glimmer of hope that the men might be found alive.*
2 a light that is not very bright: *the glimmer of a candle flame*

glimmer[2] *verb*
to shine with a light that is not very bright: *We saw a light glimmering far across the lake.*

glimpse /glɪmps/ *noun*
a very quick look at someone or something: *The fans waited outside the singer's hotel, hoping to catch a glimpse of her* (=see her for a short time).
—**glimpse** *verb* to see someone or something, but only for a very short time: *I thought I glimpsed Cindy in the crowd as I drove by.*

glis·ten /ˈglɪsən/ *verb*
to shine and look wet or oily: *Her eyes glistened with tears.*

glitch /glɪtʃ/ *noun*
a small problem, especially a technical problem, that stops something from working correctly: *The plane took off late because of a glitch in the computer system.*

glit·ter /ˈglɪtɚ/ *verb*
to shine brightly with a lot of small flashes of light: *New snow glittered in the sunlight.*
—**glitter** *noun*: *the glitter of her diamond ring*
➔ See Thesaurus box at **shine**[1]

gloat /gloʊt/ *verb*
to behave in a way that shows that you are happy that you have succeeded and that another person has failed: *The fans are still gloating over their team's victory.*

G

glob•al /ˈgloʊbəl/ Ac *adjective*
including or affecting the whole world: *The illness could spread quickly through the world and become a global problem.*
SYNONYM **worldwide**
—**globally** *adverb*

ˌglobal ˈwarming *noun*
an increase in world temperatures, caused by an increase of CARBON DIOXIDE around the Earth: *Global warming is mainly caused by pollution from cars, planes, and factories.*

globe

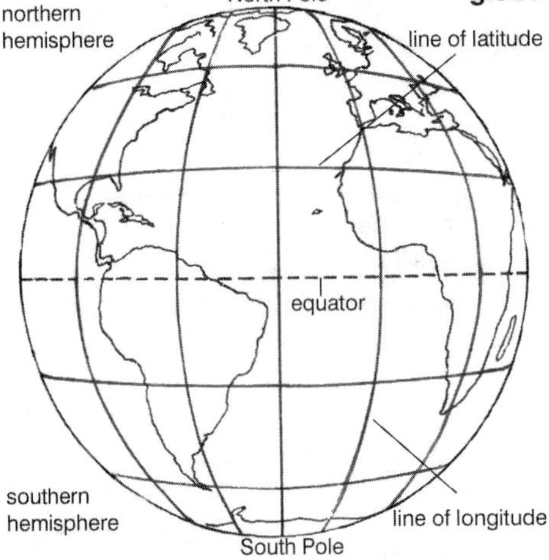

globe /gloʊb/ Ac *noun*
1 the globe = the world: *Our company has offices all over the globe.*
2 a round object that has a map of the Earth on it: *The teacher used a globe to show how the ships sailed from England to America.*

WORD FAMILY look at the words:
→ **globe** *noun*
→ **global** *adjective*
→ **globally** *adverb*

gloom /glum/ *noun*
1 a feeling of sadness, or having no hope: *The country was full of gloom after President Kennedy's death.*
2 *formal* darkness that makes it difficult for you to see: *Nobody was outside in the cold wet winter gloom.*
—**gloomy** *adjective*: *Why are you are looking so gloomy? Did something bad happen?*

glo•ri•fy /ˈglɔrəˌfaɪ/ *verb* **glorified**, third person singular **glorifies**
1 to make someone or something seem better or more important than they really are: *Too many movies glorify violence by making it seem exciting.*
2 to praise someone or something, especially God
—**glorification** /ˌglɔrəfəˈkeɪʃən/ *noun*

glo•ri•ous /ˈglɔriəs/ *adjective*
1 very beautiful or impressive: *It was a glorious day, and there wasn't a cloud in the sky.*
2 very good or successful and deserving praise and honor: *The country has a glorious history.*
—**gloriously** *adverb*

glo•ry /ˈglɔri/ *noun* plural **glories**
1 the importance, praise, and honor that people give to someone or something that they admire: *Although he was a great artist, he wasn't interested in all the glory that came with success.*
2 the beautiful and impressive appearance that something has: *Ahead of us we saw the Grand Canyon, in all its glory* (=looking very beautiful and impressive).
3 an achievement that is greatly admired or respected: *The painting is one of Rembrandt's best and one of the glories of Western art.*

gloss /glɔs/ *noun*
a shiny attractive surface: *The dog was sick, and its fur had lost its gloss.*

glos•sa•ry /ˈglɑsəri/ *noun* plural **glossaries**
a list of words with an explanation of their meaning, usually printed at the end of a book

gloss•y /ˈglɔsi/ *adjective*
1 shiny and smooth: *She had long glossy black hair.*
2 a glossy magazine, book, or photograph is printed on shiny, good-quality paper: *I saw a picture of the hotel in a glossy magazine.*

glove /glʌv/ *noun*
a piece of clothing that you wear on your hand, with separate parts to cover the thumb and each finger: *Do you have a warm pair of gloves?*
→ See picture on page A6

glow[1] /gloʊ/ *verb*
to shine with a soft steady light: *The harbor lights glowed in the distance.*
➔ See Thesaurus box at **shine**[1]

glow[2] *noun*
1 a soft steady light: *I saw the man in the glow of the street lights.*
2 the bright color your face has when you are healthy, have been exercising, or you feel happy, proud, etc.: *She was an athlete, and her face always had a healthy glow.*

glue[1] /glu/ *noun*
a sticky substance used for attaching things together: *I stuck the two pieces of wood together with glue.*

glue[2] *verb*
1 to join things together using glue: *Glue the colored shapes to the paper.*
2 be glued to the television/the screen, etc. = to be watching the television, a computer screen, etc. for a long time because you are very interested in it: *My sisters were glued to the TV all morning, watching cartoons.*
➔ See Thesaurus box at **fasten**

gnaw /nɔ/ *verb*
to keep biting at something: *The dog was gnawing on a bone.* SYNONYM **chew**

GNP *noun*
Gross National Product the total value of the goods and services produced by a country, including money from selling goods and services in other countries: *Government spending is more than 15 percent of GNP.*

go[1] /goʊ/ *verb* **went** /wɛnt/ **gone** /gɔn/ **been** /bɪn/ third person singular **goes** /goʊz/
1 to move or travel to a place: *He went home at 5 o'clock.* | *"Where's Maria?" "She had to go to the library."* | *I usually go to school by bus.* | *Have you ever been to Paris* (=have you ever visited Paris?)

GRAMMAR: go

gone and been

Gone and **been** are past participles of **go**. A past participle is a form of a verb that shows an action happening in the past.

Has gone is the usual way to say that someone has traveled to a place in the past: *George has gone to Denver* (=George has traveled to Denver and is there now.)

Has been is the way you say that someone has visited a place in the past: *George has been to Denver* (=George has visited Denver before, but is not there now.)

2 to leave: *It's time for us to go.*
3 be going to do something = used when saying that something is likely to happen or that someone will do something in the future: *It looks like it is going to rain.* | *I'm going to stay with my grandparents in New York.*
4 to do an activity in a different place from where you are now: *I want to go shopping tomorrow.* | *Do you want to go for a walk?*
5 to reach as far as a particular place: *My belt won't go around my waist.*
6 to regularly attend school, a church, etc.: *Which college did you go to?*
7 to change in some way, especially by becoming worse than before: *I'll go crazy if I have to stay here another week!* | *Her hair is starting to go gray.*

USAGE: go

Go, **get**, and **become** can all mean "to begin to be something," but they are used in different ways.

Go and **get** are less formal than **become**, and are used more often in spoken English: *Have you gone crazy?* | *I got very hungry.*

Become is used in both written and spoken English: *He's becoming a very good tennis player.* | *The area has become popular with mountain bikers.*

Go and **get** are used only in front of an adjective (=word that describes something): *It's getting dark.* | *Beethoven went deaf when he was 40 years old.*

Become can be used in front of an adjective or a noun: *It became clear that Scott was not doing his work.* | *The noise from the airport is becoming a problem.*

8 to happen in a particular way: *The party went well, and everyone had a good time.*
9 to go a) used when saying how much time there is before something happens:

Only two more days to go before our vacation (=we leave in two days)*!* **b)** food that is to go is bought from a restaurant and taken away to be eaten: *I'll have two large fries to go.*

10 How's it going?/How are things going? = used when you meet someone, to ask how he or she is: *"Hey, Jimmy, how's it going?" "I'm good. And you?"*

11 go to sleep = to start to sleep: *I went to sleep at about 11:00.*

12 go (to the bathroom) = to use the toilet: *Mommy, I have to go!*

PHRASAL VERBS

go after someone or something

to try to catch or get someone or something: *The police went after the man and arrested him.*

go ahead

1 used when giving someone permission to do something or to start speaking: *"Can I sit here?" "Go ahead!"*

2 used when encouraging someone to do something, when they seem to be unsure about doing it: *Go ahead, you'll have fun at Dan's house!*

3 to do something that you have planned to do: *They decided to go ahead with their plans to get married.*

go along with someone or something

to agree with or support someone or something: *My husband always goes along with everything I say, because he doesn't like to argue.*

go away

to leave a place or a person: *Go away, and leave me alone!* | *We're going away for two weeks in June* (=leaving to go on vacation.)

go back

1 to return to a place: *I never want to go back there again.*

2 to have existed for a long time: *The history of the school goes back over 100 years.*

go by

if time goes by, it passes: *The days went by, and he still didn't call me.*

go down

1 to become less: *The temperature went down to 15 degrees below zero.*

2 when the sun goes down, it appears to move down until you cannot see it anymore and night begins

3 if a computer system goes down, it stops working for a short time

go for

1 go for something = to try to get or win something: *He's going for his fifth gold medal at the Winter Olympics.*

2 Go for it! *informal* = used when you want to encourage someone to do something: *If you really want to go to Stanford, then go for it!*

3 go for someone or something *informal* = to usually like a particular type of person or thing: *I don't usually go for men with glasses.*

go into something

to describe or explain something thoroughly: *I don't want to go into details right now, but it was an awful experience.*

go off

1 to explode: *A bomb went off in the middle of the city.*

2 if an alarm goes off, it makes a loud noise: *My alarm clock didn't go off, and I slept until 10 o'clock.*

3 if a light or the power supply goes off, it stops working: *Suddenly, all the lights went off.*

go on

1 to continue: *He stopped for a few minutes and then went on with his work.*

2 to happen – used especially when you think something bad or unusual is happening: *I heard a strange noise downstairs, and I wondered what was going on.*

3 if a machine or light goes on, it starts working or starts shining: *The lights went on in the yard, and we saw the deer.*

go out

1 to leave your house, especially in order to do something you enjoy: *We're going out for dinner. Do you want to come?*

2 to have a romantic relationship with someone: *She has been going out with David for over a year.*

3 if the TIDE goes out, the water moves away from the land ANTONYM **come in**

4 if a light or fire goes out, it stops shining or burning: *The lights went out, and we couldn't find a candle.*

G

go through something
1 to have a very upsetting or difficult experience: *She has been through a lot in her life – both her parents died when she was only 10 years old.*
2 to look at, read, or explain something carefully: *The teacher went through all the questions and made sure that we understood them.*
go through with something
to do something you had planned or promised to do: *I'm not sure if I can go through with the wedding – I'm so scared.*
go together
to look good or taste good together: *Do you think these colors go together?*
go up
to increase in number or amount: *Our rent has gone up by almost 20%.*
go with something
1 to look good or taste good together: *White wine goes well with fish.*
2 to accept someone's idea or plan: *I'm happy to go with that idea, if everyone else agrees.*

go² *noun* plural **goes**
1 give it a go *informal* = to try doing something: *I'd never ice skated before, but I thought I'd give it a go.* SYNONYM **give it a try**
2 on the go *informal* = very busy doing a lot of things, and not stopping for a rest: *I've been on the go all morning, and I need to sit down.*

ˈgo-aˌhead *noun*
give (someone) the go-ahead/get the go-ahead *informal* = to give or be given official permission to start doing something: *The judge gave the final go-ahead for a new trial.*

goal /goʊl/ Ac *noun*
1 something that you hope to achieve in the future: *I finally achieved my goal of teaching at a university.* | *My ultimate goal is to win a medal at the Olympics.*
2 in sports such as SOCCER or HOCKEY, the action of making a point, or the point that you get by doing this: *Crespo scored both goals in Argentina's 2–0 win over Mexico.*
3 the area where you make points in SOCCER or HOCKEY
➔ See Thesaurus box at **purpose**

goal·ie /ˈgoʊli/ *noun, informal*
➔ **goalkeeper**

goal·keep·er /ˈgoʊlˌkipɚ/ *also* **goal·tend·er** /ˈgoʊlˌtendɚ/ *noun*
the player whose job is to stop the ball from going into the goal in sports such as SOCCER or HOCKEY

goat /goʊt/ *noun*
a farm animal that has horns and long hair under its chin

gob·ble /ˈgabəl/ *also* **gobble up/down** *verb, informal*
to eat something very quickly: *The kids gobbled up the cake and then asked for more.*

god /gad/ *noun*
1 God = the BEING whom Christians, Jews, and Muslims believe created and controls the universe: *Do you believe in God?*
2 one of many male spirits or BEINGS who some religions believe control the world or events that happen in it: *Shiva, the Hindu god of destruction*

god·child /ˈgadtʃaɪld/ *noun* plural **godchildren** /ˈgadˌtʃɪldrən/
a child that a GODPARENT has promised to help

god·daugh·ter /ˈgadˌdɔtɚ/ *noun*
a female godchild

god·dess /ˈgadɪs/ *noun*
one of many female spirits or BEINGS who some religions believe control the world and events that happen in it: *Athena, the Greek goddess of wisdom*

god·fa·ther /ˈgadˌfaðɚ/ *noun*
1 a male godparent
2 *informal* the leader of a criminal organization, especially the MAFIA

god·ly /ˈgadli/ *adjective*
showing that you believe in God: *He went to church every day and lived a godly life.* SYNONYM **religious**

god·moth·er /ˈgadˌmʌðɚ/ *noun*
a female godparent

god·par·ent /ˈgadˌperənt/ *noun*
someone who promises at a BAPTISM to help a child, and to teach him or her Christian values

god·son /ˈgadsʌn/ *noun*
a male GODCHILD

gog·gles /ˈgɑgəlz/ *plural noun*
special glasses that fit close to your face, so that things cannot go into your eyes: *I wear goggles when I go swimming, so that the water doesn't get into my eyes.*

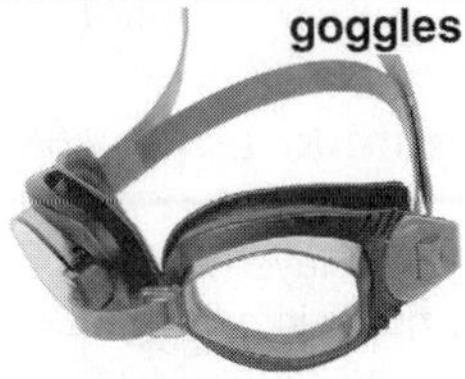
goggles

gold /goʊld/ *noun*
a valuable yellow metal that is used to make jewelry, coins, etc.: *The ring is made of pure gold* (=gold that does not have other metals mixed with it).
—**gold** *adjective* made of gold: *a gold watch*

gold·en /ˈgoʊldən/ *adjective*
1 having a bright shiny yellow color: *golden hair*
2 a golden opportunity = a good chance to be very successful or to get something important: *The team missed a golden opportunity to win the game in the last quarter.*
3 made of gold: *a golden crown*

gold·fish /ˈgoʊldˌfɪʃ/ *noun* plural **goldfish**
a small orange fish that people often keep as a pet

ˈgold ˌmine *noun*
1 a deep hole below the ground where gold is dug out from rocks
2 something that produces or achieves a lot of something: *The Internet can be a gold mine of information.*

golf /gɑlf/ *noun*
a game in which you hit a small white ball into a hole in the ground with a special stick called a golf club: *I play golf every weekend.*
—**golfer** *noun* someone who plays golf
→ See picture on page A24

gone /gɔn/ *verb*
the past participle of GO

good¹ /gʊd/ *adjective* **better, best**
1 of a high standard: *His last album was really good. | Who's the best player on the team? | His work just isn't good enough.* ANTONYM **bad**

THESAURUS: good

great *informal* very good or very enjoyable: *We had a really great time at camp.*
excellent very good: *It was an excellent concert.*
wonderful very good or enjoyable, in a way that makes you feel happy: *It was wonderful to be back home again.*
fantastic very good, in a way that makes you feel happy or excited: *The movie's special effects were fantastic.*
outstanding better than anyone or anything else: *Her work this year has been outstanding.*
exceptional *formal* very good in a way that is unusual: *She is an exceptional athlete.*

USAGE: good

Use **good** to talk about the quality of something or someone: *a good teacher | Was the movie good?*
Use **well** to talk about the way someone does something: *He plays tennis very well.*

2 useful or appropriate: *It was a good day for going to the beach.* ANTONYM **bad**
3 likely to be successful: *That's a good idea. | We have a good chance of winning.* ANTONYM **bad**
4 someone who is good at something can do it well: *I'm not a very good swimmer. | Andrea is very good at her job.*
5 enjoyable and pleasant: *good weather | It's good to see you again. | We had such a good time.* ANTONYM **bad**
6 likely to make you healthy: *Fresh fruit and vegetables are good for you.*
7 behaving well, used especially about children: *Wait for me here, and be a good girl.*
8 kind and helpful: *My friends were very good to me when my mother died. | It's good of you to give me a ride to work.*
9 as good as = almost: *The work is as good as finished.*
10 good luck = something you say to someone when you hope that he or she is going to be successful: *Good luck! I know you can do it!*

good² *noun*
1 something that makes a situation better or gives you an advantage: *A vacation would do you good* (=make you feel happier).
2 not any/much good = bad in quality: *The movie wasn't much good.*

3 no good/not much good = not useful or not successful: *It's no good trying to explain it to her – she won't listen.*
4 for good = always or permanently: *I'd like to live in Denver for good.*
5 behavior or actions that are morally right: *the struggle between good and evil*

good ˌafterˈnoon *formal*
something you say when you meet someone in the afternoon: *Good afternoon, sir. Can I help you?*

good·bye /gʊdˈbaɪ/
something you say when you are leaving, or when someone is leaving: *Goodbye, John, see you tomorrow.*

good ˈevening *formal*
something you say when you meet someone in the evening: *Good evening, ladies and gentlemen.*

ˌGood ˈFriday *noun*
the Friday before the Christian holiday of EASTER

ˌgood-ˈhearted *adjective*
someone who is good-hearted is kind and willing to help people: *My aunt was a good-hearted woman who often took care of us when my parents were having problems.*

ˌgood-ˈlooking *adjective*
someone who is good-looking is attractive to look at: *He's a good-looking guy – I'm surprised he isn't dating someone.* | *He was very good-looking when he was younger.*
➔ See Thesaurus box at **beautiful**

good ˈmorning
something you say when you meet someone in the morning: *Good morning, Debbie – how are you?*

good·ness /ˈgʊdnɪs/ *noun*
1 *also* **my goodness** you say this when you are surprised about something: *My goodness, you've gotten so tall!*
2 for goodness sake = you say this when you are annoyed about something: *For goodness sake, stop yelling.*
3 the quality of being good and kind to other people: *He gets a little angry sometimes, but there is a lot of goodness in him.*

good ˈnight
something you say when someone is leaving at night, or when someone is going to bed: *Good night. See you tomorrow.*

goods /gʊdz/ *plural noun, formal*
things such as televisions, food, or clothes, etc. that are bought and sold: *The store sells furniture and other goods for the home.*

good·will /gʊdˈwɪl/ *noun*
friendly feelings you have for other people or that two people or groups have for each other: *When a teacher treats students with respect, the goodwill of the students toward teachers grows.*

goof[1] /guf/ *also* **goof up** *verb, informal*
to make a silly mistake: *I goofed and sent the check to the wrong address.*

PHRASAL VERBS

goof around
to spend time doing silly or unimportant things: *Stop goofing around, and get your work done.*

goof off
to not do any work: *She goofed off at college and never got her degree.*

goof[2] *noun, informal*
someone who is silly: *He's such a big goof – he makes me laugh.*

goof·y /ˈgufi/ *adjective, informal*
stupid or silly: *a goofy smile*

goose /gus/ *noun* plural **geese** /gis/
a large white bird that looks like a duck, but is bigger

goose·bumps *also* **goose bumps** /ˈgusbʌmps/ *plural noun*
small raised spots on your skin that you get because you are cold, afraid, or excited: *I think I'm in love – I get goosebumps every time I see her.*

GOP *noun*
the GOP = **Grand Old Party** another name for the Republican Party

go·pher /ˈgoʊfɚ/ *noun*
a North American animal with light brown fur, fat cheeks, and a short tail, that lives in holes in the ground

gorge /gɔrdʒ/ *noun*
a narrow valley (=area between two hills or mountains) with high straight sides: *We climbed to the top and looked down at the deep gorge below.*

gor·geous /ˈgɔrdʒəs/ *adjective, informal*
very beautiful: *You look gorgeous with your new haircut!* | *Maine has gorgeous mountains and a beautiful rocky coast.*

G

go•ril•la /gəˈrɪlə/ *noun*
a large animal that looks like a monkey. Gorillas are the largest type of APE

gosh /gɑʃ/
something you say when you are surprised: *Gosh! I never expected the pool to be so big.*

gos•ling /ˈgɑzlɪŋ/ *noun*
a baby GOOSE

gos•pel /ˈgɑspəl/ *noun*
1 *also* **Gospel** one of the four books of the Christian Bible that tell the story of Christ's life
2 *also* **gospel truth** something that is completely true: *I was young and took everything people said as gospel* (=believed what people said was completely true).

G

gos•sip¹ /ˈgɑsəp/ *noun*
things that people say about other people's behavior and lives, especially things that are unkind or untrue: *It's not just Hollywood gossip; this story is really true.*

gossip² *verb*
to talk about other people's behavior and lives, often saying things that are unkind or untrue: *Everyone started gossiping about them, because we all thought they were secretly dating.*
➔ See Thesaurus box at **talk¹**

got /gɑt/ *verb*
1 the past tense of GET
2 a past participle of GET

got•ten /ˈgɑtn/ *verb*
the usual past participle of GET

gourd /gɔrd/ *noun*
a large fruit with a hard shell that was used as a container in the past

gour•met¹ /gʊrˈmeɪ/ *adjective*
relating to very good-quality food and drink: *She bought all the food for dinner from a gourmet food store, and it cost her over $100!*

gourmet² *noun*
someone who enjoys good-quality food and drink, and knows a lot about them

gov•ern /ˈgʌvən/ *verb*
1 to legally control a country, state, or city and make all the decisions about taxes, laws, etc.: *The President must work with Congress to govern the country.*
2 *formal* if laws or rules govern something, they control what happens or the way in which it happens: *the rules that govern how computers talk to each other on the Internet*

WORD FAMILY look at the words:

➔ **govern** *verb*
➔ **government** *noun*
➔ **governmental** *adjective*
➔ **governor** *noun*
➔ **governorship** *noun*

gov•ern•ment /ˈgʌvəmənt/ *noun*
1 *also* **Government** the group of people who govern a country or state: *The money will be provided by the federal government* (=the main government of the country, not a state government). | *government officials*

THESAURUS: government

democracy a political system in which the people of a country can vote to choose the government: *In 1974, Greece became a democracy again, after seven years of being ruled by the military.*

republic *formal* a country that has an elected government, and does not have a king or queen: *The United States and France are both republics.*

monarchy *formal* a country that has a king or queen as the head of state, and which may or may not also have an elected government: *The British have kept their monarchy, though the country is run by people who are elected.*

regime *formal* a government, especially one that was not elected fairly or that you disapprove of: *The regime had almost complete control of people's lives: it chose your school for you, it chose your job for you.*

2 a system of government: *I decided that I wanted to work in government, and not in a private company.*
—**governmental** /ˌgʌvənˈmentl/ *adjective* relating to government: *The EPA is the governmental agency that is responsible for protecting the environment.*

gov•er•nor *also* **Governor** /ˈgʌvənə/ *noun*
the person in charge of governing a state in the U.S.: *the Governor of California*
—**governorship** *noun* the position of being governor, or the period during which someone is governor

gown /gaʊn/ *noun*
1 a long dress worn by a woman on formal occasions: *She wore a red silk evening gown and diamonds.*
2 a long loose piece of clothing worn for formal ceremonies by people such as judges or students at GRADUATION: *The students walked across the stage in their black graduation gowns.*
3 a loose piece of clothing worn in a hospital by a doctor or a patient during an operation: *a hospital gown*

GPA *noun*
grade point average the average of all the grades that a student gets. An A is 4 points, a B is 3 points, a C is 2 points, a D is 1 point, and an F is 0: *He graduated in 2000 with a GPA of 3.3.*

grab /græb/ *verb* **grabbed, grabbing**
to take hold of someone or something in a rough or violent way: *Rob grabbed my arm and pulled me away.* | *The fish slipped out of my hands when I grabbed hold of its tail.*
➔ See Thesaurus box at **hold[1]**

grace /greɪs/ *noun*
1 a smooth way of moving that appears natural, relaxed, and attractive: *She moves with the grace of a dancer.*
2 polite behavior: *She accepted her punishment with grace; she did not cry or get angry.*
3 the kindness and love that God shows to people: *By the grace of God, I was able to walk again.*
4 a short prayer said before a meal: *Before we eat – Tom, can you please say grace?*

grace•ful /ˈgreɪsfəl/ *adjective*
moving in a way that is smooth and attractive: *The swan is a graceful swimmer.*
—**gracefully** *adverb*: *The dolphins swam gracefully through the ocean.*

gra•cious /ˈgreɪʃəs/ *adjective*
behaving in a polite and kind way: *She was gracious and invited us in, even though she did not know us.*
—**graciously** *adverb*: *Mr. Allen graciously thanked me for coming.*
—**graciousness** *noun*

grade[1] /greɪd/ Ac *noun*
1 one of the 12 years that students are in school in the U.S.: *My brother is in the third grade.* | *a fourth-grade class*
2 a number or letter that a student gets for his or her work or for a test: *His grades have started to improve.* | *Paul has to get good grades to get into college.*
3 a level of quality that shows you how good a product, material, etc. is: *The farm produces high grade eggs and milk.*
4 **make the grade** = to succeed or be as good as a particular standard: *Only a few athletes make the grade in professional sports.*

grade[2] *verb*
to give a grade to a test or to a piece of school work: *The teacher is grading the papers tonight, and giving them back tomorrow.*

ˈgrade point ˌaverage *noun*
➔ GPA

ˈgrade ˌschool *noun*
➔ elementary school

grad•u•al /ˈgrædʒuəl/ *adjective*
happening slowly over a long period of time: *There has been a gradual change in his health; he seems to be getting better slowly.*
ANTONYM **sudden**
—**gradually** *adverb*: *Spring was coming, and the temperature was gradually getting warmer.*

grad•u•ate[1] /ˈgrædʒuɪt/ *noun*
someone who has successfully completed his or her studies at a school, college, or university: *high school graduates* | *a graduate of MIT*

WORD FAMILY look at the words:
➔ **graduate** *verb*
➔ **graduate** *noun*
➔ **graduation** *noun*

grad•u•ate[2] /ˈgrædʒuˌeɪt/ *verb*
to obtain a DIPLOMA or a degree by completing your studies at a school, college, or university: *Ruth has just graduated from Princeton.* | *He graduated from college in 2003.*

grad•u•ate[3] /ˈgrædʒuɪt/ *adjective*
relating to a student who is studying to get a MASTER'S DEGREE or a PH.D.: *He did his*

graduate work at Columbia University. | *a graduate student* | *graduate classes*

ˈgraduate ˌschool *noun*
a college or university where you can study for a MASTER'S DEGREE or a PH.D. after finishing your first degree

grad•u•a•tion /ˌgrædʒuˈeɪʃən/ *noun*
a ceremony for students who have successfully finished their studies at a school, college, or university, at which they get a degree or DIPLOMA: *We went to Bobby's graduation yesterday.*

graf•fi•ti /grəˈfiti/ *noun*
writing and pictures that people draw illegally on the walls of buildings, trains, etc.

grain /greɪn/ *noun*
1 the seeds of crops such as corn, wheat, or rice that are grown for food: *Most of the grain that we grow on the farm is used to feed cattle.*
2 a very small piece of a substance: *How many grains of sand do you think there are on the beach?*
3 the grain = the natural lines or patterns you can see in wood: *Split the wood along the grain.*
4 a grain of something = a very small amount of something: *There isn't a grain of truth in his story* (=his story is completely untrue).
5 take something with a grain of salt = to realize that part of what someone says may not be true: *He always makes things seem worse than they are, so take everything he says with a grain of salt.*

gram /græm/ *noun, written abbreviation* **gm**
a unit for measuring weight. There are 1,000 grams in a kilogram.

gram•mar /ˈgræmɚ/ *noun*
the rules of a language, which control how words change tense and how sentences are formed: *The rules of English grammar are difficult.* | *There are some mistakes in your spelling and grammar.*
—**grammatical** /grəˈmætɪkəl/ *adjective* relating to grammar: *There were several grammatical errors in his English paper.*

grand /grænd/ *adjective*
1 bigger or more impressive than other similar things: *We walked past some of the grand old buildings by the river.*
2 grand total = the total you get when you add up several numbers or amounts: *We paid $300 to get the car's brakes fixed, $150 for the damage to the door, and $300 for the paint, for a grand total of $750.*
3 grand opening = a special event on the day that a business opens for the first time: *The store had its grand opening yesterday, with a band playing and free balloons for kids.*
—**grandness** *noun*

grand•child /ˈgræntʃaɪld/ *noun* plural **grandchildren** /ˈgrænˌtʃɪldrən/
the child of your son or daughter

grand•daugh•ter /ˈgrænˌdɔtɚ/ *noun*
the daughter of your son or daughter

grand•fa•ther /ˈgrændˌfɑðɚ/ *noun*
the father of your mother or father

ˈgrandfather ˌclock *noun*
a clock in a tall wooden case that stands on the floor

grand•ly /ˈgrændli/ *adverb*
in a way that is impressive or intended to attract attention: *Jessie walked grandly into the room, hoping everyone would look at her.*

grand•ma /ˈgrændmɑ/ *noun, informal*
➔ **grandmother**

grand•moth•er /ˈgrændˌmʌðɚ/ *noun*
the mother of your mother or father

grand•pa /ˈgrændpɑ/ *noun, informal*
➔ **grandfather**

grand•par•ent /ˈgrændˌperənt/ *noun*
the parent of your mother or father

grand•son /ˈgrændsʌn/ *noun*
the son of your son or daughter: *I have a grandson who is two years old.*

grand•stand /ˈgrændˌstænd/ *noun*
rows of seats outdoors where people sit to watch sports: *We watched the race from the grandstand.*

gran•ite /ˈgrænɪt/ *noun*
a type of hard gray rock, often used in buildings

G

grant[1] /grænt/ Ac *noun*
money that organizations sometimes give to people for a particular purpose: *Some students get a research grant* (=money to do research).

grant[2] *verb*
1 take it for granted (that) = to think that something is definitely true, although it may not be true: *My parents took it for granted that I would go to college, but I didn't want to.* SYNONYM **assume**
2 *formal* to allow someone to do or have something: *The witch granted the girl's wish* (=gave her what she wished for).

grape /greɪp/ *noun*
a small round green or red fruit that you can eat, and that people use for making wine: *I bought a bunch of grapes* (=a group growing together).
➔ See picture on page A13

grape•fruit /ˈgreɪpfrut/ *noun*
a big round yellow fruit with a thick skin, like a large orange but not as sweet
➔ See picture on page A13

grape•vine /ˈgreɪpvaɪn/ *noun*
the plant that GRAPEs grow on SYNONYM **vine**

graph /græf/ *noun*
a picture that shows information about different numbers or amounts, so that you can compare them: *This graph shows the amount of rain in Miami for every month of the year.*

graph•ic /ˈgræfɪk/ *adjective*
1 describing or showing something very clearly, especially something unpleasant: *One man gave a graphic description of the dead and injured people after the plane crash.*
2 relating to art that uses lines not color, for example drawing but not painting: *a graphic artist*
—**graphically** *adverb* in a way that describes or shows something very clearly: *The movie was graphically violent.*

graph•ics /ˈgræfɪks/ *noun*
pictures in books or images on screens: *Our video games are made using the latest computer graphics* (=images made using a computer).

grasp /græsp/ *verb*
1 to hold something firmly: *Grasp the rope with both hands, so that you don't drop it.*
2 to understand something: *At first, I didn't grasp what she was saying to me, but then I understood.*

grass /græs/ *noun*
a plant with thin green leaves that covers the ground in yards, parks, and fields: *The grass in the backyard needs cutting.*

grass•hop•per /ˈgræsˌhɑpɚ/ *noun*
a green or brown insect with long back legs that lives in the grass, can jump high, and makes a short loud noise

gras•sy /ˈgræsi/ *adjective*
covered with grass: *There are some grassy areas around the school where the kids play.*

grate[1] /greɪt/ *verb*
if you grate cheese, a carrot, etc., you rub it against a special tool with many holes, in a way that cuts many thin pieces off it: *Grate the cheese over the pasta.*
—**grater** *noun* a kitchen tool used in order to grate food
➔ See Thesaurus box at **cut**[1]
➔ See picture on page A14

grate[2] *noun*
1 a metal frame with bars across it, over a hole in the street or in front of a window: *Iron grates covered the prison windows.* SYNONYM **grating**
2 the metal frame that holds the wood in a FIREPLACE

grate•ful /ˈgreɪtfəl/ *adjective*
wanting to say thank you to someone because he or she has been kind or helpful to you: *I was very grateful for all his help.*
—**gratefully** *adverb*: *She gratefully accepted my offer to drive her.*

WORD FAMILY look at the words:
➔ **grateful** *adjective*
➔ **ungrateful** *adjective*
➔ **gratefully** *adverb*
➔ **gratitude** *noun*
➔ **ungratefulness** *noun*

grat•i•fy /ˈgrætəˌfaɪ/ *verb* **gratified**, third person singular **gratifies** *formal*
if you are gratified by something, it makes you feel happy and satisfied: *The actors were gratified to see that the audience loved*

the play.

—**gratification** /ˌgrætəfə'keɪʃən/ *noun* when you get pleasure and satisfaction from something: *As a teacher, I get a lot of gratification from seeing students learn.*

grat•ing /'greɪtɪŋ/ *noun*
another word for a GRATE

grat•i•tude /'grætəˌtud/ *noun*
the feeling you have when you want to thank someone because he or she has been kind or helpful to you: *Maria was full of gratitude for his support.*

gra•tu•i•tous /grə'tuətəs/ *adjective, formal*
unnecessary and likely to upset people: *The movie contained scenes of gratuitous violence* (=violence that it was not necessary to show).

G

gra•tu•i•ty /grə'tuəti/ *noun* plural **gratuities** *formal*
another word for a TIP

grave[1] /greɪv/ *noun*
a hole in the ground for burying a dead person: *My father was buried in a grave in the cemetary.*

grave[2] *adjective, formal*
very serious in a way that makes you worry: *I think Jo is making a grave mistake.*
—**gravely** *adverb*: *She was gravely ill* (=seriously ill).

grav•el /'grævəl/ *noun*
small stones that are used to make the surface of a path or road: *I heard the sound of footsteps on the gravel outside.*

grave•stone /'greɪvstoʊn/ *noun*
a stone on a grave that shows the name of the dead person, and the date he or she was born and died

grave•yard /'greɪvyɑrd/ *noun*
an area of land for burying dead people: *There was an old graveyard next to the church.*

grav•i•ty /'grævəti/ *noun*
1 the force that makes things fall to the ground: *An apple falls down from a tree because of the Earth's gravity.*
2 *formal* how bad a situation is: *Nobody understood the gravity of the situation until after the fighting started in the region.*

gra•vy /'greɪvi/ *noun*
a liquid made from the juice of cooked meat, that you serve with the meat: *We had roast beef and potatoes with gravy.*

gray[1] /greɪ/ *adjective*
1 having the color of black mixed with white: *My Dad is getting older, and he has gray hair.* | *He was wearing a gray suit.*
2 cloudy and with no sun: *It was a gray day in winter.*

gray[2] *noun*
the color that you get when you mix black with white: *You can buy the shoes in gray or red.*

graze /greɪz/ *verb*
1 if an animal grazes, it eats grass: *Some cows were grazing in the field.*
2 to slightly damage the skin on part of your body: *Billy fell and grazed his knee, but it didn't bleed much.*

grease[1] /gris/ *noun*
1 soft fat from cooked meat: *The pan was full of hot grease.*
2 oil that you put on parts of a car, bicycle, etc.: *Some of the grease from the bike came off on my hands.*

grease[2] *verb*
to put fat or oil on something: *Grease the pan with butter.*

greas•y /'grisi/ *adjective*
1 cooked in too much oil: *Greasy food is bad for you.*
2 greasy hair is very dirty and looks like there is too much oil in it: *His hair was greasy, and he looked like he needed a bath.*
SYNONYM **oily**; ANTONYM **dry**
➔ See Thesaurus box at **dirty**

great /greɪt/ *adjective*
1 very good or enjoyable: *We saw a great movie last night.* | *It's great to see you again!* | *This pasta dish is great for a quick dinner.* SYNONYM **excellent**
2 very important or famous: *Abraham Lincoln was a great American president.*
3 very big or very large in amount: *She had great big blue eyes.*
4 great-grandmother/great-grandfather = the mother or father of one of your grandparents

5 great-granddaughter/great-grandson = the daughter or son of your GRANDCHILD
→ See Thesaurus box at **good**[1]

great·ly /'greɪtli/ *adverb, formal*
very much: *If you practice a lot, it will greatly increase your chances of winning.*

greed·y /'gridi/ *adjective* **greedier, greediest**
wanting more money, food, etc., than you need: *I gave you $10 to spend already – don't be greedy and ask for more.*
—**greed** *noun* the feeling of wanting more money, food, etc., than you need: *They didn't need the money – they stole it out of greed.*
—**greedily** *adverb* in a greedy way: *Jake was looking at the chocolate greedily.*

Greek *noun* /grik/
1 someone from Greece
2 the language spoken in Greece
—**Greek** *adjective* from Greece: *a Greek woman*

green[1] /grin/ *adjective*
1 having the color of grass: *She has green eyes.*
2 covered with grass and trees: *Cities need more green areas.*

green[2] *noun*
the color of grass: *Green is my favorite color.*

ˌgreen 'card *noun*
an official card that allows people to live and work in the U.S. if they come from another country: *The man at the desk asked to see my green card.*

green·house /'grinhaʊs/ *noun*
1 a glass building for growing plants that need a warm light place
2 greenhouse gas = a gas such as CARBON DIOXIDE that stops heat from escaping from the Earth
3 the greenhouse effect = the process in which the air around the Earth is getting slowly warmer because greenhouse gases stop the heat from escaping

greet /grit/ *verb*
to welcome or say hello to someone: *He greeted her and hugged her.*

greet·ing /'gritɪŋ/ *noun*
1 something you say or do when you meet someone: *Every time I go there, I get a warm greeting* (=they greet me in a friendly way).
2 a message you send to say you hope someone has a happy birthday, Christmas, etc.: *Sara got lots of birthday greetings from all her friends.*

gre·nade /grə'neɪd/ *noun*
a small bomb that you can throw, or fire from a gun: *The soldiers all carried hand grenades* (=that you can throw).

grew /gru/ *verb*
the past tense of GROW

grey /greɪ/ *adjective, noun*
another spelling of GRAY

grey·hound /'greɪhaʊnd/ *noun*
a thin dog that can run very fast, and that often competes in races

grief /grif/ *noun*
great sadness: *Her feelings of grief lasted for months after her husband died.*

griev·ance /'grivəns/ *noun, formal*
something that you want to complain about because you think it is unfair to you: *The people who lost their jobs met to discuss their grievances.*

grieve /griv/ *verb*
to feel very sad, because someone you love has died: *The family is still grieving for their son, who died in the crash.*

griev·ous /'grivəs/ *adjective, formal*
very bad or serious: *The president of the company realized he had made a grievous mistake and offered to leave his job.*

grill[1] /grɪl/ *verb*
to cook meat, fish, etc. on a frame over a fire: *Grill the chicken for fifteen minutes.*
→ See Thesaurus box at **cook**[1]

grill[2] *noun*
a metal frame that you put meat, fish, etc. on to cook over a fire: *Let's put the steaks on the grill.*

grim /grɪm/ *adjective*
1 making you feel worried and unhappy: *The news that day was grim; it was all about war.*
2 very serious and sad: *The policeman looked grim as he explained how the accident had happened.*
—**grimly** *adverb* in a very serious way: *"The situation is dangerous," Doug said grimly.*

G

grim•ace /ˈgrɪməs/ *verb*
to twist your face because you feel pain, or you do not like something: *Lou grimaced with pain.*
—**grimace** *noun* a look on your face that shows you feel pain, or you do not like something: *She swallowed the medicine with a grimace.*

grimace

grin /grɪn/ *noun*
a big smile: *He opened the door with a big grin on his face and hugged me.*
—**grin** *verb* to give a big smile: *"It's great to see you," she said, grinning.*
→ See Thesaurus box at **smile**[1]

grind /graɪnd/ *verb* **ground** /graʊnd/
to crush or cut something into small pieces or powder: *This machine grinds the coffee beans.*
→ See Thesaurus box at **press**[1]

grind•er /ˈgraɪndɚ/ *noun*
a machine that crushes or cuts something into small pieces or powder: *Put the coffee beans in the grinder.*

grip[1] /grɪp/ *noun*
1 a strong hold on something: *He had a firm grip on my arm as he pushed me through the door.*
2 control of your feelings or of a situation: *Dee tried to get a grip on herself* (=to control her feelings).

grip[2] *verb* **gripped, gripping**
to hold something very firmly: *She gripped the rail to stop herself from falling.*
→ See Thesaurus box at **hold**[1]

grit /grɪt/ *noun*
very small pieces of dirt or stone: *Wash the vegetables to remove any grit.*

griz•zly bear /ˈgrɪzli ˌber/ *also* **grizzly** *noun*
a large brown bear that lives in parts of North America

groan /groʊn/ *verb*
to make a long deep sound, because you are in pain or not happy: *One of the players was on the ground, holding his leg and groaning.*
—**groan** *noun* a long deep sound that you make when you are in pain or not happy: *Mom read the bad news from the bank and gave a loud groan.*

gro•cer /ˈgroʊsɚ/ *noun*
someone who owns or works in a GROCERY STORE

gro•cer•ies /ˈgroʊsəriz/ *plural noun*
the food and things you use in the home that you buy in a store: *I put the groceries away in the refrigerator.*

groceries

gro•cer•y store /ˈgroʊsəri ˌstɔr/ *also* **grocery** *noun*
a store that sells food and things you use in the home: *I went to the grocery store to get some milk.*

groom /grum/ *noun*
a man who is getting married: *The groom arrived at the church first.* SYNONYM **bridegroom**

groove /gruv/ *noun*
a thin line that goes down in the surface of something: *Plant the seeds in rows in grooves in the soil.*

grope /groʊp/ *verb*
to try to find something you cannot see using your hands: *It was dark, and Mark groped for the light switch.*

gross /groʊs/ *adjective, informal*
very unpleasant: *The food in the school cafeteria is really gross – it's usually cold, and it tastes bad.*
—**grossness** *noun*

ˌgross ˌnational ˈproduct *noun*
another word for GNP

gro•tesque /groʊˈtesk/ *adjective*
ugly and very strange in a way that is frightening: *Some of the people in his paintings are grotesque.*

grouch•y /ˈgraʊtʃi/ *adjective, informal*
feeling annoyed about things, and talking to people in an annoyed way: *Dad's been grouchy all week because his car is not working.*

ground¹ /graʊnd/ *noun*
1 the surface of the Earth: *A tree had fallen to the ground.*
2 soil or land: *It was winter, and the ground was hard.*
3 a wire that connects electrical equipment to the ground, so you can use it safely

ground² *verb*
the past tense and past participle of GRIND

ground³ *adjective*
1 **ground beef/pork, etc.** = meat that is in very small pieces: *You make hamburgers with ground beef.*
2 ground coffee, pepper, etc. is a powder because you have crushed it: *Add some freshly ground pepper* (=pepper you have just crushed).

ˌground ˈfloor *noun*
the part of a building that is on the same level as the ground: *My office is on the ground floor.* SYNONYM **first floor**

Ground•hog Day /ˈgraʊndhɔg ˌdeɪ/ *noun*
February 2; in American stories, a GROUNDHOG comes out of its hole on this day, and if it sees its shadow, there will be six more weeks of winter; if it does not, good weather will come early.

grounds /graʊndz/ *plural noun*
1 an area of land or sea that is used for a particular purpose: *fishing grounds* | *The fence was built to protect the old Native American burial grounds* (=place where people were buried after they died).
2 the land or gardens that surround a large building: *You are not allowed to leave school grounds during lunch.*
3 *formal* a good reason for doing something: *Did the police have legal grounds to arrest him?*

group¹ /grup/ *noun*
1 several people or things that are together in the same place: *A fight started between two groups of men.* | *The Cyclades Islands are a group of 39 islands in the Aegean Sea.*

THESAURUS: group

Group of People

crowd a large group of people in one place: *There was a crowd of people standing around him.*

team a group of people who work together: *a team of doctors* | *Ryan's trying out for the football team.*

crew a group of people who all work together, especially on a ship or airplane: *The ship had a small crew.*

gang *informal* a group of young people, especially a group that often causes trouble and fights, but sometimes just a group of friends: *There have been gang and drug problems in this part of the city.* | *I usually hang out with the gang on Friday nights.*

mob a large noisy group of people, especially one that is angry and violent: *An angry mob was gathering outside the courtroom.*

bunch *informal* a group of people: *They're a nice bunch of kids.*

Group of Animals

herd of cows/deer/elephants

flock of sheep/birds

school/shoal of fish/dolphins/tuna, etc.

pack of dogs/wolves

litter of puppies/kittens/piglets (=a group of baby animals born from the same mother at the same time)

Group of Things

bunch of flowers/grapes/keys, etc. (=several flowers, etc. tied or held together): *He gave her a bunch of roses on their anniversary.*

bundle of papers/clothes/sticks (=several papers, etc. tied or held together): *Bundles of newspapers were stacked on the curb.*

2 several musicians who play and sing popular music together: *U2 is a famous rock group.*

group² *verb*
1 to arrange things in a group: *Books can be grouped into two basic types: fiction and non-fiction.*
2 to come together and form a group: *The cows had grouped together under the trees.*

grove /groʊv/ *noun, formal*
1 an area of land with fruit or nut trees growing on it: *an orange grove*
2 a small group of trees of the same type, without low branches

grov•el /ˈgrɑvəl/ *verb*
to try too hard to please someone to show you are sorry for something or because you are frightened of him or her: *Just apologize to your teacher in a calm way; you don't need to grovel.*

grow /groʊ/ *verb* **grew** /gru/ **grown** /groʊn/
1 to get bigger in size or amount: *Babies grow quickly in their first year.* | *The number of students at the college grew by 5% last year.*
2 if plants grow somewhere, or if you grow them there, they are alive in that place: *Not many plants can grow in the far north.* | *We grow our own vegetables.*
3 grow old, grow strong, etc. = to become old, strong, etc.: *Grandad was growing old and becoming forgetful.*

PHRASAL VERBS

grow out of something
1 if a child grows out of clothes, he or she becomes too big to wear them: *Kids grow out of their shoes so quickly.*
2 if someone grows out of something, they stop doing it as they become older: *He sucked his thumb till he was six, but grew out of it eventually.*

grow up
to gradually change from being a child to being an adult: *I grew up in San Diego.*
→ See Thesaurus box at **increase**[1]

growl /graʊl/ *verb*
if a dog, bear, etc. growls, it makes a deep angry sound: *The dog usually growls at visitors.*
—**growl** *noun* a deep angry sound made by a dog, bear, etc.: *The bear gave a loud growl.*

grown[1] /groʊn/ *adjective*
grown man/woman = used when talking about an adult who is not behaving in the way you expect an adult to behave: *I was young, and I had never seen a grown man cry before.*

grown[2] *verb*
the past participle of GROW

grown•up[1] /ˈgroʊnʌp/ *noun*
an adult – used by or to children: *My brother and I listened while the grownups talked.*

ˌ**grown-up**[2] *adjective*
someone who is grown-up is an adult: *She has two grown-up daughters – one is 25 and the other is 22.*

growth /groʊθ/ *noun*
1 an increase in amount, number, or size: *The growth of the Internet has happened very quickly.* | *There has been huge growth in the number of people who have quit smoking.*
2 the increase in the physical size and strength of a person, animal, or plant over a period of time: *A variety of good foods are necessary for the healthy growth of your body.*

grub•by /ˈgrʌbi/ *adjective, informal*
dirty: *Her hands were grubby from cleaning the mud off her bike.*

grudge /grʌdʒ/ *noun*
an unfriendly feeling towards someone because he or she did something bad to you in the past: *She criticized him months ago, and he's still holding a grudge* (=continuing to have an unfriendly feeling).

gru•el•ing /ˈgruəlɪŋ/ *adjective*
very difficult and tiring: *It was a grueling five-hour climb to the top of the mountain.*

grue•some /ˈgrusəm/ *adjective*
very unpleasant or shocking, and usually involving death or injury: *The race driver was seriously injured in a gruesome accident.*

grum•ble /ˈgrʌmbəl/ *verb*
to complain: *He's always grumbling about how expensive everything is.*

grump•y /ˈgrʌmpi/ *adjective* **grumpier, grumpiest**
if someone is grumpy, they show that they feel slightly angry: *I'm feeling grumpy because I'm tired.*
—**grumpily** *adverb*: *"Leave me alone," she said grumpily.*

grun•gy /ˈgrʌndʒi/ *adjective, informal*
dirty and sometimes smelling bad: *His clothes were grungy, and he smelled bad.*

grunt /grʌnt/ *verb*
1 to make a short low sound instead of talking: *I told him to get out of bed, but he just grunted and went back to sleep.*
2 if a pig grunts, it makes a low rough sound
—**grunt** *noun* a short low sound that you make in your throat, or a similar sound that a

pig makes: *Alex answered the question with a grunt.*

gua•ca•mo•le /ˌgwɑkəˈmoʊleɪ/ *noun*
a cold Mexican dish made with crushed AVOCADO

guar•an•tee¹ /ˌgærənˈti/ Ac *verb*
to promise to do something, or to promise that something will happen: *We guarantee we will repair your computer within 48 hours.* | *I guarantee that you'll love this movie.* SYNONYM **promise**
➔ See Thesaurus box at **promise¹**

guarantee² *noun*
a promise by a company to repair or replace something you have bought from them, for example if it breaks: *The MP3 player has a two-year guarantee.*

guard¹ /gɑrd/ *noun*
1 someone whose job is to protect a person or place, or to make sure that a person does not escape: *A security guard was standing outside the jewelry store.* | *Two armed guards stood by the door of the prison.*
2 the act of protecting a person or place, or making sure that a person does not escape: *Soldiers are always on guard outside the embassy.* | *A police officer stood guard in front of the hotel after the robbery.*

DOGS GUARD
THIS BUILDING
guard

guard² *verb*
to protect someone or something from being attacked or stolen, or to prevent a prisoner from escaping: *Two large dogs guard the building at night.*
➔ See Thesaurus box at **protect**

PHRASAL VERB
guard against something
to prevent something bad from happening: *The best way to guard against illness is to wash your hands.*

ˈguard dog *noun*
a dog that protects someone's home or property

guard•ed /ˈgɑrdɪd/ *adjective*
careful not to show your emotions or give away information: *The Senator gave a guarded answer to the reporter's question, saying "I'm not sure I can tell you anything more now."*

guard•i•an /ˈgɑrdiən/ *noun*
someone who is legally responsible for a child, but who is not the child's parent: *His parents died, and his aunt is his legal guardian.*
—**guardianship** *noun, formal* the state of being responsible for someone or something: *I have guardianship of my grandson, because his mother is in jail.*

guer•ril•la *also* **guerilla** /gəˈrɪlə/ *noun*
a member of an unofficial army that is fighting for political reasons: *The guerillas made a surprise attack on a government office building.*

guess¹ /ges/ *verb*
1 to answer a question or decide something when you are not sure if you are right: *I think he's about 40, but I'm just guessing.* | *"Guess how much this dress cost?" "I don't know, about $50? $75?"* | *Can you guess my age?*
2 keep someone guessing = to make someone feel excited or not sure about what will happen next: *The movie is a mystery that really keeps the audience guessing.*
3 I guess a) used to say that you think something is probably true: *He's not here yet, but I guess he'll be coming later.* | *"Does she make a lot of money?" " I guess so."* **b)** used to say that you will do something, even though you do not really want to: *I'm tired, so I guess I'll stay home tonight.*

guess² *noun*
an attempt to answer a question or decide something when you are not sure if you are right: *I think the painting is by Picasso, but that's just a guess.* | *I couldn't decide which answer was right, so I had to make a guess.*

guest /gest/ *noun*
1 someone who you invite to stay in your home or invite to an event: *How many guests are coming to your party?*
2 someone who is staying in a hotel: *Use of the swimming pool is free to hotel guests.*

G

guid•ance /ˈgaɪdns/ *noun*
helpful advice: *Your teacher can give you guidance on choosing a career.*

guide¹ /gaɪd/ *noun*
1 someone whose job is to show a place to tourists: *The tour guide was taking a group of tourists around the museum.*
2 a book that gives information about a particular subject or explains how to do something: *I bought him a beginner's guide to using the Internet.*
3 something that helps you make a decision: *Use your nose as a guide – if the fish is fresh, it will smell fresh.*

guide² *verb*
1 to help someone to go somewhere, for example by showing them the right direction: *He took the old lady's hand and guided her across the road.*
2 to help someone manage a difficult situation: *The school staff can guide you when you apply for colleges.*

G

guide•book /ˈgaɪdbʊk/ *noun*
a book with information about a city or country for people who are visiting it: *The guidebook gives the hotel three stars and says it has a good restaurant.*

ˈ**guide dog** *noun*
a specially trained dog that blind people use to help them go to places: *Guide dogs help safely guide blind people through traffic, crowds, and other situations.*

guide•lines /ˈgaɪdlaɪnz/ Ac *plural noun*
rules or instructions about the best way to do something: *The teacher gave the class some guidelines on writing essays for the exam.*

guilt /gɪlt/ *noun*
1 a sad feeling you have when you have done something wrong: *She felt a sense of guilt about lying to her parents.*
2 the fact that someone has broken a law: *We were sure that he had stolen the money, but we couldn't prove his guilt.* ANTONYM **innocence**
3 the state of being responsible for something bad that has happened: *I know that the guilt for the accident was mine, because I was driving too fast.* SYNONYM **fault**
4 guilt trip *informal* = the act of trying to make someone feel very sorry for something he or she has done: *My parents are giving me a guilt trip for scratching the car.*

guilt•y /ˈgɪlti/ *adjective*
1 unhappy and ashamed because you have done something that you know is wrong: *Rob felt guilty about stealing the book.*
2 find someone guilty (of something) = if a court of law finds someone guilty of a crime, it decides that they COMMITted that crime: *The jury found him guilty of murder.* ANTONYM **innocent**
—**guiltily** *adverb*: *"Yes, I took it," she said guiltily.*

guin•ea pig /ˈgɪni ˌpɪg/ *noun*
1 a small furry animal with no tail that is often kept as a pet
2 someone who is used in a scientific test to see how successful or safe a new product, system, etc. is: *The scientists are looking for guinea pigs to try out a new diet.*

gui•tar /gɪˈtɑr/ *noun*
a wooden musical instrument with strings and a long neck, which you play by pulling the strings: *an electric guitar*
—**guitarist** *noun* someone who plays the guitar: *Jimi Hendrix was a famous guitarist.*
➔ See picture at **acoustic**

gulf /gʌlf/ *noun*
a large area of ocean that is partly surrounded by land: *The Gulf of Mexico is to the west of Florida.*

gull /gʌl/ *noun*
a SEAGULL

gulp¹ /gʌlp/ *verb*
1 *also* **gulp down** to swallow food or drink quickly: *She gulped down her breakfast and ran for the bus.*
2 to swallow suddenly because you are surprised or nervous: *Ed gulped when he saw how hard the test questions were.*

gulp² *noun*
an act of quickly swallowing a large amount of drink: *He took a gulp of his lemonade.*

gum /gʌm/ *noun*
1 *also* **chewing gum** a sweet type of candy that you CHEW for a long time, but do not swallow
2 the pink parts inside your mouth that your teeth grow out of

gun /gʌn/ *noun*
1 a weapon that fires bullets: *The man was carrying a gun.* | *Someone fired a gun at the President.*
2 a tool that forces out small objects or a liquid by pressure: *He used a spray gun to paint the car.*

gun•fire /ˈgʌnfaɪɚ/ *noun*
shots fired from a gun: *The soldiers could hear gunfire in the distance.*

gun•man /ˈgʌnmən/ *noun* plural **gunmen** /ˈgʌnmən/
a criminal who uses a gun: *The gunman walked into the bank and demanded money.*

gun•point /ˈgʌnpɔɪnt/ *noun*
at gunpoint = while threatening someone or being threatened with a gun: *They were held at gunpoint while the man stole their car.*

gun•pow•der /ˈgʌnˌpaʊdɚ/ *noun*
an explosive substance used in bombs and FIREWORKS

gun•shot /ˈgʌnʃɑt/ *noun*
1 the sound made by a gun: *We heard a gunshot and a loud scream.*
2 the bullets that are shot from a gun: *He died from a gunshot wound.*

gur•gle /ˈgɚgəl/ *verb*
1 to make a low sound, especially because water is moving around: *A small stream gurgled over the rocks.*
2 if someone gurgles, he or she makes a pleasant low sound in their throat: *The baby smiled and gurgled with pleasure.*

gu•ru /ˈgʊru/ *noun*
1 *informal* someone who knows a lot about a particular subject, and whose opinions are respected by many people: *She is a fashion guru who gives advice about what clothes people should wear.*
2 a Hindu religious teacher

gush /gʌʃ/ *verb*
if liquid gushes somewhere, a large amount of it flows there: *Blood was gushing from a deep cut in his arm.*
—**gush** *noun* a large quantity of liquid that suddenly pours out of something: *a gush of cold water from the faucet*
→ See Thesaurus box at **pour**

gust /gʌst/ *noun*
a sudden strong wind: *A gust of wind blew our tent down.*
→ See Thesaurus box at **wind**[1]

gut[1] /gʌt/ *adjective*
gut feeling/gut reaction *informal* = a feeling or idea that you are sure is right, although you cannot give a reason for it: *My gut reaction is that this is a bad idea.*

gut[2] *also* **guts** *noun, informal*
your stomach and the tubes in your body that food passes through: *My guts were aching after eating too much at dinner.*

gut[3] *verb* **gutted, gutting**
to destroy the inside of a building completely: *The house was gutted by fire.*

guts /gʌts/ *noun, informal*
courage and determination to do something difficult: *He didn't have the guts to ask his boss for more money.*

gut•ter /ˈgʌtɚ/ *noun*
a part at the lowest edge of something such as a roof or a road, that collects water and waste so that it can flow away: *The gutter was blocked by leaves.*

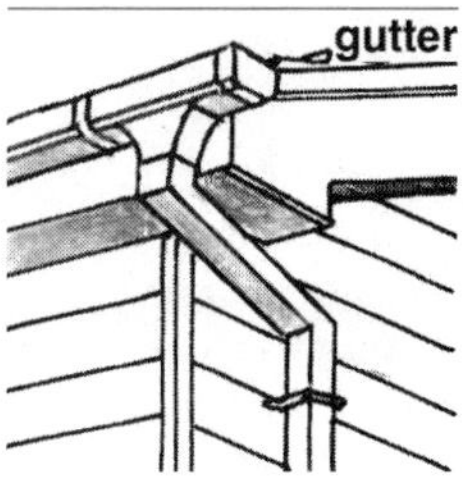

guy /gaɪ/ *noun, informal*
a man: *He's a really nice guy.*

guz•zle /ˈgʌzəl/ *verb, informal*
to drink a lot of something very quickly: *My brother and his friends were eating pizza and guzzling soda.*

gym /dʒɪm/ *noun*
a building or room that has equipment for doing physical exercise: *I go to the gym three times a week.*
→ See Thesaurus box at **exercise**[2]

gym•na•si•um /dʒɪmˈneɪziəm/ *noun*
→ **gym**

gym•nas•tics /dʒɪmˈnæstɪks/ *noun*
a sport involving skillful physical exercises and movements
—**gymnast** /ˈdʒɪmnæst/ *noun* someone who performs gymnastics: *an Olympic gymnast*
→ See picture on page A24

G

gymnastics

gy·ne·col·o·gy /ˌgaɪnəˈkɑlədʒi/ *noun*
the study and treatment of medical conditions relating to women's ability to have children
—**gynecologist** *noun* someone who studies gynecology
—**gynecological** /ˌgaɪnəkəˈlɑdʒɪkəl/ *adjective* relating to gynecology

gyp·sy /ˈdʒɪpsi/ *noun* plural **gypsies**
a member of a group of people who travel around rather than live in one place. Gypsies originally came from northern India.

G

Hh

ha /hɑ/
said when you are surprised or pleased about something: *Ha! I knew I was right.*

hab·it /ˈhæbɪt/ *noun*
something that you do often or regularly: *We got in the habit of staying up very late.* | *Smoking is a very bad habit.*

hab·i·tat /ˈhæbəˌtæt/ *noun, formal*
the place in which a plant or animal lives: *The woods are the natural habitat of foxes.*

hack /hæk/ *verb*
1 to cut something roughly or violently: *Tom hacked the branches off the tree.*
2 to use a computer to enter someone else's computer system in order to damage it or get secret information: *The criminals hacked into the bank's computer system and moved money into their bank accounts.*

hack·er /ˈhækɚ/ *noun, informal*
someone who secretly uses or changes the information in other people's computer systems: *A hacker stole some information from the company's computer system.*
—**hacking** *noun* the activity of secretly using or changing information in other people's computer systems

hack·saw /ˈhæksɔ/ *noun*
a type of cutting tool with small teeth on its blade, used especially for cutting metal
—**hacksaw** *verb* to cut something with a hacksaw

had /əd; *strong* hæd/ *verb*
the past tense and past participle of HAVE

had·n't /ˈhædnt/ *verb*
the short form of "had not": *I hadn't eaten anything all day.*

hail[1] /heɪl/ *verb*
if it hails, small hard pieces of frozen rain fall from the sky: *It was hailing when we came out of church.*

hail[2] *noun*
small hard pieces of frozen rain that fall from the sky: *There will be some hail later today.*
➔ See Thesaurus boxes at **snow**[1] and **rain**[1]

hail·stone /ˈheɪlˌstoʊn/ *noun*
a small ball of frozen rain: *Most hailstones are about the size of peas.*

hair /her/ *noun*
1 the things like thin threads that grow together on your head: *Tim has brown hair.* | *She was brushing her hair.*

> **GRAMMAR: hair**
> In this meaning, **hair** is an uncountable noun so it has no plural: *Tim has brown hair (NOT brown hairs).*

2 one of the thin threads that grow on the skin of a person or animal: *There are cat hairs all over this chair.*
3 let your hair down *informal* = to relax and enjoy yourself: *On weekends, people like to let their hair down with friends.*
➔ See picture on page A2

hair·brush /ˈherbrʌʃ/ *noun*
a brush that you use to make your hair look neat
➔ See picture at **brush**

hair·cut /ˈherkʌt/ *noun*
1 if you have a haircut, someone cuts your hair: *My hair's too long, so I'm going to have a haircut.*
2 the way your hair is cut: *Do you like my new haircut?*

hair·do /ˈherdu/ *noun* plural **hairdos** *informal*
the style in which your hair is cut or arranged: *Mom came home with a new hairdo.* SYNONYM **hairstyle**

hair·dress·er /ˈherˌdresɚ/ *noun*
someone whose job is to cut and arrange people's hair: *Marie's always been good at cutting hair, so she's training to be a hairdresser.*
➔ See picture on page A16

hair·dry·er /ˈherˌdraɪɚ/ *noun*
a machine that you use to dry your hair

hair·style /ˈherstaɪl/ *noun*
the style in which your hair is cut and arranged: *She's had the same short hairstyle for years.*

hair·y /ˈheri/ *adjective*
hairy arms, legs, etc. have a lot of hair on them: *a big man with a hairy chest*

H

Haj *also* **Hajj** /hɑdʒ/ *noun*
a trip to Mecca that all Muslims try to make for religious reasons
—**Haji** *also* **Hajji** /ˈhɑdʒi/ *noun* a Muslim who has made the trip to Mecca

ha•lal /həˈlɑl/ *adjective*
halal meat is from animals that were killed in a way that Muslim law approves

half[1] /hæf/ *noun* plural **halves** /hævz/ *pronoun*
1 one of two equal parts of something: *Half of 10 is 5.* | *Half the students spoke Spanish, the other half spoke English.* | *I cut the sandwich in half* (=in two equal pieces). | *My brother is two and a half* (=two years and six months old).
2 one of two parts of a game in some sports: *Alan scored a goal at the end of the first half.*
3 half an hour = thirty minutes: *I'll be there in half an hour.*
4 half a dozen = six: *I need half a dozen eggs.*

half[2] *adverb*
partly but not completely: *A half-empty coffee cup was on the table.*

ˈhalf-ˌbrother *noun*
a brother who is the child of only one of your parents

ˌhalf-ˈhearted *adjective*
if you do something in a half-hearted way, you do it without really trying or succeeding: *She was very upset, but she made a half-hearted attempt to smile.*

ˌhalf-ˈhour *noun*
thirty minutes: *The cake is not done – it needs another half-hour in the oven.*
—**ˈhalf-hour** *adjective* continuing for thirty minutes: *a half-hour TV show*

ˌhalf-ˈmast *adjective*
at half-mast = if a flag is at half-mast, it is in the middle of the pole and not at the top, because someone important has died: *The flag flew at half-mast for a week after the governor died.*

ˈhalf-ˌsister *noun*
a sister who is the child of only one of your parents

ˈhalf time *noun*
a time when the teams rest between two parts of a game such as football: *Our team was winning at half time, but they scored twice in the second half.*

half•way /ˌhæfˈweɪ/ *adjective, adverb*
1 in the middle between two places or things: *I live halfway between New York and Washington D.C.* | *The boat was halfway across the lake.*
2 in the middle of a period of time or an event: *Dad fell asleep halfway through the movie.*

hall /hɔl/ *noun*
1 a narrow area in a house or building with doors that lead to other rooms: *Go down the hall and turn right, and you'll see the bathrooms.* SYNONYM **hallway**
2 a room that you go through when you enter a house, with doors that lead to other rooms: *You can hang your coats in the front hall.* SYNONYM **hallway**
3 a big room or building that people use for public meetings, concerts, etc.: *The audience was coming into the concert hall.*

hal•le•lu•jah /ˌhæləˈluyə/
a word people say to praise to God

Hal•low•een /ˌhæləˈwin/ *noun*
the night of October 31, when children dress as WITCHES, GHOSTS, etc., and go to people's houses asking for candy by saying "trick or treat!": *Children love dressing up for Halloween.*

hal•lu•ci•nate /həˈlusəˌneɪt/ *verb, formal*
to see or hear something very clearly, although it is not really there: *Sometimes the drug makes people hallucinate.*
—**hallucination** /həˌlusəˈneɪʃən/ *noun* something you see or hear very clearly, although it is not really there: *The man was screaming and having hallucinations about monsters trying to kill him.*

hall•way /ˈhɔlweɪ/ *noun*
1 a room that you go through when you enter a house, with doors that lead to other rooms: *I came into the house and found Sam standing in the hallway.* SYNONYM **hall**
2 a narrow area in a house or building with doors that lead to other rooms: *The classroom is the last door on the right at the end of the hallway.* SYNONYM **hall**

halt[1] /hɔlt/ *verb, formal*
to stop: *Our taxi halted outside the airport.* | *Problems have halted work on the new building.*

halt[2] *noun, formal*
a stop: *The cars suddenly came to a halt because some children were crossing the road.*

halve /hæv/ *verb, formal*
to cut something into two equal parts: *Halve the tomato, and put the two pieces on each side of the dish.*

halves /hævz/ *noun*
the plural of HALF

ham /hæm/ *noun*
the meat from a pig with salt added to it to keep it fresh: *I put two slices of ham in the sandwich.*
➔ See Thesaurus box at **meat**

ham•burg•er /ˈhæmˌbɚgɚ/ *noun*
1 a flat piece of meat in the shape of a circle, made from very small pieces of BEEF, that you cook and eat between pieces of round bread: *He was eating a hamburger and fries.*
2 BEEF that is cut into very small pieces, used for making hamburgers and other dishes: *I bought a pound of hamburger.*

ham•mer[1] /ˈhæmɚ/ *noun*
a tool you use for hitting nails into wood

hammer[2] *verb*
to hit something with a hammer: *He hammered a nail into the fence.*

ham•mock /ˈhæmək/ *noun*
a piece of net or other material that hangs between two trees or poles that you use for sleeping in

ham•ster /ˈhæmstɚ/ *noun*
a small soft animal like a mouse with no tail, that children often keep as a pet
➔ See picture at **pet**

hand[1] /hænd/ *noun*
1 the part of your body at the end of your arm, that you use to hold things: *Go and wash your hands.* | *Most people write with their right hand.* | *Raise your hand* (=lift it up) *if you know the answer.*
2 a hand = some help: *Can you give me a hand with this box? It's really heavy.*

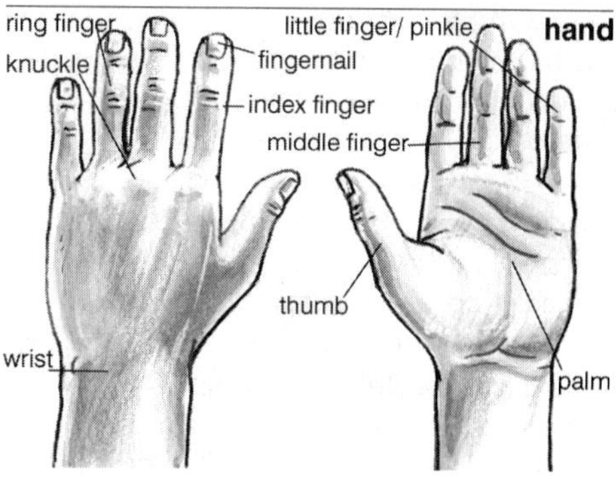

3 (on the one hand...) on the other hand = you use this for giving another idea or fact that you should consider: *The work was really hard, but on the other hand I learned a lot.*
4 by hand = done or made by a person, not a machine: *The rug was made by hand.*
5 one of the things that move to show the time on a clock: *The hands on the clock moved slowly toward noon.*
6 be/get out of hand = to be or become impossible to control: *The party was beginning to get out of hand, so I told everyone to leave.*
7 on hand = near and ready if needed: *A teacher is always on hand to help.*
8 the cards that you are holding in a game: *Tom held the winning hand.*
➔ See picture on page A2

hand[2] *verb*
to give something to someone else using your hand: *Can you hand me a towel?*
➔ See Thesaurus box at **give**[1]

PHRASAL VERBS

hand something down
to give something to a younger member of your family: *This necklace was handed down from my grandmother to me.*

hand something in
to give something to a teacher, employer, etc.: *Hand in your homework, please.*

hand something out
to give something to everyone in a group: *The teacher handed out the tests.*

hand something over
to give something to someone else using your hand: *She handed the phone over to me.*

H

hand•bag /ˈhændbæg/ *noun*
a bag that a woman uses to carry money, keys, etc.: *She was carrying a brown leather handbag.* SYNONYM **purse**
→ See picture on page A6

hand•book /ˈhændbʊk/ *noun*
a small book with information about something: *I bought a handbook for travelers in South America.*

hand•cuffs /ˈhændkʌfs/ *noun*
two metal rings joined by a chain, that hold a prisoner's wrists together: *The police took him away in handcuffs.*
—**handcuff** *verb* to put handcuffs on someone: *An officer handcuffed him, because they could not control him.*

hand•ful /ˈhændfʊl/ *noun*
1 an amount that you can hold in your hand: *She took a handful of nuts from the bowl.*
2 a handful of something = a small number of people or things: *Only a handful of people came to the meeting – I think there were five people there.*

H

hand•gun /ˈhændgʌn/ *noun*
a small gun you can hold in one hand

hand•i•cap /ˈhændiˌkæp/ *noun*
1 *formal* something that is permanently wrong with a part of your body or mind, so that you are not able to use it in the normal way: *Some diseases can cause mental handicaps* (=of the mind). SYNONYM **disability**
2 something that makes it difficult for you to do something: *If you don't speak Spanish, it will be a handicap when you travel in South America.* SYNONYM **disadvantage**

hand•i•capped /ˈhændiˌkæpt/ *adjective*
not able to use a part of your body or mind because there is something permanently wrong with it: *The school is good for physically handicapped children, because there are no stairs.* SYNONYM **disabled**

USAGE: handicapped

handicapped is old-fashioned and may offend some people. It is better to use the word **disabled**: *The hotel has special rooms on the ground floor for disabled people.*

hand•ker•chief /ˈhæŋkɚtʃɪf/ *noun*
a piece of cloth that you use for drying your nose or eyes

han•dle¹ /ˈhændl/ *verb*
1 to deal with something: *If there are any problems, I'll handle them.*
2 to pick up or touch something: *If you handle uncooked meat, you should wash your hands.*

handle² *noun*
the part of something that you have in your hand when you hold or open it: *the handle of the knife | a door handle*

han•dle•bars /ˈhændlˌbɑrz/ *noun*
the part of a bicycle or MOTORCYCLE that you hold with your hands when you are riding it

hand•made /ˌhændˈmeɪd/ *adjective*
made by a person and not a machine: *I bought a handmade rug for the bedroom.*

hand•out /ˈhændaʊt/ *noun*
1 a piece of paper with information on it, that you give to people in a class or meeting: *The teacher gave us a handout with our math homework on it.*
2 money or food that people receive because they need help: *There are a lot of poor people living on government handouts* (=that the government gives).

hand•shake /ˈhændʃeɪk/ *noun*
an act of taking someone's right hand in your hand and moving it up and down, for example when you meet or make an agreement: *People welcomed us with smiles and handshakes.*

hand•some /ˈhænsəm/ *adjective, formal*
a handsome man is attractive: *He was a handsome young man, and he worked as a model for a while.* SYNONYM **good-looking**; ANTONYM **ugly**
→ See Thesaurus box at **beautiful**

hand•writ•ing /ˈhændˌraɪtɪŋ/ *noun*
the way someone writes with a pen or a pencil: *She has very neat handwriting, which is easy to read.*

hand•writ•ten /ˈhænd,rɪtn/ *adjective*
written with a pen or pencil and not a machine: *She sent me a handwritten letter, not an email.*

hand•y /ˈhændi/ *adjective* **handier**, **handiest**
1 useful: *I earned some extra money, which came in handy* (=was useful).
2 near and easy to reach: *Do you have a pen handy?*

hand•y•man /ˈhændi,mæn/ *noun* plural **handymen** /ˈhændi,men/
someone who is good at making and repairing things: *Bruce works as a handyman at the school, and he's doing a lot of building work.*

hang[1] /hæŋ/ *verb*
1 hung /hʌŋ/ to put clothes in a cupboard, pictures on a wall, etc. by attaching the top part of them to something like a hook: *I hung my coat on a hook in the hall.* | *Do you want me to hang the picture here?*
2 hanged to kill someone by putting a rope around their neck and letting them drop down toward the ground: *The man hanged himself in prison.*

PHRASAL VERBS

hang around *informal*
to stay in one place and not do much: *On Saturdays, a lot of kids hang around downtown.*

hang on *informal*
1 to hold something carefully in order to keep it or yourself safe: *Hang on to your wallet in this part of town, or someone will take it.* SYNONYM **hold on**
2 you say this when you want someone to wait for you: *Hang on – I'm almost ready to go.* SYNONYM **hold on**

hang out *informal*
to spend a lot of time somewhere with friends and not do much: *I'm going to hang out at the beach all summer.*

hang up
to finish speaking on the telephone by putting the telephone down: *Dad wants to use the phone, so I have to hang up now.*

hang[2] *noun, informal*
get the hang of something = to learn how to do or use something: *He falls off his bike a lot, but he'll get the hang of it soon.*

hang•er /ˈhæŋɚ/ *noun*
something you use for hanging clothes on, made of some curved wire, wood, etc. with a hook on top

hang•o•ver /ˈhæŋ,oʊvɚ/ *noun*
a feeling of sickness that someone has when they have drunk too much alcohol the day before: *The morning after the party, he had a bad hangover.*

Ha•nuk•kah /ˈhɑnəkə/ *noun*
a Jewish holiday in November or December, that continues for eight days

hap•haz•ard /,hæpˈhæzɚd/ *adjective, formal*
not organized, neat, or planned: *Brian's books were lying all over his desk in a haphazard way.*
—**haphazardly** *adverb*: *She threw her clothes haphazardly onto the bed.*

hap•pen /ˈhæpən/ *verb*
1 when something happens, there is an event that no one planned or expected: *The accident happened outside my house.* | *I'm going to call Kara and tell her what happened.*

> **THESAURUS: happen**
>
> **happen** if something happens, you usually did not plan or expect it: *A strange thing happened on my way to school.*
>
> **take place** *formal* if an event takes place, it is usually because of a plan or arrangement: *The next meeting will take place on Thursday.*
>
> **occur** *formal* if an event occurs, it usually happens in a particular place or at a particular time: *The robbery occurred around 9 p.m.*

2 happen to do something = to do something by chance: *I went downtown to do some shopping, and I happened to meet Greg* (=I met him when I did not expect to meet him).

hap•pi•ness /ˈhæpinəs/ *noun*
the state of being happy: *Her happiness was easy to see from the big smile on her face.*

hap•py /ˈhæpi/ *adjective* **happier**, **happiest**
1 feeling pleased, for example because your life is good, or something good has happened: *Pete is very happy at his new*

H

school. | *I was really happy to hear your good news!* ANTONYM **sad**

THESAURUS: happy

cheerful someone who is cheerful seems happy and smiles a lot: *Tom's a very cheerful little boy.*

pleased happy because someone has done something good, or something good has happened: *Her parents were pleased that she had done so well in college.*

glad happy because something good has happened. You use **glad** especially when you are telling other people that you are happy about something: *I'm really glad you can come to the party.*

delighted *formal* very happy because something good has happened: *She will be delighted when she hears the news.*

H

2 Happy Birthday/New Year, etc. = you say this to someone on a special occasion to show that you hope they have a nice time

—**happily** *adverb* in a happy way: *They laughed happily.*

➔ See picture on page A23

ha•rass /hə'ræs/ *verb, formal*

to annoy or threaten someone by treating them in a way that is very unpleasant: *The man harassed her by writing threatening letters and calling her on the phone late at night.*

—**harassment** *noun* behavior that annoys or threatens someone: *The cases of harassment were reported to the principal.*

harbor

har•bor /'hɑrbɚ/ *noun*

an area of water next to the land, where ships can stay safely

hard¹ /hɑrd/ *adjective*

1 firm and stiff: *I didn't sleep well because the bed was so hard.* ANTONYM **soft**

THESAURUS: hard

firm not soft to touch, but not completely hard either: *Bake the cake until it is firm when you touch it.*

stiff difficult to bend: *The kids used stiff cardboard to make models of their homes.*

solid something that is solid is very hard and does not bend or move when you touch it: *solid rock* | *Outside it was snowing, and the ground was frozen solid.*

2 difficult to do or understand: *Some of the exam questions were really hard.* ANTONYM **easy**

3 needing a lot of effort, work, etc.: *There is so much hard work to do on a farm.* | *They were always poor, and they had a hard life.* ANTONYM **easy**

4 be hard on someone *informal* = to criticize someone or be unfair to them: *Don't be too hard on Mike – he's still young.*

—**hardness** *noun* the quality of being firm and stiff: *The hardness of the soil made it difficult to dig.*

hard² *adverb*

with a lot of effort or force: *He worked hard and saved his money.* | *It was raining hard.*

hard•back /'hɑrdbæk/ *noun*

a book that has a strong stiff cover: *I bought the book in hardback.*

ˌhard 'disk *also* **ˌhard 'drive** *noun*

a part of a computer on which you can keep information permanently: *You can install the software on your hard disk.*

hard•en /'hɑrdn/ *verb*

to become firm or stiff: *The glue takes about an hour to harden.*

hard•ly /'hɑrdli/ *adverb*

almost not, none, etc.: *When my family moved to this area, we hardly knew anyone.* | *I hardly ever* (=almost never) *watch that show on TV, because I don't really like it.*

USAGE: hardly

Do not use **hardly** as the adverb of hard. The adverb of **hard** is also **hard**: *The teacher made us work very hard (NOT very hardly).*

hard•ship /ˈhɑrdˌʃɪp/ *noun*
something that makes living difficult, such as not having enough food or money: *In those years of hardship, we never had enough to eat.*

hard•ware /ˈhɑrdwer/ *noun*
1 computer machinery and equipment: *First you have to buy the hardware – hard drive, keyboard, printer – then buy the software programs.*
2 tools you use to build and fix things: *a hardware store* (=where you can buy these things)

ˌhard-ˈworking *adjective*
someone who is hard-working works using a lot of effort: *a hard-working student* ANTONYM **lazy**

hare /her/ *noun*
an animal like a large rabbit, with longer ears and longer back legs

harm¹ /hɑrm/ *noun*
damage, injury, or trouble: *He spent the night in the woods without any harm.* | *Staying up late tonight won't do you any harm.*

WORD FAMILY look at the words:
- ➔ **harm** *noun*
- ➔ **harm** *verb*
- ➔ **harmful** *adjective*
- ➔ **harmless** *adjective*

harm² *verb*
to hurt or damage something: *Too much sun will harm your skin.* SYNONYM **damage**

harm•ful /ˈhɑrmfəl/ *adjective*
causing harm: *These chemicals are harmful to the environment.*

harm•less /ˈhɑrmləs/ *adjective*
something that is harmless will not hurt someone or damage something: *The snake is harmless – it will not bite you.*
—**harmlessly** *adverb*

har•mon•i•ca /hɑrˈmɑnɪkə/ *noun*
a small metal musical instrument that fits in your hand and is often used in BLUES and rock music. You blow into the holes along the side.
➔ See picture on page A21

har•mo•ny /ˈhɑrməni/ *noun* plural **harmonies**
1 a situation in which people do not argue with each other: *Why can't people live in harmony and be happy?*
2 the combination of two or more musical notes or two or more lines of music, especially ones that sound good together: *The song has beautiful harmonies.*
—**harmonious** /hɑrˈmoʊniəs/ *adjective, formal* not involving arguments: *My brother and I had a harmonious relationship – we never fought.*

har•ness /ˈhɑrnɪs/ *verb, formal*
to use a kind of energy or power to do something: *The machine harnesses the energy of waves to produce electricity.*

harp /hɑrp/ *noun*
a musical instrument like a frame with three corners, with strings stretched from the top to the bottom of the frame
—**harpist** *noun* someone who plays the harp
➔ See picture on page A21

harsh /hɑrʃ/ *adjective*
1 severe or unpleasant, in a way that is not nice to experience: *Many plants died in the harsh winter.* | *The harsh street lights made everything look greenish and ugly.*
2 unkind or too strict: *harsh criticism*
—**harshly** *adverb*
—**harshness** *noun*

har•vest¹ /ˈhɑrvɪst/ *noun*
the act of collecting crops, or the amount that is collected: *The wheat harvest has begun.* | *This year we had a good harvest* (=a large amount was collected).

harvest² *verb*
to collect crops: *They will harvest the corn later in the year.*

has /əz; *strong* hæz/ *verb*
the third person singular of the present tense of HAVE: *She has three sisters.*

hash /hæʃ/ *noun*
a dish made with cooked meat and potatoes mixed together

ˌhash ˈbrowns *plural noun*
small pieces of potato, cooked in oil

has•n't /ˈhæzənt/ *verb*
the short form of "has not": *He hasn't come home yet.*

H

has•sle /ˈhæsəl/ *noun*
something that is annoying to do or deal with: *My pasta was cold, but it was too much hassle to go back and wait in line to ask for more.*

haste /heɪst/ *noun, formal*
quick action, because you are in a hurry: *In her haste to get to the airport, Pam forgot the tickets.*

hast•y /ˈheɪsti/ *adjective, formal*
done in a hurry, or doing something in a hurry: *I made a hasty decision, and now I wish I could change it.* SYNONYM **quick**
—**hastily** *adverb*: *I hastily apologized and then ran onto the bus.* SYNONYM **quickly**

hat

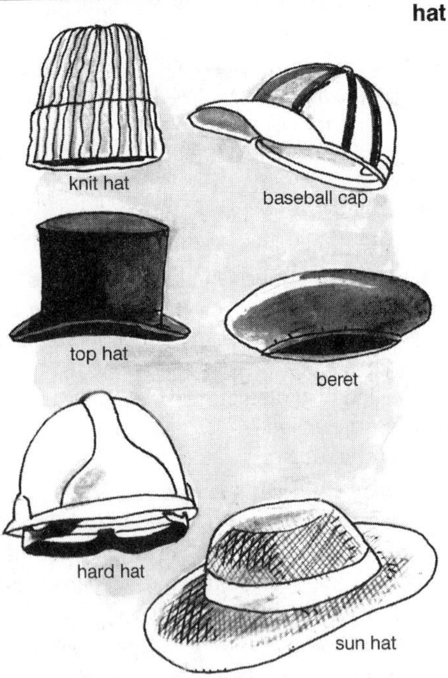

hat /hæt/ *noun*
a piece of clothing that you wear on your head: *She was wearing a black wool hat.*

hatch /hætʃ/ *verb*
if an egg hatches, a baby bird, fish, or insect comes out of it

hatch•et /ˈhætʃɪt/ *noun*
a small AX

hate¹ /heɪt/ *verb*
to dislike someone or something very much: *I hate the cold.* | *He hated the boy for laughing at him in front of the other kids.*
ANTONYM **love**

> **THESAURUS: hate**
>
> **dislike** to not like someone or something: *The only food I dislike is peanut butter.*
>
> **can't stand** to dislike someone or something very much: *I can't stand being late.*
>
> **detest** *formal* to hate someone or something very much: *I was going out with a boy my mother detested.*
>
> **despise** *formal* to hate someone very much and not respect him or her at all: *Would she despise him when she found out what he had done?*

hate² *noun*
a very strong feeling of dislike: *She felt hate for the men who had hurt her brother.*
SYNONYM **hatred**; ANTONYM **love**

hate•ful /ˈheɪtfəl/ *adjective*
very bad: *I wanted to get out of that hateful place.*

ha•tred /ˈheɪtrəd/ *noun, formal*
a very strong feeling of dislike: *He would not fight in the war because of his hatred of violence.* SYNONYM **hate**; ANTONYM **love**

haul /hɔl/ *verb*
to pull or carry something heavy: *They hauled the boat up onto the beach.*
➔ See Thesaurus box at **pull¹**

haunt /hɔnt/ *verb*
if the spirit of a dead person haunts a place, it appears there often: *The owner told us that the ghost haunts the upstairs bedrooms.*
—**haunted** *adjective* a haunted building or place is often visited by the spirits of dead people: *Would you spend the night in a haunted house?*

haunt•ing /ˈhɔntɪŋ/ *adjective*
something that is haunting is so beautiful and sad that you remember it for a long time: *The haunting tune made me want to cry.*

have¹ /həv; *strong* hæv/ *auxiliary verb* **had** /əd, strong hæd/ **having**
used with the past participle of a verb to form the perfect form of the verb. Used when talking about the period of time up to and including the present: *She has never*

been on a plane before. | *"Have you seen the new Disney movie?" "No, I haven't."* | *"What has he been doing?" "He's been working and going to school"* (=he is still working and going to school now).

have² /hæv/ *verb* **had, having**

1 to possess, own, or include something: *Do you have a car?* | *She had beautiful brown eyes.* | *I don't have any brothers or sisters.* | *The school has over 1,000 students.*

2 to eat, drink, or smoke something: *What time do you usually have breakfast?* | *Can I have another cup of coffee?*

3 to experience something: *I often have problems with my computer.* | *Did you have a good time at the party?*

4 to be sick with an illness or affected by injury: *She has a cold.* | *He has a broken leg.*

5 to be carrying something with you: *Do you have your wallet with you?*

6 to be allowed a particular amount of time to do something: *You have 30 minutes to finish the test.*

7 to think of something: *I have an idea!*

8 if a woman has a baby, the baby is born: *When is she going to have the baby?*

9 have to do something = if you have to do something, you must do it because it is important or necessary: *She has to go to a business meeting.* | *I don't have to go until tomorrow.*

10 had better do something = if you had better do something, you should do it: *You had better tell her that you're sorry.*

11 have your hair cut/your car fixed, etc. = to pay someone to do something for you, for example to cut your hair, or fix your car: *You need to have your hair cut.*

12 have your eyes closed/your mouth open, etc. = to keep part of your body in a particular position: *He had his eyes closed, and he looked like he was asleep.*

→ See Thesaurus box at **own²**

PHRASAL VERB

have something on

to be wearing something: *The man had no clothes on.*

have•n't /ˈhævənt/ *verb*

the short form of "have not": *I haven't seen him in a long time – does he still live here?*

have to /ˈhæftə; *strong* ˈhæftu/ *also* **have ˈgot to** *verb*

1 if you have to do something, you must do it: *I have to go now. I'm already late!* | *You've got to make a decision by tomorrow.*

USAGE: have to

If an action is not necessary, you can say that you **don't have to** do it: *You don't have to come with us if you don't want to.*

You can also say **don't need to** if it is not necessary for someone to do something: *I don't need to leave until 10.*

If someone **must not** do something, she or he is not allowed to do it. **Must not** is fairly formal and is used mainly in written English: *You must not take any sharp objects on the plane.* | *You mustn't tell anyone else about this.*

Do not say **don't have to** to mean **must not**.

GRAMMAR: have to

have to, have got to, must

have to – used when a rule, law, situation, etc. forces you to do something and you do not have a choice about it: *You have to pay tax on your income* (=because the law says it is necessary). | *We have to visit Grandma on Sunday* (=e.g. because my mother says it is necessary).

must – used especially in more formal writing when a law or someone who is in charge of something forces you do to something: *All students must have shorts and a t-shirt for P.E.* (=because the school says it is necessary) | *Motorcycle riders must wear helmets* (=because a law says it is necessary)

must – used when you make yourself do something because you think it is a good idea or necessary: *We must visit Grandma on Sunday* (=e.g. because we haven't seen her for a long time and it would be a good idea). | *I must study for tomorrow's test* (=because I know it is a good idea if I want to do well).

have got to – used in spoken English instead of **have to** or **must** to show how important it is to do something: *I've got to talk to him.*

2 used when saying that you are sure that

something is true or will happen: *This has to be a joke – they can't be serious.*

hawk /hɔk/ *noun*
a large bird that eats small birds and animals

hay /heɪ/ *noun*
dry grass that is fed to farm animals: *a bale of hay* (=amount of hay tied together)

ˈhay ˌfever *noun*
a condition like a bad cold that some people get from breathing in POLLEN (=dust from plants)

haz•ard /ˈhæzɚd/ *noun*
something that may be dangerous: *The smoke from the factory is a health hazard* (=a danger to people's health).
—**hazardous** *adjective* dangerous: *Snow is making the roads hazardous.*
➔ See Thesaurus box at **danger**

H

haze /heɪz/ *noun*
smoke or dust in the air that is difficult to see through: *They could almost see the sun through the haze.*

haz•y /ˈheɪzi/ *adjective*
1 air that is hazy has smoke or dust in it: *On a hazy day you cannot see the mountains.* ANTONYM **clear**
2 a hazy memory or idea is not clear: *I was very young, so my memories of that night are a little hazy.*

he /i; *strong* hi/ *pronoun*
used when talking about a man, boy, or male animal: *"That's my brother." "How old is he?"*

head[1] /hed/ *noun*
1 the top part of your body, where your eyes, mouth, and ears are: *She wrapped a scarf around her head to keep warm.* | *She shook her head* (=as a way of saying "no"). | *He was covered in mud from head to toe* (=completely covered in mud).
2 your mind: *I can't get that song out of my head.* | *Come on, use your head* (=think)! SYNONYM **brain**
3 the person who is in charge of a group or organization: *Who's the head of the biology department?* | *the head coach*
4 the top or front of something, or the most important part of it: *His mother sat at the head of the table.*
5 keep your head = to stay calm in a difficult situation: *He fell through the ice on the lake, but he kept his head and pulled himself out.*
6 lose your head = to behave stupidly in a difficult situation: *One of the boys lost his head and started yelling at the dog.*
7 go to someone's head = to make someone feel more important than he or she really is: *Don't let your success go to your head.*
8 laugh/yell/scream, etc. your head off *informal* = to laugh, shout, etc. very much: *The movie was so funny – we were laughing our heads off.*
➔ See picture on page A2

head[2] *verb*
1 to go in a particular direction: *I headed for* (=went toward) *the door.*
2 to be in charge of a group or organization: *The company is headed by David Marshall.*
3 be heading/headed for something = if you are heading for something, it is likely to happen to you: *The team has to learn how to work together, or they'll be headed for trouble when the season starts.*

head•ache /ˈhedeɪk/ *noun*
a pain in your head: *I have a bad headache.*

head•ing /ˈhedɪŋ/ *noun*
a word or words at the beginning of a piece of writing that tells what it is about: *The heading at the beginning of the paragraph said, "Fashion Tips."*

head•light /ˈhedlaɪt/ *noun*
one of the two large lights on the front of a car: *When I turned the headlights on, only one was working.*
➔ See picture on page A28

head•line /ˈhedlaɪn/ *noun*
the title of a report in a newspaper: *"President Flies Home," said the headline.*

head•phones /ˈhedfoʊnz/ *plural noun*
a piece of equipment that you wear over your ears to listen to music

headphones

head•quar•ters /ˈhedˌkwɔrtɚz/ *noun*
HQ the place from which people run a large organization or control military activities: *The company's headquarters are in New York.*

heads /hedz/ *noun*
the side of a coin that has a picture of someone's head on it: *I lost because I called heads.* ANTONYM **tails**

ˌ**head** ˈ**start** *noun*
the advantage you get by starting before other people: *We gave the younger kids a head start in the race, so that they had a chance to win against the older kids.*

head·way /ˈhedweɪ/ *noun*
make headway = to succeed in achieving part of something that is difficult: *The officers trying to solve the crime have not made much headway* (=they have not learned much about the crime). SYNONYM **make progress**

heal /hil/ *verb*
1 if a wound heals, the skin or flesh grows back together: *The scratch on her finger healed quickly.*
2 to make a sick person or a wound get better: *The cream will heal the cut faster.*
—**healer** *noun* someone who makes sick people get better, but not with ordinary medical treatment: *a religious healer*

health /helθ/ *noun*
the condition of your body and your mind: *Smoking is bad for your health.* | *My mother had a lot of mental health problems.* | *Are your grandparents in good health* (=healthy)?

ˈ**health care** *also* **health·care** /ˈhelθker/ *noun*
medical treatment and care: *the high cost of health care*

ˈ**health food** *noun*
food that is natural and good for you: *She bought some brown rice from the health food store.*

health·ful /ˈhelθfəl/ *adjective, formal*
good for your body: *fruit, vegetables and other healthful food* SYNONYM **healthy**

health·y /ˈhelθi/ *adjective*
1 physically well and strong: *We are very happy to have a healthy baby girl.* ANTONYM **sick**

THESAURUS: healthy

well healthy – used for saying how someone feels or looks: *Aren't you feeling well?*

fine healthy – used when someone has asked you how you feel and you are replying that you feel well: *"Hi, Tom, how are you?" "Fine, thanks."*

better less sick than you were, or no longer sick: *I'm feeling a lot better now.*

in shape healthy and physically strong: *He's fifty, but he runs a lot and he's in pretty good shape.*

physically fit healthy and having a strong body: *Even kids need exercise to be physically fit.*

2 good for your body or your mind: *I try to eat a healthy diet and get exercise.* | *It's not healthy to be alone so much.* ANTONYM **unhealthy**

heap[1] /hip/ *noun*
a large messy pile of things: *There was a heap of clothes on the floor.*

heap[2] *verb*
to put a lot of things on top of each other in a messy way: *He heaped his plate with food.*

hear /hɪr/ *verb* **heard** /hɚd/
1 to notice a sound, using your ears: *He heard footsteps.* | *I could hear my parents yelling downstairs.*
2 to be told some news or information: *Have you heard the news? Jen had her baby.* | *I heard that he was sick.* | *She had heard about the robbery on the radio.*
3 have heard of someone/something = to know that someone or something exists: *I've heard of the book, but I've never read it.*

PHRASAL VERB
hear from someone
to get news or information from someone: *Have you heard from John lately?*

hear·ing /ˈhɪrɪŋ/ *noun*
1 your ability to hear: *My hearing is not very good, so you'll have to speak louder.*
2 an official meeting to find out the facts about something: *The Senate began hearings on arline safety this week.*

ˈ**hearing aid** *noun*
a small object that you put in your ear if you cannot hear well, to make sounds louder

heart /hɑrt/ *noun*
1 the part inside your chest that makes blood move through your body: *Her heart beat faster.*
2 the part of you which has strong feelings

H

such as love: *I loved her with all my heart* (=very strongly). | *I knew in my heart that I wouldn't see him again.*
3 a shape that is used to mean love: *The card was decorated with pink hearts.*
4 the heart of something a) the middle of an area or thing: *Our hotel was in the heart of the city* **b)** the most important part of something: *We need to get to the heart of the problem so that we can fix it.*
5 a card used in card games, with red heart shapes on it: *the four of hearts* (=a card with four heart shapes)
6 know something by heart = to know a poem, song, etc. so well that you can say it or sing it without reading it: *I know the song by heart, so I won't need the music.*
7 break someone's heart = to make someone very unhappy: *When she asked for a divorce, she broke my heart.*
8 take heart = to have more hope and confidence than before: *"Take heart," the coach said to the team. "I know we can play much better than we did today."*
9 lose heart = to have less hope and confidence than before: *Don't lose heart – we'll find an answer to the problem!*
10 someone's heart sinks = used when saying that someone suddenly becomes very sad or loses hope: *Her heart sank when she realized how big the job was.*
11 be something at heart = used when saying what type of person someone really is: *He gets mad easily, but he's a good person at heart.*
→ See picture on page A2

'heart at,tack *noun*
a time when someone's heart suddenly stops working normally: *He had a heart attack and died.*

heart•beat /'hartbit/ *noun*
the movement or sound that someone's heart makes: *The doctor listened to the baby's heartbeat.*

heart•break /'hartbreɪk/ *noun, formal*
great sadness that you feel when something happens: *He remembered the heartbreak he felt when she married another man.*
—heartbroken /'hart,broʊkən/ *adjective* very sad because of something that has happened: *They were heartbroken when the Red Sox didn't win.*

heart•less /'hartlɪs/ *adjective, formal*
cruel or unkind: *Her husband was a stupid heartless man.*

heart•y /'harti/ *adjective, formal*
a hearty meal is very big: *Everyone was hungry, and ate a hearty dinner.*

heat[1] /hit/ *noun*
1 the warmth from something hot: *She felt the heat from the sun on her face.*
2 very hot weather: *I can't work in this heat.*
3 the heat = the system in a building that keeps it warm: *It's cold in here – I'll turn the heat on.*

heat[2] *also* **heat up** *verb*
to make something warm or hot: *I'll heat some soup for dinner.*

heat•ed /'hitɪd/ *adjective*
if an object is heated, a heater makes it warm: *The hotel has a heated swimming pool.*

heat•er /'hitɚ/ *noun*
a machine for heating air or water: *He lived in a small room with one electric heater to keep him warm.*
→ See picture on page A28

'heat wave *noun*
some days or weeks when the weather is very hot: *In August, there was a heatwave when the temperature was over 95 for a week.*

heave /hiv/ *verb*
to lift or pull something heavy: *Three men heaved the big box into the house.*

heav•en /'hevən/ *noun*
in some religions, the place where God is, and good people go after they die: *Do you think you'll go to heaven?*
→ **hell**
—heavenly *adjective* relating to heaven: *Christians sometimes call God the heavenly Father.*

heav•y /'hevi/ *adjective*
1 weighing a lot: *I couldn't lift the box – it was too heavy.* ANTONYM **light**
2 large in amount: *There was heavy snow and some roads were closed.* ANTONYM **light**

heavy

H

3 a heavy smoker/drinker = someone who smokes a lot, or drinks a lot of alcohol: *Lung cancer is more common if you are a heavy smoker.*
—**heaviness** *noun* the feeling that something weighs a lot
➔ See Thesaurus box at **fat**[1]

ˌheavy-ˈduty *adjective*
very strong and not easy to damage: *The workmen need to wear heavy-duty boots to protect their feet.*

heav·y·weight /ˈheviˌweɪt/ *noun*
in BOXING, someone who belongs in the group of people who weigh the most

hec·tic /ˈhektɪk/ *adjective*
very busy, with a lot of different things happening: *I had a hectic week, with three exams and a paper due on Friday.*

he'd /id; *strong* hid/
1 the short form of "he had": *He'd met her before.*
2 the short form of "he would": *George said he'd be late.*

heel /hiːl/ *noun*
1 the round part in the back of your foot
2 the part on the bottom of a shoe in the back: *She likes shoes with high heels for parties.*
➔ See page A2, picture at **shoe**

heft·y /ˈhefti/ *adjective, informal*
1 a hefty amount of money is very large: *They paid him a hefty salary – over 2 million dollars.*
2 someone who is hefty is large and heavy: *He was a hefty guy with dark hair.*

height /haɪt/ *noun*
1 how tall someone or something is: *First, the doctor measured her height.*
2 the level something is above the ground: *You can change the height of your chair and make it lower if that is more comfortable.*
3 the time when something is busiest or most successful: *July is the height of the tourist season, and thousands of people come here every day.*

heir /er/ *noun*
someone who gets money or other things from a person who has died: *Her son was the heir to everything she owned.*

held /held/ *verb*
the past tense and past participle of HOLD

hel·i·cop·ter /ˈhelɪˌkɑptɚ/ *noun*
an aircraft with long metal parts on top that spin to make it fly. A helicopter can go straight up into the air: *A police helicopter landed on top of the building.*
➔ See picture on page A26

he'll /il; *strong* hil/
the short form of "he will": *He'll call us when he gets there.*

hell /hel/ *noun*
in some religions, the place where bad people go when they die

hel·lo /həˈloʊ/
a word you say when you meet someone, or talk on the telephone: *Hello Paul, how are you?*

hel·met /ˈhelmət/ *noun*
a hard hat that covers and protects your head: *Don't forget to wear your bicycle helmet.*
➔ See picture on page A26

help[1] /help/ *verb*
1 to do something that makes a job, work, etc. easier for another person: *"This box is really heavy." "I can help." | Mom, can you help me with my homework?*
2 to make something bad or unpleasant better: *If you have a headache, lying down helps.*
3 can't help doing something = used in order to say that you cannot stop yourself from doing something: *She looked so funny – I couldn't help laughing.*
4 help yourself = used in order to tell someone to take as much food or drink as he or she wants to: *There's plenty of food, so help yourself.*
5 help! = a word you shout when you are in danger, and you need someone to come
—**helper** *noun* someone who helps another person: *I built the wall myself, with a few helpers.*

help[2] *noun*
something that makes a job, work, etc. easier for another person: *Could you come here for a minute – I need help. | If you don't understand, ask your teacher for help.*

help·ful /ˈhelpfəl/ *adjective*
1 useful: *The website is full of helpful information about the college.*
2 willing to help: *The librarian was very*

H

helpful and found exactly the book I wanted.
—**helpfully** *adverb* in a helpful way: *"If you need anything, just ask me," he said helpfully.*

help·ing /ˈhelpɪŋ/ *noun*
an amount of food for one person, that you put on a plate: *I ate a big helping of ice cream.*

help·less /ˈhelpləs/ *adjective*
not able to take care of yourself: *When babies are born, they are totally helpless.*
—**helplessly** *adverb*: *He could not swim, and struggled helplessly in the water.*

hem /hem/ *noun*
the bottom edge of a piece of clothing, that you make by folding it over and sewing it: *I shortened the skirt, and sewed up the hem.*

hem·i·sphere /ˈheməˌsfɪr/ *noun*
one half of the Earth: *Australia is in the southern hemisphere.*

H

hen /hen/ *noun*
a female chicken: *Hens usually lay eggs in the same place every day.*

hep·a·ti·tis /ˌhepəˈtaɪtɪs/ *noun*
a serious disease of the LIVER

her /ɚ; *strong* hɚ/ *pronoun*
a woman or girl: *I gave her $20.*
—**her** *adjective* belonging to a woman or girl: *Mom lost her purse.*

herb /ɚb/ *noun*
a plant that you use for giving more taste to food, or for making medicine: *Cook the chicken with some fresh herbs.*

herb·i·vore /ˈhɚbəˌvɔr/ *noun, formal*
an animal that only eats plants: *Rabbits are herbivores.*

herd[1] /hɚd/ *noun*
a group of big animals of the same kind: *In Kenya, we saw a herd of elephants.*
→ See Thesaurus box at **group**[1]

herd[2] *verb*
to make a group of people or animals move somewhere together: *The men herded us into a room.*

here /hɪr/ *adverb*
1 in or to this place: *How long have you lived here? | Come here, and stand next to me.*
2 if a period of time is here, it has begun: *Winter is gone and Spring is here!*
3 here you go/here you are = something you say when you are giving something to someone: *"Can I see your pictures?" "Sure, here you go."*
4 here and there = in different places: *Boats were sailing here and there on the water.*

her·it·age /ˈherətɪdʒ/ *noun, formal*
the ideas, history, art, etc. of the people in a country or group, that they pass to their children: *My family is Chinese-American, and we are proud of our Chinese heritage.*

he·ro /ˈhɪroʊ/ *noun* plural **heroes**
1 someone who people admire, who has done something very brave or good: *When he came back from the war, he was a hero.*
2 a man who is the most important character in a book, play, or movie: *The hero escapes and saves the children at the end of the movie.*
—**heroism** /ˈheroʊˌɪzəm/ *noun* when someone does something very brave or good: *My father received a medal for his heroism.*

he·ro·ic /hɪˈroʊɪk/ *adjective*
very determined or brave: *The neighbors made a heroic effort to save our house as it burned.*

her·o·ine /ˈheroʊɪn/ *noun*
a woman who is the most important character in a book, play, or movie: *In movies, the heroine is usually beautiful.*

her·on /ˈherən/ *noun*
a big bird with very long legs and a long beak, that lives near water

her·ring /ˈherɪŋ/ *noun* plural **herring** or **herrings**
a long thin silver fish that lives in the ocean

hers /hɚz/ *pronoun*
something that belongs to a woman or girl: *That's not my bag – it's hers* (=her bag).

her·self /ɚˈself; *strong* hɚˈself/ *pronoun*
1 the woman or girl who you have just mentioned: *Anna looked at herself in the mirror.*
2 used with "she" or a woman's name, to emphasize that she did something: *I know it's true, because she told me herself.*
3 (all) by herself = alone or without help: *She painted the house by herself.*

he's /iz; *strong* hiz/
1 the short form of "he is": *He's a doctor.*
2 the short form of "he has": *He's bought a new car.*

hes·i·tate /ˈhezəˌteɪt/ *verb*
to stop before you do or say something, because you are thinking about what to do or say: *She hesitated for a second before she picked up the phone.*
—**hesitation** /ˌhezəˈteɪʃən/ *noun* an act of hesitating: *He asked me to marry him, and I said "yes" without hesitation* (=immediately).

het·er·o·sex·u·al /ˌhetərəˈsekʃuəl/ *adjective, formal*
someone who is heterosexual is attracted to people of the opposite sex

hi /haɪ/ *informal*
another word for HELLO: *Hi Jen! How are you?*

hi·ber·nate /ˈhaɪbɚˌneɪt/ *verb*
if an animal hibernates, it sleeps all through the winter: *Some bears hibernate, and wake up in the spring.*
—**hibernation** /ˌhaɪbɚˈneɪʃən/ *noun* the act of hibernating

hic·cups /ˈhɪkʌps/ *plural noun*
if you get the hiccups, you start making short sounds in your throat that you cannot control: *I suddenly got the hiccups, and had to drink some water to make them go away.*

hide¹ /haɪd/ *verb* **hid** /hɪd/ **hidden** /ˈhɪdn/
1 to put something where people will not find it: *She didn't want him to see the letter, so she hid it in a drawer.*
2 to go somewhere where people cannot see or find you: *Jake hid from his mom, because he thought she would be mad.*
3 to stop other people from knowing the truth, or seeing how you feel: *Mark couldn't hide the fact that he liked Kim a lot.*

hide² *noun*
the skin of an animal, that people use for leather

ˌhide-and-ˈseek *noun*
a game in which one child tries to find all the other children, who are hiding in different places: *The kids were in the yard, playing hide-and-seek.*

hid·e·ous /ˈhɪdiəs/ *adjective*
very ugly: *A lot of people thought the new building was hideous.*

hi·er·ar·chy /ˈhaɪəˌrɑrki/ Ac *noun*
plural **hierarchies**
a system of organizing people in which some people are more important and powerful than others: *The president is at the top of the hierarchy.*

high /haɪ/ *adjective*
1 high mountains, walls, etc. are tall: *There was a high wall around the house.* | *Mount Everest is the highest mountain in the world.*
ANTONYM **low**
2 high windows, cupboards, etc. are a long way above the ground: *Keep medicine in a high cupboard that children cannot reach.*

> **USAGE: high**
>
> Use **high** to talk about mountains, walls, fences, etc.: *the highest mountain in the world* | *How high will the wall be?*
>
> Use **high** to talk about how far something is from the ground: *The shelf's too high for the kids to reach.*
>
> Use **tall** to talk about the height of people and trees: *She's only five feet tall.* | *a tall man* | *the tall trees in the park*
>
> Use **tall** to talk about other narrow objects: *an old house with tall chimneys* | *a tall flagpole*
>
> We usually use **tall** to talk about buildings: *the tall buildings in the downtown area*

3 a high amount, number, etc. is big: *I got a really high score on my math test.*
4 of a very good quality or standard: *The food in that store is very high quality.*
5 a high sound is near the top of the range of sounds that humans can hear: *She had a high voice, like a little girl's voice.*
6 be high in something = to have a lot of a substance: *Candy bars are not healthy because they are very high in fat.*
WORD FAMILY → **height** *noun*

ˌhigher eduˈcation *noun*
education at a college or university: *The school encourages its students to go on to higher education.*

ˈhigh jump *noun*
the high jump = a sport in which you jump as high as you can over a bar

high·lands /ˈhaɪləndz/ *noun*
an area with a lot of mountains: *The family traveled to the highlands where it was cooler.*

H

high·light[1] /ˈhaɪlaɪt/ Ac *verb*
to mark important words on paper or on a computer, using a color that is easy to see: *Use a colored pen to highlight information that you want to remember.*

highlight[2] *noun*
the best or most important part of something: *We can watch the highlights of the game on TV later tonight.*

high·ly /ˈhaɪli/ *adverb*
1 very: *The movie was highly successful – millions of people went to see it.*
2 highly paid/trained, etc. = very well paid, etc.: *All our teachers are highly experienced.*

High·ness /ˈhaɪnəs/ *noun*
Your/His/Her Highness = a title for a king or queen, and some other royal people

ˌhigh-ˈpitched *adjective*
a high-pitched sound is not low like a man's voice: *I could hear the high-pitched laughter of the girls upstairs.*

ˈhigh school *noun*
a school in the U.S. and Canada for students over the age of 14: *high school students* | *Wendy and I were good friends in high school.*

high-tech *also* **hi-tech** /ˌhaɪ ˈtek/ *adjective*
using very modern equipment and methods: *In Japan, there are a lot of high-tech companies that produce electronic goods.*

ˌhigh ˈtide *noun*
the time when the ocean comes a long way up the beach: *At high tide, the water covers the whole beach.*
➔ See picture at **tide**

high·way /ˈhaɪweɪ/ *noun* plural **highways**
a big fast road between cities: *There was a lot of traffic on the highway because of an accident.*
➔ See Thesaurus box at **road**

hi·jack /ˈhaɪdʒæk/ *verb*
to use violence or threats to take control of an airplane, bus, etc.: *The terrorists hijacked a plane flying from London to the U.S.*
—**hijacker** *noun* someone who hijacks a plane, bus, etc.: *A hijacker in Miami took a school bus and left the children by the side of the road.*
—**hijacking** *noun* an act of hijacking a plane, bus, etc.: *Two people were shot in the hijacking.*

hike /haɪk/ *noun*
a long walk in the country: *On Sunday, we took a hike in the mountains.*
—**hike** *verb* to walk a long way in the country: *A lot of people hike the mountain trail that runs from New Hampshire to Georgia.*
➔ See Thesaurus box at **walk**[1]

hi·lar·i·ous /hɪˈleriəs/ *adjective*
very funny: *His jokes were hilarious – I couldn't stop laughing.*
➔ See Thesaurus box at **funny**[1]

hill /hɪl/ *noun*
an area of high land, like a small mountain: *Why don't we climb to the top of the hill?*
—**hilly** *adjective* having a lot of hills: *San Francisco is a hilly city.*

him /ɪm; *strong* hɪm/ *pronoun*
a man or boy: *I gave him the letter.*

him·self /ɪmˈself; *strong* hɪmˈself/ *pronoun*
1 the man or boy who you have just mentioned: *Pete fell and hurt himself.*
2 used with "he" or a man's name to emphasize that he did something: *Dad made the boat himself.*
3 (all) by himself = alone or without help: *He likes working by himself.*

hin·der /ˈhɪndɚ/ *verb, formal*
to make it difficult for someone to do something: *The bad weather hindered their efforts to save the men.*

hind·sight /ˈhaɪndsaɪt/ *noun*
the ability to understand a situation that you can only get after it has happened: *In hindsight, I realize that he was lying to me* (=I know now that he was lying).

Hin·du·ism /ˈhɪnduˌɪzəm/ *noun*
the main religion in India
—**Hindu** *noun* someone whose religion is Hinduism
—**Hindu** *adjective* relating to Hinduism: *a Hindu temple*

hinge /hɪndʒ/ *noun*
a piece of metal that joins two parts of a door, box, etc., so that one of them can open or shut: *The door's hinges squeak every time it opens.*

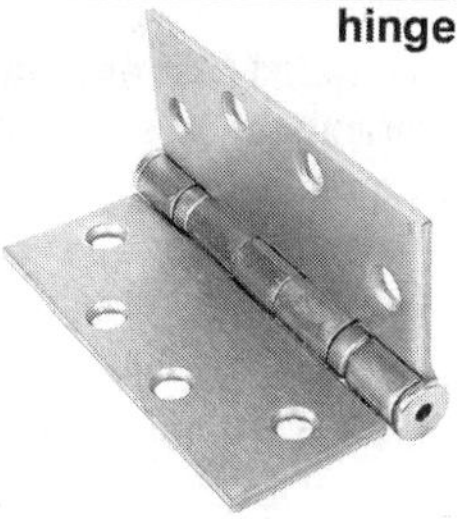

hint /hɪnt/ *noun*
1 something you say that helps someone guess something: *Mom, what am I getting for my birthday – give me a hint!*
2 something that is useful advice: *The book is full of helpful hints on how to get a job.*
—**hint** *verb* to say something that helps someone guess something: *She said she and Dan had some big news – I think she was hinting that they might get married.*

hip /hɪp/ *noun*
the part of your body where your legs join your body: *The woman was holding a baby on her hip.*
➔ See picture on page A2

ˈhip-hop *noun*
a type of popular music with a strong beat and spoken words, that people dance to

hip•pie *also* **hippy** /ˈhɪpi/ *noun*
someone from the 1960s and 1970s who had long hair and unusual clothes and who did not want war or a traditional way of living

hip•po•pot•a•mus /ˌhɪpəˈpɑtəməs/ *also* **hip•po** /ˈhɪpoʊ/ *noun* plural **hippopotamuses**
a large African animal with a fat body and thick gray skin, that lives in and near water

hire /haɪɚ/ *verb*
to pay someone to work for you: *Most hotels hire more people during the summer when it is busy.* SYNONYM **employ**

his[1] /ɪz; *strong* hɪz/ *adjective*
belonging to a man or boy: *Did he do his homework?*

his[2] *pronoun*
something that belongs to a man or boy: *That's not my jacket – it's his* (=his jacket).

His•pan•ic /hɪˈspænɪk/ *noun*
someone from a country where the people speak Spanish or Portuguese
—**Hispanic** *adjective* from a country where the people speak Spanish or Portuguese: *Hispanic students*

hiss /hɪs/ *verb*
to make a sound like "ssss": *The snake hissed at me, and I jumped.*
—**hiss** *noun* a sound like "ssss": *The elevator doors opened with a hiss.*
➔ See picture on page A22

his•to•ri•an /hɪˈstɔriən/ *noun*
someone who studies or writes about history: *She is a famous historian who knows a lot about early American history.*

his•tor•ic /hɪˈstɔrɪk/ *adjective*
important in history: *It was a historic moment when the two countries signed the peace agreement.*

his•to•ry /ˈhɪstəri/ *noun*
1 *also* **History** the study of things that happened in the past: *My favorite subject at school is History.*
2 all the things that happened in the past: *The Civil War was the most difficult time in the history of our nation.*
—**historical** /hɪˈstɔrɪkəl/ *adjective* relating to things that have happened in the past: *I like reading historical novels.*

WORD FAMILY look at the words:
- ➔ **history** *noun*
- ➔ **historic** *adjective*
- ➔ **historical** *adjective*
- ➔ **historian** *noun*
- ➔ **prehistoric** *adjective*

hit[1] /hɪt/ *verb* **hit, hitting**
1 to move your hand quickly, so that you touch something with a lot of force: *One boy hit me on the arm really hard.* | *I picked up the bat and hit the ball hard.*

THESAURUS: hit

punch to hit someone hard with your hand closed, especially in a fight: *One of the boys punched him in the stomach.*

slap to hit someone with the flat part of your hand, especially because you are angry with him or her: *I saw him slap his girlfriend.*

beat to hit someone or something many times: *He had been robbed and beaten.*

smack to hit someone or something, usually with your open hand: *The ball smacked him in the face.*

H

strike *formal* to hit someone or something very hard: *She fell and struck her head on a table.*

knock to hit a door or window with your closed hand to make a noise and get someone's attention: *Someone was knocking on the door.*

bang to make a loud noise, especially by hitting something against something hard: *A policeman was banging on the door.*

tap to gently hit your fingers or foot against something: *I tapped him on the shoulder.*

pound to knock very hard, making a lot of noise: *Scott pounded on the door with his fist.*

2 to crash into something: *Ann's car hit a tree.*

3 if a bullet or bomb hits someone or something, it goes into them and causes injury or damage: *The bullet hit him in his shoulder.*

4 hit the roof/ceiling *informal* = to become very angry: *Dad hit the roof, when I got home late.*

PHRASAL VERB

hit on something

to have a good idea about something: *Chris hit on the idea of asking our professor for help.*

hit² *noun*

1 a movie, song, play, etc. that is very successful: *The band's first song was a big hit* (=it was very popular).

2 the act of hitting the ball in a game such as baseball: *Michael played really well – he had four hits.*

hitch•hike /ˈhɪtʃhaɪk/ *verb*

to travel by asking for free rides from people who are driving past you: *I hitchhiked around Europe because I didn't have enough money for the trains.*

—**hitchhiker** *noun* someone who is hitchhiking: *I picked up a hitchhiker when I was driving home.*

hi-tech /ˌhaɪ ˈtek/ *adjective*

another spelling of HIGH-TECH

HIV *noun*

Human Immunodeficiency Virus a VIRUS people get that can cause AIDS

hive /haɪv/ *noun*

also **beehive** a place where BEEs live

HMO *noun*

Health Maintenance Organization a type of insurance organization that pays for your health care if you use doctors and hospitals that are part of the organization

hoard¹ /hɔrd/ *also* **hoard up** *verb*

to collect or hide a lot of something you will use in the future: *Animals such as squirrels hoard food for the winter.*

—**hoarder** *noun* someone who hoards something

hoard² *noun*

a large amount of something that someone has hidden to keep it safe: *People say there is a hoard of gold somewhere on the island.*

hoarse /hɔrs/ *adjective*

if you are hoarse, your voice sounds low and is not clear: *I talked so much that I was hoarse by the end of the day.*

—**hoarsely** *adverb* if you speak hoarsely, your voice sounds hoarse: *"I can't speak very well," he said hoarsely.*

—**hoarseness** *noun* the quality of sounding hoarse

hoax /hoʊks/ *noun*

an unkind trick to make people think something that is not true: *The caller said there was a bomb in the store, but it was a hoax.*

hob•ble /ˈhɑbəl/ *verb*

to walk with small steps because it is difficult to walk: *His leg was hurting badly, but he managed to hobble home.*

hob•by /ˈhɑbi/ *noun* plural **hobbies**

an activity that you enjoy doing in your free time: *My hobbies are swimming and playing the piano.*

➔ See Thesaurus box at **game**

hock•ey /ˈhɑki/ *noun*

also **ice hockey** a sport that two teams play on ice, using curved sticks to hit a hard flat object

hoe /hoʊ/ *noun*

a tool with a long handle, used for making the soil loose

hog¹ /hɔg/ *noun*

a large pig: *a hog farm*

hog² *verb*, *informal* **hogged, hogging**

to use something a lot, so it is difficult for other people to use it: *My sister always hogs the bathroom.*

hoist /hɔɪst/ *verb*
to lift something using ropes or a machine: *The soldiers came into the building and hoisted the flag.*

hold¹ /hoʊld/ *verb* **held** /held/
1 to have something in your hands or arms: *The boy was holding a $10 bill.* | *Hold my hand when we cross the street.*

THESAURUS: hold

grip to hold something firmly: *I gripped the rail and tried not to look down.*
clutch to hold something tightly: *a child clutching a bag of candy*
take/keep/grab hold of something to take something in your hands and hold it tightly: *Doug took hold of my hand and pulled me away from the crowd.*
grab to take hold of someone or something suddenly or violently: *Vince grabbed hold of my arm.*
seize *formal* to take hold of something or someone suddenly and using force: *He was seized by three young soldiers.*

2 to keep something in a position: *He held the picture up so we could see it.* | *She held the door open for me.*
3 to have a formal meeting: *The school is holding a meeting for parents and teachers next week.*
4 to have space for a number or amount of something: *The theater holds 800 people.* | *The container holds one gallon of liquid.*
5 *formal* to have a particular position, job or level of achievement: *The green card allows people from another country to hold a job in the U.S.*
6 hold it! *informal* = you say this when you are telling someone to wait or stop doing something: *"Hold it"! the teacher said, "Nobody leave the room yet – I'm still talking."*
7 hold your breath = to breathe in and not breathe out again for a short time: *I held my breath, and jumped into the water.*
➔ **hold your breath** at **breath**

PHRASAL VERBS

hold something against someone
to blame or dislike someone for something he or she did: *John got the job that she was supposed to get, and she holds that against him.*

hold something back
to stop something or someone from moving forward: *The police couldn't hold the crowds back.*

hold on
1 hold on! *informal* = used when asking someone to wait, while you do or say something: *Hold on a minute – I need to find my keys.*
2 to keep something carefully or tightly in your hand: *If you go out at night, hold on to your wallet.*

hold someone or something up
to make someone or something late: *Bad weather held us up, and we got home an hour late.*
➔ See picture on page A4

hold² *noun*
1 take/grab/keep hold of something = to take something in your hand and keep it there: *Mom took hold of the handle and pulled hard.*
2 get (a) hold of someone or something = to find someone or something that you need or want: *I need to get hold of Mike to ask him a question.*
3 on hold = if you are on hold, you are waiting to speak to someone on the telephone: *Every time I call the bank, they put me on hold* (=make me wait).
4 the hold = the bottom part of a ship, where you store goods

hold·up /ˈhoʊldʌp/ *noun*
1 a delay: *There was a holdup on the freeway because of an accident.*
2 if there is a holdup, people try to rob a store, bank, etc., using guns or other weapons: *He went to jail for driving the car in a holdup.*

hole /hoʊl/ *noun*
1 an empty space, especially where something is broken or torn: *There's a hole in my sweater.*

THESAURUS: hole

space the empty area between two things, into which you can put something: *There's a space for that box on the shelf over there.*
gap an empty space between two things or two parts of something: *She has a gap between her two front teeth.*

leak a small hole that lets liquid or gas flow into or out of something: *There was a leak in the oil tank.*

crack a very narrow space between two things or two parts of something: *He pushed the letter through the crack under the door.*

2 a space in the ground where an animal lives: *a rabbit hole*

hol•i•day /ˈhɑləˌdeɪ/ *noun* plural **holidays**
an official day when people do not have to go to school or work: *Many of the stores were closed, because it was a national holiday.*
➔ See Thesaurus box at **vacation**

hollow

hol•low /ˈhɑloʊ/ *adjective*
having an empty space inside: *The kids hid in the old tree, which was hollow inside.*

hol•ly /ˈhɑli/ *noun*
a small tree with dark green pointed leaves and small red fruits

ho•ly /ˈhoʊli/ *adjective* **holier**, **holiest**
1 relating to God or religion: *Jerusalem is a holy city for Christians, Muslims, and Jews.* SYNONYM **sacred**
2 a holy person is very good and close to God: *The priest was a very holy man.*
—**holiness** *noun* the quality of being very good and close to God

home¹ /hoʊm/ *noun*
1 the place where you live: *On Monday Mia felt sick, so she stayed at home.*

THESAURUS: home

house the house or apartment where someone lives: *Her house is always really clean.*

place *informal* the house, apartment, or room where someone lives: *We went back to my place after the movie.*

residence *formal* the place where someone lives: *There are some private residences inside the national parks.*

2 a place where people live if they need someone to take care of them: *That building is now a home for the elderly.*
3 be/feel at home = to feel happy and confident somewhere, because you know it well: *I feel at home in the city, because I've lived here all my life.*

home² *adverb*
to or at the place where you live: *I was tired, and I wanted to go home.* | *Hi Mom, I'm home.*

home³ *adjective*
1 relating to the place where you live or were born: *My home town is Chicago.*
2 playing on your team's sports field, not the field of another team: *The team has won all its home games.* ANTONYM **away**

home•land /ˈhoʊmlænd/ *noun*
the country where you were born: *When the war started, many people left their homeland.*

home•less /ˈhoʊmləs/ *adjective*
without a place to live: *There were terrible floods, and a lot of people became homeless.*
—**the homeless** *noun* people who do not have a place to live: *The money goes to medical care for the homeless.*

home•made /ˌhoʊmˈmeɪd/ *adjective*
homemade bread, jam, etc. is made at home, not in a store: *I love my mom's homemade cookies.*

ˈhome page *also* **home•page** /ˈhoʊmpeɪdʒ/ *noun*
the first page of a WEBSITE that gives you general information about the website: *This arrow will take you back to the homepage.*

home•room /ˈhoʊmrum/ *noun*
a room where groups of students go at the beginning of each school day to get general information and take ATTENDANCE: *Carrie and I sit next to each other in homeroom.*

ˌhome ˈrun *noun*
a good hit in baseball, that gives the player time to run all the way around, and get a

point: *Johnny's a good basketball player – he hit a home run in our last game.*

home•sick /'hoʊm,sɪk/ *adjective*
sad because you are away from your home: *When Jessie went to camp for three weeks, she was really homesick.*
—**homesickness** *noun*
➔ See Thesaurus box at **sad**

home•work /'hoʊmwɚk/ *noun*
work for school that students do at home: *I did all my homework, and then I went outside.*

hom•i•cide /'hɑmə,saɪd/ *noun, formal*
the crime of murder: *The police charged the man with homicide for killing two people.*

ho•mo•sex•u•al /,hoʊmə'sekʃuəl/ *adjective, formal*
sexually attracted to people of the same sex SYNONYM **gay**; ANTONYM **heterosexual**
—**homosexuality** /,hoʊmə,sekʃu'æləti/ *noun* the state of being homosexual

hon•est /'ɑnɪst/ *adjective*
an honest person is good, and does not lie or steal: *He was an honest man, who everyone liked and trusted.* ANTONYM **dishonest**
—**honestly** *adverb* behaving in an honest way: *Please answer these questions honestly.*

WORD FAMILY look at the words:
➔ **honest** *adjective*
➔ **honestly** *adverb*
➔ **honesty** *noun*
➔ **dishonest** *adjective*
➔ **dishonestly** *adverb*
➔ **dishonesty** *noun*

hon•es•ty /'ɑnɪsti/ *noun*
the quality of being good and not lying or stealing: *Thank you for telling me the truth – I admire your honesty.* ANTONYM **dishonesty**

hon•ey /'hʌni/ *noun*
a sweet sticky liquid that BEEs make, and that people eat

hon•ey•moon /'hʌni,mun/ *noun*
a vacation that people take after they get married: *Two days after the wedding, they went to Greece on their honeymoon.*

honk /hɑŋk/ *verb*
to use the horn in a car, so that it makes a loud noise: *I crossed the road in front of a cab, and the driver honked his horn.*

hon•or /'ɑnɚ/ *noun*
1 something that makes you feel proud: *It was an honor to play for this great team.*
2 in honor of someone = in order to show respect for someone or something important: *They built a memorial in honor of the Princess after she died.*
3 something that someone officially receives as a sign of praise and respect for something good he or she has done: *The medal is the highest honor that the President can give to someone.*
—**honorable** *adjective* deserving respect or praise for being good, fair, or honest: *He gave the money that he took back to the family, which was the honorable thing to do.*

hood /hʊd/ *noun*
1 the part of a jacket, SWEATSHIRT, etc. that you pull up to cover your head: *The man had pulled up his hood, so I couldn't see his face.*
2 the metal cover over the engine of a car: *I lifted the hood of the car to look at the engine.*
➔ See picture on pages A6 and A26

hoof /hʊf/ *noun*
plural **hoofs** or **hooves** /hʊvz/
the hard foot of a horse, cow, etc.

hoof

hook /hʊk/ *noun*
1 something curved that you hang things on, on a wall, door, etc.: *Kate took off her coat, and hung it on a hook behind the door.*
2 a curved piece of metal that you use for catching fish: *a fishing hook*
3 off the hook = if a telephone is off the hook, the part that you speak into is not on its base, so nobody can call you

hoop /hup/ *noun*
a round piece of wood, metal, or plastic: *a basketball hoop* (=that you throw the ball through)

hoo•ray /hʊ'reɪ/
you shout this when you are very happy about something: *Hooray! We won!*

hoot /hut/ *verb*
if an OWL hoots, it makes a loud noise: *The owl hooted and then flew away.*
—**hoot** *noun* the loud noise that an owl makes

H

hooves /hʊvz/ *noun*
the plural of HOOF

hop /hɑp/ *verb* **hopped, hopping**
1 if a bird or animal hops, it moves with short quick jumps: *The bird hopped across the grass, and ate the bread.*
2 if people hop, they jump on one leg: *Can you hop from one side of the yard to the other?*
3 *informal* to get into or out of a car: *Hop in, and I'll give you a ride to your house.*
—**hop** *noun* a short jump
➔ See Thesaurus box at **jump**[1]
➔ See picture at **jump**[1]

hope[1] /hoʊp/ *verb*
to want something to happen or be true: *I hope that you feel better soon.* | *Bill's hoping to finish his degree next year.* | *"Do you think we'll win?" "I hope so."* (=I want this to happen)

H

WORD FAMILY look at the words:
➔ **hope** *verb*
➔ **hope** *noun*
➔ **hopeful** *adjective*
➔ **hopeless** *adjective*
➔ **hopelessness** *noun*

hope[2] *noun*
1 the feeling that something good may happen: *My family were poor, but we always had hope for the future.*
2 a chance that you will succeed in doing something: *The police say there is some hope of finding the children alive.*
3 something that you hope will happen: *He talked about his hopes and dreams for his future.*

hope•ful /ˈhoʊpfəl/ *adjective*
believing that what you want will happen: *Scientists are hopeful that they will find a cure for the disease.*

hope•ful•ly /ˈhoʊpfəli/ *adverb*
1 you say this to show what you hope will happen: *Hopefully, I'll be home early.*
2 in a hopeful way: *"Can I have some icecream"? Kayla asked hopefully.*

hope•less /ˈhoʊpləs/ *adjective*
unlikely to succeed or improve: *We were lost on the mountain, and the situation seemed hopeless.*
—**hopelessness** *noun*

ho•ri•zon /həˈraɪzən/ *noun*
the horizon = the line where the land or ocean seems to meet the sky: *We looked out at the ocean and saw a ship on the horizon.*

hor•i•zon•tal /ˌhɔrəˈzɑntl/ *adjective*
flat and level: *Draw a horizontal line from one side of the paper to the other side.*
➔ See Thesaurus box at **flat**[1]
➔ See picture at **diagonal**

hor•mone /ˈhɔrmoʊn/ *noun*
a chemical that your body produces, and that makes your body grow and change

horn /hɔrn/ *noun*
1 a hard pointed part that grows on the heads of some animals: *Cows often have horns.*
2 the thing in a car, bus, etc. that makes a loud sound when you push a button: *The driver behind me was honking his horn* (=making a loud noise with the horn). SYNONYM **beep**
3 a musical instrument that you play by blowing
➔ See picture on page A28

hor•net /ˈhɔrnɪt/ *noun*
a large black and yellow insect that can sting you

hor•o•scope /ˈhɔrəˌskoʊp/ *noun*
a description of what will happen to you, that comes from the position of the stars when you were born: *My horoscope says I will have good luck today.*

hor•ri•ble /ˈhɔrəbəl/ *adjective*
very bad or frightening: *I had a horrible dream last night.* | *The food in the school cafeteria is horrible – I won't eat it.* SYNONYM **terrible, awful**
—**horribly** *adverb*: *Some of the people are suffering horribly from disease and lack of food.*
➔ See Thesaurus box at **bad**

hor•ri•fied /ˈhɔrəˌfaɪd/ *adjective*
feeling very shocked or upset: *We were horrified to hear that she had died so young.* —**horrify** *verb* to make someone feel horrified: *The news of the murder horrified me.*

hor•ror /ˈhɔrɚ/ *noun*
a feeling of great shock or fear: *I watched in horror as Ramsey hit her.*

horse /hɔrs/ *noun*
a large animal that people ride, and use in races: *I learned to ride a horse when I was a kid.*

horse•back /ˈhɔrsbæk/ *noun*
on horseback = riding a horse: *We passed two girls on horseback.*

ˈhorseback ˌriding *noun*
the activity of riding horses: *On weekends, I go horseback riding.*

horse•shoe /ˈhɔrʃ-ʃu/ *noun*
a curved piece of iron that covers and protects the bottom of a horse's foot

hor•ti•cul•ture /ˈhɔrtəˌkʌltʃɚ/ *noun, formal*
the activity or science of growing plants

hose /hoʊz/ *noun*
a long tube that water or air can travel through: *Dad was watering the yard with the hose.*

hos•pi•ta•ble /hɑˈspɪtəbəl/ *adjective, formal*
willing to welcome people who visit your home or country: *I traveled all over Europe, and the people were very hospitable.*

hos•pi•tal /ˈhɑspɪtl/ *noun*
a building where doctors and nurses help people who are sick or hurt: *Eric's dad is still in the hospital* (=getting care in a hospital). | *I went to the hospital to have some blood tests done.*

hos•pi•tal•i•ty /ˌhɑspəˈtæləti/ *noun, formal*
friendly behavior toward people who visit you: *They welcomed us into their home with great hospitality.*

host /hoʊst/ *noun, formal*
a person who organizes a party and invites people to it: *Our host greeted us at the door.*

hos•tage /ˈhɑstɪdʒ/ *noun*
someone who is the prisoner of an enemy, until other people do what the enemy asks: *The terrorists are still holding five hostages and demanding money from the U.S.*

host•ess /ˈhoʊstɪs/ *noun, formal*
a woman who organizes a party and invites people to it: *Our hostess was wearing a long black dress.*

hos•tile /ˈhɑstl/ *adjective, formal*
behaving in an angry and unfriendly way: *The prisoners were hostile toward the police officers, yelling at them and throwing things.* —**hostility** /hɑˈstɪləti/ *noun* unfriendly or angry feelings or behavior: *The two brothers had never liked each other and there was still a lot of hostility between them.*

hot /hɑt/ *adjective* **hotter, hottest**
1 having a lot of heat: *Don't touch that plate – it's hot.* | *It was summer, and the weather was hot.* ANTONYM **cold**

> **THESAURUS: hot**
>
> **warm** a little hot, especially in a pleasant way: *a warm summer evening* | *The bread was still warm from the oven.*
>
> **humid** if air or the weather is humid, it feels hot and wet: *It can be very humid in Florida in the summer.*
>
> **lukewarm** a liquid that is lukewarm is only slightly warm, and not as cold or hot as it should be: *The soup was only lukewarm.*
>
> **scalding** a scalding liquid is hot enough to burn you: *a cup of scalding coffee*

2 hot food has a burning taste: *I like pizza with hot peppers.*

ˈhot dog *also* **hot•dog** /ˈhɑtdɔg/ *noun*
a long SAUSAGE that you eat in a piece of bread

ho•tel /hoʊˈtel/ *noun*
a building where you pay to stay when you are traveling: *In Jamaica, we stayed in a hotel right next to the ocean.*

ˈhot plate *also* **hot•plate** /ˈhɑtpleɪt/ *noun*
a small electric thing with a flat top, that you use for cooking food

hour /aʊɚ/ *noun*
1 a time of 60 minutes: *The show lasted an hour.* | *I'll be home in an hour* (=when one hour has passed). | *It's a ten hour trip by car to Chicago.*
2 a time during the day when you do something: *I'll go to the store on my lunch hour*

(=during the time when I stop working to have lunch). I *Please call me during office hours* (=at the time when the office is open).
3 hours *informal* = a long time: *I've been waiting for him to get here for hours.*
4 on the hour = at exactly one o'clock, two o'clock, three o'clock, etc.: *Classes begin on the hour.*
5 at this hour = at a time that is so late: *I'm sorry to call you at this hour, but I didn't know what else to do.*

hour•ly /ˈaʊɚli/ *adjective, adverb*
happening every hour: *The bus leaves hourly from outside the airport.*

house /haʊs/ *noun* plural **houses** /ˈhaʊzɪz/
1 a building that you live in, especially with your family: *Come over to my house after school.*
2 all the people who live in a house: *Be quiet, or you'll wake up the whole house!*
3 *also* **house music** a type of modern music that you dance to
➔ See Thesaurus box at **home**[1]

H

house•hold /ˈhaʊshoʊld/ *noun*
a house and the people who live in it together: *Most households have at least one computer.*
—**household** *adjective* relating to a house and the people who live in it: *Get your kids to do some household chores* (=jobs around the house).

ˌ**House of Repreˈsentatives** *noun*
the larger of the two parts of the government in the U.S., Australia, and New Zealand

house•wife /ˈhaʊswaɪf/ *noun* plural **housewives** /ˈhaʊswaɪvz/
an old-fashioned word for a married woman who does the cooking, cleaning, etc. at home, and no other work: *Later, she quit her job and became a housewife.*

house•work /ˈhaʊswɚk/ *noun*
the work that you do to keep a house clean: *On Saturday, we all help to do the housework; my job is to clean my bedroom.*

hous•ing /ˈhaʊzɪŋ/ *noun, formal*
houses, apartments, etc. that people live in: *They are building new housing downtown.* I *low-income housing* (=houses for people who do not earn much money)

hov•er /ˈhʌvɚ/ *verb*
to stay in one place in the air: *A helicopter hovered above the crowd.*

how /haʊ/ *adverb, conjunction*
1 you say this to ask about the way you do something: *How do you spell your name?*
2 how much/how long/how old, etc. ...? = you say this to ask about the amount of something: *How much did your jeans cost?* I *How old are you?*
3 you say this to ask if someone is well and happy: *How are you?* I *How's your mother?*
4 how about ...? *informal* = you say this to suggest something: *I can't come tonight, but how about tomorrow?*
5 how come? = why?: *How come you were so late?*
6 you say this to ask someone for their opinion or to explain something: *"How do I look in this dress?" "Great!"* I *How can he be so unkind?*
7 how do you do? *formal* = you say this when you meet someone for the first time

how•dy /ˈhaʊdi/ *informal*
you can use this to say "hello" in a very informal way

how•ev•er /haʊˈevɚ/ *adverb*
1 you use this to mean "but", before saying something a little surprising: *It was a very hard test; however, everyone passed.*
2 however long/difficult, etc. ... = even if something is very long, difficult, etc. ...: *She goes swimming every day, however cold the weather is.*

howl /haʊl/ *verb*
to make a long loud sound like a dog crying: *A wild dog howled, and another one answered.*
—**howl** *noun* a sound like a dog crying

ˈ**how-to** *adjective*
a how-to book, video, etc. tells you the way to do something: *a how-to book on choosing a career*

hud•dle /ˈhʌdl/ *verb*
also **huddle together** to move very close to the other people in a small group: *We huddled around the fire to keep warm.*

hug /hʌg/ *verb* **hugged, hugging**
to put your arms around someone to show love or friendship: *My grandmother hugged me and gave me a kiss.*

—**hug** *noun* the act of hugging someone: *Come here and give me a hug!*

huge /hyudʒ/ *adjective*
very big: *Their house is huge – it has six bedrooms and a big playroom.*
➔ See Thesaurus box at **big**

huge•ly /'hyudʒli/ *adverb*
very: *The TV show was hugely popular for years.*

hum /hʌm/ *verb* **hummed, humming**
1 to sing a tune with your mouth closed: *Dad was humming as he worked.*
2 to make a low steady sound like a BEE: *High in the sky, an airplane hummed.*

hu•man /'hyumən/ *adjective*
belonging or relating to people: *Give an example of how human behavior is similar to animal behavior.* | *The accident was a result of human error* (=a mistake made by a person, not a machine).

ˌhuman 'being *also* **human** *noun*
a person, not an animal: *They have not tested the drug on human beings yet.*

hu•mane /hyu'meɪn/ *adjective, formal*
not cruel: *Farm animals should have humane treatment.* ANTONYM **inhumane**
—**humanely** *adverb*

hu•man•i•tar•i•an /hyuˌmænə'teriən/ *adjective, formal*
relating to people who are in a very bad or dangerous situation and the help that countries or organizations give them: *The U.S. sent humanitarian aid* (=food, medicine, and other help) *to the people affected by the earthquake.*

hu•man•i•ty /hyu'mænəti/ *noun, formal*
1 all the people in the world: *He thought he was different from the rest of humanity.*
2 kindness and respect toward other people: *We should treat prisoners with humanity.*

hu•man•ly /'hyumənli/ *adverb*
humanly possible = able to be done by someone who is trying very hard: *The doctors did everything humanly possible to save his life.*

ˌhuman 'race *noun*
the human race = people considered as a group: *How long has the human race existed?*

ˌhuman 'rights *plural noun*
the basic rights that everyone has to be treated well, especially by the government: *The country has a bad record on human rights; many people have been unfairly put in prison.*

hum•ble /'hʌmbəl/ *adjective*
1 someone who is humble does not think that he or she is special or important: *The great scientist was a humble man who did not want praise.* ANTONYM **proud**
2 poor and of a low social rank: *He came from humble beginnings and later became President.*
—**humbly** *adverb*

hu•mid /'hyumɪd/ *adjective*
if the weather is humid, the air feels warm and wet: *Summers here are hot and humid.*
—**humidity** /hyu'mɪdəti/ *noun* the wetness of warm air: *The heat and humidity made me feel tired.*
➔ See Thesaurus box at **hot**

hu•mil•i•ate /hyu'mɪliˌeɪt/ *verb*
to make someone feel or seem stupid or weak, in an upsetting way: *The teacher humiliated him by laughing at the answer he gave.*
—**humiliated** *adjective*
—**humiliating** *adjective*
—**humiliation** /hyuˌmɪli'eɪʃən/ *noun* when someone is humiliated: *the team's humiliation after their loss*

hu•mor /'hyumɚ/ *noun*
1 sense of humor = the ability to be funny and to understand things that are funny: *She has a great sense of humor – she really makes me laugh.*
2 funny things that someone says or writes: *There's a lot of humor in the book.*

hu•mor•ous /'hyumərəs/ *adjective, formal*
funny: *We make humorous television ads that make our product seem fun.*
—**humorously** *adverb*
➔ See Thesaurus box at **funny**[1]

hump /hʌmp/ *noun*
a large round raised part or object: *Some camels have one hump on their backs and some have two.*

H

hunch /hʌntʃ/ *noun*
a feeling that something is true or will happen, which is not based on any facts: *My hunch is that things will improve soon.*

hunched /hʌntʃt/ *adjective*
bending forward so that your back forms a curve: *He sat hunched over his desk.*

hun•dred /ˈhʌndrɪd/ *number*
100
—**hundredth** *number* 100th or 1/100

hung /hʌŋ/ *verb*
the past tense and past participle of HANG

hun•ger /ˈhʌŋgɚ/ *noun*
the state of needing or wanting to eat: *There has been no food in this town for weeks, and people are dying of hunger.*

hun•gry /ˈhʌŋgri/ *adjective* **hungrier**, **hungriest**
1 needing or wanting to eat something: *When's dinner? I'm hungry.*
2 go hungry = to not have enough food to eat: *My family was poor, but we never went hungry.*

H

hunt /hʌnt/ *verb*
1 to chase wild animals in order to kill them: *They hunted deer in the woods.*
2 to look for something or someone very carefully: *She hunted for her keys all around the house.* SYNONYM **search**
—**hunting** *noun* the activity of chasing wild animals in order to kill them: *We're going hunting in the White Mountains this weekend.*
—**hunt** *noun* an attempt to catch or find someone or something: *The hunt for the terrorists could last for years, and we may never find them.*

hunt•er /ˈhʌntɚ/ *noun*
someone who hunts wild animals: *a deer hunter*

hurl /hɚl/ *verb*
to throw something with a lot of force: *He hurled a brick through the window.*
➔ See Thesaurus box at **throw**[1]

hur•ri•cane /ˈhɚɪˌkeɪn/ *noun*
a storm with very strong fast winds that comes from the ocean: *The hurricane destroyed many buildings.*
➔ See Thesaurus box at **wind**[1]

hur•ry[1] /ˈhɚi/ *verb* **hurried**, third person singular **hurries**
to do something or go somewhere quickly: *We have to hurry or we'll miss the plane.* | *The girls hurried home to tell their parents.*
SYNONYM **rush**

PHRASAL VERB
hurry up
to do something or move somewhere more quickly than before: *Hurry up! We're going to be late!*

hurry[2] *noun*
1 be in a hurry = to need to do something or go somewhere very quickly: *He was in a hurry and couldn't stop to talk.*
2 (there's) no hurry = used when telling someone that he or she does not have to do something immediately: *You can give me the CD back any time – there's no hurry.*

hurt[1] /hɚt/ *verb* **hurt**
1 to injure yourself or someone else: *She fell and hurt her knee.* | *No one was hurt in the explosion.*

THESAURUS: hurt

To Injure Someone

Hurt and **injure** can mean the same, but **hurt** is usually used when the damage to your body is not very great: *Alex fell and hurt his knee.*

injure to damage someone's body – usually used for saying that someone has been hurt in an accident: *Three people were seriously injured in the crash.*

wound to injure someone using a weapon such as a gun or knife: *The gunman killed two people and wounded six others.*

To Feel Pain

ache to feel a continuous pain: *My back was aching.*

sting to cause a sudden sharp pain in your eyes, throat, or skin: *The soap got in my eyes and stung a lot.*

be tender if a part of your body is tender, it is painful if someone touches it: *The bruise on her leg was very tender.*

be stiff if a part of your body is stiff, your muscles hurt and it is difficult to move, usually because you have exercised too much or you are sick: *My legs are so stiff!*

be sore to be painful as a result of a wound, infection, or too much exercise: *My ankle was really sore where I'd twisted it.* | *She had a sore throat and fever.*

2 if a part of your body hurts, it is painful: *My stomach hurts.*
3 if an action hurts, it makes you feel pain: *My throat is sore, and it hurts to swallow.*
4 to make someone feel upset: *He said some terrible things that really hurt my feelings.*

hurt[2] *adjective*
1 injured: *Is he badly hurt?*
2 upset: *I felt hurt when they didn't invite me to the party.*

hurt•ful /ˈhɚtfəl/ *adjective*
making you feel upset: *That's a hurtful thing to say – you should say you're sorry.*

hus•band /ˈhʌzbənd/ *noun*
the man that a woman is married to: *This is my husband Bob.*

hush[1] /hʌʃ/
said in order to tell someone, especially a child, to be quiet or stop crying: *Hush now. It's time to go to sleep.*

hush[2] *noun, formal*
a peaceful silence: *A hush fell over the crowd* (=everyone suddenly became quiet).

hut /hʌt/ *noun*
a small simple house or building: *The village is a group of mud huts.*

hy•dro•e•lec•tric /ˌhaɪdroʊɪˈlektrɪk/ *adjective*
hydroelectric power is electricity that is produced by the force of water

hy•dro•gen /ˈhaɪdrədʒən/ *noun*
a light gas that is an ELEMENT

hy•giene /ˈhaɪdʒin/ *noun*
things you do to keep people and things clean in order to prevent diseases: *It is important to have good personal hygiene* (=keep your body clean).
—**hygienic** /haɪˈdʒenɪk/ *adjective* clean, so that people will not get diseases: *Restaurants must have hygienic kitchens, so that people who eat in them do not get sick.*

hymn /hɪm/ *noun*
a song that people sing in Christian churches

hy•phen /ˈhaɪfən/ *noun*
a mark (-) that you use to join two words or parts of a word: *The word "four-legged" has a hyphen in it.*

hyp•no•sis /hɪpˈnoʊsɪs/ *noun*
a state like sleep, in which you can remember more things, and someone can make you think or do things. A doctor usually puts you into this special state: *He remembered details about the crime while he was under hypnosis.*
—**hypnotize** /ˈhɪpnəˌtaɪz/ *verb* to put someone in a state of hypnosis
—**hypnotist** *noun* someone who hypnotizes people

hyp•o•crite /ˈhɪpəˌkrɪt/ *noun*
someone who tells people to behave in a particular way, but who does not behave in that way himself or herself: *You're such a hypocrite – you told me never to smoke, but now you're smoking!*
—**hypocritical** /ˌhɪpəˈkrɪtɪkəl/ *adjective* someone who is hypocritical is a hypocrite
—**hypocrisy** /hɪˈpɑkrəsi/ *noun* the action of being hypocritical

hy•poth•e•sis /haɪˈpɑθəsɪs/ Ac *noun*
plural **hypotheses** /haɪˈpɑθəsiz/ *formal*
an idea that no one has proved to be true yet: *The scientist did an experiment to test his hypothesis* (=find out if it could be true).
SYNONYM **theory**

hy•po•thet•i•cal /ˌhaɪpəˈθetɪkəl/ Ac *adjective*
a hypothetical situation is not real, but might happen: *I'm going to give you a hypothetical situation, and you tell me how you would deal with it if it really happened.*

hys•ter•ical /hɪˈsterəkəl/ *adjective*
so upset, excited, etc. that you cannot control yourself: *When she was told her daughter was dead, she became hysterical.*
—**hysteria** /hɪˈsteriə/ *noun* your feelings and actions when you are hysterical: *There was public hysteria when the newspaper reported that the disease was spreading.*

H

Ii

I[1] /aɪ/ *pronoun*
used as the subject of a verb when you are talking about yourself: *I saw Mike yesterday.*

I[2]
the number 1 in the system of ROMAN NUMERALS

ice /aɪs/ *noun*
water that has frozen: *Do you want some ice in your drink?* | *Ice began to cover the lake.*

ice·berg /ˈaɪsbɚg/ *noun*
a very large piece of ice floating in the ocean

ˈice cream *noun*
a sweet frozen food made from milk or cream: *chocolate ice cream*

ˈice cream ˌcone *noun*
a pointed container that you can eat, that holds ice cream

ˈice cube *noun*
a small square piece of ice that you put in a drink

ˈice skate *verb*
to move along on ice wearing special boots
—**ice skate** *noun* a special boot with a blade attached under it that you wear for moving on ice
—**ice skater** *noun* someone who ice skates

i·ci·cle /ˈaɪsɪkəl/ *noun*
a long pointed piece of ice that hangs down from something: *The water began to freeze and there were icicles hanging from the roof.*

ic·ing /ˈaɪsɪŋ/ *noun*
a sweet substance that you put on cakes, made from sugar and liquid and often butter SYNONYM **frosting**

i·con /ˈaɪkɑn/ *noun*
1 a small picture on a computer screen that you can choose with your mouse to make the computer do something
2 someone who is famous and admired by many people: *Elvis Presley is a pop icon.*
➔ See picture on page A20

ic·y /ˈaɪsi/ *adjective* **icier**, **iciest**
1 very cold: *An icy wind was blowing from the north.*
2 covered in ice: *Cars were sliding on the icy road.*
➔ See Thesaurus box at **cold**[1]

I'd /aɪd/
1 the short form of "I had": *I'd never seen her before.*
2 the short form of "I would": *I'd love to come!*

ID *noun*
an official document that shows who you are and usually has a picture on it: *You have to be 21 to come into the bar. Can I see your ID?*

i·de·a /aɪˈdɪə/ *noun*
1 a thought about something that someone could do or try: *I like the idea of getting a dog.* | *"Let's ask Jim what to do." "That's a good idea* (=the action is likely to be successful).*"*
2 understanding or knowledge of something: *I had no idea* (=did not know at all) *what the problem was.* | *Can you give me an idea of how much it will cost?*
3 an opinion or belief: *He explained his ideas about how the music should sound.*
4 the idea = the aim of an action or plan: *The idea is to make children aware of pollution by showing them how much pollution their car produces.*

i·de·al[1] /ˌaɪˈdiəl/ *adjective*
the best possible: *It's a beautiful beach – an ideal place for a vacation.* SYNONYM **perfect**
—**ideally** *adverb* used when saying what would be the best thing to happen: *Ideally, you should start learning to play soccer at the age of about five.*

ideal[2] *noun*
an idea about a way of living, way of doing something, etc. that is the very best and that you should try to achieve: *We believe strongly in the American ideals of freedom and democracy.*

i•de•al•ism /aɪ'diə,lɪzəm/ *noun*
the belief that a good world and good behavior are possible: *He is a young politician with a lot of idealism – he believes that democracy can work better than it does now.*
—**idealistic** /,aɪdiə'lɪstɪk/ *adjective* believing that a good world and good behavior are possible: *an idealistic young teacher*
—**idealist** /aɪ'diəlɪst/ *noun* someone who is idealistic

i•de•al•ize /aɪ'diə,laɪz/ *verb, formal*
to think or try to show that something is much better than it really is: *The show idealizes family life by showing a "perfect" family in a "perfect" house.*

i•den•ti•cal /aɪ'dentɪkəl/ Ac *adjective*
exactly the same: *Your dress is identical to mine.* | *identical twins* (=two brothers or sisters who were born at the same time and look exactly alike)
➔ See Thesaurus box at **similar**

i•den•ti•fi•ca•tion /aɪ,dentəfə'keɪʃən/ Ac *noun*
something that shows who you are: *You can use a passport as identification.* SYNONYM **ID**

i•den•ti•fy /aɪ'dentə,faɪ/ Ac *verb* **identified**, third person singular **identifies**
to say who someone is or what something is: *Our teacher could identify all the plants we saw.*

PHRASAL VERB

identify with someone
to feel that someone is similar to you, so that you understand the way he or she thinks or behaves: *I identified with the main character in the book.*

WORD FAMILY look at the words:
➔ **identify** *verb*
➔ **identification** *noun*
➔ **identity** *noun*

i•den•ti•ty /aɪ'dentəti/ Ac *noun* plural **identities**
1 someone's name: *The police do not know the identity of the dead man.*
2 the qualities that make one person or group different from others: *Our country has a strong national identity, and we don't want other countries to tell us how to think.*

i•de•ol•o•gy /,aɪdi'ɑlədʒi/ Ac *noun* plural **ideologies** *formal*
a set of political beliefs or ideas: *Communist ideology*
—**ideological** /,aɪdiə'lɑdʒɪkəl/ *adjective* relating to ideologies: *The two men have ideological differences.*

id•i•om /'ɪdiəm/ *noun*
a group of words which have a special meaning when they are used together: *"Get cold feet" is an idiom which means "to suddenly feel worried about doing something."*
—**idiomatic** /,ɪdiə'mætɪk/ *adjective* being an idiom, or containing idioms
➔ See Thesaurus box at **phrase**

id•i•ot /'ɪdiət/ *noun*
a stupid person: *Don't drive so fast, you idiot!*
—**idiotic** /,ɪdi'ɑtɪk/ *adjective* stupid: *Don't ask such idiotic questions.*

i•dle /'aɪdl/ *adjective*
1 not working or being used: *Machines are sitting idle because there is no one to operate them.*
2 an old-fashioned word meaning "lazy"
—**idleness** *noun*

i•dol /'aɪdl/ *noun*
1 someone, especially someone famous, who you admire very much: *President Reagan was his idol when he was a child.*
2 a STATUE of a god: *People worshiped the idol in the temple.*
—**idolize** *verb* to admire someone very much: *He idolizes his father and says he wants to be just like him.*

i.e. /,aɪ 'i/
used before explaining exactly what you mean: *The movie is for adults only, i.e. people over the age of 18.*

if /ɪf/ *conjunction*
1 used when talking about something that might happen or that might have happened: *If I find out where the party is, I'll call you.* | *If we hadn't taken him to the hospital, he would have died.*
2 whether: *I don't know if I'll be able to come.*
3 whenever: *If I drink milk, I get a stomachache.*
4 if I were you = used when giving advice: *If I were you, I'd wear something warmer because it's getting really cold.*

→ **even if** at even[1], **as if/though** at as, **if only** at only[1]

ig•nite /ɪɡˈnaɪt/ *verb, formal*
to make something start burning: *A cigarette ignited the gas, and the gas exploded.*

ig•ni•tion /ɪɡˈnɪʃən/ *noun*
the part of a car where you put a key to start the engine: *He turned the key in the ignition.*
→ See picture on page A28

ig•no•rance /ˈɪɡnərəns/ Ac *noun*
the state of not knowing something, especially something you should know: *I was embarrassed by my ignorance of their culture* (=how much I did not know about their culture).

ig•no•rant /ˈɪɡnərənt/ Ac *adjective*
not knowing something, especially something you should know: *She had just come to this country and was ignorant of her rights as a U.S. citizen.*

ig•nore /ɪɡˈnɔr/ Ac *verb*
to not pay any attention to someone or something: *I tried to talk to her, but she ignored me.*

ill /ɪl/ *adjective*
1 someone who is ill has a disease or does not feel well: *She can't go to work because she's ill.* | *He is mentally ill.* SYNONYM **sick**
2 ill at ease *formal* = nervous or embarrassed: *He felt ill at ease in this group of rich people.* SYNONYM **uncomfortable**
→ See Thesaurus box at **sick**

I'll /aɪl/
the short form of "I will": *I'll be back soon.*

il•le•gal /ɪˈliɡəl/ Ac *adjective*
not allowed by the law: *It's illegal to park here.* | *illegal drugs* ANTONYM **legal**
—**illegally** *adverb*: *They had entered the country illegally, so they were sent back to their own country.*

il•leg•i•ble /ɪˈledʒəbəl/ *adjective*
impossible to read: *I couldn't read the letter, because his writing was illegible.* ANTONYM **legible**

il•le•git•i•mate /ˌɪləˈdʒɪtəmət/ *adjective, formal*
an illegitimate child has parents who were not married when the baby was born: *He has an illegitimate son.*
—**illegitimacy** /ˌɪləˈdʒɪtəməsi/ *noun* the state of being illegitimate

il•lit•er•ate /ɪˈlɪtərət/ *adjective*
not able to read or write: *She did not know what the letter said because she was illiterate.*
—**illiteracy** /ɪˈlɪtərəsi/ *noun* when people cannot read or write

ill•ness /ˈɪlnəs/ *noun*
a disease, or a period of being ill: *She has had several serious illnesses, including cancer.* | *people with mental illness* (=problems with your mind, for example problems controlling your thoughts and feelings)

il•log•i•cal /ɪˈlɑdʒɪkəl/ Ac *adjective*
an illogical idea or action is not based on good thinking: *It is illogical to hit your computer when it does something that you do not like.* ANTONYM **logical**

il•lu•mi•nate /ɪˈluməˌneɪt/ *verb, formal*
if a light illuminates something, it makes it bright: *The fire illuminated her face, and I could see that she was crying.*
—**illumination** /ɪˌluməˈneɪʃən/ *noun* the act of making a place bright

il•lu•sion /ɪˈluʒən/ *noun*
1 something that seems to be real or true but is not: *One line looks longer than the other, but that is just an optical illusion; they are actually the same length.*
2 a false belief: *She has no illusions about winning* (=she realizes she probably will not win).

il•lus•trate /ˈɪləˌstreɪt/ Ac *verb*
1 to give or be an example that makes something clearer: *This story illustrates how important it is to tell the truth.*
2 to add pictures to a book: *She illustrates children's books.*
—**illustrator** *noun* someone who draws pictures for books

WORD FAMILY look at the words:
→ **illustrate** *verb*
→ **illustration** *noun*
→ **illustrator** *noun*

il•lus•tra•tion /ˌɪləˈstreɪʃən/ Ac *noun*
1 a picture in a book: *The book has beautiful color illustrations.*
2 an example that shows something: *The Bible gives Jesus's life as an illustration of how to live a good life.*
→ See Thesaurus box at **picture**[1]

I'm /aɪm/
the short form of "I am": *I'm hungry.*

im•age /ˈɪmɪdʒ/ Ac *noun*
1 a picture that you can see on a television, in a mirror, etc.: *We watched the images on TV of the destruction caused by the flood.*
2 the way that someone or something seems to the public: *The President wanted to improve his image, so he traveled around the country to meet people.*
3 a picture that you have in your mind: *I have a clear image of the kind of house I want to live in.*

im•age•ry /ˈɪmɪdʒri/ Ac *noun, formal*
the things described or shown in poems, books, movies, etc.: *The song's violent imagery upset many people.*

i•mag•i•nar•y /ɪˈmædʒəˌneri/ *adjective*
something that is imaginary is not real and only exists in your mind: *The book shows us an imaginary world of strange people living on other planets.*

i•mag•i•na•tion /ɪˌmædʒəˈneɪʃən/ *noun*
the ability to think of new ideas or make new pictures in your mind: *She had a vivid imagination* (=a great ability to imagine new things).
—**imaginative** /ɪˈmædʒənətɪv/ *adjective* having or showing a lot of imagination: *The boy wrote a very imaginative story.*

i•mag•ine /ɪˈmædʒɪn/ *verb*
1 to use your mind to think of new ideas, stories, pictures, etc.: *Imagine (that) you have lots of money, and you can do anything you want.*
2 to use your mind to try to understand something that is new, different, or difficult: *I can imagine how you felt – you must have been really mad.*
3 to think that something will probably happen or is probably true: *I imagine she was pretty upset.*

WORD FAMILY look at the words:

- → **imagine** *verb*
- → **imagination** *noun*
- → **imaginative** *adjective*
- → **imaginary** *adjective*

im•i•tate /ˈɪməˌteɪt/ *verb*
1 to copy the way a person or animal speaks or moves to entertain other people: *He imitated the teacher to make the other kids laugh.*
2 to copy something because you think it is good: *Other companies have tried to imitate our products, but ours are still the best.* SYNONYM **copy**
—**imitation** /ˌɪməˈteɪʃən/ *noun* the act of imitating someone or something: *She does imitations of birds' songs* (=she makes sounds to copy them).

im•i•ta•tion /ˌɪməˈteɪʃən/ *adjective*
made to look like something real: *The necklace was made of imitation pearls, not real ones.*
→ See Thesaurus box at **fake**

im•ma•ture /ˌɪməˈtʃʊr/ Ac *adjective*
behaving like someone much younger than you: *I think Jim's too immature to live by himself.* SYNONYM **childish**; ANTONYM **mature**
—**immaturity** /ˌɪməˈtʃʊrəti/ *noun* the quality of being immature

im•me•di•ate /ɪˈmidiət/ *adjective*
1 happening or coming very soon: *I wrote them an email, and I got an immediate reply.* | *What are your plans for the immediate future* (=the time that is very soon after now)*?*
2 someone's immediate family = someone's parents, children, brothers, and sisters: *We only invited our immediate families to our wedding, because we didn't want too many people there.*

im•me•di•ate•ly /ɪˈmidiətli/ *adverb*
very quickly and with no delay: *I knew immediately that something was wrong, when I saw that she had been crying.*

THESAURUS: immediately

instantly immediately – used when something happens at almost the same time as something else: *He was killed instantly when his motorcycle hit a truck.*

right away *informal* immediately and without waiting – used especially when something needs to be done urgently: *Jill called him right away.*

at once immediately or without waiting: *I realized at once that I had said the wrong thing.*

right now *informal* at this time and not later – used especially when something needs to be done urgently: *Ben! Stop that right now!*

im•mense /ɪ'mens/ *adjective, formal*
very large: *We have an immense amount of work to do.* SYNONYM **enormous, huge**

im•mense•ly /ɪ'mensli/ *adverb, formal*
very or very much: *The show is immensely popular.*

im•merse /ɪ'mɚs/ *verb, formal*
1 to put something into a liquid so that the liquid covers it completely: *Do not immerse this equipment in water.*
2 immerse yourself in something = to give all your attention to something: *She immersed herself in her school work because she didn't want to think about her problems.*
—**immersion** /ɪ'mɚʒən/ *noun* the act of putting something into a liquid so that the liquid covers it completely

im•mi•grant /'ɪməgrənt/ Ac *noun*
someone who comes to live in a country: *His grandparents were Chinese immigrants* (=they came from China).

im•mi•gra•tion /ˌɪmə'greɪʃən/ Ac *noun*
the act of coming to live in a country: *People on the Mexican border are trying to stop illegal immigration.*
—**immigrate** /'ɪməˌgreɪt/ *verb* to come to live in a country: *He immigrated to the United States from Poland.*

im•mor•al /ɪ'mɔrəl/ *adjective*
bad and wrong: *Religions teach us that killing and stealing are immoral.*
—**immorality** /ˌɪmə'rælәti/ *noun* immoral behavior

im•mor•tal /ɪ'mɔrtl/ *adjective*
living or continuing forever: *Some people believe the soul is immortal and lives after the body dies.* ANTONYM **mortal**
—**immortality** /ˌɪmɔr'tælәti/ *noun* the state of living or continuing forever: *Greek people in ancient times believed in the immortality of their gods.*

im•mune /ɪ'myun/ *adjective*
not able to be affected by something bad, especially a disease: *A small group of people are immune to the virus and have not gotten sick at all.*
—**immunity** /ɪ'myunәti/ *noun* the state of being immune to something: *The children do not have immunity to the disease.*

im'mune ˌsystem *noun*
the system by which your body protects itself against disease: *People with weakened immune systems are at risk from the disease.*

im•mu•nize /'ɪmyəˌnaɪz/ *verb*
to protect someone from disease by giving him or her a VACCINE (=weak form of the disease): *We must immunize children against these diseases.*
—**immunization** /ˌɪmyənə'zeɪʃən/ *noun* the act of immunizing someone

im•pact /'ɪmpækt/ Ac *noun*
the effect that something has: *The decision to close the school will have a major impact on the town* (=cause big changes in the town).
—**impact** /ɪm'pækt/ *verb* to affect something: *How does the disease impact on your life?*

im•pair /ɪm'per/ *verb, formal*
to make something less good, for example to make an ability less good: *The injury to her brain impaired her ability to talk.*
—**impairment** *noun* the state of being less good: *He has a hearing impairment, so you have to speak louder.*

im•par•tial /ɪm'pɑrʃəl/ *adjective*
not supporting a particular person or group: *The judge should be impartial* (=fair to both sides). SYNONYM **objective**; ANTONYM **biased**
—**impartially** *adverb*
—**impartiality** /ɪmˌpɑrʃi'ælәti/ *noun* the quality of being impartial

im•pa•tient /ɪm'peɪʃənt/ *adjective*
1 annoyed because something has not been done immediately: *The teacher gets impatient with students who do not listen to her.*
2 impatient to do something = wanting to do something immediately: *Juan was impatient to leave, because he was bored.*
—**impatience** *noun* the state of feeling impatient
—**impatiently** *adverb*

im•peach /ɪm'pitʃ/ *verb*
to say officially that a public official has committed a serious crime
—**impeachment** *noun* when someone is impeached

im•per•a•tive[1] /ɪm'perətɪv/ *noun*
the form of a verb that you use when you tell someone to do something: *In the sentence*

"Come here!" the verb "come" is in the imperative.

imperative² *adjective*
formal something that is imperative is very important and must be done: *It is imperative that we win this game.*

im•per•fect /ɪm'pɚfɪkt/ *adjective, formal*
not perfect: *We live in an imperfect world.*
—**imperfection** /ˌɪmpɚ'fekʃən/ *noun* a fault, mark, etc. that makes something not perfect: *There were some imperfections in the cloth, so they lowered the price.*

im•pe•ri•al•ism /ɪm'pɪriəˌlɪzəm/ *noun, disapproving*
a political system in which one country controls a lot of other countries
—**imperialist** *noun*
—**imperialist,** *also* **imperialistic** /ɪmˌpɪriə'lɪstɪk/ *adjective*

im•per•son•al /ɪm'pɚsənəl/ *adjective*
dealing with you in a way that is not friendly or does not show any interest in you: *I wrote an email to explain my problem to the bank, but I just got an impersonal reply.*

im•per•so•nate /ɪm'pɚsəˌneɪt/ *verb*
to copy someone's voice and behavior in order to entertain or trick people: *He impersonates many famous people on his show.*
—**impersonator** *noun* someone who impersonated someone else: *an Elvis impersonator*
—**impersonation** /ɪmˌpɚsə'neɪʃən/ *noun* the act of impersonating someone: *He does a good impersonation of the President.*

im•ple•ment¹ /'ɪmpləˌment/ Ac *verb, formal*
if you implement a plan, process, etc., you begin to make it happen
—**implementation** /ˌɪmpləmən'teɪʃən/ *noun* the act of implementing a plan

im•ple•ment² /'ɪmpləmənt/ Ac *noun*
a simple tool: *farm implements*

im•pli•ca•tion /ˌɪmplə'keɪʃən/ Ac *noun*
a possible result or effect of something: *What are the implications of the research* (=what effects does it have)?

implicit /ɪm'plɪsɪt/ Ac *adjective*
an idea that is implicit can be understood from something you say, but is not said directly: *My boss didn't say that my work was bad, but there was an implicit criticism in the way he said it.*
—**implicitly** *adverb*

im•ply /ɪm'plaɪ/ Ac *verb* **implied**, third person singular **implies**
to make someone think that something is true without saying it directly: *I think he was implying that I would get the job, but I'm not sure.*

im•po•lite /ˌɪmpə'laɪt/ *adjective*
not polite: *It's impolite to yawn when someone is talking.* SYNONYM **rude**
➔ See Thesaurus box at **rude**

im•port¹ /ɪm'pɔrt/ *verb*
to bring things into a country to sell or use: *We import a lot of oil from other countries.* ANTONYM **export**
—**importer** *noun* a person or company that imports things

im•port² /'ɪmpɔrt/ *noun*
1 something that is brought into a country to be sold or used: *The stores are full of cheap imports.* ANTONYM **export**
2 the action of bringing things into a country to sell or use: *The government stopped the import of weapons.* ANTONYM **export**

im•por•tance /ɪm'pɔrtns/ *noun*
the quality of being important: *I understand the importance of a good education, because my parents did not have one.* | *This is a matter of great importance* (=a very important matter).

im•por•tant /ɪm'pɔrtnt/ *adjective*
1 if something is important, you care about it a lot or should care about it a lot: *This is the most important part of the class.* | *My family is very important to me.* | *It's important to stay calm during an emergency.*

THESAURUS: important

crucial *formal* very important: *The U.S. plays a crucial role in the region.*

vital *formal* very important or necessary: *She was able to give the police some vital clues that helped them catch the murderer.*

essential *formal* very important and necessary: *It's essential that you buy tickets in advance.*

major very large or important, especially when compared to other things: *Several major roads were closed to any traffic.*

significant *formal* noticeable or important: *His music has had a significant influence on other musicians.*

key very important and needed for success: *One of the team's key players is injured and won't be playing this Friday.*

2 an important person has power or influence: *She is the most important person in the company.*

—**importantly** *adverb* used when mentioning something important: *The restaurant is beautiful and, more importantly, the food is excellent.*

WORD FAMILY look at the words:

→ **important** *adjective*
→ **unimportant** *adjective*
→ **importance** *noun*

im•pose /ɪm'poʊz/ Ac *verb, formal*
to force people to have a law, punishment, etc.: *The principal imposed a new rule to stop students from wearing jewelry in school.*
—**imposition** /ˌɪmpə'zɪʃən/ *noun* the act of imposing something

im•pos•ing /ɪm'poʊzɪŋ/ Ac *adjective*
large and impressive: *The White House is an imposing building.*

im•pos•si•ble /ɪm'pɑsəbəl/ *adjective*
not able to be done or to happen: *I could not do it – it was an impossible job.* | *It was so hot that it was impossible to sleep.*
—**impossibility** /ɪmˌpɑsə'bɪləti/ *noun* the fact that something is impossible, or something that is impossible: *I wanted mom's party to be a secret, but I knew that would be an impossibility because my brother would tell her.*

im•pos•ter /ɪm'pɑstɚ/ *noun*
someone who pretends to be someone else in order to trick people: *He wasn't a real soldier; he was an imposter.*

im•prac•ti•cal /ɪm'præktɪkəl/ *adjective*
an impractical plan or way of doing something is too difficult, too expensive, etc.: *It would be impractical to ask every person what he or she thinks.*

im•pre•cise /ˌɪmprɪ'saɪs/ Ac *adjective, formal*
not exact: *I believe there were about 1,500 people there, but that is an imprecise number.*

im•press /ɪm'pres/ *verb*
to make someone feel admiration and respect: *He rented a nice car to impress his girlfriend.*
—**impressed** *adjective*: *I was very impressed with the new classrooms.*

WORD FAMILY look at the words:

→ **impress** *verb*
→ **impressed** *adjective*
→ **impressive** *adjective*

im•pres•sion /ɪm'preʃən/ *noun*
1 the opinion or feeling you have about someone or something because of what you see or hear: *I got the impression that he didn't like me* (=I felt that he didn't like me). | *It's important to make a good impression at your interview* (=make people have a good opinion of you in the interview).
2 be under the impression that = to think that something is true when it is not: *I was under the impression that they were married, but they are not.*
3 the act of copying the voice or behavior of a famous person in order to entertain people: *Erin does a great impression of Britney Spears.* SYNONYM **imitation**

im•pres•sive /ɪm'presɪv/ *adjective*
if something is impressive, it is very good and you admire it: *Winning five gold medals is an impressive achievement.*

im•pris•on /ɪm'prɪzən/ *verb, formal*
to put someone in prison: *The new leader imprisoned anyone who disagreed with him.*
—**imprisonment** *noun* the state of being in prison: *His imprisonment lasted ten years.*

im•prob•a•ble /ɪm'prɑbəbəl/ *adjective, formal*
not likely to happen or to be true: *The car accident was very bad, and it is improbable that anyone survived.* SYNONYM **unlikely**; ANTONYM **probable**

im•prop•er /ɪm'prɑpɚ/ *adjective, formal*
wrong or unacceptable: *The improper use of child car seats resulted in many deaths.*
—**improperly** *adverb*: *We didn't go into the*

restaurant because it was a formal place and we were improperly dressed.

im•prove /ɪm'pruv/ *verb*
to become better, or to make something better: *Her health improved when she stopped smoking.* | *I want to improve my language skills.*

im•prove•ment /ɪm'pruvmənt/ *noun*
1 when something becomes better: *He seems happier, and there's been an improvement in his behavior.* | *Her health is showing signs of improvement.*
2 a change that makes something better: *You can borrow money to pay for home improvements such as putting in a new kitchen or painting the house.*

im•pro•vise /'ɪmprəvaɪz/ *verb*
to do or make something without any preparation: *The musicians improvised, so they did not have written music in front of them.*
—**improvisation** /ɪmˌprɑvə'zeɪʃən/ *noun* the act of improvising

im•pulse /'ɪmpʌls/ *noun*
a sudden desire to do something: *I resisted the impulse to hit him* (=I stopped myself from hitting him).

im•pul•sive /ɪm'pʌlsɪv/ *adjective*
someone who is impulsive does things suddenly, without thinking about the results: *Small children are impulsive; they will do or say anything that they think of.*
—**impulsively** *adverb*: *Impulsively, he kissed her.*

im•pure /ɪm'pyʊr/ *adjective*
1 containing another substance that is unwanted: *Impure drugs can make you very sick.* ANTONYM **pure**
2 *formal* bad, according to a religion: *impure thoughts* ANTONYM **pure**
—**impurity** /ɪm'pyʊrəti/ *noun* an unwanted substance that another substance contains: *We can remove some of the impurities from the water to make it taste better.*

in /ɪn/ *preposition, adverb*
1 inside a container or building, or surrounded by a place: *She had a pencil in her pocket.* | *Put the knives and forks in the drawer.* | *He lives in Denver.* | *Come in!*
2 during a month, year, etc.: *We moved here in September.* | *I was born in 1990.*
3 after a period of time: *Gerry should be home in an hour.*
4 using a particular language or way of speaking: *He said something in Italian.* | *They spoke in whispers.*
5 wearing: *Who's the woman in the black dress?*
6 if you are in something, you are part of it or involved in it: *I talked to the other people in the group.* | *He has appeared in several movies.* | *She's in advertising* (=she works in the business of advertising).
7 fashionable now *informal*: *Long hair is in again.* ANTONYM **out**
8 be in for something = if you are in for something, something is about to happen to you: *If you think this game is going to be easy, you're in for a shock.*
9 be in on something = to be involved in something or know about something: *Do you think he was in on the robbery?*
10 in all = used when mentioning a total amount: *There were 20 of us in all.*

in.
the written abbreviation of **inch**

in•a•bil•i•ty /ˌɪnə'bɪləti/ *noun, formal*
the fact of not being able to do something: *He was embarrassed about his inability to read.* ANTONYM **ability**

in•ac•ces•si•ble /ˌɪnək'sesəbəl/ Ac *adjective, formal*
difficult or impossible to reach: *The house is inaccessible in winter, because snow blocks the road.* ANTONYM **accessible**

in•ac•cu•rate /ɪn'ækyərɪt/ Ac *adjective, formal*
not completely correct: *He gave an inaccurate description of the house, so we did not recognize it when we saw it.* ANTONYM **accurate**
—**inaccuracy** *noun* the quality of being inaccurate
→ See Thesaurus box at **wrong**

in•ac•tive /ɪn'æktɪv/ *adjective, formal*
not doing anything: *Most fish are inactive at night.* ANTONYM **active**
—**inactivity** /ˌɪnæk'tɪvəti/ *noun* the state of not doing anything

in•ad•e•quate /ɪn'ædəkwət/ Ac *adjective, formal*
not good enough or great enough: *The medical care I received at first was*

inadequate, so I had to go back into the hospital. ANTONYM **adequate**
—**inadequately** *adverb*

in·ap·pro·pri·ate /ˌɪnəˈproʊpri-ət/ Ac *adjective*
not right for a particular situation or person: *The book is inappropriate for children, because it discusses sex.* ANTONYM **appropriate**
—**inappropriately** *adverb*

in·au·di·ble /ɪnˈɔdəbəl/ *adjective, formal*
too quiet to hear: *Her reply was almost inaudible, so I asked her to say it again.* ANTONYM **audible**

in·au·gu·rate /ɪˈnɔgyəˌreɪt/ *verb*
to have a ceremony when someone begins an important job: *The President is inaugurated in January.*
—**inaugural** /ɪˈnɔgyərəl/ *adjective* relating to an inauguration: *the President's inaugural speech*
—**inauguration** /ɪˌnɔgyəˈreɪʃən/ *noun* when someone is inaugurated

in·bound /ˈɪnbaʊnd/ *adjective*
inbound planes, trains, cars, etc. are coming toward or into a place: *Traffic is slow on the inbound lanes of the freeway.* ANTONYM **outbound**

Inc.
the written abbreviation of **incorporated**, used after the name of a big company: *General Motors Inc.*

in·ca·pa·ble /ɪnˈkeɪpəbəl/ Ac *adjective, formal*
incapable of (doing) something = not able to do something: *Since the accident, she has been incapable of moving her legs.*

in·car·cer·ate /ɪnˈkɑrsəˌreɪt/ *verb, formal*
to put or keep someone in a prison: *He has been incarcerated for 10 years in the local jail.*

in·censed /ɪnˈsenst/ *adjective, formal*
very angry: *She was incensed at his unkind words.*

in·cen·tive /ɪnˈsentɪv/ Ac *noun*
something that makes you want to do something: *If students choose their own rewards, it gives them an incentive to work hard.*

inch /ɪntʃ/ *noun* plural **inches**
written abbreviation **in.** a unit for measuring length, equal to 2.54 centimeters: *There are 12 inches in a foot.* | *The insect is about 1.5 inches long.*

in·ci·dent /ˈɪnsədənt/ Ac *noun, formal*
something unusual, serious, or violent that happens: *You should report the incident to the police.*

in·ci·den·tally /ˌɪnsəˈdentli/ Ac *adverb*
used when giving more information or starting to talk about something new: *He's an excellent player. Incidentally, he's also my cousin.*

in·cin·er·ate /ɪnˈsɪnəˌreɪt/ *verb, formal*
to burn something in order to destroy it: *We incinerate a lot of our garbage.*
—**incineration** /ɪnˌsɪnəˈreɪʃən/ *noun* the act of incinerating something
—**incinerator** /ɪnˈsɪnəˌreɪtɚ/ *noun* a machine in which you incinerate things

in·cli·na·tion /ˌɪnkləˈneɪʃən/ Ac *noun*
a feeling that you want to do something: *He showed no inclination to leave* (=he did not behave as if he wanted to leave).

in·clined /ɪnˈklaɪnd/ Ac *adjective*
be inclined to do something a) to be likely to do something: *I'm inclined to trust him because he's always been honest with me.* **b)** to often do something in a particular situation: *He's inclined to get upset over small things.*

in·clude /ɪnˈklud/ *verb*
1 if one thing includes another, the second thing is part of the first: *The trip includes a visit to the Grand Canyon.*
2 to make someone or something part of a larger group: *Did you include my name on the list?* ANTONYM **exclude**
—**inclusion** /ɪnˈkluʒən/ *noun* the act of including something

WORD FAMILY look at the words:
→ **include** *verb*
→ **exclude** *verb*
→ **including** *preposition*
→ **excluding** *preposition*
→ **inclusive** *adjective*
→ **exclusive** *adjective*
→ **inclusion** *noun*
→ **exclusion** *noun*

in·clud·ing /ɪn'kludɪŋ/ *preposition*
used when saying that someone or something is part of the group you are talking about: *There were 20 people in the room, including the teacher.* ANTONYM **excluding**

in·clu·sive /ɪn'klusɪv/ *adjective, formal*
including many different people or things: *The price for the vacation is inclusive of flight, hotel, and all taxes.*

in·co·her·ent /ˌɪnkoʊ'hɪrənt/ Ac *adjective, formal*
if you are incoherent, you are speaking in a way that is very unclear: *She was incoherent because she hadn't slept in four days.*
—**incoherently** *adverb*
—**incoherence** *noun* the quality of being incoherent

in·come /'ɪŋkʌm/ Ac *noun*
the money that you get, for example for working: *She has an income of $50,000 per year.*
→ See Thesaurus box at **pay**[2]

'income tax *noun*
money that you must give the government when you earn money

in·com·pat·i·ble /ˌɪnkəm'pætəbəl/ Ac *adjective*
too different to be able to work together well or have a good relationship: *The software is incompatible with the software I already have.* ANTONYM **compatible**
—**incompatibility** /ˌɪnkəmˌpætə'bɪləti/ *noun* the quality of being incompatible: *My parents' incompatibility led to their divorce.*

in·com·pe·tent /ɪn'kɑmpətənt/ *adjective*
not able to do your job well: *He was fired for being incompetent.* ANTONYM **competent**
—**incompetence** *noun* the quality of being incompetent: *I was shocked at the incompetence of the managers.*

in·com·plete /ˌɪnkəm'plit/ *adjective*
not having all its parts or not finished yet: *The bridge is incomplete, but it will be finished later this year.* ANTONYM **complete**

in·com·pre·hen·si·ble /ˌɪnkɑmprɪ'hensəbəl/ *adjective*
impossible to understand: *The lawyer's letter was incomprehensible to me, because he used so many legal terms.*

in·con·clu·sive /ˌɪnkən'klusɪv/ Ac *adjective, formal*
not resulting in clear information or a clear situation: *The medical tests were inconclusive; they did not show what was causing her pain.*
—**inconclusively** *adverb*

in·con·sid·er·ate /ˌɪnkən'sɪdərɪt/ *noun, formal*
not thinking or caring about what other people feel or need: *You never call to say you are going to be late, and that's inconsiderate.* ANTONYM **considerate**

in·con·sist·ent /ˌɪnkən'sɪstənt/ Ac *adjective*
not always the same or not the same as others: *He's an inconsistent player – sometimes good, sometimes terrible.* | *His answer to the first question is inconsistent with the answers he gave later* (=his first answer does not match his later answers).
—**inconsistently** *adverb*

in·con·ven·ient /ˌɪnkən'viniənt/ *adjective*
causing problems or difficulties: *If this is an inconvenient time to talk, I'll call you back later.*
—**inconvenience** *noun* problems, or something that causes problems: *We are sorry for the inconvenience caused by this delay.*

in·cor·po·rate /ɪn'kɔrpəˌreɪt/ Ac *verb*
to include something as part of something else: *I tried to incorporate the changes that my teacher suggested into my paper.*

in·cor·rect /ˌɪnkə'rekt/ *adjective, formal*
not right: *That answer is incorrect.* SYNONYM **wrong**; ANTONYM **correct**
—**incorrectly** *adverb*
→ See Thesaurus box at **wrong**

in·crease[1] /ɪn'kris/ *verb*
if an amount increases, or if something increases it, it becomes larger: *My weight had increased by five pounds.* | *Smoking increases your chances of getting cancer.* ANTONYM **decrease**

THESAURUS: increase

go up to increase in number, amount, or value: *Prices have gone up 2%.*

rise to increase in number, amount, quality, or value: *The city's population has risen to over 10 million people.*

grow to get bigger in size or amount: *The number of people working from home has grown in the last ten years.*

double to become twice as big: *The company has doubled in size in ten years.*

shoot up *informal* to quickly increase in number, size, or amount: *Her grades have shot up this semester.*

increase

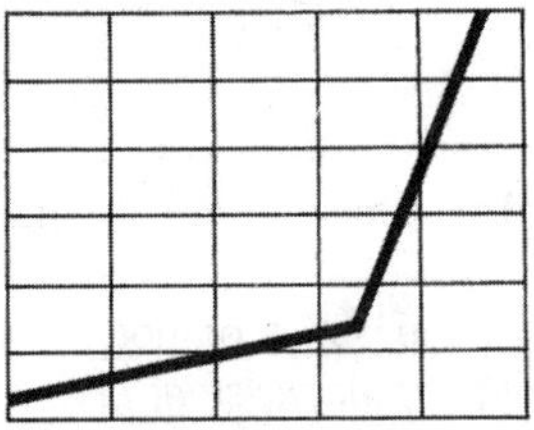

in•crease² /ˈɪŋkris/ *noun*
a rise in the amount of something: *There has been an increase in crime.* ANTONYM **decrease**

in•creas•ing•ly /ɪnˈkrisɪŋli/ *adverb*
more and more: *He wasn't home by midnight and his parents were becoming increasingly worried.*

in•cred•i•ble /ɪnˈkredəbəl/ *adjective*
1 very good or large: *The food here is incredible* (=very good)*!* | *I have an incredible amount of respect for him.*
2 very hard to believe: *It's incredible that he survived the fall from the third floor.*
—**incredibly** *adverb* very: *She works incredibly hard.*

in•crim•i•nate /ɪnˈkrɪməˌneɪt/ *verb, formal*
to make someone seem guilty of a crime: *He didn't say anything, because he didn't want to incriminate himself.*
—**incriminating** *adjective* making someone seem guilty of a crime: *They found the gun and other incriminating evidence in his house.*

in•cu•ba•tor /ˈɪŋkyəˌbeɪtɚ/ *noun*
a special container in a hospital, where very small or weak babies are put so that they stay alive

in•cur /ɪnˈkɚ/ *verb* **incurred, incurring** *formal*
if you incur something bad, it happens to you because of something you do: *A family incurs extra expenses when a child is born.*

in•cur•a•ble /ɪnˈkyʊrəbəl/ *adjective*
an incurable disease cannot be cured

in•debt•ed /ɪnˈdetɪd/ *adjective*
be indebted to someone *formal* = to be very grateful to someone for his or her help: *We are indebted to everyone who helped us write this magazine.*

in•de•cent /ɪnˈdisənt/ *adjective*
likely to shock people: *You can't wear a skirt that short – it's indecent!*
—**indecency** *noun* indecent behavior

in•de•ci•sive /ˌɪndɪˈsaɪsɪv/ *adjective*
not able to make decisions quickly: *a weak indecisive leader* ANTONYM **decisive**

in•deed /ɪnˈdid/ *adverb, formal*
1 used in order to emphasize what you are saying or to say that what someone has said is true: *It is indeed unfortunate that this happened* (=I agree that it is unfortunate).
2 used when adding information: *He liked the book. Indeed, he said it was the best one he had ever read.*

in•def•i•nite /ɪnˈdefənət/ Ac *adjective*
an indefinite period of time has no fixed end: *The police are increasing the number of officers in the area where the crimes happened for an indefinite period.*
—**indefinitely** *adverb* for a period of time that has no fixed end: *She will remain on the team indefinitely.*

inˌdefinite ˈarticle *noun*
"a" and "an"

inˌdefinite ˈpronoun *noun*
a word such as "someone" or "anything", which does not refer to a particular person or thing

in•dent /ɪnˈdent/ *verb*
to start a line of writing closer to the middle of the page than the other lines: *Indent the first line of each paragraph.*

in•de•pend•ence /ˌɪndəˈpendəns/ *noun*
1 the freedom to do what you want to do and take care of yourself: *When I got my first car, I was so excited to have more independence.* | *Having a job gives you financial independence.*
2 freedom from control by another country: *Nigeria gained independence from Britain in 1960.*

Inde'pendence ,Day *noun*
a U.S. national holiday on July 4th, when Americans celebrate the time when their country became independent from Britain

in·de·pend·ent /ˌɪndəˈpendənt/ *adjective*
1 doing what you want to do and taking care of yourself: *I wanted to move out of my parents' home and be independent.* ANTONYM **dependent**
2 not controlled by another country, organization, or group: *India became independent in 1947.*
—**independently** *adverb*

WORD FAMILY look at the words:
→ **independent** *adjective*
→ **dependent** *adjective*
→ **independence** *noun*
→ **dependence** *noun*
→ **independently** *adverb*

'in-depth *adjective*
considering or dealing with all the details of something: *The program is an in-depth look at the problem of racism.*

in·de·scrib·a·ble /ˌɪndɪˈskraɪbəbəl/ *adjective*
not possible to describe: *an indescribable smell*

in·dex /ˈɪndeks/ Ac *noun* plural **indexes** or **indices** /ˈɪndəˌsiz/
a list at the end of a book that tells you the page where each thing in the book is mentioned: *Subjects in the index are in alphabetical order.*

'index ,finger *noun*
the finger next to your thumb
→ See picture at **hand**[1]

In·di·an[1] /ˈɪndiən/ *adjective*
1 from India
2 a word meaning NATIVE AMERICAN which some people think is offensive

Indian[2] *noun*
1 someone from India
2 a word for a NATIVE AMERICAN which some people think is offensive

in·di·cate /ˈɪndəˌkeɪt/ Ac *verb*
1 to show that something is likely to be true: *Research indicates that people are becoming healthier.*
2 to say something in a way that is not direct: *She indicated that she would be willing to help us.*
—**indicator** *noun, formal* something that shows something else: *Weight is an important indicator of how healthy you are; if you are too heavy, you are likely to be unhealthy.*
—**indicative** /ɪnˈdɪkətɪv/ *adjective, formal* showing something: *The team's loss last night is indicative of how bad the season has been for them.*

WORD FAMILY look at the words:
→ **indicate** *verb*
→ **indication** *noun*
→ **indicative** *adjective*
→ **indicator** *noun*

in·di·ca·tion /ˌɪndəˈkeɪʃən/ Ac *noun*
a sign that something exists or is likely to be true: *His performance today gives an indication of* (=shows) *how talented he is.* | *There were indications that the fire was started by someone inside the house.*

in·di·ces /ˈɪndəˌsiz/ *noun*
a plural of INDEX

in·dict /ɪnˈdaɪt/ *verb, formal*
to officially say that someone may have committed a crime: *He was indicted for murder.*
—**indictment** *noun* an official written statement indicting someone

in·dif·ferent /ɪnˈdɪfrənt/ *adjective*
not interested in something, or not caring about something: *He was indifferent to their opinions.*
—**indifference** *noun* the state of being indifferent to something

in·di·ges·tion /ˌɪndɪˈdʒestʃən/ *noun*
pain that you get when your stomach cannot deal with the food you have eaten: *I ate too much, and now I have indigestion.*

in·dig·nant /ɪnˈdɪgnənt/ *adjective, formal*
angry because you feel someone has treated you in a rude or unfair way: *She was indignant at the man's offensive questions.*
—**indignantly** *adverb*
—**indignation** /ˌɪndɪgˈneɪʃən/ *noun* an indignant feeling: *Students protested to show their indignation at the high cost of a college education.*

I

in•di•rect /ˌɪndəˈrekt/ *adjective*
1 not directly caused by or relating to something: *The accident was an indirect result of the heavy rain, which had created a hole in the road.* ANTONYM **direct**
2 an indirect way of showing what you think or feel is not very clear: *His silence was an indirect way of showing his anger.* ANTONYM **direct**
3 *formal* an indirect way of getting to a place is not the straightest one: *We took an indirect route through the country.* ANTONYM **direct**
—**indirectly** *adverb*: *I was indirectly responsible for her mistake, because I forgot to check her work.*

ˌindirect ˈobject *noun*
a word or phrase referring to the person or thing that receives something: *In the sentence "Pete gave me the money," "me" is the indirect object.*

in•dis•creet /ˌɪndɪˈskrit/ *adjective*
careless about what you say or do, so that you let people know too much

in•dis•pu•ta•ble /ˌɪndɪˈspyutəbəl/ *adjective*, *formal*
definitely true: *I have indisputable evidence that he has been lying.*
—**indisputably** *adverb*

in•dis•tin•guish•a•ble /ˌɪndɪˈstɪŋgwɪʃəbəl/ *adjective*, *formal*
things that are indistinguishable are so similar that you cannot see any difference between them: *This material is indistinguishable from real silk.*

in•di•vid•u•al[1] /ˌɪndəˈvɪdʒuəl/ Ac *adjective*
1 used when talking about each person or thing, rather than the whole group: *We have to think about the needs of the individual student.*
2 for one person rather than a group: *The children had individual desks.*
—**individually** *adverb* separately: *The teacher spoke to the students individually.*

WORD FAMILY look at the words:
- → **individual** *adjective*
- → **individual** *noun*
- → **individually** *adverb*
- → **individualized** *adjective*

individual[2] *noun*, *formal*
a person, not a group: *Every individual is different.*

in•di•vid•u•al•ism /ˌɪndəˈvɪdʒuəˌlɪzəm/ Ac *noun*
the practice of allowing people to do what they want, alone, and in their own way
—**individualist** *noun* someone who believes in individualism
—**individualistic** /ˌɪndəˌvɪdʒuəˈlɪstɪk/ *adjective* doing what you want, alone, and in your own way

in•di•vid•u•al•ized /ˌɪndəˈvɪdʒuəˌlaɪzd/ *adjective*, *formal*
made or designed for a particular person: *The school has an individualized learning method in which students have more choices.*

in•door /ˈɪndɔr/ *adjective*
inside a building: *an indoor swimming pool* ANTONYM **outdoor**

in•doors /ˌɪnˈdɔrz/ *adverb*
into or inside a building: *It's raining – let's stay indoors.* SYNONYM **inside**; ANTONYM **outdoors**

in•dulge /ɪnˈdʌldʒ/ *verb*
1 to do something that you enjoy, which you do not usually do or should not do: *I had a little extra time, so indulged in an afternoon nap.*
2 to let someone do or have whatever he or she wants, even if it is bad for him or her: *Her parents indulge her, giving her toys whenever she asks for them.*
—**indulgent** *adjective* letting someone do or have whatever he or she wants: *indulgent parents*
—**indulgence** *noun* when you allow yourself or someone else to do or have something

in•dus•tri•al /ɪnˈdʌstriəl/ *adjective*
relating to industry, or having a lot of industries: *The river has been polluted by industrial waste.* | *the world's leading industrial nations*

in•dus•tri•al•ized /ɪnˈdʌstriəˌlaɪzd/ *adjective*
an industrialized country has a lot of industries
—**industrialization** /ɪnˌdʌstriələˈzeɪʃən/ *noun* the process of developing a lot of industries: *Industrialization meant that more*

people worked in factories instead of on farms.

in·dus·tri·ous /ɪn'dʌstriəs/ *adjective, formal*
an industrious person works hard
—**industriously** *adverb*

in·dus·try /'ɪndəstri/ *noun* plural **industries**
1 the making of things in factories: *He wanted a job in industry.*
2 all the businesses that make or do a particular type of thing: *She has friends in the music industry.*

WORD FAMILY look at the words:
→ **industry** *noun*
→ **industrial** *adjective*
→ **industrialized** *adjective*
→ **industrialization** *noun*

in·ed·i·ble /ɪn'edəbəl/ *adjective, formal*
dangerous to eat or tasting too bad to eat: *The cookies were so burnt they were inedible.* ANTONYM **edible**

in·ef·fec·tive /ˌɪnə'fektɪv/ *adjective*
something that is ineffective does not achieve what you want it to achieve: *The medical treatment was ineffective, and the patient did not get better.* ANTONYM **effective**
—**ineffectiveness** *noun*

in·ef·fi·cient /ˌɪnə'fɪʃənt/ *adjective*
working or done in a way that wastes time, money, or energy: *The engine is inefficient and uses a lot of fuel.* ANTONYM **efficient**
—**inefficiently** *adverb*
—**inefficiency** *noun* the quality of being inefficient

in·el·i·gi·ble /ɪn'elədʒəbəl/ *adjective*
not allowed to do or have something, according to a rule: *He is ineligible for money from the government because he earns too much money.* ANTONYM **eligible**

in·e·qual·i·ty /ˌɪnɪ'kwɑləti/ *noun* plural **inequalities**
an unfair situation in which some people in society have more money, opportunities, etc. than others: *Poor people often cannot afford a good education, and this leads to inequalities in our society.* ANTONYM **equality**

in·ev·i·ta·ble /ɪ'nevətəbəl/ [Ac] *adjective*
certain to happen and impossible to avoid: *The situation between the two countries is so bad that war seems inevitable.*
—**inevitably** *adverb* if something will inevitably happen, it will definitely happen

in·ex·pen·sive /ˌɪnɪk'spensɪv/ *adjective*
cheap: *The food is simple and inexpensive.* ANTONYM **expensive**
—**inexpensively** *adverb*

in·ex·pe·ri·enced /ˌɪnɪk'spɪriənst/ *adjective*
not having much experience: *An inexperienced teacher may have difficulty controlling his or her class.* ANTONYM **experienced**
—**inexperience** *noun* the quality of being inexperienced

in·fa·mous /'ɪnfəməs/ *adjective*
well known for being bad or evil: *an infamous murderer* SYNONYM **notorious**
—**infamy** *noun* the state of being infamous

in·fant /'ɪnfənt/ *noun, formal*
a baby: *The class is for mothers and infants.*
—**infancy** /'ɪnfənsi/ *noun* the period when someone is a baby: *Their son died in infancy.*
→ See Thesaurus box at **child**

in·fan·try /'ɪnfəntri/ *noun*
soldiers who fight on foot: *The infantry followed the tanks into the area.*

in·fat·u·at·ed /ɪn'fætʃuˌeɪtɪd/ *adjective*
having a feeling of love for someone that is too strong or not sensible: *He's infatuated with her, so he can't see any of her faults.*
—**infatuation** /ɪnˌfætʃu'eɪʃən/ *noun* a feeling of love for someone that is too strong or not sensible

in·fect /ɪn'fekt/ *verb*
to give someone a disease: *People with the disease can easily infect others.*
—**infected** *adjective*: *How many people are infected with the virus?*

WORD FAMILY look at the words:
→ **infect** *verb*
→ **infection** *noun*
→ **infectious** *adjective*
→ **infected** *adjective*

in·fec·tion /ɪn'fekʃən/ *noun*
a disease affecting a part of your body which is caused by a BACTERIA or VIRUS: *I have an ear infection, so the doctor gave me some drops to put in my ear.*

I

in•fec•tious /ɪnˈfekʃəs/ *adjective*
an infectious disease can be passed between people, without them touching each other: *Infectious diseases can spread quickly.*

in•fer /ɪnˈfɚ/ Ac *verb* **inferred, inferring**
formal
to decide that something is probably true, because of what you see or hear: *They inferred from his refusal to answer that he was guilty.*

in•fe•ri•or /ɪnˈfɪriɚ/ *adjective*
not as good as someone or something else: *The new gym is inferior to the old one, and no one is happy with it.* ANTONYM **superior**
—**inferiority** /ɪnˌfɪriˈɑrəti/ *noun* the state of being inferior to someone or something else: *He had failed twice, and his feeling of inferiority was growing.*

in•fest /ɪnˈfest/ *verb*
if insects, rats, etc. infest a place, there are a lot of them there: *The old hotel was infested with rats.*

in•field /ˈɪnfild/ *noun*
the part of a baseball field that is inside the four bases

in•fi•nite /ˈɪnfənət/ Ac *adjective*
without a limit or end: *Is the universe infinite, or does it have an edge?* ANTONYM **finite**

in•fi•nite•ly /ˈɪnfənətli/ Ac *adverb*, *formal*
very much: *Their first album was infinitely better than this one. I don't like this one at all.*

in•fin•i•tive /ɪnˈfɪnətɪv/ *noun*
the basic form of a verb, used with "to": *In the sentence "I want to go," "to go" is an infinitive.*

in•fin•i•ty /ɪnˈfɪnəti/ *noun*
1 a space or distance without a limit or end: *If you put two mirrors opposite each other, you can see reflections going into infinity.*
2 a number that is larger than all others: *It is impossible to count to infinity.*

in•flamed /ɪnˈfleɪm/ *verb*, *formal*
red, swollen, and painful: *Her throat was inflamed because of an infection.*

in•flam•ma•ble /ɪnˈflæməbəl/ *adjective*, *formal*
something that is inflammable burns very easily: *Gasoline is highly inflammable, so you should never smoke near it.* SYNONYM **flammable**

in•flam•ma•tion /ˌɪnfləˈmeɪʃən/ *noun*, *formal*
the state of being red, swollen, and painful: *There was some inflammation around the sore on her arm.*

in•flate /ɪnˈfleɪt/ *verb*
to fill something with air or gas, so that it becomes larger: *Inflate the bicycle's tires.*
—**inflatable** *adjective* something that is inflatable can be inflated: *an inflatable boat made of rubber*

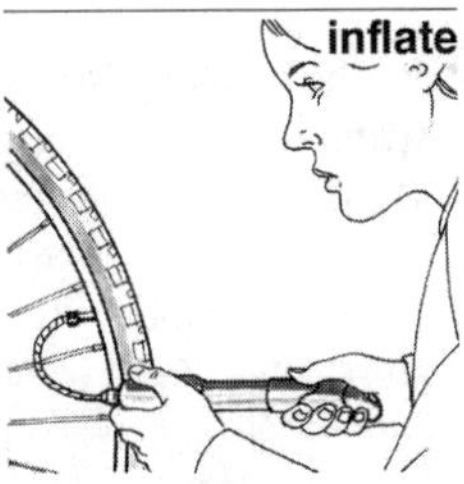

in•fla•tion /ɪnˈfleɪʃən/ *noun*
a continuing increase in prices: *When there is high inflation, people need more money just to pay for basic things.*
—**inflationary** /ɪnˈfleɪʃəˌneri/ *adjective* causing inflation

in•flict /ɪnˈflɪkt/ *verb*, *formal*
to make someone suffer something bad: *He seemed to enjoy inflicting pain on his younger brother.*

in•flu•ence[1] /ˈɪnfluəns/ *noun*
1 the power to affect what someone does or thinks: *Television has a lot of influence on young people. They often behave like people they see on TV.*
2 someone or something that affects what someone does or thinks: *Her boyfriend was a bad influence on her* (=made her behave in a worse way).
3 under the influence of alcohol/drugs *formal* = drunk or affected by drugs: *He committed the crime under the influence of alcohol.*
—**influential** /ˌɪnfluˈenʃəl/ *adjective* having a lot of influence: *He was an influential thinker, whose ideas have changed the world.*
→ See Thesaurus box at **persuade**

influence[2] *verb*
to affect what someone does or thinks: *If I tell you which college I like best, I might influence your decision, and I don't want to do that.*

in•form /ɪn'fɔrm/ *verb, formal*
to tell someone something: *I informed them that I would be arriving on June 24.* | *He did not inform me of his plans.*

WORD FAMILY look at the words:
→ **inform** *verb*
→ **information** *noun*
→ **informative** *adjective*

in•for•mal /ɪn'fɔrməl/ *adjective*
1 relaxed, and not done in an official way or according to rules: *It was an informal meeting, and no one bothered to take notes.* ANTONYM **formal**
2 appropriate for ordinary situations rather than formal ones: *"See you!" is an informal way of saying "goodbye."* ANTONYM **formal**
—**informally** *adverb*
—**informality** /ˌɪnfɔr'mæləti/ *noun* the quality of being informal

in•for•ma•tion /ˌɪnfɚ'meɪʃən/ *noun*
facts that you get from someone or give someone: *Can you give me some information about where to buy this book?* | *Before you start on the project, I have one more important piece of information for you.*

GRAMMAR: information
Do not say "an information" or "informations." Say, for example, **some/any information, a lot of information**, or **a piece of information**: *Where can I find some information about your company?* | *All of this information is in the book.* | *I need a couple more pieces of information before I can finish my report.*

in•form•a•tive /ɪn'fɔrmətɪv/ *adjective*
giving many facts: *It was a very informative program – I learned a lot.*

in•fra•struc•ture /'ɪnfrəˌstrʌktʃɚ/ Ac *noun, formal*
the basic systems that a country needs, for example roads and communication systems: *The country's roads and other infrastructure are old and need to be rebuilt.*

in•fre•quent /ɪn'frikwənt/ *adjective, formal*
not happening often: *We enjoy her infrequent visits and wish she would come more often.* SYNONYM **rare**
—**infrequently** *adverb* not often

in•fu•ri•ate /ɪn'fjʊriˌeɪt/ *verb, formal*
to make someone very angry: *He was lazy, which infuriated his parents.*
—**infuriating** *adjective*

in•ge•nious /ɪn'dʒiniəs/ *adjective*
1 an ingenious plan, machine, etc. is the result of intelligent thinking: *She had invented an ingenious machine that peeled fruit.*
2 good at thinking of new plans, machines, etc.: *He was an ingenious man and could always find a solution to his problems.*
—**ingenuity** /ˌɪndʒə'nuəti/ *noun* the quality of being ingenious

in•gre•di•ent /ɪn'gridiənt/ *noun*
one of the things that you use to make a particular food: *Mix the egg with the other ingredients and pour the mixture into a cake pan.*

in•hab•it /ɪn'hæbɪt/ *verb, formal*
if people or animals inhabit a place, they live there: *These people have inhabited the region for 800 years.*
—**inhabited** *adjective* if a place is inhabited, people live there: *They did not know if the island was inhabited because they didn't see any houses.*

in•hab•it•ant /ɪn'hæbətənt/ *noun, formal*
one of the people who live in a place: *It is a small town with only 250 inhabitants.*

inhale

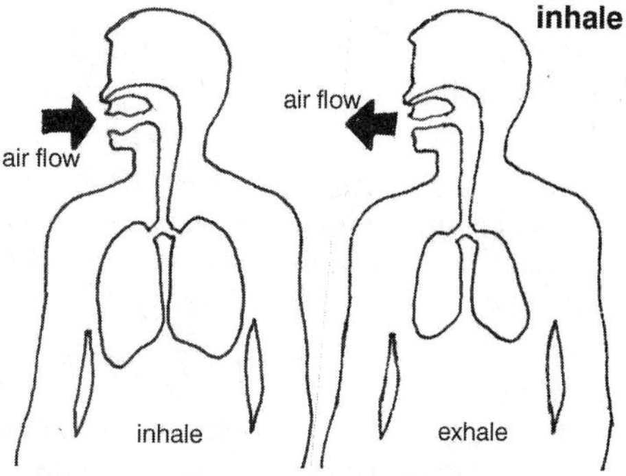

in•hale /ɪn'heɪl/ *verb, formal*
to breathe in air, smoke, or gas: *Some of the people rescued from the fire had inhaled a lot of smoke.* ANTONYM **exhale**

in•her•ent /ɪn'hɪrənt/ Ac *adjective, formal*
a quality or feature that is inherent in something cannot be removed: *The problem is inherent in the system, so we have to change*

I

the system to fix the problem.
—**inherently** *adverb, formal*: *Being a firefighter is an inherently dangerous job.*

in•her•it /ɪn'herɪt/ *verb*
1 to get something from someone after he or she has died: *I inherited the house from my uncle when he died.*
2 to get a quality or feature from one of your parents: *Anna inherited her mother's good looks.*
—**inheritance** *noun* money or things that you get from someone after he or she has died: *He spent all his inheritance on expensive cars.*

in•hu•mane /ˌɪnhyu'meɪn/ *adjective*
inhumane treatment is cruel: *We are trying to end the inhumane treatment of prisoners.*
ANTONYM **humane**
—**inhumanity** /ˌɪnhyu'mænəti/ *noun* cruel treatment

in•i•tial[1] /ɪ'nɪʃəl/ *noun*
the first letter of a name: *His name is John Smith, so his initials are J. S.*

initial[2] Ac *adjective*
happening at the beginning: *My initial reaction was shock. But then I was angry.*
SYNONYM **first**

in•i•tial•ly /ɪ'nɪʃəli/ Ac *adverb, formal*
at first: *Initially, my new job seemed very difficult, but after a few weeks it became easier.*

in•i•ti•ate /ɪ'nɪʃiˌeɪt/ Ac *verb, formal*
to start something: *I initiated the conversation by asking him what his name was.*

in•i•ti•a•tion /ɪˌnɪʃi'eɪʃən/ Ac *noun*
the action of making someone a member of a group, usually with a ceremony: *The club has an initiation ceremony for new members once a year.*

in•i•tia•tive /ɪ'nɪʃətɪv/ Ac *noun*
1 the ability to do things without waiting for someone to tell you what to do: *He showed initiative by thinking of a way to deal with the problem and then getting other people to help him do it.*
2 an important plan or way of solving a problem: *The initiative to reduce crime in the area has been a success.*
3 take the initiative = to do something rather than waiting for other people to do something: *If you want the problem to be fixed, you're going to have to take the initiative. No one else is going to do anything.*

in•ject /ɪn'dʒekt/ *verb*
to put a drug into someone's body using a special needle: *The doctor injected the patient with the new drug.* | *Chemicals were injected into the animals.*

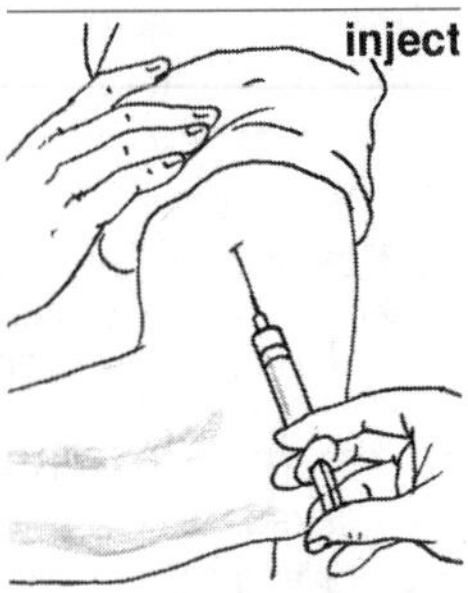

—**injection** /ɪn'dʒekʃən/ *noun, formal* if you have an injection, a drug is injected into your body: *The nurse gave me an injection of penicillin.*

in•jure /'ɪndʒɚ/ Ac *verb*
to damage someone's body: *Her father was seriously injured in a car accident.* | *I injured my knee playing football.*
—**injured** *adjective*

WORD FAMILY look at the words:
→ **injure** *verb*
→ **injured** *adjective*
→ **injury** *noun*

→ See Thesaurus box at **hurt**[1]

in•ju•ry /'ɪndʒəri/ Ac *noun* plural **injuries**
physical damage to someone's body: *Wear a helmet to prevent head injuries.* | *He suffered a serious injury to his right leg and couldn't use it for several months.*

THESAURUS: injury

wound an injury, especially a deep cut made in your skin by a knife or bullet: *Soldiers were being treated for wounds from the battle.*

bruise a black or blue mark on your skin that you get when you fall or get hit: *There was a dark bruise on her cheek.*

cut the small wound you get if a sharp object cuts your skin: *a cut on her finger*

sprain an injury to a joint in your body, caused by suddenly twisting it: *He missed the race because of an ankle sprain.*

bump an area of skin that is swollen because you have hit it on something: *How did you get that bump on your forehead?*

> **scratch** a long thin cut on your skin: *Her legs and arms were covered in scratches from where she'd pushed through the bushes.*

in·jus·tice /ɪn'dʒʌstɪs/ *noun*
a situation in which someone is treated unfairly: *He fought against the injustice of innocent people being sent to prison for crimes they were not involved in.* ANTONYM **justice**

ink /ɪŋk/ *noun*
a colored liquid used for writing or printing

'in-laws *plural noun*
the parents of your husband or wife: *We're spending Christmas with my in-laws.*

,in-line 'skating *noun*
the activity of moving along while wearing special boots with a line of wheels under them
—**in-line skates** *plural noun* special boots with a line of wheels under them

in·mate /'ɪnmeɪt/ *noun*
someone who is kept in a prison or a mental hospital: *Two of the inmates got into a fight and were sent back to their prison cells.*

inn /ɪn/ *noun*
a small hotel, usually not in a city

in·ner /'ɪnɚ/ *adjective*
1 on the inside or close to the middle of something: *An infection of the inner ear can cause problems with balance.* | *an inner room of the house with no windows* ANTONYM **outer**
2 relating to thoughts or feelings that you feel at a very basic level: *Meditation gave him a feeling of inner calm.*

,inner 'city *noun*
an area that is close to the middle of a city, where many poor people live: *The program is designed to help kids from the inner city whose families do not have a lot of money.*
—**inner-city** *adjective* existing in the inner city: *inner-city schools*

in·ner·most /'ɪnɚ,moʊst/ *adjective*
your innermost feelings or thoughts are your most private ones: *He did not tell anyone his innermost thoughts.*
→ See Thesaurus box at **private**[1]

in·ning /'ɪnɪŋ/ *noun*
one of the nine playing periods in a game of baseball

in·no·cent /'ɪnəsənt/ *adjective*
1 not guilty of a crime: *They cannot send an innocent man to jail.* | *The jury found him innocent of his wife's murder* (=they decided he was innocent). ANTONYM **guilty**
2 someone who is innocent does not have much experience of the bad things in life, and believes that everyone is good and honest: *I was young and innocent, and I trusted everyone.*
3 innocent victim/bystander/civilian, etc. = someone who gets hurt or killed in a war or during a crime, though he or she is not involved in it: *Two of the victims were members of a gang, and the other was an innocent bystander.*
—**innocently** *adverb*
—**innocence** *noun*

in·no·vate /'ɪnə,veɪt/ Ac *verb, formal*
to start to use a new idea, invention, or a new way of doing something: *We try not to repeat what we did in the past – we want to innovate.*
—**innovative** *adjective* new and better than in the past: *The company has been successful by developing innovative new products.*

> **WORD FAMILY look at the words:**
> → **innovate** *verb*
> → **innovation** *noun*
> → **innovative** *adjective*

in·no·va·tion /,ɪnə'veɪʃən/ Ac *noun*
a new idea, invention, or way of doing something: *We are constantly seeing new innovations in medicine that can improve health.*

in·oc·u·late /ɪ'nɑkyə,leɪt/ *verb, formal*
to protect someone against a disease by putting a weak form of the disease into his or her body using a needle: *Doctors are inoculating every child in the village to stop the disease.*
—**inoculation** /ɪ,nɑkyə'leɪʃən/ *noun* the act of inoculating someone

in·of·fen·sive /,ɪnə'fensɪv/ *adjective*
not causing offense or not making anyone upset: *The words of the song are inoffensive, so I let my little sister listen to it.* ANTONYM **offensive**

in·pa·tient /'ɪn,peɪʃənt/ *adjective*
relating to someone who stays in hospital while he or she is being given medical

treatment: *Inpatient care is usually much more expensive than outpatient treatment.*

in•put /ˈɪnpʊt/ Ac *noun, formal*
1 ideas that you have or things that you do to help make something succeed: *We want to get input from all the students in the class so that we can make the changes that they want.*
2 information that is put into a computer ANTONYM **output**

in•quire /ɪnˈkwaɪɚ/ *verb, formal*
to ask someone for information: *"Do you live here?" he inquired.* | *I took the pants back to the store and inquired about getting my money back.* | *A man called me to inquire whether my car was still for sale.*
—**inquirer** *noun* someone who inquires about something

in•quir•y /ɪnˈkwaɪəri/ *noun* plural **inquiries** *formal*
1 a question you ask in order to get information: *You should make inquiries about the area before you decide to move there.*
2 an official process to try to find out why something bad happened: *Relatives of the dead woman have asked for an inquiry into the crash.*

in•quis•i•tive /ɪnˈkwɪzətɪv/ *adjective*
interested in finding out about things: *Jake's an inquisitive boy; he asks questions about everything.*

in•sane /ɪnˈseɪn/ *adjective*
1 *informal* very stupid, and often dangerous: *It's insane to try to cross the ocean in such a small boat.*
2 someone who is insane is seriously mentally ill: *a hospital for the criminally insane*
—**insanely** *adverb*
—**insanity** /ɪnˈsænəti/ *noun* the state of being seriously mentally ill
➔ See Thesaurus box at **crazy**

in•sect /ˈɪnsekt/ *noun*
a small creature such as an ANT or a fly, with six legs and a body divided into three parts. Some insects also have wings.

in•sec•ti•cide /ɪnˈsektəˌsaɪd/ *noun*
a chemical substance used for killing insects

in•se•cure /ˌɪnsɪˈkyʊr/ Ac *adjective*
1 not feeling confident that other people like you, or not confident about your ability to do something: *Many teenagers feel insecure about their looks; they worry about being too fat or not having the right clothes.* ANTONYM **confident**
2 if a situation or your job is insecure, you cannot depend on it because it might be taken away at any time: *Workers at the old factory feel insecure about their economic future.*

in•sen•si•tive /ɪnˈsensətɪv/ *adjective, formal*
not noticing or caring whether something you say or do upsets someone: *The police officer was insensitive to the girl's feelings, and asked unkind questions about her dead boyfriend.*

in•sep•a•ra•ble /ɪnˈsepərəbəl/ *adjective*
1 people who are inseparable are always together because they like each other a lot: *The kids became inseparable, playing together every day.*
2 things that are inseparable cannot be considered separately: *The problems of hunger and poverty are inseparable in this area; we cannot end hunger unless we also end poverty.*

in•sert /ɪnˈsɚt/ Ac *verb, formal*
to put something inside or into something else: *Insert a CD into the CD player.*
—**insertion** /ɪnˈsɚʃən/ *noun* the action of putting something inside something else

insert

in•side¹ /ɪnˈsaɪd/ *adverb, preposition*
in a container, room, building, etc.: *Her keys were locked inside the car.* | *It's raining – let's go inside.* | *The temperature inside the building is hotter than outside.* ANTONYM **outside**

inside² *noun*
1 the inside = the inner part of something: *The skin on the inside of my ear was red and sore.* | *The door was locked from the inside and I couldn't get in.*
2 inside out = if clothing is inside out, the part that is usually on the outside is on the inside: *One of her socks was inside out.* | *Turn your jeans inside out when you wash them.*

inside³ *adjective*
on the inside of something: *He took a pen from the inside pocket of his jacket.*

in•sid•er /ɪn'saɪdɚ/ *noun*
someone who works for an organization and knows a lot about it: *Some insiders believe the company is having trouble, but there have been no public announcements.*

in•sight /'ɪnsaɪt/ Ac *noun*
the ability to understand what people and situations are really like: *Living in Paris really gave me insight into the way the French people live.*
—**insightful** *adjective* able to understand what people and situations are really like

in•sig•ni•a /ɪn'sɪgniə/ *noun* plural **insignia**
a piece of cloth or plastic showing someone's rank or the name of the organization he or she works for. It is usually worn on a shirt or jacket: *His shirt had a navy insignia on the arm.*

in•sig•nif•i•cant /ˌɪnsɪg'nɪfɪkənt/ Ac *adjective, formal*
too small or unimportant to think or worry about: *Our problems seem insignificant compared to people whose houses were destroyed.*
—**insignificantly** *adverb*
—**insignificance** *noun* the fact that something is insignificant

in•sin•cere /ˌɪnsɪn'sɪr/ *adjective*
pretending to think or feel something that you do not really think or feel: *He laughed to show that he wasn't afraid, but his laughter sounded insincere.*
—**insincerely** *adverb*
—**insincerity** /ˌɪnsɪn'serəti/ *noun* the fact that someone is pretending to think or feel something that he or she does not really think or feel

in•sist /ɪn'sɪst/ *verb*
1 to keep saying firmly that something is true, even when other people think you may not be telling the truth: *He kept insisting that Mike was driving when the accident happened.*
2 to say firmly that you will do something or that something must happen: *He insisted on going to work even though he was sick.* | *The insurance company insisted (that) I had to be checked by my doctor, or they would not pay.*
—**insistence** *noun* the act of demanding that something must happen

in•som•ni•a /ɪn'sɑmniə/ *noun*
if you have insomnia, you are not able to sleep
—**insomniac** /ɪn'sɑmniˌæk/ *noun* someone who regularly has difficulty sleeping

in•spect /ɪn'spekt/ Ac *verb*
to examine something carefully, especially as part of an official activity: *The bags will be inspected by a customs official.* | *We inspected the roof for leaks.*
—**inspector** *noun* someone whose job is to check that something is being done correctly and that rules are being obeyed: *Building inspectors checked the new building for problems.*

in•spec•tion /ɪn'spekʃən/ Ac *noun*
a careful examination of something, to make sure that something is in good condition or that something has been done correctly: *a safety inspection* | *Engineers do an inspection of the engines before the plane takes off.*

I

in•spi•ra•tion /ˌɪnspə'reɪʃən/ *noun*
something or someone that makes you want to achieve something, or that gives you new ideas: *When I was a kid I wanted to be a fighter, and Muhammad Ali was my inspiration.* | *The author said that his children were the inspiration for many of his stories* (=they gave him ideas).
—**inspirational** *adjective* giving you inspiration: *an inspirational leader*

in•spire /ɪn'spaɪɚ/ *verb*
1 to make someone feel that he or she wants to do or achieve something: *His love for the young woman inspired him to write the song.*
2 to make someone have a particular feeling: *The captain inspired confidence in the soldiers who worked with him.*

in•stall /ɪn'stɔl/ *verb*
1 *formal* to put a piece of equipment somewhere and connect it so that it is ready to be used: *It took me two hours to install the new light in the bedroom ceiling.*
2 to add new computer software onto a computer: *Download the software, and install it on your computer.*

—**installation** /ˌɪnstəˈleɪʃən/ *noun* the act of putting a new piece of equipment somewhere

in•stall•ment /ɪnˈstɔlmənt/ *noun*
a payment that you make every week, month, etc. in order to pay for something you have bought: *You can pay for the computer in monthly installments if you don't have all the money right now.*

in•stance /ˈɪnstəns/ Ac *noun*
1 for instance = for example: *In some states, for instance Nevada, gambling is legal.*
2 *formal* an example of something, especially something bad: *There are too many instances of people being cruel to animals.*

in•stant[1] /ˈɪnstənt/ *adjective*
1 happening immediately: *The movie was an instant success.*
2 instant coffee or food can be prepared very quickly by adding hot water: *instant noodles*

I

instant[2] *noun*
a very short period of time: *I saw her for an instant, and then she was gone.* SYNONYM **moment**

in•stan•ta•ne•ous /ˌɪnstənˈteɪniəs/ *adjective*
happening immediately: *With email, communication is almost instantaneous.*
—**instantaneously** *adverb*

in•stant•ly /ˈɪnstəntli/ *adverb*
very quickly: *He still looked exactly the same, and I recognized him instantly.* SYNONYM **immediately**
➔ See Thesaurus box at **immediately**

ˌinstant ˈreplay *noun*
an occasion when the action in a sports game on television is shown again, immediately after it first happens: *They used the instant replay to show that his foot went outside the lines.*

in•stead /ɪnˈsted/ *adverb*
if you do, use, or have something instead of another thing, you do, use, or have it rather than another thing: *If you don't want chicken, you can have beef instead.* | *I'll ride my bike to work instead of driving* (=I will ride, not drive).

in•stinct /ˈɪnstɪŋkt/ *noun*
a natural behavior or action that you do quickly, and that you have not learned or thought about: *I was very scared, and my instinct was to run to a safe place.*
—**instinctive** *adjective* based on instinct: *Most children have an instinctive fear of the dark.*
—**instinctively** *adverb*: *I knew instinctively that he wasn't guilty.*

in•sti•tute /ˈɪnstəˌtut/ Ac *noun*
an organization where people work on a subject related to education, especially a science: *the Massachusetts Institute of Technology*

in•sti•tu•tion /ˌɪnstəˈtuʃən/ Ac *noun*
1 a large important organization, such as a bank, hospital, or university: *banks and other financial institutions*
2 a behavior or way of doing something that people in a particular society have used for a very long time: *The institution of marriage has changed throughout history.*
—**institutional** *adjective* relating to an institution

in•struct /ɪnˈstrʌkt/ Ac *verb, formal*
1 to officially tell someone to do something: *Employees were instructed not to talk to the media.*
2 to teach someone something: *The program instructs students in English grammar.*
—**instructor** *noun* someone who teaches a skill or activity: *a swimming instructor*

WORD FAMILY look at the words:
→ **instruct** *verb*
→ **instructor** *noun*
→ **instruction** *noun*

in•struc•tion /ɪnˈstrʌkʃən/ Ac *noun*
1 a statement telling someone what they must do: *Dan shouted instructions to us, telling us to bring a rope.* | *He gave instructions that I should deliver the package to you.*
2 *formal* lessons that teach you a particular skill or subject: *She never had any instruction in music, so she can't read music.*
3 instructions = information that tells you how to do something: *Follow the instructions on the back of the box, and you can build this model car.* | *The invitation came*

with a map and instructions on how to get to the party. SYNONYM **directions**

in•stru•ment /ˈɪnstrəmənt/ *noun*
1 something such as a piano, TRUMPET, VIOLIN, etc. that you play in order to make music: *Can you play any musical instruments?*
2 a piece of scientific equipment or a medical tool: *The doctor had his surgical instruments laid out for the operation.*

in•stru•men•tal /ˌɪnstrəˈmentl/ *adjective*
1 instrumental music is played by instruments, not sung by voices
2 be instrumental in doing something = to be a person that helps to make something happen: *My biology professor was instrumental in getting me this job. He knew someone at the company.*

in•sub•stan•tial /ˌɪnsəbˈstænʃəl/ *adjective, formal*
not large or definite enough to have an important effect: *The evidence against him was insubstantial and did not convince the jury.*

in•suf•fi•cient /ˌɪnsəˈfɪʃənt/ Ac *adjective, formal*
not enough: *The amount of money in your bank account was insufficient to pay the bill.* ANTONYM **sufficient**
—**insufficiently** *adverb*

in•su•late /ˈɪnsəˌleɪt/ *verb*
1 to cover or protect something with a material that stops electricity, sound, heat, etc. getting in or out: *Insulate the pipes to stop them from freezing.*
2 to protect someone from knowing about or experiencing something bad: *Kids from wealthy families can be insulated from the type of problems that poor kids have.*
—**insulation** /ˌɪnsəˈleɪʃən/ *noun* material used to insulate something, especially a building

in•su•lin /ˈɪnsələn/ *noun*
a substance which your body makes naturally in order to change sugar into energy

in•sult¹ /ɪnˈsʌlt/ *verb*
1 to say something unkind, rude, or offensive about someone: *You insulted him when you said he didn't have enough skill to do the job himself.*
2 be insulted = to feel upset because someone has said or done something unkind, rude, or offensive: *She might be insulted if we don't come to her party.*

in•sult² /ˈɪnsʌlt/ *noun*
a rude or offensive remark or action: *The man and woman were yelling nasty insults at each other.*

in•sult•ing /ɪnˈsʌltɪŋ/ *adjective*
very rude or offensive to someone: *His jokes are insulting to women and have offended his staff, especially the women.* | *insulting remarks*
→ See Thesaurus box at **rude**

in•sur•ance /ɪnˈʃʊrəns/ *noun*
an arrangement in which you pay a company an amount of money every month or every year, and they pay you money if anything bad happens to you or something you own: *You should have health insurance in case you have a serious medical problem. Treatment can be very expensive.* | *I pay very high insurance premiums* (=the amount you pay every month, year, etc. for insurance).

inˈsurance ˌpolicy *noun*
a legal written agreement with an insurance company so that you have insurance: *If I die, my life insurance policy will pay my wife a large amount of money.*

in•sure /ɪnˈʃʊr/ *verb*
1 to buy or provide insurance for something or someone: *This painting is insured for $5,000 in case it is stolen or damaged.*
2 to make certain that something happens: *The gift of $200,000 dollars will insure that the school has enough money to build a new library.*
—**insurer** *noun* a company that provides insurance

in•tact /ɪnˈtækt/ *adjective*
not harmed or damaged: *The storm destroyed many of the wooden buildings, but the hotel was still intact.*

in•te•ger /ˈɪntədʒɚ/ *noun, formal*
a whole number, not a FRACTION (=a part of a number, such as ¼ or ½): *6, -2, and 0 are all integers.*

in•te•gral /ˈɪntəgrəl/ Ac *adjective, formal*
forming an important and necessary part of something: *Women are now an integral part*

I

of our military; we could not fight a war without them.

in·te·grate /ˈɪntəˌgreɪt/ Ac *verb*
1 to become part of a group or society and be accepted by them: *Some immigrants do not want to integrate into American life.*
2 to end the practice of separating people of different races in schools or institutions: *The Supreme Court's decision to integrate public schools allowed black children and white children to go the same schools across the U.S.*
—**integrated** *adjective* having people from different places or of different types living together: *We live in an integrated community with people of all races and religions.*
—**integration** /ˌɪntəˈgreɪʃən/ *noun* the process of becoming part of a group or society and being accepted by them

in·teg·ri·ty /ɪnˈtegrəti/ Ac *noun*
the quality of being honest and doing what you believe is right: *I admire his integrity; I have known him for 20 years, and I have never heard him lie.*

in·tel·lect /ˈɪntəˌlekt/ *noun*
the ability to understand things and think intelligently: *My professor is a woman of great intellect.*

in·tel·lec·tu·al[1] /ˌɪntəˈlektʃuəl/ *adjective*
relating to your ability to think and understand ideas and information: *In a democracy we have intellectual freedom; nobody can limit what we learn about.*

intellectual[2] *noun*
an intelligent person who spends time thinking about complicated ideas: *We live near a university, so there are lots of intellectuals and artists in the town.*

in·tel·li·gence /ɪnˈtelədʒəns/ Ac *noun*
1 the ability to learn, understand, and think about things: *He was a child of average intelligence, who got B's and C's at school.*
2 information about the secret activities of foreign governments, such as their military plans: *The President said the intelligence that was collected was too secret to be shown to the public.*

in·tel·li·gent /ɪnˈtelədʒənt/ Ac *adjective*
able to learn and understand things quickly: *an intelligent man* | *She's a good student who always asks intelligent questions.* ANTONYM **stupid**
—**intelligently** *adverb*

THESAURUS: intelligent

smart intelligent: *He's a really smart guy and he studies really hard.*

bright quick at learning things – used especially about children and young people: *Their daughter is very bright; she's only four and she's already learned to read.*

brilliant very intelligent and good at the work you do: *a brilliant scientist*

wise having a lot of experience and knowledge about people and the world, so that you can make good decisions and give good advice: *My mother was a wise woman, who helped me understand how to treat other people kindly.*

clever intelligent and good at thinking of ideas: *He's clever, and can usually figure out a way to get what he wants.*

gifted a gifted child is much more intelligent than most other children: *a special class for gifted children*

in·tend /ɪnˈtend/ *verb*
1 to plan to do something: *The work took longer than we intended.* | *Bob never intended to hurt me.* SYNONYM **mean**
2 be intended for someone/something = made for a particular person or designed for a particular purpose: *It's a movie for kids – it's not intended for adults.*

WORD FAMILY look at the words:

→ **intend** *verb*
→ **intention** *noun*
→ **intentional** *adjective*
→ **intentionally** *adverb*
→ **intent** *noun*

in·tense /ɪnˈtens/ Ac *adjective*
having a very strong effect on someone or felt very strongly: *The heat from the burning building was intense.* | *intense pain*
—**intensely** *adverb*: *Bill disliked her intensely and hated being around her.*

in•ten•si•fy /ɪn'tensəˌfaɪ/ Ac *verb, formal*
to increase in strength, size, or amount, etc.: *The pain intensified, until it was so bad that I went to the hospital.* | *Officials have intensified the search for the missing children.*

in•ten•si•ty /ɪn'tensəti/ Ac *noun*
when something is felt very strongly or has a very strong effect: *You could see the intensity of the love he felt for his children in the gentle way he took care of them.*

in•ten•sive /ɪn'tensɪv/ Ac *adjective*
involving a lot of work in a short period of time: *The team did two months of intensive training before the Olympics.*
—**intensively** *adverb*

in•tent /ɪn'tent/ *noun*
formal what you want or plan to do: *It was never my intent to hurt anybody – the bad things that happened were an accident.* SYNONYM **intention**

in•ten•tion /ɪn'tenʃən/ *noun*
something that you plan to do: *I have no intention of retiring – I'm going to continue working as long as possible.*

in•ten•tion•al /ɪn'tenʃənəl/ *adjective*
an action that is intentional is one that you plan to do: *He broke the rules, but I'm sure it wasn't intentional.*
—**intentionally** *adverb*

in•ter•act /ˌɪntə'rækt/ Ac *verb, formal*
to talk, work, or be involved in an activity with someone: *The Senator tries to interact with ordinary Americans, so that he knows how they think.*
—**interaction** /ˌɪntə'rækʃən/ *noun* the activity of talking or working with other people

in•ter•ac•tive /ˌɪntə'ræktɪv/ Ac *adjective*
if a television, piece of software, etc. is interactive, you can send and receive messages telling it what to do: *The museum has an interactive program that allows you to enter your weight and see how much you would weigh on the moon.*

in•ter•cept /ˌɪntɚ'sept/ *verb*
to stop something that is going from one place to another before it gets there: *He threw the ball to a teammate, but a member of the other team intercepted it.*
—**interception** /ˌɪntɚ'sepʃən/ *noun* the action of stopping something before it gets somewhere

in•ter•com /'ɪntɚˌkɑm/ *noun*
a system that lets people in different parts of a building, aircraft, etc. speak to each other: *I was sitting down in the plane when the captain spoke to us over the intercom.*

in•ter•con•nect•ed /ˌɪntɚkə'nektɪd/ *adjective, formal*
if two or more things are interconnected, they are related to each other or connected to each other: *Computers have thousands of interconnected parts.*

in•ter•de•pend•ent /ˌɪntɚdɪ'pendənt/ *adjective, formal*
depending on or necessary to each other: *Work and family are interdependent areas of a parent's life.*
—**interdependence** *noun* when two or more things depend on or are necessary to each other

I

in•terest¹ /'ɪntrəst/ *noun*
1 the feeling that you want to know more about a subject or person, or do more of an activity: *The girls have started to show an interest in fashion* (=become interested in fashion). | *I got bored with the book and began to lose interest* (=stopped being interested).
2 a subject or activity that you enjoy studying or doing: *My interests are music, soccer, and riding horses.*
3 money that you must pay a bank when you borrow money, or money that a bank pays you if you save money: *I haven't even paid the interest on my student loan yet.*

interest² *verb*
if a subject, activity, or person interests you, you want to find out more about them: *The idea of studying journalism interests me and I want to learn more about it.*

in•terest•ed /'ɪntrəstɪd/ *adjective*
1 if you are interested in something, you want to learn more about it because you enjoy it: *Most girls who are my age are interested in music, clothes, and boys.*
2 if you are interested in doing something, you want to do it: *I'm interested in buying your truck. How much money do you want for it?*

in·terest·ing /ˈɪntrəstɪŋ/ *adjective*
unusual or exciting in a way that makes you want to find out more: *That's an interesting story – could you tell me more about it?*

WORD FAMILY look at the words:
- → interesting *adjective*
- → interested *adjective*
- → interest *verb*
- → interest *noun*

in·ter·fere /ˌɪntəˈfɪr/ *verb*
to get involved in a situation when other people do not want you to: *It's better not to interfere in their arguments. They need to solve their problems themselves.*
—**interference** *noun* an act of interfering
PHRASAL VERB
interfere with something
to prevent something from happening in the way that is planned: *Her family problems began to interfere with her work and her boss had to talk to her about it.*

I

in·te·ri·or /ɪnˈtɪriə/ *noun*
the inside part or inside of something: *The interior of the ship was dark and noisy.* ANTONYM **exterior**
—**interior** *adjective* inside: *The interior walls of the house need to be painted.*

in·ter·jec·tion /ˌɪntəˈdʒekʃən/ *noun*
a word or phrase that is used to express surprise, shock, pain, etc. In the sentence "Ouch! That hurt!", "ouch" is an interjection.

in·ter·me·di·ate /ˌɪntəˈmidiət/ Ac *adjective*
done or happening between two other stages, levels, etc.: *First you take the beginners English class, then the intermediate class, and then the advanced class.*

in·ter·mis·sion /ˌɪntəˈmɪʃən/ *noun*
a short period of time when a play, concert, etc. stops before starting again: *The show lasts 85 minutes with a short intermission in the middle.*

in·tern¹ /ˈɪntən/ *noun*
1 a student who works without pay so that he or she can learn how to do a job
2 someone who has almost finished training as a doctor and is working in a hospital

in·tern² /ɪnˈtən/ *verb*
1 to work at an organization as an intern: *Scott's interning at a law firm during summer vacation from law school.*
2 to put someone in prison for political reasons or during a war, without charging him or her with a crime: *Thousands of people were interned at labor camps and forced to build roads.*
—**internment** *noun* the practice of keeping people in prison for political reasons or during a war, without charging them with a crime

in·ter·nal /ɪnˈtənl/ Ac *adjective*
1 existing or happening within a company, organization, or country: *The bank began an internal investigation into the illegal activity among its employees.*
2 inside your body: *the internal organs such as the heart, lungs, and stomach* ANTONYM **external**
—**internally** *adverb*

in·ter·na·tion·al /ˌɪntəˈnæʃənəl/ *adjective*
involving or existing in more than one country: *They asked the United Nations and other international organizations for help.* | *international terrorism*
—**internationally** *adverb*

in·ter·net /ˈɪntəˌnet/ *noun*
the Internet = a computer system that allows millions of computer users around the world to send and receive information: *You can buy airline tickets on the Internet.* SYNONYM **the Net, the Web**
—**Internet** *adjective*: *The phone company now provides Internet access to its customers.*

in·ter·pret /ɪnˈtəprɪt/ Ac *verb*
1 to change what someone is saying in one language into another language: *Gina speaks Spanish, so she interpreted for me when we were in Mexico.*
2 *formal* to believe that something has a particular meaning: *I interpreted his silence as a sign of guilt.*
—**interpreter** *noun* someone who changes what someone is saying in one language into another language

in•ter•pre•ta•tion /ɪnˌtɚprəˈteɪʃən/ Ac *noun, formal*
the way in which someone understands or explains something: *What is your interpretation of the end of the story? Do you think the characters are happy?*

in•ter•ra•cial /ˌɪntɚˈreɪʃəl/ *adjective*
happening or existing between different races of people: *Interracial marriage is more common now than it used to be.*

in•ter•ro•gate /ɪnˈterəˌgeɪt/ *verb*
to ask someone questions for a long time in order to get information: *The police interrogated the men for more than three hours, trying to find out exactly what happened.*
—**interrogator** *noun* a police officer or other official who asks someone questions in order to get information
—**interrogation** /ɪnˌterəˈgeɪʃən/ *noun* the act of asking someone questions for a long time in order to get information

in•ter•rupt /ˌɪntəˈrʌpt/ *verb*
1 to say or do something that stops someone else from speaking: *He got mad at me for interrupting his conversation.*
2 to make a process or activity stop for a short time: *The rain interrupted our barbecue.*
—**interruption** /ˌɪntɚˈrʌpʃən/ *noun* something that makes an activity stop for a short time

in•ter•sec•tion /ˌɪntɚˈsekʃən/ *noun*
a place where two or more roads meet and cross each other, often where there is a traffic light: *Turn left at the next intersection.*

in•ter•state[1] /ˈɪntɚˌsteɪt/ *noun*
a wide road that goes between states, on which cars can travel very fast: *The car was going south on Interstate 93.*
➔ See Thesaurus box at **road**

interstate[2] *adjective*
between different states in the U.S.: *interstate transportation*

in•ter•val /ˈɪntɚvəl/ Ac *noun*
1 a period of time or distance between two events, activities, etc.: *There was a short interval of good weather between the storms.*
2 at regular intervals = with the same amount of time or distance between each thing, activity, etc.: *The light flashes at regular intervals.*

in•ter•vene /ˌɪntɚˈvin/ Ac *verb, formal*
to do something to try to stop an argument, problem, war, etc.: *I could hear the boys arguing, but I decided not to intervene and let them solve their own problems.*
—**intervention** /ˌɪntɚˈvenʃən/ *noun* the act of intervening in something in order to change what happens: *We oppose U.S. military intervention in the area.*

in•ter•ven•ing /ˌɪntɚˈvinɪŋ/ Ac *adjective*
the intervening months/years, etc. *formal* = the time that has passed between two events: *I hadn't visited my school in a long time, and a lot had changed in the intervening years.*

in•ter•view[1] /ˈɪntɚˌvyu/ *noun*
1 an occasion when a famous person is asked a lot of questions about his or her life and opinions by a newspaper, television program, etc.: *In an interview with CBS, Jack said that he planned to get married in the fall.* | *a TV interview*
2 a formal meeting in which someone asks you questions to find out if you are a good person to work in a particular job or to study at a college, etc.: *I have an interview at Dartmouth College tomorrow.* | *a job interview*

interview[2] *verb*
to ask someone questions during an interview: *Kelly was interviewed on the radio after the game.* | *We are interviewing 15 people for the job.*
—**interviewer** *noun* the person who asks someone questions during an interview
—**interviewee** *noun* the person who answers questions in an interview

in•tes•tine /ɪnˈtestɪn/ *noun*
the long tube in your body that food passes through after it leaves your stomach and before it leaves your body
—**intestinal** *adjective* related to the intestine: *intestinal infection*
➔ See picture on page A2

in•ti•mate /ˈɪntəmət/ *adjective*
1 having a very close relationship with someone: *a small party for intimate friends*
2 relating to very private or personal matters:

I

He told her the most intimate embarrassing details of his private life.

3 intimate knowledge of something = very detailed and thorough knowledge of something, gained through experience or study: *During his four years in Mexico City, he gained an intimate knowledge of Mexican life.*

4 *formal* relating to sex: *The man and woman were close friends but had never had an intimate relationship.*

—**intimately** *adverb*

—**intimacy** /ˈɪntəməsi/ *noun* when you have a close personal relationship with someone

in•tim•i•date /ɪnˈtɪməˌdeɪt/ *verb*
to make someone feel frightened of you, so that he or she does what you want him or her to do: *The police arrested members of the gang for intimidating witnesses and trying to keep them from talking to police.*

—**intimidating** *adjective* making you feel worried or not confident: *I find job interviews quite intimidating.*

—**intimidation** /ɪnˌtɪməˈdeɪʃən/ *noun* the act of intimidating someone

in•to /ˈɪntə; *before vowels* ˈɪntʊ; *strong* ˈɪntu/ *preposition*

1 inside a container or place: *When she saw his car coming, Ruth ran into the house.* | *I put some clothes into my suitcase, and left for the airport.*

2 involved in a situation or activity: *After college, he decided to go into teaching* (=become a teacher). | *Those boys are always getting into trouble.*

3 becoming a different thing: *Caterpillars turn into butterflies.* | *They are going to make the book into a movie.*

4 hitting something, usually by accident: *Dick drove his dad's car into a tree and wrecked it.*

5 be into something *informal* = to like something very much: *I'm totally into sports, especially football.*

6 in a particular direction: *She held my face and looked into my eyes.*

7 used when dividing one number by another number: *Five goes into ten two times.*

in•tol•er•a•ble /ɪnˈtɑlərəbəl/ *adjective, formal*
more difficult, bad, or painful than you can deal with: *The pain became intolerable, so I went to the hospital.*

in•tox•i•cat•ed /ɪnˈtɑksəˌkeɪtɪd/ *adjective, formal*

1 drunk: *He was arrested for driving while intoxicated.*

2 very happy and excited by something, so that you stop thinking clearly: *He became intoxicated by dreams of winning lots of money in Las Vegas.*

—**intoxicating** *adjective* making you drunk: *intoxicating liquor*

—**intoxication** /ɪnˌtɑksəˈkeɪʃən/ *noun* the state of being drunk

in•tran•si•tive /ɪnˈtrænsətɪv/ *adjective*
an intransitive verb does not have an object. In the sentence "They arrived early," "arrive" is an intransitive verb

—**intransitive** *noun* an intransitive verb

in•tri•cate /ˈɪntrɪkət/ *adjective*
containing many small parts or details: *the intricate patterns of an Oriental rug*

in•trigue /ɪnˈtrig/ *verb, formal*
to interest someone a lot, especially by being strange or mysterious: *The title of the book intrigued me because it was so unusual.*

—**intriguing** *adjective* interesting and slightly strange or mysterious: *The experiment produced some intriguing results, and scientists are investigating them further.*

—**intrigued** *adjective* very interested in something because it seems strange or mysterious

in•trin•sic /ɪnˈtrɪnzɪk/ Ac *adjective, formal*
being an important basic quality or feature of something: *I felt the intrinsic pleasure of swimming smoothly through the water.*

—**intrinsically** *adverb, formal*: *We believe that people are intrinsically good, and that it is the troubles in their lives that make them do bad things.*

in•tro•duce /ˌɪntrəˈdus/ *verb*

1 if you introduce someone to another person, you tell each person the other person's name for the first time: *She took me home and introduced me to her parents.* | *Let me*

introduce myself – my name is Mark Wright.
2 *formal* to make something happen or be available for the first time: *Apple introduced the iPod in 2004.*

WORD FAMILY look at the words:

→ **introduce** *verb*
→ **introduction** *noun*
→ **introductory** *adjective*

in•tro•duc•tion /ˌɪntrəˈdʌkʃən/ *noun*
1 *formal* the act of making something happen or be available for the first time: *Every year we see the introduction of new more powerful computers.*
2 the act of telling two people each other's names when they meet for the first time: *Wade greeted his guests and made the introductions* (=told everyone what each person's name was).
3 a short written or spoken explanation at the beginning of a book or speech: *In the introduction, the author explains why he wrote the book.*
—**introductory** /ˌɪntrəˈdʌktəri/ *adjective*: *Write an introductory paragraph to your essay stating your main ideas.*

in•tro•vert•ed /ˈɪntrəˌvɚtɪd/ *adjective*
an introverted person is quiet and shy, and does not enjoy being with other people: *At fifteen years old, she was quiet and introverted.* ANTONYM **extroverted**
—**introvert** *noun* someone who is introverted
→ See Thesaurus box at **shy**

in•trude /ɪnˈtrud/ *verb, formal*
to interrupt someone or become involved in a private situation when people do not want you to: *"I hope I'm not intruding," she said to the people sitting around the table.* | *I don't want newspapers intruding into our private lives*
—**intrusion** /ɪnˈtruʒən/ *noun* an occasion when someone or something intrudes in your private affairs

in•trud•er /ɪnˈtrudɚ/ *noun*
1 someone who illegally enters a building or area in order to steal something: *The intruders entered the school building through a window.*
2 someone who is in a place where he or she is not wanted: *The border guards have promised to fight against foreign intruders.*

in•tu•i•tion /ˌɪntuˈɪʃən/ *noun*
the feeling that you know something is true or correct without having definite facts: *My intuition told me not to trust him, but I wasn't sure why.*
—**intuitive** /ɪnˈtuətɪv/ *adjective* based on feelings, not facts or knowledge

In•u•it /ˈɪnuɪt/ *noun*
the Inuit = a race of people who live in the very cold parts of North America

in•un•date /ˈɪnənˌdeɪt/ *verb*
be inundated with/by something = to receive too much of something, so that you cannot deal with all of it: *We were inundated with phone calls from people who wanted tickets.*

in•vade /ɪnˈveɪd/ *verb*
to enter a country with an army in order to take control of it: *Iraqi troops invaded Kuwait in 1990.*
—**invader** *noun* a country or army that invades another country

in•va•lid[1] /ˈɪnvələd/ *noun*
someone who is sick, injured, or old and needs other people to do things for them

in•val•id[2] /ɪnˈvælɪd/ Ac *adjective*
something that is invalid is not legally acceptable because it breaks a rule: *If the credit card doesn't have a signature, it is invalid and cannot be used.* ANTONYM **valid**
—**invalidate** *verb* to make something invalid

in•val•ua•ble /ɪnˈvælyəbəl/ *adjective, formal*
very useful: *His experience was invaluable to the younger players on the team.* SYNONYM **valuable**

in•va•sion /ɪnˈveɪʒən/ *noun*
an occasion when an army enters a country in order to take control of it: *The invasion of Poland marked the beginning of World War II.*

in•vent /ɪnˈvent/ *verb*
1 to make, design, or think of something that is completely new and different: *Alexander Graham Bell invented the telephone in 1876.*

THESAURUS: invent

create to make something new: *a new dish created by our chef*

think up to produce an idea, plan, etc. that is completely new: *Teachers always have to think up ways to keep the kids interested.*

come up with something to think of a new idea, plan, reply, etc.: *Carson said he came up with the idea for the book about five years ago.*

devise *formal* to invent a way of doing something: *Two scientists devised a test to measure people's intelligence.*

make up something to produce a new story, song, game, etc.: *Grandpa made up stories for us at bedtime.*

2 to think of a reason, story, etc. that is not true and tell it to people: *She invented a reason not to go to the party.*
—**inventive** *adjective* able to think of new, different, or interesting ideas

I

WORD FAMILY look at the words:

→ **invent** *verb*
→ **inventor** *noun*
→ **invention** *noun*
→ **inventive** *adjective*

→ See Thesaurus box at **lie**[2]

in•ven•tion /ɪn'venʃən/ *noun*
something that has been invented, or the act of inventing something: *The computer industry is constantly coming up with new inventions.* | *The invention of television has changed the world.*

in•ven•tor /ɪn'ventɚ/ *noun*
someone who thinks of or makes something completely new and different

in•ven•to•ry /'ɪnvənˌtɔri/ *noun* plural **inventories**
1 all the things that are for sale in a store
2 a list of all the things in a place

in•ver•te•brate /ɪn'vɚtəbrɪt/ *noun*
a creature that does not have a BACKBONE (=a row of connected bones going down its back): *Worms are invertebrates.*

in•vest /ɪn'vest/ Ac *verb*
1 to buy property, shares, goods, etc. because you hope their value will increase and you will make a profit: *I have some money that I want to invest and hopefully make a good profit.* | *We've decided to invest the money in land.*
2 to use a lot of time, effort, or money to improve something and make it succeed: *The government has invested heavily in education.*
—**investor** *noun* someone who buys property, shares, or goods because he or she hopes they will make a profit

in•ves•ti•gate /ɪn'vestəˌgeɪt/ Ac *verb*
to try to find out the truth about a crime, accident, etc.: *After investigating the case, the police arrested two men.* | *I heard a strange noise and went downstairs to investigate.*
—**investigator** *noun* someone who investigates a crime, accident, etc.

WORD FAMILY look at the words:

→ **investigate** *verb*
→ **investigation** *noun*
→ **investigator** *noun*

in•ves•ti•ga•tion /ɪnˌvestə'geɪʃən/ Ac *noun*
an official attempt to find out the reasons for something, such as a crime or accident: *an investigation into the cause of the plane crash* | *The company is under investigation* (=being investigated) *for tax fraud.*

in•vest•ment /ɪn'vestmənt/ Ac *noun*
1 the money that you use to buy property, shares, goods, etc. in order to make a profit, or the act of doing this: *People want to know that their investments are growing.* | *Foreign investment in China has increased year after year.*
2 something that you buy or do because it will be valuable or useful later: *Going back to school was a good investment of my time.*

in•vis•i•ble /ɪn'vɪzəbəl/ Ac *adjective*
something that is invisible cannot be seen: *At 5,000 feet the small plane was almost invisible; it looked like a dot in the sky.*
—**invisibly** *adverb*
—**invisibility** /ɪnˌvɪzə'bɪləti/ *noun* the fact that something is invisible

in•vi•ta•tion /ˌɪnvə'teɪʃən/ *noun*
1 a request inviting someone to go somewhere or do something: *I decided to accept Andrea's invitation to visit her.*
2 a piece of paper that someone sends you

to ask you to come to a party or event: *You have to bring the invitation with you to get into the party.*

in•vite /ɪn'vaɪt/ *verb*
to ask someone to come to a party, dinner, wedding, etc.: *"Why weren't you at Eva's party?" "I wasn't invited."* | *I invited the Rosens to dinner next Friday.* | *They've invited us for lunch.*
PHRASAL VERBS
invite someone in
to ask someone to come into your home: *We stood on the front porch for a while, but she didn't invite us in.*
invite someone over
to ask someone to come to your home for a party, meal, etc.: *They invited us over for a barbecue.*

in•vit•ing /ɪn'vaɪtɪŋ/ *adjective*
something that is inviting is attractive and makes you want to enjoy it: *The swimming pool looked inviting* (=made me want to swim in it).
—**invitingly** *adverb*

in•voice /'ɪnvɔɪs/ *noun*
a list that shows how much you must pay for goods, work, etc. SYNONYM **bill**
—**invoice** *verb* to send someone an invoice

in•voke /ɪn'voʊk/ Ac *verb, formal*
to use a law, principle, etc. to support your ideas or actions: *Stern invoked his rights and refused to answer questions in court* (=he refused to speak in court, which is his legal right).

in•vol•un•tar•y /ɪn'vɑlən,teri/ *adjective*
relating to a movement, reaction, etc. that you or your body makes but that you cannot control: *Breathing is an involuntary process – we do it without thinking about it.*
—**involuntarily** /ɪn,vɑlən'terəli/ *adverb*: *My eye was sore and red, and began to twitch involuntarily* (=make slight movements that could not be controlled).

in•volve /ɪn'vɑlv/ Ac *verb*
1 to include or affect someone or something: *Two students from our school were involved in the fight.*
2 to encourage or allow someone to take part in something, for example a game or a discussion: *It's important to involve children in sports and after-school activities.*
3 if an activity or situation involves something else, that thing is part of it or is the result of it: *It's a difficult climb, and we all knew the risks involved.* | *Taking the job involves moving to Texas.*

in•volved /ɪn'vɑlvd/ Ac *adjective*
if you are involved in an activity or event, you take part in it: *I don't want to get involved in anything that's illegal.* | *Lots of kids become involved with Little League Baseball.*

in•ward /'ɪnwɚd/ *also* **inwards** *adverb*
toward the inside or center of something: *The door opens inward.* ANTONYM **outward**
—**inward** *adjective* toward the inside or center of something

in•ward•ly /'ɪnwɚdli/ *adverb*
in a way that is not seen or noticed by other people: *I laughed inwardly, but said nothing.*

IOU *noun*
I owe you a piece of paper that you sign to say that you owe someone some money

IPA *noun*
International Phonetic Alphabet a system of signs that represent the sounds made when speaking

IQ *noun*
intelligence quotient the level of someone's intelligence. It is shown as a number, with 100 being the average: *He's extremely intelligent. He has an IQ of 130.*

I•rish[1] /'aɪrɪʃ/ *adjective*
coming from Ireland or relating to Ireland

Irish[2] *noun*
the Irish = the people of Ireland

i•ron[1] /'aɪɚn/ *noun*
1 a piece of electrical equipment used for making clothes smooth: *Be careful – the iron is still hot!*
2 a common hard metal that is used to make steel: *The old fence was made of iron.*
3 a natural substance that is in food and your blood in small amounts: *Red meat has a lot of iron in it.*

iron[2] *verb*
to make your clothes smooth using an iron: *Thanks for ironing my shirt – it looks a lot neater now.*
PHRASAL VERB
iron something out *informal*
to solve a small problem: *The embassy*

iron

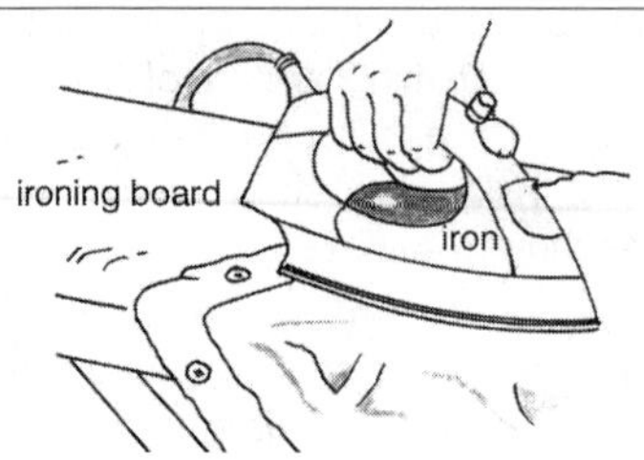

helped me iron out some problems with my visa.

iron[3] *adjective*

1 made of iron: *an iron gate*

2 do something with an iron hand/fist/grip = to do something in a way that is very strict and severe: *He ruled the country with an iron fist and did not allow any opposition.*

i•ron•ing /ˈaɪɚnɪŋ/ *noun*

the activity of making clothes smooth using an iron: *I usually do the ironing while I watch TV.*

ˈironing ˌboard *noun*

a tall narrow table used for ironing clothes

➔ See picture at **iron**[1]

i•ro•ny /ˈaɪrəni/ *noun* plural **ironies**

1 a situation that is funny or sad because something strange happens, or the opposite of what is expected happens: *People are dying from taking this drug, and the irony is that the drug is supposed to save lives.*

2 a form of humor in which you say something using words that are the opposite of what you really mean

—**ironic** /aɪˈrɑnɪk/ *adjective* relating to irony: *It's ironic that he moved all the way to Alaska and then married a girl he met there who comes from his home town.* | *ironic comments*

ir•ra•tion•al /ɪˈræʃənəl/ Ac *adjective*

irrational feelings, behavior, reasons, etc. are not sensible or reasonable because they are not based on clear thinking: *I know my fear of dogs is irrational, but I can't stop being afraid.* ANTONYM **rational**

—**irrationally** *adverb*: *He was given the drug because he was behaving irrationally and could not be controlled.*

ir•reg•u•lar /ɪˈregyəlɚ/ *adjective, formal*

1 not happening at times that are an equal distance apart: *The test showed that she had an irregular heartbeat and needed medical treatment.*

2 not happening or done at the normal time or at the same time every day, week, month, etc.: *Actors work irregular hours; often a movie will be filmed in the middle of the night.*

3 having a shape, surface, etc. that is not even or smooth: *the irregular edges of a piece of broken glass*

4 an irregular verb or noun does not change in the normal way when you use them in the past tense, the plural, etc.: *"Go" is an irregular verb and "deer" is an irregular noun.*

—**irregularly** *adverb*

ir•reg•u•lar•i•ty /ɪˌregyəˈlærəti/ *noun* plural **irregularities** *formal*

1 a situation in which the normal rules or laws have not been followed: *City officials closed the club because of financial irregularities.*

2 a situation in which something does not happen regularly in the way it should: *The drug can cause irregularities in your heartbeat.*

ir•rel•e•vant /ɪˈreləvənt/ Ac *adjective*

not useful or not relating to a particular situation, and therefore not important: *We know he can do the job, so his age is irrelevant* (=it does not matter how old he is). ANTONYM **relevant**

—**irrelevance** *noun* the quality of being irrelevant

ir•re•sist•i•ble /ˌɪrɪˈzɪstəbəl/ *adjective*

1 if someone or something is irresistible, he, she, or it is so attractive that you cannot stop yourself from wanting him, her, or it: *The cake looks irresistible. I can't wait to try it.* | *He thinks he's irresistible to women, but actually very few women find him attractive.*

2 too strong or powerful to be stopped: *She suddenly felt an irresistible urge to cry and tears began to flow down her face.*

—**irresistibly** *adverb*

ir•re•spon•si•ble /ˌɪrɪˈspɑnsəbəl/ *adjective*

behaving in a careless way, without thinking about the bad results that might happen: *It was irresponsible to go out and leave the kids alone.*

—**irresponsibly** *adverb*

—**irresponsibility** /ˌɪrɪˌspɑnsəˈbɪləti/ *noun* the quality of being irresponsible

ir•ri•gate /ˈɪrəˌgeɪt/ *verb*
to supply water to land or crops: *Egyptian farmers used water from the Nile to irrigate their land.*
—**irrigation** /ˌɪrəˈgeɪʃən/ *noun* the process of supplying land or crops with water

ir•ri•ta•ble /ˈɪrətəbəl/ *adjective*
an irritable person gets annoyed or angry very easily: *He's always irritable in the morning, so it's best not to talk to him then.*
—**irritably** *adverb*
—**irritability** /ˌɪrətəˈbɪləti/ *noun* the fact that someone is irritable

ir•ri•tate /ˈɪrəˌteɪt/ *verb*
1 to make someone angry or annoyed: *His bad jokes are starting to irritate me.*
2 to make a part of your body painful and sore: *Cigarette smoke irritates your lungs, making you cough.*
—**irritating** *adjective* making you feel angry or annoyed
—**irritated** *adjective* feeling angry or annoyed
—**irritant** *noun* something that keeps you angry or annoyed for a long period of time
—**irritation** /ˌɪrəˈteɪʃən/ *noun* the feeling of being angry or annoyed

IRS *noun*
the IRS = **the Internal Revenue Service** the government organization in the U.S. that deals with taxes

is /z, s, əz; *strong* ɪz/
the third person singular of the present tense of BE

Is•lam /ˈɪzlɑm/ *noun*
the Muslim religion which was started by Muhammad and whose holy book is the Koran
—**Islamic** /ɪzˈlɑmɪk/ *adjective* relating to the religion of Islam or to Muslim people and countries: *Their system is based on Islamic law.*

is•land /ˈaɪlənd/ *noun*
a piece of land completely surrounded by water: *a small island off the coast of Florida | You can take the ferry to Staten Island. | They live on the island and have to take a boat to the mainland.*

island

isle /aɪl/ *noun, formal*
an island: *a desert isle | the Isle of Skye*

is•n't /ˈɪzənt/ *verb*
the short form of "is not": *He isn't here right now, but he'll be back in an hour.*

i•so•late /ˈaɪsəˌleɪt/ Ac *verb*
to keep one person or thing separate from others: *The heavy snow has completely isolated the mountain town. | If a puppy becomes sick, isolate it from the other puppies, and call the vet.*

i•so•lat•ed /ˈaɪsəˌleɪtɪd/ Ac *adjective*
1 far away from other things: *They lived on an isolated farm and had no neighbors.*
2 feeling alone or unable to meet or speak to other people: *Yes, I did feel isolated when we first moved to the new neighborhood.*
3 an isolated action or event happens only once and is not likely to happen again: *The attack is not an isolated incident – there were two other attacks earlier this week.*

is•sue¹ /ˈɪʃu/ Ac *noun*
1 a subject or problem that people discuss: *The cost of health care is an issue that affects everyone. | At the next meeting, we should raise the issue* (=begin to discuss it).
2 a magazine or newspaper that is sold on a particular day, week, month, or year: *The article is in this month's issue of the magazine.*

issue² *verb, formal*
1 to make an official statement, or to give an order or a warning: *The mayor issued a statement saying that two of the schools would close.*
2 to officially provide someone with documents or equipment: *The U.S. will not issue a visa to people with a criminal record.*

it /ɪt/ *pronoun*
1 used to talk about something you have already mentioned or something that the person you are talking to already knows about: *"Did you bring your umbrella?" "No, I left it at home." | "Where's the bread?" "It's* (=it is) *on the shelf." | Don't get angry with me. It wasn't my fault.*

2 used to talk about the situation that someone is in now: *I can't stand it any longer. I'm leaving.*
3 used as the subject or object of a sentence when the real subject or object is later in the sentence: *It costs less to drive than to take the bus.*
4 used with the verb "be" to talk about the weather, time, distance, etc.: *It's cold today.* | *It was late by the time we got home.* | *It's not far to the beach from here.*
5 used in order to talk about a child or animal when you do not know what sex he or she is: *"Marilyn had a baby." "Is it a boy or girl?"*

IT *noun*
information technology the study or use of computers and other electronic equipment to store and process information

i·tal·ics /ɪˈtælɪks/ *plural noun*
a style of printed letters that lean to the right: *The examples in this dictionary are written in italics.*
—**italic** *adjective*: *italic type*

itch /ɪtʃ/ *noun*
1 an unpleasant feeling on your skin that makes you want to rub it with your nails: *I have an itch on my back – can you scratch it for me?*
2 *informal* a strong desire to do or have something: *I've got this itch to go to Australia. I think it would be a lot of fun.*
—**itch** *verb* to feel an itch: *My arms itched where the wool touched them.*

itch·y /ˈɪtʃi/ *adjective*
if your skin is itchy, it feels unpleasant in a way that makes you want to rub your nails across it: *My skin felt dry and itchy.*

it'd /ˈɪtəd/
1 the short form of "it would": *It'd be more fun if we both went.*
2 the short form of "it had": *It'd been a warm summer, but now it was growing cooler.*

i·tem /ˈaɪtəm/ Ac *noun*
1 a single thing in a set, group, or list: *There were several items of clothing on the floor.* | *I checked every item on the list.*
2 a single piece of news in a newspaper, on television, or on the radio: *I heard a news item about his arrest on the radio.*
→ See Thesaurus box at **thing**

i·tin·er·ar·y /aɪˈtɪnəˌreri/ *noun* plural **itineraries**
a plan or list of the places you will visit on a trip: *The first place on our itinerary is Las Vegas, and after that we go to the Grand Canyon.*

it'll /ˈɪtl/
the short form of "it will": *It'll be fun, I promise.*

it's /ɪts/
1 the short form of "it is": *It's snowing!*
2 the short form of "it has": *It's been so hot all week.*

its /ɪts/ *adjective*
belonging to thing, animal, or baby that has been mentioned: *The dog was barking and wagging its tail.* | *The school has had some problems with its computer systems.* | *A baby is totally dependent on its parents.*

it·self /ɪtˈself/ *pronoun*
1 the REFLEXIVE form of "it", used to say that a thing, animal, or baby is affected by its own actions: *The cat was licking itself.* | *Our country has the right to defend itself.*
2 in itself = only the thing mentioned, and not anything else: *You finished the race, and that in itself is fantastic, even if you didn't win.*
3 used to emphasize a particular thing: *The acting is good, but the movie itself is a little slow.*

I've /aɪv/
the short form of "I have": *I've never been to New York.*

i·vo·ry /ˈaɪvəri/ *noun*
the hard smooth white substance that the TUSKS (=long teeth) of an ELEPHANT are made of
—**ivory** *adjective* made of ivory: *an ivory bracelet*

i·vy /ˈaɪvi/ *noun*
a plant with dark green shiny leaves that grows up the walls of buildings: *They lived in a large old brick house, with ivy covering the walls.*
→ **poison ivy**

ˈIvy ˌLeague *adjective*
relating to a group of eight important and respected colleges in the northeast of the U.S.: *an Ivy League school*

Jj

jab[1] /dʒæb/ *verb* **jabbed, jabbing**
to push something pointed into or toward something else using short quick movements: *Mom, Laurie just jabbed her finger in my eye!*

jab[2] *noun*
a sudden hard push with a pointed object or with your hand, finger, etc.: *I gave him a jab in the ribs with my finger to get his attention.*

jack /dʒæk/ *noun*
1 a piece of equipment used for lifting something heavy, such as a car: *I got the jack out of the car and started to change the flat tire.*
2 a card used in card games which has a picture of a young man on it: *the jack of clubs*

jack•al /ˈdʒækəl/ *noun*
a wild animal like a dog that lives in Africa and Asia

jack•et /ˈdʒækɪt/ *noun*
a short light coat: *a black leather jacket* | *He took off his suit jacket and sat down to eat.*
➔ See picture on page A6

jack•ham•mer /ˈdʒækˌhæmɚ/ *noun*
a large powerful tool used for breaking hard materials such as the surface of a road

ˈjack-in-the-ˌbox *noun*
a toy shaped like a box with a toy person or animal inside that comes out on a SPRING when the lid of the box opens

jack•knife /ˈdʒæknaɪf/ *noun* plural **jackknives** /ˈdʒæknaɪvz/
a knife with a blade that folds into its handle

jack-o'-lan•tern /ˈdʒæk ə ˌlæntən/ *noun*
a PUMPKIN with holes cut into it to make it look like a face. It usually has a light inside it and is used at HALLOWEEN.

jack•pot /ˈdʒækpɑt/ *noun*
1 a very large amount of money that you can win in a game: *If you win the jackpot, you get $55 million.*
2 hit the jackpot = to win a lot of money or be very lucky: *He hit the jackpot when he married Kim – she's just right for him.*

Ja•cuz•zi /dʒəˈkuzi/ *noun, trademark*
an object like a large heated bathtub for several people to sit in. It makes bubbles that help to relax your muscles.

jade /dʒeɪd/ *noun*
a green stone used especially for making jewelry

jag•ged /ˈdʒægɪd/ *adjective*
having a rough uneven edge with a lot of sharp points: *The jagged rocks along the coast are a danger to ships.*

jag•uar /ˈdʒægwɑr/ *noun*
a large wild cat with yellow fur and black spots that lives mainly in Central and South America

jail /dʒeɪl/ *noun*
a place where criminals are sent as a punishment for a crime: *He was sentenced to 10 years in jail* (=the judge said he must spend 10 years in jail). | *You could go to jail for doing that.* | *a two-year jail sentence* SYNONYM **prison**
—**jail** *verb* to put someone in prison: *The judge jailed him for two years for stealing cars.*

jam[1] /dʒæm/ *verb* **jammed, jamming**
1 to push something into a small space using a lot of force: *I jammed all the books I needed into my backpack.*
2 if a machine jams, it stops working because a part of it stops moving: *Every time I try to use the copy machine it jams and I have to get someone to repair it.*
3 *informal* if a lot of people or things jam a place, they completely fill it and it is difficult for them to move: *It was 5:00 p.m. and the freeway was jammed with cars.*
4 if a door jams, it is stuck and will not open or close: *The bathroom door had jammed, trapping her inside.*

jam[2] *noun*
1 a thick sticky sweet food made from fruit that you eat on bread. Jam has small pieces of fruit in it: *an English muffin with butter and jam*
2 be in a jam/get into a jam *informal* = to be or become involved in a difficult or bad

J

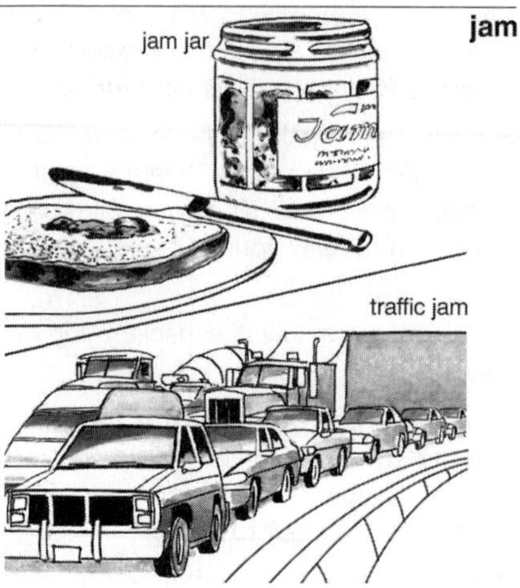

situation: *Sarah, I'm in a jam – could you help me out?*
3 a situation in which something is stuck somewhere: *There is a paper jam in the fax machine.*
➔ **traffic jam**

ˌjam-ˈpacked *adjective, informal*
completely full of people or things: *The mall was jam-packed with people shopping on the weekend.*

jan·i·tor /ˈdʒænətɚ/ *noun*
someone whose job is to clean and take care of a large building: *the school janitor* SYNONYM **custodian**

Jan·u·ar·y /ˈdʒænyuˌeri/ *noun, written abbreviation* **Jan.**
the first month of the year, between December and February: *We got married on January 12, 2000.* | *It's very cold here in January.* | *We moved to Texas last January.* | *Jack's coming to visit next January.*

Jap·a·nese¹ /ˌdʒæpəˈniz◂ / *adjective*
from Japan: *Japanese students*

Japanese² *noun*
1 the language used in Japan
2 the Japanese = the people of Japan

jar /dʒɑr/ *noun*
a round glass container with a lid, used for storing food: *He kept cookies in a jar on his desk.* | *a jar of peanut butter*

jar·gon /ˈdʒɑrgən/ *noun*
technical words and phrases that people doing the same type of work use, which other people find difficult to understand: *Legal jargon can be confusing.*
➔ See Thesaurus box at **language**

jav·e·lin /ˈdʒævəlɪn/ *noun*
1 the javelin = a sport in which you throw a long pointed stick as far as you can
2 the long pointed stick used in this sport

jaw /dʒɔ/ *noun*
the bottom part of your face that contains the two bones which your teeth are in: *He punched Ted in the jaw.*
➔ See picture on page A2

jay·walk·ing /ˈdʒeɪˌwɔkɪŋ/ *noun*
the act of walking across a street at a place where it is dangerous to cross: *The police officer fined me for jaywalking and told me to cross at the corner.*
—**jaywalker** *noun* some who walks across a street at a place where it is dangerous to cross
—**jaywalk** *verb*

jazz /dʒæz/ *noun*
a type of music that started in the early 1900s and has developed and changed many times since then. It is usually played in groups, but peformers often IMPROVISE (=play something new based on the tune that the band plays): *He began listening to jazz when he moved to New Orleans.*

jeal·ous /ˈdʒeləs/ *adjective*
1 feeling unhappy because someone else has something that you wish you had: *He was jealous of his brother's nice car.* SYNONYM **envious**
2 feeling angry or unhappy because the person you love likes another person, or another person likes the person you love: *It makes me jealous when my boyfriend dances with other women.* | *a jealous husband*
—**jealousy** *noun* a feeling of being jealous
➔ See picture on page A23

jeans /dʒinz/ *noun*
pants made from DENIM (=a strong, usually blue, cotton cloth): *She was wearing a pair of jeans and a T-shirt.*
➔ See picture on page A6

Jeep /dʒip/ *noun, trademark*
a type of car made for traveling over rough ground

jeer /dʒɪr/ *verb*
to laugh and shout rude things at someone in order to show that you do not respect him or her: *The crowd began to jeer at the soldiers and throw rocks.*
—**jeer** *noun* something rude that you shout at someone

Je•ho•vah's Wit•ness /dʒɪˌhoʊvəz ˈwɪtnəs/ *noun*
a member of a religious organization that believes the end of the world will happen soon and sends its members to people's houses to try to persuade them to join

Jell-o /ˈdʒeloʊ/ *noun, trademark*
a soft sweet food, made from fruit juice, that shakes when you move it

jel•ly /ˈdʒeli/ *noun*
a thick sticky sweet food made from fruit that you eat on bread: *a peanut butter and jelly sandwich*

jel•ly•bean /ˈdʒeliˌbin/ *noun*
a small soft candy that is shaped like a bean. Jellybeans come in different colors and flavors.

jel•ly•fish /ˈdʒeliˌfɪʃ/ *noun*
a sea animal that has a round transparent body with parts hanging down that can sting you

jeop•ard•ize /ˈdʒepɚˌdaɪz/ *verb, formal*
to risk losing or destroying something that is valuable or important: *The injury could jeopardize his career in football.*

jerk[1] /dʒɚk/ *verb*
to move with a sudden quick movement: *She fell over when the train jerked forward.* | *"Don't touch me," she said, jerking her arm away.*

jerk[2] *noun*
1 *informal* someone, especially a man, who does stupid or annoying things: *Your brother's a real jerk – he says such rude things!*
2 a sudden quick movement: *The car stopped with a jerk, and I hit by forehead on the windshield.*
—**jerky** *adjective* stopping and starting suddenly and roughly: *The elevator's jerky movements frightened me.*

jer•sey /ˈdʒɚzi/ *noun* plural **jerseys**
a shirt worn as part of a sports uniform: *The team was wearing red and white jerseys.*

Je•sus /ˈdʒizəs/ *also* ˌ**Jesus** ˈ**Christ**
the person who Christians believe was the son of God, and whose life and ideas Christianity is based on

jet /dʒet/ *noun*
1 a fast airplane with a special type of engine that pushes out hot gases: *Military jets flew overhead.*
2 a thin stream of liquid or gas that comes out of a small hole very quickly: *The fountain has a jet of water spraying from the top.*

ˈ**jet lag** *noun*
the feeling of being very tired after traveling a long distance in an airplane to a part of the world where the time is different
—**jet-lagged** *adjective* feeling the effects of jet lag

jew•el /ˈdʒuəl/ *noun*
a small valuable stone, such as a DIAMOND

jew•el•er /ˈdʒuəlɚ/ *noun*
someone who buys, sells, makes, or repairs jewelry

jewelry

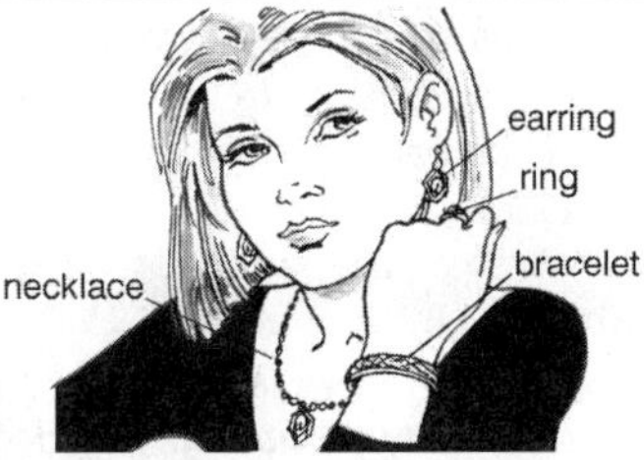

jew•el•ry /ˈdʒuəlri/ *noun*
small things that you wear for decoration, such as rings and NECKLACEs: *She was wearing a gold necklace and other expensive jewelry.* | *a beautiful piece of jewelry*

jew•els /ˈdʒuəlz/ *plural noun*
another word for jewelry

Jew•ish /ˈdʒuɪʃ/ *adjective*
relating to Judaism
—**Jew** *noun* someone whose religion is Judaism

jig•gle /ˈdʒɪgəl/ *verb* **jiggled, jiggling** *informal*
to move from side to side with short quick movements: *I jiggled the baby up and down on my knee.* | *His big belly jiggled when he laughed.*

jig•saw puz•zle /ˈdʒɪgsɔ ˌpʌzəl/ *also* **puzzle** *noun*
many small pieces of shaped wood or CARDBOARD that have pieces of a picture on

them. You try to fit the pieces together to make the whole picture

jin•gle /ˈdʒɪŋgəl/ *verb*
to shake small metal objects together so that they produce a noise: *Lucy jingled the keys in front of the kitten to get its attention.* | *I could hear coins jingling in his pocket.*

jinx¹ /dʒɪŋks/ *noun*
someone or something that brings bad luck

jinx² *verb*
to make someone have bad luck: *I don't want to talk about winning – I'm afraid I'll jinx myself.*
—**jinxed** *adjective* having a lot of bad luck

job /dʒɑb/ Ac *noun*
1 work that you do regularly in order to earn money: *Dad's always telling me to get a job and earn some money.* | *I have applied for a job at the bank.* | *After college, Cathy took a full-time job as a computer programmer.* | *I've got a part-time job at a fast-food restaurant.* | *You can live here until you find a job* (=get a job).

USAGE: job

Do not say "What is your job?" or "What is your work?" Say **"What do you do?"** or **"What kind of work do you do?"**

THESAURUS: job

Your **job** is the particular work you do regularly to earn money: *I got a job in a music store.*

Work is used in a more general way to talk about the job you do: *What kind of work do you do?*

Position is a more formal word for a job in a particular organization: *He was offered a teaching position at the college.*

Occupation is a formal word used mainly on official forms to mean your **job**: *Please give your name, age, and occupation.*

A **profession** is a job for which you need special education and training: *the legal profession*

Your **career** is the work you do for most of your life: *I'm interested in a career in journalism.*

A **vocation** is formal word for a job that you do because you enjoy it and because you feel you are the right type of person to do it: *Nursing was both my job and my vocation.*
➔ **work**

2 on the job = while at work, or while doing your job: *He was injured on the job, so his employer paid for his treatment.*
3 something that you are responsible for doing: *It's my job to watch my little brother.*
4 something that you have to do without being paid: *I have a lot of little jobs to do at home this weekend, like cleaning out the garage.* SYNONYM **task**
5 do a good/great/bad, etc. job = to do something well or badly: *You did a great job on the picture – it really looks like Sarah.*

jock•ey /ˈdʒɑki/ *noun*
someone who rides horses in races

jog /dʒɑg/ *verb* **jogged, jogging**
to run at a slow steady speed for exercise: *Julie jogs in the park every morning.*
—**jog** *noun* a slow steady run
—**jogging** *noun* the activity of running at a slow steady speed: *I went jogging around the neighborhood at about 6 a.m.*
—**jogger** *noun* someone who jogs
➔ See picture on page A4

join /dʒɔɪn/ *verb*
1 to become a member of an organization, society, or group: *He joined the army when he was nineteen.* | *We haven't lost a game since Vince joined the team.*
2 *also* **join in** to begin to take part in an activity that other people are involved in: *Other kids started to join in the laughter.* | *More police arrived to join the search.*
3 to go somewhere in order to do something with someone else: *Why don't you join us for dinner?*
4 to do something with other people, as a group: *Please join with me in welcoming tonight's speaker.*
5 to be connected or fastened together: *This is where the two rivers join to form the Ohio River.*

joint¹ /dʒɔɪnt/ *adjective*
involving two or more people, or owned or shared by two or more people: *The two Senators had a joint news conference.* | *My husband and I have a joint bank account and*

we both put our pay into it.
—**jointly** *adverb*: *The company is jointly owned by two big software makers.*

joint

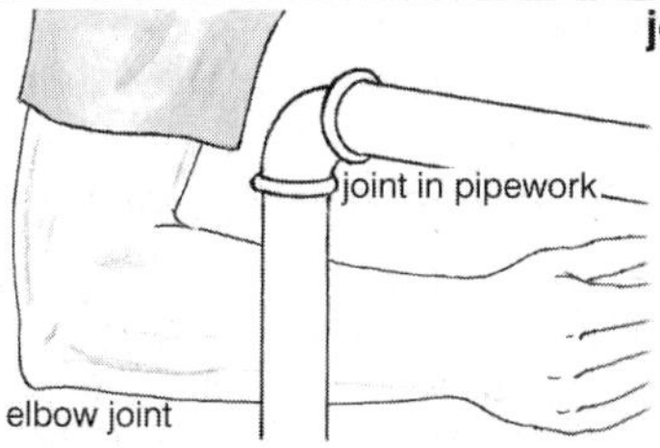

joint² *noun*
1 a part of the body where two bones meet, that can bend: *the elbow joint*
2 *informal* a cheap restaurant or club: *She works in a hamburger joint.*
3 a place where two parts of something are connected or joined together: *One of the pipe joints was leaking.*

joke¹ /dʒoʊk/ *noun*
1 something funny that you say to make people laugh: *We laughed and told jokes all night.* | *Don't make jokes about your mother!*
2 be a joke *informal* = to be completely stupid or unreasonable: *I thought his idea was a joke, but the teacher loved it.*

WORD FAMILY look at the words:
→ **joke** *noun*
→ **joke** *verb*
→ **joker** *noun*
→ **jokingly** *adverb*

joke² *verb*
to say things that are intended to be funny: *I saw him in the hall talking and joking with my girlfriend.*
—**jokingly** *adverb*
—**joker** *noun* someone who likes to tell jokes and make people laugh

jol·ly /ˈdʒɑli/ *adjective* **jollier, jolliest**
happy and friendly: *Santa Claus is a jolly old man with a long white beard.*

jolt¹ /dʒoʊlt/ *noun*
1 a sudden strong feeling, especially surprise, shock, or excitement: *The news came as a jolt to the whole family.*
2 a sudden rough or violent movement: *The car hit the tree with a jolt.*

jolt² *verb*
1 to make something move suddenly and roughly: *The earthquake jolted southern California.*
2 to give someone a sudden shock: *She was jolted awake by a loud bang.*

jos·tle /ˈdʒɑsəl/ *verb*
to push roughly against other people in a crowd, usually so that you can get somewhere or do something before them: *People in the crowd jostled for a better view of the field.*

jot /dʒɑt/ *verb* **jotted, jotting**
PHRASAL VERB
jot something down
to write something quickly on a piece of paper: *I jotted down her address and phone number.*

jour·nal /ˈdʒɚnl/ [Ac] *noun*
1 a book in which you write about the things that happen to you each day, your thoughts and opinions, etc.: *He wrote several pages in his journal that night to record everything that had happened.* SYNONYM **diary**
2 a serious magazine or newspaper produced for professional people, such as doctors: *The Wall Street Journal*

jour·nal·ist /ˈdʒɚnlɪst/ *noun*
someone who writes reports for newspapers, magazines, television, or radio: *Several journalists asked the president the same question.* SYNONYM **reporter**
—**journalism** *noun* the job or activity of writing reports for newspapers, magazines, television, or radio: *During his career in journalism he has worked for newspapers and on television.*
→ See picture on page A16

jour·ney /ˈdʒɚni/ *noun*
a trip from one place to another, especially over a long distance: *Columbus's journey from Spain to the New World* | *The book is about the two men's journey across North America.*
→ See Thesaurus box at **travel²**

joy /dʒɔɪ/ *noun*
1 a feeling of great happiness and pleasure: *Tears of joy and relief rolled down her cheek.* | *You could see the joy on the kids' faces when they saw the puppies.*
2 something or someone that gives you

J

happiness or pleasure: *The car is a joy to drive.*

—**joyful** *adjective* very happy or likely to make people happy: *The birth of a child is a joyful experience.*

—**joyous** *adjective* very happy or likely to make people happy: *The day she came home from the hospital was a joyous occasion for the family.*

joy•stick /'dʒɔɪˌstɪk/ *noun*
a handle that you use to control an aircraft or a computer game

Jr.
the written abbreviation of **Junior**

Ju•da•ism /'dʒudiˌɪzəm/ *noun*
the Jewish religion based on books called the Hebrew Scriptures, which include many of the books that are in the Old Testament of the Christian BIBLE

judge[1] /dʒʌdʒ/ *noun*
1 the person in control of a court who decides how criminals should be punished: *The judge gave Simmons six years in jail for the crime.*
2 someone who decides the result of a competition: *the judges at the Olympic ice skating competition*
3 a good/bad, etc. judge of something = someone whose opinion about something is usually right or wrong: *My father is a good judge of character* (=he can judge whether someone is a good, bad, etc. person).
➔ See picture on page A16

judge[2] *verb*
1 to decide something or form an opinion about someone or something: *You should not judge people by the color of their skin.* | *Judging from her expression, I'd say she was angry.* | *You will be judged on how many correct answers you give.*
2 to decide the result of a competition: *Kim and I will be judging the writing competition.*

judg•ment *also* **judgement** /'dʒʌdʒmənt/ *noun*
1 an opinion that you reach after thinking about something: *It's too early to make a judgment; we need more information.*
2 the ability to make decisions about situations or people: *I trust your judgment, and I know you will make the right decision.*
3 an official decision made by a judge or a court of law: *the court's final judgment*

ju•di•cial /dʒu'dɪʃəl/ *adjective, formal*
1 relating to a court of law, a judge, or a judge's decisions: *the court's judicial authority*
2 the judicial branch = the part of a government that consists of all the judges in a country

—**judiciary** /dʒu'dɪʃiˌeri/ *noun* the judicial branch

ju•do /'dʒudoʊ/ *noun*
a sport, originally from Japan, in which you try to throw your opponent onto the ground

jug /dʒʌg/ *noun*
a large deep container for liquids that has a narrow opening and a handle: *a jug of water*

jug•gle /'dʒʌgəl/ *verb*
1 to keep three or more objects moving through the air by throwing and catching them so that one or more of them is always in the air: *He threw three tennis balls into the air and started juggling them.*
2 to try to do two or more jobs, activities, etc. at the same time: *He has to juggle three jobs to support his family.*

—**juggler** *noun* someone who juggles objects in the air

juice /dʒus/ *noun*
1 the liquid that comes from fruit and vegetables, or a drink made from this: *a glass of orange juice*
2 the liquid that comes out of meat when it is cooked

juic•y /'dʒusi/ *adjective* **juicier**, **juiciest**
containing a lot of juice: *a juicy peach*

—**juiciness** *noun*

juke•box /'dʒukˌbɑks/ *noun*
a machine that plays music when you put money in it. Jukeboxes are usually in places such as bars and restaurants.

Ju•ly /dʒʊ'laɪ/ *noun, written abbreviation* **Jul.**
the seventh month of the year, between June and August: *Her birthday is on July 9.* | *Henry started working here in July.* | *We went to Seattle last July.* | *Next July is my mom's 40th birthday.*

jum•ble /'dʒʌmbəl/ *noun*
a group of things mixed together in a messy way: *There was a jumble of books and magazines next to his bed.*

—**jumble** *verb* to mix things together in a messy way

jum•bo /ˈdʒʌmboʊ/ *adjective*
larger than other things of the same type: *I ordered a plate of jumbo shrimp.*

jump¹ /dʒʌmp/ *verb*
1 to push yourself up into the air or over something using your legs: *Her horse jumped over the fence easily.* | *Some fans tried to jump onto the stage with the band.* | *Karen was waving her arms and jumping up and down* (=jumping many times) *with excitement.*

THESAURUS: jump

skip to move forward with little jumps between your steps: *Tammy skipped along ahead of her mother.*

hop to move by jumping on one leg: *For one race, we had to hop on one foot to the tree and back.*

leap to jump high into the air or to jump over something: *The dog leaped over the fence.*

dive to jump into water with your head and arms going in first: *The swimmers dived into the water at the sound of the whistle.*

2 to drop down from a place that is above the ground: *The cat jumped down and came to meet us.* | *Some kids were jumping off the wall.*

3 to move somewhere quickly or suddenly: *Paul jumped up to help me with the grocery bags.*

4 if an amount jumps, it increases suddenly and by a large amount: *The population of Arizona has jumped 500% since 1950.*

5 make someone jump = if something makes you jump, it frightens you and your body makes a sudden movement: *A branch touched my arm in the dark and made me jump.*

6 jump to conclusions = to form an opinion about something before you have all the facts: *Don't jump to conclusions – we don't have all the information yet.*

PHRASAL VERB

jump at something
to eagerly accept the chance to do something: *Heidi jumped at the chance to go to Harvard.*

jump² *noun*
1 a movement in which you push yourself up into the air using your legs
2 a movement in which you drop from a place that is above the ground: *a parachute jump*
3 a sudden large increase in an amount:

J

There's been another big jump in gas prices; they went by up 20 cents.

jump•y /ˈdʒʌmpi/ *adjective*
worried or nervous because you are expecting something bad to happen: *We'd heard that there might be an attack, and everyone was jumpy.* SYNONYM **nervous**

junc•tion /ˈdʒʌŋkʃən/ *noun*
a place where one road, track, etc. joins another: *The bakery is near the junction of Highland Avenue and Lowell Street.* SYNONYM **intersection**

June /dʒun/ *noun, written abbreviation* **Jun.**
the sixth month of the year, between May and July: *Can you come to our party on June 24?* | *Janet was born in June.* | *Last June I got my driver's license.* | *Dad's going to Europe next June.*

jun•gle /ˈdʒʌŋgəl/ *noun*
a tropical forest with many trees and large plants growing very close together: *Many unusual plants and animals are found in the Amazon jungle.*
➔ See Thesaurus box at **tree**

J

junior[1] *noun*
a student in the third year of HIGH SCHOOL or college: *I'm a junior at Van Nuys High School.*

junior[2] *adjective*
1 Junior *or* **Jr.** used after the name of a man who has the same name as his father: *Martin Luther King, Jr.*
2 younger, less experienced, or of a lower rank: *Mark's a junior partner in the firm.* ANTONYM **senior**

ˌjunior ˈcollege *noun*
a college that people can go to, usually for two years, in order to learn a skill or to prepare to go to another college or university SYNONYM **community college**

ˌjunior ˈhigh school *also* **ˌjunior ˈhigh** *noun*
a school in the U.S. and Canada for students who are between 12 and 14 or 15 years old

junk /dʒʌŋk/ *noun*
old or unwanted things that have no use or value: *Let's have a yard sale and sell all that junk in the garage.*

ˈjunk food *noun, informal*
food that is not healthy because it has a lot of fat or sugar: *He just eats junk food like French fries and hamburgers.*

junk•ie /ˈdʒʌŋki/ *noun*
informal someone who is not able to stop taking illegal drugs such as HEROIN and COCAINE

ˈjunk mail *noun*
mail that companies send to your house in order to advertise a product
➔ See Thesaurus box at **advertisement**

Ju•pi•ter /ˈdʒupətɚ/ *noun*
the largest PLANET, which is fifth from the sun

ju•ry /ˈdʒʊri/ *noun* plural **juries**
a group of 12 people who listen to a case in court and decide whether someone is guilty of a crime

just[1] /dʒʌst/ *adverb*
1 exactly: *My brother looks just like me. People are always thinking I'm him.* | *These pants fit just right. They're perfect.* | *Just then the bus came around the corner.*
2 only: *You can't blame him, he's just a kid.* | *I'll be okay – I just need a good night's sleep.* | *He's making just enough money to pay his rent and bills, but he didn't have any left over.*
3 if something has just happened, it happened only a short time ago: *I just got back from Maria's house two minutes ago.* | *He just left, but he should be back soon.*
4 just about *informal* = almost: *I go to the gym just about every day.*
5 be just about to do something = if you are just about to do something, you are going to do it soon: *I was just about to call you.*
6 just before/after = only a short time before or after something else: *Theresa got home just before us.*
7 just (barely) = if something just happens, it does happen, but it almost did not: *Kurt just barely made it home before the storm.*
8 just a minute/second/moment = used in order to ask someone to wait for a short time while you do something: *Just a second – I'm on the phone.*
9 used for emphasizing something you are saying: *I just knew he was going to be late*

again. | *Just be quiet, will you?*
→ See Thesaurus box at **recently**

just² *adjective, formal*
morally right and fair: *He received a just punishment for his crimes.* ANTONYM **unjust**

jus·tice /'dʒʌstɪs/ *noun*
1 the action of treating people in a way that is fair and right: *He murdered their daughter, and they want justice.* ANTONYM **injustice**
2 the laws of a country and the way they are used: *the criminal justice system*
3 a judge in a court of law: *a Supreme Court justice*

ˌjustice of the 'peace *noun*
someone who judges law cases that are not serious, and who can perform marriages

jus·ti·fy /'dʒʌstəˌfaɪ/ Ac *verb* **justified**, third person singular **justifies**
to give a reason for doing something that other people think is not right: *How can you justify spending so much money on shoes, when you can't pay the rent?*
—**justifiable** *adjective* an action that is justifiable is done for good reasons: *Can killing someone ever be justifiable?*
—**justification** /ˌdʒʌstəfə'keɪʃən/ *noun* a reason someone gives for doing something that other people think is wrong: *Her justification for taking the money was that the people she stole it from were rich.*

ju·ve·nile /'dʒuvənl/ *adjective*
relating to children younger than about 16. This word is used only in legal language: *There has been an increase in juvenile crime* (=crimes done by young people).
—**juvenile** *noun* a child younger than about 16

ˌjuvenile de'linquent *noun, formal*
a person under the age of 18 who breaks rules or laws: *Juvenile delinquents are sent to a special jail for young people.*

Kk

K /keɪ/

1 *informal* 1,000: *He earns $50K* (=$50,000) *a year.*

2 the written abbreviation of **kilometer**: *a 10K race*

3 the written abbreviation of **kilobyte**

kan•ga•roo /ˌkæŋgəˈru/ *noun*
an animal from Australia that has strong back legs that it uses to jump, and that carries its babies in a pocket of skin on its stomach

ka•ra•te /kəˈrɑti/ *noun*
a sport from Japan in which you fight using your hands and feet to hit and kick

karate

kay•ak /ˈkaɪæk/ *noun*
a small closed boat with two pointed ends, for one or two people. You PADDLE (=move) it using a long stick with two large flat ends on both sides

keen /kin/ *adjective*
very interested in something or wanting to do it: *He read the story with keen interest.*
—**keenly** *adjective*

keep /kip/ *verb* **kept** /kept/

1 to have something and not give it to anyone else or not get rid of it: *You can keep that sweater – it's too small for me.* | *I kept all his old letters.*

2 to make someone or something continue to be in a place or situation: *The doctors kept him in the hospital for three days.* | *Put your coat on to keep warm.*

3 keep (on) doing something = to continue doing something: *It was noisy, but she kept on reading.*

4 to put something in the same place that you always put it: *We keep the glasses in that cupboard there.*

5 keep a record/diary etc. = to write down information regularly: *The teacher keeps a record of who was in class each day.*

6 keep your promise = to do what you have promised to do: *He said he'd meet her at the restaurant, but he didn't keep his promise.*

7 keep a secret = to not tell anyone something that you have promised not to tell: *"Can you keep a secret?" "Yes." "Well, Lisa really likes Danny, but don't tell her I told you."*

8 if food keeps, it stays fresh enough to be eaten: *Eggs keep better in the refrigerator.*

9 Keep Out! = used on signs to tell people that they are not allowed to go into a place

PHRASAL VERB

keep up

1 to do something as fast or as well as someone else: *The little boy had to run to keep up with his sisters.*

2 keep something up = to continue to do something: *Keep up the good work!*

keep•er /ˈkipɚ/ *noun*
someone whose job is to take care of something: *a zookeeper*

ken•nel /ˈkenl/ *noun*
a place where you can take your dog, so that someone will take care of it while you are away

kept /kept/ *verb*
the past tense and past participle of KEEP

ker•nel /ˈkɚnl/ *noun*
a seed that you can eat: *corn kernels*

ker•o•sene /ˈkerəˌsin/ *noun*
a type of oil that people burn for heat and light

ketch•up /ˈketʃəp/ *noun*
a red sauce made from tomatoes that you can put on different foods, for example HAMBURGERs: *Do you want ketchup on your fries?*

ket•tle /ˈketl/ *noun*
a metal container used for boiling and pouring water

key[1] /ki/ *noun*

1 a shaped piece of metal that you put into a lock to open or close it, or to start the engine of a car: *I can't find my car keys.* | *Do you have a key to the front door?*

2 the part of a computer or machine that you press to make it work or to write words: *Use the Control and S keys to save your work.*
3 the part of a musical instrument such as a piano that you press to make a sound: *a piano key*
4 a set of musical notes with a particular base note: *The song was in the key of C.*
5 the key = the most important thing that helps you do something: *Exercise is the key to a healthy body.*
→ See picture on page A20

key² *adjective*
very important and needed for success: *She's a key player on the basketball team. We couldn't win without her.*
→ See Thesaurus box at **important**

key•board /ˈkibɔrd/ *noun*
1 all the keys on a computer, piano, machine, etc. that you press to make it work
2 a musical instrument that is like a small electric piano
→ See picture on page A20

key•hole /ˈkihoʊl/ *noun*
the hole in a lock that you put a key in

ˈkey ring *noun*
a metal ring that you keep keys on

kg.
the written abbreviation of **kilogram**

kha•ki /ˈkæki/ *noun*
a light brown color
—**khaki** *adjective*

kha•kis /ˈkækiz/ *noun*
pants that are a light brown color

kick¹ /kɪk/ *verb*
1 to hit something with your foot: *Juan kicked the ball into the goal.*
2 to move your legs in the air: *The baby was kicking his legs.*
PHRASAL VERBS
kick off
informal to start an event: *The Cubs kicked off the baseball season with a win against the Cincinnati Reds.*
kick someone out *informal*
to make someone leave a place: *Sean was kicked out of school for cheating.*
→ See picture on page A4

kick² *noun*
1 an act of hitting something with your foot: *Evan's kick was good, and we scored the extra point.*
2 *informal* a strong feeling of excitement or pleasure: *He gets a kick out of hearing the kids laugh at his jokes.*

kick•off /ˈkɪk-ɔf/ *noun*
1 the time when a game of football or SOCCER starts: *The stadium opens at 2:00 and kickoff is at 3:00.*
2 the first kick in a game of football or SOCCER

kid¹ /kɪd/ *noun*
1 a child: *The kids were playing outside.* | *"Do you have any kids?" "Yes, I have two sons."*
2 a young goat
→ See Thesaurus box at **child**

kid² *verb* **kidded, kidding** *informal*
to say something as a joke: *"Did you really eat all those cookies?" "No, I was just kidding!"* | *"He's always late." "No kidding* (=said when something could be a joke, but is true)*."* | *"The bear came right into our campsite!" "You're kidding* (=said when something is surprising but true)*!"*

kid•nap /ˈkɪdnæp/ *verb* **kidnapped, kidnapping** *also* **kidnaped, kidnaping**
to take someone away using force: *The group kidnapped the son of a rich man and asked for money.*
—**kidnapper** *noun* someone who kidnaps people
—**kidnapping** *noun* the crime of kidnapping people

kid•ney /ˈkɪdni/ *noun* plural **kidneys**
a part of your body that cleans waste liquid from your blood. You have two kidneys, and they are inside your body close to your lower back.
→ See picture on page A2

kill /kɪl/ *verb*
1 to make a person, plant, or animal die: *Her son was killed in the war.* | *If you don't water the plants, you'll kill them.*

THESAURUS: kill

murder to deliberately kill someone: *He murdered his wife.*

K

commit manslaughter to kill someone when you did not plan to do it: *The gun went off accidentally and killed his friend, so he was charged with committing manslaughter.*
commit suicide to deliberately kill yourself: *She committed suicide after her boyfriend left her.*
assassinate to deliberately kill an important person: *He tried to assassinate the president.*
slaughter/massacre to kill a lot of people in a violent way, especially when they cannot defend themselves: *People in the town, including women and children, were slaughtered by the soldiers.*
execute to kill someone as a punishment for a crime: *He was executed for kidnapping and killing a little boy.*

2 *informal* to be very angry at someone: *My mom will kill me if I'm late again.*

kill•er /ˈkɪlɚ/ *noun*
a person, animal, or thing that kills: *Police are still looking for the girl's killer.*

ki•lo /ˈkiloʊ/ *noun* plural **kilos**
an abbreviation of **kilogram**

ki•lo•byte /ˈkɪləˌbaɪt/ *noun*
k a unit for measuring computer information, which is around 1,000 BYTEs

kil•o•gram /ˈkɪləˌgræm/ *also* **kilo** *noun*
written abbreviation **kg** a unit for measuring weight, equal to 1,000 grams

ki•lom•e•ter /kɪˈlɑmətɚ/ *noun*
written abbreviation **km** a unit for measuring length, equal to 1,000 meters

kil•o•watt /ˈkɪləˌwɑt/ *noun*
written abbreviation **kW** a unit for measuring electrical power, equal to 1,000 WATTs

kin /kɪn/ *noun*
your family: *The police are trying to find the dead man's next of kin* (=closest relative).

kind[1] /kaɪnd/ *noun*
1 a type of person or thing: *"What kind of dog is that?" "It's an English Sheepdog."* | *I like all kinds of music – hip hop, rock, jazz, country, and other kinds too.* SYNONYM **sort, type**
2 kind of *informal* = a little bit: *I felt kind of scared.* | *It's kind of hard to explain the story.* SYNONYM **slightly**

kind[2] *adjective*
helpful, friendly, and nice to other people: *Our neighbors were very kind to us when we moved into our new house; they even made us dinner!*

THESAURUS: kind

nice friendly and kind: *My new roommate seems really nice.*
considerate *formal* a considerate person thinks about what other people feel or need: *The neighbors are very considerate; they don't play their music too loud.*
thoughtful thinking of things you can do to make other people happy: *He brought her flowers when she wasn't feeling well, which was really thoughtful.*

—**kindly** *adverb*: *She kindly drove me home.*
—**kindness** *noun*: *She showed kindness to anyone who needed help.*

kin•der•gar•ten /ˈkɪndɚˌgɑrtn/ *noun*
a class in school for children who are about five years old. Children go to kindergarten before they start first grade.

king /kɪŋ/ *noun*
a man who is the ruler of a country because he is from a royal family: *King George III was king of England during the American Revolution.*

king•dom /ˈkɪŋdəm/ *noun*
a country that has a king or queen

ˈking-size *also* **ˈking-sized** *adjective*
the largest size that something can be: *All the hotel rooms have a king-size bed.*

kiss /kɪs/ *verb*
to touch someone with your lips, to show that you love him or her or when you say hello or goodbye: *She and her boyfriend started kissing.* | *She kissed me on the cheek.*
—**kiss** *noun* the act of kissing someone: *Her mother gave her a kiss on the forehead.*

kit /kɪt/ *noun*
1 a set of tools or equipment that you keep together and that you use to do something: *There are some bandages in the first-aid kit.*
2 a set of pieces that you put together to make something: *a model airplane kit*

kitch•en /ˈkɪtʃən/ *noun*
the room where you cook food: *Jay's in the kitchen washing the dishes.*

kite /kaɪt/ *noun*
a toy that you fly in the air on the end of a long string

kit•ten /ˈkɪtn/ *noun*
a young cat

kit•ty /ˈkɪti/ *also* **kit•ty•cat** /ˈkɪtiˌkæt/ *noun* plural **kitties** *informal*
a cat: *Here, kitty kitty! Here's your food.*

ki•wi /ˈkiwi/ *also* **ˈkiwi fruit** *noun*
a soft green fruit with small black seeds and a thin brown skin
➔ See picture on page A13

Kleen•ex /ˈklineks/ *noun, trademark*
a piece of soft thin paper, that you use to clean your nose or dry your eyes: *She was crying, so I handed her a Kleenex.* SYNONYM **tissue**

km.
the written abbreviation of **kilometer**

knack /næk/ *noun, informal*
the ability to do something well: *Kelly has a knack for learning languages – she speaks Chinese, Greek, and French.*
➔ See Thesaurus box at **ability**

knead /nid/ *verb*
to press a bread mixture with your hands to make it ready to cook: *Knead the dough for ten minutes.*
➔ See picture on page A14

knee /ni/ *noun*
1 the middle part of your leg, where it can bend: *I got on my knees to look under the bed* (=with my legs bent and my knees on the floor).
2 the part of your pants that covers your knee: *Billy's jeans had holes in both knees.*
➔ See picture on page A2

knee•cap /ˈnikæp/ *noun*
the bone at the front of your knee
➔ See picture on page A2

ˌknee-ˈdeep *adjective*
deep enough to reach your knees: *The water was knee-deep.*

kneel /nil/ *also* **kneel down** *verb* **knelt** /nelt/ or **kneeled**
to put your knees on the ground, so that they are supporting your body: *She knelt down beside the bed to pray.*
➔ See picture on page A4

knew /nu/ *verb*
the past tense of KNOW

knife /naɪf/ *noun* plural **knives** /naɪvz/
a tool used to cut things or as a weapon. It has a sharp metal part and a handle: *Mom cut up the chicken with a knife.*
➔ See picture on page A9

knight /naɪt/ *noun*
a soldier in Medieval times, who fought while riding a horse

knit /nɪt/ *verb* **knit** or **knitted, knitting**
to make clothes out of thick thread using long pointed sticks: *Grandma is knitting a sweater.*
—**knitting** *noun*
something you are making that you knit: *We learned sewing and knitting from our mother.*

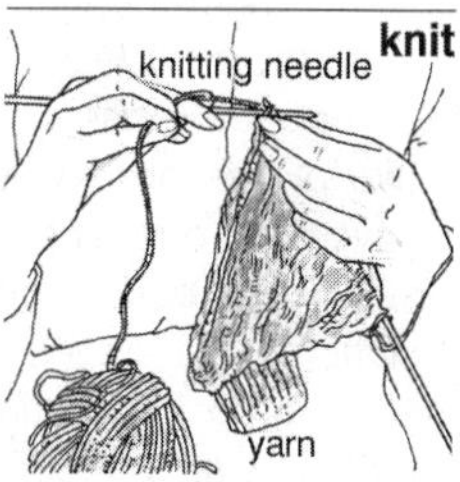

knob /nɑb/ *noun*
a round handle that you pull or turn to open a door, turn on a radio, etc.: *I tried to turn the knob, but the door was locked and it wouldn't move.*

knock¹ /nɑk/ *verb*
1 to hit a door or window with your hand to make a noise and get someone's attention: *I knocked on the door for five minutes, but nobody answered.*
2 to hit something hard so that it moves or falls down: *The dog knocked the phone off the table.*
3 knock it off *informal* = used to tell someone to stop doing something that is annoying you: *Hey, knock it off! I'm on the phone.*

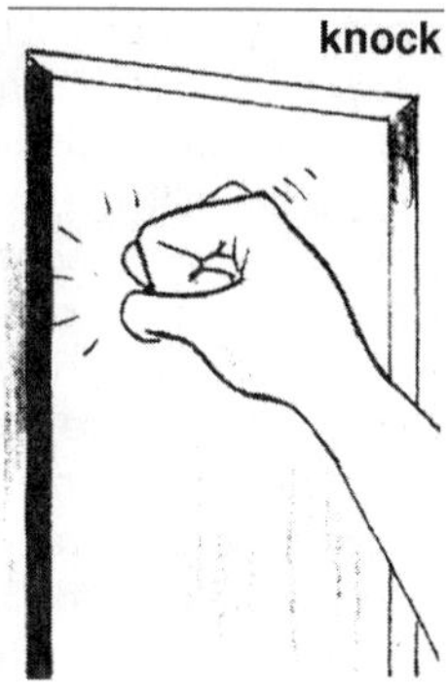

K

PHRASAL VERBS

knock something down
to hit or push something so that it falls to the ground: *The wind was so strong it knocked down trees.*

knock someone out
to hit someone hard so that he or she falls down and cannot get up: *The boxer knocked his opponent out in the fifth round.*
➔ See Thesaurus box at **hit**[1]
➔ See picture on page A3

knock[2] *noun*
the sound that is made by hitting something hard: *There was a loud knock on the door.*

knock•out /ˈnɑk-aʊt/ *noun*
an act of hitting someone so hard in the sport of BOXING that he falls down and cannot get up again

knot /nɑt/ *noun*
1 the place where you have tied together two pieces of rope or string, or where you have tied one end of a piece of rope or string: *We learned how to tie knots for rock climbing.* | *There's a knot in my shoelace.*
2 a unit for measuring the speed of a ship, that is equal to 6,080 feet or 1,853 meters in an hour
—**knot** *verb* to tie something in a knot: *She knotted the scarf around her neck.*

K

know /noʊ/ *verb* **knew** /nu/ **known** /noʊn/
1 to have information about something in your mind: *Do you know the answer?* | *Doctors don't really know much about the disease.* | *We don't know what we're supposed to be doing.* | *I knew that Andy would help us.* | *"Is Bob coming?" "I don't know."*
2 know how to do something = to be able to do something: *By age six, most kids know how to tie their shoes.*
3 if you know a person or place, you have met him or her or been there before: *I've known Ben since I was three years old.* | *She's lived in Chicago for ten years and knows the city pretty well.* | *This game will help us all get to know each other better* (=find out about each other).
4 you know a) people use this when they cannot quickly think of what to say next: *Then I said, you know, let's go to the movies on Friday.* **b)** used to make sure that someone understands what you are saying or that he or she is listening: *She just seems so angry all the time, you know?* **c)** used when you want to start talking about something: *You know Rita's cat? He hurt his foot.*
5 I know (what you mean) = used to say that you agree with or understand what someone is saying: *"Science was so boring today!" "I know."*
6 as far as I know = said when you think something is true, but you are not sure: *Tom's never been married, as far as I know.*
7 know better = to be old enough or have done something often enough that you understand that you should not do something: *You know better than to play ball in the house!*

WORD FAMILY look at the words:
➔ **know** *verb*
➔ **knowledge** *noun*
➔ **knowledgeable** *adjective*
➔ **known** *adjective*
➔ **unknown** *adjective*

ˈ**know-how** *noun, informal*
the knowledge or ability you need to do something: *He has the technical know-how to keep the computers working.*

knowl•edge /ˈnɑlɪdʒ/ *noun*
the information and understanding about something that you have in your mind: *Laura's knowledge of Spanish helped her get a job.*
—**knowledgeable** *adjective* having a lot of knowledge about something: *He's very knowledgeable about fixing cars and has helped me repair my car many times.*

known[1] /noʊn/ *verb*
the past participle of KNOW

known[2] *adjective*
if someone or something is known, many people know about them: *Ansel Adams is known for his photographs of Yosemite National Park.* SYNONYM **famous**

knuck•le /ˈnʌkəl/ *noun*
one of the places where your fingers can bend, including the places where they join your hand
➔ See picture at **hand**[1]

ko•a•la /koʊˈɑlə/ *also* **koˈala bear** *noun*
an Australian animal that looks like a small bear and that climbs trees and eats leaves

Ko•ran /kə'ræn/ *noun*
the Koran = the holy book of the Muslim religion

Ko•re•an[1] /kə'riən/ *adjective*
from Korea

Korean[2] *noun*
1 someone from Korea
2 the language spoken in Korea

ko•sher /'kouʃɚ/ *adjective*
kosher food is prepared according to Jewish law

ku•dos /'kudous/ *noun*
praise for doing something well: *The newspaper gave kudos to Jim Carrey for an excellent performance.*

kung fu /ˌkʌŋ 'fu/ *noun*
a sport from China in which you fight using your hands and feet to hit and kick

kW
the written abbreviation of **kilowatt**

Ll

lab /læb/ *noun, informal*
a LABORATORY

label

la·bel¹ /ˈleɪbəl/ Ac *noun*
a piece of paper or cloth that is attached to something and has information written on it: *Always read the instructions on the label before taking any medicine.*

label² *verb*
1 to put a label on something or write information on it: *We labeled each toy box with what was inside it: cars, blocks, dolls.*
2 to always use a particular word to describe someone even if it is not a true or fair way to describe them: *The teachers labeled him "a lazy student" and stopped trying to help him.*

la·bor¹ /ˈleɪbɚ/ Ac *noun*
1 hard work that you do using your body and hands: *He did a lot of manual labor* (=physical work) *to earn money, especially mowing lawns and raking leaves.*
2 all the people who work for a company or in a country: *The car industry needs skilled labor* (=employees who have been trained to do a job).
3 if a woman is in labor, she is pushing a baby out of her body

labor² *verb, formal*
to work very hard: *Farmers labored in the fields.*

lab·ora·to·ry /ˈlæbrəˌtɔri/ *also* **lab** *noun*
plural **laboratories**
a room or building in which scientists work: *Scientists in the laboratory are working on drugs to help cancer patients.*

L

ˈLabor Day *noun*
a holiday on the first Monday in September that shows respect for people who work

ˈlabor ˌunion *noun*
an organization that helps workers in a particular job get better pay, health insurance, money for when they stop working, etc.: *The labor union wants to make sure employees receive better healthcare.* SYNONYM **union**

lab·y·rinth /ˈlæbəˌrɪnθ/ *noun*
another word for a MAZE

lace¹ /leɪs/ *noun*
1 a type of cloth that has a pattern made of very small holes in it: *The wedding dress was covered with lace.*
2 a string that you tie your shoes with: *His laces were untied.* SYNONYM **shoelace**

lace² *also* **lace up** *verb*
to fasten something by tying a lace: *Paul put on his boots and laced them up.*

lack¹ /læk/ *noun*
the state of not having something, or of not having enough of something: *A lack of money stops these families from finding better places to live.*

lack² *verb, formal*
to not have something, or to not have enough of it: *He wants to go to college, but he lacks grades that are good enough.*

lad·der /ˈlædɚ/ *noun*
1 a piece of equipment that you use to climb up to high places, made of two long pieces of metal or wood with bars between them that you use as steps: *The painter climbed up the ladder to reach the top of the wall.*
2 a series of jobs in which each job is better than the one before, so that you get more power and money: *Nelson worked hard to climb the company ladder and get a job in management.*

ˈladies' room *noun*
a room in a public building with toilets for women

la·dle /ˈleɪdl/ *noun*
a deep spoon with a long handle, that you use to put soup into bowls
—**ladle** *verb Mom ladled the soup into each bowl.*

la·dy /ˈleɪdi/ *noun* plural **ladies**
1 a polite word for a woman: *Ladies and gentlemen, thank you for coming this evening.*
2 *informal* said when talking to a woman you do not know in an impolite way: *Hey, lady, hurry up!*

la·dy·bug /ˈleɪdiˌbʌg/ *noun*
a small insect that has red or orange wings with black spots on them

lag /læg/ *verb* **lagged, lagging**
to move or achieve things more slowly than other things or people: *Jonathan walked slowly and lagged behind the rest of the kids climbing the hill.*

la·goon /ləˈgun/ *noun*
an area of ocean that has land almost all the way around it

laid /leɪd/ *verb*
the past tense and past participle of LAY

ˌlaid-ˈback *adjective*
relaxed and not worried about anything: *My teacher is pretty laid-back. He likes to have fun in class.*

lain /leɪn/ *verb*
the past participle of LIE

lake /leɪk/ *noun*
a large area of water with land all around it: *We're going swimming in the lake.* | *Lake Michigan*

lake·front /ˈleɪkfrʌnt/ *noun*
the land next to a lake: *They built a house on the lakefront so they could go boating and fishing whenever they wanted to.*

lamb /læm/ *noun*
a young sheep, or the meat of a young sheep

lame /leɪm/ *adjective*
1 *informal* silly or not very good: *The jokes were lame, and no one laughed.*
2 *formal* not able to walk easily because your leg or foot is hurt: *The horse was lame; it had cut its leg on a fence.*

lamp /læmp/ *noun*
an object that produces light, which you put on a table or that stands on the floor: *She turned on the lamp to read.*
➔ See picture at **light**[1]

lamp·shade /ˈlæmpʃeɪd/ *noun*
a cloth or plastic cover over the light of a lamp that the light shines through
➔ See picture on page A8

land[1] /lænd/ *noun*
1 an area of ground, which people can own or use for farming: *Three houses will be built on the land.* | *Mr. Peterson owns the land near the river and grows crops there.*
2 the part of the Earth that is not covered by water: *Frogs live on land and in the water.*
3 *formal* a country or place: *They came to America from many lands.*
➔ See Thesaurus boxes at **earth** and **country**

land

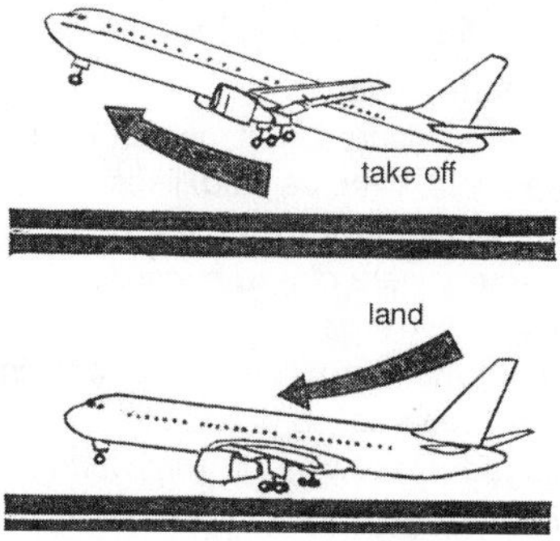

land[2] *verb*
1 to arrive somewhere in a boat or airplane: *Airplanes land and take off from the airport every few minutes.*
2 to fall onto something after moving through the air: *Chris slipped and landed on his back.*
➔ See Thesaurus box at **arrive**

land·ing /ˈlændɪŋ/ *noun*
the landing of an airplane or boat is when it arrives on land: *The plane made a safe landing.* ANTONYM **takeoff**

land·la·dy /ˈlændˌleɪdi/ *noun* plural **landladies**
a woman who owns the house or apartment that you rent

land·lord /ˈlændlɔrd/ *noun*
someone who owns the house or apartment that you rent

land·mark /ˈlændmɑrk/ *noun*
1 something that helps you know where you are, such as a famous building: *The Empire State Building is a famous landmark in New York.*

L

2 an important event: *The discovery of penicillin was a landmark in the history of medicine.*

land•own•er /ˈlændˌoʊnɚ/ *noun, formal*
someone who owns a lot of land

land•scape /ˈlændskeɪp/ *noun*
a view across an area of land: *The snow changed the landscape, making it seem soft and beautiful.*

land•slide /ˈlændslaɪd/ *noun*
1 a landslide is when a lot of dirt and rocks fall down the side of a hill or mountain: *Part of the highway is blocked by a landslide.*
2 a defeat in which someone wins an election by a very large number of votes: *Wilson won in a landslide – he had twice as many votes as his closest opponent.*

lane /leɪn/ *noun*
1 one of the long narrow areas that a road is divided into with painted lines, and along which people drive their cars: *Three lanes of the freeway were closed because of an accident.*
2 one of the narrow areas that a swimming pool or race track is divided into, and along which people swim or run during races: *Johnson will be running in lane 4.*
➔ See Thesaurus box at **road**

lan•guage /ˈlæŋgwɪdʒ/ *noun*
1 the words and grammar that people who live in a country use when they talk to each other: *the English language* | *"Do you speak any foreign languages?" "Yes, I speak Arabic."*

THESAURUS: language

dialect *formal* a form of a language that is spoken in one area, which is different from the way it is spoken in other areas: *Cantonese is only one of many Chinese dialects.*

accent a way of pronouncing words that someone has because of where he or she was born or lives: *She has a strong Southern accent.*

slang very informal spoken words: *Teenagers sometimes use slang that their parents don't understand.*

jargon technical words and phrases used by people who are doing the same type of work: *I couldn't understand the computer book; it was full of technical jargon.*

2 the type of words that someone uses: *In my classroom, I don't allow bad language* (=swear words). | *He described the experiment using scientific language* (=special words that scientists use, which people do not usually use).
3 a system used to give instructions to a computer: *Java is a computer programming language often used in making websites.*

lan•tern /ˈlæntɚn/ *noun*
a type of lamp you can carry, that has a metal frame and glass sides: *He used the lantern to find his way to the tent.*
➔ See picture at **light**[1]

lap[1] /læp/ *noun*
1 the flat area that the tops of your legs make when you are sitting down: *The little girl was sitting on her mother's lap.*
2 one trip around a race track, or a trip from one end of a swimming pool to the other: *Patty swims 30 laps every day.*

lap[2] *also* **lap up** *verb* **lapped, lapping**
if an animal laps a drink, it drinks it by touching it with its tongue: *The cat lapped up the milk.*

la•pel /ləˈpel/ *noun*
part of one of the front edges of a coat which is folded back: *He wore a pin on his lapel.*

lapse /læps/ *noun, formal*
a short period of time when you forget something or do not do something you should: *There was a lapse in security at the airport, and a man with a gun got on the plane.*

lap•top /ˈlæptɑp/ *also* **ˌlaptop comˈputer** *noun*
a small computer that you can carry with you
➔ See picture on page A20

lar•ce•ny /ˈlɑrsəni/ *noun, formal*
the crime of stealing something

large /lɑrdʒ/ *adjective*
big in size, number, or amount: *a large pizza* | *The high school has 1,500 students, so it is much larger than the middle school.* ANTONYM **small**
➔ See Thesaurus box at **big**

large•ly /ˈlɑrdʒli/ *adverb*
mostly or mainly: *Grizzly bears largely eat fruit and plants, but will also eat meat.*

lark /lɑrk/ *noun*
a small wild brown bird that sings and has long pointed wings

lar•va /ˈlɑrvə/ *noun* plural **larvae** /ˈlɑrvi/
a young insect with a soft body and no wings, that will become an insect with wings later in its life

la•ser /ˈleɪzɚ/ *noun*
a piece of equipment that produces a powerful narrow beam of light: *Doctors can use lasers to correct your eyesight.*

lash /læʃ/ *noun*
an EYELASH

lasso

las•so /ˈlæsoʊ/ *noun*
a rope with one end tied in a circle, used for catching cows and horses
—**lasso** *verb* to catch a cow or horse using a lasso

last¹ /læst/ *adjective*
1 most recent, or happening just before the one happening now: *The last time we played tennis, you won.* | *I saw Tim last week.*
2 at the end, after everyone or everything else: *We were last in line for tickets.* | *When is the last day of school?* | *He dies in the last chapter of the book.*
3 the last one is the only one that is still there from a group: *Do you want the last piece of cake?*
4 the last person/thing = a person or thing that you do not expect or want at all: *He's the last person I'd want to go on a date with!*

last² *verb*
1 to continue to happen for a period of time: *The meeting lasted only ten minutes.*
2 if something lasts, it continues to be in good condition and you can use it: *Most batteries will last for up to 8 hours before they need to be recharged.*

last³ *adverb*
1 most recently before now: *"When did you see her last?" "Three days ago."*
2 after everything or everyone else: *I run as fast as I can, but I always finish last.*
3 last but not least = said to show that the last thing you say is just as important as the other things you have said: *Last but not least, I'd like to thank my mother for all the help she has given me.*

last⁴ *noun*
1 at last = after a long time: *The rain stopped at last.*
2 the last = the person or thing that is after all the others: *Joe was the last to go to bed that night.*

last•ing /ˈlæstɪŋ/ *adjective*
continuing for a long time: *We have a lasting friendship – we've known each other 25 years.*

last•ly /ˈlæstli/ *adverb, formal*
used when telling someone the last thing you want to say: *Lastly, I'd like to thank you all for coming.*

ˈlast-ˌminute *adjective*
done or happening at the end of a period of time: *Lucas made some last-minute changes to his paper before he gave it to the teacher.*

ˈlast name *noun*
your family's name, which in English comes after your other names: *I think Julio's last name is Martinez.*

latch /lætʃ/ *noun*
a small metal object that keeps a door, gate, or window closed

late /leɪt/ *adjective, adverb*
1 after the usual or expected time: *She was late for school and got in trouble again.* | *Our flight got to Houston two hours late, so we missed our next flight.*
2 near the end of a period of time: *The house was built in the late 19th century.* | *The team finally scored late in the game.*
3 at night, or near the end of the day: *It's late and I'm tired.* | *the late show on TV*

late•ly /ˈleɪtli/ *adverb*
recently: *"Have you seen Barbara lately?" "No, not for several months."* | *Lately, I've been really busy.*
➔ See Thesaurus box at recently

L

lat•er¹ /ˈleɪtɚ/ *adverb*
1 after the time now, or after the time you are talking about: *I'll see you later.* | *They met in July, and only two months later they got married.*
2 later on = at some time in the future, or after something else: *She said she'd meet you later on this evening.*
→ See Thesaurus box at **after**

later² *adjective*
1 coming in the future, or after something else: *You can freeze the soup and use it at a later time.*
2 more recent: *Later models of the car are much improved.*

lat•est /ˈleɪtəst/ *adjective*
most recent: *I like to know the latest news, so I buy a newspaper every day.*
→ See Thesaurus box at **new**

La•tin /ˈlætn/ *noun*
an old language, used in science, law, and medicine: *The names of each plant are given in Latin.*

ˌLatin Aˈmerica *noun*
all the countries in Central America and South America
—**Latin American** *adjective* from or in Latin America: *Latin American art*

lat•i•tude /ˈlætəˌtud/ *noun*
formal the distance north or south of the EQUATOR (=an imaginary line around the middle of the Earth): *New York City is on the same latitude as Naples, Italy.*

lat•ter /ˈlætɚ/ *noun*
the latter *formal* = the second of two people or things that someone talks about: *There was tea and coffee, and I chose the latter* (=coffee).

laugh¹ /læf/ *verb*
to make a sound with your voice because you think something is funny: *No one laughs at my jokes.* | *We made her laugh by telling funny stories.*

> **THESAURUS: laugh**
>
> **giggle** to laugh quickly in a high voice: *The girls were giggling about something that had happened at school.*
>
> **chuckle** to laugh quietly: *Jim waved at her and made a silly face, and she chuckled.*
>
> **snicker** to laugh quietly in a way that is not nice: *"Stop pushing me!" she shouted, and some of the kids snickered.*

PHRASAL VERB
laugh at someone
to make jokes about someone in a way that upsets him or her: *Other kids laughed at him because he couldn't read.*

laugh² *noun*
the sound you make when you laugh: *"That's funny!" he said, with a laugh.*

laugh•ter /ˈlæftɚ/ *noun*
the sound of people laughing: *When he finished the joke, the audience roared with laughter* (=laughed very loudly).

launch /lɔntʃ/ *verb*
1 to start an important new plan or activity: *The school launched a campaign against smoking.*
2 to send a space vehicle into space: *They launched the space shuttle from Cape Canaveral.*
3 to put a boat or ship into the water: *The ship was launched in 1911.*

laun•dro•mat /ˈlɔndrəˌmæt/ *noun*
a place where you pay to wash your clothes in a machine

laun•dry /ˈlɔndri/ *noun*
1 clothes and sheets that you need to wash: *Did you do the laundry* (=wash clothes and sheets)?
2 clothes and sheets that you have washed: *a pile of clean laundry*

la•va /ˈlɑvə/ *noun*
hot liquid rock that comes out of the top of a mountain: *Lava flowed out of the volcano.*

lav•a•to•ry /ˈlævəˌtɔri/ *noun* plural **lavatories** *formal*
a room with a toilet, in a public building or airplane

lav•en•der /ˈlævəndɚ/ *noun*
a plant with purple flowers that have a pleasant smell

law /lɔ/ *noun*
1 the law = the system of rules in a country: *Driving without a seatbelt on is against the law* (=illegal). | *If you buy stolen goods you are breaking the law* (=doing something illegal).
2 a rule that everyone in a country must obey, and if they do not, they might be

L

punished by a court: *There is a law against driving too fast.*

3 the study of legal systems: *I'd like to study law.*

➔ See Thesaurus box at **rule**[1]

law•a•bid•ing /ˈlɔ əˌbaɪdɪŋ/ *adjective, formal*

a law-abiding person always obeys the law: *I am a law-abiding citizen – I have never gotten into trouble with the police.*

law•ful /ˈlɔfəl/ *adjective, formal*

allowed by the law: *He made his money through lawful means* (=doing legal things). SYNONYM **legal**; ANTONYM **illegal**

lawn /lɔn/ *noun*

an area of grass around a house or building: *Dad was mowing the lawn* (=cutting the grass).

ˈlawn ˌmower *noun*

a machine for cutting grass

law•suit /ˈlɔsut/ *noun*

formal a problem that someone takes to a court of law so that a judge can decide who is right and who is wrong: *They filed a lawsuit against the building company when it did not complete its work.*

law•yer /ˈlɔyɚ/ *noun*

someone whose job is to advise people about the law, and speak for them in court: *My lawyer told me not to give them any money until they sign the papers.* SYNONYM **attorney**

➔ See picture on page A16

lay[1] /leɪ/ *verb* **laid** /leɪd/

1 to put something in a particular place: *She laid her coat over a chair.* | *He laid the baby on the bed.*

2 to put or attach something in the correct place on the ground: *We are laying carpet in the living room.*

3 if a bird or insect lays eggs, eggs come out of its body: *The hen laid an egg.*

PHRASAL VERBS

lay someone off

if a company lays off employees, it stops employing them because it does not have enough work for them: *The company had to lay off 25 workers when business got slowed down.*

lay something out

1 to spread something out so that it is lying flat: *Pam laid out her dress for the party on the bed.*

2 to explain or describe an idea with all the details: *The mayor laid out her plans for building two new parks downtown.*

lay[2] *verb*

the past tense of LIE

USAGE: lay

Lay means to put something down in a flat position. The past tense for this is **laid**: *She laid the newspaper down and picked up the phone.*

Lie has two different meanings:

– to be or move into a flat position on the floor, a bed, etc.: *She was lying on the sofa.*

The past tense for this meaning of lie is **lay**: *He lay on the bed.*

– to say something that is not true: *Why did you lie to me?*

The past tense for this meaning of lie is **lied**: *The police think that he lied.*

lay•er /ˈleɪɚ/ Ac *noun*

1 an amount of something that covers a surface: *No one had been there for months, and there was a thick layer of dust on the table.*

2 something that you put on or between other things: *It was cold, so we wore several layers of clothing.*

lay•off /ˈleɪɔf/ *noun*

the act of ending someone's employment, because there is not enough work for them: *The factory closed down, and there were about 100 layoffs.*

lay•out /ˈleɪaʊt/ *noun*

the way things are arranged in a place or on a page: *We changed the layout of our bedroom, and put the bed under the window.* | *a newspaper's page layout*

la•zy /ˈleɪzi/ *adjective* **lazier**, **laziest**

1 not wanting to work or make any effort: *Tom is so lazy; he never helps with the housework.*

2 a lazy time is spent relaxing and not doing any work: *We spent a lazy day at the pool.* ANTONYM **busy**

—**laziness** *noun* the quality of being lazy: *She complained about his laziness, saying all he did was watch TV.*

L

lb.
the written abbreviation of **pound**: *I weigh 140 lbs.*

lead[1] /lid/ *verb* **led** /lɛd/
1 to show someone the way somewhere, by walking in front of him or her: *You lead, and we'll follow.* | *He led his horse to the barn.* ANTONYM **follow**
2 to go in front of a group of people or vehicles: *Our town's high school band is leading the parade.*
3 if a road, path, or door leads somewhere, you can get there by using it: *This road leads to Springfield.* SYNONYM **go**
4 to be winning a game or competition: *Our team was leading 8–0.*
5 to control an activity or a group of people: *Who is leading the investigation?*
6 to be more successful at an activity than other companies, countries, or people: *Our company leads the world in making cars.*
7 lead a ... life = to have a particular kind of life: *It's hard to lead a normal life when you're famous.*

PHRASAL VERBS
lead to something
to make something happen or exist: *The new factory has led to a lot of new jobs.*
lead up to something
to come before something: *In the days leading up to her operation she was very nervous.* ANTONYM **follow**

WORD FAMILY look at the words:
→ **lead** *verb*
→ **leader** *noun*
→ **leadership** *noun*

lead[2] *noun*
1 a position in front of other people or vehicles: *Barron is still in the lead, but the race is only half finished.*
2 the amount by which one person is ahead of another in a competition or race: *We are in first place with a lead of ten points.*
3 a piece of information that may help you discover something: *The police got an important lead when someone reported seeing a tall man near the murder scene.*

lead[3] /lɛd/ *noun*
1 a heavy gray metal: *lead pipes*
2 the gray substance in a pencil that makes marks when you write: *The lead on my pencil broke.*

lead•er /ˈlidɚ/ *noun*
1 someone who leads or controls other people: *The meeting will be attended by all the world leaders* (=people who lead countries' governments).
2 the person or team that is winning a race or competition: *She was the leader for the first half of the race.*
—**leadership** *noun* the quality of being good at leading people

lead•ing /ˈlidɪŋ/ *adjective*
1 *formal* most important or most successful: *The director liked him, and he got a leading part in the play.* | *the team's leading scorer*
2 a leading lady/man = the actor who has the most important female or male part in a movie: *Julia Roberts is the leading lady in many movies.*

leaf /lif/ *noun* plural **leaves** /livz/
one of the flat green parts of a plant or tree that grow from its stem or branches: *There are still some leaves on the trees, but most of them have fallen off.*

leaf•let /ˈliflɪt/ *noun*
a piece of paper with information or an advertisement printed on it: *They gave out leaflets in the street, inviting people to join their church.*

league /lig/ *noun*
1 a group of teams in a particular sport that play against each other every year in order to see who is best: *How many teams are in the National Football League?*
2 a group of people or countries that have joined together to work for a special aim: *the League of Women Voters*

leak[1] /lik/ *verb*
1 if something leaks, liquid or gas comes out of a hole in it where it is broken or damaged: *The roof leaks when it rains, and we need to get it fixed.* | *Gas was leaking out of the pipes.*
2 to give secret information to a newspaper or television company, so that people find out about something: *Details of the president's speech were leaked to reporters.*
—**leakage** *noun* liquid or gas that leaks from something

—**leaky** *adjective* something that is leaky is leaking

→ See Thesaurus box at **pour**

leak² *noun*

leak

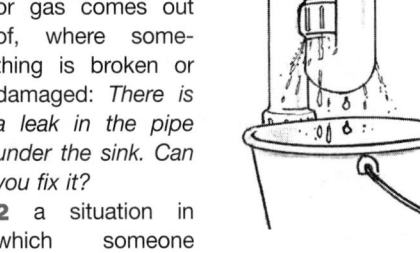

1 a hole that liquid or gas comes out of, where something is broken or damaged: *There is a leak in the pipe under the sink. Can you fix it?*

2 a situation in which someone gives secret information to a newspaper or television company, so that people find out about something: *No one knew about the deal until there was a leak from the White House.*

→ See Thesaurus box at **hole**

lean¹ /lin/ *verb*

1 to bend your body in a particular position: *She leaned forward to kiss him.*

2 to rest your body against something: *He was leaning against his car. | She leaned on her cane as she walked.*

3 to put something against something else to support it: *He leaned the ladder against the wall.*

PHRASAL VERB

lean toward something

to slightly prefer one thing when you are trying to choose from several things: *She's leaning toward majoring in history, but she hasn't decided for sure yet.*

lean

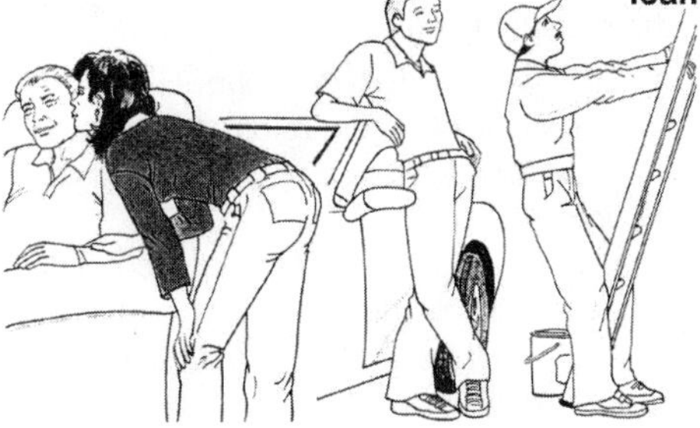

lean² *adjective*

1 thin in a healthy way: *His body was lean and athletic.* ANTONYM **fat**

2 lean meat does not have much fat on it ANTONYM **fatty**

→ See Thesaurus box at **thin**

leap /lip/ *verb* **leaped** or **leapt** /lept/

to jump into the air or to jump over something: *The dog leaped over the fence. | Jon leapt up from the chair to answer the phone.*

—**leap** *noun* an act of leaping: *With one leap, she crossed the stream.*

→ See Thesaurus box at **jump¹**

→ See picture at **jump¹**

ˈleap year *noun*

a year when February has 29 days instead of 28, which happens every four years

learn /lɚn/ *verb*

1 to study or practice a subject or activity so that you know about it or know how to do it: *I am learning to speak German. | We learned about electricity in school.*

> **USAGE: learn**
>
> You **learn** a subject or skill when you study or practice it: *I want to learn English. | Jo's learning to drive.*
>
> If you **teach** someone a subject or skill, you help him or her learn it: *Dad taught me to play the guitar.*
>
> You cannot say "Dad learned me to play the guitar."

2 to know something very well so it is easy to remember, by reading or repeating it many times: *She learned the poem and read it in front of the class.*

learn·ing /ˈlɚnɪŋ/ *noun*

the process of learning: *Learning is fun if new information is taught correctly. | Children with learning difficulties take a long time to learn to read.*

lease /lis/ *noun*

a legal agreement that allows you to live in a building or do business from it for a period of time: *The company signed a five-year lease on their new offices.*

—**lease** *verb* to have a lease on something

leash /liʃ/ *noun*

a piece of rope or leather that you attach to a dog's collar and hold when you take the dog for a walk: *Please keep your dog on a leash.*

least /list/ *pronoun, adverb, adjective*

1 less than anything or anyone else: *She doesn't have much money, so she bought the least expensive computer. | They came to my house when I least expected it* (=when I did not expect them). ANTONYM **most**

2 at least a) used for saying something good about a bad situation: *It's not good news, but at least we know now what the problem is.* **b)** not less than a number or amount: *He's tall – at least six foot.*
3 least of all = especially not: *I don't like vegetables, least of all carrots.*
4 not in the least = not at all: *The dog had escaped many times, so I wasn't in the least surprised when it happened again.*
5 the least = the smallest number or amount: *Even the least amount of this poison can hurt you.*

leath·er /ˈleðɚ/ *noun*
a material used for making shoes, bags, and belts, that is the skin of an animal: *a leather jacket*
—**leathery** *adjective* like leather: *She smoked and spent too much time in the sun, and her skin was leathery.*

leave¹ /liv/ *verb* **left** /left/ **leaving**
1 to go away from a place: *The bus leaves in five minutes – you'd better get on.* | *I leave school at 3 and I'm home by 3:30.* ANTONYM **arrive**
2 to put something somewhere and go away without it: *We left the car at the airport when we went to Washington.* | *Leave the keys on the table.*

> **USAGE: leave**
>
> When you want to talk about the place where you left something by mistake, you must use "leave": *I left my homework at home.*
>
> You can also say "I forgot my homework."
>
> Do not say "I forgot my homework at home."

3 leave a message = to tell someone something by asking someone else to tell him or her or by writing a note: *Pete was out, so I left a message with his mom.*
4 to stop living with your husband or wife, because you do not love him or her: *Mom cried all the time when dad left her.*
5 to stop doing a job or going to a school or college and not return to it: *He left school and got a job.* SYNONYM **quit**; ANTONYM **start**
6 leave someone alone = used for telling someone to stop annoying or upsetting someone: *Go away and leave me alone!*
7 leave something alone = used for telling someone to stop touching something: *Leave those glasses alone, or you'll break them.*
8 be left = if something is left after everything else has gone, it is still there: *There wasn't much food left at the end of dinner.*
9 to not do something until later: *I'm too tired to do the dishes now – let's leave them until the morning.*
10 to arrange that someone will have something you own after you die: *She left a lot of money to her son in her will.*

PHRASAL VERBS
leave something behind
to not take something with you when you go somewhere: *When we moved to the U.S. we had to leave our dog behind in Mexico.*
leave out
1 leave something out = to not include something: *Tell me everything that Colleen said, and don't leave out any details.*
2 be/feel left out = to feel as if you are not accepted or welcome in a particular group of people: *I always felt left out when my older sister's friends came to our house.*
leave something to someone
to let someone make a decision or be responsible for something and not do it yourself: *Jon likes driving and I don't, so I leave that to him.*

leave² *noun*
a period of time away from your work because you are sick or on vacation: *I took sick leave when I had the operation.*
➔ See Thesaurus box at **vacation**

leaves /livz/
the plural of LEAF

lec·ture¹ /ˈlektʃɚ/ Ac *noun*
1 a formal talk to a group of people about a subject: *The professor gave a lecture on modern art.*
2 a long serious talk with someone that criticizes him or her or warns him or her about something: *Dad gave me a lecture about my school work.*

lecture² *verb*
1 to have a long serious talk with someone, criticizing his or her behavior or warning him or her about something: *He's always lecturing me about how bad smoking is.*
2 to give a formal talk about a subject to a

group of people: *She lectures to school groups about the animals and plants that live in the area.*

—**lecturer** *noun* someone who gives lectures that teach people about a subject

led /led/ *verb*
the past tense and past participle of LEAD

ledge /ledʒ/ *noun*
a narrow flat surface either on a large rock, or like the one at the bottom of a window

ledg•er /ˈledʒɚ/ *noun*
a book in which a business records the money it receives and spends

leek /lik/ *noun*
a long vegetable with straight green leaves that tastes like an onion
➔ See picture on page A12

left¹ /left/ *verb*
the past tense and past participle of LEAVE

left² *noun*
1 the side opposite to the one with which most people write: *The school is up ahead on the left.* ANTONYM **right**
2 the left = in politics, people who think the government should pay for important things people need and that business should have less power: *More people on the left support the idea of government health care for everyone.* ANTONYM **the right**

left³ *adjective*
on or toward the left side: *He writes with his left hand, so a lot of desks are hard for him to use.* | *The store is on the left side of the street.* ANTONYM **right**

left⁴ *adverb*
toward the left side: *Turn left at the next street.* ANTONYM **right**

ˌleft-ˈhanded *adjective*
someone who is left-handed uses his or her left hand to write and throw a ball ANTONYM **right-handed**

—**left-hander** *noun* someone who is left-handed

left•ist /ˈleftɪst/ *adjective, formal*
another word for LEFT-WING: *The military did not like the leftist government.*

left•o•vers /ˈleftˌoʊvɚz/ *noun*
food that remains at the end of a meal that you can keep and eat later: *They gave the leftovers from dinner to the dog to eat.*

ˌleft-ˈwing *adjective*
people who are left-wing believe that the government should pay for the important things that people need and that business should not have too much power: *My brother is more left-wing than I am.*

leg /leg/ *noun*
1 one of the two long parts of your body on which you stand or walk: *Dogs have four legs.* | *She fell and broke her leg.*
2 one of the long parts that supports a table, chair etc.: *One of the table legs was shorter than the others, so the table wobbled.*
➔ See picture on page A2

leg•a•cy /ˈlegəsi/ *noun* plural **legacies** *formal*
1 money or property that you receive from someone after he or she dies SYNONYM **inheritance**
2 a situation that exists because of things that happened at an earlier time: *The high level of crime in the country is a legacy of the war.*

le•gal /ˈligəl/ Ac *adjective*
1 relating to laws: *the legal system* | *The company offers free legal advice.*
2 allowed by the law: *Is it legal to own a gun in every state?* ANTONYM **illegal**

—**legally** *adverb*: *You can't legally buy alcohol until you're 21.*

—**legalize** *verb* to make something legal: *a plan to legalize gambling*

—**legality** /lɪˈgæləti/ *noun* the fact of whether something is legal or not: *We have questions about the legality of the deal.*

WORD FAMILY look at the words:
- ➔ **legal** *adjective*
- ➔ **illegal** *adjective*
- ➔ **legally** *adverb*
- ➔ **illegally** *adverb*
- ➔ **legalize** *verb*

L

ˌ**legal ˈholiday** *noun*
a day when government offices, schools etc. are closed because of a law: *Christmas Day is a legal holiday.*

leg·end /ˈledʒənd/ *noun*
1 an old well-known story about people in the past, that is usually not true: *the legend of King Arthur* | *According to legend, he lived to be 125 years old.*
2 someone who is very famous for a long time because they are good at doing something: *Elvis Presley is a rock and roll legend.*
➔ See Thesaurus box at **story**

leg·end·ar·y /ˈledʒənˌderi/ *adjective*
famous and admired: *the legendary baseball player, Babe Ruth*

leg·i·ble /ˈledʒəbəl/ *adjective*
written or printed clearly enough for you to read: *The teacher gave my paper back because my writing was not legible.* ANTONYM **illegible**

le·gion /ˈlidʒən/ *noun, formal*
a large number of people or things: *The singer has legions of fans around the world.*

leg·is·late /ˈledʒəˌsleɪt/ Ac *verb, formal*
to make a law about something: *Congress will try to legislate new health care changes.*
—**legislator** *noun* someone who has the power to make new laws: *A group of legislators will meet with members of the public to discuss the issue.*

L

leg·is·la·tion /ˌledʒəˈsleɪʃən/ Ac *noun, formal*
a law or set of laws: *Congress wants to pass new legislation to* (=pass it) *reduce teenage smoking.*

leg·is·la·tive /ˈledʒəˌsleɪtɪv/ Ac *adjective, formal*
1 relating to laws or to making laws: *Congress's legislative powers*
2 the legislative branch = the part of a government that makes laws

leg·is·la·ture /ˈledʒəˌsleɪtʃɚ/ Ac *noun*
a group of people who make or change laws in a government: *the Ohio state legislature*

le·git·i·mate /ləˈdʒɪtəmət/ *adjective*
1 a legitimate feeling, reason, remark, etc. is one that is completely reasonable: *She has a legitimate reason for not coming to school – her mother is very sick.*
2 done or made in a way that is allowed by law: *It is only legitimate to use the software if you have paid for it.* ANTONYM **illegal**
—**legitimacy** *noun* the fact of whether something is legitimate or not: *We have questions about the legitimacy of the election because too many people were not allowed to vote.*
—**legitimize** *verb* to make something legitimate: *Nothing can legitimize the killing of innocent people.*

lei·sure /ˈliʒɚ/ *noun*
the time when you are not at school or working and can do things that you enjoy: *I like to play soccer and video games in my leisure time.*

lei·sure·ly /ˈliʒɚli/ *adjective*
done in a slow and relaxed way: *They took a leisurely walk around the park.*

lem·on /ˈlemən/ *noun*
a yellow fruit with a juice that tastes sour: *There was a slice of lemon with each piece of fish.* | *lemon juice*
—**lemony** *adjective* tasting or smelling of lemon
➔ See picture on page A13

lem·on·ade /ˌleməˈneɪd/ *noun*
a drink made with lemon juice, sugar, and water: *a nice cold glass of lemonade*

lend /lend/ *verb* **lent** /lent/
1 to let someone have some money or something that belongs to you for a short time: *Could you lend me your bike for the weekend? I want to go for a bike ride.*

USAGE: lend

If you **lend** something to someone, you give it to him or her so that she or he can use it for a short time: *I lent that DVD to Rick.* | *Mom, could you lend me some money?*

You cannot say "Could you borrow me some money?"

If you **borrow** something from someone, you take something that someone gives you for a short time, and then you give it back: *Can I borrow your pen?*

You cannot say "Can I lend your pen?"

2 if a bank lends you money, it gives it to you but you must pay it back within a certain time and pay an additional amount of money called "interest": *The bank lends money to people who want to start a business.*

length /leŋθ/ *noun*
1 the distance from one end of something to the other end: *The length of the room is ten feet. | The pole was about 7 feet in length.*
2 the amount of time during which something happens or continues: *The length of summer vacation is about ten weeks.*

length·en /ˈleŋθən/ *verb*
to make something longer: *I need to lengthen this dress – it's too short for me. | There are new plans to lengthen the school day from 6 and a half to 7 hours.* ANTONYM **shorten**

length·wise /ˈleŋθwaɪz/ *also* **length·ways** /ˈleŋθweɪz/ *adverb*
in the direction or position of something's longest side: *Fold the cloth lengthwise.*

length·y /ˈleŋθi/ *adjective, formal*
continuing for a long time: *We had a lengthy discussion about my work that took over an hour.*

le·ni·ent /ˈliniənt/ *adjective, formal*
punishing someone in a way that is not as severe as people expect: *I think judges are too lenient with drunk drivers; they should take the drunk driver's license away the first time.*
—**leniency** *noun* lenient behavior or a lenient attitude
—**leniently** *adverb*

lens /lenz/ *noun*
a piece of curved glass or plastic that makes things look bigger, smaller, or clearer: *His glasses had thick lenses in them. | a camera lens*

lent /lent/ *verb*
the past tense and past participle of LEND

len·til /ˈlentəl/ *noun*
a small round seed which has been dried and can be cooked

Le·o /ˈlioʊ/ *noun*
1 the fifth sign of the ZODIAC, represented by a lion
2 someone born between July 23 and August 22

leop·ard /ˈlepɚd/ *noun*
a large wild cat with yellow fur and black spots, from Africa and southern Asia

les·bi·an /ˈlezbiən/ *noun*
a woman who is sexually attracted to other women
—**lesbian** *adjective* relating to lesbians

less[1] /les/ *adverb*
1 less important/likely/busy, etc. = not so important, likely, etc.: *People who exercise regularly are less likely to develop heart disease. | This hotel is less expensive than the other one, but it's not as nice.* ANTONYM **more**
2 happening fewer times or for a shorter time: *I see him much less than I used to.* ANTONYM **more**
3 less and less = in a way that becomes less in amount: *I began to think less and less about our fight, and I finally forgot about it.*

less[2] *adjective, pronoun*
1 a smaller amount: *I'm trying to exercise more and eat less to lose weight. | He earns less money than some of his friends, but he has less stress. | She spends less of her time studying now that she has a job. | Which dress costs less? The red one or the pink one?* ANTONYM **more**

GRAMMAR: less

less, fewer
Use **less** before nouns that are things you cannot count: *There is less water in this cup than in that one. | This book has less information than the other one.*
Use **fewer** before nouns whose form shows that there is more than one: *There were fewer cars on the roads in the 1950s. | Fewer people were in the class than I expected.*

2 less and less = in a way that gets smaller in amount: *My boyfriend and I have been spending less and less time together. We might break up.*

less·en /ˈlesən/ *verb*
to become less, or to make something become less: *If you wear a seatbelt, you lessen the chances that you will be hurt in a car accident. | The little girl's fear lessened a little when she saw her mother.* ANTONYM **increase**
➔ See Thesaurus box at **reduce**

L

less•er /ˈlesɚ/ *adjective, formal*
not as large, as important, or as much as something else: *These wounds would have killed a lesser man* (=someone not as strong or brave).

les•son /ˈlesən/ *noun*
a period of time when someone teaches you something: *I have a guitar lesson today.* | *Hannah is taking swimming lessons at the YMCA pool.*

let /let/ *verb* **let**, **letting**
1 to allow someone to do something, or allow something to happen: *I wanted to go, but my mom wouldn't let me.* | *Let me finish this, and then we can go.*
2 to allow someone or something to come into or go out of a place: *Security guards refused to let reporters into the building.* | *He opened the door to let the dog out.*
3 let go = to stop holding someone or something: *The boy was holding the toy car and refused to let go.* | *You can let go of my hand after we cross the street.*
4 let someone go = to allow someone to go, after you have been keeping them somewhere: *The police let him go after asking him some questions.* SYNONYM **release**
5 let someone know = to tell someone something: *I'll let you know when dinner is ready.*
6 let me do something = said when you are offering to help someone: *Let me carry that for you.*
➔ **let's**

PHRASAL VERB
let someone down
to make someone feel disappointed because you have not done what he or she wanted or expected you to do: *You can trust John – he won't let you down.*
➔ See Thesaurus box at **allow**

let•down /ˈletdaʊn/ *noun*
something that makes you feel disappointed because it is not as good as you expected: *Our hotel was a big letdown – the rooms were very small and not very clean.* SYNONYM **disappointment**

le•thal /ˈliθəl/ *adjective*
lethal weapons or substances can kill someone: *The drug can be lethal if you take too much of it.*

let's /lets/
the short form of "let us," used when you want to suggest that someone or a group of people do something with you: *I'm hungry – let's eat.* | *Let's not talk about this right now.*

let•ter /ˈletɚ/ *noun*
1 a written message that you put into an envelope and send to someone by mail: *I wrote a letter to my mother telling her that I was coming to visit.* | *I got a letter from the college about my application.* | *Can you mail this letter on your way to work?*
2 one of the signs in writing that represents a sound in speech: *There are 26 letters in the English alphabet.*

let•tuce /ˈletɪs/ *noun*
a green vegetable with large thin leaves joined together at the bottom, that you eat raw in SALADs
➔ See picture on page A12

let•up /ˈletʌp/ *noun*
a pause or a reduction in something unpleasant or difficult: *There's no sign of a letup in the rain – it's supposed to continue all weekend.*

leu•ke•mia /luˈkimiə/ *noun*
a serious disease that affects the blood and that can cause death: *Her son had leukemia and died last year.*

lev•ee /ˈlevi/ *noun*
a wall that is built to stop a river from flooding

lev•el[1] /ˈlevəl/ *noun*
1 the amount or degree of something, compared to another amount or degree: *People have shown a high level of interest in the subject and have been asking for more information.* | *The price of gas stayed at that high level through the summer.*
2 the height or position of something in relation to the ground or to another thing: *The water level in the lake is very high and houses near the shore have flooded.*
3 a standard of skill or ability in a particular subject, sport, etc.: *Rick played football at the highest level – the Superbowl.*

level[2] *adjective*
1 flat and not sloping, with no part higher than any other part: *The floor isn't level so the furniture doesn't sit straight.*
2 at the same height as something else: *The*

top of my head was level with his chin, so I had to look up to see his face.

→ See Thesaurus box at **flat**[1]

level[3] *verb*

1 to knock down or completely destroy a building or area: *An earthquake leveled several buildings in the city.*

2 to make a surface flat and smooth: *Level the ground before putting the brick sidewalk down.*

lev•er /ˈlevɚ/ *noun*

1 a long handle that you pull or push to make a machine start

2 a long piece of metal used for lifting something heavy. You put one end under the object and push down on the other end

lev•er•age /ˈlevərɪdʒ/ *noun, formal*

influence that you can use to make people do what you want: *Small businesses have less leverage with banks than big businesses do because they don't have as much money as the big businesses.*

li•a•ble /ˈlaɪəbəl/ *adjective*

1 be liable to do something = to be likely to do something: *Remind me to call her because I'm liable to forget.*

2 legally responsible for something and having to pay money as a result: *Should cigarette companies be liable for a smoker's health problems?*

—**liability** /ˌlaɪˈbɪləti/ *noun* legal responsibility for the cost of something: *The airline tried to deny liability for the accident.*

li•ar /ˈlaɪɚ/ *noun*

someone who deliberately says something that is not true: *You're a liar! I didn't say that.*

li•bel /ˈlaɪbəl/ *noun*

the illegal act of writing or printing things about someone that are not true: *He is suing the magazine for libel because it reported that he stole something when he did not.*

lib•eral[1] /ˈlɪbərəl/ Ac *adjective*

willing to accept or respect other people's ideas and behavior even if it is different from your own: *a liberal church that welcomes people of other religions* ANTONYM **conservative**

liberal[2] *noun*

someone with liberal opinions or principles: *Political liberals want to spend more on education.* ANTONYM **conservative**

—**liberalism** *noun* the attitude or behavior of liberals

ˌliberal ˈarts *plural noun*

subjects that develop someone's general knowledge and ability to think, rather than technical skills: *liberal arts such as history and sociology* | *a liberal arts college*

lib•eral•ize /ˈlɪbrəˌlaɪz/ Ac *verb, formal*

to make a system or laws less strict so that people have more freedom: *The state government plans to liberalize gambling laws and allow more casinos.*

lib•er•ate /ˈlɪbəˌreɪt/ Ac *verb, formal*

1 to free prisoners, a city, a country, etc. from someone's control: *The U.S. army liberated the town from the Nazis in 1945.*

2 to free someone from feelings or situations that make his or her life difficult: *Machines such as dishwashers have liberated us from a lot of hard work at home*

—**liberator** *noun* someone or something that liberates people or places: *The people believed he was a liberator who could end the dictator's rule.*

—**liberation** /ˌlɪbəˈreɪʃən/ *noun* the act of liberating prisoners, a city, country, etc. *the liberation of Eastern Europe*

lib•er•ty /ˈlɪbɚti/ *noun* plural **liberties**

1 the freedom to do what you want without too much control from a government or authority: *The people of this country fought for liberty and democracy.*

2 a particular legal right: *The new law will protect religious liberties so that all people can worship as they choose.*

Li•bra /ˈlibrə/ *noun*

1 the seventh sign of the ZODIAC, represented by a SCALE

2 someone born between September 23 and October 23

li•brar•y /ˈlaɪˌbreri/ *noun* plural **libraries**

a room or building containing books that you can borrow or read there: *He borrowed a book from the school library.* | *library books*

—**librarian** /laɪˈbreriən/ *noun* someone who works in a library

lice /laɪs/ *noun*

the plural of LOUSE

li•cense[1] /ˈlaɪsəns/ Ac *noun*

an official document that gives you permission to own something or do something: *He*

L

doesn't have a driver's license so he can't drive. | *You can't carry a gun without a license.*

license² *verb*
to give official permission for someone to own or do something: *Williams is not licensed to practice law in New York.*

ˈlicense plate *noun*
one of the signs with numbers and letters on it on the back or front of a car
➔ See picture on page A28

lick /lɪk/ *verb*
to move your tongue across the surface of something: *The dog jumped up and licked her face.*

lic•o•rice /ˈlɪkərɪʃ/ *noun*
a type of black or red candy with a strong taste

lid /lɪd/ *noun*
a cover for a pot, box, or other container: *He carefully lifted the lid of the box to see what was inside.*
➔ See Thesaurus box at **cover²**
➔ See picture on page A9

lie¹ /laɪ/ *verb* **lay** /leɪ/ **lain** /leɪn/ **lying**
1 to be in a position in which your body is flat on the floor, a bed, etc.: *We lay on the beach all day.*
2 *also* **lie down** to put yourself in a position in which your body is flat on the floor, a bed, etc.: *I'm going upstairs to lie down.* | *He lay on the floor and went to sleep.*

lie² *verb* **lied** /laɪd/ **lying**
to deliberately tell someone something that is not true: *She lied about her age and said she was 30 when she was really 35.* | *Don't lie to me! I can tell if you're not telling the truth.*

THESAURUS: lie

make something up to think of and tell someone something that is not true: *"What'll you tell your mother?" "I'll make something up."*

fib *informal* to tell someone a lie about something that is not important: *Were you fibbing when you said you didn't see what happened?*

tell a lie to say something that you know is not true: *I didn't want to tell a lie, but I didn't want to get Brian in trouble, either.*

invent to think of an idea, story, etc. that is not true: *If I can't find a reason, I'll invent one.*

mislead *formal* to make someone believe something that is not true by giving him or her false or incomplete information: *The ads mislead people about how healthy the diet is.*

deceive *formal* to make someone believe something that is not true: *During the war, both sides sent false messages to deceive the enemy.*

USAGE: lie

Lie has two different meanings:
– to be or move into a flat position on the floor, a bed, etc.: *She was lying on the sofa.*
The past tense for this meaning of **lie** is **lay**: *He lay on the bed.*
– to say something that is not true: *Why did you lie to me?*
The past tense for this meaning of **lie** is **lied**: *The police think that he lied.*
Lay means to put something down in a flat position. The past tense for this is **laid**: *She laid the newspaper down and picked up the phone.*

lie³ *noun*
something that you say which you know is not true: *My teacher made me stay after school for telling her a lie.*

lieu•ten•ant /luˈtenənt/ *noun*, *written abbreviation* **Lt.** *or* **Lieut.**
1 an officer who has a fairly low rank in the Army, Air Force, Navy, or Marines: *He's a lieutenant in the Army.* | *Lieutenant Patrick Smith*
2 an officer who has a fairly high rank in the police force

life /laɪf/ *noun* plural **lives** /laɪvz/
1 the period of time between someone's birth and death: *Charles lived in New York City all his life.* | *She spent her life helping others.*
2 the state of being alive: *Surgery could save her life.* | *Firemen risked their lives to save him* (=did something that could have killed them to save him).
3 all the experiences and activities that are typical of a particular way of living: *Life in the city is very exciting.*

4 the type of experience that someone has during his or her life: *Tia had a full and happy life.* | *My social life is pretty boring right now, because I have so much studying to do.*
5 living things such as people, animals, or plants: *Do you think there is life on other planets?*
6 activity or movement: *The house looked empty, and there were no signs of life.* | *Katie was young and full of life* (=very cheerful and active).
7 human existence, and all the things that can happen during someone's life: *Life can be hard sometimes.*
8 **real life** = things that really happen, rather than things that happen in a story or in someone's imagination: *Don't believe everything you see on TV – it's not like that in real life.*

life•boat /ˈlaɪfboʊt/ *noun*
a small boat that a big ship carries, and that people go into if the big ship sinks: *The ship did not have enough lifeboats for everyone on it so many people drowned.*

ˈlife ˌcycle *noun*
all the stages in the life of an animal or plant, as it develops and changes into different forms: *In Biology today, we learned about the life cycle of the butterfly.*

ˈlife inˌsurance *noun*
a type of insurance that pays money to your family when you die

ˈlife ˌjacket *noun*
a piece of equipment that you wear around your chest to stop you from sinking in the water

life•less /ˈlaɪfləs/ *adjective*
1 not exciting or interesting: *a lifeless, boring party*
2 dead or seeming to be dead: *They pulled her lifeless body from the river.*

life•like /ˈlaɪflaɪk/ *adjective*
very much like a real person or thing: *The statue was so lifelike that I thought it was a real person.*

life•long /ˈlaɪflɔŋ/ *adjective*
continuing all through your life: *She had a lifelong interest in birds.*

ˈlife preˌserver *noun*
a thing shaped like a ring that you use in water to stop yourself from sinking

ˈlife raft *noun*
a small rubber boat filled with air, that you can use if your ship sinks or your airplane crashes

ˌlife ˈsentence *noun*
the punishment of sending someone to prison for the rest of his or her life: *The judge gave him a life sentence for the murder.*

life•style /ˈlaɪfstaɪl/ *noun*
the way in which you live, and what kinds of activities you do: *She has a very healthy lifestyle: she eats well and exercises daily.*

life•time /ˈlaɪftaɪm/ *noun*
the period of time during which someone is alive: *I never thought that there would be another big war in my lifetime.*

lift[1] /lɪft/ *verb*
1 *also* **lift up** to move something up into the air: *Lift up your feet so I can sweep the floor.*
2 to go up into the air: *The fog started to lift and the sun came out.*
3 to end a rule or a law that says that something is not allowed: *The government has lifted the ban on traveling to the area.*
4 *informal* to steal something or copy someone else's words, ideas, etc.: *Parts of her essay were lifted directly from the Internet.*
SYNONYM **copy**
➔ See picture on page A4

lift[2] *noun*
1 something that makes something more successful, or that makes someone feel happier: *The economy needs a lift, and the president hopes the tax cut will help.*
2 something that makes something else move upward: *We rode the ski lift to the top of the mountain.*
3 an occasion when you take someone somewhere in your car: *Can I give you a lift to school?* SYNONYM **ride**

ˈlift off *noun*
the moment when a space vehicle leaves the ground and rises up into the air: *After lift-off the rocket shot up into the sky.*

light[1] /laɪt/ *noun*
1 the brightness from the sun, a lamp, etc. that allows you to see things: *The room was very dark and there wasn't much light.*
ANTONYM **dark**
2 a thing that produces light, for example an

L

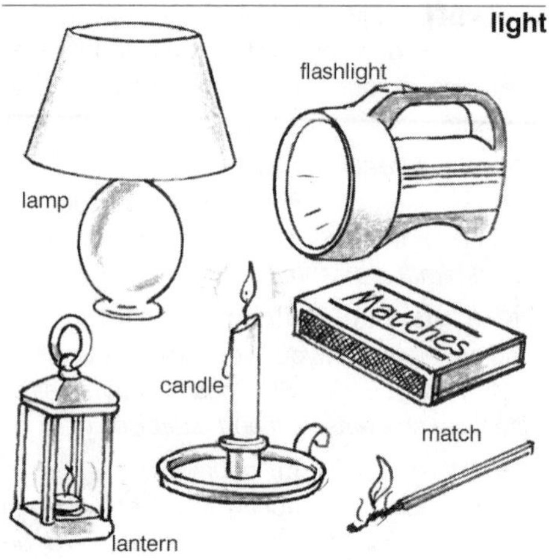

electric lamp: *Don't forget to turn off the lights.*

3 a set of red, green, and yellow lights used for controlling traffic: *Turn left at the light.*

4 **a different/new, etc. light** = a different, new, etc. way of thinking about someone or something: *I now thought of him in a different light.*

light² *adjective*

1 not weighing very much: *The box is very light.* ANTONYM **heavy**

2 a light color is not dark and seems to have a lot of white mixed into it: *a light blue dress* SYNONYM **pale**; ANTONYM **dark**

3 if it is light, the sky is not dark: *It gets light at about 5 a.m. in the summer.*

4 light clothes are thin and not very warm: *She put on a light sweater when it got cooler in the evening.* ANTONYM **thick**

5 a light wind is not strong: *a light breeze* ANTONYM **strong**

6 if something is light, there is only a small amount of it: *light rain | The traffic was light on the freeway.* ANTONYM **heavy**

7 gentle and soft: *She gave him a light kiss on the cheek.*

8 **make light of something** = to joke about something or to treat it as if it were not important: *I don't want to make light of her problems.*

—**lightness** *noun*

light³ *verb* **lit** /lɪt/ or **lighted**

1 to make something start burning or producing light: *We lit a fire to keep ourselves warm.*

2 to give light to something: *The room is lit by candles.*

PHRASAL VERB

light up

1 **light something up** = to make something become bright: *Fireworks lit up the night sky.*

2 if your face or eyes light up, you show that you are happy or excited: *Paula's eyes lit up when she saw all of her presents.*

3 to make a cigarette start burning

'light bulb *noun*
the round glass part of a lamp that uses electricity to produce light

light·en /ˈlaɪtn/ *verb*

1 *formal* to become brighter: *The sky started to lighten and the sun came out.* ANTONYM **darken**

2 to make something less heavy: *I took some boxes out of the car to lighten the load.*

PHRASAL VERB

lighten up

to stop being so serious: *He needs to lighten up and stop worrying about his work.*

light·er /ˈlaɪtɚ/ *noun*
a small object that produces a flame to light cigarettes, CIGARs, etc.

ˌlight-ˈheaded *adjective*
unable to think clearly or move steadily, for example because you have drunk alcohol or you are sick: *The wine was making me feel light-headed.* SYNONYM **dizzy**

light·house /ˈlaɪthaʊs/ *noun*
a tall building near the ocean with a very bright light at the top that warns ships of danger

light·ing /ˈlaɪtɪŋ/ *noun*
the kind of light, or the system used to produce light: *The lighting wasn't very good and it was hard to read the map.*

light·ly /ˈlaɪtli/ *adverb*
gently: *I tapped her lightly on the shoulder so as not to scare her.*

light•ning /ˈlaɪtnɪŋ/ *noun*
a bright flash of light in the sky that happens during a storm: *The tree was hit by lightning and split in two.*

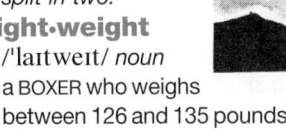

light•weight /ˈlaɪtweɪt/ *noun*
a BOXER who weighs between 126 and 135 pounds

ˈlight year *noun*
the distance that light travels in one year: *The star is millions of light years away from the Earth.*

lik•a•ble /ˈlaɪkəbəl/ *adjective*
a likable person is nice and easy to like: *She's funny and likable and has lots of friends.*

like¹ /laɪk/ *preposition, conjunction*
1 similar to another person or thing: *Ken looks like his brother.* | *The Earth is round like a ball.* ANTONYM **unlike**
2 used when you are giving examples for what you are talking about. Many teachers do not think that using like in this way is correct, and use "such as" instead: *Vegetables like broccoli and carrots are very good for you.* SYNONYM **such as**
3 typical of a person or thing, or what they usually do: *It's not like Nancy to be late* (=she is usually not late).
4 *informal* used when you are describing someone or something: *He acts like he knows everything.* | *"What was the movie like?" "It was good."*
→ See Thesaurus box at **similar**

like² *verb*
1 to think that someone or something is nice or good, or to enjoy doing something: *I never liked her brother very much.* | *She likes driving.* | *He doesn't like to talk about himself.* ANTONYM **dislike**

GRAMMAR: like

Do not say "I am liking it" or "I am liking to do it." Say "I like it" or "I like to do it."
Do not say "I am liking very much Anna." Say "I like Anna very much."

2 to think that someone is nice and attractive: *"Do you like Jeff?" "Yeah, he's really cute."*
3 **would like/'d like** = a polite way of saying "want": *I'd like a large pizza with mushrooms.*
4 **How do you like ...?** = used when asking someone's opinion about something: *"How do you like your new house?" "It's okay."*
→ See Thesaurus box at **enjoy¹**

like•ly /ˈlaɪkli/ *adjective*
if something is likely, it will probably happen or is probably true: *It's likely to rain tomorrow.*
—**likelihood** *noun* the state of being likely: *What is the likelihood of getting the disease?*

like•ness /ˈlaɪknəs/ *noun*
the image of someone in a painting, photograph, STATUE, etc.: *The stamp had a likeness of President Lincoln on it.*

ˌlikes and ˈdislikes *plural noun*
the things that you like and do not like: *Children have strong likes and dislikes about food.*

like•wise /ˈlaɪk-waɪz/ Ac *adverb*
1 *formal* in the same way: *The boss stood up, and everyone else did likewise.*
2 used when saying that you feel the same as the other person: *"It's great to see you." "Likewise."*

lik•ing /ˈlaɪkɪŋ/ *noun*
the feeling when you like someone or something: *He's always had a liking for ice cream and usually orders it for dessert.*

li•lac /ˈlaɪlək/ *noun*
1 a small tree with purple or white flowers, which has a nice smell
2 a light purple color
—**lilac** *adjective*

lil•y /ˈlɪli/ *noun* plural **lilies**
a plant with large flowers, which are usually white or yellow: *There was a beautiful bunch of lilies in a vase.*

limb /lɪm/ *noun, formal*
1 an arm or leg: *He had a fever and all his limbs were shaking.*
2 a large branch of a tree: *The cat climbed the tree and sat on one of the limbs.*

lime /laɪm/ *noun*
a small round green fruit that has a sour taste: *a lime tree* | *Squeeze some lime juice*

L

on the fish.

➔ See picture on page A13

lim·it¹ /ˈlɪmɪt/ *noun*

1 the greatest amount, number, or distance that is allowed or is possible: *The speed limit is 65 miles per hour.* | *There is a limit on how much money you can take out of the bank at one time.*

2 the edge or border of something: *Students are not allowed outside the school limits during school hours.*

3 be off limits = if a place is off limits, you are not allowed to go there: *The beach is off limits after dark.*

limit² *verb*

to stop an amount or number from getting bigger than a particular amount: *Class size is limited to 30.* | *I limit the amount of TV my kids watch. Otherwise, they would watch it all day.*

—**limited** *adjective* small in number or amount: *There are a limited number of tickets, so get yours early.*

lim·o /ˈlɪmoʊ/ *noun, informal*

a LIMOUSINE

lim·ou·sine /ˈlɪməˌzin/ *noun*

a big expensive car that is longer than a normal car, and that is driven by someone who is paid to drive: *The band arrived at the concert in a big white limousine.*

L

limp¹ /lɪmp/ *adjective*

hanging down loosely, in a way that is not stiff or firm: *The hot weather made my hair limp and unattractive.*

—**limply** *adverb*: *Her weak arm hung limply at her side.*

limp² *verb*

to walk with difficulty because your leg or foot is hurt: *He limped off the soccer field after he was knocked down.*

—**limp** *noun* a way of walking with difficulty because your leg or foot is hurt: *After the accident he always walked with a limp.*

➔ See Thesaurus box at **walk¹**

line¹ /laɪn/ *noun*

1 a long thin mark on a surface: *She drew a line across the page.* | *He reached the finish line at the end of the race.*

2 a row of people or things: *A long line of cars was waiting to buy gas.* | *Mia stood in line at the cafeteria to get her food.* | *If you want to buy tickets, you'd better get in line.*

3 a long piece of string or rope: *I hung the wet clothes on the line.* | *a fishing line* (=for catching fish)

4 a border between two states or countries: *I didn't stop driving until I crossed the state line into Kansas.*

5 the direction something travels, or the imaginary path between two points in space: *Light travels in a straight line – it doesn't curve.*

6 a single row of words in a poem, play, song, book, etc.: *I only know the first three lines of the poem.*

7 a wire or connection, for example for electricity or the telephone: *The strong winds blew the power lines down.* | *I tried to call him, but the line was busy* (=someone was already using the telephone).

8 on line = using a computer that is connected to the Internet to get information or communicate with other people: *I buy a lot of books on line from home – it's easier than going to the store.*

9 out of line *informal* = not acceptable in that situation: *What he did was out of line, and he will be punished.*

line² *verb*

1 to cover the inside of something with something else: *We lined the box with old cloths to make it soft for the kittens.* | *The coat was lined with wool.*

2 to form a line along the edge of something: *Trees line the streets.*

PHRASAL VERB

line up

to form a line of people or things: *The fans were already lining up outside the stadium.*

lin·en /ˈlɪnən/ *noun*

1 a kind of cloth used to make clothes, to cover tables, etc., that is made from a plant called flax: *a cool linen shirt*

2 bed/table linen *formal* = the sheets that you put on the bed, or the cloth that you put on a table

lin·er /ˈlaɪnɚ/ *noun*

a large ship for carrying people: *They sailed to Hawaii on an ocean liner.*

line·up /ˈlaɪnʌp/ *noun*

1 the list of players or performers who are going to take part in a game or concert: *He* *won't be in the lineup for tonight's basketball game because of an injury.*

2 a set of events, programs, etc. that have been arranged to happen one after the other: *Friday night's TV lineup includes three comedy shows.*

lin•ger /ˈlɪŋgɚ/ *also* **linger on** *verb, formal*
to stay somewhere for a long time: *The smell of onions lingered in the kitchen and Darla could not cover it up.*

lin•ge•rie /ˌlɑnʒəˈreɪ/ *noun, formal*
women's underwear

lin•guis•tics /lɪŋˈgwɪstɪks/ *noun, formal*
the study of languages, including their grammar and history

lin•ing /ˈlaɪnɪŋ/ *noun*
a piece of material covering the inside of a coat, box, etc.: *a jacket with a red lining*

link1 /lɪŋk/ Ac *verb*
1 to say or show that two things are related, so that one thing causes or affects the other: *Smoking is linked to cancer.*
2 *also* **link something up** to connect two things or places together: *You can link your computer up to the Internet with this cable.* | *The highway links two major cities.*

link2 *noun*

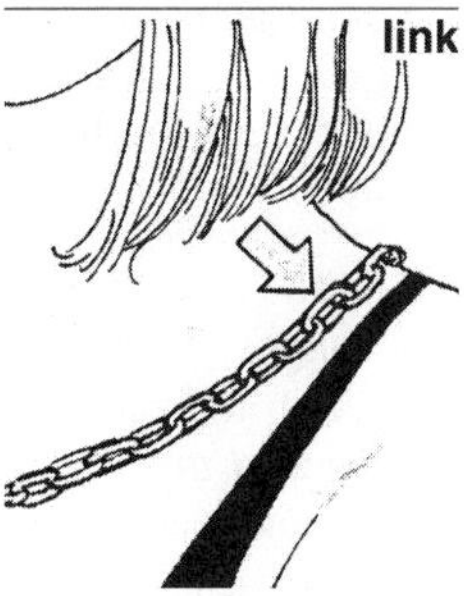

1 a relationship or connection between two or more things or people: *Do you think that there is a link between the two murders, or are they unrelated?*
2 one of the rings in a chain: *One of the links on my necklace has broken.*
3 a satellite/telephone/rail, etc. link = something that makes it possible to communicate or travel between different places: *The reporters sent the pictures back to the TV studio using a satellite link.*

li•no•le•um /lɪˈnoʊliəm/ *noun*
smooth material that is used to cover a floor: *The linoleum on the kitchen floor is easy to keep clean.*

lint /lɪnt/ *noun*
soft small pieces of thread that come off cotton, wool, or other material

li•on /ˈlaɪən/ *noun*
a large wild cat that lives in Africa: *Male lions have long thick hair around their necks.*

lip /lɪp/ *noun*
1 one of the two outer parts of your mouth: *She kissed him on the lips.*
2 the top edge of a container such as a cup or a bowl: *Soup had spilled over the lip of the bowl.*
➔ See picture on page A2

lip•stick /ˈlɪpˌstɪk/ *noun*
a substance that women use to put color on their lips, to make them look more attractive: *I usually wear lipstick if I'm going out in the evening.*

liq•ue•fy /ˈlɪkwəˌfaɪ/ *verb* **liquified**, third person singular **liquifies** *formal*
to change into a liquid: *The gas liquefies when it is cooled to a low temperature.*

liq•uid /ˈlɪkwɪd/ *noun*
a substance such as water that is not a solid or a gas: *There was still some liquid in the bottle.*
—**liquid** *adjective* not a solid or a gas: *a bottle of liquid soap*

liq•uor /ˈlɪkɚ/ *noun*
a strong alcoholic drink such as WHISKEY: *The bar sells whiskey, vodka, and other kinds of liquor.*

ˈliquor store *noun*
a store where alcohol is sold

list1 /lɪst/ *noun*
a set of things that you write one below the other: *Make a list of the things you'll need.* | *Is my name on the list?*

list2 *verb*
to write or say a list of things: *List your ten favorite movies, starting with the one you like the best.*

lis•ten /ˈlɪsən/ *verb*
1 to pay attention to what someone is saying or to a sound such as music: *Listen carefully – this is important.* | *He was listening to a CD.*
2 *informal* used when you want someone to pay attention to what you are saying: *Listen, Amanda, it's time to clean up your room.*
3 listen up! *informal* = said in order to get a

group of people's attention when you are going to say something important: *Okay, class, listen up! Turn to page 33.*

—**listener** *noun* someone who listens to what people are saying, or to a radio station: *Do you want to talk about it? I'm a good listener.*

list·ing /ˈlɪstɪŋ/ *noun*
a list, or something that is on a list: *She checked the TV listings to see if there was anything good on TV.*

lit[1] /lɪt/ *verb*
the past tense and past participle of LIGHT

lit[2] *adjective*
burning or having light: *The room was brightly lit and everyone's face was clearly visible.*

lite /laɪt/ *adjective*
used in the names of types of food and drinks that have less fat, sugar, or alcohol than other types

li·ter /ˈlitɚ/ *noun*
written abbreviation **l** a unit for measuring liquids, equal to 0.26 gallons: *a liter of water*

lit·er·a·cy /ˈlɪtərəsi/ *noun*
the ability to read and write: *We provide literacy programs* (=classes to teach reading and writing) *for adults.*

lit·er·al /ˈlɪtərəl/ *adjective*
the literal meaning of a word is its basic or first meaning: *The fight against crime is not a fight in the literal sense* (=it does not mean trying to physically hurt someone).

lit·er·al·ly /ˈlɪtərəli/ *adverb*
used when saying that you are using the basic meaning of a word, or that you mean exactly what you say: *She has literally thousands of books* (=several thousand, not just a large number).

lit·er·ar·y /ˈlɪtəˌreri/ *adjective*
relating to literature: *He wrote poems and other literary works.*

lit·er·ate /ˈlɪtərɪt/ *adjective*
able to read and write: *People who are not literate cannot read job application forms.*
ANTONYM **illiterate**

lit·er·a·ture /ˈlɪtərətʃɚ/ *noun*
good books, plays, poems, etc.: *I studied the book in my American literature class.*
➔ See Thesaurus box at **book**[1]

lit·ter /ˈlɪtɚ/ *noun*
1 waste paper, cans, etc. that people leave on the ground: *The sidewalks were covered in litter that people had thrown there.*
2 a group of baby animals born to one mother at the same time: *Our cat just had a litter of five kittens!*

—**litter** *verb* if things litter a place, they are there and make it look messy: *The floor was littered with toys.*
➔ See Thesaurus box at **group**[1], **garbage**

lit·tle[1] /ˈlɪtl/ *adjective, pronoun*
1 small: *The dog had cute little ears.* | *The mother was carrying her little girl.*
2 less, least a small amount: *I only know a little Spanish – just the basics.* | *"Would you like some gravy?" "Just a little."* | *Can I have a little bit of milk in my coffee, please?* | *Little is known about the disease, but scientists are trying to learn more.* | *We had very little money and could not afford expensive clothes.*

> **GRAMMAR: little**
>
> **little, a little**
>
> Use **little** when you mean "not much": *I have very little money left.*
>
> Use **a little** when you mean "a small amount": *I accidentally spilled a little coffee on the carpet.*
>
> **Little** and **a little** are always used with nouns that are things that you cannot count.

3 a little bit = slightly: *I wanted to play a little bit longer.*
4 short in time or distance: *I'll wait a little while and then call again.* | *Anna walked a little way down the road with him before she turned back.*
5 not important: *He gets angry over little things.*
➔ See Thesaurus box at **small**

little[2] *adverb*
1 a little = slightly: *I was a little nervous at first, but then I calmed down.*
2 not much: *I slept very little last night and I'm very tired today.*

liv·a·ble *also* **liveable** /ˈlɪvəbəl/ *adjective*
good enough to live in: *How can we make our cities more livable?*

L

live¹ /lɪv/ *verb*

1 to be alive or stay alive: *He was the best athlete who ever lived.* | *My grandmother lived to be 88* (=stayed alive until she was 88).

2 to have your home in a particular place: *I live in Atlanta.*

3 to have a particular kind of life: *I just want to live a normal life.*

PHRASAL VERBS

live on/off something

1 to eat only a particular kind of food: *These animals live on insects.*

2 to have a particular amount of money to spend on things you need: *We were living on $1,500 a month.*

live up to something

to be as good as someone expects: *The movie didn't live up to my expectations.*

live with someone

to share your home with someone, especially a boyfriend or girlfriend: *Tim's living with a girl he met in college.*

WORD FAMILY look at the words:

→ **live** *verb*
→ **life** *noun*
→ **living** *adjective*
→ **alive** *adjective*

live² /laɪv/ *adjective*

1 live animals are not dead: *He fed the snake live rats.* ANTONYM **dead**

2 a live broadcast on television or the radio lets people see or hear an event as it happens: *There was a live broadcast of the president's speech so people across the country heard it at the same time.*

3 performed for people who are there watching: *The club has live music three nights a week. The other nights, they have a DJ who plays CDs.*

—**live** *adverb* broadcast as something is actually happening: *The ceremony will be broadcast live on television.*

live-in /ˈlɪv ɪn/ *adjective*

living in the same home as the person you work for, or living in the same home as your boyfriend or girlfriend: *a live-in cook*

live•li•hood /ˈlaɪvliˌhʊd/ *noun*

the way you earn money in order to live: *Farming is their livelihood, so when crops are bad, they have no money.*

live•ly /ˈlaɪvli/ *adjective* **livelier**, **liveliest**

full of activity: *a lively dog with lots of energy* | *The discussion was lively and some people started shouting.*

liv•er /ˈlɪvɚ/ *noun*

1 a large part inside your body which cleans your blood

2 the liver of an animal, eaten as meat

→ See picture on page A2

lives /laɪvz/ *noun*

the plural of LIFE

live•stock /ˈlaɪvstɑk/ *noun*

animals that are kept on a farm: *They keep cows and other livestock.*

liv•ing¹ /ˈlɪvɪŋ/ *adjective*

alive: *The ocean is full of living things* (=animals and plants). ANTONYM **dead**

living² *noun*

1 money for things that you need in order to live, or a way of earning money: *"What does he do for a living?" "He works in an office."* | *It's hard to make a living* (=earn enough money) *as an actor.*

2 **the living** *formal* = the people who are alive: *We must help the living before burying the dead.*

→ **cost of living**

ˈliving room *noun*

the main room in a house, where you sit, watch television, etc.: *Jack was lying on the sofa in the living room, reading.*

liz•ard /ˈlɪzɚd/ *noun*

an animal that has rough skin, short legs, and a long tail: *Lizards are a kind of reptile.*

'll /l, əl/ *verb*

the short form of "will": *She'll do it tomorrow.*

load¹ /loʊd/ *noun*

1 a large amount of something that is carried by a vehicle or person: *The truck was carrying a load of fruit.*

2 a large amount of something that you have to do or deal with: *New teachers have a heavy work load – they have to teach five different classes.* | *I put a load of laundry in the washing machine.*

3 **loads of something** *informal* = a lot of something: *He must have loads of money.*

load² *verb*
1 *also* **load up** to put things on or into a vehicle: *We loaded the van with boxes to take to the new apartment.* | *They loaded all their luggage into the car.*
2 to put bullets into a gun, or film into a camera: *He loaded the gun with bullets when he heard the noise downstairs.*
3 to put a program into a computer: *It doesn't take long to load the software.*

loaf /loʊf/ *noun* plural **loaves** /loʊvz/
bread that has been cooked in one large piece: *I bought a loaf of bread.*

loan¹ /loʊn/ *noun*
an amount of money that you borrow, especially from a bank: *He had to get a loan from the bank to buy the car.*

loan² *verb*
to lend someone money: *I loaned him $200.* SYNONYM **lend**

loaves /loʊvz/ *noun*
the plural of LOAF

lob·by /ˈlɑbi/ *noun* plural **lobbies**
1 a large hall inside the entrance of a building: *Wait for me downstairs in the hotel lobby.*
2 a group of people who try to persuade the government to do something: *The environmental lobby is becoming more powerful and influential with lawmakers.*
—**lobby** *verb* to try to persuade the government to do something
—**lobbyist** *noun* someone who tries to persuade the government to do something

lob·ster /ˈlɑbstɚ/ *noun*
a sea animal which has a hard body and ten legs, two with large CLAWs: *Lobsters turn red when they are cooked.*

lobster

lo·cal /ˈloʊkəl/ *adjective*
in or relating to the area where someone lives: *We borrowed books from the local library.*
—**locally** *adverb* in the area where someone lives: *Most of the fruit we buy is grown locally.*
➔ See Thesaurus box at **near¹**

ˈlocal time *noun*
the time in a particular part of the world: *We'll arrive in Denver at four o'clock local time.*

lo·cate /ˈloʊkeɪt/ Ac *verb, formal*
1 **be located** = to be in a particular place: *The hotel is located near the airport, so it's easy to get to.*
2 to find the place where something is: *The police have located the hidden bomb.*
➔ See Thesaurus box at **find**

lo·ca·tion /loʊˈkeɪʃən/ Ac *noun*
a particular place or position: *His apartment is in a really good location close to stores and restaurants.*
➔ See Thesaurus box at **place¹**

lock¹ /lɑk/ *noun*
a thing that keeps a door, drawer, etc. shut, which you open with a key: *This key doesn't open this lock.*

lock² *verb*
to close a door, drawer, etc. with a lock: *Did you remember to lock the door when you left this morning?* | *Her parents locked her in her room* (=locked the door so she could not get out). ANTONYM **unlock**

PHRASAL VERB
lock up
1 **lock someone or something up** *also* **lock someone or something away** = to lock a door, drawer, etc. so that someone or something cannot leave or be taken out: *They should lock up criminals like that and never let them out.*
2 to lock all the doors of a building: *Don't forget to lock up when you leave.*

lock·er /ˈlɑkɚ/ *noun*
a small cupboard where you leave things you own, especially at school or when you are playing sports

ˈlocker room *noun*
a room where people change their clothes before playing sports that has lockers in it

lo·co·mo·tive /ˌloʊkəˈmoʊtɪv/ *noun*
the part of a train that pulls the other parts along SYNONYM **engine**

lodge¹ /lɑdʒ/ *verb*
1 to become stuck somewhere: *A fish bone had lodged in his throat.*
2 **lodge a complaint/protest** *formal* = to officially complain about something: *I would*

like to lodge a complaint with management about the bad service we received.

lodge² *noun*
a simple building or hotel in the country or in the mountains where people can stay for a short time: *a ski lodge*

lodg•ing /ˈlɑdʒɪŋ/ *noun*
a place to stay: *The tourist office will help you find lodging when you arrive.*

loft /lɔft/ *noun*
an area with a floor that is above a room or in a BARN: *The farmer stored hay in the loft.*

log¹ /lɔg/ *noun*
1 a thick piece of wood cut from a tree: *Put another log on the fire so the flame doesn't go out.*
2 an official record of things that have happened or been done: *The ship's captain wrote what had happened in the log.*

log² *verb* **logged, logging**
PHRASAL VERBS
log off/out
to stop using a computer, computer program, or WEBSITE: *Log off when you're finished using the program.*
log on/in
to enter information to start using a computer, computer program, or WEBSITE: *I can't log on because I've forgotten my password.*

log•ging /ˈlɔgɪŋ/ *noun*
the activity of cutting down trees in a forest

log•ic /ˈlɑdʒɪk/ Ac *noun*
a way of thinking in which you think very carefully about facts and how the facts are related: *The detective used logic to figure out who must have taken the money.*

WORD FAMILY look at the words:
→ **logic** *noun*
→ **logical** *adjective*
→ **illogical** *adjective*
→ **logically** *adverb*

log•i•cal /ˈlɑdʒɪkəl/ Ac *adjective*
sensible and based on good thinking: *It seems logical to give kids a good breakfast if we want them to be ready to learn all morning.* ANTONYM **illogical**
—**logically** *adverb*

lo•go /ˈloʊgoʊ/ *noun* plural **logos**
a picture that is the official sign of a company or organization: *The players have the team logo on their helmets.*

lol•li•pop /ˈlɑliˌpɑp/ *noun*
a hard candy on the end of a stick

lone /loʊn/ *adjective, formal*
a lone person or thing is the only one that is somewhere or does something: *The lone survivor of the crash was the driver.*

lone•ly /ˈloʊnli/ *adjective*
1 unhappy because you are alone: *He is lonely without his wife.*
2 *formal* a long way from where people live: *a lonely country road*
—**loneliness** *noun* the feeling you have when you are lonely

lone•some /ˈloʊnsəm/ *adjective*
lonely: *I felt so lonesome when she left.*

long¹ /lɔŋ/ *adjective*
1 measuring a large distance from one end to the other: *Julie has long hair.* | *A long line of people waited ahead of me.* ANTONYM **short**
2 continuing for large amount of time: *I had a long talk with him.* | *It happened a long time ago – back in 1853.* ANTONYM **short**
3 used to ask or talk about the length of something: *"How long is the movie?" "About 3 hours."* | *The snake was three feet long.*
4 a long book has a lot of pages: *The book was long and it took me months to read it.* ANTONYM **short**

long² *adverb*
1 *also* **for long** for a long time: *Have you been waiting long?* | *He didn't stay angry for long. The next day he was fine.*
2 **long before/after** = a long time before or after an event: *He died long before you were born.*
3 **as long as** = if: *You can go as long as you're back by four o'clock.*
4 **no longer** *also* **not any longer** = if a situation that existed in the past no longer exists, it does not exist now: *She no longer teaches at this school – she's now at Hansen Middle School.*
5 **before long** = soon: *Before long, we arrived at the station.*
6 **so long** = goodbye

L

long³ *verb, formal*
to want something very much: *She longed to go home and thought about it every day.*

ˌlong-ˈdistance *adjective*
1 a long-distance (telephone/phone) call = a telephone call to someone who lives far away: *Long-distance phone calls don't cost any extra on my cell phone.* ANTONYM **local**
2 traveling between places that are far away from each other: *long-distance truck drivers*
—**long-distance** *adverb* speaking by telephone to someone who is far away, or traveling long distances: *She called her boyfriend long-distance every night while she was on vacation.*

long·ing /ˈlɔŋɪŋ/ *noun, formal*
a strong feeling of wanting someone or something very much: *He was filled with longing to be back home.*
—**longingly** *adverb, formal*: *The boy looked longingly at the cookies in the jar, but his mother said "no."*

lon·gi·tude /ˈlɑndʒəˌtud/ *noun*
the distance east or west of an imaginary line going from the top of the Earth to the bottom. Longitude is measured in degrees: *The island at longitude 21° west.*

ˈlong jump *noun*
the long jump = a sport in which you jump as far as possible

L

ˌlong-ˈrunning *adjective* **longest-running**
happening continuously for a long time: *The long-running legal battle has now lasted five years.*

ˌlong-ˈterm *adjective*
relating to what will happen a long time in the future: *When I was seven years old, my long-term goal was to become a professional baseball player by age 22.* ANTONYM **short-term**

look¹ /lʊk/ *verb*
1 to move your eyes toward something or something so that you can see them: *David took $5 from her purse when she wasn't looking.* | *She looked at me and smiled.*

THESAURUS: look

Look At Something

glance to look at someone or something for a short time and then look quickly away: *Kevin glanced at the clock.*

peek to quickly look at something, especially something you are not supposed to see: *Close your eyes and don't peek – I'm going to bring you a surprise.*

peer to look very carefully, especially because you cannot see something well: *Hansen peered through the car window at the street signs.*

stare to look at someone or something for a long time, especially without closing your eyes: *That man is staring at me!*

gaze to look at someone or something for a long time, often without realizing that you are doing it: *Helen gazed out the window at the lake.*

Look For Something

search to look carefully for someone or something: *We searched the whole house for the keys.*

try to find someone/something to look for someone or something, especially when this is difficult: *He's been trying to find a job for six months.*

seek *formal* to try to find someone or something: *You should seek advice from your doctor.*

USAGE: look

You **look at** a picture, person, thing, etc. because you want to: *Hey, look at the hat that guy is wearing.* | *Maria was looking at a picture book.*

You **see** something without planning to: *Two people saw him take the woman's purse.* | *I saw a big black dog in the park.*

You **watch** TV, a movie, or something that happens for a period of time: *My parents always come to watch me play basketball.* | *The kids are watching TV.*

You can also say that you saw a movie, a program, etc., but you cannot say "see television": *I saw a great movie on TV last night.*

2 to try to find someone or something using your eyes: *I looked everywhere for my car keys but I couldn't find them.* | *"Is there any orange juice?" " Look in the refrigerator."*
3 to try to find someone or something that you need: *He says he wants a new job, but he's not looking very hard.* | *We're looking for a new secretary in my office. Do you know of anyone?*

4 to seem or appear to be something: *He doesn't look like a criminal – he seems so nice.* | *Mom's eyes were closed and she looked tired.*

5 -looking = having a particular type of appearance: *That's a strange-looking dog!*

6 Look... = said when you are annoyed and you want to emphasize what you are saying: *Look, I'm not giving you any money, so don't ask me again!*

➔ See Thesaurus box at **seem**

➔ See picture at **see**

PHRASAL VERBS

look after someone

to take care of someone or something: *Sarah asked me to look after the children while she went shopping.*

look ahead

to think about what will happen in the future: *You should forget about the past and look ahead to the future.*

look around (something)

to look at what is in a building, store, place while you are walking: *We have about three hours to look around downtown.*

look forward to something

to be excited and happy about something that is going to happen: *I'm really looking forward to seeing my dad when he comes home.*

look into something

to try to find out the truth about a crime or problem: *The police are looking into the cause of the fire.*

look on

1 to watch something, without being involved in it: *A truck pulled the car out of the mud while several people looked on.*

2 look on/upon something *formal* = to think about something in a particular way: *There are some problems that I have to solve, but I look on them as challenges.*

look out

look out! = use this to tell someone to pay attention because something dangerous is happening: *Look out! There's a car coming.*

look something over *informal*

to examine something quickly: *Can you look over this job application before I send it?*

look up

1 look something up = to try to find information in a book: *I had to look the word up in the dictionary to find out what it means.*

2 look someone up = to go to see someone you know when you are visiting the place where he or she lives: *Don't forget to look up my parents when you're in Seattle.*

look up to someone

to admire and respect someone: *He looks up to his older brothers and wants to be just like them.*

look² *noun*

1 an act of looking at something: *We decided to take a look around the museum and see what was there.*

2 an expression that you make with your eyes or face to show how you feel: *There was a look of hate in his eyes.* | *Jon gave me a strange look* (=looked at me in a strange way).

look•out /ˈlʊk-aʊt/ *noun*

1 be on the lookout (for something) *informal* = to pay attention to things around you in order to find something that you want, or to avoid something bad: *We are always on the lookout for talented singers to hire for our club.* | *Be on the lookout for snakes – they hide in the grass.*

2 someone whose job is to watch carefully for danger

looks /lʊks/ *plural noun*

how attractive someone is: *He has the good looks to be a model.*

loom /lum/ *verb, formal*

to appear as a large unclear shape that seems dangerous or frightening: *The huge house loomed over him in the darkness.*

loop¹ /lup/ *noun*

a shape like a circle in a piece of string or wire: *The keys were hanging from a loop of string.*

loop² *verb*

to put a piece of rope, string, etc. around or over something in a shape like a circle: *I looped the rope around the tree and tied a knot.*

loop•hole /ˈluphoʊl/ *noun*

a small mistake in a law that makes it possible to legally avoid doing what the law intended: *Congress plans to close this loophole in the law so that all businesses will have to pay the tax.*

loose /lus/ *adjective*

1 not firmly attached to something: *I have two loose teeth, and they'll probably fall out soon.* | *One of the buttons on my shirt is coming loose – I need to sew it on better.*

2 loose clothes do not fit tightly on your body: *My jeans are loose and comfortable.* SYNONYM **baggy**

3 free to move around, not in a CAGE, prison, etc.: *The dogs got loose and started chasing the horses.*

4 if your hair is loose, it is not tied or kept firmly in place: *Her hair was loose and hung down her back.*

—**loosely** *adverb*: *His clothes were too big and they hung loosely on her.*

—**looseness** *noun*

ˌloose-ˈleaf *adjective*

having pages that can be put in or removed easily: *You can add pages to a loose-leaf binder.*

loos•en /ˈlusən/ *verb*

to make something less tight or less firmly fastened: *He took off his shoes and loosened his tie.* | *The ropes around her wrist had started to loosen because of her movements.*

loot /lut/ *verb*

to steal things from stores or houses during a war or RIOT: *The mob started looting stores and setting fire to cars.*

—**loot** *noun* money or things that have been stolen, especially during a war

—**looting** *noun* the act of stealing things during a war or RIOT

—**looter** *noun* someone who loots

lop•sid•ed /ˌlɑpˈsaɪdɪd/ *adjective, informal*

1 having one side that is heavier, larger, or lower than the other side: *a lopsided smile*

2 not equal or fair: *The Red Sox beat Baltimore 10–0 in a lopsided game.*

lord *also* **Lord** /lɔrd/ *noun*

1 **Lord** *also* **the Lord** = a title used for God or Jesus Christ, used especially when praying: *Let us give thanks to the Lord our God.*

2 a man in Britain who has a particular position in the ARISTOCRACY: *the poet, Lord Byron*

lose /luz/ *verb* **lost** /lɔst/

1 to stop having something that is important to you or that you need: *Michelle lost her job and needs to get another one quickly.* | *Her family lost everything they owned in the storm.*

2 to be unable to find someone or something: *I think I've lost my wallet – I've been looking everywhere for it.*

3 to not win a game, war, etc.: *Napoleon's army was defeated, and France lost the war.* | *We played well, but we still lost the game by 2 points.*

4 to have less of something than before: *I need to lose weight.*

5 **lose your sight/memory/voice, etc.** = to stop being able to see, remember things, talk, etc.: *Grandpa's getting old and losing his hearing.*

6 to not have a particular quality, attitude, etc. anymore: *Marie lost interest in going to college and decided to get a job instead.*

7 **lose your temper** = to become angry: *Jake lost his temper and started yelling at everyone.*

8 you say you lose a member of your family when he or she dies: *Mrs. Keenan lost two sons in the war.*

9 **lose your life** = to die: *More than 2,000 people lost their lives in the earthquake.*

10 **lose someone** *informal* = to confuse someone when you are trying to explain something: *You lost me. Can you explain it again, please?*

WORD FAMILY look at the words:

→ **lose** *verb*
→ **lost** *adjective*
→ **loser** *noun*
→ **loss** *noun*

los•er *noun* /ˈluzɚ/

1 someone who loses a competition or game: *The losers of this game will get the silver medal, and the winners will get the gold medal.* ANTONYM **winner**

2 *informal* you use this about someone who you do not like or respect: *Don't go to the dance with him – he's such a loser.*

loss /lɔs/ *noun*

1 the fact of no longer having something: *weight loss* | *The factory is closing, and there will be many job losses.*

2 if a business makes a loss, it spends more money than it earns: *The company had huge*

losses last year, and investors were not happy.
3 an occasion when you do not win a game: *The team has 3 wins and 4 losses this season*
4 the death of someone: *We are all very sad at the loss of a dear friend.*

lost¹ /lɔst/ *adjective*
1 if you get lost, you do not know where you are or how to get somewhere: *It's easy to get lost in a city this big.* | *We were lost, so we asked a policeman for directions.*
2 if something is lost, you cannot find it: *I'm calling to report a lost credit card.*
3 Get lost! *informal* = used to tell someone rudely to go away or to stop annoying you

lost² *verb*
the past tense and past participle of LOSE

ˌlost-and-ˈfound *noun*
a place where bags, coats, etc. that people have lost are kept until someone comes to get them

lot /lɑt/ *noun*
1 a lot a) *also* **lots** *informal* a large amount or number: *A million dollars is a lot of money.* | *The police asked me lots of questions, but I couldn't answer them all.* **b)** very much: *I like her a lot – she's a very good friend.* | *We'll get there a lot faster if we drive than if we walk.*

GRAMMAR: lot

a lot of, much, many

In sentences with "not", you can use **much** or **many** instead of **a lot of**.

Much is used with nouns that are things you cannot count: *There isn't much milk left.*

Many is used with nouns that show there is more than one thing or person: *I didn't see many people there that I knew.*

A lot of can be used with both types of noun: *There isn't a lot of time to work on this.* | *She doesn't have a lot of friends.*

2 a small area of land in a town or city that is used for a particular purpose, especially for building houses: *We bought the empty lot next to our house.*
➔ **parking lot**

lo•tion /ˈloʊʃən/ *noun*
a liquid that you put on your skin in order to make it soft or to protect it: *I put hand lotion on my dry hands.*

lot•ter•y /ˈlɑtəri/ *noun* plural **lotteries**
a game in which you buy tickets with a series of numbers on them. If your number is picked, you can win a lot of money: *Maybe I'll win the lottery and never have to work again!* | *a lottery ticket*

lot•to /ˈlɑtoʊ/ *noun*
a lottery: *He won $10.5 million in the New York Lotto.*

loud /laʊd/ *adjective*
making a lot of noise: *The music was so loud that I didn't hear the phone.* | *He heard a loud bang followed by gunshots.* ANTONYM **quiet**
—**loudly** *adverb*
—**loudness** *noun*

loud•speak•er /ˈlaʊdˌspikɚ/ *noun*
a piece of equipment that makes sounds louder: *A voice on the loudspeaker told us that the flight was delayed.*

loudspeaker

lounge¹ /laʊndʒ/ *noun*
a room in a hotel, an airport, or other public building where people can relax, sit down, or have a drink: *We sat and waited for the taxi in the hotel lounge.*

lounge² *verb*
to sit or lie in a place in a very relaxed way without doing much: *My brother and his friends were lounging in front of the TV.*

louse /laʊs/ *noun* plural **lice** /laɪs/
a very small insect that can live on the skin and hair of animals and people

lous•y /ˈlaʊzi/ *adjective, informal*
very bad: *I lied to her, and now I feel lousy.* | *We had lousy seats, way in back of the theater.*
➔ See Thesaurus box at **bad**

lov•a•ble /ˈlʌvəbəl/ *adjective*
easy to love: *a sweet, lovable child*

love¹ /lʌv/ *verb*
1 to care very much about someone, especially a member of your family or a close

friend: *Mom loved us, fed us, and looked after us.*
2 to have a strong romantic feeling for someone: *I love you Amy, and I want to marry you.*
3 to enjoy doing something very much: *Tom loves to read. | I love playing hockey.*
➔ See Thesaurus box at **enjoy**

love² *noun*
1 a strong romantic feeling for someone: *He is in love with Laura. | We fell in love, got married, and had children.*
2 the strong feeling of caring very much about someone or something: *a mother's love for her child*
3 something that you like or enjoy doing very much: *My sister and I both have a love of books.*
4 someone you love romantically: *Mike was my first love.*
5 love/lots of love/all my love *informal* = written at the end of a letter to a friend, parent, husband, etc.: *Take care. Lots of love, Dad.*

ˈlove afˌfair *noun*
a romantic sexual relationship between two people who are not married to each other: *His wife divorced him when she found out about his love affair.*

love·ly /ˈlʌvli/ *adjective*
1 attractive: *She was lovely with beautiful black hair and big brown eyes.*
2 very enjoyable: *Everyone had a lovely time at the beach.*

lov·er /ˈlʌvɚ/ *noun*
1 someone who is having a sexual relationship with someone he or she is not married to
2 someone who enjoys something very much: *The park was full of dog lovers, walking their dogs.*

lov·ing /ˈlʌvɪŋ/ *adjective*
a loving mother, wife, husband, etc. behaves in a gentle and caring way toward the people she or he loves: *She has a wonderful loving husband and three great kids.*

low¹ /loʊ/ *adjective*
1 not high, or not far above the ground: *I picked an apple from one of the lower branches. | The dog jumped over the low wall easily.* ANTONYM **high**
2 small in degree or amount: *The work is hard and the pay is low. | The restaurant serves good food at low prices.* ANTONYM **high**
3 bad, or below the usual standard: *The teacher gave Kim a low grade for not turning in the assignment.* ANTONYM **high**
4 if a supply of something is low, you have used almost all of it and there is not much left: *Ali was running low on cash and needed a job. | Supplies of food are getting low.*
5 unhappy: *I've been feeling low ever since my best friend moved away.* SYNONYM **depressed**
6 a low sound is quiet: *"I am leaving now," she said in a low voice that I could barely hear.* ANTONYM **loud**

low² *adverb*
in a low position or at a low level: *It was evening, and the sun was low in the sky. | There's a lot of noise from low-flying aircraft.* ANTONYM **high**

low³ *noun, formal*
a low level: *Support for the senator has dropped to a new low.* ANTONYM **high**

low·er¹ /ˈloʊɚ/ *verb*
1 to reduce something in amount, strength, etc.: *The company has lowered the prices of many of its video games to increase sales. | She lowered her voice* (=spoke more quietly) *so that father couldn't hear us.*
2 to move something down: *The flag is lowered every evening and put away.*
➔ See Thesaurus box at **reduce**

lower² *adjective*
1 below something else of the same kind: *He cut his lower lip in a fight. | Our apartment's on one of the lower floors of the building.* ANTONYM **upper**
2 smaller in amount, level, etc. than something else: *Prices are usually lower in the supermarket. | Temperatures outside will be lower than yesterday.*

low·er·case /ˈloʊɚˌkeɪs/ *noun, formal*
letters written in their small form, such as a, b, c, etc.: *Use a capital letter for the first word in the sentence and write the rest in lowercase.* ANTONYM **uppercase**
—**lowercase** *adjective* lowercase letters are written in their small form: *a lowercase m*

ˌlower ˈclass *noun*
the lower class = the people in a country who do not have much money or power
—**lower-class** *adjective* relating to the lower class: *She was born into a a lower-class family.*

ˌlow ˈtide *noun*
the time when the ocean is at its lowest level and far away from the shore
→ **high tide**

loy•al /ˈlɔɪəl/ *adjective*
always supporting someone, an organization, country, idea etc.: *The team has loyal fans that come to every game.* | *She remained loyal to her husband even after she discovered he had been lying to her.*
—**loyalty** *noun* the quality of being loyal: *All the players feel a strong loyalty to the team.*

lu•bri•cate /ˈlubrəˌkeɪt/ *verb, formal*
to put a substance such as oil on something in order to make it move smoothly: *Lubricate the door with some oil, so that it doesn't squeak.*
—**lubrication** /ˌlubrəˈkeɪʃən/ *noun* the act of lubricating something
—**lubricant** /ˈlubrəkənt/ *noun* a substance that is put on something in order to make it move smoothly

luck /lʌk/ *noun*
1 *also* **good luck** good things that happen to people by chance: *Have you had any luck finding someone to rent the room?* | *People throw rice at the married couple for good luck.*
2 bad luck = bad things that happen to people by chance: *We've had a lot of bad luck recently – first the car broke down, then I broke my arm, and last week Julio's wallet was stolen.*
3 Good luck! = used to tell someone that you hope that he or she will be successful: *Good luck on your exam!*
4 be in luck/be out of luck = to get or not get something that you want: *You're in luck – there's one ticket left!*

luck•y /ˈlʌki/ *adjective* **luckier**, **luckiest**
1 having good luck: *It was a terrible accident, and he's lucky to be alive.* | *We were lucky (that) the plane was delayed because we got to the airport very late.* | *I look at my family, and I feel like the luckiest guy in the world.* SYNONYM **fortunate**; ANTONYM **unlucky**
2 bringing good luck: *Seven is my lucky number.*
—**luckily** *adverb*: *Luckily, no one was hurt.*

lug /lʌg/ *verb* **lugged, lugging** *informal*
to carry something with difficulty because it is very heavy: *We had to lug our bags up to the 5th floor.*

lug•gage /ˈlʌgɪdʒ/ *noun*
the bags that you carry when you are traveling: *She helped us carry our luggage to our hotel room.*
→ See picture on page A30

luke•warm /ˌlukˈwɔrm/ *adjective*
1 liquid or food that is lukewarm is slightly warm, often when it should be hot: *a cup of lukewarm tea*
2 not showing very much interest or excitement: *Critics gave the movie a lukewarm reception* (=they were not very excited about it).
→ See Thesaurus box at **hot**

lul•la•by /ˈlʌləˌbaɪ/ *noun* plural **lullabies**
a quiet slow song that you sing to children in order to make them go to sleep: *Maria sat on the edge of her son's bed and sang him a lullaby.*

lum•ber /ˈlʌmbɚ/ *noun*
wood that is used for building: *We bought some lumber to build a new porch.*

lum•ber•jack /ˈlʌmbɚˌdʒæk/ *noun*
someone whose job is cutting down trees for wood

lump /lʌmp/ *noun*
1 a small piece of something solid that does not have a definite shape: *Stir the mixture until all the lumps are gone.* | *a lump of coal*
2 a small hard swollen area just under the surface of the skin, caused by an injury or illness: *She felt a lump in her breast and decided to have an X-ray.*
→ See Thesaurus box at **piece**

lump•y /ˈlʌmpi/ *adjective* **lumpier**, **lumpiest** *informal*
something that is lumpy has small solid pieces in it when it should not: *A lumpy mattress is hard to sleep on.* | *The sauce was lumpy because it hadn't been stirred enough.*

lu•nar /ˈlunɚ/ *adjective, formal*
relating to the moon: *The spacecraft landed on the lunar surface.*

L

lu•na•tic /ˈlunətɪk/ *noun, informal*
someone who behaves in a crazy or very stupid way: *I saw him chasing his wife down the road like a lunatic.*

lunch /lʌntʃ/ *noun*
a meal that you eat in the middle of the day: *I had a sandwich for lunch.* | *"What time do you eat lunch?" "At noon."* | *Let's have lunch at the Chinese restaurant.*
➔ See Thesaurus box at **meal**

lunch•time /ˈlʌntʃtaɪm/ *noun*
the time in the middle of the day when people eat lunch: *I usually just have a sandwich at lunchtime.*

lung /lʌŋ/ *noun*
one of the two parts inside your body that you use for breathing: *Smoking is bad for your lungs.*
➔ See picture on page A2

lunge /lʌndʒ/ *verb*
to move toward someone or something quickly and using your strength: *She lunged at Jim, hitting him hard in the face.*
—**lunge** *noun* a sudden strong movement toward someone or something

lurch /lɚtʃ/ *verb*
to move forward suddenly in an uncontrolled way: *The train lurched forward, throwing some people to the floor.*
—**lurch** *noun* an uncontrolled movement forward

L

lush /lʌʃ/ *adjective, formal*
lush plants are healthy and have a lot of green leaves: *a lush green lawn*

lux•u•ry /ˈlʌkʃəri/ *noun* plural **luxuries**
1 comfort and pleasure that you get from expensive things: *They live a life of luxury in a huge house with a swimming pool.* | *a luxury car with leather seats*
2 something expensive that you want but do not need: *I can't afford to buy luxuries such as chocolates and cookies for my kids.*
—**luxurious** /lʌgˈʒʊriəs/ *adjective* very expensive, beautiful, and comfortable: *They have a luxurious home with five huge bedrooms and a formal dining room.*

ly•ing /ˈlaɪ-ɪŋ/ *verb*
the present participle of LIE

lynch /lɪntʃ/ *verb*
if a crowd of people lynches someone, they kill that person by HANGing him or her illegally: *A crowd of angry men lynched him before the trial could start.*
—**lynching** *noun* an occasion when someone is lynched

lyr•ics /ˈlɪrɪks/ *plural noun*
the words of a popular song: *I love the lyrics to this song but I don't really like the tune.*
—**lyricist** /ˈlɪrəsɪst/ *noun* someone who writes the words of a song

PICTURE DICTIONARY

Body	A2
Verbs of Movement (hands)	A3
Verbs of Movement (body)	A4
Clothing	A6
Family	A7
Living Room	A8
Kitchen	A9
Bedroom	A10
Bathroom	A11
Vegetables	A12
Fruit and Nuts	A13
Kichen Verbs	A14
Restaurant	A15
Jobs	A16
Office	A18
Computer	A20
Musical Instruments	A21
Sounds	A22
Emotions	A23
Sports	A24
Transportation	A26
Car	A28
Weights and Measures	A29
Airport	A30
Map of the United States	A32

Workbook	A33

The Body

Body

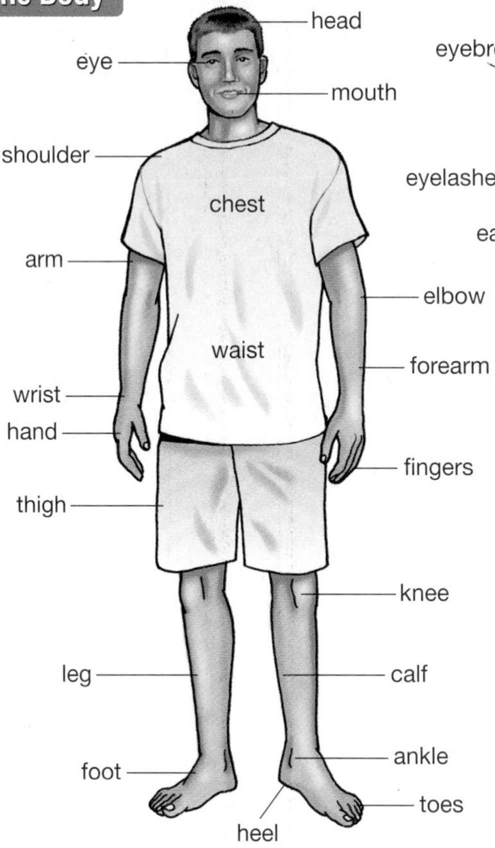

Face

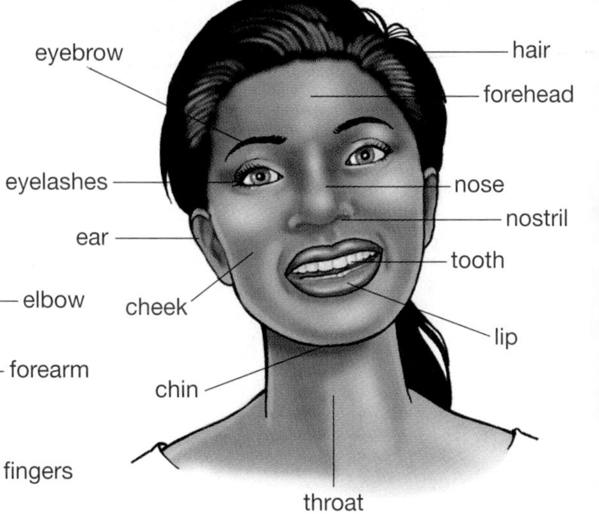

Internal organs

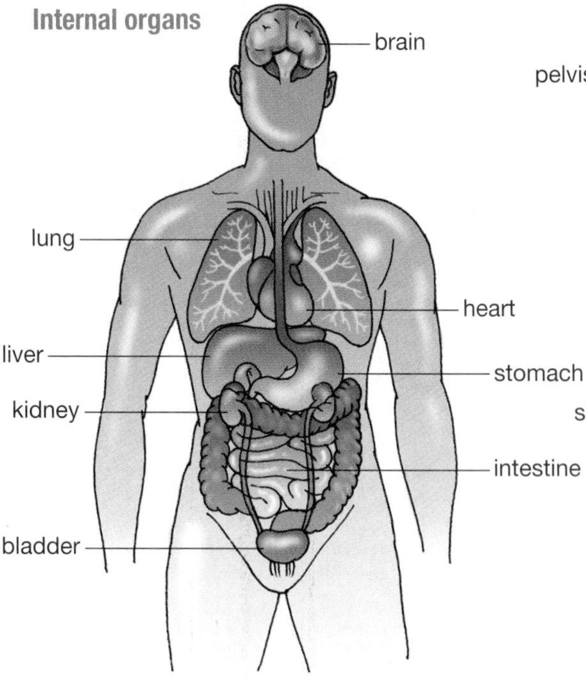

Skeleton

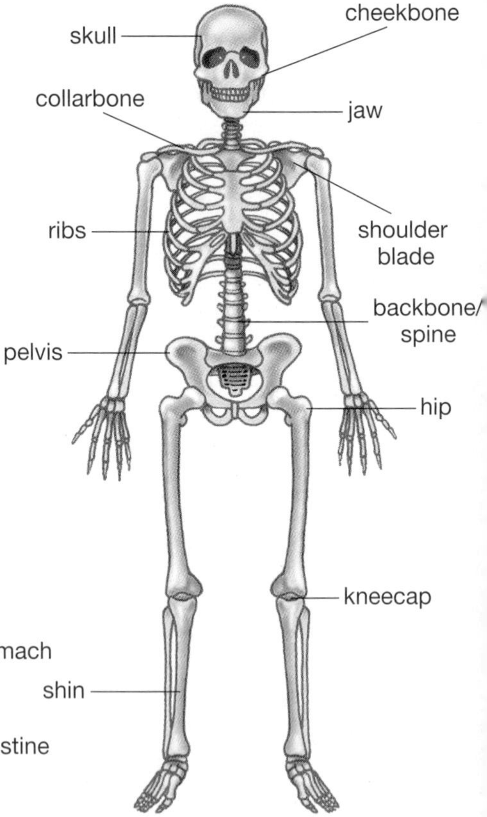

Verbs of Movement (hands)

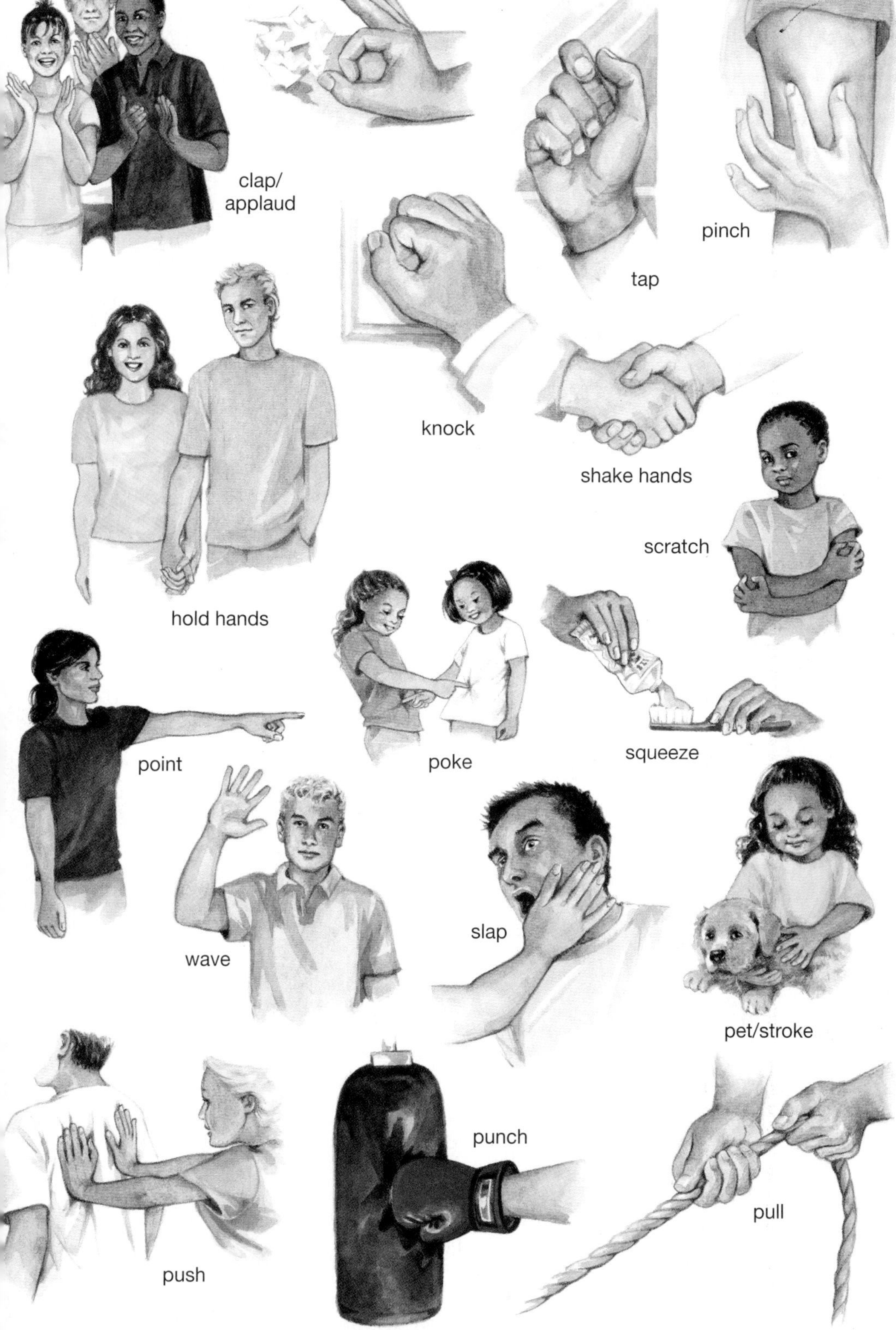

Verbs of Movement (body)

kneel
squat
crouch
trip
lean
stretch
climb
fall
hold
sit
drag
hit
throw
kick
catch

Clothing

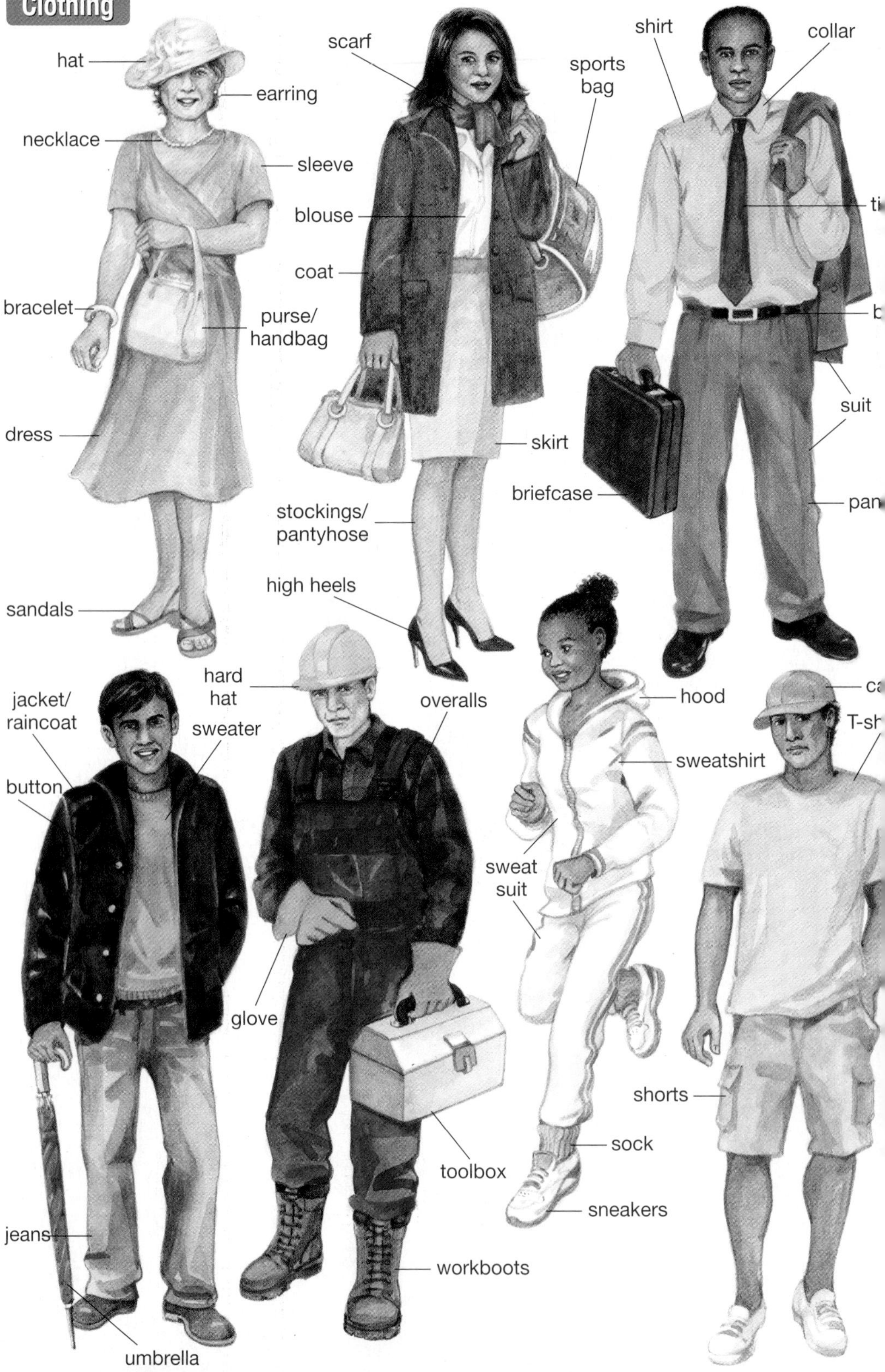
hat
earring
necklace
sleeve
bracelet
purse/
handbag
dress
sandals
scarf
blouse
coat
skirt
stockings/
pantyhose
high heels
sports
bag
shirt
collar
ti
b
suit
briefcase
pan
jacket/
raincoat
button
sweater
jeans
umbrella
hard
hat
overalls
glove
toolbox
workboots
hood
sweatshirt
sweat
suit
sock
sneakers
ca
T-sh
shorts

Family

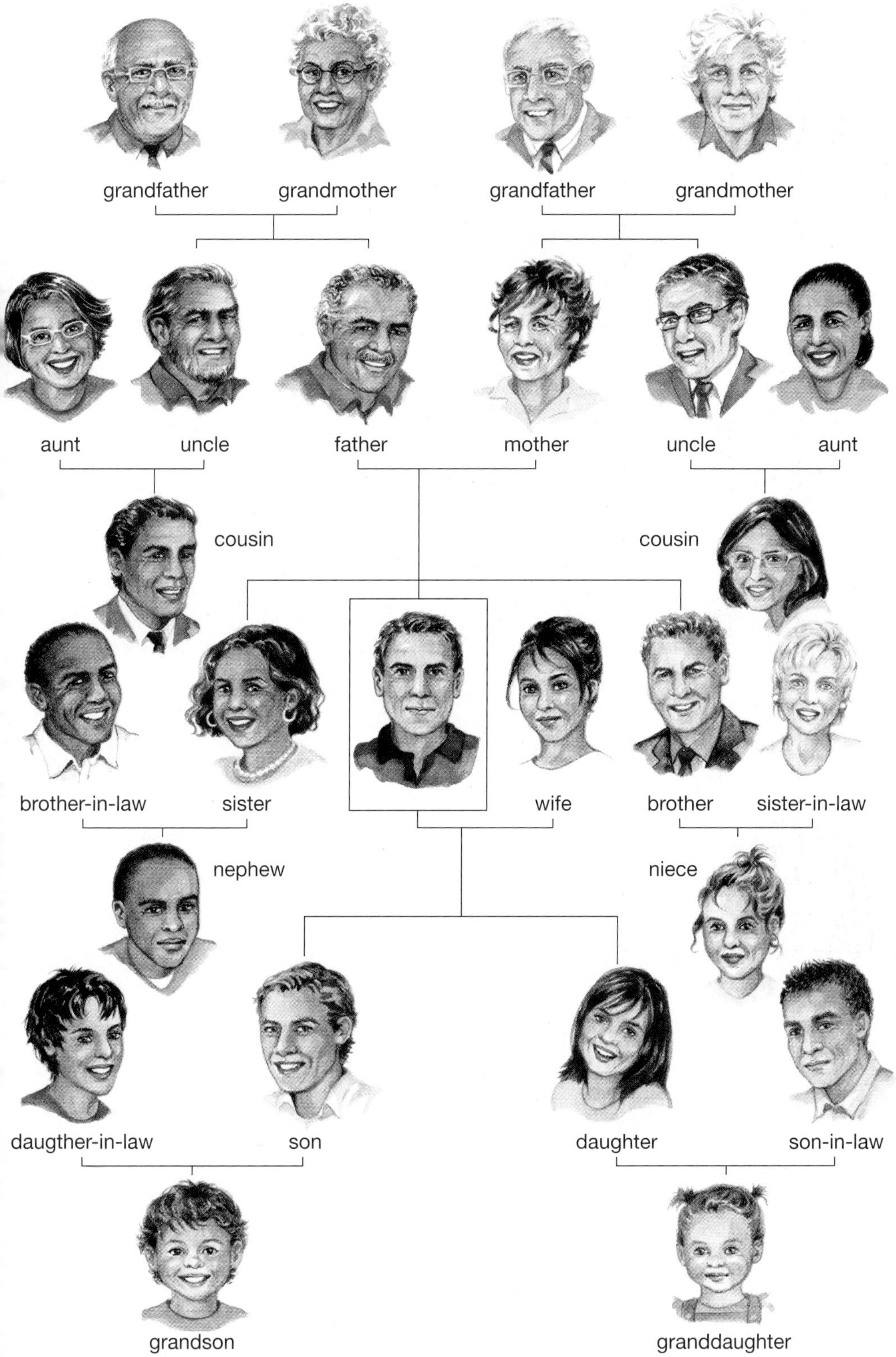

grandfather
grandmother
grandfather
grandmother
aunt
uncle
father
mother
uncle
aunt
cousin
cousin
brother-in-law
sister
wife
brother
sister-in-law
nephew
niece
daugther-in-law
son
daughter
son-in-law
grandson
granddaughter

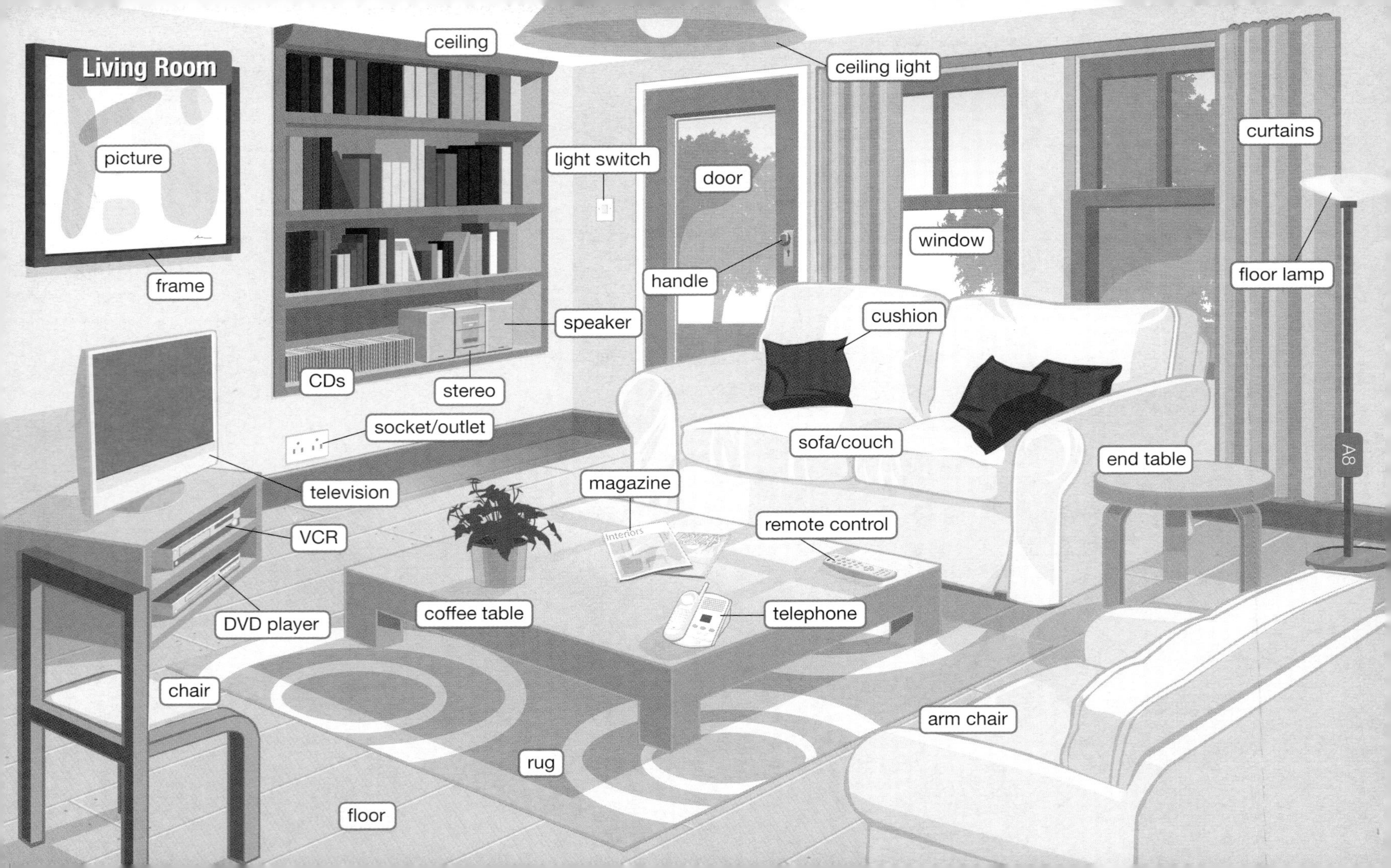
Living Room
picture
frame
ceiling
light switch
door
ceiling light
window
curtains
floor lamp
handle
speaker
cushion
CDs
stereo
socket/outlet
sofa/couch
end table
television
magazine
Interiors
remote control
VCR
coffee table
telephone
DVD player
chair
arm chair
rug
floor

Kitchen

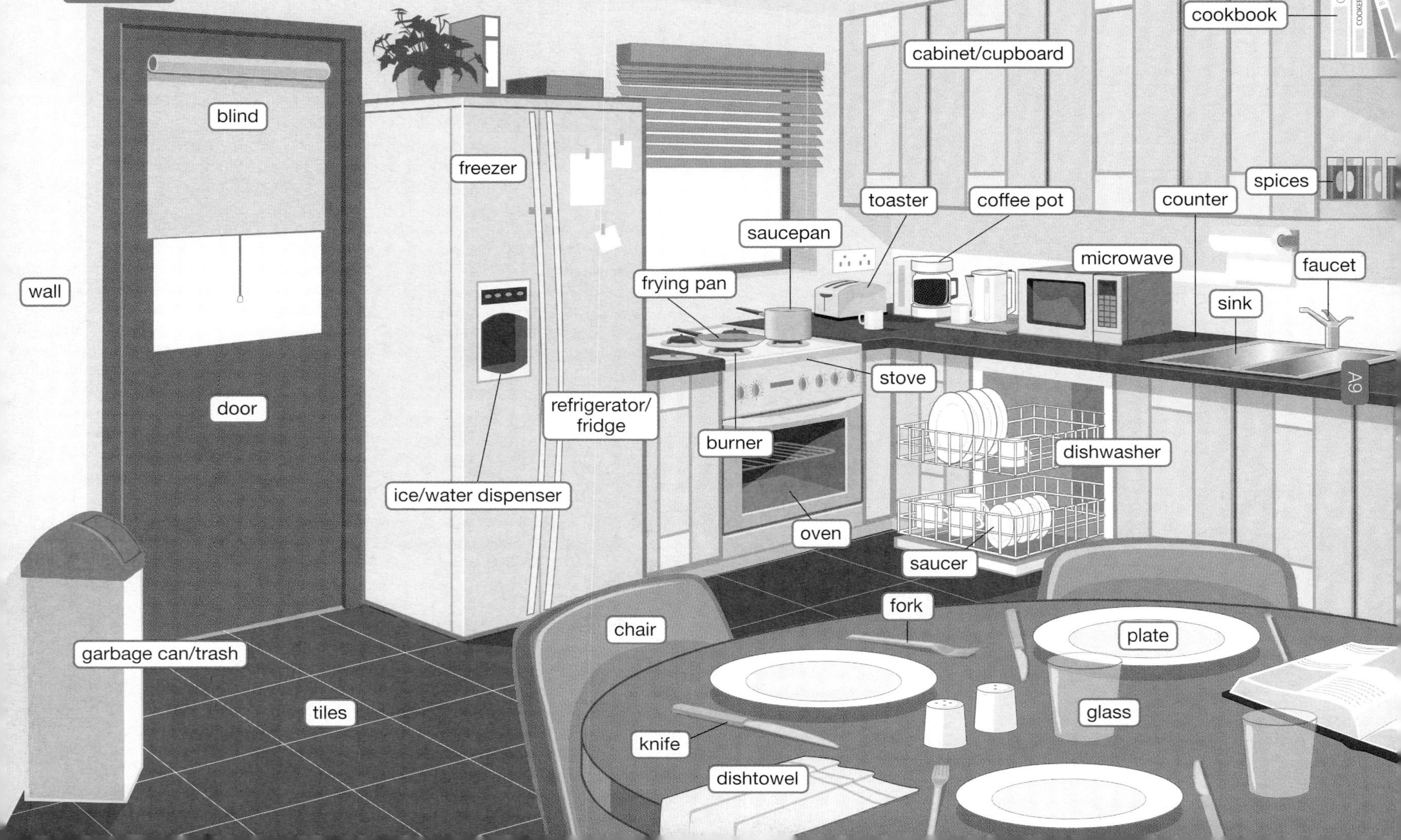

cookbook
cabinet/cupboard
blind
freezer
spices
toaster
coffee pot
counter
saucepan
microwave
faucet
wall
frying pan
sink
stove
door
refrigerator/
fridge
burner
dishwasher
ice/water dispenser
oven
saucer
fork
chair
plate
garbage can/trash
tiles
glass
knife
dishtowel
COOK
COOKERY
BAKING
A9

Bedroom

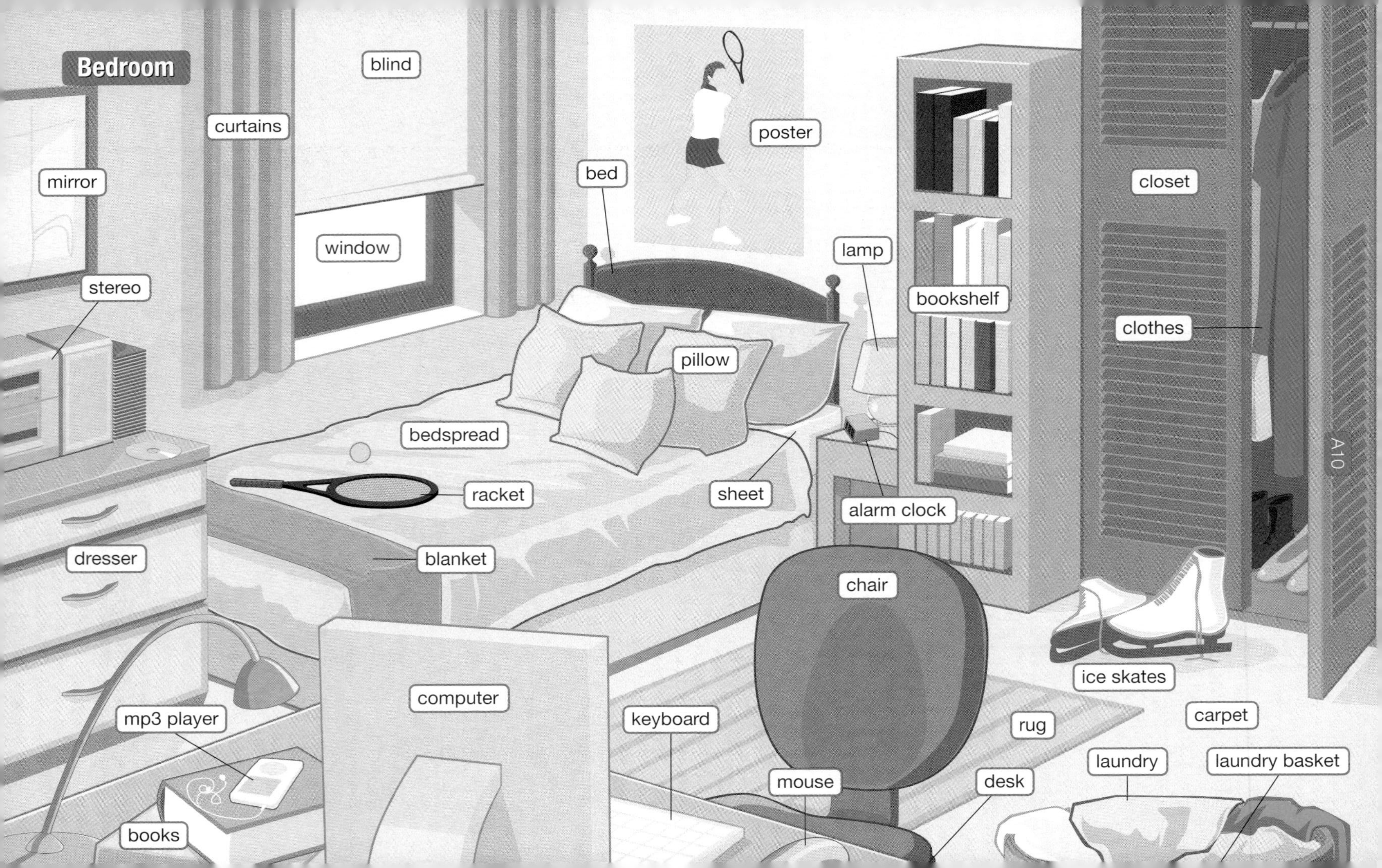
blind
curtains
mirror
window
stereo
bed
poster
closet
lamp
bookshelf
clothes
pillow
bedspread
racket
sheet
alarm clock
dresser
blanket
chair
ice skates
computer
mp3 player
keyboard
rug
carpet
laundry
laundry basket
mouse
desk
books

Bathroom

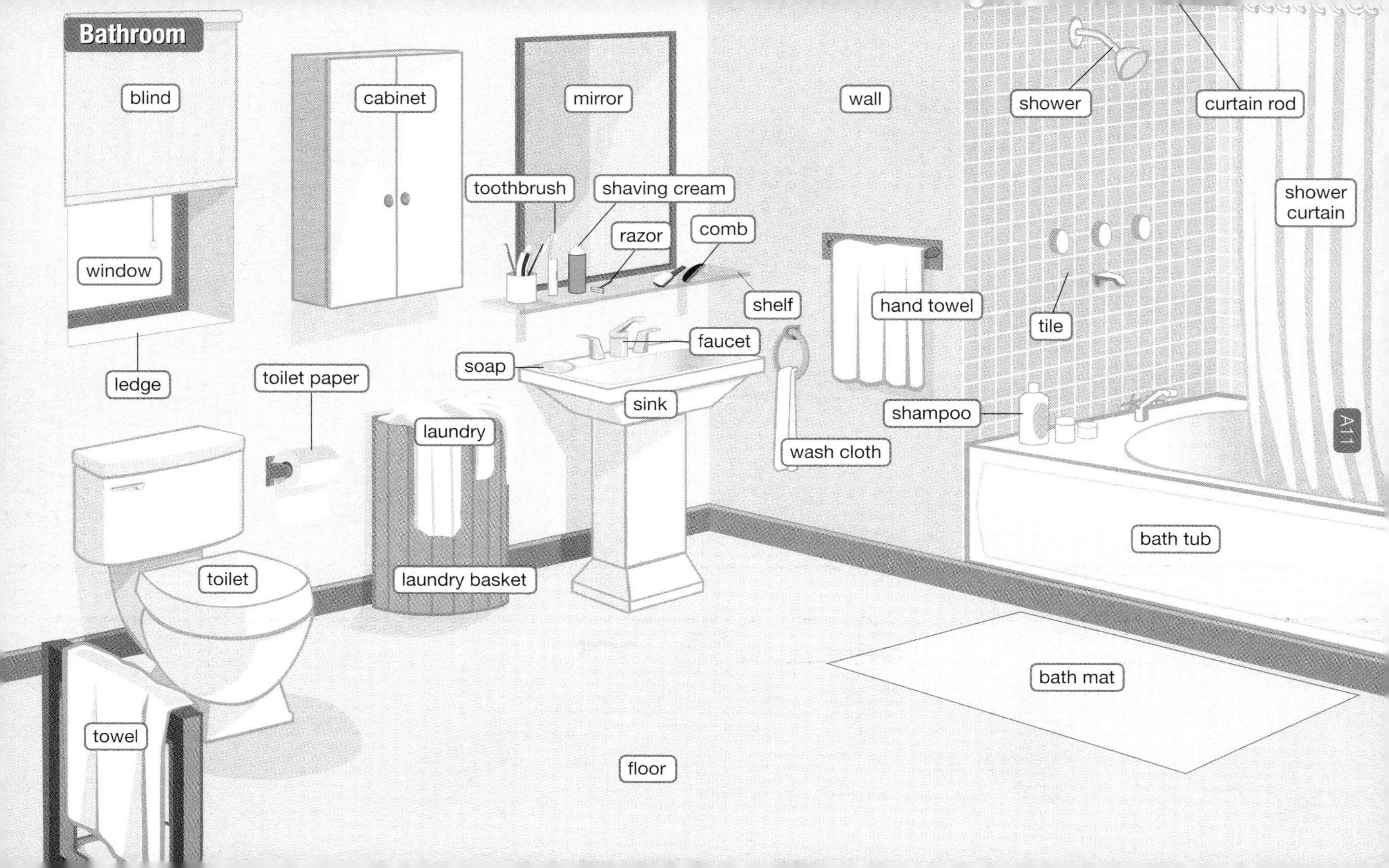
blind
cabinet
mirror
wall
shower
curtain rod
toothbrush
shaving cream
razor
comb
shower
curtain
window
shelf
hand towel
tile
faucet
soap
ledge
toilet paper
sink
shampoo
laundry
wash cloth
bath tub
toilet
laundry basket
bath mat
towel
floor

Vegetables

green onions
lettuce
potato
onion
eggplant
artichoke
radishes
green beans
leek
cucumber
squash
spinach
broccoli
mushrooms
asparagus
garlic
carrots
tomato
celery
zucchini
pumpkin
cabbage
red pepper
green pepper
corn
peas
yellow pepper

Fruit and Nuts

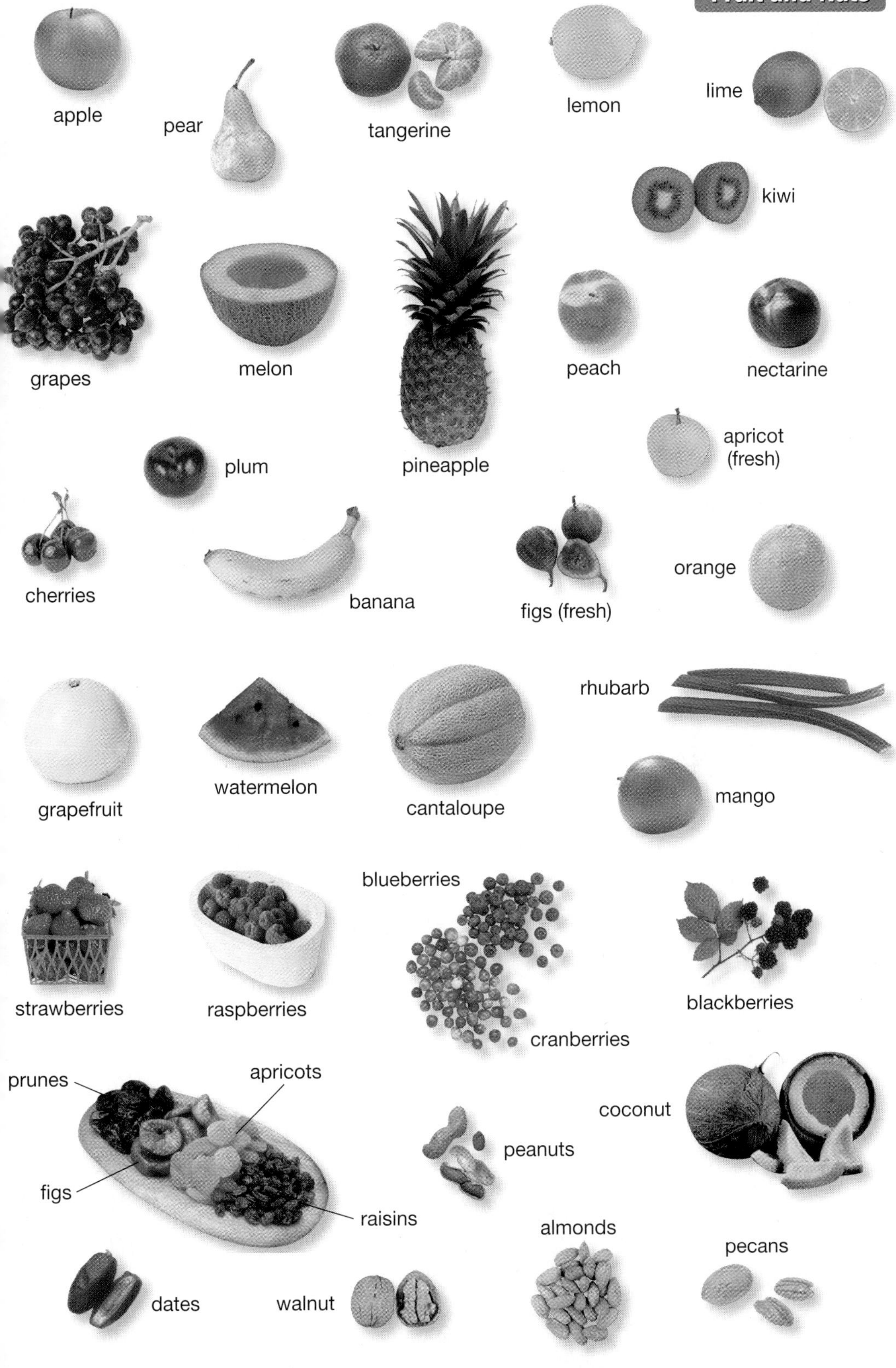
apple
pear
tangerine
lemon
lime
kiwi
grapes
melon
pineapple
peach
nectarine
plum
apricot (fresh)
cherries
banana
figs (fresh)
orange
grapefruit
watermelon
cantaloupe
rhubarb
mango
strawberries
raspberries
blueberries
cranberries
blackberries
prunes
apricots
figs
raisins
coconut
peanuts
almonds
pecans
dates
walnut

Kitchen Verbs

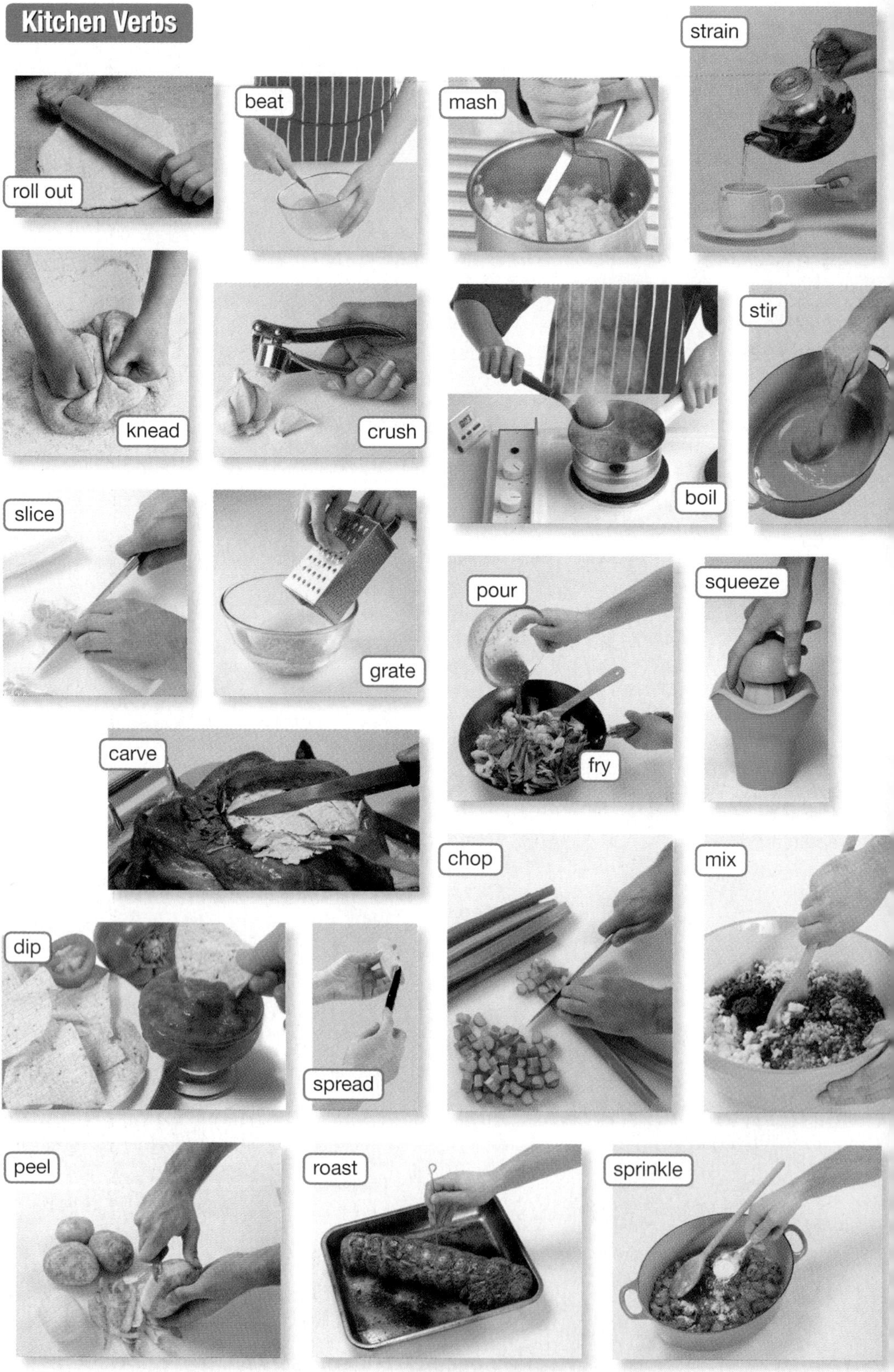

chef
spoon
kitchen
waiter
hostess
straw
cup
tray
waitress
salt
pepper
glass
knife
fork
tablecloth
menu
Beverages
Menu
candle
napkin
customer
chair
table
place mat

Jobs

mechanic
plumber
receptionist
hairdresser
baker
optician
painter
florist
electrician
waiter
chef/
cook
butcher
veterinarian
doctor

dentist
firefighter
pharmacist
teacher
police
officer
bank teller
journalist/reporter
professor
judge
lawyer
artist
photographer
salesperson

Office

bookcase
wall pegs
photocopier
flip chart
wastebasket
desk lamp
chair
screen
pencil
mug
computer (laptop)
telephone
keyboard
calculator
highlighter
pen

calendar
bulletin board
folders
file cabinet
monitor
computer (desktop)
desk
printer
fax machine
briefcase
files
drawer
cell phone

Computer

scanner
PC/personal computer/
desktop computer
printer
screen
email
CD/DVD drive
To...
Cc...
Subject
Dear Sir/Madam:
Please find attached the
document you requested
spreadsheet
socket
plug
monitor
key
cable
speakers
floppy disk
keyboard
laptop computer
mouse
mousepad
CD-ROM
pda (personal
digital assistant
desk

Musical Instruments

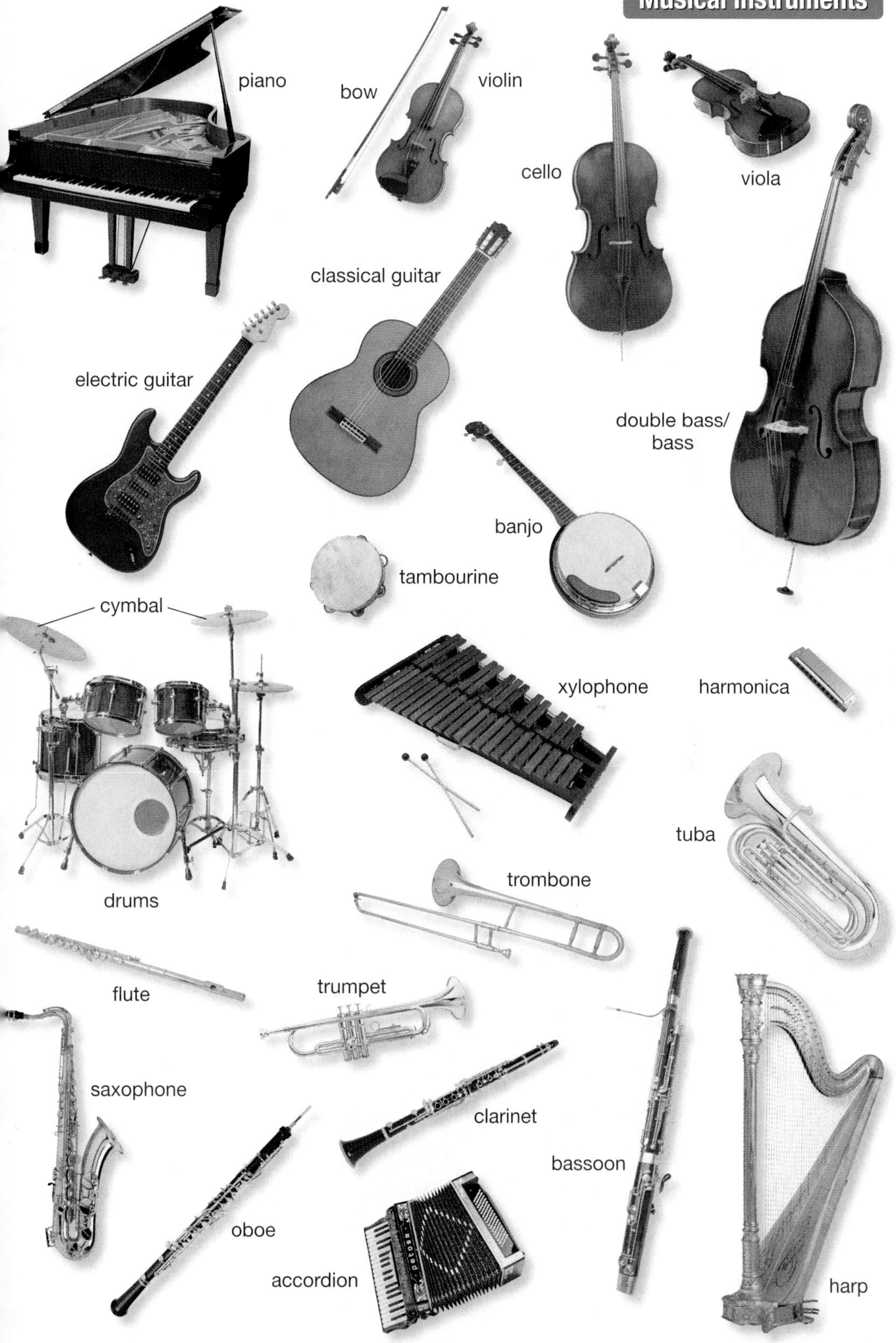
piano
bow
violin
cello
viola
classical guitar
electric guitar
double bass/
bass
banjo
tambourine
cymbal
xylophone
harmonica
tuba
trombone
drums
flute
trumpet
saxophone
clarinet
bassoon
oboe
accordion
harp

Sounds

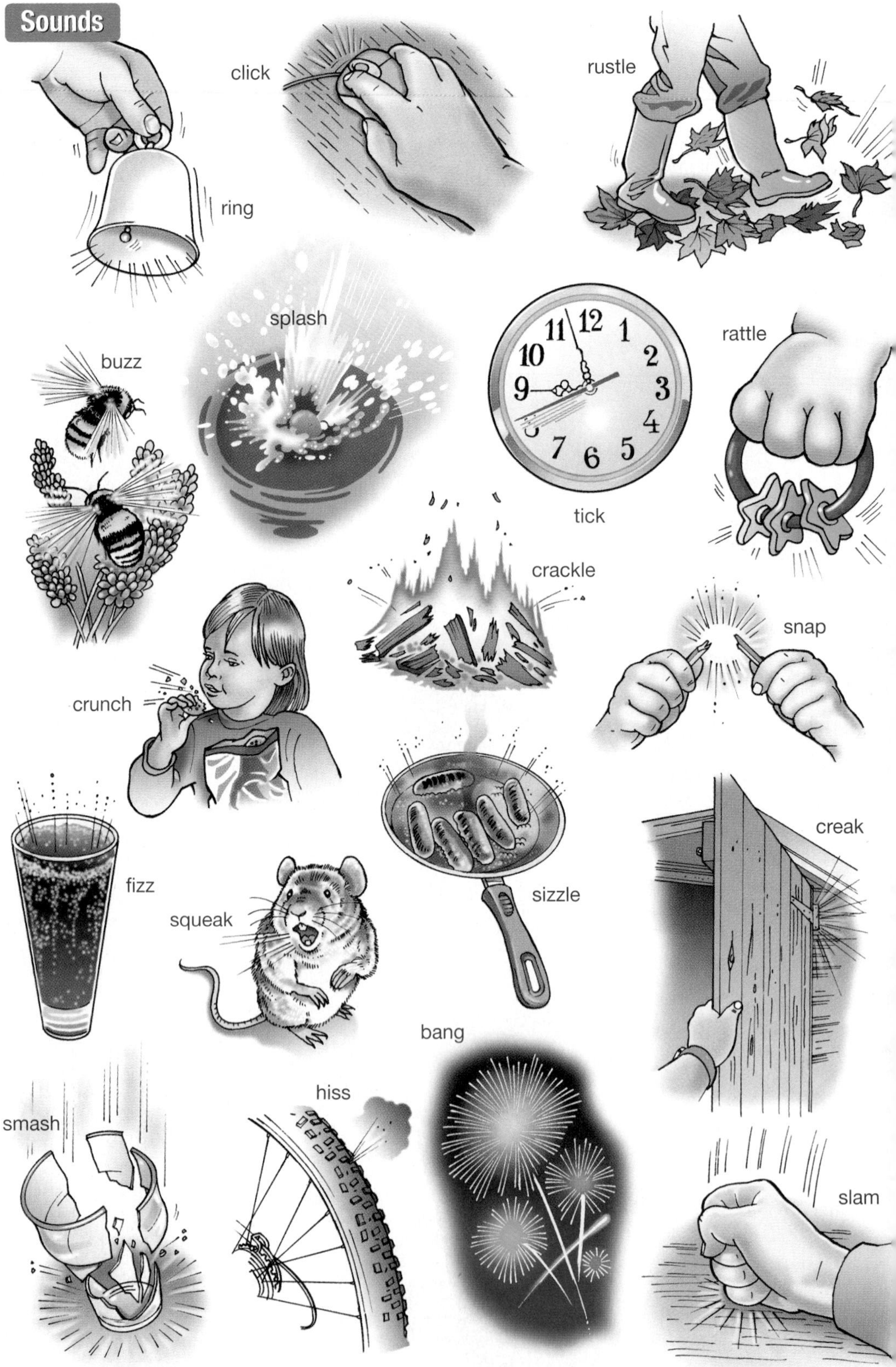
click
rustle
ring
splash
buzz
rattle
tick
crackle
snap
crunch
creak
fizz
sizzle
squeak
bang
hiss
smash
slam

Emotions

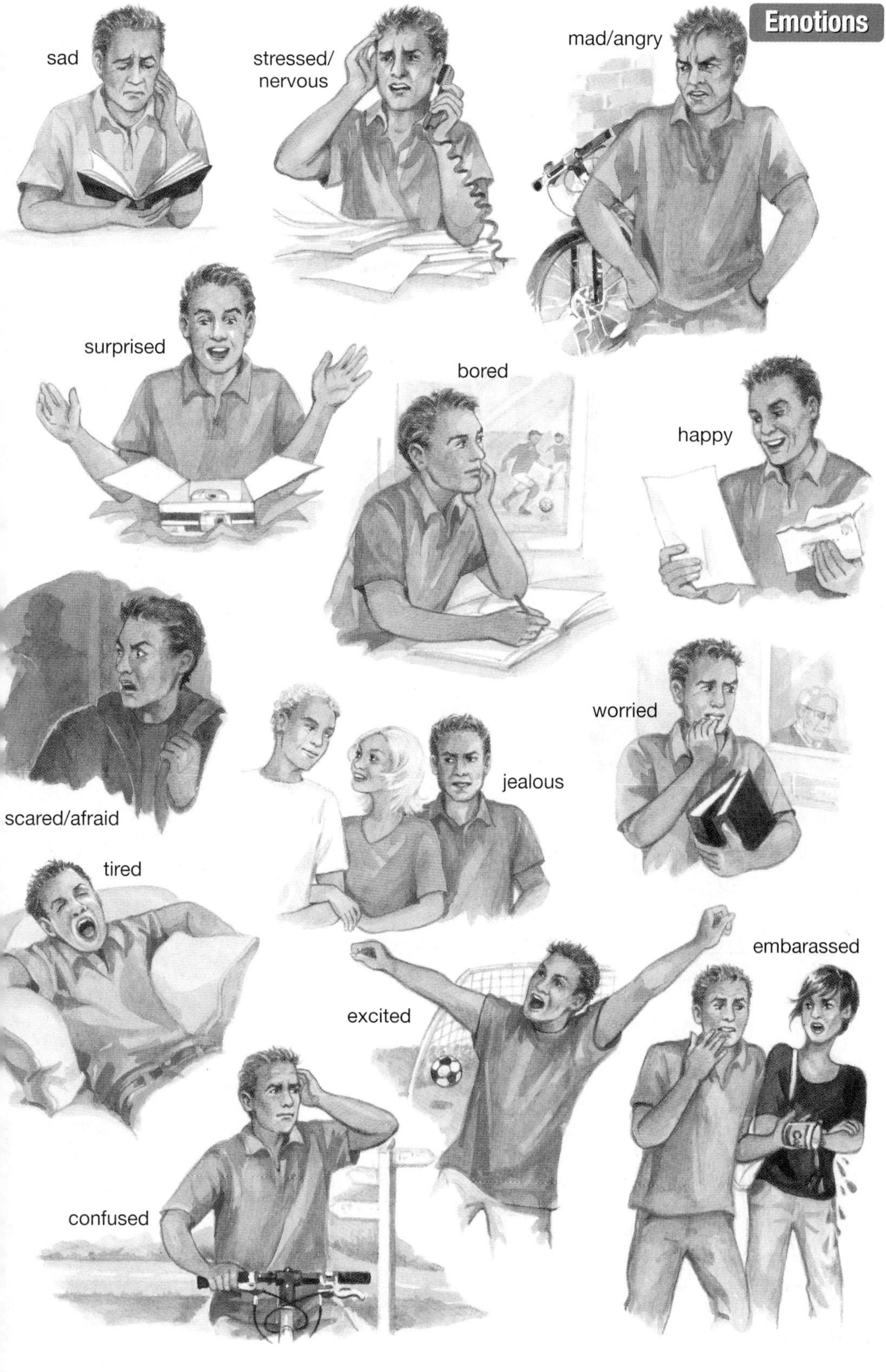
sad
stressed/
nervous
mad/angry
surprised
bored
happy
worried
jealous
scared/afraid
tired
embarassed
excited
confused

Sports

ice hockey

basketball

sailing

martial arts

tennis

football

golf

climbing

fencing

gymnastics

baseball

cycling

windsurfing

riding

swimming

volleyball

boxing

skiing

snowboarding

waterskiing

rollerblading

soccer

running

Transportation

van
UNIVERSAL

police car
NYPD
POLICE

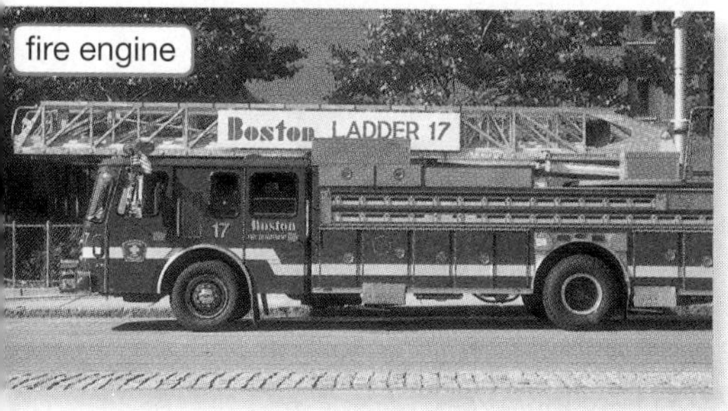
fire engine
Boston LADDER 17

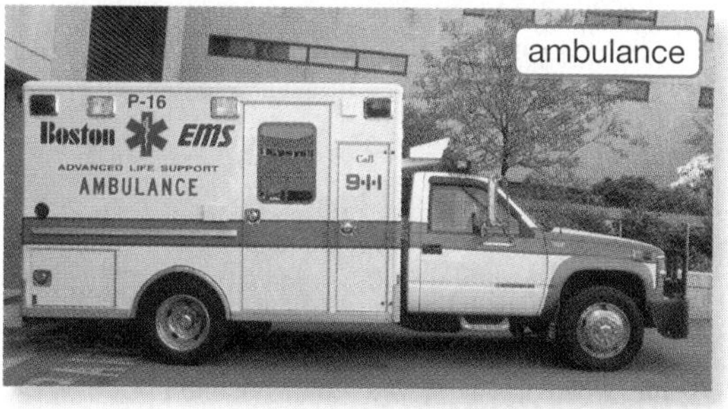
ambulance
P-16
Boston EMS
ADVANCED LIFE SUPPORT
AMBULANCE
Call 9-1-1

plane
runway

pickup truck

rowboat

ship

ferry

N22CP
helicopter

truck
northAmerican
ELECTRONICS EXHIBITS

Car

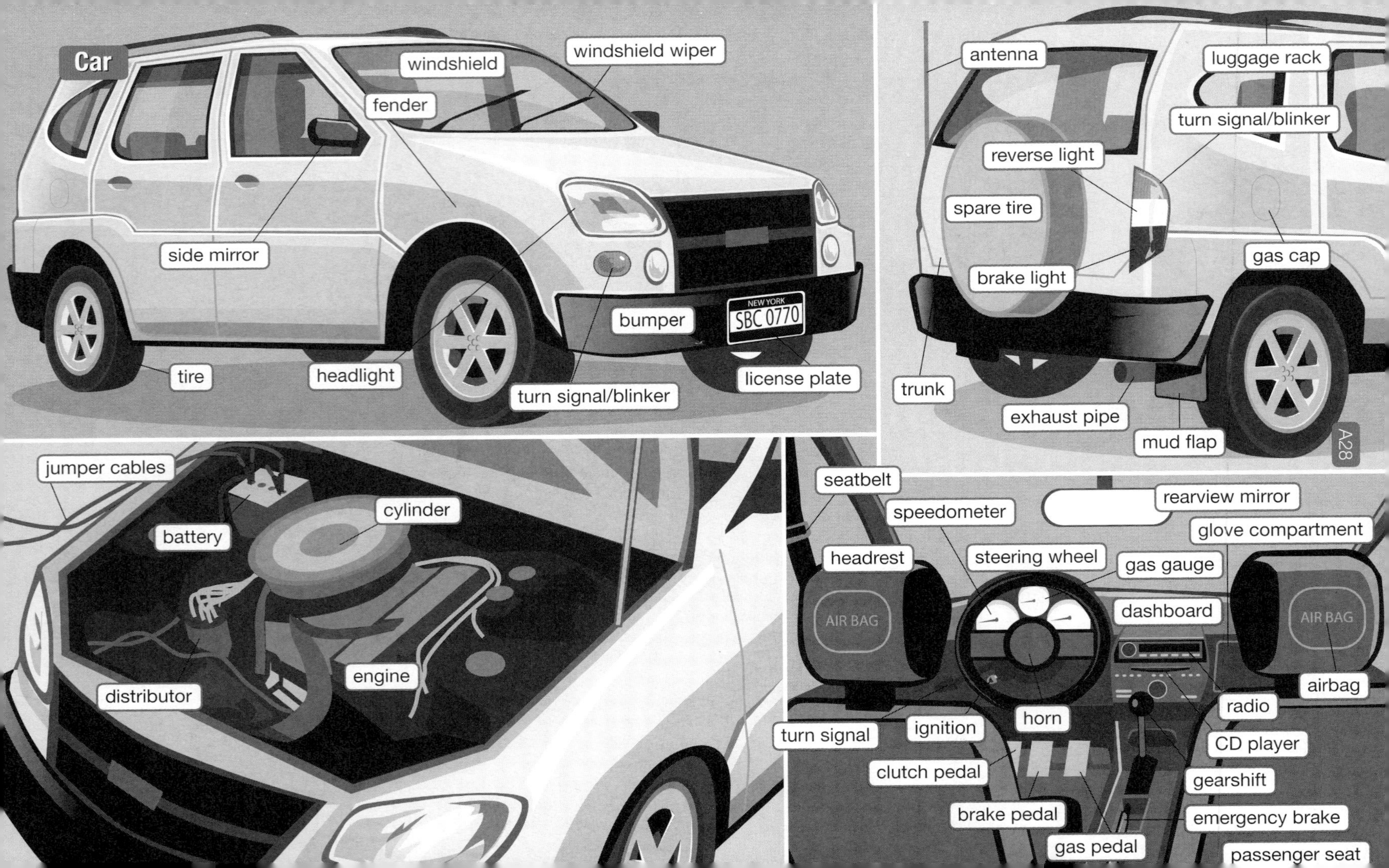
windshield
windshield wiper
fender
side mirror
tire
headlight
turn signal/blinker
bumper
license plate
NEW YORK
SBC 0770
antenna
luggage rack
turn signal/blinker
reverse light
spare tire
brake light
gas cap
trunk
exhaust pipe
mud flap
jumper cables
battery
cylinder
engine
distributor
seatbelt
speedometer
rearview mirror
glove compartment
headrest
steering wheel
gas gauge
dashboard
AIR BAG
AIR BAG
airbag
radio
CD player
gearshift
emergency brake
passenger seat
turn signal
ignition
horn
clutch pedal
brake pedal
gas pedal

Weights and Measures

(see also page 801)

Height

Metric system
m = meter
dm = decimeter
cm = centimeter
mm = millimeter

U.S. customary system
yd = yard
ft = foot
in = inch

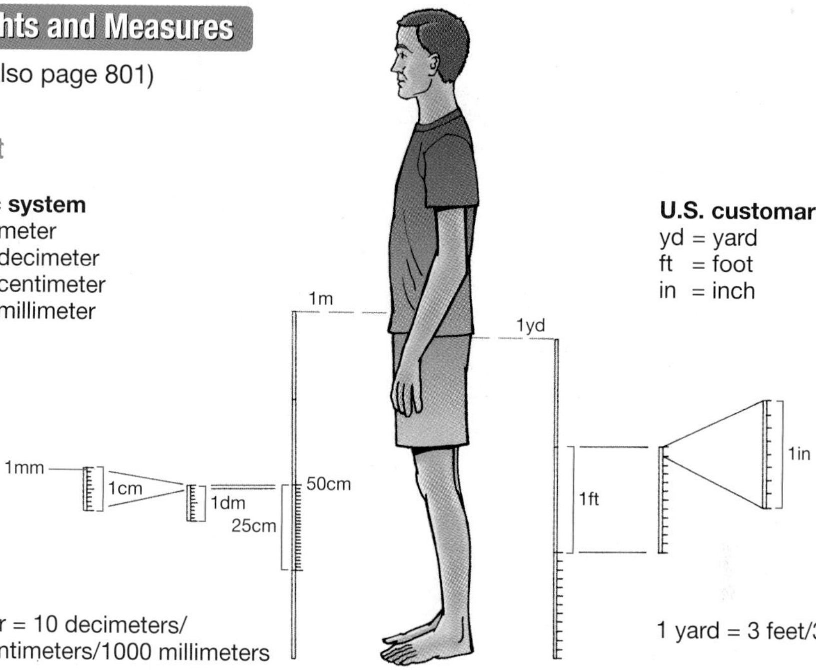

1 meter = 10 decimeters/
100 centimeters/1000 millimeters

1 yard = 3 feet/36 inches

1 yard = 0.9144 meter

Temperature

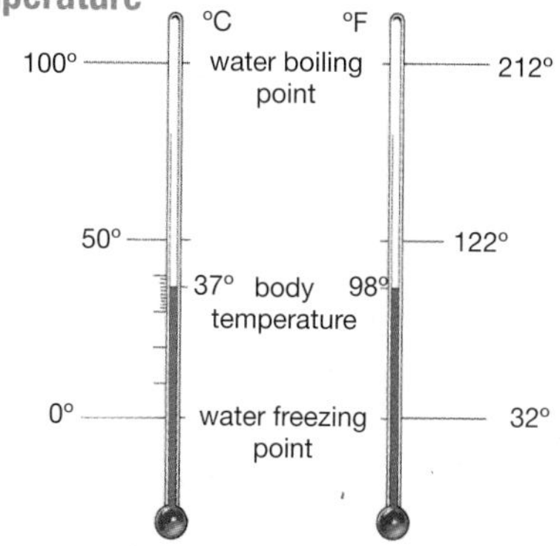

Celsius/
Centigrade

Fahrenheit

Speed

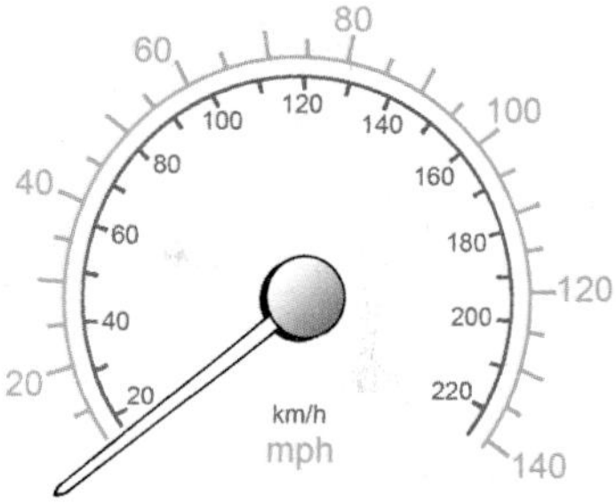

km/h = kilometers per hour
mph = miles per hour

1kilometer = 1000 meters
1 mile = 1,760 yards/1,609 meters

Weight

kg = kilogram lb = pound
1kilogram = 2.205 pounds

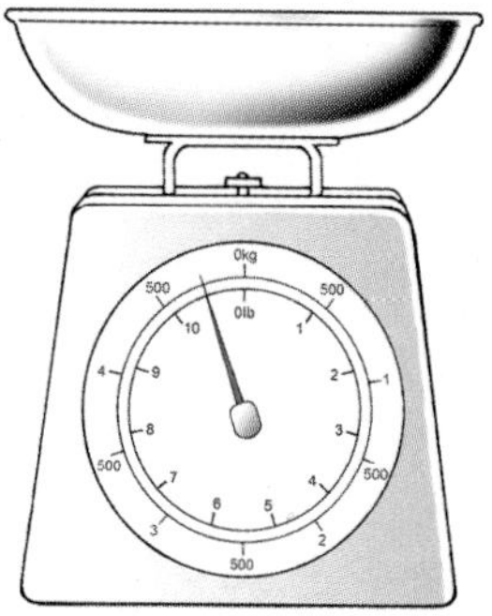

Volume

Metric system
l = liter
dl = deciliter
cl = centiliter
ml = milliliter

1 liter = 1.06 quarts
1 pint = 0.4732 liters

US customary system
pt = pint
qt = quart
fl oz = fluid ounce

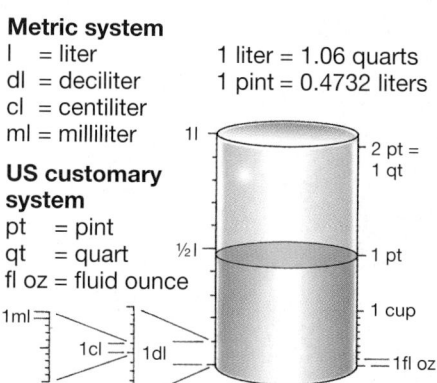

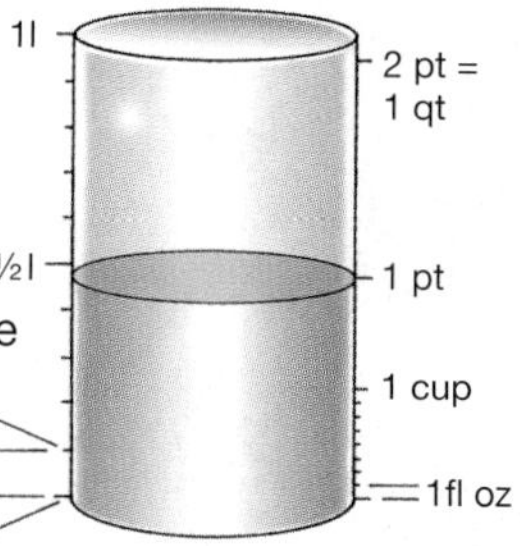

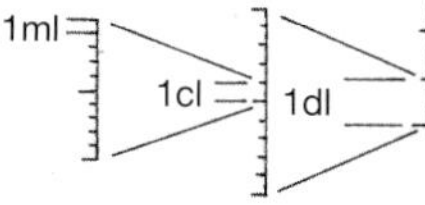

Charts

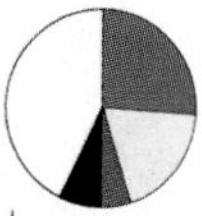

pie chart

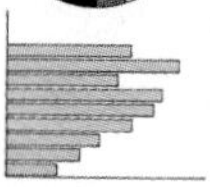

bar chart

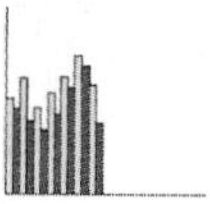

column chart

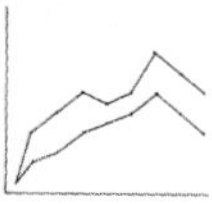

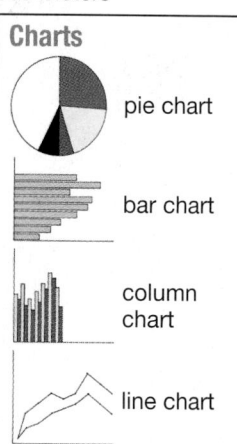

line chart

Airport

1 entrance
2 departures
3 security
4 departure lounge

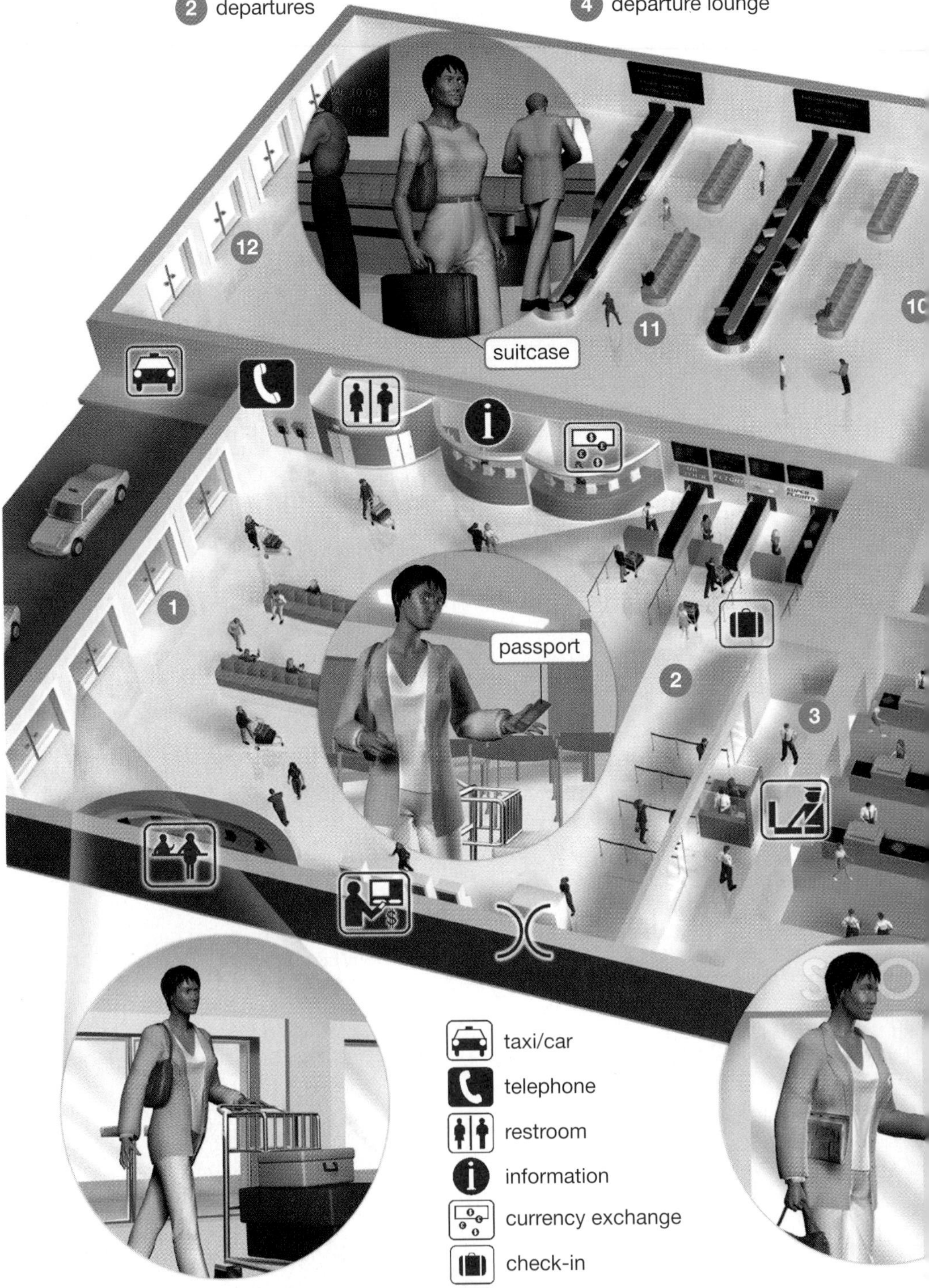

taxi/car
telephone
restroom
information
currency exchange
check-in
ATM
ticket desk

5 boarding gates
6 shops
7 seating area
8 information screens
9 café/restaurant
10 arrivals
11 baggage reclaim
12 exit

customs
internet point
café/restaurant
baggage carts

Map of the United States

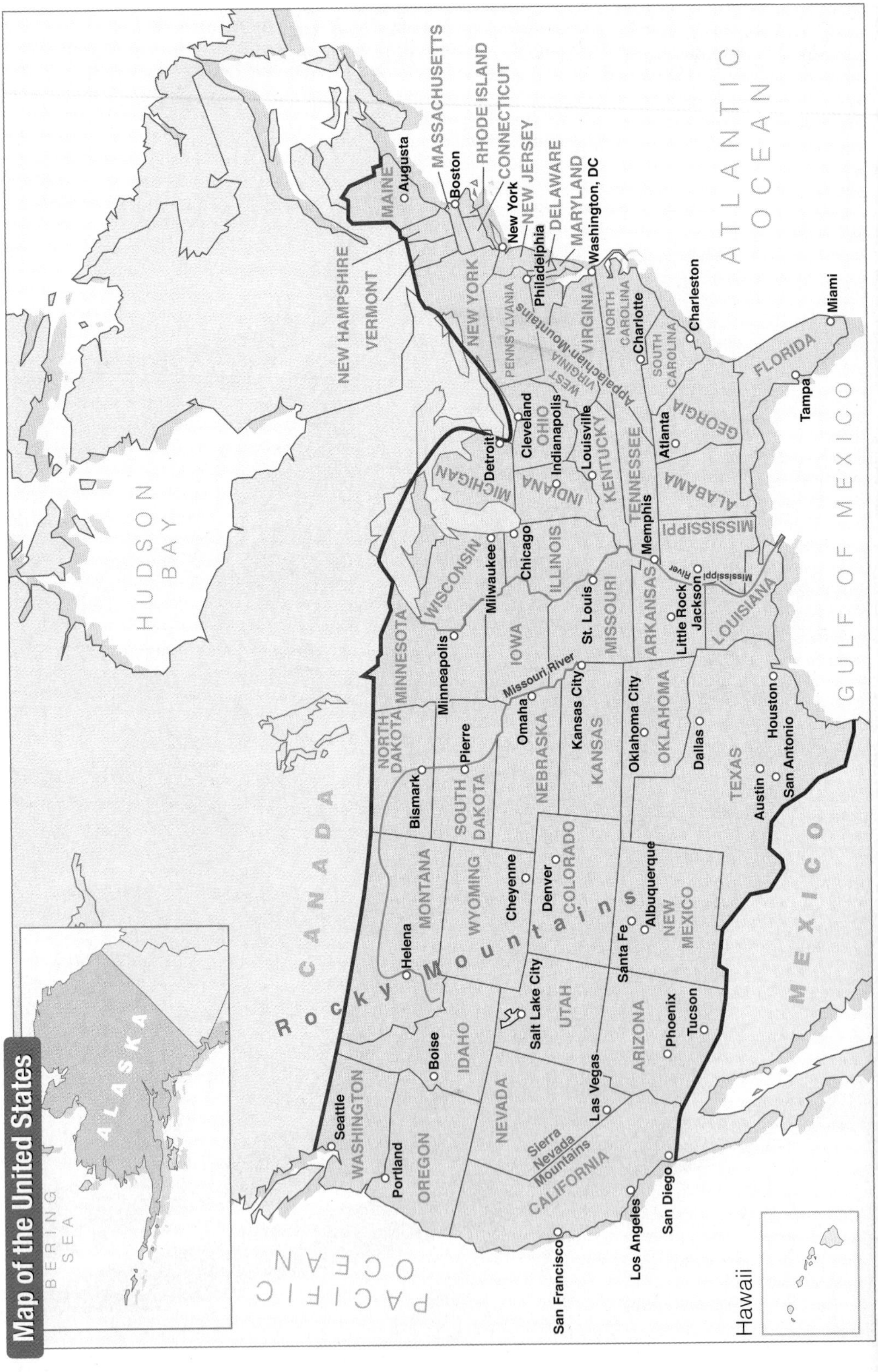

WORKBOOK

Lesson 1	Introducing the Dictionary	A34
Lesson 2	Develop accuracy in spelling	A35
Lesson 3	Develop learner understanding of grammatical functions of words	A36
Lesson 4	Develop learner awareness of multiple senses of words	A38
Lesson 5	Develop learner understanding of word usage	A40
Lesson 6	Develop learner understanding of idiomatic language	A42
Lesson 7	Expand learner vocabulary through learning words from the same family	A44
Lesson 8	Expand learner vocabulary through learning synonyms, antonyms and related words	A46
Lesson 9	Develop learner ability to use pronunciation symbols	A48
Lesson 10	Familiarize the learner with the dictionary's other resources	A50

Answer Key 805

LESSON 1

Objective: Introducing the Dictionary

Dictionary Skill: Find words in the dictionary

Tasks: Putting words in alphabetical order, Using guidewords, Recognizing key words

EXERCISE 1

The dictionary lists words in alphabetical order. These are called **main words**.
It does not matter if the word begins with a capital letter (*English*) or if it is a compound word (*ice cream* or *man-made*) or an abbreviation (*P.O.*). ▶ Number these groups of words in alphabetical order.

Group 1		Group 2		Group 3		Group 4		Group 5	
bag	2	hospital	☐	cell phone	☐	king	☐	Labor Day	☐
desk	☐	kiss	☐	circle	☐	king-size	☐	labor	☐
apple	1	jump	☐	Christmas	☐	key	☐	label	☐
electric	☐	ID	☐	carry	☐	keep	☐	labor union	☐
clock	☐	guest	☐	company	☐	kind	☐	lab	☐

EXERCISE 2

Guidewords show you the first word on the left page and the last word on the right page. ▶ Look at these guidewords for pages in the dictionary. Which word will you find on those pages? Circle it.

1 Pages 380–381: *landowner* to *lately*   a layer   b lack   c (language)

2 Pages 278–279: *generation* to *get*   a getaway   b gesture   c GED

3 Pages 310–311: *hassle* to *have to*   a hardware   b headache   c haul

4 Pages 434–435: *missionary* to *moderate*   a modem   b module   c minus

5 Pages 680–681: *sweat suit* to *sympathy*   a synonym   b survey   c syllable

6 Pages 694–695: *terminate* to *that*   a time zone   b territory   c tentacle

EXERCISE 3

The most common main words in the dictionary look like this: **case**. These are called **key words**, and they are very important words to learn. ▶ The words in each group have similar meanings, but only one is a key word. Work with a partner and use your dictionaries to find the key word in each group. Circle it.

1 awesome   (excellent)   fabulous   outstanding

2 mend   repair   restore   fix

3 mandatory   compulsory   necessary   obligatory

4 assess   evaluate   gauge   judge

5 huge   enormous   vast   gigantic

LESSON 2

Objective: Develop accuracy in spelling

Dictionary Skill: Find how to spell a word

Tasks: Using the dictionary to check spelling, Checking spelling changes in inflected words

EXERCISE 1

Use the dictionary when you are not sure how to spell a word. ▶ Each word is missing one letter. Write the correct spelling on the line.

1 adition ___addition___
2 basball ________
3 beutiful ________
4 comunicate ________
5 diffrence ________
6 fasinating ________
7 intresting ________
8 restarant ________

EXERCISE 2

Some words change their spelling when you add an ending (to make a noun plural or to change a verb to the simple past tense, for example). The dictionary shows those spelling changes. ▶ Complete each sentence with the word in parentheses plus the ending. Make other necessary spelling changes. Check your answers in the dictionary.

1 (happy + *-est*) It was the ___happiest___ day of my life.
2 (put + *-ing*) This year, they are ________ computers in all classrooms.
3 (knife + *-s*) The ________ , forks, and spoons are in that drawer.
4 (big + *-er*) Is a rhinoceros ________ than a hippopotamus?
5 (worry + *-ed*) Tom's mother ________ when he played football.
6 (frantic + *-ly*) The man searched ________ for his lost child.

EXERCISE 3

You must know the first few letters of a word to find it in the dictionary. If you cannot find a word, you might have the wrong spelling. Then you need to think about other possible ways to spell the word. ▶ These words have errors in the first few letters. Working with a partner, find the correct spelling and write it on the line.

1 foto ___photo___
2 ecsitement ________
3 olways ________
4 onesty ________
5 skedule ________
6 caracter ________
7 psicological ________
8 gard ________

LESSON 3

Objective: Develop learner understanding of grammatical functions of words

Dictionary Skill: Find what part of speech a word is

Tasks: Locating information about parts of speech, Recognizing words that can be more than one part of speech, Analyzing words for their function in sentences

EXERCISE 1

The dictionary tells you what **part of speech** a word is. That is, it tells you how the word functions in a sentence. ▶ Draw a line to match each word with its part of speech.

1 celebrate	a noun	5 and	e adjective
2 president	b pronoun	6 sometimes	f adverb
3 between	c verb	7 should	g modal verb
4 them	d preposition	8 terrible	h conjunction

EXERCISE 2

Some words can be more than one part of speech. When you see a small, raised number after a main word, like **call**[1], look for other entries for that word. ▶ Check (✔) the words that can be more than one part of speech. Write the parts of speech on the line.

1 ☐ beside	preposition	5 ☐ habit	______
2 ☑ box	noun, verb	6 ☐ friction	______
3 ☐ color	______	7 ☐ explode	______
4 ☐ direct	______	8 ☐ guarantee	______

EXERCISE 3

Sometimes a word can be two different parts of speech. The second part of speech is sometimes shown at the end of the entry for the word. For example, look at the entry for *ladle*. ▶ Find the entries for these words. Write both parts of speech shown in the entry.

1 ladle	a noun	b verb
2 maroon	a ______	b ______
3 tow	a ______	b ______
4 giggle	a ______	b ______
5 crimson	a ______	b ______
6 litter	a ______	b ______
7 shame	a ______	b ______
8 camouflage	a ______	b ______

EXERCISE 4

Read the sentences. What part of speech is the word in **bold** letters? Circle your answer.

1 I have lived here since I was a little **kid**. verb / noun
2 Don't listen to him. He's just **kidding**. verb / noun
3 **Check** your homework carefully. verb / noun
4 She wrote a **check** for $100. verb / noun
5 He changed his **mind**. verb / noun
6 Do you **mind** waiting for me? verb / noun
7 I'm taking some **hard** classes. adjective / adverb
8 She works very **hard**. adjective / adverb
9 Did you **notice** the look on his face? verb / noun
10 I read the **notice** on the door. verb / noun

EXERCISE 5

Play this game with a partner. Tell your partner a number between 1 and 782. Write down the page number your partner gives you. (It must be the number of a full page in the dictionary.) Find words on that page to write in the chart. They must be the right parts of speech. The first person to complete his or her chart is the winner.

	Page _____
a noun	
a verb	
an adjective	
a word that can be more than one part of speech	

	Page _____
a noun	
a verb	
an adjective	
a word that can be more than one part of speech	

LESSON 4

Objective: Develop learner awareness of multiple senses of words

Dictionary Skill: Understand definitions, Recognize words with multiple senses, Distinguish among definitions

Tasks: Understanding definitions, Finding the number of senses, Recognizing the more common meanings, Choosing the appropriate definition, Choosing an appropriate modal verb

EXERCISE 1

Match each word with its meaning. Write the word next to the definition.

context generate hypothesis legislate method similar

1 to produce something ___generate___
2 a way of doing something ______
3 to make a law about something ______
4 almost the same, but not exactly ______
5 an idea that no one has proved to be true yet ______
6 the situation that is related to something, and that helps you to understand it ______

EXERCISE 2

Some words have more than one meaning. Different meanings are listed after the blue numbers **1**, **2**, and so on. ▶ How many meanings does each of these words have in the dictionary? Write the number of meanings on the line. (Remember to count all the meanings of words that can be more than one part of speech.)

1 consume ___2___
2 area ______
3 source ______
4 lose ______
5 lookout ______
6 major ______
7 environment ______
8 long ______

EXERCISE 3

Each word in **bold** letters has more than one meaning in the dictionary. Find the right meaning of the word as it is used in the sentence. The small numbers indicate which entry you need to look at, for example **major**[2] – *noun*. Circle the number of the meaning.

1 The **major**[2] gave orders to the soldiers.	1	(2)	
2 Every **generation** has its own kind of popular music.	1	2	
3 In Biology, we are studying the **structure**[1] of the human body.	1	2	
4 The **core**[1] holds the seeds of the apple.	1	2	3
5 I set a **target** of five new vocabulary words a day.	1	2	3
6 When the wires come into **contact**[1], they complete the circuit.	1	2	3

EXERCISE 4

When a word has more than one meaning, the dictionary shows the most common meaning first. That is the meaning most often used, but you should read the other definitions, too. ▶ Read each pair of sentences. The words in **bold** letters have different meanings. Check (✔) the sentence that uses the more common meaning of the word.

1 ☐ a There are **gaps** in my understanding of English grammar.
☑ b His smile showed the **gap** where he had lost a front tooth.

2 ☐ a My family lives in a working **class** neighborhood.
☐ b How many students are in your **class**?

3 ☐ a Education is the **key** to success.
☐ b Turn the **key** and push open the door.

4 ☐ a In French class, we study both the language and **culture** of France.
☐ b If you are interested in **culture**, you would like New York's museums and concerts.

5 ☐ a She signed the papers to **transfer** ownership of the car to her son.
☐ b The bank **transferred** six employees from the main office to other locations.

6 ☐ a Parents are responsible for the **welfare** of their children.
☐ b Nancy's **welfare** checks made it possible for her to finish college.

LESSON 5

Objective: Develop learner understanding of word usage

Dictionary Skill: Use the dictionary to find word forms and usage information

Tasks: Finding irregular plurals, Finding irregular verb forms, Distinguishing levels of formality, Identifying academic vocabulary

EXERCISE 1

Most plural nouns end in *-s*. A few nouns do not. They have **irregular plurals**.

▶ Write the irregular plural form of each noun.

1 one child, two __children__
2 one deer, two __________
3 one foot, two __________
4 one fish, two __________
5 one mouse, two __________
6 one person, two __________
7 one tooth, two __________
8 one woman, two __________

EXERCISE 2

A **regular verb** ends in *-ed* in the simple past and past participle, for example:

Base form: Tell them to **listen**.
Simple Past: I **listened** to the weather report last night.
Past Participle: I have **listened** to Latin music all my life.

An **irregular verb** is different. The dictionary tells you its simple past form and its past participle. You can find this information in the entry for the verb and also in the chart on pages 783–785.

▶ Complete the sentences. Use (a) the simple past and (b) the past participle of the **boldfaced** verb.

1 That dog **bites**. He (a) __________ the mail carrier yesterday. He has (b) __________ two of my friends, too.

2 I usually **do** my homework right after school. I (a) __________ my math homework first today. I have not (b) __________ my English homework yet.

3 Don't **eat** all the cookies! Hey, who (a) __________ the last one? Wait, give me that cookie—I haven't (b) __________ any, and you've had a lot!

4 I never **fall** off my bike. My sister (a) __________ off once and broke her arm. Have you ever (b) __________ off a bike?

5 We always get to **choose** what kind of birthday cake we want. Last year my brother (a) __________ a carrot cake. I have always (b) __________ chocolate.

6 Mr. Lee **writes** a lot of e-mail. He (a) __________ 20 messages yesterday. He has (b) __________ 10 messages so far today.

EXERCISE 3

Most words can be used in both spoken and written English, but not all. **Formal** words are usually used in writing but not in conversation. **Informal** words are fine for conversation but not for academic writing. The dictionary tells you when a word is formal or informal. ▶ The two words in parentheses have similar meanings. Circle the less formal word. Then ask a partner the questions, using the less formal words. Check (✔) your partner's answers.

	Always	Usually	Sometimes	Never
1 Are you (grouchy/irritable) when you get up in the morning?	☐	☐	☐	☐
2 Do you (transport/lug) a heavy backpack to school?	☐	☐	☐	☐
3 Are you sorry to see the (end/close) of the school day?	☐	☐	☐	☐
4 Do you do (activities/stuff) with your family on weekends?	☐	☐	☐	☐
5 When you go shopping, can you (locate/find) exactly what you want?	☐	☐	☐	☐
6 Are you (polite/civil) to people you don't like?	☐	☐	☐	☐
7 Do you ever have to eat things you (can't stand/detest)?	☐	☐	☐	☐
8 Do you feel (weary/tired) and ready for bed by 9:00 p.m.?	☐	☐	☐	☐

EXERCISE 4

Words labeled **Ac** in the dictionary are academic words. They often occur in textbooks. These are important words to learn for the reading and writing you do in school.
▶ Choose the academic word and use it to complete the sentence.

1 (build/construct) How did the ancient Egyptians *construct* the pyramids?
2 (sector/part) There are many job openings in that ______________ of the industry.
3 (happened/occurred) According to police, the accident ______________ at 1:15 a.m.
4 (indicates/shows) Research ______________ that the drug has a success rate of 85%.
5 (guess/estimate) He could not measure the distance, but he made a good ______________ .
6 (conduct/behavior) The child received good marks for her ______________ in school.
7 (respond/answer) The police questioned him, but he refused to ______________ .
8 (made/created) The dry weather has ______________ problems for farmers.

LESSON 6

Objective: Develop learner understanding of idiomatic language

Dictionary Skill: Locate and interpret information about phrasal verbs and idioms

Tasks: Finding phrasal verb entries, Recognizing phrasal verb meanings, Matching particles to verbs to form phrasal verbs, Identifying and interpreting idiomatic expressions

EXERCISE 1

A **phrasal verb** is a special verb. It is a verb followed by one or two other words (adverbs or prepositions). The meaning of a phrasal verb can be very different from the meaning of the verb alone. ▶ Look for phrasal verbs at the end of verb entries in the dictionary. Complete the phrasal verbs in the sentences. Use a verb from the box.

come	get	give	go	make	move

1 What time do you usually ___get___ **up**?
2 Some new people are going to ______ **in** next door.
3 I hate to ______ **down with** a cold when I'm on vacation.
4 The class will be hard at first, but don't ______ **up**.
5 Please ______ **on** reading—don't stop there.
6 Ann and Lisa are mad at each other, but I'm sure they will ______ **up**.

EXERCISE 2

Write each phrasal verb from Exercise 1 next to its meaning.

1 to continue: ___go on___
2 to get an illness: ______
3 to start living in a new home: ______
4 to get out of your bed after you have been sleeping: ______
5 to stop trying to do something because it is too difficult: ______
6 to become friends with someone again, after you have had an argument: ______

EXERCISE 3

The words in **bold** letters are parts of phrasal verbs. Complete the phrasal verb in each question with the correct word from the box. Then find a partner and ask the questions. Circle your partner's answers.

down	in	on	out	up

1 Do you ever **look** ___up___ words in the dictionary? Yes, I do. / No, I don't.
2 Have you ever been in a car that **ran** ______ of gas? Yes, I have. / No, I haven't.

3 Have you ever **turned** ________ a job offer? Yes, I have. / No, I haven't.

4 Do you **try** ________ shoes before you buy them? Yes, I do. / No, I don't.

5 Have you ever **signed** ________ for a club? Yes, I have. / No, I haven't.

6 Have your friends ever **let** you ________ ? Yes, they have. / No, they haven't.

7 Do you know anyone who **dropped** ________ of school? Yes, I do. / No, I don't.

8 Have you ever **turned** ________ your homework late? Yes, I have. / No, I haven't.

EXERCISE 4

An **idiom** is a group of words with a special meaning. The meaning of the group is different from the meanings of the individual words put together. Many idioms are used mostly in informal English. ▶ Look up each word in **bold** letters in the dictionary. In the entry for that word, find the idiom and underline it in the sentence below. Then match the definition (a–f) to the idiom by writing the correct letter on the line.

1 __b__ He has quit the team before, but this time, it is for **good**.

2 _____ That car almost hit us! Wow, that was a **close** call.

3 _____ The judge gave him just a **slap** on the wrist.

4 _____ Don't worry. The test should be a piece of **cake**.

5 _____ Off the **top** of my head, I would say there are 30 or 40 countries in Africa.

6 _____ I have never changed a diaper before, but I'll give it a **shot**.

a to be very easy

b always or permanently

c to attempt to do or achieve something

d punishment that is not strong enough

e a situation you are in that is dangerous, but that you escape from

f said immediately, without thinking carefully or checking the facts

EXERCISE 5

Work with a partner. Guess if each statement is true or false, and circle your answer. Then check your answer by looking up the idioms under the words in **bold**. Underline the idioms.

	Your Guess
1 If you know something by **heart**, you remember it completely.	(True) / False
2 If you lose your **head**, you do something stupid.	True / False
3 If someone says "Stop that! **Cut** it out!," you need scissors.	True / False
4 If you make the **most** of something, you earn a lot of money.	True / False
5 If you keep your **word**, you do what you promised.	True / False
6 If you play **games** with someone, you are on the same team.	True / False

LESSON 7

Objective: Expand learner vocabulary through learning words from the same family

Dictionary Skill: Find words not listed as main words, Find words related to main words, Use Word Family Boxes

Tasks: Finding related words within the same entry, Finding related words in separate entries, Using Word Family boxes

EXERCISE 1

Words belong to families. For example, the words *whaler* and *whaling* are related. In this dictionary, you can find them in the entry for the main word *whale* because they are less common than *whale*. ▶ The words in the list are not main words in the dictionary. Write the related main word where you can find each word.

1 whiten ____white____
2 medicinal ________
3 leathery ________
4 greed ________
5 simplicity ________
6 tyrant ________

EXERCISE 2

The words in the chart are main words in the dictionary. Look in the entries for these words and find other words from the same family. Use the related words to complete the chart.

	Nouns	Verbs	Adjectives	Adverbs
1	hike	hike		
2			homesick	
3	miracle			
4			modest	
5	snob			
6		transform		

EXERCISE 3

Sometimes two or more main words are related. Look at the nearby entries for members of the same word family. Read the definitions to see if the words are related. For an example, see the entries for *assist*, *assistance*, and *assistant*. ▶ Work with a partner. Complete the word family chart.

	Nouns	Verbs	Adjectives	Adverbs
1	correction	correct	correct	correctly
2	glory			
3	magic			
4			sad	
5		tempt		

EXERCISE 4

The dictionary has **Word Family Boxes** that show words with the same root.
▶ Find the Word Family Box for each word in **bold** letters. Complete each sentence with the correct word from the box.

1 a They don't help. They just **create** problems.
  b Artists are ___creative___ people.
  c Your ideas show a lot of ______________ . Good work!

2 a A computer is a complicated **machine**.
  b He knows how to operate farm ______________ .
  c A ______________ problem caused the delay.

3 a His work never seemed to **satisfy** the boss.
  b My grades have been ______________ but not great.
  c We were very ______________ with the good deal we got on our new car.

4 a I understood the **general** idea but did not get all the details.
  b Sometimes he gets depressed, but ______________ , he is in good spirits.
  c It is not fair to ______________ about teenagers just because of a few troublemakers.

LESSON 8

Objective: Expand learner vocabulary through learning synonyms, antonyms, and related words

Dictionary Skill: Locate synonyms and antonyms, Use Thesaurus boxes

Tasks: Finding synonyms and antonyms, Determining word relationships, Comparing related words in Thesaurus Boxes

EXERCISE 1

Sometimes the entry for a word reads "another word for … ." For example, the entry for *watchdog* says, "another word for a GUARD DOG." *Watchdog* and *guard dog* are **synonyms** – words with the same meaning – but *guard dog* is more commonly used. ▶ Find synonyms for the words in this list. Write them on the line.

1 sitter babysitter
2 tidy ______
3 safety belt ______
4 gratuity ______
5 trousers ______
6 bye ______
7 sci-fi ______
8 fridge ______

EXERCISE 2

A synonym can sometimes be found at the end of an entry. ▶ Find synonyms for these words. Write them on the lines.

1 assist help
2 security ______
3 cassette ______
4 suspect ______
5 conduct ______
6 frightening ______
7 seldom ______
8 subsequent ______

EXERCISE 3

An **antonym** is a word with opposite meaning. An antonym can sometimes be found at the end of an entry. ▶ Look at these pairs of words. Do they have the same meaning or different meanings? Underline your answers. Use your dictionary to check them.

1 large – small the same meaning / different meanings
2 hurry – rush the same meaning / different meanings
3 tactful – tactless the same meaning / different meanings
4 pretty – attractive the same meaning / different meanings
5 conclude – begin the same meaning / different meanings
6 substitute – replace the same meaning / different meanings
7 majority – minority the same meaning / different meanings
8 legible – illegible the same meaning / different meanings

EXERCISE 4

The **Thesaurus Boxes** in the dictionary group together words with similar meanings or words that all relate to a particulate topic. ▶ Go to the Thesaurus Box at each word in **bold** letters. Read the definitions for the other words. Notice how they are used in sentences. Then complete the exercise.

1 **happy:** glad delighted cheerful

a I'm ___glad___ to hear you're feeling better.

b The teachers were ______________ with the students' test results.

c She is a ______________ person. She is always quick with a smile.

2 **choose:** pick decide opt

a We need to ______________ on a time and place to meet.

b The coaches ______________ the players for the teams.

c Some high school graduates ______________ for college; others go to work.

3 **money:** cash currency change

a We need ______________ for the parking meter. Do you have any quarters?

b This restaurant doesn't accept credit cards, only ______________ or checks.

c The yen is the ______________ used in Japan.

EXERCISE 5

Work with a partner. Each of you chooses a list of words. Look for synonyms for the words in your list. If there is a synonym, write it in the chart. If there is no synonym, mark an *X*. When you finish, check each other's answers.

List 1

1	cab	taxi
2	truly	
3	most	
4	satisfactory	
5	second-hand	
6	mortally	
7	link	
8	momentarily	

List 2

1	great	excellent
2	truthful	
3	type	
4	least	
5	scarcely	
6	motivation	
7	label	
8	farm	

LESSON 9

Objective: Develop learner ability to use pronunciation symbols

Dictionary Skill: Use pronunciation table, Interpret pronunciation symbols, Determine syllable stress

Tasks: Matching symbols and sounds, Interpreting pronunciation symbols, Using correct syllable stress

EXERCISE 1

The **pronunciation table** is inside the back cover of the dictionary. It shows symbols for the sounds of American English. These symbols will help you understand how to say words. The pronunciation of a main word is shown at the beginning of its entry, between slanted lines, as in **cook**[1] /kʊk/. ▶ Match each pronunciation symbol with the sound made by the **boldfaced** letters in each word in the box. Write the words on the lines.

b**a**d	ban**a**n**a**	b**oo**k	**c**ame	**ch**ur**ch**	cr**y**	**sh**ip	**th**ing

1 ə banana

2 æ ________

3 ʊ ________

4 aɪ ________

5 k ________

6 θ ________

7 ʃ ________

8 tʃ ________

EXERCISE 2

Letters represent sounds, but you cannot depend on a word's spelling to show its pronunciation. Pronunciation symbols represent sounds more reliably. ▶ Work with a partner. Look up the pronunciation of each word in the box, and say it out loud. Then write each word in the chart under the symbol for its vowel sound.

bought	do	feet	field	food	meant
red	said	saw	seat	taught	true

/ɪ/	/ɛ/	/ɔ/	/u/
feet	meant	bought	do

EXERCISE 3

Each word in the box begins with the sound /s/, /k/, or /n/. Write each word on the line after the sound it begins with.

category	ceiling	chorus	circle	contrast	cycle
gnaw	kilo	kneel	know	pneumonia	psychology

1 /s/ ceiling
2 /k/ ______
3 /n/ ______

EXERCISE 4

Sometimes words are spelled differently but sound the same, and sometimes words look almost the same but sound different. ▶ Work with a partner. Look up the pronunciation of these pairs of words. Say them out loud. Is the pronunciation the same or different? Circle your answers.

1 lesson, lessen — the same / different
2 breath, breathe — the same / different
3 wait, weight — the same / different
4 know, now — the same / different
5 cite, site — the same / different
6 mail, male — the same / different
7 dual, duel — the same / different
8 chord, cord — the same / different

EXERCISE 5

The symbol ' appears before a syllable that receives stress. For example, the pronunciation symbols for *safari*, /sə'fɑri/, show that the stress goes on the second syllable. Say that syllable with more force, so it sounds a little louder and longer. ▶ Work with a partner. Look up the pronunciation of each word. Say the word out loud. Circle the stressed syllable.

1 available
2 luxury
3 economy
4 analyze
5 income
6 invest
7 legislation
8 examination

LESSON 10

Objective: Familiarize the learner with the dictionary's other resources

Dictionary Skill: Use all sections of the dictionary

Tasks: Locating special sections of the dictionary, Looking up information in special sections of the dictionary, Reading a map

EXERCISE 1

In addition to the A to Z pages, the dictionary has several sections with specialized information. ▶ Write the page number where you can find each section.

1 Guide to the Dictionary _____

2 Picture Dictionary _____

3 Irregular Verbs _____

4 Table of Weights and Measures _____

5 School Content Vocabulary _____

6 Map of the United States _____

7 Geographical Names _____

EXERCISE 2

In which class would you probably hear and read these words? Write your answers on the lines. Then go to the section "School Content Vocabulary" and check your answers.

math	literature	general science	history	music

1 laboratory, experiment, hypothesis, research, scientist, theory: general science

2 arithmetic, addition, subtraction, division, multiplication, algebra: ______________

3 treaty, society, government, empire, revolution, election: ______________

4 note, rhythm, instrument, harmony, orchestra, conductor: ______________

5 poem, novel, narrative, satire, writer, paragraph: ______________

EXERCISE 3

Work with a partner. Find the answers to these questions. Write the answer and the page number where you found it.

1 What is the past tense of pay? ______________ (page _____)

2 Which is more, a pint or a cup? ______________ (page _____)

3 Which is more, an acre or a square mile? ______________ (page _____)

4 Which word can be a measure of either weight or volume?
______________ (page _____)

5 Which state is in the south, Missouri or Mississippi? ______________ (page _____)

6 Write the names of two cities in Texas? ______________ (page _____)

7 What do you call a person from the Netherlands? ______________ (page _____)

8 What country do Peruvians come from? ______________ (page _____)

Mm

m.
the written abbreviation of **meter**

'm *verb*
the short form of "am": *I'm late for work* (=I am late for work).

M.A. *noun*
Master of Arts a university degree in a subject such as History or Art, which is more advanced than a B.A.: *He has an M.A. in English Literature.*

ma'am /mæm/ *noun*
used in order to speak politely to a woman when you do not know her name: *May I help you, ma'am?*

mac•a•ro•ni /ˌmækəˈrouni/ *noun*
a type of PASTA in the shape of small curved tubes: *Today the school cafeteria is serving macaroni and cheese* (=macaroni cooked with a cheese sauce).

ma•chine[1] /məˈʃin/ *noun*
a piece of equipment with moving parts that uses power to do a job: *We need a new washing machine.*

THESAURUS: machine

appliance a machine that is used in the home: *kitchen appliances such as refrigerators*

device a piece of equipment that is usually small and usually electronic, that does a special job: *A seismograph is a device that measures how strong an earthquake is.*

gadget *informal* a small piece of equipment that makes a particular job easier to do: *a new gadget for opening the garage door*

WORD FAMILY look at the words:

→ **machine** *noun*
→ **machinery** *noun*
→ **mechanical** *adjective*

maˈchine gun *noun*
a gun that fires a lot of bullets very quickly

ma•chin•er•y /məˈʃinəri/ *noun*
large machines: *This piece of machinery rolls the paper flat and dries it.*

ma•cho /ˈmɑtʃou/ *adjective, informal*
a man who is macho wants to show people that he is strong and brave, and never shows that he feels sad or frightened: *He's a macho guy who thinks he has to be tough.*

mad /mæd/ *adjective* **madder, maddest**
1 *informal* angry: *I think Mom's still mad at me for breaking the vase.* | *It makes me so mad when he doesn't listen!* | *Wendy got really mad when she saw the mess we'd made.*
2 do something like mad *informal* = to do something as quickly as you can: *People were running like mad away from the fire.*
3 *formal* mentally ill: *I was afraid that I was going mad because I kept hearing voices in my head.* SYNONYM **crazy, insane**
→ See Thesaurus box at **angry**
→ See picture on page A23

mad•am /ˈmædəm/ *noun, formal*
used in order to be polite when you are talking or writing to a woman whose name you do not know: *Dear Sir or Madam: I am writing about the job you advertised in the paper.*

made /meɪd/ *verb*
the past tense and past participle of MAKE

mad•ly /ˈmædli/ *adverb*
1 madly in love (with someone) = very much in love: *They were young and madly in love with each other.*
2 *formal* in a fast uncontrolled way: *The kids ran madly out of the school gates.*

mad•man /ˈmædmən/ *noun* plural **madmen**
a man who is mentally ill

mad•ness /ˈmædnəs/ *noun*
1 very stupid and often dangerous behavior: *It's madness to spend so much money on a dress you'll only wear once.* SYNONYM **insanity**
2 mental illness: *There's a history of madness in their family – her aunt was put in an institution.* SYNONYM **insanity**

mad•wom•an /ˈmædˌwumən/ *noun* plural **madwomen** /ˈmædˌwɪmɪn/
a woman who is mentally ill

M

mag•a•zine /ˈmægəˌzin/ *noun*
a large thin book with a paper cover that has news, stories, pictures, etc., and that is sold every week or month: *a sports magazine for kids* | *Did you read that magazine article about the new Superman movie?*

mag•ic¹ /ˈmædʒɪk/ *noun*
1 a special power that makes strange or impossible things happen: *The witch turned the prince into a frog by magic.*
2 the skill of doing tricks that look like magic in order to entertain people: *He likes magic, and he's always making things disappear or finding quarters behind people's ears.*
3 a quality that makes something seem exciting and special: *There's something about the magic of Christmas.*

magic² *adjective*
1 a magic word or object has special powers that makes strange or impossible things happen: *a magic wand*
2 relating to the skill of doing tricks that look like magic in order to entertain people: *My favorite magic trick is the one where they saw a woman in half.*

mag•i•cal /ˈmædʒɪkəl/ *adjective*
1 very enjoyable and exciting, in a strange or special way: *There's something magical about these beautiful mountains.*
2 relating to magic, or done using magic: *The witch used her magical powers to make them all disappear.*

ma•gi•cian /məˈdʒɪʃən/ *noun*
someone who does magic tricks in order to entertain people

ma•gis•trate /ˈmædʒəˌstreɪt/ *noun*
a government official who decides if someone is guilty in a court that deals with less serious crimes

mag•ne•si•um /mægˈniziəm/ *noun*
a common silver-white metal

mag•net /ˈmægnət/ *noun*

magnet

1 a piece of iron or steel that makes other metal objects move toward it: *I use little magnets to hold photographs on the refrigerator door.*
2 a person or place that attracts many other people or things: *Hollywood is a magnet for young actors.*
—**magnetize** /ˈmægnəˌtaɪz/ *verb* to make a piece of iron or steel able to pull other pieces of metal to it

mag•net•ic /mægˈnetɪk/ *adjective*
relating to the way a magnet can pull metal objects toward it: *Some rocks are magnetic and can attract metal.*
—**magnetism** /ˈmægnəˌtɪzəm/ *noun* the physical force that makes metal objects move toward each other

mag•nif•i•cent /mægˈnɪfəsənt/ *adjective*
very good, because of being very big, beautiful, etc.: *We had a magnificent view of the Grand Canyon.*
—**magnificence** *noun* the fact that something is magnificent

mag•ni•fy /ˈmægnəˌfaɪ/ *verb*
magnified, third person singular **magnifies**
to make something look larger than it really is: *The microscope magnifies the drop of water so that you can see the tiny living things in it.*

magnify

—**magnification** /ˌmægnəfəˈkeɪʃən/ *noun* the process of magnifying something, or the amount to which something is magnified

ˈmagnifying ˌglass *noun*
a round piece of glass with a handle that you look through to make things seem bigger: *Grandpa has to use a magnifying glass to read the paper.*

mag•ni•tude /ˈmægnəˌtud/ *noun, formal*
1 how large or important something is: *We need to understand the magnitude of the problem of global warming before it is too late.*
2 how strong an EARTHQUAKE is

mag•pie /ˈmægpaɪ/ *noun*
a wild bird with black and white feathers that makes a loud sound

ma•hog•a•ny /mə'hɑgəni/ *noun*
a hard dark wood used to make furniture
—**mahogany** *adjective* made of mahogany: *a mahogany table*

maid /meɪd/ *noun*
a woman whose job is to clean a house or the rooms in a hotel

maid•en name /'meɪdn ˌneɪm/ *noun*
the family name that a woman has before she gets married and uses her husband's family name: *What was your mother's maiden name?*
➔ See Thesaurus box at **name**[1]

ˌmaid of 'honor *noun*
the main BRIDESMAID in a wedding

mail[1] /meɪl/ *noun*
1 the system of collecting and delivering letters and packages: *I got a letter in the mail from Joanne.* | *Your airline tickets will be delivered by mail.*
2 the letters and packages that are delivered to your house or office: *"Is there any mail for me?" "Just a postcard and a couple of bills."*
3 messages that you send and receive on a computer: *I check my computer every morning to see if I have any mail.* SYNONYM **email**
➔ **airmail**

mail[2] *verb*
1 to send a letter or package to someone: *I'll mail the check to you tomorrow.*
2 to send something to someone using a computer: *You can mail the report to me as an attachment.* SYNONYM **email**

mail•box /'meɪlbɑks/ *noun*
1 a box outside your house where letters are put when they are delivered to your house: *I'd better check the mailbox – I'm expecting a letter from Susan.*
2 a special box in the street or at a POST OFFICE where you mail letters: *There's a mailbox at the end of the street – you can mail your letters there.*
3 the part of a computer's memory where EMAIL messages are kept: *You should get rid of all the old messages from your mailbox.*

'mail ˌcarrier *noun*
someone whose job is delivering mail to people's houses

mail•man /'meɪlmæn/ *noun* plural **mailmen** /'meɪlmen/
a man whose job is delivering mail to people's houses

ˌmail 'order *noun*
a way of buying things in which the company sends you the things by mail: *You can order the jeans from a mail order catalog.*

maim /meɪm/ *verb, formal*
to injure someone very badly: *The bomb maimed hundreds of people and killed 12.*

main /meɪn/ *adjective*
bigger and more important than other things of the same kind: *The main reason we bought this house is that it's close to a good school.* | *The main character in the book is a ten-year-old girl.*

'main clause *noun*
in a sentence, a group of words with a noun and a verb that can be a complete sentence on its own. In the sentence "At four o'clock, I walked home," "I walked home" is the main clause.

main•frame /'meɪnfreɪm/ *noun*
a large powerful computer that has a lot of smaller computers connected to it

main•land /'meɪnlənd/ *noun*
the mainland = the land that forms the main part of a country, not including any islands near it: *A bridge connects the island to the mainland.*
—**mainland** *adjective*: *mainland China*

main•ly /'meɪnli/ *adverb*
mostly or almost all: *The students here are mainly from California and Oregon, but there are several from other states.*

main•stream /'meɪnstrim/ *noun*
the mainstream = the beliefs or ways of doing things that most of the people in a country think are right: *His paintings are outside the mainstream of American art* (=many people think the paintings are unusual).
—**mainstream** *adjective* accepted by or involving most people in a country: *She belongs to one of the large, mainstream political parties.*

main•tain /meɪn'teɪn/ Ac *verb*
1 to keep something in good condition by taking care of it: *The city pays to maintain the roads and keep them in good condition.*

M

2 to make something continue in the same way as before: *Students have to maintain their grades to play on the school teams.*

main•te•nance /ˈmeɪntənəns/ Ac *noun*
work that is done to keep something in good condition and working correctly: *The class teaches women about car maintenance, such as checking oil, changing tires, etc.*

ma•jes•tic /məˈdʒestɪk/ *adjective, formal*
looking very big and impressive: *The sun rose over the majestic mountains.*
—**majestically** *adverb*

maj•es•ty /ˈmædʒəsti/ *noun*
1 the quality of being impressive and beautiful: *the majesty of the pyramids in Egypt*
2 Your/His/Her Majesty *formal* = used when you are talking to a king or queen, or talking about a king or queen

ma•jor¹ /ˈmeɪdʒɚ/ *adjective*
1 very large or important: *Not everything was perfect, but we didn't have any major problems.* ANTONYM **minor**
➔ See Thesaurus box at **important**
2 based on a particular type of musical SCALE ANTONYM **minor**

major² *noun*
1 the main subject that you study in college: *His major at college was history.* | *She's a math major* (=her main subject is math).
2 *written abbreviation* **Maj.** an officer who has a middle rank in the Army, Air Force, or Marines: *Major Arnold was in charge at that time.*

major³ *verb*
PHRASAL VERB
major in something
to study something as your main subject in college: *Stewart majored in biology at Stanford.*

ma•jor•i•ty /məˈdʒɔrəti/ Ac *noun*
most of the people or things in a group: *The majority of Americans still support the president, but of course, not all of them do.* ANTONYM **minority**

ˌmajor ˈleagues *noun*
the group of teams that form the highest level of professional baseball: *Schmidt pitched in the major leagues for ten years.*
—**major-league** *adjective* relating to the major leagues: *a major-league baseball team*

make /meɪk/ *verb* **made** /meɪd/ **making**
1 to produce or build something: *The birds had made a nest in the tree.* | *Do you want to make some cookies with me?* | *It's Dad's turn to make dinner.*
2 to do something: *Anyone can make a mistake.* | *The kids are making too much noise.* | *I made a decision to go back to college.* | *I need to make an appointment to see the doctor.*
3 to cause someone or something to feel something or to happen in a particular way: *His nasty remarks make me so mad sometimes!* | *Winning an award makes you feel good.* | *The disease can make it difficult to walk.*
4 to force someone to do something: *My parents used to make me take piano lessons.* | *They make us work too hard.*
5 to earn money: *Evan's making $11 an hour at his job.* | *Some farmers don't make enough money to pay all their bills.*
6 be made of/from something = to be made from a particular substance or material: *The desk is made of solid wood and is very sturdy.*
7 to be a particular amount when added together: *2 and 2 make 4.*
8 to have the qualities that you need for a job or purpose: *John will make a good father – he's very kind and patient.* | *The book would make a good movie.*
9 make it a) to arrive somewhere or go to an event: *Did you make it to school on time?* | *I'm sorry, but I can't make it to your wedding. I'm going to be away on business.* **b)** to be successful at something: *Do you think Deon is good enough to make it in basketball?*
➔ See Thesaurus boxes at **earn** and **force¹**
➔ **make a difference** at **difference**, **make friends** at **friend**, **make fun of someone or something** at **fun**, **make sure** at **sure**, **make sense** at **sense**, **make up your mind** at **mind¹**

PHRASAL VERBS
make out
1 make something out = to be able to hear, see, or understand something: *I couldn't quite make out what he was saying, so I asked Connie if she knew what he was saying.*

2 *informal* to kiss and touch someone in a sexual way

make up

1 make something up = to think of and tell someone a story that is not true: *Later, she told the police that she had made the whole thing up.* | *The children made up stories and drew pictures to go with them.*

2 make up = to become friends with someone again, after you have had an argument: *Katie and Maria are always fighting and then making up.*

ˈmake-beˌlieve *adjective*

not real, but imagined or pretended: *The boys were flying around the room in make-believe airplanes.*

—**make-believe** *noun* the act of imagining something

—**make believe** *verb* to imagine something

make•up /ˈmeɪk-ʌp/ *noun*

colored powder and creams that some women put on their faces to look prettier: *I don't usually wear makeup unless I'm going somewhere special.*

ma•lar•i•a /məˈleriə/ *noun*

a serious disease that people get when a MOSQUITO with the disease bites them: *He got malaria when he lived in Africa and became very sick.*

male[1] /meɪl/ *adjective*

1 a male person or animal is the type that cannot have babies or lay eggs: *a male lion* | *She has many male friends.* ANTONYM **female**

2 relating to men: *a male voice* ANTONYM **female**

male[2] *noun*

1 a man or boy: *Young males are more likely to have car accidents than any other group.* ANTONYM **female**

2 a male animal: *The males have brightly colored feathers, while the female bird is brown.* ANTONYM **female**

mal•ice /ˈmælɪs/ *noun, formal*

a feeling of wanting to hurt or upset someone: *My sisters teased me, but they did it without malice – they knew I kind of liked it.*

—**malicious** /məˈlɪʃəs/ *adjective* intended to hurt or upset someone

mall /mɔl/ *noun*

a very large building with a lot of stores in it: *I'll meet you at the mall and we can go shopping together.* SYNONYM **shopping mall**

mal•nu•tri•tion /ˌmælnuˈtrɪʃən/ *noun, formal*

illness that is caused by not having enough food to eat, or by not eating healthy food: *Malnutrition is common in poor countries where there isn't enough food.*

mal•prac•tice /ˌmælˈpræktɪs/ *noun, formal*

the fact that a professional person has not done his or her job correctly or has made a serious mistake while doing it: *The doctors operated on the wrong knee, so Elaine is going to sue them for malpractice.*

ma•ma, momma /ˈmɑmə/ *noun, informal*

a MOTHER, used especially by children: *Happy birthday, Mama.*

mam•mal /ˈmæməl/ *noun*

an animal that drinks its mother's milk when it is young, for example a cow, lion, or person

man[1] /mæn/ *noun* plural **men** /men/

1 an adult male person: *Chris is an intelligent young man.* | *My father's a rich man.* | *The room was full of men watching the football game.*

2 all people, both men and women, considered as a group: *This is one of the worst diseases known to man.*

3 used to emphasize what you are saying: *Oh, man! I'm going to be really late.*

man[2] *verb* **manned, manning**

1 to operate a machine: *The helicopters were manned by American pilots.*

2 to work at or guard a particular place: *At night, five guards manned the bridge.*

man•age /ˈmænɪdʒ/ *verb*

1 to succeed in doing something difficult: *Rick managed to run the whole 10 miles!*

2 to be in charge of a business or store and the people who work there: *My daughter manages the restaurant now.*

man•age•a•ble /ˈmænɪdʒəbəl/ *adjective, formal*

able to be done or controlled: *Teachers should give a manageable amount of homework so that students don't become frustrated.*

M

man•age•ment /ˈmænɪdʒmənt/ *noun*
1 the job of controlling and organizing the work of a company or store: *I am responsible for the management of the department, and 25 employees report to me.*
2 the people who control and organize the work of a company or store: *The store has new management, so maybe it will improve.*

man•ag•er /ˈmænɪdʒɚ/ *noun*
someone whose job is to manage a business, store, sports team, etc.: *He's the manager of a bookstore.*
—**managerial** /ˌmænəˈdʒɪriəl/ *adjective* relating to the job of a manager

man•da•to•ry /ˈmændəˌtɔri/ *adjective, formal*
if something is mandatory, a law or rule says that it must be done: *It is mandatory for people riding motorcycles to wear a helmet.*

mane /meɪn/ *noun*
the long hair on the neck of a horse or male lion

ma•neu•ver /məˈnuvɚ/ *verb, formal*
to move something into a different position, using your skill: *I maneuvered the car into a small parking space.*
—**maneuver** *noun* a movement in which you maneuver something

man•go /ˈmæŋgoʊ/ *noun* plural **mangos** or **mangoes**
a sweet juicy tropical fruit that is orange inside and has a large seed
➔ See picture on page A13

ma•ni•ac /ˈmeɪniˌæk/ *noun, informal*
someone who behaves in a crazy or dangerous way: *He was driving like a maniac and scared all of us in the car.*

man•i•cure /ˈmænɪˌkyʊr/ *noun*
a treatment for your hands that includes cutting and painting your FINGERNAILS
—**manicurist** *noun* someone whose job is giving people a manicure

ma•nip•u•late /məˈnɪpyəˌleɪt/ [Ac] *verb, formal*
1 to move things into different positions: *This computer program lets you manipulate blocks of writing and pictures.*
2 to influence someone so that he or she does what you want: *She's trying to manipulate you into doing the work for her.*
—**manipulation** /məˌnɪpyəˈleɪʃən/ *noun* the act of manipulating someone
—**manipulative** /məˈnɪpyəˌleɪtɪv/ *adjective* good at manipulating people

man•kind /ˌmænˈkaɪnd/ *noun*
all people, considered as a group: *A cure for cancer would be good for all mankind.*

man•ly /ˈmænli/ *adjective*
having qualities that people think a man has, such as strength and courage: *He had a deep manly voice.*
—**manliness** *noun*

ˌman-ˈmade *adjective*
man-made things, such as plastic, are made by people, rather than being produced by animals, plants, or the Earth: *The jacket is 80% wool and 20% man-made material.*

man•ner /ˈmænɚ/ *noun, formal*
1 the way in which something is done or happens: *They greeted us in a very friendly manner.*
2 the way in which you behave with other people: *She has a calm, happy manner.*

man•ner•ism /ˈmænəˌrɪzəm/ *noun, formal*
a way of speaking or moving that a particular person often uses: *He and his father have some of the same mannerisms – they both close their eyes when they're thinking.*

man•ners /ˈmænɚz/ *plural noun*
polite ways of behaving: *Your children have very good manners – they always say "please" and "thank you." | It's bad manners to ask how old a woman is.*

man•sion /ˈmænʃən/ *noun*
a very large house: *The party will be held in the governor's mansion.*

man•slaugh•ter /ˈmænˌslɔtɚ/ *noun*
the crime of killing someone when you did not plan to do it: *He was driving drunk, hit a girl and killed her, and was arrested for manslaughter.*

man•tel /ˈmæntl/ *also* **man•tel•piece** /ˈmæntlˌpis/ *noun*
the shelf above a FIREPLACE

man•u•al[1] /ˈmænyuəl/ [Ac] *adjective*
manual work is done using your hands or your strength: *Farms employ manual laborers* (=people who work using their hands) *to pick the apples.*
—**manually** *adverb*

M

manual² *noun*

a book that gives instructions about how to do something: *What does the computer manual say to do?*

man•u•fac•ture /ˌmænyəˈfæktʃɚ/ *verb*

to use machines to make things in large amounts: *The company manufactures jet engines.*

—**manufacture** *noun* the process of manufacturing goods

—**manufacturer** *noun* a company that manufactures things

ma•nure /məˈnʊr/ *noun*

waste that animals produce, that people put into the earth to make plants grow better: *We use cow manure around the roses to help them grow.*

man•u•script /ˈmænyəˌskrɪpt/ *noun*

a piece of writing before it is printed as a book or before it is printed in a magazine or newspaper: *Writers send publishers hundreds of manuscripts every week.*

man•y /ˈmeni/ *adjective, pronoun* **more, most**

1 a large number of people or things: *We lived in New Hampshire for many years while the kids were growing up.* | *There aren't many cookies left – only about three.* | *Many of the students were unhappy and they decided to complain.* | *You have been late for work too many times* (=more than you should). ANTONYM **few**

GRAMMAR: many

much, many, a lot of

Many is used with nouns that show there is more than one thing or person: *I didn't see many people there that I knew.*

Much is used with nouns that are things you cannot count: *There isn't much milk left.*

A lot of can be used with both types of noun: *There isn't a lot of time to work on this.* | *She doesn't have a lot of friends.*

THESAURUS: many

a large number: *A large number of people came to the meeting.*

a lot/lots a large amount, quantity, or number of something: *There are lots of really good books to read.* | *He has a lot of money.*

plenty a large amount that is enough or more than enough: *Make sure you eat plenty of fruit and vegetables.*

2 how many = used for asking about the number of people or things: *How many people are coming to the party?*

map

map /mæp/ *noun*

a drawing of an area or country showing the rivers, roads, cities, etc.: *The kids drew maps of the neighborhood around the school.* | *I couldn't find the city of Fargo on the map.*

ma•ple /ˈmeɪpəl/ *noun*

a tree that grows in northern countries. It has leaves with five points that turn red and yellow in the fall.

mar•a•thon /ˈmærəˌθɑn/ *noun*

a race in which people run 26 miles and 385 yards: *She ran the Boston marathon in just over three hours.*

mar•ble /ˈmɑrbəl/ *noun*

1 a hard rock that people can cut and POLISH, and that is often used to make floors, buildings, STATUEs, etc.: *The statue was made out of marble.*

2 a small colored glass ball that children roll along the ground as part of a game: *Does anyone want to play marbles?*

march¹ /mɑrtʃ/ *verb*

1 to walk with regular steps and lift your knees up, like a soldier: *The high school band marched onto the field.*

2 to walk somewhere with a large group of

M

people in order to protest about something: *Hundreds of people marched on the White House to protest the war.*
3 to walk quickly because you are angry or determined: *My mother stood up angrily and marched out of the room.*
—**marcher** *noun* someone who walks somewhere with a large group of people in order to protest about something
➔ See Thesaurus box at **walk**[1]
➔ See picture on page A4

march[2] *noun*
1 an event in which many people walk together in order to protest about something: *Thousands of people took part in civil rights marches during the 1960s.*
2 an occasion when soldiers march somewhere: *The soldiers were tired at the end of the day's march.*
3 a piece of music with a regular beat for soldiers to march to: *Bands played marches in the parade.*

March /mɑrtʃ/ *noun, written abbreviation* **Mar.**
the third month of the year, between February and April: *We have an appointment at 3:00 p.m. on March 15.* | *I might be going to California in March.* | *Julia had her baby last March.* | *The movie will open next March.*

mare /mer/ *noun*
a female horse or DONKEY

mar•ga•rine /ˈmɑrdʒərɪn/ *noun*
a yellow food that is like butter, but is made from vegetable oil

mar•gin /ˈmɑrdʒɪn/ Ac *noun*
1 the empty space at the side of a page of writing: *In the margin, my teacher had written "Good work."*
2 the amount by which someone wins an election, competition, game, etc.: *The president's margin of victory in Florida was very small.*

mar•gin•al /ˈmɑrdʒənl/ Ac *adjective, formal*
small in importance or amount: *There has been a marginal increase in unemployment, but nothing significant.*
—**marginally** *adverb*

ma•rine /məˈrin/ *adjective*
relating to the ocean and the animals and plants that live there: *marine life* (=animals and fish that live in the ocean)

Ma•rine Corps /məˈrin kɔr/ *noun*
the Marine Corps *also* **the Marines** = a part of the U.S. armed forces in which soldiers are trained to fight on land and on ships
—**Marine** *noun* a soldier in the Marine Corps

mark[1] /mɑrk/ *verb*
1 to write a word or draw a sign on something: *The box was marked "toys."*
2 to show where something is: *Lights marked the entrance to the harbor.*
3 to be a sign of an important event: *The ceremonies marked the 50th anniversary of the end of World War II.*
4 to make a mark on something in a way that spoils or damages it: *The rubber heels of his boots had marked the floor.*

PHRASAL VERB
mark something down
to make the price of something lower: *These shoes were marked down to $10!*

mark[2] *noun*
1 a spot or dirty area on something that spoils how it looks: *Who made these black marks on the couch?*

THESAURUS: mark

Types of Dirty Marks

stain a mark that is difficult to get rid of: *There was an ink stain on his shirt pocket.*

spot a small mark: *Spots of paint covered the floor.*

smudge a dirty mark, made when something is rubbed against a surface: *The kids touch the walls when they go upstairs, leaving dirty smudges.*

Types of Marks on Someone's Skin

blemish a mark on your skin that spoils the way it looks: *Makeup covers your blemishes.*

bruise a purple or brown mark on your skin that you get because you have fallen or been hit: *His legs are covered in bruises from falling down so much.*

scar a permanent mark on your skin, caused by a cut or by something that burns you: *She has a scar under her chin, from when she fell and cut it open.*

pimple a small raised red mark or lump on your skin that teenagers often have: *There was a pimple on his nose.*

zit *informal* a pimple: *Most teenagers get zits; it's nothing to worry about.*

wart a small hard raised mark on your skin caused by a virus (=a living thing that causes an infectious illness): *He has some warts on his hands.*

blister a small area of skin that is swollen and full of liquid because it has been rubbed or burned: *My new shoes gave me blisters.*

freckle one of several small light brown marks on someone's skin: *Toby has red hair and freckles.*

mole a small usually brown mark on the skin that is often slightly higher than the skin around it: *Some moles can be a sign of cancer, so get a doctor to check them.*

2 a cut or damaged area on someone or something: *She had scratch marks on her hand from the cat.*

3 a sign or shape that is written or printed: *Put a question mark by her name—I don't know if she's coming.*

mar•ket /ˈmɑrkɪt/ *noun*

1 a place where people buy and sell goods and food: *I bought some fresh peaches at the market.*

2 on the market = available for someone to buy: *Our house has been on the market for a year now.*

3 all the people who want to buy something: *The market for online games is still growing.*

4 the job/labor market = the number of people looking for work or the number of jobs available

➔ **black market**, **flea market**

mar•ket•place /ˈmɑrkɪtˌpleɪs/ *noun*

1 the marketplace = the business of buying and selling things in competition with other companies: *A good quality product helps a company do well in the marketplace.*

2 an open area where there is a market

ma•roon /məˈrun/ *noun*

a very dark red-brown color

—**maroon** *adjective*: *a maroon T-shirt*

mar•riage /ˈmærɪdʒ/ *noun*

1 the relationship between two people who are married: *My grandparents had a long and happy marriage. They were together 60 years.*

2 the ceremony in which two people get married: *The marriage will take place in St. Augustine's Church next Saturday.* SYNONYM **wedding**

mar•ried /ˈmærid/ *adjective*

if you are married, you have a husband or a wife: *Are you married or single? | Helen is married to a lawyer.*

THESAURUS: married

If someone is **single**, they are not married.

If someone is **engaged**, they have agreed to marry someone.

If a husband and wife are **separated**, they are living apart because they are having problems in their marriage.

If a husband and wife get **divorced**, they legally end their marriage.

If two people **live with** each other, they are in a romantic relationship and share a home together, but are not married.

A **widow** is a woman whose husband has died.

mar•ry /ˈmæri/ *verb* **married**, third person singular **marries**

1 to become someone's husband or wife: *I've asked Linda to marry me. | We got married last July.*

2 to perform the ceremony at which two people get married: *Rabbi Feingold has agreed to marry us.*

WORD FAMILY look at the words:

➔ **marry** *verb*
➔ **married** *adjective*
➔ **unmarried** *adjective*
➔ **marriage** *noun*

marsh /mɑrʃ/ *noun*

an area of ground that is soft and wet: *Many animals and birds live in these marshes.*

—**marshy** *adjective* marshy land is soft and wet

—**marshland** *noun* a large area of land that is marshy

mar•shal /ˈmɑrʃəl/ *noun*

1 a police officer in the U.S. whose job is to make sure that people do what a court of law has ordered them to do: *He was arrested*

M

by federal marshals and taken back to Chicago.
2 the officer in charge of a city's fire department: *The fire marshal can close a building if it does not have enough fire exits.*

marsh•mal•low /ˈmɑrʃˌmeloʊ/ *noun*
a very soft white candy made of sugar and the white part of eggs: *We sat around the campfire toasting marshmallows.*

mar•tial /ˈmɑrʃəl/ *adjective, formal*
relating to the army, war, and fighting: *The government declared martial law* (=the government said that the army would control the country).

ˌmartial ˈarts *plural noun*
sports such as judo or karate, in which you fight with your hands and feet: *She took a martial arts course to learn to protect herself.*
➔ See picture on page A24

mar•vel•ous /ˈmɑrvələs/ *adjective, formal*
very good or enjoyable: *It's a wonderful show and the acting is marvelous.*

mas•car•a /mæˈskærə/ *noun*
a dark substance you put on your EYELASHes to make them look darker and thicker: *She started crying, which made her mascara run* (=it came off her eyelashes onto her face).

mas•cot /ˈmæskɑt/ *noun*
an animal, toy, etc. that a team or organization has to bring them good luck: *The team's mascot is an eagle.*

mas•cu•line /ˈmæskjələn/ *adjective*
1 like a man or how a man behaves: *He has a deep, masculine voice.*
2 in grammar, a masculine noun or PRONOUN has a form that means it relates to a male, such as "widower" or "him"

mash /mæʃ/ *verb*
to crush food until it is soft: *Mash the potatoes until they are nice and smooth.*
➔ See Thesaurus box at **press**[1]
➔ See picture on page A14

mask /mæsk/ *noun*
something that covers your face, that you wear to protect or hide it: *One boy wore a clown mask to the Halloween party.* | *He had a catcher's mask on so the ball couldn't hit him in the face.*

mas•quer•ade /ˌmæskəˈreɪd/ *verb, formal*
to pretend to be someone or something else: *He masqueraded as a police officer to get into the building.*

mass /mæs/ *noun*
1 a large amount of something: *The volcano sent a mass of ash and smoke up into the air.*
2 *formal* the amount of material in something: *How do scientists measure the mass of a star?*
3 *also* **Mass** the main religious ceremony in some Christian churches, especially the Roman Catholic Church: *I go to Mass every Sunday at St. Mary's.*

mas•sa•cre /ˈmæsəkɚ/ *verb*
to kill a lot of people, especially people who cannot defend themselves: *In 1890, soldiers massacred hundreds of American Indians who were at a religious ceremony.*
—**massacre** *noun* an occasion when a lot of people are massacred

mas•sage /məˈsɑʒ/ *noun*
the action of pressing and rubbing someone's body with your hands, in order to make pain better or help him or her relax: *Can you give my back a massage, please?*
—**massage** *verb* to give someone a massage

mas•sive /ˈmæsɪv/ *adjective*
very large or powerful: *There was a massive earthquake in Japan that killed 5,000 people.*

ˌmass ˈmedia *noun*
television, radio, newspapers, and magazines, which give information and news to the public: *There were some reports about the event in the mass media.*

mast /mæst/ *noun*
1 a tall pole that the sails of a ship hang from
2 a tall pole that a flag hangs from

mas•ter[1] /ˈmæstɚ/ *noun*
1 a man who has control over people or animals: *The dog stood by its master's side.*
2 someone who is very skilled at something: *Ellington was one of the masters of jazz music.*

master[2] *verb*
to learn a skill or language so well that you can do it easily: *He mastered French after living in France for only a year.*

M

ˌmaster of ˈceremonies *noun, abbreviation* **M.C.**
someone who introduces speakers or performers at an event: *He was the master of ceremonies at the Academy Awards this year.*

mas•ter•piece /ˈmæstɚˌpis/ *noun*
one of the very best works of art, pieces of writing, music, movies, etc.: *Many people consider Orson Welles's movie "Citizen Kane" to be a masterpiece of film.*

mas•ter's /ˈmæstɚz/ *noun, informal*
a master's degree

ˈmaster's deˌgree *noun*
a university degree that you get by studying for one or two years after your first degree: *She's working on a master's degree in history, after finishing her bachelor's degree last year.*

mat /mæt/ *noun*
1 a piece of thick material that covers part of a floor: *Please wipe your feet on the mat when you come in.*
2 a small piece of material that you put under a plate or glass to protect the surface of a table: *She put the hot plates down onto place mats.*
3 a piece of thick soft material used in some sports for people to fall onto: *Wrestling matches take place on a gym mat.*

match[1] /mætʃ/ *noun*
1 a small wooden or paper stick that makes a flame when you rub it against a surface, and that you use to light a fire, cigarette, etc.: *a box of matches* | *She struck a match and lit the fire.*
2 a game or competition between two people or teams, in boxing, soccer, tennis, and some other sports: *Are you going to watch the boxing match tonight?*
→ See picture at **light**[1]

match[2] *verb*
1 to be like something else in size, shape, color, etc.: *I bought a pink dress and I want to find a pink hat that matches.*
2 to be equal to something in size, value, or quality: *We're a small college, and our teams can never match the quality of the teams from big universities.*

mate[1] /meɪt/ *noun*
1 the sexual partner of an animal: *In spring, the male bears try to find a mate.*
2 a husband or wife: *He's dated a lot of women, but he's still searching for the perfect mate.*
→ **classmate, roommate**

mate[2] *verb*
if animals mate, they have sex to make babies: *The male usually mates with several females each year.*

ma•te•ri•al /məˈtɪriəl/ *noun*
1 cloth used for making clothes, curtains, etc.: *I've bought some material to make curtains.*
2 a solid substance, such as wood, plastic, or metal: *The students were testing different materials to see if they would float on water.*
3 *also* **materials** the things that you use in order to do a job or activity: *drawing materials such as paper and pencils*
4 information or ideas used in books, movies, etc.: *He's looking for material for his new book.*

ma•ter•ni•ty /məˈtɚnəti/ *adjective*
used by or relating to a woman who is PREGNANT or who has just had a baby: *a maternity dress* | *I had three months of maternity leave* (=when you do not have to go to work) *after I had the baby before going back to work.*

math /mæθ/ *noun*
the short form of the word mathematics: *The math test covered adding and subtracting.*

math•e•mat•ics /ˌmæθəˈmætɪks/ *noun, formal*
the study of numbers and shapes: *He has been teaching mathematics for several years.* SYNONYM **math**
—**mathematical** *adjective* relating to mathematics
—**mathematician** /ˌmæθməˈtɪʃən/ *noun* someone who has studied mathematics to a high level or who teaches mathematics

mat•ter[1] /ˈmætɚ/ *noun*
1 a subject or situation that you have to think about or deal with: *Bullying is a serious matter that I need to discuss with your parents.*
2 **the matter** *informal* = used to ask why something is not working or why someone

M

seems upset: *What's the matter? Why are you crying?* | *There's something the matter with the engine – it won't start.*

3 no matter how/where/what, etc. *informal* = used to say that something does not change: *No matter how hard she tried, she couldn't get the door open.*

4 as a matter of fact *informal* = used when you are telling someone something that is surprising: *"Did you just get here?" "No, as a matter of fact I got here an hour ago."*

5 the material that things are made of: *all the matter in the universe*

matter² *verb*
to be important: *She is the only person that really matters to him. He doesn't care about anyone else.* | *It doesn't matter how long it takes, as long as the work gets done.*

mat•tress /'mætrəs/ *noun*
the soft part of a bed that you lie on
➔ See picture on page A10

ma•ture¹ /mə'tʃʊr/ Ac *adjective*
1 behaving in a sensible and responsible way, like an adult: *She's mature for her age* (=she behaves sensibly, even though she is young). ANTONYM **immature**
2 fully grown and developed: *The park has many mature trees.*
—**maturity** /mə'tʃʊrəti/ *noun* the quality or state of being mature: *Rabbits reach maturity in only five weeks.*

mature² *verb*
1 to begin to behave in a sensible and responsible way, like an adult: *She has matured a lot since going to college.*
2 to become fully grown or developed: *These fish mature in three months.*

max•i•mize /'mæksəˌmaɪz/ Ac *verb, formal*
to make something as great or large as possible: *You can maximize your chances of winning by training every day.* ANTONYM **minimize**

max•i•mum /'mæksəmən/ Ac *noun*
the largest number or amount that is possible or allowed: *There is a maximum of 20 students in each class.* ANTONYM **minimum**
—**maximum** *adjective*: *The plane had a maximum speed of 130 miles per hour.*

may /meɪ/ *verb*
1 used for saying that something is possible: *I may need your help later, so don't go too far away.* | *I don't know where they are. They may have gotten lost.*
2 *formal* used for asking or giving permission: *May I speak with Anne, please?* | *You may ask questions at the end of the class.*

May /meɪ/ *noun*
the fifth month of the year, between April and June: *Our anniversary is on May 1.* | *We might be going to Texas in May.* | *We haven't seen Tania since last May.* | *Construction is scheduled to begin next May.*

may•be /'meɪbi/ *adverb*
1 used for saying that something may be true or may happen: *Maybe her phone's not working.* | *"Will you be there tomorrow night?" "Maybe."* SYNONYM **perhaps**
2 used when making a suggestion: *Maybe Jeff could help you. Why don't you ask him?*

may•on•naise /'meɪəˌneɪz/ *noun*
a thick white sauce made of egg and oil: *He mixed the tuna with the mayonnaise and spread it on the bread.*

may•or /'meɪɚ/ *noun*
someone who is elected to lead the government of a town or city: *the mayor of Chicago* | *Mayor Villaraigosa made a speech today.*

maze /meɪz/ *noun*
1 a place that has many confusing paths that are difficult to find your way through: *He led us through a maze of streets in the old part of the city.*
2 a game in which you have to find your way or draw a line through a confusing set of lines, without crossing any of them: *The book had mazes and other kinds of puzzles.*

maze

M.C.
the abbreviation of **Master of Ceremonies**

M.D. *abbreviation*
Doctor of Medicine: *Karen Johnson, M.D.*

M

me /mi/ *pronoun*
1 used after a verb or PREPOSITION when you are talking about yourself: *He doesn't like me.* | *Listen to me.*
2 me too = used when saying that you are like the person you are talking to: *"I'm hungry!" "Me too. Let's eat."*

mead•ow /ˈmedoʊ/ *noun*
a field with wild grass and flowers

meal /mil/ *noun*
the food that you eat at a particular time: *We had a nice meal at that new restaurant.* | *Most people eat three meals a day.*

THESAURUS: meal

Types of Meals

breakfast a meal that you eat in the morning: *It's important to eat breakfast before you go to school.*

lunch a meal that you eat in the middle of the day: *I had a sandwich and an apple for lunch.*

brunch a meal that you eat in the late morning, instead of breakfast or lunch: *We went to a nice restaurant for brunch on Sunday.*

dinner/supper a meal that you eat in the evening: *What's for supper, Mom?* | *I had dinner with my family.*

picnic a meal that you eat outdoors, with food that you make earlier: *We took a picnic to the park.*

barbecue a meal that you cook and eat outdoors: *It was a warm evening, so we had a barbecue.*

meal•time /ˈmiltaɪm/ *noun*
a time when you have a meal: *I only see him at mealtimes when we all sit down together to eat.*

mean¹ /min/ *verb* **meant** /ment/
1 to have a particular meaning: *What does the word "humid" mean?* | *The red light means "stop."*
2 to want to use a particular meaning when you say something: *I meant this weekend, not next weekend.* | *"He isn't coming back." "What do you mean?"*
3 to want and plan to do something or want and plan that something should happen: *Sorry, I didn't mean to scare you.* | *It was meant to be a joke!* SYNONYM **intend**
4 to have a particular result: *This injury means that he won't play Saturday.*
5 means a lot to someone = to be very important to someone: *This award means a lot to me.*
6 I mean a) used when explaining what you have just said or giving an example: *It's so unfair. I mean, he hadn't done anything wrong.* **b)** used when you have just said something wrong: *She plays the violin, I mean the viola.*

mean² *adjective*
not kind or nice: *Don't be mean to your sister.*

mean•ing /ˈminɪŋ/ *noun*
1 the idea or information that a word or sign gives you: *Look up the meaning of the word in a dictionary.*
2 the quality of being important or having a purpose: *He wanted to help people to give his life meaning.*
—**meaningful** *adjective* having some meaning: *We had a meaningful discussion about what is important in a marriage.*
—**meaningless** *adjective* without any meaning: *It's a meaningless job – I don't know why it exists.*

means /minz/ *noun* plural **means**
1 a method, object, etc. that you use to do something: *He climbed the tree by means of* (=using) *a ladder.* | *I didn't have any means of finding out who was responsible for the fight.*
2 by all means *formal* = used for saying in a strong way that someone may do something: *"May I borrow your pencil?" "By all means."*
3 by no means *formal* = not at all: *It is by no means a perfect solution, but it's the best we can do right now.*
4 *formal* the money that you have and can use: *These houses are beyond the means of most people* (=too expensive for most people).

meant /ment/ *verb*
the past tense and past participle of MEAN

mean•time /ˈmintaɪm/ *noun*
in the meantime = in the time before something happens: *John will be here soon. In the meantime, I'll get things ready.*

mean•while /ˈminwaɪl/ *adverb*
while something is happening, or before something happens: *Davis scored 12 points,*

M

but Johnson, meanwhile, made just one basket.

mea•sles /ˈmizəlz/ *also* **the measles** *noun*
an illness in which you have small red spots on your body: *Did you have measles when you were a kid?*

meas•ure¹ /ˈmeʒɚ/ *verb*
1 to find out the size or amount of something, using a piece of equipment: *She measured the piece of wood with a ruler.*
2 to be a particular size: *The table measures four feet by six feet.*
—**measurable** *adjective* able to be measured

PHRASAL VERB
measure up
to be good enough: *He is afraid he won't measure up.*

measure² *noun*
1 an official action that someone does to deal with a problem: *We have taken measures to stop bullying at school.*
2 a measure of something *formal* = something that shows what the size or amount of something is: *Test scores are a measure of a student's progress.*

meas•ure•ment /ˈmeʒɚmənt/ *noun*
the length, width, height, or amount of something: *I took measurements to see if the sofa would fit in the room.*

meat /mit/ *noun*
the flesh of animals and birds eaten as food: *Vegetarians don't eat meat.*

THESAURUS: meat

Types of Meat
beef the meat from a cow
veal the meat from a young cow
pork the meat from a pig
ham meat from a pig, that has been kept good by putting it in salt or smoke
bacon long thin pieces of meat from the back or sides of a pig, that have been kept good by putting them in salt or smoke

The meat from lamb, birds, or fish is called by the name of the animal: *We had chicken for dinner.* | *roast lamb* | *a tuna sandwich*

meat•ball /ˈmitbɔl/ *noun*
a small round ball made from very small pieces of meat: *We had spaghetti and meatballs for dinner.*

me•chan•ic /mɪˈkænɪk/ *noun*
someone whose job is to repair cars, airplanes, etc. or other kinds of machines: *What did the mechanic say was wrong with the car?*
➔ See picture on page A16

me•chan•i•cal /mɪˈkænɪkəl/ *adjective*
relating to machines: *The plane could not fly because of a mechanical problem.*
—**mechanically** *adverb*

mech•a•nism /ˈmekəˌnɪzəm/ Ac *noun*
the part of a machine that does a particular job: *The car's steering mechanism was broken, so he couldn't turn the car.*

med•al /ˈmedl/ *noun*
a piece of metal that someone gets as a prize or gets for doing something brave: *He won an Olympic gold medal.*
—**medalist** *noun* someone who has won a medal

me•di•a /ˈmidiə/ Ac *plural noun*
the media = television, radio, and newspapers: *The event was widely reported in the media.* | *The trial got a lot of media attention.*

med•ic /ˈmedɪk/ *noun*
someone in the army who is trained to give medical treatment

med•i•cal /ˈmedɪkəl/ Ac *adjective*
relating to illnesses and injuries, and ways of treating them: *She went to medical school and is now a doctor.* | *new types of medical treatment*
—**medically** *adverb*

med•i•ca•tion /ˌmedəˈkeɪʃən/ *noun, formal*
medicine: *He's on medication* (=he takes medicine) *for his heart.*
➔ See Thesaurus box at **medicine**

med·i·cine /ˈmedəsən/ *noun*
1 something that you drink or eat when you are sick, for example a drug, to help you get better: *Remember to take your medicine.*

THESAURUS: medicine

pill/tablet a small hard piece of medicine that you swallow: *The doctor gave her pills for the pain.* | *a vitamin tablet*

capsule a small object with medicine inside that you swallow whole: *She took two capsules of Tylenol for her headache.*

eye/ear drops liquid medicine that you put into your eye or ear: *The ear drops will get rid of the infection.*

drug a medicine or a substance for making medicines: *a new drug in the treatment of breast cancer*

dosage/dose *formal* the amount of medicine that you should take: *The usual dosage is 25 to 50 mg.* | *Never take more than the recommended dose of two pills every four hours.*

medication *formal* medicine: *He's on medication for his heart.*

2 the study and treatment of illnesses and injuries: *She wanted to study medicine.*
—**medicinal** /məˈdɪsənəl/ *adjective* used for treating illnesses and injuries: *medicinal herbs*

me·di·e·val /medˈivəl/ *adjective*
relating to the time between the 5th and 15th centuries A.D.: *a medieval castle*

me·di·o·cre /ˌmidiˈoʊkɚ/ *adjective*
not very good or very bad: *My grades were mediocre so I worked to improve them.*

Med·i·ter·ra·ne·an /ˌmedɪtəˈreɪniən/ *noun*
the Mediterranean = the sea between northern Africa and southern Europe, and the land around it
—**Mediterranean** *adjective*

me·di·um /ˈmidiəm/ Ac *adjective*
not big or small: *She is of medium height – about the same height as most of her classmates.* | *Use a medium-sized onion for this dish.* | *"What size T-shirt do you wear?" "Medium."*

meet /mit/ *verb* **met** /met/
1 *also* **meet up (with someone)** to come to the same place as someone else because you have planned this: *I'm meeting him for lunch downtown.* | *My mom will meet us in front of the school.*
2 to see and talk to someone for the first time: *"Paul, this is Jack." "Nice to meet you."*
3 to see and talk to someone without planning to do this: *You'll never guess who I met at the store: Diane, that girl I used to play softball with!*
4 *formal* to do or be what people need or want: *A school should meet the needs of all its students.* | *We've met our goal of raising $5,000.*
5 if things meet, they join or touch: *The two trails meet at the lake.*

PHRASAL VERB
meet with someone
to have a meeting with someone: *I met with the principal this morning to discuss Andy's behavior.*

meet·ing /ˈmitɪŋ/ *noun*
a time when people come together to discuss something: *I had a meeting with the team yesterday to talk about its performance.* | *John has been in a meeting with his coworkers all morning.*

meg·a·byte /ˈmegəˌbaɪt/ *noun*, *written abbreviation* **MB**
a unit for measuring computer information, equal to a million BYTEs

mel·an·chol·y /ˈmelənˌkɑli/ *adjective*, *formal*
sad: *I felt melancholy when she had gone.*
—**melancholy** *noun* sadness

mel·low /ˈmeloʊ/ *adjective*
1 relaxed and calm: *He's become a little more mellow as he's gotten older. He doesn't get angry as often.*
2 sounding or tasting smooth and pleasant: *His mellow voice put me to sleep.*

me·lod·ic /məˈlɑdɪk/ *adjective*, *formal*
having a pleasant tune or a pleasant sound: *Their earlier songs are more melodic and easier to sing.*

mel·o·dra·mat·ic /ˌmelədrəˈmætɪk/ *adjective*, *formal*
having or showing feelings that are very strong but also a little bit silly: *"My life is ruined!" "Stop being so melodramatic."*

M

mel•o•dy /ˈmelədi/ *noun* plural **melodies**
a set of musical notes that sound good together: *The song has a really pretty melody.* SYNONYM **tune**
➔ See Thesaurus box at **music**

mel•on /ˈmelən/ *noun*
a large juicy fruit with a thick skin and large flat seeds
➔ See picture on page A13

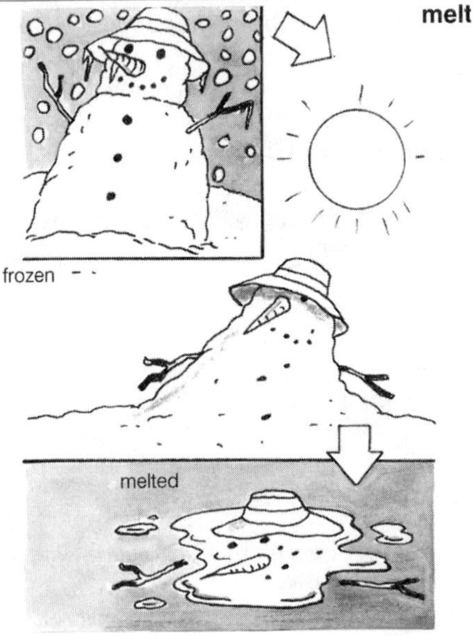

melt /melt/ *verb*
if something solid melts, or if you melt it, it changes to a liquid when it becomes warmer: *The snowman's melting.* | *Melt some butter in a pan.*

ˈmelting pot *noun*
a place where people from different countries live together and start to share common ideas and beliefs: *The U.S. is often called a melting pot because people came from all over the world and became Americans.*

mem•ber /ˈmembɚ/ *noun*
someone who belongs to a group or organization: *Are you a member of the French club?*

mem•ber•ship /ˈmembɚˌʃɪp/ *noun*
1 the state of being a member of a group or organization: *I applied for membership in the health club.* | *The membership fee is $25.*
2 the members of a group or organization: *The group's membership is around 400* (=it has around 400 members).

mem•o /ˈmemoʊ/ *also* **mem•o•ran•dum** /ˌmeməˈrændəm/ *noun* plural **memos**
a short note to another person in the same organization: *He sent a memo about the changes to everyone in the department.*

mem•o•ra•ble /ˈmemərəbəl/ *adjective*
likely to be remembered: *The day I learned to ride a bike was the most memorable day of my childhood.*

me•mo•ri•al /məˈmɔriəl/ *noun*
something that is built to remind people of someone who has died: *All the soldiers' names are carved on the war memorial.*

mem•o•rize /ˈmeməˌraɪz/ *verb*
to learn words, music, or facts so that you can remember them: *She memorized her speech so she wouldn't have to read it when she spoke.*

mem•o•ry /ˈheməri/ *noun* plural **memories**
1 the ability to remember things: *I have a good memory.* | *Could you draw the map from memory* (=by remembering it)?
2 something in the past that you remember: *I have a lot of good memories of our family's vacations.*
3 the amount of space that a computer has for keeping information: *The computer has 256 megabytes of memory.*
4 **in memory of someone** = as a way of remembering someone who has died: *They lit candles in memory of those who died in the bombing.*

WORD FAMILY look at the words:
➔ **memory** *noun*
➔ **memorize** *verb*
➔ **memorable** *adjective*
➔ **memorial** *noun*

men /men/ *noun*
the plural of MAN

men•ace /ˈmenɪs/ *noun, formal*
something or someone that is dangerous or very annoying: *This disease is a menace to people everywhere.*

mend /mend/ *verb*
to repair a damaged piece of clothing: *Your shirt is torn – let me mend it for you.*
➔ See Thesaurus box at **repair**[2]

men•o•pause /ˈmenəˌpɔz/ *noun*
the time when a woman stops being able to have a baby

ˈmen's room *noun*
a room in a public place with toilets for men

men•stru•ate /ˈmenstruˌeɪt/ *verb, formal*
if a woman menstruates, blood flows out of her body every month
—**menstruation** /ˌmenstruˈeɪʃən/ *noun* when blood flows out of a woman's body
—**menstrual** *adjective* relating to menstruation

men•tal /ˈmentl/ Ac *adjective*
1 relating to the mind: *I have a mental picture of what the house will be like. I hope that's the way it ends up!*
2 relating to illnesses of the mind: *He was put in a mental hospital when he became violent and irrational.*
—**mentally** *adverb*

men•tal•i•ty /menˈtæləti/ Ac *noun*
plural **mentalities** *formal*
a particular attitude or way of thinking: *It's hard to understand the mentality of these terrorists. What are they thinking?*

ˌmentally ˈill *adjective*
if someone is mentally ill, they have an illness in their mind that makes them behave in ways that are not normal: *She works in a hospital, taking care of people who are mentally ill.*
—**mental illness** *noun* an illness in your mind, that makes you behave in strange ways
➔ See Thesaurus box at **crazy**

men•tion /ˈmenʃən/ *verb*
1 to say something, without giving a lot of information: *I mentioned to Dad that the TV wasn't working.*
2 not to mention someone or something = used when adding something to what you have said, usually something more important: *He didn't want to disappoint his teacher, not to mention his parents.*
—**mention** *noun* the act of mentioning something: *He makes no mention of* (=does not say anything about) *his famous father in the book.*
➔ See Thesaurus box at **say**[1]

men•u /ˈmenyu/ *noun*
1 a list of the food that you can eat in a restaurant: *There was no fish on the menu, so I ordered chicken.*
2 a list of things that you can ask your computer to do: *Go to the edit menu and select "copy."*
➔ See picture on page A15

me•ow /miˈaʊ/ *verb*
if a cat meows, it makes a sound
—**meow** *noun*

mer•chan•dise /ˈmɚtʃənˌdaɪz/ *noun, formal*
things that are for sale: *The stores are full of cheap merchandise.*

mer•chan•dis•ing /ˈmɚtʃənˌdaɪzɪŋ/ *noun, formal*
the activity of trying to sell things: *The new movie offers a great merchandising opportunity – kids will want to buy things connected with it.*

mer•chant /ˈmɚtʃənt/ *noun, formal*
someone who buys and sells things: *a wine merchant*

mer•ci•ful /ˈmɚsɪfəl/ *adjective, formal*
kind and forgiving: *The king was merciful and did not punish the man.*

mer•ci•less /ˈmɚsɪləs/ *adjective*
not at all kind or forgiving: *a merciless killer*
—**mercilessly** *adverb*

mer•cu•ry /ˈmɚkyəri/ *noun*
a liquid silver-colored metal: *In some thermometers, a line of mercury shows what the temperature is.*

mer•cy /ˈmɚsi/ *noun*
kindness and a willingness to forgive people: *He said he was guilty, but begged the judge for mercy.*

mere•ly /ˈmɪrli/ *adverb, formal*
only: *Ken merely smiled in reply to her question and did not say anything.* SYNONYM **just**
—**mere** *adjective* only: *The house took a mere two weeks to build.*

merge /mɚdʒ/ *verb*
to join together to form one thing: *The school later merged with two others to form the largest school in the county.*

me•rid•i•an /məˈrɪdiən/ *noun, formal*
a line drawn from the North Pole to the South Pole on a map: *The zero meridian goes through Greenwich, England.*

M

mer•it /ˈmerɪt/ *noun*
a good quality of something: *One of the merits of this book is that it is very clear.*

mer•maid /ˈmɚmeɪd/ *noun*
a woman in stories who has a fish's tail instead of legs

mer•ry /ˈmeri/ *adjective* **merrier**, **merriest**
happy: *Merry Christmas!* (=used as a greeting at Christmas)

ˈmerry-go-ˌround *noun*
a machine that turns around and around, that children ride on for fun: *Anna rode a white horse on the merry-go-round.*

mess¹ /mes/ *noun*
1 a place or a group of things that is not organized or neat and may be dirty: *The room was a mess with books, newspapers, and clothes everywhere.* | *The kids make such a mess when they help me cook.* | *I'll help you clean up the mess.*
2 a situation in which there are a lot of problems: *How did we ever get into this mess and what can we do to get out of it?*

mess² *verb*
PHRASAL VERBS
mess around *informal*
to play or do silly things when you should be working or paying attention: *Mrs. Waxman says if you don't stop messing around in class you're going to get a bad grade.*
mess up *informal*
1 mess something up = to spoil or ruin something: *I hope I haven't messed up your plans by not coming.*
2 mess something up = to make something dirty or messy: *The wind had messed her hair up.*
3 mess (something) up = to make a mistake or do something badly: *I messed up at college and didn't graduate.* | *I know I messed up the test – I just hope I don't get an F.*

mes•sage /ˈmesɪdʒ/ *noun*
a piece of information that you leave for someone when you cannot speak to him or her: *I have a message for you: Mrs. Robinson called when you were out.* | *Mike left a message saying he would be late.* | *Sorry, Tony's not home yet. Can I take a message* (=used in a phone call when someone wants to talk to a person who is not there)? | *When I came back from my vacation, there were 115 email messages for me!*

mes•sen•ger /ˈmesəndʒɚ/ *noun*
someone who takes packages or messages to other people: *The note was delivered by messenger.*

mess•y /ˈmesi/ *adjective* **messier**, **messiest**
1 dirty or not neat: *The boys' bedroom was very messy.* | *His hands were getting messy working on the car.*
2 a messy person or activity makes things dirty or leaves things in a way that is not neat: *Cleaning the oven can be a messy job.* | *He's a very messy person and doesn't like to clean.*
3 a messy situation is complicated and hard to deal with: *She's just been through a messy divorce and is still very upset.*

met /met/ *verb*
the past tense and past participle of MEET

met•al /ˈmetl/ *noun*
a hard substance such as iron, gold, or steel: *Coins are made of metal.* | *a metal spoon*
—**metallic** *adjective* made of metal or similar to metal

met•a•phor /ˈmetəˌfɔr/ *noun, formal*
a way of describing something by comparing it to something else that has similar qualities, without using the words "like" or "as": *"A river of tears" is a metaphor.*
—**metaphorical** /ˌmetəˈfɔrɪkəl/ *adjective* relating to or using a metaphor

me•te•or /ˈmitiɚ/ *noun*
a piece of rock or metal that burns very brightly when it falls from space into the air around the Earth: *We could see a bright meteor moving across the night sky.*

me•te•or•ite /ˈmitiəˌraɪt/ *noun*
a piece of rock or metal from space that has landed on the Earth's surface

me•te•or•ol•o•gy /ˌmitiəˈrɑlədʒi/ *noun, formal*
the scientific study of the weather
—**meteorologist** *noun* someone whose job is to study the weather, especially in order to say what it will be like in the next days or weeks
—**meteorological** /ˌmitiərəˈlɑdʒɪkəl/ *adjective* relating to meteorology

meter /ˈmitɚ/ *noun*
1 *written abbreviation* **m** a unit for measuring length, equal to 100 centimeters or 39.37 inches: *She is 1.68 meters tall.*
2 a piece of equipment that measures the amount of gas, electricity, etc. you have used: *Someone from the gas company came to look at the meter.*
➔ **parking meter**

meth·ane /ˈmeθeɪn/ *noun*
a gas with no color or smell, which can be burned to give heat

meth·od /ˈmeθəd/ Ac *noun*
a way of doing something: *The school uses traditional teaching methods.* | *Using a microwave oven is a common method of cooking food.*

me·thod·i·cal /məˈθɑdɪkəl/ Ac *adjective, formal*
1 done in a careful and well organized way: *Police made a methodical search of the area making sure not to miss any spot.*
2 someone who is methodical does things in a careful and well organized way: *Scientists must be very methodical and keep careful records.*

meth·od·ol·o·gy /ˌmeθəˈdɑlədʒi/ Ac *noun* plural **methodologies** *formal*
the methods and rules you use when you are studying a subject or doing a particular type of work: *The students learn a methodology for simple science experiments.*
—**methodological** /ˌmeθədəˈlɑdʒɪkəl/ *adjective* relating to methodology

met·ric sys·tem /ˈmetrɪk ˌsɪstəm/ *noun*
the system of measuring that is based on meters, grams, and liters
—**metric** *adjective* using the metric system

met·ro·pol·i·tan /ˌmetrəˈpɑlətn/ *adjective*
in or relating to big cities: *Pollution is a big problem in metropolitan areas such as Los Angeles or Denver.*

Mex·i·can /ˈmeksɪkən/ *adjective*
from Mexico: *Mexican food*
—**Mexican** *noun* someone from Mexico

mg.
the written abbreviation of **milligram**

mice /maɪs/ *noun*
the plural of MOUSE

mi·crobe /ˈmaɪkroʊb/ *noun, formal*
a very small living thing that you cannot see without a MICROSCOPE

mi·cro·chip /ˈmaɪkroʊˌtʃɪp/ *noun*
a small object inside a computer, that contains the electronic connections which make the computer work SYNONYM **chip**

mi·cro·film /ˈmaɪkrəˌfɪlm/ *noun*
film on which there are very small photographs of documents, which you can read using a special machine: *Images of the old newspapers are stored on reels of microfilm.*

mi·cro·phone /ˈmaɪkrəˌfoʊn/ *noun*
a piece of equipment that you speak into to make your voice sound louder or to record it: *Please speak clearly into the microphone so everyone can hear you.*

microphone

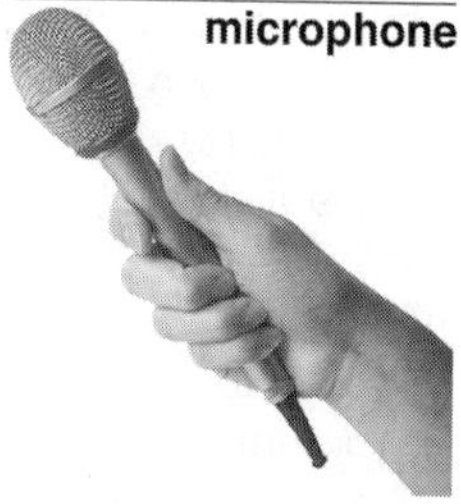

mi·cro·scope /ˈmaɪkrəˌskoʊp/ *noun*
a scientific instrument that helps you to see very small things by making them look bigger: *We looked at the insects under a microscope so we could see all their tiny parts.*

microscope

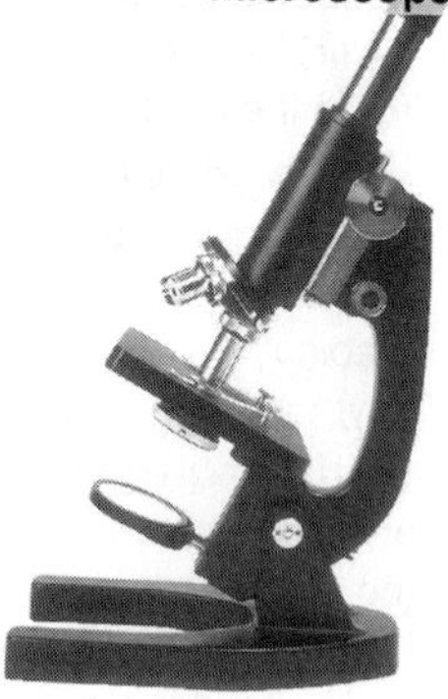

mi·cro·scop·ic /ˌmaɪkrəˈskɑpɪk/ *adjective, formal*
extremely small: *Water has microscopic creatures living in it.*

mi·cro·wave /ˈmaɪkrəˌweɪv/ *also* **microwave oven** *noun*
a type of machine that cooks food very quickly: *Cook the vegetables in the microwave for three minutes.*
—**microwave** *verb* to cook something in a microwave
➔ See picture on page A9

M

mid *also* **mid-** /mɪd/
used before other words to mean in the middle of a period of time: *It was mid-morning and the sun was starting to get hotter.* | *The weather was warm for mid December.*

mid•day /ˈmɪd-deɪ/ *noun, formal*
the middle of the day, around 12:00 p.m.: *At midday, lunch was on the table.* SYNONYM **noon**

mid•dle¹ /ˈmɪdl/ *noun*
1 the middle = the part that is closest to the center of something: *The lake is very deep in the middle.* | *There were a bunch of books in the middle of the floor.* SYNONYM **center**
2 the middle = the part that is between the beginning and the end of a period of time or an event: *He woke up suddenly in the middle of the night and couldn't get back to sleep until 3 a.m.*

middle² *adjective*
closest to the center of something: *The socks are in the middle drawer.*

ˌmiddle ˈclass *noun*
the middle class = the group of people in a country who are not rich but not poor either: *Most doctors belong to the middle class.*
—**middle-class** *adjective* belonging or relating to the middle class: *middle-class families*

ˌMiddle ˈEast *noun*
the Middle East = the part of Asia that is between the Mediterranean Sea and the Arabian Sea, and includes countries such as Egypt and Iran

ˈmiddle school *noun*
a school in the U.S. for students between the ages of 11 and 14, or in grades five or six through eight: *She's a science teacher at Rockridge Middle School.*

midg•et /ˈmɪdʒɪt/ *noun*
a rude word for someone who is very short

mid•night /ˈmɪdnaɪt/ *noun*
12 O'CLOCK at night: *The party ended at midnight.*

mid•way /ˌmɪdˈweɪ/ *adjective, adverb*
1 at the middle point between two places: *There's a gas station midway between here and Fresno.*
2 in the middle of a period of time or an event: *I left midway through the show because I wasn't feeling well.*

Mid•west /ˌmɪdˈwest/ *noun*
the Midwest = the central area of the U.S.: *The Midwest is known mainly for its farms.*
—**Midwesterner** *noun* someone who comes from the Midwest

mid•wife /ˈmɪdwaɪf/ *noun* plural **midwives** /ˈmɪdwaɪvz/
a nurse whose job is to help women when they are having a baby
—**midwifery** *noun* the job of being a midwife

might¹ /maɪt/ *verb*
1 used for talking about what was or is possible: *I might be able to get free tickets – let me check.* | *They might not be able to come to the wedding, but they'll tell us before then.* | *I don't know what happened to the bike. Someone might have taken it.*
2 used for giving advice or making a suggestion: *You might try calling the store to see if it's open.* | *You might want to see a doctor if you're still sick.*

might² *noun*
1 *formal* power, especially a country's military or economic power: *China's economic might has been growing.*
2 with all your might = if you do something with all your might, you use all your strength to do it: *She pulled on the rope with all her might.*

might•y /ˈmaɪti/ *adjective, formal*
strong and powerful: *A mighty storm hit the country causing a lot of damage.*

mi•graine /ˈmaɪgreɪn/ *noun*
a very bad HEADACHE (=pain in your head): *Emma had a migraine and had to go to bed.*

mi•grant /ˈmaɪgrənt/ Ac *noun*
someone who goes to another area or country in order to find work: *200,000 migrant workers will enter Canada this year to look for jobs.*

mi•grate /ˈmaɪgreɪt/ Ac *verb*
1 if birds or animals migrate, they travel to a different part of the world in the fall and spring: *Ducks migrate south every fall.*
2 if people migrate, they move to another area or country in order to find work: *People migrated from the countryside to the cities.*
—**migration** /maɪˈgreɪʃən/ *noun* the act of migrating somewhere
—**migratory** /ˈmaɪgrəˌtɔri/ *adjective* migratory birds or animals migrate

WORD FAMILY look at the words:

- → migrate *verb*
- → migration *noun*
- → migrant *noun*
- → migratory *adjective*

mike /maɪk/ *noun, informal*
a MICROPHONE

mild /maɪld/ *adjective*
1 not very severe or serious: *Children often have mild illnesses such as colds.* SYNONYM **slight**
2 having a taste that is not strong or spicy: *The cheese had a mild flavor that was fine with anything.*
3 mild weather is not too hot and not too cold: *The weather was mild enough to go out without a coat.*

mile /maɪl/ *noun*
1 a unit for measuring distance, equal to 5,280 feet or about 1,609 meters: *Mark jogs five miles a day.*
2 miles *informal* = a very long distance: *We walked for miles without seeing anyone.*

mile•age /ˈmaɪlɪdʒ/ *noun*
1 the number of miles that a car has traveled since it was new: *Try to buy a used car with low mileage, not one that's been driven a lot.*
2 the number of miles a car can travel using one gallon of gasoline: *Does the car get good gas mileage?*

mile•stone /ˈmaɪlstoʊn/ *noun*
a very important event in the development of something: *Winning the match was a milestone in his tennis career.*

mil•i•tant /ˈmɪlətənt/ *adjective, formal*
willing to do violent things in order to change the way a country or organization is organized: *A militant group made the attack against government buildings.*
—**militant** *noun* someone who is militant

mil•i•tar•y /ˈmɪləˌteri/ Ac *adjective*
relating to the army, navy, or air force: *military aircraft*
—**the military** *noun* a country's army, navy, or air force: *My brother is in the military.*

milk[1] /mɪlk/ *noun*
1 a white liquid that people drink, which comes from a cow: *She was drinking a glass of milk. | He put milk on his cereal.*
2 a white liquid that comes from the body of female animals, and that they use to feed their babies: *The baby woke and drank its mother's milk.*
—**milky** *adjective* containing milk

milk[2] *verb*
to take milk from a cow or goat: *The farmer was milking the cows.*

milk•shake /ˈmɪlkʃeɪk/ *noun*
a thick drink made from milk and ICE CREAM: *She drank the chocolate milkshake through a straw.*

ˌMilky ˈWay *noun*
the Milky Way = the pale white band of stars that you can see across the sky at night

mill /mɪl/ *noun*
1 a large machine used for crushing food such as corn or grain into a powder: *The farmer took his wheat to the flour mill.*
2 a building where materials such as paper, steel, or cotton cloth are made: *He worked in a steel mill.*

mil•li•gram /ˈmɪləˌgræm/ *noun, written abbreviation* **mg**
a unit for measuring weight. There are 1,000 milligrams in a gram.

mil•li•li•ter /ˈmɪləˌlitɚ/ *noun, written abbreviation* **ml**
a unit for measuring liquids. There are 1,000 milliliters in a liter.

mil•li•me•ter /ˈmɪləˌmitɚ/ *noun, written abbreviation* **mm**
a unit for measuring length. There are 1,000 millimeters in a meter.

mil•lion /ˈmɪlyən/ *number*
1 1,000,000: *$350 million | 4 million people*
2 *also* **millions** *informal* a very large number of people or things: *I've heard that excuse a million times, so don't try it again.*
3 not/never in a million years *informal* = said in order to show how impossible something is: *I never would have guessed in a million years.*
—**millionth** /ˈmɪlyənθ/ *number* 1,000,000th or 1/1,000,000

mil•lion•aire /ˌmɪlyəˈner/ *noun*
someone who is very rich and has more than one million dollars: *He's a millionaire with houses all over the world.*

M

mim•ic /ˈmɪmɪk/ *verb* **mimicked, mimicking** *formal*
to copy the way someone talks or moves in order to make people laugh: *Lily mimicked Sue's Southern accent.*
—**mimic** *noun* someone who mimics other people: *He was a good mimic and could walk just like she did.*
—**mimicry** *noun* the skill or act of mimicking someone

mind¹ /maɪnd/ *noun*
1 your thoughts, or the part of your brain you use for thinking and imagining things: *His mind was full of ideas for stories.* | *What did you have in mind* (=what have you thought of doing) *for Sara's birthday party?*
2 change your mind = to change your opinion or decision about something: *If you change your mind and want to come, just let me know.*
3 make up your mind = to decide something: *Have you made up your mind which college you want to go to?*
4 be out of your mind *informal* = to be crazy: *You lent him $10,000? Are you out of your mind?*
5 on your mind = if something is on your mind, you are thinking or worrying about it a lot: *Sorry I didn't call, but I've had a lot on my mind lately.*

mind² *verb*
1 to feel annoyed or angry about something: *Do you think she'd mind if I borrowed this book?* | *I don't mind helping you. In fact, I enjoy it.*
2 do you mind/would you mind = used to ask politely if you can do something or if someone will do something: *Do you mind if I use your phone?* | *Would you mind waiting here a minute?*
3 I wouldn't mind (doing) something = said when you would like to do something: *I wouldn't mind learning to surf. I think it might be fun.*

mind•ful /ˈmaɪndfəl/ *adjective, formal*
thinking about a rule or fact when you decide what to do: *They were mindful of the guide's warning and returned before dark.*

mine¹ /maɪn/ *pronoun*
the thing that belongs to the person who is speaking: *Theresa's coat is black. Mine is blue.* | *He doesn't have a car so I let him borrow mine.*

mine² *noun*
1 a deep hole in the ground from which people dig coal, gold, etc.: *a coal mine*
2 a type of bomb under the ground or in the ocean that explodes when someone or something touches it: *Three soldiers were hurt when their car hit a land mine.*

mine³ *verb*
1 to dig gold, coal, etc. out of the ground: *They were mining for gold.*
2 to hide bombs under the ground or in the ocean: *The area was heavily mined* (=there were a lot of bombs under the ground).

mine•field /ˈmaɪnfild/ *noun*
an area of land that has mines hidden in it

min•er /ˈmaɪnɚ/ *noun*
someone who digs into a hole in the ground for coal, gold, etc.: *a coal miner*

min•er•al /ˈmɪnərəl/ *noun*
a natural substance such as iron, coal, or salt that is in the earth and also in some foods: *Milk is full of vitamins and minerals that you need to stay healthy.*

ˈmineral ˌwater *noun*
water that comes from under the ground and has minerals in it that you can buy in bottles: *I bought a bottle of mineral water.*

min•gle /ˈmɪŋgəl/ *verb*
1 to meet and talk with a lot of different people, for example at a party: *The school fair gives parents a chance to mingle with students and teachers.*
2 if smells, sounds, or feelings mingle, they mix together: *He felt anger mingled with disappointment.*

min•i /ˈmɪni/ *noun*
another word for a MINISKIRT

mini- /mɪni/
smaller than other things of the same type: *a mini-market* (=a small food store)

min•i•a•ture /ˈmɪniətʃɚ/ *adjective*
smaller than other things of the same kind: *The miniature camera fits in your pocket.*
—**miniaturized** *adjective* made to be miniature

min•i•mal /ˈmɪnəməl/ Ac *adjective, formal*
very small in amount: *The fire caused minimal damage.*

WORD FAMILY look at the words:
→ **minimum** *noun*
→ **minimum** *adjective*
→ **minimize** *verb*
→ **minimal** *adjective*

min•i•mize /ˈmɪnəˌmaɪz/ Ac *verb, formal*
to make the amount of something as small as possible: *To minimize the risk of getting heart disease, eat well and exercise daily.* ANTONYM **maximize**

min•i•mum /ˈmɪnəməm/ Ac *noun*
the smallest possible number, amount, or size: *You should spend a minimum of* (=no less than) *30 minutes on your homework.* ANTONYM **maximum**
—**minimum** *adjective* smallest or lowest: *The minimum age for voting is eighteen.*

ˌminimum ˈwage *noun*
the lowest amount of money that the person you work for can legally pay you for one hour of work: *Jobs that pay the minimum wage are usually not very good.*

min•ing /ˈmaɪnɪŋ/ *noun*
the job or industry of digging gold, coal, etc. out of the ground: *The main industry in the state is coal mining.*

min•i•skirt /ˈmɪniˌskɚt/ *noun*
a very short skirt

min•is•ter /ˈmɪnəstɚ/ *noun*
1 a religious leader in some Christian churches: *The minister prayed for peace in the world.*
2 a politician who is in charge of a government department in some countries: *He is the Minister of Defense in Great Britain*

min•is•try /ˈmɪnəstri/ Ac *noun* plural **ministries**
1 the ministry = the work of being a church leader: *Our son joined the ministry two years ago* (=became a minister).
2 a government department in some countries: *She worked for the Ministry of Agriculture.*

mi•nor¹ /ˈmaɪnɚ/ Ac *adjective*
1 small or not very important: *They had minor injuries such as cuts and bruises.* ANTONYM **major**
2 based on a particular type of musical SCALE ANTONYM **major**

minor² *noun*
1 *formal* someone who is younger than 18, and is not allowed by law to do things such as drink alcohol or vote: *It's illegal to sell cigarettes to minors.* ANTONYM **adult**
2 the second main subject that you study for your college degree: *She has a major in physics and a minor in history.*

minor³ *verb*
minor in something = to study a second main subject as part of your college degree: *I minored in English at college.*

mi•nor•i•ty /məˈnɔrəti/ Ac *noun* plural **minorities** *formal*
1 a group of people who have a different background or religion than most people in a country: *Our organization helps African Americans and other minorities.*
2 a small group of people or things that are part of a larger group: *A minority of students failed the test, but more than 75% passed.* ANTONYM **majority**

mint /mɪnt/ *noun*
1 a candy with a strong fresh taste
2 a plant whose leaves have a strong fresh taste and that you use to flavor food
—**minty** *adjective* tasting like mint: *a minty flavor*

mi•nus¹ /ˈmaɪnəs/ *preposition*
used in mathematics to show that you are SUBTRACTing one number from another: *10 minus 2 equals 8 is written as 10–2=8.* ANTONYM **plus**

minus² *noun*
1 *also* **minus sign** the sign (–) that you write when you SUBTRACT one number from

M

another: *Negative numbers have a minus in front of them.* ANTONYM **plus**
2 something bad about a situation: *One of the minuses of living near an airport is the noise.* ANTONYM **plus**

minus³ *adjective*
1 A minus/B minus, etc. = a grade for a piece of work that is slightly lower than a grade A, a grade B, etc.: *A-, written on your work means A minus, which is lower than A but higher than B+ .*
2 minus 5/20/30, etc. = 5, 20, 30, etc. less than zero: *The temperature dropped to minus 10.*

ˈminus sign *noun*
a sign (-) showing that a number is less than zero, or that the second of two numbers should be SUBTRACTed from the first

min•ute¹ /ˈmɪnɪt/ *noun*
1 a measure of time equal to 60 seconds: *The plane will be landing in ten minutes* (=10 minutes from now). | *It was three minutes to four* (=3 minutes before four o'clock).
2 a very short period of time: *For a minute I thought he was serious, but then I realized he was joking.* | *This will only take a minute* (=last for a short time). SYNONYM **moment**
3 any minute (now) = used when saying that you expect something to happen very soon: *She should be here any minute now.*
4 at the last minute = at the last possible time, just before you have to do something: *Frank changed his mind at the last minute and decided to come with us.*
5 in a minute = used when telling someone that something will happen very soon or you will do something very soon: *I'll come and help you in a minute when I'm finished here.*
6 just a minute = used when asking someone to wait for a short time until you have done something: *"Are you coming?" "Yes, just a minute – I need to get some money."*
7 this minute = used when telling someone to do something immediately: *Come here this minute!*

mi•nute² /maɪˈnut/ *adjective*
very small: *I could hardly read the minute writing.* SYNONYM **tiny**
→ See Thesaurus box at **small**

mir•a•cle /ˈmɪrəkəl/ *noun*
1 something lucky that happens, that you did not think was possible: *It's a miracle (that) you weren't killed!*
2 a surprising event that people believe God caused: *The statue cried tears of blood and people said it was a miracle.*
—**miraculous** /mɪˈrækyələs/ *adjective* like a miracle: *He made a miraculous recovery. Even the doctors were amazed.*

mir•ror /ˈmɪrɚ/ *noun*
a flat object made of glass that you look at when you want to see yourself: *She looked at herself in the mirror.*
→ See picture on page A11

mis- /mɪs/
used at the beginning of words to mean "bad" or "wrong": *misspell* (=spell something wrong)

mis•be•have /ˌmɪsbɪˈheɪv/ *verb*
if children misbehave, they behave badly: *If the kids misbehave, teachers make them stay late after school.*
—**misbehavior** /ˌmɪsbɪˈheɪvyɚ/ *noun* bad behavior

mis•car•riage /ˈmɪsˌkærɪdʒ/ *noun*
if a pregnant woman has a miscarriage, the baby leaves her body at a time when it has not developed very much and it is too early for it to live: *She had a miscarriage last year and lost the baby.*
—**miscarry** /mɪsˈkæri/ *verb* to have a miscarriage

mis•cel•la•ne•ous /ˌmɪsəˈleɪniəs/ *adjective, formal*
miscellaneous things are all different from each other and there are many of them: *The box contained a doll, some pens, a telephone, and other miscellaneous objects.*

mis•chief /ˈmɪstʃɪf/ *noun*
bad behavior by children that causes no serious harm: *He likes to make mischief and is always hiding his friends' stuff.*
—**mischievous** /ˈmɪstʃəvəs/ *adjective* regularly making mischief: *He's a naughty, mischievous child.*

mis•con•duct /ˌmɪsˈkɑndʌkt/ *noun, formal*
bad behavior by someone in his or her job, or by someone in an important position: *The*

M

teacher was fired for misconduct after he hit a student.

mis•er•a•ble /ˈmɪzərəbəl/ *adjective*
1 very unhappy: *She's been miserable since she broke up with her boyfriend.*
2 very bad in quality: *miserable cold wet weather*
—**miserably** *adverb*: *He stared miserably at the rain.*
➔ See Thesaurus box at **sad**

mis•er•y /ˈmɪzəri/ *noun* plural **miseries** *formal*
great unhappiness: *He told us about the misery of life in prison.*

mis•for•tune /mɪsˈfɔrtʃən/ *noun, formal*
bad luck or something that happens as a result of bad luck: *He had an unhappy life that was full of misfortune.* | *We had the misfortune of being in an airport when the snowstorm hit.*

mis•in•ter•pret /ˌmɪsɪnˈtɚprɪt/ Ac *verb, formal*
to not understand the meaning of what someone says or does: *She misinterpreted my joke and thought I was criticizing her.*
—**misinterpretation** /ˌmɪsɪnˌtɚprəˈteɪʃən/ *noun* the act of misinterpreting something

mis•lead /mɪsˈlid/ *verb* **misled** /mɪsˈled/ *formal*
to make someone believe something that is not true by not giving all the information or by giving wrong information: *He misled Rachel by not telling her he was married.*
—**misleading** *adjective* tending to mislead: *The information was misleading even if it wasn't actually dishonest.*
➔ See Thesaurus box at **lie**[2]

mis•place /ˌmɪsˈpleɪs/ *verb, formal*
to put something somewhere and then forget where you put it: *The teacher had misplaced her pen again and spent several minutes looking for it.* SYNONYM **lose**

mis•print /ˈmɪsˌprɪnt/ *noun*
a word in a book or magazine that is printed wrongly: *"Coal" is a misprint and should read "coral."*

mis•rep•re•sent /ˌmɪsreprɪˈzent/ *verb, formal*
to say something about someone that is not true, when you know that it is not true: *He claims that the newspaper misrepresented what he said and made it sound worse than it was.*

miss[1] /mɪs/ *verb*
1 to not do something, because you forget about it or are doing something else: *I missed the party because I was on vacation.*
2 to arrive too late to get on a train, bus, or plane: *Hurry or we'll miss the flight.*
3 to feel sad because someone is not with you, or because you are away from a place where you feel happy: *Did you miss me while I was gone?* | *I miss living in the city, now that we live in the suburbs.*
4 to not hit or catch something: *He threw the ball to me, but I missed it.*
5 to not see, hear, or notice something: *Did you hear what he said? I missed it.* | *It's a big red house – you can't miss it* (=it is very easy to notice).
6 miss the point = to not understand the main idea of what someone is saying: *You're missing the point – taking the money is not just a bad idea, it's illegal.*

PHRASAL VERB

miss out (on something)
to not have the chance to do something that you enjoy: *You'll be missing out on a good time if you don't come to our party.*

miss[2] *noun*
1 the title of a girl or woman who is not married that comes before her family name: *Miss Harris*
2 an action in which you try to hit or catch something but fail: *He hit ten balls without a miss.*

mis•sile /ˈmɪsəl/ *noun*
a weapon that flies a long way and explodes when it hits something: *The plane fired a missile at the enemy camp.*

miss•ing /ˈmɪsɪŋ/ *adjective*
something that is missing is not in the correct place and you cannot find it: *$200 was missing from my desk drawer. Did you take it?* | *Police are looking for a missing child.*

mis•sion /ˈmɪʃən/ *noun*
1 the important aim in someone's work: *The principal's mission was to improve the test scores at the school.*
2 a trip to another country in order to do something for your country or government: *They went on a trade mission to Hong Kong.*

M

3 a trip in a space vehicle or military plane: *The spacecraft went on a mission to Mars.*

mis•sion•ar•y /ˈmɪʃəˌneri/ *noun* plural **missionaries**
someone who goes to another country in order to teach people about his or her religion: *He went to Africa as a missionary to teach about Christianity.*

mis•spell /ˌmɪsˈspel/ *verb, formal*
to spell a word incorrectly: *Students often misspell words that sound exactly like another word, for example "their" and "there."*
—**misspelling** *noun* a word spelled incorrectly

mist /mɪst/ *noun*
a light low cloud close to the ground: *We couldn't see through the mist over the field.*

mis•take¹ /mɪˈsteɪk/ *noun*
1 something which is not correct: *You have made a mistake here: this 3 should be a 5.* | *His work is full of spelling mistakes.* SYNONYM **error**
2 something you do that you later realize was not the right thing to do: *Marrying him was a big mistake.* | *I made the mistake of giving her my phone number, and now she calls me all the time.*
3 by mistake = without intending to do something: *I brought the wrong book home by mistake.* SYNONYM **accidentally**; ANTONYM **on purpose, deliberately**

mistake² *verb* **mistook** /mɪˈstʊk/ **mistaken** /mɪˈsteɪkən/
PHRASAL VERB
mistake something for something *formal*
to think that one thing is something else because the two things look, sound, or seem very similar: *I'm sorry – I mistook you for someone I know.*

mis•tak•en /mɪˈsteɪkən/ *adjective, formal*
wrong about something: *I was mistaken when I said she was a teacher. She is a doctor.*
—**mistakenly** *adverb*: *They mistakenly believed the Earth was flat.*

mis•treat /ˌmɪsˈtrit/ *verb, formal*
to treat someone in a cruel way: *The guards mistreated the prisoners, hitting them and taking away their clothes.*

mis•tress /ˈmɪstrɪs/ *noun*
a woman who a man regularly has sex with while he is married to someone else

mis•trust /mɪsˈtrʌst/ *noun, formal*
the feeling that you cannot trust someone: *He has a deep mistrust of politicians – he thinks they are all liars.*
—**mistrust** *verb* to not trust someone

mist•y /ˈmɪsti/ *adjective*
if it is misty, there is a lot of light cloud low over the ground: *a misty morning*

mis•un•der•stand /ˌmɪsʌndəˈstænd/ *verb* **misunderstood** /ˌmɪsʌndəˈstʊd/ *formal*
to not understand something correctly: *I wanted water, but the waiter misunderstood and gave me wine.*

mit•ten /ˈmɪtn/ *noun*
a piece of clothing that keeps your hand warm, with one part for your four fingers together and one part for your thumb

mix¹ /mɪks/ *verb*
to put different things together to make something new: *Mix the butter and flour together.* | *Oil and water don't mix.*

THESAURUS: mix

combine to join two or more things together: *Combine the flour and milk and beat until smooth.* | *The movie combines comedy with a mystery.*

stir to mix a liquid or food by moving a spoon around in it: *Stir the mixture over a low heat.*

blend to mix together soft or liquid foods to form a single smooth substance: *Blend the yogurt with fresh fruit for a wonderful drink.*

beat to mix food together quickly and thoroughly using a fork or kitchen tool: *Beat the eggs and add to the sugar mixture.*

PHRASAL VERB
mix up
1 mix someone up with someone = to think that someone is someone else: *I keep mixing him up with his brother because they look so much alike.* SYNONYM **confuse**
2 mix something up = to change things around so that there is no order: *Don't mix*

M

up those papers, or we'll never find the ones we need.
➔ See picture on page A14

mix² *noun*
different things or people together in a place: *There was a good mix of people – young and old, men and women.*

ˌmixed ˈup *adjective*
if you are mixed up, you are confused so you do the wrong thing because you are confused: *I got mixed up and went to the wrong restaurant.* SYNONYM **confused**

mix•ture /ˈmɪkstʃɚ/ *noun*
a substance you make by mixing different things together: *Pour the mixture into a pan.*

ˈmix-up *noun*
a situation in which arrangements or details get confused, so that the wrong thing happens: *There was a mix-up, and Tyra got on the wrong bus.*

ml.
the abbreviation of **milliliter**

mm.
the abbreviation of **millimeter**

moan /moʊn/ *verb*
1 to make a low sound because you feel pain or are sad: *A man was lying on the floor moaning in pain.* SYNONYM **groan**
2 to complain in an annoying way: *Stop moaning about your problems and get to work!*
—**moan** *noun* the act of moaning

mob /mɑb/ *noun*
a large group of people who are noisy and angry: *He was attacked by a mob of angry young men.*
➔ See Thesaurus box at **group¹**

mo•bile /ˈmoʊbəl/ *adjective, formal*
if someone is mobile, he or she can move from place to place easily: *I'm more mobile now that I have a car.*
—**mobility** /moʊˈbɪləti/ *noun* how mobile someone is: *The new wheelchair is smaller, so I have much better mobility.*

ˌmobile ˈhome *noun*
a small metal house built in a factory that a vehicle takes to the place where it will stay: *Several mobile homes were destroyed by a tornado.*

mock /mɑk/ *verb, formal*
to laugh at someone in a way that is not nice: *They mocked the strange way he dressed.*

mo•dal aux•il•i•ary /ˌmoʊdl ɔgˈzɪlyəri/ *noun, formal*
a word such as "can," "may," or "might" that comes before another verb: *In "I might go to the party," "might" is a modal auxiliary.*

mod•el¹ /ˈmɑdl/ *noun*
1 a small copy of something: *We built a model of a train in my bedroom.*
2 a beautiful person who wears new clothes in fashion shows and magazines: *She works as a model for Tommy Hilfiger.*
3 one of the types of vehicle, computer, etc. that a company makes: *The car maker has several new models this year.*
4 someone who lets an artist paint him or her: *They're looking for models for their art class.*
➔ See Thesaurus box at **type¹**

model² *adjective*
1 model airplane/train/car, etc. = a small copy of an airplane, train, etc., that you put together from separate parts
2 *formal* **model student/prisoner/employee, etc.** = a very good student, prisoner, etc.: *Joe is a model student and always works hard.* SYNONYM **perfect**

model³ *verb, formal*
1 to wear new clothes in fashion shows or magazines so that people might want to buy the clothes: *She modeled for Vogue magazine.*
2 to let an artist paint you: *An artist asked if I would model for him.*

PHRASAL VERB
model something on something
if you model one thing on another, you try to make the first thing like the second thing: *Writers often model their characters on people they know.*

mo•dem /ˈmoʊdəm/ *noun*
a piece of electronic equipment that allows your computer to use the internet

mod•er•ate /ˈmɑdərət/ *adjective, formal*
not very big but not very small, not very hot but not very cold, not very fast but not very slow, etc.: *The temperatures were moderate*

M

and comfortable. | *The train traveled at a moderate speed.* SYNONYM **medium**

mod•ern /'mɑdɚn/ *adjective*
belonging to the present time: *The old buildings are gone, and the area is much more modern.* SYNONYM **fashionable**; ANTONYM **old-fashioned, traditional**
➔ See Thesaurus box at **new**

WORD FAMILY look at the words:

➔ **modern** *adjective*
➔ **modernize** *verb*
➔ **modernization** *noun*

mod•ern•ize /'mɑdɚˌnaɪz/ *verb*
to make something less old-fashioned: *We're modernizing the house, starting with a new kitchen.*
—**modernization** /ˌmɑdɚnə'zeɪʃən/ *noun* the process of modernizing something

mod•est /'mɑdɪst/ *adjective*
1 not talking too much about your abilities or the things you do well: *She is very modest about her success – she doesn't like to brag.*
2 *formal* not very big: *They are not rich and live in a modest house.*
—**modestly** *adverb*

mod•i•fi•er /'mɑdəˌfaɪɚ/ *noun*
a word that gives extra information about another word in a sentence: *In the sentence "He walked slowly," "slowly" is a modifier.*

mod•i•fy /'mɑdəˌfaɪ/ Ac *verb* **modified**, third person singular **modifies** *formal*
1 to make small changes to something: *The car had been modified for a disabled driver.*
2 if one word in a sentence modifies another, it gives more information about it: *In the sentence, "I'm reading a good book," "good" modifies "book."*
—**modification** /ˌmɑdəfə'keɪʃən/ *noun* a small change to something

mod•ule /'mɑdʒul/ *noun, formal*
a part of something such as a building, machine, or spacecraft that has a special use: *The astronauts came back to earth in a module that came down in the ocean.*

moist /mɔɪst/ *adjective*
a little wet: *Her cheeks were moist from tears.*
—**moisten** /'mɔɪsən/ *verb* to make something moist

mois•ture /'mɔɪstʃɚ/ *noun*
small amounts of water that make something a little wet: *Plants use their roots to absorb moisture from the soil.*

mois•tur•ize /'mɔɪstʃəˌraɪz/ *verb*
to put a substance on your skin to make it soft and not dry: *This cream is good for moisturizing your skin.*

mo•lar /'moʊlɚ/ *noun, formal*
one of the large teeth in the back of your mouth

mold[1] /moʊld/ *noun*
1 a green substance that grows on old food and on things that are warm and wet: *The old bread was covered in mold.*
2 a container that you pour liquid into, so that when the liquid becomes solid, it has the shape of the container: *She poured the Jell-O into the ring-shaped mold.*
—**moldy** *adjective* covered in green mold

mold[2] *verb*
1 to make a substance into a shape by pressing it or putting it in a mold: *We molded the clay with our fingers.*
2 *formal* to have a big effect on the type of person someone becomes: *The difficult training molds them into good soldiers.*
3 to grow mold: *Some of the food in the refrigerator had been there so long it had started to mold.*

mole /moʊl/ *noun*
1 a small dark brown spot on someone's skin: *The doctor said the dark mole on my shoulder should be removed.*
2 a small animal that lives in holes in the ground: *The moles left piles of dirt all over the grass.*
➔ See Thesaurus box at **mark**[2]

mol•e•cule /'mɑləˌkyul/ *noun*
the smallest part of a substance that you cannot divide without changing its form: *A molecule of water has two hydrogen atoms and one oxygen atom.*
—**molecular** /mə'lekyəlɚ/ *adjective* relating to molecules

mo•lest /mə'lest/ *verb, formal*
to harm someone in a sexual way

mol•ten /'moʊltən/ *adjective, formal*
molten metal or rock is liquid because it is very hot: *Molten rock flowed out of the volcano.*

M

mom /mɑm/ *noun*
mother: *Do you think your mom will let you go to the movie? | Is dinner ready, Mom?*

ˌmom-and-ˈpop store *noun*
a small store that a family owns and works in: *There's a mom-and-pop store on the corner where you can buy a paper.*

mo•ment /ˈmoʊmənt/ *noun*
1 a particular point in time: *Just at that moment, Shelly came in. | He said he loved her from the moment he met her.* SYNONYM **minute**
2 at the moment = now: *Japanese food is popular at the moment.*
3 *formal* a very short period of time: *Jacob stopped talking for a moment and then started again. | Could you wait just a moment? I'm almost done. | Where did he go – he was here a moment ago.* SYNONYM **minute**
4 for the moment = happening now but maybe not in the future: *The rain has stopped for the moment.*
5 *formal* **any moment (now)** = used when saying that you expect something to happen very soon: *Susan will be here any moment now.*
6 in a moment *formal* = used when saying that you will do something or something will happen very soon: *I'll get you a drink in a moment.*

mo•men•tar•i•ly /ˌmoʊmənˈterəli/ *adverb, formal*
for a very short time: *She looked momentarily surprised but quickly regained a calm expression.* SYNONYM **briefly**

mo•men•tous /moʊˈmentəs/ *adjective, formal*
a momentous event, change, etc. is very important: *The 20th century with two world wars and huge changes in technology was a momentous time in our history.*

mo•men•tum /moʊˈmentəm/ *noun*
the force that makes something continue to move: *If you roll a ball down a hill, it goes faster as it gains momentum.*

mom•my /ˈmɑmi/ *noun* plural **mommies** *informal*
used by children to mean "mother": *"I want my mommy," the little girl cried.*

mon•arch /ˈmɑnɚk/ *noun, formal*
a king or queen: *the British monarch*

mon•arch•y /ˈmɑnɚki/ *noun*
the system of ruling a country with a king or queen: *Many British people want to keep the monarchy.*
➔ See Thesaurus box at **government**

mon•as•ter•y /ˈmɑnəsˌteri/ *noun* plural **monasteries**
a place where MONKs live

Mon•day /ˈmʌndi/ *noun, written abbreviation* **Mon.**
the second day of the week, between Sunday and Tuesday: *The results will be announced Monday. | It snowed on Monday. | We'll see you next Monday. | Kelly arrived last Monday. | I'll call you first thing Monday morning.*

mon•ey /ˈmʌni/ *noun*
1 coins and pieces of paper that you use to buy things: *I'm going to the bank to get some money.*

THESAURUS: money

Types of money

bill paper money: *a $20 bill*

coin metal money: *She gave each child a few coins to buy candy with.*

penny a coin worth 1 cent

nickel a coin worth 5 cents

dime a coin worth 10 cents

quarter a coin worth 25 cents

buck *informal* a dollar: *Mr. Levy paid me five bucks for mowing his lawn.*

cash the coins and paper money that you use for buying things: *I didn't have enough cash, so I paid by check.*

change coins, not paper money: *Do you have any change for the phone?*

change the money you get back in a store, in coins and bills, when you have paid more than something costs: *If a book costs $13.50, and you pay with a $20 bill, how much money do you get in change?*

currency the money used in a particular country: *He had $500 worth of Japanese currency.*

2 what you earn by working: *He started a business and made a lot of money.*
3 a lot of money that belongs to a person or

M

family: *His parents have money, so he doesn't really have to worry about a job.*

4 get your money's worth = to get enough use, enjoyment, etc. from something you buy, for the price you pay: *These sneakers are really expensive but good – you'll get your money's worth.*

5 for my money *informal* = in my opinion: *For my money, Williams is the best ballplayer.*

mon•i•tor[1] /ˈmɑnətɚ/ *noun*
the part of a computer or television that shows information or pictures: *Your eyes should be on the same level as your computer monitor.*
➔ See picture on page A20

monitor[2] Ac *verb*
to carefully watch or measure something to see if it changes: *Your teacher will monitor your work during the year to make sure that you understand everything.*

monk /mʌŋk/ *noun*
a man who belongs to a religious group of men who live together

mon•key /ˈmʌŋki/ *noun* plural **monkeys**
an animal that climbs trees, with a long tail and a face that is similar to a human face

mon•o•lin•gual /ˌmɑnoʊˈlɪŋgwəl/ *adjective*
using only one language: *Most of the people there were monolingual and couldn't even say hello in another language.*

mon•o•logue *also* **monolog** /ˈmɑnlˌɔg/ *noun*
something one person says that is very long, when no other people are speaking: *The main character in the play gives a ten-minute monologue about his private thoughts.*

mo•nop•o•ly /məˈnɑpəli/ *noun* plural **monopolies**
the control of all of a type of business activity by one organization: *If the last two oil companies join together, they will have a monopoly on the country's oil industry.*
—**monopolize** *verb* to have control of all of a business or activity: *The company has monopolized the music industry.*

mo•not•o•nous /məˈnɑtnəs/ *adjective*
boring and always the same: *I was working in a monotonous job in a factory and sick of doing the same thing every day.*
—**monotony** *noun* when something is boring and always the same: *It was a long trip, so we played a game to break the monotony* (=stop it from being so boring).

mon•soon /ˌmɑnˈsun/ *noun*
the time when it rains a lot in India and other parts of Asia

mon•ster /ˈmɑnstɚ/ *noun*
1 a frightening creature in stories or dreams: *The monster had two heads and six legs.*
2 a very bad cruel person: *The man was a monster, who loved to talk about how many people he had killed.*

month /mʌnθ/ *noun*
1 one of the 12 periods of time that divide a year: *January is the first month of the year.*
2 a time period of about 30 days: *I'm going on vacation for a month.*

month•ly /ˈmʌnθli/ *adjective, adverb*
happening every month: *Every teacher has to write a monthly report.* | *This magazine is published monthly.*

mon•u•ment /ˈmɑnyəmənt/ *noun*
something that is built so people will remember an important event or person: *The statue is a monument to the men who died in the war.*

mon•u•men•tal /ˌmɑnyəˈmentl/ *adjective, formal*
very big or important: *Exploring space is a monumental challenge.*

moo /mu/ *noun*
the sound that a cow makes
—**moo** *verb* to make the sound that a cow makes

mood /mud/ *noun*
the way you feel now, especially when this may change: *On Saturdays, Dad's usually in a good mood* (=feeling happy). | *She was in a bad mood, so I tried to do something to make her feel better.*
—**moody** *adjective* having feelings that change often, so you are sometimes happy, sometimes sad, etc.: *Teenagers are often moody.*

moon /mun/ *noun*
1 the moon = the round object that moves around the earth and shines at night: *When did the first person land on the moon?* | *The night was clear and the moon was shining brightly.*

M

2 a round object that moves around other PLANETs: *Saturn has several moons.*

moon•light¹ /'munlaɪt/ *noun*
the light from the moon: *The water looked silver in the moonlight.*

moonlight² *verb, informal*
to do a second job, when you are not doing your main job: *He's a firefighter, but he moonlights as a waiter to earn extra money.*

moose /mus/ *noun*
a wild animal like a very big DEER with big flat horns

mop¹ /mɑp/ *noun*
a thing for washing floors, made of a long stick with soft material on the end: *a mop and bucket*

mop² *verb* **mopped, mopping**
to wash a floor with a mop: *There was a man in the kitchen, mopping the floor.*
➔ See Thesaurus box at **clean²**

PHRASAL VERB
mop something up
to get liquid off something using a mop, cloth, etc.: *I got a paper towel to mop up the juice I had spilled.*

mor•al¹ /'mɔrəl/ *adjective*
relating to ideas about what is right and wrong: *Many people did not agree with the war for moral reasons.* ANTONYM **immoral**

WORD FAMILY look at the words:
➔ **moral** *adjective*
➔ **immoral** *adjective*
➔ **morality** *noun*

moral² *noun*
a lesson about life that you learn from a story or something that happens: *The moral of the story is that money doesn't make you happy.*

mo•rale /mə'ræl/ *noun, formal*
the level of confidence, interest, etc. that people have in their work or something they are doing: *If you don't praise people when they do good work, it causes low morale* (=little confidence, interest, etc.).

mo•ral•i•ty /mə'ræləti/ *noun*
ideas about good behavior and what is right and wrong: *Some people think changes in morality have led to more crime.*

mor•als /'mɔrəlz/ *plural noun*
the ideas about what is right and wrong that you believe and use in your life: *My father was a man with very strong morals – he was very hard-working and never lied.*

more¹ /mɔr/ *adverb*
1 more important/difficult/beautiful, etc. = having a greater amount of importance, etc.: *The second test was more difficult, and I did not do as well.* | *I think history is more interesting than math.* ANTONYM **less**
2 happening in larger amounts, more often, or for longer: *We need to practice more if we want to improve.* ANTONYM **less**
3 more and more = in a way that gets greater in degree or amount: *He got more and more angry, until he started yelling at me.*
➔ **anymore**

more² *adjective, pronoun*
1 an additional amount of something: *Would you like some more coffee?* | *Could I have a little more? I'm still hungry.*

THESAURUS: more

another one more person or thing of the same kind: *Do you want another cup of coffee?*

extra more than the usual or expected amount of something: *I gave her an extra five dollars, since she'd helped wash the car.*

additional more than you already have, or more than was agreed or expected: *You can find additional information on our website.*

further *formal* more, used especially when something happens again or is done again: *Further research is needed before the drug can be sold.*

2 a greater amount or number: *She's won more prizes than any other student.* | *We spend more of our money on food these days than we used to.* | *These jeans cost more* (=more money than some other jeans). ANTONYM **less, fewer**
3 more and more = in a way that gets greater in amount: *He's been spending more and more time at the gym. He goes a couple of hours every day.*
4 more or less = about a particular amount or number: *We've lived here for twenty*

M

years, more or less (=about twenty years). SYNONYM **approximately**

more·o·ver /mɔr'oʊvɚ/ *adverb, formal*
you use this to mean "also" when you are giving more information: *The apartment is in a good area; moreover, the rent is not too expensive.*

morgue /mɔrg/ *noun*
a building or room for keeping dead bodies, before burying or burning them

morn·ing /'mɔrnɪŋ/ *noun*
1 the time from when the sun rises until the middle of the day: *Classes start at 9 o'clock in the morning.* | *I got an email from Wayne this morning* (=today in the morning). | *See you tomorrow morning.*
2 (Good) Morning = you say this when you meet someone in the morning: *Morning, Kim.*

Morse code /ˌmɔrs 'koʊd/ *noun*
a way of sending messages using short and long signals of sound or light

mor·tal /'mɔrtl/ *adjective, formal*
not living forever: *All humans are mortal. We all will eventually die.* ANTONYM **immortal**
—**mortally** *adverb, formal* in a way that causes death: *He was mortally wounded by the gunshot.* SYNONYM **fatally**
—**mortality** /mɔr'tæləti/ *noun* the fact that you will die one day

mort·gage /'mɔrgɪdʒ/ *noun*
money that you borrow from a bank to buy a house, and pay back over a long time: *The bank agreed to give us a mortgage, so we could buy our first house.*
—**mortgage** *verb* if your house is mortgaged, you bought it using a mortgage and you have not paid the money back yet

Mos·lem /'mɑzləm/ *noun*
another word for a MUSLIM that many people think is not correct

mosque /mɑsk/ *noun*
a building where Muslims go to pray

mos·qui·to /mə'skitoʊ/ *noun*
plural **mosquitoes**
a small flying insect that bites people, drinks blood, and spreads disease

mosquito

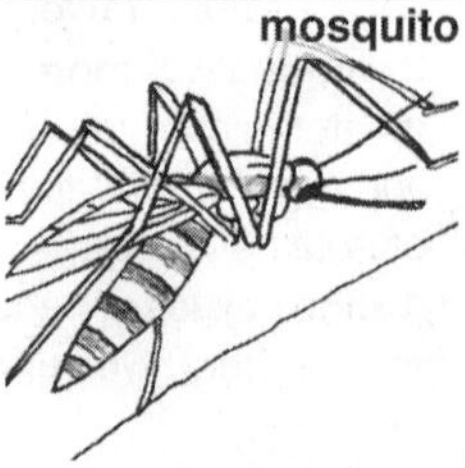

moss /mɔs/ *noun*
a soft green plant that grows on wet ground, trees, and rocks
—**mossy** *adjective* covered with moss: *a mossy bank beside the river*

most¹ /moʊst/ *adverb*
1 the most powerful/popular/important, etc. = having the greatest amount of power, etc.: *The president is the most powerful man in the U.S.* ANTONYM **least**
2 more than anything else: *Which of these three shirts do you like most?* | *Sean worried a lot, but most of all he worried about money.*

most² *adjective, pronoun*
1 the greatest amount or number of something: *Most kids come to school on the bus, but a few walk or are brought by their parents.* | *We've already eaten most of the cake, but there's still a little bit left.* | *Sam won a lot of prizes, but I won the most* (=more prizes than anyone else).

GRAMMAR: most

most, most of

When you are talking about the whole of something and not a particular example of it, use **most** before the form of a noun that shows there is more than one thing: *I like most animals.*

Also use **most** before nouns that are things that you cannot count: *He thinks most poetry is boring.*

Use **most of** before "the," "this," "my," etc. and a noun when you are talking about a particular group or thing: *I got most of the answers right.* | *He does most of his work at home.*

2 at most/at the most = not more than: *The test will take one hour at the most.*
3 make the most of something = to use a good opportunity well, so that you get a lot from it: *You're only young once, so make the most of it!*
4 for the most part *formal* = in most cases, but not always: *For the most part, everyone was friendly, but one man was kind of rude.*

most·ly /'moʊstli/ *adverb*
1 usually: *Mostly, we visit my grandparents on the weekend.*
2 almost all: *My friends are mostly in the same class as me. I don't know many other kids.*

M

mo•tel /moʊˈtel/ *noun*
a hotel you stay in when you are traveling by car, with a place for your car near your room

moth /mɔθ/ *noun*
an insect like a BUTTERFLY that flies at night

moth•er /ˈmʌðɚ/ *noun*
a female parent: *My mother is a lawyer.*
—**motherly** *adjective* kind and loving, like a good mother: *Mrs. Watts was a big, motherly woman.*
—**motherhood** /ˈmʌðɚhʊd/ *noun* the state of being a mother

ˈmother-in-ˌlaw *noun* plural **mothers-in-law**
the mother of your husband or wife

ˈMother's Day *noun*
a day when people give cards and gifts to their mothers, on the second Sunday of May in the U.S.

ˈmother ˌtongue *noun*
the first language that you learn, when you are a child: *I was born in Mexico, so my mother tongue is Spanish.*

mo•tion /ˈmoʊʃən/ *noun, formal*
1 the process of moving: *Scientists study the motion of the planets around the sun.* | *Please stay in your seats, while the bus is in motion.*
2 a movement of your hand or head: *The teacher made a motion for the class to stand up.*

mo•tion•less /ˈmoʊʃənləs/ *adjective, formal*
not moving: *The girl was lying motionless under a tree and we thought she had maybe been hurt.*

mo•ti•vate /ˈmoʊtəˌveɪt/ Ac *verb*
if something motivates you, it makes you want to do something: *If classes are interesting, it motivates students to learn.*
—**motivation** /ˌmoʊtəˈveɪʃən/ *noun, formal* a reason for wanting to do something: *What is your motivation for wanting to study physics?* SYNONYM **reason**

mo•tive /ˈmoʊtɪv/ Ac *noun*
the reason why someone does something bad: *Police are unsure about the motive for the attack.*
→ See Thesaurus box at **reason**

mo•tor /ˈmoʊtɚ/ *noun*
the part of a machine that makes it work or move: *This toy works using a small electric motor.*

mo•tor•boat /ˈmoʊtɚˌboʊt/ *noun*
a fast boat with an engine: *The motorboat moved quickly across the lake.*

mo•tor•cy•cle /ˈmoʊtɚˌsaɪkəl/ *noun*
a fast vehicle with two wheels and an engine
→ See picture on page A26

ˈmotor home *noun*
a big vehicle with beds, a kitchen, etc. in it, that people use for traveling
→ See picture on page A26

mo•tor•ist /ˈmoʊtərɪst/ *noun, formal*
someone who drives a car: *The lower price of oil is good news for motorists.* SYNONYM **driver**

ˈmotor ˌvehicle *noun, formal*
a car, bus, truck, etc.: *There's been an accident involving five motor vehicles.* SYNONYM **vehicle**

mot•to /ˈmɑtoʊ/ *noun* plural **mottoes**
a few words that state the main idea of an organization, nation, etc.: *The motto of the Boy Scouts is "Be Prepared."*

mound /maʊnd/ *noun*
1 a pile of dirt, stones, sand, etc.: *There was a mound of dirt next to a deep hole.*
2 a pile of something: *There's a mound of papers on my desk that I have to deal with.*
3 the mound = the small hill that the person throwing the ball stands on in a game of baseball

mount¹ /maʊnt/ *verb*
1 to attach something onto a wall, board, etc.: *Two TVs were mounted on the wall of the bar.*
2 *formal also* **mount up** to increase over a period of time: *Dad had no job, and our debts were mounting up.* SYNONYM **grow, increase**
3 *formal* to get on a horse or bicycle

mount² *noun*
Mount = used before the name of a mountain: *Mount Everest*

moun•tain /ˈmaʊntən/ *noun*
1 a very high hill: *It took us five hours to climb the mountain.* | *We went skiing in the Rocky Mountains.*
2 a large amount of something: *I have a*

M

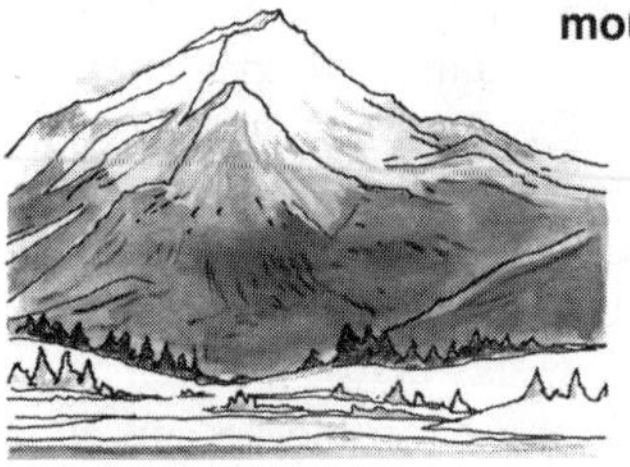

mountain of work to do so I'll be busy all weekend.

—**mountainous** *adjective* having a lot of very high hills: *the mountainous areas of Europe*

ˈmountain ˌbike *noun*
a strong bicycle with wide thick tires that can easily go over rocks or rough ground

ˈmountain ˌlion *noun*
another word for a COUGAR

ˈmountain ˌrange *noun*
a group of mountains in one area: *To get to the ocean, you have to cross a mountain range.*

mourn /mɔrn/ *verb, formal*
to feel very sad because someone has died: *She is still mourning her son's death.*
—**mourning** *noun* when you feel and show great sadness because someone has died: *The president died, and the whole nation was in mourning.*

mourn•er /ˈmɔrnɚ/ *noun, formal*
someone who is at a FUNERAL: *Hundreds of mourners came to the church for the funeral.*

mourn•ful /ˈmɔrnfəl/ *adjective, formal*
very sad: *He looked sadly at her with mournful eyes.*

mouse /maʊs/ *noun*
1 plural **mice** /maɪs/ a small animal with a long tail that lives in buildings or fields: *The cat has caught a mouse again.*
2 plural **mouses** or **mice** /maɪs/ a small thing that you use to control a computer, by moving it in your hand: *The mouse should be next to the computer keyboard.*
➔ See picture on page A20

ˈmouse pad *noun*
a flat piece of plastic or rubber on which you move a computer mouse
➔ See picture on page A20

mouse•trap /ˈmaʊstræp/ *noun*
a small trap that you use in a house to catch mice

mousse /mus/ *noun*
1 a cold sweet food made from mixing cream, eggs, and fruit or chocolate: *chocolate mousse*
2 a substance like FOAM that you put in your hair to give it a particular style: *Use this mousse to make your hair look thicker.*

mouth /maʊθ/ *noun* plural **mouths** /maʊðz/
1 the part of your face that you use for speaking and eating: *She opened her mouth to say something and then stopped.*
2 the part of a river where it joins the ocean: *The water flows out the mouth of the Mississippi into the Gulf of Mexico.*
3 the mouth of a cave = the entrance to a cave
4 keep your mouth shut *informal* = to not say what you are thinking: *I was getting really mad, but I kept my mouth shut.*
5 big mouth *informal* = used when talking about someone who often says things that he or she should not say: *Don't tell Maya any secrets – she has a very big mouth.*
➔ See picture on page A2

mouth•ful /ˈmaʊθfʊl/ *noun*
an amount of food or drink that you put in your mouth: *He took another mouthful of salad and started to chew.*

mouth•wash /ˈmaʊθwɑʃ/ *noun*
a liquid you use to clean your mouth and make it smell fresh

mov•a•ble /ˈmuvəbəl/ *adjective*
able to be moved: *The doll's arms and legs are movable.*

move¹ /muv/ *verb*
1 to go from one place or position to another: *I could hear Mom moving around downstairs.* | *I moved closer to the door, so that I could leave quickly.*
2 to put something in a different place or position: *Could you move your car, please?*
3 to go to a new place to live, work, etc.: *Our family sold the house, and moved to Texas.*
4 to make someone feel a strong emotion: *The boy told me about the death of his family, and his sad story moved me.*

PHRASAL VERBS

move away
to go to live in a different area: *Carla moved away, and I never saw her again.*

M

move in
to start living in a new home: *Has your new neighbor moved in yet, or is the house still empty?*

move out
to leave the house where you are living, and go to live somewhere else: *I'm moving out of this house, after I graduate from college.*

move over
to change position toward the left or right so that there is more space for someone or something else: *Could you move over, so I can sit next to Dan?*

move² *noun*

1 a movement toward something or someone: *Becky made a move toward the door in an attempt to leave.*

2 an act of leaving your home and going to live somewhere else: *Our move to Seattle was very hard, because my brother didn't want to go.*

3 something you decide to do in order to achieve something: *The team is practicing more this year, and that's a good move.*

4 an action that you make in a game like CHESS: *It's your move* (=it is your turn to play).

move•ment /'muvmənt/ *noun*

1 the action of moving from one position to another: *The rocking movement of the boat was making me sleepy.*

2 the action of moving part of your body: *He watched the dancer's graceful movements.*

3 a group of people who want to change something in society: *People from the environmental movement* (=who want to change things in order to protect the environment) *are fighting the new rules.*

mov•er /'muvɚ/ *noun*

someone whose job is helping people move from one house to another: *The movers came and packed up all our things to take to the new house.*

mov•ie /'muvi/ *noun*

1 something that tells a story with moving pictures and sound: *Do you want to go to the theater to see a movie tonight?*

THESAURUS: movie

Types of Movies

film a movie, especially one that people think is very good or important: *It won an Oscar as the Best Film in a Foreign Language.*

flick *informal* a movie: *I like action flicks – lots of car chases and stuff.*

comedy a funny movie that makes people laugh: *It's a comedy about three men who have to take care of a baby.*

drama a serious movie, especially one about the relationships that people have with each other: *The movie is a drama that shows what happens to a family when one of the sons dies.*

romance a movie about love: *"When Harry Met Sally" is a romance, but it's also very funny.*

thriller an exciting movie about murder, crime, or spies: *The "Mission Impossible" movies have been pretty good thrillers.*

horror movie a frightening movie about ghosts, murders, etc.: *I can't watch horror movies; they give me bad dreams.*

cartoon a movie with characters that are drawn or made using a computer: *"The Incredibles" is one of the best cartoons I've seen in a long time.*

animation the process of making movies that use drawing or computer pictures rather than real people: *"Toy Story" was one of the first movies to use computer animation only.*

People Who Make Movies

actor a man or woman who acts in a movie: *Who's your favorite actor?*

actress a woman who acts in a movie: *I think Reese Witherspoon is a really good actress.*

star a famous actor or actress: *Tom Cruise is still one of Hollywood's biggest stars.*

director the person who tells the actors and actresses in a movie what to do: *Steven Spielberg was the movie's director.*

producer the person who organizes things so that a movie can be made, and who controls the money used to make it: *A producer asked Al Pacino if he'd be in the movie.*

M

film/movie crew the people who use the camera, lights, etc. and help the director make a movie: *A film crew was setting things up in the street.*

2 the movies = the theater where you go to see a movie: *How often do you go to the movies?*

ˈmovie star *noun*
an actor or actress who is famous in movies: *Will Smith is my favorite movie star.*

ˈmovie ˌtheater *noun*
a building where you go to see movies

mov•ing /ˈmuvɪŋ/ *adjective*
1 making you feel strong emotions: *The book tells a moving story about love and death.*
2 changing from one position to another: *the moving parts of an engine*

mow /moʊ/ *verb* **mowed**, **mowed** or **mown** /moʊn/
to cut grass with a machine: *Dan usually mows the lawn on Sunday.*
—**mower** *noun* a machine that you use to cut grass
➔ See Thesaurus box at **cut**[1]

Mr. /ˈmɪstɚ/
a word you use before a man's family name: *This is Mr. Brown.*

Mrs. /ˈmɪsɪz/
a word you use before the family name of a married woman: *Mrs. Brown is on the telephone.*

M.S. *also* **M.Sc.** *noun*
Master of Science a university degree in a science subject, which is more advanced than a B.S.

Ms. /mɪz/
a word you can use before a woman's family name, that does not show if she is married or not: *Ms. Aitkins is the head of the department.*

much[1] /mʌtʃ/ *adverb*
1 a lot: *Alaska is much bigger than California.* | *This T-shirt is much too big. I need a smaller one.* | *Thank you very much. I really liked the gift.* | *"Did you like the movie?" "No, not very much."*
2 so much = used for emphasizing that something is a large amount: *My brother left home a year ago, and I miss him so much.*

much[2] *adjective, pronoun*
1 a lot of something: *Hurry up – we don't have much time.*

> **GRAMMAR: much**
>
> **much, many, a lot of**
>
> **Much** is used with nouns that are things you cannot count: *There isn't much milk left.*
>
> **Many** is used with nouns that show there is more than one thing or person: *I didn't see many people there that I knew.*
>
> **A lot of** can be used with both types of noun: *There isn't a lot of time to work on this.* | *She doesn't have a lot of friends.*
>
> In sentences that are not questions and do not use the word "not," use **a lot of** rather than **much**: *There was a lot of traffic.*
>
> Do not say "There was much traffic."

2 how much = used when asking about the amount or cost of something: *How much water is left in the bottle?* | *How much were those jeans* (=how much money did they cost)*?*
3 too much = more than you need or want: *I ate too much, and I feel sick.*
4 not much = used when saying that something is not important or interesting: *"What did you do on Saturday?" "Not much* (=nothing interesting or important).*"*
5 as much as = the same amount as: *I've done as much work as I can today. I can't do any more.*

mud /mʌd/ *noun*
wet earth that is soft and sticky: *Take your boots off – they're covered in mud!*
—**muddy** *adjective* covered with mud: *After the rain, the path was muddy.*

muf•fin /ˈmʌfən/ *noun*
a small, sweet type of bread that often has fruit in it: *I had a blueberry muffin for breakfast.*

mug[1] /mʌg/ *noun*
a large cup with straight sides and a handle: *a mug of coffee*
➔ See picture at **cup**

mug[2] *verb* **mugged**, **mugging**
if you are mugged, someone attacks and robs you: *She was mugged outside her apartment by a man with a gun.*

—**mugger** *noun* someone who attacks and robs people: *The muggers held him down and stole his wallet.*
—**mugging** *noun* an act of mugging someone: *The mugging happened Saturday night.*

mug•gy /ˈmʌgi/ *adjective* **muggier**, **muggiest** *informal*
muggy weather is hot and HUMID (=with a lot of water in the air) so that it feels uncomfortable: *It was a muggy night, and we couldn't sleep.*

mule /myul/ *noun*
an animal that has a DONKEY and a horse as parents

multi- /mʌlti/
many of something: *multicolored* (=having many colors)

mul•ti•me•di•a /ˌmʌltɪˈmidiə/ *adjective*
using pictures, sounds, and words to give information on a computer: *The multimedia learning software teaches kids with pictures, video, songs, and games.*

mul•ti•ple /ˈmʌltəpəl/ *adjective, formal*
many of something: *He fell off a ladder, and suffered multiple injuries to his arms, legs, and head.*

ˌmultiple-ˈchoice *adjective*
a multiple-choice test or question shows you a number of answers, and you must choose the right one

mul•ti•ply /ˈmʌltəˌplaɪ/ *verb* **multiplied**, third person singular **multiplies**
1 if you multiply a number, you make it bigger by adding the same number to it several times: *4 multiplied by 5 is 20* (=4 x 5 = 20)
2 *formal* to increase a lot: *Our problems have multiplied this year and I don't know what we're going to do.*
—**multiplication** /ˌmʌltəpləˈkeɪʃən/ *noun* the act of multiplying a number: *The students in this class are learning multiplication and division.*

mul•ti•ra•cial /ˌmʌltɪˈreɪʃəl/ *adjective*
including people of many different races: *We live in a multiracial society with people from all over the world.*

mum•ble /ˈmʌmbəl/ *verb*
to say something very quietly, in a way that is not clear: *If you mumble, the rest of the class can't hear or understand you.*
→ See Thesaurus box at **say**[1]

mumps /mʌmps/ *noun*
an illness that makes your throat and neck swell and become painful

munch /mʌntʃ/ *also* **munch on** *verb*
to eat something in a steady or noisy way: *The kids were munching on popcorn.*

mu•nic•i•pal /myuˈnɪsəpəl/ *adjective*
relating to the government of a town or city: *52% of the people voted in the municipal elections for mayor and city council.*

mu•ral /ˈmjʊrəl/ *noun*
a large painting that someone has done on a wall: *The school has murals on the walls that the students painted.*

mur•der[1] /ˈmɚdɚ/ *noun*
the crime of killing someone on purpose: *Wilson was 23 when he committed the murder.*
→ See Thesaurus box at **kill**, **crime**

murder[2] *verb*
to kill someone on purpose: *The police still do not know who murdered the girl.*
—**murderer** *noun* a person who murders someone: *The murderer spent the rest of his life in prison.* SYNONYM **killer**

mur•mur /ˈmɚmɚ/ *verb*
to say something in a soft quiet voice: *"Goodnight, dear," she murmured.*
—**murmur** *noun* the sound of a voice or voices speaking quietly: *I lay in bed listening to the murmur of voices downstairs.*
→ See Thesaurus box at **say**[1]

mus•cle /ˈmʌsəl/ *noun*
a part of your body under your skin that joins bones together and helps you to move: *Running will make your leg muscles stronger.*

mus•cu•lar /ˈmʌskjəlɚ/ *adjective*
1 having big strong muscles: *He had muscular arms from lifting weights.*
2 relating to the muscles: *It is a muscular disease that affects your ability to move.*

mu•se•um /myuˈziəm/ *noun*
a building that keeps old, interesting, or beautiful things for people to go and see: *We*

M

saw some interesting paintings at the Museum of Modern Art.*

mush /mʌʃ/ *noun*
something that is soft and wet in an unpleasant way: *The fruit was old and had turned to mush.*
—**mushy** *adjective* soft and wet in a way that is unpleasant: *The vegetables were overcooked and too mushy.*

mush•room /ˈmʌʃrum/ *noun*
a type of FUNGUS with a stem and a round top that people eat: *a pizza with ham and mushrooms*
➔ See picture on page A12

mu•sic /ˈmyuzɪk/ *noun*
1 the sounds that people make when they play instruments or sing: *Ben's in his room, listening to music.*

THESAURUS: music

tune a series of musical notes that are nice to listen to: *Suzy was humming a tune.*

melody a set of musical notes that sound good together: *He played a beautiful melody on the flute.*

song a short piece of music with words: *I heard a great song on the radio.*

piece/piece of music music that someone has written: *Learn these three pieces for your next lesson.*

composition *formal* a piece of music or art, or a poem: *She played one of Schubert's early compositions.*

2 the marks on paper that tell you what music to play or sing: *If you want to play the piano well, you have to learn to read music.*

mu•si•cal /ˈmjuzɪkəl/ *adjective*
1 relating to music: *"Do you play a musical instrument?" "I play the piano."*
2 good at playing music or singing: *My family is very musical. Everyone sings and plays an instrument.*

mu•si•cian /mjuˈzɪʃən/ *noun*
someone who plays or sings music well, or as a job: *He's a well-known jazz musician.*

Mus•lim /ˈmʊzləm/ *noun*
someone whose religion is Islam
—**Muslim** *adjective* relating to Islam: *Iraq is mainly a Muslim country.*

mus•sel /ˈmʌsəl/ *noun*
a small sea animal with a black shell and a soft body that you can eat

must[1] /məst; *strong* mʌst/ *modal verb*
1 used for saying that it is necessary to do something: *Everyone must give me their homework by 9 o'clock tomorrow.*

USAGE: must

If someone **must not** do something, she or he is not allowed to do it. **Must not** is fairly formal and is used mainly in written English: *You must not take any sharp objects on the plane.* | *You mustn't tell anyone else about this.*

If an action is not necessary, you can say that you **don't need to** do it: *I don't need to leave until 10.*

You can also say **don't have to** if it is not necessary for someone to do something: *You don't have to come with us if you don't want to.*

Do not say **don't need to** or **don't have to** to mean **must not**.

GRAMMAR: must

must, have to, have got to

must – used especially in more formal writing when a law or someone who is in charge of something forces you do to something: *All students must have shorts and a t-shirt for P.E. (=because the school says it is necessary)* | *Motorcycle riders must wear helmets (=because a law says it is necessary).*

must – used when you make yourself do something because you think it is a good idea or necessary: *We must visit Grandma on Sunday (=e.g. because we haven't seen her for a long time and it would be a good idea).* | *I must study for tomorrow's test (=because I know it is a good idea if I want to do well).*

have to – used when a rule, law, situation, etc. forces you to do something and you do not have a choice about it: *You have to pay tax on your income (=because the law says it is necessary).* | *We have to visit Grandma on Sunday (=e.g. because my mother says it is necessary).*

have got to – used in spoken English instead of **have to** or **must** to show how important it is to do something: *I've got to talk to him.*

2 used for saying that you think something is probably true based on information that you have: *The door's open, so she must be at home.* | *There's no more cake – Dad must have eaten it.*

must² /mʌst/ *noun*
a must = something that you must do, see, or have: *If you go to Europe, Venice is a must* (=you have to go to Venice).

mus•tache /ˈmʌstæʃ/ *noun*
hair that grows above a man's mouth: *He has a beard and a mustache.*
➔ See picture at **beard**

mus•tard /ˈmʌstəd/ *noun*
a yellow SAUCE with a hot taste, made from the seeds of a plant: *I had a burger with mustard and ketchup.*

mu•ti•ny /ˈmyutəni/ *noun* plural **mutinies**
a situation in which soldiers or SAILORs refuse to obey someone: *There was a mutiny on the ship, and the sailors took control of it.*

mut•ter /ˈmʌtə/ *verb*
to say something quietly, because you are annoyed or do not want people to hear: *"That's a lie," Lisa muttered, so no one would hear.*
➔ See Thesaurus box at **say¹**

mu•tu•al /ˈmyutʃuəl/ Ac *adjective*
1 if a feeling is mutual, two people have the same feeling toward each other: *I know he loves me, and the feeling is mutual* (=I love him too).
2 a mutual friend/interest = a friend or interest that two people share: *We both know Carrie well – she's a mutual friend.*

my /maɪ/ *adjective*
belonging to me: *It's my birthday tomorrow.*

my•self /maɪˈself/ *pronoun*
1 used after "I" and a verb to mean the person who is speaking or writing: *I looked at myself in the mirror.*
2 used for giving "I" a stronger meaning: *I told him myself* (=no one else did it) *that I wasn't going to come.*
3 (all) by myself = alone or without help: *Look, Mommy – I tied my shoes all by myself!*

mys•te•ri•ous /mɪˈstɪriəs/ *adjective*
strange and difficult to explain or understand: *A lot of people saw the mysterious light in the sky, but no one knew what it was.*
—**mysteriously** *adverb*: *The girl mysteriously disappeared while she was on vacation.*
➔ See Thesaurus box at **strange¹**

mys•ter•y /ˈmɪstəri/ *noun* plural **mysteries**
1 something that is difficult to explain or understand: *The reason why the ship sank is still a mystery.*
2 a story about a murder or other crime, in which no one knows who COMMITted (=did) the crime until the end: *I love reading murder mysteries.*

mys•ti•fy /ˈmɪstəˌfaɪ/ *verb* **mystified**, third person singular **mystifies**
if something mystifies you, it is very difficult to explain or understand: *Her death has mystified the police, and there are few clues.*

myth /mɪθ/ *noun*
1 a story from ancient times about gods, brave men, strange creatures and events: *Greek myths about the hero Hercules and the gods*
2 an idea that many people believe, but that is not true: *It's a myth that men are better drivers than women. Women are often excellent drivers.*
➔ See Thesaurus box at **story**

my•thol•o•gy /mɪˈθɑlədʒi/ *noun*
stories from ancient times about gods, brave men, strange creatures and events: *a book of Roman mythology*
—**mythological** /ˌmɪθəˈlɑdʒɪkəl/ *adjective*
relating to mythology: *dragons and other mythological creatures*

N n

nag /næg/ *verb* **nagged, nagging**
to ask someone to do something many times, in an annoying way: *Mom's been nagging me to clean up my room, but I don't want to do it.*

nail¹ /neɪl/ *noun*
1 a thin pointed piece of metal with a flat end that you hit with a hammer: *I'll need a few nails to fix this chair.*
2 the hard flat part that covers the end of your fingers and toes: *Maria had painted her nails red.*

nail² *verb*
to fasten something with a nail: *We made a boat by nailing old pieces of wood together.*

ˈnail ˌclipper *noun*
a small metal tool for cutting the nails on your fingers or toes

ˈnail file *noun*
a thin piece of metal with a rough surface that you use for shaping your nails

ˈnail ˌpolish *noun*
liquid that you paint on your nails to make them look attractive

na•ïve /nɑˈiv/ *adjective*
someone who is naïve does not have much experience or understanding of life: *She was sixteen, and still very naïve.*
—**naïvely** *adverb*: *He said he loved me, and I naïvely believed that he was telling the truth.*
—**naïvete** /nɑˌivˈteɪ/ *noun* the state of being naïve

na•ked /ˈneɪkɪd/ *adjective*
not wearing any clothes: *He had just gotten out of the shower and he was still naked.*
SYNONYM **nude**

name¹ /neɪm/ *noun*
1 the word that you call someone or something: *"What's your name?" "Carlos."* | *I can't remember the name of the hotel.* | *Her first name is Rebecca, and her middle name is Emily.*

THESAURUS: name

first name for example "Bret" in the name Bret Stern

last name/family name for example "Potter" in the name Harry Potter

middle name the name between your first and last names, for example "Ann" in Lisa Ann Smith

full name your complete name: *He wrote her full name, Mary Louise Johnson, in the space on the form.*

maiden name a woman's family name before she got married and changed it: *Mrs. Robertson's maiden name was Hansen.*

nickname a name your friends and family use for you, not your real name: *He runs so fast that his nickname is "Flash."*

pen name/pseudonym a name a writer uses that is not his or her real name: *Mark Twain is a pen name; his real name was Samuel Clemens.*

2 a big/household name = a famous or important person: *The movie made him a big name in Hollywood.*
3 a good/bad name = if you have a good or bad name, people think you are good or bad: *The company has a very good name.*
SYNONYM **reputation**

name² *verb*
to give a name to someone or something: *They named their son Jacob.*

name•ly /ˈneɪmli/ *adverb, formal*
used for giving more exact information about something you have mentioned: *There is another problem, namely, we need to raise more money.*

nan•ny /ˈnæni/ *noun* plural **nannies**
a woman that people employ to take care of their children: *The couple hired a nanny to take care of the kids while they were at work.*

nap /næp/ *noun*
a short sleep during the day: *Joe's two, so he still takes a nap after lunch.*

nap•kin /ˈnæpkɪn/ *noun*
a small piece of cloth or paper that you use for cleaning your mouth or hands when you are eating: *a paper napkin*
→ See picture on page A15

N

nar·cot·ic /nɑrˈkɑtɪk/ *noun*
a drug such as HEROIN that stops pain and makes people sleep
—**narcotic** *adjective* relating to narcotics: *The drug has a narcotic effect, so you will probably fall asleep.*

nar·rate /ˈnæreɪt/ *verb*
to be the person who describes what is happening in a movie, television program, story, etc.: *A well-known actor narrated the story in the movie.*
—**narration** /næˈreɪʃən/ *noun* the act of narrating a story or the events in a movie, etc.
—**narrator** /ˈnæreɪtɚ/ *noun* the person who narrates a story or the events in a movie, etc.: *the narrator of the story*

nar·ra·tive /ˈnærətɪv/ *noun, formal*
the description of events in a story: *The writer based the narrative on events in his own childhood.*

narrow

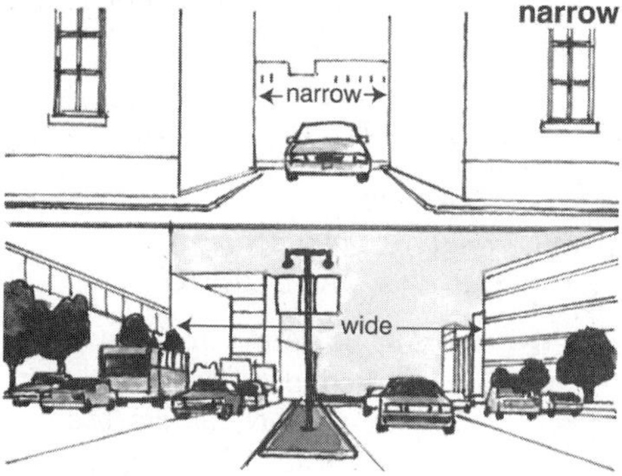

nar·row /ˈnæroʊ/ *adjective*
1 measuring only a small distance from one side to the other: *In the old part of the town, the streets were very narrow, and cars could not drive down them.* ANTONYM **wide**
2 a narrow escape = an occasion when something bad almost happens to you: *Luckily no one was hurt in the crash, but it was a narrow escape.*
—**narrowly** *adverb* if you narrowly avoid something bad, you avoid it by a very small amount: *We narrowly avoided disaster by stopping the car before it rolled down the hill.*

ˌnarrow-ˈminded *adjective*
not willing to accept ideas that are new or different: *People in very small towns are sometimes narrow-minded and unaccepting of new ideas or people.*

na·sal /ˈneɪzəl/ *adjective*
relating to the nose: *the nasal passages*

nas·ty /ˈnæsti/ *adjective* **nastier**, **nastiest**
1 unkind or unpleasant: *Don't be so nasty to your sister! She's always nice to you.*
2 unpleasant to smell, taste, or look at: *That medicine has a nasty taste. I don't like it.*

na·tion /ˈneɪʃən/ *noun*
1 all the people living in a country: *The President is addressing the nation tomorrow.*
2 a country with its own government: *He declared the republic an independent nation in 1991.*

WORD FAMILY look at the words:

→ **nation** *noun*
→ **national** *adjective*
→ **nationally** *adverb*
→ **nationality** *noun*
→ **nationalism** *noun*
→ **nationalist** *noun*

→ See Thesaurus boxes at **race**[1] and **country**

na·tion·al /ˈnæʃənəl/ *adjective*
relating to the whole of a nation: *Today is a national holiday, so no one has to go to work.* | *national elections for president*

national an·them /ˌnæʃənəl ˈnænθəm/ *noun*
the official song of a nation that people sing or play on special occasions

na·tion·al·ism /ˈnæʃənəlˌɪzəm/ *noun*
the feeling that your country is good, or better than any other country
—**nationalist** *noun* someone who is very proud of his or her country
—**nationalistic** /ˌnæʃənəlˈɪstɪk/ *adjective* relating to nationalism: *a nationalistic speech*

na·tion·al·i·ty /ˌnæʃəˈnæləti/ *noun*
plural **nationalities**
your nationality is the country that you belong to: *He has Canadian nationality* (=he is Canadian) *but he lives in the U.S.* SYNONYM **citizenship**

na·tion·al·ly /ˈnæʃənəli/ *adverb*
everywhere in a nation: *The basketball game was broadcast nationally, and people everywhere watched it.*

N

ˌnational ˈpark *noun*
a large area of natural land that the government protects, and allows people to visit: *Yellowstone National Park*

na•tion•wide /ˌneɪʃənˈwaɪd/ *adjective, adverb*
in every part of a nation: *The band went on a nationwide tour from California to Maine.*

na•tive[1] /ˈneɪtɪv/ *adjective*
1 native language/tongue = the language you learned to speak when you were born: *She speaks English well, but her native language is Japanese.*
2 *formal* used for talking about the place where you were born: *Two years later, he returned from his long trip to his native South Africa.*

native[2] *noun, formal*
someone who was born in a particular country: *Andrea is a native of Brazil, but she moved to the U.S. with her parents when she was 4.*

ˌNative Aˈmerican *noun*
someone who belongs to one of the tribes that lived in North America before Europeans arrived
—**Native American** *adjective* relating to Native Americans: *the Native American languages*

ˌnative ˈspeaker *noun*
someone who speaks a language as his or her first language: *a native speaker of English*

nat•u•ral /ˈnætʃərəl/ *adjective*
1 existing in nature, and not made by people: *I love the natural beauty of the mountains.* | *earthquakes and other natural disasters* ANTONYM **man-made**
2 normal or usual: *It's natural to feel nervous before you start at a new school.* ANTONYM **unnatural**
3 a natural leader/athlete, etc. = someone who is born with an ability to lead people, play sports, etc.: *He was tall and slim and a natural athlete.*

nat•u•ral•ize /ˈnætʃərəˌlaɪz/ *verb*
be naturalized = if you are naturalized, you get the legal right to belong to a country, although you were not born there: *He was born in Lebanon, but was naturalized as a U.S. citizen in 1994.*
—**naturalized** *adjective* having been naturalized: *a naturalized U.S. citizen*
—**naturalization** /ˌnætʃərələˈzeɪʃən/ *noun* when someone is naturalized: *the process of naturalization*

nat•u•ral•ly /ˈnætʃərəli/ *adverb*
1 caused by nature, not made by people: *Alison's hair is naturally curly – she doesn't have to do anything to make it look like that.*
2 *formal* in a way that is usual or normal and that you expect: *Naturally, we wanted to win.*

na•ture /ˈneɪtʃɚ/ *noun*
1 the world and everything in it that people have not made, such as plants, animals, or the weather: *I grew up in a small town in the mountains, and I learned to love nature.*
2 what someone's character is like: *Some people are born with a cheerful nature* (=they are cheerful).

nau•se•a /ˈnɔziə/ *noun, formal*
the feeling you have when you think you are going to VOMIT: *Stop taking the pills if they cause nausea.*

na•val /ˈneɪvəl/ *adjective*
relating to the navy: *a naval officer on the ship*

na•vel /ˈneɪvəl/ *noun, formal*
another word for a BELLY BUTTON

nav•i•gate /ˈnævəˌgeɪt/ *verb*
1 to decide which direction a car, ship, plane, etc. should travel: *Sailors used to navigate using the stars.*
2 to find your way around the Internet or a website by CLICKing on things on the computer screen: *The university's website is easy to navigate.*
3 to sail along a river or area of water: *In some places the river is too narrow to navigate.*
—**navigator** *noun* a person on a ship or airplane who decides which direction to travel
—**navigation** /ˌnævəˈgeɪʃən/ *noun* the act of deciding which direction to travel: *space navigation*

na•vy /ˈneɪvi/ *noun* plural **navies**
the organization that a country's ships and sailors belong to: *Frank is in the navy and sails around the world.*

ˌnavy ˈblue *also* **navy** *adjective*
very dark blue: *a navy blue jacket*
—**navy blue** *noun* a very dark blue color

near

near[1] /nɪr/ *adverb, preposition*
1 close to someone or something: *The hotel was near the beach so we could get there in a couple of minutes.* | *Is there a bank near here?*

THESAURUS: near

close not far from someone or something: *He sat close to his mom.*
not far/not far away not a long distance away: *The park's not far away.*
nearby near here or near a particular place: *Is there a grocery store nearby?* | *a nearby farm*
within walking distance easy to walk to from somewhere: *The school is within walking distance from their house.*
local used about stores, schools, etc. that are in the area where you live: *your local library*

2 close to a time or event: *Near the end of the game, a lot of people started to leave because it was clear who was going to win.*

near[2] *adjective*
1 a place that is near is only a short distance from you: *We quickly drove to the nearest hospital.*
2 in the near future = at a time that is close to now: *We will be hiring two new teachers in the near future.*
3 used for describing something bad that almost happens: *The project was a near disaster, but we managed to keep it from being too terrible.*

near·by /ˌnɪrˈbaɪ/ *adjective*
only a short distance from you or your home: *The kids rode their bikes to a nearby pool to go swimming.*
—**nearby** *adverb*: *My friend Amy lives nearby, so we see each other often.*
➔ See Thesaurus box at **near[1]**

near·ly /ˈnɪrli/ *adverb*
1 almost: *He's nearly ten years old. His birthday is next month.*
2 not nearly = you use this for saying that something is much less than something else: *I've saved $50, but that's not nearly enough* (=much less than I need). | *The second movie wasn't nearly as good as the first, so I was very disappointed.*

near·sight·ed /ˈnɪrˌsaɪtɪd/ *adjective*
unable to see things that are far away from you: *I'm nearsighted, so I wear glasses when I drive.* ANTONYM **farsighted**

neat /nit/ *adjective*
1 clean and in good order: *They keep their house neat and clean and it always looks great when I visit.*
2 a neat way of doing something is simple and works well: *That's a neat way of solving the problem. It's really clever.*
3 *informal* you use this to say that you like something or someone a lot: *Todd's new computer is really neat. It has a lot of great features.* SYNONYM **great**
—**neatly** *adverb* in a way that is clean and in good order: *The young women were neatly dressed in white uniforms.*
—**neatness** *noun* the state of being clean and in good order

nec·es·sar·i·ly /ˌnesəˈserəli/ *adverb, formal*
not necessarily = used for saying that something may not always be true: *Having a lot of money does not necessarily make you happy.*

nec·es·sar·y /ˈnesəˌseri/ *adjective*
if something is necessary, you need to have it or do it: *A good tent is necessary for camping outdoors.* | *It's necessary to study hard, if you want to get good grades.*
WORD FAMILY ➔ **necessity** *noun*

ne·ces·si·ty /nəˈsesəti/ *noun* plural **necessities** *formal*
something you need to have or do: *Light is a necessity for plants to grow.*

neck /nek/ *noun*
1 the part of your body between your head and your shoulders: *She was wearing a gold*

N

chain around her neck. | *Swans are large white water birds with long necks.*

2 the narrow part at the end of something such as a bottle: *He held the bottle of beer by its neck.*

3 neck and neck *informal* = having an equal chance of winning in a competition or race: *It was an exciting race, with two of the horses running neck and neck.*

4 be up to your neck in something *informal* = to be in a very difficult situation: *The company is up to its neck in debt and may have to close.*

➔ See picture on page A2

neck•lace /'nek-ləs/ *noun*

a piece of jewelry that you wear around your neck: *a silver necklace*

➔ See picture at **jewelry**

neck•tie /'nektaɪ/ *noun, formal*

another word for a TIE

nec•ta•rine /ˌnektə'rin/ *noun*

a yellow-red fruit that has a smooth skin and a big seed inside

➔ See picture on page A13

need[1] /nid/ *verb*

1 if you need something, you must have it in order to do something: *You need eggs to make pancakes.* | *I need more money if I want to buy an MP3 player.* | *I live in the city, so I don't need a car.*

2 need to do something = to have to do something: *I need to write my English paper tonight.* | *There's something I need to tell you.*

USAGE: need

Use **don't need to** when saying that an action is not necessary: *I don't need to leave until 10.*

You can also use **don't have to** when saying that it is not necesssary for someone to do something: *You don't have to come with us if you don't want to.*

Use **must not** or **mustn't** when saying that someone is not allowed to do something: *You mustn't tell anyone else about this.* | *You must not take any sharp objects on the plane.*

Must not is fairly formal and is used mainly in written English.

need[2] *noun*

1 something that it is necessary to have or do in order to improve a situation: *There's a need for more nurses in our hospitals.* | *The boys are safe now, so there is no need to worry* (=it is not necessary to worry).

2 something that you want to have or must have: *A small baby's needs are simple; they want food, sleep, and love.*

3 in need of something *formal* = needing to have something: *The house is in need of repairs.*

4 in need = not having enough food or money: *We're collecting money for children in need.*

nee•dle /'nidl/ *noun*

1 a thin pointed piece of metal with a hole at one end for thread, that you use for sewing: *a needle and thread*

2 another word for a KNITTING NEEDLE

3 a thin sharp hollow piece of metal that puts medicine or drugs into your body, or takes blood out: *The nurse stuck a big needle in my arm to take my blood.*

4 a thin pointed leaf from a PINE tree: *There were dry needles all over the carpet from the Christmas tree.*

5 a long thin part on a piece of electrical equipment that points to measurements or directions: *The needle on the car's gas gauge was pointing to "empty."*

need•less /'nidləs/ *adjective, formal*

not necessary: *Every day we see pictures of needless suffering on TV. We can and should do something to stop it.*

—**needlessly** *adverb*: *We are needlessly causing damage to the environment by putting chemicals into the river.*

need•y /'nidi/ *adjective*

not having enough money to live, eat, etc.: *There is some financial help for needy students.* | *They collect food and give it to the needy* (=people who need it). SYNONYM **poor**

➔ See Thesaurus box at **poor**

neg•a•tive[1] /'negətɪv/ Ac *adjective*

1 having a bad effect: *Too much TV can have a negative effect on kids.* ANTONYM **positive**

2 showing dislike or bad feelings toward a situation or person: *Jake had a lot of negative feelings about school because he felt the*

teachers did not understand him. ANTONYM **positive**
3 *formal* meaning "no": *I asked if he agreed, and the reply was negative* (=he said "no").
—**negatively** *adverb* in a way that shows dislike of a situation or idea: *A lot of people reacted negatively to the idea of a new airport* (=they did not like the idea).

negative² *noun*
1 a piece of film from which you print a photograph
2 *formal* a word or expression that means "no": *He replied in the negative* (=he said "no").
3 something bad about a plan, idea, etc.: *I think it's a good idea, and I can't see any negatives.* ANTONYM **positive**

ne·glect¹ /nɪˈglekt/ *verb*
1 to not give enough care or attention to someone or something: *Martin was working too hard and neglecting his family.*
2 neglect to do something *formal* = to not do something that you should do: *He neglected to tell his mother that his teacher was making him stay after school, so she didn't know why he was late coming home.*
—**neglected** *adjective* not cared for well: *She works for an organization that helps neglected children.*

neglect² *noun*
when someone or something is not cared for well: *I saw a lot of young kids suffering from neglect because their parents took drugs.*

ne·go·ti·ate /nɪˈgoʊʃiˌeɪt/ *verb, formal*
to talk about something in order to get an agreement: *Leaders from both countries met to try and negotiate an end to the war.*
—**negotiator** *noun* someone who negotiates
—**negotiation** /nɪˌgoʊʃiˈeɪʃən/ *noun* the act of negotiating: *The plan is still under negotiation* (=people are negotiating about it).

neigh /neɪ/ *verb*
if a horse neighs, it makes a long loud sound
—**neigh** *noun* the sound that a horse makes

neigh·bor /ˈneɪbɚ/ *noun*
1 someone who lives in the house next to your house, or very near you: *My neighbor came over to borrow a ladder.* | *John is my next-door neighbor* (=he lives in the house next to mine).
2 a country that is next to another country: *Canada and Mexico are neighbors of the U.S.*
3 someone who is sitting next to you: *He turned and said something to his neighbor during the meeting.*
—**neighboring** *adjective* near to a place: *We went to Indiana and the neighboring states of Ohio and Illinois.*

neigh·bor·hood /ˈneɪbɚˌhʊd/ *noun*
1 someone's neighborhood = the area where someone lives: *I know all the kids in my neighborhood.*
2 a small area of a town: *Are there any good restaurants in the neighborhood* (=in this area of town)?
➔ See Thesaurus box at **area**

nei·ther¹ /ˈniðɚ/ *adjective, pronoun*
not one and not the other other of two people or things: *It was a boring game, and neither team played well.* | *Neither of us could stop laughing.*

neither² *adverb*
you use this for agreeing with a negative statement: *"I don't like coffee." "Neither do I."* | *"Tom can't swim yet." "Neither can Sam."*

neither³ *conjunction*
neither... nor... = not one and not the other: *Neither his mother nor his father speaks English.*

ne·on /ˈniɑn/ *noun*
a gas used in electric lights and signs, that shines very brightly: *the bright neon lights of Las Vegas*

neph·ew /ˈnefju/ *noun*
1 the son of your brother or sister
2 the son of the brother or sister of your husband or wife

nerd /nɚd/ *noun, informal*
someone who is boring, and is interested only in boring things: *Alex didn't play sports, and all the cool guys at school thought he was a nerd.*
—**nerdy** *adjective* being a nerd: *Mark was a nerdy engineer.*

nerve /nɚv/ *noun*
1 the ability to do something difficult or brave: *I wanted to jump into the river, but I didn't have the nerve.*

N

2 something in your body that sends information between your brain and other parts of your body: *When we want to move, our nerves send a message to our muscles.*
3 have the nerve to do something *informal* = to do something that seems rude and might upset someone: *He had the nerve to ask me for more money!*
4 hit a nerve *informal* = to talk about a subject that upsets someone: *I hit a nerve when I asked him about his last girlfriend.*

ˈnerve-ˌracking *also* **nerve-wracking** *adjective*
worrying or frightening: *Taking tests is always nerve-racking.*

nerves /nɚvz/ *plural noun*
1 the feeling of being nervous: *I went running to try and calm my nerves* (=make the nervous feeling go away).
2 get on someone's nerves = to annoy someone: *There were some other kids in the library making a lot of noise, and it was getting on my nerves.*

nerv•ous /ˈnɚvəs/ *adjective*
1 worried or frightened: *I was really nervous before my college interview.*
2 a nervous person gets worried or upset easily: *My mother's a nervous person, so she doesn't like driving alone.*
3 relating to the nerves in your body: *The human body's nervous system is what allows us to feel heat, pressure, and pain.*
—**nervously** *adverb* in a worried or frightened way: *"I thought a heard a noise downstairs," she said nervously.*
—**nervousness** *noun* the state of being worried or frightened
➔ See Thesaurus box at **worried**
➔ See picture on page A23

ˌnervous ˈbreakdown *noun*
a mental illness in which someone is very worried and upset all the time, and cannot live normally: *He got really stressed out at work and had a nervous breakdown.*

nest /nest/ *noun*
1 a place that a bird makes to lay its eggs in: *A bird is building a nest for its eggs in that tree.*
2 a place where some small animals or insects live: *a wasps' nest*

nest

net /net/ *noun*
1 something made of string, wire, etc., with open spaces between the pieces of material: *a fishing net* | *She hit the tennis ball, and it went straight into the net* (=the thing made of string across the middle of the court).
2 the Net = another word for the INTERNET: *You can find this information on the Net.*

net•work /ˈnetwɚk/ Ac *noun*
1 a system of roads, lines of communication, etc. that connect to each other: *the university's computer network* | *The city has a complicated network of streets and highways.*
2 a radio or television company that shows the same programs across the country: *the ABC television network*

neu•rot•ic /nʊˈrɑtɪk/ *adjective*
worried or frightened about something in a way that is not normal: *Some people are neurotic about their health and always believe they are sick.*

neu•tral /ˈnutrəl/ Ac *adjective*
1 not supporting any country, person, etc. in a war or argument: *Switzerland was neutral during World War II.*
2 a neutral color is not strong or bright: *Gray is a neutral color.*
—**neutrality** /nuˈtræləti/ *noun* the state of not supporting any country, person, etc. in a war or argument: *the country's neutrality during the war*

neu•tral•ize /ˈnutrəˌlaɪz/ Ac *verb*, *formal*
to prevent something from having an effect: *This new spray helps neutralize pet smells and keep your home smelling fresh.*

nev•er /ˈnevɚ/ *adverb*
1 at no time, not ever: *I've never been to Europe, but I hope to go there soon.* | *She'll never forgive him for saying that.*
2 never mind = you use this for telling someone that something is not important:

N

"We missed the bus." "Never mind, it's not too far to walk."

nev•er•the•less /ˌnevɚðəˈles/ Ac *adverb, formal*
in spite of that: *His lawyers did a good job of defending him, but, nevertheless, the jury said he was guilty.*

new /nu/ *adjective*
1 if something is new, it did not exist before: *The city is building a new football stadium.* | *a new model of computer* ANTONYM **old**

THESAURUS: new

recent used about something that was new or that happened a short time ago: *a recent issue of the magazine*

modern used about things belonging to the present time, that are different from earlier things of the same kind: *There are a few old buildings, but most of them are modern.*

original new and different from anything that has been done or thought of before: *The book is interesting and has some original ideas.*

fresh used about food that was made, picked, etc. only a short time ago: *fresh bread*

latest used about a film, book, fashion, etc. that is the newest one: *We're going to see his latest movie.*

2 not owned or used by anyone before: *He bought a brand new car.* ANTONYM **used**
3 someone or something that is new to you is one that you have not known, had, or experienced before: *Do you like my new dress?* | *Do you like your new teacher?* | *Learning a new language is always hard.*
4 if you are new in a place, you started living, studying, etc. there recently: *Are you a new student here?*
5 a new planet, cure, etc. is one that someone has recently found: *There are a lot of new species at the bottom of the sea.*

new•com•er /ˈnuˌkʌmɚ/ *noun, formal*
someone who has recently arrived somewhere: *Are you a newcomer to San Diego or have you lived here for a while?*

new•ly /ˈnuli/ *adverb*
newly arrived/discovered, etc. = very recently arrived, discovered, etc.: *I just bought the band's newly released CD.*
➔ See Thesaurus box at **recently**

new•ly•wed /ˈnuliˌwed/ *noun*
a person who has recently got married: *The newlyweds left for a vacation in Vermont.*

new•ness /ˈnunɪs/ *noun*
1 the state of being new, and not existing before: *I was impressed by the newness of the technology.*
2 the state of being new when you have bought something recently, done something for the first time, etc.: *Liz loved the newness of her shiny black shoes.*

news /nuz/ *noun*
1 reports in the newspapers, on television, etc. about things that are happening in the world: *I like reading the sports news in the newspaper.* | *Dad turned on the TV to watch the news* (=the program that gives you reports).
2 information about things that have happened in your life recently: *My friend Diane called me to tell me all her news.*

GRAMMAR: news

News is always followed by a form of a verb that shows there is only one thing: *The news about the school trip was very exciting.*

You can say **some news**, **any news**, etc., or **a piece of news**: *Is there any interesting news in the paper?*

news•cast /ˈnuzkæst/ *noun*
a news program on television or the radio: *the evening newscast*
—**newscaster** *noun* someone who reads the news on television SYNONYM **anchor**

news•pa•per /ˈnuzˌpeɪpɚ/ *noun*
also **paper** pieces of thin paper containing news, that you can buy and read every day or week: *I read about the fair in the newspaper.*

news•stand /ˈnuzˌstænd/ *noun*
a place on a street where you can buy newspapers

ˌnew ˈyear *noun*
the year that will start soon: *We're moving to a different house in the new year* (=soon after it starts).

ˌNew Year's ˈDay *noun*
January 1: *Most offices are closed on New Year's Day.*

N

ˌNew Year's ˈEve *noun*
December 31: *Are you going to a party on New Year's Eve?*

next[1] /nekst/ *adjective, pronoun*
1 happening after the present day, week, time, etc.: *School starts next Monday.* | *I'll see you next week.* | *Be more careful next time* (=if something happens again).
2 closest to where you are now: *Turn left at the next street.*
3 the person or thing that is after the present one: *What's next on the shopping list?* | *Complete the next two exercises for homework.*
→ See Thesaurus box at **after**

next[2] *adverb*
1 after now, or after you have done something else: *We're almost finished with this. What do you want to do next?* | *Next, I'm going to show you how to make some cookies.*
2 next to someone or something = close to someone or something, with no other person or thing in between: *I sat next to Danny on the bus so we could talk.* SYNONYM **beside**
3 next to nothing = very little: *She was feeling sick and ate next to nothing.*

next ˈdoor *adverb*
in the room, building, etc. that is next to another room, building, etc.: *Her office is right next door and I can hear her talking on the phone.* | *The two boys lived next door to each other and play together often.*

ˌnext-door ˈneighbor *noun*
someone who lives in the house or apartment next to yours: *Our next-door neighbors will take care of the cats when we are on vacation.*

nib•ble /ˈnɪbəl/ *verb*
to eat food by taking small bites: *I wasn't very hungry, so I just nibbled on some potato chips.*

nice /naɪs/ *adjective*
1 pleasant, attractive, or enjoyable: *Michael looks nice in a suit.* | *Did you have a nice time at the party?* | *Their apartment is much nicer than ours, but it costs more too.*

THESAURUS: nice

enjoyable used for describing something that gives you pleasure because it is interesting, exciting, etc.: *It's an enjoyable movie.*

pleasant used for describing something that you like, especially something that is peaceful or relaxing: *It had been a pleasant evening.*

great/fantastic/wonderful used for describing something that you like very much: *"How was your vacation?" "Wonderful!"* | *We had a great time at the beach.*

2 friendly or kind: *She's a really nice old lady and fun to visit.* | *Everyone was very nice to me, and I enjoyed meeting them.*
3 used to say that you think something is good or is what you want to do: *It was nice to be back home again.* | *It would be nice if we went to visit my parents.*
—**niceness** *noun*
→ See Thesaurus box at **kind**[2]

nice•ly /ˈnaɪsli/ *adverb*
1 in a pleasant, attractive, or satisfactory way: *The girls were nicely dressed.* | *Brian's broken leg is healing nicely, and it should be completely healed soon.* SYNONYM **well**
2 in a polite or friendly way: *I'm sure he'll help if you ask him nicely.*

nick•el /ˈnɪkəl/ *noun*
1 a coin used in the U.S. and Canada that is worth 5 cents
2 a hard silver colored metal
→ See Thesaurus box at **money**

nick•name /ˈnɪkneɪm/ *noun*
a name that your friends or family use instead of your real name: *His nickname was "Tiny" because he was very tall.*
—**nickname** *verb* to give someone another name
→ See Thesaurus box at **name**[1]

nic•o•tine /ˈnɪkəˌtin/ *noun*
a dangerous substance in tobacco that makes it difficult for people to stop smoking: *Smokers are addicted to the nicotine in cigarettes.*

niece /nis/ *noun*
the daughter of your brother or sister, or the daughter of your husband's or wife's brother

or sister: *This is my niece, Kelli. She's my sister's daughter.*

night /naɪt/ *noun*
1 the part of the day when it is dark and most people are sleeping: *It was a hot night and I couldn't sleep.* | *I don't like driving at night.*
2 the evening: *We have dinner together as a family almost every night.* | *I took my girlfriend to the movies last night.*
3 night and day *also* **day and night** = all the time: *It rained day and night.*

night•club /ˈnaɪtklʌb/ *noun*
a place where people go to drink and dance that is open late at night: *There's a good band at the nightclub this Friday.*

night•fall /ˈnaɪtfɔl/ *noun, formal*
the time when it begins to get dark in the evening: *We drove until nightfall and then we stopped at a motel.* SYNONYM **dusk**

night•gown /ˈnaɪtgaʊn/ *noun*
a piece of loose clothing, like a dress, that a woman wears in bed: *She put on her nightgown, brushed her teeth, and went to bed.*

night•in•gale /ˈnaɪtɪŋˌgeɪl/ *noun*
a small wild bird that sings very beautifully, especially at night

night•life /ˈnaɪtlaɪf/ *noun*
all the entertainment that you can take part in during the evening in towns and cities, for example dancing, drinking, etc.: *New York City is famous for its exciting nightlife.*

night•ly /ˈnaɪtli/ *adjective, adverb*
happening every night: *the nightly news show*

night•mare /ˈnaɪtmer/ *noun*
1 a very frightening dream: *He still has nightmares about the accident.*
2 be a nightmare *informal* = if a situation is a nightmare, it is difficult, bad, or frightening: *The freeway can be a nightmare at rush hour.*

ˈnight school *noun*
classes taught at night, for people who work during the day: *After work, Juan goes to night school to study English.*

ˈnight shift *noun*
1 a period of time at night when people work: *My mother works the night shift as a nurse at the hospital.*
2 the group of people who work on the night shift: *The night shift starts to arrive about 9:45 p.m.*

night•time /ˈnaɪt-taɪm/ *noun*
the time during the night when the sky is dark: *The desert is hot during the day, but cold at nighttime.* ANTONYM **daytime**

nine /naɪn/ *number*
1 9: *I rode nine miles on my bicycle today.*
2 9 O'CLOCK: *I have to be in the office by nine.*
3 nine years old: *I'll be nine next Tuesday.*

nine•teen /ˌnaɪnˈtin/ *number*
1 19: *We have been married for nineteen years.*
2 nineteen years old: *He's nineteen, but he looks older.*
—**nineteenth** /ˌnaɪnˈtinθ/ *number* 19th or 1/19

nine•ty /ˈnaɪnti/ *number*
1 90: *A soccer game lasts ninety minutes.*
2 the nineties a) *also* **the '90s** the years between 1990 and 1999: *They won the World Series four times in the nineties.* **b)** *also* **the 90s** the temperatures between 90 and 99: *It was hot, with temperatures in the 90s.*
3 be in your 90s = to be aged between 90 and 99: *My grandmother is in her 90s.*
—**ninetieth** /ˈnaɪntiɪθ/ *number* 90th or 1/90

ninth /naɪnθ/ *number*
1 9th
2 1/9

nip /nɪp/ *verb* **nipped, nipping**
to bite someone or something with small sharp bites: *The puppy kept nipping my ankle.*

nip•ple /ˈnɪpəl/ *noun*
1 the dark raised circle in the middle of a woman's breast that a baby sucks in order to get milk
2 one of the two dark raised circles on a man's chest
3 the small piece of rubber on the end of a baby's bottle

ni•tro•gen /ˈnaɪtrədʒən/ *noun, written abbreviation* **N**
a gas that is the main part of the Earth's air

nit•ty-grit•ty /ˈnɪti ˌgrɪti/ *noun, informal*
the important details of how an agreement or activity can be done: *Let's get down to the nitty-gritty and talk about the cost.*

N

—**nitty-gritty** *adjective* relating to all the details of something

no¹ /noʊ/ *adverb*
1 used to answer a question when something is not true or when you do not want something: *"Is your sister married?" "No, she's not. She's still single."* | *"Do you need a ride home?" " No, thanks. I'm going to walk."* ANTONYM **yes**
2 used when you do not agree with something someone says: *"You and your sister are very alike." "No, we're not!"* ANTONYM **yes**

no² *adjective*
1 not any: *The men had no food or water.*
2 No Parking/No Smoking, etc. = signs saying that parking, smoking, etc. is not allowed
→ **no way**

no•bil•i•ty /noʊˈbɪləti/ *noun*
the group of people in some countries who have the highest social class: *His grandfather was a Duke in the Russian nobility.*

no•ble /ˈnoʊbəl/ *adjective*
1 good or generous: *The group raises money for noble causes, such as helping the poor in Africa.*
2 belonging to the group of people in some countries who have the highest social class: *He was born into a noble family.*
—**nobly** *adverb*

no•bod•y¹ /ˈnoʊˌbɑdi/ *pronoun*
no person: *We were all scared, but nobody screamed.* SYNONYM **no one**

nobody² *noun* plural **nobodies**
someone who is not important, successful, or famous: *He went from being a nobody to being a movie star.*

nod /nɑd/ *verb* **nodded, nodding**
1 to move your head up and down, to show that you agree with something or understand something: *"Yes," he said, nodding his head.*
2 to move your head up and down once in order to greet someone or to give someone instructions to do something: *"Sally's in there," Jim said, nodding toward the door.*
—**nod** *noun* an act of nodding: *He gave a nod of agreement.*

PHRASAL VERB
nod off *informal*
to begin to sleep when you do not plan to: *I keep nodding off in front of the TV.*

noise /nɔɪz/ *noun*
a loud or annoying sound: *The noise of the police siren woke the baby.* | *Why are the kids making so much noise?*

nois•y /ˈnɔɪzi/ *adjective* **noisier, noisiest**
1 making a lot of noise: *a noisy crowd of hockey fans* | *Jet engines are really noisy.*
2 filled with noise: *The restaurant was crowded and noisy.*
—**noisily** *adverb*

no•mad /ˈnoʊmæd/ *noun*
a member of a group of people that move from place to place to find food: *Nomads traveled the plains hunting and looking for food.*
—**nomadic** /noʊˈmædɪk/ *adjective* relating to nomads

nom•i•nate /ˈnɑməˌneɪt/ *verb*
to officially suggest someone or something for an important job or prize: *The movie has been nominated for three Academy Awards.* | *He's been nominated as the party's presidential candidate.*
—**nomination** /ˌnɑməˈneɪʃən/ *noun* the act of nominating someone or something for a job or prize

none /nʌn/ *pronoun*
1 not any of something: *"Can I have some more pie?" "Sorry, there's none left."* | *Luckily, none of the eggs broke.*
2 not one person or thing: *None of my friends likes baseball.* | *A little exercise is better than none at all.*

none•the•less /ˌnʌnðəˈles/ Ac *adverb, formal*
used when although what you have just said is true, something else is also true: *Everyone in the family works, but nonetheless they are still poor.* SYNONYM **however, nevertheless**

non•ex•ist•ent /ˌnɑnɪgˈzɪstənt/ *adjective, formal*
not present in a particular place: *In this small town, traffic accidents are almost nonexistent.*

non•fic•tion /ˌnɑnˈfɪkʃən/ *noun*
books or writing about real facts or events, not imagined ones: *I like reading nonfiction, especially books about animals or history.* ANTONYM **fiction**

—**nonfiction** *adjective*: *a nonfiction book about the rain forest*
➔ See Thesaurus box at **book**[1]

non•sense /ˈnɑnsens/ *noun*
1 something that someone says or thinks that is not true or that seems very stupid: *"Mom hates me." "That's nonsense!"*
2 behavior that is stupid and annoying: *She won't take any nonsense from the kids in her class.*
3 speech or writing that has no meaning: *The letter was nonsense and I couldn't figure out what she was trying to say.*

non•stick /ˌnɑnˈstɪk/ *adjective*
nonstick pans have a special surface inside that food will not stick to

non•stop /ˌnɑnˈstɑp/ *adjective, adverb*
without stopping: *It's been raining nonstop since we got here, and I just want to see the sun.* | *a nonstop flight from New York to L.A.*

noo•dles /ˈnudlz/ *plural noun*
food made from flour, eggs, and water, cut into long flat thin pieces and cooked in boiling water: *Add the noodles to the chicken soup.*

noon /nun/ *noun*
12 O'CLOCK in the middle of the day: *We ate lunch at noon.*

ˈ**no one** *pronoun*
not anyone: *I rang the doorbell, but no one came to the door.* SYNONYM **nobody**

nope /noʊp/ *adverb, informal*
no: *"Do you want to go to the movies?" "Nope, I'm too tired."*

nor /nɚ; *strong* nɔr/ *conjunction, formal*
1 neither... nor = used to say that two things are not true or possible: *My mother's family was neither rich nor poor.*
2 and not: *I didn't tell Dad, nor did John. So Dad never knew.*

norm /nɔrm/ Ac *noun, formal*
the usual or normal way of doing something: *Working during your lunch break is becoming the norm for many people.*

nor•mal /ˈnɔrməl/ Ac *adjective*
usual, typical, or expected: *Since the accident he has not been able to lead a normal life.* | *It's normal to feel nervous before an exam.*
—**normality** /nɔrˈmæləti/ *noun* a state in which something is normal

THESAURUS: normal

ordinary not special, unusual, or different in any way: *It's just an ordinary watch – it doesn't do anything extra.*

average typical of a normal person or thing, and not special or unusual: *The average family has two kids.*

standard used about things or methods that are the most usual type: *The shoes only come in standard sizes.*

routine used about something that is done regularly, not for any special or unusual reason: *a routine check of the plane*

conventional *formal* belonging to a type that had been used for a long time – used when comparing a piece of equipment, method, etc. with something that is new and different: *Microwave ovens cook food faster than conventional ovens.*

WORD FAMILY look at the words:

➔ **normal** *adjective*
➔ **abnormal** *adjective*
➔ **normally** *adverb*
➔ **normality** *noun*

nor•mal•ize /ˈnɔrməˌlaɪz/ Ac *verb, formal*
to become normal again: *Do you think the United States will ever normalize relations* (=become friendly again after a period of disagreement) *with Cuba?*

nor•mal•ly /ˈnɔrməli/ Ac *adverb*
usually or in the expected way: *I normally drive to work. But today I took the bus.*

norms /nɔrmz/ Ac *plural noun, formal*
accepted ways of behaving in society: *In school, there are norms of behavior that children must follow.*

north[1] *also* **North** /nɔrθ/ *noun*
1 the direction toward the top of a map of the world: *Which way is north?*
2 the north = the northern part of a country or area: *My family came from the north of Ireland.*
3 the North = the part of the U.S. east of the Mississippi River and north of Washington, D.C.

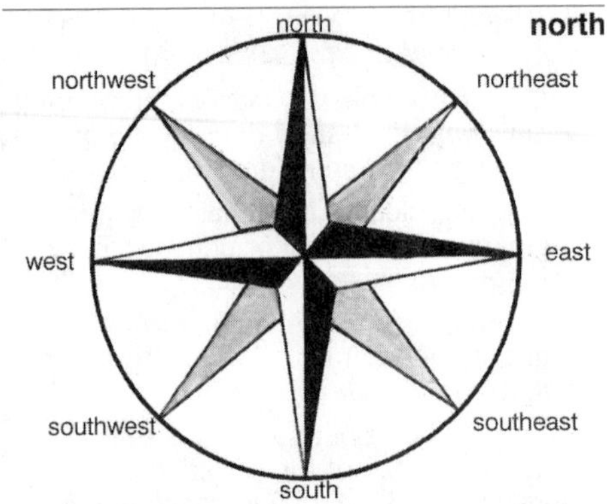

north

north[2] *adjective*
1 in, to, or facing north: *a town 20 miles north of Salem* | *the north side of Chicago*
2 north wind = a wind that comes from the north: *a cold north wind*

north[3] *adverb*
toward the north: *Drive north on the highway.*

north•east[1] /ˌnɔrθ'ist/ *noun*
1 the direction that is exactly between north and east
2 the Northeast = the northeast part of a country or area: *Boston is the largest city in the Northeast.*
—**northeastern** *adjective* in or from the northeast

northeast[2] /ˌnɔrθ'istɚn/ *adverb, adjective*
in, from, or toward the northeast: *a northeast wind*
➔ See picture at **north**

north•ern /'nɔrðɚn/ *adjective*
in or from the north: *the giant redwood trees in northern California*

north•ern•er /'nɔrðɚnɚ/ *noun*
someone who comes from the northern part of a country

ˌNorth 'Pole *noun*
the North Pole = the most northern place on the surface of the earth: *Scientists at the North Pole are studying the effects of global warming on the ice.*
➔ See picture at **globe**

northward /'nɔrθwɚd/ *adverb, adjective*
toward the north: *The ship sailed northward.*

north•west[1] /ˌnɔrθ'west/ *noun*
1 the direction that is exactly between north and west
2 the Northwest = the northwest part of a country or area: *The state of Washington is in the Northwest.*
—**northwestern** /ˌnɔrθ'westɚn/ *adjective* in or from the northwest: *the northwestern states of the U.S.*

northwest[2] *adverb, adjective*
in, from, or toward the northwest: *We drove northwest through the Rockies.*
➔ See picture at **north**

nose /noʊz/ *noun*
1 the part of a person's or animal's face that they use for smelling and breathing: *The ball hit me in the face and broke my nose.* | *He took out a tissue and blew his nose* (=cleared it by blowing).
2 (right) under someone's nose *informal* = so close to someone that he or she should notice, but does not: *I took her chocolate from right under her nose!*
3 the pointed front end of an airplane, ROCKET, boat, etc.
➔ See picture on page A2

nose•bleed /'noʊzblid/ *noun*
if you have a nosebleed, blood starts coming out of your nose: *He hit me on the nose and gave me a nosebleed.*

nos•tal•gia /nɑ'stældʒə/ *noun*
the feeling that you get when you remember a happy time in the past and wish that things had not changed: *He was full of nostalgia as he watched old home movies of the kids at the beach.*
—**nostalgic** *adjective* feeling slightly sad about a happy time you remember from the past that you wish had not changed

nos•tril /'nɑstrəl/ *noun*
one of the two holes at the end of your nose, through which you breathe
➔ See picture on page A2

nos•y /'noʊzi/ *adjective*
always trying to find out information about other people's lives: *She's really nosy, and I hate the way she asks my mother questions about my dad.*
—**nosiness** *noun* the act of being nosy

not /nɑt/ *adverb*
1 used when you want to give the opposite meaning to a word, statement, or question: *She's not very tall, and she can't reach the top shelf.* | *The room wasn't* (=was not) *crowded.* | *"Can we play ball, Dad?" "Not*

right now, son, I'm busy." | *"Is Mark still sick?" "I hope not"* (=I hope he is not still sick.)

2 not only = used to say that someone has one quality and also another quality: *She's not only funny, she's also smart.*

note¹ /noʊt/ *noun*

1 a short informal letter: *I wrote everyone a note thanking them for the present.*

2 something that you write down to help you remember something: *Let me make a note of your new address so I don't forget it.*

3 a particular musical sound, or the sign for that sound: *I can sing the low notes, but I can't reach the high notes.*

4 take note (of something) = to pay careful attention to something: *The coach took note of who was playing well during practice.*

note² *verb*

1 *formal* to notice or pay careful attention to something: *Please note that the museum is closed on Mondays.*

2 *also* **note down** to write something down so that you will remember it: *I carefully noted down the train times.*

note·book /ˈnoʊtbʊk/ *noun*

1 a book of plain paper in which you can write notes: *I wrote the answers to the math problems in my notebook.*

2 a small computer that you can carry

note·pa·per /ˈnoʊtˌpeɪpɚ/ *noun*

paper used for writing letters or notes

notes /noʊts/ *plural noun*

information that a student writes down from a class or book: *I always take notes during class and use them when I am studying for a test.*

noth·ing¹ /ˈnʌθɪŋ/ *pronoun*

1 not anything or no thing: *There was nothing in the room except a chair.* | *My girlfriend knows nothing about football so she never knows who's winning or losing.*

2 something that you do not think is important or interesting: *There's nothing on TV tonight. Let's go see a movie.*

3 *informal* zero: *We won the game three nothing* (=we had 3 points and the other team had no points).

4 for nothing *informal* **a)** without paying or being paid: *You can't ask people to work for nothing.* **b)** without getting what you expected or wanted: *"I'm sorry, he left an hour ago." "You mean, we drove all the way over here for nothing?"*

5 have nothing to do with someone or something = to not be related or involved with a situation or person: *Our argument had nothing to do with money. We were fighting about lies he told me.*

6 nothing but... *informal* = only: *I've had nothing but bad luck my whole life. I'm ready for some good luck!*

nothing² *adverb*

be nothing like someone or something *informal* = to not be at all similar to someone or something else: *Tommy is nothing like his father. They're completely different.*

no·tice¹ /ˈnoʊtɪs/ *verb*

to see, feel, or hear someone or something: *He noticed that his pants were getting tight.* | *Did you notice how tired Jean looked?*

—**noticeable** *adjective* easy to notice: *There's been a noticeable change in the weather.*

➔ See Thesaurus box at **see**

notice² *noun*

1 a written or printed paper that gives information or a warning to people: *The notice on the door said the library was closed.*

2 information or a warning about something that will happen: *You have to give two weeks' notice if you want to quit your job.*

3 take notice (of someone or something) = to pay attention to someone or something: *I told him to stop, but he didn't take any notice.*

no·ti·fy /ˈnoʊtəˌfaɪ/ *verb* **notified**, third person singular **notifies** *formal*

to tell someone something officially: *You should notify your bank if you move.* SYNONYM **inform**

no·tion /ˈnoʊʃən/ Ac *noun, formal*

an idea, belief, or opinion about something: *His beliefs are based on the notion that there is life on other planets.*

no·to·ri·ous /noʊˈtɔriəs/ *adjective*

famous for something bad: *Al Capone was a notorious criminal.*

—**notoriously** *adverb*

not·with·stand·ing /ˌnɑtwɪθˈstændɪŋ/ Ac *preposition, adverb, formal*

in spite of something: *Notwithstanding one bad teacher, Larry liked his new school.*

N

noun /naʊn/ *noun*
a word that is the name of a person, place, thing, quality, action, or idea: *In the sentence "Joe parked his car outside the store," "Joe," "car," and "store" are nouns.*

nour•ish /ˈnɚɪʃ/ *verb, formal*
to give a person, plant, or animal the food they need in order to live, grow, and be healthy: *Fertilizer nourishes the soil and helps to produce strong plants.*
—**nourishing** *adjective*: *Nourishing food makes you strong and healthy.*

nour•ish•ment /ˈnɚɪʃmənt/ *noun, formal*
food that people and other living things need in order to live and be healthy: *Fresh fruit and vegetables provide nourishment for a child's growing body.*

nov•el[1] /ˈnɑvəl/ *noun*
a book in which the story, characters, and events are not real: *"The Grapes of Wrath" is a famous novel by John Steinbeck.*
—**novelist** *noun* someone who writes novels
➔ See Thesaurus box at **book**[1]

novel[2] *adjective, formal*
new and unusual: *We need a novel solution to the problem – the old ways aren't working.*

nov•el•ty /ˈnɑvəlti/ *noun* plural **novelties**
1 something new and unusual: *I can remember when the Internet was still a novelty and a lot of people had never used it.*
2 *formal* the quality of being new and unusual: *Going to the gym was fun at first, but then the novelty wore off* (=it became boring).

No•vem•ber /noʊˈvembɚ/ *noun, written abbreviation* **Nov.**
the 11th month of the year, between October and December: *His birthday is on November 6.* | *Thanksgiving is in November.* | *My sister's baby was born last November.* | *We plan to get married next November.*

nov•ice /ˈnɑvɪs/ *noun*
someone who has just begun learning a skill or activity: *The basic class is for computer novices.*

now /naʊ/ *adverb*
1 at the present time: *I was sick yesterday, but I feel better now.* | *Judy's late – she should have been home by now* (=before now). | *Mom says I have to wash my own clothes from now on* (=starting now and continuing into the future).

> **THESAURUS: now**
>
> **at the moment** now: *The TV isn't working at the moment.*
>
> **for the moment** happening now but likely to change in the future: *I'll just leave these things here for the moment.*
>
> **at present** *formal* happening or existing now: *I'm afraid there are no jobs available at present.*
>
> **currently** happening or existing now: *I'm currently a student, but I will graduate in June.*

2 for now = for a short time: *You can leave your bag by the front door for now. But you'll have to move it before Mom gets home.*
3 immediately: *You'd better go now or you'll miss your bus.* ANTONYM **later**
4 now and then *also* **now and again** = used to say that something happens sometimes but not very often: *My son writes me letters now and then, but he never visits.*
5 now that = as a result of something: *Now that I have my own room, I'm a lot happier.* SYNONYM **since**

no ˈway *adverb, informal*
used to say that you will not agree to do something: *"You should tell your parents." "No way, they won't listen!"*

no•where /ˈnoʊwer/ *adverb*
1 not any place: *This town is so boring – there's nowhere to go and nothing to do.* | *The plants on the island grow nowhere else* (=in no other place).
2 get/go nowhere *informal* = to have no success, or make no progress: *The principal's efforts to improve the school have gone nowhere and things are still just as bad.*

nu•cle•ar /ˈnukliɚ/ Ac *adjective*
1 using or relating to nuclear energy: *nuclear power plants*
2 involving the use of nuclear weapons: *People were afraid of the possibility of nuclear war.*

ˌnuclear ˈenergy *noun*
the power produced by splitting an atom or joining two atoms together: *The main use of nuclear energy is to produce electricity.*

ˌnuclear ˈfamily *noun*
a family that includes parents and children and no other relatives

ˌnuclear ˈweapon *noun*
a very powerful bomb or other weapon that uses nuclear energy

nu•cle•us /ˈnukliəs/ *noun* plural **nuclei** /ˈnukliaɪ/
1 the central part of an atom: *The nucleus of an atom is surrounded by electrons.*
2 the central part of a cell: *The nucleus of a each cell contains genetic information.*

nude¹ /nud/ *adjective, adverb*
not wearing any clothes: *There's a special beach for people who like to sunbathe nude.*
SYNONYM **naked**
—**nudity** /ˈnudəti/ *noun* the state of not wearing any clothes

nude² *noun*
1 a painting, STATUE, etc. of someone without any clothes: *Most of his paintings are nudes.*
2 in the nude = not wearing any clothes: *He came out of the shower and stood there in the nude.*

nudge /nʌdʒ/ *verb*
to push someone gently with part of your body, especially your elbow, in order to get his or her attention: *Ken nudged me with his elbow and said, "Let's go."*
—**nudge** *noun* a movement in which you nudge someone
➔ See Thesaurus box at **push¹**

nug•get /ˈnʌgɪt/ *noun*
a small rough piece of a valuable metal found in the earth: *a gold nugget*

nui•sance /ˈnusəns/ *noun*
someone or something that annoys you or causes problems: *Jon's constant phone calls had become a nuisance.*

numb /nʌm/ *adjective*
1 if a part of your body is numb, you are not able to feel anything, usually because you are very cold: *His feet were numb from the cold.*
2 not able to react or show emotion in the normal way: *Instead of feeling jealous, I just felt numb.*
—**numbness** *noun*: *An electric shock may cause numbness.*

num•ber¹ /ˈnʌmbɚ/ *noun*
1 a word or sign that shows a quantity: *Add the numbers 7, 4, and 3.* | *an even number* (=2, 4, 6, 8, etc.) | *an odd number* (=1, 3, 5, 7, etc.)
2 a telephone number: *Give me your number and I'll call you.* | *I think I dialed the wrong number.*
3 a number showing the position of something in a list: *Try to answer question number five.*
4 a set of numbers that show who someone is: *What's your Social Security number?*
5 an amount of something that you can count: *We have been friends for a number of years* (=several years). | *I was surprised by the number of people who came.* | *There have been a large number of accidents on this road.*
WORD FAMILY ➔ **numerical** *adjective*

> **USAGE: number**
>
> Use **number** with nouns that are things you can count: *a large number of cities*
>
> Use **amount** with nouns that are things you cannot count: *a large amount of water*

number² *verb*
1 to give a number to something that is part of a set or list: *He numbered the pages one through six.*
2 if people or things number a particular amount, there are that many people or things: *General Lee's army numbered about 50,000 men.*

nu•mer•al /ˈnumərəl/ *noun, formal*
a written sign that represents a number: *10, 89, and 323 are all numerals.*

nu•me•ra•tor /ˈnuməˌreɪtɚ/ *noun*
the number that appears above the line in a FRACTION: *5 is the numerator in the fraction 5/6.*

nu•mer•i•cal /nuˈmerɪkəl/ *adjective, formal*
expressed in numbers, or consisting of numbers: *Make sure that the pages are in numerical order* (=in the order 1, 2, 3, etc.).
—**numerically** *adverb*

num•er•ous /ˈnumərəs/ *adjective, formal*
many: *I've been to Chicago numerous times, so I know the city fairly well.*

N

nun /nʌn/ *noun*
a woman who is a member of a group of religious women who live together: *Sister Agnes and the other nuns went into the church to pray.*

nurse¹ /nɚs/ *noun*
someone whose job is to take care of people who are sick or injured: *The nurse gave him his medication and asked how he was feeling.*

nurse

nurse² *verb*
1 to take care of people who are sick or injured: *Michael nursed his wife through a long illness.*
2 if a woman nurses a baby, she feeds it with milk from her breasts: *I nursed my son until he was about nine months old.*

nurs•er•y /ˈnɚsəri/ *noun* plural **nurseries**
1 a place where plants and trees are grown so that people can buy them: *We went to the nursery to buy some plants.*
2 a bedroom for a baby: *If we have a girl, we'll decorate the nursery in pink.*

ˈnursery rhyme *noun*
a short well-known poem or song for children: *She read the children nursery rhymes before they went to bed.*

ˈnursery ˌschool *noun*
a school for children from three to five years old

nurs•ing /ˈnɚsɪŋ/ *noun*
the job of taking care of people who are sick, injured, or very old: *She chose a career in nursing because she likes helping people.*

ˈnursing home *noun*
a place where people who are too old or sick to take care of themselves can live: *Grandpa's very old now, and he might have to go to live in a nursing home.*

nut /nʌt/ *noun*
1 a large seed that you can eat that usually grows in a hard brown shell: *a bowl of cashew nuts*
2 a small piece of metal with a hole in the middle that you screw onto a BOLT in order to fasten things together: *Use a wrench to loosen the nut.*

nu•tri•ent /ˈnutriənt/ *noun, formal*
a chemical or food that helps plants, animals, or people to live and grow: *These plants need soil with a lot of nutrients.*

nu•tri•tion /nuˈtrɪʃən/ *noun, formal*
the process of eating the right type of food for good health and growth: *This book teaches you about good nutrition and shows you how to cook healthy meals.*
—**nutritional** *adjective, formal* relating to the substances in food that help you to stay healthy and grow well: *Peanuts are a good snack for kids because they have a high nutrional value.*
—**nutritionist** *noun* someone who knows a lot about nutrition
—**nutritious** *adjective, formal* full of the natural substances that your body needs to stay healthy and grow well: *Fruit and vegetables are very nutritious.*

WORD FAMILY look at the words:
→ **nutrition** *noun*
→ **nutritious** *adjective*
→ **nutritional** *adjective*
→ **nutritionist** *noun*

nuts /nʌts/ *adjective, informal*
crazy or very angry: *The kids have been so noisy they're driving me nuts* (=making me annoyed).
→ See Thesaurus box at **crazy**

nut•shell /ˈnʌtʃel/ *noun*
1 (to put it) in a nutshell *informal* = used when you are telling someone the main facts about something in a short clear way: *In a nutshell, I think you should get a job and start paying rent.*
2 the hard outer part of a nut

nut•ty /ˈnʌti/ *adjective*
1 tasting like nuts: *Almonds give the sauce a nutty flavor.*
2 *informal* crazy: *Riding a bike across the country seemed like a nutty idea at first.*

ny•lon /ˈnaɪlɑn/ *noun*
a strong material that is used for making plastic, cloth, rope, etc.: *Bike shorts usually contain nylon.*

ny•lons /ˈnaɪlɑnz/ *plural noun*
a piece of clothing that women wear on their legs, that is very thin and made of nylon SYNONYM **pantyhose**

Oo

O /oʊ/ *number*
used for saying the number zero: *She lives in apartment two o four (=204).*

oak /oʊk/ *noun*
a large tree that is common in northern countries, or the hard wood of this tree: *a strong oak table*

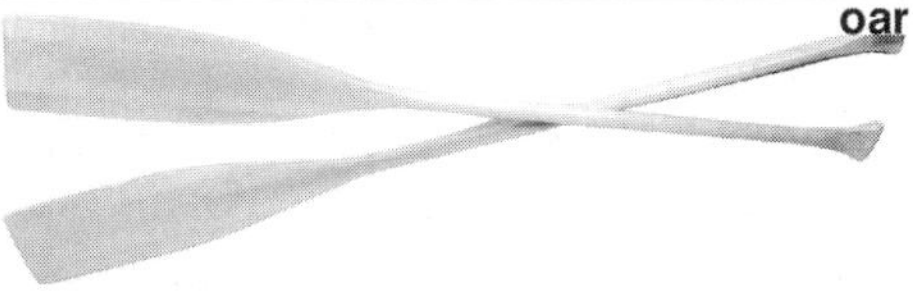

oar /ɔr/ *noun*
a long pole with a wide blade at one end, used for rowing a boat
➔ See picture at **boat**

o•a•sis /oʊˈeɪsɪs/ *noun* plural **oases** /oʊˈeɪsiz/
a place with trees and water in a desert

oath /oʊθ/ *noun* plural **oaths** /oʊðz/
1 a formal and serious promise: *I took an oath to defend the United States when I joined the army.*
2 be under oath = to have made an official promise to tell the truth in a court of law: *Remember you're under oath, so you have to tell the truth.*

oat•meal /ˈoʊtmil/ *noun*
crushed oats that are boiled and eaten for breakfast, or used in cooking: *I ate a bowl of oatmeal for breakfast.*

oats /oʊts/ *plural noun*
a grain that is used as food
—**oat** *adjective* made of oats: *oat cereal*

o•be•di•ent /əˈbidiənt/ *adjective*
always doing what a rule or someone in authority tells you to do: *I was a good, obedient child who always did as I was told.* ANTONYM **disobedient**
—**obedience** *noun* obedient behavior
—**obediently** *adverb*

o•bese /oʊˈbis/ *adjective, formal*
very fat in a way that is unhealthy: *Her doctor told her she was obese and needed to lose weight.*
—**obesity** *noun, formal* the condition of being obese
➔ See Thesaurus box at **fat**[1]

o•bey /əˈbeɪ/ *verb* **obeyed**, third person singular **obeys**
to do what a law, rule, or person in authority tells you: *If you do not obey the law, then you will be punished.* ANTONYM **disobey**

THESAURUS: obey

do what someone says/do what someone tells you: *You'd better do what the coach says if you want to stay on the team.*

do what you are told/do as you are told: *Maybe next time you'll do what you are told.*

follow someone's orders/instructions: *Follow the instructions at the top of the test.* | *You must follow your doctor's orders.*

WORD FAMILY look at the words:

➔ **obey** *verb*
➔ **disobey** *verb*
➔ **obedient** *adjective*
➔ **disobedient** *adjective*
➔ **obedience** *noun*
➔ **disobedience** *noun*

ob•ject[1] /ˈɑbdʒɪkt/ *noun*
1 a thing that you can see, hold, or touch: *Keep your back straight when lifting heavy objects.*
2 the purpose of a plan, action, or activity: *The object of the game is to score points by throwing the basketball through the hoop.*
3 in grammar, the person or thing that is affected by the action of the verb: *"Book" is*

the object in the sentence "I read the book."
→ See Thesaurus box at **thing**

ob·ject² /əb'dʒekt/ *verb*
to say that you do not like or approve of something: *Her father objected to the marriage and refused to go to the wedding.*

O

ob·jec·tion /əb'dʒekʃən/ *noun*
the reason someone gives for not approving of an idea or plan: *My main objection to your idea is that it would cost too much money.*

ob·jec·tive /əb'dʒektɪv/ Ac *noun*
something that you are working hard to achieve: *My objective is to become the next state champion.*
→ See Thesaurus box at **purpose**

ob·li·gat·ed /'ɑblə,geɪtɪd/ *adjective*
be/feel obligated to do something = to have to do something because of a rule or law or because you feel it is your duty: *You are obligated to pay your rent on time. If you don't, the landlord can make you leave.* SYNONYM **obliged**

ob·li·ga·tion /,ɑblə'geɪʃən/ *noun*
something that you must do because it is the law or your duty: *Schools have an obligation to provide a safe place for students to learn.*

o·blig·a·to·ry /ə'blɪgə,tɔri/ *adjective, formal*
something that is obligatory must be done because of a law or rule: *It is obligatory for restaurant staff to wash their hands after using the restroom.* SYNONYM **mandatory**

WORD FAMILY look at the words:
→ **obligatory** *adjective*
→ **obliged** *adjective*
→ **obligated** *adjective*
→ **obligation** *noun*

o·bliged /ə'blaɪdʒd/ *adjective*
be/feel obliged to do something *formal* = to have to do something because of a rule or law or because you feel it is your duty: *All the people in the car are obliged to wear seatbelts.* SYNONYM **obligated**

o·blique /ə'blik/ *adjective, formal*
said in a way that is not direct or clear: *The letter contained oblique references to their argument, but didn't mention it directly.*

ob·liv·i·ous /ə'blɪviəs/ *adjective, formal*
not knowing about or not noticing something that is happening around you: *The boys were oblivious to danger as they started climbing down the cliff.* SYNONYM **unaware**

ob·long /'ɑblɔŋ/ *adjective*
having a shape that is longer than it is wide: *This oblong table is 58 inches long by 36 inches wide.*

ob·nox·ious /əb'nɑkʃəs/ *adjective, formal*
very offensive or rude: *Some of the boys were so loud and obnoxious that they were asked to leave the club.*

o·boe /'oʊboʊ/ *noun*
a long thin wooden musical instrument that you play by blowing and pressing holes in it with your fingers
→ See picture on page A21

ob·scene /əb'sin/ *adjective*
showing or talking about sex in a way that is offensive or shocking: *Students who use obscene language in class will be suspended.*

ob·scure¹ /əb'skjʊr/ *adjective, formal*
1 not well known and not very important: *The paintings were done by an obscure French artist that very few people have even heard of.*
2 unclear or difficult to understand: *The library was closed at lunchtime for some obscure reason that no one could explain.*

obscure² *verb, formal*
to prevent something from being seen or heard clearly: *Clouds obscured the top of the mountain.*

ob·serv·ant /əb'zɚvənt/ *adjective*
good at noticing the things that happen around you: *Police officers are trained to be observant.*

ob·ser·va·tion /,ɑbzɚ'veɪʃən/ *noun*
1 the process of watching someone or something carefully for a long time: *Based on our past observations of the river, we expect that it will flood this fall.*
2 a remark about something that you have noticed: *He made some funny observations about the other students in the class.*

ob·serve /əb'zɚv/ *verb, formal*
to watch someone or something carefully: *Mr. Davis observed the woman entering the*

building at 9:18.
—**observer** *noun* someone who watches someone or something carefully

WORD FAMILY look at the words:

→ **observe** *verb*
→ **observer** *noun*
→ **observant** *adjective*
→ **observation** *noun*

ob•sessed /əb'sest/ *adjective*
if you are obsessed with someone or something, you think about them all the time and cannot think about anything else: *William is obsessed with making money. That's all he talks about.*

ob•ses•sion /əb'seʃən/ *noun*
something that you think about too much, in a way that is not normal: *Young girls often have an unhealthy obsession with being thin.*

ob•so•lete /ˌɑbsə'lit/ *adjective, formal*
no longer used or needed because something newer and better has been made: *Now that there are DVDs, videotapes are becoming obsolete.*

ob•sta•cle /'ɑbstɪkəl/ *noun*
1 something that stops you doing or achieving something successfully: *Lack of money was a major obstacle to buying a car.*
2 something that blocks a road, path, etc., so that you must go around it: *They had to drive around branches and other obstacles in the road.*

ob•struct /əb'strʌkt/ *verb, formal*
to block a road, passage, etc. so that nothing can get past: *The truck was on its side and obstructed two lanes of traffic.*

obstruction

ob•struc•tion /əb'strʌkʃən/ *noun, formal*
something that blocks a road, passage, etc.: *The accident caused an obstruction on the freeway.*

ob•tain /əb'teɪn/ Ac *verb, formal*
to get something that you want: *You will need to obtain a visa in order to visit the United States.*
—**obtainable** *adjective, formal* able to be obtained: *The disks are obtainable at your local computer store.*

ob•vi•ous /'ɑbviəs/ Ac *adjective*
easy to notice or understand: *It was obvious (that) he was sick from the way he looked.*
—**obviously** *adverb*: *He's obviously nervous. He keeps checking the clock and biting his nails.*
→ See Thesaurus box at **clear**[1]

oc•ca•sion /ə'keɪʒən/ *noun*
1 a time when something happens: *I met with him on several occasions.*
2 an important event or ceremony: *We only use the good plates at Christmas and other special occasions.*

oc•ca•sion•al /ə'keɪʒənəl/ *adjective*
happening sometimes but not often: *Her English is good, but she makes the occasional mistake.*
—**occasionally** *adverb*: *He looked at his watch occasionally.*

oc•cu•pa•tion /ˌɑkjə'peɪʃən/ Ac *noun*
1 a job or profession: *Write your name, address, and occupation at the top of the form.*
2 the act of entering a place and getting control of it, using military force: *The enemy's occupation of the city lasted several months.*
3 something you do in your free time, for enjoyment: *Donna's favorite occupation is shopping.*
—**occupational** *adjective, formal* related to or caused by your job: *Injuries are an occupational risk for athletes.*
→ See Thesaurus box at **job**

oc•cu•py /'ɑkjəˌpaɪ/ Ac *verb* **occupied**, third person singular **occupies** *formal*
1 to live in or use all of a particular place, building, etc.: *The same family has occupied the apartment for 20 years.*
2 if something occupies you or your time, you are busy doing it: *We played games to occupy the children's time while it rained.*
3 to enter a place and get control of it, usually by force: *Students occupied the university and refused to leave.*

O

O

4 to fill a particular amount of space: *Family photos occupied almost the entire wall.*
—**occupant** *noun, formal* someone who lives or stays in a particular place

oc·cur /əˈkɚ/ Ac *verb* **occurred, occurring** *formal*
to happen without being expected: *Earthquakes usually occur without any warning signs.*
—**occurrence** *noun, formal* something that happens: *Forest fires are a common occurrence in the summer.*

PHRASAL VERB
occur to someone *formal*
if a thought or idea occurs to you, you suddenly think of it: *It never occurred to me (that) she might be married. I just assumed she was single.*
→ See Thesaurus box at **happen**

o·cean /ˈoʊʃən/ *noun*
1 the ocean = the large amount of salt water that covers most of the Earth's surface: *We went swimming in the ocean when we visited California.*
2 a particular large area of salt water somewhere on Earth: *the Pacific Ocean*
—**oceanic** /ˌoʊʃiˈænɪk/ *adjective, formal* related to the ocean: *oceanic currents*

o'clock /əˈklɑk/ *adverb*
one/two/three, etc. o'clock = one of the times when the clock shows the exact hour as a number from 1 to 12: *I'll meet you at one o'clock for lunch.*

Oc·to·ber /ɑkˈtoʊbɚ/ *noun, written abbreviation* **Oct.**
the tenth month of the year, between September and November: *The group will be performing on October 22. | Clare's going to be two in October. | We have been in this apartment since last October. | Our membership expires next October.*

oc·to·pus /ˈɑktəpəs/ *noun* plural **octopuses** or **octopi** /ˈɑktəpaɪ/
an ocean creature with a soft body and eight TENTACLES (=arms)

odd /ɑd/ Ac *adjective*
1 strange or different from normal: *He always calls if he's going to be late, so it's odd (that) he hasn't called by now.*
2 an odd number cannot be divided by 2: *1, 3, 5, and 7 are all odd numbers.*
→ See Thesaurus box at **strange[1]**

odd·i·ty /ˈɑdəti/ *noun* plural **oddities** *formal*
a strange or unusual person or thing: *In the 1960s, foreign cars were an oddity in the U.S. Everyone had American cars.*

ˈodd jobs *noun*
small jobs of different types, for example fixing things: *I tried to earn some extra money on weekends doing odd jobs, like painting and fixing fences.*

odds /ɑdz/ Ac *plural noun*
the odds = how likely it is that something will or will not happen: *The team's odds of winning are not very good.*

ˌodds and ˈends *plural noun, informal*
various small things that have little value: *I need to stop at the store to pick up a few odds and ends.*

o·dor /ˈoʊdɚ/ *noun, formal*
a bad smell: *There's an unpleasant odor coming from the drain.*
→ See Thesaurus box at **smell[1]**

of /əv; *strong* ʌv/ *preposition*
1 used for showing who or what has a particular quality or feature: *Did you notice the color of her eyes? | the enormous size of the building*
2 used for showing what something is a part of: *I really liked the first scene of the movie.*
3 used for showing who someone or something belongs to: *She is the daughter of a famous actor.*
4 used for saying what type of people or things form a particular group: *A group of students was studying in the library. | a pack of dogs*
5 used for showing what an amount refers to: *Do you want a glass of milk?*
6 used in dates before the name of the month: *I'll see you on the 23rd of January.*
7 used in giving the time, to mean "before": *It's ten of five* (=ten minutes before 5:00). SYNONYM **to**
8 used for giving the reason or cause of something: *She died of cancer.*
9 used for saying what a picture shows: *This is a picture of my family.*
→ **of course** at **course**

off /ɔf/ *adverb, preposition, adjective*
1 not resting on or touching something: *Get your feet off the couch!* | *He took his shoes off* (=off his feet). | *He fell off his chair.* ANTONYM **on**
2 away from a place: *She waved and drove off.*
3 out of a bus, airplane, train, or boat: *The bus stopped, and she got off.* ANTONYM **on**
4 if a machine or light is off, someone has made it stop working for a time: *Turn the lights off when you leave.* ANTONYM **on**
5 a distance away, or in the future: *Off in the distance, we could see the mountains.* | *Our hotel was just off the main street* | *Summer is a long way off.*
6 not at work or school: *I'll try to finish it today because I'm off tomorrow.* | *I'm going to take a day off this week.*
7 if a planned event is off, it will not now take place: *The wedding's off. Brad and Kim aren't even speaking to each other.* ANTONYM **on**
8 if there is money off something, it is being sold at a lower price than before: *The dress was 20% off, so I bought it.*
9 off and on/on and off = for short periods of time during a longer period: *It had been raining off and on all morning.*
→ **well-off**

of•fend /ə'fend/ *verb, formal*
to make someone angry and upset: *I offended him by laughing at his haircut.*

> **WORD FAMILY look at the words:**
> → **offend** *verb*
> → **offense** *noun*
> → **offensive** *adjective*
> → **inoffensive** *adjective*

of•fend•er /ə'fendɚ/ *noun, formal*
someone who is guilty of a crime: *How should juvenile offenders* (=young offenders) *be punished?*

of•fense¹ /ə'fens/ *noun*
1 a crime: *He has committed a serious offense and will probably be sent to prison.*
2 take offense = to feel angry and upset because of what someone has said or done: *She took offense when I asked how old she was.*

of•fense² /'ɔfens/ *noun*
the action of trying to score points in a sports game, or the players who try to score points: *The team has a strong offense.*

of•fen•sive /ə'fensɪv/ *adjective, formal*
1 very impolite and likely to upset people: *He was fired for telling offensive jokes.* SYNONYM **rude**; ANTONYM **inoffensive**
2 used for attacking a person or place: *offensive weapons* ANTONYM **defensive**
→ See Thesaurus box at **rude**

of•fer¹ /'ɔfɚ/ *verb*
1 to say or show that you are willing to give someone something: *I offered him a slice of my pizza.* | *They offered us $325,000 for the house.*
2 to say that you are willing to do something for someone: *She offered to help me carry the boxes.*

offer² *noun*
a statement that you are willing to do something for someone or give someone something: *He refused all offers of help.* | *He got a job offer and will probably take the job.* | *I made him a good offer* (=offered to pay a good price) *for the bike.*

of•fice /'ɔfɪs/ *noun*
1 a building where people work at desks, or a room in this building: *Are you going to the office today?* | *Is Shaw in his office?* | *I called the doctor's office for an appointment.*
2 an important job, especially in government: *the president's first year in office* | *The mayor took office* (=started the job) *in December.*
→ **box office, post office**

of•fi•cer /'ɔfəsɚ/ *noun*
1 someone who has an important position in the army, navy, etc.: *The soldier saluted the officer.*
2 a POLICE OFFICER: *Officer Parks arrested him for drunk driving.*
3 someone who has an important position in an organization: *the chief financial officer of the company*

of•fi•cial¹ /ə'fɪʃəl/ *adjective*
done or produced by someone who has an important position in the government or in an organization: *The president was on an official visit to Mexico.* | *He got an official letter with information about the visa.*

—**officially** *adverb*: *Two days later, war was officially declared.*

official² *noun*
someone who has an important position in an organization: *Government officials say the problem is getting worse.*

O

'off-ˌseason *noun*
the time in the year when a sport is not usually played: *The football player wanted to wait until the off-season to have surgery on his knee.*

off•set /ˌɔf'set/ Ac *verb* **offset, offsetting** *formal*
if something offsets another thing, it has an opposite effect: *Higher fuel prices have offset the savings I made by driving less.*

off•shore /ˌɔf'ʃɔr/ *adjective, adverb*
in the ocean, at a distance from the coast: *an offshore oil rig*

of•ten /'ɔfən/ *adverb*
1 many times: *She often works weekends.* ANTONYM **rarely**

THESAURUS: often

a lot *informal* a large amount or number: *We go to the beach a lot in the summer.*

frequently *formal* very often: *He's frequently late for work.*

regularly often and at regular times, for example every day, every week, or every month: *You should exercise regularly.*

constantly very often over a long period of time: *He seems to eat constantly!*

continuously *formal* without stopping: *It's been raining continuously since we got here.*

again and again/over and over (again) many times, and more often than you would expect: *She has played the game again and again.* | *I get bored doing the same thing over and over again.*

2 how often = used to ask how many times something happens during a period of time: *"How often do you go to the dentist?" "About once a year."*
3 every so often = sometimes, but not regularly: *We go out to the movies every so often.*

oh /oʊ/
1 said when you are surprised, happy, upset, etc.: *Oh, no! My wallet is gone!*
2 said before you answer someone: *"Why?" "Oh, I don't know."*

ohm /oʊm/ *noun*
a unit for measuring how hard it is for electricity to flow through something

oil¹ /ɔɪl/ *noun*
1 a thick liquid from under the ground which people use for making GASOLINE, for heating, or for making machines work smoothly: *They want to start drilling for oil* (=digging into the ground to find oil) *in Alaska.*
2 a thick liquid from a plant which you use in cooking: *Fry the vegetables in olive oil.*

oil² *verb*
to put oil into or onto something: *He oiled the hinges of the door to stop them from squeaking.*

'oil rig *noun*
a large structure with equipment for digging into the ground or under the ocean to get oil

'oil well *noun*
a deep hole that people dig so that they can get oil out from under the ground

oil•y /'ɔɪli/ *adjective*
covered with oil, or containing a lot of oil: *The car mechanic wiped his hands on an oily rag.*

oint•ment /'ɔɪntmənt/ *noun*
a substance that you rub into your skin as a medicine

o•kay *also* **OK** /oʊ'keɪ/ *adjective, informal*
1 used for saying yes: *"Can I come too?" "Okay."* SYNONYM **all right**
2 used to get people's attention before saying something: *OK, let's get started.*
3 acceptable to you: *"I don't want to go out tonight." "That's okay."* SYNONYM **all right**
4 not sick, hurt, or unhappy: *That was a bad fall. Are you okay?* SYNONYM **all right**
5 fairly good: *"Was the movie good?" "It was OK, but I didn't love it."* SYNONYM **all right**
—**okay** *also* **OK** *adverb* fairly well: *She's doing okay in school, but she's not getting A's.*

old /oʊld/ *adjective*
1 having lived for a long time: *My grandmother is very old.* | *We should respect the old* (=old people). ANTONYM **young**
2 having existed for a long time: *The old building needed a lot of repairs.* ANTONYM **new**

THESAURUS: old

ancient used about buildings, cities, languages, etc. that are from a time thousands of years ago: *ancient history* | *the ancient city of Rome*

antique used about furniture, jewelry, etc. that is old and valuable: *an antique rug*

vintage *formal* used about things that are old but valuable and good quality: *vintage cars*

classic used about movies, books, television programs, songs, and cars that are old but very good quality: *The classic TV show "I Love Lucy" still makes people laugh.*

used used about cars or other things that are not new but that someone is selling: *a used car dealer*

stale used about bread, cake, cookies, etc. that are not fresh any more

rotten used about food, especially fruit or eggs, that is not good to eat any more

3 used for asking or talking about the age of someone or something: *How old are you?* | *Our dog is three years old.*

4 an old friend = a friend that you have known for a long time

5 someone's old house/job/teacher, etc. = the house, etc. that someone had before, but does not have now: *Our old house was smaller than this one.*

old 'age *noun*
the time when you are old: *He took care of his parents in their old age.*

ˌold-'fashioned *adjective*
not modern or fashionable: *an old-fashioned telephone with a dial*

ol•ive /'ɑlɪv/ *noun*
a small green or black fruit that you can eat or use for making oil: *I asked for olives on my pizza.*

O•lym•pic Games /əˌlɪmpɪk 'geɪmz/ *plural noun*
the Olympic Games *also* **the Olympics** = a sports competition that happens every four years, in which people from many different countries take part
—**Olympic** *adjective*

ome•let *also* **omelette** /'ɑmlɪt/ *noun*
eggs that have been mixed together and cooked, often with other foods inside: *a cheese omelet*

om•i•nous /'ɑmənəs/ *adjective*
making you feel that something bad is going to happen: *ominous black clouds*
—**ominously** *adverb*

o•mit /oʊ'mɪt/ *verb* **omitted, omitting** *formal*
to not include something: *My name was omitted from the list, so I didn't get a copy of the email.* SYNONYM **leave out**
—**omission** /oʊ'mɪʃən/ *noun* the act of omitting something

on /ɔn/ *preposition, adjective, adverb*

1 touching or supported by something: *There was a magazine on the table.* | *I have mud on my shoes.* | *Put your coat on* (=on your body). ANTONYM **off**

2 in a particular place: *The answer is on page 44.* | *I grew up on a farm.*

3 in or into a bus, airplane, train, or boat: *Did you sleep on the plane?* | *When the bus came, I got on.* ANTONYM **off**

4 at the side of a road, river, lake, or sea: *the stores on Main Street*

5 during a particular day: *Their next game is on March 12.*

6 if a machine or light is on, someone has made it start working: *The TV was on and I could hear it upstairs.* | *Turn on the light if you're going to read.* ANTONYM **off**

7 being broadcast by a television or radio station: *What's on TV tonight?* | *The news will be on at 6:00.*

8 about a particular subject: *a book on China*

9 used when saying that someone or something continues: *We drove on to the next town.* | *Go on, Cheryl. What happened next?*

10 using something: *I talked to him on the phone.* | *She played a tune on the piano.*

11 if you are on a trip, visit, etc., you are going somewhere or have come from somewhere: *They met on a trip to Spain.*

12 used when showing who or what is affected by something: *Should people do experiments on animals?*

13 if a planned event is on, it is going to happen: *Is the party still on? Someone said it might be canceled.* ANTONYM **off**

→ **later on** at **later**[1], **on and off** at **off**

O

once[1] /wʌns/ *adverb*
1 one time: *I've only met her once, but I remember that time very well.* | *She goes to the gym once a week* (=one time every week).
2 at a time in the past: *They were once good friends.*
3 (every) once in a while = sometimes, but not often: *We go fishing every once in a while.*
4 at once a) at the same time: *I can't do two things at once!* **b)** immediately: *He still looked the same, and I recognized him at once.*
5 all at once *formal* = suddenly: *All at once, I felt a pain in my leg.*
6 once again/more *formal* = again: *I tried once more to persuade him not to go.*
7 for once = used when something that happens is unusual: *For once, he was right.*
8 once and for all = completely and finally: *Let's settle this once and for all so we don't have to keep fighting about it.*
9 once upon a time = a long time ago. This is used at the beginning of children's stories

once[2] *conjunction*
after or when: *It's easy, once you learn how to do it.*

one[1] /wʌn/ *number*
1 1: *I have one brother and two sisters.* | *One of the windows was broken..*
2 one O'CLOCK: *I'll have to leave at one.*
3 one year old: *Katie's almost one.*
4 one or two *informal* = a few: *I have one or two things to do.*

one[2] *pronoun*
1 used instead of a noun when it is clear what kind of thing you mean: *"Do you have a bike?" "No, but I'm getting one for my birthday."* | *"Which candy bar do you want?" " That one."*
2 one by one/one after the other/one after another = first one person or thing, then the next, etc.: *One by one, people got off the bus.*
3 *formal* people in general: *One does not usually talk about one's health to strangers.*

one[3] *adjective*
1 one day/afternoon, etc. a) on a particular day, etc. in the past: *One day I got a call from my brother.* **b)** on some day, etc. in the future: *We should get together one evening.*
2 *formal* only: *My one goal is to do better in school.*

one•self /wʌn'self/ *pronoun, formal*
used when saying that people in general do something to themselves: *One must protect oneself.*

ˌone-ˈway *adjective*
1 moving or allowing movement in only one direction: *He was driving the wrong direction on a one-way street.*
2 a one-way ticket is for going from one place to another, but not back again

on•go•ing /ˈɔnˌgoʊɪŋ/ Ac *adjective, formal*
continuing: *The program is part of our ongoing anti-drug campaign that started ten years ago.*

on•ion /ˈʌnjən/ *noun*
a round vegetable with many white layers inside which has a strong taste and smell
➔ See picture on page A12

on•line *also* **on-line** /ˈɔnlaɪn/ *adjective, adverb*
using the Internet: *online shopping* | *I looked up the information online.*

on•ly[1] /ˈoʊnli/ *adverb*
1 not more than an amount or number: *Only five people came to the party.*
2 not anyone or anything else: *She eats only raw fruit and vegetables.* | *This room is for teachers only. Students aren't allowed.* SYNONYM **just**
3 not in any other way, not in any other situation, etc.: *You can only get there by boat. There are no roads to the area.* | *Eat only when you are hungry.* SYNONYM **just**
4 used for saying that something is not very important or serious: *Don't get upset – it's only a game.* SYNONYM **just**
5 if only = I wish: *If only I'd kept a copy of the letter! I'd love to read it again.*

only[2] *adjective*
1 used for saying that there is not more than one person or thing of a particular kind: *You're the only person I can trust.*
2 an only child = someone who has no brothers or sisters

only[3] *conjunction, informal*
but: *I'd help, only I'm really busy that day.*

ˈon-the-job *adjective*
on-the-job training is training you get while you are working

on·to /ˈɔntə; *before vowels* ˈɔntʊ; *strong* ˈɔntu/ *preposition*
used for showing what someone or something is on after moving: *He climbed onto the roof.*

on·ward /ˈɔnwɚd/ *also* **onwards** *adverb, formal*
1 from... onward = beginning at a particular time: *From the 1980s onward, the town got bigger.*
2 forward: *The ship sailed onward.*

ooh /u/
said when you like something, are excited, etc.: *Ooh, look at those cool shoes!*

oops /ʊps/
said when someone has fallen, dropped something, or made a small mistake: *Oops! I spilled some milk.*

ooze /uz/ *verb*
to flow from something very slowly: *Blood oozed from the cut on his knee.*
➔ See Thesaurus box at **pour**

o·paque /oʊˈpeɪk/ *adjective, formal*
impossible to see through: *You can buy special opaque glass for bathroom windows so no one can see in.* ANTONYM **clear, transparent**

o·pen[1] /ˈoʊpən/ *adjective*
1 not shut or closed: *Who left the window open? | I'm so tired I can't keep my eyes open.*
2 if a store, library, etc. is open, people can come in: *Is the library open today?*
3 if something is open to people of a particular kind, they can take part in it: *The competition is open to children aged 7 to 14.*
4 an open area is not surrounded or covered by tall things: *the wide open spaces of Nevada*
5 honest and not hiding anything: *Parents should try to be open with their children.*
➔ See picture at **ajar**

open[2] *verb*
1 to move something so that it is open, or to become open: *I opened my eyes and looked around. | The door opened, and Frank came in.* ANTONYM **close, shut**
2 when a store, library, etc. opens, people can then come in: *What time does the bookstore open on Sundays?* ANTONYM **close**
3 open an account = to start having a bank account

PHRASAL VERB
open up
1 open (something) up = to make something available, or to become available: *Education opens up all kinds of opportunities.*
2 to stop being shy and talk about your feelings

o·pen·er /ˈoʊpənɚ/ *noun*
a tool used for opening things: *a can opener*

o·pen·ing[1] /ˈoʊpənɪŋ/ *noun*
1 a time when people can start coming into a new store, library, etc.: *He invited them to the opening of his new restaurant.*
2 a hole in something that a person or thing can go through: *He went through a narrow opening in the fence.*
3 a job that is available: *Are there any openings at the store? I really need a job.*

opening[2] *adjective*
coming at the start of something: *The opening chapter of the book introduces all of the main characters.*

o·pen·ly /ˈoʊpənli/ *adverb*
not trying to hide anything: *They talk openly about their problems.*

op·era /ˈɑprə/ *noun*
a play in which the actors sing all the words: *Mozart wrote many famous operas.*

op·er·ate /ˈɑpəˌreɪt/ *verb*
1 *formal* when a machine operates it works: *Do you know how to operate this machine?*
2 to cut into someone's body in order to repair or remove a part that is damaged: *The doctors operated on her stomach.*

op·er·a·tion /ˌɑpəˈreɪʃən/ *noun*
1 the process of cutting into someone's body to repair or remove a part that is damaged: *He needs to have an operation on his knee.*
2 an organized set of actions by a number of people in order to achieve something: *The rescue operation was successful and all the people were saved.*

op·er·a·tor /ˈɑpəˌreɪtɚ/ *noun*
1 someone whose job is to connect telephone calls: *The hotel operator can connect your call.*
2 someone whose job is to use a machine or piece of equipment: *a crane operator*

O

O

o·pin·ion /ə'pɪnyən/ *noun*
what you think about something: *What's your opinion on school uniforms?* | *You did the right thing, in my opinion* (=I think you did).

o·pin·ion·at·ed /ə'pɪnyəˌneɪtɪd/ *adjective*
saying what you think too strongly: *He's very opinionated and thinks that everyone else is wrong.*

o·pos·sum /ə'pɑsəm/ *noun*
an American animal that looks like a large rat and can climb trees

op·po·nent /ə'poʊnənt/ *noun*
1 someone who tries to defeat someone else in a competition, game, or election: *The Dallas Cowboys easily beat their opponents.*
2 someone who disagrees with an idea or action: *Opponents of the plan spoke against it at the meeting.*

op·por·tu·ni·ty /ˌɑpɚ'tunəti/ *noun* plural **opportunities**
a chance to do something: *I was glad to have the opportunity to meet such a famous athlete.*

op·pose /ə'poʊz/ *verb*
to disagree with an idea or action: *They oppose the plan because they think it will cost too much money.*

WORD FAMILY look at the words:
→ **oppose** *verb*
→ **opposed** *adjective*
→ **opposition** *noun*

op·posed /ə'poʊzd/ *adjective*
be opposed to something = to disagree with an idea or action: *He was opposed to the war and joined the protest.*

op·pos·ing /ə'poʊzɪŋ/ *adjective*
opposing teams or groups are trying to defeat each other: *I think our team played better than the opposing team.*

op·po·site[1] /'ɑpəzɪt/ *adjective*
1 as different as possible: *I headed north, and he headed in the opposite direction* (=south).
2 the opposite side, end, or corner is the one that is farthest away: *We have to cross to the opposite side of the river.* SYNONYM **other**

opposite[2] *noun*
someone or something that is as different as possible from someone or something else: *Hot is the opposite of cold.*

op·po·si·tion /ˌɑpə'zɪʃən/ *noun*
strong disagreement with or protest against something: *There has been a lot of opposition to the changes.*

op·press /ə'pres/ *verb*
if people with power oppress other people, they treat them badly or do not let them do what they want: *The king oppressed the poor farmers.*
—**oppressive** *adjective* oppressing people: *an oppressive government*
—**oppressed** *adjective*: *oppressed minorities*
—**oppression** /ə'preʃən/ *noun* when people oppress other people

opt /ɑpt/ *verb, formal*
to choose to do or have one thing instead of another: *I opted for the apple pie.*

op·ti·cal /'ɑptɪkəl/ *adjective*
relating to seeing things: *One line looks longer than the other, but that is just an optical illusion* (=something that makes you think you are seeing something that you are not) – *they're the same length.*

op·ti·cian /ɑp'tɪʃən/ *noun*
someone who makes glasses
→ See picture on page A16

op·ti·mism /'ɑptəˌmɪzəm/ *noun*
a belief that good things will happen: *Because of her optimism, she was sure that things would get better.* ANTONYM **pessimism**

op·ti·mist /'ɑptəˌmɪst/ *noun*
someone who believes that good things will happen: *I'm an optimist, so I'm not worried about the future.* ANTONYM **pessimist**

op·ti·mist·ic /ˌɑptə'mɪstɪk/ *adjective*
believing that good things will happen: *I'm very optimistic about our chances of winning today.* ANTONYM **pessimistic**

op·tion /'ɑpʃən/ Ac *noun*
something that you can choose to do: *You have two options: you can come with us or stay here on your own.*

op·tion·al /'ɑpʃənəl/ Ac *adjective, formal*
if something is optional, you do not have to do it or have it: *Attendance at the meeting is optional, but most members will be there.* ANTONYM **mandatory**

op•tom•e•trist /ɑp'tɑmətrɪst/ *noun*
someone who tests people's eyes and orders glasses for them
—**optometry** /ɑp'tɑmətri/ *noun* the work of an optometrist

or /ɚ; *strong* ɔr/ *conjunction*
1 used when mentioning another possible thing: *On weekends, I usually play computer games or go to the park.*
2 used when mentioning another thing after "not," "never," etc.: *I don't like broccoli or peas.*
3 used when mentioning something bad that will happen if someone does not do something: *Hurry, or you'll be late!*

o•ral /'ɔrəl/ *adjective, formal*
1 spoken, not written: *You have to pass both a written test and an oral test.*
2 relating to the mouth: *oral cancer*
—**orally** *adverb*: *The medicine is taken orally.*

or•ange /'ɔrɪndʒ/ *noun*
1 a round juicy fruit that is a color between red and yellow and has a thick skin: *Do you want me to peel an orange for you?* | *orange juice*
2 the color of an orange
—**orange** *adjective*: *The sun was bright orange before it set.*
➔ See picture on page A13

or•bit[1] /'ɔrbɪt/ *noun*
the path of an object that is moving around another object in space: *the Moon's orbit around the Earth*

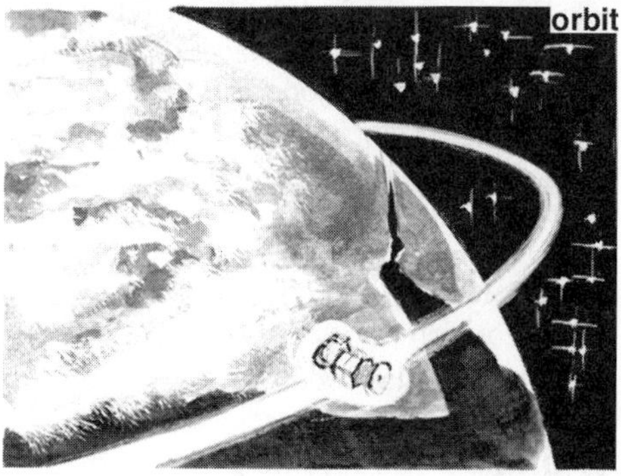

orbit

orbit[2] *verb*
to move around an object in space: *Many satellites now orbit the Earth.*

or•chard /'ɔrtʃɚd/ *noun*
a place where fruit trees are grown: *a cherry orchard*

or•ches•tra /'ɔrkɪstrə/ *noun*
a large group of musicians who play CLASSICAL MUSIC: *She plays the violin in the school orchestra.*

or•deal /ɔr'dil/ *noun, formal*
a very bad or difficult experience: *We wanted to avoid the ordeal of another trial.*

O

or•der[1] /'ɔrdɚ/ *noun*
1 in order to do something = so that you can do something: *I came here in order to see you.*
2 the way that you arrange things or put them on a list: *Write the names in alphabetical order* (=starting with names beginning with A).
3 something that you ask for from a business or in a restaurant: *The waiter came and took our order.* | *Your order will be ready soon.*
4 something that someone in authority tells you to do: *Soldiers must obey orders.* SYNONYM **command**
5 out of order = if a machine is out of order, it is not working: *The phone was out of order, so I couldn't call you.*
6 a situation in which people obey rules and do not behave violently: *When there were riots, the police soon restored order.*
➔ See Thesaurus box at **ask**

order[2] *verb*
1 to ask for something from a business or in a restaurant: *They ordered a new carpet for the bedroom.* | *Are you ready to order* (=said by a waiter or waitress in a restaurant)?
2 to tell someone to do something: *The police officer ordered him to stop.*

or•der•ly /'ɔrdɚli/ *adjective, formal*
arranged or organized in a neat way: *We arranged the seats in orderly rows.*

or•di•nal num•ber /ˌɔrdn-əl 'nʌmbɚ/ *noun*
a word that shows where something comes in a series: *"First," "second," "third," etc. are ordinal numbers.*

or•di•nar•i•ly /ˌɔrdn'erəli/ *adverb*
usually: *Ordinarily, I leave the house at 8:00, but today I left at 9:00.*

or•di•nar•y /'ɔrdnˌeri/ *adjective*
1 not different or special in any way: *It was just an ordinary day – nothing unusual happened.*
2 out of the ordinary = unusual: *Did you*

notice anything out of the ordinary?
→ See Thesaurus box at **normal**

ore /ɔr/ *noun*
rock or earth that people can get metal from: *The country exports iron ore.*

O

or•gan /ˈɔrgən/ *noun*
1 a part of your body that has a particular purpose: *The heart is the organ that makes blood move around your body.*
2 a musical instrument like a piano but with long pipes, or an electric instrument that makes similar sounds: *She plays the organ for the church.*
—**organist** *noun* someone who plays the organ

or•gan•ic /ɔrˈgænɪk/ *adjective*
1 grown or produced without using chemicals: *organic vegetables*
2 *formal* relating to living things: *You can improve your soil by adding organic matter such as leaves and grass.*
—**organically** *adverb*

or•ga•nism /ˈɔrgəˌnɪzəm/ *noun, formal*
a living thing, especially a very small one: *Pond water contains many organisms.*

or•ga•ni•za•tion /ˌɔrgənəˈzeɪʃən/ *noun*
1 a group of people such as a club or business: *I belong to several environmental organizations.*
2 the way in which something is organized: *Good organization makes your work easier.*

or•ga•nize /ˈɔrgəˌnaɪz/ *verb*
1 to put people or things into an order or system: *Can you help me organize these books?*
2 to plan an activity or event: *Who is organizing the party?*
—**organizer** *noun* someone who organizes something

WORD FAMILY look at the words:
→ **organize** *verb*
→ **organizer** *noun*
→ **organized** *adjective*
→ **disorganized** *adjective*
→ **organization** *noun*

or•ga•nized /ˈɔrgəˌnaɪzd/ *adjective*
1 planned or arranged carefully: *The book is well organized – it's easy to find the information you need.* ANTONYM **disorganized**
2 an organized person plans and arranges things carefully: *Debbie always does a good job. She's very organized.* ANTONYM **disorganized**
3 involving a group of people doing something together: *organized religion*

o•ri•ent•ed /ˈɔriˌentɪd/ Ac *adjective*
1 family-oriented / customer-oriented / goal-oriented, etc. = caring most about families, customers, etc.: *He's very goal-oriented and is always thinking about his future.*
2 get oriented = to become used to a new situation: *It always takes new students a few weeks to get oriented.*

or•i•gin /ˈɔrədʒɪn/ *noun*
1 the start of something: *There are different ideas about the origin of the universe, but no one knows for sure how it started.*
2 the place or group of people that someone comes from: *Many of the students are of Hispanic origin and speak Spanish at home.*

WORD FAMILY look at the words:
→ **origin** *noun*
→ **original** *adjective*
→ **originally** *adverb*

o•rig•i•nal /əˈrɪdʒɪnəl/ *adjective*
1 first: *Our original plan was to go to Florida, but then we decided to go to Yellowstone.*
2 new and different: *The book is very interesting and contains a lot of original ideas.*
3 not copied: *an original painting*
→ See Thesaurus box at **new**

o•rig•i•nal•ly /əˈrɪdʒɪnəli/ *adverb*
in the beginning: *I'm originally from Texas, but I've lived in Oregon for 10 years.*

or•na•ment /ˈɔrnəmənt/ *noun*
a beautiful object that you show in your home or use to decorate something: *We hung the ornaments on the Christmas tree.*
—**ornamental** /ˌɔrnəˈmentl/ *adjective* used as decoration

or•phan /ˈɔrfən/ *noun*
a child whose parents are dead

or•phan•age /ˈɔrfənɪdʒ/ *noun*
a home for children whose parents are dead

or•tho•dox /ˈɔrθəˌdɑks/ *adjective*
1 Orthodox = following the traditional beliefs of a religion: *an Orthodox Jew*
2 accepted by most people as correct or normal: *His orthodox approach to teaching*

is not very exciting, but it has been very successful.

os•trich /ˈɑstrɪtʃ/ *noun*
a very large African bird with long legs that runs fast but cannot fly

oth•er /ˈʌðɚ/ *adjective, pronoun*
1 the person, people, thing, or things in the rest of a group: *Here's one sock, but where's the other one?* | *His left hand was empty, but there was something in his other hand.* | *We're the only ones here – it looks like all the others have left.*
2 different things or people of the same kind: *Does anyone have any other questions?* | *Some computers are better than others.* SYNONYM **additional**
3 the other day = recently: *I saw Rosie the other day.*
4 other than = except for something: *Did you get anything other than lettuce in your salad?* SYNONYM **besides**
5 every other day/week, etc. = every two days, weeks, etc.: *The class meets every other Thursday.*
6 someone/something, etc. or other = used when you are not certain about something: *We'll get the money somehow or other.*
→ **each other**

oth•er•wise /ˈʌðɚˌwaɪz/ *adverb*
1 used when mentioning something bad that will happen if someone does not do something: *You have to put the fish back in the water; otherwise, it'll die.* SYNONYM **or else**
2 if the situation had been different: *Our flight was delayed. Otherwise, we would have gotten here sooner.*
3 except for what has just been mentioned: *The sleeves are too long, but otherwise the dress fits.*

ot•ter /ˈɑtɚ/ *noun*
a small animal with brown fur that eats fish and can swim

ouch /aʊtʃ/
said when you suddenly feel pain: *Ouch! That hurt!*

ought to /ˈɔtə; *strong* ˈɔtu/ *verb*
1 used for saying that someone should do something: *It's a great place – you ought to go there.* SYNONYM **should**
2 used for saying that you expect something to happen or be true: *He's really smart – he ought to be able to get a job pretty easily.* SYNONYM **should**

ounce /aʊns/ *noun, written abbreviation* **oz.**
a unit for measuring weight, equal to 28.35 grams: *There are 16 ounces in a pound.*

our /aʊɚ/ *adjective*
belonging to us: *Our house is very small.*

ours /aʊɚz/ *pronoun*
something that belongs to us: *"Whose car is that?" "It's ours."*

our•selves /aʊɚˈselvz/ *pronoun*
1 used for saying that we are affected by something that we do: *It was strange seeing ourselves on television.*
2 used for emphasizing that we did something: *We did all the work ourselves.*
3 (all) by ourselves = alone or without help: *Amy and I made supper all by ourselves.*

out /aʊt/ *adverb, adjective, preposition*
1 away from the inside of a place or container: *She went out into the yard.* | *The keys must have fallen out of my pocket.* | *He put his head out the window and looked around.* ANTONYM **in**
2 not at home or in the office where you work: *Did anyone call while I was out?* ANTONYM **in**
3 if a light is out or the electricity supply is out, it is not working: *The lights are out – I don't think anyone's home.*
4 able to be seen: *The rain stopped and the sun came out.*
5 a player who is out cannot play anymore in that game: *I caught the ball, so you're out.*
6 out of something = if you are out of something, you do not have any of it left: *We need to find a gas station soon – the car's almost out of gas.*
7 two out of three/three out of four, etc. = used for talking about part of a group: *Three out of four students think the test is too hard* (=¾ of the students think this).

out•bound /ˈaʊtbaʊnd/ *adjective*
outbound planes, trains, cars, etc. are going away from a place: *All outbound flights were delayed by the snow.* ANTONYM **inbound**

out•break /ˈaʊtbreɪk/ *noun, formal*
the start of something bad such as a war or

O

disease: *People left the country quickly at the outbreak of war.*

out·burst /ˈaʊtbɚst/ *noun*
a sudden expression of a strong emotion: *She found her father's angry outbursts very frightening.*

out·come /ˈaʊtkʌm/ Ac *noun*
the final result of something: *Did his injury change the outcome of the game?*
→ See Thesaurus box at **result**[1]

out·dat·ed /ˌaʊtˈdeɪtɪd/ *adjective*
old and no longer useful: *The textbooks are outdated and need to be replaced.*

out·do /aʊtˈdu/ *verb* **outdid** /aʊtˈdɪd/ **outdone** /aʊtˈdʌn/ third person singular **outdoes** /aʊtˈdʌz/
to be better or more successful than someone else: *The skaters were trying to outdo each other by doing more and more difficult turns.*

out·door /ˈaʊtdɔr/ *adjective*
happening or used outside: *The motel has an outdoor swimming pool.* ANTONYM **indoor**

out·doors /ˌaʊtˈdɔrz/ *adverb*
outside, not in a building: *It's a nice day – let's play outdoors.* ANTONYM **indoors**

out·er /ˈaʊtɚ/ *adjective*
on or near the outside of something: *Take off the cabbage's outer leaves.* ANTONYM **inner**

ˌouter ˈspace *noun*
the area outside the Earth's air, where the stars and PLANETs are: *The animal is so strange, it looks like a creature from outer space.*

out·field /ˈaʊtfild/ *noun*
the part of a baseball field that is farthest from the player who is BATting

out·fit /ˈaʊtˌfɪt/ *noun*
a set of clothes that you wear together: *She bought a new outfit for the party.*

out·go·ing /ˈaʊtˌgoʊɪŋ/ *adjective*
someone who is outgoing enjoys meeting and talking to people: *Sally is really outgoing and easy to talk to.* SYNONYM **friendly**
→ See Thesaurus box at **shy**

out·grow /aʊtˈgroʊ/ *verb* **outgrew** /aʊtˈgru/ **outgrown** /aʊtˈgroʊn/
if children outgrow their clothes, they grow too big for them: *Kara's already outgrown her shoes. We'll have to buy her a new pair.*

out·ing /ˈaʊtɪŋ/ *noun*
a short trip in which you go somewhere for fun: *a family outing to the beach*

out·last /aʊtˈlæst/ *verb*
to continue to exist or do something longer than something or someone else: *Some of the stuff we throw away, such as plastic bags, will outlast us by many years.*

out·law[1] /ˈaʊtlɔ/ *verb*
to say that something is illegal or not allowed: *The new law would outlaw cigarette machines.*

outlaw[2] *noun*
used in the past to mean a criminal who is hiding from the police: *the outlaws of the Wild West*

out·let /ˈaʊtlet/ *noun*
1 a place on a wall where you can connect things to the electricity supply: *The room only had one electrical outlet, so that's where we had to plug in the TV.*
2 *also* **outlet store** a store that sells things for less than the usual price: *I got these jeans at one of the outlet stores for $20.*

out·line /ˈaʊtlaɪn/ *noun*
1 a list of the main ideas or facts about something which shows the order that you will use when you talk or write about them: *Write an outline of your paper first to help organize your ideas.*
2 if you can see the outline of something, you can see its shape, but you cannot clearly see any other parts of it: *We could see the outline of the Statue of Liberty against the sky as it got dark.*

out·look /ˈaʊtlʊk/ *noun*
1 what people expect to happen in the future: *The outlook for people with this disease is good if they are treated early.*
2 the way you think about life and what happens to you: *Neil has a very positive outlook; he believes that everything that has happened to him has been good for him.*

ˌout-of-ˈdate *adjective*
another word for OUTDATED

out·pa·tient /ˈaʊtˌpeɪʃənt/ *adjective*
relating to someone who goes to the hospital for treatment from a doctor, but does not stay there for very long: *She went to an outpatient clinic for treatment for her fever.*
—**outpatient** *noun* someone who goes to

the hospital for treatment from a doctor, but does not stay there for very long

out•put /ˈaʊtpʊt/ Ac *noun, formal*
the amount of goods or work that a company or country produces: *The company has increased its output of computers.* SYNONYM **production**

out•rage /ˈaʊtreɪdʒ/ *noun*
1 a strong feeling of anger or shock: *The murder of the little girl caused outrage in the neighborhood.*
2 something that causes a strong feeling of anger and shock: *It is an outrage that people here do not have enough to eat.*

out•ra•geous /aʊtˈreɪdʒəs/ *adjective*
1 something that is outrageous is very wrong, and makes you feel very shocked and angry: *He told some really outrageous lies that really made me angry.*
2 very unusual or strange, but in a way that people like: *She wears very unusual clothes, and I love her outrageous hats*
—**outrageously** *adverb*: *The shoes were outrageously expensive.*

out•right[1] /ˈaʊtraɪt/ *adjective*
complete and very clear: *I couldn't believe he was telling me an outright lie.*

out•right[2] /aʊtˈraɪt/ *adverb*
1 clearly and directly: *Nadine laughed outright at the suggestion.*
2 buy/own something outright = to own something such as a house completely because you have paid the full price with your own money

out•set /ˈaʊtset/ *noun*
at/from the outset = at or from the beginning: *It was clear from the outset of the game that the other team would win.*

out•side[1] /ˌaʊtˈsaɪd/ *also* **outˈside of** *adverb, preposition*
1 not inside a building or room, but near it: *Mom, can I go outside and play? | She waited for him outside of his office.* ANTONYM **inside**
2 not in a city or country, but near it: *They live just outside Seattle* (=outside Seattle but very near it).
3 not in a group or organization: *Don't talk about this to anyone outside the family.*

outside[2] *adjective*
not inside a building: *We turned off the outside lights after our guest left.* ANTONYM **inside**

outside[3] *noun*
the outside = the outer part or surface of something: *They painted the outside of the building pink.* ANTONYM **inside**

out•sid•er /aʊtˈsaɪdɚ/ *noun*
someone who does not belong to a particular group, organization, etc.: *Lisa was new at the school and felt like an outsider.*

out•skirts /ˈaʊtskɚts/ *noun*
the parts of a city or town that are far away from the center: *The car sales place is on the outskirts of town.*

out•spo•ken /aʊtˈspoʊkən/ *adjective*
an outspoken person says what he or she thinks, even when it may shock people or make them angry: *Lang is an outspoken critic of the war and has given many speeches against it.*

out•stand•ing /aʊtˈstændɪŋ/ *adjective*
better than anyone or anything else: *Nikki is an outstanding basketball player – she's one of our best scorers.* SYNONYM **excellent**
➔ See Thesaurus box at **good**[1]

out•ward[1] /ˈaʊtwɚd/ *adjective*
1 relating to how someone seems to feel or think, when this might be different from what that person really feels or thinks: *I waited for his expression to change, but there were no outward signs that he was upset.* ANTONYM **inward**
2 going away from a place or toward the outside: *The outward flight was bumpy, but the trip back was fine.* SYNONYM **outbound**

outward[2] *also* **outwards** *adverb*
toward the outside of something, or away from the middle: *The person in the middle of the circle moves outward to the edge of the circle.* ANTONYM **inward**

out•weigh /aʊtˈweɪ/ *verb, formal*
to be more important or have more effect than something else: *The benefits of the new cancer drug outweigh the risks.*

o•val /ˈoʊvəl/ *noun*
a shape that is like a circle, but longer than it is wide
—**oval** *adjective*: *an oval table*
➔ See picture at **shape**[1]

O

ˌOval ˈOffice *noun*
the Oval Office = the office where the president of the U.S. works, in the White House in Washington, D.C.

o•va•ry /ˈoʊvəri/ *noun* plural **ovaries** *formal*
the part of a woman's body or a female animal's body that produces eggs

ov•en /ˈʌvən/ *noun*
a piece of equipment that you cook food inside, shaped like a metal box with a door on it. An oven is usually part of a STOVE: *Bake the cake in the oven for 30 minutes.* | *Set the oven temperature to 400 degrees.*
➔ See picture on page A9

o•ver¹ /ˈoʊvɚ/ *preposition*
1 above or higher than something: *I leaned over the desk.* | *The sign over the door said "Exit."* ANTONYM **under**
2 moving across the top of something, or from one side of it to the other: *We walked over the hill.* | *The dog jumped over the fence.* ANTONYM **under**
3 covering someone or something: *I put the blanket over the baby.* ANTONYM **under**
4 more than an amount, number, or age: *Over a hundred people came to the school play.* | *The game is for children over seven years old.* ANTONYM **under**
5 during: *Where did you go over summer vacation?*
6 all over = everywhere in a place: *Why are your clothes all over the floor?*
7 be/get over something = to feel better after being sick, upset, or angry: *I can't seem to get over this cold.*

over² *adverb*
1 down from an upright position: *Do you remember when that big tree fell over?* | *I knocked over a glass.*
2 used for showing where someone or something is, when you can point to it: *I'm over here!* | *There's a mailbox over on the corner.*
3 to or in a place: *Can I go over to Scott's house to play?*
4 again: *I got confused and had to start over.* | *She just keeps saying the same thing over and over.*
5 so that another side is showing: *Turn the test over and start writing.* | *He rolled over in bed and faced the wall.*
6 think/read/talk something over = to think, read, or talk about something carefully before deciding what to do: *I might go to summer school, but I need to talk it over with my mom first.*
7 above: *A helicopter flew over.*
8 more than a particular amount, number, or age: *a game for children ages six and over* (=six years old and older) ANTONYM **under**

over³ *adjective*
1 finished: *The game's over – Dallas won.*
➔ See Thesaurus box at **done²**
2 get something over with *informal* = to do something that you do not want to do, so that it is finished: *You have to tell her you're sorry, so call her and get it over with.*

o•ver•all /ˌoʊvɚˈɔl/ Ac *adjective, formal*
including everything: *The overall cost of the trip is $500, including food, hotel, and transportation.*

o•ver•alls /ˈoʊvɚˌɔlz/ *plural noun*
pants with a square piece that covers your chest attached, held up by two pieces of cloth that go over your shoulders
➔ See picture on page A6

o•ver•board /ˈoʊvɚˌbɔrd/ *adverb*
1 over the side of a boat into the water: *He fell overboard into the lake during the storm.*
2 go overboard = to do or say something that is too extreme for the situation: *Don't go overboard and put on too much makeup.*

o•ver•cast /ˈoʊvɚˌkæst/ *adjective*
if the sky is overcast, it is dark and cloudy

o•ver•charge /ˌoʊvɚˈtʃɑrdʒ/ *verb*
to make someone pay too much money for something: *I think the restaurant overcharged us – the bill seems way too high.*

o•ver•coat /ˈoʊvɚˌkoʊt/ *noun*
a long warm coat that you wear over other clothes

o•ver•come /ˌoʊvɚˈkʌm/ *verb* **overcame** /ˌoʊvɚˈkeɪm/ **overcome** *formal*
to succeed in controlling a feeling or solving a problem: *The city has to overcome some serious transportation problems.*

o•ver•crowd•ed /ˌoʊvɚˈkraʊdɪd/ *adjective*
a place that is overcrowded has too many people or things in it: *The room was overcrowded, and I couldn't find a chair to sit in.*

o•ver•do /ˌoʊvɚˈdu/ *verb* **overdid** /ˌoʊvɚˈdɪd/ **overdone** /ˌoʊvɚˈdʌn/ third person singular **overdoes** /ˌoʊvɚˈdʌz/
to do or use too much of something: *It's good to exercise, but don't overdo it.*

o•ver•dose /ˈoʊvɚˌdoʊs/ *noun*
too much of a drug taken at one time: *He died from a heroin overdose.*
—**overdose** *verb* to take too much of a drug at one time

o•ver•due /ˌoʊvɚˈdu/ *adjective*
late in arriving or late in being done: *My library books are overdue; I was supposed to return them last week.* SYNONYM **late**

o•ver•es•ti•mate /ˌoʊvɚˈestəˌmeɪt/ Ac *verb, formal*
to think that something is bigger, longer, more important, etc. than it really is: *I overestimated the distance to the school; it was only a mile, not three miles.*

o•ver•flow /ˌoʊvɚˈfloʊ/ *verb*
if something overflows, liquid or objects fill it completely and come over its edge: *The toilet's overflowing! How do I turn off the water?*

o•ver•grown /ˌoʊvɚˈgroʊn/ *adjective*
covered with plants that have grown without being cut: *Their yard was overgrown with weeds.*

o•ver•head /ˌoʊvɚˈhed/ *adjective, adverb*
above your head: *A plane flew overhead, and the animals looked up.*

o•ver•hear /ˌoʊvɚˈhɪr/ *verb* **overheard** /ˌoʊvɚˈhɚd/
to hear what other people are saying by accident, when they do not know that you are listening: *I overheard my parents arguing downstairs.*

o•ver•lap /ˌoʊvɚˈlæp/ Ac *verb* **overlapped, overlapping** *formal*
if two or more things overlap, part of one thing covers part of another thing: *Draw two circles that overlap, and color in the area that they share.*

o•ver•load•ed /ˌoʊvɚˈloʊdɪd/ *adjective*
if someone is overloaded, they have too many things to do or think about: *Our teachers are already overloaded; they don't need more work to do.*
—**overload** *verb* to give someone or something too many things to do

o•ver•look /ˌoʊvɚˈlʊk/ *verb, formal*
1 to not see or notice something: *It's easy to overlook mistakes in your own writing.*
2 to have a view of something from above: *Three of the windows overlook the street.*

o•ver•night /ˌoʊvɚˈnaɪt/ *adverb*
for or during the night: *She's staying overnight at a friend's house.*

o•ver•pass /ˈoʊvɚˌpæs/ *noun*
a part of a road that is like a bridge going over another road: *They drove over the overpass that crosses Market Street.*

o•ver•pow•er•ing /ˌoʊvɚˈpaʊərɪŋ/ *adjective, formal*
very strong: *The smell of garbage was overpowering.*

o•ver•rat•ed /ˌoʊvɚˈreɪtɪd/ *adjective, formal*
not as good as some people say: *I think he's overrated as a player. He's not that great.*

o•ver•seas /ˌoʊvɚˈsiz/ Ac *adjective, adverb*
to or in a country that is across the ocean: *Her dad got a job overseas, so they're moving to Europe.*

o•ver•shad•ow /ˌoʊvɚˈʃædoʊ/ *verb, formal*
to make someone seem less important: *Lori's older sister had always overshadowed her at school; she got better grades and was better at sports than Lori was.*

o•ver•sleep /ˌoʊvɚˈslip/ *verb* **overslept** /ˌoʊvɚˈslept/
to sleep for longer than you planned to: *I overslept and was late for class.*
→ See Thesaurus box at **sleep**[1]

ˌover-the-ˈcounter *adjective*
over-the-counter medicines are ones that you can buy without seeing a doctor first: *You can buy over-the-counter pain relievers without a prescription.*

o•ver•throw /ˌoʊvɚˈθroʊ/ *verb* **overthrew** /ˌoʊvɚˈθru/ **overthrown** /ˌoʊvɚˈθroʊn/ *formal*
to remove a leader or government from power by using force: *Rebels are trying to overthrow the government.*

O

o·ver·time /ˈoʊvɚˌtaɪm/ *noun*
1 extra hours that someone works in their job, in addition to the normal number of hours they work in a week: *We had to work overtime to fix the computer problems.*
2 a period added to the end of a sports game to give one of the two teams a chance to win: *The two teams were tied, so the game went into overtime.*

o·ver·turn /ˌoʊvɚˈtɚn/ *verb, formal*
if something overturns, it turns upside down or falls on its side: *The bottle overturned and spilled the juice everywhere.* | *He overturned a table to stop the men that were chasing him.*

o·ver·view /ˈoʊvɚˌvyu/ *noun*
a short description of something that gives the main ideas but not the details: *This article gives a good overview of the situation in the Middle East.*

o·ver·weight /ˌoʊvɚˈweɪt/ *adjective*
too fat: *He was 20 pounds overweight and the doctor told him to eat less and start exercising.*
➔ See Thesaurus box at **fat**[1]

o·ver·whelm·ing /ˌoʊvɚˈwelmɪŋ/ *adjective*
1 an overwhelming feeling is very strong: *After his sister's death, Jon felt overwhelming sadness.*
2 if there is an overwhelming number or amount of something, it is a big number or there is a lot of it: *There was overwhelming evidence that he was guilty of the crime* (=there was a lot of evidence).
—**overwhelmingly** *adverb*

owe /oʊ/ *verb*
1 if you owe someone money, you need to give money back to him or her because you borrowed it from him or her: *Bob owes me $20 that he borrowed from me last week.*
2 to feel that you should do something for someone because they have done something for you: *Jane will watch the kids – she owes me a favor* (=you did something for her, so she will feel she needs to do something for you).

owl /aʊl/ *noun*
a bird that hunts at night and has large eyes

own[1] /oʊn/ *adjective, pronoun*
1 belonging to a particular person: *Jeff has his own car.* | *You must make your own decision.*
2 (all) on your own = without anyone with you or helping you: *Did you write this story on your own?* | *You can't leave young kids on their own. It's not safe.*

own[2] *verb*
if you own something, it belongs to you: *The city owns the buildings.*

THESAURUS: own

have to own something: *Do you have a bike?*

belong to someone if something belongs to you, you own it: *The ring belonged to my grandmother.*

possess *formal* to own or have something: *He was arrested for possessing explosives.*

PHRASAL VERB
own up
to admit that you did something wrong: *He'll never own up to his mistakes.*

own·er /ˈoʊnɚ/ *noun*
someone who owns something: *He's the owner of the restaurant, so he makes all the big decisions.*
—**ownership** *noun* the fact of owning something: *Home ownership is very important to many people.*

ox /ɑks/ *noun* plural **oxen** /ˈɑksən/
a male cow that has had part of its sex organs cut off, and that farmers used in the past for farm work: *The two oxen pulled the plow.*

ox·y·gen /ˈɑksɪdʒən/ *noun, written abbreviation* **O**
a gas in the air that all plants and animals need in order to live: *As you breathe, your lungs send the oxygen into your blood.*

oys·ter /ˈɔɪstɚ/ *noun*
a small sea animal that has a shell and can produce a jewel called a PEARL

oz.
the written abbreviation of **ounce**

o·zone lay·er /ˈoʊzoʊn ˌleɪɚ/ *noun*
a layer of gases around the Earth that stops a type of heat from the sun from harming the Earth

Pp

pace[1] /peɪs/ *noun*
how quickly you do something, or how quickly something happens: *We walked up the hill at a fast pace so we were breathing hard when we got to the top.*

pace[2] *verb*
to walk first in one direction and then in another, when you are waiting or worried about something: *Darren paced back and forth in the hospital waiting room.*

Pa•cif•ic O•cean /pəˌsɪfɪk ˈoʊʃən/ *noun*
the Pacific Ocean, **the Pacific** = the large ocean between Asia and Australia in the west, and North and South America in the east

pac•i•fi•er /ˈpæsəˌfaɪə/ *noun*
a plastic or rubber object that a baby sucks on so that he or she does not cry

pac•i•fist /ˈpæsəfɪst/ *noun, formal*
someone who believes that wars and violence are wrong
—**pacifism** *noun* the belief that wars and violence are wrong

pack[1] /pæk/ *verb*
1 *also* **pack up** to put things into boxes or bags so you can take them somewhere: *Mr. Levy packed his suitcase and left for the airport.*
2 if a crowd of people packs a place, there are so many people that the place is full: *50,000 fans packed the stadium.*

PHRASAL VERB
pack up
informal to put things into boxes or bags and get ready to leave: *In the morning I packed up my things.*
—**packing** *noun* the act of putting things into boxes or bags so that you can take them somewhere: *Have you done your packing yet?*

pack[2] *noun*
1 a small box or paper that holds a set of things: *a pack of gum*
2 a set of things that are put or tied together, to make them easy to carry or sell: *a six-pack of soda*
3 a group of wild animals that live and hunt together: *a wolf pack*
4 a BACKPACK
→ See Thesaurus box at **group**[1]

pack•age /ˈpækɪdʒ/ *noun*

package

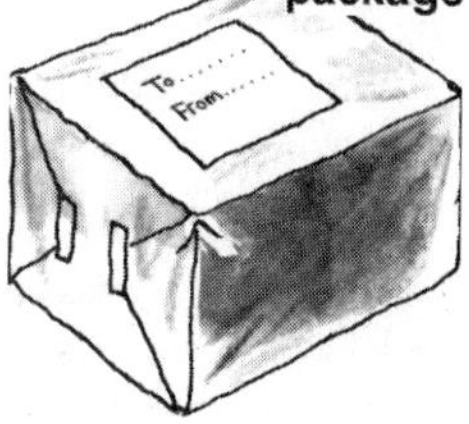

1 a box, bag, etc. that holds food or other things so they can be sold: *I bought two packages of cookies.*
2 something that you have wrapped in paper or put in a box or bag so that you can mail it: *Did you mail that package at the post office?*
3 a group of things or services that are being sold or given together: *The cable TV company offers a 31-channel package.*
—**package** *verb* to put something into a box or bag, ready to be sold or sent somewhere

pack•ag•ing /ˈpækɪdʒɪŋ/ *noun*
the box or paper that something is sold in: *The toy's packaging is colorful.*

packed /pækt/ *adjective*
full of people or things: *The theater was packed and we couldn't find seats.*
→ See Thesaurus box at **full**

pack•et /ˈpækɪt/ *noun*
an envelope that holds something: *a packet of seeds*

pact /pækt/ *noun, formal*
an agreement between two groups, countries, or people: *The U.S. signed a trade pact with Canada.*

pad /pæd/ *noun*
1 many sheets of paper fastened together at one edge: *He wrote the message on a pad of paper near the phone.*
2 a thick piece of soft material that makes something softer or more comfortable: *A football player was putting his shoulder pads on.* | *Use a mouse pad under your computer's mouse so you don't scratch the desk.*

pad•ded /ˈpædɪd/ *adjective*
covered or filled with a soft material: *a soft padded chair*
—**pad** *verb* to cover or fill something with a

soft material
—**padding** *noun* material that fills or covers something to make it softer or more comfortable

pad•dle[1] /ˈpædl/ *noun*
a short pole with a wide flat end, that you use to move a small boat across water

P

paddle[2] *verb*
to move a small boat across water, using a paddle: *They paddled up the river in their canoes.*

pad•lock /ˈpædlɑk/ *noun*
a lock with a curved bar at the top that you can put on a door, bicycle, etc.: *He unlocked the padlock on the gate.*

page /peɪdʒ/ *noun*
1 one side of a sheet of paper in a book, newspaper, etc.: *The book has 147 pages.* | *Do the exercises on page 10 for homework.*
2 all the writing and pictures that you can see at one time on a computer screen: *a web page*

pag•eant /ˈpædʒənt/ *noun*
a competition for women in which people judge them by how beautiful they are: *She is a beautiful young woman and has won several beauty pageants.*

paid /peɪd/ *verb*
the past tense and past participle of PAY

pail /peɪl/ *noun*
1 a container that is open at the top and has a handle, that you use to carry something such as water, sand, etc.: *He had a pail of water to wash the car with.* SYNONYM **bucket**
2 a container you use to carry or hold something: *a garbage pail*

pain /peɪn/ *noun*
1 the feeling you have when part of your body hurts: *He was in terrible pain* (=feeling pain). | *There was a sharp pain in his chest.* | *At first I didn't feel any pain, but then it really started to hurt.*
2 a feeling of unhappiness when something bad has happened: *Parents can help children deal with the pain of divorce.*
3 be a pain (in the neck/butt) *informal* = to be very annoying: *My brother's a real pain sometimes.*

WORD FAMILY look at the words:
→ **pain** *noun*
→ **painful** *adjective*
→ **painless** *adjective*

pain•ful /ˈpeɪnfəl/ *adjective*
1 making part of your body hurt: *a painful injury* | *After I fell on the ice, it was painful to walk.* ANTONYM **painless**
2 making you feel unhappy: *The memories were too painful to talk about.*
—**painfully** *adverb*
—**painfulness** *noun*

pain•kill•er /ˈpeɪnˌkɪlɚ/ *noun*
a medicine that stops you from feeling too much pain

pain•less /ˈpeɪnləs/ *adjective*
causing no pain: *Dentists try to make fixing your teeth as painless as possible.* ANTONYM **painful**

pains•tak•ing /ˈpeɪnzˌteɪkɪŋ/ *adjective, formal*
done very carefully: *Repairing the old paintings is painstaking work.*
—**painstakingly** *adverb*

paint[1] /peɪnt/ *noun*
a colored liquid that you use to cover surfaces or make pictures: *Mix yellow and blue paint to make green paint.* | *The kitchen needs a fresh coat of paint* (=layer of paint).

paint[2] *verb*
1 to put paint on a surface: *How much will it cost to paint the house?*
2 to make a picture using paint: *We painted pictures of our families in art class today.*

paint•brush /ˈpeɪntbrʌʃ/ *noun*
a special brush used for painting
→ See picture at **brush**

paint•er /ˈpeɪntɚ/ *noun*
1 someone who paints pictures: *Picasso was a famous painter.* SYNONYM **artist**
2 someone whose job is painting houses, rooms, etc.: *The painters are coming Tuesday to paint the garage.*
→ See picture on page A16

paint•ing /ˈpeɪntɪŋ/ *noun*
a painted picture: *a painting of the mountains*
→ See Thesaurus box at **art**

pair /per/ *noun* plural **pairs** or **pair**
1 two things of the same kind that are used together: *a pair of socks*
2 something made of two parts that are joined together: *a pair of scissors* | *a pair of jeans* | *He got a new pair of glasses.*
3 two people who are standing or doing something together: *The kids were working in pairs* (=in groups of two).

pa•ja•mas /pə'dʒɑməz/ *plural noun*
soft pants and a shirt that you wear in bed: *He put on his pajamas and got into bed.*

pal /pæl/ *noun, informal*
a friend: *Okay, pal. See you later.*

pal•ace /'pælɪs/ *noun*
a large house where a king or queen lives: *In England, the queen lives in Buckingham Palace.*
—**palatial** /pə'leɪʃəl/ *adjective, formal* a palatial house or building is very large

pal•ate /'pælɪt/ *noun, formal*
the hard top part inside your mouth

pale /peɪl/ *adjective*
1 someone who is pale looks white because they are sick or frightened: *Ellie has a fever and is very pale.*
2 a pale color is very light: *a pale blue shirt*
—**paleness** *noun*

palm /pɑm/ *noun*
1 the flat part of the inside of your hand, between your fingers and your wrist: *The camera was so small it fit in the palm of his hand.*
2 another word for a PALM TREE
➔ See picture at **hand**[1]

palm tree

'palm tree *noun*
a tree that grows in warm places. It has pointed leaves at the top and no branches: *Tall palm trees grew near the beach.*

pam•per /'pæmpɚ/ *verb, formal*
to give someone a lot of care and attention, in a way that is bad for him or her: *She was an only child, and her parents pampered her.*

pam•phlet /'pæmflɪt/ *noun*
a very thin book with a paper cover, that gives information about something: *a pamphlet about the dangers of using drugs*

pan /pæn/ *noun*
1 a metal container that you cook food in, and that often has a handle: *a large pan of boiling water* | *Heat the oil in the frying pan.* | *Pour the batter into a cake pan.*
2 a container with low sides, used for holding liquids: *a car's oil pan*

pan•cake /'pænkeɪk/ *noun*
a flat round type of bread made from flour, milk, and eggs that is cooked in a pan on top of the STOVE: *Do you want pancakes with maple syrup for breakfast?*

pan•da /'pændə/ *noun*
a large black and white animal, similar to a bear, that lives in China

pane /peɪn/ *noun*
a piece of glass in a window or door: *He hit the ball and broke one of the window panes.*

pan•el /'pænl/ Ac *noun*
1 a group of people who are chosen to talk about or decide something: *Reporters and politicians are on the panel to discuss the changes.*
2 a flat sheet of wood, glass, etc. that forms part of a door, wall, or ceiling: *a door with three wooden panels*
3 instrument/control panel = the place in an airplane, boat, or spacecraft that has the controls and things that give you information about your speed, etc.: *The pilot looked at his instrument panel to check the speed of the plane.*

pan•ic[1] /'pænɪk/ *noun*
a sudden strong feeling of fear and worry that makes you do things without thinking carefully: *The bomb warning caused panic, and people started to run in all directions.*

panic[2] *verb* **panicked, panicking**
to suddenly feel so frightened that you do things without thinking carefully first: *The crowd panicked at the sound of the guns and started running and screaming.*
—**panicky** *adjective* feeling panic

pan•o•ram•a /ˌpænə'ræmə/ *noun, formal*
a view over a wide area of land: *a panorama of the Rocky Mountains*

P

P

—**panoramic** *adjective* a panoramic view or picture shows a wide area of land

pant /pænt/ *verb*
to breathe quickly with short breaths because you have been exercising or because it is hot: *He was panting when he reached the top of the hill.*
➔ See Thesaurus box at **breathe**

pan·ther /ˈpænθɚ/ *noun*
a large wild black cat that is good at hunting

pant·ies /ˈpæntiz/ *plural noun*
a piece of underwear that girls or women wear on their bottoms

pan·try /ˈpæntri/ *noun* plural **pantries**
a large cupboard or small room in a kitchen, where you can keep food and dishes

pants /pænts/ *plural noun*
a piece of clothing that covers you from your waist to your feet and has a separate part for each leg: *Joe was wearing a new pair of pants.*
➔ See picture on page A6

pan·ty·hose /ˈpæntiˌhoʊz/ *noun*
a very thin, tight piece of clothing that covers your legs from your feet to your waist, that women wear under dresses or skirts

pa·pa /ˈpɑpə/ *noun, informal*
a name that children call their father: *Where are you going, Papa?*

pa·per /ˈpeɪpɚ/ *noun*
1 thin sheets that you write or draw on, use to wrap gifts, etc.: *Write your name at the top of a piece of paper.* | *Alison tore the paper off her birthday present.* | *a brown paper bag*
2 a newspaper: *There's an article in the paper about the school football team.*
3 a piece of writing that you do for a class: *Your paper should be three pages long.*

pa·per·back /ˈpeɪpɚˌbæk/ *noun*
a book with a stiff paper cover: *He was reading a paperback.*

ˈpaper clip *noun*
a small piece of curved wire that you use to hold sheets of paper together
➔ See picture on page A18

pa·pers /ˈpeɪpɚz/ *plural noun, formal*
official pieces of paper that give information about who you are and what you are allowed to do, for example your PASSPORT: *The border guards looked at my papers.*

pa·per·work /ˈpeɪpɚˌwɚk/ *noun*
1 the official pieces of paper that you must write information on in order to do something or get something: *I had to fill out a lot of paperwork before we could get the dog from the shelter.*
2 work such as writing letters or reports: *I have a lot of paperwork to do this weekend.*

par·a·chute /ˈpærəˌʃut/ *noun*
a large piece of cloth that you attach to your back so that you can jump out of an airplane and fall slowly and safely to the ground: *He died when he jumped from a plane and his parachute didn't open.*

parachute

pa·rade¹ /pəˈreɪd/ *noun*
a celebration in which musical bands, decorated trucks, etc. move in a long line along a street: *The school band got to march in the parade.*

parade² *verb, formal*
to walk or march together to celebrate or protest something: *The protesters paraded in front of City Hall.*

par·a·dise /ˈpærəˌdaɪs/ *noun*
1 a place that is very beautiful and enjoyable: *The island seemed like paradise.*
2 a) another word for HEAVEN **b)** the place where Adam and Eve first lived, according to the Bible

par·a·dox /ˈpærəˌdɑks/ *noun, formal*
a statement or situation that seems strange because it contains two ideas or things that are very different but are both true: *It's a paradox that such a rich country has so many poor people.*
—**paradoxical** /ˌpærəˈdɑksɪkəl/ *adjective* relating to a paradox
—**paradoxically** *adverb*

par·a·graph /ˈpærəˌgræf/ Ac *noun*
a group of sentences that starts on a new line and deals with one idea in a piece of writing: *The first paragraph of your essay should say what your main point is going to be.*

par·a·keet /ˈpærəˌkit/ *noun*
a small bird with brightly colored feathers, that some people keep as a pet

par•a•le•gal /ˌpærəˈligəl/ *noun*
someone whose job is to help a lawyer do his or her work

par•al•lel¹ /ˈpærəlel/ Ac *adjective*
lines that are parallel go in the same direction and are the same distance apart along their whole length: *The street runs parallel to the train tracks.*

parallel² *noun, formal*
if there is a parallel between events or situations, they are like each other in some way: *He talked about the parallels between his own life and the character he plays on television.*
—**parallel** *verb* if something parallels something else, it is like it in some way

pa•ral•y•sis /pəˈræləsɪs/ *noun, formal*
the lack of the ability to move or feel part of your body: *The disease can cause paralysis of the whole body.*

par•a•lyze /ˈpærəˌlaɪz/ *verb, formal*
1 to make someone unable to move part of his or her body, or to feel anything in it: *The disease paralyzed his legs and he could no longer walk.*
2 to make something or someone unable to work normally: *Heavy snow has paralyzed New York City.*
—**paralyzed** *adjective* unable to move part of your body: *The injury left him paralyzed and unable to take care of himself.*

par•a•med•ic /ˌpærəˈmedɪk/ *noun, formal*
someone whose job is to help sick or hurt people until they get to a hospital, and who works in an AMBULANCE: *The paramedics were working on a woman who had had a heart attack.*

pa•ram•et•er /pəˈræmətɚ/ Ac *noun, formal*
a limit or rule that controls the way that something should be done: *The committee has to set the parameters for how the money will be spent.*

par•a•mil•i•tar•y /ˌpærəˈmɪləˌteri/ *adjective, formal*
a paramilitary group is organized like an army, but is not part of the legal military forces of a country: *He belonged to a paramilitary group that opposed the new leaders of the country.*

par•a•noid /ˈpærəˌnɔɪd/ *adjective, formal*
believing that you cannot trust other people, or that they are trying to harm you: *He was so paranoid he thought everyone was watching him.*
—**paranoia** /ˌpærəˈnɔɪə/ *noun* the illness or feeling of being paranoid

par•a•phrase /ˈpærəˌfreɪz/ *verb, formal*
to say or write what someone else has said in a way that uses different words and is often clearer: *Write a paragraph that paraphrases the story.*
—**paraphrase** *noun* a piece of writing or something that you say that paraphrases something

par•a•site /ˈpærəˌsaɪt/ *noun, formal*
a plant or animal that lives on or in another plant or animal and gets food from it

par•cel /ˈpɑrsəl/ *noun*
something that has been wrapped in paper so that it can be sent through the mail: *The mailman left a parcel for you.* SYNONYM **package**

par•don¹ /ˈpɑrdn/ *verb*
1 pardon me *spoken* **a)** used to politely say you are sorry: *Pardon me, I didn't mean to push you.* | *Pat burped and said, "Pardon me."* SYNONYM **excuse me b)** *also* **Pardon?** used to politely ask someone to say something again: *"Are you and Ken going together?" "Pardon me?" "Are you and Ken going to the party together?"* SYNONYM **excuse me? c)** used to politely get someone's attention: *Pardon me, do you know what time it is?* SYNONYM **excuse me**
2 to allow someone who has done something bad not to be punished for it: *The men were in jail, but the president later pardoned them.*

pardon² *noun*
an official order that allows someone who has done something bad not to be punished for it: *The governor gave him a pardon for his involvement in the crime.*
→ **I beg your pardon** at **beg**

par•ent /ˈperənt/ *noun*
a father or mother: *I have to call my parents and tell them if I'm going to be out late.*
—**parental** /pəˈrentl/ *adjective* relating to being a parent
—**parenthood** /ˈperəntˌhʊd/ *noun* the fact of being a parent

P

P

pa•ren•the•ses /pə'renθə,siz/ *plural noun*
the signs ( ). Parentheses are used around words that give you more information, for example in the sentence "The book is old (written in 1879) but very good.": *The dates in parentheses tell you when the people were born and when they died.*

park¹ /pɑrk/ *noun*
1 a large area with grass and trees, where people can walk, play games, etc.: *The kids were climbing trees in the park.*
2 a large area of land that has been kept in its natural state to protect the plants and animals there: *Yellowstone is a national park.*

park² *verb*
to put your car in a particular place and leave it there for a period of time: *Can I park in your driveway?*

par•ka /'pɑrkə/ *noun*
a thick warm coat with a HOOD (=part that goes over your head): *It was snowing, and the children had their parkas on.*

,park and 'ride *noun*
a system in which you leave your car in a special parking lot and take a bus or train to another part of a city

park•ing /'pɑrkɪŋ/ *noun*
1 the act of putting your car somewhere and leaving it there for a period of time: *Parking in the red zone is illegal.*
2 spaces in which you can leave a car: *We found a parking space near the door.* | *There is lots of parking behind the store.*

'parking lot *noun*
a large area where you can leave your car: *The parking lot was almost full.*

'parking ,meter *noun*
a machine that you put money into to pay for parking your car next to it: *I put fifty cents into the parking meter, so that I could park for an hour.*

park•way /'pɑrkweɪ/ *noun*
a wide road, with grass and trees in the middle or along the sides: *Traffic was slow on the parkway this morning.*

par•lia•ment /'pɑrləmənt/ *noun*
a group of people who are elected to make laws, in countries such as Canada or Great Britain
—**parliamentary** /,pɑrlə'mentri/ *adjective* relating to what is done in a parliament

par•lor /'pɑrlɚ/ *noun*
ice cream/beauty/funeral etc. parlor = a store or business that sells a particular thing or provides a particular service: *I went to the beauty parlor today to get my hair cut.*

pa•ro•chi•al school /pə'roʊkiəl ,skul/ *noun*
a school that is run by or connected with a church: *Mary goes to a Catholic parochial school.*

par•o•dy /'pærədi/ *noun* plural **parodies** *formal*
a piece of writing, a movie, etc. that copies someone else's way of doing something in a funny way: *The stories are parodies of fairy tales, so the story of "The Gingerbread Man" becomes "The Stinky Cheese Man."*
—**parody** *verb* to copy something or how someone does something in a funny way

pa•role /pə'roʊl/ *noun, formal*
if a prisoner gets parole, he or she is allowed to leave prison if he or she behaves well outside of prison: *He is now on parole after being in prison for five years.*
—**parole** *verb* to give someone parole

par•rot /'pærət/ *noun*
a tropical bird with colored feathers and a curved beak. You can teach some parrots to say words

pars•ley /'pɑrsli/ *noun*
a plant with green curled leaves, that you use in cooking or as a decoration on food

part¹ /pɑrt/ *noun*
1 one piece or amount of something: *Which part of town do you live in?* | *The fight was the best part of the whole movie.*

THESAURUS: part

piece a part of something that is separate from the rest of it: *One of the pieces of the jigsaw puzzle was missing.* | *a piece of pie*

section one of the parts that something is divided into: *the sports section of the newspaper*

chapter one of the parts that a book is divided into: *I've read the first two chapters.*

scene one of the parts that a play or movie is divided into: *The best scene is when he fights the dragon.*

department one part of a business, college, government, etc. which is responsible for a particular kind of work: *the history department at the school* | *He works in the men's clothes department.*

2 one of the pieces that a machine is made of: *Do you sell parts for Ford cars?*

3 take part = to do an activity with other people: *Twenty runners took part in the race.* SYNONYM **participate**

4 a character in a play, movie, or television show, that an actor will play: *She got a big part in a new TV series.*

5 the things that one person does in an activity that is done by several people: *Teachers have an important part in children's lives.*

6 the line on your head that you make when you divide your hair with a comb: *Your part isn't straight.*

7 for the most part = mostly or most of the time: *The kids get along well, for the most part.*

part² *verb*

1 if you part your hair, you comb some of your hair in one direction and the rest in the other direction, so that there is a line on your head: *Her hair is parted in the middle.*

2 to move the two sides of something apart: *He parted the curtains and looked out.*

part³ *adverb*

if something is part one thing and part another thing, some of it is the first thing, and some of it is the second thing: *He drew an animal that was part snake and part bird.*

par•tial /ˈpɑrʃəl/ *adjective*

not complete: *This is a partial list of the available classes this semester; we'll have the rest of the list next week.* ANTONYM **full**

—**partially** *adverb*

par•tic•i•pant /pɑrˈtɪsəpənt/ Ac *noun, formal*

someone who does an activity with other people: *Each participant in the competition sang two songs.*

par•tic•i•pate /pɑrˈtɪsəˌpeɪt/ Ac *verb, formal*

to do an activity with other people: *I want to thank everyone who participated in the festival.* SYNONYM **take part**

par•ti•ci•ple /ˈpɑrtəˌsɪpəl/ *noun, formal*

the form of a verb that you use to make verb tenses or as an adjective: *The past participle of "sing" is "sung" and the present participle is "singing."*

par•ti•cle /ˈpɑrtɪkəl/ *noun, formal*

a very small piece of something that you cannot see: *The air is full of particles of dust.*

par•tic•u•lar /pɚˈtɪkyələ/ *adjective*

1 special or important: *Did you have a particular reason for coming here today?*

2 a particular thing is the one you are talking about and not any other: *I've read some Harry Potter books, but not that particular one.*

3 *formal* very careful about choosing exactly what you like: *She's very particular about what she wears and only buys black clothes.* SYNONYM **picky**

4 in particular a) used when talking about one thing and not something more general: *I know you're having problems, but is there anything in particular I can help you with?* **b)** *formal* most of all: *I like sports, baseball in particular.*

par•tic•u•lar•ly /pɚˈtɪkyələli/ *adverb, formal*

1 most of all: *I like bright colors, particularly red.* SYNONYM **especially**

2 more than usual: *It had been hot all week, but it was particularly hot on Tuesday.* | *She's not particularly pretty.* SYNONYM **especially**

part•ly /ˈpɑrtli/ *adverb*

a little, but not completely: *Her face was partly covered by a scarf, but I could see her eyes.*

part•ner /ˈpɑrtnɚ/ Ac *noun*

1 someone with whom you do an activity that involves two people, such as dancing: *His partner kept stepping on his toes as they danced.*

2 one of the owners of a business: *She's a partner in a law firm.*

3 your husband or wife or your girlfriend or boyfriend: *Discuss things with your partner before you decide.*

P

P

—**partnership** *noun* a relationship between partners: *He went into partnership with another lawyer.*

ˌpart of ˈspeech *noun* plural **parts of speech**
one of the groups that you can divide words into, such as "noun" or "verb"

ˌpart-ˈtime *adjective, adverb*
if you work or study part-time, you do it for only part of each day or week: *a part-time student* | *I work part-time in a bookshop, so I'm not home on Tuesdays or Wednesdays.*

par·ty /ˈpɑrti/ *noun* plural **parties**
1 an occasion when people enjoy themselves by eating, drinking, and dancing together in a group, for example when it is someone's birthday: *We're having a party on Saturday. Do you want to come?* | *Can you come to my birthday party?*

THESAURUS: party

get-together *informal* a small informal party: *I'm having a get-together with some friends on Friday. Want to come?*

bash *informal* a party: *His wife is planning a big bash for his fiftieth birthday.*

birthday party a party to celebrate someone's birthday, especially a child's: *How many kids did you invite to Chris's birthday party?*

baby/wedding/bridal shower a party at which people give presents to a woman who is going to have a baby or get married: *A lot of her friends came to her baby shower.*

reception a large formal party, for example after a wedding: *There was dinner and dancing at the reception.*

celebration a party that is organized in order to celebrate something: *Please join us for our son's 21st birthday celebration!*

2 a group of people with the same political views, that you can vote for in elections: *the Democratic Party*

pass¹ /pæs/ *verb*
1 to go past someone or something: *She waved at me as she passed our house.*
2 to move from one place to another, following a particular direction: *We passed through Texas on our way to Mexico.* | *A plane passed over the fields.* SYNONYM **go**
3 to take something and put it in someone's hand: *Pass the salt, please.* | *Can you pass me a pen?*
4 to kick, throw, or hit a ball to someone on your own team during a game: *Dad taught me how to pass a football.*
5 if time passes, it moves forward: *Time passes very slowly when you're waiting.* SYNONYM **go by**
6 to succeed in a test or class: *Did you pass your driving test?* | *You won't pass if you don't study.* ANTONYM **fail**
7 to officially accept a law by voting: *The new law was passed, 15 votes to 3.*
8 to end or finish: *The storm soon passed.* | *Ann will be upset for a while, but it'll pass.*
➔ See Thesaurus boxes at **give¹** and **throw¹**

PHRASAL VERBS

pass something around
to give something to each person in a group: *Pass these dictionaries around so that everyone has one.*

pass away
formal to die: *He was very old when he passed away.*

pass something on
to tell someone information that someone told you: *I will pass the message on to her.*

pass out
to suddenly become unconscious: *The pain was so strong that I passed out.* SYNONYM **faint**

pass² *noun*
1 the act of kicking, throwing, or hitting a ball to someone on your team in a game: *He made a great pass to this teammate, half the length of the football field.*
2 a special piece of paper that allows you to go somewhere or do something: *You need a pass to use the ski-lifts.* | *a bus pass*
3 a road or path high up in the mountains: *We walked to the other side of the mountain along a narrow mountain pass.*

pas·sage /ˈpæsɪdʒ/ *noun*
1 a short piece of writing or music, from a longer piece: *He read a passage from the Bible.*
2 a long narrow place in a building that connects one room with another: *There was a short passage connecting the two hotel rooms.*

3 *formal* a tube in your body that air or liquid passes through: *When you have a cold, the passages in your nose become blocked.*

pas•sen•ger /ˈpæsəndʒɚ/ *noun*
someone who travels in a car, bus, plane, etc., but is not driving it: *There were 10 passengers on the bus.*

pass•ing /ˈpæsɪŋ/ *adjective*
1 *formal* going past: *I couldn't hear for a minute because of noise from a passing truck.*
2 continuing for only a short time: *Her interest in religion was just a passing phase* (=it lasted a short time).

pas•sion /ˈpæʃən/ *noun*
1 a very strong feeling such as love, hate, or anger: *He spoke with passion about feeding the poor.*
2 a strong feeling of liking something: *He has a passion for golf and plays three times a week.*

pas•sion•ate /ˈpæʃənət/ *adjective*
showing very strong feelings such as love, hate, or anger: *a passionate kiss* | *She is passionate about animals and has several pets.*
—**passionately** *adverb*

pas•sive /ˈpæsɪv/ Ac *adjective*
1 *formal* a passive person accepts things as they are and does not try to change them: *Dan was a passive person who had never disagreed with his teachers before.*
2 in a passive sentence, the form of the verb shows that someone else did the action: *In the sentence "The ball was kicked by John," "was kicked" is a passive verb.* ANTONYM **active**
—**passively** *adverb*: *She passively accepted all the bad things that happened to her.*
—**passivity** /pæˈsɪvəti/ *noun* passive behavior

pass•port /ˈpæspɔrt/ *noun*
a small book with your photograph inside which you must have to leave one country and go to another: *They checked my passport and let me onto the plane.*
➔ See picture on page A30

pass•word /ˈpæswɚd/ *noun*
a secret group of letters or numbers that you need to get into a computer system: *Type in your password and press enter.*

past[1] /pæst/ *noun*
1 **the past** = all the time before now: *Traveling is much easier now than it was in the past.* ANTONYM **the future**
2 **someone's past** = someone's life before now: *I don't know anything about his past.*

past[2] *adjective*
1 used when talking about an earlier time that has been happening until now: *He's tired because he's been working hard the past few weeks.* SYNONYM **last**
2 past events happened before now: *Our current problems are the result of past mistakes.* ANTONYM **future**

past[3] *adverb, preposition*
1 up to and beyond someone or something: *We walked past slowly.* | *Do you drive past the school when you go home?*
2 after a particular time: *It's just past four o'clock – about 4:05 or so.*

pas•ta /ˈpɑstə/ *noun*
an Italian food made from flour and water that you can buy in different shapes: *My favorite kind of pasta is spaghetti.*

paste[1] /peɪst/ *noun*
1 a type of thick glue: *We used wallpaper paste to stick the paper to the wall.*
2 a soft wet mixture that you can spread easily: *Mix the water and the powder into a smooth paste.*

paste[2] *verb*
1 to put words in a new place on a computer screen after moving or copying them from another place: *Cut and paste your address into a new file.*
2 to stick one thing to another using thick glue: *The kids were pasting pieces of colored paper together.*

pas•tel /pæˈstel/ *adjective*
1 a soft pale color such as pale blue or pale pink: *The baby's room was painted in pastels.*
2 a small colored stick used for drawing pictures, similar to CHALK
—**pastel** *adjective*: *pastel colors*

pas•time /ˈpæstaɪm/ *noun*
formal something that you do to have fun or relax when you are not working: *His pastimes include watching TV and reading.* SYNONYM **hobby**

P

pas•tor /'pæstɚ/ *noun*
a minister in a church: *He is a pastor in a Baptist church.*

ˌpast 'participle *noun*
the form of a verb that shows an action happening in the past: *"Fallen" is the past participle of the verb "fall."*

pas•try /'peɪstri/ *noun* plural **pastries**
1 a mixture of flour, butter, and water which makes the outer part of a PIE: *Roll out the pastry and put it in a pie pan.*
2 a small sweet cake: *We had a cup of coffee and a pastry.*

ˌpast 'tense *noun*
the past tense = the form of a verb that shows past time: *The past tense of the verb "go" is "went."*

pas•ture /'pæstʃɚ/ *noun*
land covered with grass for cows and sheep to eat: *There was a herd of cows in the pasture.*

pat /pæt/ *verb* **patted, patting**
to touch something lightly several times, with your hand flat: *He patted the dog.* | *She patted me on the back and said, "Don't worry."*
—**pat** *noun* an act of patting something: *She gave the boy a pat on the head.*
➔ See Thesaurus box at **touch**[1]

patch[1] /pætʃ/ *noun*
1 a small piece of material that covers a hole in clothes: *His pants had patches on the knees where the holes had been.*
2 a part of an area that is different from the parts around it: *The sky was gray, except for a small patch of blue between the clouds.*

patch[2] *verb*
to put a small piece of material over a hole to cover it: *I patched the bicycle tire with a piece of rubber.*

pa•tent /'pætnt/ *noun, formal*
if you have a patent on something, only you can make it or sell it by law: *He applied for a patent on his new machine.*
—**patent** *verb* to get a patent on something

path /pæθ/ *noun* plural **paths** /pæðz/
1 a narrow road for walking on: *There is a narrow path through the forest.*
2 the direction in which something is moving: *The storm destroyed everything in its path.* SYNONYM **way**

pa•thet•ic /pə'θetɪk/ *adjective*
very bad, useless, or weak: *Your excuses are pathetic. I'm not even going to listen to them.* | *The sick animals looked pathetic in their cages.*
—**pathetically** *adverb*: *He looked pathetically scared.*

pa•tience /'peɪʃəns/ *noun*
the ability to deal with a problem or wait for something without becoming angry or upset: *After two hours waiting for the bus, I finally lost my patience* (=stopped being patient).
ANTONYM **impatience**

pa•tient[1] /'peɪʃənt/ *noun*
someone who is getting medical treatment from a doctor or hospital: *There are 150 patients in the hospital.*

patient[2] *adjective*
able to deal with a problem or wait for something without getting angry or upset: *Be patient – the taxi will be here soon.*
ANTONYM **impatient**
—**patiently** *adverb*: *She waited patiently for a reply to her email.*

WORD FAMILY look at the words:
➔ **patient** *adjective*
➔ **patiently** *adverb*
➔ **patience** *noun*

pat•i•o /'pætiˌoʊ/ *noun* plural **patios**
a hard flat area outside of a house, where you can sit or eat: *It was a warm morning, so we had breakfast on the patio.*

pa•tri•ot /'peɪtriət/ *noun, formal*
someone who loves his or her country and will defend it: *These soldiers are patriots who will go to war for their country.*

pa•tri•ot•ic /ˌpeɪtri'ɑtɪk/ *adjective, formal*
someone who is patriotic loves his or her country: *He is very patriotic and has his country's flag outside his house.*
—**patriotically** *adverb*

pat•rol[1] /pəˈtroʊl/ *verb* **patrolled, patrolling**
to go around a place checking for problems or crime: *Every hour the police patrol our street.*

patrol[2] *noun*
1 on patrol = going around a place checking for problems or crime: *Guards were on patrol throughout the night.*
2 used in the names of some groups of police officers or soldiers that patrol a place: *The California Highway Patrol reported an accident on Interstate 5.*

paˈtrol car *noun*
a police car that drives around the streets of a city

pa•tron /ˈpeɪtrən/ *noun, formal*
someone who helps an organization, artist, or performer by giving money: *He is a patron of the arts who has given thousands of dollars to public art galleries.*

pa•tron•iz•ing /ˈpeɪtrəˌnaɪzɪŋ/ *adjective, formal*
a patronizing person treats you as though you are less important or less intelligent than him or her: *It is patronizing to say that women can't survive without men.*

pat•ter /ˈpætɚ/ *noun, formal*
the sound of something light hitting a hard surface: *I heard the patter of rain on the roof.*

pat•tern /ˈpætɚn/ *noun*
1 an arrangement of shapes, lines, and colors that decorates a material, picture, etc.: *The dress has a pattern of flowers on it.*
2 the regular way that something happens: *There is a pattern to his headaches – they usually come in the morning before he eats breakfast.*
3 a shape that you copy onto cloth or paper to make clothing: *She used the pattern to make a skirt.*

pause[1] /pɔz/ *verb*
1 to stop speaking or doing something for a short time: *Tom paused for a moment, and then continued speaking.* | *When he reached the top of the hill, he paused to rest.*
2 to push a button on a CD PLAYER or a DVD PLAYER to make a CD or DVD stop playing for a short time: *Pause the movie while I go get a drink.*
➔ See Thesaurus box at **stop**[1]

pause[2] *noun*
a short time when you stop speaking or doing something: *There was a pause in the conversation, so I decided to offer everyone another drink.*

pave /peɪv/ *verb*
1 to cover a road with a hard surface such as CONCRETE: *They paved the yard so the kids could play basketball.*
2 pave the way for something = to do something that will make something else possible in the future: *My parents' worked hard and paved the way for our success in life.*

pave•ment /ˈpeɪvmənt/ *noun*
the hard surface of a road: *She fell off the bike, and her arm hit the pavement hard.*

paw /pɔ/ *noun*
the foot of an animal such as a dog or cat: *The cat hurt its paw and is walking strangely now.*

pay[1] /peɪ/ *verb* **paid** /peɪd/ third person singular **pays**
1 to give money to someone when you buy something or when someone has done work for you: *Who paid for lunch?* | *I haven't paid you for those tickets.* | *He gets paid $10 an hour.* | *Dad pays me to wash his car.*
2 if something pays, it has a good result for you: *Crime doesn't pay.* | *It pays to get there early, because you get the best seats.*
3 pay attention = to listen or watch something carefully: *I wasn't paying attention. What did you say?*
4 pay your way = to pay for things you need, without asking for money from anyone else: *My friends are rich but I always pay my way.*

PHRASAL VERBS

pay someone back
to give someone the money that you owe him or her: *Can I borrow $10? I'll pay you back tomorrow.* SYNONYM **repay**

pay off
to have a good result: *All her hard work paid off, because she got into law school.*

pay something off
to pay all the money that you owe for something: *She's paid off all her debts.*

pay² *noun*
money you get for work you have done: *You will get your pay on Friday.* | *She asked her boss for a pay raise* (=more money).

> **THESAURUS: pay**
>
> **income** money that you receive from working, investments, etc.: *families on a low income*
>
> **salary** the pay that you get every month for the work that you do, especially for work such as a teacher or manager: *The president of the company earns a salary of $145,000 a year.*
>
> **wages** the pay that someone earns every hour or every week: *Her wages barely cover the rent.*
>
> **earnings** *formal* all the money that you earn by working: *Women's earnings still tend to be lower than men's earnings.*

P

pay•a•ble /ˈpeɪəbəl/ *adjective, formal*
1 if an amount of money is payable, you must pay it: *$200 is payable in July, and the rest of the rent is payable when you arrive.*
2 payable to someone = if you make a check payable to someone, you write his or her name on it so he or she gets the money

pay•check /ˈpeɪtʃek/ *noun*
a small piece of paper you get as pay for work you have done: *I get a paycheck from my employer every week.*

pay•day /ˈpeɪdeɪ/ *noun*
the day when you get your money for work you have done: *I can't pay the bill until payday. I don't have any money in my account.*

pay•ment /ˈpeɪmənt/ *noun*
1 an amount of money that you pay, often one of many amounts in a series: *My last credit card payment was $50.*
2 *formal* the act of paying: *Late payment of this bill will result in a $10 fine.*

ˈpay phone *noun*
a telephone you can use by putting coins or a card into it: *There's a pay phone on the corner of the street where you can make the call.*

pay•roll /ˈpeɪroʊl/ *noun, formal*
a list of all the people who work for a company and the amounts of money the company pays them: *We have 127 employees on the payroll.*

PC¹ *noun*
personal computer a type of computer that people have at home: *I play games and do my homework on my PC.*
→ See picture on page A20

PC² *adjective*
politically correct someone who is PC uses careful language to avoid upsetting anyone because of his or her religion, sex, etc.: *It's not PC to call a woman "baby."*

pea /pi/ *noun*
a very small round green vegetable: *Eat your peas.*

peace /pis/ *noun*
1 a time when there is no war or fighting: *We all hope for world peace.*
2 a situation that is quiet and calm: *I went to the library to work in peace.*

> **WORD FAMILY look at the words:**
>
> → **peace** *noun*
> → **peaceful** *adjective*
> → **peacefully** *adverb*

peace•ful /ˈpisfəl/ *adjective*
1 quiet and calm: *The house is peaceful in the early morning, when everyone's still asleep.*
2 without fighting or violence: *Leaders from several countries met to try and find a peaceful solution to the conflict.*
—**peacefully** *adverb*: *The baby was sleeping peacefully.*

peace•keep•ing /ˈpisˌkipɪŋ/ *noun*
the process of trying to stop people from fighting each other: *The soldiers are being sent to the country on a peacekeeping operation.*
—**peacekeeper** *noun* someone who tries to stop people from fighting each other: *United Nations peacekeepers*

peach /pitʃ/ *noun*
a juicy yellow and red fruit with a soft skin and one large rough seed
→ See picture on page A13

pea•cock /ˈpikɑk/ *noun*
a large male bird with long blue and green feathers that spread out

peak /pik/ *noun*
1 the pointed top of a mountain: *The peak of the mountain was covered in snow.*

2 the time when something is most successful, best, etc.: *Rob was 45 and at the peak of his career.*

peal /pil/ *noun, formal*
a long loud sound of someone laughing, thunder, or church bells ringing: *There was a flash of lightning and then a peal of thunder.*

pea•nut /ˈpinʌt/ *noun*
1 a small light brown nut with a soft shell that people eat: *He bought a soda and a pack of peanuts.*
➔ See picture on page A13
2 peanuts *informal* = a very small amount of money: *I'm tired of working for peanuts – I want to make more money.*

ˈpeanut ˌbutter *noun*
a soft food made from crushed peanuts, that you eat on bread: *a peanut butter sandwich*

pear /per/ *noun*
a sweet juicy fruit, usually green or yellow, that is round and wide at the bottom and thin at the top
➔ See picture on page A13

pearl /pɚl/ *noun*
a small round white object that forms inside an OYSTER, and is a valuable jewel: *She was wearing a necklace made of pearls.*

peas•ant /ˈpezənt/ *noun*
a word used in past times for a poor person who works on the land

peb•ble /ˈpebəl/ *noun*
a small smooth stone on a beach or in a river: *The boys were throwing pebbles in the water.*

pe•can /pɪˈkɑn/ *noun*
a long brown sweet nut: *pecan pie*
➔ See picture on page A13

peck /pek/ *verb*
if a bird pecks something, it quickly moves its head to eat or hit that thing: *A bird was pecking at the berries on the tree.*

pe•cu•liar /pɪˈkyulyɚ/ *adjective*
1 strange or unusual: *This cheese has a peculiar smell and I didn't want to taste it.*
2 be peculiar to someone or something = if something is peculiar to one place or person, only that place or person has it: *Both these animals are peculiar to Alaska – you won't find them anywhere else.*
—**peculiarly** *adverb* in a strange or unusual way: *Ben's been behaving very peculiarly – he won't talk to anyone and just goes around singing.*
—**peculiarity** /pɪˌkyuliˈærəti/ *noun* something that is strange, unusual, or special: *His love of reading stories about death is one of his peculiarities.*
➔ See Thesaurus box at **strange**[1]

ped•al[1] /ˈpedl/ *noun*
a part of a bicycle, car, etc. that you push with your foot: *She stepped on the gas pedal, and the car moved forward.*
➔ See picture at **bicycle**

pedal[2] *verb*
to ride a bicycle by pushing the pedals with your feet: *It was hard work pedaling the bike up the hill.*

pe•des•tri•an /pəˈdestriən/ *noun*
someone who is walking in a town: *It was Saturday, and the sidewalks were crowded with pedestrians.*

pe•di•a•tri•cian /ˌpidiəˈtrɪʃən/ *noun*
a doctor who treats children
➔ See Thesaurus box at **doctor**

ped•i•gree /ˈpedəˌgri/ *noun*
the parents and other past family members of an animal or person: *We bought the dog because it has a very good pedigree* (=its mother, father, etc., are good).

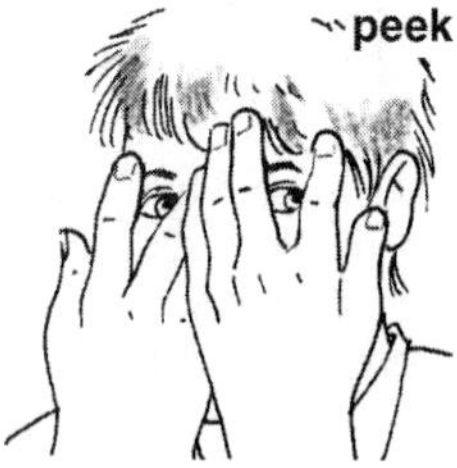

peek /pik/ *verb*
to quickly look at something that you should not look at: *He opened her bag and peeked inside.*
—**peek** *noun* a quick look: *I took a quick peek at her diary when she was not at home.*
➔ See Thesaurus box at **look**[1]

peel[1] /pil/ *verb*
to take off the skin of a fruit or vegetable: *I'll peel the potatoes.*
➔ See Thesaurus box at **cut**[1]
➔ See picture on page A14

peel[2] *noun*
the skin of a fruit or vegetable: *a banana peel*

peep /pip/ *verb*
to look somewhere quickly in a secret way: *I saw someone peeping through the window.*

peer[1] /pɪr/ *noun, formal*
your peers are people who are the same age as you: *Teenagers usually want to spend time with their peers, not adults or little kids.*
➔ See Thesaurus box at **look**[1]

peer[2] *verb*
to look very carefully, because it is dark or you cannot see well: *The old lady peered at me through her glasses.*

P

peg /peg/ *noun*
1 a short piece of wood or metal that you fasten to a wall and use for hanging things: *Marty hung her towel on a peg.*
2 *also* **tent peg** a pointed piece of wood or metal that you push into the ground to keep a tent in the right place

pel•i•can /ˈpelɪkən/ *noun*
a big bird that has a bag of skin under its beak, where it stores fish before it eats them

pel•let /ˈpelɪt/ *noun*
a small hard ball made from metal, food, etc.: *The farmer gives the cattle special food pellets.*

pelt[1] /pelt/ *verb*
to throw a lot of things at someone: *Two kids were pelting each other with snowballs.*

pelt[2] *noun*
the skin of a dead animal with the fur on it: *Hunters killed the animals and sold their pelts.*

pel•vis /ˈpelvɪs/ *noun*
the wide curved bones at the base of your SPINE, and at the top of your legs
—**pelvic** *adjective* relating to the pelvis: *the pelvic bones*
➔ See picture on page A2

pen /pen/ *noun*
1 something you use for writing and drawing in ink: *Can I borrow your pen to write this postcard?* | *Fill out the form with a black pen* (=one with black ink).
2 a small area with a fence around it where a farmer keeps animals: *The lambs are kept in indoor pens.*
➔ See picture on page A18

pe•nal•ize /ˈpinlˌaɪz/ *verb*
1 to punish someone for not obeying a rule or law: *His teacher penalized him because his paper was too short* (=by giving him a lower grade).
2 to punish a player or team in sports by giving an advantage to the other team: *The player was penalized for his illegal play.*

pen•al•ty /ˈpenlti/ *noun* plural **penalties**
1 a punishment for not obeying a law or rule: *The penalty for the crime is five years in prison.* | *I don't agree with the death penalty* (=killing someone as a punishment).
2 a disadvantage that a player or team in sports gets for not obeying the rules: *There was a penalty against the Cowboys.*

pen•cil /ˈpensəl/ *noun*
something you use for writing and drawing, with a gray substance that is not ink: *Write in pencil so you can erase it if you make a mistake.*
➔ See picture on page A18

pend•ing /ˈpendɪŋ/ *preposition, formal*
until something happens, or while something is happening: *The judge delayed his decision, pending further investigation.*

pen•du•lum /ˈpendʒələm/ *noun*
a long stick with a weight on the end that swings from side to side in a large clock

pen•e•trate /ˈpenəˌtreɪt/ *verb, formal*
to pass into or through something that is deep or thick: *The bullet penetrated his brain and killed him instantly.*
—**penetration** /ˌpenəˈtreɪʃən/ *noun* the act of penetrating something

pen•guin /ˈpeŋgwɪn/ *noun*
a big black and white sea bird that swims very quickly under water but cannot fly

pen•i•cil•lin /ˌpenəˈsɪlən/ *noun*
a medicine that cures infections by destroying BACTERIA

pe•nin•su•la /pəˈnɪnsələ/ *noun*
a piece of land that has water on most sides, but is joined to a bigger area of land: *Most of the state of Florida is a peninsula.*

pen•i•ten•tia•ry /ˌpenəˈtenʃəri/ *noun* plural **penitentiaries**
a prison: *He was sent to the state penitentiary for the crime.*

pen•knife /ˈpen-naɪf/ *noun* plural **penknives** /ˈpen-naɪvz/
another word for a POCKET KNIFE

ˈpen name *noun*
a name a writer uses instead of his or her real name: *Samuel Clemens wrote his books using "Mark Twain" as his pen name.* SYNONYM **pseudonym**

pen•ni•less /ˈpenɪləs/ *adjective*
having no money: *I had no job, and I was penniless.*

pen•ny /ˈpeni/ *noun* plural **pennies**
a coin that is worth 1 cent (=1/100 of a dollar): *The kids keep their pennies in a box.*
➔ See Thesaurus box at **money**

ˈpen pal *noun*
someone in another country that you write letters to, as a way of becoming friends: *I have a pen pal in Mexico. We write to each other once a month.*

pen•sion /ˈpenʃən/ *noun*
the money that a company pays regularly to someone who has stopped working: *He started receiving a pension when he retired.*

Pen•ta•gon /ˈpentəˌgɑn/ *noun*
the Pentagon = the building in Washington, D.C. where the people work who control the U.S. army, navy, etc.

pent•house /ˈpenthaʊs/ *noun*
an expensive apartment on the top floor of a tall building: *She lived in a penthouse on Fifth Avenue.*

peo•ple /ˈpipəl/ *noun*
1 the plural of PERSON: *There were about one hundred people at the party.*

THESAURUS: people

the public all the people in an area or country: *The museum is open to the public from 10 a.m. to 6 p.m.*

society all the people who live in a country, and the way they live: *Is American society too violent?*

the human race/mankind all the people in the world, considered as a group: *Is mankind harming our environment?*

population the number of people who live in a a place: *What's the population of Los Angeles?*

2 the people = all the ordinary people in a country or a state: *In my country, the people vote for the government they want.*
3 *formal* a race or nation: *The French are a proud people.*
➔ See Thesaurus box at **race**[1]

pep•per /ˈpepɚ/ *noun*
1 a powder that tastes a little hot, that you use with food to give it more flavor: *Add some salt and pepper.*
2 a red, green, or yellow vegetable that you eat uncooked or add to other food: *a pizza with onions and green peppers*
➔ See picture on page A15

pep•per•mint /ˈpepɚˌmɪnt/ *noun*
1 a plant with a strong sweet taste and smell, that people use for making tea, candy, etc.: *peppermint tea*
2 a candy that tastes like peppermint: *Would you like a peppermint?*

pep•pe•ro•ni /ˌpepəˈroʊni/ *noun*
an Italian SAUSAGE with a strong taste

per /pɚ/ *preposition*
for or during each: *Tickets are $10 per person.* | *The park has four million vistors per year.*

per•ceive /pɚˈsiv/ Ac *verb, formal*
1 to think about something in a particular way: *In the past, people perceived the world as flat.*
2 to see or hear something: *Cats cannot perceive color.*

per•cent /pɚˈsent/ Ac *noun*
five percent (5%)/10 percent (10%), etc. = five, ten, etc. in every hundred: *60% of the students are boys and 40% are girls.*

per•cent•age /pɚˈsentɪdʒ/ Ac *noun*
an amount that you express as part of one hundred: *What percentage of students go to college after high school?*

per•cep•tion /pɚˈsepʃən/ Ac *noun, formal*
the way you think about something and your ideas about it: *Our perception of the role of women has changed over the last 100 years.*

per•cep•tive /pɚˈseptɪv/ *adjective*
good at understanding what is happening, and what people are feeling: *She was only 8, but she was very perceptive and could tell when others were upset.*

perch /pɚtʃ/ *verb*
to sit on something: *A bird perched on the branch.*

per•cus•sion /pɚˈkʌʃən/ *noun*
drums and other musical instruments which you play by hitting them

per•fect[1] /ˈpɚfɪkt/ *adjective*
1 the best possible: *Lori wanted a perfect wedding.*
2 without any mistakes or problems: *Your English is perfect.*

P

3 exactly right for something: *The weather was perfect for a picnic.*

WORD FAMILY look at the words:

→ **perfect** *adjective*
→ **perfect** *verb*
→ **perfectly** *adverb*
→ **perfection** *noun*

per•fect² /pɚˈfekt/ *verb*
to make something very good and without any mistakes: *She spent a year in France to perfect her French.*

per•fec•tion /pɚˈfekʃən/ *noun*
1 the state of being perfect and without any mistakes: *Dan's piano teacher expected perfection from him; she stopped him every time he made a mistake.*
2 to perfection = if something is done to perfection, it is done in the best possible way: *The food was delicious, and it was cooked to perfection.*
—**perfectionist** *noun* someone who wants everything to be completely perfect

per•fect•ly /ˈpɚfɪktli/ *adverb*
1 without any mistakes or problems: *He speaks Spanish perfectly. Everyone thinks he's from Spain.*
2 completely or very: *If you feel nervous before your test, that's perfectly normal.*

per•form /pɚˈfɔrm/ *verb*
1 to act in a play, play music, etc. to entertain people: *The drama club is performing a new play next week.*
2 *formal* to do a job or piece of work: *In the hospital, the surgeons performed a difficult operation.*

per•form•ance /pɚˈfɔrməns/ *noun*
1 an occasion when someone performs a play, piece of music, etc.: *The performance begins at 8 o'clock, so let's get to the theater about 7:30.*
2 someone's/something's performance = how well someone or something does something: *Linda's performance at school has gotten much better; she's getting A's and B's instead of C's.*

per•form•er /pɚˈfɔrmɚ/ *noun*
someone who acts, plays music, etc. to entertain people: *We stopped to watch the street performers* (=people acting, playing music, etc. on the street).

per•fume /ˈpɚfyum/ *noun*
1 a liquid with a pleasant smell that women put on their skin: *She was wearing a lot of perfume, and I could smell it across the room.*
2 *formal* a pleasant sweet smell: *The air was full of the perfume of flowers.*

per•haps /pɚˈhæps/ *adverb, formal*
1 possibly: *Perhaps it will snow later today. We'll have to wait and see.* SYNONYM **maybe**
2 you use this for suggesting something politely: *Perhaps you should see a doctor.* SYNONYM **maybe**

per•il /ˈperəl/ *noun, formal*
great danger: *A storm began, and the ship was in peril.*
—**perilous** *adjective, formal* very dangerous: *a perilous trip*

pe•rim•e•ter /pəˈrɪmətɚ/ *noun*
the length of the border around an area or shape: *Find the perimeter of the triangle* (=the total length of its sides).

perimeter

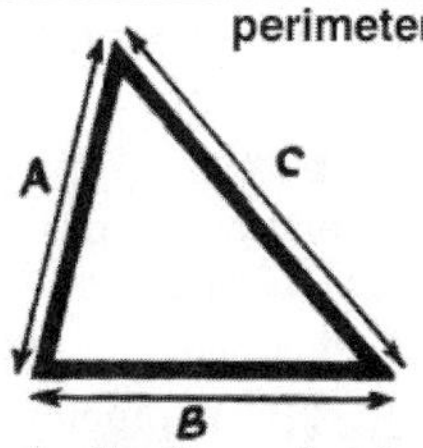

A+B+C=perimeter

pe•ri•od /ˈpɪriəd/ Ac *noun*
1 a length of time: *The disease usually lasts for a period of two weeks.* | *The stores are very busy during the Christmas period* (=the time around Christmas).
2 the mark (.) that you use in writing at the end of a sentence, or after an abbreviation
3 one of the equal times that divide the school day: *I have a history test during first period on Tuesday.*
4 one part of a game in some sports: *They scored four goals in the third period.*
5 the time when blood comes out of a woman's body once a month

pe•ri•od•ic /ˌpɪriˈɑdɪk/ Ac *adjective, formal*
happening at different times again and again: *Dave gets periodic headaches, but he doesn't get them as often as he used to.*
—**periodically** *adverb* in a periodic way: *The river floods periodically – usually every two or three years.*

ˌperiodic ˈtable *noun*
the periodic table = a list of the ELEMENTS (=simple chemical substances)

pe•riph•e•ral /pəˈrɪfərəl/ *adjective, formal*
less important than others: *He had only a peripheral role in what happened – he was hardly involved at all.* SYNONYM **minor**

per•i•scope /ˈperəˌskoʊp/ *noun*
a long tube with mirrors in it that you use for looking over the top of something, especially in a SUBMARINE

per•ish /ˈperɪʃ/ *verb, formal*
to die: *Hundreds perished when the ship sank.*

per•ju•ry /ˈpɚdʒəri/ *noun*
the crime of telling a lie in a court of law: *He had committed perjury when he said he had not met her. In fact, he knew her very well.*

perk•y /ˈpɚki/ *adjective, informal*
happy and confident: *She was a cute little girl with a perky voice.*

perm /pɚm/ *noun*
a treatment for hair that makes it curly: *I hate my straight hair, so I got a perm.*

per•ma•nent /ˈpɚmənənt/ *adjective*
continuing for a long time or for always: *In young children, the illness can cause permanent damage.* ANTONYM **temporary**
—**permanence** *noun* the state of being permanent
—**permanently** *adverb*: *The business has closed permanently – it won't reopen.*

per•mis•si•ble /pɚˈmɪsəbəl/ *adjective, formal*
allowed by law or the rules: *Smoking in school is not permissible.* ANTONYM **forbidden**

per•mis•sion /pɚˈmɪʃən/ *noun*
agreement from someone like a parent, teacher, the government, etc. that allows you to do something: *You have to ask permission if you want to leave class early.*

per•mit[1] /pɚˈmɪt/ *verb* **permitted, permitting** *formal*
1 to allow someone to do something: *You are permitted to bring a dictionary into the examination room.*
2 weather permitting/time permitting, etc. = if the weather is good enough, if there is enough time, etc. for you to do something: *Weather permitting, we're planning to eat outside.*

WORD FAMILY look at the words:
→ **permit** *verb*
→ **permit** *noun*
→ **permission** *noun*
→ **permissible** *adjective*

→ See Thesaurus box at **allow**

per•mit[2] /ˈpɚmɪt/ *noun*
an official piece of paper that allows you to do something: *You can't park here without a permit.*

per•se•cute /ˈpɚsɪˌkyut/ *verb, formal*
to treat someone in a bad way because of his or her ideas: *In Roman times, the rulers persecuted Christians.*
—**persecution** /ˌpɚsɪˈkyuʃən/ *noun* the act of persecuting someone

per•se•vere /ˌpɚsəˈvɪr/ *verb, formal*
to continue trying to do something in a determined way, although it is difficult: *Tanya thought physics was the hardest class she'd ever taken, but she persevered.*

per•sist /pɚˈsɪst/ Ac *verb, formal*
to continue to do something in a steady way, although it is difficult: *He didn't reply to her emails, but she persisted in trying to contact him.*
—**persistent** *adjective* persisting in trying to do something: *Sometimes you have to be persistent if you want to get a job and call them again and again.*
—**persistence** *noun* the quality someone has when he or she persists in trying to do something: *I admired her persistence.*

per•son /ˈpɚsən/ *noun* plural **people** /ˈpipəl/
1 a man, woman, or child: *Diane is a really nice person.* | *In this game, each person has to think of an animal.*
2 in person = if you do something in person, you do it by going to a place, not by writing or using the telephone: *You may have to apply for a visa in person.*
→ **first person, third person**

per•son•al /ˈpɚsənəl/ *adjective*
1 belonging or relating to you: *She's had some personal problems recently – I think she broke up with her boyfriend.* | *Rich packed all his personal belongings in a small suitcase.*

2 doing something yourself, instead of asking someone else to do it: *The president made a personal visit to the scene of the accident.*

➔ See Thesaurus box at **private**[1]

ˌpersonal comˈputer *noun*, *abbreviation* **PC**

a type of computer that people have at home: *I do all my work on a personal computer.*

➔ See picture on page A20

per·son·al·i·ty /ˌpɚsəˈnæləti/ *noun* plural **personalities**

1 someone's character and how he or she behaves toward other people: *She has a great personality – she's always very friendly and funny.*

2 someone who is well-known because he or she is often on TV or radio: *TV personality Jon Stewart was the host of the show.*

per·son·al·ly /ˈpɚsənəli/ *adverb*

1 used when saying what you think about something, not what anyone else thinks: *Many people like spicy food. Personally, I hate it.*

2 if you do something personally, you do it and no one else does it for you: *I know she has the letter because I gave it to her personally.*

3 if you know someone personally, you have met him or her: *I don't know her personally, but I've read her books.*

4 **take something personally** = to get upset by the things other people say because you think they are saying them because they do not like you: *He's mean to everyone, so don't take the things he said personally.*

ˌpersonal ˈpronoun *noun*

a word that you use for the person who is speaking, the person you are speaking to, or the person you are talking about: *"I," "you," and "they" are personal pronouns.*

per·son·nel /ˌpɚsəˈnel/ *noun*, *formal*

people who work in an organization: *The ship was full of military personnel.* SYNONYM **staff**

per·spec·tive /pɚˈspektɪv/ Ac *noun*, *formal*

1 your way of thinking about something, because of the things that have happened to you: *Having a job gave her a new perspective on life.* | *The book is written from a child's perspective using the words a child would use.* SYNONYM **viewpoint**

2 the ability to think about something sensibly, so that it does not seem worse than it is: *You've got to keep things in perspective and not get too upset – we lost a football game, that's all.*

per·spire /pɚˈspaɪɚ/ *verb*, *formal*

if you perspire, water comes out of your skin because you are hot SYNONYM **sweat**

—**perspiration** /ˌpɚspəˈreɪʃən/ *noun* water from your skin when you perspire

perspire

per·suade /pɚˈsweɪd/ *verb*

to make someone decide to do something by giving him or her good reasons: *We persuaded him to wear a suit by telling him he looked cool.*

THESAURUS: persuade

talk someone into something *informal* to persuade someone to do something: *Can you talk Ken into playing tomorrow? We need another player.*

get someone to do something *informal* to persuade someone to do something: *I'm trying to get the kids to help around the house more.*

encourage to persuade someone to do something, especially by telling him or her that it is good for him or her: *My parents always encouraged me to try new things.*

influence to have an effect on what someone does or thinks: *Sports players influence kids' ideas about what's cool.*

convince *formal* to persuade someone to do something, especially something her or she does not want to do: *Kim convinced him to take the day off.*

coax *formal* to persuade someone to do something by talking gently and kindly: *"Come for Christmas," Jody coaxed over the phone.*

WORD FAMILY look at the words:

→ **persuade** *verb*
→ **persuasion** *noun*
→ **persuasive** *adjective*
→ **persuasively** *adverb*

per•sua•sion /pɚ'sweɪʒən/ *noun, formal*
the act of persuading someone to do something: *After a lot of persuasion, she agreed to go.*

per•sua•sive /pɚ'sweɪsɪv/ *adjective*
able to persuade people to do things: *She is very persuasive and got Angela to agree to help us.*
—**persuasively** *adverb*: *He argued persuasively about changing the system and convinced many people.*

pes•si•mis•m /'pesəˌmɪzəm/ *noun, formal*
the feeling that bad things will happen, not good things: *Some students are sure they will fail, and this pessimism is a problem.* ANTONYM **optimism**

pes•si•mist /'pesəmɪst/ *noun, formal*
someone who thinks that bad things will happen, not good things: *Ray is a pessimist: every time he gets on a plane, he's sure there will be an accident.* ANTONYM **optimist**

pes•si•mis•tic /ˌpesə'mɪstɪk/ *adjective, formal*
someone who is pessimistic thinks that bad things will happen, not good things: *I'm pessimistic about the future – I think things will get worse.* ANTONYM **optimistic**

pest /pest/ *noun*
1 an animal or insect that harms crops or damages places where people live: *Farmers put chemicals on their crops to kill pests.*
2 *informal* someone who annoys you: *That kid is a pest! I wish he would stay at home.*

pes•ti•cide /'pestəˌsaɪd/ *noun, formal*
a chemical that kills insects that destroy crops: *Farmers spray pesticides on their crops to kill insects.*

pet[1] /pet/ *noun*
an animal that you keep at home: *I have three pets – a dog, a cat, and a rabbit.*

pet[2] *verb* **petted, petting**
to move your hand over an animal's fur to show that you like it: *Can I pet your dog?*
→ See picture on page A3

pet

pet•al /'petl/ *noun*
one of the brightly colored parts of a flower: *The flower has purple petals.*

pe•tite /pə'tit/ *adjective, formal*
a woman who is petite is short and thin in a nice way SYNONYM **small**

pe•ti•tion /pə'tɪʃən/ *noun*
a piece of paper that a lot of people sign in order to ask for something or complain about something: *I signed a petition against the closing of the school.*
—**petitioner** *noun* someone who organizes or signs a petition: *Petitioners collected 500 signatures.*

pet•ri•fied /'petrəˌfaɪd/ *adjective*
very frightened: *I'm petrified of dogs. When I see one, I can hardly move.* SYNONYM **terrified**
—**petrify** *verb* to make someone petrified
→ See Thesaurus box at **frightened**

pe•tro•le•um /pə'troʊliəm/ *noun*
oil from beneath the ground for making GASOLINE

pet•ty /'peti/ *adjective*
caring too much about things that are not important or serious: *They had a petty argument about who had nicer shoes.*

pew /pyu/ *noun*
a long wooden seat in a church

phan•tom /'fæntəm/ *noun, formal*
the spirit of a dead person that some people believe you can see SYNONYM **ghost**

P

phar•ma•ceu•ti•cal /ˌfɑrməˈsutɪkəl/ *noun, formal*
a medicine: *The drug company sells pharmaceuticals to hospitals and doctors.* SYNONYM **drug**
—**pharmaceutical** *adjective* relating to pharmaceuticals: *pharmaceutical companies*

phar•ma•cist /ˈfɑrməsɪst/ *noun*
someone whose job is to prepare and sell medicines: *The pharmacist at the drugstore gave me my pills.*
➔ See picture on page A16

phar•ma•cy /ˈfɑrməsi/ *noun* plural **pharmacies**
a store that sells medicines: *I bought some cough medicine from the pharmacy.*

phase¹ /feɪz/ Ac *noun*
one part of a process in which something develops: *The first phase of the building work will be to clear the ground.* SYNONYM **stage**

phase² *verb*
PHRASAL VERB
phase something in
to gradually start using a new way of doing something: *The changes will be gradually phased in over the next two years.*

Ph.D. /ˌpi eɪtʃ ˈdi/ *noun*
the highest possible university degree: *It took her about eight years to complete her Ph.D. in history.* SYNONYM **doctorate**

phe•nom•e•nal /fɪˈnɑmənəl/ Ac *adjective*
big or extreme in a surprising and good way: *His new business was a phenomenal success and he made a lot of money.*
—**phenomenally** *adverb*: *He is phenomenally intelligent and got the highest score ever on the test.*

phe•nom•e•non /fɪˈnɑmənən/ Ac *noun* plural **phenomena** /fɪˈnɑmənə/ *formal*
something that happens in society or in nature: *Homelessness is not a new phenomenon – it has always existed.*

phi•lan•thro•pist /fɪˈlænθrəpɪst/ *noun*
a rich person who gives money to help poor people

phi•los•o•pher /fɪˈlɑsəfɚ/ Ac *noun*
someone who studies or teaches philosophy: *Socrates was a Greek philosopher.*

phi•los•o•phy /fɪˈlɑsəfi/ Ac *noun* plural **philosophies**
the study of life and what it means: *She has a degree in philosophy.*
—**philosophical** /ˌfɪləˈsɑfɪkəl/ *adjective* relating to philosophy: *a philosophical discussion*

WORD FAMILY look at the words:
➔ **philosophy** *noun*
➔ **philosopher** *noun*
➔ **philosophical** *adjective*

pho•bi•a /ˈfoʊbiə/ *noun, formal*
a strong fear of something that most people are not afraid of: *She has a phobia about the dark and sleeps with the light on.*

phone¹ /foʊn/ *noun*
a piece of equipment you use to speak to someone in another place: *The phone's ringing.* | *I got up to answer the phone.* | *Karen's on the phone* (=talking to someone using a phone). SYNONYM **telephone**

phone² *verb*
to talk to someone using a phone: *I'll phone you tomorrow.* SYNONYM **call**

ˈphone book *noun*
a book that has the names, addresses, and telephone numbers of all the people living in a particular area

ˈphone booth *noun*
a small structure with a telephone inside that you pay to use: *She called me from a phone booth on Polk Street.*

ˈphone ˌnumber *noun*
a set of numbers that you push on a telephone when you call someone: *What's your phone number?*

pho•net•ic /fəˈnetɪk/ *adjective, formal*
relating to the sounds you make when you speak: *This dictionary uses a phonetic alphabet to show you how to say words.*

pho•net•ics /fəˈnetɪks/ *noun, formal*
the study of sounds you make when you speak: *He studies phonetics as part of his linguistics degree.*

pho•ny /ˈfoʊni/ *adjective, informal*
false or not real: *He gave the police a phony address so they wouldn't know where he lived.* SYNONYM **fake**
➔ See Thesaurus box at **fake**

pho•to /ˈfoʊtoʊ/ *noun* plural **photos**
a photograph: *There was a photo of the man and his family in the paper.* | *Who's the girl in the photo?* SYNONYM **picture**

pho•to•cop•i•er /ˈfoʊtəˌkɑpiɚ/ *noun*
a machine for copying pieces of writing or pictures: *I made three copies of the letter on the photocopier.* SYNONYM **copier**
➔ See picture on page A18

pho•to•cop•y¹ /ˈfoʊtəˌkɑpi/ *noun* plural **photocopies**
a copy of a piece of writing or picture that you make on a photocopier: *Here's a photocopy of the letter. I'm going to keep the original.* SYNONYM **copy**

photocopy² *verb*
to make a copy of a piece of writing or picture on a photocopier: *Photocopy your work when you finish it so you have any extra copy in case something happens.* SYNONYM **copy**

pho•to•graph¹ /ˈfoʊtəˌgræf/ *noun, formal*
a picture you make using a camera: *Here's a photograph of my dad.* | *You can't take photographs* (=use a camera) *in the church.* SYNONYM **picture**
➔ **picture¹**
➔ See Thesaurus box at **art**

photograph² *verb, formal*
to make a picture of someone or something using a camera: *He has photographed many famous people.*

pho•tog•ra•pher /fəˈtɑgrəfɚ/ *noun*
someone whose job is to make pictures using a camera: *The wedding photographer took the bride's picture.*
➔ See picture on page A16

pho•tog•ra•phy /fəˈtɑgrəfi/ *noun*
the art or business of making pictures with a camera: *I'm taking a class in photography and learning to use my camera better.*
—**photographic** /ˌfoʊtəˈgræfɪk/ *adjective* relating to photography: *a photographic image*

ˌphrasal ˈverb *noun*
a verb made of a verb and a word such as 'off',' 'up,' or 'down': *"Take off" and "give up" are phrasal verbs.*

phrase /freɪz/ *noun*
a group of words that is not a complete sentence: *"Later that day" and "on the way home" are phrases.*

THESAURUS: phrase

expression a word or phrase that has a particular meaning: *It was the first time I'd heard the expression, and I didn't know what it meant.*

idiom *formal* a group of words that have a special meaning that is different from the usual meaning of each word: *Many common phrases are idioms. For example "I'm tied up right now" means "I'm busy," not that I have ropes tying my hands together.*

cliché a phrase that has been used so often that it is boring: *It's a cliché, but we really do have to take this one day at a time.*

saying/proverb a phrase that many people know, that gives advice or information about life: *And the car wouldn't start this morning. It's like the old saying says, "It never rains but it pours!"* (=a lot of bad things always happen at the same time) | *There's a Japanese proverb that says, "If you want rice cakes, go to the rice cake maker." In other words, if you need something, go to someone who knows what they're doing.*

phys•i•cal¹ /ˈfɪzɪkəl/ Ac *adjective, formal*
1 relating to your body, not your mind or soul: *Physical activity such as walking or swimming is good for you.*
2 relating to things that you can see, touch, smell, or taste: *An emotion is not a physical thing.*
—**physically** *adverb*: *He was not physically fit and needed to exercise more.*

physical² *noun*
a medical examination by a doctor to check that you are healthy: *She had a physical before she started running on the track team.*

phy•si•cian /fɪˈzɪʃən/ *noun, formal*
a doctor
➔ See Thesaurus box at **doctor**

phys•ics /ˈfɪzɪks/ *noun*
the study of natural forces, such as heat, light, and movement: *We're learning about gravity in physics.*

P

P

—**physicist** /ˈfɪzəsɪst/ *noun* someone who studies or teaches physics

phys·i·ol·o·gy /ˌfɪziˈɑlədʒi/ *noun, formal* the study of how the bodies of living things work

phys·i·o·ther·a·py /ˌfɪzioʊˈθerəpi/ *noun*
a way of treating an illness or injury by moving or touching someone's body: *She needed physiotherapy after she broke her leg.*

phy·sique /fəˈzik/ *noun, formal*
the shape and size of someone's body: *He has a strong physique from playing a lot of sports.*

pi·an·ist /piˈænɪst/ *noun*
someone who plays the piano

pi·an·o /piˈænoʊ/ *noun* plural **pianos**
a large musical instrument that you play by pressing narrow black and white parts
➔ See picture on page A21

pick[1] /pɪk/ *verb*
1 to choose something: *If you ask kids whether they want fries or vegetables, they pick fries.*
2 to pull a flower or fruit from a plant or tree: *She picked an apple from the tree.*
3 to remove small pieces from something with your fingers: *If you pick pimples on your face, you make them worse.*
4 pick a fight = to begin an argument or fight with someone: *He's always picking fights with younger kids.*
5 pick your nose = to remove small pieces from inside your nose with your finger: *Stop picking your nose!*
—**picker** *noun* someone who picks flowers or fruit: *fruit pickers*

PHRASAL VERBS

pick on someone
to treat someone in an unfair or unkind way: *Other children pick on him, laughing at him and calling him names.*

pick up
1 pick something up = to hold something and lift it up from a surface: *He bent down to pick up his keys.*
2 pick someone up = to go somewhere and get someone: *Dad came to pick me up from school in his truck.*
3 pick something up = to learn something by watching or listening to other people: *I picked up a little Spanish when I went to Mexico.*
4 pick something up *informal* = to buy something: *Will you pick up some bread on the way home?*
➔ See picture on page A4

pick up on something
to notice something about the way someone is behaving, when it is difficult to notice: *I was worried about my grades, but my parents didn't pick up on it.*
➔ See picture on page A4

pick[2] *noun*
take your pick = used when telling someone to choose anything from a group of things: *There are four kinds of cake, so take your pick.*

pick·et /ˈpɪkɪt/ *noun*
a group of people who stand outside the place where they work to show they want more money or better work conditions: *He joined the picket line* (=group of people in a picket) *protesting job cuts.*
—**picket** *verb* to take part in a picket: *Workers are threatening to picket for better working conditions.*

pick·le /ˈpɪkəl/ *noun*
a green vegetable kept in a liquid with a sour taste: *Would you like pickle on your burger?*

pick·pock·et /ˈpɪkˌpɑkɪt/ *noun*
someone who steals things from people's pockets

pick·up /ˈpɪkʌp/ *noun*
a small truck with a part with no roof in the back, used for carrying large things
➔ See picture on page A26

pick·y /ˈpɪki/ *adjective* **pickier**, **pickiest**
someone who is picky is difficult to make happy because there are a lot of things he or she does not like: *I'm not picky about food – I'll eat anything.*

pic·nic /ˈpɪknɪk/ *noun*
an occasion when you take food and eat it outdoors: *We had a picnic with sandwiches and fruit by the lake.*
➔ See Thesaurus box at **meal**

pic·ture[1] /ˈpɪktʃɚ/ *noun*
1 a drawing, painting, or photograph: *She drew a picture of me.* | *His picture was in the*

newspaper. | *Can I look at the pictures of the wedding?*

THESAURUS: picture

sketch a picture that is drawn quickly and does not have a lot of details: *He drew a sketch of the house.*

snapshot a photograph that is taken quickly: *Show us your vacation snapshots!*

portrait a painting, drawing, or photograph of a person: *The painting is a portrait of a woman with her baby.*

cartoon a funny drawing in a newspaper or magazine that tells a story or a joke or comments on a news story: *The cartoon shows the President in a cowboy hat, riding on a horse into the meeting.*

illustration a picture in a book: *The illustrations in this children's book are wonderful.*

poster a large picture printed on paper, that advertises something or that you use as a decoration: *a poster for Tom Cruise's new movie*

2 take a picture = to take a photograph: *She took a picture of the waterfall.*
3 an idea of what a situation is like that you get when someone tells you about it: *After speaking with Lynn, I got a clearer picture of what was going on.*
4 the image that you see on a television or in a movie: *The picture's not very clear on this TV set.*
➔ See picture on page A8

picture² *verb*
1 to imagine something: *I can't picture myself as a mother.*
2 to show something or someone in a photograph, painting, or drawing: *She was pictured in a magazine with Brad Pitt.*

pie /paɪ/ *noun*
a PASTRY with fruit inside that you cook in an oven: *Would you like some apple pie?*

piece /pis/ *noun*
1 a part of something that is separate from the rest of it: *He took a piece of cake.* | *I dropped a glass and it broke into pieces.*

THESAURUS: piece

scrap a small piece of paper, cloth, etc.: *She wrote her phone number on a scrap of paper.*

chunk a thick piece of something that does not have an even shape: *The soup had large chunks of chicken in it.*

lump a small piece of something solid that does not have a definite shape: *a lump of metal*

fragment *formal* a small piece that has broken off something, especially glass or metal: *Fragments of glass from the car crash were still on the street.*

crumb a very small piece of bread, cake, etc.: *There were crumbs all over the floor.*

slice a thin, flat piece of bread, meat, etc. cut from a larger piece or from a whole thing: *a slice of blueberry pie*

2 a piece of writing/music/art = something that someone has written, drawn, or made: *I did a piece of writing about our family.*
3 a piece of advice/information, etc. = some advice, information, etc.: *She gave me one piece of advice: don't smoke.*
➔ See Thesaurus box at **part¹**

pier /pɪr/ *noun*
a long structure you can walk along that goes from the land into the ocean: *We stood on the pier watching the boats.*

pierce /pɪrs/ *verb*
to make a hole in something with a sharp object: *The needle pierced her skin.* | *I want to have my ears pierced* (=have holes for jewelry put in my ears).

pierc•ing¹ /ˈpɪrsɪŋ/ *adjective*
a piercing sound is loud and not nice: *I heard a piercing scream.*

piercing² *noun*
a hole that you put in your body for jewelry: *He has several tattoos and piercings.*

pig /pɪg/ *noun*
1 a fat pink farm animal: *The pigs were rolling in the mud.*
2 *informal* someone who eats too much or takes more than his or her share: *Don't be such a pig – leave some for everyone else.*
3 *informal* someone who behaves in an unkind way toward other people: *He's a pig and I hate him!*

pi•geon /ˈpɪdʒən/ *noun*
a gray bird that you often see in cities: *There were pigeons eating crumbs on the side-walk.*

P

ˈpiggy bank *noun*
a container in the shape of a pig in which children save coins

pig•let /ˈpɪglət/ *noun*
a young pig

pig•tail /ˈpɪgteɪl/ *noun*
if a girl's hair is in pigtails, she has pulled it together and tied it so that it hangs in two pieces, one on each side of her head

pile¹ /paɪl/ *noun*
1 a group of things on top of each other: *There was a pile of books on the table.* | *She sorted her clothes into piles.*
2 an amount of something in the shape of a small hill: *There were piles of snow by the side of the road.* SYNONYM **mound**

pile² *verb*
1 *also* **pile up** to put things together in a pile: *They piled the boxes in a corner.* | *Our suitcases were piled up on a cart.*
2 be piled with something = be filled or covered with something: *The shelves were piled with toys.*

pil•grim /ˈpɪlgrəm/ *noun*
a religious person who travels a long way to a holy place: *Thousands of pilgrims travel to Mecca each year.*
—**pilgrimage** *noun* a trip by pilgrims: *They went on a pilgrimage to Jerusalem.*

pill /pɪl/ *noun*
a small hard piece of medicine that you eat: *If you have a headache, take a pill* (=eat a pill). SYNONYM **tablet**

pil•lar /ˈpɪlɚ/ *noun*
a tall piece of stone that supports a building: *Ten pillars support the roof of the building.*
SYNONYM **column**

pil•low /ˈpɪloʊ/ *noun*
a soft square thing that you rest your head on in bed
➔ See picture on page A10

pil•low•case /ˈpɪloʊˌkeɪs/ *noun*
a cover for a pillow: *She changed the sheets and pillowcases.*

pi•lot /ˈpaɪlət/ *noun*
someone who flies an aircraft: *The pilot flew the plane very well.*

pim•ple /ˈpɪmpəl/ *noun*
a small red spot on your skin: *Teenagers often get pimples on their faces.*
—**pimply** *adjective* covered with pimples: *pimply skin*
➔ See Thesaurus box at **mark²**

pin¹ /pɪn/ *noun*
1 a short piece of metal with a sharp point, that you use to fasten pieces of material together: *She turned up the bottom of the skirt and put pins in it.*
2 a piece of metal that you fasten to your clothes, with jewels, a picture, or writing on it: *He wore a pin with a Canadian flag on it.*
3 one of the things you try to knock down in a game of BOWLING: *He knocked down all ten pins.*
➔ **clothespin**, **safety pin**

pin² *verb* **pinned, pinning**
1 to use a pin to attach something somewhere: *She pinned a flower on my coat.*
2 to hold someone so he or she cannot move: *He pinned her against the wall and wouldn't let her move.*

pinch¹ /pɪntʃ/ *verb*
to take a piece of someone's skin between your finger and thumb and press it: *My grandmother always pinches my cheeks and kisses me.*
➔ See picture on page A3

pinch² *noun*
1 the act of taking someone's skin between your finger and thumb and pressing it: *I gave her a pinch on the arm, and she yelled "Ouch!"*
2 a pinch of salt = a small amount of salt that you can hold between your finger and thumb: *Put a pinch of salt in the soup.*

pine /paɪn/ *noun*
1 *also* **pine tree** a tree with long leaves like needles and pine cones: *Some pine trees are used for Christmas trees.*
2 a soft, light-colored wood from pine trees: *a pine kitchen table*

pine•ap•ple /ˈpaɪnˌæpəl/ *noun*
a large yellow fruit that is rough on the outside and grows in hot places: *We ate a lot of pineapple when we were in Hawaii.*
➔ See picture on page A13

ˈpine cone *noun*
the brown seed container of a pine tree

ping-pong /ˈpɪŋpɑŋ/ *noun*
a game in which two people hit a ball across a net on a table

pink /pɪŋk/ *adjective*
a color that is a mixture of red and white: *pink lipstick*
—**pink** *noun*: *Baby girls often wear pink.*

pink•ie /ˈpɪŋki/ *noun, informal*
the smallest finger on your hand
➔ See picture at **hand**[1]

pin•na•cle /ˈpɪnəkəl/ *noun, formal*
the most successful part of something: *At 40, she had reached the pinnacle of her law career.*

pin•point /ˈpɪnpɔɪnt/ *verb, formal*
to say exactly when, where, or what something is: *I can pinpoint the moment I first met Steve – it was on my 12th birthday.* | *The doctors know there's something wrong, but they can't pinpoint what it is.*

pint /paɪnt/ *noun*
a measure of liquid, equal to 0.47 litres: *a pint of milk* | *He lost two pints of blood in the accident.*

pi•o•neer /ˌpaɪəˈnɪr/ *noun, formal*
1 one of the first people to do something that has a big effect on people's lives: *Bill Gates is a pioneer of computer software.*
2 one of the first people to go to a new place and start living there: *The pioneers crossed the American plains in wagons.*
—**pioneering** *adjective* doing new work that has a big effect on people's lives: *a pioneering heart surgeon*

pipe[1] /paɪp/ *noun*
1 a tube for carrying water or gas: *One of the water pipes broke and flooded the basement.*
2 an object for smoking tobacco that has a long part with a small bowl at the end: *My grandfather smoked a pipe.*

pipe[2] *verb*
to send a liquid or gas through a pipe: *They pipe water into the fields from the river.*

pipe•line /ˈpaɪp-laɪn/ *noun*
1 a system of pipes that carry oil or gas over long distances: *The pipeline carries oil from Russia to western Europe.*
2 be in the pipeline *formal* = if something is in the pipeline, people are planning it: *A new movie is in the pipeline, and filming should start next year.*

pi•rate[1] /ˈpaɪrət/ *noun*
someone who sails on the ocean attacking other ships and stealing from them: *He was dressed as a pirate, with a patch on his eye.*

pirate[2] *verb, formal*
to copy and sell movies, music, or computer programs in a way that is not legal: *Pirated copies of the movie were being sold illegally on the streets.*
—**piracy** *noun* the act of pirating something

Pis•ces /ˈpaɪsiz/ *noun*
1 the twelfth sign of the ZODIAC, represented by two fish
2 someone born between February 19 and March 20

pis•tol /ˈpɪstl/ *noun*
a small gun

pit /pɪt/ *noun*
1 a large hole in the ground: *They dug a pit and buried the garbage in it.*
2 a large hard seed in some fruits: *a peach pit*

pitch[1] /pɪtʃ/ *verb*
1 to throw the ball for a player to hit in baseball: *Who's pitching in tonight's baseball game?*
2 pitch a tent = to prepare a tent so that you can go inside it and use it: *We pitched our tent near the river.*

PHRASAL VERB
pitch in
to help other people with a job: *Everyone pitched in so that we could finish the cleaning and go home.*
➔ See Thesaurus box at **throw**[1]

pitch[2] *noun*
1 a throw of the ball for a player to hit in baseball: *His next pitch was high, and the batter let it pass.*
2 the pitch of a musical note is how high or low it is: *Trumpet players use their lips to change the pitch of a note.*

pitch•er /ˈpɪtʃɚ/ *noun*
1 a container used for holding and pouring liquids: *a pitcher of cold water* SYNONYM **jug**
2 the baseball player who throws the balls for other players to hit

pit•fall /ˈpɪtfɔl/ *noun, formal*
a common problem in a situation: *One of the pitfalls of being famous is having no privacy.* SYNONYM **disadvantage**

P

pit•i•ful /ˈpɪtɪfəl/ *adjective, formal*
very bad, in a way that makes you sad: *Children begging for money is a pitiful sight.*
—**pitifully** *adverb*: *Their pay is pitifully low.*

pit•y[1] /ˈpɪti/ *noun*
1 the sadness you feel when someone is in a bad situation: *I feel pity for people who have nowhere to live.*
2 take/have pity on someone = to help someone who is in a bad situation: *When she said she had no money, I took pity on her and gave her $50.*
3 a pity = used when saying that you wish a situation was different: *What a pity (that) you can't come with us.*

pity[2] *verb* **pitied**, third person singular **pities** *formal*
to feel sadness for someone because he or she is in a bad situation: *I pity people who have no family.*

piz•za /ˈpitsə/ *noun*
a round flat food with tomato, cheese and other things on top: *We ordered a sausage pizza and had it delivered.*
—**pizzeria** *noun* a restaurant that sells pizzas

plac•ard /ˈplækɚd/ *noun*
a sign with writing on that people carry when they are protesting about something: *They carried placards saying, "Stop the War."*

place[1] /pleɪs/ *noun*
1 an area, building, city, or country: *He lives in a place called Maple Meadows.* | *This is the place where I first saw her.* | *I couldn't find a place to park the car.*

> **THESAURUS: place**
>
> **position** the exact place where someone or something is, in relation to other things: *The shortstop's position is between second and third base.*
>
> **spot** *informal* a place, especially a pleasant one where you spend time: *It's a favorite spot for picnics.*
>
> **location** *formal* a place where something is, especially a hotel, store, office, etc., or the place where a movie is made: *The hotel is in a great location, right near the beach.*
>
> **site** a place where something is going to be built, or where something important happened: *the site for the new airport* | *This is the site where Lewis and Clark, the explorers, spent the winter after their trip across America.*
>
> **point** a particular place, for example on a map: *At this point the two roads cross.*

2 the right or usual position for something: *Put the CDs back in their place.*
3 a position in a line of people: *I had to leave the line for a minute, so I asked the man in front of me to save my place* (=make sure that I could come back to the same place).
4 *informal* someone's home: *Do you want to study at my place?* SYNONYM **house**
5 all over the place *informal* = everywhere: *I dropped a vase, and pieces of glass went all over the place.*
6 in first/second/last, etc. place = first, second, etc. at the end of a race or competition: *Joe finished the race in third place.*
7 in place *formal* = if something is in place, it is ready if people need it: *The college has a good security system in place.*
8 out of place = if something is out of place in a particular situation, it does not belong there: *She felt out of place, because all the other people were men.*
9 in place of = instead of someone or something: *I use honey in place of sugar in tea.*
10 take place *formal* = to happen: *The meeting will take place on Friday.*
11 take someone's place = to be as important as someone: *My mother married again, but no one could ever take my father's place.*
➔ See Thesaurus box at **home**[1]

place[2] *verb, formal*
1 to put something somewhere carefully: *Rachel placed the box on the table.*
2 place an order = to say that you want to buy something that you will get at a later time: *He placed an order for a new computer, and it was delivered one week later.* SYNONYM **order**

pla•gia•rism /ˈpleɪdʒəˌrɪzəm/ *noun, formal*
the act of copying someone else's words or ideas and pretending they are your own work: *His whole paper was copied from the*

Internet, and a teacher discovered his plagiarism.

—**plagiarize** /ˈpleɪdʒəˌraɪz/ *verb* to use plagiarism

plague /pleɪg/ *noun, formal*

a disease that kills people and spreads quickly: *Thousands of people died in a plague called "The Black Death."*

plaid /plæd/ *noun*

a pattern of squares and lines on material for clothing: *a plaid work shirt*

plain¹ /pleɪn/ *adjective*

1 something that is plain does not have a pattern on it or anything extra on it: *He wore a plain blue suit.* | *a sheet of plain paper* (=with no lines on it) ANTONYM **fancy**

2 easy to see, hear, or understand: *He made it plain (that) he didn't like me.* | *Why don't you tell me what you mean in plain English* (=without using difficult words)? SYNONYM **clear**

3 a plain woman or girl is not beautiful: *She was a plain girl with thin brown hair and sad eyes.*

—**plainness** *noun*

plain² *noun*

a large area of flat land: *Farmers grow wheat in the plains of America.*

plain·ly /ˈpleɪnli/ *adverb, formal*

1 in a way that is easy to see, hear, or understand: *He was plainly embarrassed because he was turning bright red.* SYNONYM **clearly, obviously**

2 in a simple way: *She was plainly dressed in jeans and a T-shirt.*

plan¹ /plæn/ *noun*

1 something you have decided to do: *Do you have any plans for Friday night?* | *I have no plans to leave school.*

2 a set of actions for doing something in the future: *The city has a plan for dealing with a big earthquake.*

3 a drawing showing all the parts of a building, room, machine, etc.: *The builder showed me the plans for the new library.*

plan² *verb* **planned, planning**

1 to think about something you want to do and about how to do it: *Carla's planning a party for her sixteenth birthday.*

2 to intend to do something: *How long do you plan on staying?* | *I plan to be an actor when I'm older.*

plane /pleɪn/ *noun*

a vehicle that flies using wings and an engine: *What time does your plane take off* (=leave)? | *The plane landed* (=arrived) *at O'Hare Airport.* | *It was time to board the plane* (=get on the plane). SYNONYM **airplane**

➔ See picture at **airplane**

plan·et /ˈplænət/ *noun*

1 a large round object in space, like the Earth, that moves around a star like the Sun: *Mercury is the smallest planet of our Sun.*

2 the planet = the Earth: *Pollution is destroying the planet.*

—**planetary** /ˈplænəˌteri/ *adjective* relating to planets: *planetary movements*

plank /plæŋk/ *noun*

a long flat piece of wood used for building something: *He made a table from planks of wood he found in the old house.*

plank·ton /ˈplæŋktən/ *noun*

very small plants and animals that float in the ocean: *Fish eat plankton.*

plant¹ /plænt/ *noun*

1 a living thing that has leaves and roots and grows in the ground: *I'm going to water the plants* (=give them water). | *They have some beautiful plants and trees in their yard.*

2 a factory and all its equipment: *The car plant produces thousands of vehicles every year.*

plant² *verb*

to put plants or seeds in the ground to grow: *Spring is the best time to plant flowers.*

plan·ta·tion /plænˈteɪʃən/ *noun*

a large farm in a hot country where a crop such as tea, cotton, or sugar is grown: *a sugar plantation*

plaque /plæk/ *noun*

1 a piece of flat metal or stone with writing on it: *A plaque on the house said: Walt Whitman was born here.*

2 a harmful substance that forms on your teeth: *Brushing your teeth every day helps to stop plaque.*

plas·ter¹ /ˈplæstɚ/ *noun*

a substance used for covering walls and ceilings to give them a smooth surface

plaster[2] *verb*

1 to cover a surface by spreading or sticking something all over it: *The walls of the restaurant were plastered with pictures of movie stars.*

2 to cover a wall or ceiling with plaster: *We need to plaster the cracks in the ceiling before we paint it.*

—**plasterer** *noun* someone whose job is to plaster walls and ceilings

P

plas•tic /ˈplæstɪk/ *noun*

a light strong substance made from chemicals, that is used for making many things: *Many children's toys are made of plastic.*

—**plastic** *adjective* made from plastic: *a plastic bag* | *plastic bottles*

ˌplastic ˈsurgery *noun*

medical operations that some people have, either in order to look better or to repair injuries: *She needed plastic surgery after being attacked by a dog.*

plate /pleɪt/ *noun*

1 a flat dish that you eat from or serve food on: *He put some rice and beans on his plate.*

2 *also* **plateful** /ˈpleɪtfʊl/ the amount of food on a plate: *He was eating a plate of pasta.*

➔ See picture on page A9

pla•teau /plæˈtoʊ/ *noun*

a large area of flat land that is higher than the land around it

plat•form /ˈplætfɔrm/ *noun*

1 a raised structure for people to stand or work on: *He climbed onto the platform and began to speak to the crowd.*

2 the place in a railroad station where you get on and off a train: *We were waiting on the platform.* | *The train leaves from platform 9.*

3 the main ideas and aims that a political party or politician states before an election: *The party is running on a platform of better education and healthcare.*

➔ See picture on page A26

plat•ing /ˈpleɪtɪŋ/ *noun*

a thin layer of metal that covers a metal object: *The box was metal with gold plating.*

plat•i•num /ˈplætn-əm/ *noun*

an expensive silver-white metal that is used for making jewelry

—**platinum** *adjective* made from platinum: *a platinum ring*

plat•ter /ˈplætɚ/ *noun*

1 a large plate, used for serving food: *Arrange the lettuce leaves on a large serving platter.*

2 *also* **platterful** /ˈplætɚfʊl/ the amount of food on a platter: *a platter of sliced beef*

play[1] /pleɪ/ *verb*

1 to take part in a game or sport: *I played baseball in school.* | *We're playing against a team from Indiana.*

> **GRAMMAR: play**
>
> Do not use a preposition (=a word such as "at," "on," or "in") or "the" after **play** when you are talking about playing a game or sport. Say: *They're playing football.*
>
> Do not say "They're playing at football" or "They're playing the football."

2 if children play, they enjoy themselves with toys and games: *The kids were playing outside in the yard.* | *She likes playing with dolls.*

3 to perform a piece of music on an instrument: *He plays the violin in an orchestra.* | *The band will be playing here tomorrow night.*

4 to act as one of the characters in a movie, television, or theater performance: *Kidman plays the part of Virginia Woolf in the movie.* | *In the movie, Potts plays a high school teacher.*

PHRASAL VERB

play with something

to keep touching or moving something: *He sat at the table playing with his glass of water.*

play[2] *noun*

1 a story that actors perform in a theater or on the radio: *He was a good actor and usually got the main part in the school plays.* | *The play is about two men on trial for murder.* | *Each year the drama department puts on a play* (=performs a play).

2 the actions of the people who are playing a game or sport: *The first play of the game was very exciting.*

3 the things that children do for fun, such as using toys or playing games: *Children learn through play.*

play•er /ˈpleɪɚ/ *noun*
someone who plays a game, sport, or musical instrument: *a piano player* | *a basketball player*

play•ful /ˈpleɪfəl/ *adjective*
1 intended to be fun or friendly rather than serious: *She gave him a playful poke.*
2 very active and happy: *Young cats are usually very playful.*
—**playfully** *adverb*
—**playfulness** *noun*

play•ground /ˈpleɪgraʊnd/ *noun*
an area where children can play, in a park or next to a school: *The neighborhood playground is a place for children to run, climb, and swing.*

ˈ**playing card** *noun*
one of a set of 52 cards that you use for playing games SYNONYM **card**

play•mate /ˈpleɪmeɪt/ *noun*
a friend that a child plays with: *There are a lot of kids in the neighborhood, so my son has lots of playmates.*

play•wright /ˈpleɪraɪt/ *noun*
someone who writes plays

pla•za /ˈplɑzə/ *noun*
an outdoor area with a lot of stores and small businesses: *They have a store in the Horton Plaza.*

plea /pli/ *noun, formal*
a strong or emotional request for something: *Nobody heard her pleas for help.* | *The charity has made a plea for more money to help the homeless children.*

plead /plid/ *verb, formal*
1 to ask for something you want very much, in an urgent and emotional way: *The woman pleaded for help to find her daughter.* | *I pleaded with him not to leave me alone.* SYNONYM **beg**
2 *formal* to officially say to a court of law whether you are guilty of a crime: *Parker pleaded not guilty to four charges of theft.*

pleas•ant /ˈplezənt/ *adjective, formal*
1 enjoyable, nice, or good: *It had been a pleasant evening.* | *a pleasant surprise* SYNONYM **nice**; ANTONYM **unpleasant**
2 polite, friendly, or kind: *The hotel manager was very pleasant and helpful.* SYNONYM **nice**; ANTONYM **unpleasant**
—**pleasantly** *adverb*: *We were pleasantly surprised by how friendly everyone was.*
—**pleasantness** *noun*
➔ See Thesaurus box at **nice**

please[1] /pliz/
1 a word you say to be polite when you are asking someone to do something: *Could you come here, please?* | *Can I have a cookie, please?*
2 a word you say to politely accept something that someone offers you: *"Would you like some coffee?" "Yes, please."*

please[2] *verb*
to make someone feel happy or satisfied: *I've tried to give him things he might like, but he's very hard to please.*

WORD FAMILY look at the words:
➔ **please** *verb*
➔ **pleased** *adjective*
➔ **pleasing** *adjective*
➔ **pleasant** *adjective*
➔ **pleasure** *noun*

pleased /plizd/ *adjective, formal*
happy or satisfied: *We're very pleased with the students' good grades.* | *Ellen was pleased that he remembered her birthday.*
➔ See Thesaurus box at **happy**

pleas•ing /ˈplizɪŋ/ *adjective, formal*
making you feel pleasure, happiness, or enjoyment: *The pictures in the book are visually pleasing* (=nice to look at).
—**pleasingly** *adverb*

pleas•ure /ˈpleʒɚ/ *noun*
a feeling of happiness, satisfaction, or enjoyment: *I get a lot of pleasure from traveling.* | *We encourage students to read for pleasure, not just because the teacher tells them to.*
—**pleasurable** *adjective, formal* giving you pleasure: *Schools should make reading a pleasurable experience for children.*

pleat /plit/ *noun*
a permanent fold in a piece of clothing
—**pleated** *adjective* a pleated skirt, dress, etc. has pleats in it

pledge[1] /pledʒ/ *noun*
a formal promise to do something: *The Republicans have made a pledge to cut taxes.*

P

pledge[2] *verb*
to make a formal promise to do something: *The government pledged to provide medical help to the people hurt in the storm.*

plen•ti•ful /ˈplentɪfəl/ *adjective*
more than enough in amount: *The birds come to the area because of the plentiful supply of food.*
—**plentifully** *adverb*

P

plen•ty /ˈplenti/ *pronoun*
a large amount that is enough or more than enough: *Eat plenty of fruit and vegetables to stay healthy.* | *There's plenty to see in New York City.*
➔ See Thesaurus boxes at **many** and **enough**

pli•ers /ˈplaɪɚz/ *plural noun*
a small metal tool used for bending or cutting wire: *a pair of pliers*

pliers

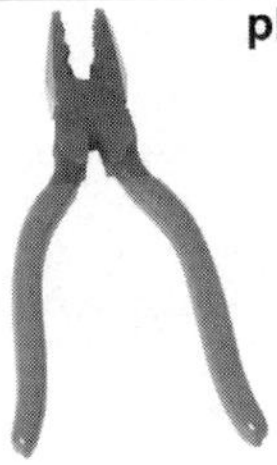

plot[1] /plɑt/ *noun*
1 the story of a book, movie, or play: *The movie has a very complicated plot – lots of things happen.*
2 a secret plan to do something illegal: *He was involved in a plot to kill the president.*
3 a small piece of land for building or growing things on: *a two-acre plot of land*

plot[2] *verb* **plotted, plotting**
to make a secret plan to do something illegal: *She was put in jail for plotting to kill her husband.*

plow[1] /plaʊ/ *noun*
1 a large piece of equipment used on farms, that cuts up the ground so that seeds can be planted
2 another word for a SNOWPLOW

plow[2] *verb*
to use a plow in order to cut up the ground so seeds can be planted: *He was out plowing the field.*

pluck /plʌk/ *verb*
1 *formal* to pull something quickly in order to remove it: *He plucked a flower from the bush.* SYNONYM **pick**
2 to pull the feathers off a chicken or other bird before cooking it

plug[1] /plʌg/ *noun*
1 the object at the end of a wire, that you put into a wall to get electricity for a piece of equipment: *She put the plug in the socket and turned the TV on.*
2 a round flat piece of rubber used for blocking the hole in a bathtub or SINK: *He pulled the plug out of the drain and the water went down.*
➔ See picture on page A20

plug[2] *verb* **plugged, plugging**
also **plug up** to fill a hole or block it: *We managed to plug the hole in the pipe.*

PHRASAL VERB
plug something in
to connect a piece of electrical equipment to a supply of electricity: *Is the TV plugged in? It's not working.* ANTONYM **unplug**

plum /plʌm/ *noun*
a soft round red or purple fruit with one large seed: *a plum tree*
➔ See picture on page A13

plumb•er /ˈplʌmɚ/ *noun*
someone whose job is to put in and repair water pipes, SINKs, toilets, etc.
➔ See picture on page A16

plumb•ing /ˈplʌmɪŋ/ *noun*
1 the system of water pipes in a building: *The plumbing in the bathroom leaks and needs to be replaced.*
2 the job that a plumber does

plum•met /ˈplʌmɪt/ *verb*
1 if a price, amount, or rate plummets, it suddenly and quickly becomes lower: *House prices have plummeted, and you can buy homes really cheaply now.* SYNONYM **plunge**
2 to fall suddenly and very quickly from a high place: *The plane plummeted to the ground.* SYNONYM **plunge**
➔ See Thesaurus box at **decrease**[1]

plump /plʌmp/ *adjective*
1 large and round in an attractive way: *plump juicy strawberries*
2 a polite way of describing someone who is fat: *He was 67, short, and a little plump.* | *the baby's plump fingers*
➔ See Thesaurus box at **fat**[1]

plunge /plʌndʒ/ *verb*
1 to fall suddenly and quickly from a high place: *The plane plunged into the Atlantic ten minutes after takeoff.* SYNONYM **plummet**

2 if an amount or level plunges, it suddenly becomes lower: *Profits plunged by 25%, and the company had to lay off workers.* SYNONYM **plummet**

PHRASAL VERB

plunge something into something
to quickly push something deeply into something else: *She plunged the knife into his chest and killed him.*

plu·ral /'plʊrəl/ *noun*
the plural = in grammar, the form of a word that you use when talking about more than one person or thing: *"Dogs" is the plural of "dog."*
—**plural** *adjective*: *a plural noun*

plus¹ /plʌs/ Ac *preposition*
used when one number or amount is added to another: *Three plus six equals nine* (=3+6=9). | *The jacket costs $49.95 plus tax.* ANTONYM **minus**

plus² *noun*
something good about a situation: *One of the pluses of riding a bike to work is that I don't have to worry about the price of gasoline.* ANTONYM **minus**

plus³ *adjective*
A plus/B plus, etc. *also* **A/B, etc.** = a grade for a piece of work that is slightly higher than a grade A, a grade B, etc.: *I got a C plus. If I'd answered two more questions right, I would have gotten a B minus.*

'plus sign *noun*
the sign (+), for example used in mathematics

Plu·to /'plutoʊ/ *noun*
the ninth PLANET from the Sun

plu·to·ni·um /plu'toʊniəm/ *noun*
a metal that is used for making NUCLEAR power

ply·wood /'plaɪwʊd/ *noun*
a type of board made from thin pieces of wood that have been stuck together: *They nailed a sheet of plywood over the broken window.*

p.m. /ˌpi 'em/
used when talking about times in the afternoon or evening, from 12 o'clock NOON until 12 o'clock MIDNIGHT: *I get out of work at 5:30 p.m.*

pneu·mat·ic /nʊ'mætɪk/ *adjective, formal*
1 filled with air: *a pneumatic tire*
2 a pneumatic tool or machine works by using air pressure: *a pneumatic drill*

pneu·mo·nia /nʊ'moʊnjə/ *noun*
a serious illness that affects your lungs and makes it difficult to breathe

poach /poʊtʃ/ *verb*
to cook food such as eggs or fish in a small amount of boiling liquid: *poached eggs*

P.O. box /pi 'oʊ ˌbɑks/ *noun* plural **P.O. boxes**
a numbered box in a post office where you can receive mail, instead of at your home

pock·et /'pɑkɪt/ *noun*
the part of a coat, skirt, pair of pants, etc. that you can put things in: *He had a few coins in his pocket.* | *He reached into his coat pocket and pulled out a small notebook.*

pock·et·book /'pɑkɪtˌbʊk/ *noun*
another word for a woman's PURSE SYNONYM **handbag**

'pocket knife *noun*
a small knife with a blade that you can fold into its handle

pod /pɑd/ *noun*
the long part of plants such as beans and PEAs that the seeds grow in

po·di·um /'poʊdiəm/ *noun*
1 a small raised area where someone stands to give a speech or CONDUCT a group of musicians: *She stepped up on the podium to make her speech.*
2 a tall narrow desk that you stand behind when giving a speech to a lot of people

po·em /'poʊɪm/ *noun*
a piece of writing that uses a pattern of lines and sounds to express emotions, experiences, and ideas: *He read a poem by Robert Frost.*

WORD FAMILY look at the words:
→ **poem** *noun*
→ **poet** *noun*
→ **poetry** *noun*
→ **poetic** *adjective*

po·et /'poʊɪt/ *noun*
someone who writes poems

po•et•ic /poʊ'etɪk/ *adjective*
relating to poetry, or typical of poetry: *He used poetic language to describe the sunset.*

po•et•ry /'poʊətri/ *noun*
poems: *She writes poetry about her feelings.*

point¹ /pɔɪnt/ *noun*
1 an idea or opinion in an argument or discussion: *He made a lot of good points in his report.*
2 the point = the most important fact or idea: *Come on, Charlie, get to the point* (=say your idea directly)*!* | *The point is (that) I don't want to stay here any more.* | *I think you're missing the point* (=you do not understand the most important thing).
3 the purpose or aim of doing something: *The whole point of traveling is to experience new things.* | *There's no point in worrying about things if you can't change them.*
4 a particular moment or time: *He started yelling, and at that point I decided to leave.* | *She had reached a point in her life when she wanted to do something new.*
5 a particular position or place: *the point where two lines cross each other*
6 a unit used for showing the SCORE in a game or sport: *The Rams beat the Giants by six points.*
7 the way you say the sign (.) used for separating a whole number from the DECIMALs that follow it: *four point five percent* (=4.5%)
8 the sharp end of something: *The point of a needle went through her skin.*
9 up to a point = partly, but not completely: *He believed her story, up to a point.*
→ **point of view**
→ See Thesaurus boxes at **end¹** and **place¹**

point² *verb*
1 to show someone something by holding your finger out toward it: *John pointed to the house and said, "That's where I used to live."* | *"That's my car," she said, pointing at a large white Ford.*
2 to aim something in a particular direction: *He pointed a gun at my head.*
PHRASAL VERB
point something out
to tell someone something that he or she does not already know or has not yet noticed: *He pointed out that the costs could be very high.*
→ See picture on page A3

point•ed /'pɔɪntɪd/ *adjective*
having a point at the end: *The shoes had pointed toes and I could hardly squeeze my feet in.*

point•er /'pɔɪntɚ/ *noun*
1 a helpful piece of advice: *I gave him some pointers on how to swing a golf club.*
SYNONYM **tip**
2 a small ARROW on a computer screen that you move to the place that you want to work: *Move the pointer to the picture and click.*
3 a long stick used for pointing at things on a map, board, etc.

point•less /'pɔɪntləs/ *adjective*
having no purpose, or not likely to have any effect: *It's pointless trying to call him – he isn't home.*

ˌpoint of 'view *noun*
1 your opinion about something: *My parents never seem to understand my point of view.*
2 a particular way of thinking about or judging a situation: *The project was not successful from a financial point of view.*

poi•son¹ /'pɔɪzən/ *noun*
a substance that can kill you or make you sick: *We used rat poison to kill the rats.*
WORD FAMILY → **poisonous** *adjective*

poison² *verb*
to kill or harm someone by using poison: *She was put in jail after she tried to poison her husband.*

ˌpoison 'ivy *noun*
a plant that makes your skin hurt when you touch its leaves

ˌpoison 'oak *noun*
a plant that makes your skin hurt when you touch its leaves

poi•son•ous /'pɔɪzənəs/ *adjective*
containing poison: *She died after breathing in poisonous gas.*

poke /poʊk/ *verb*
to push your finger or something pointed into something or someone: *Polly poked me in the stomach with her finger.*
→ See Thesaurus box at **push¹**
→ See picture on page A3

pok•er /ˈpoʊkɚ/ *noun*
a card game that people play to win money

po•lar /ˈpoʊlɚ/ *adjective*
relating to the North Pole or the South Pole: *polar ice*

ˈpolar bear *noun*
a large white bear that lives near the North Pole

pole /poʊl/ *noun*
1 a long post made of wood or metal: *The telephone poles held up telephone wires along the road.*
2 the most northern or southern point of the Earth: *There is a lot of snow and ice at the North Pole.*

Pole /poʊl/ *noun*
someone from Poland

ˈpole vault *noun*
the pole vault = a sport in which you jump over a high BAR using a long pole

po•lice /pəˈlis/ *noun*
the group of people whose job is to catch criminals and make sure that people obey the law: *I saw someone stealing a car and called the police.* | *a police car*
➔ See page A27

poˈlice force *noun*
the group of police in a particular country or place: *Jones joined the Los Angeles police force in 2003.*

po•lice•man /pəˈlismən/ *noun* plural **policemen** /pəˈlismən/
a male police officer

poˈlice ˌofficer *noun*
a member of the police: *Police officers arrested the man for selling drugs.*
➔ See picture on page A16

poˈlice ˌstation *noun*
the office of the police in a town or city: *He went to the police station to report the attack.*

po•lice•wom•an /pəˈlisˌwʊmən/ *noun* plural **policewomen** /pəˈlisˌwɪmɪn/
a female police officer

pol•i•cy /ˈpɑləsi/ Ac *noun* plural **policies**
a set of ideas and methods that a government, business, or organization agrees to use when it is dealing with a situation: *The school has a strict policy on smoking – no one is allowed to smoke.*

po•li•o /ˈpoʊliˌoʊ/ *noun*
a serious infectious disease that can permanently stop someone from moving some muscles

pol•ish[1] /ˈpɑlɪʃ/ *verb*
to make something shiny by rubbing it: *He polished his shoes each night.*
—**polished** *adjective* shiny after being polished: *a smooth, polished wooden floor*

polish[2] *noun*
a substance that you rub on something to make it shiny: *shoe polish*
➔ **nail polish**

Po•lish[1] /ˈpoʊlɪʃ/ *adjective*
from Poland

Polish[2] *noun*
the language spoken in Poland

po•lite /pəˈlaɪt/ *adjective*
behaving or speaking in a pleasant way that is correct for the social situation you are in: *It's not polite to talk with your mouth full.*
ANTONYM **impolite, rude**
—**politely** *adverb*
—**politeness** *noun*

po•lit•i•cal /pəˈlɪtɪkəl/ *adjective*
relating to the government or politics of a country: *The U.S. has two main political parties: the Republicans and the Democrats.*
—**politically** *adverb*

poˌlitically corˈrect *adjective*, *abbreviation* **PC**
very careful to treat people equally whatever their skin color, sex, etc. is and not to offend or insult anyone: *Children's stories are more politically correct now, and often have girls doing adventurous things.*

pol•i•ti•cian /ˌpɑləˈtɪʃən/ *noun*
someone who is an elected member of a government: *Most Democratic politicians voted for the new law.*

pol•i•tics /ˈpɑlətɪks/ *noun*
1 ideas and activities relating to getting and using power in a country, city, etc.: *I'm not very interested in politics, but I do vote.*
2 the job of being a politician: *Smith went into politics as a young man.*

WORD FAMILY look at the words:
➔ **politics** *noun*
➔ **politician** *noun*
➔ **political** *adjective*

pol•ka /ˈpoʊlkə/ *noun*
a fast dance for people dancing in pairs

poll /poʊl/ *noun*
the process of asking a lot of people questions in order to find out what they think about something: *A recent opinion poll shows that more than 50% of people do not like the president's plan.*
—**poll** *verb* to do a poll: *They polled over 2,000 people to get their opinions.*

pol•len /ˈpɑlən/ *noun*
a powder that flowers produce, which is carried by the wind or insects to other flowers so they can make seeds: *Pollen from some flowers makes me sneeze.*

pol•li•nate /ˈpɑləˌneɪt/ *verb*
to make a flower produce seeds by giving it pollen: *Bees and other insects pollinate the flowers.*
—**pollination** /ˌpɑləˈneɪʃən/ *noun* the process of pollinating a flower

pol•lute /pəˈlut/ *verb*
to make air, water, or soil dangerously dirty: *Smoke from the factory pollutes the air.*
—**polluted** *adjective* with a lot of harmful and dirty substances in the air, water, or soil: *It is one of the country's most polluted cities, with lots of factories and traffic.*
—**pollutant** *noun, formal* something that pollutes air, water, or soil: *We need to reduce the amount of pollutants that cars produce.*

pollution

pol•lu•tion /pəˈluʃən/ *noun*
1 substances that have a harmful effect on air, water, or soil: *Heavy traffic produces a lot of air pollution.*
2 the process of making air, water, or soil dangerously dirty: *The pollution of lakes and rivers is killing fish.*

pol•y•es•ter /ˈpɑliˌestɚ/ *noun*
an artificial material used to make cloth: *The shirt was made from cotton and polyester.*

pomp•ous /ˈpɑmpəs/ *adjective, formal*
trying to make people think you are important by using a lot of formal words: *He made a long and pompous speech about his achievements.*

pon•cho /ˈpɑntʃoʊ/ *noun* plural **ponchos**
a type of coat that is a piece of thick cloth with a hole in the middle for your head

pond /pɑnd/ *noun*
a small area of water that is smaller than a lake: *There were some ducks swimming on the pond.*

pon•der /ˈpɑndɚ/ *verb, formal*
to think carefully about something: *She pondered the question before she gave her answer.*

po•ny /ˈpoʊni/ *noun* plural **ponies**
a small horse: *The children were riding ponies.*

po•ny•tail /ˈpoʊniˌteɪl/ *noun*
long hair that you tie together at the back of your head: *Chrissy pulled her hair back in a ponytail.*

poo•dle /ˈpudl/ *noun*
a dog with thick curly hair

pool /pul/ *noun*
1 *also* **swimming pool** a structure that is filled with water for people to swim in: *He was swimming in the pool in their backyard.*
2 a game in which you use a stick to hit numbered balls into holes in the sides and corners of a table: *Let's play a game of pool.*
3 a pool of blood/water/oil, etc. = a small area of blood, water, etc. on the ground or another surface: *He had been shot and was lying in a pool of blood.*

poor /pʊr/ *adjective*
1 having very little money: *They were so poor that they couldn't buy new shoes for the children.* | *a poor country* ANTONYM **rich**

THESAURUS: poor

needy not having enough food or money: *The program provides health care to needy families.*

broke *informal* not having any money for a period of time: *He was broke and hungry.*

disadvantaged *formal* having social problems, such as a lack of money, that make it difficult to succeed: *Students from disadvantaged groups may need more help in school.*

underprivileged *formal* poor and not having the same education, health care, safety, etc. of other people in society: *The center is a place where underprivileged kids can go for help.*

deprived *formal* not having the things that you need for a comfortable or happy life: *a deprived area in the inner city*

2 not very good: *Many people are unable to work because of poor health.* ANTONYM **good**
3 said in order to show that you feel sorry for someone: *The poor girl looked very scared.*

poor•ly /ˈpʊrli/ *adverb*
badly: *The article was poorly written and contained lots of mistakes.*

pop[1] /pɑp/ *verb* **popped, popping**
to make a short loud sound, for example by bursting: *Jody squeezed the balloon until it popped.*
➔ See Thesaurus box at **break[1]**

pop[2] *noun*
1 *also* **ˈpop ˌmusic** modern music that is popular with young people: *a pop concert*
2 a sudden short sound like a small explosion: *She heard the pop of a gun.*

pop•corn /ˈpɑpkɔrn/ *noun*
a type of corn that swells and bursts open when you cook it: *They ate popcorn while they watched the movie.*

Pope /poʊp/ *noun*
the leader of the Roman Catholic Church: *Pope Benedict XVI*

pop•u•lar /ˈpɑpyələ˞/ *adjective*
liked by a lot of people: *Tom is very popular with women and always has a girlfriend.* ANTONYM **unpopular**
—**popularize** *verb, formal* to make something become popular

pop•u•lar•i•ty /ˌpɑpyəˈlærəti/ *noun*
the quality of being liked by a lot of people: *The growing popularity of Internet shopping is badly affecting many downtown stores.*

pop•u•lat•ed /ˈpɑpyəˌleɪtɪd/ *adjective, formal*
a populated area has people living in it: *The weapons tests are done away from populated areas.*
—**populate** *verb, formal* if groups of people populate an area, they live there

pop•u•la•tion /ˌpɑpyəˈleɪʃən/ *noun*
the number of people who live in a place: *Chicago has a population of nearly 3 million.*
➔ See Thesaurus box at **people**

pop•u•lous /ˈpɑpyələs/ *adjective, formal*
a populous place has a lot of people living in it: *China and India are the world's most populous countries.*

por•ce•lain /ˈpɔrsəlɪn/ *noun*
a hard shiny white substance that is used for making expensive plates, cups, etc.: *a valuable porcelain cup*

porch /pɔrtʃ/ *noun*
a structure with a floor and roof that is built onto a house at its front or back door: *On summer evenings, he sat on the porch reading a book.*

por•cu•pine /ˈpɔrkyəˌpaɪn/ *noun*
an animal with long, sharp, needle-like parts growing all over its back and sides

pork /pɔrk/ *noun*
the meat from pigs: *The sausage is made from pork.*
➔ See Thesaurus box at **meat**

por•poise /ˈpɔrpəs/ *noun*
a large ocean animal, like a DOLPHIN, that breathes air

port /pɔrt/ *noun*
1 a place where ships stop and people put goods onto them or take goods off: *The ship was getting ready to leave the port.*
2 a town or city with a port: *Hong Kong is the world's largest port.*

port•a•ble /ˈpɔrtəbəl/ *adjective*
light and easy to move or carry: *Portable computers make it easy to take work with you when you travel.*
—**portability** /ˌpɔrtəˈbɪləti/ *noun* the quality of being portable

por•ter /ˈpɔrtə˞/ *noun*
someone whose job is to carry travelers' bags at airports, hotels, etc.

P

port·fo·li·o /pɔrtˈfoʊliˌoʊ/ *noun* plural **portfolios**
1 a large flat case for carrying pictures or documents
2 a collection of paintings, photographs, or pieces of writing that an artist or writer shows people as an example of his or her work: *Art students will have to produce a portfolio of work.*

por·tion /ˈpɔrʃən/ Ac *noun, formal*
1 a part of something larger: *He agreed to pay a small portion of the total bill.* SYNONYM **part**
2 an amount of food for one person: *The food was good, but the portions were very small.*

por·trait /ˈpɔrtrɪt/ *noun*
a painting, drawing, or photograph of someone: *He painted a portrait of his daughter.*
➔ See Thesaurus box at **picture**[1]

por·tray /pɔrˈtreɪ/ *verb* **portrayed**, third person singular **portrays** *formal*
1 portray someone or something as something = to describe or show someone or something in a particular way: *The governor tries to portray himself as a man who understands and cares about people.*
2 to act the part of a character in a play or movie: *In the movie, he portrays a college professor.* SYNONYM **play**
—**portrayal** *noun, formal* the way that someone or something is portrayed: *The article's portrayal of young people as troublemakers is unfair.*

Por·tu·guese[1] /ˌpɔrtʃəˈgiz/ *adjective*
from Portugal

Portuguese[2] *noun*
1 the language spoken in Portugal and Brazil
2 the Portuguese = people from Portugal in general

pose[1] /poʊz/ Ac *verb*
1 pose a problem/threat/challenge etc. *formal* = to cause a problem, danger, difficulty, etc.: *Nuclear waste poses a threat to the environment.*
2 to sit or stand in a particular position so that someone can photograph you or do a painting of you: *The president posed for photographs before going inside for the meeting.*
3 pose a question *formal* = to ask a question that people need to think about: *Nielsen's essay poses some tough questions.*

pose[2] *noun*
the position that you stand or sit in when someone is doing a painting of you or taking a photograph of you: *She sat in a strange pose, with her head to one side.*

po·si·tion /pəˈzɪʃən/ *noun*
1 the way someone stands, sits, or lies: *You should be in a comfortable position when driving.* | *This exercise is done in a sitting position.*
2 the situation that someone or something is in: *I'm not sure what I would do if I were in your position.* SYNONYM **situation**
3 the place where someone or something is, in relation to other things: *She changed the position of the furniture in the room.*
4 *formal* a job: *He decided to give up his position as coach of the football team.*
➔ See Thesaurus boxes at **job** and **place**[1]

pos·i·tive /ˈpɑzətɪv/ Ac *adjective*
1 very sure that something is right or true: *I'm positive (that) I told her to meet us here at 2:00.*
2 hopeful and confident, and thinking about what is good in a situation rather than what is bad: *She has a very positive attitude, even though she has health problems.* ANTONYM **negative**
3 good or useful: *At least something positive has come out of all these problems – we've become better friends.* ANTONYM **negative**
4 expressing support, agreement, or approval: *So far, we've had mostly positive reactions to the new show.* ANTONYM **negative**
5 a medical test that is positive shows that someone has a disease or condition: *Her pregnancy test came back positive* (=showed she was going to have a baby). ANTONYM **negative**
—**positively** *adverb*

pos·sess /pəˈzɛs/ *verb, formal*
to own or have something: *They lost everything they possessed in the fire.*
—**possessor** *noun* someone who possesses something
➔ See Thesaurus box at **own**[2]

pos•ses•sion /pə'zeʃən/ *noun, formal*
1 something that you own: *One small bag held all his possessions.* SYNONYM **belongings**
2 the state of having or owning something: *He was arrested for possession of illegal drugs.*

pos•ses•sive /pə'zesɪv/ *adjective, formal*
relating to words that show who something belongs to: *Add 's to a noun to make the possessive form: This is John's bike.*
—**possessive** *noun* words that show who something belongs to: *Words such as "my" and "theirs" are possessives.*

pos•si•bil•i•ty /ˌpɑsə'bɪləti/ *noun* plural **possibilities**
something that might happen or be true: *There's a possibility that Jim won't be able to play in Saturday's game.*

pos•si•ble /'pɑsəbəl/ *adjective*
1 something that is possible may happen or be true: *"Will Ron be at the party?" "It's possible."* | *Some math problems have more than one possible answer.*
2 if something is possible, people can do it: *It is possible to send people to Mars, but no country has done it.* ANTONYM **impossible**
3 as soon as possible/as long as possible/as much as possible, etc. = as soon as you can, as long as you can, etc.: *She needs to see a doctor as soon as possible.*

WORD FAMILY look at the words:
→ **possible** *adjective*
→ **possibly** *adverb*
→ **possibility** *noun*

pos•si•bly /'pɑsəbli/ *adverb*
1 used when saying that something may be true or may happen: *"How long will the rehearsal be?" "Two hours, possibly three."* SYNONYM **perhaps, maybe**
2 used to emphasize what someone can or cannot do. The words "can" and "could" are used with "possibly" in this meaning: *I can't possibly be there by six o'clock – I don't finish work until then.*

pos•sum /'pɑsəm/ *noun, informal*
another word for an OPOSSUM

post¹ /poʊst/ *noun*
1 a wood or metal pole that you put into the ground to support something: *a fence post*
2 *formal* an important job in the government: *She decided to leave her post at the Justice Department.*
3 something that you write on a website that allows people to talk about different subjects: *Have you been reading the posts about the last Harry Potter book?*

post² *verb*
to put a message or notice about something on a wall or website: *The school rules are posted on the bulletin board in each classroom.*

post•age /'poʊstɪdʒ/ *noun*
the money that you pay for sending something by mail: *How much was the postage for that package you sent to Dan?*

'postage stamp *noun, formal*
another word for a STAMP

post•al /'poʊstl/ *adjective, formal*
relating to the organization that takes letters from one place to another: *Postal workers are very busy at Christmas.*

post•card /'poʊskɑrd/ *noun*
a card with a picture on the front, that you can send in the mail without an envelope: *Emily sent me a postcard from Yellowstone National Park.*

post•er /'poʊstɚ/ *noun*
a large printed notice or picture, that advertises something or that you use as a decoration: *Did you see the poster advertising the school play?*
→ See Thesaurus boxes at **picture¹** and **advertisement**
→ See picture on page A10

post•man /'poʊstmən/ *noun* plural **postmen** /'poʊstmən/
a man whose job is delivering mail to people's houses SYNONYM **mailman**

post•mark /'poʊstmɑrk/ *noun*
a mark on a letter or package that shows the place and time it was sent: *The letter had a New York postmark, so she must have mailed it when she was there.*
—**postmark** *verb* to put a postmark on a letter or package

P

P

ˈpost ˌoffice *noun*
a place where you can buy stamps and send letters and packages: *I'm going to the post office to mail this package.*

ˈpost office ˌbox *noun*, *abbreviation* **P.O. box**
a numbered box in a post office where you can receive mail, instead of at your home

post•pone /poʊsˈpoʊn/ *verb*, *formal*
to change the time of an event to a later time or date: *The game was postponed because of rain.*
—**postponement** *noun* the act of postponing something

pos•ture /ˈpɑstʃɚ/ *noun*
the way you hold your body when you sit or stand: *Back exercises will help his bad posture.*

pot /pɑt/ *noun*
1 a round container that you cook things in: *Mom made a big pot of chicken soup.*
2 a container with a handle and a lid, that you use to make and pour coffee or tea: *a coffee pot*
→ **flowerpot**
→ See picture on page A9

po•tas•si•um /pəˈtæsiəm/ *noun*
a silver-white soft metal that is in some types of food in very small amounts: *Bananas have potassium in them.*

po•ta•to /pəˈteɪtoʊ/ *noun* plural **potatoes**
a hard round white vegetable with brown, red, or yellow skin, that grows under the ground: *Peel the potatoes and boil them.*
→ See picture on page A12

poˈtato chip *noun*
a thin hard piece of potato that was cooked in oil: *He opened a bag of potato chips.*

po•ten•tial /pəˈtenʃəl/ Ac *noun*, *formal*
a quality or an ability that has not developed completely yet: *He has the potential to be one of our best players.*
—**potential** *adjective* possible, but not yet completely developed: *We need to be ready for any potential problems.*
—**potentially** *adverb*

pot•hole /ˈpɑthoʊl/ *noun*
a hole in a road that makes driving harder: *The street has a lot of big potholes and is hard to drive on.*

pot•luck /ˌpɑtˈlʌk/ *adjective*
a meal for which everyone brings food to share: *Can you bring a chicken dish for the potluck?*

pot•ter•y /ˈpɑtəri/ *noun*
1 the activity of making objects out of clay and then baking them: *She's taking a pottery class.*
2 plates, cups, and other objects that are made out of clay that you bake: *Jill makes and sells bowls and other pottery.*
—**potter** *noun* someone who makes pottery

poul•try /ˈpoʊltri/ *noun*, *formal*
birds such as chickens and ducks that are kept on farms for their eggs and meat: *Poultry should be completely cooked before you eat it.*

pounce /paʊns/ *verb*
to suddenly jump on someone or something in order to catch him, her, or it: *The cat pounced on a bird.*

pounce

pound¹ /paʊnd/ *noun*
1 *written abbreviation* **lb.** a unit for measuring weight, equal to 16 OUNCEs or 453.6 grams: *Jim weighs 175 pounds.*
2 the standard unit of money in Great Britain and some other countries
3 **the pound** = a place where a city keeps lost dogs and cats
→ See Thesaurus box at **hit¹**

pound² *verb*
1 to hit something many times: *Someone was pounding on the door, trying to wake the people inside.*
2 if your heart pounds, it beats very quickly: *I was scared, and my heart was pounding.*

pour /pɔr/ *verb*
1 to make a liquid or other substance flow out of or into a container: *Will you pour me another cup of coffee, please? | Pour the batter into a cake pan.*

THESAURUS: pour

flow to move in a steady stream: *The river flows into the sea.*

drip if a liquid drips or if something drips liquid, the liquid falls in drops: *Water dripped onto the floor.*

leak if a liquid leaks or something leaks a liquid, the liquid passes through a hole or crack: *The car is leaking oil.*

ooze to flow from something very slowly: *Blood oozed through the bandages.*

gush to flow or pour out quickly in large quantities: *One of the pipes broke, and water gushed out of it.*

run to flow: *Tears ran down her cheeks.*

2 if a liquid pours somewhere, it flows there quickly: *Sweat was pouring down my forehead.*
3 to rain a lot: *It's been pouring all afternoon.*
➔ See picture on page A14

pov•er•ty /ˈpɑvɚti/ *noun, formal*
the state of being poor: *They live in poverty and don't have enough money to buy food every day.*

poverty-strick•en /ˈpɑvɚti ˌstrɪkən/ *adjective, formal*
very poor: *They live in poverty-stricken communities with no running water.*

pow•der /ˈpaʊdɚ/ *noun*
a soft dry substance in the form of very small grains: *Add one teaspoon of chili powder to the meat mixture.*
—**powdery** *adjective* feeling or looking like powder

pow•er /ˈpaʊɚ/ *noun*
1 the ability to control people or control what happens: *The president has a lot of power.* | *Teachers have the power to punish you if you do not behave well.*
2 energy such as electricity that is used to make a machine work, or to give light, heat, etc.: *The flashlight went out because there was no power left in the batteries.*
3 to the power of 3/4/5, etc. = used to say the number of times a number is multiplied by itself: *2 to the power of 3 (2x2x2) equals 12.*

pow•er•boat /ˈpaʊɚˌboʊt/ *noun*
a boat that people use for racing

pow•er•ful /ˈpaʊɚfəl/ *adjective*
1 a powerful person or country is important and has a lot of control over other people or over what happens: *The president is one of the most powerful men in the world.*
2 something that is powerful is very strong or has a strong effect: *The car has a powerful engine.* | *Television has a powerful influence on our lives.*
—**powerfully** *adverb*

pow•er•less /ˈpaʊɚləs/ *adjective, formal*
not having strength or control: *I wanted to help her, but I was powerless to do anything.*

ˈpower plant *also* **ˈpower ˌstation** *noun*
a building where electricity is made for people to use in their homes, businesses, etc.

P

prac•ti•cal /ˈpræktɪkəl/ *adjective*
1 sensible and likely to work correctly or do something in a way that works well: *He's a very practical person.* | *A sports car isn't practical for a family with three kids.*
2 relating to doing things rather than thinking or talking about them: *The students do practical work in the chemistry lab.*

ˌpractical ˈjoke *noun*
a trick that surprises someone and makes other people laugh: *He put a mouse in her desk drawer as a practical joke.*

prac•ti•cally /ˈpræktɪkli/ *adverb, informal*
almost: *These shoes are practically new – I bought them a month ago.*

prac•tice[1] /ˈpræktɪs/ *noun*
1 a regular activity that you do in order to improve your skill at it: *It takes a lot of practice to be a good piano player.* | *What time is baseball practice?*
2 in practice = used say what the real situation is rather than what seems to be true: *Jess is supposed to be the leader, but in practice Lisa runs everything.*
3 be out of practice = to not be able to do something well because you have not done it for a long time: *I used to play the guitar, but I'm really out of practice now.*
4 *formal* the work or business of a doctor or lawyer: *He started his own legal practice when he finished law school.*

practice[2] *verb*
1 to do something regularly in order to improve your skill at it: *Kate practices the piano for half an hour every day.*

THESAURUS: practice

rehearse to practice something such as a play or concert before people come to see it: *The band was rehearsing for the show that night.*

work on something to practice a skill, musical instrument, etc. in order to improve: *Jessie has been working on her tennis serve.*

train to prepare for a sports event by exercising and practicing: *Olympic swimmers train for hours every day.*

drill to teach people something by making them repeat the same thing many times: *The teacher was drilling the kids on their multiplication tables.*

2 *formal* to work as a doctor or lawyer: *Bill is practicing medicine in Ohio now.*

prag•mat•ic /præg'mætɪk/ *adjective, formal*
dealing with situations in a sensible way that is likely to work: *The article had some pragmatic ideas for getting kids to eat vegetables.*
—**pragmatism** /'prægmə,tɪzəm/ *noun* the quality of being pragmatic

prairie

prai•rie /'preri/ *noun*
a large area of land in the middle part of North America that is covered in grass and does not have many trees: *In the 1860s, they moved to a small farm on the Iowa prairie.*

praise¹ /preɪz/ *verb*
1 to say that someone has done something well, or that something is good: *The coach praised them for playing so well.*
2 to give your thanks and respect to God: *They sang songs to praise God.*

praise² *noun*
1 words that you say or write to praise someone or something: *The movie has gotten praise from the critics.*
2 respect or thanks that you give to God: *Let us give praise to the Lord.*

pray /preɪ/ *verb*
to talk to God or other gods to ask for help or give thanks: *We prayed for Nancy when she was in the hospital.*

prayer /prer/ *noun*
the act of praying, or the words that you say when you pray: *I said a prayer for my mother when she got on the plane.*

preach /pritʃ/ *verb*
to talk about a religious subject in church: *The minister preached about helping strangers.*

preach•er /'pritʃɚ/ *noun*
someone who talks about religious subjects in a church SYNONYM **minister**

pre•car•i•ous /prɪ'keriəs/ *adjective, formal*
a precarious situation may become worse very suddenly: *His health is in a precarious condition and his family is very worried.*
—**precariously** *adverb*

pre•cau•tion /prɪ'kɔʃən/ *noun, formal*
something that you do to stop something bad or dangerous from happening: *I took the precaution of locking the door when I left.*
—**precautionary** *adjective* relating to something you do as a precaution

pre•cede /prɪ'sid/ Ac *verb, formal*
to be or happen before something else: *A loud explosion preceded the fire.*

pre•cinct /'prisɪŋkt/ *noun, formal*
one of the parts that a city is divided into: *Only three of the city's twelve precincts supported him.*

pre•cious /'preʃəs/ *adjective*
1 very valuable and important: *Diamonds are precious stones.*
2 very important or special to you: *The doll is precious because it was my grandmother's.*

pre•cip•i•ta•tion /prɪ,sɪpə'teɪʃən/ *noun, formal*
rain or snow

pre•cise /prɪ'saɪs/ Ac *adjective, formal*
exact and correct: *There were more than a hundred people there, but I don't know the precise number.*
—**precisely** *adverb*: *He arrived precisely at 4:00.*

WORD FAMILY look at the words:

→ **precise** *adjective*
→ **imprecise** *adjective*
→ **precisely** *adverb*
→ **precision** *noun*

pre•ci•sion /prɪˈsɪʒən/ Ac *noun, formal*
the quality of being very exact and correct: *The clock measures time with precision – it tells you exactly what time it is.*
—**precision** *adjective* made in a very exact way, or doing something in a very exact way: *precision instruments*

pre•con•cep•tion /ˌprikənˈsepʃən/ *noun, formal*
an idea that you have about something before you know what it is really like: *I had a lot of preconceptions about the U.S. from watching American movies.*

pred•a•tor /ˈpredətɚ/ *noun, formal*
an animal that kills and eats other animals: *Sharks are predators that eat fish in the ocean.*

pred•e•ces•sor /ˈpredəˌsesɚ/ *noun, formal*
someone that did a job or something that existed before the person who does the job now or thing that exists now: *This computer is much faster than its predecessors.*

pre•dic•a•ment /prɪˈdɪkəmənt/ *noun, formal*
a difficult situation in which you do not know what is the best thing to do: *We were lost and frightened about our predicament.*

pred•i•cate /ˈpredɪkɪt/ *noun, formal*
in grammar, the part of a sentence that has the main verb, and that tells what the subject is doing or describes the subject. In the sentence "He ran out of the house," "ran out of the house" is the predicate.

pre•dict /prɪˈdɪkt/ Ac *verb, formal*
to say what is going to happen before it happens: *The weatherman predicted rain this weekend.*
—**predictable** *adjective* happening in the way that you expect

pre•dic•tion /prɪˈdɪkʃən/ Ac *noun, formal*
a statement saying what is going to happen before it happens: *It's too early to make predictions about who will win the competition.*

pre•dom•i•nant /prɪˈdɑmənənt/ Ac *adjective, formal*
most common, most noticeable, or strongest: *Red was the predominant color in the painting, but other colors were used as well.*
—**predominate** /prɪˈdɑməˌneɪt/ *verb* to be predominant

pre•dom•i•nant•ly /prɪˈdɑmənəntli/ Ac *adverb, formal*
mostly or mainly: *They are the only Asian family in a predominantly white neighborhood.*

pref•ace /ˈprefəs/ *noun*
a part of a book that comes before the main part, and that tells you about the book or the writer: *The preface to the novel tells the reader a little bit about Mark Twain's life.*

pre•fer /prɪˈfɚ/ *verb* **preferred, preferring**
to like someone or something better than someone or something else: *Which color do you prefer?*

pref•er•a•ble /ˈprefərəbəl/ *adjective, formal*
better or more appropriate: *Classes with only 20 children are preferable to larger ones.*
—**preferably** *adverb*

pref•er•ence /ˈprefərəns/ *noun*
if someone has a preference for something, he or she likes it better than another thing: *Even small babies show preferences for some kinds of food – they like some, and dislike others.*

pre•fix /ˈprifɪks/ *noun, formal*
a group of letters that you add to the beginning of a word in order to make a new word: *If we add the prefix "un" to the word "happy," we make the word "unhappy."*

preg•nan•cy /ˈpregnənsi/ *noun* plural **pregnancies**
the state of having a baby growing inside your body: *Women sometimes feel sick at the start of a pregnancy.*

preg•nant /ˈpregnənt/ *adjective*
having a baby growing in your body: *Kathy got pregnant soon after she and Todd were married.*

P

P

pre·his·tor·ic /ˌprihɪˈstɔrɪk/ *adjective*
relating to the time thousands of years ago, before anything was written down: *People lived in these caves in prehistoric times.*

prej·u·dice /ˈpredʒədɪs/ *noun*
an unfair belief that someone who is a different race, sex, religion, etc. is not as good as you are: *Black people still have to deal with prejudice against them.*

THESAURUS: prejudice

racism unfair treatment of people because they belong to a different race: *Racism is still a problem in American society.*

sexism unfair treatment of women: *Sexism kept women out of good jobs.*

discrimination the practice of treating one group of people differently from another in an unfair way: *At that time, there was a lot of discrimination against Jews.*

prej·u·diced /ˈpredʒədɪst/ *adjective*
believing unfairly that someone who is a different race, sex, religion, etc. is not as good as you are: *He's prejudiced and would never hire a woman for an important job.*

pre·lim·i·nar·y /prɪˈlɪməˌneri/ Ac *adjective, formal*
done at the beginning of something, to get ready for it: *Joe made a preliminary drawing before starting to paint.*

prel·ude /ˈpreɪlud/ *noun, formal*
be a prelude to something = to happen just before something else: *The rain was a prelude to a terrible storm.*

pre·ma·ture /ˌpriməˈtʃʊr/ *adjective, formal*
happening too early or before the right time: *The baby was six weeks premature and was very small.*
—**prematurely** *adverb*

pre·mier[1] *also* **Premier** /prɪˈmɪr/ *noun*
the leader of the government in some countries: *The president met with the Chinese premier.*

premier[2] *adjective, formal*
best or most important: *The Superbowl is football's premier event.*

pre·mi·um /ˈprimiəm/ *noun*
the money that you pay for insurance every month or year: *"How much are your health insurance premiums?" "I pay $200 a month."*

pre·oc·cu·pied /priˈɑkyəˌpaɪd/ *adjective, formal*
thinking about something a lot, so that you do not pay attention to other things: *She seemed preoccupied, so I asked if something bad had happened at school.*
—**preoccupation** /priˌɑkyəˈpeɪʃən/ *noun*
the state of being preoccupied

prep·a·ra·tion /ˌprepəˈreɪʃən/ *noun*
1 the act of getting something or someone ready for something: *We cleaned the house in preparation for their visit.*
2 preparations = the things that you do to get ready for something: *The soldiers made preparations to attack.*

pre·par·a·to·ry /prɪˈpærəˌtɔri/ *adjective, formal*
done in order to get ready for something: *She's taking college preparatory classes.*

pre·pare /prɪˈper/ *verb, formal*
1 to make something ready: *Wash your hands before you prepare food.*
2 to make yourself or another person ready to do something: *Angie was preparing for a math test.*

WORD FAMILY look at the words:

→ **prepare** *verb*
→ **preparation** *noun*
→ **preparatory** *adjective*
→ **prepared** *adjective*
→ **unprepared** *adjective*

pre·pared /prɪˈperd/ *adjective*
1 ready to do something or to be used: *He wasn't prepared for their questions and didn't know how to answer them.*
2 be prepared to do something = to be willing to do something: *I'm prepared to stay and help if you need me.*
—**preparedness** /prɪˈperɪdnɪs/ *noun*

prep·o·si·tion /ˌprepəˈzɪʃən/ *noun, formal*
a word such as "to," "for," "on," "by," etc. which is put in front of a noun to show where, when, or how: *In the sentence "I'm going to the store," "to" is a preposition.*

—**prepositional** *adjective* relating to prepositions and how they are used: *a prepositional phrase*

pre•school /ˈpriskul/ *noun*
a school that children between the ages of 2 and 5 can go to, where they learn things that help make them ready to go to a school for older children: *Look at the painting Andy did at preschool.*
—**preschool** *adjective* relating to a preschool: *preschool education*

pre•scribe /prɪˈskraɪb/ *verb*
to say what medicine or treatment a sick person should have: *The doctor prescribed pills for the pain.*

pre•scrip•tion /prɪˈskrɪpʃən/ *noun*
a piece of paper on which a doctor writes what medicine a sick person should have: *The doctor wrote a prescription for antibiotics.*

pres•ence /ˈprezəns/ *noun*
1 the state of being in a particular place at a particular time: *Tests showed the presence of blood on the carpet.* ANTONYM **absence**
2 in someone's presence/in the presence of someone *formal* = with someone, or in the same place as him or her: *He never uses swear words in the presence of his children.*

pres•ent¹ /ˈprezənt/ *adjective*
1 be present *formal* = to be in a particular place: *All twenty-eight children were present in class.* ANTONYM **absent**
2 happening or existing now: *What is your present job?*

present² *noun*
1 something that you give someone: *What are you giving Anne as a birthday present?* SYNONYM **gift**
2 the present = the time that is happening now: *The family has lived on the farm from 1901 until the present.*
3 at present *formal* = at this time: *There are no jobs available at present.*

pre•sent³ /prɪˈzent/ *verb*
1 *formal* to give something to someone: *He presented a gold cup to the winning team.*
2 to give or show information: *Groups of students presented their work to the rest of the class.*

pre•sen•ta•tion /ˌprizənˈteɪʃən/ *noun*
1 *formal* the act of giving someone something in a formal ceremony: *The presentation of the awards will take place after dinner.*
2 a formal talk about a particular subject: *Each student gave a short presentation about the book they had read.*

ˌpresent ˈparticiple *noun*
the form of a verb that ends in "-ing," which you use for showing an action that is continuing, or as an adjective: *In the sentences "The child is sleeping" and "I woke the sleeping child," "sleeping" is a present participle.*

ˌpresent ˈperfect *noun*
the present perfect = the form of a verb made by adding the verb "have" to the PAST PARTICIPLE of a verb, which you use to talk about a time up to and including the present time: *In the sentence, "I have eaten the cake," "have eaten" is in the present perfect.*

ˌpresent ˈtense *noun*
the form of a verb that shows what exists or happens now: *In the sentence, "I leave for school at 7:45," "leave" is in the present tense.*

pre•serv•a•tive /prɪˈzɚvətɪv/ *noun*
a chemical that food companies add to food to stop it from going bad: *The bread has preservatives in it to stop it from becoming stale too quickly.*

pre•serve¹ /prɪˈzɚv/ *verb*
to keep something from being harmed or damaged: *The fish is preserved with salt.* | *The group is working to preserve the rain forests.*
—**preservation** /ˌprezɚˈveɪʃən/ *noun* the act of preserving something
→ See Thesaurus box at **protect**

preserve² *noun*
an area of land or water in which the government protects animals, fish, or trees: *The area where the seals live is a marine preserve* (=a preserve in the ocean).

pres•i•den•cy /ˈprezədənsi/ *noun* plural **presidencies**
the job or time of being a president: *The election for the presidency is held in November.*

P

pres·i·dent /ˈprezədənt/ *noun*

1 the leader of the government in some countries, including the U.S.: *President Washington was our first president.* | *He was the president of Mexico.*

2 someone who is in charge of a business, bank, club, college, etc.: *She won the election for president of the student council.*

—**presidential** /ˌprezəˈdenʃəl/ *adjective* relating to a president

P

ˈ**President's ˌDay** *noun*

a U.S. holiday that shows respect for two of America's most important presidents, George Washington and Abraham Lincoln. The holiday is on the third Monday in February, because both presidents were born in February

press[1] /pres/ *verb*

1 to push something with your finger: *Press the blue button to turn the TV on.*

THESAURUS: press

push to press a button or switch with your finger to make a machine start or stop working: *Push this red button, here, to start recording.*

squash to press something and damage it by making it flat: *Put the tomatoes at the top of the bag, where they won't get squashed.*

crush to press something very hard so that it breaks or is damaged: *The car rolled over his leg, crushing it.*

mash to press fruit or cooked vegetables until they are soft and smooth: *Mash the potatoes well.*

grind to press something into powder using a special machine: *Can you grind the coffee beans?*

squeeze to press something from both sides, usually with your fingers: *Squeeze the toothpaste tube from the bottom.* | *fresh-squeezed orange juice*

2 to push something hard against something else: *Mike pressed the phone against his ear.* SYNONYM **push**

3 to make clothes smooth using an iron: *I need to press a shirt for tomorrow.* SYNONYM **iron**

press[2] *noun*

the press = newspapers and magazines and the people who work for them: *Members of the press were not allowed in the courtroom.*

press·ing /ˈpresɪŋ/ *adjective, formal*

a pressing problem, question, etc. needs to be dealt with very soon: *The country's most pressing problem is that there is not enough food for everyone.* SYNONYM **urgent**

pres·sure /ˈpreʃɚ/ *noun*

1 the use of strong words or arguments to try to make someone do something: *Her parents put a lot of pressure on her to do well at school.*

2 the things that are happening in your life that make you worry and feel that you have a lot to do: *I've been under a lot of pressure at work because of all the projects.*

3 the force that something causes when it pushes on another thing: *The air pressure in the tires might be low.* | *I could feel the pressure of his hand on my shoulder.*

—**pressure** *verb* to make someone feel that he or she must do something, when he or she does not really want to: *Kids sometimes try to pressure their friends into smoking.*

→ See Thesaurus box at **force**[1]

pres·tige /preˈstiʒ/ *noun, formal*

if you have prestige, people respect and admire you because of your job or something that you have achieved: *His work as the head of a company gives him power and prestige.*

—**prestigious** /preˈstidʒəs/ *adjective* having prestige: *a prestigious job*

pre·sum·a·bly /prɪˈzuməbli/ Ac *adverb*

used when you think that something is probably true: *Presumably, he's going to come back to our house to get his car.*

pre·sume /prɪˈzum/ Ac *verb, formal*

to think that something is probably true: *I left a message with the man who answered the phone. I presumed it was Tony's father.* SYNONYM **assume**

—**presumption** /prɪˈzʌmpʃən/ *noun* the belief that something is probably true

pre·sup·pose /ˌprisəˈpoʊz/ *verb, formal*

to depend on something you believe may happen or be true: *The math lesson presupposed that the children could add and subtract.* SYNONYM **assume**

pre·tend /prɪ'tend/ *verb*
to behave as if something is true or real, when it is not: *Terry pretended to be asleep so Lydia would go away.* | *The kids are pretending that they are lions.*
—**pretense** /'pritens/ *noun* the act of pretending that something is true

pre·ten·tious /prɪ'tenʃəs/ *adjective, formal*
trying to seem more important, rich, or smart than you really are: *He used a lot of big words, so he sounded pretentious.*
—**pretension** /prɪ'tenʃən/ *noun* the act of trying to seem more important, rich, or smart than you really are

pre·text /'pritekst/ *noun, formal*
a false reason that you give for doing something, in order to hide the real reason: *I called Gina on the pretext of asking about the homework, when really I wanted to hear about her date with Ron.*

pret·ty¹ /'prɪti/ *adjective* **prettier, prettiest**
nice to look at or listen to: *Jenny is so pretty she could be a model.* | *That's a pretty dress. It looks really good on you.* | *That's a really pretty song – sing it again.*
➔ See Thesaurus box at **beautiful**

pretty² *adverb*
1 if something is pretty easy, pretty fast, pretty good, etc., it is easier or faster or better than usual, but not very easy, very fast or very good: *I thought the test was pretty easy. But a couple of the questions were hard.* | *Dad was pretty angry about it, but he didn't yell or anything.* SYNONYM **fairly**
2 pretty much *informal* = almost completely: *I'm pretty much done with my homework. I'll be finished in five minutes.*

pret·zel /'pretsəl/ *noun*
a type of bread, baked in the shape of a loose knot and that you eat as a SNACK (=food you eat that is not part of a main meal)

pre·vent /prɪ'vent/ *verb*
to stop something from happening, or stop someone from doing something: *To prevent accidents, don't run near the swimming pool.* | *A knee injury prevented him from playing.*
—**preventable** *adjective* able to be prevented
—**preventive** *adjective* done in order to prevent something

WORD FAMILY look at the words:
- ➔ **prevent** *verb*
- ➔ **prevention** *noun*
- ➔ **preventable** *adjective*
- ➔ **preventive** *adjective*

pre·ven·tion /prɪ'venʃən/ *noun*
the things you do in order to stop something happening: *Clean water is important for the prevention of disease.*

pre·vi·ous /'priviəs/ Ac *adjective*
happening before the one that exists or is happening now: *She has two children from a previous marriage and one child with her current husband.*

pre·vi·ous·ly /'priviəsli/ Ac *adverb*
before now: *It isn't as cold today as it was previously.*
➔ See Thesaurus box at **before¹**

prey /preɪ/ *noun, formal*
an animal that another animal kills and eats: *A spider catches its prey in its web.*

price /praɪs/ *noun*
the amount of money that you must pay in order to buy something: *The price of gas has gone up again.* | *I like the clothes they sell, and their prices are really low.* | *Is there a big difference in price between the two computers?*
➔ See Thesaurus box at **cost¹**

price·less /'praɪsləs/ *adjective*
very valuable: *The museum has many priceless works of art.*

pric·ey, pricy /'praɪsi/ *adjective, informal*
costing a lot of money, or making you pay a lot of money for something: *We ate at a pricey restaurant. Luckily, he paid for everything.* SYNONYM **expensive**

prick /prɪk/ *verb*
to make a small hole in something with a sharp point: *She pricked her finger on the needle.*

pride /praɪd/ *noun*
a feeling of happiness and respect for yourself, because you have done something well or have something good: *Joey took a lot of pride in the bird house he had made.* | *She looked at her daughter with pride.*

P

priest /prist/ *noun*
someone who performs religious duties and ceremonies in some religions: *a Catholic priest*

pri•mar•i•ly /praɪˈmerəli/ Ac *adverb, formal*
mainly: *The children primarily speak English, but they occasionally speak Spanish.*

P

pri•mar•y /ˈpraɪˌmeri/ Ac *adjective, formal*
most important: *Our primary concern is the safety of the children.* SYNONYM **main**

ˌprimary ˈcolor *noun*
one of the three colors – red, yellow, and blue – that you can mix together to make any other color

prime /praɪm/ Ac *adjective, formal*
1 most important: *Smoking is the prime cause of lung disease.* SYNONYM **primary, main**
2 very good: *Soccer is a prime example of a game that girls and boys can play together.*

ˌprime ˈminister *noun*
the leader of the government in some countries, for example Great Britain

ˌprime ˈnumber *noun*
a number that can only be divided by itself and the number one: *7 is a prime number.*

prim•i•tive /ˈprɪmətɪv/ *adjective*
1 primitive people live in the way that people lived thousands of years ago, without any modern things: *Some primitive people lived in caves.* ANTONYM **modern**
2 very simple and without anything modern: *The houses were primitive, and did not have running water.*

prince /prɪns/ *noun*
1 the son of a king or queen: *In the story, the prince falls in love with Cinderella.*
2 a male ruler of some countries: *the Prince of Monaco*

prin•cess /ˈprɪnses/ *noun*
the daughter of a king or queen, or the wife of a prince: *In the story of "Snow White," the princess runs away from the evil queen.*

prin•ci•pal[1] /ˈprɪnsəpəl/ Ac *noun*
someone who is in charge of a school: *Helen Davies is the principal of Ferry Elementary School.*

principal[2] Ac *adjective*
most important: *New York is one of America's principal cities.* SYNONYM **main**

prin•ci•ple /ˈprɪnsəpəl/ Ac *noun*
an idea that you believe is right, and that helps you to decide how to behave: *One of our school's principles is that we treat every child fairly.*

print[1] /prɪnt/ *verb*
1 to put words, numbers, or pictures on paper, using a machine: *He wrote his report on the computer and printed it.*
2 to write words without joining the letters together: *Please print your name clearly.*
—**printable** *adjective* able to be printed

PHRASAL VERB

print something out
to make a printed copy of something from a computer: *I printed out a picture of a shark from a website.*

print[2] *noun*
1 the letters that are printed in books, newspapers, and magazines: *Children's books often have big print.*
2 a mark that something makes on a surface or in something soft: *The dog had made muddy paw prints on the floor.*
3 a picture or painting that has been printed on paper: *Do you want extra prints of your photographs?*

print•er /ˈprɪntɚ/ *noun*
1 a machine that puts the words or pictures from a computer onto paper
2 a person or business whose work is printing books, magazines, etc.: *We sent the text to the printer.*
➔ See picture on page A20

print•ing /ˈprɪntɪŋ/ *noun*
the process of printing words and pictures in a book, magazine, etc. using a machine: *The spelling mistake was made during printing.*

print•out /ˈprɪntˌaʊt/ *noun*
a piece of paper with information on it, that you print from a computer: *The teacher gave a printout of the story to each student.*

pri•or /ˈpraɪɚ/ Ac *adjective, formal*
1 prior to something = before: *He went back to Washington two days prior to the election.*
2 done, given, etc. at an earlier time: *The*

school needs the parents' prior agreement before children can go on the trip.

pri·or·i·ty /praɪˈɔrəti/ Ac *noun, formal*
the thing that you think is most important and that needs your attention first: *The governor said that education is his top priority.*
—**prioritize** *verb, formal* to decide how important a number of things are, so that you can do the most important first: *Try to prioritize your work and deal with the most important things first.*

pris·on /ˈprɪzən/ *noun*
a building where people must stay as a punishment for a crime: *He attacked an old lady, and spent four years in prison.* SYNONYM **jail**

pris·on·er /ˈprɪzənɚ/ *noun*
someone who must stay in a prison as a punishment for a crime: *Some of the prisoners are here for life.* SYNONYM **convict**

ˌprisoner of ˈwar *noun, abbreviation* **P.O.W.**
a member of the military who the enemy catches and keeps during a war

pri·va·cy /ˈpraɪvəsi/ *noun*
1 the state of being able to be alone when you want to be: *Teenagers need privacy and a room of their own.*
2 the state of being able to keep your life secret: *Movie stars have very little privacy. Reporters and photographers are always following them.*

pri·vate¹ /ˈpraɪvət/ *adjective*
1 secret and not for other people to know about: *She wrote all her private thoughts in her journal.*

THESAURUS: private

secret known or felt only by you, and not talked about or shown to anyone else: *Her secret belief was that her parents had not wanted her.*

personal if something is personal, it is about you and private, and other people do not need to know about it: *He asked a lot of personal questions.*

innermost *formal* your innermost feelings, desires, etc. are the ones you feel most strongly and keep private: *Collins expressed her innermost feelings in her poetry.*

be none of someone's business *informal* if something is none of your business, it is private and you should not ask about it: *I don't know how much money he makes, and really it's none of my business.*

2 for one person or group, and not for everyone: *The band flew to Miami in a private jet.*
3 owned by a person or business, and not a government: *The museum is a private organization.* ANTONYM **public**
4 quiet and without other people: *Is there a private place where we can talk?*

private² *noun*
1 in private = without other people listening or watching: *I need to talk to you in private.*
2 someone who has the lowest position in the army: *He started as a private, and worked his way up to colonel.*

pri·vate·ly /ˈpraɪvətli/ *adverb*
1 secretly, so that other people do not know about something: *He told me privately how unhappy he was.*
2 in a quiet place without other people: *Is there someplace we can meet privately?*
3 privately owned/funded/run, etc. = owned, etc. by a person or business and not a government: *The company is privately owned.*

ˈprivate school *noun*
a school where parents pay for their children's education

priv·i·lege /ˈprɪvəlɪdʒ/ *noun*
a special advantage that only one person or group gets: *Students at the school get more privileges as they get older.*

priv·i·leged /ˈprɪvəlɪdʒd/ *adjective, formal*
having more money, opportunities, better jobs, etc. than other people: *Benjamin came from a privileged background* (=his family had money, good education, etc.).

prize /praɪz/ *noun*
something that you win in a game, competition, or race: *I entered a competition, and won first prize!* | *a prize of $3,000*

pro¹ /proʊ/ *noun*
1 *informal* someone who is paid to do something, such as play a sport, act, play music,

etc. that other people do for fun: *a tennis pro* SYNONYM **professional**

2 *informal* someone who has had a lot of experience with a particular type of situation: *These guys are real pros, so you know they'll do a good job.*

3 an advantage of something: *You should consider the pros and cons* (=advantages and disadvantages) *of the plan before you act.* ANTONYM **con**

P

pro² *adjective, informal*

paid to do something such as a sport, that other people do for fun: *pro basketball players* SYNONYM **professional**; ANTONYM **amateur**

prob·a·bil·i·ty /ˌprɑbəˈbɪləti/ *noun*

the amount of chance that something will happen: *The team has a high probability* (=good chance) *of winning.*

prob·a·ble /ˈprɑbəbəl/ *adjective*

likely to happen or be true: *It is probable that there will be more forest fires this year.*

prob·a·bly /ˈprɑbəbli/ *adverb*

likely to happen or be true: *Mom will probably call me later today, so I need to stay near the phone.*

WORD FAMILY look at the words:

→ **probably** *adverb*
→ **probably** *adjective*
→ **probability** *noun*

probe¹ /proʊb/ *verb*

1 to ask questions in order to find things out: *reporters probing into the personal lives of politicians*

2 to look for something or examine something, using a long thin instrument

—**probing** *adjective*: *probing questions*

probe² *noun*

a SPACECRAFT without people in it that goes into space to get information: *They sent a space probe to Mars.*

prob·lem /ˈprɑbləm/ *noun*

1 a difficult situation: *When Dad lost his job, it was a serious problem.* | *She's had some problems with her son.*

2 a question that you must answer using numbers or other information: *Mom, can you help me solve this math problem?*

3 no problem *informal* = used for saying that you are willing to do something: *"Can you open this window?" "Sure, no problem."*

prob·lem·at·ic /ˌprɑbləˈmætɪk/ *also* **prob·le·mat·i·cal** /ˌprɑbləˈmætɪkəl/ *adjective, formal*

full of problems or causing problems: *Mike and Lisa's relationship was very problematic and they were always arguing.*

pro·ce·dure /prəˈsidʒɚ/ Ac *noun, formal*

the correct or normal way of doing something: *You must follow the correct procedure for installing the software or it won't work.*

—**procedural** *adjective* relating to a procedure

pro·ceed /prəˈsid/ Ac *verb, formal*

1 to do something that you have planned to do: *The college will proceed with plans to build a new library.*

2 to move in a particular direction: *Please proceed to the nearest exit.*

pro·cess /ˈprɑses/ Ac *noun*

1 a series of things you do to get a particular result: *Education is the process of teaching and learning.*

2 a series of changes that happen naturally: *Growing up is a natural process.*

pro·ces·sion /prəˈseʃən/ *noun, formal*

a line of people or cars moving slowly as part of a ceremony: *A procession of cars went by on the way to a funeral.*

pro·cras·ti·nate /prəˈkræstəˌneɪt/ *verb, formal*

to delay doing something that you ought to do: *Just do your homework and stop procrastinating.*

—**procrastinator** *noun* someone who procrastinates

—**procrastination** /prəˌkræstəˈneɪʃən/ *noun* the act of procrastinating

pro·duce¹ /prəˈdus/ *verb*

1 to make something happen or have a particular effect: *What kind of effects does alcohol produce in the body?*

2 to make something naturally: *Plants produce oxygen.*

3 to make or grow something in order to sell it: *Japan produces a lot of electronic goods.* | *Coffee is produced in South America.*

4 to make something using a skill or art: *The kids have produced some fantastic paintings.*

5 to control the making of a movie, play, or television show: *Walt Disney produced the movie "Snow White."*

WORD FAMILY look at the words:
→ **produce** *verb*
→ **producer** *noun*
→ **product** *noun*
→ **production** *noun*
→ **productive** *adjective*

prod•uce² /'prɑdus/ *noun, formal*
food that people grow to sell, especially fruits and vegetables: *Good restaurants always use fresh produce.*

pro•duc•er /prə'dusɚ/ *noun*
1 a person, company, or country that makes or grows something to sell: *The company is an important producer of computer equipment.*
2 someone whose job is to control how a movie, play, or television program is prepared: *He's a Hollywood producer and has made many successful movies.*
→ See Thesaurus box at **movie**

prod•uct /'prɑdʌkt/ *noun*
1 *formal* something that people grow or make in order to sell it: *The price of food products goes up all the time.*
2 the number you get when you multiply numbers: *The product of 3 x 3 is 9.*

pro•duc•tion /prə'dʌkʃən/ *noun*
1 the process of making or growing things in order to sell them: *the production of cotton in California*
2 a movie, play, etc.: *We went to the new theater to see a production of "Death of a Salesman."*

pro•duc•tive /prə'dʌktɪv/ *adjective, formal*
producing or achieving a lot: *If people are happy at work, they are more productive.*
—**productively** *adverb*

pro•fes•sion /prə'feʃən/ *noun*
a job that needs special education and training: *People in the medical profession have studied for many years before becoming doctors.*

WORD FAMILY look at the words:
→ **profession** *noun*
→ **professional** *adjective*
→ **professional** *noun*
→ **professionalism** *noun*

→ See Thesaurus box at **job**

pro•fes•sion•al¹ /prə'feʃənəl/ Ac *adjective*
1 relating to a job that needs special education and training: *A lawyer can give you professional advice.*
2 professional sports players, writers, artists, etc. do their sport or other activity as a job: *He's a professional football player and earns lots of money.* ANTONYM **amateur**

professional² *noun, formal*
someone who works in a job that needs a lot of education or training: *Trained professionals can earn plenty of money.*
—**professionalism** *noun* the skill that a professional person has

pro•fes•sor /prə'fesɚ/ *noun*
a teacher at a university: *a professor of economics* | *Professor Davis teaches American history.*
→ See picture on page A16

pro•fi•cient /prə'fɪʃənt/ *adjective, formal*
able to do something very well: *Most kids are proficient at using the Internet.* | *Are you proficient in English* (=able to speak it well)?
—**proficiency** *noun* the state of being able to do something very well

pro•file /'proʊfaɪl/ *noun, formal*

profile

1 a view of someone's head from the side: *The painting was of a young girl in profile* (=looked at from the side).
2 a short description that gives important details about what someone or something is like: *The students write profiles of themselves to go in the book.*

prof•it /'prɑfɪt/ *noun*
1 money that you get when you sell something for more than you paid: *We made a big profit when we sold our house.*
2 the money that a company makes by

P

doing business: *The company's profits rose to $23 million.*

prof•it•a•ble /ˈprɑfɪtəbəl/ *adjective, formal*
making enough or a lot of money: *Her father had a profitable business and a comfortable life.*
—**profitably** *adverb* in a way that is profitable

P

pro•found /prəˈfaʊnd/ *adjective, formal*
having a very great effect: *The story had a profound effect on me and made me want to become a writer.*

pro•gram¹ /ˈproʊgræm/ *noun*
1 a show on television or radio: *What's your favorite TV program? | We watched a program about whales.*
2 a set of instructions for a computer that makes it do something: *The students are learning how to write computer programs.*
3 a set of organized activities that people do in order to achieve something: *Members of the team have to follow an exercise program. | the U.S. space program*
4 a piece of paper or short book that you get at a play, event, or concert, that has information about the event and the performers: *The program gave the names of all the performers.*

program² *verb* **programmed, programming**
to give a set of instructions to a computer to make it do something: *You can program a computer to play chess.*
—**programming** *noun* the act or job of writing instructions for a computer: *He's studying computer programming.*

pro•gram•mer /ˈproʊˌgræmɚ/ *noun*
someone whose job is writing programs for computers: *a computer programmer*

prog•ress¹ /ˈprɑgrəs/ *noun*
1 the process of getting better at doing something: *Bob has made good progress in math this year.*
2 the process of getting closer to achieving something: *There has been progress toward peace in the area.*
3 movement toward a place: *The traffic was bad, so we made slow progress.*
4 in progress = happening now: *Please be quiet – there is a test in progress.*

pro•gress² /prəˈgres/ *verb, formal*
1 to continue to get better and develop: *Technology is progressing all the time.*
2 to happen or move forward slowly: *I got more and more bored as the meeting progressed.*

pro•gres•sion /prəˈgreʃən/ *noun, formal*
a process of changing and developing: *You can see the progression of the artist's work during these years.*

pro•gres•sive /prəˈgresɪv/ *adjective, formal*
liking or using modern ideas and ways of doing things: *Our new teacher is very progressive and is always trying new ideas.*
—**progressive** *noun* someone who is progressive

pro•hib•it /proʊˈhɪbɪt/ Ac *verb, formal*
if you are prohibited from doing something, the law does not allow you to do it: *If you are under 21, you are prohibited from buying alcohol.* ANTONYM **permit**
—**prohibition** /ˌproʊhɪˈbɪʃən/ *noun* the act of not allowing people to do something
→ See Thesaurus box at **forbid**

pro•hib•i•tive /proʊˈhɪbətɪv/ Ac *adjective, formal*
preventing people from doing or buying something: *The cost of the trip was prohibitive* (=too expensive for people to do).

proj•ect¹ /ˈprɑdʒekt/ Ac *noun*
some work that you plan carefully, and that often takes a long time: *I'm still working on my school science project. | a three-year research project*

pro•ject² /prəˈdʒekt/ Ac *verb*
1 to calculate what the amount, cost, etc., of something will be in the future: *The population is projected to increase to 26 million in a few years.*

2 to shine a light through a movie or photograph so that it shows on a screen or flat surface: *The movie is projected onto the screen from the back of the theater.*

pro•jec•tion /prəˈdʒekʃən/ Ac *noun, formal*
1 a statement that says what is likely to happen in the future: *Some projections of future weather show that the ice at the North Pole will melt.*
2 the movie or picture that you see when someone shines a light through it so that it shows on a screen or flat surface

pro•jec•tor /prəˈdʒektɚ/ *noun*
a machine that makes a movie or photograph show on a screen by shining a light through it: *a movie projector*
→ See picture at **project**²

pro•lif•ic /prəˈlɪfɪk/ *adjective, formal*
producing a lot of books, songs, paintings, etc.: *He's a prolific writer and has published about 20 books.*

pro•long /prəˈlɔŋ/ *verb, formal*
to make something continue for longer: *Modern medicine is prolonging our lives.*

prom /prɑm/ *noun*
a formal dance party for students in HIGH SCHOOL: *Who are you going to the prom with?*

prom•i•nent /ˈprɑmənənt/ *adjective, formal*
famous or important: *a prominent politician*
—**prominence** *noun* the state of being prominent: *He rose to prominence* (=became famous or important) *in the business world.*

prom•ise¹ /ˈprɑmɪs/ *verb*
1 to say that you will definitely do something: *Lou promised to give me a ride to the dance.* | *I promise that I'll call you every day.*

THESAURUS: promise

swear to make a very serious promise: *Do you swear to tell the truth?*

take/swear an oath *formal* to make a very serious promise in public: *You must take an oath of loyalty to your country.*

vow *formal* to make a serious promise, often to yourself: *She vowed that she would never drink alcohol again.*

guarantee to promise something that you feel very sure about: *I guarantee that you'll love this book.*

give someone your word to promise someone very sincerely that you will do something: *He gave us his word that he wouldn't do it again.*

2 to seem likely to be good, exciting, etc.: *The game on Saturday promises to be exciting.*

promise² *noun*
a statement saying that you will definitely do something: *Mom made a promise to take me to Disneyland on my birthday.*

prom•is•ing /ˈprɑmɪsɪŋ/ *adjective, formal*
likely to be good or successful: *She's a promising young singer and certain to have a great career.*

pro•mote /prəˈmoʊt/ Ac *verb*
1 to give someone a better position at work: *Her boss promoted her to senior salesperson.*
2 to help something be successful or sell in large numbers: *She promoted her new book on the show.*
WORD FAMILY → **promotion** *noun*

pro•mo•tion /prəˈmoʊʃən/ Ac *noun*
1 a move to a better position at work: *Dean got a promotion to manager.*
2 something you do to make people want to buy or do something: *The music company spends a lot of money on promotion for its bands.*

prompt /prɑmpt/ *adjective*
done without delay: *I wrote to the company last week, and received a prompt reply.*
—**promptly** *adverb* without delay: *Callan dealt with the problem promptly before it got any worse.*
—**promptness** *noun* the quality of being prompt

prone /proʊn/ *adjective, formal*
likely to do or have something bad: *This river is prone to flooding when there is a lot of rain.*

pro•noun /ˈproʊnaʊn/ *noun*
a word like "he," "she," "it," etc., which you use instead of using a noun

pro•nounce /prəˈnaʊns/ *verb*
to make the sound of a word or letter: *It is hard for Japanese people to pronounce the letter "r" in English.*

P

P

pro•nun•ci•a•tion /prəˌnʌnsiˈeɪʃən/ *noun*
1 the way in which a word or letters should sound in a language: *The pronunciation of some words is different in America and England.*
2 the way a particular person says a word or letters: *I need to improve my pronunciation in Spanish.*

proof /pruf/ *noun*
facts that prove something is true: *There is no proof that humans can get this disease.*

proof•read /ˈprufrid/ *verb* **proofread** /ˈprufred/
to read a letter, book, etc. in order to correct any mistakes: *A team of people proofread the book to make sure there were no mistakes.*

prop /prɑp/ *verb* **propped, propping**
to make something stay in a particular position, by using something to support it: *He propped his bike against the fence.*

prop•a•gan•da /ˌprɑpəˈgændə/ *noun, formal*
information which is not completely correct, that a government or organization uses to try to make people agree with them: *Propaganda is often used during a war.*

pro•pel•ler /prəˈpelɚ/ *noun*
a piece of equipment with curved parts that turn around to make an airplane or ship move: *The helicopter's propellers began to spin.*

prop•er /ˈprɑpɚ/ *adjective*
1 right or correct: *Our teacher showed us the proper way to throw the ball.*
2 appropriate: *You can't go skiing without the proper clothes or you'll get wet and cold.*
3 *formal* showing that you know how to behave well: *I wanted a drink, but I didn't think it was proper to ask.*

prop•er•ly /ˈprɑpɚli/ *adverb*
in the right way: *My camera isn't working properly. I need to get it fixed.* SYNONYM **correctly**

ˌproper ˈnoun *also* **ˌproper ˈname** *noun*
a noun that is the name of a particular person, place, or thing: *"Tom," "Boston," and "Christmas" are proper nouns.*

prop•er•ty /ˈprɑpɚti/ *noun, formal*
1 something that someone owns: *The floods caused a lot of damage to personal property.*

THESAURUS: property

possessions *formal* the things that you own: *The fire destroyed most of their possessions.*
things *informal* the things that you own or are carrying: *Just put your things over there.*
stuff *informal* the things that you own or are carrying with you: *I don't want my little brother to touch my stuff.*
belongings things you own, especially things you are carrying with you: *Each child has a drawer to keep their belongings in.*

2 land or buildings: *They're going to build a house on the property.*
3 a quality that something has: *In science, children learn about the physical properties of materials, such as whether something is hard or soft.*

proph•e•cy /ˈprɑfəsi/ *noun* plural **prophecies** *formal*
a statement that says what will happen in the future: *There is an old prophecy about how the world will end.*

proph•et /ˈprɑfɪt/ *noun*
1 someone who tells people about God or what will happen in the future: *the prophets in the Bible*
2 the Prophet = Muhammad, who began the religion of Islam
—**prophetess** *noun* a woman who tells people about what will happen in the future

pro•por•tion /prəˈpɔrʃən/ Ac *noun*
an amount of something compared to something else: *The proportion of girls to boys in science classes is getting higher.*
—**proportional** *adjective, formal* relating one amount to another amount: *A punishment should be proportional to the crime.*

pro•pos•al /prəˈpoʊzəl/ *noun*
1 *formal* a plan or suggestion: *The city is considering a proposal to build a new sports stadium.*
2 the act of asking someone to marry you: *Did she accept his proposal* (=agree to marry him)?

pro•pose /prə'poʊz/ *verb*
1 *formal* to suggest something: *The principal proposed another meeting next week.*
2 *formal* to intend to do something: *I'll explain the problem, and tell you what we propose to do.*
3 to ask someone to marry you: *Has he proposed to you yet?*

prop•o•si•tion /ˌprɑpə'zɪʃən/ *noun, formal*
1 a statement in which you express an idea: *Do you agree with the proposition that money can buy you happiness?*
2 a new law that people in a state or city vote on: *If the proposition passes, there will be more money for building new schools.*

pro•pri•e•tor /prə'praɪətɚ/ *noun, formal*
an owner of a business: *My uncle was the proprietor of a small hotel.*

prose /proʊz/ *noun*
ordinary language, not poetry: *He was a poet, but he also wrote in prose.*

pros•e•cute /'prɑsəˌkyut/ *verb*
to take someone to a court of law because he or she may be guilty of a crime: *The police decided to prosecute him for theft.*

pros•e•cu•tion /ˌprɑsə'kyuʃən/ *noun*
the prosecution = the lawyers in a court of law who are trying to show that someone is guilty of a crime: *The prosecution will question witnesses this week.*
—**prosecutor** /'prɑsəˌkyutɚ/ *noun* a lawyer who is trying to prove that someone is guilty of a crime

pros•pect /'prɑspekt/ Ac *noun, formal*
the thought of something that will probably happen in the future: *The prospect of getting married frightened Alice.*

pro•spec•tive /prə'spektɪv/ Ac *adjective, formal*
prospective customer/buyer, etc. = someone who may become a customer, a buyer, etc.: *A lot of prospective buyers came to look at the house.*

pros•per /'prɑspɚ/ *verb, formal*
to be successful or become rich: *Matt worked hard, and his business prospered.*

pros•per•i•ty /prɑ'sperəti/ *noun, formal*
the state of having money and being successful: *The country had many years of peace and prosperity.*

pros•per•ous /'prɑspərəs/ *adjective, formal*
rich and successful: *She was a prosperous businesswoman and drove an expensive car.*
➔ See Thesaurus box at **rich**

pros•ti•tute /'prɑstəˌtut/ *noun*
someone who has sex with people to earn money

pro•tect /prə'tekt/ *verb*
to stop someone or something from being harmed or damaged: *Bike riders should wear helmets to protect their heads.*

THESAURUS: protect

guard to protect someone or something from being attacked or stolen: *Soldiers guarded the camp.*

shield to protect someone or something from being hurt, damaged, or upset: *She put up her arms to shield her face.*

give/offer/provide protection to protect someone from something harmful: *A hat gives some protection from the sun.*

shelter *formal* to protect someone from the weather or from danger: *At great risk to themselves, they sheltered Jews from the Nazis.*

preserve to keep someone or something from being harmed, destroyed, or changed too much: *National Parks help to preserve our wilderness.*

pro•tec•tion /prə'tekʃən/ *noun*
something that protects someone or something: *The animals need some protection from the wind.*

pro•tein /'proʊtin/ *noun*
a substance in food such as meat or eggs that helps your body to grow and be healthy: *Make sure you eat plenty of fruit, vegetables, and protein.*

pro•test¹ /'proʊtest/ *noun*
1 an action or words that show you do not agree with something: *I turned off the TV, despite the kids' protests.*
2 an occasion when a group of people show in public that they do not agree with something that is happening: *There have been protests against the war.*

pro•test² /prə'test/ *verb*
if a group of people protest, they show in public that they do not agree with

something: *Teachers have protested against the larger class sizes.*
—**protester** *also* **protestor** *noun* someone who protests about something in public, with a group of other people: *Over 1,000 protesters marched to the Capitol.*

Prot•es•tant /ˈprɑtəstənt/ *adjective*
relating to Christian churches that are not Roman Catholic or Orthodox: *There are several Protestant churches in town – a Lutheran one, a Baptist one, and a Methodist one.*
—**Protestant** *noun* someone who belongs to a Protestant church

pro•to•col /ˈproʊtəˌkɔl/ Ac *noun, formal*
rules for the correct way to behave: *Any organization has its own protocol that members must follow.*

pro•trude /proʊˈtrud/ *verb, formal*
to stick out from somewhere: *A gun was protruding from his pocket.*
—**protruding** *noun* sticking out from somewhere: *She had protruding teeth and had to wear braces to correct them.*

proud

proud /praʊd/ *adjective*
1 feeling pleased because you think that you, someone in your family, your country, etc. has done something good: *When my son graduated, I was very proud of him.*

THESAURUS: proud

conceited *formal* very proud of how you look or what you can do, in a way that other people do not like: *I don't want to sound conceited, but school was easy for me.*
big-headed *informal* very proud of yourself and thinking that you are very good, in a way that people do not like: *Don't go getting big-headed – you've only won two games.*
vain very proud of the way you look, in a way that other people do not like: *There were all these vain guys at the gym, looking at themselves in the mirrors.*
arrogant behaving in a rude and unfriendly way because you think that you are better than other people: *He's arrogant and won't listen to anyone else's ideas.*

2 wanting to do things for yourself so that you get respect from other people: *They were proud people, who always worked hard and who wouldn't accept any help.*
—**proudly** *adverb* in a way that shows you feel pleased about something you, your family, etc. have done: *Johnny proudly showed me his test score.*
➔ **pride**

prove /pruv/ *verb* **proved**, **proved** or **proven** /ˈpruvən/
1 to show that something is true: *The police were able to prove that she was guilty.*
2 *formal* to have a particular result or quality: *Getting a job proved difficult.*

prov•en /ˈpruvən/ *adjective, formal*
shown to be good or true: *He's a player of proven ability* (=he has shown that he has ability as a player in a sport).

prov•erb /ˈprɑvɚb/ *noun*
a short statement that most people know, that gives advice about life: *There's an old African proverb that says, "It takes a village to raise a child."*

pro•vide /prəˈvaɪd/ *verb*
to give something that someone needs: *The school provides books for the children.*
PHRASAL VERB
provide for someone
to be able to buy the food, clothes, and other things that someone needs: *Dad worked hard, but it wasn't easy to provide for five children.*

pro•vid•ed /prəˈvaɪdɪd/ *also* **pro•vid•ing** /prəˈvaɪdɪŋ/ *conjunction*
provided/provided that = if something happens: *You'll pass the class, provided that you do the work.*

prov•ince /ˈprɑvɪns/ *noun*
a large area of a country, with its own local government: *British Columbia and Alberta are two of the western provinces of Canada.*

—**provincial** /prə'vɪnʃəl/ *adjective* relating to a province: *the provincial capital*

pro•vi•sions /prə'vɪʒənz/ *noun, formal* food supplies: *We had enough provisions for at least two weeks in the woods.*

pro•voke /prə'voʊk/ *verb, formal* to make someone angry: *She provoked him by kissing another guy.*

prowl /praʊl/ *verb* to move around quietly, especially to hunt: *Cats go out at night to prowl around.*

pru•dent /'prudənt/ *adjective, formal* sensible and careful: *It is prudent to save some of your money.*

prune /prun/ *noun* a dried PLUM (=type of fruit)
➔ See picture on page A13

pry /praɪ/ *verb* **pried**, third person singular **pries**
1 to open or remove something using force: *Jim used a metal bar to pry the door open.*
2 to try to find out about someone's life in a rude way: *Movie stars always have people prying into their lives.*

psalm /sɑm/ *noun* a song or poem praising God: *a psalm from the Bible*

pseu•do•nym /'sudn,ɪm/ *noun, formal* a name that a writer or artist uses instead of his or her real name: *"George Eliot" is the pseudonym that the writer Mary Ann Evans used.*

psy•chi•a•try /saɪ'kaɪətri/ *noun* the study and treatment of mental illness: *He studied psychiatry because he wanted to understand the human mind.*
—**psychiatrist** *noun* a doctor who treats people who have a mental illness

psy•chic[1] /'saɪkɪk/ *adjective* relating to unusual mental abilities, for example being able to bend spoons without touching them, that science cannot explain: *Some people say they have psychic powers, such as being able to see what will happen in the future.*

psychic[2] *noun* someone who has strange mental abilities such as knowing what other people are thinking

psy•chol•o•gy /saɪ'kɑlədʒi/ Ac *noun* the study of the mind and how it affects behavior: *He's interested in child psychology, especially how children learn.*
—**psychologist** *noun* someone who has studied psychology
—**psychological** /,saɪkə'lɑdʒɪkəl/ *adjective* relating to the mind: *He had some psychological problems.*

psy•cho•path /'saɪkə,pæθ/ *noun* someone who has a mental illness and behaves in a violent way: *Her killer was a psychopath who had killed several times before.*

PTA *noun* **Parent-Teacher Association** an organization of the teachers and parents at a particular school

pub /pʌb/ *noun* a BAR that often serves food: *We went to a pub when we were in London for lunch and a beer.*

pu•ber•ty /'pyubəti/ *noun* the time when your body changes from a child to an adult: *Puberty usually takes place from about ages 10 to 15.*

pub•lic[1] /'pʌblɪk/ *adjective*
1 relating to all the people in an area or country: *Dirty drinking water is a danger to public health.*
2 for anyone to use: *A lot of people use cars rather than public transportation.* ANTONYM **private**
3 make something public = to tell something to all the people in an area or country: *The White House did not make this information public.*

public[2] *noun*
1 the public = all the people in an area or country: *The museum is open to the public five days a week.*
2 in public = in a place where anyone can see or hear: *They tried not to argue in public.*

pub•li•ca•tion /,pʌblə'keɪʃən/ Ac *noun*
1 the process of printing a book, newspaper, or magazine and sending it to stores for people to read and buy: *She was in New York for the publication of her new book.*
2 a book, magazine, or newspaper: *I read "Sports Illustrated" and some other publications.*

P

P

pub•lic•i•ty /pʌˈblɪsəti/ *noun*
the attention that newspapers, television, or radio gives to someone or something: *His new movie has received a lot of publicity.*
—**publicize** /ˈpʌbləˌsaɪz/ *verb* if newspapers, television, or the radio publicize something, they tell people about it: *When the two actors got divorced, it was highly publicized* (=there was a lot of information about it).

ˌpublic ˈschool *noun*
a school that everyone can go to, because the government pays for it

ˌpublic ˈservice *noun*
jobs that help people, especially jobs in the government: *She spent many years in public service serving on the school board and on the city council.*

pub•lish /ˈpʌblɪʃ/ Ac *verb*
to print a book, magazine, or newspaper and make it available for people to read and buy: *The book was first published in 1968.*

WORD FAMILY look at the words:
→ **publish** *verb*
→ **publication** *noun*
→ **publisher** *noun*

pub•lish•er /ˈpʌblɪʃɚ/ Ac *noun*
a person or company that produces and sells books, newspapers, or magazines

pud•ding /ˈpʊdɪŋ/ *noun*
a thick sweet food that you make with milk, eggs, and sugar: *chocolate pudding*

puddle

pud•dle /ˈpʌdl/ *noun*
a small pool of water on the ground or road: *The kids splashed in the puddles after it rained.*

puff¹ /pʌf/ *verb*
to breathe quickly after running, carrying something heavy, etc.: *Grandpa was puffing after climbing the stairs.*

puff² *noun*
a small amount of air, smoke, or wind: *Some puffs of smoke were coming from the chimney.*

puff•y /ˈpʌfi/ *adjective*
puffy eyes, cheeks, or faces are swollen: *Her eyes were red and puffy from crying.*

pull¹ /pʊl/ *verb*
1 to use your hands to move something toward you: *I pulled the door shut to block the wind.* | *Stop pulling my hair!* ANTONYM **push**

THESAURUS: pull

tug to pull something suddenly, especially several times with small movements: *The little boy was tugging at her sleeve.*

drag to pull something heavy somewhere, along the ground: *She dragged a chair over to their table.*

haul to pull something heavy, sometimes using a rope: *The guys hauled all the furniture upstairs.*

tow if a vehicle or boat tows another one, it pulls the other vehicle or boat along behind it: *He parked in a red zone, and they towed his car away.*

2 to make something move behind you in the direction you are moving: *The truck was pulling a trailer.* ANTONYM **push**
3 to remove something from its place, especially by using force: *The dentist pulled out the tooth.*
4 pull someone's leg *informal* = to tell someone something that is not true, as a

joke: *I don't think he was serious – he was just pulling your leg.*

5 pull a gun/knife (on someone) = to take out a gun or knife and be ready to use it: *The man suddenly pulled a gun and began shooting.*

PHRASAL VERBS

pull away

to start to drive away from a place: *She watched the cars slowly pull away.*

pull back

to move away from a place or person: *The general gave the order for his soldiers to pull back.*

pull for someone *informal*

to want someone to succeed and encourage them to do this: *The fans were all pulling for their team.*

pull in (something)

if a car pulls in, it drives into a place and stops: *I looked out the window, just as Reggie was pulling in the driveway.*

pull off

1 pull something off = to quickly take off some clothes: *He pulled off his wet clothes and put them by the fire.*

2 pull off (a road) = to leave a road in order to stop or to turn into another road: *They pulled off the freeway and went to get some lunch.*

3 pull off something *informal* = to succeed in doing something difficult: *Tom thinks he can win, but I don't think he will pull it off* (=succeed).

pull something on

to quickly put clothes on your body: *She pulled on her sweater and ran downstairs.*

pull out

1 to drive onto a road, especially when other cars are driving more quickly than you are: *Another car suddenly pulled out in front of me, and I had to brake.*

2 to leave a dangerous place or situation: *Firefighters had to pull out, because the fire was too dangerous.*

pull over

to drive to the side of a road and stop your car: *The police officer told us to pull over.*

pull through *informal*

to stay alive after a serious injury or illness: *He's very weak after his operation, but his doctor says that he will pull through.*

pull yourself together

to stop being upset or frightened: *Stop crying and pull yourself together – you're going to be fine.*

pull up

1 pull up = if a car pulls up, it stops: *The car pulled up at the stop lights.*

2 pull up a chair/stool, etc. = to get a chair and sit down near someone who is already sitting

pull² *noun*

1 the action of holding something and using force to make it move toward you: *Give the rope a good pull.* ANTONYM **push**

2 *informal* power and influence: *He is a very wealthy businessman, and he has a lot of pull in this city.*

pul•ley /ˈpʊli/ *noun* plural **pulleys**

a piece of equipment with a rope and a wheel, that you use for lifting heavy things: *They raised the boat from the bottom of the lake on a pulley.*

pulp /pʌlp/ *noun*

1 the soft inside part of a fruit or vegetable: *The orange juice had a lot of pulp in it.*

2 a soft substance that is almost liquid: *Mash the bananas to a pulp.*

pulse /pʌls/ *noun*

the regular beat that you can feel as your heart moves blood around your body: *A nurse came in and took my pulse* (=counted the number of beats in a minute).

pu•ma /ˈpumə/ *noun*

another word for a COUGAR

pump¹ /pʌmp/ *noun*

a machine that makes liquid or gas go into or out of something: *a gas pump | a bicycle pump* (=for putting air in the tires)

pump² *verb*

1 to make liquid or gas move in a particular direction using a pump: *The farmers pumped water from the river onto their fields.*

2 pump money into something = to supply a lot of money for something: *The state pumped money into the research project.*

pump•kin /ˈpʌmpkɪn/ *noun*
a very large orange fruit that grows on the ground: *At Halloween, children cut faces in pumpkins and put candles inside.*
➔ See picture on page A12

punch¹ /pʌntʃ/ *verb*
1 to hit someone hard with your hand closed: *He punched me in the stomach, and I bent over in pain.*
2 to make a hole in something using something sharp: *I punched a hole in the bottom of the plastic cup so the water would run out.*
➔ See Thesaurus box at **hit¹**

punch² *noun*
1 a hard hit with your hand closed: *I'll give you a punch on the nose!*
2 a drink made from fruit juice, sugar, and water: *We made a bowl of punch for the party.*

punc•tu•al /ˈpʌŋktʃuəl/ *adjective, formal*
someone who is punctual arrives at exactly the right time: *She's very punctual and has never been late for school.*
—**punctually** *adverb*: *He's a good customer who pays his bills punctually.*
—**punctuality** /ˌpʌŋktʃuˈæləti/ *noun* the quality of being punctual

punc•tu•ate /ˈpʌŋktʃuˌeɪt/ *verb, formal*
to use punctuation marks in your writing: *The students are learning how to punctuate a sentence correctly.*

punc•tu•a•tion /ˌpʌŋktʃuˈeɪʃən/ *noun*
the use of punctuation marks in your writing: *Learning the rules of punctuation will make your writing better.*

ˌpunctuˈation mark *noun*
a sign such as . ; , : or ?, that you use in your writing to make sentences clearer: *A period is the punctuation mark you use at the end of a sentence.*

punc•ture /ˈpʌŋktʃɚ/ *verb, formal*
to make a small hole in something, so that air or liquid comes out: *He punctured the balloon with a pin.*
—**puncture** *noun, formal* a hole made by puncturing something

pun•ish /ˈpʌnɪʃ/ *verb*
to make someone suffer because he or she has done something wrong: *I came home late, so my father punished me by not giving me my allowance.*

pun•ish•ment /ˈpʌnɪʃmənt/ *noun*
something bad that someone makes you do when you have done something wrong: *The punishment for his crime was four years in prison.*

punk /pʌŋk/ *noun*
1 *informal* a young man who often has fights and does illegal things: *Some punks started a fight in the street.*
2 a type of loud rock music that was popular in the 1970s and 1980s, or someone who likes this type of music: *a punk with pink hair*

pu•pil /ˈpyupəl/ *noun*
1 *formal* a child in school: *There are 500 pupils in my school.*
2 the small black part in the middle of your eye: *In bright light, your pupils get smaller.*
➔ See picture at **eye**

pup•pet /ˈpʌpɪt/ *noun*
a figure of a person or animal that you move by pulling the strings on it or by putting your hand inside it: *He had a puppet on each hand and was making them talk to each other.*
—**puppeteer** /ˌpʌpəˈtɪr/ *noun* someone who makes and uses puppets

pup•py /ˈpʌpi/ *noun* plural **puppies**
a young dog

pur•chase¹ /ˈpɚtʃəs/ Ac *verb, formal*
to buy something: *You can purchase tickets over the phone.*
—**purchaser** *noun* someone who purchases something
➔ See Thesaurus box at **buy**

purchase² *noun, formal*
1 the act of buying something: *I made a purchase using my credit card.*
2 something you bought: *The store will deliver your purchases.*

pure /pyʊr/ *adjective*
1 not mixed with anything else: *The ring was made of pure gold.* ANTONYM **impure**
2 clean, without anything harmful: *The water is pure, so you can drink it.* ANTONYM **impure**
3 used when describing a strong feeling, that is not mixed with any other feeling: *She gave a smile of pure joy.* SYNONYM **complete, total**

—**purity** *noun* the quality of being pure: *I love the purity of the air in the moutains.*

WORD FAMILY look at the words:

→ **pure** *adjective*
→ **impure** *adjective*
→ **purify** *verb*
→ **purity** *noun*

pure•ly /ˈpyʊrli/ *adverb, formal*
in every way: *I found the money purely by accident – someone had dropped it in the street.* SYNONYM **completely, totally**

pu•ri•fy /ˈpyʊrəˌfaɪ/ *verb, formal* **purified,** third person singular **purifies**
to take the dirty parts out of something such as water or air: *Use a filter to purify water.*
—**purification** /ˌpyʊrəfəˈkeɪʃən/ *noun* the process of purifying something

pur•ple /ˈpɚpəl/ *noun, adjective*
a dark color that is a mixture of red and blue: *She had a purple bruise on her leg.*

pur•pose /ˈpɚpəs/ *noun*
1 *formal* a reason for doing something, because you want to achieve something: *The purpose of exercise is to keep you healthy.* | *The Red Cross sent supplies for medical purposes.*

THESAURUS: purpose

aim something that you want to achieve: *Her aim is to have enough money for college.*

goal something that you hope to achieve in the future: *My goal is to run in the Olympics.*

objective *formal* something that you are working hard to achieve: *The state set an objective for schools: every child should be reading by age 9.*

2 on purpose = if you do something on purpose, you intend to do it and it is not an accident: *I left the lights on on purpose, so people would think I was home.* SYNONYM **deliberately**; ANTONYM **accidentally**

pur•pose•ful /ˈpɚpəsfəl/ *adjective, formal*
showing that you have a reason for doing something: *Children work harder when their work is purposeful.*

pur•pose•ly /ˈpɚpəsli/ *adverb, formal*
if you do something purposely, you plan to do it and it is not an accident: *I purposely closed the door so no one could hear our conversation.* SYNONYM **on purpose, deliberately**; ANTONYM **accidentally**

purr /pɚ/ *verb*
if a cat purrs, it makes a soft low sound when it is happy
—**purr** *noun* the sound a cat makes when it is happy

purse /pɚs/ *noun*
a bag that women use to carry money and other things: *She took her keys out of her purse.*
→ See picture at **bag**

pur•sue /pɚˈsu/ Ac *verb, formal*
1 to chase someone in order to catch him or her: *The police pursued the man who had stolen the car.*
2 to work hard in order to achieve something: *He wanted to pursue a career in acting.* SYNONYM **follow**

pur•suit /pɚˈsut/ Ac *noun, formal*
1 the act of chasing someone in order to catch him or her: *A truck drove by fast, with a police car in pursuit.*
2 an activity that you spend a lot of time doing: *She enjoys pursuits such as reading and sewing.*
3 the act of trying to get something: *He'd spent his adult life in the pursuit of money; he ended up rich, but lonely.*

pus /pʌs/ *noun*
a yellow liquid that comes out of an infected part of your body: *The wound had pus in it.*

push¹ /pʊʃ/ *verb*
1 to move a person or thing away from you by pressing him, her, or it with your hands: *We pushed the car out of the garage.* | *She pushed her sister into the swimming pool.* ANTONYM **pull**

THESAURUS: push

poke to push someone or something with your finger or something sharp: *Jill poked Miguel in the arm to get his attention.*

shove to push someone or something roughly: *He shoved her out of the way.*

P

nudge to push someone gently with your elbow to get their attention: *"Move over," she said, nudging my arm.*

2 to press a button, SWITCH, etc. to make a machine start or stop working: *Push the green button to start the engine.*
3 to move somewhere by pushing people away from you: *The men pushed their way to the front of the crowd.*
4 to try hard to persuade someone to do something: *My parents pushed me into going to college.*
5 to make someone work very hard: *He has been pushing himself too hard in order to make straight A's.*
➔ See Thesaurus box at **press**[1]

PHRASAL VERBS

push someone around
informal to tell someone what to do in a rude or threatening way: *Tell the big kids to stop pushing you around.*

push something through
to get a plan, law, etc. officially accepted, especially quickly: *The president tried to push his plan through.*

push something up
to make something increase: *The high oil prices pushed up the cost of traveling.*

push[2] *noun*
1 the act of pushing someone or something: *I'm sure that the door will open if you give it a good push.* ANTONYM **pull**
2 a situation in which someone works very hard to get or achieve something: *The school is making a big push to get parents to help at the school.*
➔ See picture on page A3

'push-up *noun*
an exercise in which you lie facing the floor, and push yourself up with your arms: *I do push-ups to make my arms and chest stronger.*

push·y /ˈpʊʃi/ *adjective*
trying hard to get what you want, in a rude way: *The salesman was pushy, and wouldn't go away when I said I didn't want to buy anything.*

put /pʊt/ *verb* **put, putting**
1 to move someone or something into a place or position: *"Where did you put my shoes?" "They're by the door."* | *She put the money in the bank.*
2 to write or print something: *Put your name at the top of your answer sheet.*
3 to make someone be in a situation or make someone have a feeling: *The sunshine put everyone in a good mood.*
4 to say something in a particular way: *If you don't understand what I'm saying, I'll put it another way.*
5 put an end to something/put a stop to something = to stop an activity that is bad or not acceptable: *The city authorities want to put an end to the violence.*
6 put the blame on someone = to decide that someone caused something bad to happen: *You shouldn't always put the blame on yourself.*
7 put something behind you = to try to forget about a bad experience or a mistake so that it does not affect you now: *I had some problems, but now I have to put them behind me.*

PHRASAL VERBS

put something away
to put something in the place where it is usually kept: *Make sure that you put all your clothes away before you go to bed.*

put something forward
to suggest a plan, idea, etc.: *I wanted to put forward a suggestion.*

put off
1 put something off = to delay something: *We decided to put off our trip to Europe until next year.* SYNONYM **postpone**
2 put someone off (something) = to make you dislike something or not want to do something: *The fruit has a strong smell, which puts some people off.*

put on
1 put something on = to put a piece of clothing on your body: *He put on his best suit for the wedding.* ANTONYM **take off**
2 put on weight/5 pounds, etc. = to become fatter and heavier: *She put on a lot of weight after she had the baby.*

put out
1 put out a fire/cigarette = to make a fire, cigarette, etc. stop burning: *It took almost three hours to put out the fire.* SYNONYM **extinguish**

2 put out a book/record, etc. = to produce a new book, record, etc., which is available for people to buy

3 put out your hand/foot/arm = to move your hand, foot, etc. away from your body: *She put out her hand and touched the baby's face.*

put someone through something

to make someone do something that is very bad or difficult: *The soldiers are put through eight weeks of basic training.*

put together

1 put something together = to make something by joining its different parts together: *It took a long time to put the toy together.*

2 put together = combined: *He earns more money than the rest of us put together.*

put up

1 put something up = to build something such as a building, a wall, etc.: *We put up a new fence last summer.*

2 put something up = to attach a picture, notice, or decorations to a wall, so that people can see them: *Someone had put up a sign on the wall advertising free puppies.*

3 put someone up *informal* = to let someone stay in your house: *One of my friends offered to put me up while I was in town.*

put up with someone or something

to accept a bad situation or person without complaining: *He's so annoying – I don't know how his wife puts up with him.*

puz•zle[1] /ˈpʌzəl/ *noun*

1 a picture that has been cut into pieces that you can put back together again for fun: *We put together a 100-piece puzzle of a map of the United States.*

2 a game in which you have to think hard to solve a problem: *Sudoku is a type of number puzzle.*

puzzle

3 something that is difficult to understand or explain: *The way the stock market works is a puzzle to me.*

puzzle[2] *verb*

if something puzzles you, it confuses you because you cannot understand it: *It puzzled me that he hadn't asked for help sooner.*

—**puzzled** *adjective* confused, because you cannot understand something: *He had a puzzled expression on his face when I asked him about the money.*

—**puzzling** *adjective* making you puzzled: *a puzzling problem*

PHRASAL VERB

puzzle over

to think for a long time about something because you do not understand it: *He sat puzzling over his homework.*

py•lon /ˈpaɪlɑn/ *noun*

a tall metal structure that supports wires carrying electricity

pyr•a•mid /ˈpɪrəmɪd/ *noun*

1 a solid shape with a flat base and four sides that form a point at the top: *The sides of a pyramid are triangles.*

2 a very large building in the shape of a pyramid, in Mexico or Egypt: *We visited the pyramids near Mexico City.*

→ See picture at **shape**[1]

py•thon /ˈpaɪθɑn/ *noun*

a large snake that kills animals for food by curling around them and pressing them

P

Qq

Q-tip /ˈkyu tɪp/ *noun*
a small thin stick with cotton at each end: *She cleaned the baby's ears with a Q-tip.*

Q

quack¹ /kwæk/ *verb*
if a duck quacks, it makes a short loud sound

quack² *noun*
1 the sound a duck makes
2 *informal* someone who pretends to be a doctor: *The doctor was a quack and had never been to medical school.*

quad•ru•ple /kwɑˈdrupəl/ *verb, formal*
to become four times as big as before: *The number of children at the school has quadrupled, from 100 to 400.*
—**quadruple** *adjective* four times as big as before: *a quadruple increase in price*

quail /kweɪl/ *noun*
a small bird that people hunt for food or as a sport

quaint /kweɪnt/ *adjective*
a quaint place is pretty, in an old-fashioned way: *Douglas, Arizona, is a quaint little town.*

quake¹ /kweɪk/ *verb, formal*
to shake because you are afraid: *She was quaking with fear.* SYNONYM **tremble**

quake² *noun, informal*
a strong and sudden shaking of the ground: *Many buildings were destroyed in the quake.* SYNONYM **earthquake**

qual•i•fi•ca•tion /ˌkwɑləfəˈkeɪʃən/ *noun*
experience or skills that make you able to do a particular job: *He had all the qualifications that he needed to be a teacher.*

qual•i•fied /ˈkwɑləˌfaɪd/ *adjective*
having the right knowledge or skills to do something: *College graduates are qualified for higher paying jobs.*

qual•i•fi•er /ˈkwɑləˌfaɪɚ/ *noun, formal*
1 someone who has proved that he or she is good enough to be in a race or competition: *The fastest qualifier will run in the middle lane.*
2 a word or phrase that tells you more about another word or phrase: *In the phrase "her new red bike," "new" and "red" are qualifiers.*

qual•i•fy /ˈkwɑləˌfaɪ/ *verb, formal* **qualified**, third person singular **qualifies**
1 to have the education or skills that you need to do a particular job: *A high-school diploma qualifies you for a lot of jobs.*
2 to be able to have or do something, because of something you have done or because you are in a particular situation: *Poor children qualify for free school lunches.*

WORD FAMILY look at the words:

→ **qualify** *verb*
→ **qualification** *noun*
→ **qualified** *adjective*
→ **unqualified** *adjective*
→ **disqualify** *verb*

qual•i•ty /ˈkwɑləti/ *noun* plural **qualities** *formal*
1 how good something is: *The quality of his work is excellent.* | *All the books we use are of high quality* (=good quality). | *They complained about the poor quality of the food* (=it was not good).
2 something good that is part of someone's character: *His greatest quality is his kindness.*

quan•ti•fy /ˈkwɑntəˌfaɪ/ *verb, formal* **quantified**, third person singular **quantifies**
to measure something and say how big it is in numbers: *The damage to the company is difficult to quantify in a dollar amount.*

quan•ti•ty /ˈkwɑntəti/ *noun* plural **quantities** *formal*
an amount of something: *He drank a large quantity of water.*

quar•an•tine /ˈkwɔrənˌtin/ *noun, formal*
in quarantine = if a person or animal is in quarantine, they must stay in a place away from other people or animals so they do not pass on a dangerous disease: *His dog was kept in quarantine for 120 days after arriving in Hawaii.*
—**quarantine** *verb, formal* to put a person or animal in quarantine

quar•rel[1] /ˈkwɔrəl/ *noun*
an angry argument: *We had a quarrel about money.*

quarrel[2] *verb*
to have an angry argument: *The children are always quarreling over something.*

quar•ry /ˈkwɔri/ *noun* plural **quarries**
a place where vehicles and machines dig stone or sand out of the ground: *The marble comes from a quarry in Colorado.*

quart /kwɔrt/ *noun*
a unit for measuring liquid, equal to 0.95 liters: *There are two pints in one quart.* | *a quart of milk*

quar•ter /ˈkwɔrtɚ/ *noun*
1 one of four equal parts of something: *A quarter of 44 is 11.* | *Cut the sandwiches into quarters.*
2 a coin worth 25 cents: *He put a quarter in the machine.*
3 15 minutes: *I left home at a quarter after* (=15 minutes after) *7.* | *I'll meet you at quarter to* (=15 minutes before) *three.* | *The bus leaves at quarter of* (=15 minutes before) *ten.* | *The baby cried for a quarter of an hour.* | *Can you be ready to go in three-quarters of an hour* (=45 minutes)*?*
4 one of the four equal periods that a basketball or football game is divided into: *The score was 66–58 in the third quarter.*
5 one of the four periods during a year in which you can take classes at college: *I'm taking three classes this quarter.*
6 a period of three months, which businesses use to divide the year: *The company's profits fell in the first quarter.*
→ See Thesaurus box at **money**

quar•ter•back /ˈkwɔrtɚˌbæk/ *noun*
the player in football who throws the ball or tries to move the ball forward toward the goal: *The quarterback passed the ball to the receiver.*

quar•ter•ly /ˈkwɔrtɚli/ *adjective, adverb, formal*
every three months, or four times a year: *The first quarterly report comes at the end of March.*

quar•tet /kwɔrˈtet/ *noun*
a group of four musicians or singers: *A string quartet has two violin players, one viola player, and one cello player.*

quartz /kwɔrts/ *noun*
a hard rock used in electronic watches and clocks

quay /keɪ/ *noun, formal*
a place where you can tie up boats or put things on them: *We went to the quay and got on the boat.* SYNONYM **dock**

quea•sy /ˈkwizi/ *adjective*
feeling that you are going to be sick: *The sight of blood makes me queasy.*

queen /kwin/ *noun*
1 the female ruler of a country, or the wife of a king: *Elizabeth became Queen of England in 1588.*
2 a card with a picture of a queen on it, in the game of cards: *He put down the queen of diamonds.*

ˈqueen-size *adjective*
a queen-size bed is a bed for two people that is bigger than the usual size

queer /kwɪr/ *adjective, formal*
strange and not normal: *I had this queer feeling, as if I was in someone else's body.* SYNONYM **peculiar, odd**

quench /kwentʃ/ *verb, formal*
quench your thirst = to drink something so that you stop feeling thirsty: *I drank some water to quench my thirst.*

que•ry /ˈkwɪri/ *noun* plural **queries** *formal*
a question asking for more information about something: *Here is your bill – if you have any queries, call me.*
—**query** *verb, formal* to ask a question about something, because you want more information: *I queried the price, because it seemed too high.*

ques•tion[1] /ˈkwestʃən/ *noun*
1 a group of words that ask for information: *Can I ask you a question – how old are you?* | *You didn't answer my question.* | *She asked some questions about the math homework.* ANTONYM **answer**
2 a part of a test that asks you to give information: *The history test had twenty questions.*
3 *formal* a problem that people need to talk about and deal with: *We discussed the question of where Jon should live.* SYNONYM **issue**
4 be out of the question = to not be

Q

possible or allowed: *No, you're not going. It's out of the question!*

question² *verb, formal*
1 to ask someone about something: *Police questioned him about the crime.*
2 to start to have doubts about something: *I'm not questioning your honesty because I know I can trust you.*
➔ See Thesaurus box at **ask**

ques·tion·a·ble /ˈkwestʃənəbəl/ *adjective, formal*
not certain: *It's questionable whether she will pass the test because she hasn't done much studying.* SYNONYM **doubtful**

ˈquestion mark *noun*
the mark ?, used in writing at the end of a question

ques·tion·naire /ˌkwestʃəˈner/ *noun*
a written set of questions that someone gives to a large number of people in order to collect information: *I filled out a questionnaire about where I buy my clothes.*

quiche /kiʃ/ *noun*
a mixture of eggs, cheese, and vegetables cooked in a pie CRUST

quick /kwɪk/ *adjective*
1 something that is quick takes only a short time: *It was just a quick visit – I was only there for five minutes.* SYNONYM **brief**; ANTONYM **long**
2 someone or something that is quick moves fast or does things fast: *He's a quick worker and always finishes first.* | *a quick sports car* SYNONYM **fast**; ANTONYM **slow**

quick·ly /ˈkwɪkli/ *adverb*
1 fast: *Driving too quickly is dangerous.*
2 after a very short time: *I quickly discovered I'd made a mistake.* SYNONYM **soon**
➔ See Thesaurus box at **fast²**

quicksand

quick·sand /ˈkwɪksænd/ *noun*
wet sand that is difficult to get out of if you walk in it: *In the movie, he gets sucked into quicksand.*

qui·et¹ /ˈkwaɪət/ *adjective*
1 not making a lot of noise: *Be quiet – I'm on the phone!* | *It's very quiet in the middle of the night.* ANTONYM **noisy, loud**
2 without a lot of activity: *I had a quiet day at home.* ANTONYM **busy**
—**quietly** *adverb*: *They talked quietly.*

quiet² *noun*
the state of being quiet: *I love the peace and quiet of the morning.* ANTONYM **noise**

quilt /kwɪlt/ *noun*
a cover for a bed, made by sewing two large pieces of cloth together and putting feathers or cotton inside: *A patchwork quilt is made from squares of material.*

quit /kwɪt/ *verb* **quit, quitting** *informal*
1 to stop doing something: *I quit smoking cigarettes last year.* | *Quit hitting your sister!* ANTONYM **start**

THESAURUS: quit

give up to stop doing something, or stop trying to do something: *It's hard at first, but don't give up.*

resign *formal* to officially leave your job or position: *Garcia resigned from the committee.*

drop out *informal* to stop going to school or stop an activity before you have finished it: *Tucker dropped out of high school when he was 16.*

2 to leave your job: *Betty quit her job to stay home with the kids.* | *I hated my boss, so I quit.* SYNONYM **resign**

quite /kwaɪt/ *adverb*
1 very, but not extremely: *The house is quite big, but not huge.* SYNONYM **pretty**
2 not quite = not completely: *I'm not quite ready – I still have to brush my teeth.*

quiv·er /ˈkwɪvɚ/ *verb, formal*
to shake a little because you are afraid or upset: *The little girl quivered with fear.* SYNONYM **tremble**

quiz /kwɪz/ *noun* plural **quizzes**
1 a short test: *Every week, the teacher gives us a math quiz.*
2 a set of questions that you answer, to see how much you know about something or to find out something about yourself: *There's a quiz about finding your perfect boyfriend in the magazine.*

quo•ta /ˈkwoʊtə/ *noun, formal*
1 an amount of something that is the most that an official organization allows someone to have: *There is a quota on the number of fish that you are allowed to catch.* SYNONYM **limit**
2 an amount of something that someone must do in a period of time: *He has to sell 30 washing machines a week to meet his quota* (=achieve his quota). SYNONYM **target**

quo•ta•tion /kwoʊˈteɪʃən/ Ac *noun*
1 words from a book or speech that you repeat in your own speech or writing: *"To be or not to be" is a famous quotation from Shakespeare.* SYNONYM **quote**
2 a written statement of how much something will cost: *He gave us a quotation for repairing the roof.* SYNONYM **quote**

quoˈtation ˌmarks *plural noun*
the marks "...", which you write before and after what someone says

quote¹ /kwoʊt/ Ac *verb*
1 to say or write exactly what someone else has written: *She quoted President Roosevelt, "You have nothing to fear but fear itself."*
2 to tell someone how much he or she will have to pay you for something: *The airline quoted me $400 for a ticket to New York.*

WORD FAMILY look at the words:
→ **quote** *verb*
→ **quote** *noun*
→ **quotation** *noun*

quote² *noun*
another word for QUOTATION

Q

Rr

rab·bi /ˈræbaɪ/ *noun* plural **rabbis**
a Jewish religious leader and teacher

rab·bit /ˈræbɪt/ *noun*
a small animal with long ears that lives in holes in the ground or that people keep as a pet
→ See picture at **pet**

R

rac·coon /ræˈkun/ *noun*
an animal with black fur around its eyes and black and white lines around its tail: *A raccoon was looking for food in the trash can.*

race[1] /reɪs/ *noun*
1 a competition to find out who can do something fastest, for example running, driving, or swimming: *Who won the race?*
2 a group of humans that is different from other groups in skin color, hair color, size, etc.: *People from many different races live in America.*

WORD FAMILY look at the words:
→ **race** *noun*
→ **racial** *adjective*
→ **racist** *noun*
→ **racism** *noun*
→ **multiracial** *adjective*

THESAURUS: race
nation a country and its government: *The leaders of several Western nations are meeting in Paris this week.*
people a race or group of people that live in a particular country. The plural of this meaning of "people" is "peoples": *the native peoples of the United States*
tribe a group of people within a country who are the same race, and who have the same language and traditions and the same leader: *The Navajo tribe is the second largest in the U.S.*
ethnic group *formal* a group of people of the same race, nation, or tribe: *Many different ethnic groups live in New York.*

→ **human race**

race[2] *verb*
1 to compete in a race: *She'll be racing against some of the best athletes.*
2 to go somewhere very quickly: *I raced home to see if the letter had arrived.*
→ See Thesaurus box at **run**[1]

race·horse /ˈreɪsˌhɔrs/ *noun*
a horse that competes in races: *He bet $100 on a racehorse.*

race·track /ˈreɪs-træk/ *noun*
a special road where horses, cars, or people compete in races: *I went to the racetrack to watch the horse racing.* SYNONYM **track**

ra·cial /ˈreɪʃəl/ *adjective*
relating to someone's RACE: *I totally oppose racial discrimination* (=treating people unfairly because of their race).
—**racially** *adverb*

rac·ism /ˈreɪsɪzəm/ *noun*
the act of treating people unfairly because they belong to a different RACE than you do: *They accused him of racism when he fired a black woman.*
→ See Thesaurus box at **prejudice**

rac·ist /ˈreɪsɪst/ *noun*
someone who believes that his or her own RACE of people is better than any other: *She said the police were racists who didn't trust anyone with brown skin.*
—**racist** *adjective* relating to the things a racist does or says: *He made racist remarks about a Chinese student.*
→ See Thesaurus box at **prejudice**

rack /ræk/ *noun*
a thing like a shelf or bar, used for holding things: *She decided she didn't want to buy the dress and put it back on the sales rack.*

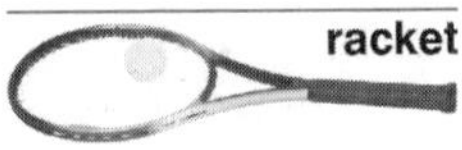

rack·et /ˈrækɪt/ *noun*
1 *informal* a loud noise: *The kids were making such a racket I didn't hear the doorbell.*
2 something you use to hit the ball in games such as tennis: *One of the strings on his tennis racket broke.*

rack·et·ball /ˈrækɪtˌbɔl/ *noun*
an indoor game in which two players hit a ball against the walls of a special room

ra·dar /ˈreɪdɑr/ *noun*
a way of finding out where ships and airplanes are in the ocean or sky, using radio

waves: *The radar showed that two ships were coming closer.*

ra•di•ant /ˈreɪdiənt/ *adjective, formal*
looking very very happy: *The bride had a radiant smile.*

ra•di•a•tion /ˌreɪdiˈeɪʃən/ *noun*
a form of energy that is dangerous to living things if there is too much of it: *Radiation killed many people when the nuclear bomb exploded.*

ra•di•a•tor /ˈreɪdiˌeɪtɚ/ *noun*
1 a flat metal object on a wall, which hot water passes through to make a room warm: *The radiators were turned off, so the house was cold.*
2 the part of a car that keeps the engine cool: *He put some more water in the radiator to cool the engine.*

rad•i•cal /ˈrædɪkəl/ [Ac] *adjective, formal*
1 making something very different: *He made a radical change in his life, leaving his job and becoming a priest.* SYNONYM **big**; ANTONYM **slight**, **small**
2 having beliefs that are very different from what most people believe: *Radical political groups supported the use of violence.* ANTONYM **moderate**
—**radically** *adverb*: *Many African countries are radically different from the U.S.A.*

ra•di•o /ˈreɪdiˌoʊ/ *noun*
1 a piece of electrical equipment that you use to listen to music, news, and other programs: *I was listening to the radio in the car.* | *There was country music on the radio.*
2 the activity of making programs that people listen to on the radio: *He wants to get a job in radio.*
3 the use of electrical waves to send and receive messages: *Ships send messages to each other by radio.*
➔ See picture on page A28

ra•di•o•ac•tive /ˌreɪdioʊˈæktɪv/ *adjective*
something that is radioactive produces a type of energy that is dangerous to living things if there is too much of it: *Nuclear power stations produce a lot of radioactive waste.*
—**radioactivity** /ˌreɪdioʊækˈtɪvəti/ *noun* the quality of being radioactive

rad•ish /ˈrædɪʃ/ *noun*
a small red or white vegetable with a hot taste that grows in the ground and that you do not cook: *Radishes are great in salads.*
➔ See picture on page A12

ra•di•us /ˈreɪdiəs/ *noun* plural **radii** /ˈreɪdiaɪ/ *formal*
1 the distance from the center of a circle to the edge
2 within a 10-mile/100-meter, etc. radius (of something) = up to a distance of 10 miles, etc. in all directions from somewhere: *All our students live within a 15-mile radius of the school.*
➔ See picture at **diameter**

raf•fle /ˈræfəl/ *noun*
a competition in which people buy tickets with numbers on them in order to try to win prizes: *Kelly won a bike in the raffle the school held to raise money.*

raft /ræft/ *noun*
a flat boat that you make by tying pieces of wood together: *They made a raft and left the island.*
➔ **life raft**

rag /ræg/ *noun*
1 a small piece of old cloth: *He cleaned the machine with an oily rag.*
2 in rags = wearing old torn clothes: *The children were very poor and were dressed in rags.*

rage /reɪdʒ/ *noun*
very strong anger: *She was filled with rage when she realized Steve had lied to her.* SYNONYM **fury**

raid[1] /reɪd/ *noun*
1 an occasion when the police come to search a place for something illegal, when the people there are not expecting it: *Police officers found drugs during a raid on the apartment.*
2 a sudden attack on a place during a war: *He flew planes on bombing raids during the war.*

raid[2] *verb*
1 if the police raid a place, they go there to search for something illegal when the people there are not expecting it: *Police found guns and drugs when they raided his home.*

R

2 to attack a place suddenly, in a war: *Soldiers raided the village.*
—**raider** *noun* someone who raids a place

rail /reɪl/ *noun*
1 a bar that is fastened along or around something, that stops you from falling over an edge or that you can hold when going up and down stairs: *I held onto the rail and looked down at the tiny cars on the street below us.*
2 one of the two long metal bars on which a train moves: *Snow on the rails stopped the train from leaving.* SYNONYM **track**
—**rail** *adjective* relating to traveling using a train: *rail service between New York and Philadelphia*

R

rail•ing /ˈreɪlɪŋ/ *noun*
a low fence with a bar and upright posts, that stops you from falling over an edge or that you can hold when going up or down stairs: *The steps were steep, so I held onto the railing.*

rail•road /ˈreɪlroʊd/ *noun*
the system of tracks, equipment, etc. that trains use: *I took him to the railroad station.* | *The train moved along the railroad tracks.*

rail•way /ˈreɪlweɪ/ *noun*
another word for RAILROAD

rain¹ /reɪn/ *noun*
water that falls from the sky: *The weather man said there would be rain.* | *During the night, there was heavy rain* (=a lot of rain).

THESAURUS: rain

drizzle light rain with very small drops of water: *They walked along the street in a cold drizzle.*

shower a short period of rain: *There will be a few light showers during the day.*

downpour a lot of rain that falls in a short period of time: *The downpour made driving difficult.*

storm very bad weather with a lot of wind and rain: *Storms are forecast for this weekend.*

hail small hard drops of frozen rain that fall from the clouds: *A hail storm flattened crops.*

sleet a mixture of snow and rain: *There will be sleet and snow showers.*

rain² *verb*
if it rains, drops of water fall from the sky: *Is it still raining?* | *It started raining hard* (=raining a lot).

rainbow

rain•bow /ˈreɪnboʊ/ *noun*
a large curve of different colors in the sky, after it has rained

rain•coat /ˈreɪnkoʊt/ *noun*
a coat that keeps you dry in the rain
➔ See picture on page A6

rain•drop /ˈreɪndrɑp/ *noun*
a single drop of rain: *There were raindrops on the window.*

rain•fall /ˈreɪnfɔl/ *noun*
the amount of rain that falls somewhere: *Rainfall in the Amazon is around 20 meters a year.*

ˈrain ˌforest *noun*
a thick forest in a part of the world that is hot and wet: *The rain forests are being destroyed by people cutting down trees for wood.*
➔ See Thesaurus box at **tree**

rain•y /ˈreɪni/ *adjective*
having a lot of rain: *On rainy days, Dad drives me to school.*

raise¹ /reɪz/ *verb*
1 to move something to a higher position: *He raised his arms above his head.* | *Raise your hand if you know the answer.* SYNONYM **lift**; ANTONYM **lower**
2 to increase something: *They raised the price from $1.99 to $3.99.* ANTONYM **lower**
3 to take care of children, animals, or crops until they are grown: *She raised three sons on her own.*
4 to collect money to help people: *The kids raised $400 for the school by washing cars.*
5 to begin to talk or write about something that you want people to think about: *The students raised several interesting questions during the discussion.*

raise[2] *noun*
an increase in the money you earn: *She asked her boss for a raise after she had been there a year.*

rai•sin /ˈreɪzən/ *noun*
a dried GRAPE: *The cookies had raisins in them.*
→ See picture on page A13

rake[1] /reɪk/ *noun*
a tool that you use for moving leaves off of grass

rake[2] *also* **rake up** *verb*
to use a rake to move leaves off of grass: *He spends hours raking leaves every fall.*

ral•ly[1] /ˈræli/ *noun* plural **rallies**
a large public meeting to support a political idea or a sports team: *The school had a pep rally* (=a rally to make people excited) *before the football game.*

rally[2] *verb* **rallied**, third person singular **rallies** *formal*
to join other people in order to support a person or idea: *Republicans rallied to the president after Democrats criticized his leadership.*

ram /ræm/ *verb* **rammed, ramming**
if a car, truck, or something hard rams something, it hits it with a lot of force: *A truck rammed into a line of cars, crushing them all.*

ramp /ræmp/ *noun*
1 a road for driving onto or off a main road: *There was a line of cars on the exit ramp.*
2 a slope that connects two places that are at different levels: *The building has ramps for wheelchair users.*

ramp•ant /ˈræmpənt/ *adjective, formal*
if something bad is rampant, there is a lot of it and it is difficult to control: *Violent crime is rampant in the city and no one feels safe.*

ran /ræn/ *verb*
the past tense of RUN

ranch /ræntʃ/ *noun*
a large farm with cows, horses, or sheep: *He owns a sheep ranch in Australia.*
—**rancher** *noun* someone who owns or works on a ranch
—**ranching** *noun* the job of owning or working on a ranch

R & B /ˌɑr ən ˈbi/ *noun*
rhythm and blues a type of popular music that is a mixture of BLUES and JAZZ

ran•dom /ˈrændəm/ Ac *adjective*
happening or chosen without using any reason or pattern: *The teacher picked six people at random to help her.*
—**randomly** *adverb*: *The lottery numbers are randomly chosen.*

rang /ræŋ/ *verb*
the past tense of RING

range /reɪndʒ/ Ac *noun*
1 a group of things that are different, but are the same type of thing: *The store sells a wide range of shoes, so I'm sure you can find something you like.*
2 the amounts or numbers between two limits: *The games are good for the 8–12 age range.* | *The car is out of our price range* (=it is too expensive for us).
3 a line of mountains or hills: *The Alps are the largest mountain range in Europe.*
4 the distance that something can reach or travel: *The missiles have a range of more than 300 miles.*

rank[1] /ræŋk/ *noun*
the position or level that someone has in an organization: *A general is an army officer with a very high rank.*

rank[2] *verb*
to have a particular position in a list that shows how good someone or something is: *The team ranks 12th in the league after losing their last six games.*

ran•som /ˈrænsəm/ *noun*
money that is paid to criminals who are keeping someone prisoner, so that the criminals will let that person go: *The kidnappers wanted a $200,000 ransom to release the businessman's wife.*

rap /ræp/ *also* **ˈrap ˌmusic** *noun*
a type of popular music in which someone speaks words rather than singing them
—**rapper** *noun* someone who performs rap

rap•id /ˈræpɪd/ *adjective*
done very quickly, or happening in a short time: *David has made rapid progress in learning to read – he's already reading simple books.* SYNONYM **fast, quick**; ANTONYM **slow**
—**rapidly** *adverb*: *The number of people using cell phones has grown rapidly.*
—**rapidity** /rəˈpɪdəti/ *noun* the quality of being rapid

R

rare /rer/ *adjective*
1 not happening or seen very often: *The rare birds are found in only two or three places in the world.* ANTONYM **common**
2 meat that is rare is not completely cooked: *a medium rare steak*

rare·ly /'rerli/ *adverb*
not often: *He's very sick and rarely leaves his home.* ANTONYM **frequently**

rash¹ /ræʃ/ *adjective*
done too quickly and without thinking carefully: *She made a rash decision to leave her parents' home and get her own apartment.*

R

rash² *noun*
red spots on someone's skin, caused by an illness or by something he or she has eaten or touched: *He had a fever and a rash on his chest.*

rasp·ber·ry /'ræzˌberi/ *noun* plural **raspberries**
a soft sweet red BERRY: *Raspberries grow on bushes.*
→ See picture on page A13

rat /ræt/ *noun*
an animal that looks like a large mouse with a long tail: *I saw a big rat run across the basement of the old house.*

rate /reɪt/ *noun*
1 the number of times that something happens in a period of time: *Utah has one of the lowest crime rates* (=there are not many crimes in a period of time) *in the U.S.*
2 the amount of money that you earn or pay for something: *The hourly rate of pay for the job is $15.* | *What is the interest rate* (=the money the bank gives you for keeping your money there) *on that savings account?*
3 the speed at which something happens: *Children learn at different rates.*
4 at any rate = said when a particular fact is important in a situation: *"How many people are coming?" "I don't know, but Grandma and Grandpa are, at any rate."*

rath·er /'ræðɚ/ *adverb*
1 rather than = instead of: *Let's go out tonight rather than tomorrow night.*
2 would rather = used when you would like to do or have one thing more than another: *I hate having nothing to do; I'd rather be busy.* | *Dave would rather have a dog than a cat.*
3 a little bit: *He was rather tired after his long trip.* SYNONYM **fairly, quite, somewhat**

rat·ing /'reɪtɪŋ/ *noun*
a measurement of how good or popular something is: *The hotel was given a low rating for its food.*

ra·ti·o /'reɪʃiˌoʊ/ Ac *noun* plural **ratios** *formal*
a relationship between two amounts, in which you use two numbers to show how much bigger one amount is than the other: *The ratio of boys to girls in the class is 2:1* (=two boys for each girl).

ra·tion /'ræʃən/ *noun, formal*
the amount of something such as food or gas that you are allowed to have when there is not much available: *During the war, the weekly meat ration was very small.*
—**ration** *verb* to limit the amount of something such as food or gas that people can have because there is not much available: *Rice and sugar are rationed by the government.*

ra·tion·al /'ræʃənəl/ Ac *adjective, formal*
doing things based on facts rather than on your feelings: *It's not easy to make a rational decision about when to have a baby.* ANTONYM **irrational**
—**rationally** *adverb*: *We were too shocked to think rationally.*
—**rationality** /ˌræʃə'næləti/ *noun*

ra·tion·ale /ˌræʃə'næl/ *noun, formal*
the reasons that you use when you make a decision, plan, etc.: *The judge gave no rationale for his decision, and many people were confused by it.*

rat·tle¹ /'rætl/ *verb*
to shake and make a knocking sound: *There was something rattling around in the trunk.*

rattle² *noun*
a baby's toy that makes a noise when you shake it
→ See picture on page A22

rat·tle·snake /'rætlˌsneɪk/ *noun*
an American snake that makes a noise with its tail and that can make you very sick if it bites you

ra·ven /'reɪvən/ *noun*
a large black bird

ra•vine /rə'vin/ *noun*
a deep narrow valley with steep sides: *The river is at the bottom of a deep ravine.*

raw /rɔ/ *adjective*
not cooked: *Wash your hands after touching raw meat.*

ray /reɪ/ *noun*
a narrow beam of light from the sun or a lamp: *A ray of light came through a gap in the curtains.*

ra•zor /'reɪzɚ/ *noun*
a sharp tool for removing hair from your body: *He shaved off his beard with an electric razor.*
➔ See picture on page A11

'razor blade *noun*
a small, flat, sharp piece of metal, used in razors

Rd.
the written abbreviation of **road**, used when you are writing someone's address: *John Smith, 5421 Hill Rd.*

're /ɚ/ *verb*
the short form of "are": *We're late.*

reach[1] /ritʃ/ *verb*
1 to move your hand or arm to touch or pick up something: *I can't reach the cans on the top shelf.* | *David reached for his glass.*

reach

2 to get to a particular amount or level: *The temperature will reach 95° today.*
3 reach a decision/agreement/verdict, etc. = to succeed in deciding something, agreeing on something, etc.: *Have you reached a decision about what to do?*
4 to arrive at a particular place: *We reached home before it was dark.*
5 to be able to talk to someone on the telephone: *I tried calling him at home, but I couldn't reach him.*
➔ See Thesaurus box at **arrive**

reach[2] *noun*
the distance that you can stretch out your arm to touch something: *The ball rolled under the bed, just out of reach.* | *Babies try to grab everything within reach.*

re•act /ri'ækt/ Ac *verb*
to behave in a particular way because of what someone has done or said to you: *How did she react to the news?* | *The audience reacted by shouting and booing.*
WORD FAMILY ➔ **reaction** *noun*

re•ac•tion /ri'ækʃən/ Ac *noun*
something that you feel or do because of something that has happened or something that someone has said: *Crying is a very natural reaction to sad news.*

re•ac•tion•ar•y /ri'ækʃəˌneri/ Ac *adjective, formal*
strongly opposed to social or political change: *Reactionary politicians voted against the new welfare plan.*

read /rid/ *verb* **read** /red/
1 to look at words and understand them: *He's only four and he can already read.* | *She was reading a magazine.*
2 to say written words to other people: *She was reading a story to her kids.* | *He read me the letter.*

read•a•ble /'ridəbəl/ *adjective*
interesting, enjoyable, or easy to read: *The book is very readable, and I enjoyed it a lot.*
—**readability** /ˌridə'bɪləti/ *noun* the fact of being easy or enjoyable to read

read•er /'ridɚ/ *noun*
1 someone who reads a lot, or reads in a particular way: *She's an avid reader* (=someone who likes to read a lot). | *I'm a slow reader.*
2 someone who reads a particular book, newspaper, or magazine: *The magazine's readers are mostly women.*

read•i•ly /'redəli/ *adverb*
quickly and easily: *The information is readily available on the Internet.*

read•i•ness /'redinəs/ *noun, formal*
the state of being ready to deal with something that might happen and willing to do it: *The army was waiting in readiness for an attack.*

read•ing /'ridɪŋ/ *noun*
the activity of looking at words and understanding them: *Paula loves reading and is always buying books.*

read•y /'redi/ *adjective*
1 someone who is ready is prepared or able to do something: *Aren't you ready yet?* |

R

We're just about ready to eat. | *Go get ready for bed.*
2 something that is ready has been prepared and you can use or eat it immediately: *Is supper ready?* | *The computer is now set up and ready to use.* | *Is everything ready for the party?*
3 willing or likely to do something: *She's always ready to help.*

real /rɪəl/ *adjective*
1 not imaginary but actually existing: *Monsters and ghosts are not real.* | *War became a very real possibility.*
2 true and not pretended: *What's the real reason you were late?* | *Everyone called him Johnny but his real name was David.*
3 not false or artificial: *His shoes were real leather.* ANTONYM **fake**
4 *informal* used to emphasize what you are saying: *The kids have made a real mess in here.*

R

WORD FAMILY look at the words:
→ real *adjective*
→ unreal *adjective*
→ reality *noun*
→ really *adverb*

ˈreal esˌtate *noun*
property such as houses or land: *She sells houses and other real estate.*
—**real estate** *adjective* relating to property such as houses or land: *Real estate prices fell last year, but we still can't afford a new house.*

ˈreal eˌstate ˌagent *noun*
someone whose job is to sell houses or land

re•al•is•tic /rɪəˈlɪstɪk/ *adjective*
1 someone who is realistic accepts the facts about a situation and understands what is possible and what is not possible: *You have to be realistic about your chances of winning* (=realize that you may not win).
2 showing things as they are in real life: *His paintings are so realistic, they look like photographs.*
—**realistically** *adverb*

re•al•i•ty /riˈæləti/ *noun* plural **realities**
what is true or what actually happens, and not what you imagine or would like: *It took time to understand the reality of my mother's death.* | *The color looks green, but in reality it is made of tiny blue and yellow dots.*

re•al•i•za•tion /ˌrɪələˈzeɪʃən/ *noun, formal*
the act of understanding or realizing something that you did not know before: *I finally came to the realization that I would have to study harder if I wanted to do well at school.*

re•al•ize /ˈrɪəˌlaɪz/ *verb*
to know or understand something that you did not know before: *I suddenly realized that someone was watching me.* | *I didn't realize how late it was.*

real•ly /ˈrɪəli/ *adverb*
1 very or very much: *Tom's a really nice guy – everyone likes him.* | *His letter really annoyed me.*
2 used for saying what is true, rather than what seems to be true: *He's not really angry – he's just pretending.*
3 really? = used when you are surprised about or interested in what someone has said: *"Meg's getting married." "Really? When?"*
4 not really = used in order to say "no": *"Are you okay?" "Not really, my back hurts."*

real•tor /ˈriltɚ/ *noun*
someone whose job is to sell houses and land SYNONYM **real estate agent**

rear[1] /rɪr/ *noun*
1 the back part of an object, car, building, etc.: *There is a parking lot at the rear of the restaurant.*
2 *also* **rear end** your bottom: *Your rear end's all dirty. What did you sit in?*

rear[2] *adjective*
relating to the back of something: *He got into the rear seat of the taxi.* | *the rear entrance of the hospital* ANTONYM **front**

re•ar•range /ˌriəˈreɪndʒ/ *verb*
1 to change where you put things: *We rearranged the furniture in the living room and put the couch by the window.*
2 to change the time or day that a meeting or event will happen on: *The meeting has been rearranged so that more people can come.*
—**rearrangement** *noun* the act of rearranging things

rear•view mir•ror /ˌrɪrvyu ˈmɪrɚ/ *noun*
the mirror in a car that you use to see what is behind you
➔ See picture on page A28

rea•son /ˈrizən/ *noun*
1 a fact that explains why something happens or why someone does something: *Did he give any reason for quitting?* | *There are many reasons why people develop heart disease.* | *One of the reasons that she moved to Boston is her family.*

THESAURUS: reason

explanation a reason that you give for why something happened or why you did something: *Did she give any explanation for why she went home early?*

excuse a reason that you give for why you did something bad: *I hope she has a good excuse for being late again.*

motive *formal* a reason that makes someone do something, especially something bad: *The police have found no motive for the attack.*

2 a fact that makes it right or fair to do something: *I had no reason to think she was lying.*
3 the ability to think, understand, and make good judgments: *Students are encouraged to use reason to solve the problem.*

rea•son•a•ble /ˈrizənəbəl/ *adjective*
1 fair and sensible: *The idea sounds perfectly reasonable – let's try it.* | *He seemed like a reasonable guy who would be easy to work with.* ANTONYM **unreasonable**
2 a reasonable amount, number, or price is not too much or too big: *The restaurant serves good food at a reasonable price.*

rea•son•a•bly /ˈrizənəbli/ *adverb*
1 fairly but not very: *I did reasonably well on the test, but I didn't get an A.* SYNONYM **fairly, quite**
2 in a way that is fair or sensible: *"I'm sure we can find an answer," Steve said reasonably.*

re•as•sess /ˌriəˈses/ Ac *verb, formal*
to think about something again, in order to decide if you should change your opinion or decision: *If this doesn't work, we will have to reassess the situation.*

re•as•sure /ˌriəˈʃʊr/ *verb*
to make someone feel less worried about something: *She reassured me that everything was going to be okay.*
—**reassurance** *noun* something that reassures someone: *Children often need reassurance when they first start school.*

re•bate /ˈribeɪt/ *noun*
an amount of money that is paid back to you after you have bought something, or because you have paid too much rent or tax: *The company offered a $600 rebate on all its new cars.*

reb•el[1] /ˈrebəl/ *noun*
someone who fights against a leader or government: *Rebels have overthrown the government.*

re•bel[2] /rɪˈbel/ *verb* **rebelled, rebelling**
to disobey or fight against someone who has power over you, such as parents or the government: *Teenagers sometimes rebel against their parents.*
➔ See Thesaurus box at **disobey**

re•bel•lion /rɪˈbelyən/ *noun*
an attempt to remove a government or political leader by using violence: *He led an armed rebellion against the government.*

re•bel•lious /rɪˈbelyəs/ *adjective*
someone who is rebellious disobeys people who have power over him or her, such as parents or the government: *Anne became very rebellious as a teenager.*

re•boot /riˈbut/ *verb*
if you reboot a computer, you start it again after it has stopped working: *The computer crashed, so I had to reboot it.*

re•call /rɪˈkɔl/ *verb, formal*
to remember something from the past: *I recall that he looked very nervous on that day.* | *I don't recall meeting him before. Are you sure we've met?*

re•ceipt /rɪˈsit/ *noun*
a piece of paper that you get from someone to show that you have paid him or her money or bought something: *If you keep the receipt, you can take the shirt back to the store if it doesn't fit him.*

re•ceive /rɪˈsiv/ *verb, formal*
to get or be given something: *Have you received my letter?* | *He received an award from the college.* SYNONYM **get**

re•ceiv•er /rɪˈsivɚ/ *noun*
the part of a telephone that you hold next to your mouth and ear: *The phone rang and he picked up the receiver.*

re•cent /ˈrisənt/ *adjective*
happening or done a short time ago: *He still hasn't completely recovered from his recent illness.* | *The situation has improved in recent months.*
➔ See Thesaurus box at **new**

re•cent•ly /ˈrisəntli/ *adverb*
not long ago: *We recently moved from Ohio.* | *He worked as a teacher until recently.*

R

THESAURUS: recently

just only a few minutes, hours, or days ago: *The show just started.* | *He just got home from school.*

a little while ago only a few minutes, hours, or days ago: *I talked to Mark a little while ago.*

lately in the recent past: *Have you seen Angie lately?*

freshly used to say that something was recently made, picked, etc.: *freshly baked bread* | *freshly cut flowers*

newly used to say that something happened or has been done recently: *a newly married couple* | *newly built homes*

re•cep•tion /rɪˈsepʃən/ *noun*
1 a large formal party to celebrate something or to welcome someone: *They got married in church and had the wedding reception at a hotel.*
2 reception desk/area = the desk or area where visitors who are arriving in a hotel or business go first: *He was waiting for me in the reception area.*
3 the quality of the signal that gives you a picture or sound on a television, radio, or CELL PHONE: *The TV reception was poor, and the picture kept disappearing.*
➔ See Thesaurus box at **party**

re•cep•tion•ist /rɪˈsepʃənɪst/ *noun*
someone whose job is to answer the telephone and welcome people when they arrive at an office or hotel
➔ See picture on page A16

re•cess /ˈrises/ *noun*
a time in the school day when children go outside to play: *Charlie got into a fight with another kid during recess.*

re•ces•sion /rɪˈseʃən/ *noun*
a period of time when businesses and industries are not very successful and many people do not have a job: *When a country is in a recession, more people borrow money.*

re•charge /ˌriˈtʃɑrdʒ/ *verb*
to put a new supply of electricity into a BATTERY: *I need to recharge my cell phone – the battery is dead.*

rec•i•pe /ˈresəpi/ *noun*
a set of instructions that tells you how to cook something: *He gave me a recipe for chocolate cake.*

re•cip•i•ent /rɪˈsɪpiənt/ *noun, formal*
someone who receives something: *Bauer has been the recipient of many awards for his work.*

re•cite /rɪˈsaɪt/ *verb*
to say something such as a poem or story, that you have learned and can remember without reading the words: *She recited a poem at the school concert.*

reck•less /ˈrekləs/ *adjective*
doing something in a dangerous way, without thinking about the bad things that could happen: *The accident was caused by his reckless driving.*
—**recklessness** *noun*

rec•og•ni•tion /ˌrekəgˈnɪʃən/ *noun*
1 the act of knowing someone because you have seen him or her before: *She hoped to avoid recognition by wearing dark glasses.*
2 public praise and thanks for what someone has done: *She was given an award in recognition of her bravery.*

rec•og•nize /ˈrekəgˌnaɪz/ *verb*
to know someone or something because you have seen or heard him, her, or it before: *He'd lost so much weight that I didn't recognize him.* | *I recognized his voice immediately.*
—**recognizable** /ˌrekəgˈnaɪzəbəl/ *adjective*
if someone or something is recognizable, you can recognize him, her, or it

re•com•mence /ˌrikəˈmens/ *verb, formal*
to begin something again after it has stopped: *Work on the building recommenced in June after a short pause.*

rec•om•mend /ˌrekəˈmend/ *verb*
1 to say that someone should do something: *Dentists recommend that you get a new toothbrush every few months.*
2 to say that you think someone or something is good: *A friend recommended this restaurant to me; I hope it's as good as he says.*

rec•om•men•da•tion /ˌrekəmenˈdeɪʃən/ *noun*
1 an official suggestion about what someone should do: *Doctors have made the recommendation that babies should sleep on their backs.*
2 a suggestion that someone should choose a person or thing because he, she, or it is good: *We took the tour on a friend's recommendation – he thought it was great.*

re•con•sid•er /ˌrikənˈsɪdɚ/ *verb, formal*
to think again about something in order to decide if you should change your opinion or decision: *I wish you'd reconsider your decision to leave school.*

re•con•struc•tion /ˌrikənˈstrʌkʃən/ Ac *noun, formal*
work that people do to repair a building or place that has been almost destroyed: *He helped in the reconstruction of the city after the war.*

re•cord¹ /ˈrekɚd/ *noun*
1 information which you write on paper or store on a computer: *Keep a record of how much you spend.* | *His medical records showed he'd had a heart attack in 2002.*
2 the best that anyone has ever achieved, in something such as a race: *She holds the world record for the 1,500 meter run* (=she is faster than anyone else has ever been). | *The movie broke all box office records* (=it was more popular than any other movie has been).
3 a round flat piece of black plastic on which music is stored: *She has a huge collection of old records.*

re•cord² /rɪˈkɔrd/ *verb*
1 to write down information or store it on a computer so that you can look at it later: *She recorded all the events in her diary.*
2 to store music, sound, television programs, etc. on tape or DISKs so that people can listen to them or watch them again: *The band has just recorded a new album.*

re•cord•er /rɪˈkɔrdɚ/ *noun*
another word for a TAPE RECORDER

re•cord•ing /rɪˈkɔrdɪŋ/ *noun*
a piece of music, speech, etc. that has been recorded: *We listened to a recording of Mozart's music.*

ˈrecord ˌplayer *noun*
a piece of equipment for playing music stored on records

re•cov•er /rɪˈkʌvɚ/ Ac *verb*
1 to get better after an illness or injury: *Have you recovered from your cold?*
2 to get back something that had been stolen or had disappeared: *The stolen paintings have been recovered.*

re•cov•er•y /rɪˈkʌvəri/ Ac *noun*
the process of getting better after an illness or injury: *Doctors expect Kelly to make a full recovery from his heart attack.*

re•cre•ate /ˌrikriˈeɪt/ Ac *verb, formal*
to make something like it was in the past or like something in another place: *The zoo tries to recreate the places the animals would naturally live in.*

rec•re•a•tion /ˌrekriˈeɪʃən/ *noun*
an activity that you do for fun: *The parks are a great place for outdoor recreation such as soccer games or barbecues.*
➔ See Thesaurus box at **game**

re•cruit¹ /rɪˈkrut/ *verb*
to find new people to work in a company or join an organization: *We need to recruit new police officers.*
—**recruitment** *noun* the process of finding new people to work in a company or join an organization: *The company is trying to improve its recruitment of new lawyers.*
—**recruiter** *noun* someone whose job is to find new people to work in a company or join an organization: *He was a recruiter for the army.*

recruit² *noun*
someone who has recently joined a company or an organization: *The new recruits are sent on a training course.*

rec•tan•gle /ˈrekˌtæŋgəl/ *noun*
a shape with four straight sides, two of which are longer than the other two
➔ See picture at **shape¹**

R

rec•tan•gu•lar /rek'tæŋgyələ/ *adjective*
having a shape like a RECTANGLE: *a rectangular table*

rec•ti•fy /'rektəˌfaɪ/ *verb* **rectified**, third person singular **rectifies** *formal*
to correct something that is wrong: *All attempts to rectify the problem have failed.*

re•cu•per•ate /rɪ'kupəˌreɪt/ *verb, formal*
to get better after an illness or injury: *Jan is still recuperating from her operation.*
—**recuperation** /rɪˌkupə'reɪʃən/ *noun* the process of recuperating

recycle

re•cy•cle /ˌri'saɪkəl/ *verb*
to put something that is thrown away through a special process so that it can be used again: *The city is recycling glass, plastic bottles, cans, and paper.*
—**recycled** *adjective*: *The fleece jackets are made of recycled plastic bottles.*

re•cy•cling /ri'saɪklɪŋ/ *noun*
the process of treating glass, plastic bottles, newspapers, etc. so that they can be used again: *The city runs a recycling program.*

red /red/ *noun, adjective*
1 the color of blood: *Strawberries are red.* | *a red dress*
2 red hair is an orange-brown color

re•deem /rɪ'dim/ *verb, formal*
to give a store, bank, etc. a piece of paper that is worth an amount of money, so that you do not have to pay as much when you buy something or so that they give you that amount of money: *You can redeem the coupon for $1 off a pack of diapers.*

ˌred-'handed *adjective*
catch someone red-handed *informal* = to catch someone at the moment when he or she is doing something wrong: *She was caught red-handed stealing money.*

red•neck /'rednek/ *noun, informal*
someone who lives in a country area and who does not have much education and does not think or behave in a way that people in cities think is acceptable: *The bar was filled with drunk rednecks.*

re•do /ri'du/ *verb* **redid** /ri'dɪd/ **redone** /ri'dʌn/ third person singular **redoes** /ri'dʌz/
to do something again: *The essay wasn't good enough so I had to redo it.*

ˌred 'tape *noun*
official rules that seem unnecessary and that delay something: *We had to deal with a lot of red tape to get the visa.*

re•duce /rɪ'dus/ *verb*
to make the amount or size of something less than it was before: *Eating healthy food reduces your risk of getting cancer.* | *The jacket was reduced from $75 to $35.*

THESAURUS: reduce

To Reduce Prices, Numbers, or Amounts

lower to make the amount of something less than it was before: *The drug helps to lower your blood pressure.*

decrease to become less or make an amount become less: *You can decrease the size of the letters on the computer using this, see?*

cut to reduce the amount of something: *Stores often cut prices after Christmas.*

slash to make a price, amount, or size much lower, especially suddenly: *A few years ago they slashed class sizes to only 20 students in each class.*

To Reduce Pain

relieve to make pain less bad: *Aspirin is good for relieving headaches.*

ease to make pain less bad and make someone feel more comfortable: *A hot bath can ease the pain from tight muscles.*

lessen to make something less bad: *The drugs lessen the effects of the disease, but do not cure it.*

re•duc•tion /rɪ'dʌkʃən/ *noun, formal*
when the amount or size of something becomes less than it was before: *There's been a reduction in the number of accidents on this part of the freeway.* | *a 25% price reduction*

red•wood /ˈredwʊd/ *noun*
a very tall tree that grows near the coast in Oregon and California: *redwood forests*

reed /rid/ *noun*
a tall plant that looks like grass and grows near water

reef /rif/ *noun*
a line of sharp rocks or a raised area of sand near the surface of the sea

reel /ril/ *noun*
a round object onto which you wind things such as film or string: *30,000 reels of movie film are stored in the library.*

re•e•lect /ˌriəˈlekt/ *verb*
to choose the same person again to do a job, by voting: *Bush was elected as president in 2000 and then reelected in 2004.*
—**reelection** /ˌriəˈlekʃən/ *noun* the act of reelecting someone

re•fer /rɪˈfɚ/ *verb* **referred, referring**
PHRASAL VERB
refer to
1 refer to someone/something = to talk about someone or something: *He referred to Jack in his letter.*
2 refer to something = to look at a book, map, etc. to get information: *Refer to page 14 for instructions.*

ref•er•ee /ˌrefəˈri/ *noun*
someone who makes sure that players in a sports game obey the rules: *The referee called a foul.*

THESAURUS: referee

Referee and **umpire** mean the same thing but are used for different sports.

Use **referee** when you are talking about football, soccer, ice hockey, basketball, boxing, wrestling, or volleyball.

Use **umpire** when you are talking about baseball or tennis.

ref•erence /ˈrefərəns/ *noun*
1 the act of looking at something for information: *I keep the dictionary on my desk for reference.*
2 a letter that someone who knows you writes, which says what your character and abilities are, and which is then sent to someone who might give you a job or let you come to a school: *Your teachers will write references for you when you apply to college.*
3 something you say or write that talks about another person or thing: *Her writing is full of references to his hometown.*

ˈreference ˌbook *noun*
a book such as a dictionary that you look at to find information
➔ See Thesaurus box at **book**[1]

ref•er•en•dum /ˌrefəˈrendəm/ *noun* plural **referenda** /ˌrefəˈrendə/ or **referendums** *formal*
an occasion when people in a state or country vote in order to make a decision about a particular subject: *Quebec held a referendum on independence from Canada, but it failed and Quebec remained part of the country.*

re•fill[1] /ˌriˈfɪl/ *verb*
to fill something again: *A waiter refilled our glasses with water.*

re•fill[2] /ˈrifɪl/ *noun*
another drink to fill your cup or glass again: *You get free refills for all the soft drinks.*

re•fine /rɪˈfaɪn/ Ac *verb*
to make a substance more pure using a special process: *Oil is refined to make gasoline.*
WORD FAMILY ➔ **refinery** *noun*

re•fin•er•y /rɪˈfaɪnəri/ *noun* plural **refineries**
a factory where something such as oil, sugar, or metal is treated to make it more pure: *an oil refinery*

reflect

re•flect /rɪˈflekt/ *verb*
1 if a mirror or water reflects something, you can see that thing in it: *We could see the mountains reflected in the lake.*
2 if a surface reflects light, heat, or sound, it

R

sends back the light, etc. that hits it: *The sunlight reflected off the windows of the building.*
3 to show or be a sign of a particular situation, idea, or feeling: *His home reflected his love of art and was full of paintings.*
4 *formal* to think carefully: *Please take some time to reflect on our offer.*

re•flec•tion /rɪˈflekʃən/ *noun*
1 the thing that you see when you look in a mirror or water: *She was looking at her reflection in the mirror.*
2 *formal* careful thought, or an idea or opinion that you have after careful thought: *A church can be a place for quiet reflection and prayer.*
3 something that shows or is a sign of a particular situation, fact, or feeling: *The rise in crime is a reflection of a violent society.*

R

re•form[1] /rɪˈfɔrm/ *verb*
to improve an organization, law, or system by making changes to it: *There are plans to reform the way young children are educated.*
➔ See Thesaurus box at **change**[1]

reform[2] *noun*
a change that improves an organization, law, or system: *There have been calls for a reform of the health care system.*

re•fresh /rɪˈfreʃ/ *verb, formal*
to make someone feel less tired or hot: *A shower will refresh you.*
—**refreshed** *adjective* less tired or hot: *I felt refreshed after a good night's sleep.*

re•fresh•ing /rɪˈfreʃɪŋ/ *adjective*
1 making you feel less tired or less hot: *We went for a refreshing swim.*
2 different from usual, in a good way: *It was a refreshing change to go out for dinner because usually I cook.*

re•fresh•ments /rɪˈfreʃmənts/ *plural noun, formal*
food and drinks that you get at a meeting, show, sports game, or party: *During the break, they served sandwiches and other refreshments.*

re•frig•er•ate /rɪˈfrɪdʒəˌreɪt/ *verb, formal*
to put food into a refrigerator to keep it cold and fresh: *Milk will go bad if you do not refrigerate it.*
—**refrigeration** /rɪˌfrɪdʒəˈreɪʃən/ *noun* the process of refrigerating food

re•frig•er•a•tor /rɪˈfrɪdʒəˌreɪtə˞/ *noun*
a large piece of kitchen equipment used for keeping food cold and fresh: *I took some cheese out of the refrigerator.* SYNONYM **fridge**
➔ See picture on page A9

ref•uge /ˈrefyudʒ/ *noun, formal*
a place where you are safe from bad weather or danger: *When the storm started, we took refuge in a store* (=we went there so that we would not get wet). SYNONYM **shelter**

ref•u•gee /ˌrefyʊˈdʒi/ *noun*
someone who has to leave his or her own country because it is dangerous for him or her to be there: *During the war, many refugees crossed the border into neighboring countries.*

re•fund[1] /riˈfʌnd/ *verb*
to give someone back the money he or she paid for something, for example because the thing that person bought is not good enough: *If the toaster breaks within six months, we will refund your money.*

re•fund[2] /ˈrifʌnd/ *noun*
if you get a refund, you get back the money that you paid for something, because it is not good enough: *The clock I bought was broken, so I asked for a refund.*

re•fus•al /rɪˈfyuzəl/ *noun, formal*
an act of saying that you will not do something or will not allow something: *His refusal to pay the fine means he may go to jail.* ANTONYM **agreement**

re•fuse[1] /rɪˈfyuz/ *verb*
to say that you will not do something or will not allow something: *I asked her to marry me, but she refused.* | *Steve refused to answer any questions.* ANTONYM **agree**

ref•use[2] /ˈrefyus/ *noun, formal*
things that are thrown away, such as old food and dirty paper: *A truck comes to collect the refuse.* SYNONYM **garbage**
➔ See Thesaurus box at **garbage**

re•gain /rɪˈgeɪn/ *verb, formal*
to get back something that you used to have: *After the accident, she did not regain the use of her legs.*

re•gard¹ /rɪˈgɑrd/ *verb, formal*
to think about someone in a particular way: *I regard you as my friend.*

regard² *noun, formal*
1 respect for someone or something: *Most people have a high regard for* (=a lot of respect for) *doctors and think they do an important job.*
2 with/in regard to something = used when saying what you are talking or writing about: *I am writing to you with regard to your son.* SYNONYM **regarding**

re•gard•ing /rɪˈgɑrdɪŋ/ *preposition, formal*
used when saying what you are talking or writing about: *I wrote you a letter regarding my daughter's school progress.* SYNONYM **about**

re•gard•less /rɪˈgɑrdlɪs/ *adverb, formal*
if something happens regardless of other things, those things do not affect it: *He does what he wants regardless of what I say.*

re•gards /rɪˈgɑrdz/ *plural noun, formal*
good wishes: *Give my regards to your parents.*

reg•gae /ˈregeɪ/ *noun*
a type of popular music from Jamaica: *I love reggae, especially Bob Marley.*

re•gime /reɪˈʒim/ Ac *noun, formal*
a government of a particular type, or that has a particular leader, usually one that is not elected: *Saddam Hussein was the leader of a brutal regime.*
➔ See Thesaurus box at **government**

reg•i•ment /ˈredʒəmənt/ *noun*
a large group of soldiers who are part of an army: *There are 400 soldiers in the regiment.*

re•gion /ˈridʒən/ Ac *noun*
a large area: *The Great Lakes region includes eight U.S. states.*
—**regional** *adjective* relating to regions: *There are regional differences in the way Americans talk.*
➔ See Thesaurus box at **area**

reg•is•ter¹ /ˈredʒəstɚ/ Ac *noun, formal*
1 an official list or record of something: *The museum is on the National Register of Historic Places.*
2 another word for a CASH REGISTER

register² *verb*
1 to put a name or details on an official list: *The car is registered in my name.* | *How many students registered for the American history class?*
2 *formal* if an instrument registers an amount, it shows that amount: *The thermometer registered 74°F.*

ˌregistered ˈnurse *noun*
a nurse who has a college degree and has worked in a hospital as part of his or her training SYNONYM **R.N.**

reg•is•trar /ˈredʒəˌstrɑr/ *noun*
someone in a school or college who takes care of official records: *The registrar keeps a record of students' grades.*

reg•is•tra•tion /ˌredʒəˈstreɪʃən/ Ac *noun*
1 the act of putting names or details on an official list: *Registration for classes will take place on Monday.* | *Do you support the registration of guns?*
2 a piece of paper that shows you have registered something on an official list: *Can I see your car registration, please?*

reg•is•try /ˈredʒəstri/ *noun* plural **registries** *formal*
a place where there are official records: *The Registry of Motor Vehicles keeps the addresses of car owners.*

re•gret¹ /rɪˈgret/ *verb* **regretted, regretting**
1 to wish that you had not done something: *I regret leaving home, because I miss my family.*
2 *formal* to be sorry about a situation: *The letter read, "I regret that I will not be able to attend your wedding."*

regret² *noun*
sadness that you feel about something, because you wish you had not done it: *I have no regrets about selling the car; it was a very good decision.*

reg•u•lar /ˈregyəlɚ/ *adjective*
1 happening or repeated at the same time every second, hour, day, etc.: *His heartbeat is strong and regular.* | *We have a regular meeting every Monday.* ANTONYM **irregular**
2 normal or usual, and not special or different: *I saw Dr. Stein, because my regular doctor was on vacation.* | *He didn't want a*

R

regular job; he wanted to do something exciting.
3 of a standard size: *Do you want a large or regular Coke?*
4 a regular verb or noun changes its forms in the same way as most verbs or nouns: *The verb "walk" is regular, but the verb "be" is not.* ANTONYM **irregular**

reg·u·lar·i·ty /ˌregyəˈlærəti/ *noun, formal*
the fact that something happens or is repeated at the same time every second, hour, day, etc.: *I listened to the regularity of the clock's ticking.*

R

reg·u·lar·ly /ˈregyələ·li/ *adverb*
1 at the same time every second, hour, day, etc.: *Take the medicine regularly three times a day.*
2 often: *When using a computer, save your work regularly.*
→ See Thesaurus box at **often**

reg·u·late /ˈregyəˌleɪt/ Ac *verb, formal*
1 to control activities or people by having rules: *The Medical Board regulates doctors*
2 to make a machine or your body work at a particular speed, temperature, etc.: *People sweat to regulate their body heat, so they don't get too hot.*
—**regulatory** /ˈregyələˌtɔri/ *adjective* for regulating something: *regulatory laws*

WORD FAMILY look at the words:
→ **regulate** *verb*
→ **regulation** *noun*
→ **regulatory** *adjective*

reg·u·la·tion /ˌregyəˈleɪʃən/ Ac *noun, formal*
1 an official rule: *Fire regulations say that you must not block the exits.*
2 the act of controlling something, using rules: *The Internet has little regulation, so people can put almost anything they want on it.*
→ See Thesaurus box at **rule**[1]

re·hears·al /rɪˈhə·səl/ *noun*
a practice of a play, concert, etc. before people come to see it: *Rehearsals for the play will take place after school.*

re·hearse /rɪˈhə·s/ *verb*
to practice for a play, concert, etc. before people come to see it: *They rehearsed the song many times before the performance.*
→ See Thesaurus box at **practice**[2]

reign /reɪn/ *noun, formal*
the time when a king or queen rules a country: *The king led the country in two wars during his reign.*
—**reign** *verb* to be the king or queen of a country: *The king reigned for 52 years.*

re·im·burse /ˌriɪmˈbə·s/ *verb, formal*
to give someone back the money that he or she paid for something, so that a company or someone else pays for it: *I pay the hotel bill, and then my company reimburses me.*

rein·deer /ˈreɪndɪr/ *noun*
a large animal with long horns on its head that lives in cold places: *In the Christmas story, Rudolph is a reindeer with a red nose.*

re·in·force /ˌriɪnˈfɔrs/ Ac *verb, formal*
1 to make an idea, opinion, or feeling that someone already has even stronger: *Paying attention to your son when he is behaving well will help reinforce his good behavior.*
2 to make a part of a building or a piece of clothing stronger: *They reinforced the wall with concrete.* SYNONYM **strengthen**

reins /reɪnz/ *plural noun*
long pieces of leather that you hold to control a horse when you are riding it: *She pulled on the reins, and the horse stopped.*

re·ject /rɪˈdʒekt/ Ac *verb, formal*
to decide that you do not want something or someone: *She rejected my offer of help.* ANTONYM **accept**

THESAURUS: reject

reject to say firmly that you do not want an offer or suggestion: *A lot of publishers rejected the book, but when one finally printed it the book was a hit.*

turn down *informal* to say that you do not want something that you have been offered – use this especially when this is surprising: *They offered her a job, but she turned it down.*

say no *informal* to say you do not want something or will not accept a suggestion: *I asked him if he wanted a drink, but he said no.*

decline *formal* to say politely that you cannot or will not accept an offer: *Mr. and Mrs. Forester declined the invitation.*

re•jec•tion /rɪˈdʒekʃən/ Ac *noun, formal*
the act of saying or showing that you do not want something or someone: *He was afraid of rejection, and didn't ask her for a date in case she said no.* ANTONYM **acceptance**

re•joice /rɪˈdʒɔɪs/ *verb, formal*
to feel or be very happy: *His parents rejoiced when he came home safely.*

re•late /rɪˈleɪt/ *verb, formal*
1 if two things relate to each other, there is a connection between them: *The teacher showed how the math problems relate to what people who work in a bank have to do every day.*
2 to tell someone about something that happened: *He later related the whole story to us.*

re•lat•ed /rɪˈleɪtɪd/ *adjective*
1 if two people are related, they are in the same family: *I'm related to John – he's my uncle.*
2 if two things are related, there is a connection between them: *Lung cancer is related to smoking.* | *Politics and economics are closely related.* SYNONYM **connected**

WORD FAMILY look at the words:

➔ **related** *adjective*
➔ **unrelated** *adjective*
➔ **relate** *verb*
➔ **relation** *noun*
➔ **relationship** *noun*

re•la•tion /rɪˈleɪʃən/ *noun*
1 relations = the way people, countries, etc. behave toward each other: *After my parents' divorce, relations between them were not good.*
2 a connection between two or more things: *There is a direct relation between the gene and breast cancer.* SYNONYM **relationship**
3 a member of your family: *All my aunts, uncles, and other relations came to the wedding.* SYNONYM **relative**
➔ See Thesaurus box at **family**

re•la•tion•ship /rɪˈleɪʃən,ʃɪp/ *noun*
1 the way in which two people or groups feel and behave toward each other: *My mother and I have a good relationship and enjoy spending time together.* | *The relationship between the two countries is friendly.*
2 a situation in which two people are together because they love each other: *It's been a while since I was in a relationship with anyone.*
3 the way in which two things are connected: *The relationship between health and exercise is clear.*

rel•a•tive¹ /ˈrelətɪv/ *noun*
a member of your family: *Her parents, sister and other close relatives visited her in the hospital.* SYNONYM **relation**
➔ See Thesaurus box at **family**

relative² *adjective, formal*
having a particular quality when compared with something else: *After a week of sleeping on the floor, I enjoyed the relative comfort of the sofa.*

ˌrelative ˈclause *noun*
a part of a sentence that has a verb in it and begins with a word such as "who," "which," or "that": *In the sentence, "The dress that I bought is too small," "that I bought" is a relative clause.*

rel•a•tive•ly /ˈrelətɪvli/ *adverb, formal*
when compared with something else: *Compared with gold, silver is relatively cheap.*

ˌrelative ˈpronoun *noun*
a word such as "who," "which," or "that," which connects a RELATIVE CLAUSE to the rest of the sentence: *In the sentence, "The dress that I bought is too small," "that" is the relative pronoun.*

re•lax /rɪˈlæks/ Ac *verb*
1 to become less worried or angry or busy, and more calm: *Don't worry about it – try to relax.*
2 to become less tight or stiff: *He felt his muscles relax as he lay in the bathtub.*

WORD FAMILY look at the words:

➔ **relax** *verb*
➔ **relaxed** *adjective*
➔ **relaxing** *adjective*
➔ **relaxation** *noun*

re•lax•a•tion /ˌrilækˈseɪʃən/ Ac *noun*
the state of being less worried, less busy, or less stiff in your body: *Yoga is good for relaxation.*

re•laxed /rɪˈlækst/ Ac *adjective*
calm and not worried: *Gail was lying in the sun, looking happy and relaxed.* ANTONYM **tense**

re•lax•ing /rɪ'læksɪŋ/ Ac *adjective*
making you feel calm, or less stiff in your body: *A hot bath is very relaxing.*

re•lay[1] /'rileɪ/ *verb* **relayed**, third person singular **relays** *formal*
to send information from one person or place to another: *Could you relay a message to Mary for me?* SYNONYM **pass**

relay[2] *noun*
a race in which each member of a team runs or swims part of the distance: *Smith ran the first 400 meters of the relay.*

re•lease[1] /rɪ'lis/ Ac *verb*
1 to let someone go free: *Four prisoners have been released. | I released the horse, and it ran away.*
2 to let people know about something that has happened: *The police have not released details of the crime.*
3 to make a movie, CD, etc. available for people to buy or see: *The band has just released a new album and it is available in stores.*

release[2] *noun, formal*
1 the act of letting someone go free: *After his release, he talked about the men who kidnapped him.*
2 a new movie, book, or music that is available for people to see or buy: *The band's new release is on sale now.*

re•lent•less /rɪ'lentləs/ *adjective, formal*
if something bad is relentless, it continues without stopping or getting better: *The pressure at work has been relentless.*

rel•e•vant /'reləvənt/ Ac *adjective*
directly relating to what you are discussing or doing: *The information she had was relevant to our investigation of the crime.* ANTONYM **irrelevant**
—**relevance** *noun* the fact that something is relevant

WORD FAMILY look at the words:

→ **relevant** *adjective*
→ **irrelevant** *adjective*
→ **relevance** *noun*
→ **irrelevance** *noun*

re•li•a•ble /rɪ'laɪəbəl/ Ac *adjective*
1 reliable people do what they say they will do: *He's a good worker, and very reliable.* SYNONYM **dependable**; ANTONYM **unreliable**
2 something that is reliable does what it should do: *I need a reliable car that won't break down.* ANTONYM **unreliable**
—**reliably** *adverb*: *This washing machine has worked reliably for 10 years.*
—**reliability** /rɪˌlaɪə'bɪləti/ *noun* the state of being reliable

re•li•ant /rɪ'laɪənt/ Ac *adjective, formal*
be reliant on someone = if you are reliant on someone, you cannot do something without him or her: *She does not have a job, so she's reliant on her parents for money.* SYNONYM **dependent**
—**reliance** *noun* the state of being reliant on someone

rel•ic /'relɪk/ *noun, formal*
something old from the past that still exists: *They discovered pots, bones, and other relics in the ground.*

re•lief /rɪ'lif/ *noun*
1 happiness because something bad did not happen or has finished: *I hate tests, and it was a relief when they were over.*
2 *formal* the act of making pain go away: *Drugs are used for pain relief.*
3 *formal* help that organizations give to people who are suffering because of a war, flood, EARTHQUAKE, etc.: *Relief workers gave out food to people affected by the tornado.*

re•lieve /rɪ'liv/ *verb*
to make pain or trouble less bad: *The medicine relieved his headache. | We sang songs to relieve the boredom* (=stop being bored).
→ See Thesaurus box at **reduce**

re•lieved /rɪ'livd/ *adjective*
happy because something bad did not happen or is finished: *We were relieved when Gary called to tell us he was safe.*

re•li•gion /rɪ'lɪdʒən/ *noun*
1 belief in one or more gods: *Religion is very important to me, and I pray every day.*

THESAURUS: religion

faith belief in God, or a particular religion: *Her faith helped her get through a really difficult time. | the Jewish faith*
belief an idea that you think is true or right: *He has strong religious beliefs.*

2 a particular set of beliefs in one or more

gods: *Hinduism and Buddhism are important religions in India.*

re•li•gious /rɪˈlɪdʒəs/ *adjective*
1 relating to religion: *We have different religious beliefs, because I am a Muslim and he is a Christian.*
2 a religious person believes in a god or gods and obeys the rules of his or her religion: *My mother is very religious, and goes to church every week.* SYNONYM **holy**

re•li•gious•ly /rɪˈlɪdʒəsli/ *adjective*
if you do something religiously, you always do it: *I run five miles religiously every day.*

rel•ish /ˈrelɪʃ/ *verb, formal*
to enjoy something or like it: *She relished the chance to go to Mexico.*

re•lo•cate /riˈloʊˌkeɪt/ Ac *verb, formal*
to move to a new place: *I lived in New York until our company relocated to California.*
—**relocation** /ˌriloʊˈkeɪʃən/ *noun* the act of relocating

re•luc•tant /rɪˈlʌktənt/ Ac *adjective, formal*
if you are reluctant to do something, you do not want to do it: *I was reluctant to let the man in because I didn't know him.* ANTONYM **eager**
—**reluctance** *noun* the state of being reluctant
—**reluctantly** *She reluctantly gave all her money to Mark.*

re•ly /rɪˈlaɪ/ Ac *verb* **relied**, third person singular **relies**
PHRASAL VERB
rely on someone
to know that someone will help you or do something: *Ann is a good friend – I can rely on her.*

WORD FAMILY look at the words:
- → **rely** *verb*
- → **reliable** *adjective*
- → **unreliable** *adjective*
- → **reliability** *noun*

re•main /rɪˈmeɪn/ *verb, formal*
1 to stay in the same place: *The others left, while I remained at home.*
2 to stay in the same state or condition: *They met in high school, and remained friends for years.*

re•main•der /rɪˈmeɪndɚ/ *noun, formal*
the part of something that is still there after all the other parts are gone: *I'll go with you; the remainder of the group can stay here.* SYNONYM **rest**

re•main•ing /rɪˈmeɪnɪŋ/ *adjective, formal*
the remaining things or people are the ones that are still there when all the others are gone: *I took an apple and put the remaining fruit in the bowl.*

re•mains /rɪˈmeɪnz/ *plural noun, formal*
1 the parts of something that are left after the rest is gone: *We visited the remains of the old city.*
2 a person's body after he or she has died: *His remains are buried in the graveyard.*

R

re•mark[1] /rɪˈmɑrk/ *noun*
something that you say: *He made a rude remark about the woman.* SYNONYM **comment**

remark[2] *verb*
to say something: *One woman remarked that he was handsome.*

re•mark•a•ble /rɪˈmɑrkəbəl/ *adjective, formal*
unusual or surprising, especially in a good way: *It's remarkable that your old car is still going.*
—**remarkably** *adverb*: *Steven is only eight, but he plays chess remarkably well.*

re•marry /ˌriˈmæri/ *verb* **remarried**, third person singular **remarries**
to get married again: *After her husband's death, Carol never remarried.*
—**remarriage** *noun* the act of getting married again

re•me•di•al /rɪˈmidiəl/ *adjective, formal*
for students who are having problems learning something and need to improve: *Remedial math is for children who find number work difficult.*

rem•e•dy /ˈremədi/ *noun* plural **remedies** *formal*
1 a successful way of dealing with a problem: *The best remedy for a bad mood is a good night's sleep.* SYNONYM **cure**
2 a medicine or drink that stops pain or makes an illness better: *Honey and lemon is a remedy for colds.* SYNONYM **cure**

re•mem•ber /rɪˈmembɚ/ *verb*
to think of something and keep it in your mind: *Did you remember to feed the cat?* | *He suddenly remembered that he had left the stove on when he left the house.* ANTONYM **forget**

re•mem•brance /rɪˈmembrəns/ *noun, formal*
the act of remembering and showing respect to someone who has died: *She planted a tree in remembrance of her husband.*

re•mind /rɪˈmaɪnd/ *verb*
to make someone remember something that he or she must do: *Remind me to mail that letter tomorrow.*
PHRASAL VERB
remind someone of someone or something
if someone or something reminds you of another person or thing, he, she, or it makes you think of that person or thing by being very similar to him, her, or it: *Julia reminds me of my sister; they have the same smile.*

re•mind•er /rɪˈmaɪndɚ/ *noun*
something that makes you remember something else: *The damaged buildings were a reminder of the recent war.*

rem•nant /ˈremnənt/ *noun, formal*
a small part of something that is still there after the rest has gone: *These woods are only a remnant of what was once a very big forest.*

re•morse /rɪˈmɔrs/ *noun*
a feeling that you are sorry for doing something very bad: *The thief showed no remorse for his crime.*

re•mote /rɪˈmoʊt/ *adjective*
1 far away from other places: *They lived on a remote farm, many miles away from the nearest town.*
2 very small: *The doctors have a remote chance of saving the injured man's life.*
3 far away in time: *In the remote past, dinosaurs lived on Earth.*

re,mote con'trol *also* **remote** *noun*
a thing that you use to control a television, DVD player, etc. from a distance, for example to turn it on and off: *Where's the remote control for the TV?*
➔ See picture on page A8

re•mote•ly /rɪˈmoʊtli/ *adverb, formal*
used for emphasizing that someone or something does not have any of the qualities you are talking about: *I'm not even remotely interested in computer games; I never play them.*

re•mov•al /rɪˈmuvəl/ Ac *noun*
the act of taking something away: *His mouth hurt from the removal of four teeth.*

re•move /rɪˈmuv/ Ac *verb*
1 to take something away from a place: *Please do not remove these books from the library.*
2 *formal* to take off a piece of clothing: *He removed his hat.*
—**removable** *adjective* easy to take away: *The seat has a removable cover.*

re•new /rɪˈnu/ *verb*
1 to do the things you need to do so that an official document or agreement continues: *I need to renew my passport; it's expired.*
2 *formal* to begin to do something again: *The police will renew their search for the missing boy in the morning.* SYNONYM **resume**

re•new•a•ble /rɪˈnuəbəl/ *adjective*
1 if an official document or agreement is renewable, you can make it continue: *The visa is renewable one time.*
2 renewable things are made by natural processes, and people can never use them until they are completely gone: *Wind power is a renewable source of energy.*

ren•o•vate /ˈrenəˌveɪt/ *verb, formal*
to fix a building so that it looks new: *The company renovated the hotel.*
—**renovation** /ˌrenəˈveɪʃən/ *noun* the process of fixing a building so that it looks new: *The museum is closed for renovation.*
➔ See Thesaurus box at **repair**[2]

re•nowned /rɪˈnaʊnd/ *adjective, formal*
famous for something: *The restaurant is renowned for its excellent food.*

rent[1] /rent/ *verb*
1 to pay money to live in a place: *We rent the apartment from my uncle.*
2 to pay money to use something for a short time: *They're going to rent a car.*
3 *also* **rent out** if you rent something that you own, you allow someone else to use it, and they pay you money: *They rent the*

house out to tourists in the summer.
—**renter** *noun* someone who pays money to live in a place: *I have two renters living in the apartment.*

rent² *noun*
1 money that you pay to use a house, car, etc. that belongs to someone else: *I pay the rent for the house at the beginning of each month.*
2 for rent = available to be rented: *Do you have any apartments for rent?*
➔ See Thesaurus box at **cost¹**

rent•al /'rentl/ *noun*
an arrangement in which you pay to use something that belongs to someone else: *a car rental company* | *Ski rental is $14.*

re•paid /ri'peɪd/ *verb*
the past tense and past participle of REPAY

re•pair¹ /rɪ'per/ *noun*
something that you do to fix something that is damaged or not working: *He's doing repairs on my car.* | *The roof is badly in need of repair* (=needs to be repaired).

repair² *verb*
to fix something that is damaged or not working: *How much will it cost to repair the TV?* | *We need to get the car repaired* (=arrange for someone to fix it).

THESAURUS: repair

fix to repair something that is broken or not working correctly: *Someone's coming to fix the washing machine.*

mend to repair a hole in a piece of clothing: *She was mending a pair of jeans.*

renovate *formal* to repair a building, room, or furniture so that it looks new again: *We want to renovate the kitchen.*

restore *formal* to repair something so it is as good as when it was new: *He restores old cars.*

re•pair•man /rɪ'permæn/ *noun*
someone whose job it is to fix something that is damaged or not working: *a TV repairman*

re•pay /rɪ'peɪ/ *verb* **repaid** /ri'peɪd/ third person singular **repays**
1 to give money back to someone you have borrowed it from: *I'll repay the money you lent me next week.*
2 to do something for someone because he or she has helped you: *I'd like to buy him something to repay him for his kindness.*
—**repayment** *noun* the act of giving back money that you have borrowed: *The repayment of the loan took several years.*

re•peal /rɪ'pil/ *verb, formal*
to officially end a law: *They voted to repeal the law banning this type of gun.*
—**repeal** *noun* the act of officially ending a law: *The president supports the repeal of the law.*

re•peat¹ /rɪ'pit/ *verb*
to say or do something again: *Could you repeat what you just said?* | *Repeat the exercises twice a day.*

WORD FAMILY look at the words:

➔ **repeat** *verb*
➔ **repeat** *noun*
➔ **repetition** *noun*
➔ **repeated** *adjective*
➔ **repeatedly** *adverb*
➔ **repetitive** *adjective*

repeat² *noun*
something that happens in exactly the same way as it happened before: *This year's game was a repeat of last year's: Houston Rockets won 82 to 80 again.*

re•peat•ed /rɪ'pitɪd/ *adjective, formal*
done several times: *He made repeated attempts to lose weight, but he only lost a pound or two each time.*
—**repeatedly** *adverb*: *I asked him repeatedly to leave, but he wouldn't go.*

rep•e•ti•tion /ˌrepə'tɪʃən/ *noun, formal*
the act of saying or doing the same thing again, or doing it many times: *We don't want a repetition of past mistakes.*

re•pet•i•tive /rɪ'petətɪv/ *also* **rep•e•ti•tious** /ˌrepə'tɪʃəs/ *adjective, formal*
something that is repetitive is boring because the same thing is done or said many times: *Many factory jobs are very repetitive and boring.*

re•place /rɪ'pleɪs/ *verb*
to get a new person or thing to use instead of the one you use now: *When the TV stopped working, we had to replace it.* | *He left the company in June, and they still*

R

haven't replaced him with anyone (=employed someone else to do his job).
—**replaceable** *adjective* able to be replaced

re•place•ment /rɪˈpleɪsmənt/ *noun*
a new person or thing that you can see instead of the one you used before: *Who will be the boss's replacement when she retires?*

re•play /ˈripleɪ/ *noun*
an action in a sports game on television that is shown again right after it happens: *You can see on the replay that the player dropped the ball.*
—**replay** /riˈpleɪ/ *verb* to show a replay on television

R

rep•li•ca /ˈreplɪkə/ *noun*
an exact copy of something: *The model was an exact replica of the palace.*

re•ply¹ /rɪˈplaɪ/ *verb* **replied** /rɪˈplaɪd/ third person singular **replies** /rɪˈplaɪz/
to answer: *"Yes, that's true," she replied.* | *He didn't reply to my letter.* | *I asked him about the movie, and he replied that he didn't like it.*

reply² *noun* plural **replies**
something that you say or write as an answer: *I am still waiting for a reply to my letter.* | *I asked her if she was okay, but she made no reply* (=did not answer).
➔ See Thesaurus box at **answer¹**

re•port¹ /rɪˈpɔrt/ *noun*
something that gives facts about a situation or event: *Each child wrote a report on the class's visit to the museum.* | *There is a report in the newspaper about the accident.*

report² *verb*
1 to tell people about something that has happened: *The newspaper reported that several people had been killed in the fire.*
2 to tell the police that a crime or accident has happened: *Did you report the theft to the police?*

PHRASAL VERB
report to someone
to work for someone: *All the salesmen report to Greg Shaw, who is the manager of the sales department.*

reˈport card *noun*
a piece of paper with a student's grades on it, and statements from teachers about how hard he or she has worked: *He had three A's, two B's, and a C on his report card.*

reˌported ˈspeech *noun*
in grammar, the style of speech or writing that is used for telling people what someone says, without repeating the actual words: *The sentence "She said she didn't feel well" is an example of reported speech.*

re•port•er /rɪˈpɔrtɚ/ *noun*
someone who writes news stories: *a newspaper reporter*
➔ See picture on page A16

rep•re•sent /ˌreprɪˈzent/ *verb*
1 if someone represents you, he or she officially speaks for you or does a job for you because you cannot do it yourself: *Each class elects two students to represent them on the School Council.*
2 to show or mean something: *The red lines on the map represent the railroad.*
—**representation** /ˌreprɪzenˈteɪʃən/ *noun* the state of having someone to represent you: *Each state has equal representation in the Senate.*

WORD FAMILY look at the words:
➔ **represent** *verb*
➔ **representation** *noun*
➔ **representative** *noun*

rep•re•sent•a•tive /ˌreprɪˈzentətɪv/ *noun*
1 someone who people have chosen to do things for them: *Two representatives from the church are going to the meeting.*
2 Representative = a member of the House of Representatives in the U.S. Congress: *She is one of California's Representatives.*

re•prieve /rɪˈpriv/ *noun*
an official order to change or delay a decision to kill a prisoner as an official punishment: *The governor granted the prisoner a reprieve at the last minute and saved his life.*

rep•ri•mand /ˈreprəˌmænd/ *verb, formal*
to tell someone officially that he or she has done something wrong: *The teacher reprimanded him for being late.*
—**reprimand** *noun* the act of reprimanding someone

re•pris•al /rɪˈpraɪzəl/ *noun, formal*
something that you do to punish an enemy: *He didn't tell the police because he was afraid of reprisals* (=he was afraid the criminals would punish him if he told the police).

re•proach /rɪˈproʊtʃ/ *verb, formal*
to say something that makes someone feel sorry for what he or she has done: *Ben's daughter reproached him for not telling her the truth.*

re•pro•duce /ˌriprəˈdus/ *verb, formal*
1 if a person, animal, or plant reproduces, it has babies: *Most fish reproduce by laying eggs.*
2 to make a copy of something such as a work of art: *Picasso's paintings are reproduced in this book.*

re•pro•duc•tion /ˌriprəˈdʌkʃən/ *noun*
1 the act of producing babies, young animals or plants: *We learned about human reproduction in biology class.*
2 a copy of something such as a work of art: *The picture is a reproduction of a painting by Van Gogh.*

rep•tile /ˈreptaɪl/ *noun*
an animal such as a snake or a LIZARD: *The body temperature of a reptile changes when the temperature around it changes.*

re•pub•lic /rɪˈpʌblɪk/ *noun*
a country that elects its government and does not have a king or queen: *France is a republic.*
→ See Thesaurus box at **government**

Re•pub•li•can /rɪˈpʌblɪkən/ *noun*
a member of the Republican Party: *Most Republicans in the House voted for a change in the law.*
—**Republican** *adjective* relating to the Republican Party: *a Republican politician*

Reˈpublican ˌParty *noun*
one of the two main political parties of the U.S.: *The Republican Party supports laws that help businesses.*

rep•u•ta•ble /ˈrepyətəbəl/ *adjective, formal*
respected for being honest and doing good work: *If you want a used car, go to a reputable dealer.*

rep•u•ta•tion /ˌrepyəˈteɪʃən/ *noun*
the opinion that people have of someone or something: *This school has a very good reputation and many parents want to send their children here.*

re•quest¹ /rɪˈkwest/ *noun, formal*
the act of asking for something politely or formally: *He has made a request for a pay raise.*

request² *verb, formal*
to ask for something politely or formally: *To request further information, please call this phone number.*
→ See Thesaurus box at **ask**

re•quire /rɪˈkwaɪə/ Ac *verb*
1 to need something: *Pets require a lot of care.*
2 *formal* to say officially that someone must do something: *The law requires all drivers to wear seat belts.*

re•quire•ment /rɪˈkwaɪəmənt/ Ac *noun, formal*
something that you need: *The new computer system will meet all our requirements* (=do everything we need it to). | *Three years of math is a requirement for graduation* (=you must have studied it for three years to graduate).

re•run /ˈrirʌn/ *noun*
a television program that is being shown again: *We watched a rerun of "Friends."*
—**rerun** /riˈrʌn/ *verb* to show a television program again

re•sched•ule /riˈskedʒəl/ Ac *verb*
to arrange for something to happen at a different time: *We've rescheduled Tuesday's meeting; it will now take place on Friday.*

rescue

res•cue¹ /ˈreskyu/ *verb*
to save someone when they are in danger: *He rescued two people from the burning car.*
—**rescuer** *noun* someone who rescues someone else

rescue² *noun*
an act of saving someone from danger: *The newspaper reported on the rescue of a small boy from the river.* | *Firefighters came to the rescue of* (=saved) *the people in the burning building.*

re•search¹ /'risɚtʃ/ Ac *noun*
a study of a subject in order to find out new information: *Scientists are doing research into the causes of the disease.*

re•search² /rɪ'sɚtʃ/ Ac *verb*
to study a subject so you can find out new facts about it: *Scientists are researching ways of reducing pollution.*
—**researcher** *noun* someone who researches a subject: *Medical researchers have discovered a new treatment for the illness.*

re•sem•blance /rɪ'zembləns/ *noun*
if there is a resemblance between two things or people, they look similar to each other: *There's a resemblance between Mike and his cousin* (=they look like each other).

re•sem•ble /rɪ'zembəl/ *verb, formal*
to look like or be similar to someone or something: *She resembles her mother in many ways; they are both tall with dark hair and green eyes.*

re•sent /rɪ'zent/ *verb, formal*
to feel angry and upset about something unfair that someone has done to you: *I resent having to work such long hours.*
—**resentful** *adjective* angry and upset about something unfair that someone has done to you: *She was resentful that her sister got more attention than she did.*

re•sent•ment /rɪ'zentmənt/ *noun, formal*
a feeling of anger about something that you think is unfair: *My grandpa always liked Sam better than me, and so I felt a lot of resentment.*

res•er•va•tion /ˌrezɚ'veɪʃən/ *noun*
1 an arrangement that you make for something to be kept for you to use, for example a seat on an airplane or a table in a restaurant: *Have you made reservations at the restaurant yet?*
2 *formal* a feeling of doubt about something: *She has reservations about Tim's ability to do the job; she says he doesn't know the subject well enough.*
3 an area of land that is kept separate for Native Americans to live on: *a Navajo reservation*

re•serve¹ /rɪ'zɚv/ *verb*
1 to arrange for something to be kept for you to use, for example a seat on an airplane or a room in a hotel: *Tom reserved a table for two people at 8:00 at the restaurant.*
2 to keep something for a particular purpose: *This parking area has been reserved for buses, so cars cannot park here.*

reserve² *noun*
1 a supply of something that you can use if you need it: *We always keep some money in reserve for emergencies.* | *the oil reserves in Alaska*
2 an area of land where wild animals, plants, etc. are protected: *The monkeys live on a wildlife reserve.*

re•served /rɪ'zɚvd/ *adjective*
not liking to show or talk about your thoughts and feelings: *He is a quiet, reserved man, who never shows much emotion.*
➔ See Thesaurus box at **shy**

res•er•voir /'rezɚˌvwɑr/ *noun*
a lake that people have made for storing water: *The water is stored in the reservoir before it goes to people's houses.*

res•i•dence /'rezədəns/ Ac *noun, formal*
1 a house where someone lives: *The White House is the president's official residence.*
2 the state of living in a place: *He took up residence in* (=began living in) *Atlanta later that year.*
➔ See Thesaurus box at **home¹**

res•i•dent /'rezədənt/ Ac *noun*
someone who lives in a particular place: *Local residents have complained about the noise from the factory.*

res•i•den•tial /ˌrezə'denʃəl/ Ac *adjective, formal*
a residential area has houses in it, not offices or businesses: *We live in a quiet, residential neighborhood.*

res•i•due /ˈrezəˌdu/ *noun*
a substance that is still there after the rest of it has gone: *Soap can leave a residue on your skin.*

re•sign /rɪˈzaɪn/ *verb*
to say officially that you are going to leave your job: *I've decided to resign from my job, and look for a new one.*
➔ See Thesaurus box at **quit**

res•ig•na•tion /ˌrezɪgˈneɪʃən/ *noun*
the act of officially saying that you are going to leave your job: *Matt handed in his resignation* (=gave a letter to his manager saying that he wanted to leave his job).

re•signed /rɪˈzaɪnd/ *adjective*
be resigned to something/be resigned to doing something = to accept calmly a situation that is bad, but cannot be changed: *He's resigned to spending Christmas alone, because his wife has left him.*

re•sist /rɪˈzɪst/ *verb*
1 to not want to accept something and try to stop it: *He resists anything that is new in his life, because he's afraid of change.*
2 to stop yourself doing something you would like to do, but should not: *I couldn't resist eating the chocolate – it looked so good!*
3 to not be changed or harmed by something: *Vitamin C helps you resist colds.*

re•sist•ance /rɪˈzɪstəns/ *noun*
the act of not wanting to accept something and trying to stop it: *There was resistance to the idea of making the school day longer; most of the students did not like the idea.*

res•o•lu•tion /ˌrezəˈluʃən/ Ac *noun, formal*
1 a promise that you make to yourself to do something: *I made a New Year's resolution to stop smoking.*
2 a solution to a problem or difficulty: *There is no easy resolution to this argument.*

re•solve /rɪˈzɑlv/ Ac *verb, formal*
1 to do something that ends a problem or disagreement: *Another accident could happen unless we resolve these safety problems.*
2 to decide to do something: *He resolved to work harder.*
➔ See Thesaurus box at **decide**

re•sort /rɪˈzɔrt/ *noun*
1 a place where a lot of people go for a vacation: *Acapulco is one of Mexico's most popular resorts.*
2 as a last resort = if everything else fails: *The police only use guns as a last resort.*

re•source /ˈrisɔrs/ Ac *noun*
something that is available for people to use: *The Internet is a useful resource for finding information.* | *The country is rich in natural resources* (=oil, coal, gold, etc.).

re•sour•ces /ˈriˌsɔrsɪz/ Ac *plural noun*
all the money, people, skills, etc. that you have available to use: *Some students do not have the financial resources* (=money) *to go to college.*

R

re•spect[1] /rɪˈspekt/ *noun*
1 if you have respect for someone, you admire him or her and have a very good opinion of him or her: *He is a very good teacher and I have great respect for him.*
2 a polite way of behaving toward other people: *We expect everyone at this school to treat each other with respect.* | *Children should show respect for older people* (=treat them in a polite way).

respect[2] *verb*
1 to admire someone and have a good opinion of him or her: *The students respect their teacher because he knows a lot about his subject.* | *She respected him for his honesty.*
2 if you respect other people's feelings, you show that you understand and care about them: *Parents should respect a teenager's need for privacy.*
3 if you respect a law or rule, you obey it: *It is important to respect local customs and laws when you are traveling in other countries.*
➔ See Thesaurus box at **admire**

re•spect•a•ble /rɪˈspektəbəl/ *adjective*
1 someone who is respectable is good and honest: *They are a respectable family and they work hard.*
2 clean and neatly dressed: *He wore a suit and tie so that he would look respectable.*
—**respectably** *adverb*: *Jane always dressed respectably when she went to church.*
—**respectability** /rɪˌspektəˈbɪləti/ *noun* the quality of being considered respectable

re•spect•ful /rɪ'spektfəl/ *adjective, formal*
showing respect for someone or something: *The people in the church listened in respectful silence to the minister.*
—**respectfully** *adverb*: *Treat other people respectfully.*

re•spec•tive /rɪ'spektɪv/ *adjective, formal*
belonging to each of the people or things that you have just mentioned: *I asked my sisters, Amy and Colleen, and their respective husbands to the wedding.*
—**respectively** *adverb, formal*: *The shirt and pants cost $30 and $25 respectively.*

R

res•pira•to•ry /'resprə,tɔri/ *adjective, formal*
relating to breathing and your lungs: *Smoking can cause respiratory illness.*

re•spond /rɪ'spand/ Ac *verb*
1 *formal* to say or write something after someone has said or written something to you: *I responded that I did not believe her.*
SYNONYM **reply**
2 to do something because of something that has happened: *Police usually respond to a 911 call in less than five minutes.*
SYNONYM **react**

WORD FAMILY look at the words:
→ **respond** *verb*
→ **response** *noun*
→ **responsive** *adjective*

→ See Thesaurus box at **answer**[1]

re•sponse /rɪ'spans/ Ac *noun, formal*
1 something you say or write as a reply to something: *"No," he said in response to my question* (=as an answer to my question).
2 something you do as a reaction to something: *His quick response to the accident saved the child's life.*

re•spon•si•bil•i•ty /rɪ,spansə'bɪləti/ *noun* plural **responsibilities**
1 something that you do because it is your duty or your job: *It is the parents' responsibility to protect their children.*
2 blame for something bad that has happened: *Mike took responsibility for the mistakes in the report; he said that nobody else should be blamed.*

re•spon•si•ble /rɪ'spansəbəl/ *adjective*
1 if you are responsible for something bad, you caused it to happen: *The person who is responsible for breaking the window will be punished.*
2 if you are responsible for doing something, it is your duty to do it: *Who is responsible for feeding the dog?*
3 a responsible person behaves in a sensible way and can be trusted: *The children are being cared for by responsible adults.*
—**responsibly** *adverb*: *You can trust Lori to act responsibly.*

WORD FAMILY look at the words:
→ **responsible** *adjective*
→ **responsibly** *adverb*
→ **responsibility** *noun*

re•spon•sive /rɪ'spansɪv/ Ac *adjective, formal*
quick to react in a good or helpful way: *A good company must be responsive to the needs of its customers and answer any questions they have as quickly as possible.*

rest[1] /rest/ *noun*
1 the rest = the part of a thing or group that still remains: *Two of the boys moved slowly forward and the rest followed.* | *What would you like to do for the rest of the day?*
2 a period of time when you can relax or sleep: *You've got a busy day tomorrow, so you'd better get some rest.*

rest[2] *verb*
1 to spend time relaxing or sleeping: *Let your mom rest when she gets home from work – she'll be tired.*
2 *formal* to put an object or part of your body on or against something that will support it: *He rested his right hand on his knee.*

res•tau•rant /'restə,rant/ *noun*
a place where you can buy and eat a meal: *Have you eaten at this restaurant before?*

rest•ful /'restfəl/ *adjective*
peaceful and quiet: *He was feeling better after a restful night's sleep.*

rest•less /'restləs/ *adjective*
unable to relax and keep still because you are nervous or bored: *The young children were beginning to get restless after sitting for a half and hour.*

re•store /rɪˈstɔr/ Ac *verb, formal*
1 to make something exist again: *My friends' love and support restored my confidence* (=made me feel confident again).
2 to repair something so that it is as good as when it was new: *They're restoring an old house in town, and it looks so much better.*
—**restoration** /ˌrestəˈreɪʃən/ *noun, formal* the act of restoring something
➔ See Thesaurus box at **repair**[2]

re•strain /rɪˈstreɪn/ Ac *verb*
to prevent someone or something from moving or from doing something: *He put his hand on her shoulder to restrain her from getting up.*

re•strained /rɪˈstreɪnd/ Ac *adjective, formal*
calm and controlled, and not showing any strong emotion: *He answered her in a restrained voice, but I knew he was mad.*

re•straint /rɪˈstreɪnt/ Ac *noun, formal*
calm and controlled behavior in a difficult situation: *She showed a lot of restraint by not yelling at him even though she was very angry.*

re•strict /rɪˈstrɪkt/ Ac *verb, formal*
to control or limit something: *State law restricts the sale of guns.*
—**restricted** *adjective* limited or controlled by a law or rule: *The restricted parking is for employees only.*
—**restrictive** *adjective, formal* stopping people from doing something: *restrictive rules*

WORD FAMILY look at the words:
➔ **restrict** *verb*
➔ **restricted** *adjective*
➔ **restriction** *noun*
➔ **restrictive** *adjective*

re•stric•tion /rɪˈstrɪkʃən/ Ac *noun, formal*
a rule that limits what you are allowed to do: *There are very severe restrictions on cigarette advertising, for example you cannot advertise in magazines anymore.*
➔ See Thesaurus box at **rule**[1]

rest•room /ˈrestrum/ *noun*
a room with a toilet, in a public place such as a restaurant or a theater: *I need to use the restroom.*

re•sult[1] /rɪˈzʌlt/ *noun*
1 something that happens or exists because of something that has already happened: *He died as a result of the accident.*

THESAURUS: result
consequences *formal* the things that happen as a result of an action, event, etc.: *What are the possible consequences of drinking and driving?*
effect a change that is the result of something: *the harmful effects of pollution on the Earth*
outcome the final result of a meeting, election, game, war, etc.: *We were pleased with the outcome of the election.*
upshot the final result of a situation: *The upshot of all this was that Kate and Luisa stopped talking to each other.*

2 the final number of points, votes, etc. at the end of a competition, election, etc.: *The election results will be announced today.*
3 information or answers that are produced by examining something carefully: *We are waiting for the results of your blood test.*

result[2] *verb, formal*
to happen or exist because of something: *The flooding resulted from all the rain last weekend.*
PHRASAL VERB
result in something
to make something happen: *The fire resulted in the building being destroyed.* SYNONYM **cause**

re•sume /rɪˈzum/ *verb, formal*
to start again after stopping: *We resumed the meeting after lunch.*

ré•su•mé /ˈrezəˌmeɪ/ *noun*
a written document that lists your education and previous jobs, that you send to employers when you are looking for a job: *Send your résumé to our Human Resources department.*

re•tail /ˈriteɪl/ *verb*
retail for/at something *formal* = to be sold at a particular price in stores: *The wine retails for $8.95 a bottle.*
—**retail** *noun* the business of selling goods to people in stores

re•tail•er /ˈriˌteɪlɚ/ *noun*
a person or business that sells goods to people in a store

R

re•tain /rɪ'teɪn/ Ac *verb, formal*
to keep something or to continue to have something: *Pine trees retain their leaves all year.*
—**retention** /rɪ'tenʃən/ *noun, formal* the act of keeping something

re•tal•i•ate /rɪ'tæliˌeɪt/ *verb, formal*
to do something bad to someone because he or she has done something bad to you: *Joe hit his brother, who retaliated by hitting him back.*
—**retaliation** /rɪˌtæli'eɪʃən/ *noun, formal* the act of retaliating

R

ret•i•na /'retənə/ *noun*
the area at the back of your eye that receives light and sends an image of what you see to your brain

re•tire /rɪ'taɪɚ/ *verb*
to stop working at the end of your working life: *I plan to retire when I'm 70.*
—**retiree** /rɪˌtaɪə'ri/ *noun* someone who has retired from work

WORD FAMILY look at the words:
→ **retire** *verb*
→ **retirement** *noun*
→ **retiree** *noun*

re•tire•ment /rɪ'taɪɚmənt/ *noun*
the period of time after you have retired: *While you're working, you should be saving money for your retirement.*

re•treat[1] /rɪ'trit/ *verb*
if an army retreats, it stops fighting and moves away from the enemy: *The soldiers had to retreat when the much larger army attacked them.*

retreat[2] *noun*
an occasion when an army moves away from the enemy after they have been beaten in a battle: *Some soldiers were shot during their retreat from the city.*

ret•ri•bu•tion /ˌretrə'byuʃən/ *noun, formal*
severe punishment for doing something: *Neighbors were worried about retribution if they told police about the gang members.*

re•turn[1] /rɪ'tɚn/ *verb, formal*
1 to go or come back to a place where you were before: *Kevin has just returned from Texas after visiting his parents there.* SYNONYM **come back**
2 to give something back to someone: *Will you return these books to the library for me?*
3 if a feeling or situation returns, it starts happening again: *I felt my anger returning.* SYNONYM **come back**

return[2] *noun*
1 the act of giving something back: *She was willing to pay $500 for the return of her stolen necklace.*
2 *formal* the act of going or coming back to a place where you were before: *We were so excited about Mom's return from her trip.*

re•un•ion /ri'yunyən/ *noun*
a meeting of people who have not met for a long time: *The class of 1987 is having a reunion at the school.*

re•u•nite /ˌriyu'naɪt/ *verb*
to bring people together again after they have been separated: *She was reunited with her mother after the war.*

Rev.
the written abbreviation of REVEREND

re•veal /rɪ'vil/ Ac *verb, formal*
1 to tell people information that was secret: *He refused to reveal the location of the money.* ANTONYM **conceal**
2 to show something that could not be seen before: *He opened his shirt to reveal a scar across his chest.* ANTONYM **conceal**

WORD FAMILY look at the words:
→ **reveal** *verb*
→ **revealing** *adjective*
→ **revelation** *noun*

re•veal•ing /rɪ'vilɪŋ/ Ac *adjective*
1 showing something about someone's true character, thoughts, or feelings: *The book tells revealing stories about the actress's life.*
2 revealing clothes show parts of your body that you usually keep covered: *a revealing swimsuit*

rev•e•la•tion /ˌrevə'leɪʃən/ Ac *noun, formal*
a surprising fact about someone or something, that people are suddenly told about: *Shocking revelations about her private life appeared in the newspapers.*

re•venge /rɪ'vendʒ/ *noun*
something you do in order to punish someone who has done something bad to you:

He took revenge on the men who killed his father by killing them.

rev•e•nue /ˈrevəˌnu/ [Ac] *noun, formal*
money that a company earns or a government receives from tax: *The state will receive revenue from selling the land.*

Rev•erend /ˈrevrənd/ *noun, written abbreviation* **Rev.**
used in the title of a minister in a Christian church: *The pastor of the church is Reverend Stephen Dyer.*

re•verse¹ /rɪˈvɚs/ [Ac] *verb, formal*
to change something such as a decision or process so that it is the opposite of what it was before: *It will take years to reverse the damage done by pollution.*
—**reversal** *noun* the act of changing something such as an action to do the opposite: *the reversal of the principal's decision*
—**reversible** *adjective* able to be reversed: *The damage to the forest may not be reversible.*

reverse² *noun*
1 the control in a vehicle that makes it go backward: *I started the car and put it in reverse to back out of the driveway.*
2 the reverse *formal* = the opposite: *It rains every day in a rainforest, but in a desert the reverse is true.*

reverse³ *adjective*
the opposite of what is usual, or the opposite of what you expected: *He was trying to help, but his advice had the reverse effect* (=it did not help).

re•view¹ /rɪˈvyu/ *noun*
1 an article in a newspaper or magazine that says what is good and bad about a new book, play, movie, etc.: *The movie got very good reviews, so I really want to see it.*
2 the process of thinking carefully about something or examining it again in order to decide how to change it: *The governor is considering a review of the state's education programs because many people are unhappy with the schools.*

review² *verb*
1 to write an article in a newspaper or magazine saying what is good and bad about a new book, play, movie, etc.: *He reviewed the movie and gave it five stars.*
2 to prepare for a test by studying books, notes, etc. again: *I spent the weekend reviewing my notes for the final exam.*
3 to think carefully about something or examine it again in order to decide how to change it: *We will review your problem and decide how we can help you.*
—**reviewer** *noun* someone whose job is reviewing new books, plays, films, etc. in a newspaper or magazine SYNONYM **critic**

re•vise /rɪˈvaɪz/ [Ac] *verb*
1 to change your opinions, plans, etc. because you have new information or ideas: *We had to revise our vacation plans when Kelly decided not to go.* SYNONYM **change**
2 to improve a piece of writing by adding new information or removing mistakes: *Revise your paper before you turn it in again.*
—**revision** /rɪˈvɪʒən/ *noun* the process of changing something in order to improve it

re•vive /rɪˈvaɪv/ *verb, formal*
1 to make someone conscious or alive again: *He was taken to hospital, where doctors were able to revive him.*
2 to make something successful or popular again: *Older people are teaching classes to children to try to revive old traditions.*
—**revival** *noun* a process in which something becomes successful or popular again

re•volt¹ /rɪˈvoʊlt/ *verb*
1 if people revolt, they refuse to obey a government and use violence to try to change it: *Rebel forces in the south revolted against the government.* SYNONYM **rebel**
2 to refuse to obey someone in authority or a rule, law, etc.: *Young people often revolt against authority.* SYNONYM **rebel**
3 to make you feel sick and shocked: *The thought of kissing him revolted me.*

revolt² *noun*
strong and often violent action by a lot of people against their ruler or government: *Local leaders started a revolt against the central government.*

rev•o•lu•tion /ˌrevəˈluʃən/ [Ac] *noun*
1 a time when people change a ruler or political system by using force or violence: *During the American Revolution, Americans fought against their British rulers.*
2 a complete change in the way people think or do something: *In the past 10 years there has been a revolution in the education system and everything has changed.*

R

3 one complete circular movement around a central point: *The earth makes one revolution around the sun each year.*

rev•o•lu•tion•ar•y /ˌrevəˈluʃəˌneri/ Ac *adjective*
completely new and different in a way that leads to great improvements: *This revolutionary new treatment for the disease could save thousands of lives every year.*

rev•o•lu•tion•ize /ˌrevəˈluʃəˌnaɪz/ Ac *verb*
to completely change the way people think or do something: *The Internet has revolutionized the way people find information.*

R

re•volve /rɪˈvɑlv/ *verb*
to make a circular movement around a central point: *The Earth revolves around the Sun, going completely around it once a year.*

re•volv•er /rɪˈvɑlvɚ/ *noun*
a small gun with a container for bullets that moves around: *He pulled out a revolver and shot her.*

re•ward¹ /rɪˈwɔrd/ *noun*
1 something that you are given because you have done something good: *His parents bought him a bike as a reward for getting good grades.*
2 money that is offered to people for helping the police to solve a crime: *The police are offering a reward for information about the people who stole the cars.*

reward² *verb*
to give something to someone because he or she has done something good: *The company rewarded him with a big pay rise.*

re•ward•ing /rɪˈwɔrdɪŋ/ *adjective*
a rewarding activity makes you feel happy and satisfied: *Nursing is hard work, but it can be very rewarding.*

re•wind /riˈwaɪnd/ *verb* **rewound** /riˈwaʊnd/
to make a TAPE go back to the beginning: *Rewind the videotape when you're done watching it.*

re•write /ˌriˈraɪt/ *verb* **rewrote** /riˈroʊt/ **rewritten** /riˈrɪtn/
to change a piece of writing in order to improve it or make it correct: *I rewrote the last chapter of the book and changed the ending completely.*
—**rewrite** /ˈriraɪt/ *noun* a piece of writing that has been rewritten

rhi•noc•er•os /raɪˈnɑsərəs/ *also* **rhi•no** /ˈraɪnoʊ/ *informal noun* plural **rhinoceros** or **rhinoceroses**
a large heavy animal with thick rough skin and one or two horns on its nose

rhu•barb /ˈrubɑrb/ *noun*
a plant with long thick red stems that are cooked and eaten as a fruit
➔ See picture on page A13

rhyme¹ /raɪm/ *verb*
if two words or lines of poetry rhyme, they end with the same sound: *"Door" rhymes with "floor."*

rhyme² *noun*
1 a short children's poem or song that uses words that rhyme
2 a word that ends with the same sound as another word, such as "big" and "dig"

rhythm /ˈrɪðəm/ *noun*
a regular repeated pattern of sounds or movements: *Dancers moved to the rhythm of the drums.*
—**rhythmic** /ˈrɪðmɪk/ *adjective, formal* having a rhythm: *the rhythmic motion of the waves*

ˌrhythm and ˈblues *noun*
another word for R & B

rib /rɪb/ *noun*
one of the pairs of curved bones in your chest: *She was so thin you could see her ribs under the skin.*
➔ See picture on page A2

rib•bon /ˈrɪbən/ *noun*
1 a long narrow piece of cloth, used for tying things and making them look pretty: *Karen tied a red ribbon in her daughter's hair.*
2 a decoration made of colored ribbons, given as a prize in a competition: *Kelli's pony won the blue ribbon at the state fair.*

ˈrib cage *noun*
the structure of ribs inside your chest around your lungs and heart

rice /raɪs/ *noun*
a white or brown grain grown in wet fields that you eat after it has been boiled: *I always have rice when I eat Chinese food.*

rich /rɪtʃ/ *adjective*
1 having a lot of money: *He's very rich and drives a big expensive car.* ANTONYM **poor**

THESAURUS: rich

wealthy having a lot of money: *He's a wealthy businessman.*

well-off having enough money to have a good life, with all the things you want: *His parents are fairly well-off.*

prosperous *formal* rich and successful: *one of the world's most prosperous nations*

well-to-do *formal* rich and having a high position in society: *Most of these kids come from well-to-do families.*

2 rich foods contain a lot of butter, cream, or eggs, and make you feel full very quickly: *You'll gain weight if you keep eating all that rich food.* ANTONYM **light**

rich•es /ˈrɪtʃɪz/ *plural noun, formal*
a lot of money or expensive things that someone owns: *The king had many riches.*

rich•ly /ˈrɪtʃli/ *adverb, formal*
in a beautiful or expensive way: *The bedroom was richly decorated with silk and velvet.*

ric•o•chet /ˈrɪkəˌʃeɪ/ *verb, formal*
if something flying through the air ricochets, it changes direction when it hits a surface: *The bullet ricocheted off the wall and hit the woman.* SYNONYM **bounce**

rid /rɪd/ *adjective*
get rid of something = to throw away or remove something you do not want: *I got rid of some old books and bought some new ones.*

rid•den /ˈrɪdn/ *verb*
the past participle of RIDE

rid•dle /ˈrɪdl/ *noun*
a funny question that you must guess the answer to: *Here's a riddle: What clothing does a house wear? Answer: Address.*

ride¹ /raɪd/ *verb* **rode** /roʊd/ **ridden** /ˈrɪdn/ **riding**
1 to sit on a bicycle or horse and make it move forward: *She rode her bicycle to school.* | *The cowboys were riding horses.*
2 to travel in a car, truck, or bus: *We rode the bus into New York City.* | *I don't want to drive, so can I ride with you?*

ride² *noun*
1 a trip in a vehicle or on an animal: *Do you want to go for a ride in my new car?* | *He took me for a ride on his horse.*
2 a large machine with moving parts that people sit in at a FAIR or AMUSEMENT PARK: *I went on a scary ride at the state fair.*

rid•er /ˈraɪdɚ/ *noun*
someone who rides a horse or bicycle: *The rider fell off his horse.*

ridge /rɪdʒ/ *noun*
a long narrow part of something such as the top of a mountain: *He stood on the ridge looking at the valley below.*

rid•i•cule /ˈrɪdɪˌkyul/ *verb, formal*
to make jokes about someone or something in a way that makes him, her, or it seem stupid: *When I moved down south, they ridiculed the way I spoke and said I had a funny accent.*
—**ridicule** *noun, formal* jokes or remarks that are not nice and are intended to make someone or something seem stupid

ri•dic•u•lous /rɪˈdɪkyələs/ *adjective*
very silly: *He looked ridiculous dressed in women's clothes.*
—**ridiculously** *adverb*

rid•ing /ˈraɪdɪŋ/ *noun*
the sport of riding horses: *Let's go riding.*
➔ See picture on page A24

ri•fle /ˈraɪfəl/ *noun*
a long gun that you hold up to your shoulder to shoot: *He went hunting with his rifle.*

rig¹ /rɪg/ *verb* **rigged, rigging**
to make dishonest changes to an election or competition, so that the person you want to win wins: *They rigged the election by letting some people vote more than once.*

rig² *noun*
a large structure that makes a hole for getting oil out of the ground: *an oil rig*

right¹ /raɪt/ *adjective*
1 correct: *Did you get the right answer?* | *I thought there was a problem, and I was right.* ANTONYM **wrong**

THESAURUS: right

correct used about answers, facts, etc. that are right: *Is this information correct?*

accurate *formal* used about measurements, descriptions, etc. that are completely right: *This type of clock gives a very accurate measurement of time.*

2 on the side of the body that has the hand most people write with: *Take the next right turn.* | *Raise your right hand.* ANTONYM **left**
3 if something is right, people should do it, because it is good or fair: *It's not right to kill people.* ANTONYM **wrong**
4 *informal* used when saying that you agree with someone or when asking if someone agrees with you: *You're Steve, right?*
—**rightly** *adverb*: *He rightly decided to call the police.*
→ **all right**

R

right² *noun*
1 something that the law allows you to do or what the law should allow you to do: *Everyone should have equal rights* (=the same rights). | *In 1920, women got the right to vote.*
→ **civil rights, human rights**
2 the side of your body that has the hand that most people write with: *In the U.S., we drive on the right.* ANTONYM **left**
3 behavior that is good or fair: *You have to teach children the difference between right and wrong.* ANTONYM **wrong**
4 the right = people who believe that the government should not make too many rules to control businesses and social problems: *Politicians on the right are opposed to welfare increases.* SYNONYM **conservative**; ANTONYM **the left**
5 the rights to something = if someone has the rights to a story, song, etc., people have to ask him or her if they want to use it in another form: *Michael Jackson bought the rights to most of The Beatles' songs.*

right³ *adverb*
1 exactly in a particular position or place: *He's right behind you!* | *I left the keys right there.*
2 correctly: *He has a long name that no one spells right.* ANTONYM **wrong**
3 toward the right side: *Turn right at the lights.* ANTONYM **left**
4 all the way: *The nail went right through his shoe.*
5 I'll/he'll, etc. be right there = I am, he is, etc. coming now: *Tell Sarah I'll be right there.*
6 right away = without waiting: *When she got his message, she called him back right away.* SYNONYM **immediately**
7 right now = at this time, not later: *Come here right now!* SYNONYM **immediately**

ˈright ˌangle *noun*
the shape that two sides of a square make where they meet: *There are 90 degrees in a right angle.*

right•ful /ˈraɪtfəl/ *adjective, formal*
correct and fair, or legally correct: *The police returned the stolen painting to its rightful owner.* SYNONYM **proper**
—**rightfully** *adverb*: *She took back the money that was rightfully hers.*

ˌright-ˈhanded *adjective*
someone who is right-handed uses his or her right hand to write or throw a ball: *Most of the school desks are made for right-handed people.*

ˌright-ˈwing *adjective*
believing that the government should not make too many rules to control businesses and social problems: *Her father was right-wing and always voted Republican.* SYNONYM **conservative**; ANTONYM **left-wing**

rig•id /ˈrɪdʒɪd/ Ac *adjective, formal*
1 not easy to bend or move: *The box has rigid sides to protect the glasses inside.* SYNONYM **stiff**; ANTONYM **flexible**
2 rigid rules, ideas, methods, etc. are strict and difficult to change: *My parents are strict and have lots of rigid rules.* ANTONYM **flexible**
—**rigidly** *adverb*
—**rigidity** /rɪˈdʒɪdəti/ *noun* the quality of being rigid

rig•or•ous /ˈrɪgərəs/ *adjective, formal*
involving a lot of work or effort: *Athletes have to do rigorous training, and run for miles every day.* SYNONYM **strict**
—**rigorously** *adverb*

rim /rɪm/ *noun*
the outside edge of something round: *There was lipstick on the rim of the glass.*

rind /raɪnd/ *noun*
the hard outer skin of oranges, LEMONs, or MELONs

ring¹ /rɪŋ/ *noun*
1 a piece of jewelry that you wear on your finger: *She wore a diamond ring.* | *When people get married, they usually exchange*

wedding rings.
→ See picture at **jewelry**
2 a circle: *The hot cup made a ring on the table.*
3 a group of people who do an illegal activity together: *The drug ring sold drugs all over the state.*
4 the sound that a bell makes: *There was a ring at the door.*

ring² *verb* **rang** /ræŋ/ **rung** /rʌŋ/
1 to make a bell make a sound: *I rang the doorbell.* | *The telephone's ringing.*
2 ring a bell *informal* = if something rings a bell, you think you have heard it before: *His name rings a bell, but I can't remember what he looks like.*
→ See picture on page A22

rink /rɪŋk/ *noun*
a place where people slide on ice wearing special shoes: *We went skating at the ice rink.*

rinse /rɪns/ *verb*
to use water to get soap or dirt off something: *I washed my hands, then rinsed them.*

ri•ot¹ /ˈraɪət/ *noun*
violent behavior by a crowd of people: *During the riot, people shot at police and set fire to buildings.*

riot² *verb*
if a crowd of people riots, they behave in a violent way: *The crowd rioted, turning over cars and breaking store windows.*

rip¹ /rɪp/ *verb* **ripped, ripping**
to tear something quickly: *I ripped my pants on a nail, and now I have to sew up the hole.*
PHRASAL VERB
rip something up
to tear something into several pieces: *I ripped up the letter and threw it away.* SYNONYM **tear up**

rip² *noun*
a hole in material where something has torn it: *Oh no! There's a hole in my jeans.*

ripe /raɪp/ *adjective*
ripe fruit is ready to be eaten: *Bananas turn yellow when they are ripe.*

rip•en /ˈraɪpən/ *verb*
if fruit ripens, it becomes softer and ready to eat: *The peaches ripened in the fruit bowl.*

ˈrip-off *noun, informal*
a situation in which someone pays more for something than it is worth: *She paid $200 dollars for a pair of sneakers – what a rip-off!*

rise¹ /raɪz/ *verb, formal* **rose** /roʊz/ **risen** /ˈrɪzən/ **rising**
1 to get bigger in number or amount: *The temperature rose from 70 to 75 degrees.* | *Unemployment is rising; more and more people are losing their jobs.* SYNONYM **increase, go up**; ANTONYM **fall**
2 to go up: *Smoke rose from the chimney.* ANTONYM **fall**
3 if the sun or moon rises, it appears in the sky: *The sun rose at 7:00 in the morning.* ANTONYM **set**
4 *formal* to stand up: *He got off his chair and rose to his feet.*
→ See Thesaurus box at **increase¹**

rise² *noun, formal*
an increase in number or amount: *There was a rise in crime, with more robberies and more drug dealing.* SYNONYM **increase**; ANTONYM **fall**

ris•en /ˈrɪzən/ *verb*
the past participle of RISE

risk¹ /rɪsk/ *noun*
1 the chance that something bad might happen: *If you buy an old car, there is a risk (that) it will not work well.*
2 take a risk = to do something even though there is a chance that something bad will happen: *People who do dangerous sports enjoy taking risks.*
→ See Thesaurus box at **danger**

risk² *verb*
to put something in a situation where something could harm it or damage it: *He risked his life going into a burning building to save a child.*

risk•y /ˈrɪski/ *adjective*
involving a risk that something bad will happen: *Operating on very sick people is risky, because they could die.* SYNONYM **dangerous**; ANTONYM **safe**

rit•u•al /ˈrɪtʃuəl/ *noun, formal*
a set of actions that people do in the same way at an important event or time of year:

R

Part of the ritual of Christmas is giving presents.

ri•val /ˈraɪvəl/ *noun, formal*
a person, company, or team that tries to do better than another one: *The company made more money than all its rivals.* SYNONYM **competitor**

ri•val•ry /ˈraɪvəlri/ *noun* plural **rivalries** *formal*
a situation in which two people, companies, or teams are tring to do better than each other: *There is a lot of rivalry between the two players, because they both want to be the best on the team.*

R

river

riv•er /ˈrɪvɚ/ *noun*
a long wide flow of water that goes into the ocean or a lake: *The longest river in Africa is the Nile.*

R.N. *noun, formal*
registered nurse a nurse: *She's an R.N. at a Dallas hospital.*

roach /routʃ/ *noun*
a large insect that often lives where there is food: *We used poison to kill the roaches in our kitchen.* SYNONYM **cockroach**

road /roud/ *noun*
1 a hard surface that vehicles travel on: *Find a safe place to cross the road.*

THESAURUS: road

street a road in a town, with houses or stores on each side: *I crossed the street and walked to the library.*

main street a road in the middle of a town where many stores, offices, etc. are: *There's a motel on the main street.*

avenue a road in a town – used in street names: *I got a taxi on Third Avenue.*

boulevard a wide road in a town – used in street names: *We drove down Sunset Boulevard.*

lane one of the long narrow areas that a road is divided into with painted lines, that keep cars apart: *One of the lanes on the freeway was closed because of an accident.*

main road a large and important road: *Stay on the main road until you get to Las Vegas.*

highway a very wide road for traveling fast over long distances: *The highway runs along the coast for most of the way.*

freeway/expressway a very wide road in a city or between cities, on which cars can travel very fast without stopping: *Take the freeway downtown.* | *I went north on the expressway.*

interstate a wide road that goes between states, on which cars can travel very fast: *The interstate goes from California, through Oregon and Washington, up to the Canadian border.*

2 on the road = traveling for a long distance in a car or truck: *We've been on the road since 7 a.m.*

roam /roum/ *verb, formal*
to walk or travel in a place freely: *Bears and other wild animals roamed through the woods.*

roar¹ /rɔr/ *verb*
to make a deep loud sound, like a lion: *Jets flew over the crowd, their engines roaring.*

roar² *noun*
a deep loud noise: *I heard the roar of the race car's engine.*

roast¹ /roust/ *verb*
to cook meat or vegetables in an OVEN: *We roasted a chicken for dinner.*
→ See Thesaurus box at **cook¹**
→ See picture on page A14

roast² *noun*
meat that you roast: *I'm making a pork roast for dinner.*

roast³ *adjective*
roast meat or vegetables have been cooked in an OVEN: *roast beef*

rob /rɑb/ *verb* **robbed, robbing**
to take something that is not yours from a person or place: *They robbed a bank and stole $100,000.*

WORD FAMILY look at the words:
→ **rob** *verb*
→ **robber** *noun*
→ **robbery** *noun*

rob•ber /ˈrɑbɚ/ *noun*
someone who goes to a place and takes something that is not theirs: *The robbers stole money and jewelry from the house.* SYNONYM **thief**

rob•ber•y /ˈrɑbəri/ *noun* plural **robberies**
a crime in which someone goes to a place and takes something that is not theirs: *The robbery happened at about 4:00 a.m. while the family was asleep.* SYNONYM **burglary**
→ See Thesaurus box at **crime**

robe /roʊb/ *noun*
a long loose piece of clothing that covers most of your body: *The judge wore a black robe.*

rob•in /ˈrɑbɪn/ *noun*
a bird with a red chest and a dark gray back: *Robins are often the first birds you see in the spring.*

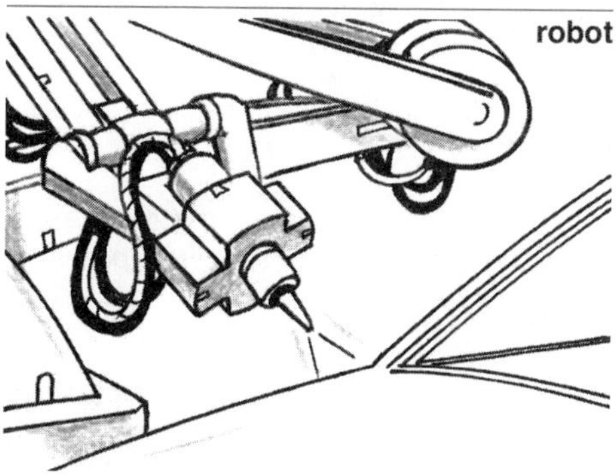
robot

ro•bot /ˈroʊbɑt/ *noun*
a machine that can move and do things people can do: *Robots are used in factories for making cars.*

ro•bust /roʊˈbʌst/ *adjective, formal*
strong and not likely have problems: *She was robust and healthy at 65 and still liked to take long walks.* ANTONYM **weak**

rock[1] /rɑk/ *noun*
1 stone that forms part of the Earth's surface: *You can see the different layers of rock in the Grand Canyon.*
2 a piece of stone: *He sat on a big rock next to the river.*
3 a type of loud modern music, that uses drums and GUITARS: *My favorite music is rock, and my favorite band is U2.*

rock[2] *verb*
to move gently from one side to another: *The boat rocked gently on the water.* | *She rocked the baby until he fell asleep.*

rock•et /ˈrɑkɪt/ *noun*
1 a long tall vehicle that travels into space: *The rocket took them to the Moon.*
2 a long thin weapon that is fired at things and explodes when it hits them: *The army fired rockets at the enemy.*
3 a long thin object that goes high into the sky and explodes into bright colors

ˈrocking chair *noun*
a chair that moves backward and forward on two curved pieces of wood

rock 'n' roll /ˌrɑk ən ˈroʊl/ *also* **ˌrock and ˈroll** *noun*
a type of modern music with a strong loud beat that became popular in the 1950s: *They called Elvis "the King of Rock'n'roll."*

rock•y /ˈrɑki/ *adjective*
ground that is rocky has a lot of rocks on it: *The beach was rocky, so I kept my shoes on.*

rod /rɑd/ *noun*
a long thin piece of metal or wood: *Men with fishing rods sat by the river.*

rode /roʊd/ *verb*
the past tense of RIDE

ro•dent /ˈroʊdnt/ *noun, formal*
a type of animal that includes rats and mice: *The drug has been tested on mice and other rodents.*

ro•de•o /ˈroʊdiˌoʊ, roʊˈdeɪoʊ/ *noun* plural **rodeos**
a competition in which people ride horses and catch cows with ropes

role /roʊl/ Ac *noun, formal*
1 the position or job that someone has in a situation or activity: *His science teacher played an important role in his decision to become a doctor* (=his teacher influenced

R

his decision in an important way). SYNONYM **part**
2 a character in a play or movie: *He played the role of the king in our play.* SYNONYM **part**

ˈrole ˌmodel *noun, formal*
someone who other people want to be like because they think he or she is good: *Pop stars who take drugs are bad role models for teenagers.*

roll¹ /roʊl/ *verb*
1 if something round rolls somewhere, it moves by turning over and over: *The ball rolled under the couch.*
2 to move on wheels: *The car rolled backward down the hill.*
3 *also* **roll up** to make something into the shape of a tube or ball by turning it over and over: *Roll up the carpet so we can carry it.*
4 *also* **roll out** to make something in a ball or tube flat and straight: *He took his sleeping bag out of its bag, and rolled it out on the floor.*
PHRASAL VERB
roll over
to turn your body so you are lying in a different position: *She rolled over so that she was lying on her back.*

roll² *noun*
1 a long amount of something that is curled into a tube: *a roll of toilet paper*
2 a small round piece of bread: *I put some butter on my roll.*

Roll•er•blade /ˈroʊlɚˌbleɪd/ *noun, trademark*
a boot with a row of wheels on the bottom: *She put on a pair of rollerblades and skated away.*
—**rollerblading** *noun* the sport of moving wearing rollerblades
➔ See picture on page A24

ˈroller ˌcoaster *noun*
a ride at a FAIR or AMUSEMENT PARK in which people sit in special cars that move along a track that goes up very high and suddenly down again

roll•er•skate /ˈroʊləˌskeɪt/ *noun*
a boot with four wheels on the bottom: *He went down the street on rollerskates.*
—**rollerskating** *noun* the sport of moving wearing rollerskates

Ro•man /ˈroʊmən/ *noun*
someone from ancient Rome: *The Romans built many roads and bridges.*
—**Roman** *adjective* relating to ancient Rome: *He dressed up as a Roman soldier with a helmet and shield.*

ˌRoman ˈCatholic *adjective*
relating to the church whose leader is the Pope: *Roman Catholic priests are not allowed to marry.* SYNONYM **Catholic**

ro•mance /ˈroʊmæns/ *noun*
1 an exciting relationship between two people who love each other: *The couple's romance began when they were in high school.*
2 a story about love between two people: *Her latest novel is a romance.*
➔ See Thesaurus box at **movie**

ˌRoman ˈnumeral *noun*
a number in a system that people used in ancient Rome, that uses letters instead of numbers: *X is the Roman numeral for 10.*

ro•man•tic¹ /roʊˈmæntɪk/ *adjective*
showing strong feelings of love: *My boyfriend is very romantic and often buys me flowers.*

romantic² *noun*
someone who is not practical and imagines that everything is better, more exciting, etc. than it really is: *Todd is a romantic who thought that being married would be easy because he was in love.*

ro•man•ti•cize /roʊˈmæntəˌsaɪz/ *verb, formal*
to make something bad seem good or exciting: *It's easy to romanticize the past and forget about all the problems we've had.*

roof /ruf/ *noun*
1 the top surface of a house, car, etc.: *There was a hole in the roof, and rain was coming into the house.*
2 the roof of your mouth = the top part of the inside of your mouth: *Some peanut butter was stuck to the roof of my mouth.*

rook•ie /ˈrʊki/ *noun, informal*
someone who has just started doing a job and does not know much about it: *He started as a rookie and is now Chief of Police.*

room /rum/ *noun*
1 one of the parts of a building that has walls and doors: *There are three rooms upstairs: two bedrooms and a bathroom.*
2 enough space: *Do you have room for me in your car?*

ˌroom and ˈboard *noun*
a room to sleep in and food to eat that you must pay for: *Room and board at college costs $600 a month.*

room•mate /ˈrumˌmeɪt/ *noun*
someone you share a room or house with: *Jo and I are roommates at college.*

room•y /ˈrumi/ *adjective, informal*
with plenty of space: *The car is roomy enough for six people.* SYNONYM **spacious**

roost /rust/ *noun*
a branch of a tree or a small building where birds rest and sleep

roost•er /ˈrustɚ/ *noun*
a male chicken: *The rooster woke us up early in the morning.*

root¹ /rut/ *noun*
the part of a plant or tree that grows under the ground: *The plant had long roots, and it was hard to pull it out of the ground.*
➔ **square root**

root² *verb*
PHRASAL VERB
root for someone
to want a person or team to win a game or competition: *I'm rooting for UCLA to win.*

ˈroot beer *noun*
a sweet drink made from the roots of some plants

rope /roʊp/ *noun*
1 a strong thick string: *They tied a rope around the tree branch, and pulled it out of the road.*
2 the ropes = the things someone needs to know in order to do a job: *Alex showed me the ropes when I first started working at the company.*

rose¹ /roʊz/ *noun*
a flower with a beautiful smell that grows on a plant with sharp points on the stem: *He sent me a bunch of red roses.*

rose² *verb*
the past tense of RISE

ros•y /ˈroʊzi/ *adjective* **rosier**, **rosiest**
1 if the skin on someone's face is rosy, it is pink: *Healthy people have rosy cheeks.* ANTONYM **pale**
2 *formal* successful or happy: *We expect a rosy future – things are going well for us.* ANTONYM **bleak**

rot /rɑt/ *verb* **rotted, rotting**
to slowly become bad or soft through natural chemical changes: *After a week, the fruit began to rot.* | *Sugar will rot your teeth.* SYNONYM **decay**

ro•tate /ˈroʊteɪt/ *verb, formal*
to go around like a wheel: *The Earth rotates every 24 hours.* | *Rotate the handle to the right.*

ro•ta•tion /roʊˈteɪʃən/ *noun, formal*
a movement around something: *I watched the rotation of the fan.*

rote /roʊt/ *noun, formal*
learn something by rote = to learn something by repeating it until you remember it: *We learned the poem by rote, and I can still remember it.*

rot•ten /ˈrɑtn/ *adjective*
1 food, wood, etc. that is rotten, is bad and soft because of natural chemical changes: *The rotten fish smelled terrible.* ANTONYM **fresh**
2 *informal* very bad: *I had a bad cold and felt rotten.* ANTONYM **great**
➔ See Thesaurus box at **old**

rough /rʌf/ *adjective*
1 not even or smooth: *His skin was hard and rough from the wind and sun.*
2 using force or violence: *Don't be too rough with the baby – you'll hurt her.* ANTONYM **gentle**
3 not exact: *I can only give you a rough idea of the cost, not an exact figure.*
4 difficult to deal with: *I've had some rough times, like when my mother died.* SYNONYM **hard**
—**roughness** *noun*

rough•ly /ˈrʌfli/ *adverb*
1 used when giving a figure that is not exact: *There's enough food for roughly 10 people.* SYNONYM **approximately**, **about**; ANTONYM **exactly**
2 not gently or carefully: *Don't pet the cat so*

roughly!
➔ See Thesaurus box at **about**

round¹ /raʊnd/ *adjective*
shaped like a circle or a ball: *The berries were small and round.* | *a round table*

round² *noun*
1 a number of events that are related: *The first round of meetings went well.*
2 one of the parts of a competition that you must win or do well in to get to the next part: *The winners of this round will play against each other tomorrow.*
3 a bullet that is shot from a gun: *Police fired several rounds into the building.*

round³ *verb, formal*
to go around a bend or the corner of a building: *The car rounded the bend quickly.*

ˈround-trip *adjective*
a round-trip ticket is for taking a trip from one place to another and back again ANTONYM **one-way**

route /rut, raʊt/ Ac *noun*
the way from one place to another: *What is the shortest route from here to the airport?*

rou•tine¹ /ruˈtin/ *noun*
the usual way in which you do things: *His morning routine is a shower, breakfast, and then work.*

routine² *adjective*
happening regularly, not for any special reason or problem: *They discovered her heart problem during a routine medical exam.* ANTONYM **special**
➔ See Thesaurus box at **normal**

rou•tin•ely /ruˈtinli/ *adverb*
happening regularly, not for any special reason or problem: *We routinely test patients for high blood pressure.* SYNONYM **normally**

row¹ /roʊ/ *noun*
1 a line of things or people: *There was a row of trees along the street.* | *When I go to the movies, I like to sit in the front row* (=in the first row of seats).
2 three/four, etc. in a row = happening three times, four times, etc. without anything different in between: *We've lost four games in a row, but I think we can win the next one.*

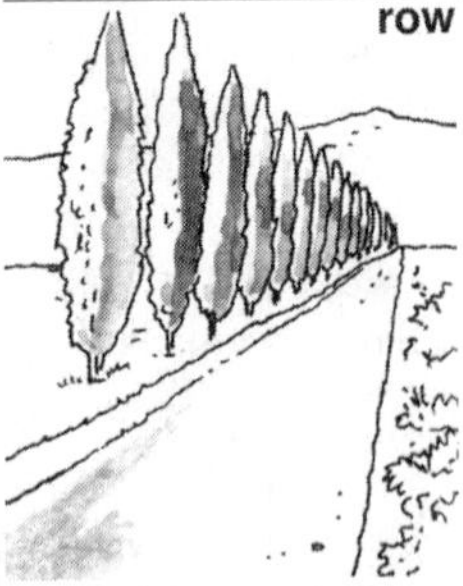
row

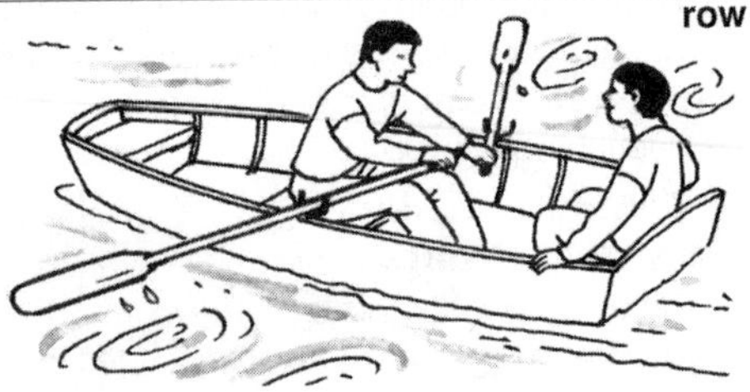
row

row² *verb*
to make a boat move through water using two long sticks with flat ends: *He took the oars and rowed across the lake.*
—**rowing** *noun* the activity of rowing a boat

row•boat /ˈroʊboʊt/ *noun*
a small boat that you move through water using long sticks with flat ends: *I watched the rowboats on the lake.*
➔ See picture on page A26

row•dy /ˈraʊdi/ *adjective*
a rowdy group of people is making a lot of noise: *A group of rowdy students went into the bar, yelling and singing.* SYNONYM **noisy**; ANTONYM **quiet**
—**rowdiness** *noun*

roy•al /ˈrɔɪəl/ *adjective*
relating to or belonging to a king or queen: *Prince Charles is a member of the British royal family.*

roy•al•ty /ˈrɔɪəlti/ *noun, formal*
members of the family of a king or queen: *The palace was built for royalty.*

RSVP
used on invitations for asking someone to reply

rub /rʌb/ *verb* **rubbed, rubbing**
to move your hand or a cloth backward and forward over a surface: *She rubbed her sore arm.*
➔ See Thesaurus box at **touch¹**

rub•ber /ˈrʌbɚ/ *noun*
a soft substance that comes from a tree and is used for making tires, boots, and other things: *She wears rubber gloves to wash the dishes.*

ˌrubber ˈband *noun*
a thin piece of rubber like a circle that holds things together: *He gave me a pile of dollar bills with a rubber band around it.*

ru•by /ˈrubi/ *noun* plural **rubies**
a dark red jewel: *The ring had a single ruby.*

rud·der /ˈrʌdɚ/ *noun*
a flat part at the back of a boat that helps the boat to change direction when it is moving
➔ See picture at **boat**

rude /rud/ *adjective*
speaking or behaving in a way that is not polite: *It's rude not to say thank you for a gift.*

THESAURUS: rude

impolite *formal* not polite: *Eating with your mouth open is very impolite.*

insulting saying or doing something unkind, rude, or offensive about someone, so that he or she feels upset: *His jokes are insulting to women.*

tactless saying or doing things that are likely to upset someone, because you have not thought carefully about what you are saying: *It was pretty tactless to ask her if she was trying to lose weight.*

offensive very impolite and likely to upset or offend people: *He made some offensive remark about how anyone who'd clean houses for a living wasn't very smart.*

—**rudely** *adverb*: *He rudely interrupted me.*
—**rudeness** *noun*

rug

rug /rʌg/ *noun*
a thick piece of cloth that covers part of a floor: *The rug covered most of the bedroom floor.*

rug·ged /ˈrʌgɪd/ *adjective*
rough, uneven and with a lot of rocks: *The rugged mountains are hard to climb.*

ru·in /ˈruɪn/ *verb*
to spoil something completely: *I spilled ink on my dress and ruined it.*

ru·ins /ˈruɪnz/ *plural noun*
1 ruins = the part of a building that is left when the rest has been destroyed: *We saw the ruins of an old church.*
2 in ruins = very badly damaged: *After the bombing, the whole city was in ruins.*

rule¹ /rul/ *noun*
1 a statement of what you can or cannot do: *In soccer, it's against the rules to pick up the ball* (=you cannot do it).

THESAURUS: rule

law a rule that people in a particular country, city, or state must obey: *The law says that motorcyclists must wear helmets.*

regulation *formal* an official rule or order: *Safety regulations say that all cars must have seat belts.*

restriction *formal* a rule or law that limits what you can do or what is allowed to happen: *Will there be new restrictions on immigration?*

2 a situation in which a particular group of people control a country: *Vietnam was under French rule before World War II.* SYNONYM **control**

rule² *verb*
1 to control a country: *The king ruled for 30 years.*
2 to make an official decision about something: *The judge ruled that the action was illegal.* SYNONYM **decide**

rul·er /ˈrulɚ/ *noun*
1 someone who controls a country: *The country had a military ruler who did not want democracy.*
2 a long piece of wood or plastic that you use for measuring or for drawing straight lines: *Use a ruler to measure how long your book is.*

rum /rʌm/ *noun*
a strong drink that contains alcohol and is made from sugar

rum·ble /ˈrʌmbəl/ *verb*
to make a long low sound: *Thunder rumbled across the sky.*

ru·mor /ˈrumɚ/ *noun*
something that people tell each other but that may not be true: *I heard a rumor that Kathy was having a baby – is that true?*

run¹ /rʌn/ *verb* **ran** /ræn/ **run, running**
1 to move very quickly using your legs: *He ran all the way to school.* | *Who's running in the race?*

R

THESAURUS: run

sprint to run as fast as you can for a short distance: *I sprinted toward the end zone.*

dash to run very fast: *The kids dashed in and out of the house.*

jog/go jogging to run at a slow steady speed for exercise: *She jogs five miles three times a week.*

race to go somewhere very quickly: *I raced home from school.*

2 to control a business or other organization: *Ann has run her family's restaurant since her father died.* SYNONYM **operate**

3 if a machine runs, it works or operates: *The car's engine was running and smoke was coming out of it.*

4 to go somewhere quickly, either walking or in a car: *Can you run to the store for me?*

5 to be in a particular place or continue in a particular direction: *A road runs along the river bank.*

6 to use a computer program: *You can run this software on any computer.*

7 to try to get a job or position by winning an election: *She is running for president.*

8 if liquid runs somewhere, it goes there in a steady stream: *Tears ran down her face.* SYNONYM **flow**

➔ See Thesaurus box at **pour**
➔ See picture on page A4

PHRASAL VERBS

run after someone or something
to chase someone or something: *He started to leave, but Kim ran after him.*

run around
to be busy doing many small jobs: *She's been running around all day getting things ready for the party.*

run away
to go away from a place because you are unhappy or afraid: *He ran away from home when he was 13.*

run into
1 run into someone = to meet someone when you were not expecting to: *I ran into an old friend at the supermarket.*

2 run into someone or something = to hit someone or something with a car you are driving: *He lost control and ran into another car.*

run off
1 to leave a person or place when you should stay where you are: *The dog kept running off, so we had to tie it up.*
2 run something off = to make copies of something using a machine: *Can you run off 20 copies of this for me?*

run out (of something)
to use all of something, so that there is none left: *If you run out of paper, there's some in my office.*

run over someone or something
to hit someone or something with a car and drive over them: *I think you just ran over some broken glass.*

run[2] *noun*
1 a period of time you spend running: *I went for a five-mile run.*
2 a point in a baseball game: *The hitters scored a lot of runs.*
3 in the long run = from now until a time far into the future: *Buying good quality equipment saves you money in the long run.*
4 make a run for it = to suddenly start running in order to get away from someone or something: *He made a run for it and escaped.*

ˈrun-down *adjective*
a run-down building or area is in very bad condition: *He lives in a run-down part of town where the buildings are old and need painting.*

rung[1] /rʌŋ/ *verb*
the past participle of RING

rung[2] *noun*
one of the steps of a LADDER: *I stood on the bottom rung, to keep the ladder from tipping.*

run•ner /ˈrʌnɚ/ *noun*
someone who runs as a sport: *The runners have to go around the track twice.*

run•ning /ˈrʌnɪŋ/ *noun*
the activity of running as a sport: *I go running every day for exercise.*

ˌrunning ˈwater *noun*
water that comes from a FAUCET: *Some of the houses do not have running water.*

run•ny /ˈrʌni/ *adjective*
1 if you have a runny nose, liquid comes out of your nose because you are sick: *I need a tissue for my runny nose.*
2 a runny liquid is not as thick as it should be: *If you add too much water, your sauce will be runny.*

run•way /ˈrʌnweɪ/ *noun*
a long wide road that an aircraft leaves from and comes down on

rup•ture /ˈrʌptʃɚ/ *verb, formal*
if something ruptures, it breaks so that it has a hole or tear in it: *A gas pipe ruptured and caused an explosion.*

ru•ral /ˈrʊrəl/ *adjective, formal*
relating to the country, not the city: *Most people who live in rural areas are farmers.* ANTONYM **urban**

rush¹ /rʌʃ/ *verb*
to move or do something quickly, because you do not have much time: *Everyone was rushing to catch the last bus.*
PHRASAL VERB
rush into something
to do something without thinking carefully about it first: *Don't rush into buying the first computer you see.*

rush² *noun*
1 a sudden fast movement of people or things: *There was a rush for the door, as everyone tried to get away from the fire.*
2 in a rush = trying to do things quickly, because you do not have much time: *I'm in a rush, because my flight leaves in an hour.*

ˈrush hour *noun*
the time of day when there are a lot of vehicles on the road because people are going to and from work: *It was rush hour, so it took us a long time to get home.*

Rus•sian¹ /ˈrʌʃən/ *adjective*
from Russia: *Russian soldiers*

Russian² *noun*
1 someone from Russia
2 the language spoken in Russia

rust¹ /rʌst/ *noun*
the brown substance that forms on metal when it has been wet: *The old car has a lot of rust on it.*

rush hour

rust² *verb*
to become covered with rust: *He painted the gates to stop them from rusting.*

rus•tle /ˈrʌsəl/ *verb*
if something such as dry leaves or papers rustle, they make a noise as they rub against each other: *Leaves rustled in the wind.*
—**rustle** *noun* the sound of something rustling
➔ See picture on page A22

rust•y /ˈrʌsti/ *adjective*
1 covered with RUST: *The old nails were rusty, so I pulled them out and put in new ones.*
2 if a skill that you have is rusty, you are not as good at it as you used to be because you have not done it for a long time: *My tennis is a little rusty, because I haven't played for a while.*

rut /rʌt/ *noun*
in a rut = living or working in a situation that does not change and is boring: *I was in a rut at school, so my teacher gave me a special project to work on.*

ruth•less /ˈruθləs/ *adjective*
not caring if you harm other people to get what you want: *He is a ruthless businessman who has made many enemies.*
—**ruthlessness** *noun*

Rx *noun*
a piece of paper that a doctor gives you so that you can get medicine SYNONYM **prescription**

rye /raɪ/ *noun*
1 the seeds of a crop used for making flour and beer
2 a type of bread that has a dark color and is made from rye flour: *My favorite sandwich is tuna on rye.*

R

Ss

's /z, s/
1 the short form of "is": *What's your name?*
2 the short form of "has": *She's been here before.*
3 the short form of "us": *Let's go, or we'll be late.*
4 used for showing who owns something: *Those are Tom's books* (=they belong to Tom).

S

Sab•bath /'sæbəθ/ *noun*
the Sabbath = the day of the week that is for resting and praying for Jews or Christians: *They don't work on the Sabbath.*

sab•o•tage /'sæbə,tɑʒ/ *verb, formal*
to damage or spoil something so that someone cannot do what he or she wants to do: *He tried to sabotage the wedding by telling guests it was canceled.*
—**sabotage** *noun* an action of sabotaging something

sack /sæk/ *noun*
a large bag made of strong material: *The truck carried sacks of rice.*

sa•cred /'seɪkrɪd/ *adjective, formal*
relating to a god or religion: *A church is a sacred building.* SYNONYM **holy**

sac•ri•fice[1] /'sækrə,faɪs/ *noun, formal*
1 something that you decide not to have or do so that you can have something more important: *My parents made a big sacrifice for me; they sold their house so they could pay for me to go to college.*
2 something that you offer to a god: *They killed a sheep as a sacrifice to God.*

sacrifice[2] *verb, formal*
to stop having or doing something so that you can have something more important: *She sacrificed her job to take care of her children.*

sac•ri•le•gious /,sækrə'lɪdʒəs/ *noun, formal*
treating something holy in a way that does not show respect: *Some of the jokes were sacrilegious and offended religious people.*
—**sacrilege** /'sækrəlɪdʒ/ *adjective, formal* an occasion when someone treats something holy in a way that does not show respect

sad /sæd/ *adjective* **sadder**, **saddest**
not happy, because a happy time has ended or something bad has happened: *She's sad because her parents are getting a divorce.* | *I'll be sad to leave all my friends.* ANTONYM **happy**

THESAURUS: sad

unhappy not happy, because you are in a bad situation that seems likely to continue being bad: *an unhappy marriage* | *I was really unhappy at school.*

miserable very sad, especially because you are lonely or sick: *He was miserable after he broke up with his girlfriend.*

upset sad because something bad or disappointing has happened: *She's still very upset about her father's death.*

depressed sad for a long time because things are wrong in your life: *She was really depressed after her husband left her.*

down/low *informal* a little sad about things in your life: *Whenever I felt down, I'd read his letter.* | *I guess I've been feeling a little low because of my grandma being sick.*

homesick sad because you are away from your home, family, and friends: *Many college students get homesick in their first year.*

→ See picture on page A23

sad•den /'sædn/ *verb, formal*
to make someone sad: *We were deeply saddened by her death* (=very sad about it).

sad•dle /'sædl/ *noun*
a leather seat that you sit on when riding a horse

sad•ly /'sædli/ *adverb*
1 in a way that shows you are sad: *She watched sadly, as he left.* SYNONYM **unhappily**; ANTONYM **happily**
2 used when talking about something that you wish were not true: *Sadly, her mother died when she was a baby.* SYNONYM **unfortunately**; ANTONYM **happily**

sad•ness /ˈsædnəs/ *noun*
an unhappy feeling: *His sadness grew stronger as he said goodbye to his brother.* SYNONYM **unhappiness**; ANTONYM **happiness**

sa•fa•ri /səˈfɑri/ *noun*
a trip through a place to watch wild animals: *We went on safari in Africa and saw elephants and lions.*

safe[1] /seɪf/ *adjective*
1 if someone or something is safe, no one will harm or destroy him, her, or it: *I don't feel safe driving home alone.* | *Keep important papers in a safe place.*
2 not likely to harm you: *Is it safe to cross the street here?* ANTONYM **dangerous**
—**safely** *adverb*: *Drive safely!*

safe[2] *noun*
a strong metal box with a lock on it, where you keep money and important things: *You need to know a special number to open the the safe.*

safe•guard /ˈseɪfgɑrd/ *noun, formal*
an action, law, etc. that protects someone or something: *Save your computer files regularly as a safeguard against losing information* (=to protect yourself from losing information).
—**safeguard** *verb* to do something that protects someone or something: *We are working to safeguard everyone from this new disease.*

safe•ty /ˈseɪfti/ *noun*
the state of being safe from danger or harm: *A lot of parents worry about the safety of their children.*

ˈ**safety belt** *noun*
another word for a SEAT BELT

ˈ**safety pin** *noun*
a pin with a cover that its point fits into, so that it cannot hurt you: *The strap on my dress is broken – do you have a safety pin?*

sag /sæg/ *verb* **sagged, sagging**
if something sags, it hangs or bends down in the middle because of weight or pressure: *The couch was very old, and it sagged in the middle.*

sa•ga /ˈsɑgə/ *noun*
a long story or description of events: *The story is the saga of a family that traveled across America in the 1880s.*

Sag•it•tar•i•us /ˌsædʒəˈteriəs/ *noun*
1 the ninth sign of the ZODIAC, represented by a man with a BOW and ARROWS
2 someone born between November 22 and December 21

said /sed/ *verb*
the past tense and past participle of SAY

sail

sail[1] /seɪl/ *verb*
to travel on water in a boat or ship: *He got in the boat and sailed across the lake.*
—**sailing** *noun* the activity of sailing in boats: *We went sailing last weekend.*
→ See picture on page A24

sail[2] *noun*
a large cloth that helps to make a boat move along, using the wind

sail•boat /ˈseɪlboʊt/ *noun*
a small boat with one or more sails: *A lot of sailboats were out on the lake.*
→ See picture on page A26

sail•or /ˈseɪlɚ/ *noun*
someone who works on a ship

saint /seɪnt/ *noun*
1 *written abbreviation* **St.** someone who lived a very good and religious life, and who the Christian church named "Saint" after he or she died: *St. Paul helped spread the Christian religion.*
2 *informal* someone who is very good and kind: *Thank you so much, Gail – you're a saint!*

sake /seɪk/ *noun*
1 for someone's sake = in order to help or please someone: *I know you don't really want to come to the party, but will you come for my sake?*
2 for the sake of something = in order to try to achieve or improve something: *He moved to the desert for the sake of his health* (=to improve it).
3 for goodness'/heaven's sake *informal* = you use this for showing that you are

S

annoyed or surprised: *Why didn't you tell me she's sick, for heaven's sake?*

sal•ad /ˈsæləd/ *noun*
a mixture of raw vegetables that you eat cold: *I put three different kinds of lettuce in the salad.*

ˈsalad ˌdressing *noun*
a mixture of liquids that you put on a salad to make it taste better

sa•la•mi /səˈlɑmi/ *noun*
a type of SAUSAGE that you eat cold in thin pieces

sal•a•ry /ˈsæləri/ *noun* plural **salaries**
money that you receive every month as payment for the job you do: *In my new job, I will get a higher salary* (=more money).
➔ See Thesaurus box at **pay**[2]

S

sale /seɪl/ *noun*
1 *formal* the act of selling something: *The sale of cigarettes to children is illegal.*
2 for sale = if something you own is for sale, you want to sell it: *Their house is for sale, and they are moving to California.*
3 go on sale = to become available for people to buy in stores: *The band's new CD went on sale last week.*
4 on sale = available for people to buy at a lower price than usual: *I bought this sweater because it was on sale for $8.99 – it usually costs $30!*
5 a time when stores sell things at lower prices than usual: *A lot of stores are having sales this week.*

ˈsales clerk *noun*
someone whose job is to help customers in a store

sales•person /ˈseɪlzˌpɚsən/ *noun* plural **salespeople** /ˈseɪlzˌpipəl/
someone whose job is to sell things to people: *One of the salespeople helped us choose a car.*
—**salesman** /ˈseɪlzmən/ *noun* a man whose job is to sell things to people
—**saleswoman** /ˈseɪlzˌwʊmən/ *noun* a woman whose job is to sell things to people
➔ See picture on page A16

ˈsales repreˌsentative *also* **sales rep** /ˈseɪlz rep/ *informal noun*
someone whose job is to travel around and sell a company's products: *He works as a sales rep for a major drug company.*

ˈsales tax *noun*
a tax that you pay that is added to the cost of something you are buying: *Sales tax is 8.5% in this city.*

sa•li•va /səˈlaɪvə/ *noun, formal*
the liquid that you produce naturally in your mouth: *The smell of food made her mouth fill with saliva.*

salm•on /ˈsæmən/ *noun*
a large ocean fish with pink flesh that you can eat

sa•lon /səˈlɑn/ *noun*
a place where you can get your hair cut, or have special treatments for your skin, nails, etc.: *She went to the beauty salon to get her hair cut.*

sal•sa /ˈsælsə/ *noun*
1 a strong-tasting Mexican sauce that you make from onions, tomatoes, PEPPERs, etc.: *Buy some chips and salsa for the party.*
2 a type of Latin American dance music or dance

salt /sɔlt/ *noun*
a white mineral that you add to food to make it taste better: *Put some salt and pepper on the meat before you cook it.*
➔ See picture on page A15

salt•y /ˈsɔlti/ *adjective*
tasting of salt: *I don't like this soup – it's too salty.*
➔ See Thesaurus box at **taste**[1]

sa•lute /səˈlut/ *verb*
to move your right hand to your head to show respect to a military officer: *He turned around and saluted the captain.*
—**salute** *noun* an act of saluting: *He raised his hand in a salute.*

sal•vage /ˈsælvɪdʒ/ *verb, formal*
to save something, when other things have been damaged or lost: *Many houses were damaged, and people were trying to salvage their things from inside.*
—**salvage** *noun* the act of salvaging things

same /seɪm/ *adjective*
1 the same a) one particular thing, and not a different one: *Kim and I go to the same school.* **b)** exactly like another person or thing: *All the little girls were wearing the same dress.* | *These two pictures are exactly the same – one is a copy of the other.* **c)** not changing: *He used to make jokes all the*

time, and he's still the same (=he has not changed). ANTONYM **different**

2 at the same time = if two things happen at the same time, they happen together: *We both started to speak at the same time, so I stopped and let him speak.*

—**the same** *adverb* in the same way: *I try to treat all the kids at school the same.*

sam•ple¹ /ˈsæmpəl/ *noun*
a small amount of something that shows you what the rest is like: *Can I see a sample of your work?* SYNONYM **example**

sample² *verb, formal*
to taste food or drink to see what it is like: *We sampled four different kinds of ice cream before we chose the one we wanted.* SYNONYM **try**

sanc•tion /ˈsæŋkʃən/ *noun*
sanctions = orders or laws that stop trade or communication with another country: *Both countries were threatening trade sanctions against each other.*

sanc•tu•ar•y /ˈsæŋktʃuˌeri/ *noun* plural **sanctuaries**
a safe area for birds or animals where people cannot hunt them: *a wildlife sanctuary*

sand /sænd/ *noun*
the very small grains of rock that are on the ground on beaches and in deserts: *The kids wanted to swim in the ocean and play in the sand.*

san•dal /ˈsændl/ *noun*
an open shoe that you wear in warm weather: *I wore a pair of sandals on the beach.*
➔ See picture at **shoe¹**

sand•pa•per /ˈsændˌpeɪpɚ/ *noun*
strong paper with a rough layer on one side, that you use for rubbing wood to make it smooth

sand•wich /ˈsændwɪtʃ/ *noun*
two pieces of bread with cheese, meat, etc. between them: *We had ham sandwiches for lunch.*

sand•y /ˈsændi/ *adjective*
covered with sand: *a sandy beach*

sane /seɪn/ *adjective, formal*
mentally healthy and able to think in a normal way: *Doctors say he was not sane when he killed his wife.* ANTONYM **insane**

sang /sæŋ/ *verb*
the past tense of SING

san•i•tar•y /ˈsænəˌteri/ *adjective, formal*
clean and healthy for people to use: *The bathrooms in the apartment buildings are not sanitary.*
—**sanitation** /ˌsænəˈteɪʃən/ *noun* the process of keeping places clean and healthy

san•i•ty /ˈsænəti/ *noun, formal*
the state of having a normal healthy mind: *Sometimes he became violent, and I thought he was losing his sanity.* ANTONYM **insanity**

sank /sæŋk/ *verb*
the past tense of SINK

San•ta Claus /ˈsæntə ˌklɔz/ *also* **Santa** *noun*
an old man with red clothes and a white BEARD, who children believe brings presents at Christmas

S

sap /sæp/ *noun*
the liquid that carries food through a plant: *Syrup is made of sap from maple trees.*

sap•phire /ˈsæfaɪɚ/ *noun*
a bright blue jewel: *a ring with sapphires and diamonds*

sar•casm /ˈsɑrˌkæzəm/ *noun*
an unkind or annoyed way of speaking, in which people say the opposite of what they mean: *"She's early as usual," Jim said, with sarcasm* (=Jim really means that she is late, as usual).
—**sarcastic** /sɑrˈkæstɪk/ *adjective* involving sarcasm: *"This is fun," she said, in a sarcastic voice.*

sar•dine /sɑrˈdin/ *noun*
a small silver fish that people eat, that is often packed in flat metal boxes: *a can of sardines*

sat /sæt/ *verb*
the past tense and past participle of SIT

Sa•tan /ˈseɪtn/ *noun*
another word for the DEVIL, a spirit that many people believe to be the most evil power in the world
—**satanic** /səˈtænɪk/ *adjective* relating to Satan: *a satanic symbol*

sat•el•lite /ˈsætlˌaɪt/ *noun*
1 a machine that goes into space to receive radio, television signals, etc., and send them to other parts of the world: *Television shows*

can be sent by satellite to anywhere in the world.

2 *formal* a moon that moves around a PLANET: *The planet Jupiter has four satellites.*

sat·in /ˈsætn/ *noun*
a type of cloth that is very smooth and shiny: *Her dress was made of satin.*

S

sat·ire /ˈsætaɪɚ/ *noun*
a book, play, etc. that criticizes someone or something in a funny way: *The book is a satire of American politics.*
—**satirist** /ˈsætərɪst/ *noun* someone who writes satires

sat·is·fac·tion /ˌsætɪsˈfækʃən/ *noun*
the pleased feeling you get when you achieve something: *Ted finished painting, and looked at the painting with satisfaction.*

sat·is·fac·to·ry /ˌsætɪsˈfæktəri/ *adjective, formal*
good enough, but not very good: *Stella's progress in science has been satisfactory.*

THESAURUS: satisfactory

good enough as good as you need something to be for a particular purpose or situation: *Is he good enough to play in the major leagues?*

acceptable good enough for a particular purpose: *The quality of your work is not acceptable.*

adequate *formal* enough in number or amount, or a good enough quality, for a particular purpose: *Plants need adequate sunlight to grow.*

all right/okay *informal* acceptable, but not very good: *The food was okay.* | *I thought the movie was all right.*

sat·is·fied /ˈsætɪsˌfaɪd/ *adjective*
pleased because something is good or because you have achieved something: *I am very satisfied with my grades – I got all A's and B's.* ANTONYM **dissatisfied**

sat·is·fy /ˈsætɪsˌfaɪ/ *verb* **satisfied**, third person singular **satisfies**
to make someone pleased by providing what he or she wants: *We work hard to satisfy our customers.*
—**satisfying** *adjective* making you pleased by providing you with what you want: *a satisfying meal*

WORD FAMILY look at the words:

→ **satisfy** *verb*
→ **satisfied** *adjective*
→ **satisfying** *adjective*
→ **satisfactory** *adjective*
→ **satisfaction** *noun*

sat·u·rat·ed fat /ˌsætʃəreɪtɪd ˈfæt/ *noun*
a type of fat that comes from meat and milk: *Too much saturated fat is not good for your body.*

Sat·ur·day /ˈsætɚdi/ *noun, written abbreviation* **Sat.**
the seventh day of the week, between Friday and Sunday: *My birthday is Saturday.* | *Jim's going to Phoenix on Saturday.* | *Would next Saturday be a good time for me to visit?* | *I went out and played golf last Saturday.* | *What are you doing Saturday night?*

sauce /sɔs/ *noun*
a thick liquid that you serve with food to give it a good taste: *spaghetti with tomato sauce*

sauce·pan /ˈsɔspæn/ *noun*
a deep metal container with a handle, that you use for cooking: *Heat the soup in a saucepan.*
→ See picture on page A9

sau·cer /ˈsɔsɚ/ *noun*
a small round plate that you put a cup on: *The saucer has a special place for the cup to sit so that it does not slide.*
→ See picture on page A9

sau·na /ˈsɔnə/ *noun*
a special room that is very hot, where people sit and relax: *The new health club has a big swimming pool and a sauna.*

sau·sage /ˈsɔsɪdʒ/ *noun*
a mixture of meat that is cooked inside a skin like a tube

sav·age /ˈsævɪdʒ/ *adjective, formal*
very cruel and violent: *She was badly hurt in a savage attack.*

—**savagery** /ˈsævɪdʒəri/ *noun, formal* the quality of being savage

save /seɪv/ *verb*

1 to make someone or something safe from danger, harm, etc.: *Firefighters saved three children from the fire.* | *The new medical treatment could save his life.*

2 *also* **save up** to keep money, so that you can use it later: *I'm saving up to buy a new computer.*

3 to use less time or money, and not waste it: *It will save time if we each do part of the work.*

4 to keep something, and not use it or throw it away: *She saved all his old letters in a special box.*

5 to make a computer keep the work that you have done on it: *Don't forget to save your work before you turn the program off.*

sav•ings /ˈseɪvɪŋz/ *plural noun*
all the money you have saved: *He used his savings to travel around the world.*

ˈsavings acˌcount *noun*
a bank account that pays you some money when you keep money in it

sav•ior /ˈseɪvyɚ/ *noun*
someone or something that can save you, when you are in a difficult or dangerous situation: *They were hoping that the new managers would be the saviors of the company.*

saw[1] /sɔn/ *verb*
the past tense of SEE

saw[2] *noun*
a tool that you use for cutting wood, with a flat blade and a row of sharp points

saw[3] *verb* **sawed, sawed** or **sawn** /sɔn/
to cut something using a saw: *He sawed the wood into three pieces.*
➔ See Thesaurus box at **cut**[1]

saw•dust /ˈsɔdʌst/ *noun*
very small pieces of wood that fall to the ground when you cut wood with a SAW

saw•mill /ˈsɔmɪl/ *noun*
a factory where machines cut trees into long thin pieces

sax /sæks/ *noun, informal*
another word for a SAXOPHONE

sax•o•phone /ˈsæksəˌfoʊn/ *noun*
a metal musical instrument that you play by blowing into it and pressing buttons on it
➔ See picture on page A21

say[1] /seɪ/ *verb* **said** /sed/ third person singular **says** /sez/

1 to speak words: *"I'll see you later," she said.* | *He said that he wasn't feeling well.* | *Did she say where she was going?*

THESAURUS: say

mention to say something but without giving many details: *He mentioned something about a party.*

add to say something more about something: *"And it's too far," she added.*

express to say how you feel about something: *Young children can't always express what they feel.*

point out to say something that other people had not noticed or thought of: *"It's upside down," Liz pointed out.*

suggest/imply if someone suggests or implies something, he or she says it in a way that is not direct, but that makes you think that it is true: *He seemed to be suggesting that I'd stolen it!*

whisper to say something very quietly: *"Is the baby asleep?" she whispered.*

mumble to say something quietly and without saying the words clearly: *Robbie mumbled an answer.*

mutter to say something quietly, because you are annoyed or do not want anyone to hear: *"It's not fair," she muttered.*

murmur to say something in a soft quiet voice: *She held her son close to her. "It's okay, you'll be okay," she murmured.*

USAGE: say

You **say** words to someone. You cannot say "say me": *She said to me that she was going home.*

You **tell** a person facts or information: *She told me that she was going home.*

You **talk** about a particular subject: *Each student had to talk about his or her family.*

2 to give information in writing, pictures, or numbers: *The clock said 6:45.* | *What did the newspapers say about the accident?*

S

say² *noun*
the right to help decide something: *The kids should have a say in where we go for our vacation.*

say•ing /ˈseɪ-ɪŋ/ *noun*
a phrase that most people know that gives advice or information about life: *There is an old saying, "A penny saved is a penny earned* (=if you save your money you will have more money)."

scab /skæb/ *noun*
a hard layer of dried blood that forms over a cut or wound: *The girl had a scab on her knee where she had scraped it.*

scaf•fold•ing /ˈskæfəldɪŋ/ *noun*
poles and boards on the outside of a building, for people to stand on while they work on the building: *They put up scaffolding so they could paint the top of the building.*

S

scald /skɔld/ *verb*
to burn yourself with hot liquid or steam: *She spilled a pan of boiling water and scalded her arm.*
—**scalding** *adjective* extremely hot: *scalding water*

scale /skeɪl/ *noun*
1 a piece of equipment for weighing people or objects: *I weighed myself on the scale in the bathroom.*
2 how big or important something is: *At first we didn't understand the scale of the problem or how much work we would have to do.*
3 a system for measuring something or comparing it with something else: *Your performance will be judged on a scale of 1 to 10, with 1 being very bad and 10 being very good.*
4 the relationship between the size of a map and the actual size of the place it represents: *The map has a scale of 1 inch equals 1 mile.*
5 a set of marks on a tool or instrument for measuring something: *I need a ruler with a metric scale.*
6 a series of musical notes that have a fixed order and become gradually higher or lower in sound: *She was playing the scale of C major.*
7 one of the small flat pieces of hard skin that covers the body of a fish, snake, etc.

scal•lop /ˈskæləp/ *noun*
a small sea animal that you can eat which has a hard flat shell

scalp /skælp/ *noun*
the skin under the hair on your head: *This shampoo is good for your hair and scalp.*

scal•pel /ˈskælpəl/ *noun*
a small sharp knife that a doctor uses for doing an operation: *The doctor cut open the patient's stomach with a scalpel.*

scam /skæm/ *noun, informal*
a dishonest plan to get money: *The scam involved getting other people's bank account information and taking money from their accounts.*

scan¹ /skæn/ *verb* **scanned, scanning**
1 *also* **scan through** to read something quickly to find important information: *He scanned the menu, looking for something he liked.*
2 if a machine scans an object or a part of your body, it produces a picture of what is inside: *All luggage has to be scanned at the airport in order to find dangerous objects and weapons.*
3 to copy a picture or piece of writing onto a computer by putting it into a machine attached to the computer: *You can scan the pictures and email them to your brother.*

scan² *noun*
a medical test in which a machine produces a picture of something inside your body: *He had a brain scan at the hospital to see if there was something wrong.*

scan•dal /ˈskændl/ *noun*
something very bad or shocking that a famous or important person does: *There was a big scandal when they found out the mayor had taken the money.*
—**scandalize** *verb* to do something that shocks someone: *Donna scandalized her father by living with her boyfriend.*

scan•dal•ous /ˈskændl-əs/ *adjective*
shocking and involving very bad behavior: *The newspapers printed scandalous stories about the senator's secret girlfriend.*

scan•ner /ˈskænɚ/ *noun*
1 a piece of equipment that copies a picture or document onto a computer
2 a piece of equipment that produces a picture of what is inside an object or a part of your body: *luggage scanners at the airport*
→ See picture on page A20

scape•goat /ˈskeɪpgoʊt/ *noun*
someone who people blame for something bad that happens, even if it is not his or her fault: *They made me the scapegoat for their mistakes because they didn't want to admit they had done anything wrong.*

scar[1] /skɑr/ *noun*
a permanent mark on your skin from a cut or wound: *The burn left a scar on her hand.*
➔ See Thesaurus box at **mark**[2]

scar[2] *verb* **scarred, scarring**
to have or leave a permanent mark on your skin from a cut or wound: *The accident had scarred his face.*

scarce /skers/ *adjective*
if something is scarce, there is not much of it and it is difficult to get: *Fresh fruit was scarce during the winter.*
—**scarcity** *noun* the quality of being scarce: *the scarcity of fuel*

scarce•ly /ˈskersli/ *adverb, formal*
almost not at all, or almost none at all: *The town has scarcely changed in the last 20 years.* SYNONYM **barely, hardly**

scare[1] /sker/ *verb*
to make someone feel afraid: *The sudden loud noise scared me.* SYNONYM **frighten**

WORD FAMILY look at the words:
➔ **scare** *verb*
➔ **scared** *adjective*
➔ **scary** *adjective*

scare[2] *noun*
1 a sudden feeling of fear: *The dog gave me a scare when it jumped up at me.*
2 a situation that frightens or worries people because they think something bad will happen: *There was a bomb scare at the subway station and everyone had to leave.*

scare•crow /ˈskerkroʊ/ *noun*
something that looks like a person, that a farmer puts in a field to keep birds away

scared /skerd/ *adjective*
afraid or nervous about something: *A lot of people are scared of flying.* | *She was scared (that) she might slip and fall on the ice.* SYNONYM **afraid, frightened**
➔ See Thesaurus box at **frightened**
➔ See picture on page A23

scarf /skɑrf/ *noun* plural **scarves** /skɑrvz/ or **scarfs**
a piece of material that you wear around your neck to keep you warm or to make you look attractive: *It was cold, so she put on a hat, scarf, and gloves.*
➔ See picture on page A6

scar•let /ˈskɑrlɪt/ *adjective, formal*
having a very bright red color
—**scarlet** *noun, formal* a very bright red color

scar•y /ˈskeri/ *adjective* **scarier, scariest**
making you feel afraid: *It's a scary movie about ghosts.* ANTONYM **frightening**

scat•ter /ˈskætɚ/ *verb*
1 to throw or drop a lot of things over a wide area: *Scatter the flower seeds over the soil, and then cover them with the dirt and water them.*
2 to make people or things move quickly in different directions: *The sound of gunfire made the crowd scatter.*

sce•nar•i•o /sɪˈneriˌoʊ/ Ac *noun* plural **scenarios** *formal*
a situation that could possibly happen: *Doctors say that the worst-case scenario is that he will never walk again after this injury to his back* (=that is the worst thing that could happen).

scene /sin/ *noun*
1 a short part of a play or movie during which the events happen in the same place: *The main character dies in the last scene of the play.*
2 the place where an accident or crime happened: *Police are examining the scene of the crime for clues.*
3 a view or picture of a place: *He painted a beautiful scene of mountains and a lake.*
➔ See Thesaurus box at **part**[1]

sce•ner•y /ˈsinəri/ *noun*
1 the natural things you can see in a place, such as mountains, forests, etc.: *The scenery is very beautiful in this part of Canada.*
2 the background and furniture on a theater stage: *They have to change the scenery between each scene of the play, from the apartment scenery to the office.*

sce•nic /ˈsinɪk/ *adjective*
with beautiful views of natural things such as mountains, forests, oceans, etc.: *We took a*

S

scenic route along California's coastline, where we could see the ocean.

scent /sent/ *noun*
1 a pleasant smell: *The scent of flowers filled the room.*
2 the smell that a person or animal leaves behind: *Police dogs are trained to pick up people's scent.*
—**scented** *adjective* having a pleasant smell: *scented candles*
→ See Thesaurus box at **smell**[1]

sched•ule /ˈskedʒəl/ Ac *noun*
1 a plan of what you will do and when you will do it: *I have a very busy schedule this week* | *Everything is going well, and we expect to finish ahead of schedule* (=before the time that was planned).
2 a list showing the times that buses, trains, etc. arrive at and leave a place: *The schedule showed that the train was due to arrive 16:50.*

S

scheme[1] /skim/ Ac *noun*
a plan, especially to do something bad or illegal: *He thought of a scheme to avoid paying taxes.*

scheme[2] *verb*
to secretly make dishonest plans to get or achieve something: *He had been scheming to steal his uncle's money.* SYNONYM **plot**
—**schemer** *noun* someone who schemes to do something

schiz•o•phre•ni•a /ˌskɪtsəˈfriniə/ *noun*
a serious mental illness in which someone's thoughts and feelings are different from what is really happening around him or her: *He had schizophrenia and sometimes heard voices when no one was there.*
—**schizophrenic** /ˌskɪtsəˈfrenɪk/ *adjective* relating to or having schizophrenia
—**schizophrenic** *noun* someone who has schizophrenia

schol•ar /ˈskɑlɚ/ *noun*
1 someone who studies a subject and knows a lot about it: *Legal scholars disagree about the meaning of the law.*
2 someone who has been given money to study at a school or university: *Clinton was a Rhodes scholar at Oxford University, which only very smart people are chosen to do.*
—**scholarly** *adverb*: *scholarly research into the causes of the Civil War*

schol•ar•ship /ˈskɑlɚˌʃɪp/ *noun*
an amount of money that an organization gives someone to help pay for his or her education: *Michael got a scholarship to Harvard University, which will pay for his books and tuition.*

school /skul/ *noun*
1 a place where children go to learn: *Which school do you go to?* | *I can get some work done while the kids are at school* (=studying in the school building).
2 the time you spend at school: *What are you doing after school?*
3 a group of fish: *Many fish swim in schools for protection.*

sci•ence /ˈsaɪəns/ *noun*
study of and knowledge about the physical world that is based on testing and proving ideas: *There have been great developments in science and technology.* | *science courses such as chemistry and biology*

> **WORD FAMILY look at the words:**
> → **science** *noun*
> → **scientist** *noun*
> → **scientific** *adjective*

ˌscience ˈfiction *noun*
books and stories about the future, for example about traveling in time and space: *I'm reading a science fiction book about a boy living on Mars.*

sci•en•tif•ic /ˌsaɪənˈtɪfɪk/ *adjective*
relating to or based on science: *There is no scientific evidence that the drug is safe.* | *scientific research into the way the weather is changing*

sci•en•tist /ˈsaɪəntɪst/ *noun*
someone who works in science: *Scientists have shown that smoking causes cancer.*

sci-fi /ˌsaɪˈfaɪ/ *noun, informal*
another word for SCIENCE FICTION

scis•sors /ˈsɪzɚz/ *plural noun*
a tool for cutting paper, cloth, etc., that has two sharp blades fastened together in the middle, and handles with holes for your

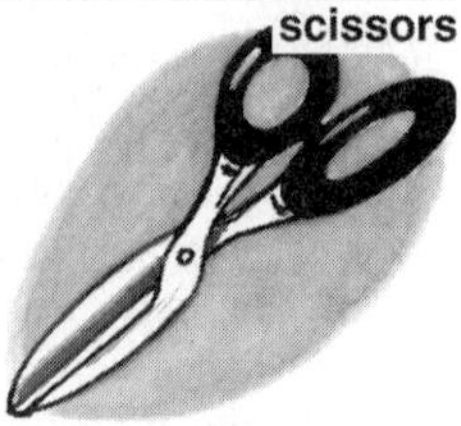
scissors

finger and thumb: *I need a pair of scissors to cut this package open.*

scold /skoʊld/ *verb*
to tell someone in an angry way that he or she has done something wrong: *Mom scolded us for taking the candy without asking first.*

scoop[1] /skup/ *noun*
a deep spoon for serving food: *She put two scoops of ice cream in a bowl.*

scoop[2] *verb*
to pick up or remove something using a spoon or your curved hand: *Cut the melon and scoop out the seeds.*

scoot·er /ˈskutɚ/ *noun*
1 a children's vehicle which has two wheels, an upright handle, and a board that the child stands on with one foot while the other foot pushes against the ground
2 a vehicle that has two small wheels and an engine: *A scooter is less powerful than a motorcycle.*

scope /skoʊp/ [Ac] *noun, formal*
the range of things that a subject, activity, book, etc. deals with: *You should limit the scope of your paper to the most important issues.*

scorch /skɔrtʃ/ *verb*
to burn the surface of something and make it change color: *Turn down the iron or you'll scorch your shirt.*

score[1] /skɔr/ *noun*
1 the number of points that you get in a game or on a test: *He got a score of 85 out of a possible 100 on the math test.* | *The final score of the game was 35 to 17.*
2 keep score = to write down how many points each person or team has in a game: *Who's going to keep score?*

score[2] *verb*
1 to get points in a game or on a test: *How many goals has he scored this year?*
2 to give a particular number of points in a game, competition, or test: *The tests will be scored by computer.*

scorn /skɔrn/ *noun, formal*
a complete lack of respect for someone or something because you think he, she, or it is not important or good: *He felt scorn for the people who did not understand his ideas.*
—**scorn** *verb, formal* to treat a person or idea as if he, she, or it is stupid and not worth considering: *They scorned her ideas and laughed at her.*

Scor·pi·o /ˈskɔrpiˌoʊ/ *noun*
1 the eighth sign of the ZODIAC, represented by a SCORPION
2 someone born between October 24 and November 21

scor·pi·on /ˈskɔrpiən/ *noun*
a small animal that stings with its tail: *Scorpions live in hot countries.*

Scotch tape /ˈskɑtʃ teɪp/ *noun, trademark*
sticky clear plastic in a long band, that you use for sticking paper together: *She used Scotch tape to fix the tear in the picture.*

Scot·tish /ˈskɑtɪʃ/ *adjective*
from Scotland

scout[1] /skaʊt/ *noun*
1 a member of the GIRL SCOUTS or BOY SCOUTS
2 someone who is sent out to get information about an area for the group they are with: *The captain sent out three scouts to check for enemy soldiers.*

scout[2] *verb also* **scout around**
to look for something in a particular area: *I'll scout around for a place to eat.*

scowl[1] /skaʊl/ *verb*
to look at someone in an angry or disapproving way: *I took another cookie and Mom scowled at me.*

scowl[2] *noun*
an angry or disapproving look that you give someone: *"That's not true," she said with a scowl.*

scram·ble /ˈskræmbəl/ *verb*
1 to climb up or over something quickly, using your hands to help you: *The kids were scrambling over the rocks.*
2 to try to do something very quickly: *We're scrambling to finish the project on time.*

ˈscrambled ˌeggs *plural noun*
eggs that have been cooked after mixing the white and yellow parts together

scrap /skræp/ *noun*
a small piece of paper, cloth, etc.: *He wrote his address on a scrap of paper.*
➔ See Thesaurus box at **piece**

S

S

scrap•book /ˈskræpbʊk/ *noun*
a book with empty pages in which you can stick pictures, newspaper articles, or other things you want to keep: *He kept a scrapbook of pictures his children had painted when they were young.*

scrape /skreɪp/ *verb*
1 to remove something from a surface, using the edge of a knife, stick, etc.: *Scrape the mud off your boots.*
2 to damage something by rubbing it against a rough surface: *She fell and scraped her knee.*

scratch¹ /skrætʃ/ *verb*
1 to rub your skin with your FINGERNAILS (=hard part at the end of each finger): *Her hand itched so she scratched it.*
2 to damage a surface or slightly cut someone's skin by pulling something sharp across it: *Don't drag the chair – you'll scratch the floor.* | *The tree branch scratched her arm.*
→ See Thesaurus box at **touch¹**
→ See picture on page A3

scratch² *noun*
a long thin cut or mark on the surface of something or on someone's skin: *She had a scratch on her face from the cat.* | *a scratch on the car door*
→ See Thesaurus box at **injury**

scratch•y /ˈskrætʃi/ *adjective*
scratchy clothes or materials have a rough surface and are uncomfortable to wear or touch: *The sweater was made of scratchy wool and made her skin itch.*

scream¹ /skrim/ *verb*
to make a loud high noise with your voice because you are afraid, hurt, excited, etc.: *There was a loud bang and people started screaming.* | *She was screaming at her husband and saying she was going to leave him.*
→ See Thesaurus box at **shout¹**

scream² *noun*
a loud high noise that you make when you are afraid, hurt, excited, etc.: *We heard screams coming from inside the burning house.*

screech /skritʃ/ *verb*
1 to shout loudly in a high voice because you are upset: *"Get out of my way!" she screeched.*
2 if a vehicle screeches, its wheels make a loud high noise: *The car screeched around the corner.*

screen /skrin/ *noun*
1 the flat glass part of a television or a computer: *The computer has an 18-inch screen.*
2 a large flat white surface that movies are shown on in a movie theater: *I don't like to sit too close to the screen at the movies.*
3 a wire net that covers an open door or window so that air can get inside a house but insects cannot: *The screens on the windows keep insects out.*
4 a piece of material on a frame that you use for dividing one part of a room from another part: *The doctor asked him to undress behind the screen.*
→ See picture on page A20

ˈscreen ˌsaver *noun*
a moving picture that appears on your computer screen when you are not using the computer

screw¹ /skru/ *noun*
a thin pointed piece of metal that you push and turn, in order to fasten pieces of wood or metal together: *Tighten the screws in the bookcase with a screwdriver.*

screw² *verb*
1 to fasten one thing to another, using a screw: *Screw the shelf to the wall.*
2 to fasten or close something by turning it: *Screw the lid back on the jar.*

screw•driv•er /ˈskruˌdraɪvɚ/ *noun*
a tool that you use to turn screws: *She used a screwdriver to put the furniture together.*

scrib•ble /ˈskrɪbəl/ *also* **scribble down** *verb*
to write something quickly in a messy way: *He scribbled down his phone number on a piece of paper.*

script /skrɪpt/ *noun*
the written words of a movie, play, or speech: *He's written a script for a new movie.*

scrip•ture /ˈskrɪptʃɚ/ *noun*
1 *also* **the (Holy) Scriptures** the Bible
2 the holy books of any religion: *Buddhist scriptures*

scroll /skroʊl/ *verb*
to move information up or down a computer screen so that you can read it: *You can scroll*

up and down using the arrows at the right of the screen.

scrub /skrʌb/ *verb* **scrubbed, scrubbing**
to clean something by rubbing it very hard: *Tom was on his knees, scrubbing the floor.*
→ See Thesaurus box at **clean**[2]

scru•ple /ˈskrupəl/ *noun, formal*
a belief about what is right and wrong that prevents you from doing something bad: *He's very dishonest and clearly has no scruples about lying.*

scru•pu•lous /ˈskrupyələs/ *adjective, formal*
careful to be completely honest, fair, and correct: *He was too scrupulous to cheat on a test.*
—**scrupulously** *adverb, formal*

scu•ba div•ing /ˈskubə ˌdaɪvɪŋ/ *noun*
the sport of swimming under water while breathing from a container of air on your back: *We went scuba diving in Hawaii and saw so many beautiful fish.*

sculp•tor /ˈskʌlptɚ/ *noun*
an artist who makes shapes and objects from stone, wood, or metal
—**sculpt** *verb* to make shapes and objects from stone, wood, or metal: *He sculpted the statue of the woman from marble.*

sculp•ture /ˈskʌlptʃɚ/ *noun*
1 a shape or object that someone has made from stone, wood, or metal as art: *There is a bronze sculpture of a lion in front of the library.*
2 the art of making objects out of stone, wood, or metal: *The sculpture class is working on making figures of people out of clay.*
→ See Thesaurus box at **art**

sea /si/ *noun*
1 a large area of salty water that is smaller than an ocean: *the Mediterranean Sea*
2 the ocean: *The boat was heading out to sea* (=away from land).

sea•food /ˈsifud/ *noun*
ocean animals such as fish and SHELLFISH that you can eat: *I love seafood like lobster and crab.*

sea•gull /ˈsigʌl/ *noun*
a common gray and white bird that lives near the sea and has a loud cry

seal[1] /sil/ *noun*
1 a large animal that lives near the ocean, swims, has smooth fur, and eats fish
2 an official mark that is put on documents or objects in order to prove that they are legal or real: *The visa had a government seal on it.*
3 a piece of plastic or paper that you have to break in order to open a bottle for the first time: *Do not use this medicine if the seal on the bottle is broken.*

seal[2] *verb*
1 *also* **seal up** to close an entrance, container, or hole with something that stops air, water, etc. from coming in or out of it: *How can I seal the crack in the bathtub?*
2 to close an envelope or package with something sticky: *She put the letter in the envelope and sealed it.*

seam /sim/ *noun*
the line where two pieces of cloth have been sewn together: *His shirt was torn along the seam.*

search[1] /sɚtʃ/ *noun*
1 an attempt to find someone or something by looking very carefully: *Police are continuing their search for the missing girl.* | *The tiger goes in search of food.*
2 an attempt to find information or an answer: *I did a search on the Internet for information on the disease.*

search[2] *verb*
1 to try to find someone or something by looking very carefully: *Police searched the house for weapons.* | *I searched through the papers on my desk, looking for the letter.*
2 to try to find information or an answer to a problem: *He was searching the Web for cheap flights.*
→ See Thesaurus box at **look**[1]

ˈsearch ˌengine *noun*
a computer program that helps you find information on the Internet: *I used a search engine to find the address of an old friend from high school.*

search•light /ˈsɚtʃlaɪt/ *noun*
a large bright light used for finding people or things at night: *The searchlight from the police helicopter lit up the whole field.*

S

sea•shell /ˈsiʃel/ *noun*
an empty shell of a small sea animal: *The kids were collecting seashells on the beach.*

sea•shore /ˈsiʃɔr/ *noun*
the seashore = the land along the edge of the ocean: *She was looking for shells on the seashore.*
➔ See Thesaurus box at **shore**

sea•sick /ˈsiˌsɪk/ *adjective*
feeling sick because of the movement of a boat: *I always get seasick on ships if the ocean is rough.*
—**seasickness** *noun*

sea•son /ˈsizən/ *noun*
1 one of the four periods in the year, which are winter, spring, summer, and fall: *Summer is my favorite season because I like hot weather.*
2 a time in a year when something usually happens or when people usually do something: *The football season starts next month.* | *Will you be seeing your parents during the holiday season* (=the period from Thanksgiving to New Year)?
—**seasonal** *adjective* relating to particular seasons: *There are seasonal changes in temperature – it is hot in summer and cold in winter.*

S

sea•son•ing /ˈsizənɪŋ/ *noun*
salt, pepper, SPICEs, etc. that you add to food to make it taste better

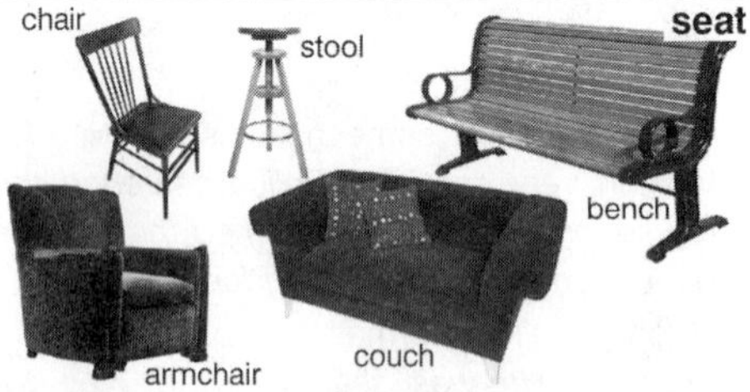

seat /sit/ *noun*
1 something you can sit on: *He made a speech and then went back to his seat.* | *I was driving and the kids were sitting in the back seat.*
2 take a seat/have a seat = to sit down: *She took a seat next to him on the sofa.*
3 the part of something that you sit on: *the toilet seat*

ˈseat belt *noun*
a belt that holds you in your seat in a car or airplane: *Fasten your seat belt when the plane is taking off and landing.*
➔ See picture on page A28

sea•weed /ˈsiwid/ *noun*
a green or brown plant that grows in the ocean

se•clud•ed /sɪˈkludɪd/ *adjective, formal*
a secluded place is very private and quiet: *We spent a quiet afternoon on a secluded beach.*
—**seclusion** /sɪˈkluʒən/ *noun, formal* the state of being in a quiet place away from other people

sec•ond¹ /ˈsekənd/ *number, pronoun*
2nd; someone or something that is after the first one: *September 2nd* | *Jane's second husband* | *She came in second in the race* (=one person was faster).

second² *noun*
1 a unit for measuring time. There are 60 seconds in a minute: *He finished the 100-meter race in 10.03 seconds.*
2 *informal* a very short period of time: *I'll be ready in a second!*

sec•ond•ar•y /ˈsekənˌderi/ *adjective*
not as important as something else: *For John, school was secondary to his friends.*

ˈsecondary ˌschool *noun, formal*
a school for children over 11 or 12 years old after ELEMENTARY SCHOOL

ˌsecond-ˈclass *adjective*
considered to be less important or good than other people or things: *In school, some of the kids treated me badly and made me feel like a second-class citizen* (=someone who is less important in society), *just because I couldn't afford to buy the right kind of clothes.*

ˌsecond-ˈhand *adjective*
something that is second-hand has already been used by someone before you buy it: *We bought a second-hand car that was two years old.* SYNONYM **used**; ANTONYM **new**

ˌsecond ˈperson *noun*
the second person = "you", and the verb forms you use with "you": *The instructions are written in the second person* (=using "you").

ˌsecond-ˈrate *adjective*
not very good: *He was just a second-rate actor that no one remembers anymore.*

se•cre•cy /ˈsikrəsi/ *noun*
a situation in which people keep something secret: *The trial took place in secrecy and no one knew what happened.*

se•cret¹ /ˈsikrət/ *adjective*
if something is secret, only you or only a few people know about it: *He hid the money in a secret place.* | *He kept his marriage secret because his parents didn't approve.*
—**secretly** *adverb*: *I secretly recorded our conversation.*
➔ See Thesaurus box at **private¹**

WORD FAMILY look at the words:
➔ **secret** *adjective*
➔ **secretly** *adverb*
➔ **secrecy** *noun*

secret² *noun*
1 an idea, plan, etc. that you do not tell other people about: *Don't tell anyone about this. It's a secret.* | *Can you keep a secret* (=not tell anyone else)?
2 in secret = doing something or happening without other people knowing: *They met in secret without telling even their closest friends.*

sec•re•tar•y /ˈsekrəˌteri/ *noun* plural **secretaries**
1 someone whose job is to answer the telephone, write letters, arrange meetings, etc. in an office: *You can talk to my secretary to make an appointment.*
2 an official who is in charge of a large U.S. government department: *the Secretary of Defense*

se•cre•tive /ˈsikrətɪv/ *adjective*
not wanting to tell people things: *She is very secretive about her past, so I don't know much about her.*

ˌsecret ˈservice *noun*
the Secret Service = the U.S. government department whose job is to protect the president

sect /sekt/ *noun*
a religious group that has separated from a larger group: *There are many sects of Islam, each of which follows the Koran but has slightly different beliefs.*

sec•tion /ˈsekʃən/ Ac *noun*
a part of something: *the children's section of the library* | *The rocket is built in sections and then put together later.*
➔ See Thesaurus box at **part¹**

sec•tor /ˈsektɚ/ Ac *noun*
a part of a country's industry or business: *The country's manufacturing sector has grown.*

se•cure /sɪˈkyʊr/ Ac *adjective*
1 not likely to change or be at risk: *It's nice to have a secure job and not have to worry about the future.*
2 safe from damage or attack: *People tried to make their houses secure before the storm hit.* SYNONYM **safe**
3 firmly fastened: *Make sure the rope is secure before you start climbing.*
—**securely** *adverb*: *For safety, guns should be kept in a securely locked cabinet.*

WORD FAMILY look at the words:
➔ **secure** *adjective*
➔ **securely** *adverb*
➔ **security** *noun*

S

se•cu•ri•ty /sɪˈkyʊrəti/ Ac *noun*
1 things that a government or organization does to protect people and places from crime or attack: *They increased security at airports after the attack, for example by having more guards and searching more bags.*
2 the state of being safe from damage or attack: *Terrorism is a threat to world peace and security.* SYNONYM **safety**

se•dan /sɪˈdæn/ *noun*
a large car that has seats for at least four people and has a TRUNK

sed•a•tive /ˈsedətɪv/ *noun*
a drug that makes someone sleepy or calm: *The doctor gave me a sedative to help me relax.*

se•duce /sɪˈdus/ *verb*, *formal*
1 to persuade someone to do something by making it seem very attractive or interesting: *Shoppers are often seduced into buying something by its attractive packaging.*
2 to persuade someone to have sex with you

see /si/ *verb* **saw** /sɔ/ **seen** /sin/
1 to notice someone or something, using your eyes: *He saw her go into the house.* | *I can't see anything without my glasses.*

see

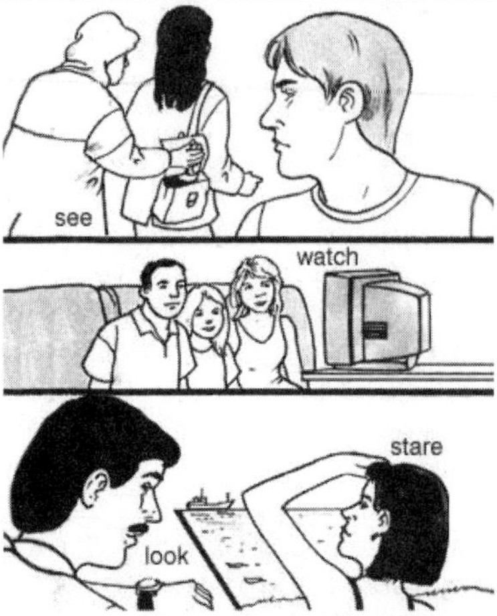

THESAURUS: see

notice to see something interesting or unusual: *I noticed a police car outside their house.*

spot to notice or recognize someone or something that is difficult to see: *At the dance, Mark spotted Carrie standing with her friends.*

catch a glimpse of something/someone to see something or someone, but only for a short time: *I caught a glimpse of his face as he ran past the window.*

make something out to see something, when this is difficult to do: *You could hardly make out the cars ahead of you in the fog.*

witness to see something, such as an accident or a crime happen: *Several people witnessed the attack.*

USAGE: see

You **see** something without planning to: *Two people saw him take the woman's purse.* | *I saw a big black dog in the park.*

You **look at** a picture, person, thing, etc. because you want to: *Hey, look at the hat that man is wearing.* | *Maria was looking at a picture book.*

You **watch** TV, a movie, or something that happens for a period of time: *My parents always come to watch me play basketball.* | *The kids are watching TV.*

You can also say that you **saw** a movie, a program, etc., but you cannot say "see television": *I saw a great movie on TV last night.*

2 to understand or realize something: *Do you see what I mean?* | *I could see (that) she didn't like me.* | *"It goes in the red box." "Oh, I see* (=I understand)*."*

3 to meet or visit someone: *I saw Rob on Saturday.* | *You ought to see a doctor.*

4 to find out information or a fact: *Plug the radio in and see if it's working.*

5 to watch a television program, play, or movie: *Have you seen his new movie yet?*

6 see you (later) = used in order to say goodbye to someone you will meet again: *Okay, I'll see you later, Ben.*

7 let's see/let me see = said when you are thinking about something, or trying to remember something: *Let me see, there will be 12 people so we need two more chairs.*

8 I'll see/we'll see = said when you do not want to make a decision immediately: *"Can Denise come too?" "We'll see."*

PHRASAL VERBS

see someone off
to go to an airport, station, etc. to say goodbye to someone who is leaving: *My friends came to see me off at the airport.*

see to something
to deal with something or make sure that it happens: *I'll make the food for the party, and you see to the drinks.*

seed /sid/ *noun*
a small grain that a new plant grows from: *She was planting sunflower seeds.*

seek /sik/ Ac *verb* **sought** /sɔt/ *formal*
to try to find or get something: *He was sick and sought help from a doctor.*
➔ See Thesaurus box at **look**[1]

seem /sim/ *verb*
to appear to be something or appear to have a particular quality or feeling: *It seems strange that he didn't call.* | *He seems to like his job – he hasn't complained.* | *She seems to be much happier at her new school.*

THESAURUS: seem

appear *formal* to seem to have particular qualities: *Light colors make a room appear bigger than it is.*

look to seem to be something, especially by having a particular appearance: *Rick looked very tired.*

sound to seem to have a particular quality when you hear or read about someone or something: *The book sounded really interesting.*

—**seemingly** *adverb* used to say that something seems to be true but is not really true: *We had the seemingly impossible job of preparing food for everyone.*

seen /sin/ *verb*
the past participle of SEE

seep /sip/ *verb*
if a substance seeps somewhere, it flows slowly through small holes in something: *Water that splashed out of the bathtub started to seep through the floor.*

see•saw /ˈsisɔ/ *noun*
a long board that two children play on, and when one end goes up, the other end goes down

seesaw

seg•ment /ˈsegmənt/ *noun, formal*
a part of something: *His comments were offensive to a large segment of the population.*

seg•re•gat•ed /ˈsegrəˌgeɪtɪd/ *adjective, formal*
segregated places or institutions are only for people of a particular race, religion, or sex: *The schools were racially segregated in the past, so black and white children went to different schools.*
—**segregation** /ˌsegrəˈgeɪʃən/ *noun* the state of keeping people of different races, religions, or sexes apart: *Segregation of students is no longer permitted here.*

seize /siz/ *verb, formal*
1 to take hold of something quickly and in a forceful way: *Thomas seized her hand and dragged her out of the water.* SYNONYM **grab**
2 to take control of something using force: *Rebel soldiers have seized control of the city.*
3 if an official organization such as the police seizes illegal goods, it takes them away from someone: *Police seized the drugs that the man was carrying.*
→ See Thesaurus box at **hold**[1]

sei•zure /ˈsiʒɚ/ *noun*
1 *formal* the action of an official organization such as the police when it takes illegal goods away from someone: *The police investigation led to the seizure of the illegal weapons.*
2 a short time when someone is unconscious and cannot control the movements of his or her body: *She had an epileptic seizure, in which she fell to the ground with her legs kicking.*

sel•dom /ˈseldəm/ *adverb*
not often: *She is old now and seldom travels.* SYNONYM **rarely**

se•lect /sɪˈlekt/ Ac *verb*
to choose something or someone: *The other students selected him to represent them at the meeting.* SYNONYM **choose, pick**

WORD FAMILY look at the words:
→ **select** *verb*
→ **selection** *noun*
→ **selective** *adjective*

→ See Thesaurus box at **choose**

se•lec•tion /sɪˈlekʃən/ Ac *noun*
1 the action of choosing someone or something: *Make a selection from the list.* | *the selection of a new captain for the team* SYNONYM **choice**
2 a group of things that you can choose from: *The restaurant offers a wide selection of dishes, including some vegetarian food.* SYNONYM **choice, range**

se•lec•tive /sɪˈlektɪv/ Ac *adjective*
careful about what you choose to do, buy, read, etc.: *I'm being very selective about the jobs I apply for – I want to make sure I get a good job.*

self /self/ *noun* plural **selves** /selvz/
the type of person you are, including what you feel and think, how you behave, etc.: *I was sick for a long time, but now I'm starting to feel like my old self* (=feel normal again).

ˌself-ˈconfident *adjective*
feeling sure that you can do things well, that people like you, etc.: *He came back from college more self-confident than when he left home.* SYNONYM **confident**; ANTONYM **shy**
—**self-confidence** *noun* a belief that you can do things well, that people like you, etc.

S

ˌself-ˈconscious *adjective*
worried and embarrassed about what you look like or what other people think of you: *Lou's very self-conscious about his baldness.*

ˌself-conˈtrol *noun*
the ability to control your feelings and behavior even when you are angry, excited, or upset: *She lacks self-control and often shouts at her children.*

ˌself-deˈfense *noun*
the use of force to protect yourself when you are attacked: *He attacked her, and she shot him in self-defense.*

ˌself-emˈployed *adjective*
working for yourself, not employed by a company: *Self-employed people have to pay for their own health insurance and retirement plans.*
—**self-employment** *noun* the state of being self-employed

ˌself-esˈteem *noun, formal*
a feeling that you are pleased with your own abilities, and that you deserve to be liked or respected: *Children who don't have many friends often have low self-esteem* (=not very much self-esteem).

ˌself-ˈinterest *noun, formal*
a feeling of caring about what is best for you instead of what is best for other people: *It was his own self-interest that made him tell the teacher about his friends' plan – he didn't want to get in trouble himself.*

self•ish /ˈselfɪʃ/ *adjective*
caring only about yourself and not about other people: *Eating all the pie was a very selfish thing to do.* ANTONYM **unselfish**
—**selfishness** *noun*
—**selfishly** *adverb*

ˌself-ˈpity *noun*
the state of feeling sorry for yourself: *A lot of bad things have happened to her, but her self-pity is stopping her from improving her life.*

ˌself-reˈspect *noun*
a feeling that you are pleased with yourself and your abilities and that other people should treat you well: *She lost her job, then her home, and finally her self-respect.*

ˌself-ˈrighteous *adjective, formal*
very sure that your beliefs, attitudes, etc. are right, in a way that annoys other people: *He's one of those self-righteous people who always think they are right.*

ˌself-ˈservice *also* **ˌself ˈserve** *adjective*
a self-service store, restaurant, etc. is one where you get things for yourself, rather than being served by someone else: *I put gas in my car at a self-service gas station.*

ˌself-sufˈficient *adjective*
able to provide all the things you need without help from other people: *The country is self-sufficient in oil.*
—**self-sufficiency** *noun* the fact that someone or something is self-sufficient

sell /sel/ *verb* **sold** /soʊld/
to give something to someone in exchange for money: *We sold the house and moved to Florida.* | *I sold my car for $5,000.* | *It is illegal to sell alcohol to minors.* | *Does the store sell milk?* ANTONYM **buy**

PHRASAL VERB

sell out
if a product sells out, all of it is sold and there is none left: *All the tickets for tonight's concert have sold out.*

sell•er /ˈselɚ/ *noun*
a person or company that sells something ANTONYM **buyer**

se•man•tics /səˈmæntɪks/ *noun*
formal the meaning of words and phrases
—**semantic** *adjective, formal* relating to semantics

se•mes•ter /səˈmestɚ/ *noun*
one of two equal periods into which a year at school or college is divided: *I'm taking Algebra I this semester, and Algebra II next semester.*

semi- /semi/
1 partly but not completely: *He's semi-retired, but he does some part-time work.*
2 exactly half: *a semicircle*

sem•i•cir•cle /ˈsemiˌsɚkəl/ *noun*
half a circle: *Students sat in a semicircle, facing the teacher.*

sem•i•co•lon /ˈsemiˌkoʊlən/ *noun*
the mark (;) that you use in writing to separate different parts of a sentence or list

sem·i·fi·nal /ˌsemiˈfaɪnl/ *noun*
one of the two sports games that are played in a competition before the final game. The winners of the two semifinals play each other in the last game to decide the winner of the competition.

sem·i·nar /ˈseməˌnɑr/ *noun*
a class in which a small group of students talk about a particular subject: *I went to several seminars on creative writing when I was in college.*

sen·ate *also* **Senate** /ˈsenɪt/ *noun*
the smaller of the two government groups that make laws, in some countries such as the U.S. and in most U.S. states: *The Senate voted 74 – 22 for the bill.*

sen·a·tor /ˈsenətɚ/ *also* **Senator** *noun*
a member of a senate: *a senator from Ohio*

send /send/ *verb* **sent** /sent/
1 to arrange for something to go or be taken to another place: *I sent you an email yesterday.* | *Do you want me to send the bill to you?*
2 to make someone go somewhere: *They sent their children to a school in Massachusetts.*

PHRASAL VERB

send for someone or something
to ask someone to come to you: *He was very sick, so his wife sent for the doctor.*

se·nile /ˈsinaɪl/ *adjective*
mentally confused or behaving strangely, because of old age: *My grandfather is going senile and barely knows who I am.*
—**senility** /sɪˈnɪləti/ *noun* the fact of being senile

senior¹ /ˈsinyɚ/ *noun*
1 a student in the last year of HIGH SCHOOL or college: *The high school seniors are deciding which college to go to.*
2 another word for SENIOR CITIZEN

senior² *adjective*
having a higher position or rank: *The case is being looked at by a senior police officer.*

Se·nior /ˈsinyɚ/ *adjective, written abbreviation* **Sr.**
used after the name of a man who has the same name as his son: *Michael Henderson, Sr., is usually called Mike, while people usually use his son's full name, Michael.*

ˌsenior ˈcitizen *noun*
someone who is over 60 years old: *The restaurant has special prices for senior citizens.*

se·nior·i·ty /ˌsinˈyɔrəti/ *noun, formal*
someone's rank or position in a company or organization that is based on how long he or she has worked there: *Wages are based on seniority, so people who have worked here longer make more money.*

sen·sa·tion /senˈseɪʃən/ *noun*
1 a physical feeling that you get from one of your five senses: *Matt felt a burning sensation in his eyes from the smoke.*
2 a feeling that is difficult to describe, caused by a particular event, experience, or memory: *I had a strange sensation that I was being watched.*

S

sen·sa·tion·al /senˈseɪʃənəl/ *adjective*
1 very good, interesting, or exciting: *You look sensational in that dress!*
2 intended to excite or shock people: *The magazine has sensational stories about movie stars' private lives – their marriages, affairs, and divorces.*

sense¹ /sens/ *noun*
1 the ability to make good decisions and do the thing that is most sensible or practical: *I hope he had the sense to lock the door when he left.*
2 a feeling about something: *We all felt a great sense of relief when the plane landed safely.*
3 make sense a) to have a clear meaning and be easy to understand: *These instructions just don't make sense.* **b)** if it makes sense to do something, it is a reasonable or sensible thing to do: *It makes sense to call first before we drive all the way there.*
4 one of the five natural powers of sight, hearing, touch, taste, and smell: *Dogs have a very good sense of smell.*
5 sense of humor = the ability to understand and enjoy things that are funny, or to make people laugh: *Jack's got a terrific sense of humor – he's a funny guy.*
6 the meaning of a word, phrase, sentence, etc.: *The word "record" has many senses.*

sense² *verb*
to feel or know that something is true without being told or having proof: *I could sense*

that something was wrong – she just didn't seem happy.

sense•less /'sensləs/ *adjective*
1 happening or done for no good reason or with no purpose: *It was a senseless killing. The killer did not know his victim and took no money.*
2 unconscious: *They beat him senseless and stole his money.*

sen•si•ble /'sensəbəl/ *adjective*
1 showing good judgment and able to make practical decisions: *I always get sensible advice from my mother.*
2 appropriate for a particular purpose, and practical rather than fashionable: *It's a long walk, so wear sensible shoes.*
—**sensibly** *adverb*

S

sen•si•tive /'sensətɪv/ *adjective*
1 a sensitive person is able to understand the feelings, problems, etc. of other people: *Good nurses are sensitive to their patients' feelings.* ANTONYM **insensitive**
2 easily upset by the things that other people do or say: *Christy is very sensitive about her weight, so don't say anything about how she looks.*
3 easily hurt or damaged by a substance or by hot or cold temperatures: *My teeth are sensitive to cold water.* | *This soap is for people with sensitive skin.*
—**sensitively** *adverb*
—**sensitivity** /ˌsensə'tɪvəti/ *noun* the fact of being sensitive

sent /sent/ *verb*
the past tense and past participle of SEND

sen•tence¹ /'sentəns/ *noun*
1 a group of words with a subject and a verb, that makes a statement or asks a question: *Please write your answers in complete sentences. For example, do not just write "Twain." Instead, write "The book was written by Mark Twain."*
2 a punishment that a judge gives to someone who is guilty of a crime: *He is serving a 10-year prison sentence for robbery* (=spending 10 years in jail).

sentence² *verb*
if a judge sentences a guilty person, he or she gives the person an official punishment: *The judge sentenced the drug dealer to five years in prison.*

sen•ti•ment /'sentəmənt/ *noun, formal*
an opinion or feeling that you have about something: *There was strong public sentiment against the new law* (=the opinion of most people was against it).

sen•ti•men•tal /ˌsentə'mentl/ *adjective*
showing emotions such as love, pity, and sadness too strongly: *sentimental love songs*
—**sentimentality** /ˌsentəmen'tæləti/ *noun* the quality of being sentimental

sep•a•rate¹ /'seprɪt/ *adjective*
1 different: *Write each list on a separate sheet of paper.*
2 not joined to or touching something else: *Keep the blue cards separate from the green cards.*
3 not related to or not affected by something else: *My personal life is separate from my work life.*

sep•a•rate² /'sepəˌreɪt/ *verb*
1 to divide something into two or more parts: *Ms. Barker separated the class into four groups.*
2 to be between two things and keep them apart: *A fence separates the house from the parking lot.*
3 to stop living with your husband, wife, or partner: *My parents separated last year, but they're not divorced.*
➔ See Thesaurus box at **divorce²**

sep•a•rate•ly /'seprɪtli/ *adverb*
not together with other people or things: *They arrived separately, but they left together.*

sep•a•ra•tion /ˌsepə'reɪʃən/ *noun*
1 *formal* when someone or something is separated from someone or something else: *The separation of church and state means that religion and government should not affect each other.*
2 a situation in which a husband and wife decide to live apart even though they are still married: *We agreed to a separation and I moved out.*

Sep•tem•ber /sep'tembɚ/ *noun, written abbreviation* **Sept.**
the ninth month of the year, between August and October: *We have to turn in the papers on September 2.* | *School starts in September.* | *Laura moved here last September.* | *They're getting married next September.*

se•quel /ˈsikwəl/ *noun*
a movie, book, etc. that continues the story of an earlier one: *I don't think the sequel is as good as the original movie.*

se•quence /ˈsikwəns/ [Ac] *noun*
a series of related events, actions, etc. that happen in a particular order: *The book explains the sequence of events that led to the war.*

se•quin /ˈsikwɪn/ *noun*
a small shiny flat round piece of metal that is sewn on clothes for decoration: *The sequins on her dress glittered as she danced across the stage.*

se•quoi•a /sɪˈkwɔɪə/ *noun*
another word for a REDWOOD

se•rene /səˈrin/ *adjective, formal*
very calm or peaceful: *The surface of the lake was serene, with no waves nor any movement.*
—**serenely** *adverb, formal*

se•ren•i•ty /səˈrenəti/ *noun, formal*
calmness and peace: *Her bedroom is a place of serenity away from the noise of the children.*

ser•geant /ˈsɑrdʒənt/ *noun, written abbreviation* **Sgt.**
an officer of a fairly low rank in the Army, Air Force, police, etc.

se•ri•al /ˈsɪriəl/ *adjective*
a story that is shown on television, broadcast on radio, or printed in a newspaper in several separate parts

se•ries /ˈsɪriz/ [Ac] *noun* plural **series**
1 a series of something = several events, actions, or things of the same kind that happen one after the other: *There have been a series of robberies on this block.*
2 a set of television programs with the same characters or on the same subject: *"I Love Lucy" is still a popular TV comedy series.*
3 a set of sports games played between the same two teams: *There are seven games in baseball's World Series, so a team has to win four games to win the series.*
→ See Thesaurus box at **television**

se•ri•ous /ˈsɪriəs/ *adjective*
1 a serious problem, situation, etc. is extremely bad or dangerous: *Drugs are a serious problem in many cities.*
2 saying what you really mean, and not joking or pretending: *If you are serious about becoming a doctor, you need to study harder.*
3 important and deserving a lot of attention: *We had a serious conversation about our future.*
—**seriousness** *noun*

se•ri•ous•ly /ˈsɪriəsli/ *adverb*
1 in a way that is bad or dangerous: *He got seriously ill and died a few days later.*
2 in a way that shows that you think something is important: *Mike doesn't take his job too seriously* (=think that it is very important) *– he keeps taking days off or going in late.*

ser•mon /ˈsɚmən/ *noun*
a talk about a religious subject given at a church

serv•ant /ˈsɚvənt/ *noun*
someone who is paid to work in someone's house, cleaning, cooking, etc.: *The rich man had many servants to take care of his house.*

serve /sɚv/ *verb*
1 to give someone food or drinks as part of a meal: *We'll serve lunch about noon.*
2 *formal* to be used for a particular purpose: *The sofa can also serve as a bed.*
3 to spend time doing a particular job: *Kelly served in the Army for three years.*
4 it serves someone right *informal* = used for saying that someone deserves something unpleasant that happens because he or she has done something bad: *"I failed my test." "It serves you right for not studying."*

WORD FAMILY look at the words:
→ serve *verb*
→ service *noun*
→ servant *noun*
→ server *noun*

serv•er /ˈsɚvɚ/ *noun*
1 a computer in a connected group of computers that all the other computers get information from: *So many people use our Web site that we need a more powerful server.*
2 someone who brings you food in a restaurant

serv•ice[1] /ˈsɚvɪs/ *noun*
1 the help that people who work in a restaurant, hotel, store, etc. give you: *The restaurant's food was good, but the service was awful. The waiter took a long time to take our*

S

order. | *Call the store's customer service department if you have any problems with your new washing machine.*
2 the work that you do for a person or organization over a long period of time: *He retired after 20 years of service in the army.*
3 a business that provides help or does jobs for people rather than producing things: *Their delivery service brings the groceries to your door.*
4 a formal religious ceremony: *The funeral service was held at his local church.*
5 a regular examination of a car or machine to make sure that it keeps working correctly: *The car needs a service every 10,000 miles.*

service² *verb*
to look at a machine, car, etc. and repair it if necessary: *A mechanic should service your car regularly.*

S

ˈservice ˌstation *noun*
another word for a GAS STATION

ses·sion /ˈseʃən/ *noun*
1 a period of time when people work or do a particular activity: *a computer training session*
2 a formal meeting or group of meetings of a court of law or government organization: *The court is now in session* (=the meeting of the court is happening now).

set¹ /set/ *verb* **set, setting**
1 to put something down somewhere carefully: *Just set that bag of groceries down on the table.*
2 if a movie, story, etc. is set in a place or at a particular time, the events takes place there or at that time: *Science fiction movies are usually set in the future.*
3 to decide and show how something should be done so that other people can continue doing it that way: *Try to set an example for your children by being polite.*
4 to do something to the controls on a clock or a machine so that it will do something at a particular time: *I set my alarm for 6:30 every day.*
5 set something on fire *also* **set fire to something** = to make something start burning: *The angry crowd set the building on fire.*
6 set the table = to put knives, forks, etc. on a table so that you can eat a meal: *Help me set the table – dinner's almost ready.*
7 when the sun or moon sets, it moves lower in the sky and disappears: *The sun sets about 7:00 this time of year.* ANTONYM **rise**
8 set someone or something free = to let a person or animal go free: *The army set some of the prisoners free.*
9 if a substance sets, it becomes hard: *Concrete will usually set in less than two hours.*

PHRASAL VERBS

set something off
to make something start happening or doing something: *When he hit the car, he set off the car alarm.*

set something up
1 to build or put something somewhere in order to prepare for something: *It took us two hours to set up all of the equipment before the dance.*
2 to start a company or organization: *His parents set up a small business that became very successful.*

set² *noun*
1 a group of similar things that belong together: *a new set of dishes, with flowers on the plates, bowls, and cups* | *a chess set*
2 a television: *a TV set*
3 a place where a movie or television program is filmed: *The two actors met on the set of their last movie.*
4 one part of a game such as tennis or VOLLEYBALL

set³ *adjective*
1 a set time, amount, price, etc. is fixed and is never changed: *I pay a set amount each month to use the gym.*
2 *informal* ready for something: *I'm all set, so we can leave anytime.*

set·back /ˈsetbæk/ *noun*
a problem that stops you from making progress: *The patient suffered a major setback when he had a second heart attack.*

set·ting /ˈsetɪŋ/ *noun*
1 the place where something is or happens, and the things around it: *The house is in a beautiful mountain setting.*
2 the place or time in which the events in a book, movie, etc. happen: *Mexico is the setting for the story.*
3 the position that you move the controls to on a machine or instrument: *Turn the oven to its lowest setting.*

seventy

4 the part of a piece of jewelry that holds a stone

set·tle /ˈsetl/ *verb*
1 to end an argument or a disagreement: *Everyone wants to settle the case before it goes to court.* | *I hope they can settle their differences* (=agree to stop arguing).
2 to decide or arrange the details of something: *"Bill isn't going." "That settles it – I'm not going either* (=the information that Bill is not going helps make the decision)*."*
3 to begin to live in a place where you live for a long time: *He worked in several cities before he finally settled in Atlanta, where he has lived ever since.*
4 to move into a comfortable position: *Dave settled back on the sofa and turned on the TV.*
5 if snow, dust, etc. settles, it falls on a surface and stays there: *Dust had settled on the furniture while they were gone.*
6 if you settle a bill, account, debt, etc., you pay all the money that you owe: *Please settle your bill before leaving the hotel.*

PHRASAL VERBS

settle down
1 to become quiet and calm: *Kids, settle down and eat your dinner.*
2 to start living a quiet and calm life in one place, especially when you get married: *I think I'm ready to settle down and start a family.*

settle for something
to accept something that is less than what you wanted: *We wanted the big truck, but it was too expensive. So we settled for the smaller one.*

settle in *also* **settle into something**
to become happier in a new situation or place than you were at the beginning: *Adam seems to have settled in at his new school. He's made a few friends.*

settle on/upon something
to decide or agree on something: *We need to settle on a plan of action.*

set·tled /ˈsetld/ *adjective*
feel/be settled = to feel comfortable about living or working in a particular place: *We don't feel settled in our new house yet. We still have boxes everywhere.*

set·tle·ment /ˈsetlmənt/ *noun*
1 an official agreement or decision that ends an argument: *Steve and his ex-wife have reached a divorce settlement* (=made an agreement).
2 a group of houses and buildings where people live, in a place where no group lived before: *Scientists are studying what is left of an early Native American settlement in the hills.*

set·tler /ˈsetlɚ/ *noun*
someone who goes to live in a new place, usually where there were few people before: *The early settlers of the American West had to work very hard to stay alive.*

set·up /ˈsetʌp/ *noun*
1 a way of organizing or arranging something: *We moved all the desks to this side of the classroom – do you like the new setup?*
2 *informal* a dishonest plan that is intended to trick someone: *The phone call was part of a setup to get her out of the house, so they could steal the computer.*

sev·en /ˈsevən/ *number*
1 7: *You start the game by giving each player seven cards.*
2 7 O'CLOCK: *The movie starts at seven.*
3 seven years old: *Janis is seven already.*

sev·en·teen /ˌsevənˈtin/ *number*
1 17: *There were seventeen books in the pile.*
2 seventeen years old: *Her brother is seventeen.*
—**seventeenth** /ˌsevənˈtinθ/ *number* 17th or 1/17

sev·enth /ˈsevənθ/ *number*
1 7th
2 1/7

sev·en·ty /ˈsevənti/ *number*
1 70
2 seventy years old: *she is almost seventy*
3 the seventies a) *also* **the '70s** the years between 1970 and 1979: *My dad had really long hair in the '70s.* **b)** *also* **the 70s** the numbers between 70 and 79, especially when used for measuring temperature: *Temperatures will be in the 70s tomorrow.*
4 be in your seventies = to be aged between 70 and 79 years old: *Grandma's in her early seventies.*
—**seventieth** /ˈsevəntiɪθ/ *number* 70th or 1/70

S

sev•er /ˈsevɚ/ *verb, formal*
1 to cut through something completely: *The knife slipped as he was cutting the meat and severed his fingers.*
2 to end a relationship or agreement with someone: *The two countries have severed all ties* (=ended all types of relationships between them).

sev•eral /ˈsevrəl/ *adjective, pronoun*
a number of people or things that is more than a few, but not a lot: *I've been to Miami several times.* | *Several of my friends offered to help.*

se•vere /səˈvɪr/ *adjective*
1 very bad or serious: *I've had some severe headaches recently.* | *Severe weather, with bad storms, kept the plane from landing.*
2 very strict or extreme: *There are very severe punishments for selling drugs.*
3 not kind or friendly: *She had a severe look on her face.*
—**severity** /səˈverəti/ *noun* the state of being severe

S

se•vere•ly /səˈvɪrli/ *adverb*
very badly or very much: *Fire severely damaged the building.*

sew /soʊ/ *verb* **sewed**, **sewn** /soʊn/ or **sewed**
to use a needle and thread to make or repair clothes, or to attach something such as a button to them: *She sews some of her own clothes.* | *Can you sew a button on this shirt for me?*

sew•age /ˈsuɪdʒ/ *noun*
the used water and waste that is carried away from houses by sewers: *Sewage is treated with chemicals before it is put in the river.*

sew•er /ˈsuɚ/ *noun*
a pipe or passage under the ground that carries away used water and waste from houses, factories, etc.

sew•ing /ˈsoʊɪŋ/ *noun*
the activity of joining pieces of cloth together using a needle and thread, or attaching something to a piece of cloth using a needle and thread: *My sister is very good at sewing. She makes a lot of her own clothes.*

ˈsewing ˌmachine *noun*
a machine used for sewing pieces of cloth together

sex /seks/ Ac *noun*
1 the physical activity that people do together in order to produce babies or for pleasure: *Rosa is waiting until she is married to have sex.*
2 the condition of being male or female: *Do you want to know what the baby's sex is before it is born?*
3 one of the two groups of people or animals, male and female: *He was always shy around members of the opposite sex* (=people that are not his own sex).
—**sexuality** /ˌsekʃuˈæləti/ *noun* the things people do and feel about having sex

sex•ism /ˈsekˌsɪzəm/ Ac *noun*
unfair treatment of one sex, usually women, that comes from the belief that one sex is weaker, less intelligent, or less important than the other: *Sue believed that her boss's sexism kept her from getting a better job.*
→ See Thesaurus box at **prejudice**

sex•u•al /ˈsekʃuəl/ Ac *adjective*
relating to sex: *They are too young to be having a sexual relationship.*
—**sexually** *adverb*

ˌsexual ˈharassment *noun*
sexual remarks, looks, or touching done to someone who does not want it

ˌsexual ˈintercourse *noun, formal*
the physical act of sex between two people

sex•y /ˈseksi/ *adjective* **sexier**, **sexiest**
sexually exciting or attractive: *She was wearing a sexy miniskirt.*

Sgt.
the written abbreviation of SERGEANT

shab•by /ˈʃæbi/ *adjective*
1 shabby clothes, places, or objects are old and in bad condition: *They lived in a shabby apartment that needed painting and new carpet.*
2 unfair or wrong: *I don't deserve this kind of shabby treatment.*
—**shabbily** *adverb*

shack /ʃæk/ *noun*
a small building that has not been built very well: *The old man lived in a shack made out of scraps of wood and metal.*

shack•le[1] /ˈʃækəl/ *noun*
one of a pair of metal rings joined by a chain, that is used for keeping a prisoner's hands

or feet together: *The prisoner came to court with shackles on his ankles.*

shackle[2] *verb*
to put shackles on someone: *Guards shackled the prisoners and took them away.*

shade[1] /ʃeɪd/ *noun*

1 an area that is cooler and darker because the light of the sun cannot reach it: *We sat in the shade under a tree.*
2 a particular form of a color: *I like this dark shade of red better than this bright one.*
3 a cover for a window that blocks light: *The sun's in my eyes. Could you pull the shades* (=close them).
4 shades *informal* = another word for SUNGLASSES

shade[2] *verb*
to protect something from direct light or heat: *She used her hand to shade her eyes from the sun.*

shad•ow[1] /ˈʃædoʊ/ *noun*

1 a dark shape or area that is caused when someone or something blocks the light: *We stood in the shadow of the building to cool down a little.*
2 without/beyond a shadow of a doubt = without any doubt at all: *The new evidence proved he was guilty beyond a shadow of a doubt.*

shadow[2] *verb*
to follow someone in order to watch what they are doing: *Two police officers shadowed him when he came out of the casino.*

shad•ow•y /ˈʃædoʊi/ *adjective*
mysterious and secret: *He lived in the shadowy world of terrorists.*

shad•y /ˈʃeɪdi/ *adjective*
1 protected from the sun: *Let's find a nice shady spot under the trees for our picnic.*
2 *informal* not honest or legal: *I don't want to be involved in any shady business deals.*

shaft /ʃæft/ *noun*
1 a long narrow passage that goes up through a building or down into the ground: *an elevator shaft*
2 a shaft of light/sunlight *formal* = a narrow beam of light
3 a long thin part of a tool, SPEAR, etc. that does not include the end: *The shaft of the spear is made of wood.*

shake[1] /ʃeɪk/ *verb* **shook** /ʃʊk/ **shaken** /ˈʃeɪkən/ **shaking**
1 to move up and down or from side to side with quick movements: *She was so cold her whole body started to shake.* | *Shake the juice before you pour it.*
2 shake your head = to move your head from side to side as a way of saying no: *"I can't do it," Bill said, shaking his head.*
3 shake someone's hand *also* **shake hands (with someone)** = to hold someone's hand in your hand and move it up and down, as a greeting or a sign that you have agreed on something: *Ron introduced the two women, and they shook hands.*
4 if your voice shakes, it sounds unsteady, because you are upset, frightened, nervous, or angry: *Mom's voice started to shake with anger.*
5 to make someone feel less confident or sure about something: *Losing the first match has really shaken her confidence.*

PHRASAL VERB
shake up
1 shake someone up = if an unpleasant experience shakes someone up, he or she is shocked or upset by it: *The accident really shook her up.*
2 shake something up = to make changes to an organization, country, etc. to make it more effective: *The new manager has promised to shake up the department.*

shake[2] *noun*
1 an act of shaking: *Give the juice a shake before you pour it.*
2 a MILKSHAKE: *a hamburger and a chocolate shake*

shak•en /ˈʃeɪkən/ *adjective*
be/look/feel shaken = to be frightened, shocked, or upset: *Mark looked shaken as*

he put down the phone. "Dad's been in an accident," he said.

shake•up /ˈʃeɪk-ʌp/ *noun*
a process in which an organization, company, etc. makes a lot of changes in a short time in order to be more effective: *A few employees lost their jobs in the department shakeup.*

shak•y /ˈʃeɪki/ *adjective*
1 weak and unsteady because of illness, old age, or shock: *I was sick yesterday, and I still felt shaky when I got up this morning.*
2 not very good and likely to fail or be unsuccessful: *I was late for the interview, so things got off to a shaky start* (=they started badly).

S

shall /ʃəl; *strong* ʃæl/ *modal verb, formal*
1 shall I/we...? = used to suggest something, offer help, or ask someone what to do: *Shall I turn on the air conditioner?*
2 used in official documents to state an order, law, promise, etc.: *No changes shall be made without written permission.*

shal•low /ˈʃæloʊ/ *adjective*
1 measuring only a short distance from the top to the bottom: *You have to stay in the shallow end of the pool until you can swim better.* ANTONYM **deep**
➔ See picture at **deep**[1]
2 not interested in important or serious matters: *She's very shallow and only cares about money.* ANTONYM **deep**

sham /ʃæm/ *noun*
something that tricks people by seeming good, real, or true, when it is not: *Our marriage is a sham – he doesn't really love me.*

shame /ʃeɪm/ *noun*
1 used when you feel disappointed because you wish a situation had happened in a different way: *It's a shame (that) you couldn't come to the wedding.*
2 the feeling of being guilty or embarrassed that you have after doing something that is wrong: *She felt a deep sense of shame for stealing from her mother.*
3 Shame on you! *spoken* = you use this to tell someone that he or she should feel ashamed of something that he or she has done: *Shame on you, Jim. You know you're not supposed to use my car without asking.*
4 a loss of respect or honor: *His behavior brought shame on the whole family.*
—**shame** *verb* to make someone feel ashamed: *It shamed her to admit that she had lied.*

WORD FAMILY look at the words:
➔ **shame** *noun*
➔ **ashamed** *adjective*
➔ **shameful** *adjective*

shame•ful /ˈʃeɪmfəl/ *adjective*
so bad that someone should be ashamed: *It's shameful that they leave their dogs outside in the cold.*
—**shamefully** *adverb*

sham•poo /ʃæmˈpu/ *noun*
a liquid soap used for washing your hair
—**shampoo** *verb* to wash your hair with a liquid soap
➔ See picture on page A11

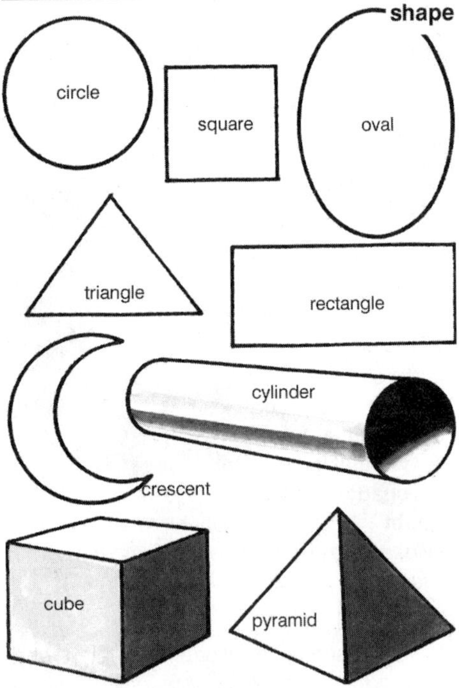

shape[1] /ʃeɪp/ *noun*
1 the outer form of something: *She made him a cake in the shape of a football.* | *His old hat had completely lost its shape.*
2 in good/bad/poor shape = in good, bad, etc. condition or health: *The old car's still in good shape.*
3 in shape/out of shape = used in order to

say that someone's body and muscles are healthy and strong or not healthy and strong: *I'm trying to get in shape by going to the gym more often.*

4 take shape = if an idea or plan takes shape, you begin to develop it into something clear and definite: *Plans for the party began to take shape; we decided where it would be and what kind of music we would play.*

5 a person or thing that you cannot see clearly enough to recognize: *A dark shape moved through the fog in front of them.*

shape[2] *verb*

1 to influence the way something develops or changes: *His mother's early death shaped the rest of his life.*

2 to make something have a particular shape: *Shape the dough into small balls.*

PHRASAL VERB

shape up *informal*

to improve your behavior or work: *You better shape up, Greg, or I'll have to call your parents.*

share[1] /ʃer/ *verb*

1 to have or use something with someone else: *There's only one book – we'll have to share.* | *I shared an apartment with my cousin for two years.*

2 to let someone have or use something that belongs to you: *My sister doesn't like to share her toys with me.*

3 to be responsible for something along with someone else: *We agreed to share the cost of the trip.*

4 to have the same interest, opinion, etc. as someone else: *My wife and I get along well because we share the same ideas about the world.*

5 to tell someone else about an idea, secret, problem, etc.: *I was afraid to share some of my ideas with the rest of the class.*

share[2] *noun*

1 the part of something that you own, deserve, or are responsible for: *I paid my share of the bill and left.* | *You'll all get your fair share of the money.*

2 one of the equal parts into which the OWNERSHIP of a company is divided: *He sold 500 shares in the company.*

share•hold•er /ˈʃerˌhoʊldɚ/ *noun*

someone who owns STOCK in a company: *a meeting of company shareholders*

shark /ʃɑrk/ *noun*

a large ocean fish with very sharp teeth

shark

sharp /ʃɑrp/ *adjective*

1 with a very thin edge or point that can cut things easily: *You need a sharp knife to cut the meat.* ANTONYM **dull**

2 a sharp feeling is sudden and very bad: *I had a sudden sharp pain in my chest.*

3 changing or turning suddenly and to a great degree: *Slow down. There's a sharp turn in the road ahead.* | *a sharp increase in prices*

4 intelligent and able to notice and understand things quickly: *You won't be able to fool her – she's very sharp.*

5 if an image or picture is sharp, you can see all the details very clearly: *The picture on the TV wasn't very sharp and it was hard to see who the people were.*

6 attractive and STYLISH: *He always has great looking clothes – he's a very sharp dresser.*

7 F/C/D, etc. sharp = a musical note that is a half STEP higher than the note F, C, D, etc., and is shown by the sign # ANTONYM **flat**

—**sharply** *adverb*

—**sharpness** *noun*

sharp•en /ˈʃɑrpən/ *verb*

to make something sharper, or become sharper: *Can you sharpen these pencils for me?*

sharp•en•er /ˈʃɑrpənɚ/ *noun*

a tool or machine that makes pencils, knives, etc. sharp

sharp•ly /ˈʃɑrpli/ *adverb*

changing suddenly: *Prices have risen sharply.*

shat•ter /ˈʃætɚ/ *verb*

1 to break suddenly into very small pieces: *The plate hit the floor and shattered into tiny pieces.*

2 to completely destroy someone's hopes,

S

beliefs, or confidence: *The accident shattered her dreams of becoming a professional athlete.*
→ See Thesaurus box at **break**[1]

shave[1] /ʃeɪv/ *verb*
to cut off hair very close to the skin using a RAZOR: *Aren't you going to shave before you go to work? | She shaves her legs once a week.*

shave[2] *noun*
an act of shaving: *He rubbed his chin and said, "I need a shave."*

shav·er /ˈʃeɪvɚ/ *noun*
a tool used for shaving: *My husband uses an electric shaver.*

ˈshaving ˌcream *noun*
a special thick substance that you put on your skin to make shaving easier
→ See picture on page A11

S

shawl /ʃɔl/ *noun*
a piece of cloth that someone wears around the shoulders or head: *She wrapped her wool shawl around her.*

she /ʃi/ *pronoun*
a female person or animal who has been mentioned or is known about: *"Where's Kate?" "She went inside."*

shear /ʃɪr/ *verb* **sheared**, **sheared** or **shorn** /ʃɔrn/
to cut the wool off a sheep: *How long does it take to shear a sheep?*

PHRASAL VERB
shear something off
to cut or separate something from something else: *The tornado sheared off part of the roof.*

shears /ʃɪrz/ *noun*
a tool like a large pair of scissors: *a pair of garden shears for trimming bushes*

she'd /ʃid/
1 the short form of "she had": *She knew she'd seen the man before.*
2 the short form of "she would": *She said she'd like to come.*

shed[1] /ʃed/ *noun*
a small building used especially for storing things: *The tool shed has his saws, hammers, and things in it.*

shed[2] *verb* **shed**
1 if a plant sheds its leaves or an animal sheds its hair or skin, they fall off as part of a natural process: *Snakes regularly shed their skin.*
2 shed light on something = to make something easier to understand: *The new research sheds light on the causes of the disease.*
3 shed tears *formal* = to cry: *Members of the dead man's family shed tears and hugged.*

sheep /ʃip/ *noun* plural **sheep**
a farm animal that is kept for its wool and its meat

sheep·ish /ˈʃipɪʃ/ *adjective*
embarrassed because you have done something silly or wrong: *Al looked sheepish when he told us he still hadn't finished the work.*
—**sheepishly** *adverb*

sheer /ʃɪr/ *adjective*
1 sheer joy/luck/bliss, etc. = complete or total joy, luck, etc.: *It was sheer luck that we saw each other at the airport.*
2 the sheer size/weight/numbers, etc. = used in order to emphasize that something is very big, heavy, etc.: *The sheer size of the building impressed us. It was at least 70 stories tall.*
3 sheer material is fine or thin, so that you can almost see through it: *The sheer curtains did not keep out much sunlight.*

sheet /ʃit/ *noun*
1 a large piece of thin cloth that you put on a bed to lie on or under: *You can sleep in my bed, but let me change the sheets* (=put clean sheets on the bed) *first.*
2 a thin flat piece of something such as paper, metal, or glass: *Can I borrow a sheet of paper to write this down on?*
3 a large flat area of something such as ice or water that is spread over a surface: *The road was covered with a sheet of ice, so driving was very dangerous.*
→ See picture on page A10

shelf /ʃelf/ *noun* plural **shelves** /ʃelvz/
a long flat board for putting things on, that is attached to a wall or is part of a piece of furniture: *Put the vase on the top shelf of the bookcase where the kids can't reach it.*
→ See picture on page A11

she'll /ʃil/
the short form of "she will": *She says she'll be here at 6.*

shell¹ /ʃel/ *noun*

1 the hard outer part that protects nuts, eggs, seeds, and some types of animals: *A turtle can pull its head inside its shell to protect itself.* | *We took the peanut shells off and ate the peanuts.*

2 a metal tube containing a bullet and an explosive substance, which is fired from a gun: *Police found three empty shells where the shooting happened.*

shell² *verb*

to take the hard outer part off nuts, eggs, seeds, etc. in order to eat them: *Mom was in the kitchen, shelling peas.*

shell·fish /ˈʃelˌfɪʃ/ *noun* plural **shellfish**

a small sea or water animal that has a shell, or this animal eaten as a food: *Crabs and shrimp are shellfish.*

shel·ter¹ /ˈʃeltɚ/ *noun*

1 protection from danger or the weather: *They took shelter from the storm under a big tree.*

2 a place where people or animals can go if they have no home or are in danger from someone who treats them badly: *He lived in homeless shelters for a few years until he found a job and an apartment.*

shelter² *verb*

to protect someone or something from danger or the weather: *A row of trees sheltered the house from the wind.*

➔ See Thesaurus box at **protect**

shelve /ʃelv/ *verb*

to decide not to continue with a plan, although you might continue with it later: *Plans to build the stadium have been shelved until more money can be found.*

shep·herd /ˈʃepɚd/ *noun*

someone whose job is to take care of sheep

sher·bet /ˈʃɚbət/ *noun*

a frozen sweet food made from water, fruit, sugar, and milk

sher·iff /ˈʃerɪf/ *noun*

a chief police officer in a COUNTY who is elected

she's /ʃiz/

1 the short form of "she is": *She's my English teacher.*

2 the short form of "she has": *She's already seen the movie twice.*

shield¹ /ʃild/ *noun*

1 something that protects someone or something from being hurt or damaged: *The animal's thick fur is a shield against the cold.*

2 a broad piece of metal or leather used in past times by soldiers to protect themselves in battle: *He blocked the other soldier's sword with his shield.*

shield² *verb*

to protect someone or something from being hurt, damaged, or upset: *Parents cannot shield their children from every danger.*

➔ See Thesaurus box at **protect**

shift¹ /ʃɪft/ Ac *verb*

1 to move from one place or position to another: *The wind shifted from the west to the east.*

2 to change the GEARs when you are driving: *When you slow down, you need to shift into a lower gear.*

3 to change a situation, opinion, attitude, etc.: *Public support has shifted away from the president's plan.*

shift² *noun*

1 one of the periods during each day and night when workers in a factory, hospital, etc. are at work: *I don't like to work the night shift – I can't stay awake.*

2 a change in the way most people think about something, or in the way something is done: *There has been a big shift in attitudes toward women's roles in the past 50 years. Women now have many more jobs that they can do, rather than simply working in the house.*

➔ **gear shift**

shim·mer /ˈʃɪmɚ/ *verb*

to shine with a soft light that seems to shake slightly: *The lake shimmered in the moonlight.*

—**shimmer** *noun*

➔ See Thesaurus box at **shine¹**

shin /ʃɪn/ *noun*

the front part of your leg between your knee and your foot

➔ See picture on page A2

shine /ʃaɪn/ *verb* **shone** /ʃoʊn/ **shining**

1 to produce light: *The sun was shining brightly.*

S

THESAURUS: shine

flash to shine brightly for a very short time: *Lightning flashed across the sky.*

flicker to shine with a light that is not steady: *The wind made the fire flicker.*

twinkle to shine in the dark with a light that keeps changing from bright to less bright: *stars twinkling in the sky*

glow to shine with a warm soft light: *I could see a lamp glowing in the window.*

sparkle to shine with many small bright points of light: *The glasses were so clean they sparkled.*

shimmer to shine with a soft light that seems to shake slightly: *The lake shimmered in the moonlight.*

glitter to shine brightly with a lot of small flashes of light: *Her jewelry glittered in the sun.*

S

2 **shined** or **shone** to point a light in a particular direction: *Don't shine the flashlight in my eyes*

3 **shined** to make something bright by rubbing it: *I need to shine my shoes before the party.*

shin•gle /ˈʃɪŋgəl/ *noun*
one of many thin pieces of wood or other material used for covering a roof or a wall

shin•y /ˈʃaɪni/ *adjective* **shinier**, **shiniest**
bright and smooth looking: *The car was clean and shiny.*

ship¹ /ʃɪp/ *noun*
1 a large boat used for carrying people and things on the ocean: *The ship was sailing to the Bahamas.* | *Supplies came by ship.*
2 a space vehicle: *The ship went around the moon but did not land.*
➔ See picture on page A26

ship² *verb* **shipped**, **shipping**
to send or deliver goods to customers: *Your order will be shipped to you the next day.*

PHRASAL VERB

ship out
to leave on a ship: *The sailors are going to ship out tomorrow morning.*

ship•ment /ˈʃɪpmənt/ *noun*
1 an amount of goods that are being delivered: *We received a shipment of art supplies this morning.*
2 an act of sending or delivering goods: *The books are packed and ready for shipment to the customer.*

ship•ping /ˈʃɪpɪŋ/ *noun*
1 the activity or cost of sending or delivering goods: *There is no charge for shipping on orders over $100.*
2 the business of carrying goods in ships: *The canal has been closed to shipping, so no ships will go through until it reopens.*

ship•wreck /ˈʃɪp-rek/ *noun*
an accident in which a ship is destroyed: *Luckily, nobody died in the shipwreck.*

shirt /ʃɚt/ *noun*
a piece of clothing that covers the upper part of your body: *He was wearing a clean white shirt and a tie.*
➔ See picture on page A6

shiv•er /ˈʃɪvɚ/ *verb*
to shake slightly because you are cold or frightened: *You're shivering – come sit by the fire.*

shoal /ʃoʊl/ *noun*
1 a large group of fish that swim together: *a shoal of tuna*
2 a small hill of sand just below the surface of water that is dangerous for boats

shock¹ /ʃɑk/ *noun*
1 an unexpected and unpleasant event or piece of news that makes you extremely upset: *It was a big shock to everyone when Chuck died suddenly.*
2 the feeling of surprise you have when something very bad happens that you do not expect: *I was in shock when I realized that my boyfriend was still seeing his old girlfriend.*
3 a medical condition that makes someone very weak and unable to think clearly because they have been injured or have been in a very dangerous or frightening situation: *After the bus crashed, many people were suffering from shock.*
4 a sudden painful feeling caused by a flow of electricity passing through your body: *Ow! The light switch gave me a shock.*

shock² *verb*
1 to make someone feel very surprised and upset: *Mrs. Worth's decision to leave shocked the whole school. No one expected it.*

2 to give someone an electric shock: *Doctors shocked him to get his heart beating again.*
—**shocked** *adjective*: *We were shocked at how poor the people were.*

shock•ing /ˈʃɑkɪŋ/ *adjective*
very surprising, upsetting, or offensive: *The pictures of the dead soldiers were shocking.*

shoe /ʃu/ *noun*
1 something that you wear to cover your feet, that is made of leather or some other strong material: *Billy needs a new pair of shoes for school.* | *high-heeled shoes*
2 be in someone's shoes = to be in the situation that someone else is in: *She's in so much trouble – I wouldn't want to be in her shoes.*

shoe•lace /ˈʃuleɪs/ *noun*
a thin piece of string or leather that you use to tie your shoes: *Your shoelaces are untied.*
SYNONYM **lace**

shone /ʃoʊn/ *verb*
a past tense and past participle of SHINE

shook /ʃʊk/ *verb*
the past tense of SHAKE

shoot¹ /ʃut/ *verb* **shot** /ʃɑt/
1 to make a bullet come out of a gun: *Stop or I'll shoot!* | *He pulled out a gun and shot her in the leg.* | *They shot at the deer but it ran away.*
2 to move quickly in a particular direction: *The cat shot across the yard and into the house.*
3 to throw, kick, or hit a ball toward the place where you can make points in a sport: *He shot the ball at the basket and scored!*
4 to take photographs or make a movie: *The movie was shot in New Zealand.*

PHRASAL VERB
shoot up
to quickly increase in number, size, or amount: *Prices shot up by 60%.*

shoot² *noun*
a new part of a plant: *The first shoots of the flowers were just coming up out of the ground.*

shoot³
you say this when you are slightly annoyed because of something you have done: *Shoot! I forgot to call Chris about the party.*

shoot•ing /ˈʃutɪŋ/ *noun*
a situation in which someone is killed or injured by a gun: *There have been three shootings downtown this week, and two men have died.*

shop¹ /ʃɑp/ *noun*
1 a small store that sells only a particular type of goods: *a card shop*
2 a place or business where things are made or repaired: *The car is in the repair shop for a week.*

shop² *verb* **shopped, shopping**
to go to one or more stores to buy things: *We shopped all day for Christmas presents.*

PHRASAL VERB
shop around
to compare the price and quality of different things before you decide which to buy: *It's a good idea to shop around for the best deal when you're buying a computer.*

shop•lift•ing /ˈʃɑpˌlɪftɪŋ/ *noun*
the crime of stealing things from a store: *Dina was arrested for shoplifting. A store detective caught her taking a sweater.*
—**shoplifter** *noun* someone who shoplifts: *The police arrested two shoplifters in the store.*
→ See Thesaurus box at **crime**

shop•per /ˈʃɑpɚ/ *noun*
someone who is shopping: *The sidewalks were full of Christmas shoppers.*

shop•ping /ˈʃɑpɪŋ/ *noun*
the activity of going to stores to buy things: *Let's go shopping at the mall this afternoon.* | *I need to do some grocery shopping this weekend.*

ˈshopping ˌcenter *noun*
a group of stores built together in one area

S

ˈshopping mall *noun*
another word for a MALL

shore /ʃɔr/ *noun*
the land along the edge of a large area of water: *The boat sank a few miles from shore.* | *the shores of Lake Michigan*

THESAURUS: shore

coast the land next to the ocean: *There are many small islands off the coast of Florida.*

beach an area of sand or small stones at the edge of an ocean or lake: *We spent the day at the beach.*

seashore the area of land next to the ocean: *She was looking for shells at the seashore.*

bank the land along the edge of a river: *the banks of the Mississippi river*

S

shore•line /ˈʃɔrlaɪn/ *noun*
the edge of a large area of water: *We had a cabin on the shoreline of Lake Michigan.*

short /ʃɔrt/ *adjective*
1 not very long in length or distance: *Short hair is a lot easier to take care of.* | *a short skirt* | *The store is only a short distance away.* ANTONYM **long**
2 happening for only a little time or for less time than usual: *a short meeting* | *She worked here for only a short time.* ANTONYM **long**
3 not very tall: *Sarah is too short to reach the shelf.* ANTONYM **tall**
4 not using many letters, words, or pages: *He left a short note to tell us where he was.* ANTONYM **long**
5 in the short run/term = during a short period of time after the present: *They may make a little money in the short run, but over time the business will fail.*
6 short of breath = unable to breathe easily: *Dad was short of breath after climbing the stairs.*
—**shortness** *noun*

short•age /ˈʃɔrtɪdʒ/ *noun*
a situation in which there is not enough of something that people need: *After the hurricane, there was a shortage of medicine, and it took time to get supplies where they were needed.*

ˌshort ˈcircuit *noun*
a bad electrical connection that makes a machine stop working correctly
—**short circuit** *verb*

short•com•ing /ˈʃɔrtˌkʌmɪŋ/ *noun*
a fault in someone or something, that makes him, her, or it less effective: *The accident showed some of the shortcomings of our safety rules.*

short•cut /ˈʃɔrtkʌt/ *noun*
1 a quicker more direct way of going somewhere: *We took a shortcut across the field, rather than going around it.*
2 a quicker way of doing something: *There aren't really any shortcuts to learning English.*

short•en /ˈʃɔrtn/ *verb*
to become shorter: *These pants are too long. How much will it cost to shorten them?* | *In the fall the days begin to shorten.* ANTONYM **lengthen**

short•fall /ˈʃɔrtfɔl/ *noun*
the difference between the amount you have and the amount you need or expect: *The city needs $1 million to pay for shortfalls in the budget.*

short•hand /ˈʃɔrthænd/ *noun*
a fast way of writing using special signs and short forms of words: *She took notes in shorthand, and typed them up in full words after the meeting.*

ˈshort list *noun*
a list of the most appropriate people or things for a job, prize, etc., chosen from all the people or things that were first considered for it: *The book is on the short list for this year's Pulitzer Prize.*

short-lived /ˌʃɔrtˈlaɪvd/ *adjective*
existing only a short time: *Our family's problems were short-lived, because my father soon found a new job.*

short•ly /ˈʃɔrtli/ *adverb*
very soon: *I expect him to come home shortly.* | *We arrived shortly before 5:00.*

ˌshort-ˈrange *adjective*
short-range weapons are designed to travel or be used over a short distance: *short-range missiles*

shorts /ʃɔrts/ *plural noun*
pants that end at or above the knee: *It's so hot – I'm going to wear shorts.*
➔ See picture on page A6

short·sight·ed *also* **short-sighted** /ˌʃɔrtˈsaɪtɪd/ *adjective*
not considering the future effects of something: *It was very short-sighted to spend the money instead of saving it.*

ˌshort ˈstory *noun*
a short written story about imaginary events: *a book of short stories*

ˌshort-ˈterm *adjective*
continuing for only a short time into the future: *This is a short-term solution, but what will we do in the future?* ANTONYM **long-term**

short·wave /ˈʃɔrtˌweɪv/
a range of radio waves used for broadcasting around the world

shot[1] /ʃɑt/ *verb*
the past tense and past participle of SHOOT

shot[2] *noun*
1 an act of making a bullet come out of a gun: *Where were you when you heard the shot?* | *Police fired shots into the air to get the crowd's attention.*
2 an attempt to throw, kick, or hit a ball toward the place where you can make points in a sport: *He tried several times to get the ball into the basket before he made the shot* (=was successful).
3 a photograph or a view of something in a movie or television program: *I'd like to get a shot of you with your mother.*
4 *informal* an attempt to do or achieve something: *I've never snowboarded before, but I'll give it a shot.*
5 the act of putting medicine into your body using a needle: *Have you gotten a flu shot this year?*
6 a small amount of a strong alcoholic drink: *a shot of whiskey*
7 **like a shot** *informal* = very quickly: *She ran out of the house like a shot.*

shot·gun /ˈʃɑtgʌn/ *noun*
a long gun, used for shooting animals and birds

should /ʃəd; *strong* ʃʊd/ *modal verb*
1 used when giving or asking for advice or an opinion: *What classes should I take this semester?* | *They should have called the police sooner.*
2 used to say what you expect to happen or be true: *We should be done by 5:00.*

shoul·der /ˈʃoʊldɚ/ *noun*
1 one of the two parts of your body on each side of your neck above your arms: *She rested her head on his shoulder during the movie.* | *I asked what happened, but he just shrugged his shoulders* (=moved them up and down to show that he didn't know).
➔ See picture on page A2
2 an area of ground beside a road where drivers can stop their cars if they are having trouble: *He drove the car onto the shoulder to change the tire.*

ˈshoulder blade *noun*
one of the two flat bones on each side of your back
➔ See picture on page A2

should·n't /ˈʃʊdnt/ *modal verb*
the short form of "should not": *You shouldn't walk around alone at night – it's dangerous.*

should've /ˈʃʊdəv/ *modal verb*
the short form of "should have": *You should've called me – I would have helped you.*

shout[1] /ʃaʊt/ *verb*
to say something very loudly: *"Help me!" she shouted.* | *Stop shouting at me.*

THESAURUS: shout

yell to shout something very loudly: *Someone yelled at them to be quiet.*

call to shout in order to get someone's attention: *They called for help.*

scream to shout in a very loud high voice because you are angry, excited, etc.: *She burned her hand and screamed in pain.*

cry/cry out to shout something suddenly or loudly: *"There's Grandpa!" the little boy cried.*

cheer to shout to show that you like a team, performance, etc.: *The audience clapped and cheered.*

PHRASAL VERB
shout something out
to say something suddenly in a loud voice: *Don't shout out the answer – raise your hand.*

shout² *noun*
a loud call that expresses anger, excitement, etc.: *There were shouts of anger from the crowd.*

shove /ʃʌv/ *verb*
to push someone or something in a rough or careless way, using your hands or shoulders: *People were pushing and shoving so that they could see the band.*
—**shove** *noun* the act of shoving something *We gave the door a shove to open it.*
➔ See Thesaurus box at **push¹**

shov•el¹ /ˈʃʌvəl/ *noun*
a tool with a wide piece of metal at the bottom and a long handle, that you use for digging, moving snow, etc.

S

shovel² *verb*
to dig, move snow, etc. using a shovel: *Dad was outside shoveling snow from the driveway.*

show¹ /ʃoʊ/ *verb* **showed, shown** /ʃoʊn/
1 to let someone see something: *Will you show me your photos? | I showed the letter to Ruth.*
2 to tell or teach someone how to do something: *Can you show me how to make these cookies?*
3 to go with someone to a place, so that he or she knows where to go: *I'll show you the way to the cafeteria.*
4 *formal* to make something clear, by giving facts or information: *Studies show that children are spending less time outdoors than in the past.*
5 if you show what you are feeling, other people can see it easily: *Alan tried not to show his disappointment. | Her anger showed on her face.*
6 if a theater shows a movie, people can go and see it there: *The theater's showing the new James Bond movie.*

PHRASAL VERBS

show off
to try to make people admire you, in an annoying way: *The boys were showing off in front of the girls.*

show up
informal to arrive somewhere, when other people are waiting or you are late: *Paula finally showed up an hour later.*
➔ See Thesaurus box at **explain**

show² *noun*
1 a play, performance, program on television, etc.: *What's your favorite T.V. show? | The show starts at 8 p.m., and tickets are $10.*
2 an event that people go to where they can see a special group of things: *The art show has paintings, photographs, and sculptures that the students have made. | a Paris fashion show*

show biz /ˈʃoʊ bɪz/ *noun, informal*
another word for SHOW BUSINESS

ˈshow ˌbusiness *noun*
the business that makes money from movies, plays, acting, etc.: *She's always wanted to be an actress and have a career in show business.*

show•down /ˈʃoʊdaʊn/ *noun, informal*
the final argument, fight, or competition between two people or groups that have argued or competed for a long time: *The final showdown between the two armies came three months later.*

show•er /ˈʃaʊɚ/ *noun*
1 a thing that you stand under to wash your body: *Craig's in the shower right now.*
2 an act of washing your body by standing under a shower: *I usually take a shower in the morning.*
3 a short time in the day when it rains: *There were a few showers during the day.*
4 a party at which you give presents to a woman who is going to marry or have a baby: *We're having a baby shower for Karen on Friday.*
—**shower** *verb* to wash yourself by standing under a shower: *Tom showered and put on clean clothes.*
➔ See Thesaurus box at **rain¹**
➔ See picture on page A11

shown /ʃoʊn/ *verb*
the past participle of SHOW

ˈshow-off *noun, informal*
someone who tries to make other people admire him or her, in an annoying way: *Daniel's always telling us how rich his Dad is – he's such a show-off!*

show•room /ˈʃoʊrum/ *noun*
a large room where you can look at things that are for sale: *a car showroom*

show•y /ˈʃoʊi/ *adjective*
very big, bright, or expensive in a way that people notice: *She was wearing a showy diamond ring.*

shrank /ʃræŋk/ *verb*
the past tense of SHRINK

shrap•nel /ˈʃrapnəl/ *noun*
small pieces of metal from a bomb or bullet that has exploded: *The bomb exploded, and a piece of shrapnel hit his chest.*

shred /ʃred/ *noun*
a small piece that is torn or cut from something: *Michael tore the letter to shreds* (=into small pieces).

shrewd /ʃrud/ *adjective*
good at understanding situations, and knowing how to get what you want: *He was a shrewd politician who said all the right things.*
—**shrewdness** *noun* the quality of being shrewd

shriek /ʃrik/ *verb*
to shout in a high voice because you are frightened, excited, or angry: *"I can't swim," she shrieked.* SYNONYM **scream**

shrill /ʃrɪl/ *adjective*
a shrill voice, cry, etc. is high and loud in a way that sounds bad: *"There's a spider in my room," Lucy cried in a shrill voice.*

shrimp /ʃrɪmp/ *noun*
a very small sea animal with a soft shell, that you can eat

shrine /ʃraɪn/ *noun*
a holy place that people visit for religious reasons: *the shrine of Saint Nicholas*

shrink /ʃrɪŋk/ *verb* **shrank** /ʃræŋk/ **shrunk** /ʃrʌŋk/
to become smaller: *Oh no! I washed my favorite sweater, and it's shrunk.* | *In many places in the ocean, the number of fish is shrinking.*

shrink•age /ˈʃrɪŋkɪdʒ/ *noun, formal*
the act of becoming smaller: *Wash the sweater in cold water to prevent shrinkage.*

shriv•el /ˈʃrɪvəl/ *also* **shrivel up** *verb*
if something shrivels, it becomes smaller, because it is dry or old: *After a few days, the flowers shriveled up.*
—**shriveled** *adjective*: *The old man had brown, shriveled hands.*

shroud[1] /ʃraʊd/ *noun*
a cloth that you wrap around a dead person's body before burying it

shroud[2] *verb, formal*
1 be shrouded in darkness/mist/clouds, etc. = to be hidden by darkness, mist, etc.: *The tops of the mountains were shrouded in clouds.*
2 be shrouded in mystery/secrecy, etc. = if an event is shrouded in mystery, etc., people have not been able to find out anything about it: *His death was shrouded in mystery.*

shrub /ʃrʌb/ *noun*
a small bush: *The park is full of beautiful trees and shrubs.*
—**shrubbery** *noun* shrubs that are grown close together

S

shrug /ʃrʌg/ *verb* **shrugged, shrugging**
to move your shoulders up and down to show that you do not know something, or do not care about it: *I asked Dan if he knew the answer, but he just shrugged.*

shrunk /ʃrʌŋk/ *verb*
the past participle of SHRINK

shud•der /ˈʃʌdɚ/ *verb*
to shake because you are frightened, shocked, or very cold: *Liz looked at the picture of the dead man and shuddered.*

shuf•fle /ˈʃʌfəl/ *verb*
1 to walk without lifting your feet off the ground: *The old lady stood up and shuffled into the kitchen.*
2 to mix playing cards or papers into a different order: *Murphy shuffled the cards for a game of poker.*

shun /ʃʌn/ *verb* **shunned, shunning** *formal*
to avoid someone or something deliberately: *Micky was lazy, and he shunned any hard work.*

shunt /ʃʌnt/ *verb*
to move someone or something to another place or position, in a way that does not seem fair: *Some of the children were shunted aside into slower classes, even though they had been doing their work.*

shut[1] /ʃʌt/ *verb* **shut, shutting**
to close: *Could you shut the window?* | *I heard the door shut.* | *Shut your eyes and go to sleep.* ANTONYM **open**

PHRASAL VERBS

shut down

1 to stop a company, factory, etc. from working, so that it never starts working again: *A lot of factories had to shut down when the company started selling fewer cars.*

2 shut something down = to stop a computer, a program, etc. from working: *How do I shut down this computer?*

shut something off

to stop electricity, water, a machine, etc. from working: *Tom stopped the car and shut off the lights.*

shut up

informal a rude way of telling someone to stop talking: *Shut up! I'm watching TV.*

S

shut² *adjective*

closed: *Are all the windows shut?* ANTONYM **open**

shut•down /ˈʃʌtdaʊn/ *noun*

a situation in which a factory, business, etc. stops operating: *Many people were sad about the shutdown of the newspaper.*

shut•off /ˈʃʌtɔf/ *noun*

when the flow of water, gas, etc. to a place stops: *If families keep paying their bills, they won't face a shutoff of their electricity.*

shut•ter /ˈʃʌtɚ/ *noun*

1 a cover that closes over the outside of a window, usually made of wood: *In some countries, houses have shutters to keep out the heat.*

2 a part of a camera that lets in light

shut•tle /ˈʃʌtl/ *noun*

1 a SPACE SHUTTLE

2 an airplane, bus, or train that makes regular short trips between two places: *We got the shuttle from the airport to the car rental place.*

shut•tle•cock /ˈʃʌtlˌkɑk/ *noun*

another word for a BIRDIE

shy /ʃaɪ/ *adjective*

nervous about meeting people and talking to them: *His brother is shy and never says very much.* | *Don't be shy about asking questions.*

THESAURUS: shy

Shy

timid shy, and not brave or confident: *She was too timid to raise her hand in class.*

bashful shy and embarrassed, and not wanting to talk to other people very much: *Rachel blushed and gave me a bashful smile.*

reserved not liking to show or talk about your feelings or thoughts: *a quiet, reserved man*

introverted *formal* quiet and shy, and not liking to be with other people: *He was an introverted boy who didn't join in with the other children very easily.*

Not Shy

outgoing liking to meet and talk to new people: *an outgoing, popular girl*

extroverted *formal* confident, and enjoying being with other people: *an extroverted salesman*

—**shyness** *noun*: *Shyness is very common in teenagers.*

sib•ling /ˈsɪblɪŋ/ *noun*

formal a brother or sister: *Do you have any siblings?*

sick /sɪk/ *adjective*

1 having a disease or illness: *His mother's very sick – she has cancer.* | *She got sick and had to stay home from school.* ANTONYM **well**

THESAURUS: sick

not feel good/well to feel sick: *Mommy, I don't feel good.*

ill *formal* sick: *His grandmother's very ill.*

not very well not healthy: *You don't look very well.*

2 be sick = to bring food up from your stomach and out of your mouth: *Stop the car – I think I'm going to be sick.* SYNONYM **vomit**

3 feel sick = to feel that you might bring food up from your stomach and out of your mouth: *I feel sick after eating all that candy.* SYNONYM **queasy**

4 be sick of something *informal* = to be angry about something and want it to stop: *I'm sick of the way he treats me.*

5 make me sick *informal* = if something

makes you sick, it makes you feel angry because you think it is wrong: *When people tell lies, it makes me sick.*

sick•en /'sɪkən/ *verb*
to make you feel angry and shocked: *Pictures of starving people sickened the whole world.*
—**sickening** *adjective* making you feel angry, shocked, or sick: *He fell to the ground with a sickening thud.*

'sick leave *noun*
the time when you are away from work because you are sick: *I haven't taken any sick leave this year.*

sick•ness /'sɪknəs/ *noun*
the state or feeling of being sick: *The drinking water was dirty, and there was a lot of sickness.*

'sick pay *noun*
money that the person or company you work for pays you when you are sick and cannot work

side /saɪd/ *noun*
1 a part of something that is not the front, back, top, or bottom: *There's a bad scratch on the side of the car.*
2 one of the flat surfaces of something: *A cube has six sides.* | *Write your name on both sides of the paper.*
3 one of the areas of something, especially when there are only two areas: *Jim grew up on the east side of the city.* | *He was driving on the wrong side of the road.* | *the left side of the brain*
4 the part of an area that is near the edge, not in the middle: *Our teacher told us to stand at the side of the room.*
5 the part of your body from your shoulder to the top of your leg: *Turn over, and lie on your right side.*
6 one of the people, groups, countries, etc. in an argument or fight: *Neither side trusted each other, so it was hard to get them to agree on anything.* | *I wanted to hear her side of the story* (=hear what she thinks happened during the argument). | *Nancy's on our side* (=agrees with us and supports us).
7 side by side = next to each other: *The sisters were walking side by side.*

side•burns /'saɪdbɚnz/ *plural noun*
hair that grows on the sides of a man's face, in front of his ears

'side ef,fect *noun*
an effect that medicine has on your body that you did not want: *This drug may have side effects such as headaches and tiredness.*

side•walk /'saɪdwɔk/ *noun*
a path with a hard surface, that you walk on next to a street: *A couple of boys were running down the sidewalk.*

side•ways /'saɪdweɪz/ *adverb*
toward one side: *He stepped sideways to let me pass.*

siege /sidʒ/ *noun*
a situation in which an army surrounds a place, and stops food and weapons from getting to it: *The city was under siege* (=surrounded by an army).

si•es•ta /si'estə/ *noun*
a short sleep in the afternoon, especially in warm countries: *It was very hot in Spain, and so we all took a siesta.*

sigh /saɪ/ *verb*
to breathe out loudly and slowly, because you are tired, sad, etc.: *Phil read the letter slowly, and sighed. "They won't be coming to visit," he said.*
—**sigh** *noun* an act of sighing: *"We're home at last," she said with a sigh.*

sight /saɪt/ *noun*
1 the ability to see: *My sight is worse than it used to be.*
2 the act of seeing something: *A lot of people don't like the sight of blood.*
3 in sight = in the area that you can see: *There was nobody in sight.*
4 out of sight = outside the area that you can see: *I watched his car until it was out of sight.*
5 the sights = the famous buildings and places to visit in a city, area, etc.: *I was in San Francisco, and I wanted to see the sights.*

sight•see•ing /'saɪt,siɪŋ/ *noun*
the activity of visiting famous or interesting places: *On our first day in Egypt, we went sightseeing and saw the pyramids.*

sign[1] /saɪn/ *noun*
1 something that has words or a picture on it to give people information, that you see in a

S

public place: *The sign says, "No smoking."* | *It's against the law to drive through a stop sign without stopping.*

2 a picture or shape that has a particular meaning: *"$" is the dollar sign.* SYNONYM **symbol**

3 an action without words that you make in order to tell someone something: *He nodded at her as a sign that he understood.*

4 something different or unusual that shows what is starting to happen: *Her work is showing signs of improvement.*

sign² *verb*

1 to write your name, for example at the end of a letter: *Please fill out this form and sign it.*

2 to move your hands and fingers as a way of telling someone something: *She signed to us to get out of the way.*

PHRASAL VERB

sign up

to put your name on a list to show that you want to do something: *If you want to join the drama club, you need to sign up today.*

sig•nal¹ /ˈsɪgnəl/ *noun*

1 a sound or action that tells someone to do something: *He blew on a whistle to give the signal for the race to begin.*

2 a light or sound WAVE that carries information to radios, television, etc.: *The spacecraft sends signals back to Earth, with information about the planets it is near.*

signal² *verb*

to make a movement or sound that tells someone to do something: *Tom signaled with his hand to the waiter for the check.*

sig•na•ture /ˈsɪgnətʃɚ/ *noun*

your name the way you usually write it, at the end of a letter, on a check, etc.: *My father's signature was at the bottom of the page.*

sign•er /ˈsaɪnɚ/ *noun, formal*

someone who signs his or her name on something: *the signers of the Declaration of Independence*

sig•nif•i•cance /sɪgˈnɪfɪkəns/ Ac *noun, formal*

1 the importance of something: *His research was of great significance* (=was very important) *in the development of the atomic bomb.*

2 the meaning of something: *In class, we discussed the significance of the poem.*

sig•nif•i•cant /sɪgˈnɪfɪkənt/ Ac *adjective, formal*

1 important: *There have been significant changes in her behavior. She is quiet in class now and her grades have improved.* ANTONYM **insignificant**

2 a significant number or amount is fairly large: *Some meat contains a significant amount of fat.*

→ See Thesaurus box at **important**

sig•ni•fy /ˈsɪgnəˌfaɪ/ Ac *verb* **signified**, third person singular **signifies** *formal*

to mean or be a sign of something: *"X" signifies the number 10 in Roman numerals.*

ˈsign ˌlanguage *noun*

a language that uses hand movements and not words, used by people who cannot hear

sign•post /ˈsaɪnpoʊst/ *noun*

a post with a street sign on top that shows you which way to go

si•lence /ˈsaɪləns/ *noun*

1 when nobody is talking: *They drove home in silence.*

2 when there is no sound: *the silence of the night*

si•lent /ˈsaɪlənt/ *adjective*

1 not talking: *Mom fell silent* (=stopped talking), *and I knew she was upset.*

2 without any sound: *The house was dark and silent.*

sil•hou•ette /ˌsɪluˈet/ *noun, formal*

a dark figure that you see in front of a light background: *The picture was a little silhouette of a woman.*

silk /sɪlk/ *noun*

a soft cloth made from the threads that a type of CATERPILLAR produces: *a silk shirt*

silk•y /ˈsɪlki/ *adjective*

soft and smooth like silk: *Sally had silky blond hair.*

sill /sɪl/ *noun*

the narrow shelf at the bottom of a window SYNONYM **windowsill**

sil•ly /'sɪli/ *adjective* **sillier**, **silliest**
not sensible or serious: *Stop asking silly questions! Of course you can't go; the party is for grown-ups only.* | *You're being silly – you can't wear your princess dress to school.*

sil•ver /'sɪlvɚ/ *noun*
1 a shiny white metal that people use for making jewelry and other valuable things: *a necklace made of silver*
2 the color of this metal: *Her new car is silver*
—**silver** *adjective* made of silver: *a silver necklace*

ˌsilver anniˈversary *noun*
the date that is exactly 25 years after someone got married, or after another important event: *It's Mom and Dad's silver anniversary in July.*

sil•ver•ware /'sɪlvɚˌwer/ *noun*
knives, forks, and spoons that are made of silver or a similar metal: *The table looked pretty, with bright silverware.*

sim•i•lar /'sɪmələ/ Ac *adjective*
almost the same, but not exactly: *She has blond hair, similar to mine.* | *These two cheeses are similar in taste.*
—**similarly** *adverb* of a similar type, size, etc.: *All the restaurants here charge similarly high prices.*

THESAURUS: similar

like similar in some way to something else: *It tastes a little like chicken.*
alike very similar: *She and her sister look alike.*
identical exactly the same: *The two pictures were identical.*

WORD FAMILY look at the words:

→ **similar** *adjective*
→ **dissimilar** *adjective*
→ **similarly** *adverb*
→ **similarity** *noun*

sim•i•lar•i•ty /ˌsɪmə'lærəti/ Ac *noun*
plural **similarities**
something that is the same about two people or things: *There are some similarities between the two men. Both are tall, for example.*

sim•i•le /'sɪməli/ *noun, formal*
a way of describing something by comparing it to something else, using the words "like" or "as": *She looked like a movie star – to use a simile.*

sim•ple /'sɪmpəl/ *adjective*
1 easy to do or understand: *This cake is very simple to make.* SYNONYM **easy**
2 not having a lot of details or decoration: *She wore a simple white dress.*
—**simplicity** /sɪm'plɪsəti/ *noun* the quality of being simple: *I was surprised by the simplicity of the math problem.* | *the simplicity of her clothes*

WORD FAMILY look at the words:

→ **simple** *adjective*
→ **simply** *adverb*
→ **simplicity** *noun*
→ **simplify** *verb*

sim•pli•fy /'sɪmpləˌfaɪ/ *verb* **simplified**, third person singular **simplifies** *formal*
to make something easier to do or understand: *The book is really long, so the movie people had to simplify the story to make it understandable.*

sim•plis•tic /sɪm'plɪstɪk/ *adjective, formal*
dealing with a difficult subject in a way that does not include important details, so that the subject is not dealt with well: *He has a simplistic view of the problem.*

sim•ply /'sɪmpli/ *adverb*
1 only: *Don't buy it simply because it's cheap.* SYNONYM **just**
2 in a way that is easy to understand or do: *My teacher's good at explaining things simply.* | *I solved the argument fairly simply, by getting the kids to take turns using the computer.*
3 used for emphasizing what you are saying: *This homework is simply impossible.*

sim•u•late /'sɪmyəˌleɪt/ Ac *verb, formal*
to make something that seems as though it is real, although it is not: *It is possible to simulate conditions in space.*
—**simulation** /ˌsɪmyə'leɪʃən/ *noun* something that copies a real situation: *People can learn to fly a plane using a computer simulation* (=using a computer to copy what you do when you are flying).

S

si•mul•ta•ne•ous /ˌsaɪməlˈteɪniəs/ *adjective, formal*
happening at the same time: *The two explosions were almost simultaneous. The first was at 6 a.m., and the second only three seconds later.*
—**simultaneously** *adverb* at the same time: *Ginny and I started speaking simultaneously.*

sin /sɪn/ *noun*
something you do that religious rules do not allow: *Stealing is a sin.*

since /sɪns/ *preposition, conjunction, adverb*
1 from a time in the past until now: *I've been waiting for him since 2 o'clock.* | *I met Steve two years ago, and we've been together ever since.*

S

GRAMMAR: since

Since, **for**, and **ago** are all used to talk about time.

Since is used to say when something started. The exact day, date, or time comes after it: *He's been here since Sunday.* | *I've been going to school here since 2006.*

For is used to say how long something has lasted. It comes before a length of time: *My aunt has been here for three days.* | *The meeting continued for five hours.*

Ago is used to say how far back in the past something happened. It comes after a length of time: *My grandfather died two years ago.*

2 *formal* because: *I decided to walk, since it was a sunny day.* SYNONYM **as**

sin•cere /sɪnˈsɪr/ *adjective*
honest and meaning what you say: *He said he was sorry, and he seemed sincere.* ANTONYM **insincere**
—**sincerity** /sɪnˈserəti/ *noun, formal* the quality of being sincere: *She spoke with great sincerity about how the group had helped her.*

sin•cere•ly /sɪnˈsɪrli/ *adverb, formal*
1 in an honest way, and meaning what you say: *I sincerely hope that you succeed.*
2 Sincerely = something you write at the end of a formal letter, before you write your name: *Sincerely, Hilary Walsh.*

sin•ful /ˈsɪnfəl/ *adjective, formal*
behaving in a way that is wrong: *I knew that lying is sinful, but I didn't know what to do.*

sing /sɪŋ/ *verb* **sang** /sæŋ/ **sung** /sʌŋ/
to make musical sounds with your voice: *Nick played the guitar and sang a song.* | *I can hear the birds singing.*

sing•er /ˈsɪŋɚ/ *noun*
someone who sings: *He's a singer in a band.*

sin•gle¹ /ˈsɪŋgəl/ *adjective*
1 only one: *We lost the game by a single point.*
2 not married: *I'm married, but my sister's single.*
3 every single = used for emphasizing that you mean every person or thing: *I've read every single book that he has written.*
4 a single bed/a single room = a bed or room for one person only

single² *noun*
1 one song, which you can buy on a record or CD that only has two or three songs on it, or which you can DOWNLOAD: *The band's latest single sold 3 million copies.*
2 a one-dollar bill: *Do you have any singles?*
3 singles = people who are not married: *a bar for singles*

ˌsingle ˈfile *noun*
a line with one person behind the other: *Our teacher told us to walk in single file.*

sin•gu•lar /ˈsɪŋgyəlɚ/ *noun*
the singular = the form of a word for only one person or thing: *"Child" is the singular, and "children" is the plural.*

sin•is•ter /ˈsɪnɪstɚ/ *adjective, formal*
seeming bad, or intending to do bad things: *I noticed a man watching the house, which seemed a little bit sinister.*

sink¹ /sɪŋk/ *verb* **sank** /sæŋk/ or **sunk** /sʌŋk/ **sunk**
1 if a ship, boat, etc. sinks, it goes down below the surface of water: *The ship hit some rocks, and it sank.*
→ See picture at **float**
2 to move down to a lower level: *It was the evening, and the sun was slowly sinking behind the hills.*

sink² *noun*
the container in a kitchen or bathroom that you fill with water to wash dishes or your

hands: *There were some dirty dishes in the sink.*
→ See picture on page A9

sin•ner /ˈsɪnɚ/ *noun*
someone who does bad things that religious rules do not allow

sip /sɪp/ *verb* **sipped, sipping**
to drink something slowly in small amounts: *Marcia sipped her hot tea slowly.*
—**sip** *noun* a very small amount of a drink: *Can I have a sip of your Coke?*

sir /sɚ/ *noun*
1 used for speaking politely to a man: *Can I help you, sir?* | *"Have you finished your homework?" "Yes, sir."*
2 Dear Sir = used at the beginning of a formal letter to a man, if you do not know his name

si•ren /ˈsaɪrən/ *noun*
a thing on police cars, fire engines, etc. that makes a very loud warning sound: *A police car went past with its siren on.*

sir•loin /ˈsɚlɔɪn/ *also* ˌ**sirloin** ˈ**steak** *noun*
a good piece of meat from a cow

sis•ter /ˈsɪstɚ/ *noun*
1 a girl or woman who has the same parents as you: *My sister is two years older than me.* | *My little sister* (=younger sister) *is so annoying!*
2 a NUN: *Sister Frances*

ˈ**sister-in-law** *noun* plural **sisters-in-law**
1 the sister of your husband or wife
2 the wife of your brother

sit /sɪt/ *verb* **sat** /sæt/ **sitting**
1 to put your bottom on a chair or the ground, with your body upright: *I usually sit at the front of the class.*
2 if something is sitting on or in a place, that is where it is: *Your keys are sitting on the kitchen table.*
3 to BABYSIT: *I need someone to sit the kids on Saturday.*
PHRASAL VERBS
sit around
to sit or rest somewhere, and not do anything useful: *Teenagers spend a lot of time sitting around in their rooms.*
sit down
to move so that you are sitting on something, after you have been standing up: *Sam came in and sat down beside me.*
sit up
to move so that you are sitting, after you have been lying down: *She heard a noise downstairs, and she sat up in bed.*
→ See picture on page A4

sit•com /ˈsɪtkɑm/ *noun*
a funny television program that has the same people in different situations each week
→ See Thesaurus box at **television**

site /saɪt/ Ac *noun*
1 a place where something important or interesting happened: *This field is the site of a famous battle.*
2 an area where people build something: *They're building two new hotels on this site.*
3 another word for a WEBSITE
→ See Thesaurus box at **place**[1]

sit•ter /ˈsɪtɚ/ *noun*
another word for a BABYSITTER

sit•u•at•ed /ˈsɪtʃuˌeɪtɪd/ *adjective, formal*
be situated = to be in a particular place: *The college is situated outside the city.*

sit•u•a•tion /ˌsɪtʃuˈeɪʃən/ *noun*
the things that are happening at a particular time, or the things that are happening in someone's life: *The company lost a lot of money, and it was a difficult situation.* | *What would you do in that situation* (=if those things were happening to you)?

six /sɪks/ *number*
1 6: *There should be six eggs in the box.*
2 six O'CLOCK: *I get out of class at six.*
3 six years old: *We moved to Houston when I was six.*

ˈ**six-pack** *noun*
six bottles or cans of a drink, that you buy together: *a six-pack of soda*

six•teen /ˌsɪkˈstin/ *number*
1 16: *There were sixteen fish in the tank.*
2 sixteen years old: *You can drive a car once you're sixteen.*
—**sixteenth** /ˌsɪkˈstinθ/ *number* 16th or 1/16

sixth /sɪksθ/ *number*
1 6th
2 1/6

S

six·ty /ˈsɪksti/ *number*
1 60
2 sixty years old: *he is almost sixty*
3 the sixties a) *also* **the '60s** the years between 1960 and 1969 **b)** *also* **the 60s** the numbers between 60 and 69, especially when used for measuring temperature
4 be in your sixties = to be between 60 and 69 years old: *He's in his early/mid/late sixties.*
—**sixtieth** /ˈsɪkstiɪθ/ *number* 60th or 1/60

siz·a·ble *also* **sizeable** /ˈsaɪzəbəl/ *adjective, formal*
fairly large: *A sizable number of people – at least fifty – agreed to help.*

size /saɪz/ *noun*
1 how big or small something is: *Your house and mine are around the same size.*
2 a number or letter that tells you how big or small clothes are: *These jeans are too small – do you have a bigger size?* | *I wear size 10 shoes.*
3 large-sized/small-size/king-size, etc. = large, small, very big, etc. in size: *a medium-sized car* | *a queen-size bed*

S

siz·zle /ˈsɪzəl/ *verb*
to make the sound of food cooking in hot oil: *The sausages were sizzling in the pan.*
➔ See picture on page A22

skate¹ /skeɪt/ *noun*
a special boot with wheels or a blade on the bottom of it: *roller skates* (=for moving over ground) | *ice skates* (=for moving on ice)

skate² *verb*
to move on ice or over ground wearing skates: *In the winter, the lake is frozen and you can skate on it.*

skate·board /ˈskeɪtbɔrd/ *noun*
a short board with wheels under it, that you stand on to ride along the ground
—**skateboarding** *noun* the activity of riding on a skateboard: *Let's go skateboarding in the park.*

skat·ing /ˈskeɪtɪŋ/ *noun*
the activity or sport of moving over ice or over the ground wearing SKATEs: *Do you want to go skating with us?*

skel·e·ton /ˈskelətən/ *noun*
all the bones in a person or animal: *In the museum, I saw the skeleton of a dinosaur.*

skep·ti·cal /ˈskeptɪkəl/ *adjective, formal*
not believing that something is true or right: *Sometimes I'm skeptical about what I read in the newspaper. Reporters don't always get all the facts.*
—**skeptic** *noun* someone who is skeptical

sketch¹ /sketʃ/ *noun*
a quick drawing that does not have a lot of details: *I did a sketch of the bird, before it flew away.*
➔ See Thesaurus box at **picture¹**

sketch² *verb*
to draw a picture quickly and without a lot of details: *Rob quickly sketched the view from the top of the hill.*

ski¹ /ski/ *noun* plural **skis**
a long narrow piece of wood or plastic that you wear on your boots for moving easily on snow: *a pair of skis*

ski² *verb* **skied**
to move over snow on skis: *She skied down the mountain.*
—**skier** *noun* someone who skis: *He's a good skier.*

skid /skɪd/ *verb* **skidded, skidding**
if a vehicle skids, it suddenly slides sideways: *A car skidded on the ice.*
➔ See picture at **slide¹**

ski·ing /ˈskiɪŋ/ *noun*
the activity or sport of moving over snow on SKIs: *We're going skiing in the mountains.*
➔ See picture on page A24

skill /skɪl/ *noun*
an ability to do something very well, because you have learned it: *For this job, you'll need good language skills* (=the ability to speak or learn languages). | *He was proud of his skill as a basketball player.*
➔ See Thesaurus box at **ability**

skilled /skɪld/ *adjective*
having the training and ability to do a job well: *Skilled workers are able to earn more money, so it's worth taking training courses.*
ANTONYM **unskilled**

skil·let /ˈskɪlɪt/ *noun*
another word for a FRYING PAN

skill·ful /ˈskɪlfəl/ *adjective*
good at doing something: *He's a skillful photographer – even his snapshots look great.*

skim /skɪm/ *verb* **skimmed, skimming**
1 to remove oil, cream, etc. that is floating on top of a liquid: *Skim the fat off the soup.*
2 *also* **skim through** to read something very quickly: *I only had time to skim through the newspaper.*

ˈskim milk *noun*
milk without much fat in it

skin /skɪn/ *noun*
1 the outer covering of a person's or animal's body: *Maria has beautiful dark skin.* | *a purse made from snake skin*
2 the outer layer of some fruits and vegetables: *Bananas have yellow skins.*

skin•ny /ˈskɪni/ *adjective* **skinnier, skinniest**
very thin or too thin: *He was a tall, skinny kid.*
➔ See Thesaurus box at **thin**

skip /skɪp/ *verb* **skipped, skipping**
1 to not do something that you would usually do or that you should do: *I was late so I skipped breakfast.* | *Brad got in trouble for skipping school.*
2 to move forward with quick jumps from one foot to the other: *The girls were skipping down the street.*
3 to not do something, and do the next thing instead: *I skipped question four and went on to question five.*
➔ See Thesaurus box at **jump**[1]
➔ See picture on page A4

skirt /skɚt/ *noun*
a piece of clothing for a girl or woman, that hangs down from her waist and covers part of her legs: *She was wearing a short black skirt and a white top.*
➔ See picture on page A6

skull /skʌl/ *noun*
the bones of a person's or animal's head
➔ See picture on page A2

skunk /skʌŋk/ *noun*
a small black and white animal that makes a very bad smell when it is afraid

sky /skaɪ/ *noun* plural **skies**
the space above the earth where the sun, clouds, and stars are: *It was a beautiful day with a clear blue sky.* | *There were a few clouds in the sky.*

sky•div•ing /ˈskaɪˌdaɪvɪŋ/ *noun*
the sport of jumping from an airplane and falling through the sky before opening a PARACHUTE
—**skydiver** *noun* someone who does skydiving

sky•line /ˈskaɪlaɪn/ *noun*
the shape that tall buildings or hills make against the sky: *From the boat we could see the New York City skyline.*

sky•scrap•er /ˈskaɪˌskreɪpɚ/ *noun*
a very tall building in a city: *He works at the top of a 30-story skyscraper in Manhattan.*

slab /slæb/ *noun*
a thick flat piece of something: *a thick slab of bread with butter and jam on it*

slack /slæk/ *adjective*
loose and not pulled tight: *The rope was slack, and the clothes hung on it almost touched the ground.*

slacks /slæks/ *plural noun*
a pair of nice-looking pants: *Other boys wore jeans, but he looked good dressed in blue slacks, a shirt, and a sweater.*

slam /slæm/ *verb* **slammed, slamming**
1 to shut a door, lid, etc. with a loud noise: *She was angry and slammed the door as she went out.* | *The gate slammed shut in the wind.*
2 to put something somewhere quickly and with a lot of force: *He slammed his fist on the desk angrily.*
➔ See picture on page A22

slan•der /ˈslændɚ/ *noun, formal*
something bad and not true that someone says about another person: *The newspaper was guilty of slander when it said she had taken drugs, because she proved that she had not taken them.*
—**slander** *verb* to say something about someone which is bad and not true

S

slang /slæŋ/ *noun*
very informal spoken words: *"The clink" is a slang word for prison.* | *Students have their own slang, such as "mick" meaning an easy class.*
➔ See Thesaurus box at **language**

slant /slænt/ *verb*
to be at an angle, rather than straight up and down or flat: *Light from the sun slanted through the window.*
—**slant** *noun* an angle, not straight up and down or flat: *Her writing went on a slant across the page.*

slap[1] /slæp/ *verb* **slapped, slapping**
to hit someone quickly with the flat part of your hand: *She slapped his face when he was rude to her.*
➔ See Thesaurus box at **hit**[1]
➔ See picture on page A3

S

slap[2] *noun*
1 a quick hit with the flat part of your hand: *I was so angry that I felt like giving him a slap.*
2 a slap on the wrist = a punishment that is not strong enough: *He hit somebody with his car and only got a slap on the wrist!*
3 a slap in the face = something that insults you: *His statement about learning English was a slap in the face to Mexican immigrants.*

slash /slæʃ/ *verb*
1 to cut something in a very violent way: *He killed her by slashing her throat with a knife.*
2 *informal* to make something such as prices or amounts much lower: *Stores have slashed prices in their after-Christmas sales.*
➔ See Thesaurus box at **reduce**

slat /slæt/ *noun*
a thin flat piece of wood, plastic, or metal, that is part of a piece of furniture or a window BLIND: *Sunlight was coming through the slats of the blind.*

slate /sleɪt/ *verb*
be slated to do something/be slated for something = if something is slated to happen, it is planned to happen in the future: *The school was slated to be closed.*

slaugh•ter /ˈslɔtɚ/ *verb*
1 to kill a lot of people in a violent way: *Hundreds of innocent people had been slaughtered by the army.*
2 to kill an animal for food: *The cows are slaughtered for their meat.*
—**slaughter** *noun* the act of slaughtering people or animals

slave[1] /sleɪv/ *noun*
someone who belongs to another person and must work for no money: *Millions of Africans were taken to America as slaves to work in the fields.*

slave[2] *also* **slave away** *verb*
to work very hard: *I've been slaving away in the kitchen all day!*

slav•er•y /ˈsleɪvəri/ *noun*
the system of having slaves: *One of the reasons for the Civil War was to stop slavery in the Southern states.*

slea•zy /ˈslizi/ *adjective* **sleazier, sleaziest**
1 a sleazy place is dirty and not pleasant, and dishonest people go there: *a sleazy bar full of cigarette smoke*
2 not honest, and willing to do things that are not really right: *The sleazy landlord took their rent, but never fixed anything.*

sled /sled/ *noun*
something you sit or lie on to slide over snow, that children often use: *They pulled the sled back up to the top of the hill and slid down again.*

sleek /slik/ *adjective*
1 sleek hair or fur is smooth and shiny: *The cat had sleek black fur.*
2 having a modern and attractive shape: *a sleek new office building*

sleep[1] /slip/ *verb* **slept** /slept/
1 to rest by lying down with your eyes closed, and not hearing any sounds or being able to say anything to anyone: *"Did you sleep well?"* | *I couldn't sleep last night because I was so worried.*

THESAURUS: sleep

doze to sleep lightly for a short time, especially when you did not intend to: *He was dozing in front of the TV.*
doze off to fall asleep, especially when you did not intend to: *I tried to read, but I kept dozing off.*
take a nap to sleep for a short time during the day: *Young babies need to take two naps a day.*

oversleep to sleep for longer than you intended: *I overslept and was late for school.*

USAGE: sleep

Use **sleep** when you are talking about something such as how long someone sleeps, or where she or he sleeps: *Young children need to sleep for about 12 hours each night.* | *We slept on the floor.*

Do not use **sleep** to talk about starting to sleep. Use **fall asleep** or **go to sleep**: *She fell asleep in front of the TV.* | *Ben and Adam, stop talking and go to sleep!*

2 to have enough beds or room for a particular number of people: *The tent sleeps six people.*

PHRASAL VERBS

sleep over
to sleep at someone's house for a night: *Mom, can I sleep over at Ann's tonight?*

sleep through something
to continue sleeping while something noisy is happening: *How could you have slept through the earthquake?*

sleep² *noun*
1 the state of being asleep: *I didn't get much sleep last night because of the noise.* | *Ed sometimes talks in his sleep* (=while he is sleeping).
2 a period when you are sleeping: *You'll feel better after a good night's sleep* (=a night when you sleep well).
3 **go to sleep/get to sleep** = to start sleeping: *What time did you get to sleep last night?*

'sleeping bag *noun*
a large warm bag for sleeping in, especially in a tent

sleep•less /ˈsliplәs/ *adjective*
a sleepless night = a night when you cannot sleep: *He had a sleepless night worrying about the test.*

sleep•y /ˈslipi/ *adjective* **sleepier**, **sleepiest**
tired and wanting to sleep: *The warmth of the sun made him feel sleepy.*

sleet /slit/ *noun*
a mixture of rain and snow
➔ See Thesaurus box at **snow¹**, **rain¹**

sleeve /sliv/ *noun*
the part of a piece of clothing that covers your arm or part of your arm: *The shirt had short sleeves.*
➔ See picture on page A6

sleigh /sleɪ/ *noun*
a thing you sit in that has metal bars under it, which horses pull across snow: *We went for a sleigh ride.*

slen•der /ˈslendɚ/ *adjective*
thin in a way that looks good: *She is tall and slender.* SYNONYM **slim**
➔ See Thesaurus box at **thin**

slept /slept/ *verb*
the past tense and past participle of SLEEP

slice¹ /slaɪs/ *noun*
a flat piece of bread, meat, etc. that you cut from a whole thing: *He was eating a slice of bread with butter on it.* | *Cut the tomato into thick slices.*
➔ See Thesaurus box at **piece**

slice² *also* **slice up** *verb*
to cut meat, bread, etc. into thin flat pieces: *Slice the onion thinly.*
➔ See Thesaurus box at **cut¹**
➔ See picture on page A14

slick /slɪk/ *adjective*
1 good at persuading people, often in a way that does not seem honest: *A slick salesman may get you to buy things you don't really need.*
2 done with a lot of skill and good to look at: *The movie is slick and beautifully filmed.*
3 smooth and wet or shiny: *His hands were slick with sweat.* SYNONYM **slippery**

slide¹ /slaɪd/ *verb* **slid** /slɪd/
1 to move smoothly over a surface: *The kids were sliding on the ice.* | *She slid the door open.*
2 to go somewhere quietly without other people noticing: *She slid out of the house without waking anyone.*

slide² *noun*
1 something for children to play on which has a slope that they slide down
2 a photograph in a frame that you shine a light through to show a picture on a screen: *They showed us some slides of their vacation.*

S

slight /slaɪt/ *adjective*
small and not serious or important: *There's been a slight increase in prices.* | *There was a slight problem with the engine, but it was easily fixed.*

slight·ly /ˈslaɪtli/ *adverb*
a little: *She turned her head slightly.* | *We painted the room a slightly different color. It's still blue, but it's a little lighter.*

slim¹ /slɪm/ *adjective*
1 thin in a way that looks good: *His wife was tall and slim.* SYNONYM **slender**; ANTONYM **fat**
2 very small in amount: *We have only a slim chance of winning.*
➔ See Thesaurus box at **thin**

slim² *verb*
PHRASAL VERB
slim down
to become thinner by eating less and exercising more: *He had slimmed down from 194 pounds to 150 pounds.*

slime /slaɪm/ *noun*
a thick, wet substance that is not nice to touch: *She came out of the pond covered in mud and slime.*
—**slimy** *adjective* covered with slime: *The worm felt slimy.*

sling /slɪŋ/ *noun*
a piece of cloth tied around your neck to support your arm or hand when it is hurt: *Emily broke her arm and it was in a sling for six weeks.*

slip¹ /slɪp/ *verb* **slipped, slipping**
1 to accidentally slide and fall: *Be careful not to slip on the ice.*
2 to slide out of the correct position or out of your hand: *The knife slipped and cut her finger.*
3 to go somewhere without other people noticing: *I managed to slip out of the office before 5:00.*
4 to put something somewhere or give someone something quietly or secretly: *Someone slipped a note under my door.*
PHRASAL VERB
slip up
to make a mistake: *They slipped up and sent me the wrong form.*
➔ See Thesaurus box at **fall¹**
➔ See picture at **slide¹**

slip² *noun*
1 a small piece of paper: *She wrote her phone number on a slip of paper and gave it to me.*
2 a piece of underwear that a woman wears under a dress or skirt

slip·per /ˈslɪpɚ/ *noun*
a soft shoe that you wear in your house: *The floor was cold, so I put on a pair of slippers.*
➔ See picture at **shoe**

slip·per·y /ˈslɪpəri/ *adjective*
something that is slippery is difficult to walk on or hold because it is wet or covered with something such as oil or ice: *He had just washed the floor and it was slippery.*

slit¹ /slɪt/ *noun*
a narrow cut or space in something: *He looked out through a slit in the curtains.*

slit² *verb* **slit, slitting**
to make a narrow cut in something: *He slit the envelope open.*

slob /slɑb/ *noun, informal*
someone who is lazy and messy: *He was a fat slob who sat on the sofa watching TV all day.*

slo·gan /ˈsloʊgən/ *noun*
a short phrase that is easy to remember, used in advertisements and politics: *The posters against smoking had the slogan "Smokers die younger."*

slope¹ /sloʊp/ *noun*
a piece of ground or a surface that is higher at one end than the other: *People were skiing down the ski slope.*

slope² *verb*
if a surface or piece of ground slopes, it is higher at one end than the other: *The field sloped down to the lake.*

slop·py /ˈslɑpi/ *adjective*
1 not done neatly or carefully: *His handwriting is sloppy and hard to read.*
2 wet and not pleasant: *He gave her a sloppy kiss on the cheek.*
—**sloppily** *adverb*

slot /slɑt/ *noun*
a long narrow hole that you put something in: *Put the coins in the slot and pick up the candy bar at the bottom of the machine.*

ˈslot maˌchine *noun*
a machine in which you put coins so that you can play games or try to win money

slow¹ /sloʊ/ *adjective*
1 not moving quickly, not being done quickly, or not happening quickly: *The buses are slow and don't come on time.* | *There has been slow growth in the number of customers, of about 2% every three months.* | *The police were slow to respond* (=took too long to do something). ANTONYM **fast**
2 if a clock or watch is slow, it shows a time that is earlier than the true time: *My watch is a few minutes slow; it says 13:50 but the real time is 13:56.* ANTONYM **fast**
—**slowness** *noun*

slow² *verb*
PHRASAL VERB
slow down
to go less fast than before: *Slow down. You're driving too fast!*

slow·ly /ˈsloʊli/ *adverb*
at a slow speed: *He was walking slowly because his feet hurt.* ANTONYM **quickly**

slug /slʌg/ *noun*
a small creature with a soft body and no legs, that moves very slowly: *Slugs eat garden plants.*

slug·gish /ˈslʌgɪʃ/ *adjective*
less good or fast than usual: *The team's performance was sluggish. They couldn't seem to move the ball down the court quickly enough.*

slum /slʌm/ *noun*
an area of a city where the houses are in bad condition and many poor people live: *She grew up in the slums of L.A.*

slum·ber par·ty /ˈslʌmbɚ ˌpɑrti/ *noun*
a party at which a group of children sleep at one child's house

slump /slʌmp/ *verb*
1 to sit with the top part of your body leaning forward and down: *Stop slumping and sit up straight!*
2 to suddenly not do as well as before: *Car sales have slumped recently. Five percent fewer cars have been sold in March than in February.*

slur /slɚ/ *verb* **slurred, slurring**
to speak in a way that is not clear because you are drunk or sick: *After a few drinks, he started to slur his words.*

slush /slʌʃ/ *noun*
snow on the ground that has started to melt
→ See Thesaurus box at **snow¹**

S

sly /slaɪ/ *adjective* **slier** or **slyer**, **sliest** or **slyest**
good at getting what you want by tricking people or doing unfair things: *He was sly and made sure he got some of the money.*

smack /smæk/ *verb*
to hit someone or something in a way that makes a noise: *Stop it or I'll smack you!*
→ See Thesaurus box at **hit¹**

small /smɔl/ *adjective*
1 not large in size or amount: *There were only a small number of people at the party.* | *Rhode Island is the smallest state in the U.S.* | *This jacket is too small.* ANTONYM **big**

THESAURUS: small
little small in size: *a little piece of cake*
tiny very small: *a tiny baby*
minute *formal* very small: *Even in minute amounts, the chemical is very harmful.*

2 not important or easy to deal with: *We've had a few small problems with the new car.* SYNONYM **minor**; ANTONYM **big**
3 a small child is young: *She was my best friend when I was small.* SYNONYM **little**

small·pox /ˈsmɔlpɑks/ *noun*
a disease that killed a lot of people in the past: *People don't get smallpox any more, because of vaccinations* (=shots that stop diseases).

smart /smɑrt/ *adjective*
1 intelligent: *Jill's a smart kid and always gets good grades.* | *He's smart enough not to waste a good opportunity.* ANTONYM **stupid**
2 trying to seem intelligent or funny, in a way that annoys someone: *He made some smart comment about her clothes, saying that she was only dressing that way to impress the boss.*
➔ See Thesaurus box at **intelligent**

smarty-pants /ˈsmɑrti ˌpænts/ *noun, informal*
someone who tries to seem intelligent or funny in a way that you think is annoying: *OK, smarty-pants, if you know all the answers, why are you asking me?*

S

smash /smæʃ/ *verb*
1 to break into many small pieces: *The plates fell onto the floor and smashed.* | *People smashed store windows and set fire to cars.*
2 to hit something in a violent way: *Murray smashed his fist against the wall.* | *He died when his motorcycle smashed into a car.*
➔ See Thesaurus box at **break**[1]

smear[1] /smɪr/ *verb*
to spread a liquid or soft substance on something in a messy way: *She smeared the bread with jam.*

smear[2] *noun*
a dirty mark where something has been rubbed on something else: *There was a smear of blood on his cheek.*

smell[1] /smel/ *noun*
1 the quality that you recognize by using your nose: *I love the smell of fresh bread.* | *There was a strong smell of gas before the explosion.*

THESAURUS: smell

aroma *formal* a strong good smell, especially of food: *the aroma of fresh coffee*
scent a nice smell: *He could smell the scent of wood smoke.*
fragrance/perfume *formal* a nice smell, especially of flowers, plants, or trees: *the fragrance of the roses*
stink *informal* to smell very bad: *The dog really stinks.*
odor *formal* a bad smell: *The odor of yesterday's fish dinner was in the air.*

2 a bad smell: *What's that smell in the basement?*
3 the ability to notice or recognize smells: *Dogs have an excellent sense of smell.*

smell[2] /smel/ *verb*
1 to have a particular smell: *The coffee smells good.* | *This drink smells like strawberries.*
2 to have a bad smell: *His feet smelled because he'd been wearing sneakers without socks.* SYNONYM **stink**
3 to use your nose to notice something: *Come smell these roses.* | *I can smell something burning.*

smell·y /ˈsmeli/ *adjective*
having a bad smell: *smelly socks*

smile[1] /smaɪl/ *verb*
to raise the corners of your mouth because you are happy or being friendly: *Keith smiled at me.*

THESAURUS: smile

grin to smile with a very big smile: *He was grinning with excitement.*
beam to smile in a very happy way: *Jenny ran to him, beaming with pleasure.*

smile[2] *noun*
a happy expression on your face: *He had a big smile on his face so I knew he had passed his driving test.*

smog /smɑg/ *noun*
dirty air caused by smoke from cars and factories in cities

smoke[1] /smoʊk/ *noun*
the white, gray, or black gas that something produces when it burns: *cigarette smoke* | *The fire sent up a huge cloud of smoke.*

smoke[2] *verb*
1 to put a cigarette in your mouth and suck in the smoke: *I smoke but I'm trying to quit.*
2 to produce smoke: *The fire was still smoking the next morning.*

smok·er /ˈsmoʊkɚ/ *noun*
someone who smokes: *She used to be a heavy smoker* (=someone who smokes a lot).

smok·ing /ˈsmoʊkɪŋ/ *noun*
the activity of using cigarettes: *Smoking is not allowed in school.*

smok•y /ˈsmoʊki/ *adjective*
filled with smoke: *The room was smoky from all the people with cigarettes.*

smol•der /ˈsmoʊldɚ/ *verb*
to burn slowly with smoke but no flame: *The factory is still smoldering after last night's fire.*

smooth /smuð/ *adjective*
1 having an even surface, without any LUMPs or rough areas: *Babies have beautiful smooth skin.* | *Mix the butter and sugar together until it's soft and smooth.* ANTONYM **rough**
2 with no sudden movements or changes of direction: *Swing the tennis racket in one smooth movement.*
3 happening without problems: *Women are still usually responsible for the smooth running of the home.*
—**smoothness** *noun*
➔ See Thesaurus box at **flat**[1]

smooth•ly /ˈsmuðli/ *adverb*
well and without problems or difficulties: *Everything went very smoothly on our trip. We didn't have car problems and we didn't get lost.*

smoth•er /ˈsmʌðɚ/ *verb*
1 to kill someone by putting something over his or her face so that he or she cannot breathe: *He had smothered her with a pillow.*
2 to cover the whole surface of something with something else: *The cake was smothered in chocolate.*

smudge[1] /smʌdʒ/ *noun*
a dirty mark: *There was a smudge of lipstick on the cup.*
➔ See Thesaurus box at **mark**[2]

smudge[2] *verb*
if a substance such as ink or paint smudges, it becomes messy or unclear because someone has touched or rubbed it: *Oh no, I smudged my writing!* | *Your lipstick is smudged.*

smug /smʌg/ *adjective*
too happy about how smart, lucky, or good you are, in a way that annoys other people: *We were standing in the rain, and he drove past us, looking very smug about being in a nice dry car.*
—**smugly** *adverb*: *"My kids always eat healthy food," she said smugly.*

smug•gle /ˈsmʌgəl/ *verb*
to take someone or something illegally from one place to another: *They were trying to smuggle guns into the country.*
—**smuggling** *noun* the activity of taking something illegally from one place to another: *He was jailed for drug smuggling.*

smug•gler /ˈsmʌglɚ/ *noun*
someone who takes something illegally from one place to another: *Police caught the drug smugglers.*

snack[1] /snæk/ *noun*
something that you eat between meals: *It's bad to eat too much candy and other sugary snacks.*

snack[2] *verb*
to eat food between meals: *You'll get fat if you snack on cookies all the time.*

ˈsnack bar *noun*
a place where you can buy drinks, snacks, and small meals: *The hospital has a snack bar which serves coffee and sandwiches.*

snag /snæg/ *noun, informal*
a small problem: *The job pays well. The only snag is that I don't finish until 2 in the morning.*

snail /sneɪl/ *noun*
a small soft creature with no legs, that moves very slowly and has a hard shell on its back

ˈsnail mail *noun*
the system of sending letters through the mail, rather than by email: *Please give your email and snail mail addresses.*

snake /sneɪk/ *noun*
a long thin animal with no legs, that slides along the ground: *Watch out for snakes; if they bite you, you could die.*

snap[1] /snæp/ *verb* **snapped, snapping**
1 to break with a short loud noise: *Dry branches snapped under their feet.* | *He snapped the chalk in two* (=into two pieces).
2 to move into a particular position with a short loud noise: *The Lego pieces just snap together like this.*
3 to suddenly speak to someone in an angry way: *"Don't be stupid," she snapped.*
4 snap your fingers = to move two of your

S

fingers together to make a noise: *"It could happen this fast," Jake said, snapping his fingers.*
→ See Thesaurus box at **break**[1]

snap[2] *noun*
1 a sudden short loud noise of something breaking: *I heard the snap of a twig behind me.*
→ See picture on page A22
2 cold snap = a time when the weather suddenly becomes very cold: *There was an early cold snap and snow in December.*

snap•shot /ˈsnæpʃɑt/ *noun*
a photograph that you take quickly: *He showed us some snapshots of his kids.*
→ See Thesaurus box at **picture**[1]

S

snare /sner/ *noun*
a trap for catching an animal
—**snare** *verb* to catch an animal using a snare

snarl /snɑrl/ *verb*
1 to say something in an angry way: *"Shut up!" he snarled.*
2 if an animal snarls, it makes a low angry sound and shows its teeth: *The two dogs snarled at each other and started fighting.*

snatch[1] /snætʃ/ *verb*
to take something from someone very quickly: *I saw two kids snatch her purse and run off.* SYNONYM **grab**

snatch[2] *noun*
a snatch of conversation/song, etc. = a short part of something that you hear: *I could hear snatches of conversation from across the room.*

sneak /snik/ *verb* **sneaked** or **snuck** /snʌk/
to go somewhere quietly because you do not want people to see or hear you: *She snuck out of the house once her parents were asleep.*

sneak•er /ˈsnikɚ/ *noun*
a soft shoe that you wear for playing sports: *She was wearing a pair of white sneakers.*
→ See picture at **shoe**[1]

sneak•y /ˈsniki/ *adjective*
doing things secretly in a way that is not fair or honest: *He's kind of sneaky – I mean, he acts really nice, then he goes and tells his friends all the things you said.*

sneer /snɪr/ *verb*
to smile or speak in a way that is not nice and shows you have no respect for someone: *He sneered at her taste in music, saying that country music was silly.*

sneeze /sniz/ *verb*
to make air suddenly come out of your nose and mouth, for example because you have a cold: *All the dust in the air made her sneeze.*
—**sneeze** *noun* the act or sound of sneezing

snick•er /ˈsnɪkɚ/ *verb*
to laugh quietly in a way that is not nice: *The teacher tripped, and some of the students snickered.*
→ See Thesaurus box at **laugh**[1]

sniff /snɪf/ *verb*
1 to breathe in through your nose in order to smell something: *The dog sniffed the bone.*
2 to breathe air into your nose with a loud sound, for example when you are crying or when you have a cold: *Stop sniffing and blow your nose!*

snip /snɪp/ *verb* **snipped, snipping**
to cut something with scissors, making quick small cuts: *She snipped off the flower with some scissors.*
—**snip** *noun* a quick small cut that you make with scissors

snip•er /ˈsnaɪpɚ/ *noun*
someone who shoots at people from a hidden place

snip•pet /ˈsnɪpɪt/ *noun*
a small piece of news, information, or conversation: *I only heard a few snippets of their conversation, not the whole thing.*

snob /snɑb/ *noun*
someone who thinks that he or she is better than other people: *I guess I was a snob – I thought going to Harvard for college made me somebody special.*
—**snobbish** *also* **snobby** *adjective* behaving like a snob: *Her snobbish parents thought she should marry someone rich.*
—**snobbery** *noun* the attitudes and behavior of snobs: *He'll only eat fancy French food and won't touch a hamburger – it's just snobbery.*

snoop /snup/ *verb*
to try to find out about someone's life or activities by secretly looking at his or her

things: *I caught her snooping around in my office, looking in my drawers.*

snooze¹ /snuz/ *verb*
to sleep for a short time: *Dad was snoozing in front of the TV.* SYNONYM **doze**

snooze² *noun*
a short sleep: *I always have a snooze after lunch, and then I work some more.* SYNONYM **nap**

snore /snɔr/ *verb*
to make a loud noise each time you breathe when you are sleeping: *I couldn't sleep because my husband was snoring so loudly.*
—**snore** *noun* the sound you make when you snore

snor•kel /ˈsnɔrkəl/ *noun*
a tube that allows a swimmer to breathe air when his or her face is under water

snort /snɔrt/ *verb*
to make a sudden loud noise through your nose, for example because you are angry or laughing: *He snorted with laughter.*

snout /snaʊt/ *noun*
the long nose of a pig or similar animal

snow¹ /snoʊ/ *noun*
soft white pieces of frozen water that fall from the sky when it is very cold: *It was winter and snow was falling.* | *High winds and heavy snow* (=a lot of snow that is falling) *caused problems on the roads.*

THESAURUS: snow

snowflakes pieces of falling snow
sleet a mixture of snow and rain
slush snow on the road that has started to melt and is very wet
blizzard a storm with a lot of snow and a strong wind
frost a white powder of ice that covers the ground when it is cold
hail balls of frozen rain

snow² *verb*
1 it snows = if it snows, snow falls from the sky: *Look, it's snowing!*
2 be snowed in = to not be able to leave a place because so much snow has fallen: *We were snowed in for a week.*

snow•ball /ˈsnoʊbɔl/ *noun*
a ball that children make from snow and throw at each other: *The kids were having a snowball fight outside.*

snow•board /ˈsnoʊbɔrd/ *noun*
a large board that you stand on with both feet and use to slide down a hill that is covered in snow
—**snowboarding** *noun* the activity of using a snowboard
➔ See picture on page A24

snow•bound /ˈsnoʊbaʊnd/ *adjective*
surrounded by so much snow that traveling is impossible: *They were trapped in a snowbound car.*

snow•drift /ˈsnoʊˌdrɪft/ *noun*
a deep pile of snow which the wind has blown into one place

snow•fall /ˈsnoʊfɔl/ *noun*
a time when snow falls from the sky, or the amount that falls in a particular period of time: *We had the first snowfall of winter last night.*

snow•flake /ˈsnoʊfleɪk/ *noun*
a soft white piece of frozen water that falls from the sky when it is very cold

snow•man /ˈsnoʊmæn/ *noun* plural **snowmen** /ˈsnoʊmen/
two or three large balls of snow that children put on top of each other to look like a person: *The kids were in the yard building a snowman.*

snow•plow /ˈsnoʊplaʊ/ *noun*
a vehicle used for pushing snow off roads

snow•storm /ˈsnoʊstɔrm/ *noun*
a storm with strong winds and a lot of snow

snow•y /ˈsnoʊi/ *adjective*
covered in snow, or with a lot of snow: *It was a snowy January day.* | *snowy fields*

snug /snʌg/ *adjective*
warm and comfortable: *The children were safe and snug in their beds.*

snug•gle /ˈsnʌgəl/ *verb*
to get into a warm comfortable position: *I snuggled down in my sleeping bag and tried to get warm.*

so¹ /soʊ/ *adverb*
1 used for emphasizing what you are saying: *The party was so boring!* | *He was so weak that he could hardly stand up.*
2 used in place of what someone has just

S

said, to avoid repeating it: *If you have not paid yet, please do so now.* | *"Will I need my coat?" "I don't think so."*

3 so do I/so is he/so would John, etc. = used for saying that something is also true about someone else: *"I have a lot to do today." "So do I."* | *Ann was there and so was Mary.*

4 used for getting someone's attention or before you ask him or her a question: *So, Lisa, how's the new job going?* | *So you aren't actually leaving until Friday?*

5 or so = used when you are not giving an exact number or amount: *He left a week or so ago.* | *The trip takes an hour or so.*

6 and so on = used after a list to show that there are other similar things that you have not mentioned: *He does all the cooking, cleaning, and so on.*

7 so long! = used in order to say goodbye: *So long, George, and good luck!*

8 say so/tell someone so = used for saying that this is what someone says: *You have to turn the TV off; Mom said so.*

9 So?/so what? = used for saying in an impolite way that you do not think something is important: *"I don't like it." "So? Eat it anyway."* | *Yeah, I'm late. So what?*

so[2] *conjunction*

1 used for showing why something happens: *I got hungry, so I ate a sandwich.*

2 in order to do something or make something happen: *I put your keys in the drawer so that they wouldn't get lost.* | *We got up early so we could go swimming.*

soak /soʊk/ *verb*

1 to leave something in water for a time: *Soak the beans overnight.* | *I left the pans to soak.*

2 to make something completely wet: *The big wave soaked them.*

PHRASAL VERB

soak something up

if something soaks up a liquid, it takes the liquid into itself: *The bread will soak up the milk.* SYNONYM **absorb**

soaked /soʊkt/ *adjective*

very wet: *I got soaked in the rain.*

soak·ing /ˈsoʊkɪŋ/ *also* **ˌsoaking ˈwet** *adjective*

very wet: *I fell in the pool and my clothes are soaking wet.*

soap /soʊp/ *noun*

1 a substance that you use with water to wash yourself: *a bar of soap* | *Wash your hands with soap.*

→ See picture on page A11

2 *informal* a SOAP OPERA

ˈsoap ˌopera *noun*

a story on television about the lives of a group of people: *She watches her favorite soap opera, "All My Children," every day.*

→ See Thesaurus box at **television**

soap·y /ˈsoʊpi/ *adjective*

containing soap: *soapy water in the bathtub*

soar /sɔr/ *verb, formal*

1 to go up quickly to a high level: *It was cool at night, but during the day the temperature soared to 97°F.*

2 to fly high in the air: *They could see an eagle soaring above them.*

sob /sɑb/ *verb* **sobbed, sobbing**

to cry with quick, noisy breaths: *She was stroking the dead cat and sobbing.*

—**sob** *noun* the act of crying loudly: *I could still hear my mother's sobs.*

→ See Thesaurus box at **cry**[1]

so·ber /ˈsoʊbɚ/ *adjective*

not having drunk too much alcohol: *You're not sober enough to drive.* ANTONYM **drunk**

ˈso-called *adjective*

used for showing that you think someone or something is not what people say they are: *These so-called experts don't really know anything.*

soc·cer /ˈsɑkɚ/ *noun*

a game in which two teams of 11 players try to kick a ball into a large net at each end of a field

→ See picture on page A24

so·cia·ble /ˈsoʊʃəbəl/ *adjective*

someone who is sociable is friendly and enjoys being with other people: *She was very sociable and loved going to parties.*

so·cial /ˈsoʊʃəl/ *adjective*

1 relating to the people in a society and the way they live: *Social problems such as poverty and crime are difficult to solve.*

2 relating to spending time with people for fun: *He has a lot of friends and a good social life.*

—**socially** *adverb*

S

so·cial·is·m /ˈsoʊʃəˌlɪzəm/ *noun*
a system of government that tries to make people more equal, and in which many businesses belong to the government
—**socialist** *noun* someone who agrees with socialism

so·cial·ize /ˈsoʊʃəˌlaɪz/ *verb*
to spend time with people for fun: *We don't socialize much with our neighbors.*

ˌsocial ˈscience *noun*
a subject such as history, politics, or ECONOMICS

ˌSocial Seˈcurity *noun*
money which the government pays to people who are old or cannot work: *He's 75 and lives on Social Security.*

ˈsocial work *noun*
the job of helping people who are poor or have problems
—**social worker** *noun* someone who does social work: *A social worker visited her because her kids looked like they'd been hit.*

so·ci·e·ty /səˈsaɪəti/ *noun* plural **societies**
1 all the people who live in a country, and the way they live: *There is too much violence in our society.*
2 an organization of people with the same interest or purpose: *He belongs to the local Historical Society, which tries to find information about the history of our area.*
➔ See Thesaurus box at **people**

WORD FAMILY look at the words:
➔ **society** *noun*
➔ **social** *adjective*
➔ **sociology** *noun*
➔ **sociologist** *noun*

so·ci·o·ec·o·nom·ic /ˌsoʊsioʊˌekəˈnɑmɪk/ *adjective, formal*
relating to both the group of people someone belongs to in society and how much money they have: *children from different socioeconomic backgrounds* (=from families of different classes and with different amounts of money)

so·ci·ol·o·gy /ˌsoʊsiˈɑlədʒi/ *noun*
the study of the way people behave
—**sociologist** *noun* someone who studies the way people behave: *Sociologists have been studying the effect of television on children's behavior.*

sock /sɑk/ *noun*
a piece of clothing that you wear on your foot inside your shoe: *a pair of socks*

sock·et /ˈsɑkɪt/ *noun*
a place in a wall where you can connect a piece of equipment to the supply of electricity SYNONYM **outlet**

so·da /ˈsoʊdə/ *noun*
a sweet drink with bubbles that does not contain alcohol SYNONYM **soft drink, pop**

so·di·um /ˈsoʊdiəm/ *noun*
a silver-white chemical ELEMENT that you need in small amounts in your body: *Salt is a combination of sodium and chlorine.*

so·fa /ˈsoʊfə/ *noun*
a comfortable seat that is wide enough for two or three people: *Her sister was lying on the sofa in the living room.* SYNONYM **couch**
➔ See picture on page A8

soft /sɔft/ *adjective*
1 not hard or firm, but easy to press: *a soft pillow* ANTONYM **hard**
2 smooth and nice to touch: *She stroked the cat's soft fur.* ANTONYM **rough**
3 a soft sound is quiet: *Her voice was soft and gentle.* ANTONYM **loud**
4 soft colors or lights are not too bright: *the soft light from the candles* ANTONYM **harsh**
5 *informal* not strict enough: *He accused the Democrats of being soft on crime.*
—**softness** *noun*

soft·ball /ˈsɔftbɔl/ *noun*
a game similar to baseball, but played with a larger and softer ball: *She played softball in high school.*

ˈsoft drink *noun*
a sweet drink with bubbles that does not contain alcohol: *cola and other soft drinks* SYNONYM **soda**

soft·en /ˈsɔfən/ *verb*
1 to become less hard: *Soften the butter by leaving it at room temperature.* | *Cook until the onions soften.* ANTONYM **harden**
2 to become gentler or kinder: *His voice softened as he talked to the little girl.*

soft·ly /ˈsɔftli/ *adverb*
quietly: *"Are you awake?" she said softly.*

S

ˌsoft-ˈspoken *adjective*
having a quiet, gentle voice: *He's a soft-spoken man in his forties.*

soft•ware /ˈsɔft-wer/ *noun*
a set of programs that tells a computer to do something: *I need to install some new software* (=put it into the computer) *that will help me do my taxes.*

sog•gy /ˈsɑgi/ *adjective*
too wet and soft: *The pie crust was kind of soggy and didn't seem cooked.*

soil /sɔɪl/ *noun*
the substance in which plants grow: *The plants did not grow well because the soil was too dry.* SYNONYM **dirt**

S

so•lar /ˈsoʊlɚ/ *adjective*
relating to the sun: *They use solar energy* (=energy from sunlight) *to heat their water.*

ˈsolar ˌsystem *noun*
the solar system = the sun and the PLANETs that move around it: *The Earth is part of the solar system.*

sold /soʊld/ *verb*
the past tense and past participle of SELL

sol•dier /ˈsoʊldʒɚ/ *noun*
someone in the army: *The soldiers fought bravely.*

sole[1] /soʊl/ Ac *adjective, formal*
only: *Their sole source of heat was the stove.*

sole[2] *noun*
the bottom of your foot or shoe: *There was gum stuck to the sole of my shoe.*
➔ See picture at **shoe**

sole•ly /ˈsoʊli/ Ac *adverb, formal*
only: *He is interested solely in money.*

sol•emn /ˈsɑləm/ *adjective*
serious or formal: *The funeral was a solemn event.*
—**solemnly** *adverb*
—**solemnity** /səˈlemnəti/ *noun* the quality of being solemn

sol•id[1] /ˈsɑlɪd/ *adjective*
1 hard or firm, and not a liquid or gas: *He was too sick to eat solid food.* | *The lake was frozen solid.*
2 having no space or holes inside: *We could not hear what they were saying through the solid wall.* ANTONYM **hollow**
3 solid gold/silver/oak, etc. = completely made of gold, etc.: *a solid gold necklace*
—**solidify** /səˈlɪdəˌfaɪ/ *verb* if a liquid solidifies, it becomes hard or firm
➔ See Thesaurus box at **hard**[1]

solid[2] *noun, formal*
a substance that is not a liquid or gas: *Wood is a solid.*

sol•i•tar•y /ˈsɑləˌteri/ *adjective, formal*
1 done or experienced alone: *She enjoyed her solitary walks.* | *In prison, he was kept in solitary confinement* (=he was kept alone in a room).
2 only one: *A solitary tree stood in the field.*

sol•i•tude /ˈsɑləˌtud/ *noun, formal*
the state of being alone, usually because you want to be: *Most writers work in solitude.*

so•lo[1] /ˈsoʊloʊ/ *adjective*
done alone, without anyone else helping you: *This is his first solo album* (=he is not now a member of a band).
➔ See Thesaurus box at **alone**

solo[2] *noun*
a piece of music performed by one person: *a violin solo*
—**soloist** /ˈsoʊloʊɪst/ *noun* a musician or singer who performs alone

sol•u•ble /ˈsɑlyəbəl/ *adjective, formal*
a soluble substance can be mixed with a liquid until it becomes part of the liquid: *Salt is soluble in water.*

so•lu•tion /səˈluʃən/ *noun*
1 a way of stopping a problem: *We must find a solution to this problem.* | *If you really cannot control your dog, the only solution is to get rid of it.*
2 the right answer to a PUZZLE or a difficult question: *The solution to the puzzle is on page 14.*
3 a liquid which has a substance mixed completely into it: *a solution of sugar and water*

solve /sɑlv/ *verb*
1 to find or be a way of stopping a problem: *Mike thinks money will solve all his problems.*
2 to find the correct answer to a PUZZLE or a

difficult question: *Police are still trying to solve the mystery.*
WORD FAMILY → **solution** *noun*

sol•vent /ˈsɑlvənt/ *noun*
a chemical into which a substance can mix completely: *Some solvents are used for cleaning things, because the dirt mixes into the chemical and comes off the surface.*

some /səm; *strong* sʌm/ *adjective, pronoun, adverb*
1 an amount of something, or a number of people or things: *Would you like some ice cream?* | *If you need a pen, there are some* (=a small number of pens) *in the drawer.*
2 part of a group or thing: *Some people believe in ghosts.* | *Some of my friends can skate, and some can't.* | *I'd like some of that pie, please.*
3 used instead of "a" when you do not know who someone is or what something is: *Some guy called while you were out.* | *He doesn't like her, for some reason.*

some•bod•y /ˈsʌmˌbɑdi/ *pronoun*
another word for SOMEONE

some•day /ˈsʌmdeɪ/ *adverb*
at some time in the future: *Someday I'm going to have my own boat.*

some•how /ˈsʌmhaʊ/ *adverb*
1 in some way, although you do not know how: *We'll get the money somehow.*
2 for a reason which you cannot explain clearly: *Somehow it seemed like the right thing to do.*

some•one /ˈsʌmwʌn/ *pronoun*
a person: *Be careful! Someone could get hurt.* | *"Is she still going out with Dave?" "No, she's dating someone else."* SYNONYM **somebody**

GRAMMAR: someone

In questions and sentences with "not" in them, we usually use **anyone** and not **someone**: *Have you told anyone about this?* | *I didn't see anyone there.*

some•place /ˈsʌmpleɪs/ *adverb, informal*
another word for SOMEWHERE

som•er•sault /ˈsʌmɚˌsɔlt/ *noun*
a movement in which you roll or jump forward, so that your feet go over your head: *She did a somersault in gymnastics.*

some•thing /ˈsʌmθɪŋ/ *pronoun*
1 a thing: *There's something in my eye.* | *Let's talk about something else.* | *Do you want to get something to eat?*

GRAMMAR: something

In questions and sentences with "not" in them, we usually use **anything** and not **something**: *Did you see anything you liked?* | *I didn't have anything to eat.*

If you are offering someone some food, a drink, etc., it sounds more polite to use **something**: *Would you like something to eat?*

2 or something *informal* = said when you cannot remember or are not sure: *She might be shopping or something.*
3 something like 100/2,000, etc. = around 100, 2,000, etc.: *He earns something like $80,000 a year.*
→ See Thesaurus box at **thing**

some•time /ˈsʌmtaɪm/ *adverb*
at some time in the past or future: *I'll call you sometime next week.*

some•times /ˈsʌmtaɪmz/ *adverb*
on some occasions, but not always: *Sometimes I don't go to bed until midnight.*

THESAURUS: sometimes

occasionally sometimes, but not often: *Let the soup cook for 30 minutes, stirring it occasionally.*

(every) once in a while/every so often sometimes, but not regularly: *We like to go out for dinner every so often.* | *Every once in a while I just don't play very well.*

from time to time sometimes, but not often or regularly: *I guess you have to expect problems from time to time.*

some•what /ˈsʌmwʌt/ Ac *adverb, formal*
slightly: *I feel somewhat responsible for what happened. After all, I let him use the car.*

some•where /ˈsʌmwer/ *adverb*
1 in or to some place: *I still have that book somewhere.* | *Let's go somewhere else.*
2 somewhere between 30 and 40/$50 and $80, etc. = more than 30 but less than 40, etc.: *It'll take somewhere between three and four hours.*

S

GRAMMAR: somewhere

In questions and sentences with "not" in them, we usually use **anywhere** and not **somewhere**: *I haven't seen it anywhere.*

son /sʌn/ *noun*
someone's male child: *My son is 12 years old.* | *She has two daughters and one son.*

so·na·ta /sə'nɑtə/ *noun*
a piece of CLASSICAL MUSIC for one instrument, or for one instrument and a piano: *a violin sonata*

song /sɔŋ/ *noun*
a short piece of music with words: *We sang a few songs.*
→ See Thesaurus box at **music**

S

'son-in-law *noun*
the husband of someone's daughter: *Our son-in-law, Jenny's husband, is a lawyer.*

son·net /'sɑnɪt/ *noun*
a poem that has 14 lines that RHYME with each other in a particular pattern: *Shakespeare wrote sonnets as well as plays.*

soon /sun/ *adverb*
1 after a short time: *Dinner will be ready soon.* | *I met her soon after I started college.* | *Get him to the hospital as soon as possible.* | *I took the cake out of the oven too soon.*
2 as soon as = immediately after something has happened: *I tried to call you as soon as I heard the news.*
3 sooner or later = used for saying that something will definitely happen, but you are not sure when: *She's going to find out sooner or later.*
4 no sooner had ... than *formal* = used for saying that something happened almost immediately after something else: *No sooner had I stepped in the shower than the phone rang.*

soot /sʊt/ *noun*
the black powder that is left on things by smoke: *After the fire, the walls of the kitchen were covered in soot.*

soothe /suð/ *verb*
1 to make someone feel less worried, angry, or upset: *Lucy soothed the baby by rocking him in her arms.*
2 to make something less painful: *The medicine soothed my sore throat.*
—soothing *adjective*: *gentle, soothing music*

so·phis·ti·cat·ed /sə'fɪstəˌkeɪtɪd/ *adjective*
1 confident and knowing a lot about art, fashion, food, etc.: *She admired her rich, sophisticated cousin.*
2 complicated, and needing a lot of intelligence and skill to make: *The airport now has sophisticated security equipment.*
—sophistication /səˌfɪstə'keɪʃən/ *noun* the quality of being sophisticated

sopho·more /'sɑfmɔr/ *noun*
a student in the second year of high school or college

so·pra·no /sə'prænoʊ/ *noun* plural **sopranos**
a female singer or boy singer with a very high voice

sore[1] /sɔr/ *adjective*
painful: *I have a sore throat.*
—soreness *noun*

sore[2] *noun*
a place where your skin is painful or infected: *Her body was covered with sores.*

sore·ly /'sɔrli/ *adverb*, *formal*
very much: *He will be sorely missed by everyone.*

sor·row /'sɑroʊ/ *noun*
great sadness, or an event that makes you feel great sadness: *He expressed his sorrow at her mother's death.* ANTONYM **joy**

sor·ry /'sɑri/ *adjective* **sorrier**, **sorriest**
1 sorry/I'm sorry = used for telling someone that you feel bad about doing something: *"You forgot to lock the door." "Sorry."* | *I'm sorry that I lied to you.* | *I'm sorry to call you so late, but this is important.* | *Sorry about the mess.*
2 disappointed or sad about something: *I'm sorry that you can't come to the party.* | *I was sorry to hear you're leaving.* ANTONYM **glad**
3 feel sorry for someone = to feel sad for someone because he or she is in a bad situation: *He was lonely and I felt sorry for him.*

sort[1] /sɔrt/ *noun*
1 a type of person or thing: *What sort of music do you like?* SYNONYM **type**, **kind**
2 sort of *informal* = used to say that something is partly true but not totally true: *I felt*

sort of tired, so I went to bed. | "Do you like him?" "Sort of."

sort² *verb*
to put things in a particular order or into groups: *I've sorted the dirty clothes into different piles – white, red, and dark.*

PHRASAL VERBS

sort something out
to find an answer to a problem: *We still have a few problems to sort out before we agree.*

sort through something
to look at a lot of things in order to find something: *She sorted through the photos to find one of the wedding.*

SOS *noun*
a signal or message that a ship or airplane is in danger and needs help: *The captain sent out an SOS just before the ship sank.*

ˈso-so *adjective, adverb, informal*
neither very good nor very bad: *"How was the movie?" "So-so."*

sought /sɔt/ Ac *verb*
the past tense and past participle of SEEK

soul /soʊl/ *noun*
the part of you that is not your body but contains your most important thoughts and feelings, which many people believe continues to exist after you die: *When Grandpa died, his soul went to heaven.*

sound¹ /saʊnd/ *noun*
1 something that you hear: *I heard the sound of birds outside. | She didn't make a sound until she knew the men were gone.*
2 from/by the sound of something *informal* = judging by what you have heard or read about something: *From the sound of it, our neighbors are having marriage problems.*

sound² *verb*
1 if someone or something sounds good, bad, etc., he, she, or it seems good, bad, etc. to you when you hear or read about him, her, or it: *Surfing sure sounds like fun.*
2 to produce a noise: *Church bells sounded in the distance.*
➔ See Thesaurus box at **seem**

sound³ *adverb*
sound asleep = completely asleep: *The children were sound asleep and didn't hear anything.*

sound⁴ *adjective, formal*
sensible and likely to produce good results: *She gave her daughters some sound advice about men.*

sound·ly /ˈsaʊndli/ *adverb*
1 sleep soundly = to sleep well and peacefully: *I slept soundly and woke up rested.*
2 completely or severely: *We were soundly defeated 24–3 by the other team.*

sound·proof /ˈsaʊndpruf/ *adjective*
a soundproof wall, room, etc. is one that sound cannot pass into or out of: *The recording studio walls must be soundproof.*
—**soundproof** *verb* to make a room or building soundproof

sound·track /ˈsaʊndtræk/ *noun*
the music that is played during a movie: *I like a lot of the songs on the soundtrack to the movie.*

soup /sup/ *noun*
a hot liquid food that usually has pieces of meat or vegetables in it: *a bowl of chicken soup*

sour /saʊɚ/ *adjective*
1 having a strong taste, like the taste of a LEMON: *the sour taste of bad coffee*
2 sour milk is not fresh and has a bad taste and smell: *How old is the milk? I think it's gone sour.*
➔ See Thesaurus box at **taste¹**

source /sɔrs/ Ac *noun*
1 the thing, place, person, etc. where something comes from: *My job is my main source of income.*
2 a person, book, or document that you get information from: *The Internet is a good source of information, but you have to choose the information carefully.*

south¹ *also* **South** /saʊθ/ *noun*
1 the direction toward the bottom of a map of the world: *Which way is south?*
2 the southern part of a country or area: *My father owns a villa in the south of France.*
3 the South = the southeastern part of the U.S.

south² *adjective*
1 in to, or facing south: *a town 30 miles south of Phoenix | the south side of the island*
2 south wind = a wind that comes from the south

S

south[3] *adverb*
toward the south: *We left Dallas and flew south to San Antonio.*
➔ See picture at **north**

south•east[1] /ˌsaʊθ'ist/ *noun*
1 the direction that is exactly between south and east
2 the Southeast = the southeast part of a country or area
—**southeastern** /saʊθ'istərn/ *adjective* in or from the southeast

southeast[2] *adverb, adjective*
in, from, or toward the southeast: *We drove southeast till we reached the ocean.*
➔ See picture at **north**

S

south•ern /'sʌðərn/ *adjective*
in or from the south: *southern New Mexico*

south•ern•er /'sʌðərnər/ *noun*
someone who comes from the southern part of a country

ˌSouth 'Pole *noun*
the South Pole = the most southern point on the surface of the Earth
➔ See picture at **globe**

south•ward /'saʊθwərd/ *adverb, adjective*
toward the south: *The ship sailed southward.*

south•west[1] /ˌsaʊθ'west/ *noun*
1 the direction that is exactly between south and west
2 the Southwest = the southwest part of a country or area
—**southwestern** /saʊθ'westərn/ *adjective* in or from the southwest
➔ See picture at **north**

southwest[2] *adverb, adjective*
in, from, or toward the southwest: *We drove southwest.*

sou•ve•nir /ˌsuvə'nɪr/ *noun*
an object that you buy in order to remember a special occasion or a place that you have visited: *I bought a small Statue of Liberty as a souvenir of New York.*

sow[1] /soʊ/ *verb* **sowed, sown** /soʊn/ or **sowed** *formal*
to put seeds into the ground so that they will grow into plants: *He sowed the seeds in the field in the late spring.*

sow[2] /saʊ/ *noun*
a female pig

soy•bean /'sɔɪbin/ *noun*
a bean from a plant from which oil, TOFU, etc. is produced

spa /spɑ/ *also* **health spa** *noun*
a place that people go to in order to improve their health or beauty

space[1] /speɪs/ *noun*
1 the area of a room, container, etc. that is empty and available to be used: *Now that we have children, we need an apartment with more space.*
2 an empty area that is used for a particular purpose: *I found a parking space right across the street.*
3 the area beyond the Earth where the stars and PLANETs are: *The astronauts spent several days in space.* SYNONYM **outer space**
4 the empty area between two things: *The dog squeezed through the space between the fence posts.*
➔ See Thesaurus box at **hole**

space[2] *verb*
to put objects somewhere with a particular amount of space between them: *Space the tomato plants two feet apart.*

space•craft /'speɪsˌkræft/ *noun* plural **spacecraft**
a vehicle that can travel in space

space•ship /'speɪsˌʃɪp/ *noun*
a vehicle in stories that can carry people through space

'space ˌshuttle *noun*
a vehicle that can carry people into space and return to Earth more than once

spa•cious /'speɪʃəs/ *adjective, formal*
a spacious room, apartment, car, etc. is large and has a lot of space to move around in: *He has a spacious 3-bedroom apartment.*

spade /speɪd/ *noun*
1 a tool with a handle and a flat metal end that you use for digging: *She used a spade to dig in the garden.*
2 a playing card with one or more black shapes like pointed leaves on it: *the King of spades*

spa•ghet•ti /spə'geti/ *noun*
long thin pieces of PASTA (=Italian food made from flour, eggs, and water), that look like strings: *spaghetti with tomato sauce and meatballs*

spam /spæm/ *noun*
email messages and advertisements that you receive but do not want to read: *His mailbox was full of spam.*
➔ See Thesaurus box at **advertisement**

span[1] /spæn/ *noun*
1 a period of time: *Many insects have a very short life span – they live only a day or two.*
2 the distance from one side of something to the other: *The golden eagle has a wing span of seven feet.*

span[2] *verb* **spanned, spanning** *formal*
1 to include all of a period of time: *Her acting career spanned 25 years.*
2 to go from one side of something to the other: *The bridge spans the river.*

Span•ish[1] /ˈspænɪʃ/ *adjective*
from Spain

Spanish[2] *noun*
1 the language spoken in Spain, Mexico, South America, etc.: *He went to Costa Rica to learn Spanish.*
2 the Spanish = the people of Spain

spank /spæŋk/ *verb*
to hit a child on the BUTTOCKS with your open hand: *My parents only spanked me if I did something very bad.*
—**spanking** *noun* an action of spanking someone

spare[1] /sper/ *adjective*
1 spare key/clothes, etc. = an extra key, set of clothes, etc. that you have available for a time when it might be needed: *I gave a spare key to my neighbor in case I lock myself out of the house.*
2 not being used by anyone now and available to be used: *If you stay, you can sleep in the spare bedroom.*
3 spare time = time when you are not working: *She spent her spare time reading.*

spare[2] *verb*
1 time/money, etc. to spare *informal* = the time or money that still remains after the time or money you have already used or spent: *We made it to the airport with 10 minutes to spare.*
2 to be able to give or lend someone something, especially when this is difficult: *"Can you lend me some money, Grandma?" "I guess I can spare a few dollars if it will help you out."*
3 *formal* to not harm someone when you could hurt or kill them: *In the end, the king spared the prisoners' lives.*

spark /spɑrk/ *noun*
a very small piece of burning material that comes from a fire: *He kicked a log in the campfire and sparks flew into the air.*

spar•kle /ˈspɑrkəl/ *verb*
to shine in small bright lights: *The snow and ice sparkled in the sunlight.*
—**sparkle** *noun* a bright shiny appearance that something has
➔ See Thesaurus box at **shine**[1]

spar•row /ˈspæroʊ/ *noun*
a common small brown or gray bird

sparse /spɑrs/ *adjective, formal*
existing in small amounts that are spread over a large area: *The population becomes sparser as you go farther north. The large cities and farms are all in the south.*
—**sparsely** *adverb*

spat /spæt/ *verb*
a past tense and the past participle of SPIT

speak /spik/ *verb* **spoke** /spoʊk/ **spoken** /ˈspoʊkən/
1 to talk to someone about something: *Hello, can I speak to Mr. Sherwood, please?* | *The principal would like to speak with you after school.* | *He never speaks about his sister's death – it's too upsetting.*
2 to use your voice to say words: *He spoke so softly I could hardly hear him.*
3 to be able to talk in a particular language: *I cannot speak French.*

PHRASAL VERBS

speak out
to say publicly what you think about something: *Many students spoke out against the school's new uniform rules.*

speak up
to speak more loudly: *Could you speak up please, I can't hear you.*

speak•er /ˈspikɚ/ *noun*
1 someone who makes a speech: *The main speaker at the conference is Professor Sinclair.*
2 the part of a radio, television, etc. where the sound comes from
➔ See picture on page A20

S

spear /spɪr/ *noun*
a pole with a sharp pointed blade at one end, used as a weapon: *He threw a spear at the deer and killed it.*

spe•cial¹ /ˈspeʃəl/ *adjective*
1 different from ordinary things, and better in some way: *I wanted to do something special for your birthday.* | *Dad only wears a suit on special occasions, like weddings.*
2 very important and deserving your love, attention, etc.: *I invited a few special friends to dinner.* | *He bought me presents and made me feel special.*

special² *noun*
1 a price for something that is cheaper than usual: *The store's announced a special on a four-pound box of cookies.*
2 a television show that is only on television once and is not part of a series: *The TV special will be shown on Christmas Eve.*

S

spe•cial•ist /ˈspeʃəlɪst/ *noun*
someone who knows a lot about a particular subject, or is skilled at doing it: *Dr. Diaz is a skin cancer specialist.*
→ See Thesaurus box at **doctor**

spe•cial•ize /ˈspeʃəˌlaɪz/ *verb*
to study only one subject or do only one activity, so that you have special knowledge of it: *The company specializes in building inexpensive homes.*

spe•cial•ly /ˈspeʃəli/ *adverb*
for one particular purpose: *Pilots have to be specially trained to fly the plane.*

spe•cial•ty /ˈspeʃəlti/ *noun* plural **specialties**
a subject that you know a lot about or an activity that you are skilled at doing: *The doctor's specialty is treating sports injuries.*

spe•cies /ˈspiʃiz/ *noun* plural **species**
a group of animals or plants of the same kind who can produce young animals or plants with each other: *Three different species of deer live in the forest.*

spe•cif•ic /spəˈsɪfɪk/ Ac *adjective*
1 detailed or exact: *He gave us specific instructions about what we could and couldn't do.*
2 used when talking about one particular thing, person, time, etc.: *I'm looking for a specific type of cheese – I don't want any other kind.*

spe•cif•i•cally /spəˈsɪfɪkli/ Ac *adverb*
1 for a particular type of person or thing: *The book was written specifically for teenagers.*
2 in a detailed or exact way: *I specifically asked you to call me when you got to Ramon's house.*

spe•ci•fy /ˈspesəˌfaɪ/ Ac *verb* **specified**, third person singular **specifies** *formal*
to state something in an exact and detailed way: *He didn't specify how much he had paid for the house.*

spec•i•men /ˈspesəmən/ *noun, formal*
a small amount or piece of something that is taken so that it can be tested or examined: *The doctors need to take a blood specimen.*
SYNONYM **sample**

speck /spek/ *noun*
a very small mark, spot, or piece of something: *I brushed some specks of dust off my jacket.*

spec•ta•cle /ˈspektəkəl/ *noun, formal*
a very impressive or unusual thing that you see: *The tornado was an amazing spectacle.*

spec•tac•u•lar /spekˈtækyələ˞/ *adjective*
very impressive or exciting: *a spectacular view of the Grand Canyon*

spec•ta•tor /ˈspekˌteɪtə˞/ *noun*
someone who watches an event, game, etc.: *There were over 50,000 spectators at the football game.*

spec•trum /ˈspektrəm/ *noun* plural **spectra** /ˈspektrə/
1 *formal* a complete range of opinions, ideas, people, etc.: *I felt a wide spectrum of emotions, from happiness to sadness.*
2 the set of different colors that light separates into when it passes through a clear block of glass

spec•u•late /ˈspekyəˌleɪt/ *verb, formal*
to guess the reason or cause for something, without knowing all the facts: *The police speculate that the same person stole all the cars.*
—**speculation** /ˌspekyəˈleɪʃən/ *noun, formal* the act of speculating about something

sped /sped/ *verb*
a past tense and past participle of SPEED

speech /spitʃ/ *noun*
1 a formal talk about a particular subject that someone gives to a group of people: *The*

class president gave a speech to the whole school.

2 the act of speaking words: *A young baby isn't capable of speech.*

speed¹ /spid/ *noun*

1 the rate at which something moves or travels: *The car was moving at a speed of 60 miles an hour.*

2 five-speed/ten-speed, etc. = used to talk about the number of GEARs a car, truck, or bicycle has: *a ten-speed racing bike*

speed² *verb* **sped** /sped/ or **speeded**

1 to move or happen quickly: *The police car sped past us on the way to the accident.*

2 be speeding = to be driving faster than the legal limit: *The officer said I was speeding and gave me a ticket.*

PHRASAL VERB

speed up

to move or happen faster: *The train began to speed up as we left the station.*

speed·boat /ˈspidboʊt/ *noun*

a small boat with a powerful engine that can go very fast

speed·ing /ˈspidɪŋ/ *noun*

the action of driving faster than you are allowed to drive on that road: *The police stopped him for speeding. He was going 50 mph on a 35 mph street.*

ˈspeed ˌlimit *noun*

the fastest speed that you are allowed to drive on a particular road: *The speed limit is 40 miles per hour.*

speed·om·e·ter /spɪˈdɑmətɚ/ *noun*

an instrument in a vehicle that shows the driver how fast it is going

➔ See picture on page A28

speed·y /ˈspidi/ *adjective* **speedier**, **speediest**

happening or doing something quickly: *I hope you have a speedy recovery from your illness.*

spell¹ /spel/ *verb*

1 to say or write the letters of a word in the correct order: *"How do you spell your name?" "J-O-N-E-S."*

2 if letters spell a word, they make that word: *C-A-T spells "cat."*

spell² *noun*

1 a series of words or actions, that someone says or does in order to make magic things happen: *In the story, the witch casts a spell* (=makes a spell) *on the girl, and turns her into an old woman.*

2 a period of something, for example weather: *a dry spell* (=a period when there is no rain)

spell·ing /ˈspelɪŋ/ *noun*

1 the ability to spell words in the correct way: *I'm not very good at spelling.*

2 the way that a word is spelled: *What is the correct spelling of the word "Mississippi"?*

spend /spend/ *verb* **spent** /spent/

1 to use your money to buy or pay for something: *She spends all her money on clothes.*

2 to use a period of time in order to do something or stay somewhere: *We spent the day relaxing at the beach.*

S

spent /spent/ *verb*

the past tense and past participle of SPEND

sperm /spɚm/ *noun* plural **sperm**

a male cell or cells that can join with a female egg to produce new life

sphere /sfɪr/ Ac *noun*

the shape of a ball: *The earth is a sphere.*

—**spherical** /ˈsfɪrɪkəl/ *adjective* in the shape of a ball: *a spherical object*

spice /spaɪs/ *noun*

a seed or powder from plants that you put into food to give it a special taste: *Indian food uses a lot of spices, such as garlic and chili powder.*

—**spicy** *adjective* food that is spicy contains a lot of spices: *The Mexican food was hot and spicy.*

spi·der /ˈspaɪdɚ/ *noun*

a small creature with eight legs that makes WEBs (=sticky nets) to catch insects

spied /spaɪd/ *verb*

the past tense and the past participle of SPY

spike /spaɪk/ *noun*

a thin piece of metal with a sharp point: *The fence has spikes on the top to stop people from climbing over.*

spill /spɪl/ *verb*

if you spill a liquid, it flows over the edge of a container by accident: *I spilled coffee on my shirt.*

—**spill** *noun* an occasion when a liquid accidentally flows out of something: *an oil spill*

spin /spɪn/ *verb* **spun** /spʌn/ **spinning**
to turn around and around very quickly: *The wheels started spinning on the ice.*

spin•ach /ˈspɪnɪtʃ/ *noun*
a vegetable with large dark green leaves: *a spinach salad*
➔ See picture on page A12

spine /spaɪn/ *noun*
1 the long row of bones down the center of your back
2 a stiff sharp point on an animal or plant: *cactus spines*
➔ See picture on page A2

spi•ral /ˈspaɪrəl/ *noun*
a curve in the form of a continuous line that goes many times around a central point, for example on a screw
—**spiral** *adjective*: *a spiral staircase* (=one that curves upward around a central point)

spir•it /ˈspɪrɪt/ *noun*
1 a person's attitudes, thoughts, and feelings: *I'm 85, but I still feel young in spirit.*
2 a creature such as a GHOST or an ANGEL that does not have a physical body: *They were worried that there was some kind of evil spirit in the house.*

spir•it•u•al /ˈspɪrɪtʃuəl/ *adjective*
1 relating to religion: *spiritual leaders*
2 relating to your attitudes, thoughts and feelings, rather than to your body: *Yoga is not only good for your body, it's good for your spiritual health.*

spit /spɪt/ *verb* **spit** or **spat** /spæt/ **spitting**
to force a small amount of liquid or food from your mouth: *He tasted the drink and immediately spit it out.*

spite /spaɪt/ *noun*
1 in spite of something = even though something else is true: *In spite of her age, she is still beautiful.* SYNONYM **despite**
2 a feeling of wanting to upset or hurt someone: *He said some very mean things out of spite* (=because of spite).

spite•ful /ˈspaɪtfəl/ *adjective*
very unkind, and only doing or saying something because you want to upset or hurt someone: *She made some nasty spiteful remarks.*

splash[1] /splæʃ/ *verb*
1 if a liquid splashes, it falls or hits against something: *The water splashed against the rocks.*
2 to make water move through the air by hitting it, jumping in it, etc.: *The children were splashing around in the pool.*
➔ See picture on page A22

splash[2] *noun*
the sound or movement when something hits the water: *Jerry jumped into the water with a loud splash.*

splen•did /ˈsplendɪd/ *adjective, formal*
excellent or impressive: *There's a splendid view from the top of the building.*

splen•dor /ˈsplendɚ/ *noun, formal*
impressive beauty: *We were amazed by the splendor of the mountains.*

splin•ter /ˈsplɪntɚ/ *noun*
a small sharp piece of wood, glass, or metal that has broken off of a larger piece: *Help me get this splinter out of my finger.*

split[1] /splɪt/ *verb* **split, splitting**
1 *also* **split up** to divide something into two or more groups, parts, etc.: *The teacher split the class into two groups.* | *We decided to split the money between us.*
2 to tear or break into different parts: *The wood had split in two.*

PHRASAL VERB
split up
to end a marriage or a relationship: *Her parents split up when she was three.*

split[2] *noun*
1 a situation in which people disgree and separate into two groups: *A split in the organization led to two separate political parties.*
2 a cut or tear in something: *There was a split in the seat of his pants.*

spoil /spɔɪl/ *verb*
1 to make something less attractive, enjoyable, useful, etc.: *I didn't want to spoil her enjoyment of the movie, so I didn't tell her how it ended.*
2 if you spoil a child, you give the child everything he or she wants, and this has a bad effect on the child's behavior: *Some parents spoil their kids by buying them too many presents.*
—**spoiled** *adjective* a spoiled child is rude

S

and behaves badly because the child's parents give the child everything he or she wants

spoke[1] /spoʊk/ *verb*
the past tense of SPEAK

spoke[2] *noun*
one of the thin pieces of metal or wood that connect the outer edge of a wheel to the center
➔ See picture at **bicycle**

spok·en /ˈspoʊkən/ *verb*
the past participle of SPEAK

spokes·per·son /ˈspoʊksˌpɚsən/ *noun*
someone who speaks officially for a group, organization, government, etc.: *A company spokesperson said that the drug was completely safe.*
—**spokesman** /ˈspoʊksmən/ *noun* a man who speaks for a group, organization, government, etc.
—**spokeswoman** /ˈspoʊksˌwʊmən/ *noun* a woman who speaks for a group, organization, government, etc.

sponge /spʌndʒ/ *noun*
a soft piece of a substance that is full of small holes and is used for washing or cleaning something: *I used a sponge to wash the dishes.*

spon·sor /ˈspɑnsɚ/ *noun*
a person or company that provides money to help pay for a television show, sports team, sports event, etc.: *The team is looking for a new sponsor.*
—**sponsor** *verb* to provide money to help pay for something: *The show is sponsored by a sportswear company.*

spon·ta·ne·ous /spɑnˈteɪniəs/ *adjective*
if something is spontaneous, people suddenly decide to do it, and it is not planned: *It was a spontaneous decision – we hadn't discussed it at all.*
—**spontaneously** *adverb*

spook·y /ˈspuki/ *adjective, informal*
strange or frightening: *a spooky old house*

spool /spul/ *noun*
an object shaped like a small wheel that you wind wire, thread, film, etc. around: *a spool of thread*

spoon /spun/ *noun*
a thing that you use for eating food such as soup or ice cream, which consists of a small bowl and a handle: *I used a spoon to get the honey out of the jar.*
➔ See picture on page A15

spoon·ful /ˈspunfʊl/ *noun*
the amount that a spoon can hold: *a spoonful of sugar*

sport /spɔrt/ *noun*
a physical activity in which people compete against each other: *What's your favorite sport? | Soccer and basketball are team sports.*
➔ See Thesaurus box at **game**

ˈsports car *noun*
a low fast car

ˈsports ˌjacket *also* **ˈsports coat** *noun*
a man's comfortable jacket, worn on informal occasions

spot[1] /spɑt/ *noun*
1 a place: *We found a good spot for the picnic near the river.*
2 a small round area of color, that is a different color from the area around it: *a white dog with black spots*
3 a small mark on something: *There are spots of paint on the floor.*
➔ See Thesaurus boxes at **mark**[2] and **place**[1]

spot[2] *verb* **spotted, spotting**
to notice or recognize someone or something: *Someone spotted the criminals at Los Angeles airport.*
➔ See Thesaurus box at **see**

spot·less /ˈspɑtləs/ *adjective*
completely clean: *Her apartment is always spotless – she must spend all her time cleaning.*

spot·light /ˈspɑtlaɪt/ *noun*
a powerful light that is pointed at someone or something, for example on the stage in a theater: *She walked on to the stage under all the spotlights.*

spot·ted /ˈspɑtɪd/ *adjective*
covered in round areas of color or marks: *a spotted dog*

spot·ty /ˈspɑti/ *adjective*
good only in some parts, and bad in others: *a spotty performance*

spouse /spaʊs/ *noun, formal*
a husband or wife: *Employees may bring their spouses to the party.*

spout /spaʊt/ *noun*
a small pipe on the side of a container that you pour liquid out through: *the spout of a coffee pot*

sprain /spreɪn/ *verb*
to injure a joint in your body by suddenly twisting it: *He fell down and sprained his ankle.*
—**sprain** *noun*
→ See Thesaurus box at **injury**

sprang /spræŋ/ *verb*
the past tense of SPRING

sprawl /sprɔl/ *also* **sprawl out** *verb*
to lie or sit with your arms or legs stretched out: *They sprawled out on the sofa in front of the TV.*

S

spray[1] /spreɪ/ *verb*
to make a liquid come out of something in very small drops: *She sprayed some perfume on her wrist.*
→ See picture at **squirt**

spray[2] *noun*
liquid that comes out of a container in a stream of very small drops: *hair spray*

spread /spred/ *verb* **spread**
1 *also* **spread out** to open something so that it covers a big area: *She spread the map out on the floor.* | *The bird spread its wings.*
2 if something such as a disease spreads, it affects more people: *Scientists are worried that the disease could spread.*
3 if news spreads, more people find out about it: *The news spread quickly and soon everyone was talking about it.*
4 to put a soft substance onto a surface in order to cover it: *She spread some butter on the bread.*

PHRASAL VERB
spread out
if a group of people spread out, they move apart from each other: *OK, everyone, spread out so you all have enough space.*

spree /spri/ *noun*
a short period in which someone spends a lot of money or drinks a lot of alcohol: *She went on a shopping spree and spent $500.*

spring[1] /sprɪŋ/ *noun*
1 the season between winter and summer, when leaves and flowers appear: *The birds make their nests in the spring.*
2 a twisted piece of metal that returns to its original shape after it has been pressed down: *The springs in the old mattress poked me in the back.*
3 a place where water comes up naturally from the ground: *a hot spring*

spring[2] *verb* **sprang** /spræŋ/ also **sprung** /sprʌŋ/ **sprung**
1 to jump or move suddenly and quickly in a particular direction: *He sprang out of bed and ran down the stairs.*
2 spring a leak = if a boat or a container springs a leak, it begins to let liquid in or out through a crack or hole

PHRASAL VERB
spring up
to suddenly appear or start to exist: *New buildings are springing up everywhere.*

spring·time /ˈsprɪŋtaɪm/ *noun*
the time of year when it is spring

sprin·kle[1] /ˈsprɪŋkəl/ *verb*
1 to scatter small drops of liquid or small pieces of something onto something else: *We sprinkled cheese on the pizza.*
2 it is sprinkling = used to say that it is raining lightly
→ See picture on page A14

sprinkle[2] *noun*
1 a few small pieces or drops of something, especially food: *a sprinkle of pepper*
2 a short period of light rain

sprin·kler /ˈsprɪŋklɚ/ *noun*
a piece of equipment used for scattering water on grass

sprint[1] /sprɪnt/ *noun*
a race in which you run fast for a short distance
—**sprinter** *noun* someone who takes part in a sprint

sprint[2] *verb*
to run quickly for a short distance: *She sprinted up the stairs.*
→ See Thesaurus box at **run[1]**

sprout[1] /spraʊt/ *verb*
to start to grow: *The seeds are already sprouting.*

sprout[2] *noun*
a new growth on a plant: *bean sprouts*

spruce /sprus/ *noun*
a tree with short leaves shaped like needles

sprung /sprʌŋ/ *verb*
the past tense and past participle of SPRING

spun /spʌn/ *verb*
the past tense and past participle of SPIN

sput·ter /ˈspʌtɚ/ *verb*
if an engine sputters, it makes sounds like very small explosions because it is not working correctly: *The old truck sputtered as it went up the hill.*

spy¹ /spaɪ/ *noun*
someone whose job is to try to find out secret information about another country, group, etc.: *The spy was passing secret military plans to the enemies of the U.S.*

spy² /spaɪ/ *verb* **spied**, third person singular **spies**
to secretly watch people or collect information about them: *I think that someone is spying on us through that window.*

squad /skwɑd/ *noun*
a group of people who work together and do a job that needs special skills: *The police bomb squad removed the strange package.*

squan·der /ˈskwɑndɚ/ *verb*
to carelessly waste money, time, opportunities, etc.: *He squandered all his money on gambling.*

square¹ /skwer/ *adjective*
1 having four equal straight sides and four right angles: *a square window*
2 a square inch/mile, etc. = the measurement of an area that is a square shape with sides of an inch, a mile, etc. long: *The room was about 100 square feet.*
➔ See picture at **shape¹**

square² *noun*
1 a shape with four straight equal sides, all at RIGHT ANGLEs to each other: *The picture is in the shape of a square.*
2 a broad open area with buildings around it in the middle of a town: *Thousands of people marched to the city's main square.*
3 the result of multiplying a number by itself: *The square of 5 is 25.*

square³ *verb*
to multiply a number by itself: *If you square 10, you get 100.*

ˈsquare root *noun*
the square root of a number is the number which, when you multiply it by itself, equals the first number: *5 is the square root of 25.*

squash¹ /skwɑʃ/ *verb*
to press something into a flat shape, often damaging it: *Someone sat on the box and squashed all the chocolates.*
➔ See Thesaurus box at **press¹**

squash² *noun*
a type of large vegetable with solid flesh and a hard skin: *A pumpkin is a type of squash.*
➔ See picture on page A12

squat /skwɑt/ *also* **squat down** *verb*
to bend your knees and lower your body near the ground, resting on the backs of your legs: *He squatted down next to the car and checked the tire.*
➔ See picture on page A4

squeak¹ /skwik/ *verb*
to make a short high sound: *The door squeaks when I open it.*
➔ See picture on page A22

squeak² *noun*
a short high sound: *The mouse gave a squeak.*
—**squeaky** *adjective* making short high sounds: *She had a funny squeaky voice.*

squeal /skwil/ *verb*
to make a long high sound or cry: *The children squealed with excitement when they saw their presents.*
—**squeal** *noun* a long loud high sound or cry: *a squeal of delight*

squeeze /skwiz/ *verb*
1 to press something firmly together with your fingers or hands: *He squeezed her hand and said that he was glad to meet her.* | *Squeeze some lemon juice onto the salad.*
2 to go into or through a small space: *She squeezed past the other people.*
➔ See Thesaurus box at **press¹**
➔ See picture on page A3

squid /skwɪd/ *noun*
a sea creature with a long soft body and ten arms, or the meat from this creature: *fried squid*

squint /skwɪnt/ *verb*
to look at something with your eyes partly closed in order to see better: *The sunlight was very bright and made him squint.*

squir·rel /ˈskwɚəl/ *noun*
a small animal with a long furry tail that lives in trees and eats nuts

S

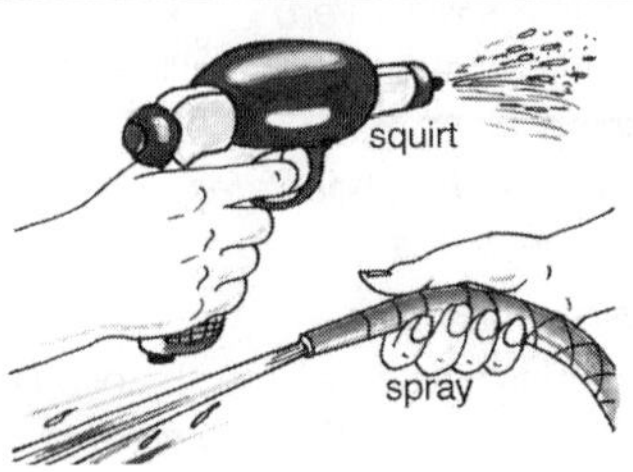

squirt

squirt /skwɚt/ *verb*
if liquid squirts it comes out of a narrow hole very quickly: *Orange juice squirted all over her dress.*

squish•y /ˈskwɪʃi/ *adjective, informal*
very soft and easy to press: *The peaches were brown and very squishy.*

St.
1 the written abbreviation of **street**, used when you are writing someone's address
2 the written abbreviation of **Saint**

stab /stæb/ *verb* **stabbed, stabbing**
to push a sharp object into someone or something: *Someone stabbed him with a knife in a fight.*

sta•bi•lize /ˈsteɪbəˌlaɪz/ Ac *verb*
to become steady and stop changing: *The doctors say that his condition has stabilized and he is no longer in danger.*

sta•ble¹ /ˈsteɪbəl/ Ac *adjective*
1 staying in the same position and not moving: *Be careful – the ladder doesn't look very stable.* ANTONYM **unstable**
2 remaining the same and with no big changes or problems: *a stable marriage* ANTONYM **unstable**
3 calm, reasonable, and not easy to upset: *He was a stable person, and she knew she could rely on him.* ANTONYM **unstable**
—**stability** /stəˈbɪləti/ *noun* conditions in which there is no sudden change

stable² *noun*
a building where horses are kept: *She led the horses back into the stable.*

stack¹ /stæk/ *noun*
a group of things that have been placed on top of each other: *There was a stack of magazines on the table.* SYNONYM **pile**

stack² *also* **stack up** *verb*
to put things into a neat pile: *Can you help me stack the chairs?*

sta•di•um /ˈsteɪdiəm/ *noun* plural **stadiums** or **stadia** /ˈsteɪdiə/
a building used for sports games, concerts, etc., that consists of a field surrounded by rows of seats: *The football stadium can hold 25,000 people.*

staff /stæf/ *noun*
the people who work for an organization: *There was a meeting for all the teaching staff at the school.*

stage /steɪdʒ/ *noun*
1 a particular time during the development of something: *The disease is still in its early stages and easier to treat.*
2 the raised floor in a theater, where actors, singers, musicians, etc. perform: *The crowd cheered when the band came on stage.*

stag•ger /ˈstægɚ/ *verb*
to walk or move in an unsteady way, almost falling over: *He staggered home from the bar.*

stag•nant /ˈstægnənt/ *adjective*
stagnant water does not move and often smells bad: *The water in the pond was stagnant, and it was impossible for anything to live in it.*

stain¹ /steɪn/ *noun*
1 a mark that is difficult to remove: *The table cloth was covered in coffee stains.*
2 a liquid that you use to change the color of wood: *We covered the table in a dark brown stain.*
➔ See Thesaurus box at **mark²**

stain² *verb*
to accidentally make a colored mark that is difficult to remove on something: *The wine had stained the carpet.*

ˌstainless ˈsteel *noun*
a type of steel that does not RUST: *a stainless steel sink*

stair•case /ˈsterkeɪs/ *noun*
a set of stairs inside a building, and the structure that supports it

stairs /sterz/ *noun*
a set of steps built for going from one level of a building to another: *He ran up the stairs to the second floor.*
➔ **downstairs, upstairs**

stair•way /ˈsterweɪ/ *noun*
a set of stairs and the structure that supports it, either inside or outside a building

stake[1] /steɪk/ *noun*
1 a pointed piece of wood, metal, etc. that is pushed into the ground to hold a rope, mark a particular place, etc.: *She put stakes in the garden to mark where she planted different seeds.*
2 be at stake = if something important is at stake, you could lose it if a plan or action is not successful: *We have to raise the money – the future of the school is at stake.*
3 have a stake in something = if you have a stake in something, you want it to succeed because you will lose money or other things if it is not successful: *Everyone in the company has a stake in the success of the plan.*

stake[2] *verb*
1 to risk losing money, or something valuable or important, if a plan or action is not successful: *He staked all his money on the horse race.* SYNONYM **bet**
2 stake a claim = to say publicly that you think you have a right to have or own something: *Both countries staked a claim to the islands.*

stale /steɪl/ *adjective*
no longer fresh: *stale bread* ANTONYM **fresh**
➔ See Thesaurus box at **old**

stale•mate /ˈsteɪlmeɪt/ *noun, formal*
a situation in which neither side in an argument, battle, etc. can win: *Negotiations have reached a stalemate – neither side wants to compromise.*

stalk[1] /stɔk/ *noun*
the long narrow part of a plant, that supports the leaves or the flowers: *celery stalks*

stalk[2] *verb*
to follow a person or animal secretly or quietly in order to attack him, her, or it: *I was worried that the man was stalking me.*

stall[1] /stɔl/ *noun*
1 a table or a small store with an open front, especially outdoors, where goods are sold: *At the fair there were lots of stalls selling art.*
2 a small enclosed area in a room, for washing or using the toilet: *a shower stall*
3 an enclosed area in a building for an animal such as a horse

stall[2] *verb*
1 if a car engine stalls, it suddenly stops working: *The car kept stalling and I had to get it fixed.*
2 to deliberately delay doing something: *Quit stalling and answer my question!*

stal•lion /ˈstælyən/ *noun*
a fully grown male horse

stam•i•na /ˈstæmənə/ *noun*
physical or mental strength that lets you continue doing something for a long time without getting tired: *You need a lot of stamina to run 20 miles.*

stam•mer /ˈstæmɚ/ *verb*
to speak or say something with a lot of pauses and repeated sounds: *"I, uh, need, uh, I need more time," he stammered.*
—**stammer** *noun* the condition of stammering

stamp[1] /stæmp/ *noun*
1 a small piece of paper that you stick onto an envelope or package that shows you have paid to mail it: *a 37-cent stamp*
2 an official mark, or a special tool for making this mark: *They put a stamp in my passport when I crossed the border.*

stamp[2] *verb*
1 to put your foot down hard onto the ground: *The little boy screamed and stamped his feet.*
2 to put an official mark on a piece of paper using a special tool: *The customs officer stamped her passport.*

PHRASAL VERB
stamp something out
to prevent something bad from continuing: *The police are trying to stamp out this new sort of crime.*

stam•pede /stæmˈpid/ *noun*
an occasion when a lot of people or animals suddenly start running together: *When the fire started, there was a stampede toward the exit of the building.*
—**stampede** *verb* if a lot of people or animals stampede, they suddenly start running together

stand[1] /stænd/ *verb* **stood** /stʊd/
1 to be on your feet, in an upright position: *We stood outside the theater and waited to go in.*
2 *also* **stand up** to move so that you are on your feet, after you have been sitting or lying down: *He stood up and walked toward the door.*

S

3 *formal* to be in a place: *The house stood on top of a hill.*
4 to accept somthing very painful or unpleasant: *He couldn't stand the pain any more.* SYNONYM **tolerate**
5 can't stand someone or something = to dislike someone or something very much: *I can't stand the smell of cigarette smoke.*
6 stand on your head/hands = to support yourself on your head or hands in an upright position, with your feet in the air
7 stand on your own two feet *informal* = to be independent and not need help from other people: *As kids get older, they need to learn to stand on their own two feet.*
8 know where you stand = to know what people really think about you: *You always know where you stand with Joe – he tells you what he thinks.*
9 know where someone stands = to know what someone's opinion about something is: *Voters need to know where the politicians stand.*

PHRASAL VERBS

stand back
to move back away from someone or something: *Stand back so that the doctor can get through.*

stand by
1 stand by something = to continue to believe that something you said or did was right: *I stand by what I said earlier.*
2 stand by someone = to stay loyal to someone and support him or her in a difficult situation: *His friends all stood by him when he was in prison.*
3 to be waiting, ready to do something: *Firefighters are now standing by.*

stand for something
1 to mean something, or be a short way of writing something: *CD stands for "compact disc."*
2 to support an idea, principle, etc.: *Martin Luther King stood for justice and equality.*

stand up
1 to move so that you are on your feet, after you have been sitting or lying down: *We stood up when the judge came in.*
2 if something stands up, it is shown to be true: *His argument doesn't stand up if you look at it carefully.*
3 stand someone up = to not meet someone when you have promised to meet him or her: *My date stood me up last night.*

stand up for someone or something
to support or defend someone or something that is being attacked or criticized: *Don't be afraid to stand up for what you believe in.*

stand up to someone
to be brave and refuse to do or say what someone is trying to make you do or say: *He finally stood up to the older boys and told them he wouldn't help them steal.*

stand² *noun*
1 a piece of furniture that you use to put something on: *a music stand* (=for sheets of paper with music written on them)
2 a table or small building, used for selling things to people: *a hotdog stand*
3 an opinion that you state publicly: *She took a stand against the war* (=she said publicly that she thought it was wrong).

stan·dard¹ /ˈstændɚd/ *noun*
1 a level that measures how good something is, or how well someone does something: *The standard of the service wasn't very good.* | *The college has high standards* (=it expects students to produce very good work).
2 by ... standards = compared to the level that you usually expect: *The house was small by American standards.*
➔ See Thesaurus box at **normal**

standard² *adjective*
normal or usual: *A work week of 40 hours is standard in the U.S.*

stan·dard·ize /ˈstændɚˌdaɪz/ *verb*
to make all the things of one type be the same as each other: *The tests of all schools in the area have been standardized.*

ˌstandard of ˈliving *noun* plural
standards of living
the kind of life that people have, based on the amount of money they have to pay for things such as houses, cars, education, etc.: *Most people in Japan have a high standard of living.*

stand·by /ˈstændbaɪ/ *noun* plural
standbies
1 someone or something that is ready to be used when needed: *a standby generator*
2 on standby a) if you are on standby for

an airplane ticket, you will be allowed to travel if there are any seats that are not being used **b)** ready to be used when needed: *The police are on standby in case of trouble.*

stand•ing /ˈstændɪŋ/ *noun*
someone's position, based on the way that other people think of him or her: *The bad news about the economy could affect the president's standing among voters.*

stand•point /ˈstændpɔɪnt/ *noun*
one way of thinking about a situation: *Let's look at this from a different standpoint.* SYNONYM **point of view**

stand•still /ˈstændˌstɪl/ *noun*
a situation in which there is no movement or activity at all: *The traffic came to a standstill because of the accident.*

stank /stæŋk/ *verb*
the past tense of STINK

sta•ple /ˈsteɪpəl/ *noun*
a small piece of thin metal that is used in order to fasten pieces of paper together
—**staple** *verb* to fasten pieces of paper together with a staple
➔ See Thesaurus box at **fasten**

sta•pler /ˈsteɪplɚ/ *noun*
a tool used for putting STAPLEs into paper

star[1] /stɑr/ *noun*
1 a very large amount of burning gases in space, that looks like a point of light in the sky at night: *They looked up at the stars in the night sky.*
2 a famous performer: *a movie star*
3 a shape with five or six points, that is supposed to look like a star in the sky: *The stars on the U.S. flag represent the 50 states.*
➔ See Thesaurus box at **movie**

star[2] *verb* **starred, starring**
to be the main character in a movie, TV program, etc.: *Johnny Depp has starred in many Hollywood movies.*

starch /stɑrtʃ/ *noun*
1 a substance in foods such as bread, rice, and potatoes: *His doctor told him to eat less starch and more green vegetables.*
2 a substance used for making cloth stiff: *He used starch to keep his shirt collars stiff.*
—**starch** *verb* to make cloth stiff by using starch: *These shirts need to be starched.*
—**starchy** *adjective* containing a lot of a substance found in foods such as bread, rice, and potatoes: *starchy foods*

star•dom /ˈstɑrdəm/ *noun*
the situation of being a famous actor, singer, sports player, etc.: *Many young actors hope for stardom.*

stare /ster/ *verb*
to look at someone or something for a long time without moving your eyes: *It's rude to stare at people.*
—**stare** *noun* the act of looking at someone or something for a long time without moving your eyes: *She gave him an angry stare.*
➔ See Thesaurus box at **look[1]**
➔ See picture at **see**

star•fish /ˈstɑrˌfɪʃ/ *noun*
a flat sea animal that is shaped like a star

Star-Span•gled Ban•ner /ˌstɑr ˌspæŋgəld ˈbænɚ/ *noun*
the Star-Spangled Banner = the U.S. national ANTHEM (=song)

start[1] /stɑrt/ *verb*
1 to begin happening or doing something: *Have you started making dinner?* | *What time does the party start?* | *Open your umbrella – it's starting to rain.* | *Mark's starting college in the fall.* SYNONYM **begin**
2 *also* **start up** to make a new company or organization: *Brad left his father's company to start a business of his own.*
3 if a car or an engine starts, it begins to work: *My car wouldn't start this morning, so I had to take the bus.*

PHRASAL VERBS

start off
to begin doing something: *Let's start off by introducing ourselves.*

start over
to start doing something again from the beginning: *When I'm drawing, if I make just one mistake, I have to start over.*

start[2] *noun*
the beginning of something: *Hurry – I don't want to miss the start of the movie.* SYNONYM **beginning**

start•le /ˈstɑrtl/ *verb*
to surprise someone by suddenly appearing in an unexpected way: *I didn't hear him come into the room and he startled me.*
—**startled** *adjective* surprised because something has suddenly happened: *I was*

S

startled to see a woman standing outside my window.
—**startling** *adjective* very unusual or surprising: *startling news*

star·va·tion /stɑrˈveɪʃən/ *noun*
a situation in which someone has little or no food to eat: *People are dying of starvation because there is not enough food for everyone.*

starve /stɑrv/ *verb*
to become sick or die because you do not have enough to eat: *He got lost in the desert and starved to death.*

starv·ing /ˈstɑrvɪŋ/ *adjective*
1 someone who is starving is sick or dying because he or she has not had enough food for a long time: *The country is full of starving people because there is no rain and no food.*
2 *also* **starved** *informal* very hungry: *After the long walk, we were all starving.*

S

state¹ /steɪt/ *noun*
1 the condition that someone or something is in: *The general state of his health is not too bad.*
2 *also* **State** one of the parts that the U.S. and some other countries are divided into: *the state of Texas*
3 *formal* a country that has its own government: *the member states of the European Union*
➔ See Thesaurus box at **country**

state² *verb, formal*
to say something publicly or officially: *When the police asked him, he stated that he had never seen the woman before.*

state·ly /ˈsteɪtli/ *adjective, formal*
impressive in style and size: *a stately old house*

state·ment /ˈsteɪtmənt/ *noun*
something that you say or write publicly and officially: *The president is going to to make a statement to reporters later today.*

States /steɪts/ *noun*
the States *informal* = the United States: *We're going back to the States in the summer.*

states·man /ˈsteɪtsmən/ *noun* plural **statesmen** /ˈsteɪtsmən/
an experienced and respected politician: *Lincoln was a great statesman.*

stat·ic /ˈstætɪk/ *noun*
1 noise caused by electricity in the air that spoils the sound from a radio or TV: *I couldn't hear the song on the radio because there was too much static.*
2 *also* **ˌstatic elecˈtricity** electricity that is not flowing in a current, but collects on the surface of an object and gives you a small electric shock

sta·tion¹ /ˈsteɪʃən/ *noun*
1 a place where trains or buses stop so that people can get on and off: *I'm getting off at the next station.* | *a train station*
2 a building that is a center for a particular type of service or activity: *Which gas station has the lowest prices?* | *a police station*
3 a company that broadcasts on radio or television: *He was listening to the local radio station.*

station² *verb, formal*
to put someone in a particular place in order to do a job or military duty: *Her father was stationed in Germany while he was in the army.*

sta·tion·a·ry /ˈsteɪʃəˌneri/ *adjective, formal*
not moving: *The truck hit a stationary vehicle.*

sta·tion·er·y /ˈsteɪʃəˌneri/ *noun*
things such as paper and envelopes that you use for writing: *Her desk drawers were filled with stationery.*

ˈstation ˌwagon *noun*
a large car with space at the back for carrying things: *The kids were riding in the back of the station wagon.*

sta·tis·tic /stəˈtɪstɪk/ Ac *noun*
1 a number that represents a fact or measurement: *These statistics show that the population is still increasing.*
2 statistics = the science of studying sets of numbers that represent facts or measurements: *He's studying statistics at college.*
—**statistical** *adjective* relating to statistics: *statistical analysis*
—**statistician** /ˌstætəˈstɪʃən/ *noun* someone who works with statistics

stat•ue /ˈstætʃu/ *noun*
a stone or metal model of a person or animal: *There is a statue of Thomas Jefferson in the center of the room.*

statue

ˌStatue of ˈLiberty *noun*
the Statue of Liberty = a very large statue of a woman in New York harbor

sta•tus /ˈsteɪtəs/ Ac *noun, formal*
1 the legal and official position of a person, group, country, etc.: *Please write your name, age, and marital status* (=whether or not you are married).
2 the social or professional rank of a person, job, etc. in relation to other people, jobs, etc.: *The status of women in society has improved and they are treated with more respect.*

ˈstatus ˌsymbol *noun*
something you own that shows you are rich or important, for example an expensive car: *Expensive cars are seen as status symbols.*

stat•u•to•ry /ˈstætʃəˌtɔri/ *adjective, formal*
fixed or controlled by law: *The statutory age for starting school is five years old.*

stay¹ /steɪ/ *verb*
1 to continue to be in the same place and not leave: *Do you want to come with me or stay here?*
2 to continue to be in the same condition or position and not change: *I was very sleepy, and it was hard to stay awake.*
3 to spend a short period of time in a place: *He stayed at a hotel while he was in town.*

PHRASAL VERB
stay up
to not go to bed: *We stayed up late last night, and I was very tired this morning.*

stay² *noun*
a period of time that you spend somewhere: *We're planning a two-week stay in Florida.*

stead•i•ly /ˈstedəli/ *adverb*
at a speed or level that does not change very much: *His work has improved steadily.*

stead•y¹ /ˈstedi/ *adjective*
1 something that is steady does not move or shake: *It's important to hold the camera steady when you take a photograph.*
2 continuing at the same rate, speed, or level without stopping or changing: *They drove along at a steady 50 miles per hour.* | *a steady heartbeat*
3 a steady job/relationship, etc. = a good job, relationship, etc. that is likely to continue for a long time: *My parents want me to find a steady job.*

steady² *verb*
1 to hold or control something to stop it from moving about: *He steadied the boat with his hand as Sarah got in it.*
2 to steady your nerves = to make yourself feel calmer: *She took a deep breath to steady her nerves before diving into the water.*

S

steak /steɪk/ *noun*
a thick flat piece of meat or fish: *a grilled steak*

steal /stil/ *verb* **stole** /stoʊl/ **stolen** /ˈstoʊlən/
to take something that belongs to someone else: *Someone stole $5 from her purse.*

steam¹ /stim/ *noun*
1 the gas that hot water produces: *The bathroom was full of steam.*
2 let/blow off steam = to get rid of your anger or energy by doing something active: *Doing physical exercise is a good way of letting off steam without hurting anyone.*

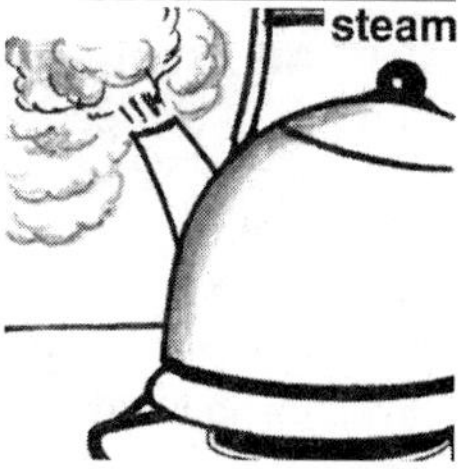
steam

steam² *verb*
1 to produce steam: *The cup of coffee was steaming.*
2 to cook something using steam: *Steam the vegetables for five minutes.*
—**steaming** *adjective* hot and producing steam
➔ See Thesaurus box at **cook¹**

steel /stil/ *noun*
a strong metal that is used for making knives, cars, etc.: *The bridge is made of steel.*

steep /stip/ *adjective*
a steep road or hill goes up or down very quickly: *The road was too steep for us to ride our bicycles up.*

stee·ple /ˈstipəl/ *noun*
a tall pointed tower on the roof of a church: *a church steeple*

steer[1] /stɪr/ *verb*
to control which way a vehicle goes: *He steered the car into the driveway.*

steer[2] *noun*
a young male cow whose sex organs have been removed

ˈ**steering wheel** *noun*
the round thing in a car, boat, etc. that you turn to make it go right or left: *He was driving with one hand on the steering wheel.*
➔ See picture on page A28

S

stem[1] /stem/ *noun*
a long thin part of a plant, from which leaves or flowers grow: *This rose has a long stem.*

stem[2] *verb*
PHRASAL VERB
stem from something
to happen as a result of something: *All their problems stemmed from their lack of money.*

sten·cil /ˈstensəl/ *noun*
a piece of stiff paper or plastic with shapes cut out of it, which you use to paint a design on something: *He used a stencil to paint the designs on the wall.*
—**stencil** *verb* to paint a design on something using a stencil

step[1] /step/ *noun*
1 a movement in which you put one foot down in front of the other: *He took a few steps and then stopped.*
2 one of a series of things that you do in order to achieve something: *This agreement between the two countries is an important step toward peace.*
3 a surface that you put your foot onto so that you can go up or down to another level: *Ellen ran up the steps and knocked on the front door.*

step[2] *verb* **stepped, stepping**
to move somewhere by putting one foot down in front of the other: *She stepped carefully over the dog.*
PHRASAL VERB
step out
to go out for a short time: *Sandy just stepped out – may I take a message?*

step·broth·er /ˈstepˌbrʌðɚ/ *noun*
the son of someone who has married one of your parents

ˌ**step-by-ˈstep** *adjective*
a step-by-step plan, method, etc. explains or does something carefully and in a particular order: *This is a step-by-step guide to making a birdhouse.*

step·child /ˈstepˌtʃaɪld/ *noun* plural **stepchildren** /ˈstepˌtʃɪldrən/
a stepdaughter or stepson

step·daugh·ter /ˈstepˌdɔtɚ/ *noun*
a daughter that your husband or wife has from a relationship before your marriage

step·fa·ther /ˈstepˌfɑðɚ/ *noun*
a man who is married to your mother but who is not your father

step·lad·der /ˈstepˌlædɚ/ *noun*
a LADDER with two sloping parts joined at the top: *He climbed up the stepladder to change the light bulb.*

step·moth·er /ˈstepˌmʌðɚ/ *noun*
a woman who is married to your father but who is not your mother

step·par·ent /ˈstepˌperənt/ *noun*
a stepfather or stepmother

step·sis·ter /ˈstepˌsɪstɚ/ *noun*
the daughter of someone who has married one of your parents

step·son /ˈstepsʌn/ *noun*
a son that your husband or wife has from a relationship before your marriage

ster·e·o /ˈsteriˌoʊ/ *noun* plural **stereos**
a machine for playing CDs, tapes, etc. that produces sound from two SPEAKERs
➔ See picture on page A8

ster·e·o·type /ˈsteriəˌtaɪp/ *noun, formal*
a common idea of what a particular type of person is like, which is often not correct: *The movie is full of racial stereotypes that aren't true at all.*
—**stereotype** *verb* to decide, usually unfairly, that some people have particular qualities because they belong to a particular race, sex, or social class: *Too many children's books stereotype girls as being weak.*

ster•ile /ˈsterəl/ *adjective*
1 completely clean and not containing any BACTERIA: *Put a sterile bandage on the wound.*
2 unable to have children: *His wife is sterile, so they can't have children.*

ster•ling /ˈstɚlɪŋ/ *noun*
very pure silver: *This ring is made of sterling silver.*

stern[1] /stɚn/ *adjective*
very serious or strict: *The teacher gave me a stern look when I got the answer wrong.*
—**sternly** *adverb*

stern[2] *noun*
the back part of a ship: *The captain stood at the stern of the ship, looking back at the port.*

steth•o•scope /ˈsteθəˌskoʊp/ *noun*
an instrument that a doctor uses to listen to your heart or breathing: *The doctor put the stethoscope on my chest to listen to my heart.*

stew /stu/ *noun*
a meal made of pieces of meat and vegetables that you cook slowly in liquid: *beef stew*

stew•ard /ˈstuɚd/ *noun*
a man whose job is to serve food and drinks to people on a ship or plane: *a ship's steward*

stew•ard•ess /ˈstuɚdɪs/ *noun*
a woman whose job is to serve food and drinks to people on a ship or plane: *The stewardess brought him his drink.*

stick[1] /stɪk/ *verb* **stuck** /stʌk/
1 to join two things together using glue: *I stuck a label on the bottle.*
2 if something sticks to a surface, it stays on it because it has glue on it, is wet, etc.: *The wet leaves were sticking to my shoes.*
3 to push a pointed object into something: *The nurse stuck a needle in my arm.*

PHRASAL VERBS

stick out
1 if something sticks out, it comes out from a surface: *Mike's ears stick out.*
2 stick something out = to deliberately move part of your body forward: *The boy stuck his tongue out at me.*

stick to something
to continue doing something in the way you planned to do it: *I think we should stick to what we decided and not make any changes.*

stick together *informal*
if people stick together, they continue to support each other when they have problems: *The two sisters have always stuck together despite all their problems.*

stick up
if something sticks up, it is not flat and comes up above a surface: *Your hair is sticking up – you should comb it.*

stick[2] *noun*
1 a long thin piece of wood from a tree: *They collected sticks to build a fire.*
2 a long thin piece of wood or plastic that you use for a particular purpose: *She used a walking stick during the hike.*
3 a long thin piece of something: *a stick of gum*

stick•er /ˈstɪkɚ/ *noun*
a small piece of paper or plastic with a picture or writing on it, that you can stick onto something: *Kerry put colored stickers all over her notebook.*

stick•y /ˈstɪki/ *adjective* **stickier**, **stickiest**
1 made of or covered with a substance that sticks to surfaces: *The floor in the theater was sticky from sodas that people had spilled.* | *This is a special kind of tape that is sticky on both sides.*
2 *informal* sticky weather is very hot and the air feels wet: *It was a hot and sticky summer day.* SYNONYM **humid**
—**stickiness** *noun*

stiff[1] /stɪf/ *adjective*
1 if a part of your body is stiff, your muscles hurt and it is difficult to move: *I've been using a heating pad on my stiff neck.*
2 difficult to bend or move: *The signs were printed on stiff pieces of cardboard.*
3 more difficult, strict, or severe than usual: *There are stiff fines for speeding in this county.*
—**stiffly** *adverb* moving in a stiff way: *The old woman moved stiffly across the room.*
—**stiffness** *noun* the quality of being stiff so that you cannot move easily: *There is still some stiffness in my leg where I broke it.*
→ See Thesaurus box at **hard**[1]

S

stiff[2] *adverb, informal*
scared/bored/worried stiff = very frightened, bored, or worried: *I was scared stiff when the doctor told me I had to have an operation.*

stiff•en /ˈstɪfən/ *verb*
if you stiffen, your body suddenly becomes firm, straight, or still because you are angry, frightened, or worried: *When he touched her, she stiffened.*

stig•ma /ˈstɪgmə/ *noun*
a strong feeling in society that a type of behavior or a particular illness or condition is something to be ashamed of: *There is still a stigma in our society about having a mental illness.*

S

still[1] /ˈstɪl/ *adverb*
1 used to say that something is continuing to happen or be true at a particular moment: *Tom's still at school.*

> **USAGE: still**
>
> **Still** is used to say that a situation that began in the past has not changed and is continuing: *He still lives with his parents.*
>
> **Always** means "all the time" or "every time": *Her clothes are always so nice. I I always see him on Tuesdays.*
>
> **Yet** is used in sentences with "not" in them and in questions to talk about something that you expect to happen, but which has not happened: *I haven't finished the book yet. I Is Mark back from lunch yet?*

2 not moving: *When he heard the sound, the dog stood still and listened.*
3 in spite of what has just been said or done: *I studied hard, but I still failed the test.* SYNONYM **nonetheless, nevertheless**

still[2] *adjective*
quiet and calm: *In the early morning, the town was still.*
—**stillness** *noun*

stim•u•late /ˈstɪmyəˌleɪt/ *verb*
1 to help an activity or process begin, develop, or improve: *The warm sun in Spring stimulates the plants to grow.*
2 to make someone excited about and interested in something: *We hope to stimulate students' interest in art with trips to the museum.*
—**stimulating** *adjective* making you feel excited or interested: *The preschool is a fun and stimulating place for young children.*
—**stimulation** /ˌstɪmyəˈleɪʃən/ *noun* something that makes you feel excited or interested

stim•u•lus /ˈstɪmyələs/ *noun* plural **stimuli** /ˈstɪmyəlaɪ/
something that causes a development or reaction: *Music can be a powerful stimulus to a baby's brain.*

sting

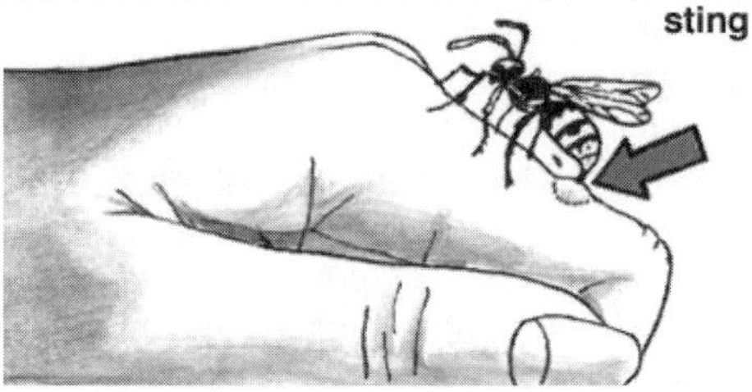

sting[1] /stɪŋ/ *verb* **stung** /stʌŋ/
1 if an insect or plant stings you, it makes a small hole in your skin and causes a sharp pain: *Ouch! That bee just stung me.*
2 to cause a sudden sharp pain on your skin or in your eyes for a short time: *The smoke was stinging my eyes.*
→ See Thesaurus box at **hurt**[1]

sting[2] *noun*
a wound made when an insect or plant stings you: *a bee sting*

stin•gy /ˈstɪndʒi/ *adjective*
not willing to spend money or share something even though you have enough: *Don't be so stingy – pay for your sister's birthday dinner.* ANTONYM **generous**
—**stinginess** *noun* the quality of being stingy

stink /stɪŋk/ *verb* **stunk** or **stank** /stæŋk/ **stunk** /stʌŋk/
1 to have a very strong bad smell: *Wash your jeans – they really stink.*
2 something stinks *informal* = said when you think something is bad or unfair: *It stinks that I have to do all the work.*
—**stinky** *adjective* having a very strong bad smell: *stinky cheese*

PHRASAL VERB
stink something up *informal*
to fill a place with a very strong bad smell:

The cigarettes stunk up the whole apartment.
➔ See Thesaurus box at **smell**[1]

stir /stɚ/ *verb* **stirred, stirring**
to mix a liquid or food by moving a spoon around in it: *Stir the sauce until it is smooth.*
➔ See Thesaurus box at **mix**[1]
➔ See picture on page A14

ˈstir-fry *verb* **stir-fried**, third person singular **stir-fries**
to quickly cook meat, vegetables, etc. in a little oil over very high heat: *Stir-fry the vegetables in a large pan.*
—**stir-fry** *noun* food that has been stir-fried

stitch[1] /stɪtʃ/ *noun*
1 one of the small lines of thread where a piece of cloth has been sewn: *She sewed the quilt with tiny neat stitches.*
2 a piece of special thread that a doctor uses to sew together a cut or wound: *Steven had to have three stitches in his chin after he fell down.*

stitch[2] *verb*
to sew two pieces of cloth together: *She stitched the lace onto the shirt.*
—**stitching** *noun* a line of stitches on a piece of cloth

stock[1] /stɑk/ *noun*
1 a supply of something that is kept to be sold or used later: *The hospital keeps large stocks of the blood for emergencies.*
2 in stock/out of stock = available for sale or not available for sale: *The book is out of stock right now, but we can order a copy for you.*
3 SHAREs of OWNERSHIP in a company: *She sold all her stock in the company just before the price dropped.*

stock[2] *verb*
to have a supply of something available to be sold or used: *Does the store stock camping equipment?*
PHRASAL VERB
stock up
to buy a lot of something that you intend to use later: *I need to stock up on snacks for the party.*

stock·brok·er /ˈstɑkˌbroʊkɚ/ *noun*
a person or company whose job is to buy and sell STOCKs, BONDs, etc. for other people

ˈstock exˌchange *noun*
a place where people buy and sell STOCKs: *We visited the New York Stock Exchange on Wall Street.*

stock·ing /ˈstɑkɪŋ/ *noun*
1 stockings = a thin close-fitting piece of clothing that covers a woman's feet and legs: *She was wearing a black dress and black stockings.*
2 a large sock that people hang up before Christmas to be filled with presents: *We hung our stockings by the fireplace on Christmas Eve.*
➔ See picture on page A6

stock·pile /ˈstɑkpaɪl/ *noun*
a large supply of something that you collect in order to use it in the future: *Police found a stockpile of weapons in the man's basement.*
—**stockpile** *verb* to collect a large supply of something to use in the future: *People were stockpiling food and supplies before the storm.*

S

stock·y /ˈstɑki/ *adjective*
having a short, heavy, strong-looking body: *a stocky policeman*

stole /stoʊl/ *verb*
the past tense of STEAL

sto·len /ˈstoʊlən/ *verb*
the past participle of STEAL

stom·ach /ˈstʌmək/ *noun*
1 the organ in your body that DIGESTs the food you eat: *After dinner I started having pains in my stomach.*
2 the front part of your body, below your chest: *He never exercises, and he has a really big stomach.*
➔ See picture on page A2

stom·ach·ache /ˈstʌməkˌeɪk/ *noun*
a pain in your stomach: *He had a bad stomachache, so he went home from school early.*

stone /stoʊn/ *noun*
1 rock, or a hard mineral substance: *The wall around the yard is made of stone.*
2 a small rock: *A few of the protesters began throwing stones at the police.* SYNONYM **rock**
3 a jewel: *She had necklaces with diamonds and other precious stones* (=expensive and rare stones).

stood /stʊd/ *verb*
the past tense and past participle of STAND

stool /stul/ *noun*
a seat that has three or four legs, but no back or arms: *We sat on stools at the counter and ate our sandwiches.*
→ See picture at **seat**

stoop /stup/ *verb*
to bend your body forward and down: *Tom stooped to pick up his pencil.*

stop[1] /stɑp/ *verb* **stopped, stopping**
1 to end an action, activity, or event: *He finally stopped smoking.* | *I wish that noise would stop.*
2 to make someone or something not move any farther: *You're supposed to stop the car at a red light.* | *She stopped me as I was leaving to ask a question.*
3 to pause during an activity, trip, etc. in order to do something: *Let's stop and have lunch before we finish painting the room.*

THESAURUS: stop

have/take a break to stop doing something for a short time in order to rest: *Okay, everyone, take a break and get a drink of water.*

break to stop for a short time in order to rest or eat something: *We broke for lunch about one o'clock.*

pause to stop speaking or doing something for a short time before starting again: *He paused for a moment to think.*

4 to prevent someone from doing something: *We can't stop him from coming if he really wants to be there.*
5 stop it/that! *spoken* = said when you want someone to stop annoying or upsetting you: *Stop it! That hurts!*
6 stop short of something = to stop before you do one more thing that would be too dangerous, risky, etc.: *Tom said she wasn't very honest, but he stopped short of calling her a liar.*

PHRASAL VERBS

stop by
to make a short visit to a person or place when you are going somewhere else: *Carol stopped by to return your CD.*

stop in *informal*
to make a short visit to a person or place when you are going somewhere else: *Let's stop in at Gary's on the way home.*

stop off
to make a short visit to a place when you are going somewhere else: *I need to stop off at the post office.*

stop[2] *noun*
1 the action of stopping moving, happening, or doing something: *The taxi came to a stop outside his hotel.*
2 a place where you stop during a trip, or the short period you spend at that place: *Memphis was the first stop on our trip.*
3 a place where a bus or train regularly stops for its passengers: *I need to get off the train at the next stop.*

stop•light /ˈstɑplaɪt/ *noun*
a set of red, yellow, and green lights used for controlling traffic

stop•o•ver /ˈstɑpˌoʊvɚ/ *noun*
a short time between parts of a long airplane trip: *We had a three-hour stopover in Chicago before we flew to Denver.*

stor•age /ˈstɔrɪdʒ/ *noun*
the state of keeping something in a special place when it is not being used: *All of Ken's furniture is in storage until he finds a place to live.*

store[1] /stɔr/ *noun*
1 a building where goods are sold to the public: *I'm going to the grocery store – is there anything you need for dinner?*
2 *formal* a supply of something that you keep to use later: *Computers can hold very large stores of information.*
3 in store (for someone) = about to happen to someone: *There's a surprise in store for you!*

store[2] *verb*
1 to put things away and keep them there until you need them: *I store all of my winter clothes in these boxes.*
2 to keep facts or information in your brain, a computer, etc.: *She stored her research papers on CDs.*

storm[1] /stɔrm/ *noun*
a period of bad weather when there is a lot of wind, rain, snow, etc.: *There was a bad snow storm and we couldn't leave the house all day.*
—stormy *adjective* stormy weather is when there is a lot of wind, rain, snow, etc.: *It's*

been stormy all week, so we haven't gone outside to play.

→ See Thesaurus boxes at **rain**[1] and **wind**[1]

storm[2] *verb*

1 to attack a place and enter it using a lot of force: *Police officers stormed the building and arrested the men inside.*

2 to go somewhere in a fast, noisy way because you are very angry: *Angela got mad and stormed out of the room.*

sto·ry /ˈstɔri/ *noun* plural **stories**

1 a description of an event that is intended to entertain people: *Juan told us a funny story about his trip to Las Vegas.* | *a love story*

THESAURUS: story

tale *formal* a story about events that are not real: *Many of the tales begin with the line, "Once upon a time."*

myth a very old story abut gods, magical creatures, etc.: *the Greek myths about Zeus and the other gods*

legend an old story about brave people or magical events: *the legend of King Arthur*

fable a story, especially one with animals, that teaches us a lesson: *The fable about the race between the tortoise and the hare shows that hard steady work can have good results.*

2 a report in a newspaper or news broadcast about a recent event: *The newspaper published a long story on the flood.*

3 a floor or level of a building: *Our apartment is on the sixth story of the building.* SYNONYM **floor**

4 it's a long story *spoken* = said when you think something will take too long to explain: *It's a long story – I'll tell you later.*

5 to make a long story short *spoken* = said when you want to finish explaining something quickly: *To make a long story short, she got mad and left.*

6 an excuse, explanation, or lie: *I don't believe his story about where he was last night.*

stove /stoʊv/ *noun*

1 a large piece of kitchen equipment on which you cook food. It usually also contains an OVEN: *The soup is in a pot on the stove.*

2 a piece of equipment inside which you burn wood, coal, etc. in order to heat a room: *The cabin has an old wood stove.*

→ See picture on page A9

straight[1] /streɪt/ *adverb*

1 in a line or direction that is not bent, curved, or leaning: *Just keep going straight ahead, and you'll see the library on the left.* | *Stand up straight!*

2 immediately and without any delay: *Come straight home after the concert.*

3 happening one after the other in a series: *We drove five hours straight without stopping.*

4 not see/think straight = to be unable to see or think clearly: *It was so noisy, I could hardly think straight.*

straight[2] *adjective*

1 not bent or curved: *She has long straight hair, but her sister has curly hair.* | *a straight line*

2 level or upright, and not bent or leaning: *Is the picture on that wall straight?* | *straight teeth*

3 honest and direct: *Just give me a straight answer and stop avoiding the question.*

4 one after the other: *The team has had three straight wins.*

5 get/keep something straight *spoken* = to correctly understand the facts about a situation without being confused: *There are so many kids in the class, I can't keep all their names straight.*

6 get straight A's/B's, etc. = to earn the GRADE "A", "B," etc. in all of your school subjects: *Susan studies hard and always gets straight A's.*

7 *informal* another word for HETEROSEXUAL: *No, Mike's straight – he has a girlfriend.*

straight·en /ˈstreɪtn/ also **straighten out** *verb*

to make something straight: *She had to wear braces to straighten her teeth.*

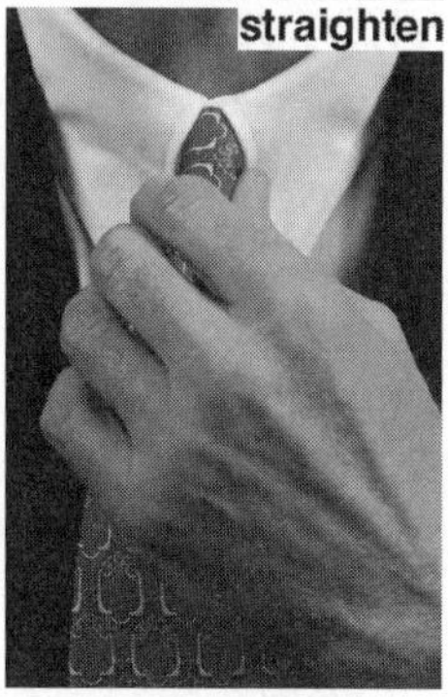

straighten

PHRASAL VERBS

straighten out

1 straighten something out = to deal successfully with a difficult situation or problem: *I'll talk to* *him about the disagreement and see if I can straighten things out.*

2 straighten someone out = to deal successfully with someone's bad behavior or personal problems: *A few years in the army will straighten him out.*

straighten up

1 to clean a room that is messy: *You need to straighten up your room before you go to the mall.*

2 to make your back straight, or to stand up straight after bending down: *The students straightened up in their seats when the principal walked in the room.*

3 to start behaving well: *You'd better straighten up or you'll be in big trouble.*

S

straight•for•ward /ˌstreɪtˈfɔrwɚd/ Ac *adjective*

1 simple or easy to understand: *The directions are fairly straightforward, so you shouldn't have problems understanding them.*

2 honest and not hiding what you think: *Greg has always been straightforward and honest with me.*

strain¹ /streɪn/ *verb*

1 to injure part of your body by stretching it or using it more than you should: *Rob strained his back lifting boxes.*

2 to try very hard to do something using a lot of effort: *She was straining to hear what they were saying.*

3 to cause problems or difficulties for someone or something by being too much to deal with: *The increase in rent will strain my finances.*

strain² *noun*

1 worry or pressure that you feel because of a difficult situation, job, etc.: *The strain of working long hours was making him sick.*

2 an injury to part of your body that you have used too much: *Lee couldn't play in the game because of a muscle strain.*

strained /streɪnd/ *adjective*

1 unfriendly, not relaxed, and showing a lack of trust: *Our relationship has been strained since I said I would not loan him money.*

2 worried and tired: *Linda's voice sounded strained.*

strait /streɪt/ *noun*

a narrow passage of water that joins two larger areas of water: *the Strait of Gibraltar*

strand /strænd/ *noun*

a single thin piece of thread, hair, wire, etc.: *She brushed a few loose strands of hair from her face.*

strand•ed /ˈstrændɪd/ *adjective*

needing help because you are unable to move from a particular place: *After the flight was canceled, I was stranded at the airport without any money.*

strange /streɪndʒ/ *adjective*

1 unusual or surprising, in a way that is difficult to understand: *Strange noises were coming from outside.* | *It was strange to see someone else wearing my clothes.* ANTONYM **normal**

THESAURUS: strange

funny a little strange or unusual: *The washing machine is making a funny noise.*

weird strange and different from what you are used to: *She wears weird clothes that never match.*

odd strange or different from normal, especially in a way that you do not approve of or cannot understand: *It seemed like an odd thing to say.*

peculiar *formal* strange, unfamiliar, or a little surprising: *The fish had a peculiar taste.*

mysterious strange in a way that is hard to explain or understand: *There were mysterious lights in the sky.*

bizarre very unusual and strange in a way that is hard to explain or understand: *His bizarre behavior was starting to worry me a lot.*

eccentric *formal* an eccentric person behaves in a way that is different from most people, in a way that makes you want to laugh a little bit: *She was an eccentric woman, who made her dresses out of old curtains and smoked a small pipe.*

2 not familiar: *I was in a strange neighborhood and didn't know anyone.*

—**strangeness** *noun*

strang•er /ˈstreɪndʒɚ/ *noun*

someone you do not know: *Never talk to strangers.*

stran•gle /ˈstræŋgəl/ *verb*
to kill someone by tightly pressing his or her throat with your hands, a rope, etc.: *Someone had strangled the woman to death.*

strap¹ /stræp/ *noun*
a strong band of cloth, leather, or plastic that is used to fasten, hang, or hold onto something: *The strap on my purse broke, and it fell onto the ground.*
→ See picture at **watch²**

strap² *verb*
to fasten something in place using a belt or band of material: *He strapped a flashlight to his head so he could keep his hands free.* | *Don't forget to strap yourself in* (=fasten your seat belt in a car).

stra•te•gic /strəˈtidʒɪk/ Ac *adjective*
1 done as part of a plan to achieve something: *The company made a strategic decision to move its headquarters to a less expensive place.*
2 strategic arms/weapons/bombing, etc. = weapons or attacks that are designed to reach an enemy area from your own area and destroy the enemy's ability to fight

strat•e•gy /ˈstrætədʒi/ Ac *noun* plural **strategies**
a planned series of actions for achieving something: *We need a strategy for getting money for our club.*

straw /strɔ/ *noun*
1 dried stems of wheat or similar plants, used for animals to sleep on, or for making things such as baskets: *The floor of the barn was covered with straw.*
2 a thin tube of plastic used for sucking a drink from a bottle or cup: *Do you want a straw for your drink?*
3 the last/final straw = the last problem in a series of problems that finally makes you get angry or stop trying to achieve something: *When she asked me to babysit for free again, that was the last straw.*
→ See picture on page A15

straw•ber•ry /ˈstrɔˌberi/ *noun* plural **strawberries**
a soft sweet red berry with small pale seeds on its surface
→ See picture on page A13

stray¹ /streɪ/ *verb*
to move away from the place where you should be, especially without intending to: *The dog had strayed from its neighborhood and was lost.*

stray² *adjective*
1 a stray animal is lost or has no home: *There were stray dogs running around in the street.*
2 accidentally separated from a larger group: *A stray bullet hit a woman who was standing nearby.*

streak /strik/ *noun*
1 a colored line or thin mark: *There were dirty streaks on the windows.*
2 a quality you have that seems different from the rest of your character: *She's very nice, but she has an independent streak and won't like me telling her what to do.*
3 a period of time when you are always successful or always failing: *The team is on a four-game winning streak* (=they have won the last four games).

stream¹ /strim/ *noun*
1 a natural flow of water that is smaller than a river: *They drank water from a mountain stream.*
→ See picture at **river**
2 a flow of water, gas, smoke, etc.: *A stream of hot air blew out of the machine.*
3 a long continuous series of people, vehicles, events, etc.: *A steady stream of trucks drove by all night and kept me awake.*

stream² *verb*
if a large amount of something or a large group of people streams somewhere, it moves quickly in one direction for a long time: *Thousands of students streamed out of the college auditorium after the speech.* | *Tears were streaming down her face as she watched the wedding.*

street /strit/ *noun*
1 a road in a town or city with houses, stores, etc. on one or both sides: *Watch for cars when you cross the street.* | *I live across the street from the park.*
2 the street/the streets = the busy public parts of a city, where there is a lot of activity, excitement, and crime: *He left home at 16 and lived on the street for two years.*
→ See Thesaurus box at **road**

S

street•light /ˈstritlaɪt/ *noun*
a light on a tall pole that is next to the street

strength /streŋθ/ *noun*
1 the physical power and energy that makes someone strong: *I was so tired that I didn't have the strength to walk home.* ANTONYM **weakness**
2 the quality of being brave or determined in dealing with difficult situations: *My parents' support gave me the strength to look for a new job.*
3 the power of an organization, country, or system: *The country's military strength helped it win the war.*
4 how strong a feeling, belief, or relationship is: *The strength of a mother's love can be very powerful.*
5 a quality or ability that makes someone or something successful: *Her intelligence is her greatest strength.*

S

strength•en /ˈstreŋθən/ *verb*
1 to make something such as a feeling, belief, or relationship stronger: *Her belief in God strengthened as she became older.* | *Eating together can strengthen family relationships.* ANTONYM **weaken**
2 to make something such as your body or a building stronger: *This exercise helps strengthen your arms.* ANTONYM **weaken**
3 to increase in value or improve: *The new laws should strengthen the economy.* ANTONYM **weaken**

stren•u•ous /ˈstrenyuəs/ *adjective*
using a lot of effort, strength, or determination: *The doctor told him not to do any strenuous exercise until he felt stronger.*
—**strenuously** *adverb*

stress¹ /stres/ Ac *noun*
1 strong feelings of worry that stop you from being happy or healthy: *Students are under a lot of stress before final exams.*
2 special attention or importance that you give to an idea or activity: *Mom always put stress on having good manners.* SYNONYM **emphasis**
3 the physical force or pressure on an object: *If you put too much stress on the table it might break.*
4 the amount of force you use when you say a word or part of a word: *In the word "after," the stress is on the first syllable.*
→ See picture on page A23

WORD FAMILY look at the words:

→ stress *noun*
→ stress *verb*
→ stressful *adjective*

stress² *verb*
1 to emphasize a statement, fact, or idea: *Ricardo stressed that everyone was welcome to come.*
2 to say a word or part of a word loudly or with more force: *"Don't do that," she said, stressing the word "don't."*

PHRASAL VERB
stress (someone) out
to feel worried and not relaxed, or to make someone feel worried and not relaxed: *I was stressing out before my biology test because I hadn't studied.* | *Visiting the dentist stresses her out.*

stress•ful /ˈstresfəl/ Ac *adjective*
making you worry a lot: *He has a stressful job and has to work a lot.*

stretch¹ /stretʃ/ *verb*
1 *also* **stretch out** to become bigger or looser as a result of being pulled: *The jeans will stretch after you start wearing them.* | *You're too big to wear my sweater – you'll stretch it out.*
2 to reach out your arms, legs, or body to full length: *Kim sat up in bed and stretched.*
3 to spread out over a large area: *The line of people waiting for the store to open stretched down the sidewalk.*
4 to pull something so it is tight: *They stretched a rope between two trees to hang their wet clothes on.*
5 stretch your legs *informal* = to go for a walk: *A few people got off the bus to stretch their legs.*
→ See picture on page A4

PHRASAL VERB
stretch out
informal to lie down so you can rest or sleep: *He stretched out on the bed.*

stretch² *noun*
1 an area of land or water: *This stretch of the road is steep and dangerous.*
2 a period of time that continues without stopping: *Two years is a long stretch of time if you're not happy.* | *We worked for ten hours at a stretch* (=without stopping).

3 an action in which you stretch part of your body: *It's good to do a few stretches before you exercise.*

stretch•er /ˈstretʃɚ/ *noun*
a frame that is used to carry someone who is injured or too sick to walk

strict /strɪkt/ *adjective*
1 expecting people to obey rules or do what you say: *Her parents are very strict – she's not allowed to go out at all during the week.*
2 a strict rule, order, etc. must be obeyed: *The school has strict rules about being late.*

strict•ly /ˈstrɪktli/ *adverb*
1 in a way that must be obeyed: *Smoking is strictly forbidden.*
2 used in order to emphasize that only one thing is true or possible, and nothing else: *I play the piano strictly for fun. I never perform.*

stride[1] /straɪd/ *verb* **strode** /stroʊd/ **stridden** /ˈstrɪdn/ **striding**
to walk with quick long steps: *He strode confidently across the room.*
➔ See Thesaurus box at **walk**[1]

stride[2] *noun*
a long step that you make when you walk: *He reached the door in three long strides.*

strike[1] /straɪk/ *verb* **struck** /strʌk/
1 *formal* to hit someone or something: *Ron struck his head on the table as he fell.* | *She struck him hard across the face.*
2 if a thought or idea strikes you, you suddenly realize it or think of it: *It suddenly struck me that I was the youngest person at the meeting.*
3 strike someone as something = to seem to someone to have a particular quality: *She strikes me as a very intelligent woman.*
4 if a group of workers strikes, they stop working for a while because they do not like something about their jobs: *The nurses are striking for higher pay.*
5 to attack quickly and suddenly: *Police fear the killer will strike again.*
6 if something bad strikes, it happens suddenly: *Most people were asleep when the earthquake struck.*
➔ See Thesaurus box at **hit**[1]

strike[2] *noun*
1 a time when a group of workers STRIKES: *The hotel workers went on strike for health insurance.*
2 a military attack: *Air strikes have destroyed large parts of the city.*

strik•ing /ˈstraɪkɪŋ/ *adjective*
1 unusual or interesting enough to be noticed: *The most striking part of the performance was the beautiful music.*
2 very attractive, often in an unusual way: *Even at age 75, she is still a striking woman.*
➔ See Thesaurus box at **clear**[1]

string[1] /strɪŋ/ *noun*
1 a strong thread made of several threads twisted together, used for tying things: *The pen was attached to the desk by a long piece of string.*
2 a number of similar things or events that happen one after the other: *There has been a string of accidents along this part of the highway.*
3 a string of pearls/beads, etc. = a lot of PEARLs, BEADs etc. on a string, chain, etc.: *They put a string of colored lights on the Christmas tree.*
4 one of the long thin pieces of wire that is stretched across a musical instrument to produce sound: *One of the strings on her guitar broke.*
5 the strings = the people in an ORCHESTRA who play instruments such as the VIOLIN, CELLO, etc.

string[2] *verb*
1 to hang things in a line using string, wire, etc.: *A woman was stringing the wash out on the wire.*
2 to put strings on a musical instrument: *Do you know how to string a guitar?*

string•y /ˈstrɪŋi/ *adjective*
1 stringy food has long thin pieces in it that are difficult to eat: *The meat was stringy and hard to chew.*
2 stringy hair is thin, dirty, and unpleasant looking: *He had a messy beard and long stringy hair.*

strip[1] /strɪp/ *verb* **stripped, stripping**
1 to take off your clothes: *He stripped and got into the shower.*
2 to remove something that is covering the surface of something else: *We need to strip off the wallpaper before we start painting.*

strip[2] *noun*
1 a long narrow piece of cloth, paper, etc.: *Tear the paper into one-inch strips.*

2 a long narrow area of land: *They own a strip of land by the lake.*

stripe /straɪp/ *noun*
a long narrow line of color: *a shirt with blue and red stripes*

striped /straɪpt/ *adjective*
having a pattern of stripes: *Do you like the striped tie or the solid blue one?*

strive /straɪv/ *verb* **strove** /stroʊv/ or **strived, striven** /ˈstrɪvən/ or **strived, striving** *formal*
to try very hard to get or do something: *The school is striving to improve its students' test scores.*

stroke[1] /stroʊk/ *noun*
1 an occasion when an ARTERY (=tube carrying blood) in your brain bursts or becomes blocked: *After Grandma had a stroke she couldn't move her left arm.*
2 a repeated movement of your arms when you are swimming or rowing a boat: *We learned the back stroke in swimming lessons today.*
3 a single movement of a pen or brush, or a line made by doing this: *If you look closely at the painting you can see the artist's brush strokes.*

stroke[2] *verb*
to move your hand gently over something: *He gently stroked the cat in his lap.*
➔ See picture on page A3
➔ See Thesaurus box at **touch**[1]

stroll /stroʊl/ *verb*
to walk in a slow relaxed way: *We strolled along the street and looked in the store windows.*
—**stroll** *noun* a slow relaxed walk: *We went for a stroll after dinner.*
➔ See Thesaurus box at **walk**[1]

stroll·er /ˈstroʊlɚ/ *noun*
a chair on wheels for a small child to be pushed along in

strong /strɔŋ/ *adjective*
1 having a lot of physical power: *He's so strong that he can move the refrigerator by himself.* | *strong legs* ANTONYM **weak**
2 not easily broken or damaged: *The plastic bags are very strong and can carry a lot.* | *a strong branch* ANTONYM **weak**
3 having a lot of power, influence, or ability: *We need a strong leader that people will listen to.* | *a strong army* ANTONYM **weak**
4 strong feelings, ideas, etc. are ones that you are very sure and serious about or that affect you a lot: *She has a strong belief that people are good.* | *He made a strong impression on everyone he met.* ANTONYM **weak**
5 a strong reason, opinion, etc. is one that is likely to persuade other people: *There's strong evidence that he's innocent, but many people still do not believe it.* ANTONYM **weak**
6 determined and able to deal with problems without becoming upset or worried by them: *Lola is very strong – she'll help the kids understand the bad news.*
7 a strong relationship or friendship is likely to last a long time: *They have a very strong friendship, so little arguments are not a big problem.*
8 having a taste, smell, color, etc. that is easy to notice: *The smell of her perfume was so strong it made me feel sick.*
9 likely to succeed or happen: *There's a strong chance it will rain, so you'd better take an umbrella.*
—**strongly** *adverb*: *I strongly agree with everything he said.*

WORD FAMILY look at the words:
➔ **strong** *adjective*
➔ **strongly** *adverb*
➔ **strength** *noun*
➔ **strengthen** *verb*

struck /strʌk/ *verb*
the past tense and past participle of STRIKE

struc·ture[1] /ˈstrʌktʃɚ/ Ac *noun*
1 the way in which the parts of something connect with each other to make a whole: *The structure of the brain is extremely complex.*
2 something that has been built: *The museum is a huge structure of steel and glass.*

structure[2] Ac *verb*
to organize something carefully so that all the parts connect together to make a whole: *The teacher structured the lesson so that the children would have time to learn about magnets and time to try to use them.*

strug•gle¹ /ˈstrʌgəl/ *verb*
1 to try very hard to do or achieve something, even though it is difficult: *She's struggling to raise her children alone.*
2 to fight someone who is attacking you or holding you: *She struggled with her attackers and screamed for help.*
3 to move somewhere with a lot of difficulty: *The old man struggled up the stairs.*

struggle² *noun*
1 a long hard fight for freedom, political rights, power, etc.: *the struggle for equal rights for all people*
2 a fight or argument between two people for something: *One of the men was stabbed during the struggle.*

strut /strʌt/ *verb* **strutted, strutting**
to walk in a proud way with your head up and your chest pushed forward: *He strutted around as if he was better than everyone else.*

stub /stʌb/ *noun*
1 the part of a ticket that is returned to you as proof that you have paid: *You need to show your ticket stub to get back inside.*
2 the short part of something that is left after the rest has been used: *a cigar stub*

stub•born /ˈstʌbən/ *adjective*
determined not to change your opinions, beliefs, etc., because you believe you are right: *He's so stubborn – there's nothing you can say to change what he thinks.*

stuck¹ /stʌk/ *verb*
the past tense and past participle of STICK

stuck² *adjective*
1 not able to move: *I can't open the drawer – it's stuck. | We got stuck in traffic.*
2 not able to continue working on something because it is too difficult: *Can you help me with my homework? I'm stuck on question 7.*
3 not able to get away from a boring or unpleasant situation: *I hate being stuck in the house on a rainy day.*

stu•dent /ˈstudnt/ *noun*
someone who is studying at a school, university, etc.: *She has 30 students in her class. | high school students*

stu•di•o /ˈstudiˌoʊ/ *noun*
1 a room where television and radio programs are made and broadcast, or where music is recorded: *a recording studio*
2 a movie company or the place where movies are made: *He works for one of the big Hollywood studios.*
3 a room where a painter or photographer works: *an art studio*
4 *also* **studio apartment** a small apartment with one main room

stud•y¹ /ˈstʌdi/ *verb* **studied**, third person singular **studies**
1 to spend time going to classes, reading, etc. to learn about a subject: *I need to study for my biology test. | She wants to go to college to study psychology.*
2 to examine something carefully to find out more about it: *Scientists are studying how cars affect the earth's temperatures.*

study² *noun* plural **studies**
1 a piece of work that is done to find out more about a particular subject or problem, and that is usually written in a report: *a scientific study | The study shows the dangerous effects of the drug.*
2 the process of learning about a subject: *the study of ancient history*
3 a room in a house that is used for work or study
4 **studies** = the work you do in order to learn about something: *After he finished his studies, he got a job with the government.*

stuff¹ /stʌf/ *noun, informal*
1 a substance or material of any type: *What's this sticky stuff on the table?*
2 a number of different things: *Where's the camping stuff? | You can put your stuff over here for now.*
3 different activities that someone does: *I have a lot of stuff to do. | He likes camping and fishing and stuff like that.*
4 different subjects, information, or ideas: *You don't believe all the stuff he says, do you?*
→ See Thesaurus boxes at **property** and **thing**

stuff² *verb*
1 to push things into a small space quickly: *He stuffed some clothes into a bag and left.*
2 to fill something until it is full: *They stuff the dolls' bodies with cotton.*

stuff•ing /ˈstʌfɪŋ/ *noun*
1 a mixture of bread, rice, etc. that you put inside a chicken, vegetable, etc. before cooking it

S

2 material that is used for filling something such as a PILLOW

stuff•y /'stʌfi/ *adjective*
not having enough fresh air: *The room was hot and stuffy.*

stum•ble /'stʌmbəl/ *verb*
1 to almost fall down while you are walking: *Larry got out of bed and stumbled over a book on the floor.*
2 to stop or make a mistake when you are reading or speaking to people: *He was nervous and stumbled over the words as he read his speech.*
PHRASAL VERB
stumble across/on/upon someone or something
to discover someone or something by chance: *I stumbled across some old pictures while I was cleaning my room.*
→ See Thesaurus box at **fall**[1]

S

stump /stʌmp/ *noun*
1 the part of a tree that is still in the ground after the rest has been cut down: *He sat on a tree stump to rest.*
2 the part of an arm, leg, etc. that remains when the rest has been cut off

stun /stʌn/ *verb* **stunned, stunning**
1 to surprise or shock someone so much that he or she cannot react immediately: *My sister stunned the family when she told us she was leaving home.*
2 to make someone almost unconscious for a short time by hitting him or her on the head: *The blow to his head stunned him for several minutes.*

stung /stʌŋ/ *verb*
the past tense and past participle of STING

stunk /stʌŋk/ *verb*
the past tense and past participle of STINK

stun•ning /'stʌnɪŋ/ *adjective*
1 extremely attractive or beautiful: *You look stunning in that dress.*
2 very surprising or shocking: *The team's stunning victory surprised everyone.*

stu•pid /'stupɪd/ *adjective*
not intelligent or showing good sense: *It was stupid of me to leave the tickets at home.* | *Stop asking stupid questions.* SYNONYM **dumb**; ANTONYM **smart**
—**stupidity** /stu'pɪdəti/ *noun* stupid behavior

stur•dy /'stɚdi/ *adjective* **sturdier, sturdiest**
strong and not likely to break: *sturdy walking boots* ANTONYM **fragile, delicate**

stut•ter /'stʌtɚ/ *verb*
to speak with difficulty, repeating the first sound of some words: *"My n-n-n-name is Joe," he stuttered.*
—**stutter** *noun* a way of talking in which you stutter

style /staɪl/ Ac *noun*
1 a particular way of doing something: *Her style of cooking is very simple.*
2 a design for clothes, hair, furniture, etc.: *I'm tired of my hair – I need a new style.*
3 if someone has style, he or she has a special way of dressing or doing things that people think is good: *She dresses with a lot of style, and always wears attractive clothes.*

styl•ish /'staɪlɪʃ/ Ac *adjective*
stylish people or things look good in a fashionable way: *She was wearing a stylish black dress.*

styl•ist /'staɪlɪst/ *noun*
someone whose job is to cut or arrange people's hair

sub•dued /səb'dud/ *adjective, formal*
more quiet than usual: *He seemed subdued, and only spoke when I asked him questions.* ANTONYM **talkative**

sub•ject[1] /'sʌbdʒɪkt/ *noun*
1 something that you talk or write about: *We need to talk about your grades – stop trying to change the subject* (=talk about something different)*!*
2 something that you study at school: *My favorite subject is math.*
3 the person or thing that does the action of a verb in a sentence: *In the sentence "Jane bought the bread," "Jane" is the subject.*

sub•ject[2] /səb'dʒekt/ *verb, formal*
PHRASAL VERB
subject someone to something
to make someone experience something bad: *The guards subjected prisoners to beatings.*

sub•jec•tive /səb'dʒektɪv/ *adjective, formal*
something that is subjective depends on your feelings or opinions, not on facts: *The scores were very subjective and based on*

only one judge's opinions. ANTONYM **objective**

ˈsubject ˌmatter *noun, formal*
the subject matter of a book, class, movie, etc. is what it is about: *The subject matter of the movie is not intended for children.*

sub·let /sʌbˈlet/ *verb* **sublet, subletting** *formal*
to pay money to someone so you can live in a place he or she is renting from its owner: *I moved out of my rented aprtment for the summer and sublet it.*

sub·ma·rine /ˈsʌbməˌrin/ *noun*
a ship that travels under water

sub·merge /səbˈmɚdʒ/ *verb, formal*
to put something under the surface of water: *Many cars were submerged by the flood.* SYNONYM **sink**

sub·mit /səbˈmɪt/ Ac *verb* **submitted, submitting** *formal*
to give something such as a plan or a piece of work to someone so that he and she can make a decision about it: *He failed the course because he submitted his work late.*

sub·scribe /səbˈskraɪb/ *verb, formal*
to pay money so that you get a magazine or newspaper every day, week, etc.: *I subscribe to a monthly computer magazine.*
—**subscription** /səbˈskrɪpʃən/ *noun* an agreement to subscribe to something

sub·se·quent /ˈsʌbsəkwənt/ Ac *adjective, formal*
coming after something: *This topic will be discussed again in subsequent chapters.* SYNONYM **following**
—**subsequently** *adverb* after something: *He had a heart attack and subsequently died.*

sub·side /səbˈsaɪd/ *verb, formal*
to become less strong or loud: *He took a pill, and soon the pain subsided.* ANTONYM **increase**

sub·stance /ˈsʌbstəns/ *noun, formal*
any type of solid or liquid: *Glue is a sticky substance.* SYNONYM **stuff**

sub·stan·tial /səbˈstænʃəl/ *adjective, formal*
large in amount or number: *$100,000 is a substantial amount of money.*

sub·sti·tute¹ /ˈsʌbstəˌtut/ Ac *noun*
someone or something that does what another person or thing usually does: *Our teacher, Miss Stein, was sick, so we had a substitute.* SYNONYM **replacement**

substitute² *verb*
to use something new or different instead of something else: *You can substitute margarine for butter in this recipe.* SYNONYM **replace**
—**substitution** /ˌsʌbstəˈtuʃən/ Ac *noun* the act of substituting one thing for another

sub·ti·tles /ˈsʌbˌtaɪtlz/ *noun*
words written at the bottom of a movie or television screen that tell you what a foreign actor is saying: *We watched a French movie with English subtitles.*

sub·tle /ˈsʌtl/ *adjective, formal*
not easy to notice: *There are subtle differences in the way people from different parts of the state talk.* SYNONYM **small**; ANTONYM **obvious**

sub·tle·ty /ˈsʌtlti/ *noun* plural **subtleties** *formal*
the quality of being important but difficult to notice: *I didn't understand all the subtleties of the play.*

sub·to·tal /ˈsʌbˌtoʊtl/ *noun, formal*
the amount you get when you add some but not all of a set of numbers: *Add the subtotals of each column of figures to get the total.*

sub·tract /səbˈtrækt/ *verb, formal*
to take a number or amount from a larger number or amount: *If you subtract 3 from 5 you get 2.* SYNONYM **take away**; ANTONYM **add**

sub·trac·tion /səbˈtrækʃən/ *noun, formal*
the act of subtracting one number or amount from another: *15 – 5 involves basic subtraction.* ANTONYM **addition**

sub·urb /ˈsʌbɚb/ *noun*
an area away from the center of a city, where a lot of people live: *She lives in a quiet suburb of Chicago.*
➔ See Thesaurus box at **area**

sub·way /ˈsʌbweɪ/ *noun* plural **subways**
a railroad that is under the ground in cities: *He rode the subway around New York City.*
➔ See picture on page A26

suc·ceed /səkˈsid/ *verb*
1 to do something that you wanted to do or tried to do: *The climbers finally succeeded in reaching the top of the mountain.* ANTONYM **fail**

S

2 to do well at school or in your job: *You don't need a college degree to succeed in business.*

WORD FAMILY look at the words:

→ **succeed** *verb*
→ **success** *noun*
→ **successful** *adjective*
→ **successfully** *adverb*

suc·cess /sək'ses/ *noun*
1 if you have success, you do what you wanted to do or what you tried to do: *He had no success in finding a job and is still unemployed.* ANTONYM **failure**
2 someone or something that is as good as you wanted it to be: *The party was a big success, and everyone had a good time.* ANTONYM **failure**

S

suc·cess·ful /sək'sesfəl/ *adjective*
1 someone who is successful has done what he or she wanted or tried to do: *She is very successful, and owns her own business.* ANTONYM **unsuccessful**
2 giving the result that you wanted: *It was a successful shopping trip, because we came back with everything on our list.* ANTONYM **unsuccessful**
—**successfully** *adverb*

such /sʌtʃ/ *adverb, adjective*
1 used when making what you say stronger: *I had such a bad headache (that) I had to lie down.*
2 *formal* like the one you have just mentioned: *He hates weddings, so he doesn't go to such events.*
3 *formal* **such as** = used when giving an example of something: *I like team sports, such as basketball.* SYNONYM **for example**

suck /sʌk/ *verb*
1 to hold something in your mouth and pull on it with your lips and tongue: *Lots of kids suck their thumbs.*
2 to pull liquid into your mouth with your lips: *The baby sucked milk from a bottle.*

sud·den /'sʌdn/ *adjective*
1 a sudden thing happens quickly, when you did not expect it: *I was shocked by his sudden change of attitude.*
2 **all of a sudden** = suddenly: *It was warm and sunny, then all of a sudden, it started to rain.*

sud·den·ly /'sʌdnli/ *adverb*
if something happens suddenly, it happens quickly, when you are not expecting it: *Smith died suddenly of a heart attack.*

sue /su/ *verb*
to try to make someone pay you money in a court of law, because he or she has made something bad happen to you: *She sued the man for damaging her car.*

suede /sweɪd/ *noun*
soft leather with a slightly rough surface: *a suede jacket*

suf·fer /'sʌfɚ/ *verb*
1 to feel pain or another bad feeling: *Drugs make sick people suffer less.*
2 *formal* if you suffer an injury or difficult situation, you experience it: *The team suffered a bad defeat.*
3 to become worse in quality: *He studied less, and his work began to suffer.*
—**sufferer** *noun* someone who has a particular disease

PHRASAL VERB

suffer from something
to have a disease or medical condition: *People who suffer from asthma sometimes find it difficult to breathe.*

suf·fer·ing /'sʌfərɪŋ/ *noun*
great pain or trouble that you experience: *It is terrible to watch the suffering of people who have no food.*

suf·fi·cient /sə'fɪʃənt/ Ac *adjective, formal*
enough: *One chicken is sufficient to feed four people.* ANTONYM **insufficient**
—**sufficiently** *adverb*: *He wasn't sufficiently interested to listen any more.*
→ See Thesaurus box at **enough**

suf·fix /'sʌfɪks/ *noun*
letters that you add to the end of a word to make a new word, such as adding the suffix "ness" to the word "kind" to make "kindness"

suf·fo·cate /'sʌfə,keɪt/ *verb*
to die because there is not enough air to breathe: *There was no air in the room, and I thought I was going to suffocate.*
—**suffocation** /,sʌfə'keɪʃən/ *noun* death by suffocating

sug·ar /ˈʃʊgɚ/ *noun*
a sweet white or brown substance used to make food or drinks sweet: *Do you want sugar in your coffee?*
—**sugary** *adjective* containing a lot of sugar

sug·gest /səgˈdʒest/ *verb*
1 to tell someone you think he or she should do something: *He suggested (that) I go see a doctor, but I don't think I need to.* | *They suggested meeting at 6.30.*
2 *formal* to make it seem that something is true: *Her red face suggested that she was embarrassed.*

sug·ges·tion /səgˈdʒestʃən/ *noun*
an idea about what someone should do: *I made a suggestion that we take a break.*

su·i·cide /ˈsuəˌsaɪd/ *noun*
the act of killing yourself: *Alan's brother was depressed before he committed suicide* (=killed himself).

suit¹ /sut/ *noun*
1 a set of clothes made of the same material, including a short coat and pants or a short coat and a skirt: *He wears a suit for work.*
2 a problem that someone brings to a court of law so that a judge can make a decision about it: *He filed a suit against the company that fired him.* SYNONYM **lawsuit**
➔ See picture on page A6

suit² *verb*
1 to be right for someone: *"Can you come tomorrow?" "That suits me fine."*
2 if clothes or colors suit you, they make you look nice because they go well with your skin color, shape, etc.: *Short skirts don't suit people with fat legs.*

suit·able /ˈsutəbəl/ *adjective*
right for a person or situation: *Violent movies are not suitable for small children.* SYNONYM **appropriate**; ANTONYM **unsuitable**

suit·case /ˈsutkeɪs/ *noun*
a large bag with a handle, in which you carry clothes when you travel: *She carried a small suitcase with her onto the plane.*
➔ See picture on page A30

suite /swit/ *noun*
a group of rooms in a hotel that cost a lot of money to stay in: *The band was staying in a suite at the best hotel in town.*

sul·fur /ˈsʌlfɚ/ *noun*
a yellow chemical substance: *Sulfur mixed with hydrogen has a bad smell.*

sulk /sʌlk/ *verb*
to show that you are annoyed about something by not saying anything and looking sad: *He sulks when he doesn't get what he wants.*

sul·len /ˈsʌlən/ *adjective, formal*
sad and not saying anything: *Her sullen face showed she was annoyed.*

sul·phur /ˈsʌlfɚ/
another spelling of SULFUR

sum¹ /sʌm/ Ac *noun*
1 an amount of money: *$5,000 is a large sum of money.*
2 the sum of something = the amount you get when you add two numbers together: *The sum of 4 and 5 is 9.*

sum² *verb* **summed, summing** *formal*
PHRASAL VERB
sum up
to end a speech by giving the main information about it again: *He spoke for an hour about his father, then summed up by saying, "He was a great man."*

sum·ma·rize /ˈsʌməˌraɪz/ Ac *verb*
to give the main information about something, not all the details: *We had to summarize the chapter in five sentences.*

sum·ma·ry /ˈsʌməri/ Ac *noun* plural **summaries**
a short statement that gives the main information about something, not all the details: *Read the article and write a short summary of it.*

sum·mer /ˈsʌmɚ/ *noun*
the season between spring and fall, when the weather is hottest: *The pool is open in the summer.*

sum·mer·time /ˈsʌmɚˌtaɪm/ *noun*
the time of year when it is summer: *In summertime, the days are longer.*

sum·mit /ˈsʌmɪt/ *noun, formal*
the top of a mountain: *He climbed to the summit of Mount Everest.*

sum·mon /ˈsʌmən/ *verb, formal*
to order someone to come to a place: *The principal summoned us to her office.* SYNONYM **call**

S

S

sun /sʌn/ *noun*
1 *also* **Sun** the large ball of fire in the sky that gives us light and heat: *The Earth moves around the Sun.*
2 the heat and light that come from the sun: *We went to the beach to lie in the sun.*

sun•bathe /ˈsʌnbeɪð/ *verb*
to lie in the sun so that your skin becomes brown: *We sunbathed by the pool.*

sun•block /ˈsʌnblɑk/ *noun*
a cream that you put on your skin to stop the sun from burning you

sun•burn /ˈsʌnbɚn/ *noun*
if you have a sunburn, your skin is red and sore because you have spent too much time in the sun: *You'd better come inside now, or you'll get a sunburn.*
—**sunburned** *also* **sunburnt** *adjective* having a sunburn

sun•dae /ˈsʌndeɪ/ *noun*
a dish of ICE CREAM, fruit, nuts, and a sweet liquid: *For dessert, I had a chocolate sundae.*

Sun•day /ˈsʌndi/ *noun*, *written abbreviation* **Sun.**
the first day of the week, between Saturday and Monday: *Anna is coming back Sunday.* | *I have to work on Sunday.* | *We're going to a baseball game next Sunday.* | *We had friends over last Sunday.* | *She usually wakes up early on Sunday morning.*

sun•flow•er /ˈsʌnˌflaʊɚ/ *noun*
a tall plant with a large yellow flower and seeds that you can eat

sung /sʌŋ/ *verb*
the past participle of SING

sunglasses

sun•glass•es /ˈsʌnˌglæsɪz/ *plural noun*
dark glasses that you wear to protect your eyes when the sun is bright

sunk /sʌŋk/ *verb*
a past tense and the past participle of SINK

sunk•en /ˈsʌŋkən/ *adjective, formal*
on the bottom of the ocean: *Divers discovered a sunken ship.*

sun•light /ˈsʌnlaɪt/ *noun*
light from the sun: *She opened the curtains, and sunlight filled the room.*

sun•ny /ˈsʌni/ *adjective*
if it is sunny, the sun is bright and there are few clouds: *It was a sunny day, and the sky was blue.* ANTONYM **cloudy**

sun•rise /ˈsʌnraɪz/ *noun*
the time in the morning when the sun first appears: *We got up at sunrise and started making breakfast.*

sun•screen /ˈsʌnskrin/ *noun*
a cream that you put on your skin to stop the sun from burning you

sun•set /ˈsʌnset/ *noun*
the time when the sun disappears and night begins: *We watched the beautiful pink and orange sunset.*

sun•shine /ˈsʌnʃaɪn/ *noun*
the light and heat from the sun: *I left the clothes to dry in the sunshine.*

sun•tan /ˈsʌntæn/ *noun*
if you have a suntan, your skin is brown because the sun has changed its color: *She came back from vacation with a suntan.* SYNONYM **tan**

su•per /ˈsupɚ/ *adjective, informal*
very good: *You did a super job on your homework – you get an A+!* SYNONYM **great**

su•perb /sʊˈpɚb/ *adjective, formal*
very good: *The hotel was superb, with big rooms and great food.* SYNONYM **excellent**; ANTONYM **terrible**

su•per•fi•cial /ˌsupɚˈfɪʃəl/ *adjective, formal*
not thorough or complete: *My knowledge of the subject is superficial – I only know what I've read in the newspapers.*

su•per•flu•ous /sʊˈpɚfluəs/ *adjective, formal*
not needed or wanted: *Remove superfluous information from the report to make it shorter.*

su•per•in•tend•ent /ˌsupɚɪnˈtendənt/ *noun*
1 someone who is responsible for all the schools in an area: *The superintendent of schools makes decisions for the whole school district.*
2 *also* **super** *informal* someone who takes care of an apartment building

su•pe•ri•or[1] /sə'pɪriɚ/ *adjective, formal*
better than other people or things: *The new computers are superior to the old ones.* ANTONYM **inferior**
—**superiority** /səˌpɪri'ɔrəti/ *noun, formal* the quality of being better than other people or things

superior[2] *noun, formal*
someone who has a higher position than you in your job: *His superiors told him he needed to work harder.*

su•per•la•tive /sʊ'pɚlətɪv/ *noun*
a form of a word that shows that something is the best, worst, biggest, smallest, etc.: *"Fastest" is the superlative of "fast."*

su•per•mar•ket /'supɚˌmɑrkɪt/ *noun*
a large store that sells food and things that people need for the house: *I bought some bread, meat, and milk at the supermarket.*

su•per•nat•u•ral /ˌsupɚ'nætʃərəl/ *adjective*
supernatural things do not seem real and you cannot explain them using science: *The boy in the movie has supernatural powers, and can talk to ghosts.*

sup•er•pow•er /'supɚˌpaʊɚ/ *noun*
a large powerful country, with a big army: *The U.S.A. is now the world's only military superpower.*

su•per•son•ic /ˌsupɚ'sɑnɪk/ *adjective, formal*
faster than the speed of sound: *The planes can fly at supersonic speeds.*

su•per•sti•tion /ˌsupɚ'stɪʃən/ *noun*
a belief that some things are lucky and some are not: *There is a superstition that the number 13 is unlucky.*
—**superstitious** *adjective* having many superstitions

su•per•vise /'supɚˌvaɪz/ *verb*
to watch people in order to make sure they do the right things while they work: *Mr. Stanyan supervises the younger employees.*
—**supervisory** /ˌsupɚ'vaɪzəri/ *noun* relating to supervising people: *a supervisory job*

su•per•vi•sion /ˌsupɚ'vɪʒən/ *noun, formal*
the activity of watching people in order to make sure they do the right things while they work: *Some students need a lot of supervision or they don't finish their work.*

su•per•vis•or /'supɚˌvaɪzɚ/ *noun*
someone who watches people to make sure they do the right things while they work: *Report any problems with the machines to your supervisor.*

sup•per /'sʌpɚ/ *noun*
an evening meal: *We had a light supper of soup and salad.* SYNONYM **dinner**

sup•ple•ment /'sʌpləˌment/ Ac *verb, formal*
to add one thing to another in order to make it better: *He took a night job to supplement his income.*
—**supplement** /'sʌpləmənt/ *noun* something that supplements another thing

sup•pli•er /sə'plaɪɚ/ *noun*
a company that provides things for businesses to buy: *The bakery called its supplier to order more flour.*

sup•ply[1] /sə'plaɪ/ *noun* plural **supplies**
1 an amount of something that you can use when you need it: *The country has a large supply of oil, but it won't last forever.* SYNONYM **store**
2 supplies = food and other things that people need every day: *The truck was carrying food, medicine, and other supplies for the soldiers.*

supply[2] *verb* **supplied**, third person singular **supplies**
to give or sell something to someone who needs it: *The farmers supply milk and vegetables to people in the town.* SYNONYM **provide**

sup•port[1] /sə'pɔrt/ *verb*
1 to hold something so that it does not fall: *Six wooden posts support the roof.*
2 to say that you agree with a person, group, or idea and want it to succeed: *Which political group do you support?*
3 to give money and food for someone to live: *He earns enough money to support his family.*
4 to help someone by being kind and giving advice when he or she has a problem: *She supported me when my mother was very sick.*

support[2] *noun*
1 if you give someone or something your support, you help them or say that you hope they will be successful: *They showed their*

S

support for the president by clapping and waving flags.
2 something that holds something else so that it does not fall: *Metal supports hold up the roof.*

sup•port•er /sə'pɔrtɚ/ *noun*
someone who supports a person, group, or plan: *The mayor's supporters love him.* SYNONYM **fan**

sup•port•ive /sə'pɔrtɪv/ *adjective*
a supportive person gives you help and advice when you have a problem: *My parents were very supportive when I broke up with my boyfriend.*

sup•pose /sə'poʊz/ *verb*
1 be supposed to do something = used when saying what someone should do, or what should happen: *You're supposed to stop your car at a red light.* | *When is the movie supposed to start?*
2 be supposed to be something = if something is supposed to be something, people say that it is like that: *I've never read it, but it's supposed to be a good book.*
3 I suppose = used when you think that something is probably true or that it might happen: *He's not here, so I suppose he went home.*
4 suppose (that) = used when talking about what might happen: *Suppose someone found out about our plan. What would you do?*

sup•pos•ed•ly /sə'poʊzɪdli/ *adverb, formal*
used when saying what other people say about someone or something, when you do not think they are right: *How could a supposedly intelligent person make so many stupid mistakes?*

sup•pos•ing /sə'poʊzɪŋ/ *conjunction*
used when talking about what might happen or be true: *Supposing it really was a ghost – that would be really scary!*

sup•press /sə'pres/ *verb, formal*
to control a feeling, so that you do not show it: *He could not suppress his anger, and started shouting.*
—**suppression** /sə'preʃən/ *noun, formal* the act of suppressing something

su•preme /sə'prim/ *adjective, formal*
highest, best, or most important: *The king was still the supreme political power in the country.*

Su,preme 'Court *noun*
the most important court in the country or in a state

sure[1] /ʃʊr/ *adjective*
1 certain about something: *I'm sure (that) he was there because I saw him.* | *I'm not sure what happened, but I can tell you what I heard.*
2 be sure to do something = to be certain to do something: *Whatever he decides to do, he's sure to be successful.*
3 for sure = if you know something for sure, you know that it is definitely true: *I think he's married, but I don't know for sure.*
4 make sure (that) a) to check that something is true or that something has been done: *He called to make sure that we got home okay.* **b)** to do something because it is important if you want a particular result: *If you want to get a good seat, make sure you get to the theater early.*

sure[2] *adverb*
1 *informal* used when saying yes to someone: *"Can I read your paper?" "Sure."*
2 *informal* used when emphasizing something you are saying: *It sure is cold today!* SYNONYM **certainly**
3 sure enough = used when saying that something that you expected to happen happened: *I thought she would be angry, and sure enough, she was.*

sure•ly /'ʃʊrli/ *adverb, formal*
used when you are surprised about something: *Surely you're not leaving so soon?*

surf

surf[1] /sɚf/ *verb*
1 to ride on ocean waves while standing on a board
2 surf the Internet/Net/Web = to look quickly at different pages on the Internet: *I*

was surfing the Internet and found this really interesting website.

—**surfing** *noun* the activity of surfing: *We went surfing in Hawaii.*

surf[2] *noun*

white waves that come onto the beach: *The surf wet my feet as I walked along the beach.*

sur•face[1] /ˈsɚfɪs/ *noun*

1 the outside or top part of something: *The Earth's surface is covered with land and oceans. | Leaves floated on the surface of the lake.*

2 used when talking about what someone or something seems to be like until you learn more about him, her, or it: *On the surface she seems very friendly, but when you get to know her better, she can be very mean.*

surface[2] *verb, formal*

1 if something surfaces, people start to know about it: *News reports began to surface that the leader was sick.* SYNONYM **appear**

2 to rise to the surface of water: *He went under the water and surfaced a few seconds later.* SYNONYM **come up**; ANTONYM **sink**

surf•board /ˈsɚfbɔrd/ *noun*

a board that you stand on to ride on ocean waves

surge[1] /sɚdʒ/ *verb, formal*

to suddenly move very quickly in a particular direction: *The crowd surged forward.* SYNONYM **push, press**

surge[2] *noun, formal*

a sudden large increase in something: *There is always a surge in demand for toys at Christmas.*

sur•geon /ˈsɚdʒən/ *noun*

a doctor who cuts open someone's body to fix or replace something inside: *Surgeons performed an operation on Mary's heart.*

➔ See Thesaurus box at **doctor**

sur•ger•y /ˈsɚdʒəri/ *noun*

the act of cutting open someone's body to fix or replace something inside: *She had surgery to repair her broken leg.*

sur•plus /ˈsɚpləs/ *noun, formal*

more of something than you need or can use: *We had a surplus of food, so we gave some of it away.* SYNONYM **excess**; ANTONYM **shortage**

—**surplus** *adjective*: *The army sells its surplus equipment.*

sur•prise[1] /sɚˈpraɪz/ *noun*

1 the feeling you have when something unusual or unexpected happens: *She stepped back in surprise, as a man came out of the women's bathroom.*

2 something that is unusual or that you did not expect: *I didn't know you were coming. What a surprise!*

3 take someone by surprise = if something takes you by surprise, you did not expect it: *The rain took me by surprise, and I didn't have an umbrella.* SYNONYM **surprise**

—**surprise** *adjective* unusual or not expected: *a surprise party*

WORD FAMILY look at the words:

➔ **surprise** *noun*
➔ **surprise** *verb*
➔ **surprised** *adjective*
➔ **surprising** *adjective*

surprise[2] *verb*

to make someone have a feeling of surprise: *His gift surprised me – I didn't expect anything from him.*

—**surprised** *adjective* having a feeling of surprise: *I'm surprised you're here – I thought you were working today.*

THESAURUS: surprised

amazed very surprised, because something seems unlikely: *I was amazed by how well she played, since she is so young.*

shocked feeling surprised, and often upset or offended: *We were all shocked by the news.*

astonished *formal* very surprised, because something seems unlikely: *Her lawyer was astonished that the jury found her guilty.*

startled surprised because something has suddenly happened: *She looked startled, as though she hadn't expected me to be there.*

—**surprising** *adjective* giving you a feeling of surprise: *surprising news*

➔ See picture on page A23

sur•ren•der /səˈrendɚ/ *verb, formal*

to stop fighting because you know that you cannot win: *Finally, the army surrendered to*

S

the stronger enemy.
—**surrender** *noun* the act of surrendering

sur•round /sə'raʊnd/ *verb*
to be or go all around something: *The school is surrounded by a fence.* | *Police officers surrounded the house.*

sur•round•ings /sə'raʊndɪŋz/ *plural noun*
the place that you are in and all the things in it: *When I moved to the new house, I missed my old surroundings.*

sur•vey¹ /'sɚveɪ/ Ac *noun*
a set of questions that you ask a large number of people to find out about their opinions and behavior: *They did a survey to see what kind of shampoo people buy.*

S

sur•vey² /sɚ'veɪ/ Ac *verb, formal*
to ask a large number of people a set of questions to find out about their opinions or behavior: *They surveyed 1,000 students to find out what foods they eat.*

sur•viv•al /sɚ'vaɪvəl/ Ac *noun*
the state of continuing to live after a difficult or dangerous time: *His chances of survival are not good* (=he will probably die).

sur•vive /sɚ'vaɪv/ Ac *verb*
to continue to live after an accident or illness: *Three people survived the car accident.*
—**survivor** *noun* someone who survives

WORD FAMILY look at the words:

→ **survive** *verb*
→ **survival** *noun*
→ **survivor** *noun*

sus•cep•ti•ble /sə'septəbəl/ *adjective, formal*
if you are susceptible to an illness or problem, you are likely to get it or experience it: *Young children are susceptible to coughs and colds.*

sus•pect¹ /sə'spekt/ *verb*
1 to think that someone may be guilty of a crime: *They suspected her of taking the money and told their teacher.*
2 to think that something is probably true: *I suspect (that) they lost my letter because I never got a reply.* SYNONYM **think**

WORD FAMILY look at the words:

→ **suspect** *verb*
→ **suspect** *noun*
→ **suspicion** *noun*
→ **suspicious** *adjective*

→ See Thesaurus box at **think**

sus•pect² /'sʌspekt/ *noun*
someone who the police think may have committed a crime: *The police interviewed the murder suspect.*

sus•pend /sə'spend/ Ac *verb*
1 to officially stop someone from going to school for a period of time, because he or she has done something bad: *He was suspended from school for attacking a teacher.*
2 *formal* to officially stop something from continuing for a short time: *Bad weather caused the airport to suspend flights.*
3 *formal* if something is suspended somewhere, it hangs there: *They suspended a light from the ceiling.*

sus•pense /sə'spens/ *noun*
a feeling of not knowing what is going to happen next: *Don't keep us in suspense – what happened?*
—**suspenseful** *adjective* giving you a feeling of suspense

sus•pen•sion /sə'spenʃən/ Ac *noun*
1 the act of officially stopping someone from going to school because he or she has done something bad: *He got a three-day suspension for starting a fight at school.*
2 *formal* the act of officially stopping something for a period of time: *Successful peace talks led to the suspension of fighting.*

sus•pi•cion /sə'spɪʃən/ *noun*
1 a belief that something may be true: *I had a suspicion (that) Joe was telling lies, but I wasn't sure.*
2 a feeling that you do not trust someone: *Police officers treat everyone with suspicion.*

sus•pi•cious /sə'spɪʃəs/ *adjective*
1 not trusting someone or something: *She wouldn't tell me who gave her the money, and that made me suspicious.* | *He's suspicious of strangers.*
2 making you think that something bad or wrong is happening: *There was something suspicious about the way he kept hiding his face.*

sus•tain /sə'steɪn/ Ac *verb, formal*
1 to make something continue to exist or happen: *John is doing well in school now, but will he be able to sustain his progress?* SYNONYM **maintain**
2 if you sustain an injury or damage, something hurts or damages you: *He sustained minor injuries, when his car crashed.* SYNONYM **suffer**

sus•tain•a•ble /sə'steɪnəbəl/ Ac *adjective, formal*
if something is sustainable, it can continue for a long time: *Their level of effort was not sustainable, and eventually they stopped working so hard.*

swal•low¹ /'swɑloʊ/ *verb*
to make food or drink go down your throat: *I put a pill in my mouth and swallowed it.*

swallow² *noun*
1 an act of making food or drink go down your throat: *Mike drank his milk in one swallow.*
2 a small bird with a tail that has two points

swam /swæm/ *verb*
the past tense of SWIM

swamp /swɑmp/ *noun*
land that is always soft and very wet: *Alligators live in the swamp.*
—**swampy** *adjective* like a swamp: *swampy ground*

swan /swɑn/ *noun*
a large white bird with a long neck, that swims on lakes

swap /swɑp/ *verb* **swapped, swapping**
to exchange something you have for something someone else has: *Can I swap seats with you so I can sit next to Ben?* SYNONYM **trade**
—**swap** *noun* an act of swapping things

swarm¹ /swɔrm/ *noun*
a large group of insects that move together: *A swarm of bees came out of the tree.*

swarm² *verb*
1 to move in a large group: *The crowd swarmed into the building.*
2 be swarming with = if a place is swarming with people, there are many of them there: *The beach is swarming with people on the weekend.*

sway /sweɪ/ *verb*
1 to move slowly from one side to the other: *The trees swayed in the wind.*
2 to influence someone's decision: *She has decided to leave, and nothing you say will sway her.*

swear /swer/ *verb* **swore** /swɔr/ **sworn** /swɔrn/
1 to say very rude words: *Don't swear in front of the children; we don't want them to use words like that.*
2 to promise that you will do something: *At the beginning of a court case, he had to swear to tell the truth.*
➔ See Thesaurus box at **promise¹**

PHRASAL VERBS

swear by something
to strongly believe that something is good for something: *Some people think that face cream doesn't make your skin softer, but I swear by it.*

swear someone in
to officially give someone an important job in a ceremony: *The new governor was sworn in today.*

sweat¹ /swet/ *verb*
if you sweat, water comes out of your skin because you are hot: *She was sweating when she reached the top of the hill.* SYNONYM **perspire**

sweat² *noun*
water that comes out of your skin when you are hot: *Sweat poured down his face as he ran.* SYNONYM **perspiration**
—**sweaty** *adjective* covered in sweat: *a sweaty towel*

sweat•er /'swetɚ/ *noun*
a piece of warm clothing for the top part of your body: *She put her sweater on over her shirt.*
➔ See picture on page A6

sweats /swets/ *plural noun*
1 another word for SWEAT SUIT
2 pants made of thick soft cotton that you wear when you play sports

sweat•shirt /'swet-ʃɚt/ *noun*
a soft thick piece of clothing for the top part of your body

S

'sweat suit *noun*
a set of clothes made of thick soft cotton that you wear when you play sports SYNONYM **sweats**
➔ See picture on page A6

sweep /swip/ *verb* **swept** /swept/
1 to clean the dirt from something using a brush: *I swept the floor with an old broom.*
2 *formal* to move quickly: *The crowd swept through the gates into the stadium.*
➔ See Thesaurus box at **clean[2]**

sweep•stakes /'swipsteɪks/ *noun* plural **sweepstakes**
a competition in which the winner wins a very big prize: *The winners of the sweepstakes are announced on TV.*

sweet /swit/ *adjective*
1 containing sugar or tasting like sugar: *I love sweet foods like chocolate and ice cream.* ANTONYM **sour**
2 pleasant, kind, and friendly: *It was sweet of you to help.* | *She has a sweet smile.* SYNONYM **nice**
—**sweeten** *verb* to make something sweet
➔ See Thesaurus box at **taste[1]**

sweet•heart /'swithɑrt/ *noun*
1 a way of talking to someone you love: *Good night, sweetheart.*
2 the person that you love: *He married his childhood sweetheart* (=someone he loved since he was very young).

swell /swel/ *also* **swell up** *verb* **swelled, swollen** /'swoʊlən/
to get bigger and rounder, especially because of being hurt: *My ankle swelled up like a balloon after I twisted it playing football.*
—**swelling** *noun* an area on your body that becomes larger than usual because of injury or sickness

swept /swept/ *verb*
the past tense and past participle of SWEEP

swerve /swɚv/ *verb*
to move suddenly to the left or right, especially so that you do not hit something: *The car swerved across the road to avoid hitting the boy.*

swift /swɪft/ *adjective*
happening or moving very quickly: *The army's swift victory surprised many people.*
—**swiftly** *adverb*

swim[1] /swɪm/ *verb* **swam** /swæm/ **swum** /swʌm/ **swimming**
to move through the water, using your arms and legs: *We swam in the ocean.*
—**swimming** *noun*: *Can we go swimming today?*
—**swimmer** *noun*: *She's a very good swimmer.*
➔ See picture on page A24

swim[2] *noun*
a time when you swim: *Do you want to go for a swim in the lake?*

'swimming pool *noun*
a structure that is filled with water for people to swim in SYNONYM **pool**

swim•suit /'swɪmsut/ *noun*
a piece of clothing worn for swimming SYNONYM **bathing suit**

swin•dle /'swɪndl/ *verb*
to get money from someone by tricking him or her: *He swindled his customers out of millions of dollars by selling them vacation homes that had never been built.*
—**swindle** *noun* the act of getting money from people by tricking them
—**swindler** *noun* someone who gets money from people by tricking them

swing[1] /swɪŋ/ *verb* **swung** /swʌŋ/
to move backward and forward: *The sign was swinging in the wind.* | *The door swung open when he pushed it.*
➔ See picture on page A4

swing[2] *noun*
1 a seat hanging from ropes or chains, which you sit on and make move backward and forward: *The kids were playing on the swings.*
2 take a swing at someone or something = to try to hit someone or something: *The boy took a swing at the ball.*

swipe /swaɪp/ *verb*
1 to pull a plastic card through a machine that can read the electronic information on it: *I swiped my security card in the machine.*
2 *informal* to steal something that is small or that does not cost much money: *He swiped a candy bar from the store and felt guilty about it later.*

Swiss¹ /swɪs/ *adjective*
relating to or coming from Switzerland: *a Swiss watch*

Swiss² *plural noun*
the Swiss = people from Switzerland: *The Swiss did well in the skiing competition.*

switch¹ /swɪtʃ/ *verb*
to change from one thing to another: *Some people switch jobs every couple of years.*
PHRASAL VERBS
switch something off
to make a light, machine, etc. stop working by pressing a switch: *Don't forget to switch off your computer when you're finished.* SYNONYM **turn off**
switch something on
to make a light, machine, etc. start working by pressing a switch: *Could you switch the radio on – there's a program I want to hear.*

switch² *noun*
a thing that you press to make a light, machine, etc. start or stop working: *a light switch*

switch•board /ˈswɪtʃbɔrd/ *noun*
a piece of equipment that connects all the telephone calls made to or from a hotel, company, etc.

swol•len¹ /ˈswoʊlən/ *verb*
the past participle of SWELL

swollen² *adjective*
a part of your body that is swollen is bigger than usual because of injury or sickness: *The side of his face was all swollen where he'd been hit by the ball.*

swoop /swup/ *verb*
to move down through the air, in order to catch or attack something: *The bird swooped down to catch a fish.*

sword /sɔrd/ *noun*
a weapon with a long sharp blade and a handle, which was used for fighting in past times: *He cut off the other man's arm with a sword.*

swore /swɔr/ *verb*
the past tense of SWEAR

sworn /swɔrn/ *verb*
the past participle of SWEAR

swum /swʌm/ *verb*
the past participle of SWIM

swung /swʌŋ/ *verb*
the past tense and past participle of SWING

syl•la•ble /ˈsɪləbəl/ *noun*
one of the parts that a word can be divided into. Each syllable has a single vowel sound: *"Cat" has one syllable, and "butter" has two syllables.*

syl•la•bus /ˈsɪləbəs/ *noun* plural **syllabi** /ˈsɪləbaɪ/ or **syllabuses**
a plan that shows what students will be studying during a class: *The syllabus covers American literature from 1900 to the present day.*

S

sym•bol /ˈsɪmbəl/ Ac *noun*
a sign, picture, object, etc. that represents something else: *The dove is a symbol of peace.*
—**symbolize** *verb* to be the symbol of something: *The shape of the heart symbolizes love.*

sym•met•ri•cal /sɪˈmetrɪkəl/ *adjective*
having two sides that are exactly the same size and shape: *The plant's leaves are perfectly symmetrical.*
—**symmetry** /ˈsɪmətri/ *noun* the condition of having two sides that are exactly the same

sym•pa•thet•ic /ˌsɪmpəˈθetɪk/ *adjective*
kind to someone who has problems or worries, and showing that you understand how he or she feels: *The nurse was very sympathetic and told me that I would soon feel better.* ANTONYM **unsympathetic**

sym•pa•thize /ˈsɪmpəˌθaɪz/ *verb*
to understand how sad, hurt, lonely, etc. someone feels: *I sympathized with the book's main character because I know how hard starting over can be.*

sym•pa•thy /ˈsɪmpəθi/ *noun* plural **sympathies**
1 the feeling you have when you understand and feel sad for someone because something bad has happened to him or her: *She felt a lot of sympathy for him when his parents died.*

2 the feeling that you agree with someone's opinion: *I have some sympathy for her point of view.*

WORD FAMILY look at the words:

- → **sympathy** *noun*
- → **sympathetic** *adjective*
- → **sympathize** *verb*

sym•pho•ny /'sɪmfəni/ *noun* plural **symphonies**
a long piece of music written for an ORCHESTRA

symp•tom /'sɪmptəm/ *noun*
something that shows you may have a disease or sickness: *The usual symptoms of a cold are a sore throat and a runny nose.*

S

syn•a•gogue /'sɪnəˌgɑg/ *noun*
a building where Jewish people go to have religious services

syn•di•cate /'sɪndəkət/ *noun*
a group of people or companies that join together to achieve something: *The land was bought by a syndicate of buyers.*

syn•o•nym /'sɪnəˌnɪm/ *noun, formal*
a word with the same meaning as another word: *"Sad" and "unhappy" are synonyms.*
ANTONYM **antonym**

syn•tax /'sɪntæks/ *noun, formal*
the way words are arranged in order to form sentences or phrases

syn•thet•ic /sɪn'θetɪk/ *adjective*
made from substances that are not natural, but are made by people in a factory: *The shoes were made from some kind of synthetic material, not leather.*

sy•ringe /sə'rɪndʒ/ *noun*
a hollow tube attached to a needle, which is used for giving medicine or taking out liquids through the skin: *The doctor got a syringe and gave me an injection of antibiotics.*

syr•up /'sɚəp/ *noun*
a thick sweet liquid made from sugar: *Can I have some more syrup on my pancakes?*

sys•tem /'sɪstəm/ *noun*
1 a group of things or parts that work together for a particular purpose: *a computer system | the city's transportation system*
2 a way of organizing or doing something: *a filing system*

sys•tem•at•ic /ˌsɪstə'mætɪk/ *adjective, formal*
done in a carefully organized way: *We need a systematic way of measuring the children's progress, not just random scores here and there.*
—**systematically** *adverb, formal*

Tt

tab /tæb/ *noun*

1 an amount of money that you must pay for something, when the amount is made of small amounts added together: *Hi John, will you put two coffees on my tab, and I'll pay you on Friday?*

2 a key that you press on a computer, to make the CURSOR move to a new place or move a particular number of spaces

tab•by /ˈtæbi/ *noun*

a cat with light and dark lines on its fur

ta•ble /ˈteɪbəl/ *noun*

1 a piece of furniture with a flat top supported by legs: *We all sat down at the table for dinner.*

2 a list of numbers or other information, arranged in rows on a page: *The table shows the average height and weight of children at different ages.*

→ See picture on page A15

ta•ble•cloth /ˈteɪbəlˌklɔθ/ *noun*

a large piece of cloth used for covering a table

→ See picture on page A15

ta•ble•spoon /ˈteɪbəlˌspun/ *noun*

1 a special large spoon used for measuring food: *Add two tablespoons of sugar.*

2 a large spoon used for eating food

—**tablespoonful** /ˈteɪbəlspunˌfʊl/ *noun* the amount this spoon holds

tab•let /ˈtæblɪt/ *noun*

1 a small round piece of medicine that you swallow: *I have to take two tablets after every meal.* SYNONYM **pill**

2 a set of pieces of paper for writing on that are glued together at the top: *a tablet of writing paper*

tack /tæk/ *noun*

a small nail with a flat top: *They fixed the carpet down with tacks.*

tack•le[1] /ˈtækəl/ *verb*

1 to try to deal with a difficult problem: *What do you think is the best way to tackle the problem of bullying on the playground?*

2 to make a player fall to the ground in football, so that he or she cannot carry the ball forward: *He was tackled by two players from the other team.*

tackle[2] *noun*

1 the act of making a player fall to the ground in football: *He made 52 successful tackles this year.*

2 a football player who tries to make other players fall to the ground

3 equipment you use for fishing

tack•y /ˈtæki/ *adjective*

1 something that is tacky shows that you do not know what is fashionable or what is acceptable behavior in a social situation: *He left the price tag on the present! That is just so tacky!*

2 cheaply made, not of good quality, and not looking good: *ugly, tacky furniture*

tact /tækt/ *noun*

the ability to say or do things carefully and politely so that you do not upset someone: *You need to use a lot of tact when you're dealing with customers.*

WORD FAMILY look at the words:

→ **tact** *noun*
→ **tactful** *adjective*
→ **tactless** *adjective*

tact•ful /ˈtæktfəl/ *adjective*

careful not to say or do something that will upset someone: *Doctors have to be tactful when they are asking people about their personal problems.* ANTONYM **tactless**

—**tactfully** *adverb*

tac•tic /ˈtæktɪk/ *noun*

a plan or way of organizing something that you use in order to do something: *We tried everything, but none of our tactics worked.*

tact•less /ˈtæktləs/ *adjective*

saying or doing things that are likely to upset someone, because you have not thought carefully about what you are saying: *It was tactless to say that she needed to lose some weight.* ANTONYM **tactful**

→ See Thesaurus box at **rude**

tad•pole /ˈtædpoʊl/ *noun*

a small creature with a long tail that lives in water and grows into a FROG or TOAD

tag /tæg/ *noun*
1 a small piece of paper, plastic, etc. that is attached to something and gives information about it: *It says $50 on the price tag.*
2 a children's game in which one player chases and tries to touch the others: *The kids were playing tag out on the playground.*

tail /teɪl/ *noun*
a part of an animal's body that the animal can move and that sticks out from just above their bottom: *Monkeys use their tails for climbing trees.* | *The dog was wagging its tail.*

tail·light /ˈteɪl-laɪt/ *noun*
one of the two red lights at the back of a car
➔ See picture on page A28

tai·lor /ˈteɪlɚ/ *noun*
someone whose job is to make clothes, especially men's clothes: *His suits came from a very expensive tailor in New York.*

T

tails /teɪlz/ *noun*
the side of a coin that does not have a picture of someone's head on it. This is used in a game in which one person throws a coin and other people guess which side will land facing up: *I won, because I called tails* (=guessed the coin would land with the tails side showing). ANTONYM **heads**

Tai·wan·ese[1] /ˌtaɪwɑˈniz/ *adjective*
relating to or coming from Taiwan

Taiwanese[2] *noun* plural **Taiwanese**
someone from Taiwan

take /teɪk/ *verb* **took** /tʊk/ **taken** /ˈteɪkən/
1 to move someone or something from one place to another: *The ambulance took him to the hospital.*

> **THESAURUS: take**
>
> **take** to move something from one place to another, or help someone go from one place to another: *You'd better take your jacket – it's getting cold.* | *I can take you home after the concert.*
>
> **bring** to take something or someone to a place: *You should bring her some flowers.* | *Elise brought her friend with her to the party.*
>
> **get** to go to another place and come back with something or someone: *Just a minute while I get my jacket.*

2 to remove something from a place: *He took the gun slowly out of his pocket.*
3 to get hold of something in your hands: *Let me take your coat.*
4 to steal or borrow something without asking someone's permission: *The thieves took all her money.*
5 used with some nouns when saying that someone does something: *Take a look at this!* | *I usually take a shower before breakfast.* | *I'm taking my driver's test next week.*
6 to need something in order to do something: *The game takes a lot of skill.* | *It takes about three hours to drive to Los Angeles.*
7 to accept something that someone has offered you: *Are you going to take the job?*
8 to drink or swallow some medicine or a drug: *"I have a headache." "Why don't you take an aspirin?"*
9 to use a car, bus, train, etc.: *I'll take the subway home.*
10 to react to something in a particular way: *"How did she take the news?" "She took it pretty badly."*
11 can't take something *informal* = use in order to say that you are becoming upset because a bad situation has been happening for too long: *I can't take it anymore – she just yells at us all the time.*
12 *also* **take down** to write down information: *He's not here; can I take a message* (=said when someone calls on the phone for someone who is not there)?
13 to measure the amount, level, or rate of something: *My mother took my temperature.*
14 to have enough space to contain a particular number of people or things: *The hall can take up to 300 people.*
15 to wear a particular size of clothing or shoes: *"What size shoes do you take?" "I take a size 8."*
16 to SUBTRACT a number from another number: *If you take 8 away from 20, you get 12.*
17 Do you take sugar/milk/cream, etc.? *spoken* = used when asking someone if they want to have sugar, milk, etc. in their coffee or tea
18 I'll take it = used when saying that you want to buy something
➔ **take care, take care of something** at **care**[2], **take effect** at **effect**, **take notice** at **notice**[2], **take part** at **part**[1], **take place** at **place**[1]

PHRASAL VERBS

take after someone
to look or behave like another person in your family: *She takes after her mother.*

take something away
to remove something: *They took away all our furniture.*

take something back
to return something to the store where you bought it because it does not fit, is not what you wanted, etc.: *If you don't like the dress, you can take it back.*

take in
1 take someone/something in = to give a home to a person or animal who has nowhere to live: *He had nowhere to live, but luckily one of his friends took him in.*
2 be taken in = to be deceived by someone who tells lies to you: *I was taken in by her story and gave her $20.*

take off
1 take something off = to remove a piece of clothing: *She took off her coat and sat down in a chair.* ANTONYM **put on**
2 take off = if a plane takes off, it leaves the ground and goes up into the air
3 take off *informal* = to leave a place quickly: *They took off without saying goodbye.*
4 take time off/take a week off, etc. = to not go to work for a period of time: *You look tired – you should take some time off.*
5 take off = to suddenly become successful: *He died just as his film career was taking off.*

take out
1 take someone out = to go with someone to a restaurant, movie, etc., and pay for this: *His girlfriend is taking him out for dinner on his birthday.*
2 take out a loan = to borrow money from a bank

take over something
to take control of something: *His son will take over the business.*

take up something
1 to begin doing a job or activity: *He took up swimming in order to try to lose weight.*
2 to fill a particular amount of time or space: *Our new car takes up the whole garage.*
3 to make a piece of clothing shorter: *Can you take up this dress for me?*

ˈtake-home ˌpay *noun*
the amount of money you get for doing your job after taxes have been taken away: *After taxes and Social Security, my take-home pay was less than I expected.*

tak•en /ˈteɪkən/ *verb*
the past participle of TAKE

take•off /ˈteɪk-ɔf/ *noun*
the time when an airplane leaves the ground and begins to fly: *They served the meal shortly after takeoff.* ANTONYM **landing**

take•out /ˈteɪk-aʊt/ *noun*
a meal or food that you buy at a restaurant to eat at home: *I don't feel like cooking tonight – let's get some takeout.*

tale /teɪl/ *noun, formal*
a story about events that are not real: *The book tells a tale of love and adventure during the war.* SYNONYM **story**
➔ See Thesaurus box at **story**

tal•ent /ˈtælənt/ *noun*
an ability to do something well: *Vinny has a real talent for for photography and has won many competitions.*
—**talented** *adjective* someone who is talented is very good at something: *He's a very talented actor; you really believe that he is the character.*
➔ See Thesaurus box at **ability**

talk¹ /tɔk/ *verb*
to say things to someone: *We spent the whole evening talking.* | *Who's he talking to on the phone?* | *They were talking about their classes and teachers.* | *Parents should find time to talk with their kids.*

THESAURUS: talk

have a conversation to talk to another person or people: *It's so noisy in here that it's hard to have a conversation.*

chat to talk to someone in a friendly way about things that are not very important: *She and her friends were chatting on the school bus.*

visit with someone *informal* to talk to someone you know well in a friendly way: *Mom was visiting with one of the neighbors.*

discuss to talk seriously about something: *I need to discuss this with your parents.*

T

gossip to talk about other people's behavior and lives, when they are not there, and often in an unkind way: *People were gossiping about Alan and Kim.*

whisper to talk quietly, when you do not want other people to hear what you are saying: *He turned to his mother and whispered something in her ear.*

converse *formal* to have a conversation with someone: *Students like her because she can converse with them in their own language.*

USAGE: talk

You **talk** about a particular subject: *Each student had to talk about his or her family.*

You **tell** a person facts or information: *She told me that she was going home.*

You **say** words to someone. You cannot say "say me": *She said to me that she was going home.*

T

—**talker** *noun* someone who talks a lot, or talks in a particular way

PHRASAL VERBS

talk back

to answer a parent, teacher, etc. in a rude way: *Don't talk back to your father!*

talk someone into doing something

to persuade someone to do something: *The kids talked us into getting a dog.*

talk someone out of (doing) something

to persuade someone not to do something: *His Mom talked him out of his plan to travel the world.*

talk something over

to discuss something with someone before deciding what to do: *It sounds like a good idea, but we should talk it over with everyone else before we do anything.*

WORD FAMILY look at the words:

→ **talk** *verb*
→ **talk** *noun*
→ **talkative** *adjective*

talk² *noun*

1 a conversation: *I need to have a talk with Suzanne about the way she's been behaving.*
2 a speech to a group of people: *Ms. Mason will be giving a talk on how to find a job.*

talk•a•tive /ˈtɔkətɪv/ *adjective*

someone who is talkative talks a lot: *He's very talkative and doesn't seem to listen to other people.*

ˈtalk show *noun*

a television show in which famous people answer questions about themselves

→ See Thesaurus box at **television**

tall /tɔl/ *adjective*

1 higher than most other people or things: *John is a lot taller than his younger brother.* | *The tallest building in town has 24 floors.* ANTONYM **short**

USAGE: tall

Use **tall** to talk about the height of people and trees: *She's only five feet tall.* | *a tall man* | *the tall trees in the park*

Use **tall** to talk about other narrow objects: *an old house with tall chimneys* | *a tall flagpole*

Use **high** to talk about mountains, walls, fences, etc.: *the highest mountain in the world* | *How high will the wall be?*

Use **high** to talk about how far something is from the ground: *The shelf's too high for the kids to reach.*

We usually use **tall** to talk about buildings: *the tall buildings in the downtown area*

2 having a particular height: *My brother's almost 6 feet tall.*

tam•bou•rine /ˌtæmbəˈrin/ *noun*

a musical instrument that you shake or hit with your hand. It looks like a small drum with metal pieces around the edge.

→ See picture on page A21

tame¹ /teɪm/ *adjective*

a tame animal is one that is not afraid of people because it has been near them a lot: *The bird was very tame, and flew right onto my hand.* ANTONYM **wild**

tame² *verb*

to train a wild animal so that it will not hurt people: *They tamed the monkeys and taught them to live with people.*

tam•per /ˈtæmpɚ/ *verb*

PHRASAL VERB

tamper with something

to touch or change something secretly, in order to cause damage: *Someone had tampered with his parachute, and he fell to his death.*

tam•pon /ˈtæmpɑn/ *noun*
a tube-shaped piece of cotton that a woman puts in her vagina during her PERIOD (=monthly flow of blood)

tan[1] /tæn/ *noun*
1 the darker skin that you get after you have been in the sun: *Monica got a nice tan during her trip to Hawaii.* SYNONYM **suntan**
2 a pale yellow-brown color

tan[2] *adjective*
1 someone who is tan has darker skin than usual because he or she has been in the sun: *You're really tan – have you been to the beach?*
2 pale yellow-brown in color: *He was wearing a pair of tan shoes.*

tan•ger•ine /ˌtændʒəˈrin/ *noun*
a sweet fruit that looks like a small orange
➔ See picture on page A13

tan•gi•ble /ˈtændʒəbəl/ *adjective, formal*
if something is tangible, you can be certain that it exists because you can see it, touch it, or prove it: *His hard work was starting to produce tangible results that everyone can see.*

tan•gle /ˈtæŋgəl/ *verb*
to twist hair or threads together into messy knots: *The strong wind tangled her long hair.*
—**tangle** *noun* a messy knot of hairs, threads, wires, etc.: *Mom combed the tangles out of my hair.*
—**tangled** *adjective* twisted together into messy knots: *tangled threads*

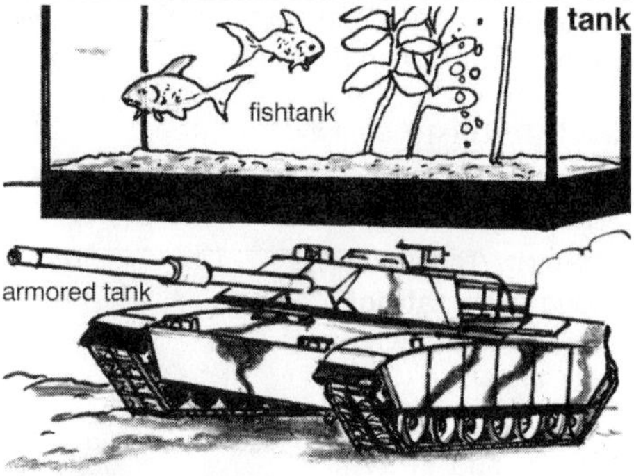

tank /tæŋk/ *noun*
1 a large container for holding liquid or gas: *She filled up the car's gas tank.* | *a fish tank*
2 a heavy military vehicle with guns on it and metal belts over its wheels

tank•er /ˈtæŋkɚ/ *noun*
a large ship or truck that carries liquids: *an oil tanker*

tanned /tænd/ *adjective*
another word for TAN: *tanned legs*

tan•trum /ˈtæntrəm/ *noun*
a time when a young child suddenly becomes angry and starts shouting and crying: *Jimmy had a big temper tantrum in the supermarket because I wouldn't buy him any candy.*

tap[1] /tæp/ *verb* **tapped, tapping**
to gently hit your fingers or foot against something: *She tapped her fingers on the table as she listened to the music.*
➔ See Thesaurus box at **hit**[1]
➔ See picture on page A3

tap[2] *noun*
1 an act of hitting something gently: *I turned when I felt a tap on my shoulder.*
2 an object that starts and stops the flow of liquid out of a pipe or container

ˈtap ˌdancing *noun*
a type of dancing in which you wear special shoes that make a sound as you dance

tape[1] /teɪp/ Ac *noun*
1 a long thin band of plastic in a small case that you use for recording sounds or pictures: *Put the tape in the VCR and press the "play" button.*
2 sticky clear plastic in a long band that you use for sticking things together: *The picture was stuck to the wall with tape.*

tape[2] *verb*
1 to record sounds or pictures onto a tape: *If we tape the movie, we can watch it later.*
2 to stick something onto something else using tape: *He has lots of postcards taped to his wall.*
➔ See Thesaurus box at **fasten**

ˈtape deck *noun*
the part of a piece of equipment in which you can play tapes with music on them: *I replaced the tape deck in my car with a CD player.*

ˈtape ˌmeasure *noun*
a long band of cloth or metal with inches or CENTIMETERs, etc. marked on it, that you use for measuring things

ˈtape reˌcorder *noun*
a machine that records and plays music and other sounds
—**tape recording** *noun* something that has been recorded using a tape recorder: *Police made a tape recording of the interview.*

tap·es·try /ˈtæpəstri/ *noun* plural **tapestries**
a picture that someone makes by weaving colored threads into heavy cloth: *There were many tapestries hanging on the walls in the palace.*

tar /tɑr/ *noun*
a black substance that is thick and sticky, and is used for making roads: *The men had put fresh tar on the road and it was still sticky.*

tar·get /ˈtɑrgɪt/ Ac *noun*
1 an object that you aim at if you are shooting: *Pete shot the arrow and missed the target by two inches.*
2 an object, person, or place that someone chooses to attack: *The building was the target of a terrorist bomb.*
3 the aim or result that you try to achieve: *We're trying to reach a target of $2 million in sales.*

tar·iff /ˈtærɪf/ *noun, formal*
a tax on goods that enter or leave a country: *The government may put new tariffs on imports to protect its own industries.*

tart /tɑrt/ *adjective*
having a sharp sour taste: *Add some sugar to the berries if they're too tart.*

task /tæsk/ Ac *noun, formal*
a job or particular thing that you have to do: *The competition judges had the difficult task of choosing a winner.*

taste¹ /teɪst/ *noun*
1 the feeling that you get when your tongue touches a particular food or drink: *Chocolate has a sweet taste.* | *I don't like the taste of garlic.* | *When you have a cold, your sense of taste and smell is not very good.*

THESAURUS: taste

delicious very good: *a delicious apple pie*
disgusting/horrible/awful very bad: *The food was disgusting – nothing seemed to be cooked right.*
sweet like sugar: *a sweet banana*
sour like a lemon: *The orange wasn't ripe so it was really sour.*
salty containing a lot of salt: *salty potato chips*
hot/spicy containing spices that give you the feeling that your mouth is burning: *Some Mexican food can be really spicy.*
bland not having very much taste: *The soup was really bland.*

2 the type of clothes, music, etc. that someone likes: *We have similar tastes in clothes and often buy the same things.*
3 a small amount of a food or drink that you have to find out what it is like: *Can I have a taste of your ice cream?*

taste² *verb*
1 to have a particular type of taste: *The chicken tastes really good – how did you make it?*
2 to put a small amount of food or drink in your mouth in order to find out what it is like: *Taste this and see if it needs more salt.*

taste·ful /ˈteɪstfəl/ *adjective, formal*
something that is tasteful looks attractive and shows that you have good judgment in choosing things: *The furniture was old but tasteful.* ANTONYM **tasteless**
—**tastefully** *adverb, formal*: *The apartment was tastefully decorated.*

taste·less /ˈteɪstləs/ *adjective, formal*
slightly offensive and not suitable for the situation: *She made some tasteless jokes about death when Ben's Dad had just died.*

tast·y /ˈteɪsti/ *adjective*
having a very good taste: *The fish was fresh and tasty.*

tat·too /təˈtu/ *noun* plural **tattoos**
a permanent picture or word on your skin, done using a needle and ink: *He has a tattoo of a snake on his left arm.*

tattoo
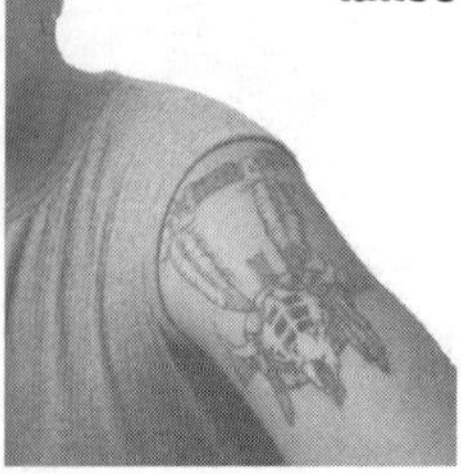

taught /tɔt/ *verb*
the past tense and past participle of TEACH

taunt /tɔnt/ *verb, formal*
to try to make someone upset or angry by saying cruel things: *The other kids taunted him about his weight.*

Tau•rus /ˈtɔrəs/ *noun*
1 the second sign of the ZODIAC, represented by a BULL
2 someone born between April 20 and May 20

taut /tɔt/ *adjective*
stretched tight: *The rope should be taut, not loose.*

tax¹ /tæks/ *noun*
the money you have to pay the government, based on how much you earn, what you buy, where you live, etc.: *There is a tax on gasoline.* | *Everyone who earns money is suppposed to pay tax.*

WORD FAMILY look at the words:
→ **tax** *noun*
→ **tax** *verb*
→ **taxation** *noun*
→ **taxable** *adjective*

tax² *verb*
to make people pay tax: *The government taxes people to pay for schools, roads, and many other things.*
—**taxable** *adjective* if something is taxable, you have to pay tax on it: *taxable income*

tax•a•tion /tækˈseɪʃən/ *noun*
the system of charging taxes, or the money a government gets from taxes

tax•i /ˈtæksi/ *noun*
a car with a driver whom you pay to take you somewhere: *I took a taxi to the airport.* | *a taxi driver* SYNONYM **cab**, **taxicab**
→ See picture on page A26

tax•i•cab /ˈtæksiˌkæb/ *noun*
another word for a TAXI

tea /ti/ *noun*
a hot drink that you make by pouring boiling water onto dried leaves: *Would you like a cup of tea or coffee?* | *herbal tea*

teach /titʃ/ *verb* **taught** /tɔt/
1 to give someone lessons in a school or college: *She teaches math at Jackson High School.* | *We teach all of our students basic computer skills.*
2 to tell or show someone how to do something: *My dad taught me how to swim.*

USAGE: teach
If you **teach** someone a subject or skill, you help him or her learn it: *Dad taught me to play the guitar.*
You cannot say "Dad learned me to play the guitar."
You **learn** a subject or skill when you study or practice it: *I want to learn English.* | *Jo's learning to drive.*

teach•er /ˈtitʃɚ/ *noun*
someone whose job is to teach: *She's a history teacher.*
→ See picture on page A16

ˌteacher's ˈpet *noun, informal*
a child who everyone thinks is the teacher's favorite student, so the other children do not like him or her

teach•ing /ˈtitʃɪŋ/ *noun*
the job of being a teacher: *I'd like to go into teaching* (=become a teacher) *when I finish college because I really like working with children.*

tea•ket•tle /ˈtiˌketl/ *noun*
a container that you boil water in to make drink

team /tim/ Ac *noun*
1 a group of people who compete against another group in a sport or game: *Which team is winning?* | *Greg is on the baseball team.*
2 a group of people who work together to do something: *A team of scientists is searching for a cure for the disease.*
→ See Thesaurus box at **group¹**

team•mate /ˈtim-meɪt/ *noun*
someone who plays or works on the same team as you

team•work /ˈtimwɚk/ *noun*
the ability of a group of people to work well together: *The success of the project will depend on good communication and teamwork.*

tea•pot /ˈtipɑt/ *noun*
a container used for serving tea

tear¹ /ter/ *verb* **tore** /tɔr/ **torn** /tɔrn/
1 to make a hole in paper or cloth by pulling it or by making it touch something sharp: *She tore her shirt on a nail.* | *The thin paper tears very easily.* SYNONYM **rip**
2 to pull something violently from a person

T

or place: *The strong wind tore the door off its hinges.*

PHRASAL VERBS

tear something down

to deliberately destroy a building: *The old train station was torn down in 1990.*

tear something up

to tear a piece of paper or cloth into small pieces: *He tore up the pictures of his ex-girlfriend.*

➔ See Thesaurus box at **break**[1]

tear[2] /ter/ *noun*

a hole in a piece of paper or cloth where someone or something has torn it: *I offered to sew up the tear in his shirt.*

tear[3] /tɪr/ *noun*

a drop of liquid that comes out of your eyes when you cry: *I had tears in my eyes as we said goodbye.* | *Garner left the courtroom in tears* (=crying).

—**tearful** *adjective* crying, or feeling as if you want to cry: *He said a tearful goodbye to his mother.*

T

tear•drop /ˈtɪrdrɑp/ *noun*

one drop of liquid that has come out of your eyes when you are crying

tease /tiz/ *verb*

to make jokes about someone in order to embarrass or annoy him or her: *His friends teased him about his accent.*

tea•spoon /ˈtispun/ *noun*

1 *written abbreviation* **tsp.** a special small spoon used for measuring food

2 a small spoon used for eating or putting sugar in drinks

tech•ni•cal /ˈteknɪkəl/ Ac *adjective*

relating to the knowledge of science or machines: *We offer technical support if you are having problems with your computer.*

tech•ni•cal•i•ty /ˌteknɪˈkæləti/ *noun*

plural **technicalities** *formal*

a small detail in a law or rule: *The police believed he was guilty, but they had to let him go because of a technicality.*

tech•ni•cian /tekˈnɪʃən/ *noun*

someone whose job involves using special machines or scientific equipment: *Lab technicians were testing all the blood samples.*

tech•nique /tekˈnik/ Ac *noun*

a special way of doing something: *Learning some relaxation techniques can help you deal with stress.*

tech•nol•o•gy /tekˈnɑlədʒi/ Ac *noun*

plural **technologies**

scientific knowledge and the way people use it to make machines: *New technology has meant that cell phones are much smaller than they used to be.*

—**technological** /ˌteknəˈlɑdʒɪkəl/ *adjective* relating to technology: *Technological developments have allowed more people to work from home.*

ted•dy bear /ˈtedi ˌber/ *noun*

a soft toy that looks like a bear

te•di•ous /ˈtidiəs/ *adjective, formal*

boring, and continuing for a long time: *I had the tedious job of typing all of the information into the computer.*

➔ See Thesaurus box at **boring**

teen /tin/ *noun*

another word for a TEENAGER

teen•ag•er /ˈtiˌneɪdʒɚ/ *noun*

someone who is between 13 and 19 years old: *The mall is full of teenagers after school.*

—**teenage** *adjective* between the ages of 13 and 19: *The magazine is intended for teenage girls.*

➔ See Thesaurus box at **child**

teens /tinz/ *plural noun*

the period of time when you are between 13 and 19 years old: *She got married when she was still in her teens.*

tee•ny /ˈtini/ *adjective, informal*

very small: *I'll just have a teeny bit of ice cream, please – I'm already pretty full.*

SYNONYM **tiny**

teeth /tiθ/

the plural of TOOTH

➔ See picture on page A2

tel•e•com•mu•ni•ca•tions

/ˌteləkəˌmyunəˈkeɪʃənz/ *noun, formal*

the process of sending and receiving messages by telephone, radio, SATELLITE, etc.: *Telecommunications companies provide telephone services.*

tel•e•gram /ˈteləˌgræm/ *noun*

a message that someone sends by telegraph

tel•e•graph /ˈtelə,græf/ *noun*
an old way of sending messages through wires using electrical signals
—**telegraph** *verb* to send a message by telegraph

tel•e•phone /ˈtelə,foʊn/ *noun*
another word for a PHONE: *Can you answer the telephone if it rings?*
—**telephone** *verb*, *formal* to call someone on a PHONE
➔ See picture on page A18

ˈtelephone di,rectory *noun*, *formal*
another word for a PHONE BOOK

ˈtelephone ,number *noun*
another word for PHONE NUMBER

tel•e•scope /ˈtelə,skoʊp/ *noun*
a piece of equipment shaped like a long tube that makes things that are far away look bigger: *Scientists use telescopes to study the moon and the planets.*

telescope

tel•e•vise /ˈtelə,vaɪz/ *verb*
to broadcast something on television: *The concert will be televised, so if you can't get tickets, let's watch it on TV.*

tel•e•vi•sion /ˈtelə,vɪʒən/ *noun*
1 *also* **television set** an object with a screen that shows moving pictures and produces sounds: *Lucy turned on the television to watch the news.* SYNONYM **TV**

THESAURUS: television

movie/film a TV program that is usually two hours long, and that tells a story: *There's a good movie on Channel 7 at 9 o'clock.*

soap opera a program that is on TV regularly, often every day, about the same group of people: *She was watching one of the daytime soap operas.*

sitcom a funny TV program which has the same people in it every week in a different story: *"I Love Lucy" was a popular sitcom about a woman and her husband.*

game show a program in which people play games in order to try and win prizes: *He won a trip to Hawaii on a game show.*

talk show a program in which famous people answer questions about themselves: *David Letterman's late night talk show*

cartoon a program with characters that are drawn and not real: *What's you favorite Saturday morning cartoon?*

series a set of TV programs about the same group of people or about a particular subject, that is shown regularly: *a new drama series about cops and lawyers*

documentary a program that gives information about a subject: *a documentary about wolves*

the news a program that gives reports about things that are happening in the world: *the 6 o'clock news*

2 the programs that you can watch and listen to on a television: *He's been watching television all day.* | *What's on television tonight?* SYNONYM **TV**
3 the activity of making and broadcasting programs on television: *Jean works in television.*
➔ See picture on page A8

tell /tel/ *verb* **told** /toʊld/
1 to give someone facts or information by talking or writing to them: *I can't tell you – it's a secret.* | *She wrote to tell me that she was getting married.* | *Tell me about your trip to New York.*

USAGE: tell

You **tell** a person facts or information: *She told me that she was going home.*

You **say** words to someone. You cannot say "say me": *She said to me that she was going home.*

You **talk** about a particular subject: *Each student had to talk about his or her family.*

2 to say that someone should do something: *She told Mike not to call her anymore.* | *His doctor told him that he needs to get more exercise.*
3 can tell/could tell = to know that something is true because you can see something that shows you it is true: *You can tell that they're sisters – they look so much alike.* | *I could tell that she was lying by the guilty look on her face.*
➔ See Thesaurus box at **explain**

tell•er /ˈtelɚ/ *noun*
someone whose job is to receive and pay out money in a bank: *The bank teller counted out the money and gave it to the customer.*

temp /temp/ *noun, informal*
someone who works for different companies for short periods of time: *We'll need a temp while Janet is on vacation.*

tem•per /ˈtempɚ/ *noun*
1 someone who has a temper gets angry easily or suddenly: *Julie has a terrible temper – she often shouts and throws things.*
2 lose your temper = to suddenly become very angry: *Al lost his temper and started screaming at us.*
➔ **temper tantrum**

T

tem•pera•ment /ˈtempərəmənt/ *noun, formal*
the type of character you have, for example whether you are usually happy, sad, friendly, etc.: *He has a calm temperament and is easy to be around.*

tem•pera•men•tal /ˌtempərəˈmentl/ *adjective, formal*
someone who is temperamental changes suddenly from being happy to being angry, sad, etc.: *My boss is temperamental, which makes him really hard to work for.*

tem•perate /ˈtempərət/ *adjective, formal*
weather or a part of the world that is temperate is never very hot or very cold: *I prefer a temperate climate to a tropical one.*

tem•pera•ture /ˈtemprətʃɚ/ *noun*
1 how hot or cold something is: *The temperature at night can drop to as low as 10° F.* | *Check the temperature of the water before you get into the tub.*
2 take someone's temperature = to measure the temperature of someone's body, to find out whether they are sick: *The nurse took my temperature with a thermometer.*
3 have a temperature = to be hot because you are sick: *He had a temperature and had to stay in bed.*

ˈtemper ˌtantrum *noun*
another word for a TANTRUM

tem•plate /ˈtempleɪt/ *noun*
something that you use as a model to make other similar things: *The software has easy-to-use templates for letters, reports, and brochures.*

tem•ple /ˈtempəl/ *noun*
1 a building where people in some religions go to pray: *a Buddhist temple*
2 the area on the side of your head, between your ear and your eye: *His dark hair is gray at the temples.*

tem•po /ˈtempoʊ/ *noun* plural **tempos**
the speed at which a person or band plays a piece of music: *He played the music at the wrong tempo – it was way too slow.*

tem•po•rar•y /ˈtempəˌreri/ Ac *adjective*
existing or happening for a short time only: *She got a temporary job during the summer.*
ANTONYM **permanent**
—**temporarily** /ˌtempəˈrerəli/ *adverb*: *The museum will be temporarily closed for repairs.*

tempt /tempt/ *verb*
to make someone want something that they should not have: *I was tempted to go with her, even though I hadn't asked Mom if I could.*

temp•ta•tion /tempˈteɪʃən/ *noun*
a strong feeling of wanting to have or do something that you should not: *I wanted another cookie, but I resisted the temptation* (=did not do what I wanted to do).

tempt•ing /ˈtemptɪŋ/ *adjective*
something that is tempting seems good and you would like to have it: *At Christmas, there are a lot of tempting foods around, and it's hard to stay on a diet.*

ten[1] /ten/ *number*
1 10: *The bill came to ten dollars.*
2 ten O'CLOCK: *I have a meeting at ten.*
3 ten years old: *She was ten when she came to New England.*

ten[2] *noun*
a piece of paper money worth $10: *I paid with a ten.*

ten•ant /ˈtenənt/ *noun*
someone who pays rent to live in a room or house: *Have you found any tenants for your house yet?*

tend /tend/ *verb*
tend to do something = to be likely to do a particular thing: *People tend to need less sleep as they become older.*
WORD FAMILY → **tendency** *adjective*

tend•en•cy /ˈtendənsi/ *noun* plural **tendencies** *formal*
if you have a tendency to do something, you often do it: *He has a tendency to talk too much and he often annoys his friends.*

ten•der /ˈtendɚ/ *adjective*
1 gentle and loving: *She gave him a tender kiss.*
2 tender food is soft and easy to cut and eat: *a tender steak* ANTONYM **tough**
3 a tender part of your body is painful if someone touches it because something has injured it: *My arm is still tender where I hurt it when I fell off my bicycle.*
—**tenderly** *adverb* in a gentle and loving way: *He kissed her tenderly.*
—**tenderness** *noun* a gentle and careful quality that shows love: *He took care of his sick wife with great tenderness.*

ten•nis /ˈtenɪs/ *noun*
a game in which two or four people use RACKETs to hit a ball to each other across a net: *We played tennis all afternoon.*
→ See picture on page A24

ˈtennis shoe *noun*
a shoe used for sports: *a pair of tennis shoes*

ten•or /ˈtenɚ/ *noun*
a male singer with a high voice: *Luciano Pavarotti is a famous tenor.*

tense¹ /tens/ Ac *adjective*
1 nervous and worried: *He felt very tense before the test.* ANTONYM **calm**
2 a tense situation makes people feel nervous or worried: *It was a tense game which either team could have won.*
WORD FAMILY → **tension** *noun*

tense² *noun*
in grammar, one of the forms of a verb that shows whether you are talking about the past, the present, or the future. For example, "he studied" is in the past tense and "he studies" is in the present tense: *Which tense is used in each of the sentences in this exercise?*

ten•sion /ˈtenʃən/ Ac *noun*
a nervous feeling that you have when you do not know what is going to happen: *The room was filled with tension as the students waited for the test to begin.*

tent /tent/ *noun*
a thing that you sleep in when you are camping, which is made of cloth and held up by poles and ropes: *We put up the tent in the campground.*

ten•ta•cle /ˈtentəkəl/ *noun*
one of the long soft arms of a sea animal such as an OCTOPUS

ten•ta•tive /ˈtentətɪv/ *adjective, formal*
not definite or certain: *We have tentative plans to meet for lunch on Tuesday, but we'll make definite plans on Monday.*

tenth /tenθ/ *number*
1 10th
2 1/10

te•pee *also* **teepee** *or* **tipi** /ˈtipi/ *noun*
a large round tent with a pointed top, used in past times by some Native Americans

te•qui•la /təˈkilə/ *noun*
a strong alcoholic drink made in Mexico

term¹ /tɚm/ *noun*
1 a word or expression that has a particular meaning: *The book contains a lot of difficult scientific terms.*
2 a period of time during which someone does a job: *The president is hoping to win a second term of office* (=a second period of time as president).
3 one of the periods that the school or college year is divided into: *She'll graduate after spring term.*
4 **in terms of something** = in relation to something: *Is the schedule realistic in terms of time and money?*
5 **terms** = the things that you accept or agree to do as part of a legal agreement: *Both sides have accepted the terms of the peace agreement.*

term² *verb, formal*
to use a word to describe something or give it a name: *Very bad headaches of this type are termed "migraines."*

ter•min•al /ˈtɚmənəl/ Ac *noun*
1 a building where people get on airplanes, buses, or ships: *Our plane leaves from Terminal 4.*

2 a screen and KEYBOARD that are connected to a computer: *She was sitting at a computer terminal, typing a report.*
3 one of the points at which you can connect wires in an electrical CIRCUIT: *Each battery has a positive and a negative terminal.*

ter•mi•nate /ˈtɚməˌneɪt/ Ac *verb, formal*
to end something: *The company decided to terminate his employment* (=no longer had a job for him).
—**termination** /ˌtɚməˈneɪʃən/ *noun, formal* the act of ending something

ter•mite /ˈtɚmaɪt/ *noun*
an insect that eats wood from trees and buildings, so that they are damaged: *Check your house regularly for termites.*

ˈterm ˌpaper *noun*
a long piece of written work by a student for a particular class: *I'm writing a term paper on the Civil War for my history class.*

T

ter•race /ˈterɪs/ *noun*
a flat area next to a building or on a roof, where you can sit: *We sat and had drinks on the terrace.*

ter•rain /təˈreɪn/ *noun, formal*
a particular type of land: *You need a strong pair of boots when walking over this rocky terrain.*

ter•ri•ble /ˈterəbəl/ *adjective*
very bad: *The food at the restaurant was terrible; I'm never going back.* | *I have a terrible headache.* SYNONYM **awful**
➔ See Thesaurus box at **bad**

ter•ri•bly /ˈterəbli/ *adverb*
1 very badly: *She sang terribly – the music was almost painful to listen to.*
2 *formal* very: *It's terribly important that I talk to him today.*

ter•rif•ic /təˈrɪfɪk/ *adjective, informal*
very good: *That's a terrific idea! Let's get started!* | *You look terrific in that dress.* SYNONYM **wonderful**

ter•ri•fy /ˈterəˌfaɪ/ *verb* **terrified**, third person singular **terrifies**
to make someone very frightened: *Flying terrifies me – I hate airplanes.*
—**terrified** *adjective* very frightened: *She was terrified of the big barking dog.*
—**terrifying** *adjective* making someone very frightened: *Being in jail was a terrifying experience.*

ter•ri•to•ry /ˈterəˌtɔri/ *noun* plural **territories**
1 land that is owned or controlled by a particular country: *Hong Kong became Chinese territory in 1997.*
2 an area of land: *This part of the mountains was unknown territory to me.*

ter•ror /ˈterɚ/ *noun*
1 a feeling of great fear: *She ran away in terror when she saw that the man had a gun.*
2 violent actions that are done to achieve a political purpose: *The president said he was doing everything possible to protect the country from terror.* SYNONYM **terrorism**

WORD FAMILY look at the words:
➔ **terror** *noun*
➔ **terrorize** *verb*
➔ **terrorist** *noun*
➔ **terrorism** *noun*

ter•ror•ism /ˈterəˌrɪzəm/ *noun*
the use of violent actions, usually against ordinary people, to try to force a government to do something: *The bombing was an act of terrorism.*

ter•ror•ist /ˈterərɪst/ *noun*
someone who uses violent actions, usually against ordinary people, to try to force a government to do something: *Terrorists use bombs to kill people.*

ter•ror•ize /ˈterəˌraɪz/ *verb, formal*
to deliberately frighten people by threatening to hurt them so that they will do what you want: *Some of the older children terrorized the younger kids.*

test¹ /test/ *noun*
1 a set of questions or activities to show how much you know or how well you can do something: *I passed my history test with a C.* | *She had to take her driving test three times before she passed.*
2 a short medical check on part of your body: *Children should have an eye test every year.*
3 something that scientists do to examine a substance: *Scientists are doing tests on the water to see if bacteria are present.*

test² *verb*
1 to ask someone questions or make him or her do things to show how much he or she knows or how well he or she can do something: *You'll be tested on everything we've learned this semester.*
2 to use something to find out whether it works: *The company is testing its new computer software before selling it.*
3 to do a medical check on part of someone's body: *The doctor tested her for heart disease.*
4 to check a substance to see what is in it: *The kids tested the water in the river for pollution.*

tes•ti•fy /ˈtestəˌfaɪ/ *verb* **testified**, third person singular **testifies** *formal*
to say in a law court what you know about something: *She testified that she had seen O'Brien leaving the house where the murder took place.*

tes•ti•mo•ny /ˈtestəˌmoʊni/ *noun* plural **testimonies** *formal*
the things you say in a law court about what you know about a crime: *The mother of the victim will give testimony on Friday.*

ˈtest tube *noun*
a small glass narrow container that is used in scientific tests: *The scientist poured the liquid into the test tube.*

Tex-Mex /ˌteks ˈmeks/ *adjective, informal*
relating to the music, cooking, etc. of Mexican-American people in Texas: *a Tex-Mex restaurant*

text /tekst/ Ac *noun*
1 the writing in a book, magazine, etc., rather than the pictures: *The report contains both pictures and text.*
2 a book about a subject which students use: *a math text* SYNONYM **textbook**

text•book /ˈtekstbʊk/ *also* **text** *noun*
a book about a subject which students use: *a history textbook*
➔ See Thesaurus box at **book¹**

tex•tile /ˈtekstaɪl/ *noun, formal*
any material that you make by crossing threads over and under each other: *The country exports textiles, especially silk and cotton.*

tex•ture /ˈtekstʃɚ/ *noun*
the way that something feels when you touch it: *Silk has a very smooth texture.*

than /ðən; *strong* ðæn/ *preposition*
used when comparing people or things: *My brother's older than me.* | *These shoes are cheaper than the other ones.* | *I can swim better than you.*

thank /θæŋk/ *verb*
1 to tell someone that you are happy or pleased about something he or she has done or has given you: *She thanked the boy for helping her.*
2 thank you = said when you want to thank someone: *Thank you for the birthday present!* | *"Here's your dinner." "Thank you."*

thank•ful /ˈθæŋkfəl/ *adjective*
glad about something: *We're thankful (that) nobody was hurt in the accident.*
—**thankfully** *adverb*: *Thankfully, it didn't rain during our picnic.*

thanks¹ /θæŋks/
said when you want to thank someone: *Thanks for taking the time to explain this to me.* | *"What time is it?" "Six o'clock." "Thanks."* | *"Would you like something to drink?" "No, thanks."*

thanks² *plural noun*
1 something that you say or do to thank someone: *I wrote him a letter of thanks.*
2 thanks to someone or something = because of someone or something: *We arrived late thanks to the traffic.*

Thanks•giv•ing /ˌθæŋksˈgɪvɪŋ/ *noun*
a holiday in the U.S. and Canada in the fall when families have a large meal together to show their thanks for food, families, health, etc.: *My whole family was here for Thanksgiving, and of course we had turkey and pumpkin pie.*

ˈthank-you *noun*
something that you say or do to thank someone: *They gave her some flowers as a thank-you.*

that¹ /ðæt/ *adjective, pronoun* plural **those** /ðoʊz/
1 used for talking about someone or something that is farther away from you, often in a place you point at: *My office is in that building.* | *Who are those boys over there?* | *Give me that!*

T

2 used for saying something about the thing you are already talking about: *I've never seen that movie.* | *Who told you that?* | *Do you have those old photographs of Dad?*
3 /ðət/ used instead of "who" or "which": *He's the boy that hit me.* | *There are lots of things that I need to do before I leave.*

that² /ðət; *strong* ðæt/ *conjunction*
1 used for joining two parts of a sentence: *He promised that he would be here.* | *Is it true that you are leaving?*
2 used after a phrase with "so" or "such" to say what the result of something is: *I was so tired that I could hardly walk.* | *They were making so much noise that I didn't hear the phone.*

that³ /ðæt/ *adverb*
1 so or very: *It won't cost all that much.* | *I didn't realize things were that bad.*
2 that long/that much/that big, etc. = as long, much, big, etc. as you show, using your hands: *The car missed us by about that much.*

T

thaw /θɔ/ *also* **thaw out** *verb*
if something frozen thaws, it becomes warmer until all the ice is gone: *The snow began to thaw in the warmer weather.* | *The freezer broke and all the food thawed out.*
ANTONYM **freeze**
—**thaw** *noun* a time when ice or snow thaws

the /ðə; *before a vowel* ði; *strong* ði/ *article*
1 used before a noun to show that you are talking about a particular person or thing: *The boy was riding a blue bicycle.* | *That's the dress I want to buy.* | *He went to the store to buy some milk.*
2 used before the names of rivers, oceans, and seas and before the names of groups of mountains: *the Mississippi River* | *the Atlantic Ocean* | *the Mediterranean Sea*
3 used before the names of certain countries: *the Philippines* | *the United States* | *the Czech Republic*
4 used for talking about all the people in a particular type of group: *a school for the deaf* | *The Germans are well-known for their cars.*
5 used for talking about a particular time or date: *Today is the fifth of May.* | *The 1960s were a time of great change in America.*
6 used for saying that something is important or famous: *This is the movie to see this year.*

USAGE: the

Do not use **the** when you are talking about all or every one of something, using a noun that is something you cannot count or a noun that shows there is more than one person or thing in the group: *I like ice cream.* | *Cats often hunt at night.*

Use **the** when you are talking about a particular thing: *I like the ice cream you bought.* | *The cats on our street make a lot of noise.*

Do not use **the** before the names of airports, train stations, or streets: *We arrived at O'Hare.* | *The train leaves from Grand Central.* | *She lives on Carr Avenue.*

Use **the** when you are talking about a particular airport, train station, or street without naming it: *We arrived at the airport.* | *The train was just leaving the station.* | *They live on the same street.*

the·a·ter /ˈθiətɚ/ *noun*
1 a building where actors perform plays: *the Apollo Theater*
2 a building where you go to see movies: *There's a good movie showing at the theater.*
3 the business of writing or performing plays: *I'd love to have a career in theater.*
—**theatrical** /θiˈætrɪkəl/ *adjective* relating to writing and performing plays: *a theatrical company*

theft /θeft/ *noun*
the crime of stealing something: *Police caught the boys in the stolen car and arrested them for theft.*
➔ See Thesaurus box at **crime**

their /ðɚ; *strong* ðer/ *adjective*
belonging to particular people or animals: *My neighbors are selling their house.*

theirs /ðerz/ *pronoun*
the thing or things that belong to particular people or animals: *The white house with the tree in front is theirs.*

them /ðəm ; *strong* ðem/ *pronoun*
used for talking about the people or things that have already been mentioned: *We made some cookies, and then we ate them all.*

theme /θim/ Ac *noun*
the main subject or idea in a book, movie, speech, etc.: *Love is the central theme of the book.*
—**thematic** /θiˈmætɪk/ *adjective, formal* relating to a theme: *the thematic content of the poem*
—**thematically** *adverb* in a way that relates to a theme

ˈ**theme park** *noun*
an AMUSEMENT PARK where the rides relate to one subject, for example water or space travel

them·selves /ðəmˈselvz/ *pronoun*
1 used when the same people or animals that you have just mentioned do an action: *The elephants were washing themselves in the river.*
2 used for emphasizing that particular people do something: *Kids should clean their rooms themselves.*
3 (all) by themselves = alone or without help: *Many old people live by themselves.*

then /ðen/ *adverb*
1 used for saying what you do next: *I get up at 7:30, and then I have breakfast.*
2 at a particular time in the past: *We lived in New York back then.*
3 used for saying what the result of a situation is: *"I'm going to be late!" "Then you'd better hurry up."*

the·ol·o·gy /θiˈɑlədʒi/ *noun*
the study of religion

the·o·ret·i·cal /ˌθiəˈretɪkəl/ Ac *adjective*
relating to something that is only an idea, and is not definitely true or right: *Life on other planets is only a theoretical possibility – there is no direct evidence for it.*
—**theoretically** *adverb*

the·o·ry /ˈθiəri/ Ac *noun* plural **theories**
an idea that tries to explain why something happens, but that may not be true: *Scientists are testing a theory that listening to Mozart's music before a test will help you do better.*
—**theorist** *noun* someone who thinks of ideas that explain why things happen
—**theorize** *verb* to think of a possible explanation for something that happens: *Scientists theorize about how the universe began.*

WORD FAMILY look at the words:
→ **theory** *noun*
→ **theoretical** *adjective*
→ **theoretically** *adverb*
→ **theorist** *noun*
→ **theorize** *verb*

ther·a·py /ˈθerəpi/ *noun* plural **therapies**
treatment for mental or physical problems, which can take weeks, months, or years: *After her son died, she had therapy for depression.*
—**therapist** *noun* someone whose job is treating mental or physical problems: *A physical therapist gave me a program of exercises to do.*

there[1] /ðer/ *pronoun*
there is/there are, etc. = used for describing what is in a place, or what happens: *There's a big truck parked outside.* | *There was an accident on the highway this morning.* | *Is there a store around here?*

there[2] *adverb*
1 in or to another place, not the place where you are: *I know Seattle well because I used to live there.* | *Jamie's having a party at 8, so I'm going over there about 8:30.*
2 hello there/hi there *informal* = said to greet someone

there·by /ðerˈbaɪ/ Ac *adverb, formal*
with the result that something happens: *Cars produce poisonous gas, thereby polluting the air.*

there·fore /ˈðerfɔr/ *adverb, formal*
for the reason that you have mentioned: *This house is smaller, and therefore cheaper.*

ther·mal /ˈθɚməl/ *adjective*
relating to or caused by heat: *The air contains thermal energy from the sun.*

ther·mom·e·ter /θɚˈmɑmətɚ/ *noun*
an instrument that measures how hot or cold something is, for example your body or the air: *When I was sick, the nurse took my temperature with a thermometer.*

Ther·mos *also* **thermos** /ˈθɚməs/ *noun, trademark*
a special type of bottle that keeps drinks hot or cold: *I always take a thermos of hot coffee on a trip.*

T

ther•mo•stat /ˈθɚməˌstæt/ *noun*
an instrument that controls how hot or cold a room or machine is: *I turned down the thermostat to 65° to save energy.*

the•sau•rus /θɪˈsɔrəs/ *noun* plural **thesauruses** or **thesauri** /θɪˈsɔraɪ/
a book in which words are put into groups with other words that have a similar meaning

these /ðiz/ *adjective, pronoun*
the plural form of THIS

the•sis /ˈθisɪs/ Ac *noun* plural **theses** /ˈθisiz/
a long piece of writing that you do in college, especially for a MASTER'S DEGREE: *He wrote his thesis on 18th century literature.*

they /ðeɪ/ *pronoun*
the people or things that you have just mentioned: *I called Carl and Tammy, but they weren't home.* | *Look at these flowers – aren't they beautiful?*

T

they'd /ðeɪd/
1 the short form of "they had": *When I arrived, they'd already left.*
2 the short form of "they would": *They said they'd help us.*

they'll /ðeɪl/
the short form of "they will": *If they are late, they'll miss the plane.*

they're /ðɚ; *strong* ðer/
the short form of "they are": *I love cats – they're so cute.*

they've /ðeɪv/
the short form of "they have": *They've lived in this neighborhood for twenty years.*

thick

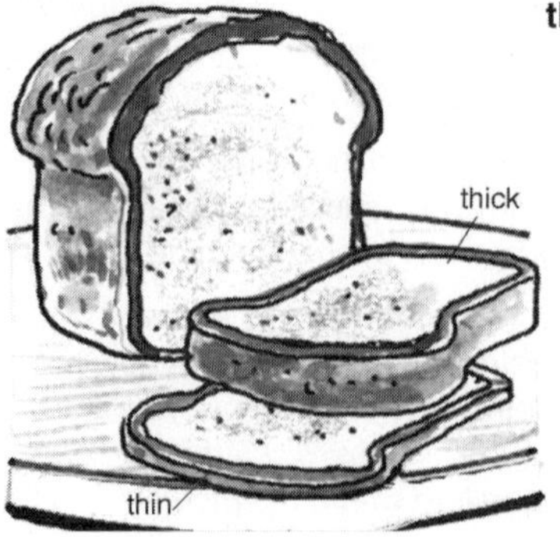

thick /θɪk/ *adjective*
1 having a large distance between one side and the other: *The old building had thick stone walls.* | *Dad cut a a thick slice of bread.* ANTONYM **thin**
2 if you have thick hair, you have a lot of hair: *He has thick black hair.* ANTONYM **thin**
3 a thick liquid does not have much water in it: *If the paint is too thick, add a little water.*
4 difficult to see through or breathe in: *There was thick fog outside.*

thick•en /ˈθɪkən/ *verb*
1 if a liquid thickens, it becomes more solid, with less water: *Stir the sauce until it thickens.*
2 if fog, snow, or smoke thickens, it becomes more difficult to see through: *Outside, the fog had thickened.*

thick•ly /ˈθɪkli/ *adverb*
in thick pieces, or in a thick layer: *The ham was thickly sliced.* | *He spread the butter thickly on his bread.* ANTONYM **thinly**

thick•ness /ˈθɪknəs/ *noun*
how thick and solid something is: *Cook the meat for 15–20 minutes, depending on its thickness.*

thief /θif/ *noun* plural **thieves** /θivz/
someone who steals things: *A thief grabbed my purse and ran away with it.* | *a car thief*

thigh /θaɪ/ *noun*
the top part of your leg above your knee
➔ See picture on page A2

thin /θɪn/ *adjective* **thinner**, **thinnest**
1 not having much fat on your body: *He's tall and thin.* ANTONYM **fat**

THESAURUS: thin

slim and **slender** used about someone who is thin in a way that looks good: *a slim young woman*

skinny used about someone who is very thin in a way that does not look good: *a tall, skinny boy*

lean used about someone who is thin in a healthy way: *His body was lean and he looked strong.*

2 having a small distance between one side and the other: *She cut a thin slice of cheese.* | *a thin layer of snow* ANTONYM **thick**
3 if you have thin hair, you do not have a lot of hair: *an old man with thin gray hair* ANTONYM **thick**
4 a liquid that is thin has a lot of water in it: *This soup's too thin.* ANTONYM **thick**
—**thinness** *noun* the state of having very

little fat on your body: *I was shocked by her thinness.*

➔ See picture at **thick**

thing /θɪŋ/ *noun*

1 an object: *What's that thing on the table?*

THESAURUS: thing

object *formal* a thing, especially a hard solid thing: *a sharp metal object*

something a thing, used especially when you do not know its name or what it is: *There's something in my eye.*

item *formal* one of the things in a set, group, or list: *He saved a few items and threw away the rest.*

article *formal* a thing, especially one of a group of things: *an article of clothing*

stuff a number of different things: *Where did you put my painting stuff?*

2 an event, statement, action, etc.: *A funny thing happened last week.* | *That's a terrible thing to say.* | *The best thing to do if you burn yourself is to put cold water on the burn.*

3 things = the events that are happening in your life, and how they affect you: *How are things with you?* | *I hope things will get better soon.*

4 things = the objects that you own: *I packed all my things and put them in the car.*

5 for one thing = used for giving one of the reasons for something: *We can't go. For one thing, we don't have the money.*

6 first thing = at the beginning of the day or morning: *I'll do that first thing tomorrow.*

think /θɪŋk/ *verb* **thought** /θɔt/

1 to use your mind to have ideas or solve problems: *I've just thought of an excellent idea!* | *What are you thinking about?* | *Think carefully before you answer this question.*

THESAURUS: think

believe to think that something is true: *We believe that the risk is small.*

suspect to think that something, especially something bad, is true, but to not be sure: *She suspected that he was seeing another woman.*

consider *formal* to think about something carefully before deciding what to do: *Have you considered going to a community college?*

figure to think that something is likely to be true: *I figure he's at least 19.*

guess to try to answer a question or decide something without knowing all the facts: *I guessed at the answer and got it right!*

2 to have an opinion or belief about something: *Do you think it's going to rain?* | *I think that Mr. Anderson is a great teacher.* | *"Will you see Ben on the weekend?" "I think so (=I believe I will)."*

3 be thinking about doing something/be thinking of doing something = to consider the idea of doing something in the future: *I'm thinking about studying to be a teacher.*

PHRASAL VERBS

think something over

to consider something carefully before you decide about it: *They offered me the job, and I have a week to think it over.*

think something up

to have an idea, plan, etc. that is completely new: *He's always thinking up crazy ideas for making money.*

think•er /ˈθɪŋkɚ/ *noun*

someone who uses his or her mind in a particular way: *She's a very creative thinker with some great ideas.*

thin•ly /ˈθɪnli/ *adverb*

1 in thin pieces, or in a thin layer: *Slice the meat thinly.* | *Spread the butter thinly.* ANTONYM **thickly**

2 thinly populated = having only a small number of people living in an area: *The mountains are thinly populated.* ANTONYM **densely**

third /θɚd/ *number*

1 3rd; someone or something that is after the second one

2 1/3

ˌthird ˈperson *noun*

the pronouns "he," "she," "it," and "they," or the forms of the verbs you use with them: *The verb "speaks" is in the third person singular.*

ˌThird ˈWorld *noun*

the Third World = the poor countries of the world that do not have a lot of industry

T

thirst /θɚst/ *noun*
the feeling of wanting or needing a drink: *I drank some water to quench my thirst* (=stop me being thirsty).

thirst·y /ˈθɚsti/ *adjective* **thirstier, thirstiest**
feeling that you want to drink something: *We were all very thirsty, so we stopped and drank some water.*
—**thirstily** *adverb* in a way that shows that you want to drink something very much: *Evie drank the water thirstily.*

thir·teen /ˌθɚˈtin/ *number*
1 13: *It took thirteen hours to get to Miami.*
2 thirteen years old: *Most of the kids in my class are still thirteen.*
—**thirteenth** /ˌθɚˈtinθ/ *number* 13th or 1/13

thir·ty /ˈθɚti/ *number*
1 30
2 the thirties a) *also* **the '30s** the years between 1930 and 1939 **b)** *also* **the 30s** the numbers between 30 and 39, especially when used for measuring temperature
3 be in your thirties = to be aged between 30 and 39: *She's in her early thirties and just had her first baby.*
—**thirtieth** /ˈθɚtiɪθ/ *number* 30th or 1/30

T

this[1] /ðɪs/ *adjective, pronoun* plural **these** /ðiz/
1 the one that is close to you, or that you are holding: *This is my book, and that's yours.* | *My grandmother gave me this necklace.* | *These are the best shoes I have.*
2 this Monday/this week/this month, etc. = the day, week, etc. that is closest to today: *We're going to see a movie this Friday* (=on Friday of the present week)
3 *informal* used for talking about something that someone has just mentioned: *Where is this party you're going to?*

this[2] *adverb*
this big/tall/hard, etc. = as big, tall, etc. as the one you are talking about: *I've never seen an apple this big before.*

this·tle /ˈθɪsəl/ *noun*
a wild plant with leaves that have sharp points

thongs /θɔŋz/ *noun*
shoes that do not have a top part, and that are held on your feet by a band shaped like a V that fits between your toes
➔ See picture at **shoe**

thorn /θɔrn/ *noun*
a sharp point that grows on a plant such as a rose: *I scratched my hand on the bush's thorns.*

thorn·y /ˈθɔrni/ *adjective*
1 a thorny problem/issue, etc. = a problem that is very difficult to deal with: *Heavy traffic in the downtown area is a thorny issue.*
2 having a lot of THORNS: *a thorny bush*

thor·ough /ˈθɚoʊ/ *adjective*
very careful and checking everything: *The police made a thorough search of the house looking for clues.*
—**thoroughly** *adverb*: *Make sure you prepare thoroughly for your tests.*
—**thoroughness** *noun*: *The doctor impressed me with his thoroughness.*

thor·ough·bred /ˈθɚəˌbred/ *noun*
a horse that has both parents of one very good breed

those /ðoʊz/ *adjective, pronoun*
the plural of THAT

though /ðoʊ/ *conjunction*
1 even if one fact is true: *My family was very happy, though we were poor.*
2 but: *I think I passed my test, though I'm not completely sure.*
3 as though = as if: *You look as though you need a vacation.*

thought[1] /θɔt/ *verb*
the past tense and past participle of THINK

thought[2] *noun*
1 an idea that you think of: *The thought of food was making me hungry.* | *Let me know if you have any other thoughts on this.*
2 the act of thinking about something carefully: *I'll have to give your idea some thought.*

thought·ful /ˈθɔtfəl/ *adjective*
1 serious and quiet because you are thinking about something: *Dad was sitting in the kitchen with a thoughtful look on his face.*
2 kind and thinking how to make other people happy: *It was thoughtful of you to call me on my birthday.*
➔ See Thesaurus box at **kind**[2]

thought·less /ˈθɔtləs/ *adjective*
not kind and not thinking about the feelings of other people: *He made a thoughtless remark about fat people.*

thou•sand /ˈθaʊzənd/ *number*
1 1,000
2 thousands *informal* = a lot of: *We've received thousands of letters from fans.*
—**thousandth** *adjective* 1,000th or 1/1,000

thread¹ /θred/ *noun*
a long thin string of cotton, silk, etc. that you use for sewing cloth: *She began sewing with a needle and thread.*

thread² *verb*
to put thread through a hole: *Can you thread this needle for me?*

threat /θret/ *noun*
a statement that you will do something violent if someone does not do what you want: *They used threats of violence to control the prisoners.* | *a bomb threat*

threat•en /ˈθretn/ *verb*
to say that you will do something bad or violent if someone does not do what you want: *He threatened to tell the teacher if we didn't stop being mean to him.*
—**threatening** *adjective* seeming to threaten someone: *a threatening letter*

three /θri/ *number*
1 3: *I've got three sisters.* | *She lost three of her CDs at the party.*
2 three O'CLOCK: *I'll meet you at three.*
3 three years old: *My sister's three.*

ˌthree-diˈmensional *also* **3-D** /ˌθri ˈdi/ *adjective*
having length, depth, and height: *A cube is a three-dimensional shape.*

threw /θru/ *verb*
the past tense of THROW

ˈthrift store *noun*
a store that sells used things and old clothes at low prices

thrif•ty /ˈθrɪfti/ *adjective, formal*
good at using money carefully and not wasting any: *He's hardworking and thrifty and has managed to save a lot of money.*

thrill¹ /θrɪl/ *noun*
a strong feeling of excitement and pleasure: *It was a thrill to meet a professional basketball player.*

thrill² *verb, formal*
to make someone feel great excitement and pleasure: *The idea of studying in Europe thrilled her.*

thrilled /θrɪld/ *adjective*
very excited, pleased, or happy: *My parents were thrilled when I graduated from college.*

thrill•er /ˈθrɪlɚ/ *noun*
a movie or book that tells an exciting story about murder or crime
➔ See Thesaurus box at **movie**

thrill•ing /ˈθrɪlɪŋ/ *adjective*
exciting and interesting: *It was a thrilling game with lost of action!*

thrive /θraɪv/ *verb* **thrived** or **throve** /θroʊv/ **thrived, thriving** *formal*
1 to become very successful: *Their business is thriving and they're going to hire more people.*
2 to become very strong and healthy: *These plants thrive in dry conditions.*

throat /θroʊt/ *noun*
1 the passage at the back of your mouth, where you swallow: *I have a sore throat, and it hurts when I swallow.*
2 the front part of your neck: *The man held me by the throat, so I couldn't move.*
➔ See picture on page A2

throne /θroʊn/ *noun*
the special chair on which a king or queen sits

through¹ /θru/ *preposition, adverb*
1 in one side of something, and out the other side: *The train went through a tunnel.* | *I managed to open a window and climb through.*
2 because of someone or something: *He got the job through a friend.*
3 from the beginning to the end of something: *I've looked through the book but I haven't read it carefully.*

through² *adjective, informal*
be through with something = to have finished using something, doing something, etc.: *Are you through with the phone yet?*
➔ See Thesaurus box at **done²**

through•out /θruˈaʊt/ *adverb, preposition*
1 in every part of a place: *The band is famous throughout the world.*
2 during all of a time: *She stayed with him in the hospital throughout the day.*

T

through•way *also* **thruway** /ˈθruˌweɪ/ *noun*
a big wide road for traffic that is traveling fast: *He took the throughway to get to work faster.*

throw¹ /θroʊ/ *verb* **threw** /θru/ **thrown** /θroʊn/
to force something out of your hand and through the air: *He threw the ball to me, and I caught it.*

THESAURUS: throw

To Throw Something

toss to throw something, especially in a careless way: *She tossed her coat onto the bed.*

hurl to throw something with a lot of force: *They hurled a brick through his window.*

fling to throw something somewhere with a lot of force, often in a careless way: *One night she flung the cooking pans out of the window.*

To Throw a Ball in a Sport

pass to throw, kick, or hit a ball to another member of your team: *Rodriguez passed to Johnson, who scored.*

pitch to throw the ball toward the person who is trying to hit the ball in a game of baseball: *Mitchell will pitch in Friday's game.*

PHRASAL VERBS

throw something away
to get rid of old food, paper, empty cans, etc.: *We used paper plates, so we could throw them away after the party.*

throw out
1 throw something out = to get rid of old things that you do not want or need: *I'm throwing out some of my old clothes.*
2 throw someone out = to make someone leave a place quickly because he or she is behaving badly: *Jay got drunk and they threw him out of the restaurant.*

throw² *noun*
an action of throwing something such as a ball: *That was a good throw – the ball came right to me!*

thrown /θroʊn/ *verb*
the past participle of THROW

thrust /θrʌst/ *verb* **thrust** *formal*
to push something somewhere suddenly or with force: *He thrust his hands into his pockets, and walked away angrily.*

thud /θʌd/ *noun*
the low sound of something heavy hitting the ground: *Mark fell off the horse, and landed with a thud.*

thug /θʌg/ *noun*
someone who is violent and may attack people: *A gang of thugs* (=a group) *attacked the man and stole his money.*

thumb /θʌm/ *noun*
1 the short thick finger on your hand that helps you hold things: *She held the coin between her finger and thumb.*
2 give someone or something the thumbs up = to show that you approve of someone or something: *A lot of people voted, and gave the idea the thumbs up.*
➔ See picture at **hand¹**

thumb•tack /ˈθʌmtæk/ *noun*
a short pin with a round flat top, that you use for attaching papers to walls: *I used thumbtacks to put the sign on the board.*

thump /θʌmp/ *verb*
to hit something in a way that makes a low sound: *Someone was outside the house, thumping on the door.*

thun•der /ˈθʌndɚ/ *noun*
the loud noise that you hear in the sky during a storm: *There was a storm last night, and the thunder woke me up.*

thun•der•storm /ˈθʌndɚˌstɔrm/ *noun*
a storm with THUNDER and LIGHTNING: *Did you hear the thunderstorm yesterday?*

Thurs•day /ˈθɚzdi/ *noun, written abbreviation* **Thurs.**
the fifth day of the week, between Wednesday and Friday: *I tried to call you Thursday.* | *Kim is leaving for Chicago on Thursday.* | *He was arrested last Thursday.* | *I made the appointment for next Thursday.* | *Jason arrived late Thursday night.*

thus /ðʌs/ *adverb, formal*
1 as a result of what you have just said: *There will be more and more cars, and thus pollution will increase.* SYNONYM **so**
2 thus far = until now: *Thus far, the disease has spread slowly, but it is uncertain what will happen in the future.*

thy•roid /ˈθaɪrɔɪd/ *also* **ˈthyroid ˌgland** *noun*
an organ in your neck that produces HORMONEs (=substances that affect your body and your behavior)

tick[1] /tɪk/ *noun*
1 a small creature like an insect that goes into your skin and sucks your blood: *After you go hiking, check your arms and legs for ticks.*
2 the short sound that a clock or watch makes: *The loud tick of the clock was keeping me awake.*
➔ See picture on page A22

tick[2] *verb*
if a clock or watch ticks, it makes a short sound every second: *In the silence, I could hear the clock ticking.*

tick•et /ˈtɪkɪt/ *noun*
1 a small piece of paper that shows that you have paid to see a movie, travel on a bus, etc.: *Tickets for the concert cost $15.* | *Do you have your plane ticket?*
2 a legal note saying that you must pay some money because you drove or parked your car in the wrong way: *I got a parking ticket for parking in a red zone.*
➔ See picture on page A30

ˈticket ˌoffice *noun*
a place that sells tickets: *I called the airline's ticket office about flying to Minneapolis.*

tick•le /ˈtɪkəl/ *verb*
to move your fingers lightly on parts of someone's body to try and make him or her laugh: *Dad was playing with the kids and tickling them under their arms.*
—**ticklish** *adjective* if you are ticklish, you laugh easily when someone tickles you: *Don't touch my feet – I'm ticklish!*
➔ See Thesaurus box at **touch**[1]

tic-tac-toe /ˌtɪk tæk ˈtoʊ/ *noun*
a children's game in which two players draw X's and O's in nine squares and try to get three of the same letter in a row

tide

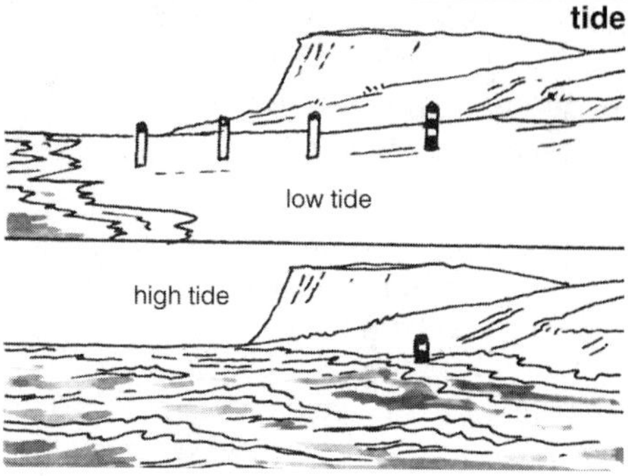

tide /taɪd/ *noun*
the change in the level of the ocean that happens because of the moon: *The ocean covers the whole beach at high tide* (=when the level is the highest).

ti•dy /ˈtaɪdi/ *adjective*
another word for NEAT

tie[1] /taɪ/ *verb* **tied, tying,** third person singular **ties**
1 to fasten something using rope, string, etc.: *I tied the dog to a tree so it wouldn't run away.* ANTONYM **untie**
2 if two players, teams, etc. tie, they have the same number of points at the end of a game or the same time at the end of a race: *The two runners tied for first place.*
—**tied** *adjective* having the same number of points during a game: *The score was tied at the end of the first half of the game.*

PHRASAL VERB

tie up
1 tie someone up = to tie someone's arms, legs, etc. so that he or she cannot move: *They tied the prisoners up, and left them.*
2 tie something up = to fasten something together using string or rope: *The box broke, so I tied it up with some string.*
3 be tied up = to be very busy: *He was tied up all day in a meeting.*
➔ See Thesaurus box at **fasten**

T

tie² *noun*
1 a narrow piece of cloth that men tie around their neck and wear outside their shirts: *He wears a suit and tie in the office.*
➔ See picture on page A6
2 a relationship between two people, groups, etc.: *Their family ties are strong, and they see their grandparents every week.*
3 the result of a game in which two people or teams get the same number of points: *He finished in a tie for third place.*

ti•ger /ˈtaɪgɚ/ *noun*
a large wild cat that has orange fur with black lines

tight¹ /taɪt/ *adjective*
1 tight clothes fit your body very closely: *If those jeans are too tight, try a bigger size.* ANTONYM **loose**
2 firmly fixed in position, and difficult to move: *Make sure the screws are tight.* | *He had a tight grip on her arm.*
3 air-tight/water-tight = not allowing air or water to get in: *This container is air-tight.*

tight² *adverb*
very firmly: *Hold on tight so you don't fall off.* SYNONYM **tightly**

tight•en /ˈtaɪtn/ *verb*
to fasten something firmly so that it is not loose: *A screw was loose, so I tightened it.*

tight•ly /ˈtaɪtli/ *adverb*
very firmly: *He tied the rope tightly around the tree, so it wouldn't become loose.* SYNONYM **tight**

tights /taɪts/ *noun*
a piece of clothing for girls or women that fits closely over the feet and legs and goes up to the waist: *a girl wearing a skirt and a pair of blue tights*

tile /taɪl/ *noun*
a thin square piece of baked clay that you use for covering floors or walls: *We're putting new floor tiles in the kitchen.*
➔ See picture on page A9

till¹ /tɪl/ *preposition, conjunction*
until: *I was at a party till 1:00 in the morning.* | *Wait there till I get back.*

till² *noun*
another word for a CASH REGISTER

tilt /tɪlt/ *verb*
to move something so that its position is not straight or upright: *You can tilt this chair back when you want to relax.*
—**tilt** *noun* a position that is not straight or upright

tim•ber /ˈtɪmbɚ/ *noun*
trees that people cut down and use for building things SYNONYM **lumber**

time¹ /taɪm/ *noun*
1 the thing that people measure in minutes, hours, years, etc.: *I like to spend time relaxing with my friends.* | *You don't need to hurry – we have plenty of time.*
2 the exact hour and minute in a day that you can see on a clock: *"What time is it?" "It's 12:15."*
3 an occasion when you do something: *When was the first time you met Kelly?* | *Next time I go downtown, I'll take the bus.* | *I go swimming three times a week* (=on three occasions every week).
4 a period of time: *Learning a new language takes a long time.*
5 a particular period of history: *Life was not easy during pioneer times.*
6 on time = at the right time, and not early or late: *The train arrived on time.*
7 in time = early enough to do something: *We got to the concert in time to get a seat.*
8 all the time = without stopping or very often: *Todd listens to music in his room all the time.*
9 have a good/great time = to enjoy yourself: *Did you have a good time at the party?*
10 it's (about) time... = you use this for saying that something should happen now or soon: *It's time for dinner.* | *It's time to go.*
11 from time to time = sometimes, but not very often: *I only see Lou from time to time, because he doesn't live nearby.*
12 in no time = soon or quickly: *If you help me, we'll be done in no time.*
13 one/two etc. ... at a time = one, two, etc. on the same occasion or at the same moment: *You can borrow three books at a time.*
14 ahead of time = before an event or before you need to do something: *We finished ahead of time and got to relax.*
15 take your time = to do something slowly

or carefully without hurrying: *Take your time to answer the questions.*

16 for the time being *formal* = for a short time, but not permanently: *For the time being, she's living with her father.*

time² *verb*

1 to arrange for something to happen at a particular time: *The bomb was timed to go off at 4:00.*

2 to measure how long it takes someone to do something: *Jill ran one hundred meters, and I timed her.*

ˌtime and a ˈhalf *noun*

one and a half times the normal rate of pay: *We get time and a half for working on Sundays, so instead of making $5.75 an hour, I get an extra $2.87, which makes $8.62 an hour.*

ˈtime card *noun*

a card on which the hours you have worked are recorded by a machine: *At the beginning and end of each day the workers put their time cards in the machine.*

ˈtime-conˌsuming *adjective, formal*

taking a long time to do: *Buying a house can be a time-consuming process.*

time•less /ˈtaɪmləs/ *adjective, formal*

not affected by changes over time: *The picture shows the timeless beauty of the city of Venice, which has not really changed much in two hundred years.*

ˈtime ˌlimit *noun*

the longest time in which you are allowed to do something: *The time limit for the test is three hours.*

time•ly /ˈtaɪmli/ *adjective, formal*

done or happening at exactly the right time: *The fight ended with the timely arrival of the police.*

ˌtime ˈoff *noun*

time when you do not have to be at work or school: *I asked my boss if I could have some time off this week.*

ˌtime ˈout *noun*

a short break during a sports game to let the players rest or plan how they will play the rest of the game: *The L.A. Lakers took a time out after the other team scored ten points in a row.*

tim•er /ˈtaɪmɚ/ *noun*

a part of a machine or system that you use to make it stop or start at a particular time: *You can set the timer to turn the oven on and off to cook food when you aren't at home.*

times /taɪmz/ *preposition*

multiplied by: *Two times two equals four (2 x 2=4).*

ˈtime sheet *noun*

a piece of paper on which you write the hours you have worked during a particular period of time: *Have you filled in your time sheet?*

ˈtime zone *noun*

one of the 24 areas that the world is divided into, each of which has its own time: *When you fly across the U.S. you cross four time zones.*

tim•id /ˈtɪmɪd/ *adjective, formal*

shy and nervous: *He was a timid boy who almost never spoke.* SYNONYM **shy**

—**timidly** *adverb*: *She timidly asked if she could borrow the book.*

➔ See Thesaurus box at **shy**

tin /tɪn/ *noun*

a soft white metal that is often used to cover and protect iron and steel: *The can was made of tin.*

tin•gle /ˈtɪŋgəl/ *verb*

if a part of your body tingles, the skin feels slightly uncomfortable: *Her face tingled from the cold wind.*

ti•ny /ˈtaɪni/ *adjective* **tinier**, **tiniest**

very small: *They live in a tiny house, with only three rooms.*

➔ See Thesaurus box at **small**

tip¹ /tɪp/ *noun*

1 the end of something long, narrow, and pointed: *He touched the flower with the tip of his finger.*

2 a useful piece of advice: *He gave me some tips on how to lose weight.*

3 an additional amount of money that you give to someone who has done a job for you as a way of thanking him or her: *I usually leave a 15 or 20% tip in a restaurant.*

➔ See Thesaurus box at **end¹**

tip² *verb* **tipped**, **tipping**

1 to move something so that one side of it is higher: *The boat kept tipping to one side.* | *The dentist told Joe to tip his head back.*

T

2 to give an additional amount of money to someone who has done a job for you as a way of thanking him or her: *I tipped the waiter $5.*

tip•sy /ˈtɪpsi/ *adjective, informal*
slightly drunk: *The wine had made her tipsy.*

tip•toe[1] /ˈtɪptoʊ/ *noun*
on tiptoe = if you stand or walk on tiptoe, you stand or walk just on your toes: *Matt stood on tiptoe to see over the crowd.*

tiptoe

on tiptoe

tiptoe[2] *verb*
to walk quietly and carefully on your toes: *She tiptoed down the stairs, trying not to make any noise.*

T

tire[1] /taɪɚ/ *noun*
a thick round piece of rubber that fits around the wheel of a car, bicycle, etc.: *I had a flat tire* (=all the air went out of it) *on the way home.*
➔ See picture on page A28

tire[2] *also* **tire someone out** *verb*
if something tires you, it makes you feel very tired: *As people become older, they tire more easily.* | *All that dancing has tired me out.*

tired /taɪɚd/ *adjective*
1 someone who is tired feels that they want to sleep or rest: *I had been working hard all week, and I felt really tired.*
2 tired of (doing) something = bored or annoyed with something: *I'm tired of waiting.*
➔ See picture on page A23

tir•ing /ˈtaɪərɪŋ/ *adjective*
making you feel tired: *The long trip was very tiring.*

tis•sue /ˈtɪʃu/ *noun*
1 a piece of soft thin paper that you use to blow your nose: *She used a whole box of tissues when she had a cold.*
2 the cells and other material in the body that form the skin, nerves, and muscles in the body: *brain tissue*

ti•tle /ˈtaɪtl/ *noun*
1 the name given to a book, painting, play, etc.: *The title of the book is "Easy Computing."*
2 a word such as "Mr.," "Mrs.," or "Dr." that you use before someone's name: *Many women use the title "Ms."*
3 the legal right to own something: *Who has the title to this land?*
WORD FAMILY ➔ **entitle** *verb*

to[1] /tə; *before vowels* tʊ; *strong* tu/
used with verbs to make the INFINITIVE: *It's starting to rain.* | *She asked the teacher to help her.* | *Sarah seems to be very happy.* | *It's great to see you!*

to[2] *preposition*
1 used to say where someone or something goes: *He ran to the door.* | *We're going on vacation to Hawaii.* | *I went to a party last night.*
2 used to say who receives something: *I gave my old jacket to my sister.*
3 used to say who someone is talking to: *Mark is talking to Steve.*
4 used to say when something ends: *The museum is open from 10:30 to 5* (=it opens at 10:30 and closes at 5).
5 used when telling the time: *It's ten to four* (=it's ten minutes before four). SYNONYM **of**

toad /toʊd/ *noun*
a brown animal like a large FROG: *Toads have dry bumpy skin and live mainly on land.*

toast[1] /toʊst/ *noun*
1 bread that has been heated until it is brown: *He ate a slice of toast for breakfast.*
2 if you make a toast to someone, you drink something in order to thank him or her, wish him or her luck, etc.: *They drank a toast to the newly married couple.*

toast[2] *verb*
1 to heat bread until it is brown: *She toasted a slice of bread.*
2 if you toast someone, you drink something in order to thank him or her, wish him or her luck, etc.: *They toasted the soldiers who had come back from the war.*

toast•er /ˈtoʊstɚ/ *noun*
a machine used for making toast: *She put two slices of bread in the toaster.*
➔ See picture on page A9

to•bac•co /təˈbækoʊ/ *noun*
dried brown leaves that people smoke in cigarettes and pipes: *pipe tobacco*

to•day[1] /təˈdeɪ/ *adverb*
1 on this day: *David has his piano lesson today.* | *I'm going swimming today.*

2 during the present period of time: *Today, half of all marriages end in divorce.*

today² *noun*

1 this day: *What's today's date? | Today is Wednesday.*

2 the present period of time: *Today's computers are very powerful.*

toe /toʊ/ *noun*

1 one of the five parts at the end of your foot: *These shoes hurt my toes.*

2 on your toes = ready for anything that might happen: *We give the students a test every week to keep them on their toes.*

➔ See picture on page A2

TOEFL /ˈtoʊfəl/ *noun*

Test of English as a Foreign Language a test of English that students can take if their first language is not English

toe•nail /ˈtoʊneɪl/ *noun*

the hard flat part at the end of your toe: *She painted her toenails red.*

tof•fee /ˈtɔfi/ *noun*

a sticky brown candy: *The toffee made his teeth stick together.*

to•geth•er /təˈgeðɚ/ *adverb*

1 if two or more people do something together, they all do it as a group, not alone: *They wrote all the songs together. | We worked together to solve the problem.*

2 if two substances or objects are together, they are mixed or joined: *I glued the pieces of wood together. | Mix the eggs and the cream together.*

3 if people or things are together, they are with or next to each other: *The girls were standing together in a group. | Felipe and I went to school together. | I put all the books together in a box.*

to•geth•er•ness /təˈgeðɚnɪs/ *noun, formal*

the pleasant feeling you have when you are part of a group of people who have a close relationship with each other: *Our family has a strong sense of togetherness.*

toi•let /ˈtɔɪlɪt/ *noun*

a large bowl that you sit on to get rid of waste substances from your body

➔ See picture on page A11

ˈtoilet ˌpaper *noun*

soft thin paper that you use to clean yourself after you have used the toilet: *a roll of toilet paper*

toi•let•ries /ˈtɔɪlətriz/ *plural noun, formal*

things such as soap, TOOTHPASTE, etc. that you use when you wash yourself

to•ken /ˈtoʊkən/ *noun*

1 a round piece of metal that you use instead of money in some machines: *You can buy subway tokens so that you don't have to stand in line in the morning.*

2 *formal* something that represents a feeling, fact, event, etc.: *We gave him a present as a token of our appreciation* (=sign of thanks).

told /toʊld/ *verb*

the past tense and past participle of TELL

tol•er•ance /ˈtɑlərəns/ *noun, formal*

1 willingness to allow people to do, say, or believe what they want: *He has no tolerance for people with different opinions; he just won't listen to them.*

2 the degree to which someone or something can suffer pain, difficulty, etc. without being harmed: *These plants have a low tolerance for the cold and usually die if it gets too cold in the spring.*

tol•er•ant /ˈtɑlərənt/ *adjective*

letting other people do or say what they want, even if you do not approve of it: *We should be tolerant of other people's beliefs.*

tol•er•ate /ˈtɑləˌreɪt/ *verb, formal*

to accept behavior or a situation that you do not like, and not do anything about it: *The teacher will not tolerate bad behavior in class.*

WORD FAMILY look at the words:

➔ **tolerate** *verb*
➔ **tolerant** *adjective*
➔ **tolerance** *noun*

toll¹ /toʊl/ *noun, formal*

1 the number of people that have been killed by something: *The death toll from the earthquake has risen to 200.*

2 money that you pay so that you can use a road, bridge, etc.: *The highway toll is $2.*

3 a bad effect that something has on someone or something over a long period of time: *Smoking has taken a toll on his health; he now has lung cancer.*

T

toll² *verb, formal*
if a large bell tolls, or you toll it, it keeps ringing slowly: *The church bell tolled.*

to·ma·to /tə'meɪtoʊ/ *noun* plural **tomatoes**
a soft round red vegetable: *Do you like tomatoes in your salad?*
→ See picture on page A12

tomb /tum/ *noun*
a large GRAVE or room where a dead person is buried: *the tomb of an Egyptian king*

to·mor·row¹ /tə'mɑroʊ/ *adverb*
on or during the day after today: *He's leaving tomorrow.*

tomorrow² *noun*
the day after today: *Today is Wednesday, and tomorrow is Thursday.* | *Do you have any plans for tomorrow?*

T

ton /tʌn/ *noun*
a unit for measuring weight, equal to 2,000 pounds: *The ship weighs 62,000 tons.*

tone /toʊn/ *noun*
1 the way that someone sounds, especially a person's voice: *"Come on in," he said in a friendly tone.*
2 the general feeling or quality that something has: *We were all happy, so the tone of the dinner party was very relaxed.*
3 one of the sounds that you hear on the telephone: *Please leave a message after the tone.* SYNONYM **beep**

ˌtone-'deaf *adjective*
unable to hear the difference between different musical notes: *I can't sing at all because I'm tone-deaf.*

tongs /tɑŋz/ *plural noun*
a tool for picking things up, which has two thin pieces of metal joined together at the top: *She picked up the hot dogs with a pair of tongs.*

tongue /tʌŋ/ *noun*
the soft part inside your mouth that moves when you eat and speak: *The taste of chocolate was still on her tongue.*

ˌtongue-in-'cheek *adjective*
a tongue-in-cheek remark is said as a joke, not seriously: *He made a tongue-in-cheek comment about how excited he was to be going back to work after his vacation.*

'tongue-tied *adjective*
unable to speak easily because you are nervous: *I always feel tongue-tied when I have to say something in class.*

'tongue ˌtwister *noun*
a word or phrase with many similar sounds that is difficult to say quickly: *"She sells sea shells by the sea shore" is a well-known tongue twister.*

to·night¹ /tə'naɪt/ *adverb*
during the night of this day: *I think I'll go to bed early tonight.*

tonight² *noun*
the night of this day: *Here is tonight's news.*

too /tu/ *adverb*
1 use "too" when you want to add a new fact or to show that something is true about two people or things: *Jan plays the guitar, and she plays the piano too.* | *"I'm really hungry." "Me too."* (="I am also.")

USAGE: too

Too, **also**, and **as well** mean the same thing, but you use them in different ways.

Too and **as well** are less formal than **also**, and you use them more often in spoken English: *Tom's hungry, and I am too.* | *Oh, are you coming as well?*

Also is more formal and is used more often in writing than in speech: *Tom was very tired, and he was also hungry.*

In sentences with "not" or "nothing," use **either** rather than **also** or **too**. Do not say "Tom was also not hungry." or "Tom was not hungry too." Say "Tom was not hungry either."

2 use "too" to show that something is more than you need or more than you want: *It's too hot in here.* | *He was driving much too fast.* | *This house is too small for six people.*

USAGE: too

Too is usually used to show that you do not like or approve of something: *This happens too often.* | *You're too young to go out by yourself.* | *We were too late and missed the bus.*

Very is used to emphasize something which can be either good or bad: *It's very hot today.* | *She's always very busy.*

took /tʊk/ *verb*
the past tense of TAKE

tool /tul/ *noun*
any object that you hold in your hand and use for doing a particular job: *I didn't have the right tools to fix the car.* | *gardening tools such as shovels and lawn mowers*

tooth /tuθ/ *noun* plural **teeth** /tiθ/
1 one of the hard white things in your mouth that you use for biting food: *Did you brush your teeth* (=clean them)*?*
2 one of the pointed parts that sticks out from a comb or saw

tooth·ache /ˈtuθeɪk/ *noun*
a pain in a tooth: *I have a toothache – I'll have to go to the dentist.*

tooth·brush /ˈtuθbrʌʃ/ *noun*
a small brush for cleaning your teeth
➔ See picture at **brush**

tooth·paste /ˈtuθpeɪst/ *noun*
a substance that you use for cleaning your teeth: *a tube of toothpaste*

tooth·pick /ˈtuθˌpɪk/ *noun*
a very small pointed stick of wood that you use for removing pieces of food from between your teeth

top[1] /tɑp/ *noun*
1 the highest part of something: *The cat climbed to the top of the tree.* | *Write your name at the top of the page.* ANTONYM **bottom**
2 the top = the best or most important position in a company, etc.: *He worked hard and got to the top of his profession.*
3 the lid or cover for a container, pen, etc.: *I can't get the top off this jar.*
4 a piece of clothing that you wear on the top part of your body: *She was wearing a pink top.*
5 off the top of your head *informal* = if you say something off the top of your head, you say it immediately, without thinking carefully about it or checking the facts: *Off the top of my head, I'd say it will cost about $50.*
➔ See Thesaurus box at **cover**[2]

top[2] *adjective*
1 highest: *My family lived on the top floor of the building.* ANTONYM **bottom**
2 best or most successful: *He won the top prize of $500.*

top·ic /ˈtɑpɪk/ Ac *noun*
a subject that people talk or write about: *The topic we will discuss in class today is President Abraham Lincoln and a speech he made called the Gettysburg Address.*

top·i·cal /ˈtɑpɪkəl/ Ac *adjective, formal*
related to events that are happening now: *Terrorism is a topical issue that all the newspapers and magazines have articles on.*

ˈtopic ˌsentence *noun*
the sentence in a PARAGRAPH that states the main idea you are writing about: *The topic sentence is usually the first sentence in a paragraph.*

tops /tɑps/ *adverb, informal*
at the most: *It should cost $500 tops to repair the car.*

ˌtop-ˈsecret *adjective*
top-secret documents or information must be kept completely secret: *a top-secret report to be read only by the president*

top·sy-tur·vy /ˌtɑpsi ˈtɚvi/ *adjective, informal*
completely messy or completely out of order: *He left his room topsy-turvy, with the bed not made and clothes all over the floor.*

torch[1] /tɔrtʃ/ *noun*
a long stick that you burn at one end for light or as a symbol: *The Olympic torch is lit before every Olympic Games.*

torch[2] *verb, formal*
to deliberately make a building, vehicle, etc. start to burn: *Protesters torched several government buildings.*

tore /tɔr/ *verb*
the past tense of TEAR

tor·ment /tɔrˈment/ *verb, formal*
to deliberately hurt, upset, or annoy someone: *He was always tormenting his little sister by stealing her toys.*

torn /tɔrn/ *verb*
the past participle of TEAR

tor·na·do /tɔrˈneɪdoʊ/ *noun* plural **tornadoes**
a violent storm with strong winds that go around and around: *A tornado tore the roof off of the building.*
➔ See Thesaurus box at **wind**[1]

T

tor•pe•do /tɔr'pidoʊ/ *noun* plural **torpedoes**
a weapon that is fired from a ship or SUBMARINE and travels under the water: *The ship was hit by a torpedo.*

tor•toise /'tɔrtəs/ *noun*
a slow-moving animal that can put its legs and head inside the shell that covers its body

tor•ture[1] /'tɔrtʃɚ/ *verb*
to deliberately hurt someone a lot for a long time: *He was tortured during the war.*

torture[2] *noun*
1 the act of deliberately hurting someone a lot for a long time: *They used torture to make the prisoners give them information.*
2 mental or physical suffering: *It was torture having to wait for the test results.*

T

toss /tɔs/ *verb*
to throw something somewhere in a careless way: *He tossed the keys to me.*
→ See Thesaurus box at **throw**[1]

to•tal[1] /'toʊtl/ *adjective*
1 used to emphasize that something is complete: *The business was a total failure, and they lost all of their money.*
2 including everything: *The total cost of the building will be $6 million.*

total[2] *noun*
the number that you get when you have added everything together: *The city spent a total of two million dollars on the library.*
—**total** *verb* to be a particular total after all the amounts have been added together: *The expenses totaled over $3,000.*

to•tal•i•tar•i•an /toʊˌtælə'teriən/ *adjective, formal*
based on a political system in which ordinary people have no power and are completely controlled by the government: *In a totalitarian state people are not free to say what they think.*
—**totalitarianism** *noun* a political system in which ordinary people have no power and are completely controlled by the government

to•tal•ly /'toʊtl-i/ *adverb*
completely: *I totally agree.* | *Los Angeles is totally different from New York.*

touch[1] /tʌtʃ/ *verb*
1 to put your finger, hand, etc. on something or someone: *She touched his arm gently.* | *Don't touch the paint – it's still wet!*

THESAURUS: touch

feel to touch something with your fingers to find out about it: *I could feel something rough under the water.*

stroke to move your hand gently over something: *Ellie stroked the cat.*

rub to move your hand or fingers over a surface while pressing it: *Bill yawned and rubbed his eyes.*

scratch to rub your fingernails on part of your skin: *Try not to scratch those mosquito bites.*

pat to touch someone or something lightly again and again, with your hand flat: *Todd patted him on the back and told him he'd done a good job.*

brush to touch someone or something lightly as you pass by: *Her hand brushed mine.*

caress to gently move your hand over a part of someone's body in a way that shows love: *Miguel gently caressed her hair.*

tickle to move your fingers lightly over someone's body to try to make him or her laugh: *Dad tried to tickle us as we ran past.*

2 if two things touch, there is no space in between them: *Their legs touched under the table.*
3 to affect someone's emotions and make him or her feel grateful, sad, or sorry for someone: *The boy's sad situation touched the hearts of people around the world.*
—**touching** *adjective* making you feel grateful, sad, or sorry for someone: *The movie has some touching moments.*

touch[2] *noun*
1 the ability to know what something is like when you feel it with your fingers: *We take in information through sight, sound, taste, touch, and smell.*
2 the action of putting your finger, hand, etc. on someone or something: *Rita felt the touch of his hand on her shoulder.*
3 get in touch/be in touch = to write to or call someone: *George decided to get in*

touch with an old friend of his and he sent him a postcard.

4 keep in touch/stay in touch = to continue to speak or write to someone who does not live near you: *Jane and I keep in touch by email.*

5 a touch of something = a small amount of something: *Add a touch of lemon juice to the salad.*

touch·down /ˈtʌtʃdaʊn/ *noun*

1 an act of taking the ball over the other team's line in football: *Brown scored the first touchdown.*

2 the moment when a plane or spacecraft lands on the ground: *The spacecraft is three minutes away from touchdown.*

tough /tʌf/ *adjective*

1 difficult to do or deal with: *Joining the army was a tough decision.* | *The game will be tough, but I'm sure we can win.* SYNONYM **hard**; ANTONYM **easy**

2 a tough person is strong, brave, or determined: *You have to be tough if you want to be successful in business.*

3 very strict: *We need tougher laws to fight crime.*

4 tough material is not easily broken or damaged: *Sails are made of tough cloth.*

5 tough meat is difficult to cut or bite: *a tough steak* ANTONYM **tender**

—**toughness** *noun*

tough·en /ˈtʌfən/ *also* **toughen up** *verb*

1 to make a rule or law more strict: *The state has toughened the laws against drunk driving.*

2 to make someone stronger physically or emotionally: *He made his son play football to toughen him up.*

tou·pée /tuˈpeɪ/ *noun*

a piece of artificial hair that a man can wear when he has no hair on part of his head: *You could tell that he was wearing a toupée.*

tour¹ /tʊr/ *noun*

1 a trip to several different places in a country, area, etc.: *We went on a tour of Italy, and visted Rome, Naples, and Venice.*

2 a trip around the different parts of a building, city, etc.: *Would you like a guided tour of the museum?*

3 a trip to different places to give concerts, perform plays, etc.: *The band is on tour in Europe right now.*

tour² *verb*

to travel around an area, visiting different places: *We're going to tour New England this summer, and see lots of historical places.*

tour·ism /ˈtʊrɪzəm/ *noun*

the business of providing tourists with places to stay and things to do: *The island's main industry is tourism.*

tour·ist /ˈtʊrɪst/ *noun*

someone who visits a place for pleasure: *San Francisco is always full of tourists from all over the world in the summer.*

tour·na·ment /ˈtʊrnəmənt/ *noun*

a competition in which many players or teams compete against each other until there is one winner: *She is playing in a tennis tournament next week.*

➔ See Thesaurus box at **competition**

T

tow /toʊ/ *verb*

if one vehicle tows another one, it pulls the other vehicle along behind it: *Our car had to be towed away when it stopped working.*

—**tow** *noun* an act of pulling a vehicle with a rope or chain: *The truck gave the car a tow to the repair shop.*

➔ See Thesaurus box at **pull¹**

➔ See picture at **pull¹**

to·ward /tɔrd/ *also* **towards** *preposition*

1 in a particular direction: *I saw a man coming toward me.*

2 just before a particular time: *I always feel tired toward the end of the day.*

3 showing how you behave to someone: *He's always been quite friendly toward me.*

tow·el /ˈtaʊəl/ *noun*

a piece of cloth used for drying something: *Here's a towel for when you finish your shower.* | *Find a dish towel and help me dry the dishes.*

➔ See page A11

tow·er /ˈtaʊɚ/ *noun*

a tall narrow building or part of a building: *There are fire towers on some of the mountains, so that the rangers can watch for forest fires.* | *the Eiffel Tower in Paris, France*

tow·er·ing /ˈtaʊərɪŋ/ *adjective, formal*

very tall: *towering mountains*

town /taʊn/ *noun*
a place with many buildings and streets, where people live and work, and which is smaller than a city: *We live in a small town.*

ˌtown ˈhall *noun*
a public building used for a town's local government: *The mayor held a meeting in the town hall.*

tox•ic /ˈtɑksɪk/ *adjective, formal*
poisonous: *We must keep toxic chemicals out of our water.*

tox•in /ˈtɑksɪn/ *noun, formal*
a poisonous substance

toy /tɔɪ/ *noun*
a thing for children to play with: *The children were playing with their toys.* | *a toy car*

trace¹ /treɪs/ Ac *verb*
1 to copy a picture by drawing on a thin piece of paper that you put over it: *I traced the map by using a piece of transparent paper.*
2 to find someone or something that has disappeared: *Police are still trying to trace the missing child.*
3 to find out when something began or where it came from: *They traced their family history back to the 17th century.*
→ See Thesaurus box at **find**

T

trace² *noun*
1 a sign that someone or something has been in a place: *There was no trace of the missing child.*
2 a very small amount of something that is difficult to notice: *The police found traces of poison in the food.*

track¹ /træk/ *noun*
1 tracks = marks on the ground that were made by someone or something that was moving: *You could see the tire tracks in the dirt.*
2 keep/lose track of something = to pay attention to something so you know what is happening to it, or to fail to do this: *She quickly lost track of all the money she was spending on Christmas presents, and spent way too much.*
3 a course with a special surface on which people, cars, horses, etc. race: *The car reached 190 mph on the track.*
4 the sport of running races on a track: *He ran track in high school.*
5 *also* **track and field** sports such as running, jumping, and throwing things: *She's on the track team; she runs the hurdles.*
6 be on the right/wrong track = to think in a way that is likely to lead to the correct or incorrect result: *"A chili pepper?" "Keep guessing – you're on the right track. It is small, red, and you can eat it." "A tomato." "Yes!"*
7 the two metal lines that a train travels on: *train tracks*

track² *verb*
PHRASAL VERB
track someone/something down
to find someone or something by searching or asking questions: *Police were unable to track down the killer.*

ˈtrack ˌrecord *noun*
all the things that a person or organization has done in the past that show how well he, she, or it is likely to do in the future: *The company has a track record of treating its employees well.*

trac•tor /ˈtræktɚ/ *noun*
a strong vehicle with large wheels that is used on farms: *He drove the tractor through the field, pulling a load of hay.*
→ See picture on page A26

trade¹ /treɪd/ *noun*
1 the act of exchanging something you have for something that someone else has: *Let's make a trade – my baseball cap for your soccer ball.*
2 the business of buying and selling things, especially between countries: *Last year we increased our trade with Saudi Arabia.*
3 a particular job, especially one in which you work with your hands: *Jerry's a plumber by trade* (=that is his job).

trade² *verb*
1 to exchange one thing for another: *I'll trade my apple for your candy bar.*
2 to buy and sell goods and services: *The two countries have traded with each other for hundreds of years, selling and buying everything from cloth to cars.*
PHRASAL VERB
trade something in
to give something that you own as part of

the payment when you buy something similar: *You can trade your old computer games in for new ones.*

trade•mark /'treɪdmɑrk/ *noun*
a special word or picture on a product that shows it is made by a particular company: *"Coca-Cola" is a trademark.*

trad•er /'treɪdɚ/ *noun*
someone who buys and sells goods or STOCKS

tra•di•tion /trə'dɪʃən/ Ac *noun*
something that people have done for a long time, and continue to do: *We have a tradition of eating a special meal on Thanksgiving.*

WORD FAMILY look at the words:
→ **tradition** *noun*
→ **traditional** *adjective*
→ **traditionally** *adverb*

tra•di•tion•al /trə'dɪʃənəl/ Ac *adjective*
traditional beliefs or activities are shared by a group of people and have existed for a long time: *It is traditional to exchange gifts at Christmas.*
—**traditionally** *adverb*: *Women are now doing jobs that were traditionally done by men in the past, such as being in the police or managing companies.*

traf•fic /'træfɪk/ *noun*
1 the vehicles moving along a particular road: *We left early to avoid the traffic during rush hour.* | *I got stuck in traffic and missed the meeting.*
2 the movement of aircraft, ships, or trains from one place to another: *There has been an increase in air traffic as flights have gotten cheaper.*

'traffic jam *noun*
a long line of vehicles on the road moving very slowly: *We were stuck in a traffic jam for two hours.*
→ See picture at **jam**[1]

traf•fick•ing /'træfɪkɪŋ/ *noun*
drug/arms trafficking = the activity of buying and selling illegal drugs or weapons
—**trafficker** *noun* someone who buys and sells illegal drugs or weapons: *a drug trafficker*

'traffic ˌlight *also* **'traffic ˌsignal** *noun*
a set of colored lights at the side of the road that show when cars are allowed to move: *He stopped because the traffic lights turned red.*
→ See picture on page A26

trag•e•dy /'trædʒədi/ *noun* plural **tragedies** *formal*
1 a very sad event: *They suffered a terrible tragedy when their son was killed in an car accident.*
2 a serious play with a sad ending

tra•gic /'trædʒɪk/ *adjective, formal*
very sad: *He died in a tragic accident.*
—**tragically** *adverb*

trail /treɪl/ *noun*
1 a rough path across open country or through a forest: *The trail led through the forest to the lake.*
2 a long line or a series of marks that has been left by someone or something: *The injured man left a trail of blood behind him on the ground.*

trail•er /'treɪlɚ/ *noun*
1 *also* **trailer home** a large vehicle like a box on wheels, which can be moved, but that people live in permanently: *We live in a trailer home.*
2 a vehicle that can be pulled behind a car, used for living in during a vacation: *We have a tent trailer that we use for camping during our vacations.*
3 a vehicle that can be pulled behind another vehicle, used for carrying something heavy: *They loaded the boat onto the trailer.*

'trailer ˌpark *noun*
an area where trailers are parked and used as people's homes: *He lives in a trailer park.*

train[1] /treɪn/ *noun*
a line of vehicles that are connected together and travel along a railroad: *I took the train to Baltimore.* | *Should we drive or go by train?*
→ See picture on page A26

train[2] *verb*
1 to teach someone the skills they need to do something difficult: *They trained us how to use computers.* | *He trained for two years to become a teacher.*
2 to prepare for a sports competition by exercising and practicing: *He is training for the Olympics.*
→ See Thesaurus box at **practice**[2]

T

train•ee /ˌtreɪˈni/ *noun*
someone who is being trained for a job: *a trainee in the sales department*

train•ing /ˈtreɪnɪŋ/ *noun*
activities that help you learn how to do a job or play a sport: *He is on a management training course.*

trai•tor /ˈtreɪtɚ/ *noun*
someone who helps the enemies of his or her country or group: *He was a traitor to his country who sold secrets to the enemy.*

tramp¹ /træmp/ *noun*
someone poor who has no home or job and moves from place to place

tramp² *verb*
to walk somewhere with heavy steps: *The kids were tramping through the snow.*

tram•ple /ˈtræmpəl/ *verb*
to step heavily on something: *Don't trample on the flowers!*

T

tram•po•line /ˌtræmpəˈlin/ *noun*
a piece of sports equipment that you jump up and down on, made of a sheet of material tightly stretched across a large frame: *She was bouncing up and down on the trampoline.*

trance /træns/ *noun*
a state in which you seem to be asleep, but you are still able to hear and understand things: *Listening to the doctor's soft voice, she went into a trance, and he gave her instructions about stopping smoking.*

tran•qui•liz•er /ˈtræŋkwəˌlaɪzɚ/ *noun*
a drug that makes someone calm or sleepy: *The doctor gave him a tranquilizer to help him calm down.*
—**tranquilize** *verb* to make someone calm or sleepy by giving him or her a drug: *They tranquilized the lion before moving him.*

trans•ac•tion /trænˈzækʃən/ *noun, formal*
a business deal, such as buying or selling something: *Keep a record of all financial transactions, especially things such as buying a car or house.*

trans•at•lan•tic /ˌtrænzətˈlæntɪk/ *adjective*
1 crossing the Atlantic Ocean: *a transatlantic flight from New York to London*
2 involving countries on both sides of the Atlantic: *a transatlantic agreement between Canada and Great Britain*

trans•con•ti•nen•tal /ˌtrænskɑntənˈentl/ *adjective, formal*
crossing a CONTINENT: *The transcontinental railroad went from the Atlantic coast to the Pacific coast.*

trans•fer¹ /ˈtrænsfɚ/ Ac *verb* **transferred, transferring** *formal*
1 to move someone or something from one place to another: *They transferred the patient to a special children's hospital.*
2 to move money from one account or institution to another: *I'd like to transfer $500 to my checking account from my savings account.*
3 to officially give property or land to someone else: *He transferred ownership of the land to his son.*
—**transferable** /trænsˈfɚəbəl/ *adjective* able to be used by someone else, on a different date, in a different organization, etc. from the original person, date, organization, etc.: *Air tickets are not transferable.*

transfer² *noun, formal*
1 the process of moving someone or something from one place to another: *She was given a transfer from Houston to the office in Chicago.*
2 a ticket that allows a passenger to change from one bus, train, etc. to another without paying more money: *You should ask the bus driver for a transfer, because you need to change buses.*

trans•form /trænsˈfɔrm/ Ac *verb, formal*
to change someone or something completely: *The new owners of the building have transformed it into a hotel.*
—**transformation** /ˌtrænsfɚˈmeɪʃən/ *noun* a complete change in someone or something: *The transformation of a caterpillar into a butterfly takes several weeks.*
→ See Thesaurus box at **change¹**

tran•sit /ˈtrænzɪt/ Ac *noun, formal*
the process of moving people or goods from one place to another: *The painting was damaged in transit* (=while it was being moved).

tran•si•tion /trænˈzɪʃən/ Ac *noun, formal*
the process of changing from one form or state to another: *Making the transition from*

being a child to being an adult can be very difficult.

—**transitional** *adjective* relating to a period of transition: *A transitional government is running the country until new elections are held.*

tran·si·tive /'trænsətɪv/ *adjective, formal* a transitive verb must have an object: *In the sentence "She makes her own clothes," "makes" is a transitive verb.*

trans·late /trænz'leɪt/ *verb*
1 to change speech or writing from one language to another: *He translated the book from English into German.*
2 *formal* if one thing translates into another, the second thing happens as a result of the first: *The new factory will translate into more jobs for local people.*
—**translator** *noun* someone whose job is to translate things from one language into another

trans·la·tion /trænz'leɪʃən/ *noun*
1 something that has been changed from one language into another: *This is an English translation of a French poem.*
2 the process of changing the words of one language into another: *Translation is not easy to do well.*

trans·mit /trænz'mɪt/ Ac *verb*
transmitted, transmitting *formal*
to send out radio or television signals: *They transmitted the message by radio.* SYNONYM **broadcast**
—**transmitter** *noun* a machine that sends out radio or television signals: *a radio transmitter*
—**transmission** /trænz'mɪʃən/ *noun* the act of transmitting something

trans·par·ent /træn'spærənt/ *adjective* if something is transparent, you can see through it: *The box is made of transparent plastic so you can see what is inside.*

trans·plant /træns'plænt/ *verb, formal* to move a body part from one person to another as a medical treatment: *The doctor transplanted the kidney from the dead man to the patient.*
—**transplant** /'trænsplænt/ *noun* a body part that has been moved from one person to another as a medical treatment: *a heart transplant*
—**transplantation** /ˌtrænsplæn'teɪʃən/ *noun* the act of moving a body part from one person to another

trans·port /træns'pɔrt/ Ac *verb* to move things or people from one place to another in a vehicle: *The coal is transported by train to all parts of the country.*

trans·por·ta·tion /ˌtrænspɚ'teɪʃən/ Ac *noun*
1 vehicles that people use to travel from one place to another: *If public transportation, such as buses and subways, was cheaper, more people would use it.*
2 the activity of moving people or things from one place to another: *There are strict rules about the transportation of dangerous chemicals.*

trap[1] /træp/ *noun*
1 a piece of equipment for catching animals: *a mouse trap*
2 a trick for catching or harming someone: *The police set a trap for the thieves.*

trap[2] *verb* **trapped, trapping**
1 be trapped = to not be able to escape from a bad place or situation: *Three people were trapped in the burning building.*
2 to catch an animal in a trap

trap·e·zoid /'træpəˌzɔɪd/ *noun, formal* a shape with four sides, two of which are parallel

trash /træʃ/ *noun*
1 waste food, paper, etc., or the container you put it in: *Put that banana peel in the trash.* | *Will someone please take out the trash* (=put it outside the house)? SYNONYM **garbage**
2 *informal* something of very bad quality: *He spends all day watching trash on TV.*
➔ See Thesaurus box at **garbage**
➔ See picture on page A9

'trash can *noun* a large container outside your house in which you put waste SYNONYM **garbage can**

trash·y /'træʃi/ *adjective, informal* of very bad quality: *Why do you read those trashy novels? They aren't written very well and the stories are stupid.*

T

trau•ma /ˈtrɔmə/ *noun, formal*
a state of being extremely upset, or an experience that causes this: *He never recovered from the trauma of seeing his parents killed.*

trau•mat•ic /trɔˈmætɪk/ *adjective, formal*
extremely upsetting: *She went through many traumatic experiences during the war.*

trav•el[1] /ˈtrævəl/ *verb*
1 to go from one place to another: *He hates traveling by bus.* | *The band has traveled the world.*
2 to move a particular distance or at a particular speed: *Sound travels at 330 meters per second.*

travel[2] *noun*
1 the activity of traveling: *His job involves a lot of travel.*

> **THESAURUS: travel**
>
> **trip** the time spent and the distance traveled in going from one place to another: *a trip to the grocery store* | *They're planning a trip to Hawaii.*
>
> **journey** *formal* a trip that is long or difficult: *Lewis and Clark's journey across America took many months.*
>
> **travels** *formal* trips to places that are far away: *her travels in South America*
>
> **voyage** *formal* a long trip in a ship or a spacecraft: *Columbus's voyage across the ocean*

2 someone's travels *formal* = someone's trips to different places: *She saw many interesting things on her travels through Asia.*

ˈtravel ˌagency *noun*
a business that arranges travel and vacations

ˈtravel ˌagent *noun*
someone who works in a travel agency: *A travel agent can help you plan your vacation.*

trav•el•er /ˈtrævələ˞/ *noun, formal*
someone who goes on a trip: *Travelers can now buy plane tickets online.*

ˈtraveler's ˌcheck *noun*
a special check for a specific amount that you can use as money when you travel

tray /treɪ/ *noun*
a flat piece of plastic, metal, or wood that is used for carrying plates, glasses, etc.: *The waiter brought their drinks on a tray.*

treach•er•ous /ˈtretʃərəs/ *adjective, formal*
1 dangerous: *Ice made the roads treacherous, and there were several accidents.*
2 *formal* someone who is treacherous secretly intends to harm his or her friends: *A treacherous member of the gang had told the police what they were planning.*
—**treachery** *noun, formal* the actions of a treacherous person

tread /tred/ *noun*
the lines in the surface of a tire or the bottom of a shoe: *The tread on the tire should be at least a quarter of an inch deep.*

trea•son /ˈtrizən/ *noun*
the crime of helping your country's enemies: *He was accused of treason for selling government secrets to other countries.*

treas•ure[1] /ˈtreʒə˞/ *noun*
a group of valuable things, such as gold, silver, jewels, etc.: *The map shows where the buried treasure is.*

treasure[2] *verb*
to keep or love something that is very important to you: *She treasures the necklace her grandmother gave her.*

treas•ur•er /ˈtreʒərə˞/ *noun*
the person who takes care of an organization's money

treas•ur•y /ˈtreʒəri/ *noun* plural **treasuries**
the government office that controls a country's money: *The Treasury has decided to print more money.*

treat[1] /trit/ *verb*
1 to behave toward someone in a particular way: *You should treat people fairly.* | *Stop treating me like an idiot* (=behaving toward me as if I were an idiot)*!*
2 to do something to make a sick or injured person better: *Doctors are treating the people who were hurt in the crash.*
3 to deal with something in a particular way: *The police are treating the death as murder* (=dealing with it as if it were murder).
4 to buy something special for someone: *We're treating Mom to dinner for her birthday.*

WORD FAMILY look at the words:

→ **treat** *verb*
→ **treatment** *noun*
→ **mistreat** *verb*

treat² *noun*
something nice and special: *Mom bought us an ice cream cone as a treat.*

treat•ment /ˈtritmənt/ *noun*
1 a way of making a sick or injured person better: *a new treatment for cancer*
2 a way of behaving toward someone: *His treatment of his wife was terrible – he used to hit her.*

trea•ty /ˈtriti/ *noun* plural **treaties**
a formal written agreement between two or more countries: *The countries signed a peace treaty to end the war.*

tree /tri/ *noun*
a tall plant that has a TRUNK (=thick wooden stem), branches, and leaves: *an apple tree*

THESAURUS: tree

the woods a large area of land with many trees: *We took a walk in the woods on the edge of town.*

woodland *formal* an area of land that is covered with trees: *the type of woodland you find in the mountains*

forest a very large area of land with a lot of trees growing closely together: *the bears that live in the forest*

rain forest a forest with a lot of very tall trees, in an area of the world where it rains a lot and is hot: *This is one of the many types of birds that live in the rain forest.*

jungle a forest with trees and large plants growing close together, in a part of the world where it is hot: *tribes that live in the jungle near the Amazon River*

trem•ble /ˈtrembəl/ *verb*
to shake because you are very afraid, excited, etc.: *He began to tremble with fear.*

tre•men•dous /trɪˈmendəs/ *adjective*
1 very large in size, amount, or power: *I have tremendous respect for her.*
2 very good: *He's a tremendous player.*
—**tremendously** *adverb* very or very much

trench /trentʃ/ *noun*
a long narrow hole that is dug in the ground: *The men were digging a trench for a new gas pipe.*

trend /trend/ Ac *noun*
the way that a change in society is developing: *There is a trend toward smaller families around the world.*

trend•y /ˈtrendi/ *adjective* **trendier**, **trendiest** *informal*
fashionable: *He wanted to impress her so he took her to a trendy restaurant.*

tres•pass /ˈtrespæs/ *verb*
to go onto someone's land without permission: *He said we were trespassing and told us to get out of his yard.*
—**trespasser** *noun* someone who trespasses
→ See Thesaurus box at **enter¹**

T

tri•al /ˈtraɪəl/ *noun*
1 the process by which a court of law decides whether someone is guilty of a crime: *The murder trial was shown on television.* | *He is on trial for robbery.*
2 a test to find out if someone or something is good or effective: *Researchers have begun trials of the new drug.*

tri•an•gle /ˈtraɪˌæŋgəl/ *noun*
a flat shape with three straight sides: *She cut the sandwich into two triangles.*
—**triangular** /traɪˈæŋgyələ˞/ *adjective* shaped like a triangle
→ See picture at **shape¹**

tri•ath•lon /traɪˈæθlɑn/ *noun*
a sports competition in which you run, swim, and ride a bicycle

trib•al /ˈtraɪbəl/ *adjective*
relating to a tribe: *We learned about the different tribal customs of Western Africa.*

tribe /traɪb/ *noun*
a group of people with a particular language and a traditional way of life: *He was the chief of a Native American tribe.*
→ See Thesaurus box at **race¹**

trib•ute /ˈtrɪbyut/ *noun*
something that you do to show that you respect and admire someone a lot: *The song is a tribute to his wife.*

trick¹ /trɪk/ *noun*
1 something that you do to deceive someone, in order to get something or for fun: *My*

brother played a trick on me by putting a plastic spider in my bed.
2 a skillful action that you do to entertain people: *He did magic tricks, like making coins disappear.*

trick² *verb*
to deceive someone in order to make him or her do something: *He tricked me into telling him the secret, by making it seem as though he already knew it.*
—**trickery** *noun* actions by which you deceive someone

trick•le /ˈtrɪkəl/ *verb*
to flow slowly in a thin line: *Sweat trickled down his face.*
—**trickle** *noun* a small amount of liquid that is flowing slowly: *a trickle of blood from a small cut*

trick•y /ˈtrɪki/ *adjective* **trickier**, **trickiest** *informal*
difficult: *Some of the test questions were tricky, so I don't know how I did.*

tri•cy•cle /ˈtraɪsɪkəl/ *noun*
a vehicle like a bicycle, but with one wheel at the front and two wheels at the back

tried /traɪd/ *verb*
the past tense and past participle of TRY

trig•ger¹ /ˈtrɪgɚ/ Ac *noun*
the part of a gun that you move with your finger to fire it: *Carter aimed the gun and pulled the trigger.*

trigger² *verb, formal*
to make something happen: *A shocking event can trigger a heart attack.*

trig•o•nom•e•try /ˌtrɪgəˈnɑmətri/ *noun*
the study of the relationships between the angles and sides of TRIANGLEs

tril•lion /ˈtrɪlyən/ *number*
1,000,000,000,000

tril•o•gy /ˈtrɪlədʒi/ *noun* plural **trilogies**
a set of three books, plays, or movies that are about the same characters: *I really like the "Lord of the Rings" trilogy.*

trim /trɪm/ *verb* **trimmed**, **trimming**
to cut a small amount off something to make it look neater: *She trimmed his hair.*
➔ See Thesaurus box at **cut¹**

tri•o /ˈtrioʊ/ *noun*
a group of three people, especially musicians: *a jazz trio with a piano player, a clarinet player, and a bass player*

trip¹ /trɪp/ *noun*
a visit to a place: *We're going on a trip to Florida.* | *He made two trips to Japan last year.* | *a camping trip*
➔ See Thesaurus box at **travel²**

trip² *verb* **tripped**, **tripping**
1 to hit your foot against something so that you fall or almost fall: *I tripped on a rock and fell.*
2 to make someone fall by putting something in front of his or her foot: *Brian stuck out his foot and tripped Joe.*
➔ See picture on page A4
➔ See Thesaurus box at **fall¹**

tri•ple¹ /ˈtrɪpəl/ *adjective*
involving three similar things: *a triple gold medal winner*

triple² *verb*
to become three times as big: *The landlord tripled the rent.*

tri•umph /ˈtraɪəmf/ *noun, formal*
a great win or success: *The team is celebrating its 100–88 triumph over Philadelphia.*
SYNONYM **victory**, **win**; ANTONYM **defeat**
—**triumphant** /traɪˈʌmfənt/ *adjective, formal* very happy and proud because you have won or succeeded

triv•i•al /ˈtrɪviəl/ *adjective, formal*
not important: *We shouldn't be arguing over something so trivial as whose turn it is to wash the dishes.*
—**trivia** *noun* unimportant things or facts: *He knows lots of trivia about celebrities.*

trol•ley /ˈtrɑli/ *noun*
an electric vehicle that takes people along the street on metal tracks
➔ See picture on page A30

trom•bone /trɑmˈboʊn/ *noun*
a metal musical instrument that you play by blowing into it and moving a long sliding part
—**trombonist** *noun* someone who plays the trombone
➔ See picture on page A21

troop /trup/ *noun*
1 **troops** = soldiers: *The U.S. will be sending more troops to the area.*
2 a group of people or animals: *a Girl Scout troop*

troop•er /ˈtrupɚ/ *noun*
a member of a state police force in the U.S.: *A state trooper pulled him over for speeding.*

tro•phy /ˈtroʊfi/ *noun* plural **trophies**
a metal cup or other object that someone gets for winning a game or race: *He's won many trophies for tennis.*

trophy

trop•i•cal /ˈtrɑpɪkəl/ *adjective*
in or from the hottest and wettest parts of the world: *tropical fruits such as pineapples and bananas*

trop•ics /ˈtrɑpɪks/ *noun*
the tropics = the hottest and wettest parts of the world: *Some plants grow only in the tropics.*

trot /trɑt/ *verb* **trotted, trotting**
to run with quick short steps: *The horse trotted along.*
—**trot** *noun* the speed of a person or animal that is trotting

trou•ble[1] /ˈtrʌbəl/ *noun*
1 problems or difficulty: *She's been having trouble with her computer.* | *I have trouble sleeping.* | *He has heart trouble* (=a physical problem with his heart).
2 the trouble with someone or something = what is not good about someone or something: *The trouble with you is you don't listen.*
3 in trouble a) if you are in trouble, you have done something wrong and someone in authority knows about it: *He got in trouble at school, and the principal called his parents.* **b)** having a lot of problems: *Their marriage was in trouble and she was afraid that her husband might leave her.*
4 an effort that you must make to do something: *She took the trouble to explain it to us again.* | *"Could you help me carry this?" "Sure, it's no trouble* (=I am happy to help)."

trouble[2] *verb, formal*
to make someone feel worried: *It was clear that something was troubling him, because he looked worried.* SYNONYM **bother**
—**troubling** *adjective, formal*: *His behavior is troubling; I'm worried that he may be taking drugs.*

trou•bled /ˈtrʌbəld/ *adjective, formal*
1 worried: *He was troubled about his mother's health problems.*
2 having a lot of problems: *Greg's troubled childhood, with a father who hit him, has affected his adult life.*

trou•ble•mak•er /ˈtrʌbəlˌmeɪkɚ/ *noun*
someone who deliberately causes problems: *A teacher needs to know how to deal with troublemakers who try to interrupt the class.*

trou•ble•shoot /ˈtrʌbəlˌʃut/ *verb*
to deal with problems in an organization, system, etc.: *His job is to troubleshoot computer problems.*
—**troubleshooter** *noun* someone who troubleshoots problems

trough /trɔf/ *noun*
a long narrow open container that holds water or food for animals: *The pigs were all eating at the trough.*

trou•sers /ˈtraʊzɚz/ *plural noun*
another word for PANTS

trout /traʊt/ *noun*
a common river fish

truce /trus/ *noun*
an agreement between two enemies to stop fighting or arguing for a time: *The two gangs called a truce* (=said they should stop fighting for a time).

truck /trʌk/ *noun*
a large vehicle that people use for carrying things: *They loaded the furniture into the truck.*
→ See picture on page A26

true /tru/ *adjective*
1 correct and based on facts: *Is it true (that) you're changing schools next year?* | *a true story*
2 real: *A true friend would be completely honest with you.*
3 come true = if a dream or wish comes true, what you hope for happens: *She has always wanted to be a singer, and now her dream has come true.*

WORD FAMILY look at the words:
→ **true** *adjective*
→ **untrue** *adjective*
→ **truth** *noun*
→ **truthful** *adjective*
→ **truthfully** *adverb*

T

tru•ly /ˈtruli/ *adverb, formal*
used for emphasizing what you are saying: *I truly believe we can win.* SYNONYM **really**

trum•pet /ˈtrʌmpɪt/ *noun*
a metal musical instrument that you play by blowing into it and pressing three buttons
—**trumpeter** *noun* someone who plays the trumpet
➔ See picture on page A21

trunk /trʌŋk/ *noun*
1 the thick wooden stem of a tree: *The squirrel ran up the tree trunk.*
2 a covered space in the back of a car where you can carry things: *Put the suitcases in the trunk.*
3 a large box in which you store or carry things: *She kept some blankets in a trunk at the end of her bed.*
4 the long nose of an ELEPHANT
➔ See picture on page A28

T

trunks /trʌŋks/ *plural noun*
short pants that men wear when they swim: *He needs a new pair of swimming trunks.*

trust[1] /trʌst/ *verb*
1 to believe that someone is honest and will not harm you: *I don't trust her, because she lied to me before.*
2 to believe that something is correct: *I trust his judgment.*

trust[2] *noun*
the belief that you can trust someone or something: *They have a good relationship that is based on trust.* ANTONYM **distrust**

WORD FAMILY look at the words:

➔ **trust** *noun*
➔ **trust** *verb*
➔ **trustworthy** *adjective*
➔ **distrust** *verb*
➔ **mistrust** *noun*

trust•ful /ˈtrʌstfəl/ *adjective*
believing that other people are good and honest and will not harm you: *He's too trustful of strangers and should be more careful.*

trust•wor•thy /ˈtrʌstˌwɚði/ *adjective*
someone who is trustworthy is honest, and you can trust him or her to do something: *Let John take care of the money; he's trustworthy.*
—**trustworthiness** *noun*

truth /truθ/ *noun*
the true facts about something: *Do you think he's telling the truth about what happened?*

truth•ful /ˈtruθfəl/ *adjective, formal*
giving the true facts about something: *It's better to be truthful about what happened, even if you get into trouble for it.* SYNONYM **honest**
—**truthfully** *adverb*

try[1] /traɪ/ *verb* **tried**, third person singular **tries**
1 to make an effort to do something: *I tried to lift the box, but it was too heavy.* SYNONYM **attempt**

THESAURUS: try

attempt to try to do something, especially something difficult: *He missed three of the five baskets he attempted during the game.*

see if you can do something *informal* to try to do something: *I'll see if I can get you a ticket.*

do your best to try very hard to do something, even if it is difficult: *They'll do their best to get it finished by Friday.*

make an effort to do something to try to do something, especially something difficult: *He has made a real effort to change his behavior.*

2 to do, use, taste, etc. something, in order to find out if it is good or successful: *Try some of this cake – it's delicious.* | *If the computer isn't working, try turning it off and turning it on again.*
3 to examine and judge someone in a court of law: *Three men were tried for the murder.*

PHRASAL VERBS

try something on
to put on a piece of clothing to find out if it fits or makes you look attractive: *I tried on three dresses, but I didn't like any of them.*

try something out
to use something in order to find out if it works or is good: *I bought a new bike last week, but I haven't had a chance to try it out yet.*

try[2] *noun* plural **tries**
an attempt to do something: *I passed the test on my first try.*

T-shirt /ˈti ʃɚt/ *noun*
a soft cotton shirt, with short SLEEVEs: *He was wearing a T-shirt and jeans.*
➔ See picture on page A6

tsu•na•mi /tsuˈnɑmi/ *noun*
a very large ocean wave that destroys buildings and kills people: *An earthquake under the ocean caused a tsunami that killed nearly 30,000 people.*

tub /tʌb/ *noun*
1 another word for BATHTUB: *He got in the tub and started to wash himself.*
2 a plastic or paper container with a lid, that food is sold in: *He bought a tub of popcorn at the movie theater.*

tu•ba /ˈtubə/ *noun*
a large metal musical instrument that you play by blowing, and which produces very low sounds
➔ See picture on page A21

tube /tub/ *noun*
1 a pipe made of metal, plastic, glass, or rubber: *The water passes through this rubber tube into this glass jar.*
2 a long container for a soft substance, that you press between your fingers to get the substance out: *a tube of toothpaste*

tu•ber•cu•lo•sis /tʊˌbɚkyəˈloʊsɪs/ *noun*
a serious infectious disease that affects someone's lungs

tuck /tʌk/ *verb*
1 to push the edge of a cloth or piece of clothing into something else: *He tucked his shirt into his pants.*
2 to put something in a small space or a safe place: *She tucked the money into her pocket.*

PHRASAL VERB
tuck someone in
to make a child feel comfortable in bed by arranging the covers around him or her: *You kids get in bed, and I'll come up to tuck you in.*

Tues•day /ˈtuzdi/ *noun*, *written abbreviation* **Tues.**
the third day of the week, between Monday and Wednesday: *He'll be back Tuesday.* | *Martha is going to St. Louis on Tuesday.* | *I'll see you next Tuesday.* | *We had the exam last Tuesday.* | *The meeting is scheduled for Tuesday afternoon.*

tug¹ /tʌg/ *verb* **tugged, tugging**
to pull something suddenly and hard: *Annie tugged at his hand and said, "Look over here, Dad."*
➔ See Thesaurus box at **pull¹**

tug² *noun*
1 *also* **tug boat** a small powerful boat used for pulling ships
2 a sudden strong pull: *I gave the rope a tug.*

ˌtug-of-ˈwar *noun*
a competition in which two teams pull on the opposite ends of a rope

tu•i•tion /tuˈɪʃən/ *noun*
the money you pay for someone to teach you: *Jeff worked while he was in college to help pay his tuition.*

tu•lip /ˈtulɪp/ *noun*
a tall brightly colored garden flower, shaped like a cup

tum•ble /ˈtʌmbəl/ *verb*
to fall with a rolling movement: *Everything tumbled out when I opened the closet door.*

tum•bler /ˈtʌmblɚ/ *noun*
a glass with a flat bottom and no handle

tum•my /ˈtʌmi/ *noun* plural **tummies** *informal*
your stomach: *Mommy, I have a tummy ache.*

tu•mor /ˈtumɚ/ *noun*
a group of cells in someone's body that grows too quickly and makes him or her sick: *He had an operation to remove a brain tumor.*

tu•na /ˈtunə/ *noun*
a large common ocean fish, or the meat from this fish: *She opened a can of tuna and made a sandwich.*

tune¹ /tun/ *noun*
a series of musical notes that are nice to listen to: *He picked up his flute and played a tune.*
➔ See Thesaurus box at **music**

tune² *verb*
to make small changes to a musical instrument so that it makes the correct sounds: *We paid a man to tune the piano.*

PHRASAL VERB
tune in
to watch or listen to a particular television or radio program: *Millions of people tuned in to watch the game.*

T

'tune-up *noun*
an occasion when someone cleans and makes small changes to a car's engine so that it works better: *I'm taking the car to the mechanic for a tune-up next week.*

tun•nel[1] /'tʌnl/ *noun*
a passage through a mountain or under the ground, for cars or trains to go through: *The train went through a tunnel in the mountain.*

tunnel[2] *verb, formal*
to dig a passage through a mountain or under the ground: *They tunneled through solid rock to make this mountain road.*

T

tur•ban /'tɚbən/ *noun*
a long piece of cloth that men from some religions wrap around their heads: *Many men in India have long beards and wear turbans.*

tur•bu•lent /'tɚbyələnt/ *adjective, formal*
1 a turbulent time or situation is one that has a lot of sudden changes: *Life was difficult during the turbulent years of the war.*
2 turbulent water or air has strong currents which change direction: *The turbulent ocean sent waves up over the deck of the ship.*
—**turbulence** *noun* the quality of being turbulent: *There was a lot of turbulence during the flight so we kept our seat belts on.*

turf /tɚf/ *noun*
short grass and the soil under it: *Artificial turf is used on some football fields.*

tur•key /'tɚki/ *noun*
a bird similar to a chicken but larger, or the meat from this bird: *Who's cooking the turkey for Thanksgiving?*

turn[1] /tɚn/ *verb*
1 to move your body so that you are looking in a different direction: *She turned and looked at me.*
2 to go in a new direction when you are walking, driving, etc.: *Turn right at the next light.*
3 to move an object so that it is facing in a different direction: *She turned the key and opened the door.*
4 to keep going around: *The wheels of the train began to turn slowly.*
5 to change and become different from before: *The weather turned colder.*
6 to become a particular age: *He has just turned 40.*
7 turn a page = to move a page in a book or magazine so that you can see the next one
8 turn your back on someone = to stop being friendly with someone and refuse to help him or her: *After she became famous, she turned her back on all her old friends.*
9 turn over a new leaf = to decide that you will change your behavior to make it better
10 turn someone or something loose = to allow a person or animal to be free: *She turned the dogs loose in the yard.*

PHRASAL VERBS

turn someone against someone/something
to make someone dislike or disagree with someone or something: *His experiences in Vietnam turned him against the war.*

turn someone away
to refuse to let people into a theater, restaurant, etc., for example because it is too full: *The concert was so popular that they had to turn people away.*

turn back
to stop going in a particular direction and start going in the opposite direction: *We had to turn back because of the snow.*

turn down
1 turn something down = to make a machine such as a television or an OVEN produce less sound, heat, etc.: *The TV's very loud. Can you turn it down?* ANTONYM **turn up**
2 turn someone/something down = to refuse someone's offer, request, or invitation: *He didn't ask her for a date, because he was worried that she would turn him down.*

turn in
1 turn something in = to give work that you have done to your teacher: *Have you turned in your homework?*
2 turn in *informal* = to go to bed: *It's getting late – I think I'll turn in.*
3 turn someone in = to tell the police where a criminal is

turn into

1 turn into something = to change or develop into something different: *The argument turned into a fight.*

2 turn someone/something into something = to make someone or something change into something different: *They're planning to turn the building into a museum.*

turn off

1 turn something off = to make a machine or light stop working, especially by pushing a button: *Don't forget to turn off your computer.* ANTONYM **turn on**

2 turn off a road = to drive off one road and onto another, often a smaller one: *We turned off the highway looking for a place to eat.*

3 turn someone off (something) = to make someone not like someone or something: *Young people are often turned off politics because they don't think that it has any connection with their lives.*

turn on

turn something on = to make a machine or light start working, for example by pushing a button: *She turned on the light.* ANTONYM **turn off**

turn out

1 turn out = to happen in a particular way, or to have a particular result: *Don't worry. I'm sure that everything will turn out fine.*

2 turn out a light = if you turn out a light, you push a button to stop the flow of electricity ANTONYM **turn on**

3 turn out = if people turn out for an event, they go to it: *Only about 30 people turned out for the show.*

turn something over to someone

to give someone the right to have something: *He turned the business over to his children.*

turn to someone/something

to try to get help, advice, or sympathy from someone or something: *I had no money, and I turned to my parents for help.*

turn up

1 turn something up = to make a machine such as a radio, OVEN, etc. produce more sound, heat, etc.: *Can you turn up the radio? I can't hear it.*

2 turn up *informal* = to arrive: *Danny turned up late as usual.*

3 turn up = if something you have lost turns up, you find it by chance: *The keys turned up in the kitchen drawer.*

4 turn up = if an opportunity or situation turns up, it happens, especially when you are not expecting it: *Don't worry, a job will turn up soon.*

turn² *noun*

1 the time when it is your chance or duty to do something that a group of people are doing, one after another: *It's your turn to pick a card.*

2 take turns = if a group of people take turns doing something, one person does it, then another person does it, etc.: *We took turns driving.*

3 a change in the direction you are moving in: *Make a right turn at the end of the road.*

4 a place where a road joins another road: *Take the second turn on the left.*

5 the action of moving something around: *Give the wheel another turn.*

ˈturning ˌpoint *noun*

the time when an important change starts to happen: *After losing so many times, the win was a turning point in his athletic career.*

turn•pike /ˈtɚnpaɪk/ *noun*

a large road for fast traffic that drivers have to pay to use: *the New Jersey Turnpike*

ˈturn ˌsignal *noun*

one of the lights on a car that flash to show that the car is going to turn left or right

➔ See picture on page A28

tur•quoise /ˈtɚkwɔɪz/ *noun*

a bright blue-green color

—**turquoise** *adjective* having a bright blue-green color

tur•tle /ˈtɚtl/ *noun*

an animal with a hard shell over its body that lives mainly in water

tusk /tʌsk/ *noun*

one of the two very long teeth that stick out of the mouth of an animal such as an ELEPHANT

tusk

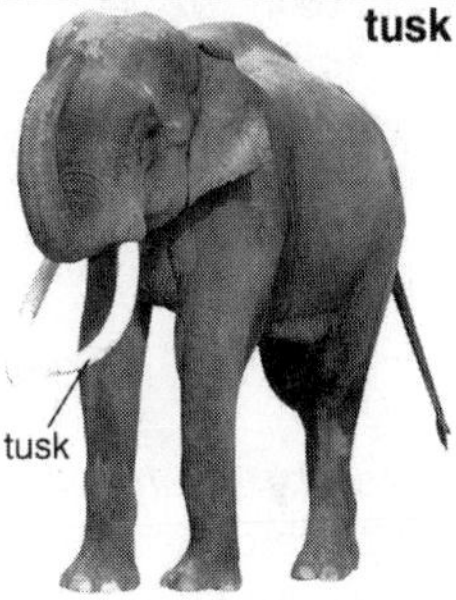

tu•tor¹ /ˈtutɚ/ *noun*

someone who teaches a subject to one student or only

T

a few students: *Mom hired a math tutor for me.*

tutor² *verb*
to teach a subject to one student or only a few students: *He's tutoring me in French.*

tu•to•ri•al¹ /tu'tɔriəl/ *noun*
a computer program that tells you how to do something: *There is an online tutorial showing you how to use the software.*

tutorial² *adjective*
relating to a tutor or his or her teaching: *They offer an after-school tutorial program for kids whose parents work full-time.*

tux•e•do /tʌk'sidoʊ/ *noun* plural **tuxedos**
a suit, usually a black one, that a man wears at formal events: *He rented a tuxedo to wear to the prom.*

TV *noun*
television: *It's time to buy a new TV – this one's too old.* | *What's on TV* (=being shown on the television)? | *The kids were watching TV.* | *a good TV show*

T

tweez•ers /'twizɚz/ *plural noun*
a small tool made from two thin metal pieces that are joined at one end, used for holding or pulling very small things: *She was removing hairs from her eyebrows with a pair of tweezers.*

twelfth /twelfθ/ *number*
1 12th
2 1/12

twelve /twelv/ *number*
1 12: *The table had twelve chairs around it.*
2 twelve O'CLOCK: *I'm going to lunch at twelve.*
3 twelve years old: *He's twelve.*

twen•ty¹ /'twenti/ *number*
1 20
2 twenty years old: *She's almost twenty.*
3 the twenties a) *also* **the '20s** the years between 1920 and 1929 **b)** *also* **the 20s** the numbers between 20 and 29, especially when used for measuring temperature
4 be in your twenties = to be aged between 20 and 29 years old: *a woman in her early twenties*
—**twentieth** /'twentiiθ/ *number* 20th or 1/20

twenty² *noun*
a piece of paper money worth $20: *Do you have two ten-dollar bills for a twenty?*

ˌtwenty-'first *noun, adjective*
21st

ˌtwenty-'one *number*
1 21
2 21 years old

twice /twaɪs/ *adverb*
two times: *I go swimming twice a week.* | *He makes twice as much money as I do. He makes $14 an hour and I make $7.*

twig /twɪg/ *noun*
a very thin branch that grows on a larger branch of a tree: *I had to pick up the twigs that blew out of the tree during the storm.*

twi•light /'twaɪlaɪt/ *noun, formal*
the time between day and night when the sky starts to become dark, or the pale light at this time: *It was twilight, and you could only see the dark outlines of the trees.*

twin /twɪn/ *noun*
one of two children who are born at the same time to the same mother: *Jenny and Julie are identical twins* (=twins who look exactly the same). | *I have a twin brother.*

'twin bed *noun*
a bed for one person

twin•kle /'twɪŋkəl/ *verb*
if a star or light twinkles, it shines with a light that keeps changing from bright to less bright: *The stars were twinkling in the sky.*
→ See Thesaurus box at **shine¹**

twirl /twɚl/ *verb*
to turn around several times very quickly: *The dancers were twirling on the dancefloor.* | *She was twirling the glass in her fingers.*

twist¹ /twɪst/ *verb*
1 to bend or wind something around something else several times: *Twist the ends of the wire together.*
2 to turn something so that it moves around in a circle: *He twisted the lid off the bottle.*
3 to change the position of your body by turning: *He twisted around to look at me.*
4 if you twist a part of your body, such as your knee, you injure it by bending it too much or in the wrong way: *I fell and twisted my ankle.*
5 if a road, river, etc. twists, it has a lot of curves in it: *The road twisted between the mountains.*

twist² *noun*

1 an unexpected change in a story or situation: *There was final twist in the movie that surprised everyone.*

2 a bend in a road, river, etc.: *There was a sharp twist in the path.*

3 a movement in which you turn something in a circle: *He put the key in the lock and gave it a twist.*

twitch /twɪtʃ/ *verb*

if a part of your body twitches, it makes a sudden small movement that you cannot control: *His eye twitches when he's tired.*

—**twitch** *noun* a small movement a part of your body makes, that you cannot control

two /tu/ *number*

1 2: *Most families in the neighborhood have two cars.* | *Two of my classmates live in my street.*

2 two O'CLOCK: *The game begins at two.*

3 two years old: *She'll be two in April.*

ty·ing /ˈtaɪ-ɪŋ/ *verb*

the present participle of TIE

type¹ /taɪp/ *noun*

a group of people or things that are similar to each other in some way: *What type of music do you like?*

THESAURUS: type

kind/sort a type of person or thing: *What kind of fish is this?* | *The store has all sorts of toys.*

category a group of people or things that are all of the same type: *The books are divided into three categories: romances, mysteries, and science fiction.*

brand a type of product made by a particular company – used about things you use every day, such as food, drinks, or cleaning products: *They sell a lot of different brands of cereal, including Kellogg's, Nestlé, and Post.*

model one particular type of a car, machine, weapon, etc.: *Ford's new models come out in September.*

type² *verb*

to write something using a computer or TYPEWRITER: *I need to type my book report.*

type·writ·er /ˈtaɪpˌraɪtɚ/ *noun*

a machine that prints letters, numbers, etc. onto paper when you press the buttons on it

ty·phoid /ˈtaɪfɔɪd/ *also* **ˌtyphoid ˈfever** *noun*

a serious disease that is caused by BACTERIA in food or water

ty·phoon /taɪˈfun/ *noun*

a violent tropical storm: *A typhoon struck the island, causing a lot of damage.*

typ·i·cal /ˈtɪpɪkəl/ *adjective*

having the usual qualities of a particular person, group, or thing: *It's typical of Rob to forget our appointment.*

—**typically** *adverb*: *Typically, students finish the program in two years.*

ty·po /ˈtaɪpoʊ/ *noun, informal*

a small mistake in the way something has been TYPEd or printed: *There's a typo on page 3 – it says "frim" instead of "firm."*

tyr·an·ny /ˈtɪrəni/ *noun*

government by a cruel ruler who has complete power: *Many people tried to escape from the tyranny of the government.*

—**tyrant** /ˈtaɪrənt/ *noun* a cruel ruler who has complete power

T

Uu

UFO *noun*
unidentified flying object a strange moving object in the sky that some people believe is a SPACESHIP from another world: *Many people thought the bright lights in the skies were UFOs.*

ug•ly /ˈʌgli/ *adjective* **uglier**, **ugliest**
not nice to look at: *Their dog is so ugly! It looks like its face has been squashed.* | *an ugly building painted gray* ANTONYM **beautiful**
—**ugliness** *noun*

ul•cer /ˈʌlsɚ/ *noun*
a sore area on your skin or inside your body: *a stomach ulcer*

ul•ti•mate /ˈʌltəmət/ Ac *adjective*
1 most important and last in a process or series: *His ultimate goal is to become a doctor, so he's majoring in biology before going to medical school.*
2 better, bigger, worse, etc. than all other people or things of the same kind: *The Olympics are the ultimate test of an athlete's ability, because you have to be the best to be selected for the Olympic team.*

ul•ti•ma•tum /ˌʌltəˈmeɪtəm/ *noun*
a statement saying that if someone does not do what you want, he or she will be punished: *Mom gave me an ultimatum: either improve my grades or quit football.*

ultra- /ʌltrə/
extremely or beyond what is usual: *an ultra-fast connection to the Internet*

ul•tra•vi•o•let /ˌʌltrəˈvaɪələt/ *adjective*, *abbreviation* **UV**
ultraviolet light cannot be seen but makes your skin darker when you are in the sun: *The sunglasses block ultraviolet light.*

um•brel•la /ʌmˈbrelə/ *noun*
a piece of cloth or plastic on a metal frame, that you hold above your head to protect yourself from the rain: *He opened his umbrella when it started to rain.*
➔ See picture on page A6

umbrella

um•pire /ˈʌmpaɪɚ/ *noun*
the person who makes sure that the players obey the rules in sports such as baseball and tennis: *The umpire said the runner was out.*
➔ See Thesaurus box at **referee**

un•a•ble /ʌnˈeɪbəl/ *adjective*
not able to do something: *After the accident, she was unable to walk.* ANTONYM **able**

un•ac•cept•a•ble /ˌʌnəkˈseptəbəl/ *adjective*
something that is unacceptable is wrong or bad and should not be allowed to continue: *Darrin's rude behavior is unacceptable, and if it does not improve, he will have to change schools.* ANTONYM **acceptable**
—**unacceptably** *adverb*

un•ac•cus•tomed /ˌʌnəˈkʌstəmd/ *adjective, formal*
not used to something: *He was from the country and unaccustomed to city life.* ANTONYM **accustomed**

un•af•fect•ed /ˌʌnəˈfektɪd/ Ac *adjective*
not changed or influenced by something: *Carla had lots of energy and seemed unaffected by the hot weather.*

un•af•ford•a•ble /ˌʌnəˈfɔrdəbəl/ *adjective*
costing too much for someone to be able to pay: *Tickets to the game are unaffordable for most families.* ANTONYM **affordable**

un•a•fraid /ˌʌnəˈfreɪd/ *adjective, formal*
not afraid: *The horses were big, but she was unafraid.* ANTONYM **afraid**, **scared**

u•nan•i•mous /yuˈnænəməs/ *adjective*
a unanimous decision or vote is one on which everyone agrees: *It was a unanimous decision to go to the lake, so we were all happy.*

—**unanimously** *adverb*: *They voted unanimously to make Juan the class president.*

un·armed /ˌʌnˈɑrmd/ *adjective*
not carrying any weapons: *The men were unarmed, but the soldiers shot them anyway.* ANTONYM **armed**

un·at·trac·tive /ˌʌnəˈtræktɪv/ *adjective*
not nice to look at: *He was very unattractive, with long greasy hair, and never had a girlfriend.* SYNONYM **ugly**; ANTONYM **attractive**

un·a·void·a·ble /ˌʌnəˈvɔɪdəbəl/ *adjective*
impossible to prevent: *Because of an unavoidable delay, we arrived late.*

un·a·ware /ˌʌnəˈwer/ Ac *adjective*
not knowing or seeing what is happening: *The girl was unaware that she was being watched.* ANTONYM **aware**

un·bear·a·ble /ʌnˈberəbəl/ *adjective*
too bad, painful, or annoying for you to deal with: *Her pain had become unbearable, and she wanted to die.* ANTONYM **bearable**
—**unbearably** *adverb*

un·be·liev·a·ble /ˌʌnbəˈlivəbəl/ *adjective*
1 very difficult to believe and probably not true: *Yvonne's excuse was totally unbelievable. She said her dog ate her homework!* ANTONYM **believable**
2 used for emphasizing how good, bad, surprising, etc. something is: *He has unbelievable talent and will be very successful.*
—**unbelievably** *adverb*

un·bi·ased /ʌnˈbaɪəst/ Ac *adjective*
fair and not influenced by someone's personal opinions: *We need unbiased information to make the right decision.* SYNONYM **impartial**; ANTONYM **biased**

un·born /ˌʌnˈbɔrn/ *adjective*
not yet born: *an unborn child* ANTONYM **born**

un·but·ton /ʌnˈbʌtn/ *verb*
to unfasten a piece of clothing that is closed with a BUTTON: *She unbuttoned her coat and took it off.* ANTONYM **button**

un·cer·tain /ʌnˈsɚtn/ *adjective*
1 not sure or feeling doubt: *I'm uncertain about what to do, so I called you for some advice.* ANTONYM **certain**
2 not clear, definite, or decided: *Because the club keeps losing members, its future is uncertain.*
—**uncertainty** *noun* the quality of being uncertain
—**uncertainly** *adverb*

un·changed /ʌnˈtʃeɪndʒd/ *adjective*
not having changed: *The little town was unchanged; everything was exactly how she remembered it.*

un·chang·ing /ʌnˈtʃeɪndʒɪŋ/ *adjective, formal*
always staying the same: *the unchanging desert*

un·cle /ˈʌŋkəl/ *noun*
the brother of your mother or father, or the husband of your AUNT: *My aunt and uncle and all my cousins came for Thanksgiving.* | *Uncle Bill*

un·clean /ˌʌnˈklin/ *adjective, formal*
dirty: *Unclean drinking water made a lot of people sick.* ANTONYM **clean**

un·clear /ˌʌnˈklɪr/ *adjective*
difficult to understand or know about: *The directions were unclear and I couldn't understand the assignment.* ANTONYM **clear**

Uncle Sam /ˌʌŋkəl ˈsæm/ *noun, informal*
a picture of a man with a white BEARD and a tall hat that represents the U.S., or the U.S. government

un·com·fort·a·ble /ʌnˈkʌmftɚbəl/ *adjective*
1 not nice to wear, sit on, or lie in: *These shoes are uncomfortable. They're too tight.* ANTONYM **comfortable**
2 feeling a little bit worried or embarrassed: *I'm a little shy, and I feel uncomfortable talking to strangers.*
—**uncomfortably** *adverb*

un·com·mon /ʌnˈkɑmən/ *adjective*
unusual, and not happening or seen very often: *Nowadays it is not uncommon for women in their late 30s and early 40s to have babies* (=it is fairly common for this to happen). SYNONYM **rare**; ANTONYM **common**
—**uncommonly** *adverb*

un·con·scious /ʌnˈkɑnʃəs/ *adjective*
not able to see, move, feel, or hear because you are not conscious (=awake and aware of what is happening): *The branch hit him on the head and knocked him unconscious.* ANTONYM **conscious**
—**unconsciously** *adverb*
—**unconsciousness** *noun*

U

un•con•sti•tu•tion•al /ˌʌnkɑnstəˈtuʃənəl/ Ac *adjective*
not allowed by the rules of a country or organization: *The Supreme Court said the law was unconstitutional and had to be changed.* ANTONYM **constitutional**

un•con•trol•la•ble /ˌʌnkənˈtroʊləbəl/ *adjective*
impossible to control or stop: *Olivia's body was shaking with uncontrollable laughter.*

un•con•ven•tion•al /ˌʌnkənˈvenʃənəl/ Ac *adjective*
very different from the usual way people do things: *Her unconventional style of clothes makes people notice her.* ANTONYM **conventional**

un•con•vinced /ˌʌnkənˈvɪnst/ *adjective*
not certain that something is true or good: *We told Tania that the trip would be fun, but she was unconvinced.* ANTONYM **convinced**

un•cool /ˌʌnˈkul/ *adjective, informal*
not fashionable or acceptable: *My parents are so uncool – they always embarrass me.* ANTONYM **cool**

U

un•couth /ʌnˈkuθ/ *adjective, formal*
behaving or speaking in a way that is rude and not acceptable: *The workers' uncouth talk shocked Mrs. Hill.*

un•cov•er /ʌnˈkʌvɚ/ *verb*
1 to discover something that has been kept secret or hidden: *Police uncovered a secret plan to rob the bank.*
2 to remove the cover from something: *Uncover the dish and let the food cool.* ANTONYM **cover**

un•de•cid•ed /ˌʌndɪˈsaɪdɪd/ *adjective*
not having made a decision about something: *I'm still undecided about which shoes I want to buy – can I try them on again?*

un•de•ni•a•ble /ˌʌndɪˈnaɪəbəl/ Ac *adjective*
definitely true or certain: *an undeniable fact*
—**undeniably** *adverb*

un•der /ˈʌndɚ/ *preposition, adverb*
1 below something or covered by it: *Your shoes are under the bed.* | *She's hiding under the blanket.*
2 less than a particular age, number, amount, or price: *What can I buy for under $20?* | *The toy is for children six and under.* ANTONYM **over**
3 controlled or governed by a particular leader, government, system, etc.: *The country was under communist rule for many years.*
4 be under discussion/construction/attack, etc. = to be in the process of being discussed, built, etc.: *The new plan is under consideration* (=being thought about)*, and a decision will be made next week.*
5 under way = happening or in the process of being done: *Construction is already under way on the new airport.*
6 affected by an influence, condition, or situation: *We're under pressure to finish the work this week.* | *He was arrested for driving under the influence of alcohol.*

un•der•class•man /ˌʌndɚˈklæsmən/ *noun* plural **underclassmen** /ˌʌndɚˈklæsmən/
a student in the first two years of HIGH SCHOOL or college

un•der•cov•er /ˌʌndɚˈkʌvɚ/ *adjective*
working or done secretly, in order to catch criminals or find out information: *Undercover police officers bought drugs to catch the drug dealers.*

un•der•de•vel•oped /ˌʌndɚdɪˈveləpt/ *adjective*
an underdeveloped country or area is poor and does not have a lot of modern industry: *Developed nations have promised to lend money to the underdeveloped world.* SYNONYM **developing**; ANTONYM **developed**

un•der•dog /ˈʌndɚˌdɔg/ *noun*
the person or team in a competition that is not expected to win: *Everyone was surprised when the underdogs won the game.*

un•der•es•ti•mate /ˌʌndɚˈestəˌmeɪt/ Ac *verb*
1 to think that something is smaller, cheaper, easier, etc. than it really is: *They underestimated the cost of the trip.* ANTONYM **overestimate**
2 to think that someone is not as good at something or intelligent as he or she really is: *Don't underestimate Sheila – she's very smart.*

un•der•go /ˌʌndɚˈgoʊ/ Ac *verb* **underwent** /ˌʌndɚˈwent/ **undergone** /ˌʌndɚˈgɔn/
to experience a change or something bad or difficult: *He underwent surgery to remove the cancer.*

un•der•grad•u•ate /ˌʌndɚˈgrædʒuət/ *noun*
a student in college, who is working for his or her BACHELOR'S DEGREE: *She's an undergraduate at Notre Dame University.*
—**undergraduate** *adjective* relating to undergraduates and the work they do: *undergraduate classes*

un•der•ground /ˌʌndɚˈgraʊnd/ *adjective, adverb*
under the earth's surface: *An underground tunnel connects the two buildings.* | *They bury the waste underground.*

un•der•growth /ˈʌndɚˌgroʊθ/ *noun*
bushes, small trees, etc. that grow around and under bigger trees: *I couldn't push my way through the dense undergrowth.*

un•der•hand /ˈʌndɚˌhænd/ *adjective, adverb*
thrown with your arm under the level of your shoulder: *The ball will be easier for me to catch if you throw it underhand.*

un•der•line /ˈʌndɚˌlaɪn/ *verb*
to draw a line under a word: *She underlined the important sentences on the page.*

un•der•ly•ing /ˈʌndɚˌlaɪ-ɪŋ/ Ac *adjective, formal*
relating to something that is most important but that is often not easy to notice: *Stress is the underlying cause of the illness.*

un•der•mine /ˈʌndɚˌmaɪn/ *verb*
to do or say something that makes someone or something less strong or effective over a period of time: *All the bad stories about Wilson undermined people's respect for him.*

un•der•neath /ˌʌndɚˈniθ/ *preposition, adverb*
directly below or under something: *He stood underneath the bridge to get out of the rain.* | *We turned some rocks over to see what was underneath.*

un•der•nour•ished /ˌʌndɚˈnɚɪʃt/ *adjective, formal*
not healthy because you have not eaten enough food or enough of the right type of food: *Many of the children in the camp were undernourished and sick.*

un•der•paid /ˌʌndɚˈpeɪd/ *adjective*
earning less money than you should: *Nurses here are underpaid for their hard work.*
—**underpay** /ˌʌndɚˈpeɪ/ *verb* to pay someone less money than he or she deserves

un•der•pants /ˈʌndɚˌpænts/ *plural noun*
a short piece of clothing that covers your bottom and is worn under your clothes

un•der•pass /ˈʌndɚˌpæs/ *noun*
a road or place to walk that goes under another road: *We took the underpass to get to the other side of the highway.*

un•der•priv•i•leged /ˌʌndɚˈprɪvəlɪdʒd/ *adjective, formal*
very poor and not having the same education, health care, safety, etc., that most other people in society have: *The program helps underprivileged children get a good education.* ANTONYM **privileged**
➔ See Thesaurus box at **poor**

un•der•shirt /ˈʌndɚˌʃɚt/ *noun*
a soft piece of clothing that you wear under a shirt: *It's cold today; put on an undershirt.*

un•der•stand /ˌʌndɚˈstænd/ *verb* **understood** /ˌʌndɚˈstʊd/
1 to know the meaning of what someone is saying: *Do you understand Spanish?* | *I'm sorry, I didn't understand – could you say that again?*
2 to know how someone feels and why he or she behaves in a particular way: *I understand how you feel – the same thing happened to me before.*
3 to know how something works or why something happens, because you have learned about it or experienced it: *I don't understand how television works.* | *Her mother has died, but she's too young to understand why her mother isn't here.*
4 to believe that something you have heard or read is true: *I understand that you're planning to move.*
—**understanding** *noun* an ability to understand someone or something: *He has a good understanding of what he has read.*

WORD FAMILY look at the words:
➔ **understand** *verb*
➔ **misunderstand** *verb*
➔ **understanding** *noun*

un•der•stand•ing /ˌʌndɚˈstændɪŋ/ *adjective*
someone who is understanding is kind and knows how you feel when you have problems: *Her parents were very understanding when she decided to quit her job.*

un•der•state•ment /ˈʌndɚˌsteɪtmənt/ *noun*
a statement that is not strong enough to say how good or bad something really is: *To say the movie wasn't very good is an understatement – it was horrible!*

un•der•stood /ˌʌndɚˈstʊd/ *verb*
the past tense and past participle of UNDERSTAND

un•der•tak•er /ˈʌndɚˌteɪkɚ/ *noun, formal*
someone whose job is to prepare a dead person to be buried and organize the funeral

un•der•tak•ing /ˈʌndɚˌteɪkɪŋ/ Ac *noun*
an important job or piece of work that you agree to do: *Planning the dance was a big undertaking, but the kids did a great job.*

U

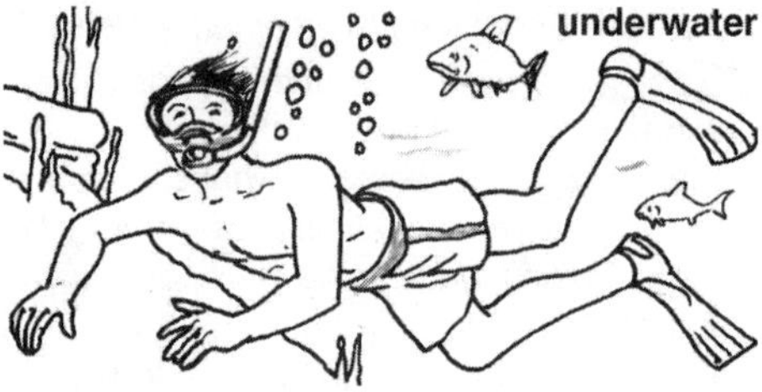

un•der•wa•ter /ˌʌndɚˈwɔtɚ/ *adjective, adverb*
below the surface of the water: *I don't like to open my eyes underwater.*

un•der•wear /ˈʌndɚˌwer/ *noun*
clothes that you wear next to your body, under your other clothes

un•der•went /ˌʌndɚˈwent/ Ac *verb*
the past tense of UNDERGO

un•der•world /ˈʌndɚˌwɚld/ *noun*
the criminals in a particular place and the activities they are involved in: *She had become involved in the city's dangerous criminal underworld.*

un•de•sir•a•ble /ˌʌndɪˈzaɪrəbəl/ *adjective, formal*
bad or harmful and not wanted: *The drug can produce undesirable side effects such as headaches.* ANTONYM **desirable**

un•do /ʌnˈdu/ *verb* **undid** /ʌnˈdɪd/ **undone** /ʌnˈdʌn/ third person singular **undoes** /ʌnˈdʌz/
1 to open something that is fastened, tied, wrapped, etc.: *He undid his shoelaces and took off his shoes.*
2 to change something back to the way it was before: *You can't undo what you've already done.*

un•do•ing /ʌnˈduɪŋ/ *noun*
be someone's undoing = to cause someone's failure, defeat, shame, etc.: *Not listening to other people's advice was his undoing.*

un•done /ˌʌnˈdʌn/ *adjective*
1 not fastened, tied, wrapped, etc.: *Your zipper's undone.*
2 not finished or completed: *A lot of the work was still undone when they left.* ANTONYM **done**

un•doubt•ed•ly /ʌnˈdaʊtɪdli/ *adverb*
used for emphasizing that something is definitely true or accepted by everyone: *Your parents will undoubtedly be pleased about how well you've done.*

un•dress /ʌnˈdres/ *verb*
to take your clothes off: *Yvonne undressed and got into bed.* ANTONYM **dress**
—**undressed** *adjective* not wearing any clothes

un•eas•y /ʌnˈizi/ *adjective*
worried because you think something bad might happen: *I was uneasy about driving through the mountains by myself.*
—**uneasiness** *noun*
—**uneasily** *adverb*
→ See Thesaurus box at **worried**

un•ed•u•cat•ed /ʌnˈdʒəˌkeɪtɪd/ *adjective*
not having a lot of education: *Uneducated people have trouble finding good jobs.* ANTONYM **educated**

un•em•ployed /ˌʌnɪmˈplɔɪd/ *adjective*
without a job: *My father has been unemployed since the factory closed last year.*

un•em•ploy•ment /ˌʌnɪmˈplɔɪmənt/ *noun*
1 the condition of not having a job: *There is a lot of unemployment in this part of the country.* ANTONYM **employment**
2 money that the government gives people who do not have jobs, to help them: *He's*

been on unemployment since he was laid off from his job.

un•e•qual /ʌn'ikwəl/ *adjective*
not the same or not equal in size, amount, the way someone is treated, etc.: *The rooms were of unequal size.* | *Rich people and poor people are often treated in unequal ways.* ANTONYM **equal**
—**unequally** *adverb*

un•e•ven /ʌn'ivən/ *adjective*
1 not flat or smooth: *The ground was uneven and hard to walk on.* ANTONYM **even**
2 not having the same qualities, sizes, amounts, etc.: *The quality of his work is uneven* (=some of it is good, but some is not).
—**unevenly** *adverb*

un•ex•pect•ed /ˌʌnɪk'spektɪd/ *adjective*
surprising because of not being expected: *He had to leave college because of his father's unexpected death.* ANTONYM **expected**
—**unexpectedly** *adverb*: *She arrived unexpectedly after we were all in bed.*

un•fair /ˌʌn'fer/ *adjective*
not right or fair: *It's unfair to punish me for something Eric did.* ANTONYM **fair**
—**unfairly** *adverb*
—**unfairness** *noun*

un•faith•ful /ʌn'feɪθfəl/ *adjective*
someone who is unfaithful has sex with someone who is not his or her wife, husband, or usual partner: *She left her husband because he was unfaithful to her and had a secret relationship with his secretary.* ANTONYM **faithful**

un•fa•mil•iar /ˌʌnfə'mɪlyɚ/ *adjective*
1 not known to you: *A lot of the vocabulary was unfamiliar to me, but I could understand most of it.* ANTONYM **familiar**
2 be unfamiliar with something = to not have any knowledge of or experience with something: *We were unfamiliar with the neighborhood and didn't know where to eat.* ANTONYM **be familiar with something**

un•fash•ion•a•ble /ʌn'fæʃənəbəl/ *adjective*
not popular at the present time: *Her clothes were old and unfashionable.* ANTONYM **fashionable**

un•fas•ten /ʌn'fæsən/ *verb*
to open something that is fastened, tied, buttoned, etc.: *Lewis unfastened his seat belt and got out of the car.* SYNONYM **undo**; ANTONYM **fasten**

un•fa•vor•a•ble /ʌn'feɪvərəbəl/ *adjective*
not good, and not making people like or approve of something: *The movie got a lot of unfavorable reviews, so we decided not to go.* ANTONYM **favorable**

un•fin•ished /ʌn'fɪnɪʃt/ *adjective*
not complete or finished: *When she died, the book she was writing was still unfinished.* ANTONYM **finished**

un•fit /ʌn'fɪt/ *adjective*
not good enough to do something or to be used for something: *The judge said she was an unfit mother and took her children away.* ANTONYM **fit**

un•fold /ʌn'foʊld/ *verb*
to open something that was folded: *She unfolded the map and spread it out on the table.* ANTONYM **fold**

U

un•fore•seen /ˌʌnfɔr'sin/ *adjective*, *formal*
an unforeseen situation is one that you did not expect to happen: *We had to cancel the trip because of unforeseen problems.*

un•for•tu•nate /ʌn'fɔrtʃənət/ *adjective*
1 an unfortunate situation is not good and you wish it was different: *It's unfortunate that no one wanted to help us.* ANTONYM **fortunate**
2 happening because of bad luck: *Three people were killed in the unfortunate accident.* SYNONYM **unlucky**; ANTONYM **lucky**

un•for•tu•nate•ly /ʌn'fɔrtʃənətli/ *adverb*
used when you wish something were not true and you feel sad or disappointed about it: *Unfortunately, I won't be able to come to your birthday party.* ANTONYM **fortunately**

un•friend•ly /ʌn'frendli/ *adjective*
not kind or friendly: *Most of the neighbors were unfriendly and we did not feel welcome.* ANTONYM **friendly**
—**unfriendliness** *noun*

un•grate•ful /ʌn'greɪtfəl/ *adjective*
not thanking someone for something he or she has given to you or done for you: *He's*

so ungrateful – he didn't even thank us for our help. ANTONYM **grateful**
—**ungratefulness** *noun*

un·hap·py /ʌn'hæpi/ *adjective* **unhappier, unhappiest**
1 not happy: *I was very unhappy when Lora moved away.* | *an unhappy childhood* SYNONYM **sad**; ANTONYM **happy**
2 not thinking something is good enough: *Our teacher was unhappy with our test scores and said we should have studied harder.* ANTONYM **pleased, satisfied**
—**unhappiness** *noun*
—**unhappily** *adverb*
➔ See Thesaurus box at **sad**

un·health·y /ʌn'helθi/ *adjective*
1 not physically healthy, and often sick: *He was an unhealthy baby, but he has become a very strong boy.* ANTONYM **healthy**
2 likely to make you sick: *Eating a lot of junk food is very unhealthy.* ANTONYM **healthy**

U

un·heard-of /ʌn'hɚd ʌv/ *adjective*
something that is unheard-of is very unusual, or has never happened before: *They paid him the unheard-of sum of $125,000!*

unhelpful /ʌn'helpfəl/ *adjective*
not helping someone: *The sales clerk was pretty unhelpful.* ANTONYM **helpful**
—**unhelpfulness** *noun*

u·ni·corn /'yunəˌkɔrn/ *noun*
a white horse with a horn on its head, that exists only in stories

u·ni·form¹ /'yunəˌfɔrm/ *noun*
special clothes that people wear for some jobs, schools, or sports: *Police officers have to wear a uniform.*

uniform² *adjective, formal*
exactly the same in size, shape, color, etc.: *Make sure all the pieces are a uniform length.*
—**uniformly** *adverb* always in the same way: *All the food at the hotel is uniformly excellent.*
—**uniformity** /ˌyunə'fɔrməti/ Ac *noun* the state of being uniform

u·ni·fy /'yunəˌfaɪ/ Ac *verb* **unified**, third person singular **unifies** *formal*
to join the different parts of a country, organization, etc. together: *They signed an agreement that unified Germany.*
—**unification** /ˌyunəfə'keɪʃən/ *noun* the act of unifying a country, organization, etc.: *the unification of Europe*

un·im·por·tant /ˌʌnɪm'pɔrtnt/ *adjective*
not important: *I'm not going to worry about unimportant details.* ANTONYM **important**

un·in·hab·it·ed /ˌʌnɪn'hæbɪtɪd/ *adjective*
an uninhabited place has no one living there: *an uninhabited island* ANTONYM **inhabited**

un·in·ter·est·ed /ʌn'ɪntrəstɪd/ *adjective*
not interested: *Larry was always uninterested in sports and rarely exercised.* ANTONYM **interested**

un·in·ter·est·ing /ʌn'ɪntrɪstɪŋ/ *adjective*
not interesting: *He had a very uninteresting job in a factory.* ANTONYM **interesting**

un·ion /'yunyən/ *noun*
1 *also* **labor union** an organization that employees form to protect their rights: *The teacher's union is asking for smaller classes and better pay.*
2 a group of countries or states with the same central government: *the European Union*
3 *formal* the act of joining countries, people, etc. together: *Marriage is the union of two people who have decided to spend the rest of their lives together.*
—**unionized** *adjective* unionized employees have formed or joined a union: *About 50% of workers are unionized.*

u·nique /yu'nik/ Ac *adjective*
1 very special and good: *I got the chance to study abroad, and it was a unique opportunity.*
2 not like anything else: *It's hard to describe the flavor of the fruit, because it's unique.*
—**uniquely** *adverb*: *This tradition is uniquely Mexican.*

u·ni·sex /'yunɪˌseks/ *adjective*
suitable for men and women: *a pair of unisex pajamas*

u·nit /'yunɪt/ *noun*
1 one part in something larger: *Our science textbook has ten units, each about a different topic.* | *The apartment building is divided into eight units.*
2 a standard that people use to measure amounts: *A kilowatt is a unit of energy.*

u•nit•ed /yunaɪtɪd/ *adjective*
1 a united country is formed by two or more countries or states joining together: *the United States of America*
2 if people are united, they have the same aims: *We are all united in our desire to improve the school.*
—**unite** *verb* to join together with other people to achieve something: *The nation united behind their leader.*
—**unity** *noun* when everyone in a group or country has the same aims: *The flag is the symbol of our national unity.*

U,nited 'Nations *noun*
the United Nations *also* **the U.N.** = an organization of many countries that tries to solve world problems in a peaceful way

u•ni•ver•sal /ˌyunəˈvɚsəl/ *adjective, formal*
involving all the people in a group or in the world: *There is a universal education system for all children in the country.*
—**universally** *adverb*: *Education should be universally available.*

u•ni•verse /ˈyunəˌvɚs/ *noun*
the universe = all the space, stars, and PLANETs that exist: *There are billions of stars in the universe.*

u•ni•ver•si•ty /ˌyunəˈvɚsəti/ *noun* plural **universities**
a school where you study at a high level to get a DEGREE: *She attended the University of California.*

un•just /ˌʌnˈdʒʌst/ *adjective, formal*
not fair: *People thought that the new law was unjust and tried to change it.* ANTONYM **just**
—**unjustly** *adverb*: *Greta felt that she had been unjustly punished and complained.*

un•jus•ti•fied /ˌʌnˈdʒʌstəˌfaɪd/ Ac *adjective, formal*
done without a good reason: *Snyder's criticism was unjustified, and he should not have said anything.* ANTONYM **justified**
—**unjustifiable** /ʌnˌdʒʌstəˈfaɪəbəl/ *adjective* very wrong in a way that no one can give a reason for: *The way the prisoners were treated was unjustifiable.*

un•kind /ˌʌnˈkaɪnd/ *adjective*
unpleasant or cruel to other people: *One of the girls said that Sally was fat, which was very unkind.* SYNONYM **mean**; ANTONYM **kind**
—**unkindly** *adverb*
—**unkindness** *noun*

un•known /ˌʌnˈnoʊn/ *adjective, formal*
not known: *The cause of the disease is unknown, which makes it scarier.*

un•law•ful /ʌnˈlɔfəl/ *adjective, formal*
against the law: *The U.S. is trying to stop unlawful entries into the country.* SYNONYM **illegal**
—**unlawfully** *adverb*

un•lead•ed /ʌnˈledɪd/ *adjective*
unleaded gas does not contain any LEAD

un•less /ənˈles/ *conjunction*
you use this for saying that something will happen if another thing does not happen: *You'll miss your bus, unless you leave now.*

un•like /ˌʌnˈlaɪk/ *preposition*
1 different from another person or thing: *Japanese is completely unlike English.* ANTONYM **like**
2 not typical of someone: *It's unlike Judy to leave without telling us.* ANTONYM **like**

un•like•ly /ʌnˈlaɪkli/ *adjective*
not likely to happen: *It's a long trip, so it's unlikely that we'll get there before 6:00.*

un•load /ʌnˈloʊd/ *verb*
1 to remove goods from a vehicle: *Outside the store, some men were unloading a truck.* ANTONYM **load**
2 to take things off a machine or piece of equipment: *Can you unload the dishwasher and put the clean dishes away?* ANTONYM **load**

un•lock /ʌnˈlɑk/ *verb*
to open a door, box, etc. with a key: *He unlocked the door and went in.* ANTONYM **lock**

un•luck•y /ʌnˈlʌki/ *adjective*
not lucky: *Many people believe that 13 is an unlucky number.* ANTONYM **lucky**

un•mar•ried /ˌʌnˈmærid/ *adjective*
not married: *Maggie was 30 and still unmarried.* SYNONYM **single**

un•mis•tak•a•ble /ˌʌnmɪˈsteɪkəbəl/ *adjective*
easy to recognize: *Garlic has an unmistakable taste.*
—**unmistakably** *adverb*

U

un•nat•u•ral /ˌʌnˈnætʃərəl/ *adjective*
different from what is normal or natural: *It's unnatural for someone his age to sleep so much.* ANTONYM **natural**

un•nec•es•sar•y /ʌnˈnesəˌseri/ *adjective*
not needed: *The writer uses too many unnecessary big words.* ANTONYM **necessary**
—**unnecessarily** /ʌnˌnesəˈserəli/ *adverb*: *I try not to spend money unnecessarily.*

un•of•fi•cial /ˌʌnəˈfɪʃəl/ *adjective*
if a statement, report, etc. is unofficial, no one has formally approved or accepted it yet: *According to unofficial reports, eight people were arrested.* ANTONYM **official**
—**unofficially** *adverb*

un•pack /ʌnˈpæk/ *verb*
to take everything out of a suitcase or box: *We arrived at our hotel, and unpacked our suitcases.* ANTONYM **pack**

un•paid /ˌʌnˈpeɪd/ *adjective*
not paid: *There were unpaid bills all over his desk.*

U

un•pleas•ant /ʌnˈplezənt/ *adjective*
not nice or enjoyable: *We had an unpleasant trip because the car stopped working.* ANTONYM **pleasant**
—**unpleasantly** *adverb*: *The water was unpleasantly cold.*
—**unpleasantness** *noun*

un•plug /ʌnˈplʌg/ *verb* **unplugged, unplugging**
to remove a PLUG from a wall, and stop something electrical from working: *My computer wasn't working because someone had unplugged it.* ANTONYM **plug in**

un•pop•u•lar /ʌnˈpɑpyələ˞/ *adjective*
not liked by many people: *Difficult subjects are often unpopular with students.* ANTONYM **popular**
—**unpopularity** /ʌnˌpɑpyəˈlærəti/ *noun* the state of being unpopular

un•pre•pared /ˌʌnprɪˈperd/ *adjective*
not ready to deal with something: *I was totally unprepared for the question and didn't know what to say.* ANTONYM **prepared, ready**

un•pro•fes•sion•al /ˌʌnprəˈfeʃənəl/ *adjective*
not obeying the rules for what is appropriate behavior for people in particular jobs: *It is unprofessional to criticize the people that you work with.*
—**unprofessionally** *adverb*

un•prof•it•a•ble /ʌnˈprɑfɪtəbəl/ *adjective, formal*
not making a profit: *Many small businesses became unprofitable and had to close.* ANTONYM **profitable**
—**unprofitably** *adverb*

un•qual•i•fied /ʌnˈkwɑləˌfaɪd/ *adjective*
not having the knowledge, experience, or education to do something: *We never hire people who are unqualified for the job.* ANTONYM **qualified**

un•ques•tion•a•bly /ʌnˈkwestʃənəbli/ *adverb, formal*
used for emphasizing that something is certainly true: *The team is unquestionably better this year, and we've won a lot more games.*
—**unquestionable** *adjective, formal* completely certain or true

un•real /ˌʌnˈril/ *adjective*
1 not really happening or existing: *While I was on vacation, all my problems back home began to seem unreal.* ANTONYM **real**
2 *informal* very unusual or special: *Ten of us went on a trip to the Andes – it was unreal!*

un•rea•son•a•ble /ʌnˈrizənəbəl/ *adjective, formal*
1 not fair or sensible: *It's unreasonable to expect you to work all weekend.* ANTONYM **reasonable**
2 unreasonable prices are too high: *The prices in that store are unreasonable, so I don't shop there.* ANTONYM **reasonable**
—**unreasonably** *adverb*

un•re•lat•ed /ˌʌnrɪˈleɪtɪd/ *adjective*
if events are unrelated, they are not connected with each other: *The two crimes were similar, but probably unrelated.* ANTONYM **related**

un•re•li•a•ble /ˌʌnrɪˈlaɪəbəl/ Ac *adjective*
not possible for you to believe or trust: *Some of the information on the Internet is unreliable, so check it carefully before you use it as a source for your research.* ANTONYM **reliable**

un•rest /ʌn'rest/ *noun, formal*
a situation in which people protest or behave violently: *There was not enough food, which caused unrest across the country.*

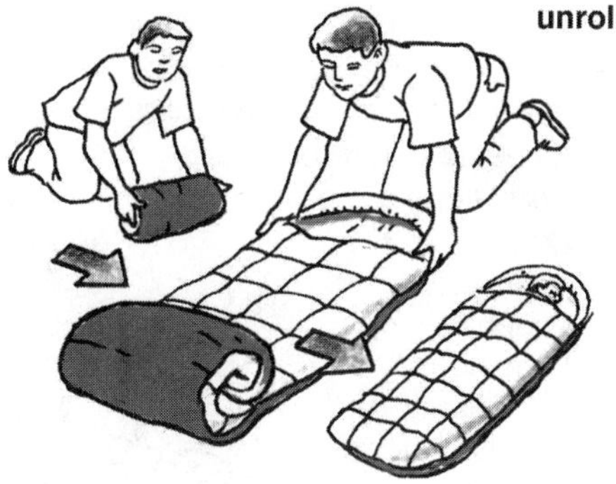

un•roll /ʌn'roʊl/ *verb*
to open something that is in the shape of a tube, and make it flat: *He unrolled the sleeping bag and climbed inside.* ANTONYM **roll up**

un•ru•ly /ʌn'ruli/ *adjective, formal*
behaving badly or violently, and difficult to control: *Teachers have to learn to deal with unruly children.*

un•safe /ˌʌn'seɪf/ *adjective*
dangerous: *It's unsafe to swim in the river.* ANTONYM **safe**
—**unsafely** *adverb*: *The police stopped him because he was driving unsafely.*

un•san•i•tar•y /ʌn'sænəˌteri/ *adjective, formal*
dirty and likely to cause disease: *In some areas, the people are living in unsanitary conditions.* ANTONYM **sanitary**

un•sat•is•fac•to•ry /ˌʌnsætɪs'fæktəri/ *adjective, formal*
not good enough: *Janie's work in class this year has been unsatisfactory, and she may have to repeat the year.* ANTONYM **satisfactory**
—**unsatisfactorily** *adverb*

un•screw /ʌn'skru/ *verb*
to open something by twisting it: *Turn off the light before unscrewing the bulb.* ANTONYM **screw in**

un•self•ish /ʌn'selfɪʃ/ *adjective*
doing things for other people, rather than just doing things for yourself: *She is an unselfish girl who likes making her friends happy.* ANTONYM **selfish**

un•set•tling /ˌʌn'setlɪŋ/ *adjective, formal*
making you feel worried or nervous: *I got a letter from Amy with some unsettling and disturbing news.*
—**unsettled** /ˌʌn'setld/ *adjective, formal*
worried or nervous: *Going to a new school often makes kids feel unsettled.*

un•skilled /ˌʌn'skɪld/ *adjective, formal*
without any special training for a job: *It's hard for unskilled workers to find a job.* ANTONYM **skilled**

un•sta•ble /ʌn'steɪbəl/ Ac *adjective, formal*
1 not steady, safe, or reliable: *Be careful – the ladder's a little unstable.* ANTONYM **stable**
2 not always able to think or behave in a normal, controlled way: *The woman was mentally unstable and often started fights with strangers.* ANTONYM **stable**

un•stead•y /ʌn'stedi/ *adjective*
shaking and likely to fall, drop something, etc.: *A baby's first steps are always a little unsteady.* ANTONYM **steady**
—**unsteadily** *adverb*
—**unsteadiness** *noun*

un•suc•cess•ful /ˌʌnsək'sesfəl/ *adjective*
not succeeding in doing something: *I applied for the job, but I was unsuccessful.* ANTONYM **successful**
—**unsuccessfully** *adverb*: *He tried unsuccessfully to become an actor.*

un•suit•a•ble /ʌn'sutəbəl/ *adjective*
not good for a particular person or purpose: *This movie is unsuitable for young children.* SYNONYM **inappropriate**; ANTONYM **suitable**

un•sure /ˌʌn'ʃʊr/ *adjective*
not sure about something: *If you're unsure about anything, ask the teacher.*

un•sym•pa•thet•ic /ˌʌnsɪmpə'θetɪk/ *adjective*
not kind to someone who has problems or worries: *The teacher was unsympathetic when I got a D on the test, and said it was my own fault.* ANTONYM **sympathetic**

U

un•tan•gle /ʌnˈtæŋgəl/ *verb*
to separate pieces of string, hair, etc. that are twisted together: *Untangle your hair with a comb before you dry it.* ANTONYM **tangle**

un•tie /ʌnˈtaɪ/ *verb*
to undo string, rope, etc. that someone has tied in a knot: *I untied the rope and got into the boat.* ANTONYM **tie**

un•til /ʌnˈtɪl/ *preposition, conjunction*
1 continuing to a particular time and then stopping: *I have classes until 4 p.m. today.*
2 not until = not before a particular time or event: *The movie doesn't start until 8 p.m.* | *You can't leave until you finish the test.*

un•time•ly /ʌnˈtaɪmli/ *adjective, formal*
an untimely death = a situation in which someone dies when he or she is still young: *Blanche died an untimely death at the age of 19.*

un•true /ʌnˈtru/ *adjective*
not true: *He said he loved me, but it was untrue.* SYNONYM **false**; ANTONYM **true**

U

un•used /ˌʌnˈyuzd/ *adjective, formal*
not used: *The upstairs rooms of the old house were empty and unused.*

un•u•su•al /ʌnˈyuʒuəl/ *adjective*
different from what is usual or normal: *It's unusual for Dave to be late; I wonder where he is.* | *I like this color because it's unusual.*
—**unusually** *adverb* more than usual: *Ben was 13, and unusually tall.*

un•veil /ʌnˈveɪl/ *verb, formal*
to tell people about a new plan for the first time: *The mayor unveiled plans for a new park.*

un•wel•come /ʌnˈwelkəm/ *adjective, formal*
not wanted: *All the other people ignored me, and I felt unwelcome.* ANTONYM **welcome**

un•will•ing /ʌnˈwɪlɪŋ/ *adjective, formal*
not wanting to do something: *Rickie was unwilling to spend any more money, so I had to pay for everything.* ANTONYM **willing**
—**unwillingly** *adverb*: *I unwillingly agreed to stay at home and take care of my brother.*
—**unwillingness** *noun*

un•wind /ʌnˈwaɪnd/ *verb* **unwound** /ʌnˈwaʊnd/
1 to relax, especially when you stop working: *Sometimes I watch TV after work to unwind.*
2 to undo rope, string, etc. that is wrapped around something else: *I took the roll of wire and unwound it.* ANTONYM **wind**

un•wise /ˌʌnˈwaɪz/ *adjective, formal*
not sensible: *I left school at 16, and that was an unwise decision.* ANTONYM **wise**
—**unwisely** *adverb*: *I unwisely told her the secret, and she told everyone else.*

un•wound /ʌnˈwaʊnd/ *verb*
the past tense and past participle of UNWIND

un•wrap /ʌnˈræp/ *verb* **unwrapped, unwrapping**
to remove the paper, plastic, etc. that is around something: *Beth was unwrapping her birthday presents.* ANTONYM **wrap**

un•zip /ʌnˈzɪp/ *verb* **unzipped, unzipping**
to unfasten clothing, a bag, etc. by opening the ZIPPER on it: *Lucy unzipped her jacket.* ANTONYM **zip up**

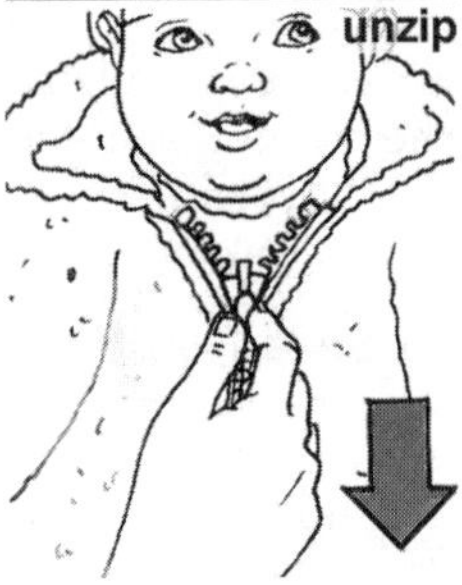

up¹ /ʌp/ *adverb, preposition*
1 toward or in a higher place: *We rode the elevator up to the fourth floor.* | *The cat ran up the tree.* | *Billy was so excited that he was jumping up and down* (=into the air and down again). ANTONYM **down**
2 to a larger level, amount, or number than before: *Can you turn up the TV? I can barely hear it.* | *The number of children at the school has gone up, and it's about twice as big as when you were here.* ANTONYM **down**
3 into a more upright position: *The teacher came in and we all sat up straight.*
4 to a place that is further along the road: *Ted lives up the street from me.* SYNONYM **down**
5 very close to someone or something: *He came up to me and asked me for some money.*
6 until something is completely gone: *I've used up all the food in the fridge.* | *The books burned up in the fire.*

7 it's up to someone = used for saying who has to make a decision: *Only you can decide what you want to study – it's up to you.*
8 up to 20 people/10 dollars, etc. = as many as 20 people, as much as 10 dollars, etc.: *We can take up to six people in our car.*
9 up to now = until this time: *Up to now, we've always gone to Florida for our vacation, but we may go somewhere new this year.*
10 be up to something = to be doing something secret or bad: *He comes home late every day, and I'm sure he's up to something.*

up² *adjective*
1 awake or out of bed: *I'm usually up at 7:00 every day.*
2 if a period of time is up, it is finished: *I didn't finish the test before the two hours were up.*
3 what's up? *informal* = used in order to greet someone, or to ask if there is a problem: *You look worried. What's up?*
4 be up on something = to know about something: *I've been on vacation, so I'm not really up on what's happening back home.*
5 be up and running = working and ready to use: *The new computer system is up and running now.*

ˌup-and-ˈcoming *adjective*
likely to become successful: *an up-and-coming young singer*

up•beat /ˌʌp'bit/ *adjective*
cheerful and making you feel that good things will happen: *She has an upbeat attitude, which is really encouraging.*

up•bring•ing /'ʌpˌbrɪŋɪŋ/ *noun*
the way that your parents care for you and teach you to behave: *Mandy had loving parents and a very good upbringing.*

up•com•ing /'ʌpˌkʌmɪŋ/ *adjective*
happening soon: *Here are some details of the museum's upcoming events for the rest of the year.*

up•date /ʌp'deɪt/ *verb*
to add the most recent information to something: *We need to update our computer records with the new data.*
—**update** /'ʌpdeɪt/ *noun* the most recent information about something: *hourly news updates*

up•front /ʌp'frʌnt/ *adverb*
paid before someone does any work: *The builder wants $300 upfront before he'll even start working.*
—**'up-front** *adjective* up-front costs, payments, etc. are ones you pay before someone does any work: *He charges an upfront fee of $500.*

up•grade /ʌp'greɪd/ *verb*
to improve something, or to exchange it for something better: *The company is upgrading its computer system, so in a few weeks everything will be done much faster.*

up•heav•al /ʌp'hivəl/ *noun, formal*
a very big change that causes problems: *Going to live in a new place can be a big upheaval.*

up•hill /ˌʌp'hɪl/ *adjective, adverb*
toward the top of a hill: *The road began to go uphill.* | *an uphill climb* ANTONYM **downhill**

up•hold /ʌp'hoʊld/ *verb* **upheld** /ʌp'held/ *formal*
to support a law or decision: *The court upheld the other judge's decision.*

up•hol•ster•y /ə'poʊlstəri/ *noun*
material that people use for covering chairs: *Our car seats have leather upholstery.*

up•keep /'ʌpkip/ *noun*
the process of keeping houses, machines, etc. in good condition: *The upkeep of a big house can be very expensive.*

up•load /ʌp'loʊd/ *verb*
to move information from your computer to the Internet or to another piece of equipment: *How do I upload this file to the network?*

up•on /ə'pɑn/ *preposition, formal*
on: *The movie is based upon a true story.* | *There was a big castle upon the hill.*

up•per /'ʌpɚ/ *adjective*
in a higher position than another part of something: *His upper lip was bleeding.* ANTONYM **lower**

ˌupperˈcase *noun*
letters written in their large form, such as A, B, D, G, J, etc.: *The names were printed in uppercase.* ANTONYM **lowercase**
—**uppercase** *adjective* uppercase letters are written in their large form: *an uppercase M*

U

ˌupper ˈclass *noun*
the upper class = the group of people in a country who are very rich or who have a lot of power
—**upper-class** *adjective* belonging or relating to the upper class

up·per·class·man /ˌʌpɚˈklæsmən/ *noun* plural **upperclassmen** /ˌʌpɚˈklæsmən/
a student in the last two years of HIGH SCHOOL or college

up·per·most /ˈʌpɚˌmoʊst/ *adjective, formal*
highest: *The uppermost part of a house is the roof.* SYNONYM **top**

up·right /ˈʌp-raɪt/ *adjective, formal*
1 straight up, not lying, sitting, or leaning: *Stand the bottle upright on the table.* | *She sat upright to eat her breakfast in bed.*
2 honest and good: *The people in his family were upright people who always obeyed the law.*

U

up·ris·ing /ˈʌpˌraɪzɪŋ/ *noun*
a situation in which people in a country fight against their government because they disagree with it: *Hundreds of people have been killed in the recent uprising.* SYNONYM **rebellion**

up·roar /ˈʌp-rɔr/ *noun*
if there is uproar, people complain in an angry way about something: *The movie was very violent, and caused uproar among parents.*

ˌups and ˈdowns *plural noun*
good things and bad things that happen: *Every marriage has its ups and downs.*

up·set¹ /ʌpˈset/ *adjective*
sad because something bad has happened: *She was upset because her cat had died.*
➔ See Thesaurus box at **sad**

upset² *verb* **upset, upsetting**
1 to make someone feel sad: *He upset me by saying I was fat.*
2 if something upsets a plan, it changes it and causes problems: *The rain upset our plans, and we had to cancel the picnic.* SYNONYM **spoil**

up·side down /ˌʌpsaɪd ˈdaʊn/ *adverb*
with the top at the bottom, and the bottom at the top: *He turned the bag upside down and dumped everything out.*
—**upside-down** *adjective*: *I sat on an upside-down box.*

up·stairs /ˌʌpˈsterz/ *adjective, adverb*
on an upper level of a building, or toward an upper level: *I went upstairs to bed.* ANTONYM **downstairs**

ˌup to ˈdate *also* **up-to-date** *adjective*
1 knowing about all the most recent things that have happened: *The president's advisors keep him up to date on events around the world.*
2 including all the newest information, technology, or fashions: *The map is not up-to-date and some new roads aren't on it.* ANTONYM **out-of-date**

ˌup-to-the-ˈminute *adjective*
including the newest information about what has been happening: *up-to-the-minute news*

up·town /ˌʌpˈtaʊn/ *adjective, adverb*
in the northern area of a city, or toward the northern area: *Rich people live in uptown Manhattan.*

up·ward /ˈʌpwɚd/ *adverb*
1 toward a higher place or position: *The balloon moved slowly upward into the sky.* ANTONYM **downward**
2 increasing to a higher level or amount: *The cost of the building work is moving upward, and we have no more money.* ANTONYM **downward**

u·ra·ni·um /yʊˈreɪniəm/ *noun*
a substance used for producing NUCLEAR energy and weapons: *The atomic bomb was made out of uranium.*

U·ra·nus /yʊˈreɪnəs/ *noun*
the seventh PLANET from the sun

ur·ban /ˈɚbən/ *adjective*
relating to a town or city: *People moved to urban areas in order to look for work.* ANTONYM **rural**
—**urbanization** /ˌɚbənəˈzeɪʃən/ *noun* a process in which urban areas get bigger

urge¹ /ɚdʒ/ *verb, formal*
to try hard to persuade someone to do something: *His parents urged him not to join the army, but he did it anyway.*

urge² *noun*
a strong feeling that you want to do something very much: *I suddenly felt the urge to go back home.*

ur•gent /ˈɚdʒənt/ *adjective*
if something is urgent, it is very important and someone needs to deal with it immediately: *an urgent message*
—**urgently** *adverb*: *He needs to see a doctor urgently or he could die.*
—**urgency** /ˈɚdʒənsi/ *noun* the need to do something as soon as possible

u•rine /ˈyʊrɪn/ *noun, formal*
liquid that comes out of your body when you go to the toilet
—**urinate** /ˈyʊrəˌneɪt/ *verb, formal* to let urine out of your body

us /əs; *strong* ʌs/ *pronoun*
the object form of "we": *We went to the movies and Jack came with us.*

U.S. *noun*
the U.S. = the United States of America: *She lives in the U.S.*

us•a•ble /ˈyusəbəl/ *adjective, formal*
if something is usable, you can use it: *The equipment was old and broken, and not usable.*

us•age /ˈyusɪdʒ/ *noun, formal*
1 the way that people use words in a language: *The usage of the word "gay" has changed: it used to mean "happy or bright"; now it usually means "homosexual."*
2 the amount of something that is used: *The usage of oil continues to increase.*

use[1] /yuz/ *verb*
1 to do something with something for a purpose: *They used candles to light the room.* | *I use the car for driving to work.*
2 to take something so that some or all of it is gone: *Big cars use a lot of gas.*
3 to treat someone in an unfair way in order to get something that you want: *He was using me to get to know my friend.*

PHRASAL VERB
use something up
to use all of something: *Someone's used all the toothpaste up, so I can't clean my teeth.*

use[2] /yus/ *noun*
1 the act of using something: *When will the machine be ready for use?*
2 a way in which something is used, or what it is used for: *The room's main use is for meetings.*
3 if you have the use of something, you can use it: *He gave me the use of his car.* | *After the accident, she lost the use of both her legs.*
4 it's no use = used when stopping doing something because you do not think it will be successful: *It's no use. I can't fix it.*
5 make use of something *formal* = to use something that is there for you to use: *Can you make use of these old clothes?*
6 in use = if something is in use, someone is using it: *I couldn't use the computer, because it was already in use.*

used /yuzd/ *adjective*
1 used cars, clothes, etc. are not new and have already had an owner: *We bought a used car because we couldn't afford a new one.* SYNONYM **second-hand**
➔ See Thesaurus box at **old**
2 /yust/ **be used to something** = if you are used to something, you have experienced it many times before so it does not seem strange or difficult: *He delivers newspapers, so he's used to getting up early.*

used to /ˈyustə; *final or before a vowel* ˈyustu/ *verb*
if something used to happen, it happened in the past but it does not happen now: *I used to live in New York before I moved to Madison.*

> **USAGE: used to**
>
> **Used to** is used in order to talk about something that someone did regularly in the past but does not do anymore: *I used to play tennis twice a week, but I don't have time now.*
>
> **Be used to** and **get used to** are used in order to talk about being or becoming more comfortable with a situation or activity, so that it does not seem surprising, difficult, etc. anymore: *Are you used to the cold winters yet?* | *It was hard to get used to being in a different country.*

use•ful /ˈyusfəl/ *adjective*
helping you to do or to get what you want: *A cell phone is useful when you're away from home.* ANTONYM **useless**
—**usefully** *adverb*
—**usefulness** *noun*: *Everyone knows the usefulness of the Internet.*

U

use•less /ˈyusləs/ *adjective*
not helpful or useful: *There's no ink in this pen – it's useless.* ANTONYM **useful**

us•er /ˈyuzɚ/ *noun, formal*
someone who uses a product, service, etc.: *Prices are falling for telephone users.*

ˌuser-ˈfriendly *adjective*
easy to use: *This program is difficult to use and we need to make it more user-friendly.*

u•su•al /ˈyuʒuəl/ *adjective*
1 done or happening most often, as you expect it to happen: *Let's meet at the usual place.* | *I woke up later than usual.*
2 as usual = in the way that happens most of the time: *They were late, as usual.*

u•su•al•ly /ˈyuʒuəli/ *adverb*
used when saying what happens most of the time: *I'm usually at school early, but today I was late.* SYNONYM **normally**

U

u•ten•sil /yuˈtensəl/ *noun, formal*
a tool or object that you use for preparing and eating food: *Knives, pots, and other kitchen utensils lay on the counter.*

u•til•i•ty /yuˈtɪləti/ Ac *noun* plural **utilities** *formal*
a service such as gas or electricity: *Is the cost of utilities included in the rent?*

u•til•ize /ˈyutlˌaɪz/ Ac *verb, formal*
to use something: *They showed us how to utilize waste water.*
—**utilization** /ˌyutl-əˈzeɪʃən/ *noun* the act of utilizing something

u•to•pi•a /yuˈtoʊpiə/ *noun, formal*
a perfect world where everyone is happy, but that does not really exist: *They dream of a utopia of world peace.*
—**utopian** *adjective* relating to a utopia: *a utopian society*

ut•ter[1] /ˈʌtɚ/ *adjective, formal*
complete or extreme: *We watched in utter amazement, unable to say anything.*
—**utterly** *adverb, formal* completely or extremely: *He felt utterly exhausted.*

utter[2] *verb, formal*
to say something: *No one uttered a word.*

U-turn /ˈyu tɚn/ *noun*
if you make a U-turn in a vehicle, you turn around and drive in the direction you came from

Vv

V /vi/
the number 5 in the system of ROMAN NUMERALS

va•can•cy /ˈveɪkənsi/ *noun* plural **vacancies**
1 a room in a hotel that is available for someone to stay in: *We tried to get a room in a motel, but there were no vacancies.*
2 *formal* a job that is available for someone to start doing: *They are advertising a vacancy for a driver.*

va•cant /ˈveɪkənt/ *adjective*, *formal*
empty and available for someone to use: *There's a vacant apartment in my building if you're looking for a place.*

va•ca•tion /veɪˈkeɪʃən/ *noun*
a time away from work and school when you can relax: *They're on vacation for the next two weeks.* | *We took a vacation to the Virgin Islands.*

> **THESAURUS: vacation**
>
> **holiday** a day when no one officially has to go to work or to school: *the Thanksgiving holiday*
>
> **break** a time when you stop working or studying in order to rest, or a short vacation from school: *a ten-minute coffee break* | *We went to Florida for spring break.*
>
> **leave** a time when you are allowed not to work for a special reason: *Angela is on maternity leave* (=she is not working because she has just had a baby).

vac•cine /vækˈsin/ *noun*
a medicine that stops you from getting a disease: *There is no vaccine for cancer.*
—**vaccinate** /ˈvæksəˌneɪt/ *verb* to give someone a vaccine: *Babies are vaccinated against polio.*
—**vaccination** /ˌvæksəˈneɪʃən/ *noun* the act of putting a vaccine into someone

vac•uum¹ /ˈvækyum/ *noun*
1 *also* **vacuum cleaner** a machine for cleaning floors by sucking up the dirt
2 a space that has no air or gas in it: *Sound cannot travel through a vacuum.*

vacuum² *verb*
to clean a floor with a machine that sucks up dirt: *She vacuumed the living room before the guests arrived.*
➔ See Thesaurus box at **clean²**

vague /veɪg/ *adjective*
not clear in your mind because of not having enough details: *My mother died when I was small, and I only have a vague memory of her.* SYNONYM **unclear**
—**vaguely** *adverb*: *His face was vaguely familiar.*
—**vagueness** *noun*

vain /veɪn/ *adjective*
too proud of the way you look or what you can do: *She was very vain and always looking at herself in the mirror.*
—**vainly** *adverb*: *He vainly thought they were talking about him.*
—**vainness** *noun*
➔ See Thesaurus box at **proud**

Val•en•tine's Day /ˈvæləntaɪnz ˌdeɪ/ *noun*
February 14, a day when people give cards, candy, or flowers to people they love
—**valentine** *noun* someone you give a card or gift to on Valentine's Day

val•id /ˈvælɪd/ Ac *adjective*
1 if a ticket or official document is valid, you can use it: *You need a valid passport to travel overseas.* ANTONYM **invalid**
2 based on good reasons: *There must be a valid reason why you miss school, for example illness.* SYNONYM **good**
—**validate** /ˈvæləˌdeɪt/ *verb* to make something valid
—**validity** /vəˈlɪdəti/ *noun* the state of being valid: *Scientists are questioning the validity*

V

of his research; they think he may have deliberately lied.

val•ley /ˈvæli/ *noun*
a low area of land between hills or mountains: *A river runs through the bottom of the valley.*

val•u•a•ble /ˈvælyəbəl/ *adjective*
1 worth a lot of money: *Diamonds are very valuable.* ANTONYM **worthless**
2 very useful: *He gave me a lot of valuable advice.*
—**valuables** *plural noun* things that are valuable: *Keep valuables in a safe place.*

val•ue[1] /ˈvælyu/ *noun*
1 the amount of money that something is worth: *The value of the house is $1 million.*
2 the importance or usefulness of something: *His research was of great value to cancer doctors.*
3 be good/great value = to be worth the amount you pay for something: *At $20, these coats are great value.*
4 values = your beliefs about what is right and wrong, or about what is important in life: *My parents have traditional values, and don't agree with divorce.*

V

WORD FAMILY look at the words:

→ **value** *noun*
→ **value** *verb*
→ **valuable** *adjective*
→ **invaluable** *adjective*
→ **valuables** *noun*

value[2] *verb*
1 to think that something is important and useful to you: *I value your friendship.*
2 to say how much something is worth: *They valued the painting at $5 million.*

valve /vælv/ *noun*
a part of a pipe that opens and closes to control the flow of liquid or gas passing through it: *A fuel valve in the engine was leaking.*

vam•pire /ˈvæmpaɪɚ/ *noun*
in stories, a dead person who bites people's necks and sucks their blood

van /væn/ *noun*
a small truck with an enclosed back part, used for carrying goods or people: *A van took us from the hotel to the airport.*
→ See picture on page A26

van•dal /ˈvændl/ *noun*
someone who damages public property deliberately: *Vandals had broken store windows.*
—**vandalize** *verb* to damage property deliberately
—**vandalism** *noun* the crime of damaging property deliberately

va•nil•la /vəˈnɪlə/ *noun*
a substance used for making the most popular flavor of ice-cream: *vanilla ice cream*

van•ish /ˈvænɪʃ/ *verb*
to disappear suddenly, in a way that you cannot explain: *He was there, but when I looked again, he'd vanished.*

van•i•ty /ˈvænəti/ *noun, formal*
the quality of being too proud of the way you look or what you can do: *He should wear glasses, but his vanity stops him.*

va•por /ˈveɪpɚ/ *noun*
many small drops of liquid that float in the air: *Steam is water vapor.*
—**vaporize** *verb* to become vapor

var•i•a•ble /ˈveriəbəl/ Ac *adjective, formal*
something that is variable changes a lot: *The weather is variable: one day it's raining and the next it's bright sunshine.* ANTONYM **constant**
—**variability** /ˌveriəˈbɪləti/ *noun* the condition of being variable

var•i•a•tion /ˌveriˈeɪʃən/ Ac *noun*
a difference between similar things: *There are big variations in price from store to store.*

var•ied /ˈverid/ Ac *adjective*
including many different types of things or people: *He eats a varied diet, with many different kinds of food.*

va•ri•e•ty /vəˈraɪəti/ *noun* plural **varieties**
1 the differences within something that make it interesting: *I need a job with variety because I get bored doing the same thing all the time.*
2 a type of something that is different from other similar things: *There are many different varieties of apples.*
3 a variety of something = a lot of different things: *These shirts come in a variety of colors, from red to green to light blue.*

var•i•ous /ˈveriəs/ *adjective*
several different: *We buy food from various stores, but I prefer the supermarket on 16th Street.*

var•nish /ˈvɑrnɪʃ/ *noun*
a clear liquid that you paint onto wood to give it a shiny surface
—**varnish** *verb* to put varnish on something

var•si•ty /ˈvɑrsəti/ *noun* plural **varsities**
the varsity team at a school or college is its main team

var•y /ˈveri/ Ac *verb* **varied**, third person singular **varies**
1 to change often: *His mood varied: sometimes he was cheerful, sometimes he was miserable.*
2 to be different from other things of the same type: *The wines vary in quality: some are good and some are bad.*
—**varying** *adjective*: *There were children of varying ages.*

WORD FAMILY look at the words:
→ **vary** *verb*
→ **variety** *noun*
→ **varied** *adjective*
→ **various** *adjective*
→ **variable** *adjective*
→ **variation** *noun*

vase /veɪs/ *noun*
a container for putting flowers in

vast /væst/ *adjective*
extremely large: *The Sahara is a vast desert.*
SYNONYM **enormous, huge**; ANTONYM **tiny**
—**vastly** *adverb*: *The two countries are vastly different.*
—**vastness** *noun*: *the vastness of outer space*

vault /vɔlt/ *noun*
a room with thick walls where money, jewels, etc. are kept safely: *The gold is stored in a vault under the bank.*

VCR *noun*
a machine used for recording television shows or watching VIDEOTAPES
→ See picture on page A8

've /v, əv/ *verb*
the short form of "have": *I've hurt my leg.* | *We've decided to sell the car.*

veal /vil/ *noun*
meat from a young cow: *The veal was very tender.*
→ See Thesaurus box at **meat**

ve•gan /ˈvigən/ *noun*
someone who does not eat meat, fish, eggs, or milk: *Vegans will not eat anything that comes from an animal.*

vege•ta•ble /ˈvedʒtəbəl/ *noun*
a plant such as corn or potatoes, which you can eat: *Fruit and vegetables are very good for you.*

veg•e•tar•i•an /ˌvedʒəˈteriən/ *also* **veggie** *noun, informal*
someone who does not eat meat: *I made a vegetable dish for the vegetarians.*

veg•e•ta•tion /ˌvedʒəˈteɪʃən/ *noun, formal*
the plants in an area: *We entered the thick green vegetation of the woods.*

ve•hi•cle /ˈviɪkəl/ Ac *noun, formal*
something such as a car or bus that carries people or things: *There were a lot of vehicles on the road.*
—**vehicular** /vɪˈhɪkyələ-/ *adjective* relating to vehicles: *The road is closed to vehicular traffic.*

veil /veɪl/ *noun*
a thin piece of material that women wear to cover their faces: *The bride wore a veil over her face.*

veil

vein /veɪn/ *noun*
one of the tubes in your body that carry blood to your heart: *Your veins look blue under your skin.*

ve•loc•i•ty /vəˈlɑsəti/ *noun* plural **velocities** *formal*
the speed at which something moves in a particular direction: *wind velocity*

vel•vet /ˈvelvɪt/ *noun*
thick cloth with a soft surface on one side: *A pair of velvet drapes hung at the window.*
—**velvety** *adjective* soft like velvet

V

vend•ing ma•chine /ˈvendɪŋ məˌʃin/ *noun*
a machine that you can get cigarettes, candy, drinks, etc. from: *I put my money in the vending machine and selected a candy bar.*

ve•ne•tian blind /vəˌniʃən ˈblaɪnd/ *noun*
an object that you pull down to cover a window, made from many long wooden or plastic parts

venge•ance /ˈvendʒəns/ *noun, formal*
if you want vengeance, you want to do something harmful to someone, because he or she has done something harmful to you: *A desire for vengeance made him kill his brother's murderer.* SYNONYM **revenge**
—**vengeful** *adjective* wanting vengeance

vent /vent/ *noun*
a hole or pipe through which gas, smoke, or liquid can go in or out: *There's an air vent in the roof of the tent.*

ven•ti•la•tion /ˌventlˈeɪʃən/ *noun, formal*
a way of letting fresh air into a room or building: *We opened the windows for ventilation.*
—**ventilate** /ˈventlˌeɪt/ *verb, formal* to let fresh air into a room or building

V

ven•ti•la•tor /ˈventlˌeɪtɚ/ *noun*
a machine that helps a very sick person to breathe: *He's in the hospital on a ventilator.*

ven•ture /ˈventʃɚ/ *noun*
a new business activity that someone starts doing: *The new theme park is a joint venture between two companies.*

ven•ue /ˈvenyu/ *noun*
a place where an organized meeting, concert, etc. takes place: *The venue for the concert was Madison Square Garden.*

verb /vɚb/ *noun*
a word such as "run," "give," or "feel," used for showing that someone does something or experiences something: *In the sentence, "She wrote a letter," "wrote" is a verb.*

ver•bal /ˈvɚbəl/ *adjective, formal*
1 spoken, not written: *There was no written contract, just a verbal agreement.*
2 relating to words or using words: *Her verbal skills make her very good in interviews.*
—**verbally** *adverb*: *He accepted the offer verbally.*

ver•dict /ˈvɚdɪkt/ *noun*
if a JURY reaches a verdict, it decides whether or not someone is guilty of a crime

verge /vɚdʒ/ *noun*
be on the verge of (doing) something = to be going to do something very soon: *She was very upset and on the verge of tears* (=she was going to cry).

ver•i•fy /ˈverəˌfaɪ/ *verb* **verified**, third person singular **verifies** *formal*
to make sure that something is correct or true: *There was no way to verify his story, so we had to trust him.*
—**verification** /ˌverəfəˈkeɪʃən/ *noun* the process of verifying something

ver•sa•tile /ˈvɚsətl/ *adjective*
able to do a lot of different things or to be used in a lot of different ways: *He's a versatile actor who makes both serious and funny movies.*
—**versatility** /ˌvɚsəˈtɪləti/ *noun* the quality of being versatile

verse /vɚs/ *noun*
1 a set of lines that forms one part of a poem or song: *We sang the first two verses of the song.*
2 *formal* poetry: *a book of verse*

ver•sion /ˈvɚʒən/ Ac *noun*
1 a form of something that is slightly different from other forms: *The new version of the software is much better than the original one.*
2 one person's description of something that has happened: *I'm not sure I believe Bobby's version of what happened.*

ver•sus /ˈvɚsəs/ *preposition, written abbreviation* **vs.** *or* **v.**
used for showing that two people or teams are against each other in a game or a court case: *Tonight's game is the Knicks versus the Lakers.*

ver•te•bra /ˈvɚtəbrə/ *noun* plural **vertebrae** /ˈvɚtəbreɪ/ *formal*
one of the small bones down the center of your back

ver•ti•cal /ˈvɚtɪkəl/ *adjective*
pointing straight upward: *He drew a vertical line from the top to the bottom of the page.* ANTONYM **horizontal**

—**vertically** *adverb*
➔ See picture at **diagonal**

ve•ry /ˈveri/ *adverb*
1 used for emphasizing another word: *It's a very good book; you should read it.* | *She speaks English very well – I thought she was American.*
2 not very = used before a word to mean the opposite of that word: *I'm not very good at math* (=I'm bad at it).
3 very much = a lot: *It didn't cost very much.* | *I enjoyed my visit very much.*

USAGE: very

Very is used to emphasize something which can be either good or bad: *It's very hot today.* | *She's always very busy.*

Too is usually used to show that you do not like or approve of something: *This happens too often.* | *You're too young to go out by yourself.* | *We were too late and missed the bus.*

ves•sel /ˈvesəl/ *noun*
a tube in your body that liquid flows through: *blood vessels*

vest /vest/ *noun*
1 a piece of clothing with buttons down the front and no SLEEVEs that you wear over a shirt
2 a piece of special clothing with no SLEEVEs that you wear to protect your body: *Police officers wear bulletproof vests.*

vet /vet/ *noun, informal*
1 another word for a VETERINARIAN
2 another word for a VETERAN
➔ See picture on page A16

vet•er•an /ˈvetərən/ *noun*
someone who has been a soldier in a war: *veterans of the Korean War*

vet•er•i•nar•i•an /ˌvetərəˈneriən/ *noun*
a doctor for animals: *We're going to take the dog to the veterinarian for shots.* SYNONYM **vet**
—**veterinary** /ˈvetərəˌneri/ *adjective* relating to the work of a veterinarian: *a veterinary clinic*

ve•to /ˈvitoʊ/ *verb* **vetoed**, third person singular **vetoes**
if someone in a powerful position vetoes something, he or she refuses to allow it: *The president vetoed the plan, so Congress had to try something else.*
—**veto** *noun* an action of vetoing something

vi•a /ˈvaɪə/ Ac *preposition, formal*
1 traveling through a place on the way to another place: *I flew from New York to Miami via Washington.*
2 using a particular method or person to send or receive something: *The concert was broadcast around the world via satellite.* SYNONYM **by**

vibe /vaɪb/ *noun*
the general feeling that you get from a person or place: *The club has a good vibe and a lot of young people go there.*

vi•bra•tion /vaɪˈbreɪʃən/ *noun*
a continuous slight shaking movement: *On deck, you could feel the vibration of the boat's engine.*
—**vibrate** /ˈvaɪbreɪt/ *verb* to make vibrations: *The washing machine began to vibrate.*

vice /vaɪs/ *noun*
1 criminal activities that involve sex or drugs
2 a bad habit: *Her only vice was eating too much candy.* ANTONYM **virtue**

ˌvice ˈpresident *noun*
1 the person who is next in rank to the president of a country: *If the president dies, the vice president becomes president.*
2 someone who is responsible for a particular part of a company: *She's the vice president of marketing.*

vi•ce ver•sa /ˌvaɪs ˈvɚsə/ *adverb*
used when the opposite of a situation you have just described is also true: *The girls may refuse to play with the boys and vice versa* (=and the boys may refuse to play with the girls).

vi•cin•i•ty /vəˈsɪnəti/ *noun, formal*
in the vicinity (of something) = in the area near a particular place: *The bomb damaged 300 buildings in the vicinity.*

vi•cious /ˈvɪʃəs/ *adjective, formal*
1 violent and likely to hurt someone: *It was a vicious attack on an old woman.* | *a vicious dog*
2 cruel and deliberately trying to upset someone: *Her vicious remarks had upset him.*

V

—**viciously** *adverb, formal*
—**viciousness** *noun, formal*

vic·tim /ˈvɪktɪm/ *noun*
someone who has been hurt or killed by someone or something, or who has been affected by a bad situation: *The organization helps victims of crime.* | *a cancer victim* | *an aid program for earthquake victims*

vic·tim·ize /ˈvɪktɪˌmaɪz/ *verb, formal*
to deliberately treat someone in an unfair way: *He felt he had been victimized by the police.*

vic·to·ry /ˈvɪktəri/ *noun* plural **victories** *formal*
the act of winning a battle, game, election, etc.: *Our team's victory over our opponents surprised everyone.* ANTONYM **defeat**
—**victorious** /vɪkˈtɔriəs/ *adjective, formal* having won a battle, game, election, etc.: *a victorious army*

vid·e·o /ˈvɪdioʊ/ *noun* plural **videos**
1 a copy of a movie or television program that is recorded on VIDEOTAPE: *Let's watch a video tonight.*
2 a short recording of moving images: *My cousin emailed me a funny video.*
3 a short recording like a movie of a singer or band performing a song: *We watched music videos on MTV.*
4 the process of recording or showing moving images: *video equipment*

ˈvideo ˌcamera *noun*
a special camera that can be used to film moving images: *Nick has a video camera, so he agreed to videotape the wedding.*

ˈvideo ˌgame *noun*
a game in which you press electronic controls to move pictures on a screen: *My brother just sits at home and plays video games all day.*

vid·e·o·tape /ˈvɪdioʊˌteɪp/ *noun*
a long band in a plastic case that you record television programs and movies onto: *We have a videotape of the graduation ceremony.* SYNONYM **tape**
—**videotape** *verb* to record something onto videotape: *His interview with police was videotaped.*

view¹ /vyu/ *noun*
1 your opinion about something: *We have different views on religion, so we don't discuss it.*
2 the ability to see something from a particular place: *We had a really good view of what was happening.*
3 the things that you can see from a particular place: *The view from the top of the hill was beautiful.*

view² *verb, formal*
1 to think of someone or something in a particular way: *Yes, he's only 16, but I don't view his age as a problem for this job.* SYNONYM **regard**
2 to look at or watch something: *To view the new apartments, please contact our office.*

view·er /ˈvyuɚ/ *noun*
someone who watches a television program: *The TV show has more than five million viewers.*

view·point /ˈvyupɔɪnt/ *noun*
a particular way of thinking about something: *From a scientific viewpoint, the explanation doesn't make any sense.* SYNONYM **point of view**

vig·i·lant /ˈvɪdʒələnt/ *adjective, formal*
watching what is happening, so that you will notice if something bad happens: *Doctors should remain vigilant for signs of infection.*
—**vigilance** *noun* the state of being vigilant

vig·or·ous /ˈvɪgərəs/ *adjective, formal*
1 using a lot of energy or effort: *Experts recommend 20 minutes of vigorous exercise every day.*
2 strong and very healthy: *He was a vigorous young man with lots of energy.*
—**vigorously** *adverb*

vil·lage /ˈvɪlɪdʒ/ *noun*
a very small town: *My parents live in a small village in Mexico.*
—**villager** *noun* someone who lives in a village

vil·lain /ˈvɪlən/ *noun*
the bad character in a movie, play, or story: *The evil queen is the villain of the story.* ANTONYM **hero**

vin·dic·tive /vɪnˈdɪktɪv/ *adjective, formal*
very mean to someone because you think he or she has harmed you: *His ex-wife was a bitter and vindictive woman.*

V

vine /vaɪn/ *noun*
a plant with long stems that attach themselves to other plants, buildings, etc.: *The side of the building was covered in vines.*

vin•e•gar /ˈvɪnɪgɚ/ *noun*
a very sour liquid that is made from wine, and used in cooking: *He made a salad dressing from olive oil, vinegar, and sugar.*

vine•yard /ˈvɪnjɚd/ *noun*
a piece of land where someone grows GRAPEs for making wine

vin•tage /ˈvɪntɪdʒ/ *adjective*
1 vintage wine is good-quality wine that has been stored for several years to improve it
2 made a long time ago but still valuable: *He drove a vintage car from the 1940s.*
➔ See Thesaurus box at **old**

vi•nyl /ˈvaɪnl/ *noun*
a type of strong plastic: *We put a vinyl tablecloth on the picnic table.*

vi•o•la /viˈoʊlə/ *noun*
a musical instrument that looks like a large VIOLIN but has a lower sound
➔ See picture on page A21

vi•o•late /ˈvaɪəˌleɪt/ Ac *verb, formal*
to do something that does not obey a law, rule, agreement, etc.: *The military action violated international law.*
—**violation** /ˌvaɪəˈleɪʃən/ *noun, formal* an act of violating something: *Importing these drugs was a clear violation of federal law.*
➔ See Thesaurus box at **disobey**

vi•o•lence /ˈvaɪələns/ *noun*
1 behavior that hurts someone in a physical way: *There's too much violence on TV – I'm tired of seeing people get beaten up or killed.*
2 *formal* very great force: *The car was lifted into the air by the violence of the explosion.*

vi•o•lent /ˈvaɪələnt/ *adjective*
1 involving actions that hurt someone physically: *There's been an increase in violent crimes, such as rape and murder.*
2 someone who is violent is likely to attack and hurt other people: *He's a violent and dangerous criminal.*
3 a violent storm, EARTHQUAKE, etc. is one that happens with a lot of force and causes a lot of damage: *The roof blew off during a violent storm.*
—**violently** *adverb*: *She was violently attacked by a man with a knife.*

WORD FAMILY look at the words:
➔ **violent** *adjective*
➔ **violently** *adverb*
➔ **violence** *noun*

vi•o•let /ˈvaɪəlɪt/ *noun*
1 a small purple flower with a sweet smell
2 a purple color

vi•o•lin /ˌvaɪəˈlɪn/ *noun*
a musical instrument with four strings, that you hold under your chin and play by pulling a special stick across the strings: *Sarah plays the violin.*
—**violinist** *noun* someone who plays a violin
➔ See picture on page A21

vi•ral /ˈvaɪrəl/ *adjective*
relating to or caused by a VIRUS: *A cold is a viral infection.*

vir•gin /ˈvɚdʒɪn/ *noun*
someone who has never had sex

Vir•go /ˈvɚgoʊ/ *noun*
1 the sixth sign of the ZODIAC, represented by a VIRGIN
2 someone born between August 23 and September 22

vir•tu•al /ˈvɚtʃuəl/ Ac *adjective*
1 almost a particular thing: *They sat together in virtual silence, only speaking one or two words at a time.*
2 made, done, or seen on a computer, rather than in the real world: *The website allows you to take a virtual tour of the art gallery.*
—**virtually** *adverb* almost: *He goes away virtually every weekend; he's hardly ever around.*

ˌvirtual reˈality *noun*
pictures and sounds that a computer produces to make you feel as if you are in a particular place: *Virtual reality makes video games exciting.*

vir•tue /ˈvɚtʃu/ *noun, formal*
a good quality that someone has: *Honesty is one of his virtues – he never lies.* ANTONYM **vice**

vi•rus /ˈvaɪrəs/ *noun*
1 a very small living thing that causes infectious illnesses, or the illness caused by this: *The doctor says I have a virus.* | *the AIDS virus*

V

2 a program that destroys or damages information on your computer: *Computer viruses are usually spread through the Internet.*

vi•sa /ˈvizə/ *noun*
an official document or mark in your PASSPORT, that allows you to enter or leave another country: *He applied for a tourist visa to visit China.*

vis•i•ble /ˈvɪzəbəl/ Ac *adjective*
if something is visible, you can see it: *The house is behind a wall and isn't visible from the road.* ANTONYM **invisible**
—**visibly** *adverb*: *She was visibly upset by the news.*
—**visibility** /ˌvɪzəˈbɪləti/ *noun* the distance that you can see because of the weather or the place where you are: *Visibility was poor because of the fog.*

WORD FAMILY look at the words:

→ **visible** *adjective*
→ **invisible** *adjective*
→ **visibly** *adverb*
→ **visibility** *noun*

V

vi•sion /ˈvɪʒən/ Ac *noun*
1 the ability to see: *She has poor vision and wears glasses all the time.* SYNONYM **sight**
2 an idea of what you think something should be like: *He has a clear vision of what he wants to do in the future.*

vis•it¹ /ˈvɪzɪt/ *verb*
1 to go and see a person or place: *Eric went to Seattle to visit his cousins.* | *My aunt is coming to visit next week.* | *I want to visit the Grand Canyon while I'm in the U.S.*

THESAURUS: visit

You **go to** a movie, museum, theater, etc.: *Did you go to the football game on Friday night?*

You **go to see** or **go and see** a person or place: *We went to see my aunt last week.*

If you **go sightseeing**, you visit places of interest in a country: *On our trip to New York, we went sightseeing and saw the Statue of Liberty.*

If someone **comes over**, he or she visits you in your home in a friendly way: *Mom, can Barbara come over and play?*

If someone **drops in/by** or **stops by/in**, he or she visits you in your home, especially on the way to another place: *Paul stopped by on his way home from work.*

2 to look at a website on the Internet: *Over 1,000 people visit our site every week.*
3 *informal* to talk to someone in a friendly way: *We watched TV while Mom visited with Mrs. Levinson.*

visit² *noun*
an occasion when someone goes and sees a place or person: *This is my first visit to Atlanta.*

vis•i•tor /ˈvɪzətɚ/ *noun*
someone who comes to visit a place or a person: *The park attracts 100,000 visitors a year.* | *a guidebook for visitors to Rio de Janeiro*

vi•sor /ˈvaɪzɚ/ *noun*
1 the part of a hat that sticks out over your eyes
2 the flat object in a car that you pull down to keep the sun out of your eyes

visor

vis•u•al /ˈvɪʒuəl/ Ac *adjective*
relating to seeing or to your sight: *The movie has a strong visual impact.*
—**visually** *adverb*

vis•u•al•ize /ˈvɪʒuəˌlaɪz/ Ac *verb*
to form a picture of someone or something in your mind: *I tried to visualize the house as he described it.* SYNONYM **imagine**

vi•tal /ˈvaɪtl/ *adjective*
extremely important or necessary: *Regular exercise is vital for your health.*
—**vitally** *adverb*: *It is vitally important that you follow the instructions exactly.*
→ See Thesaurus box at **important**

vi•ta•min /ˈvaɪtəmɪn/ *noun*
a chemical substance in food that is important for good health: *Oranges contain vitamin C.*

viv•id /ˈvɪvɪd/ *adjective*
1 vivid memories, dreams, descriptions, etc. are very clear in your mind: *I have very vivid memories of my first day at school; I can still see my teacher's face in my mind.*

2 a vivid imagination = an ability to imagine unlikely situations very clearly: *Young children have very vivid imaginations.*
3 *formal* vivid colors are very bright: *She had vivid blue eyes.*
—**vividly** *adverb*: *I can vividly remember my first visit to Tokyo.*
—**vividness** *noun*

vo·cab·u·lar·y /voʊ'kæbyəˌleri/ *noun* plural **vocabularies**
1 all the words that you know and use: *Reading is one of the best ways to improve your vocabulary.*
2 the words that people use for talking about a particular subject: *Most technical jobs use a special vocabulary.*

vo·cal /'voʊkəl/ *adjective*
1 relating to the voice: *Do you prefer vocal music or instrumental music?*
2 expressing your opinion strongly: *He's a vocal critic of the president.*
—**vocals** *plural noun* the part of a piece of music that someone sings rather than plays on a musical instrument

'vocal cords *also* **vocal chords** *plural noun*
the thin muscles in your throat that produce sound when you speak or sing

vo·cal·ist /'voʊkəlɪst/ *noun*
someone who sings with a band: *The band is looking for a new drummer and vocalist.*
SYNONYM **singer**

vo·ca·tion /voʊ'keɪʃən/ *noun, formal*
a job that you do because you enjoy it and feel you are the right type of person to do it: *Teaching isn't just a job to her – it's her vocation.*
➔ See Thesaurus box at **job**

vo'cational ˌschool *noun*
a school where you learn skills for doing a job: *She's learning to cut hair at a vocational school.*

vogue /voʊg/ *noun*
be in vogue *formal* = to be fashionable and popular: *Long skirts are back in vogue.*

voice /vɔɪs/ *noun*
1 the sound you make when you speak or sing: *I thought I heard voices downstairs.*
2 lose your voice = to be unable to speak: *He had a cold and had lost his voice.*
3 raise your voice = to speak loudly because you are angry or want someone to hear you: *She raised her voice to interrupt him.*

'voice mail *noun*
a system that records a telephone message from someone so that you can listen to it later: *He wasn't there when I called, so I left a message on his voice mail.*

void¹ /vɔɪd/ *noun, formal*
1 a feeling of great sadness that you have when someone you love dies or when something important is missing from your life: *Work helped to fill the void after his wife died.*
2 an empty space where nothing exists: *the void between Earth and the Moon*
—**void of** *preposition, formal* without any amount of something: *The presentation was void of any real new ideas.*

void² *verb*
to officially make something have no legal effect: *If the money is not paid, the contract will be voided.*

vol·ca·no /vɑl'keɪnoʊ/ *noun* plural **volcanoes** or **volcanos**
a mountain with a large hole at the top that burning rocks sometimes come out of: *The volcano erupted and covered the surrounding area in ash.*

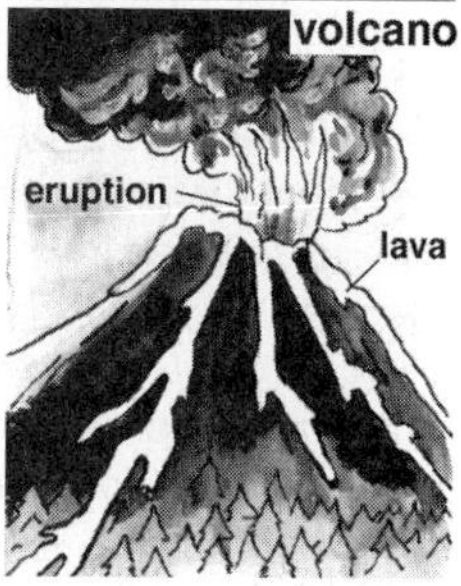

—**volcanic** /vɑl'kænɪk/ *adjective* relating to or coming from volcanoes: *volcanic rocks*

vol·ley·ball /'vɑliˌbɔl/ *noun*
1 a game in which two teams hit a ball across a net with their hands, and try not to let it touch the ground: *They were playing volleyball on the beach.*
2 the ball used in the game of volleyball
➔ See picture on page A24

volt /voʊlt/ *noun*
a unit for measuring an electric current: *a 9-volt battery*
—**voltage** /'voʊltɪdʒ/ *noun* the amount of power in an electric current: *Both heaters use the same voltage.*

vol•ume /ˈvɑlyəm/ Ac *noun*
1 the amount of sound that a television, radio, etc. produces: *I can't hear the TV. Can you turn the volume up please?*
2 the total amount of something: *There's been an increase in the volume of traffic over the last 20 years.*
3 a book that is one of a set of books: *a 12-volume set of poetry*
4 the amount of space that a substance fills or an object contains: *What's the volume of the gas tank?*

vol•un•tar•y /ˈvɑlənˌteri/ Ac *adjective*
done because you want to and not because you must: *The payment is voluntary.* ANTONYM **compulsory**
—**voluntarily** /ˌvɑlənˈterəli/ *adverb*

WORD FAMILY look at the words:
→ **voluntary** *adjective*
→ **voluntarily** *adverb*
→ **volunteer** *verb*
→ **volunteer** *noun*

vol•un•teer /ˌvɑlənˈtɪr/ Ac *noun*
someone who does something without being paid: *We need volunteers to help serve meals to old people.*
—**volunteer** *verb* to offer to do something: *He volunteered to help clean up after the party.*
—**volunteer** *adjective* volunteer work is work that you do for no money: *She does volunteer work in a hospital.*

V

vom•it /ˈvɑmɪt/ *verb, formal*
if you vomit, food comes up from your stomach and out through your mouth: *He vomited after eating some bad meat.*
—**vomit** *noun, formal* food that someone has vomited

vote[1] /voʊt/ *verb*
to show who you want to choose or which plan you support by marking a piece of paper, pressing a button, or raising your hand: *Who did you vote for in the election?* | *Most people voted against the plan.*
—**voter** *noun* someone who votes: *The voters will decide who becomes president.*

vote[2] *noun*
1 a choice or decision that you make by voting: *There were 1,079 votes for Swanson, and 766 for Reynolds.*
2 an act of making a choice or decision by voting: *We couldn't decide, so we took a vote on it.*

vouch•er /ˈvaʊtʃɚ/ *noun*
a piece of paper that you can use instead of money to buy goods, pay for travel, etc.: *They gave me a $100 gift voucher to use at the department store.*

vow /vaʊ/ *noun, formal*
a serious promise: *She made a vow to herself that she would never go back.* | *marriage vows*
—**vow** *verb* to make a vow
→ See Thesaurus box at **promise[1]**

vow•el /ˈvaʊəl/ *noun*
one of the letters a, e, i, o, or u, and sometimes y

voy•age /ˈvɔɪ-ɪdʒ/ *noun*
a long trip in a ship or a space vehicle: *The voyage from England to Hong Kong took several weeks.*
→ See Thesaurus box at **travel[2]**

vs.
the written abbreviation of VERSUS

vul•gar /ˈvʌlgɚ/ *adjective, formal*
mentioning or involving sex in a way that people think is rude and offensive: *She was offended by his vulgar jokes.*
—**vulgarity** /vəlˈgærəti/ *noun, formal* the quality of being vulgar

vul•ner•a•ble /ˈvʌlnərəbəl/ *adjective*
easy to harm, hurt, or attack: *Small birds are vulnerable to attack by cats.*
—**vulnerability** /ˌvʌlnərəˈbɪləti/ *noun* the quality of being vulnerable

vul•ture /ˈvʌltʃɚ/ *noun*
a large wild bird that eats dead animals

Ww

wack·y /ˈwæki/ *adjective, informal*
unusual in a funny or silly way: *He has some very wacky ideas, and everyone thinks he's a little crazy.*

wad /wɑd/ *noun*
a thick pile of papers or paper money: *He had a big wad of dollar bills in his pocket.*

wade /weɪd/ *verb*
to walk through water that is not deep: *She waded through the flood water.*
➔ See Thesaurus box at **walk**[1]

waf·fle /ˈwɑfəl/ *noun*
a sweet flat cake with a pattern of deep squares in it, that people eat for breakfast

waffle

wag /wæg/ *verb*
wagged, wagging
if a dog wags its tail, it shakes it from one side to another: *The dog was pleased to see us and was wagging his tail.*

wage /weɪdʒ/ *noun*
1 the amount of money you earn for each hour that you work: *He is paid a wage of $7 per hour.*
2 wages = the money that you get each day, week, or month for doing a job: *Poor people often work for very low wages.*

wag·on /ˈwægən/ *noun*
1 a vehicle that horses pull, used for carrying heavy things
2 a child's toy that is a container on four wheels with a long handle for pulling it
3 *informal* another word for a STATION WAGON

wail /weɪl/ *verb, formal*
to shout or cry with a long high sound because you are in pain or very sad: *"You're hurting me!" she wailed.*
—**wail** *noun, formal* the sound of wailing

waist /weɪst/ *noun*
the part in the middle of your body just above your HIPs: *The belt will only fit someone with a small waist.*
➔ See picture on page A2

waist·line /ˈweɪstlaɪn/ *noun*
the measurement around your waist: *Eating too much candy will put inches on your waistline.*

wait /weɪt/ *verb*
1 to stay somewhere or not do something until something else happens: *There were a lot of people waiting for the bus.* | *Her father was waiting to meet her at the airport.* | *Wait right here until I come back.*
2 wait a minute/second = used for asking someone to wait for a short time: *Wait a second – I'll get my coat and come with you.*
3 someone can't wait = used for saying that someone is very excited about something that is going to happen: *I'm so excited! I can't wait to see her again.*
—**wait** *noun* a time when you wait for something to happen: *We had a long wait for the bus.*

PHRASAL VERBS

wait on someone
to serve food to someone in a restaurant: *We sat at the table a long time before anyone waited on us.*

wait up
to wait for someone to come home before you go to bed: *I'll be home late so don't wait up for me.*

wait·er /ˈweɪtɚ/ *noun*
a man who brings food to the tables in a restaurant: *The waiter took our order and went back to the kitchen.*
➔ See picture on page A16

ˈwaiting room *noun*
a room for people to wait in, for example to see a doctor

wait·ress /ˈweɪtrɪs/ *noun*
a woman who brings food to the tables in a restaurant: *The waitress brought our food very quickly.*

wake /weɪk/ *also* **wake up** *verb* **woke** /woʊk/ **woken** /ˈwoʊkən/ **waking**
to stop sleeping: *Try not to wake the baby.* | *I woke up early this morning.*

W

walk¹ /wɔk/ *verb*
to move forward by putting one foot in front of the other: *Do you walk to school? | John walked into the room and sat down.*
→ See picture on page A4

THESAURUS: walk

march to walk with regular steps in a determined way, sometimes lifting your knees like soldiers do: *Leon marched past them into the hallway. | The band marched onto the field.*

stride to walk with quick long steps in a determined way: *A policeman strode toward me.*

stroll to walk slowly in a relaxed way, especially for pleasure: *She strolled down the street, looking in the store windows.*

wander to walk slowly around in a place, often when you are not going to any particular place: *We wandered around the museum for a few hours.*

creep/sneak to walk quietly when you do not want to be seen or heard: *Sam crept out of the house after his parents were asleep. | Two of the boys sneaked into the movie theater.*

limp to walk with difficulty because your leg or foot is hurt: *Jess limped off the court.*

wade to walk through water that is not deep: *The soldiers waded to the shore from the boat.*

hike to take a long walk in the country, mountains, etc.: *We hiked to a little lake in the woods.*

W

PHRASAL VERBS

walk away
to leave a bad or difficult situation: *You can't just walk away from the project – we need you to help us finish it.*

walk in on someone
to go into a room and see someone doing something that he or she does not want you to see: *He walked in on her while she was taking a shower.*

walk off
to leave someone by walking away from him or her: *He turned and walked off.*

walk out
1 to leave a place because you are angry about something: *The service in the restaurant was so bad that we walked out in the middle of the meal.*
2 to leave your husband, wife, etc. suddenly: *Mary walked out on him after 20 years of marriage.*

walk² *noun*
a trip that you make by walking: *Let's go for a walk. | I like to take a walk after lunch. | The school is a ten-minute walk from here.*

walk•ie-talk•ie /ˌwɔki ˈtɔki/ *noun*
a small radio that you carry with you, and use to speak to someone who has the same type of radio

wall /wɔl/ *noun*
1 one of the sides of a room or building: *There were lots of pictures on the walls.*
2 a structure made of bricks or stones, that divides one area from another: *There was a brick wall between the two yards.*
→ See picture on page A9

wal•let /ˈwɑlɪt/ *noun*
a small flat case that you keep paper money or plastic cards in, and carry in your pocket or PURSE: *She put her credit card back in her wallet.*

wall•pa•per /ˈwɔlˌpeɪpɚ/ *noun*
1 paper that you stick onto the walls of a room in order to decorate them
2 the picture that you have as the background on your computer screen

ˈWall Street *noun*
1 a street in New York City where the New York STOCK EXCHANGE is
2 the New York STOCK EXCHANGE: *The company's profits were better than Wall Street expected.*

ˌwall-to-ˈwall *adjective*
covering the whole floor: *The room has wall-to-wall carpeting.*

wal•nut /ˈwɔlnʌt/ *noun*
a nut with an uneven shape and a large shell: *a walnut tree*
→ See picture on page A13

wal•rus /ˈwɔlrəs/ *noun*
a large animal that lives in the ocean and has two long teeth that stick out of its mouth

waltz /wɔlts/ *noun*
a dance for two people that has a regular pattern of three beats, or the music for this dance

wand /wɑnd/ *noun*
a thin stick you hold in your hand to do magic tricks: *The magician waved his wand and the rabbit disappeared.*

wan•der /ˈwɑndɚ/ *verb*
1 to walk slowly around somewhere without having a clear idea of where you want to go: *We spent the whole day wandering around the city.*
2 *also* **wander off** to move away from where you are supposed to stay: *The kids got bored and started to wander off.*
3 if your mind, thoughts, etc. wander, you stop paying attention to something and start thinking about something else: *Class was boring and his mind started to wander.*
—**wanderer** *noun* someone who travels around rather than living in one place
➔ See Thesaurus box at **walk**[1]

wan•na•be /ˈwɑnəˌbi/ *noun, informal*
someone who tries to look, behave, or do something like a famous person: *an Elvis wannabe*

want[1] /wʌnt/ *verb*
to feel that you will be happy if you have or do something: *I want a bicycle for my birthday.* | *I want to be a teacher when I grow up.* | *Do you want me to help you?*

want[2] *noun, formal*
something that you need or that would make you happy, but that you do not have: *Supermarkets try to satisfy all the needs and wants of shoppers by providing many types of products.*

ˈwant ad *noun*
a small advertisement that you put in a newspaper if you want to buy something or find someone to do a job

war /wɔr/ *noun*
a time when countries fight each other: *World War II* | *Many soldiers were killed in the war.* | *The country is preparing to go to war* (=start fighting). ANTONYM **peace**
—**warring** *adjective* involved in a war: *warring countries*

THESAURUS: war

warfare *formal* the activity of fighting in a war – used especially when talking about particular ways of fighting: *Everyone was frightened about the chance of nuclear warfare.*

conflict *formal* fighting or a war: *the conflict in the Middle East*

combat fighting during a war: *The soldiers were wounded in combat.*

WORD FAMILY look at the words:
➔ **war** *noun*
➔ **warfare** *noun*
➔ **warrior** *noun*
➔ **warring** *adjective*

ward /wɔrd/ *noun*
a room in a hospital with beds for people to stay in: *She works on the children's ward of the hospital.*

war•den /ˈwɔrdn/ *noun*
the person in charge of a prison

war•drobe /ˈwɔrdroʊb/ *noun*
1 the clothes that someone has: *She has a large wardrobe of dresses and shoes.*
2 a large piece of furniture that holds hanging clothes
➔ See picture on page A10

ware•house /ˈwerhaʊs/ *noun*
a large building where a company stores goods before it sells them: *There are thousands of computers in the company's warehouse.*

war•fare /ˈwɔrfer/ *noun*
the activity of fighting in a war using a particular method or type of weapon: *chemical warfare*
➔ See Thesaurus box at **war**

warm[1] /wɔrm/ *adjective*
1 slightly hot in a pleasant way: *The water in the pool was nice and warm.* | *We stood close together to keep warm.* ANTONYM **cool**
2 warm clothes and buildings keep heat in and stop you from feeling cold: *Put a warm sweater on – it's cold out here.*
3 friendly: *They gave us a very warm welcome.*
➔ See Thesaurus box at **hot**

warm[2] *also* **warm up** *verb*
to make someone or something warmer: *Let me warm some soup for you.*

PHRASAL VERB
warm up
to prepare for an activity or sport by doing gentle exercises or practicing just before the

W

activity or game starts: *The team is warming up before the game.*

ˌwarm-ˈblooded *adjective*
warm-blooded animals have a body temperature that stays warm whether the temperature around them is hot or cold: *Mammals are warm-blooded animals, unlike reptiles.*

warm•ly /ˈwɔrmli/ *adverb*
1 in a friendly way: *He greeted us very warmly with a smile and a hug.*
2 in a way that keeps you warm: *He was warmly dressed in a thick sweater and coat.*

warmth /wɔrmθ/ *noun*
1 the heat that something produces: *The warmth of the sun felt wonderful on her face.*
2 friendliness: *The warmth of her smile made him feel good.*

ˈwarm-up *noun*
1 a set of exercises that you do just before you do a sport: *We did several stretching exercises as a warm-up.*
2 something that you do as practice for a more important activity or event: *Thursday's game was a warm-up for the main competition next week.*
—**warm-up** *adjective* done to prepare you for another activity or event: *warm-up exercises*

W

warn /wɔrn/ *verb*
to tell someone that something bad or dangerous may happen, so that he or she can avoid it: *I warned you not to walk home alone.* | *A sign warned drivers of long delays on the freeway.*

warn•ing /ˈwɔrnɪŋ/ *noun*
something that tells you that something bad or dangerous might happen, so that you can avoid it: *There are warnings about the dangers of smoking on every pack of cigarettes.* | *The enemy attacked without warning.*

warped /wɔrpt/ *adjective*
1 bent or twisted into the wrong shape: *The door is warped and won't close anymore.*
2 *informal* having ideas or thoughts that most people think are unpleasant or not normal: *He has a very warped sense of humor, and sometimes I don't understand him at all.*

war•rant /ˈwɔrənt/ *noun*
an official paper that allows the police to do something: *Officials have issued a warrant for his arrest.*

war•ran•ty /ˈwɔrənti/ *noun* plural **warranties**
a written promise that a company will fix something if it breaks after you have bought it: *The TV comes with a 3-year warranty, so if it doesn't work right, the company will fix or replace it.* SYNONYM **guarantee**

war•ri•or /ˈwɔriɚ/ *noun*
a soldier from a long time ago who was very brave

wart /wɔrt/ *noun*
a small hard raised spot on your skin caused by a VIRUS: *He had a wart on the bottom of his foot.*
➔ See Thesaurus box at **mark**²

was /wəz; *strong* wʌz/ *verb*
the past tense of BE that we use after "I," "he," "she," and "it"

wash¹ /wɑʃ/ *verb*
1 to clean something using water: *She helped Peggy wash the dishes.*
2 if water, a river, the ocean, etc. washes somewhere, it flows or pushes something there: *Strong waves washed the boat onto the shore.*
—**washable** *adjective* if something is washable, you can wash it without damaging it

PHRASAL VERBS

wash off
if a substance washes off, you can remove it from the surface of something by washing it: *Will this paint wash off?*

wash up
to wash your hands: *Go wash up for dinner.*

wash² *noun*
clothes, sheets, etc. that you have washed or that you need to wash: *I did three loads of wash this morning.* SYNONYM **laundry**

wash•cloth /ˈwɑʃklɔθ/ *noun*
a small square piece of cloth that you use for washing yourself

wash•er /ˈwɑʃɚ/ *noun*
another word for a WASHING MACHINE

ˈwashing maˌchine *noun*
a machine that washes clothes: *She put the dirty clothes in the washing machine.* SYNONYM **washer**

wash•room /ˈwɑʃrum/ *noun*, *old-fashioned*
another word for a RESTROOM

was•n't /ˈwʌzənt/
the short form of "was not": *He wasn't there.*

wasp /wɑsp/ *noun*
a black and yellow flying insect that can sting you: *Wasps and bees look quite similar.*

waste¹ /weɪst/ *verb*
to use something in a way that is not effective, or to use too much of it: *You're wasting electricity if you leave the light on when you're not in the room.*

waste² *noun*
1 the use of something in a way that is not effective or sensible: *The meeting was a complete waste of time because no decisions were made.*
2 things that are left after you have used something: *We should recycle more household waste such as empty bottles and cans.*
→ See Thesaurus box at **garbage**

waste•bas•ket /ˈweɪstˌbæskɪt/ *noun*
a container into which you put paper and other things that you want to get rid of: *She threw the candy wrapper into the wastebasket.*
→ See picture on page A18

wast•ed /ˈweɪstɪd/ *adjective*
not used effectively, or not having a useful result: *It was a wasted trip because the store was closed.*

waste•ful /ˈweɪstfəl/ *adjective*
using more of something than you need or using it badly, so that it is wasted: *Spending millions of dollars for a road no one wants is very wasteful.*
—**wastefulness** *noun*

waste•land /ˈweɪstlænd/ *noun*
an area of land that is empty or that cannot be used for anything: *a desert wasteland*

waste•pa•per bas•ket /ˈweɪstˌpeɪpɚ ˌbæskɪt/ *noun*
another word for WASTEBASKET

watch¹ /wɑtʃ/ *verb*
1 to look at something and see how it changes or moves: *Steve was watching television.* | *I watched her leave.*
→ See picture at **see**

USAGE: watch

You **watch** TV, a movie, or something that happens for a period of time: *My parents always come to watch me play basketball.* | *The kids are watching TV.*

You **look at** a picture, person, thing, etc. because you want to: *Hey, look at the hat that man is wearing.* | *Maria was looking at a picture book.*

You **see** something without planning to: *Two people saw him take the woman's purse.*

You can also say that you **saw** a movie, a program, etc., but you cannot say "see television": *I saw a great movie on TV last night.*

2 to be careful not to hurt yourself or to hurt someone else: *Watch that knife – it's sharp.* | *He never watches where he's going, so he's always bumping into things.*
3 watch your language/mouth = to be careful not to use swear words or not to talk in a rude way: *Watch your language! I don't want to hear any more bad words!*
4 watch your weight = to be careful not to get too fat: *I'm not eating cookies, because I'm watching my weight.*

PHRASAL VERBS

watch for something
to look for something so that you will be ready to deal with it: *Doctors are watching for any signs of the disease.*

watch out
to look for something and be careful of it, so that it does not hurt you: *Watch out for the cars when you cross the street.*

watch over someone
to take care of someone: *The older kids watch over the younger ones.*

watch² *noun*
1 a small clock that you wear on your wrist: *I looked at my watch: it was 2:30.*
2 keep watch = to look around so that you will notice if someone is coming and tell other people: *Jay hid all of his sister's toys, and I kept watch to tell him if she was coming back.*
3 keep a watch on something = to keep looking at something carefully, to see what happens: *Police kept a close watch on the house.*

W

watch

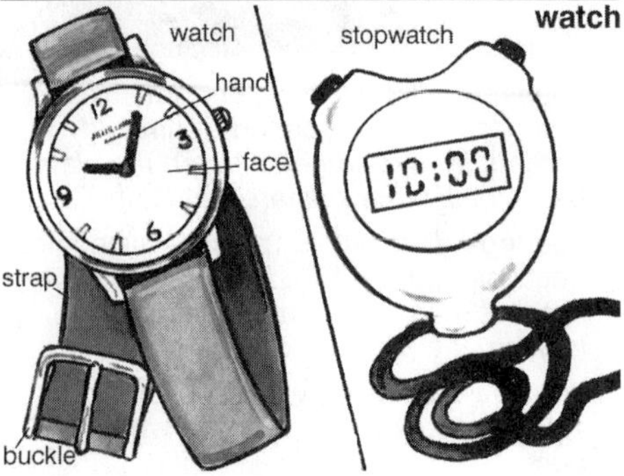

watch·dog /ˈwɑtʃdɔg/ *noun*
another word for a GUARD DOG

watch·ful /ˈwɑtʃfəl/ *adjective, formal*
under someone's watchful eye/under the watchful eye of someone = with someone watching you carefully: *She learned to cook under the watchful eye of her mother.*

wa·ter¹ /ˈwɔtɚ/ *noun*
1 a clear liquid that you drink and use for washing: *Would you like a glass of water?*
2 in hot water = if you are in hot water, you are in a situation in which you have a lot of trouble: *He's in hot water, because his mother caught him smoking a cigarette.*

W

water² *verb*
1 to pour water on a plant or seeds in the ground: *The plant died, because I never watered it.*
2 if your eyes water, they fill with water because something is hurting them: *The smoke made my eyes water.*
3 if your mouth waters, it fills with water because you see something that looks good to eat

ˈwater ˌbuffalo *noun*
a large Asian animal that pulls farm equipment: *The milk of water buffalo is used to make mozzarella cheese.*

wa·ter·col·or /ˈwɔtɚˌkʌlɚ/ *noun*
1 a type of paint mixed with water, used for making pictures
2 a painting made using paint mixed with water

ˈwater ˌcooler *noun*
a large container in an office where you can fill a cup with drinking water

wa·ter·fall /ˈwɔtɚˌfɔl/ *noun*
water that falls down over high rocks: *We looked up and saw a beautiful waterfall coming down the side of the mountain.*

waterfall

ˈwater ˌfountain *noun*
a piece of equipment in a public place that gives you water to drink when you push a button or turn a handle: *I pushed the button on the water fountain and the water shot up and hit me in the face.* SYNONYM **drinking fountain**

wa·ter·front /ˈwɔtɚˌfrʌnt/ *noun*
land at the edge of a lake, river, or ocean: *There are several restaurants on the waterfront.*

ˈwater ˌlily *noun*
a plant that floats on top of a lake or river: *The frog sat on the leaves of a water lily.*

wa·ter·logged /ˈwɔtɚˌlɔgd/ *adjective*
something that is waterlogged is very wet and cannot hold any more water: *We couldn't plant our seeds in the waterlogged soil.*

ˈwater main *noun*
a large pipe under the ground that carries water: *The water main carries water to all the houses in our street.*

wa·ter·mel·on /ˈwɔtɚˌmelən/ *noun*
a large round green fruit that is pink inside, with black seeds: *He ate a slice of watermelon.*
→ See picture on page A13

ˈwater pipe *noun*
a pipe that carries water: *Copper water pipes carry water around the house.*

wa·ter·proof /ˈwɔtɚˌpruf/ *adjective*
waterproof clothes or materials keep people dry, because water cannot go through them: *a waterproof raincoat*

ˈwater ˌskiing *noun*
a sport in which you wear two long narrow pieces of plastic on your feet, as a boat pulls you along the water: *We went waterskiing on the lake.*

—**water skier** *noun* someone who does waterskiing

→ See picture on page A24

ˈwater supˌply *noun*
water that goes to all the buildings in an area or city, through a system of pipes: *Dangerous chemicals got into the water supply.*

wa•ter•tight /ˈwɔtɚˌtaɪt/ *adjective*
if an object is watertight, water cannot get into it: *The boat has a watertight storage box.*

wa•ter•way /ˈwɔtɚˌweɪ/ *noun, formal*
a river or other area of water that boats can go through: *The Panama Canal is a waterway that connects two oceans.*

watt /wɑt/ *noun*
a measure of electrical power: *Do you have a 60-watt light bulb?*

wave[1] /weɪv/ *noun*
1 high water that moves on the surface of the ocean: *A big wave turned the boat over.*
2 a movement of your hand from side to side: *She gave us a wave as she drove away.*
3 a sudden increase in a particular feeling or activity: *A wave of sadness passed over him as he thought about his family who were so far away.* | *During the crime wave, many cars were stolen.*
→ **heat wave**
→ See picture on page A3

wave[2] *verb*
1 to move your hand from side to side, to say hello or goodbye or to tell someone to do something: *We waved goodbye to them.* | *I stopped the car because a man was waving at me and yelling.*
2 to move from side to side: *The flag waved in the wind.* | *She waved the letter in front of my face.*

wav•y /ˈweɪvi/ *adjective*
wavy hair has curved shapes in it ANTONYM **straight**

wax[1] /wæks/ *noun*
a hard substance used for making CANDLEs

wax[2] *verb*
to put wax on something to protect it or make it shine: *My brother was washing and waxing his car.*

way /weɪ/ *noun*
1 the road or path you follow to get somewhere: *Which way should we go?* | *Can you tell me the way to the school?* | *I'll drive you home, if you tell me the way* (=tell me how to get there).
2 a particular direction: *Look both ways before you cross the street.* | *Take two steps this way.*
3 a method of doing something: *The best way to get in shape is by walking.* | *He has a funny way of talking.*
4 the distance between two places: *Houston is a long way from New York.* | *I drove her home, and she talked all the way* (=for the whole distance).
5 by the way = used when you want to talk about a new subject: *Oh, by the way, your Mom called earlier.*
6 have your way/get your way = to do what you want, even if someone else wants something different: *That kid is spoiled – he always gets his way!*
7 in a way/in some ways = used when saying that something is partly true: *In a way, I'd like to be old, because old people know a lot about life.*
8 in the way/in your way = if something is in the way, it is in front of you and you cannot pass it: *I couldn't put my bicycle in the garage because the car was in the way.*
9 no way! = used when you will not do something, or when you are very surprised by something: *"Will you help me clean my room?" "No way!"* | *She's 30? No way – she looks like she's 19!*
10 on the way/on your way = while going somewhere: *I went home, and bought some food on the way.*

wavy

11 out of the way/out of your way = if something moves out of the way, it moves so it is not in front of you and you can pass it: *I can't get past – get out of the way!*
12 under way *formal* = happening or moving: *Building work has not started yet, but it will soon be under way.*
13 way around/up = used when talking about what position something should be in: *Which way around does this skirt go* (=which part is the front and which part is the back?) | *The boat turned over, and we couldn't get it the right way up.*
14 way to go! = used when you think someone has done something very well: *"I got an A on my science test." "Way to go!"*

ˌway of ˈlife *noun* plural **ways of life**
the way someone lives: *They moved away from the city to have a more relaxed way of life.*

ˌway-ˈout *adjective*
new and strange: *I like some jazz, but not the way-out stuff.*

we /wi/ *pronoun*
the person who is speaking and one or more other people: *I know John. We are friends.*

W

weak /wik/ *adjective*
1 not strong in your body: *She was too weak to lift the box.* ANTONYM **strong**
2 if someone is weak, people can easily persuade him or her to do things: *He is a weak leader who cannot control his own people.* ANTONYM **strong**

weak•en /ˈwikən/ *verb, formal*
to make someone or something less strong: *Decay weakened the tree, and made it fall down.* ANTONYM **strengthen**

weak•ling /ˈwik-lɪŋ/ *noun*
someone who is not physically strong: *The other kids called him a weakling because he couldn't carry his own suitcase.*

weak•ness /ˈwiknəs/ *noun*
1 a fault in someone or something: *Spending too much money on clothes is her weakness.* ANTONYM **strength**
2 the state of not having a lot of strength in your body: *Not eating enough can cause weakness.* ANTONYM **strength**

wealth /welθ/ *noun, formal*
1 a large amount of money that someone owns: *The family had great wealth, and owned three homes.*
2 a wealth of something = a lot of something useful or good: *There is a wealth of information on the Internet.*

wealth•y /ˈwelθi/ *adjective* **wealthier, wealthiest** *formal*
having a lot of money: *A wealthy businessman bought the plane.* SYNONYM **rich**; ANTONYM **poor**
➔ See Thesaurus box at **rich**

weap•on /ˈwepən/ *noun*
something that people fight with, for example a knife or a gun: *A gun is a dangerous weapon.*
—**weaponry** /ˈwepənri/ *noun* weapons

wear[1] /wer/ *verb* **wore** /wɔr/ **worn** /wɔrn/
1 to have clothes or jewelry on your body: *She wore a pretty dress.*
2 to make something thinner or weaker by using it or wearing it a lot: *You've worn a hole in your sock.*
3 to have your hair in a particular style: *He wears his hair short.*
4 wear well = to stay in good condition after a period of time: *These shoes have worn well. They still look new.*

PHRASAL VERBS
wear down
if something wears down, it becomes smaller or weaker because you use it a lot: *The heels on my shoes are worn down.*
wear off
to become less and less: *The pain wore off, and I felt much better.* ANTONYM **increase**
wear something out
to use something so much that it becomes weak, broken, or not good enough to use any more: *He walks a lot, so he is always wearing his shoes out.*

wear[2] *noun, formal*
1 a particular kind of clothes, or clothes for a particular activity: *The store sells evening wear* (=formal clothes for parties).
2 normal damage that something has because it has been used a lot: *The tire was showing signs of wear, so we got a new one.*

wea•ry /ˈwɪri/ *adjective* **wearier**, **weariest** *formal*
very tired: *I felt weary after working all day.*
—**wearily** *adverb*: *He sat down wearily.*
—**weariness** *noun*

wea•sel /ˈwizəl/ *noun*
an animal like a long thin rat: *The weasel chased a rabbit into a hole.*

weath•er /ˈweðɚ/ *noun*
if you talk about the weather, you talk about whether it is raining, snowing, etc. or how warm or cold it is: *The airport was closed because of bad weather.* | *What's the weather like in Atlanta this time of year?*

ˈweather ˌforecast *noun*
a report on the television or radio that says what the weather will be like: *According to the weather forecast, it will rain tomorrow.*

ˈweather vane *noun*
a metal object on the top of a building that moves to show the direction of the wind

weave /wiv/ *verb*
1 **wove** /woʊv/ **woven** /ˈwoʊvən/ to make threads into cloth, by moving one thread over and under another: *They used special machines to weave wool into carpets.*
2 **weaved** to move somewhere by turning and changing direction a lot: *The car was weaving in and out of traffic.*
—**weaver** *noun* someone who weaves cloth
—**weaving** *noun* the activity of weaving

web /web/ *noun*
1 **the Web** = the system that makes it easy for you to see and use information on the Internet: *You can find out about anything on the Web.* SYNONYM **World Wide Web**
2 a thing that a SPIDER makes to catch insects: *A spider was spinning a web.*

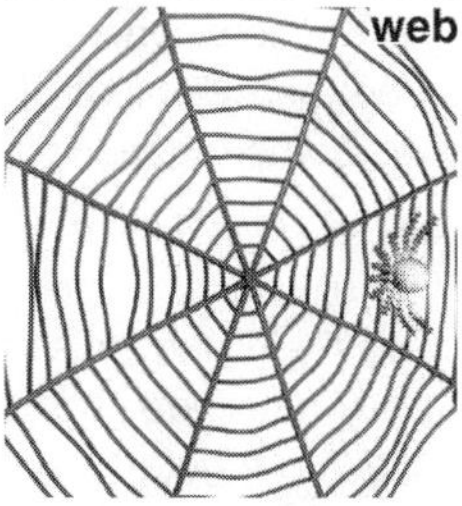

web•cam /ˈwebkæm/ *noun*
a video camera on a computer that you can use to put pictures on the Internet

web•site /ˈwebsaɪt/ *noun*
a set of pages on the Internet about a particular subject or belonging to a particular organization: *You will find information about the company on its website.*

we'd /wid/
1 the short form of "we had": *We'd forgotten our map.*
2 the short form of "we would": *We'd love to come to your party.*

wed /wed/ *verb* **wedded** or **wed** *formal*
to marry someone: *She wed Jeremiah Wooton in 1896.*

wed•ding /ˈwedɪŋ/ *noun*
an event at which two people get married: *I've been invited to their wedding in June.* | *She wore a white wedding dress.*

wedge /wedʒ/ *noun*
a piece of wood or metal with one thick edge and one pointed edge: *They put a wedge under the door to keep it open.*

Wednes•day /ˈwenzdi/ *noun*, *written abbreviation* **Weds.**
the fourth day of the week, between Tuesday and Thursday: *Classes start Wednesday.* | *What time are you coming on Wednesday?* | *I have to work next Wednesday.* | *Eva had surgery last Wednesday.* | *We're all going out to dinner on Wednesday night.*

weed¹ /wid/ *noun*
a wild plant that grows where you do not want it to grow: *The garden was full of weeds and looked very messy.*

weed² *verb*
to remove weeds from the ground: *She cut the grass and weeded the flower beds.*

week /wik/ *noun*
1 a period of seven days: *We went on vacation for two weeks.* | *I'll see you next week.*
2 the part of a week when you work on a job or go to school, from Monday to Friday: *I live with my mom during the week and go to my dad's house on the weekends.*

week•day /ˈwikdeɪ/ *noun*
any day of the week except Saturday and Sunday: *Most people work on weekdays.*

week•end /ˈwikend/ *noun*
Saturday and Sunday: *What did you do over the weekend* (=during the weekend)? | *Do you want to come over to my house this weekend* (=the weekend that is coming)? | *I usually play soccer and baseball on the weekends* (=during weekends).

W

week•ly /ˈwikli/ *adverb, adjective*
once a week, or every week: *The newspaper is printed weekly, on Fridays.* | *We have weekly meetings.*

week•night /ˈwiknaɪt/ *noun*
any night except Saturday or Sunday: *I go to bed early on weeknights, but stay up late on weekend nights.*

weep /wip/ *verb, formal* **wept** /wept/
to cry: *She wept when she heard he had died.*
→ See Thesaurus box at **cry**[1]

weigh

weigh /weɪ/ *verb*
1 to have a particular weight: *The baby weighs 12 pounds.*
2 to measure how heavy someone or something is: *I weighed the fish. It was two pounds.*
3 to think about something carefully: *You have to weigh whether or not you agree with him.*

W

weight /weɪt/ *noun*
1 how heavy something is: *The baby's weight was 9 pounds.*
2 a heavy piece of metal that people lift to make their muscles bigger: *He was in the gym lifting weights.*
3 something that is heavy: *I put a weight on the paper to stop it from blowing away.*
4 lose weight = to become thinner: *If you eat less food, you will lose weight.*
5 gain weight/put on weight = to become fatter: *I gained some weight, and now my clothes don't fit.*

weight•lift•ing /ˈweɪtˌlɪftɪŋ/ *noun*
the sport of lifting a bar with heavy metal objects on each end
—**weight-lifter** *noun* someone who does weightlifting

weird /wɪrd/ *adjective, informal*
unusual and strange: *I had a weird feeling, like I was in someone else's body.* SYNONYM **strange**
—**weirdly** *adverb*: *His head was weirdly shaped and hats didn't fit him.*
—**weirdness** *noun*
→ See Thesaurus box at **strange**[1]

weird•o /ˈwɪrdoʊ/ *noun* plural **weirdos** *informal*
a strange person who people do not like or are afraid of: *They called him a weirdo because he wore strange clothes and had green hair.*

wel•come[1] /ˈwelkəm/ *adjective*
1 if you are welcome in a place, the people there are happy that you have come: *They made us feel welcome by bringing us food.*
2 you're welcome! = used when someone has said thank you to you for something: *"Thanks for the ride." "You're welcome."*
3 be welcome to do something = used when telling someone that he or she can do something: *You're welcome to stay for lunch – there's plenty of food.*

welcome[2] *verb*
1 to say hello in a friendly way to someone who has just arrived: *He welcomed his guests at the door.*
2 *formal* to be glad to hear what someone wants to say: *I would like to know what you think about my idea, and would welcome your comments.*

welcome[3] *noun*
the way someone greets you when you arrive somewhere: *They seemed happy to see us, because they gave us a warm welcome* (=a friendly welcome).

weld /weld/ *verb*
to join metal objects to each other by heating them and pressing them together when they are hot: *The parts of the ship are welded together.*
—**welder** *noun* someone who welds metal

wel•fare /ˈwelfer/ Ac *noun*
1 money that the government gives to poor people: *Most people in this poor neighborhood are on welfare.*
2 *formal* someone's health or happiness: *My parents are worried about my welfare and want me to move back home.*

we'll /wil/
the short form of "we will": *We'll have to leave soon.*

well[1] /wel/ *adverb* **better, best**

1 in a good way: *Did you sleep well? | Mary can read very well.* ANTONYM **badly**

USAGE: well

Use **well** to talk about the way someone does something: *He plays tennis very well.*

Use **good** to talk about the quality of something or someone: *a good teacher | Was the movie good?*

2 very much: *It was late – well after 10 o'clock.*

3 in a thorough way: *Mix the paint well before you use it.* SYNONYM **thoroughly**

4 as well = also: *I'd like a cup of coffee and some cake as well.* SYNONYM **too**

USAGE: well

As well, **too**, and **also** mean the same thing, but you use them in different ways.

As well and **too** are less formal than **also** and you use them more often in spoken English: *Oh, are you coming as well? | Tom's hungry, and I am too.*

Also is more formal and is used more often in writing than in speech: *Tom was very tired, and he was also hungry.*

5 as well as = if you do one thing as well as another, you do them both: *I'm learning Spanish as well as Chinese.*

6 well done *formal* = said when someone has done a good thing or done something well: *"I won the competition." "Well done!"*

well[2] *adjective* **better, best**

healthy and not sick: *He's sick, but we hope he will be well again soon.*

➔ See Thesaurus box at **healthy**

well[3]

1 used when pausing before you say something or when you are surprised: *Well, I suppose we should go now. | Well, I'm surprised you're here.*

2 *also* **oh well** used when accepting a situation, even though it is not a good one: *"I failed the test." "Oh well, you can't do anything about it now."*

3 Well? = used when asking someone to answer your question or tell you what happened: *Well? What did he say?*

well[4] *noun*

a deep hole in the ground from which you get water or oil: *She lowered the bucket into the well.*

ˌwell-beˈhaved *adjective*

behaving in a good or polite way: *She was a well-behaved child who got along well with other children and her teachers.* SYNONYM **good**

ˌwell-ˈbeing *noun, formal*

a feeling of being comfortable, healthy, and happy: *Running gives me a feeling of well-being.*

ˌwell-ˈdone *adjective*

well-done meat has been cooked thoroughly: *He likes his steak well done, even black on the outside.* ANTONYM **rare**

W

ˌwell-ˈdressed *adjective*

wearing clothes that look good and are fashionable: *A well-dressed man wearing a suit and tie came into the room.*

ˌwell-ˈknown *adjective*

1 if someone is well known, a lot of people know about him or her: *Everyone knows who Madonna is – she's very well known.* SYNONYM **famous**; ANTONYM **unknown**

2 if something is well known, most people know it: *It's a well-known fact that smoking is bad for your health.*

ˌwell-ˈmeaning *adjective, formal*

a well-meaning person tries to help, but makes a problem worse: *I didn't want to see Todd, but a well-meaning neighbor told him where to find me.*

ˌwell-ˈoff *adjective*

having enough money to have a good life, with all the things you want: *My parents weren't very well-off, so we lived in a small house.* SYNONYM **rich**; ANTONYM **poor**

➔ See Thesaurus box at **rich**

ˌwell-ˈpaid *adjective*
getting a lot of money as pay for the job that you do: *Professional football players are very well paid, and some earn millions of dollars.*

ˌwell-ˈtimed *adjective, formal*
said or done at the best possible time: *My arrival wasn't very well timed, because Rob and Lisa were fighting.*

ˌwell-to-ˈdo *adjective, formal*
having a lot of money: *The big houses are owned by well-to-do families.* SYNONYM **rich**; ANTONYM **poor**
➔ See Thesaurus box at **rich**

Welsh¹ /welʃ/ *adjective*
from Wales: *a Welsh singer*

Welsh² *noun*
1 the language spoken in Wales
2 the Welsh = the people from Wales

went /went/ *verb*
the past tense of GO

wept /wept/ *verb*
the past tense and past participle of WEEP

we're /wɪr/
the short form of "we are": *We're almost finished.*

were /wɚ/ *verb*
the past tense of BE that we use after "you", "we" and "they"

W

weren't /wɚnt/
the short form of "were not": *I tried to call you, but you weren't home.*

were•wolf /ˈwerwʊlf/ *noun*
a person in stories who changes into a WOLF

west¹, **West** /west/ *noun*
1 the direction in which the sun goes down: *The sun sets in the west.*
2 the west = the western part of a country or area: *El Paso is in the west of Texas.*
3 the West = the countries in North America and the western part of Europe: *Countries in the West are richer than the rest of the world.*
➔ See picture at **north¹**

west² *adjective*
1 in, to, or facing toward the west: *Our hotel was west of the river.*
2 west wind = a wind that comes from the west

west³ *adverb*
toward the west: *We left New York and drove west to Virginia.*

west•ern¹ /ˈwestɚn/ *adjective*
1 in or from the west: *Vancouver is in western Canada.* ANTONYM **eastern**
2 Western = in or from the countries in North America and the western part of Europe: *William Shakespeare is very important in Western literature.*
—**westernized** *adjective* having Western ideas or attitudes: *Japanese people are very westernized.*

western² *noun*
a movie about life in the western part of the USA in the 19th century

west•er•ner /ˈwɛstɚnɚ/ *noun*
1 someone who comes from the western part of a country
2 someone who comes from the U.S. or Europe, rather than from Africa or Asia

west•ward /ˈwestwɚd/ *adverb, adjective*
toward the west: *The ship sailed westward.*

wet¹ /wet/ *adjective* **wetter**, **wettest**
1 covered in or containing liquid: *It had been raining and the ground was wet.* | *My clothes were soaking wet* (=very wet) *after I fell in the pool.* ANTONYM **dry**
2 not yet dry: *Don't touch the paint – it's still wet.* ANTONYM **dry**
3 if the weather is wet, it is raining or it has been raining: *It's been a very wet spring.* SYNONYM **rainy**; ANTONYM **dry**
—**wetness** *noun*

wet² *verb* **wet** or **wetted**, **wetting**
to make something wet: *Wet your hair before you use the shampoo.* ANTONYM **dry**

wet•land /ˈwetlənd/ *noun*
a very wet area of land: *Wetlands have a lot of different birds in them.*

ˈwet suit *noun*
a piece of rubber clothing that keeps you warm when you go swimming or diving

we've /wiv/
the short form of "we have": *We've met before, haven't we?*

whale /weɪl/ *noun*
a large animal that swims in the ocean and breathes through a hole in the top of its head
—**whaling** *noun* the activity of hunting whales
—**whaler** *noun* someone who hunts whales

wharf /wɔrf/ *noun* plural **wharves** /wɔrvz/
a long structure that sticks out into the water so that boats can stop next to it: *His boat was tied up at the wharf.* SYNONYM **pier**

what /wət; *strong* wʌt/ *pronoun*
1 used when asking about something that you do not know: *What is your name?* | *What time is it?* | *What do you do* (=what is your job)?
2 *informal* used when you did not hear what someone said: *"Is it hot?" "What?" "I said, is it hot?"* SYNONYM **excuse me, pardon**
3 *informal* used when someone has said your name and you are asking what he or she wants: *"Jane!" "What?" "Come and see this."* SYNONYM **yes**
4 used when describing a specific thing: *Show me what you bought.* | *I believe what he told me.*
5 used when showing surprise: *You gave all your money away? What a stupid thing to do!*
6 what about ...? = used when telling someone that he or she could try doing something: *What about walking instead of driving?*
7 what for? *informal* = used when asking the reason for something: *"Can I have this?" "What for?"* SYNONYM **why**
8 what if ...? = used when asking what will happen if you are in a particular situation after doing something: *What if he's not home when we get there?*

what•ev•er /wət'evɚ/ *pronoun*
1 any or all of the things that someone needs or wants: *Take whatever you need.*
2 used when saying that it is not important what happens, because it does not change a situation: *Whatever I say, she always disagrees.*
3 *informal* used as a reply to say that you do not care what happens: *"Do you want a pizza?" "Oh, whatever."*

wheat /wit/ *noun*
a plant that farmers grow in fields, that is used for making flour

wheel /wil/ *noun*
1 one of the round things under a car, bicycle, etc. that turns and makes it move: *The front wheel fell off his bike.*
2 a round object that you hold and turn to make a car move to the left or right: *He had an accident when he fell asleep at the wheel* (=while driving). SYNONYM **steering wheel**
➔ See picture at **bicycle**

wheel•bar•row /'wil͵bæroʊ/ *noun*
an object with one wheel at the front and two handles at the back, that you use outdoors for carrying things: *He took the dirt away in a wheelbarrow.*

wheel•chair /'wil-tʃer/ *noun*
a chair with wheels for people who cannot walk: *He broke his back, and is now in a wheelchair* (=he has to use a wheelchair).

wheeze /wiz/ *verb*
to breathe with difficulty, making a sound in your chest: *He has a lung disease and wheezes when he breathes.*
➔ See Thesaurus box at **breathe**

when /wen/ *adverb*
1 at what time: *When are we leaving?* | *I'll tell you when to stop.*
2 at a particular time: *I moved to the U.S. when I was young.*
3 even though something is true: *Why do you walk to work when you have a car?*
4 immediately after something happens: *I'll call you when I get home.*

when•ev•er /wen'evɚ/ *adverb*
1 every time: *Whenever we come here, we see someone we know.*
2 at any time: *Come and visit whenever you want.*

where /wer/ *adverb*
1 in or to what place: *"Where does he live?" "On 7th Street."* | *"Where are you going?" "To the store."*
2 in or to a particular place: *This is the place where I met Gayle.*
3 used when asking or talking about the state of something: *Where will it all end?*

where•a•bouts /'werə͵baʊts/ *plural noun*, *formal*
the place where someone is: *The police are searching for a man, but do not know his whereabouts.*

where•as /wer'æz; *weak* werəz/ Ac *conjunction*, *formal*
used when saying that two situations are very different: *Jane's family is poor, whereas Jason's is rich.*

W

where•by /wer'baɪ/ Ac *adverb, formal*
used when giving the details of a system, plan, process, etc.: *The store has a system whereby you can return empty bottles and get money.*

where•u•pon /ˌwerə'pɑn/ *conjunction, formal*
after the thing you have just mentioned: *The president arrived, whereupon everyone started shouting.*

wher•ev•er /wer'evə/ *adverb*
at or to any place: *Sit wherever you like.* | *I will drive you wherever you want to go.*

wheth•er /'weðə/ *conjunction*
1 used when talking about a choice between different things: *I don't know whether he'll come or not.* SYNONYM **if**
2 used when saying that it is not important what someone wants or decides because something will happen anyway: *Whether you like it or not, we're going home.*

which /wɪtʃ/ *pronoun, adjective*
1 what person or thing: *Which color do you like better – blue or green?* | *Which of you is taller: Mary or Jane?*
2 used when adding more information about a noun: *We went to Plano, which is just outside Dallas.*

W

which•ev•er /wɪ'tʃevə/ *adjective*
used when saying that it is not important which person or thing you choose, because the result will be the same: *Whichever car you buy, it will be expensive.*

whiff /wɪf/ *noun*
a smell of something that you notice for only a short time: *As she walked past, I caught a whiff of her perfume* (=smelled her perfume).

while[1] /waɪl/ *conjunction*
1 during the time that something is happening: *They arrived while we were having dinner.* | *While she works, she listens to music.*
2 *formal* although: *While it was a good school, I was not happy there.*

while[2] *noun*
a while = a short period of time: *After a while, she fell asleep.* | *We talked for a while.*

whim /wɪm/ *noun, formal*
on a whim = if you do something on a whim, you do it because you suddenly want to do it: *I quit my job on a whim, without thinking about how I would pay my bills.*

whim•per /'wɪmpə/ *verb*
to make low crying sounds: *The dog was whimpering because it had hurt its paw.*

whine /waɪn/ *verb*
1 to complain about something in a sad annoying voice: *She was whining about how hard her life is.*
2 to make a long high sound because you feel pain or are unhappy: *The dog whines at the door when he wants to come in.*

whip[1] /wɪp/ *noun*
a long thin piece of leather used for hitting a horse

whip[2] *verb* **whipped, whipping**
1 to hit a person or animal with a whip: *He whipped the horse to make it run faster.*
2 *informal* to defeat someone easily: *They whipped the other team 35–0.*
3 to move something suddenly: *He whipped a gun out of his pocket.*
4 to quickly mix cream or the clear part of an egg until it becomes stiff SYNONYM **beat**

whirl /wəl/ *verb*
to make someone or something move around quickly: *He whirled her around the dance floor.* SYNONYM **spin**

whirl•pool /'wəlpul/ *noun*
1 a bathtub that makes currents of water move around your body
2 water that moves around and down quickly: *There's a whirlpool at the bottom of the waterfall.*

whirl•wind[1] /'wəlˌwɪnd/ *noun*
a very strong wind that moves quickly around in a circle, causing a lot of damage SYNONYM **tornado**

whirlwind[2] *adjective*
a whirlwind situation or event happens very quickly: *We had a whirlwind romance and were married a month after we met.*

whisk•ers /'wɪskəz/ *plural noun*
1 long hairs that grow near the mouth of a cat or mouse
2 the hair on a man's face when he needs to cut it off: *His whiskers tickled her face when he kissed her.*

whis•key /'wɪski/ *noun*
a drink made from grain that contains a lot of alcohol

whis•per /ˈwɪspɚ/ *verb*
to speak very quietly: *She whispered the answer to me because she didn't want anyone to hear.*
—**whisper** *noun* the act of whispering: *He spoke in a whisper to avoid disturbing the others.*
➔ See Thesaurus boxes at **talk**[1] and **say**[1]

whisper

whistle /ˈwɪsəl/ *noun*
1 a small object that produces a high sound when you blow into it: *The gym teacher blew a whistle to start the race.*
2 a high sound that you make by blowing air through your lips: *When he gave a whistle, his dog ran to him.*
—**whistle** *verb* to make a high sound with a whistle or with your lips: *He whistled a song for me.*

white[1] /waɪt/ *adjective*
1 having the color of milk, salt, or snow: *a white wedding dress*
2 having light-colored skin: *Her father is white, and her mother is Asian.*
—**whiten** *verb* to make something white: *This toothpaste will whiten your teeth.*

white[2] *noun*
1 the color of milk, salt, or snow: *She was dressed in white* (=in white clothes).
2 whites = people who have light-colored skin: *Blacks, whites, Hispanics, and Asians all live together in this city.*
3 the part of an egg that becomes white when you cook it: *Mix two egg whites together.*

ˌwhite-ˈcollar *adjective, formal*
white-collar workers have jobs in offices, banks, etc., not in factories, on building sites, etc.

ˈWhite House *noun*
1 the White House = the official home in Washington, D.C., of the president of the U.S.: *We took a tour of the White House and the Capitol.*
2 the president of the U.S. and the people who work with the president: *The White House did not comment on the issue.*

whit•tle /ˈwɪtl/ *verb*
1 *also* **whittle down** to gradually make something smaller: *I've whittled down the list of guests from 30 to 16.*
2 to cut small pieces off a piece of wood: *He whittled a tiny statue of a man out of the branch.*

whiz[1] /wɪz/ *verb* **whizzed, whizzing,** third person singular **whizzes** *informal*
to move very quickly: *A motorcycle whizzed by.*

whiz[2] *noun, informal*
someone who is very good at something: *My brother's a math whiz – he can solve any math problem.*

who /hu/ *pronoun*
1 what person or people: *Who locked the door? | Who are those people? | I know who sent you that card.*
2 used for giving information about someone you have mentioned: *That's the girl who lives next door to us. | My uncle, who is a teacher, gave me this book.*

who'd /hud/
1 the short form of "who had": *The teacher asked who'd written on the board.*
2 the short form of "who would": *Do you know anyone who'd be interested in going?*

who•ev•er /huˈevɚ/ *pronoun*
1 used for saying "the person who": *Whoever broke this is going to be in trouble.*
2 used for saying "it does not matter who": *Whoever wins, it's going to be a great game.*

whole[1] /hoʊl/ *adjective*
all of something: *He ate a whole box of candy and got sick. | We spent the whole day at the beach.* SYNONYM **entire**
—**wholly** *adverb, formal* completely: *His ideas are not wholly new, but it's the first time they've all been put together.*

whole[2] *noun, formal*
1 the whole of something = all of something: *The floods affected the whole of the city.*
2 on the whole = generally: *On the whole, I like school, but I don't like everything about it.*
3 as a whole = used when you are considering all of something: *Education benefits society as a whole.*

W

whole•heart•ed•ly /ˌhoʊlˈhɑrtɪdli/ *adverb, formal*
if you believe, feel, or support something wholeheartedly, you believe, feel, or support it completely: *I agree with him wholeheartedly, and I will tell his professor that I think he's right.*

whole•sale /ˈhoʊlseɪl/ *adjective*
relating to selling things in large quantities to stores: *Wholesale prices are cheaper than retail prices* (=prices charged in stores).
—**wholesale** *adverb*
—**wholesaler** *noun* a person or company that sells things to stores

whole•some /ˈhoʊlsəm/ *adjective*
1 good for your health: *a good wholesome breakfast*
2 having or showing behavior that is right and acceptable: *It's a wholesome family show that everyone will enjoy.*

ˈ**whole wheat** *adjective*
whole wheat flour or bread is made using every part of the grain

who'll /hul/
the short form of "who will": *Who'll be here tomorrow?*

W

whom /hum/ *pronoun*
1 *formal* who – used as the object of a verb or PREPOSITION: *To whom am I speaking?*
2 some/all/one, etc. of whom = some, all, etc. of the people just mentioned: *He has two sisters, one of whom is in college.*

whoop /hup/ *verb*
to shout loudly and in a happy way: *The audience whooped and cheered when the comedian came on stage.*
—**whoop** *noun*

who's /huz/
1 the short form of "who is": *Who's coming to the party?*
2 the short form of "who has": *Who's got my math book?*

whose /huz/ *adjective, pronoun*
1 used for asking or saying who something belongs to: *Whose jacket is this?*
2 used for giving information about something that belongs to someone you have mentioned: *That's the man whose house burned down.*

who've /huv/
the short form of "who have": *People who've seen the show say it's fantastic.*

why /waɪ/ *adverb*
1 for what reason: *Why is she crying?* | *I don't know why he left.* | *"I haven't done my homework." "Why not* (=why haven't you done it)*?"*
2 why not ...? *informal* = used for making a suggestion: *Why not just ask him to help you?*
3 why not? *informal* = used for saying "yes" to a suggestion or invitation: *"Do you want to come with us?" "OK, why not?"*

wick /wɪk/ *noun*
the string in a CANDLE which burns

wick•ed /ˈwɪkɪd/ *adjective*
bad or evil: *The wicked witch turned the boy into a frog.*
—**wickedness** *noun* bad or evil actions

wick•er /ˈwɪkɚ/ *adjective*
made from thin branches woven together: *a wicker chair*

wide[1] /waɪd/ *adjective*
1 measuring a large distance from one side to the other: *The path was wide enough for two bicycles.* ANTONYM **narrow**
2 used for asking or talking about the distance between the two sides of something: *How wide is the door?* | *The bed is five feet wide.*
3 including a lot of different things or people: *The store has a wide range of clothes.*
➔ See picture at **narrow**

wide[2] *adverb*
completely, or as much as possible: *The door was wide open.* | *It was only 5:30 a.m., but I was wide awake so I got up.* | *He spread his arms wide.*

wide•ly /ˈwaɪdli/ *adverb*
1 in a lot of places or by a lot of people: *The product is widely available; you can buy it at any computer store.* | *a widely used textbook*
2 vary/differ widely = to be very different: *Taxes vary widely from state to state.*

wid•en /ˈwaɪdn/ *verb*
to become wider, or to make something wider: *The river widens here.* | *They are going to widen the road to add new lanes of traffic.*

wide•spread /ˈwaɪdspred/ Ac *adjective, formal*
happening in a lot of places: *The widespread use of computers has changed the way we live.*

wid•ow /ˈwɪdoʊ/ *noun*
a woman whose husband has died
➔ See Thesaurus box at **married**

wid•ow•er /ˈwɪdoʊɚ/ *noun*
a man whose wife has died

width /wɪdθ/ *noun*
the distance from one side of something to the other: *They measured the width of the window.* | *The table is three feet in width.*

wife /waɪf/ *noun* plural **wives** /waɪvz/
the woman that a man is married to: *This is a picture of my brother and his wife.*

wig /wɪg/ *noun*
something that has been made for someone to wear as hair: *The actress wore a blond wig.*

wig•gle /ˈwɪgəl/ *verb*
to move something, a little up and down or from side to side: *She wiggled her toes inside her shoes.*

wild¹ /waɪld/ *adjective*
1 wild animals are not kept by people: *A herd of wild horses galloped past.* ANTONYM **tame**
2 wild plants are not grown by people: *We picked some wild mushrooms.*
3 very angry, excited, etc. and not able to control yourself: *The kids were wild with excitement.*
4 *informal* very exciting or unusual: *a wild party* | *a wild haircut*
5 not based on any facts: *It was just a wild guess – it may be wrong.*
6 not wild about something/someone *informal* = not liking something or someone very much: *I'm not wild about the color they painted their house.*

wild² *noun*
in the wild = in an area that is natural and not looked after by people: *Scientists study the behavior of animals in the wild.*

wil•der•ness /ˈwɪldɚnəs/ *noun*
a large natural area of land where there is nothing made by humans: *They got lost in the wilderness.*

wild•flow•er /ˈwaɪldˌflaʊɚ/ *noun*
a flower that has not been grown by people

ˌwild ˈgoose ˌchase *noun*
a situation in which you waste a lot of time looking for something that cannot be found: *We went on a wild goose chase looking for that book – it isn't in the library.*

wild•life /ˈwaɪldlaɪf/ *noun*
animals that are not kept by people: *We must protect the birds and other wildlife of this area.*

will¹ /wɪl/ *verb*
1 used for talking about the future: *It will probably rain tomorrow.* | *I will call you when I hear any news.*
2 will you ...? = used for asking someone to do something: *Will you turn the TV off, please?*
3 used for saying what is possible: *The stadium will hold 20,000 people.* SYNONYM **can**

will² *noun*
1 a strong wish to do something or that something should happen: *He does not have the will to live anymore.* | *No one can force him to stay here against his will* (=if he does not want to).
2 a legal document in which you say who will have your money and property after you die: *My grandma left me $7,000 in her will.*

will³ *verb*
to try to make something happen by thinking about it very hard: *He willed the ball to go through the hoop.*

will•ful *also* **wilful** /ˈwɪlfəl/ *adjective*
doing what you want, even though people tell you not to: *How can you control a willful teenager?*
—**willfully** *adverb*
—**willfulness** *noun*

will•ing /ˈwɪlɪŋ/ *adjective*
1 be willing to do something = if you are willing to do something, you do not mind doing it: *Are you willing to help?* ANTONYM **unwilling**
2 doing something because you want to do it, not because you have to: *We had a lot of willing helpers.*

W

—**willingly** *adverb* if you do something willingly, you do it because you want to do it: *He willingly shared his food with us.*
—**willingness** *noun*

wil•low /ˈwɪloʊ/ *noun*
a tree with long thin branches, that grows near water

will•pow•er /ˈwɪlˌpaʊɚ/ *noun*
the ability to make yourself do something that is difficult or unpleasant: *I don't have the willpower to stay on a diet.*

wimp /wɪmp/ *noun, informal*
someone who is afraid to do things: *He's such a wimp that he'll never have the courage to ask her out.*

win[1] /wɪn/ *verb* **won** /wʌn/ **winning**
1 to be the best in a competition, game, etc.: *Who won the election?* | *Our team won by 3 points.* ANTONYM **lose**

THESAURUS: win

beat to get more points, votes, etc. than other people in a game or competition: *New York beat Boston, 4–1.* | *I beat Dad at chess!*
defeat *formal* to beat someone in a war, sport, competition, etc.: *It was a very close election in 2000, but Bush defeated Gore.* | *UCLA defeated Arizona State in Thursday's game.*

2 to get money or a prize by doing well in a competition, game, etc.: *She won a gold medal at the Olympics.*
—**winning** *adjective* the winning team or player is the one that has won

win[2] *noun*
an occasion when you win a competition, game, etc.: *The college is still happy about their 64–57 win over Oregon State.* SYNONYM **victory**; ANTONYM **loss**

wince /wɪns/ *verb*
to suddenly change your expression when you see, feel, hear, or remember something unpleasant: *She winced at the sight of the wound.*

wind[1] /wɪnd/ *noun*
air outside that moves quickly along: *The trees swayed in the wind.* | *A cold wind was blowing.* | *a strong east wind* (=coming from the east)

THESAURUS: wind

breeze a light wind: *A nice breeze came off the ocean.*
gust a sudden strong movement of wind: *A gust of wind blew open the door.*
gale a very strong wind: *Several trees blew down in the gale.*
storm a period of bad weather when there is lot of wind, rain, snow, etc.: *The storm lasted all night.*
hurricane a storm with fast strong winds that come from the ocean: *The hurricane badly damaged the city of New Orleans.*
tornado a violent storm with strong winds that go around and around: *The wind in the tornado was moving at 200 miles per hour.*

wind[2] /waɪnd/ *verb* **wound** /waʊnd/
1 to put a piece of string, cloth, etc. around and around something: *He wound his scarf around his neck.*
2 *also* **wind up** to turn a handle around and around in order to make a clock or machine able to work: *I forgot to wind my watch and it stopped.*
3 if a road, path, or river winds somewhere, it has a lot of curves: *The road winds up the hill to the top.*

PHRASAL VERBS
wind down
to become less active before ending: *The party is winding down – everyone will go home soon.*
wind up
to be in a bad situation or place after a lot has happened: *Most of the guys I knew in high school wound up in prison.*

wind•chill fac•tor /ˈwɪndtʃɪl ˌfæktɚ/ *noun*
the cooling effect of the wind: *It feels very cold today because of the windchill factor.*

wind•ing /ˈwaɪndɪŋ/ *adjective*
a winding road, path, or river has a lot of curves

wind in•stru•ment /ˈwɪnd ˌɪnstrəmənt/ *noun*
a musical instrument that you blow, such as a FLUTE or CLARINET

wind•mill /ˈwɪndˌmɪl/ *noun*
a tall structure with parts that are turned by the wind, which crushes grain or makes electricity

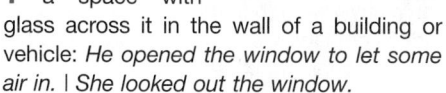

win•dow /ˈwɪndoʊ/ *noun*
1 a space with glass across it in the wall of a building or vehicle: *He opened the window to let some air in.* | *She looked out the window.*
2 an area on a computer screen where you can use a particular program: *You can change the size of the window if you want to look at two programs at one time.*
➔ See picture on page A8

ˈwindow ˌshopping *noun*
the activity of looking at things in store windows without intending to buy them

win•dow•sill /ˈwɪndoʊˌsɪl/ *noun*
a shelf at the bottom of a window: *There was a vase of flowers on the windowsill.*

wind•shield /ˈwɪndʃild/ *noun*
the large window at the front of a vehicle: *He scraped the ice off his windshield.*
➔ See picture on page A28

ˈwindshield ˌwiper *noun*
a long thin object that moves across a windshield to remove rain
➔ See picture on page A28

wind•surf•ing /ˈwɪndˌsɚfɪŋ/ *noun*
the sport of sailing across water by standing on a board and holding onto a sail
—**windsurfer** *noun*
➔ See picture on page A24

wind•y /ˈwɪndi/ *adjective*
if it is windy, there is a lot of wind: *a windy day*

wine /waɪn/ *noun*
an alcoholic drink made from GRAPEs: *a glass of red wine*
—**winery** /ˈwaɪnəri/ *noun* a place where a company makes wine

wing /wɪŋ/ *noun*
1 one of the parts of a bird's or insect's body that it uses to fly: *The duck flapped its wings* (=it moved them up and down).
2 one of the two flat parts that stick out of the sides of an airplane
➔ See picture at **airplane**
3 part of a large building that is not the main part: *They built a new wing on the museum for the Asian art.*

wing•span /ˈwɪŋspæn/ *noun*
the distance from the end of one wing to the end of the other: *The plane had a wingspan of 80 feet.*

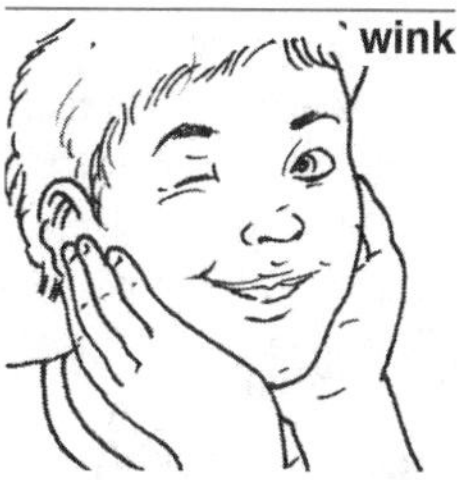

wink /wɪŋk/ *verb*
to close and open one eye quickly, usually to show that you are joking or being friendly: *"Don't tell Mom," he said, winking at her.*
—**wink** *noun He gave her a wink to let her know he'd seen her.*

win•ner /ˈwɪnɚ/ *noun*
someone who wins a competition, game, etc.: *The winner of the race gets a prize of $1,000.*

win•ter /ˈwɪntɚ/ *noun*
the season between fall and spring, when the weather is coldest: *We get a lot of snow here in the winter.* | *I'm going skiing this winter.*
—**wintry** *adjective* cold: *a wintry day*

wipe /waɪp/ *verb*
1 to remove dirt, water, etc. from something by moving a cloth or your hand across it: *She wiped her eyes with a tissue.* | *He wiped the sweat from his face.* | *Could you wipe off the table?*
2 to dry or clean something by rubbing it on something soft: *She wiped her wet hands on a towel.*

PHRASAL VERBS

wipe something out
informal to destroy or remove something completely: *Entire villages were wiped out by the floods.*

wipe something up
to remove liquid from a surface using a cloth: *I wiped up the water I spilled.*

wip•er /ˈwaɪpɚ/ *noun*
another word for WINDSHIELD WIPER

W

wire /waɪɚ/ *noun*
1 metal that is long and thin like string or thread: *a wire fence*
2 a long thin piece of metal that carries electricity: *a telephone wire*
—**wiring** *noun* all the electrical wires in a building or machine

wire·tap /ˈwaɪɚˌtæp/ *noun*
the act of secretly listening to someone's telephone calls by connecting something to the wires of his or her telephone: *The FBI gathered information about the criminals' plans using wiretaps.*

wis·dom /ˈwɪzdəm/ *noun*
good judgment and sensible ideas: *She knew her parents had more wisdom than she did.*

ˈwisdom tooth *noun*
one of the four large teeth at the back of an adult's mouth

wise /waɪz/ *adjective*
1 sensible: *I think you've made a wise decision. I would do the same thing.* ANTONYM **stupid**
2 able to make good decisions and give good advice: *a wise leader*
—**wisely** *adverb*: *He wisely refused to say anything while she was yelling at him.*
➔ See Thesaurus box at **intelligent**

W

wish¹ /wɪʃ/ *verb*
1 to want something to happen, even though it is unlikely: *I wish (that) I had a million dollars.* | *He wished for a more exciting life.*
2 wish someone something = to say that you hope someone will be happy, lucky, etc.: *Wish me luck!*
3 wish to do something *formal* = to want to do something: *I wish to make a complaint.*

wish² *noun*
1 *formal* the state of wanting to do something or wanting something to happen: *He quit school against his parents' wishes* (=his parents did not want him to quit school). | *I had no wish to see him.*
2 something that you want to happen: *She wanted to be famous, and she got her wish* (=what she wanted actually happened).
3 the act of saying that you want something to happen, believing that magic or luck will make it happen: *Close your eyes and make a wish!*
4 best wishes = a friendly phrase that you write before your name in cards and letters

ˌwishful ˈthinking *noun*
a belief or hope that something will happen, when it is not possible: *I hope he'll be well enough to play in the game next week, but maybe that's just wishful thinking.*

wish·y-wash·y /ˈwɪʃi ˌwɑʃi/ *adjective, informal*
a wishy-washy person does not have firm ideas or plans: *He's too wishy-washy to be a good leader.*

wit /wɪt/ *noun*
the ability to say things that are funny and smart: *He was famous for his wit and for telling wonderful stories.*

witch /wɪtʃ/ *noun*
a woman who has magic powers, especially one who does bad things: *The old witch knew many magic spells.*
—**witchcraft** /ˈwɪtʃˌkræft/ *noun* the use of magic powers: *She was accused of witchcraft.*

with /wɪθ/ *preposition*
1 used for saying that people or things are together: *She walks to school with her sister.* | *Put this bag with the others.* | *Serve the fish with rice.*
2 using something: *Stir the sauce with a wooden spoon.*
3 having or carrying something: *I'd like a room with a nice view.* | *The man with the gun ran off.*
4 used for saying what covers or fills something: *His hands were covered with blood.*
5 *formal* because of something: *She was shaking with fear.*
6 used for saying who or what a feeling or attitude is related to: *I was pretty angry with her.*
7 used for saying who else is involved in an activity: *Have you talked about it with her?* | *He gets into fights with people.*
8 used for saying how someone does something: *They spoke to the senator with great respect.*
9 used for talking about the position of someone's body: *He was standing with his hands in his pockets.*
10 supporting someone: *You're either with me or against me.*

with•draw /wɪθ'drɔ/ *verb* **withdrew** /wɪθ'dru/ **withdrawn** /wɪθ'drɔn/
1 to take money out of a bank account: *I withdrew $200 from the bank.* ANTONYM **deposit**
2 if soldiers withdraw from an area, they leave it: *U.S. troops withdrew from the south of the country.*
3 to stop taking part in a competition, race, etc.: *She withdrew from the race because she hurt her leg.*

with•draw•al /wɪθ'drɔəl/ *noun*
1 the act of taking money out of your bank account: *During that week, I made two withdrawals from my savings account.*
2 when soldiers leave an area: *the troop withdrawal from the region*
3 the act of stopping taking part in a competition, race, etc.: *He announced his withdrawal from the race.*

with•er /'wɪðɚ/ *also* **wither away** *verb*
if a plant withers, it becomes dry and it starts to die: *It was very hot, and a lot of the plants withered.*

with•hold /wɪθ'hoʊld/ *verb* **withheld** /wɪθ'held/ *formal*
to refuse to give someone something: *The police accused him of withholding information when he first talked to them.*

with•in /wɪ'ðɪn/ *adverb, preposition, formal*
1 before a period of time ends: *Please pay your bill within two weeks.*
2 less than a particular distance from somewhere: *The hotel is within a mile of the beach, so you can walk between the two.*
3 inside an organization or group: *There have been a lot of changes within the company.*

with•out /wɪ'ðaʊt/ *preposition*
1 not having something or someone with you: *Billy went to school without his books so I had to take them to him.* | *I don't want to go to the party without you.*
2 without doing something = not doing a particular thing: *He left without saying goodbye.*
3 go/do without something = to not have something that you need or want: *I don't like going without enough sleep.*

with•stand /wɪθ'stænd/ *verb* **withstood** /wɪθ'stʊd/ *formal*
to not be harmed or affected by something: *This plant can withstand very hot dry conditions.*

wit•ness /'wɪtnəs/ *noun*
someone who saw an accident or a crime happen: *Were there any witnesses to the accident who can tell us what happened?*
—**witness** *verb* to see an accident or a crime happen
➔ See Thesaurus box at **see**

wits /wɪts/ *plural noun*
1 your ability to think and make good decisions quickly: *He survived on the street by using his wits.*
2 scare someone out of his or her wits = to frighten someone very much

wit•ty /'wɪti/ *adjective* **wittier**, **wittiest**
good at talking in a funny or interesting way: *Max is really witty and makes everyone laugh.*
➔ See Thesaurus box at **funny**[1]

wives /waɪvz/ *noun*
the plural of WIFE

wiz•ard /'wɪzɚd/ *noun*
1 a man who has magic powers: *It's a story about witches and wizards.*
2 *also* **wiz** /wɪz/ *informal* someone who is very good at doing something: *He's a computer wizard and writes computer games in his spare time.*
—**wizardry** /'wɪzɚdri/ *noun* great skill at doing something difficult: *technical wizardry*

wob•ble /'wɑbəl/ *verb*
to move from side to side in an unsteady way: *The bicycle wobbled and Freddie fell off.*
—**wobbly** *adjective* moving from side to side in an unsteady way: *Be careful – the chair's a little wobbly.*

wok /wɑk/ *noun*
a large round pan, that you use for Chinese cooking

woke /woʊk/ *verb*
the past tense of WAKE

wo•ken /'woʊkən/ *verb*
the past participle of WAKE

W

wolf /wʊlf/ *noun* plural **wolves** /wʊlvz/
a wild animal that is like a large dog: *I thought I heard a wolf howl* (=make a loud crying sound).

wom•an /ˈwʊmən/ *noun* plural **women** /ˈwɪmɪn/
an adult female person: *His mother is a very kind woman.*

wom•en /ˈwɪmɪn/ *noun*
the plural of WOMAN

won /wʌn/ *verb*
the past tense and past participle of WIN

won•der[1] /ˈwʌndɚ/ *verb*
to want to know something that you are not sure about: *I wonder if I passed the test.* | *Molly wondered why he hadn't called her.*

wonder[2] *noun*
1 *formal* a feeling of admiration and surprise: *Sam and I looked in wonder at the paintings on the walls.*
2 no wonder = used for saying that something is not surprising: *No wonder you feel sick – you ate too much!*
3 *formal* something that people admire a lot: *the wonders of nature*

won•der•ful /ˈwʌndɚfəl/ *adjective*
very good or enjoyable: *It was a wonderful party and we had a great time!* SYNONYM **great**
—**wonderfully** *adverb, formal*: *The book is wonderfully written and fun to read.*
➔ See Thesaurus box at **good**[1]

W

won't /woʊnt/ *verb*
the short form of "will not": *I won't tell you what he said.*

wood /wʊd/ *noun*
the hard material that trees are made of: *The floor is made of solid wood.* | *a piece of wood*

wood•en /ˈwʊdn/ *also* **wood** *adjective*
made from wood: *a little wooden table*

wood•land /ˈwʊdlənd/ *noun, formal*
land with a lot of trees growing on it: *In the north, there are large areas of woodland.*
➔ See Thesaurus box at **tree**

wood•peck•er /ˈwʊdˌpekɚ/ *noun*
a bird with a long beak that it uses to make holes in trees

woods /wʊdz/ *plural noun*
a small forest: *We saw a deer when we were walking in the woods.*

wood•winds /ˈwʊdˌwɪndz/ *plural noun*
the group of musical instruments that are made of wood, and that you play by blowing into them

wood•work /ˈwʊdwɚk/ *noun*
the parts of a building that are made of wood: *We painted the woodwork around the windows white.*

wool /wʊl/ *noun*
the hair on a sheep, that people use for making clothes, etc.: *This coat is made of wool.*
—**wooly** *adjective* made of wool or like wool: *a soft wooly material*
—**woolen** *adjective* made of wool

word /wɚd/ *noun*
1 a group of sounds or letters that have a particular meaning: *You can look up the words you don't know in a dictionary.*
2 words = the words of a song and not the music: *I don't know all the words to the song.*
3 a short quick talk with someone: *Peter, could I have a word with you?*
4 give someone your word = to promise someone that something is true: *I'll do it tomorrow – I give you my word.*
5 keep your word = to do what you have promised: *We can trust Jake to keep his word.*
6 some news or a message that you get: *Andy went to Texas a week ago, but we haven't had any word from him yet.*
7 a short thing that you say: *Can I give you a word of advice?*
8 not say/hear/understand/believe a word (of something) = to not say, hear, etc. anything: *I can't understand a word of this poem.*
9 in other words = used for saying something again in a clearer way: *These two pictures are identical. In other words, they are exactly the same.*
10 in your own words = describing something in your own way, rather than repeating what you have read or heard: *I want you to listen to the story, and then write it in your own words.*
11 word for word = in exactly the same words: *Tell me what he said to you, word for word.*

ˈword ˌprocessor *also* **ˈword ˌprocessing ˌprogram** *noun*
a computer program that you use for writing —**word processing** *noun* the activity of writing using a computer

word·y /ˈwɚdi/ *adjective*
using more words than is necessary: *Her descriptions are too wordy – they could be a lot shorter.*

wore /wɔr/ *verb*
the past tense of WEAR

work¹ /wɚk/ *verb*
1 to do a job to earn money: *She works in a bank.* | *I work for a computer company.* | *Lisa works as a nurse.*
2 if a plan, method, etc. works, it has the effect that you want: *I've tried that diet, but it doesn't work. I didn't lose any weight.*
3 to use time and effort to try to achieve something: *Kimiko is working hard to improve her English.*
4 to operate a machine: *Do you know how to work the printer?*
5 if a machine works, it is operating correctly: *The car radio isn't working – it needs to be fixed.*
6 be/get worked up *informal* = to be upset: *It's only a small problem, so don't get worked up about it.*
PHRASAL VERBS
work against someone or something
to not help someone or something to be successful: *If you don't have any experience, it will work against you.*
work on something
to try to repair or improve something: *I need to work on my essay before I give it to the teacher.*
work out
1 if a problem works out, it stops being a problem: *I was very worried, but everything worked out in the end.*
2 to do exercises for your body: *Sue works out in the gym twice a week.*
3 work something out = to find the answer to a question or problem, by thinking about it carefully: *Have you worked out how much the trip will cost?*

work² *noun*
1 a job that you do to earn money: *Rob's still looking for work.* | *What time do you start work in the morning?*

USAGE: work
Do not say "What is your work?" or "What is your job?". Say **"What do you do?"** or **"What kind of work do you do?"**

2 at work = doing a job, or in the place where you do your job: *At 8 o'clock, the builders were already at work.* | *I'll see you at work on Monday.*
3 something you do that uses a lot of time and effort: *Taking care of kids can be hard work.*
4 the things you produce when you are working, studying, etc.: *My teacher said that she was pleased with my work.*
5 something that an artist, writer, etc. produces that is very good or beautiful: *This painting is a work of art.*
6 out of work = if you are out of work, you do not have a job, but you want one: *Dad was out of work for six months before he found a job.*
➔ See Thesaurus box at **job**

work·a·ble /ˈwɚkəbəl/ *adjective, formal*
a workable plan, method, etc. is one you can use to achieve what you want: *This is a workable solution to the problem that will satisfy everyone.*

work·a·hol·ic /ˌwɚkəˈhɔlɪk/ *noun*
someone who chooses to work all the time: *Tom's still at the office as usual – he's a workaholic.*

work·book /ˈwɚkbʊk/ *noun*
a school book with questions and exercises in it: *student workbooks*

work·er /ˈwɚkɚ/ *noun*
someone who does a job, but who is not a manager: *Farm workers do not earn a lot of money.*

work·force /ˈwɚkfɔrs/ *noun, formal*
all the people who work in a particular country or company: *Today there are many more women in the workforce than 50 years ago.*

work·ing /ˈwɚkɪŋ/ *adjective*
1 having a job: *A lot of families have two working parents.*
2 relating to work: *The pay was bad, and there were poor working conditions.*

W

ˌworking ˈclass *noun*
the working class = all the people who usually work with their hands, and who do not have much money or power: *Children from the working class have to work harder to be successful.*
—working-class *adjective* relating to the working class: *a working-class neighborhood*

work•ings /ˈwɚkɪŋz/ *plural noun, formal*
the system that controls something: *We still don't understand the inner workings of the human brain.*

work•load /ˈwɚkloʊd/ *noun*
the amount of work that you must do: *This week I have a heavy workload* (=a lot of work to do).

work•man /ˈwɚkmən/ *noun* plural **workmen** /ˈwɚkmən/
a man who works with his hands building or repairing things: *Some workmen were repairing the road.*

work•out /ˈwɚk-aʊt/ *noun*
a time when you do exercises to keep your body healthy: *Dan does a workout at the gym every morning.*
➔ See Thesaurus box at **exercise**[2]

W

work•sheet /ˈwɚkʃit/ *noun*
a piece of paper with questions, exercises, etc. for students: *The teacher gave the students some worksheets for homework.*

work•shop /ˈwɚkʃɑp/ *noun*
1 a class where people learn how to do something: *I went to a pottery workshop on Saturday.*
2 a room or building where people make or repair things: *Dad had a workshop in the garage where he made things out of wood.*

work•week /ˈwɚkwik/ *noun*
the number of days or hours in a week that you spend working: *You will be paid for a 40-hour workweek.*

world /wɚld/ *noun*
1 the world = the Earth that we live on: *Mount Everest is the highest mountain in the world.* SYNONYM **earth**
2 all the people or countries on the Earth: *This terrible event shocked the world.*
3 the way that people live and behave in our society: *I want a better world for my kids.*
4 the animal/plant/insect world = all animals, plants, etc. as a group: *a program about the animal world*
➔ See Thesaurus box at **earth**

ˌworld ˈrecord *noun*
the fastest time, highest jump, etc. which anyone has ever achieved: *He set the world record in speed skating.*

ˌWorld ˈSeries *noun*
the World Series = the baseball games that decide the best team in the U.S. and Canada each year

world•wide /ˌwɚldˈwaɪd/ *adjective, adverb*
everywhere in the world: *The disease affects thousands of people worldwide.*

ˌWorld Wide ˈWeb *noun, written abbreviation* **WWW**
another word for the INTERNET

worm /wɚm/ *noun*
a long thin creature with a soft body and no legs that lives in the ground: *A bird was eating a worm.*

worn[1] /wɔrn/ *verb*
the past participle of WEAR

worn[2] *adjective*
if old clothes and other things look worn, they look like someone has used them a lot: *That jacket looks old and worn now.*

ˌworn ˈout *also* **worn-out** *adjective*
1 very tired: *At the end of the day, I was worn out.* SYNONYM **exhausted**
2 something that is worn out is old and does not look good any more: *Throw that old sweater away – it's worn out.*

wor•ried /ˈwɚid/ *adjective*
unhappy or anxious because you think something bad might happen: *His mother's sick, and he's worried about her.* | *I was worried that you'd had an accident.*
➔ See picture on page A23

THESAURUS: worried

anxious very worried and unable to relax: *She was anxious about her children, as they were having problems at school.*

concerned worried about a social problem, or about someone's health, safety, etc.: *Many scientists are concerned about global warming.*

nervous worried or frightened about something, and unable to relax: *I get really nervous before speaking in front of a group of people.*

uneasy worried because you think something bad might happen: *Lois felt uneasy leaving the kids alone, even though Gary was 15 and Hannah was 13.*

stress someone (out) to make someone so worried that he or she cannot relax: *I'm getting totally stressed out about work – everything has to be done by Friday.*

wor•ry¹ /ˈwɚi/ *verb* **worried**, third person singular **worries**
to feel unhappy or anxious because you think something bad might happen: *She's always worrying about getting fat.* | *I'm worried that I might fail my tests.*
—**worrier** *noun* someone who worries a lot: *My mom's a worrier.*
—**worrying** *also* **worrisome** *adjective* making you worry: *Carl's strange behavior was worrying.*

worry² *noun* plural **worries**
1 the feeling of being unhappy or anxious about something: *You could see the worry in her face.*
2 a problem that makes you feel unhappy or anxious: *Just relax for a while and try to forget your worries.*

worse¹ /wɚs/ *adjective*
1 not as good in quality as something else: *My writing is bad, but yours is worse!* ANTONYM **better**
2 more unpleasant or severe: *During the night, the storm got worse.* ANTONYM **better**
3 sicker than before: *If you're feeling worse, go see the doctor.* ANTONYM **better**

worse² *adverb*
not as well as someone or something else: *He plays baseball worse than I do.* ANTONYM **better**

worse³ *noun*
something worse: *The situation was bad, but worse was to come* (=it was going to get worse).

wors•en /ˈwɚsən/ *verb, formal*
to become worse: *The pain worsened, and we called the doctor.*

ˌworse ˈoff *adjective*
poorer, or in a worse situation: *Our family was poor, but there were people worse off than us.*

wor•ship /ˈwɚʃɪp/ *verb* **worshiped** or **worshipped**, **worshiping** or **worshipping**
to show great respect and pray to God or a god: *People come to church to worship God.*
—**worship** *noun* the act of worshiping God or a god: *Praying is an act of worship.*
—**worshiper** *also* **worshipper** *noun* someone who worships God or a god

worst¹ /wɚst/ *adjective*
1 not as good in quality than anything or anyone else: *This is the worst book I've ever read.* ANTONYM **best**
2 the most unpleasant or severe: *My headache is worst in the morning.*

worst² *adverb*
the worst/worst of all = less well or more severely than anyone or anything else: *When she died, it affected my brother the worst.*

worst³ *noun*
1 someone or something that is the most bad: *My painting was the worst and I was embarrassed to have other people see it.*
2 at worst = in a situation that is as bad as possible: *The trip will take two hours, or two and a half hours at worst.*

worth¹ /wɚθ/ *preposition*
1 if something is worth an amount, it has that value: *This painting is worth $500,000.* | *Each question is worth 4 points.*
2 used for saying that something is interesting, good, etc. to do: *The movie was definitely worth seeing.*

worth² *noun*
1 $5/25 cents', etc. worth of something = an amount of something that has a value of five dollars, 25 cents, etc.: *I bought $5 worth of apples.*
2 ten minutes'/a week's, etc. worth of something = something that takes ten minutes, a week, etc. to happen, do, or use: *There's about a week's worth of work here.*

worth•less /ˈwɚθlɪs/ *adjective, formal*
having no value: *These coins are worthless because they are not used any more.*

W

worth•while /ˌwɚθˈwaɪl/ *adjective, formal*
if something is worthwhile, it is useful or enjoyable: *It is worthwhile to check the price of the camera in several stores before you buy it.*

wor•thy /ˈwɚði/ *adjective, formal*
1 good enough to have your respect or attention: *They raised money to fight cancer, which is a worthy cause.*
2 be worthy of something = to deserve something: *He is a leader who is worthy of respect.*

would /wəd, əd; *strong* wʊd/ *verb*
1 used instead of "will" when describing what someone said or thought in the past: *She told me she wouldn't come.* | *I didn't think she would marry him.*
2 if you say that something would happen, you think it will happen if something unlikely happens first: *If I won the lottery, I would spend the money on a huge house.*
3 would have done something = if something would have happened, it might have happened, but it did not happen: *Dad would have loved this place if he'd still been alive.*
4 someone would not/wouldn't do something = used when saying that someone refused to do something: *He would not answer my question.*
5 would you ...? a) used when asking for something politely: *Would you open the door please?* **b)** used when offering someone something politely: *Would you like something to drink?*
6 used for saying that something happened regularly in the past: *When I was a kid, we would visit my grandmother every summer.*
SYNONYM **used to**

would•n't /ˈwʊdnt/ *verb*
the short form of "would not": *She wouldn't help me, even though I asked several times.*

would've /ˈwʊdəv/ *verb*
the short form of "would have": *You would've enjoyed the movie if you had seen it.*

wound[1] /wund/ *noun*
a deep cut made in your skin by a knife or bullet: *He had a knife wound in his side.*
➔ See Thesaurus box at **injury**

wound[2] *verb*
1 to injure someone, especially with a knife or gun: *Several people were wounded in the attack.*
2 to make someone feel unhappy or upset: *His cruel remarks wounded her.*
—**wounded** *adjective* injured by a weapon such as a gun or a knife: *a wounded soldier*
➔ See Thesaurus box at **hurt**[1]

wound[3] /waʊnd/ *verb*
the past tense and past participle of WIND

wove /woʊv/ *verb*
the past tense of WEAVE

wo•ven /ˈwoʊvən/ *verb*
the past participle of WEAVE

wow /waʊ/ *informal*
said when you think something is impressive or surprising: *Wow, what a beautiful house!*

wrap /ræp/ *verb* **wrapped, wrapping**
1 to cover a present with attractive paper: *I haven't wrapped the Christmas presents yet.*
2 to put a piece of cloth or paper around something: *She wrapped the baby in a blanket.*
3 wrap your arms around someone = to hold someone by putting your arms around him or her: *She wrapped her arms around him and squeezed tight.*
—**wrapping** *noun* paper or cloth that is put around something

wrap•per /ˈræpɚ/ *noun*
the paper or plastic that covers something you buy: *a candy wrapper*
➔ See Thesaurus box at **cover**[2]

ˈwrapping ˌpaper *noun*
colored paper that you use to wrap presents: *a roll of wrapping paper*

wrath /ræθ/ *noun, formal*
very great anger: *They all hoped to avoid the king's wrath.*
—**wrathful** *adjective, formal* very angry

wreath /riθ/ *noun*
a circle of leaves or flowers that you use as a decoration: *They put a wreath on their front door around Christmas.*

wreck[1] /rek/ *verb, informal*
to destroy something completely: *The truck was wrecked in the accident.* | *His constant lying wrecked his marriage.*

wreck[2] *noun*
1 a bad accident involving cars or airplanes: *He was killed in a car wreck.* SYNONYM **crash**
2 a car, airplane, or ship that has been very badly damaged in an accident: *He was still alive when they pulled him from the wreck.*

wreck•age /ˈrekɪdʒ/ *noun, formal*
the broken parts of a vehicle or building that has been destroyed: *She pulled the driver from the wreckage of the truck after the accident.*

wren /ren/ *noun*
a very small brown bird

wrench[1] /rentʃ/ *verb*
1 to twist and pull something from somewhere, using force: *Tom wrenched the nail out of the wall.*
2 to injure a part of your body by twisting it suddenly: *He wrenched his neck when he turned his head suddenly.*

wrench[2] *noun*
a metal tool that you use for turning metal parts and making them tighter: *I used a wrench to fix the faucet.*

wres•tle /ˈresəl/ *verb*
1 to fight by holding someone and trying to push him or her to the ground: *The two men wrestled with each other.*
2 to wrestle with someone as a sport: *He's very strong – he wrestled in high school.*
—**wrestling** *noun* a sport in which two people wrestle
—**wrestler** *noun* someone who wrestles as a sport

wretch•ed /ˈretʃɪd/ *adjective*
1 very unhappy or in a very bad situation: *These wretched people have lost their homes in the floods.*
2 *informal* very bad: *wretched weather*

wrig•gle /ˈrɪgəl/ *verb*
to twist quickly from side to side: *She wriggled into the tight dress.*

wring /rɪŋ/ *also* **wring out** *verb* **wrung** /rʌŋ/
to twist wet cloth to remove water from it: *Wring out the cloth when you've finished washing the dishes.*

wrin•kle /ˈrɪŋkəl/ *noun*
1 a line on your face that you get when you are old: *The old woman's face was covered in wrinkles.*
2 a fold in a piece of clothing that you do not want: *You'll have to iron the shirt to get rid of the wrinkles.*
—**wrinkled** *adjective* covered with wrinkles: *My clothes were wrinkled when I took them out of my suitcase.*

wrist /rɪst/ *noun*
the joint between your hand and your arm: *She had a bracelet on her wrist.*
➔ See picture at **hand**[1]

write /raɪt/ *verb* **wrote** /roʊt/ **written** /ˈrɪtn/ **writing**
1 to make letters or words on paper, using a pen or pencil: *We're teaching the children to read and write.* | *Please write your name on this piece of paper.*
2 to produce a letter to send to someone: *Have you written to Mom yet?* | *He wrote me a letter.*
3 to produce a story, book, song, etc.: *He wrote several books.*

PHRASAL VERB

write something down
to write something on a piece of paper: *I wrote down her phone number so I wouldn't forget it.*

writ•er /ˈraɪtɚ/ *noun*
someone who writes books: *She's a writer of children's books.*

writ•ing /ˈraɪtɪŋ/ *noun*
1 words that are written by hand or printed: *I can't read the writing on the label – it's very small.*
2 the activity of writing stories, books, etc.: *Writing is fun if you have an interesting story to tell.*
3 the particular way someone writes with a pen or pencil: *I recognized Sue's writing on the envelope, so I knew the letter was from her.* SYNONYM **handwriting**

writ•ten /ˈrɪtn/ *verb*
the past participle of WRITE

wrong /rɔŋ/ *adjective*
1 not correct: *You're wrong – I don't live on Northwest Avenue; I live on North Street.* | *the wrong answer* ANTONYM **right**

W

THESAURUS: wrong

incorrect *formal* used about facts, answers, etc. that are completely wrong: *The date given in the book was incorrect – it happened in 1974, not 1977.*

inaccurate *formal* used about information, a number, etc. that is not completely right: *The reports about the event in the newspapers were inaccurate.*

misleading *formal* used about information that makes people believe something that is not true: *The TV commercial is misleading, because it makes kids think the juice is good for you. Really, the juice has too much sugar in it.*

false used about facts that are not true and wrong: *The rumor that Mrs. Hudson was leaving the school was false.*

be mistaken *formal* used about a person who thinks something is true when it is not: *No, I've never been to Chicago. You must be mistaken.*

2 not morally right: *Some people think it's wrong to kill animals for food.* ANTONYM **right**
3 not appropriate: *You're wearing the wrong shoes for an exercise class.* ANTONYM **right**

wrong•do•ing /ˌrɔŋˈduɪŋ/ *noun, formal*
illegal actions or immoral behavior: *Police are investigating whether there was any actual wrongdoing.*
—**wrongdoer** *noun, formal* someone who does something illegal or immoral: *All wrongdoers will be punished.*

wrong•ly /ˈrɔŋli/ *adverb*
in a way that is incorrect, unfair, or immoral: *He was wrongly accused of stealing.*

wrote /roʊt/ *verb*
the past tense of WRITE

wrung /rʌŋ/ *verb*
the past tense and past participle of WRING

WWW *noun*
the abbreviation for WORLD WIDE WEB

X

Xx

X[1]
the number 10 in the system of ROMAN NUMERALS

X[2] /eks/
PHRASAL VERB
X something out
to put an X on top of something in a piece of writing: *She X'd out the misspelled word and wrote it correctly above the X.* SYNONYM **cross something out**

X•mas /ˈkrɪsməs/ *noun, informal*
an informal way of writing "Christmas": *Merry Xmas!*

X-ray[1] /ˈeks reɪ/ *noun*
1 a special kind of light that doctors can use to take photographs of the inside of the body: *X-rays can damage human cells.*
2 a photograph of the inside of someone's body, made using an X-ray: *The X-ray showed that her leg was not broken.*

X-ray

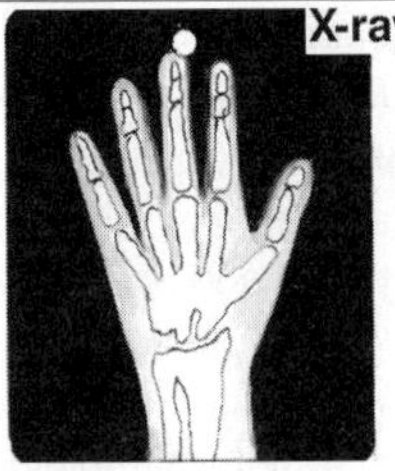

X-ray[2] *verb*
to photograph part of someone's body using X-RAYS: *The doctor X-rayed his arm to see if it was broken.*

xy•lo•phone /ˈzaɪləˌfoʊn/ *noun*
a musical instrument with flat metal wooden bars that you hit with a stick
➔ See picture on page A21

Yy

yacht /yɑt/ *noun*
a large expensive boat used for sailing, racing, or traveling for pleasure: *He was sailing his yacht.*

yacht

y'all /yɔl/ *pronoun, informal*
a word meaning "all of you," used mainly in the southern U.S.: *How are y'all doing?*

yam /yæm/ *noun*
another word for a SWEET POTATO

yank /yæŋk/ *verb*
to pull something quickly and with force: *One of the boys grabbed her hair and yanked on it.*

Yan•kee /ˈyæŋki/ *noun*
1 a soldier who fought on the side of the Union (=the northern states) during the American Civil War
2 a name for someone from the U.S., used by people from other countries
3 a name for someone from the northern states of the U.S., used by people from the southern states

yard /yɑrd/ *noun*
1 the land around a house, usually covered with grass: *The kids were playing in the front yard.*
2 *written abbreviation* **yd.** a unit for measuring length, equal to 3 feet or 0.9144 meters: *The beach was only a hundred yards from my back door.*

yard•age /ˈyɑrdɪdʒ/ *noun*
the size of something measured in yards or square yards: *What yardage of this fabric do you need?*

ˈyard sale *noun*
a sale of used clothes, furniture, toys, etc. from someone's house that takes place in his or her yard: *We sold a lot of our old stuff at the yard sale last Saturday.*

yard•stick /ˈyɑrdˌstɪk/ *noun*
1 *formal* something that you compare another thing with, in order to judge how good or successful it is: *The test results are used as a yardstick for measuring the children's progress.*
2 a special stick that is exactly one yard long, which you use for measuring

yarn /yɑrn/ *noun*
thick thread that you use for KNITting: *She used pink yarn to knit a scarf.*

yawn /yɔn/ *verb*
to open your mouth wide and breathe deeply because you are tired or bored: *He was so tired that he couldn't stop yawning.*
—**yawn** *noun* an act of yawning: *"I'm going to bed," Steve said with a yawn.*

yawn

yd.
the written abbreviation of YARD

yeah /yəe/ *adverb, informal*
yes: *"Do you want to come with us?" "Yeah, OK."*

year /yɪr/ *noun*
1 a period of 12 months or 365 days: *I have lived here for two years.* | *Next year I will be sixteen.* | *Julie is seven years old.*
2 **in/for years** = for a very long time: *I haven't talked to Mark in years.*

year•book /ˈyɪrbʊk/ *noun*
a book that a school produces every year with information about its students and activities: *He asked her to sign his high school yearbook.*

year•ly /ˈyɪrli/ *adjective, adverb*
every year: *Every athlete should have a yearly physical.* | *How much do you spend yearly on clothes?*

ˈyear-round *adjective, adverb*
continuing through the whole year: *The good weather here allows visitors to play golf year-round.* | *year-round school*

yeast /yist/ *noun*
a substance that you use when you are making bread in order to make it rise

yell /yel/ *verb*
to shout something very loudly: *"Come back!" he yelled.* | *Don't yell at me! Speak to me in a calm voice.*
—**yell** *noun* a loud shout: *He gave a yell when his team scored.*
→ See Thesaurus box at **shout**[1]

yel•low /ˈyeloʊ/ *adjective*
something that is yellow is the color of a LEMON or a BANANA: *a yellow flower*
—**yellow** *noun* a yellow color: *Yellow is my favorite color.*

ˈYellow ˌPages *noun*
the Yellow Pages = a book that contains the telephone numbers and addresses of businesses and organizations in a particular area: *All the local restaurants are listed in the Yellow Pages.*

yes /yes/ *adverb*
1 said to answer a question and show that something is true: *"Are you Ann?" "Yes, I am."* ANTONYM **no**
2 said when you agree with something: *"This is fun!" "Yes, it is."* ANTONYM **no**
3 said when you disagree with someone's negative question or statement: *"There isn't any bread left." "Yes, there is. It's on the table."*
4 said to show that you are excited about something that has happened: *Yes! Yes! We won!*

yes•ter•day /ˈyestɚdi/ *adverb, noun*
the day before today: *I went swimming yesterday.* | *How did you do on yesterday's test?*

yet[1] /yet/ *adverb*
1 used in questions and negative sentences to say that something that you expect to happen has not happened: *Have you eaten yet?* | *I don't think she's awake yet; she's still in her bedroom.*

USAGE: yet

Yet is used in questions and in sentences with "not" in them to talk about something that you expect to happen, but which has not happened: *I haven't finished the book yet.* | *Is Mark back from lunch yet?*

Still is used to say that a situation that began in the past has not changed and is continuing: *He still lives with his parents.*

Always means "all the time" or "every time": *Her clothes are always so nice.* | *I always see him on Tuesdays.*

2 *formal* used for saying that something could still happen: *She may yet call me before the end of the week.*
3 used to emphasize that something is in addition to what has already existed or happened: *Bob made yet another mistake – he needs to be more careful.* | *You were late yet again this morning – that's the fourth time this week.*
4 the best/biggest/most important, etc. yet = used to say that something is the best, biggest, most important, etc. that has existed up to the present time: *This is his best movie yet.*

yet[2] *conjunction*
used to introduce something that is surprising after what you have just said: *Tanner was a criminal, yet many people admired him.*

yield[1] /yild/ *verb*
1 *formal* to do what someone wants, although you do not want to: *He yielded to pressure from his family to return home.*
2 to allow cars from another road to go first: *If other cars are coming, you have to yield.*
3 *formal* to produce something: *Our research has yielded some interesting results.*

yield[2] *noun, formal*
the amount that something produces: *Scientists are trying to find out how to produce higher yields from crops.*

yo•ga /ˈyoʊgə/ *noun*
a system of exercises that relax you and make your muscles stronger: *She does yoga for half an hour every morning to stretch her muscles.*

yoga

yo•gurt /ˈyoʊgɚt/ *noun*
a thick liquid food that is made from milk and has a slightly sour taste: *strawberry yogurt*

yoke /youk/ *noun*
a wooden bar used for keeping two animals together when they are pulling heavy loads: *The farmer attached the yoke to the two horses.*
—**yoke** *verb* to put a yoke on two animals

yolk /youk/ *noun*
the yellow part of an egg: *He dipped his toast in the egg yolk.*

you /yə; *before vowels* yʊ; *strong* yu/ *pronoun*
1 the person or people someone is talking to: *Would you like some coffee?* | *I can't hear you.* | *What do you all* (=more than one person) *want to do tonight?*
2 people in general: *Smoking is bad for you.*

you'd /yəd; *strong* yud/
1 the short form of "you would": *You'd be surprised at how much money she spends on clothes.*
2 the short form of "you had": *If you'd been more careful, the accident would never have happened.*

you'll /yəl; *strong* yul/
the short form of "you will": *You'll have to fill out this form.*

young[1] /yʌŋ/ *adjective*
someone who is young has only lived for a short time: *You're too young to get married.* | *a young child* | *My father is 60, but he still looks young.* ANTONYM **old**

young[2] *plural noun*
1 the young = young people in general: *The young often know more about computers than their parents.*
2 young animals: *A mouse can produce 150 young a year.*

young·ster /ˈyʌŋstɚ/ *noun*
a child, or a young person who is not an adult: *A lot of youngsters enjoy going to summer camp.*

your /yɚ; *strong* yʊr/ *adjective*
belonging to the person or people you are speaking to: *Is this your sweater?* | *I want you to turn in your essays on Friday.*

you're /yɚ; *strong* yʊr/
the short form of "you are": *You're taller than I am.*

yours /yɔrz/ *pronoun*
something belonging or relating to you: *Is this bicycle yours?* | *A friend of yours called this morning.*

your·self /yɚˈself/ *pronoun* plural **yourselves** /yɚˈselvz/
1 used as an object to show that the someone you are talking to is affected by his or her own action: *Be careful, or you'll hurt yourself.* | *Make yourself a cup of coffee.*
2 used to emphasize "you": *You told me that joke yourself – don't blame Beth.*
3 by yourself = alone or without help: *Don't try to lift that box by yourself.*

youth /yuθ/ *noun* plural **youths** /yuðz, yuθs/ *formal*
1 the time when you are young: *She was very pretty in her youth, but she got much heavier when she got older.*
2 a boy or young man: *A police officer arrested two youths for vandalism.*
3 young people: *The youth of today have grown up with computers.*

youth·ful /ˈyuθfəl/ *adjective, formal*
typical of young people: *The students were full of youthful energy.*

you've /yəv; *strong* yuv/
the short form of "you have": *You've eaten all the cake!*

yo-yo /ˈyouyou/ *noun*
a small toy that goes up and down on a string that you hold and move

yuck·y /ˈyʌki/ *adjective, informal*
you use this for describing something that you think is very unpleasant: *This juice tastes yucky – I'm not going to drink it.*

yum·my /ˈyʌmi/ *adjective, informal*
tasting very good: *The cookies are yummy – can I have more?*

yup /yʌp/ *informal*
another word for YES

yup·pie /ˈyʌpi/ *noun, informal*
a young person who earns a lot of money and buys expensive things: *A lot of wealthy yuppies live downtown.*

Y

Zz

zeal /zil/ *noun, formal*
the state of being very eager to do something: *Other people did not share his zeal for the project.*
—**zealous** *adjective, formal* full of zeal: *She was zealous in doing her job, showing up early and staying late.*

ze•bra /ˈzibrə/ *noun*
a wild African animal like a horse with black and white lines on its body

ze•ro[1] /ˈzɪroʊ/ *number*
1 the number 0
2 0° in the FAHRENHEIT or CELSIUS systems: *It was 5° below zero last night.*
3 a situation in which there is none of something: *It's very safe – the risk is almost zero.*

zero[2] *verb*
PHRASAL VERB
zero in on someone or something
to direct all your attention to one person or thing: *The teacher looked around the room, and zeroed in on me.*

Z

zig•zag /ˈzɪgzæg/ *noun*
a line or pattern that is like a row of z's: *The road went in a zigzag up the mountain.*

zil•lion /ˈzɪlyən/ *number, informal*
an extremely large number: *My brother has a zillion DVDs at home.* | *There were zillions of mosquitoes in the woods.*

zinc /zɪŋk/ *noun*
a white metal that has many uses

zip /zɪp/ *verb* **zipped, zipping**
1 *also* **zip up** to close or fasten something with a ZIPPER: *Zip up your coat; it's cold outside.* ANTONYM **unzip**
2 to go somewhere very quickly: *Two police cars zipped past.*
➔ See Thesaurus box at **fasten**

ˈzip code *noun*
a number that you put below the address on an envelope, which shows the exact area to deliver it

zip•per /ˈzɪpɚ/ *noun*
something you use for fastening clothes, bags, etc., with two lines of metal or plastic that slide together: *The zipper on my coat is broken, so I can't close it.*
➔ See picture on page A6

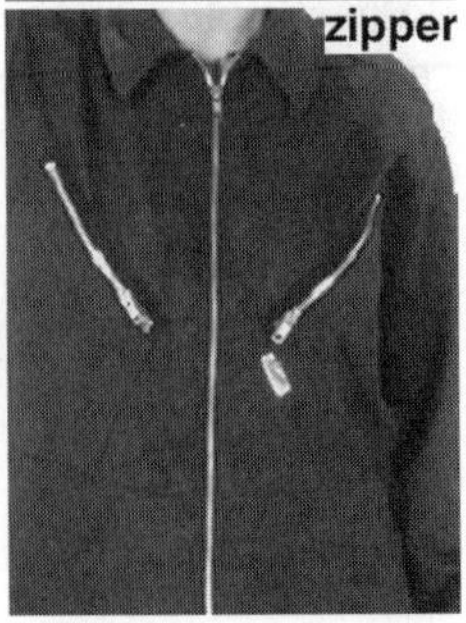
zipper

zit /zɪt/ *noun, informal*
another word for a PIMPLE: *She says that if she eats chocolate, she gets more zits.*
➔ See Thesaurus box at **mark**[2]

zo•di•ac /ˈzoʊdiˌæk/ *noun*
the zodiac = a circle of twelve areas in the sky through which the Sun, Moon, stars, etc. appear to travel, which some people believe influence our lives: *Libra is one of the signs of the zodiac.*

zom•bie /ˈzɑmbi/ *noun*
a dead body that moves, walks, etc. by magic: *a movie about monsters and zombies*

zone /zoʊn/ *noun*
an area with a particular purpose or quality, or special rules: *You can't park there – it's a no-parking zone.*
➔ **time zone**
➔ See Thesaurus box at **area**

zoo /zu/ *noun*
a place where many different animals are kept, so people can go and see them: *We saw elephants and monkeys at the zoo.*

zo•ol•o•gy /zoʊˈɑlədʒi/ *noun, formal*
the study of animals and their behavior

zoom /zum/ *verb, informal*
1 to go somewhere very quickly: *An airplane zoomed into the air.*
2 if a camera zooms in or out, it makes the thing you are taking a picture of seem larger or smaller: *He zoomed in on the deer on the other side of the river.*
—**zoom** *also* **ˈzoom lens** *noun* a feature on a camera that allows it to make things that are far away look like they are closer

zuc•chi•ni /zuˈkini/ *noun*
a long smooth green vegetable
➔ See picture on page A12

IRREGULAR VERBS

This chart shows the verbs that have irregular forms for the **Past Tense**, **Past Participle**, or **Present Participle**. When a verb has more than one form that is used, the most common form is given first.

Verb	Past Tense	Past Participle	Present Participle
arise	arose	arisen	arising
awake	awoke	awoken	awaking
be	was/were	been	being
bear	bore	borne	bearing
beat	beat	beaten	beating
become	became	become	becoming
begin	began	begun	beginning
bend	bent	bent	bending
bet	bet	bet	betting
bid[2]	bid	bid	bidding
bite	bit	bitten	biting
bleed	bled	bled	bleeding
blow	blew	blown	blowing
break	broke	broken	breaking
breed	bred	bred	breeding
bring	brought	brought	bringing
broadcast	broadcast *or* broadcasted	broadcast *or* broadcasted	broadcasting
build	built	built	building
burn	burned *or* burnt	burned *or* burnt	burning
burst	burst	burst	bursting
buy	bought	bought	buying
cast	cast	cast	casting
catch	caught	caught	catching
choose	chose	chosen	choosing
cling	clung	clung	clinging
come	came	come	coming
cost	cost	cost	costing
creep	crept	crept	creeping
cut	cut	cut	cutting
deal	dealt	dealt	dealing
dig	dug	dug	digging
dive	dived *or* dove	dived	diving
do	did	done	doing
draw	drew	drawn	drawing
dream	dreamed *or* dreamt	dreamed *or* dreamt	dreaming
drink	drank	drunk	drinking
drive	drove	driven	driving
dwell	dwelled *or* dwelt	dwelled *or* dwelt	dwelling
eat	ate	eaten	eating
fall	fell	fallen	falling
feed	fed	fed	feeding
feel	felt	felt	feeling
fight	fought	fought	fighting
find	found	found	finding
fit	fit or fitted	fit or fitted	fitting
flee	fled	fled	fleeing
fling	flung	flung	flinging
fly	flew	flown	flying
forbid	forbid *or* forbade	forbidden	forbidding
foresee	foresaw	foreseen	foreseeing
forget	forgot	forgotten	forgetting
forgive	forgave	forgiven	forgiving
freeze	froze	frozen	freezing

Verb	Past Tense	Past Participle	Present Participle
get	got	gotten	getting
give	gave	given	giving
go	went	gone	going
grind	ground	ground	grinding
grow	grew	grown	growing
hang	hung	hung	hanging
have	had	had	having
hear	heard	heard	hearing
hide	hid	hidden	hiding
hit	hit	hit	hitting
hold	held	held	holding
hurt	hurt	hurt	hurting
keep	kept	kept	keeping
kneel	knelt *or* kneeled	knelt *or* kneeled	kneeling
knit	knit *or* knitted	knit *or* knitted	knitting
know	knew	known	knowing
lay	laid	laid	laying
lead	led	led	leading
leap	leaped *or* leapt	leaped *or* leapt	leaping
leave	left	left	leaving
lend	lent	lent	lending
let	let	let	letting
lie[1]	lay	lain	lying
lie[2]	lied	lied	lying
light	lit *or* lighted	lit *or* lighted	lighting
lose	lost	lost	losing
make	made	made	making
mean	meant	meant	meaning
meet	met	met	meeting
mislead	misled	misled	misleading
mistake	mistook	mistaken	mistaking
misunderstand	misunderstood	misunderstood	misunderstanding
outdo	outdid	outdone	outdoing
overcome	overcame	overcome	overcoming
overdo	overdid	overdone	overdoing
overhear	overheard	overheard	overhearing
overthrow	overthrew	overthrown	overthrowing
pay	paid	paid	paying
prove	proved	proved *or* proven	proving
put	put	put	putting
read	read	read	reading
redo	redid	redone	redoing
repay	repaid	repaid	repaying
rewrite	rewrote	rewritten	rewriting
ride	rode	ridden	riding
ring[2]	rang	rung	ringing
rise	rose	risen	rising
run	ran	run	running
saw	sawed	sawed *or* sawn	sawing
say	said	said	saying
see	saw	seen	seeing
seek	sought	sought	seeking
sell	sold	sold	selling
send	sent	sent	sending
set	set	set	setting
sew	sewed	sewn *or* sewed	sewing
shake	shook	shaken	shaking
shed	shed	shed	shedding
shine	shone	shone	shining

Verb	Past Tense	Past Participle	Present Participle
shoot	shot	shot	shooting
show	showed	shown	showing
shrink	shrank	shrunk	shrinking
shut	shut	shut	shutting
sing	sang	sung	singing
sink	sank *or* sunk	sunk	sinking
sit	sat	sat	sitting
sleep	slept	slept	sleeping
slide	slid	slid	sliding
slit	slit	slit	slitting
sow	sowed	sown *or* sowed	sowing
speak	spoke	spoken	speaking
speed	sped *or* speeded	sped *or* speeded	speeding
spend	spent	spent	spending
spin	spun	spun	spinning
spit	spit *or* spat	spit *or* spat	spitting
split	split	split	splitting
spread	spread	spread	spreading
spring	sprang	sprung	springing
stand	stood	stood	standing
steal	stole	stolen	stealing
stick	stuck	stuck	sticking
sting	stung	stung	stinging
stink	stank *or* stunk	stunk	stinking
stride	strode	stridden	striding
strike	struck	struck *or* stricken	striking
string	strung	strung	stringing
strive	strove *or* strived	striven *or* strived	striving
swear	swore	sworn	swearing
sweep	swept	swept	sweeping
swell	swelled	swollen	swelling
swim	swam	swum	swimming
swing	swung	swung	swinging
take	took	taken	taking
teach	taught	taught	teaching
tear	tore	torn	tearing
tell	told	told	telling
think	thought	thought	thinking
throw	threw	thrown	throwing
thrust	thrust	thrust	thrusting
undergo	underwent	undergone	undergoing
understand	understood	understood	understanding
undo	undid	undone	undoing
unwind	unwound	unwound	unwinding
uphold	upheld	upheld	upholding
upset	upset	upset	upsetting
wake	woke	woken	waking
wear	wore	worn	wearing
weave	wove	woven	weaving
weep	wept	wept	weeping
wet	wet *or* wetted	wet *or* wetted	wetting
win	won	won	winning
wind	wound	wound	winding
withdraw	withdrew	withdrawn	withdrawing
withhold	withheld	withheld	withholding
withstand	withstood	withstood	withstanding
wring	wrung	wrung	wringing
write	wrote	written	writing

SCHOOL CONTENT VOCABULARY

1 Art

abstract, *adjective*
architecture, *noun*
art, *noun*
artist, *noun*
artistic, *adjective*
background, *noun*
ceramics, *plural noun*
chalk, *noun*
composition, *noun*
craft, *noun*
crayon, *noun*
creative, *adjective*
criticism, *noun*
design, *noun*
design, *verb*
draw, *verb*
drawing, *noun*
easel, *noun*
exhibit, *verb*
exhibit, *noun*
genre, *noun*
graphic, *adjective*
illustrate, *verb*
illustration, *noun*
imagery, *noun*
landscape, *noun*
nude, *noun*
paint, *noun*
paint, *verb*
painter, *noun*
painting, *noun*
passage, *noun*
pastel, *adjective*
pattern, *noun*
photograph, *noun*
photograph, *verb*
photography, *noun*
picture, *noun*
picture, *verb*
piece, *noun*
portfolio, *noun*
portrait, *noun*
pose, *verb*
pose, *noun*
pottery, *noun*
primary color, *noun*
print, *noun*
produce, *verb*
profile, *noun*
realistic, *adjective*
reproduction, *noun*
sculptor, *noun*
sculpture, *noun*
shade, *noun*
show, *noun*
sketch, *noun*
sketch, *verb*
statue, *noun*
stencil, *verb*
stroke, *noun*
studio, *noun*
symbol, *noun*
tapestry, *noun*
title, *noun*
watercolour, *noun*
weave, *verb*
work, *noun*

2 Biology

abdomen, *noun*
acute, *adjective*
adult, *noun*
AIDS, *noun*
allergic, *adjective*
allergy, *noun*
amoeba, *noun*
amphibian, *noun*
anatomy, *noun*
anemia, *noun*
anesthesia, *noun*
anesthetic, *noun*
animal, *noun*
antenna, *noun*
antibiotic, *noun*
antihistamine, *noun*
appendicitis, *noun*
appendix, *noun*
artery, *noun*
arthritis, *noun*
aspirin, *noun*
asthma, *noun*
backbone, *noun*
bacteria, *plural noun*
beak, *noun*
biologist, *noun*
biology, *noun*
bird, *noun*
birth, *noun*
bladder, *noun*
bleed, *verb*
blind, *adjective*
blood, *noun*
blood pressure, *noun*
blood vessel, *noun*
bloodstream, *noun*
body, *noun*
bone, *noun*
botany, *noun*
bowel, *noun*
brain, *noun*
branch, *noun*
breast, *noun*
breathe, *verb*
breed, *noun*
breed, *noun*
bruise, *verb*
bud, *verb*
bug, *noun*
butterfly, *noun*
calorie, *noun*
cancer, *noun*
carbohydrate, *noun*
carnivore, *noun*
cat, *noun*
caterpillar, *noun*
cell, *noun*
caesarean, *noun*
chemotherapy, *noun*
cholesterol, *noun*
chromosome, *noun*
circulate, *verb*
circulation, *noun*
citrus, *noun*
claw, *verb*
clone, *verb*
clot, *verb*
cold, *noun*
cold-blooded, *adjective*
colon, *noun*
coma, *noun*
conceive, *verb*
conception, *noun*
concussion, *noun*
condition, *noun*
cone, *noun*
conscious, *adjective*
consciousness, *noun*
conservation, *noun*
conservationist, *noun*
conserve, *verb*
constipation, *noun*
contagious, *adjective*
contract, *verb*
coral, *noun*
core, *noun*
cough, *noun*
cub, *noun*
curable, *adjective*
cure, *noun*
cure, *verb*
cycle, *noun*
cyclic, *adjective*
deaf, *adjective*
death, *noun*
decay, *verb*
decay, *noun*
decompose, *verb*
decomposition, *noun*
dehydrated, *adjective*
dehydration, *noun*
den, *noun*
dental, *adjective*
develop, *verb*
development, *noun*
diabetes, *noun*
diabetic, *noun*
diagnose, *verb*
diagnosis, *noun*
diarrhea, *noun*
diet, *verb*
digest, *verb*
digestion, *noun*
disease, *noun*

DNA, *noun*
drug, *noun*
duct, *noun*
egg, *noun*
embryo, *noun*
endangered species, *noun*
enzyme, *noun*
epidemic, *noun*
epilepsy, *noun*
evergreen, *adjective*
evolution, *noun*
evolutionary, *adjective*
exhale, *verb*
extinct, *adjective*
extinction, *noun*
eyesight, *noun*
farsighted, *adjective*
fat, *noun*
feline, *adjective*
female, *noun*
female, *adjective*
fetus, *noun*
fever, *noun*
fiber, *noun*
fin, *noun*
fir, *noun*
fish, *noun*
flipper, *noun*
flower, *verb*
flu, *noun*
fly, *noun*
foliage, *noun*
fossil, *noun*
fracture, *noun*
fracture, *verb*
fruit, *noun*
fungus, *noun*
fur, *adjective*
gender, *noun*
gene, *noun*
genetics, *noun*
germ, *noun*
gill, *noun*
gland, *noun*
grass, *noun*
grow, *verb*
gynecology, *noun*
habitat, *noun*
hatch, *verb*
heal, *verb*
health, *noun*
healthy, *adjective*
hear, *verb*
hearing, *noun*
heart, *noun*
heart attack, *noun*
heartbeat, *noun*
hepatitis, *noun*
herb, *noun*
herbivore, *noun*
herd, *noun*
heterosexual, *adjective*
hibernate, *verb*
hibernation, *noun*
HIV, *noun*
hormone, *noun*
horn, *noun*
human, *adjective*
human being, *noun*
hygiene, *noun*
hygienic, *adjective*
illness, *noun*
immune, *adjective*
immune system, *noun*
immunity, *noun*
immunization, *noun*
immunize, *verb*
indigestion, *noun*
inedible, *adjective*
infect, *verb*
infected, *adjective*
infection, *noun*
infectious, *adjective*
inflamed, *verb*
inflammation, *noun*
inhale, *verb*
inherit, *verb*
inject, *verb*
injection, *noun*
injure, *verb*
injury, *noun*
inner, *adjective*
inoculate, *verb*
inoculation, *noun*
insect, *noun*
insomnia, *noun*
instinct, *noun*
instinctive, *adjective*
insulin, *noun*
intelligence, *noun*
intelligent, *adjective*
internal, *adjective*
intestinal, *adjective*
intestine, *noun*
invertebrate, *noun*
involuntary, *adjective*
iron, *noun*
jaw, *noun*
joint, *noun*
kidney, *noun*
larva, *noun*
leaf, *noun*
leukemia, *noun*
life, *noun*
life cycle, *noun*
limb, *noun*
liver, *noun*
lung, *noun*
malaria, *noun*
male, *adjective*
male, *noun*
malnutrition, *noun*
mammal, *noun*
marine, *adjective*
mate, *noun*
mate, *verb*
mature, *adjective*
mature, *verb*
measles, *noun*
medical, *adjective*
medication, *noun*
medicinal, *adjective*
medicine, *noun*
memory, *noun*
menopause, *noun*
menstrual, *adjective*
menstruate, *verb*
menstruation, *noun*
mental, *adjective*
mental illness, *noun*
mentally, *adverb*
mentally ill, *adjective*
microbe, *noun*
migraine, *noun*
migrate, *verb*
migratory, *adjective*
mold, *noun*
mold, *verb*
molecular, *adjective*
molecule, *noun*
nasal, *adjective*
nature, *noun*
nausea, *noun*
nearsighted, *adjective*
nerve, *noun*
nervous, *adjective*
nostril, *noun*
nourish, *verb*
nourishment, *noun*
nucleus, *noun*
nut, *noun*
nutrient, *noun*
nutrition, *noun*
nutritional, *adjective*
nutritious, *adjective*
obese, *adjective*
obesity, *noun*
operate, *verb*
operation, *noun*
oral, *adjective*
organ, *noun*
organic, *adjective*
organism, *noun*
ovary, *noun*
pack, *noun*
pain, *noun*
palate, *noun*
paralysis, *noun*
paralyze, *verb*
parasite, *noun*
pass out, *phrasal verb*
passage, *noun*
pelvis, *noun*
penicillin, *noun*
period, *noun*
perspire, *verb*
petal, *noun*
pharmaceutical, *adjective*
physical, *adjective*
physiology, *noun*
physiotherapy, *noun*
physique, *noun*
plague, *noun*
plankton, *noun*
plant, *noun*
plaque, *noun*
plastic surgery, *noun*
pneumonia, *noun*
pod, *noun*
polio, *noun*
pollen, *noun*
pollinate, *verb*
predator, *noun*
pregnancy, *noun*
pregnant, *adjective*

prey, *noun*
protein, *noun*
psychiatry, *noun*
psychology, *noun*
puberty, *noun*
pulse, *noun*
pupil, *noun*
pus, *noun*
rash, *noun*
remedy, *noun*
reproduce, *verb*
reproduction, *noun*
reptile, *noun*
retina, *noun*
revive, *verb*
rib, *noun*
rib cage, *noun*
ripe, *adjective*
ripen, *verb*
rodent, *noun*
root, *noun*
rot, *verb*
rotten, *adjective*
saliva, *noun*
sap, *noun*
saturated fat, *noun*
scale, *noun*
scan, *noun*
scar, *noun*
schizophrenia, *noun*
school, *noun*
sedative, *noun*
seed, *noun*
seizure, *noun*
sense, *noun*
sensitive, *adjective*
sex, *noun*
sexual, *adjective*
shed, *verb*
shell, *noun*
shellfish, *noun*
shoal, *noun*
shock, *noun*
shoot, *noun*
shrub, *noun*
sick, *adjective*
sickness, *noun*
side effect, *noun*
sight, *noun*
skeleton, *noun*
skin, *noun*
skull, *noun*
smallpox, *noun*
smell, *noun*
snout, *noun*
species, *noun*
sperm, *noun*
spine, *noun*
sprout, *verb*
sprout, *noun*
stalk, *noun*
starch, *verb*
starve, *verb*
stem, *noun*
sterile, *adjective*
stimulate, *verb*
stimulus, *noun*
sting, *verb*
sting, *noun*
stomach, *noun*
stomachache, *noun*
stroke, *noun*
suffocate, *verb*
sugar, *noun*
surgery, *noun*
survival, *noun*
sweat, *verb*
sweat, *noun*
symptom, *noun*
tadpole, *noun*
tail, *noun*
tame, *adjective*
taste, *noun*
temperature, *noun*
tentacle, *noun*
test, *noun*
test, *verb*
therapy, *noun*
throat, *noun*
thyroid, *noun*
tissue, *noun*
tongue, *noun*
tooth, *noun*
toothache, *noun*
touch, *noun*
tranquilizer, *noun*
transplant, *noun*
treat, *verb*
treatment, *noun*
tree, *noun*
trunk, *noun*
tuberculosis, *noun*
tumor, *noun*
tusk, *noun*
twin, *noun*
typhoid, *noun*
unconscious, *adjective*
undernourished, *adjective*
unhealthy, *adjective*
vaccine, *noun*
vein, *noun*
vertebra, *noun*
vessel, *noun*
viral, *adjective*
virus, *noun*
vitamin, *noun*
warm-blooded, *adjective*
wild, *adjective*
wild, *noun*
wildflower, *noun*
wildlife, *noun*
wing, *noun*
wisdom tooth, *noun*
world, *noun*
wound, *noun*
wound, *verb*
x-ray, *noun*
x-ray, *verb*
young, *noun*
zoology, *noun*

3 Business

administrator, *noun*
agency, *noun*
agenda, *noun*
banking, *noun*
bankrupt, *adjective*
blue-collar, *adjective*
board, *noun*
boom, *noun*
branch, *noun*
budget, *noun*
budget, *verb*
capital, *noun*
chain, *noun*
charge card, *noun*
check, *noun*
checkbook, *noun*
client, *noun*
commerce, *noun*
commercial, *adjective*
company, *noun*
competitor, *noun*
consumer, *noun*
contract, *noun*
corporate, *adjective*
corporation, *noun*
crash, *noun*
deal, *noun*
dealer, *noun*
demand, *noun*
economic, *adjective*
economy, *noun*
empire, *noun*
employ, *verb*
employee, *noun*
employer, *noun*
employment, *noun*
enterprise, *noun*
entrepreneur, *noun*
export, *noun*
exporter, *noun*
fail, *verb*
fax, *noun*
fax, *verb*
firm, *noun*
goods, *plural noun*
manage, *verb*
management, *noun*
manager, *noun*
managerial, *adjective*
manufacture, *noun*
manufacturer, *noun*
memo, *noun*
monopolize, *verb*
monopoly, *noun*
negotiate, *verb*
negotiation, *noun*
partner, *noun*
patent, *verb*
pay, *verb*

pay, *noun*
payable, *adjective*
paycheck, *noun*
payment, *noun*
payroll, *noun*
personnel, *noun*
plant, *noun*
practice, *noun*
practice, *verb*
president, *noun*
price, *noun*
producer, *noun*
product, *noun*
production, *noun*
productive, *adjective*
profession, *noun*
professional, *adjective*
professional, *noun*
profit, *noun*
profitable, *adjective*
promote, *verb*
promotion, *noun*
proprietor, *noun*
purchase, *verb*
purchase, *noun*
quarter, *noun*
raise, *noun*
rate, *noun*
real estate, *adjective*
realtor, *noun*
rebate, *noun*
receipt, *noun*
recruit, *verb*
refund, *verb*
refund, *noun*
rent, *verb*
rent, *noun*
rental, *noun*
repay, *verb*
retail, *noun*
retailer, *noun*
run, *verb*
salary, *noun*
sale, *noun*
sales clerk, *noun*
sales representative, *noun*
salesperson, *noun*
sector, *noun*
self-employed, *adjective*
sell, *verb*
service, *noun*
share, *noun*
shareholder, *noun*
ship, *verb*
shipment, *noun*
shipping, *noun*
shop, *noun*
shopping mall, *noun*
shut down, *phrasal verb*
shutdown, *noun*
skilled, *adjective*
sponsor, *verb*
staff, *noun*
start, *verb*
steel, *noun*
stock, *noun*
stock, *verb*
stock exchange, *noun*
stockbroker, *noun*
store, *noun*
strike, *verb*
strike, *noun*
supermarket, *noun*
supplier, *noun*
syndicate, *noun*
tourism, *noun*
trade, *noun*
trade, *verb*
trademark, *noun*
trader, *noun*
trainee, *noun*
transaction, *noun*
underpaid, *adjective*
unprofitable, *adjective*
unskilled, *adjective*
value, *noun*
value, *verb*
venture, *noun*
vice president, *noun*
wage, *noun*
Wall Street, *noun*
warehouse, *noun*
well-paid, *adjective*
white-collar, *adjective*
wholesale, *adverb*
work, *verb*
work, *noun*
worker, *noun*
workforce, *noun*
working, *adjective*
worth, *noun*
worthless, *adjective*

4 Chemistry

absorb, *verb*
absorbent, *adjective*
acid, *noun*
alloy, *noun*
aluminum, *noun*
antiseptic, *adjective*
calcium, *noun*
carbon, *noun*
carbon dioxide, *noun*
carbon monoxide, *noun*
chemical, *noun*
chemical, *adjective*
chemist, *noun*
combine, *verb*
compound, *noun*
copper, *noun*
dilute, *verb*
dilution, *noun*
dissolve, *verb*
distillation, *noun*
distilled, *adjective*
element, *noun*
explosive, *adjective*
explosive, *noun*
fat, *noun*
filter, *noun*
filter, *verb*
fuel, *verb*
gas, *noun*
gas, *noun*
hydrogen, *noun*
inflammable, *adjective*
iron, *noun*
lead, *noun*
magnesium, *noun*
mercury, *noun*
metal, *noun*
metallic, *adjective*
methane, *noun*
molten, *adjective*
narcotic, *adjective*
neon, *noun*
nickel, *noun*
nitrogen, *noun*
oil, *noun*
organic, *adjective*
organically, *adverb*
oxygen, *noun*
periodic table, *noun*
petroleum, *noun*
plutonium, *noun*
potassium, *noun*
preservative, *noun*
purify, *verb*
radioactive, *adjective*
refine, *verb*
residue, *noun*
rust, *noun*
rust, *verb*
sodium, *noun*
soluble, *adjective*
solution, *noun*
solvent, *noun*
substance, *noun*
sulfur, *noun*
tin, *noun*
uranium, *noun*
zinc, *noun*

5 Computers

access, *noun*
access, *verb*
application, *noun*
attach, *verb*
attachment, *noun*
backup, *noun*
bug, *noun*
byte, *noun*
checker, *noun*
chip, *noun*
click, *noun*
computer, *noun*
connect, *verb*
crash, *verb*
cursor, *noun*
cyberspace, *noun*
database, *noun*
default, *verb*
delete, *verb*
deletion, *noun*
desktop computer, *noun*
digital, *adjective*
directory, *noun*
disc, *noun*
disk, *noun*
disk drive, *noun*
down, *adjective*
download, *verb*
drive, *noun*
DVD, *noun*
email, *noun*
email, *verb*
enter, *verb*
erase, *verb*
file, *noun*
floppy disk, *noun*
folder, *noun*
format, *noun*
forward, *adjective*
gigabyte, *noun*
graphics, *noun*
hard disk, *noun*
hardware, *noun*
icon, *noun*
install, *verb*
installation, *noun*
interactive, *adjective*
internet, *noun*
IT, *noun*
key, *noun*
keyboard, *noun*
kilobyte, *noun*
language, *noun*
laptop, *noun*
load, *verb*
mail, *noun*
mail, *verb*
mailbox, *noun*
mainframe, *noun*
megabyte, *noun*
memory, *noun*
menu, *noun*
message, *noun*
microchip, *noun*
modem, *noun*
monitor, *noun*
mouse, *noun*
mouse pad, *noun*
navigate, *verb*
net, *noun*
network, *noun*
notebook, *noun*
online, *adjective*
page, *noun*
paste, *verb*
PC, *noun*
personal computer, *noun*
pointer, *noun*
post, *noun*
program, *noun*
program, *verb*
programmer, *noun*
reboot, *verb*
run, *verb*
save, *verb*
scan, *verb*
scanner, *noun*
screen, *noun*
screen saver, *noun*
scroll, *verb*
search, *noun*
search engine, *noun*
server, *noun*
shut down, *phrasal verb*
site, *noun*
software, *noun*
spam, *noun*
store, *verb*
surf, *verb*
tab, *noun*
terminal, *noun*
tutorial, *noun*
upload, *verb*
virtual, *adjective*
virtual reality, *noun*
virus, *noun*
visit, *verb*
web, *noun*
webcam, *noun*
website, *noun*
window, *noun*
word processor, *noun*
World Wide Web, *noun*
WWW, *noun*

6 Drama

act, *noun*
act, *verb*
acting, *noun*
actor, *noun*
actress, *noun*
audience, *noun*
audition, *noun*
backstage, *adverb*
balcony, *noun*
ballet, *noun*
cast, *verb*
cast, *noun*
choreography, *noun*
comedy, *noun*
co-star, *verb*
costume, *noun*
dialogue, *noun*
director, *noun*
drama, *noun*
dramatic, *adjective*
dramatist, *noun*
farce, *noun*
monologue, *noun*
opera, *noun*
part, *noun*
perform, *verb*
performance, *noun*
performer, *noun*
play, *verb*
play, *noun*
playwright, *noun*
portray, *verb*
produce, *verb*
producer, *noun*
production, *noun*
recite, *verb*
rehearsal, *noun*
rehearse, *verb*
role, *noun*
scene, *noun*
scenery, *noun*
screen, *noun*
script, *noun*
series, *noun*
set, *noun*
show business, *noun*
sitcom, *noun*
soap opera, *noun*
stage, *noun*
star, *verb*
star, *noun*
subtitles, *noun*
theater, *noun*
tragedy, *noun*

7 General Science

analysis, *noun*
analyze, *verb*
apparatus, *noun*
C, *abbreviation*
cc, *abbreviation*
centimeter, *noun*
classification, *noun*
classify, *verb*
cm, *abbreviation*
data, *noun*
diagram, *noun*
discover, *verb*
discovery, *noun*
disprove, *verb*
effect, *noun*
evaluate, *verb*
evidence, *noun*
evolve, *verb*
experiment, *noun*
experiment, *verb*
fact, *noun*
factual, *adjective*
false, *adjective*
find, *verb*
fluctuate, *verb*
fluctuation, *noun*
foot, *noun*
formula, *noun*
funnel, *noun*
gallon, *noun*
hypothesis, *noun*
inch, *noun*
indicate, *verb*
indicator, *noun*
instrument, *noun*
invent, *verb*
invention, *noun*
inventor, *noun*
kg, *abbreviation*
kilogram, *noun*
kilometer, *noun*
km, *abbreviation*
laboratory, *noun*
liter, *noun*
measure, *verb*
meter, *noun*
method, *noun*
methodology, *noun*
metric system, *noun*
microscope, *noun*
microscopic, *adjective*
mile, *noun*
milligram, *noun*
milliliter, *noun*
millimeter, *noun*
ml, *abbreviation*
mm, *abbreviation*
ounce, *noun*
phenomenon, *noun*
pint, *noun*
pound, *noun*
property, *noun*
quart, *noun*
research, *noun*
research, *noun*
science, *noun*
scientific, *adjective*
scientist, *noun*
specimen, *noun*
study, *verb*
study, *noun*
technician, *noun*
technology, *noun*
test, *noun*
test, *verb*
test tube, *noun*
theoretical, *adjective*
theory, *noun*
ton, *noun*
volume, *noun*
weigh, *verb*
weight, *noun*
yard, *noun*

8 Geography and Earth Science

acid rain, *noun*
African, *adjective*
African, *noun*
African American, *noun*
African American, *adjective*
agricultural, *adjective*
agriculture, *noun*
air, *noun*
algae, *noun*
American, *adjective*
American, *noun*
Antarctic, *adjective*
Antarctic, *noun*
Arab, *adjective*
Arab, *noun*
Arctic, *noun*
arid, *adjective*
Asia, *noun*
Asian, *adjective*
Asian, *noun*
Atlantic, *noun*
atlas, *noun*
atmosphere, *noun*
autumn, *noun*
avalanche, *noun*
axis, *noun*
bank, *noun*
barley, *noun*
basin, *noun*
bay, *noun*
beach, *noun*
bean, *noun*
bed, *noun*
biodegradable, *adjective*
blizzard, *noun*
boulder, *noun*
boundary, *noun*
British, *adjective*
British, *noun*
Canadian, *noun*
canal, *noun*
canyon, *noun*
cape, *noun*
capital, *noun*
Caribbean, *adjective*
cattle, *plural noun*
cave, *noun*
channel, *noun*
chart, *noun*
Chinese, *adjective*
Chinese, *adjective*
city, *noun*
clay, *noun*
cliff, *noun*
climate, *noun*
climatic, *adjective*
cloud, *noun*
cloudy, *adjective*
coal, *noun*
coast, *noun*
coastal, *adjective*
coastline, *noun*
compass, *noun*
conservation, *noun*
conserve, *verb*
contaminate, *verb*
continent, *noun*
continental, *adjective*
contour, *noun*
core, *noun*
corn, *noun*
cotton, *noun*
country, *noun*
county, *noun*
crater, *noun*
crevice, *noun*
crop, *noun*
crude, *adjective*
crust, *noun*
cultivate, *verb*
cultivation, *noun*
D.C., *abbreviation*
dairy, *noun*
dam, *noun*
Danish, *adjective*
delta, *noun*
depth, *noun*
desert, *noun*
dew, *noun*
dike, *noun*
district, *noun*
ditch, *noun*
drought, *noun*
dune, *noun*
Dutch, *adjective*
earthquake, *noun*

east, *adjective*
east, *adverb*
east, *noun*
eastern, *adjective*
eastward, *adverb*, *adjective*
ecology, *noun*
elevation, *noun*
emissions, *plural noun*
English, *adjective*
environment, *noun*
environmental, *adjective*
environmentally, *adverb*
equator, *noun*
equatorial, *adjective*
equinox, *noun*
erode, *verb*
erosion, *noun*
erupt, *verb*
eruption, *noun*
Europe, *noun*
European, *adjective*
European, *noun*
export, *noun*
export, *verb*
fall, *noun*
fall, *verb*
Far East, *noun*
farm, *noun*
farming, *noun*
farmland, *noun*
fault, *noun*
fertilize, *verb*
fertilizer, *noun*
field, *noun*
find, *verb*
flood, *noun*
flood, *verb*
fog, *noun*
foggy, *adjective*
forest, *noun*
formation, *noun*
fresh, *adjective*
frost, *noun*
fumes, *plural noun*
gale, *noun*
geographical, *adjective*
geological, *adjective*
geologist, *noun*
geology, *noun*
German, *adjective*
glacier, *noun*
global, *adjective*
global warming, *noun*
globe, *noun*
gold, *adjective*
gold mine, *noun*
gorge, *noun*
grain, *noun*
granite, *noun*
Greek, *adjective*
Greek, *noun*
greenhouse, *noun*
gulf, *noun*
harvest, *noun*
harvest, *verb*
hemisphere, *noun*
highlands, *noun*
hill, *noun*
Hispanic, *adjective*
Hispanic, *noun*
humid, *adjective*
humidity, *noun*
hurricane, *noun*
iceberg, *noun*
icicle, *noun*
Indian, *adjective*
Indian, *noun*
industrial, *adjective*
industrialized, *adjective*
industry, *noun*
inhabit, *verb*
inhabitant, *noun*
inhabited, *adjective*
inner city, *noun*
Inuit, *noun*
Irish, *adjective*
Irish, *noun*
irrigate, *verb*
irrigation, *noun*
island, *noun*
isolated, *adjective*
Japanese, *adjective*
Japanese, *noun*
jungle, *noun*
Korean, *adjective*
Korean, *noun*
lagoon, *noun*
lake, *noun*
land, *noun*
landslide, *noun*
Latin American, *adjective*
Latin American, *noun*
latitude, *noun*
lava, *noun*
levee, *noun*
lightning, *noun*
line, *noun*
livestock, *noun*
local, *adjective*
local time, *noun*
longitude, *noun*
lowtide, *noun*
magnitude, *noun*
mainland, *adjective*
manure, *noun*
marble, *noun*
marsh, *noun*
marshland, *noun*
marshy, *adjective*
Mediterranean, *adjective*
meridian, *noun*
meterorological, *adjective*
meterorology, *noun*
metropolitan, *adjective*
Mexican, *noun*
Mexican, *adjective*
Middle East, *noun*
Midwest, *noun*
Midwesterner, *noun*
mill, *noun*
mine, *noun*
mineral, *noun*
mining, *noun*
mist, *noun*
misty, *adjective*
monsoon, *noun*
mount, *noun*
mountain, *noun*
mountainous, *adjective*
mountain range, *noun*
mouth, *noun*
national park, *noun*
nationality, *noun*
nationally, *adverb*
native, *adjective*
native, *noun*
Native American, *adjective*
neighbor, *noun*
neighboring, *adjective*
nomad, *noun*
nomadic, *adjective*
north, *adjective*
north, *adverb*
north, *noun*
North Pole, *noun*
northeast, *adverb*, *adjective*
northeast, *noun*
northeastern, *adjective*
northern, *adjective*
northerner, *noun*
northward, *adverb*, *adjective*
northwest, *noun*
northwest, *adverb*, *adjective*
northwestern, *adjective*
oasis, *noun*
ocean, *noun*
oceanic, *adjective*
offshore, *adjective*
oil rig, *noun*
ore, *noun*
origin, *noun*
outskirts, *noun*
ozone layer, *noun*
Pacific Ocean, *noun*
pasture, *noun*
peak, *noun*
pebble, *noun*
peninsula, *noun*
pest, *noun*
pesticide, *noun*
plain, *noun*
planet, *noun*
plant, *verb*
plantation, *noun*
plateau, *noun*
plow, *noun*
plow, *verb*
polar, *adjective*
pole, *noun*

Pole, *noun*
Polish, *adjective*
pollute, *verb*
pollution, *noun*
pond, *noun*
population, *noun*
populous, *adjective*
port, *noun*
Portuguese, *adjective*
poultry, *noun*
prairie, *noun*
precinct, *noun*
precipitation, *noun*
province, *noun*
quake, *noun*
quarry, *noun*
quartz, *noun*
quicksand, *noun*
rain, *noun*
rain, *verb*
rain forest, *noun*
rainbow, *noun*
rainfall, *noun*
rainy, *adjective*
ranch, *noun*
range, *noun*
ravine, *noun*
reef, *noun*
region, *noun*
reservoir, *noun*
residential, *adjective*
resort, *noun*
rice, *noun*
ridge, *noun*
river, *noun*
rock, *noun*
rocky, *adjective*
rugged, *adjective*
rural, *adjective*
Russian, *adjective*
Russian, *noun*
rye, *noun*
sand, *noun*
sandy, *adjective*
sea, *noun*
seashore, *noun*
season, *noun*
settlement, *noun*
shore, *noun*
shoreline, *noun*
shower, *verb*
silver, *adjective*
sky, *noun*
sleet, *noun*
smog, *noun*
snow, *noun*
snow, *verb*
snowdrift, *noun*
snowfall, *noun*
snowflake, *noun*
snowstorm, *noun*
snowy, *adjective*
soil, *noun*
south, *adjective*
south, *adverb*
south, *noun*
South Pole, *noun*
southeast, *adverb*, *adjective*
southeast, *noun*
southern, *adjective*
southerner, *noun*
southward, *adverb*, *adjective*
southwest, *adverb*, *adjective*
southwest, *noun*
sow, *verb*
Spanish, *adjective*
spring, *noun*
state, *noun*
States, *noun*
storm, *noun*
strait, *noun*
stream, *noun*
suburb, *adjective*
summer, *noun*
summit, *noun*
sun, *noun*
sunlight, *noun*
swamp, *noun*
Swiss, *adjective*
Swiss, *plural noun*
Taiwanese, *adjective*
Taiwanese, *noun*
temperate, *adjective*
terrain, *noun*
territory, *noun*
thaw, *noun*
Third World, *noun*
thunder, *noun*
thunderstorm, *noun*
tide, *noun*
timber, *noun*
time zone, *noun*
tornado, *noun*
town, *noun*
tractor, *noun*
transatlantic, *adjective*
transcontinental, *adjective*
transportation, *noun*
tropical, *adjective*
tropics, *noun*
tsunami, *noun*
typhoon, *noun*
uninhabited, *adjective*
union, *noun*
urban, *adjective*
valley, *noun*
vegetation, *noun*
village, *noun*
vineyard, *noun*
volcano, *noun*
waste, *noun*
wasteland, *noun*
water, *noun*
water, *verb*
waterfall, *noun*
waterlogged, *adjective*
waterway, *noun*
wave, *noun*
weather, *noun*
weather forecast, *noun*
weed, *noun*
well, *noun*
Welsh, *adjective*
west, *adjective*
west, *adverb*
west, *noun*
western, *adjective*
westward, *adverb*, *adjective*
wet, *adjective*
wetland, *noun*
wheat, *noun*
whirlpool, *noun*
whirlwind, *noun*
wilderness, *noun*
wind, *noun*
windchill factor, *noun*
windy, *adjective*
winter, *noun*
wipe something out, *phrasal verb*
woodland, *noun*
woods, *plural noun*
world, *noun*
yield, *noun*

9 History, Politics and Social Science

abolish, *verb*
act, *noun*
administration, *noun*
age, *noun*
air raid, *noun*
alliance, *noun*
ally, *noun*
ambassador, *noun*
amend, *verb*
amendment, *noun*
amnesty, *noun*
ancient, *adjective*
approval, *noun*
approve, *verb*
archaeological, *adjective*
archaeology, *noun*
armed forces, *plural noun*
army, *noun*
assassinate, *verb*
assassination, *noun*
ballot, *noun*
ban, *noun*
ban, *verb*
battle, *noun*
battleship, *noun*
bill, *noun*

Bill of rights, *noun*
bloodshed, *noun*
bomb, *noun*
bomb, *verb*
bomber, *noun*
borough, *noun*
boycott, *noun*
bureau, *noun*
bureaucracy, *noun*
cabinet, *noun*
campaign, *noun*
campaign, *verb*
cannon, *noun*
capital punishment, *noun*
capitalism, *noun*
capitalist, *adjective*
cast, *verb*
catastrophe, *noun*
catastrophic, *adjective*
Caucasian, *adjective*
cavalry, *noun*
ceasefire, *noun*
censor, *verb*
censorship, *noun*
census, *noun*
century, *noun*
chancellor, *noun*
Chicana, *noun*
Chicano, *noun*
chief, *noun*
chronological, *adjective*
citizen, *noun*
citizenship, *noun*
city hall, *noun*
civic, *adjective*
civil liberties, *plural noun*
civil rights, *plural noun*
civil war, *noun*
civilian, *adjective*
civilization, *noun*
civilized, *adjective*
class, *noun*
classical, *adjective*
clergy, *plural noun*
colonization, *noun*
colonize, *verb*
colony, *noun*
combat, *noun*
command, *noun*
command, *verb*
commander, *noun*
commemorate, *verb*
committee, *noun*
communism, *noun*
communist, *adjective*
community, *noun*
company, *noun*
conflict, *noun*
Congress, *noun*
congressman, *noun*
congresswoman, *noun*
conquer, *verb*
conquest, *noun*
conservative, *adjective*
conspiracy, *noun*
constitution, *noun*
constitutional, *adjective*
consul, *noun*
context, *noun*
council, *noun*
coup, *noun*
court, *noun*
courthouse, *noun*
court-martial, *verb*
courtroom, *noun*
crime, *noun*
criminal, *adjective*
criminal, *noun*
custom, *noun*
death penalty, *noun*
debate, *verb*
decade, *noun*
decorate, *verb*
defect, *verb*
defection, *noun*
defendant, *noun*
defense, *noun*
defensive, *adjective*
delegation, *noun*
democracy, *noun*
Democrat, *noun*
democratic, *adjective*
Democratic Party, *noun*
democratically, *adverb*
demonstration, *noun*
demonstrator, *noun*
department, *noun*
deport, *verb*
depression, *noun*
descend, *verb*
descendant, *noun*
descent, *noun*
deserter, *noun*
destroyer, *noun*
developed, *adjective*
developing, *adjective*
dictator, *noun*
dictatorship, *noun*
disarm, *verb*
disarmament, *noun*
discriminate, *verb*
discrimination, *noun*
discriminatory, *adjective*
dissident, *noun*
district attorney, *noun*
document, *noun*
domestic, *adjective*
draft, *noun*
draft, *verb*
education, *noun*
elect, *verb*
election, *noun*
eligible, *adjective*
emancipate, *verb*
emancipation, *noun*
embassy, *noun*
emblem, *noun*
emigrate, *verb*
emigration, *noun*
emperor, *noun*
empire, *noun*
express, *noun*
enact, *verb*
enemy, *noun*
enlist, *verb*
enlistment, *noun*
equal, *adjective*
equality, *noun*
era, *noun*
ethic, *noun*
ethical, *adjective*
ethnic, *adjective*
ethnicity, *noun*
evidence, *noun*
execute, *verb*
execution, *noun*
exile, *verb*
exile, *noun*
expedition, *noun*
extended family, *noun*
family, *noun*
famine, *noun*
federal, *adjective*
federation, *noun*
federally, *adverb*
felony, *noun*
feminism, *noun*
feminist, *adjective*
figure, *noun*
first lady, *noun*
first-generation, *adjective*
flag, *noun*
force, *noun*
forefathers, *plural noun*
fort, *noun*
fortress, *noun*
found, *verb*
foundation, *noun*
founder, *noun*
Fourth of July, *noun*
freedom, *noun*
frontier, *noun*
general, *noun*
generation, *noun*
ghetto, *noun*
GNP, *noun*
govern, *verb*
government, *noun*
governmental, *adjective*
governor, *noun*
governorship, *noun*
guilty, *adjective*
hierarchy, *noun*
historic, *adjective*
historical, *adjective*
history, *noun*
homeland, *noun*
House of Representatives, *noun*
human race, *noun*
human rights, *plural noun*
ideological, *adjective*
ideology, *noun*

illegal, *adjective*
illiteracy, *noun*
illiterate, *adjective*
immigrant, *noun*
immigrate, *verb*
immigration, *noun*
imperialism, *noun*
inaugural, *adjective*
inaugurate, *verb*
inauguration, *noun*
income tax, *noun*
independence, *noun*
Independence Day, *noun*
independent, *adjective*
indict, *verb*
indictment, *noun*
industrialization, *noun*
inequality, *noun*
infantry, *noun*
inflation, *noun*
infrastructure, *noun*
injustice, *noun*
innocent, *adjective*
institution, *noun*
insurance, *noun*
integrate, *verb*
integration, *noun*
international, *adjective*
interracial, *adjective*
invade, *verb*
invader, *noun*
invasion, *noun*
investment, *noun*
Ivy League, *adjective*
jail, *verb*
judge, *noun*
judgment, *adjective*
judicial, *noun*
jury, *noun*
justice, *noun*
justice of the peace, *noun*
juvenile, *noun*
juvenile delinquent, *noun*
king, *noun*
kingdom, *noun*
knight, *noun*
labor, *noun*
Labor Day, *noun*
labor union, *noun*
landslide, *noun*
law, *noun*
lawsuit, *noun*
lawyer, *noun*
leader, *noun*
leadership, *noun*
league, *noun*
left, *verb*
leftist, *adjective*
left-wing, *adjective*
legal, *adjective*
legality, *noun*
legalize, *verb*
legally, *adverb*
legislate, *verb*
legislation, *noun*
legislative, *adjective*
legislator, *noun*
legislature, *noun*
liberal, *noun*
liberty, *noun*
lieutenant, *noun*
lower class, *noun*
magistrate, *noun*
majesty, *noun*
major, *noun*
majority, *noun*
mandatory, *adjective*
march, *noun*
march, *verb*
marcher, *noun*
Marine Corps, *noun*
marriage, *noun*
martial, *adjective*
mayor, *noun*
medieval, *adjective*
memorial, *noun*
middle class, *noun*
migrant, *noun*
migrate, *verb*
migration, *noun*
militant, *noun*
military, *adjective*
military, *noun*
minor, *noun*
minority, *noun*
missile, *noun*
monarch, *noun*
monarchy, *noun*
monument, *noun*
movement, *noun*
nation, *noun*
national, *adjective*
national anthem, *noun*
nationalism, *noun*
nationalist, *noun*
naturalization, *noun*
naturalize, *verb*
naturalized, *adjective*
naval, *adjective*
navy, *noun*
neutral, *adjective*
nuclear family, *noun*
offender, *noun*
offense, *noun*
office, *noun*
official, *adjective*
official, *noun*
outbreak, *noun*
pacifist, *noun*
pact, *noun*
palace, *noun*
paramilitary, *adjective*
pardon, *verb*
pardon, *noun*
parliament, *noun*
parole, *verb*
party, *noun*
pass, *verb*
past, *noun*
past, *adjective*
patriot, *noun*
patriotic, *adjective*
patrol, *noun*
peace, *noun*
peaceful, *adjective*
peacekeeping, *noun*
peasant, *noun*
penalty, *noun*
penitentiary, *noun*
Pentagon, *noun*
people, *noun*
persecute, *verb*
petition, *noun*
pioneer, *noun*
police, *noun*
police force, *noun*
political, *adjective*
politically correct, *adjective*
politician, *noun*
politics, *noun*
power, *noun*
powerful, *adjective*
prehistoric, *adjective*
prejudice, *noun*
premier, *noun*
presidency, *noun*
president, *noun*
prime minister, *noun*
primitive, *adjective*
prince, *noun*
princess, *noun*
prison, *noun*
prisoner, *noun*
prisoner of war, *noun*
progress, *noun*
prohibit, *verb*
propaganda, *noun*
prosecute, *verb*
protest, *noun*
public, *adjective*
public, *noun*
queen, *noun*
race, *noun*
racial, *adjective*
racism, *noun*
racist, *adjective*
radical, *adjective*
raid, *noun*
rate, *noun*
reactionary, *adjective*
rebel, *verb*
rebel, *noun*
rebellion, *noun*
recession, *verb*
reelect, *noun*
referendum, *noun*
reform, *verb*
reform, *noun*
refugee, *noun*
regime, *noun*
regiment, *noun*
regulate, *verb*
regulation, *noun*
reign, *noun*
reign, *verb*
relic, *noun*
remains, *plural noun*
repeal, *noun*
representative, *noun*
reprieve, *noun*
republic, *noun*

Republican, *adjective*
Republican Party, *noun*
restrict, *verb*
restriction, *noun*
retreat, *verb*
retreat, *noun*
revolt, *verb*
revolt, *noun*
revolution, *noun*
revolutionize, *verb*
right, *noun*
right-wing, *adjective*
riot, *noun*
riot, *verb*
ritual, *noun*
Roman, *adjective*
Roman, *noun*
royal, *adjective*
royalty, *noun*
rule, *noun*
rule, *verb*
ruler, *noun*
run, *verb*
secretary, *noun*
security, *noun*
segregated, *adjective*
senate, *noun*
senator, *noun*
sentence, *noun*
sentence, *verb*
settler, *noun*
sexism, *noun*
sheriff, *noun*
shield, *noun*
shift, *noun*
shooting, *noun*
siege, *noun*
site, *noun*
slave, *noun*
slavery, *noun*
slum, *noun*
social, *adjective*
social science, *noun*
Social Security, *noun*
social work, *noun*
socialism, *noun*
society, *noun*
socioeconomic, *adjective*
sociology, *noun*
soldier, *noun*
spear, *noun*
standard of living, *noun*
statesman, *noun*
status, *noun*
status symbol, *noun*
statutory, *adjective*
strategic, *adjective*
strike, *noun*
struggle, *noun*
sue, *verb*
superpower, *noun*
Supreme Court, *noun*
surrender, *noun*
suspect, *noun*
sword, *noun*
tariff, *noun*
tax, *noun*
tax, *verb*
taxation, *noun*
term, *noun*
terrorism, *noun*
terrorist, *noun*
topical, *adjective*
totalitarian, *adjective*
town hall, *noun*
tradition, *noun*
traditional, *adjective*
traitor, *noun*
treason, *noun*
treaty, *noun*
trend, *noun*
trial, *noun*
tribal, *adjective*
tribe, *noun*
troop, *noun*
truce, *noun*
try, *verb*
tyranny, *noun*
unconstitutional, *adjective*
underdeveloped, *adjective*
underprivileged, *adjective*
underworld, *noun*
unemployed, *adjective*
unemployment, *noun*
unify, *verb*
union, *noun*
United Nations, *noun*
unity, *noun*
unlawful, *adjective*
unrest, *noun*
upper class, *noun*
uprising, *noun*
utopia, *noun*
veto, *noun*
vice president, *noun*
violate, *verb*
violence, *noun*
vote, *noun*
vote, *verb*
war, *noun*
warfare, *noun*
warrior, *noun*
way of life, *noun*
weapon, *noun*
welfare, *noun*
White House, *noun*
working class, *noun*
Yankee, *noun*

10 Languages and Literature

abridged, *adjective*
accent, *noun*
active, *adjective*
adjective, *noun*
adverb, *noun*
alphabet, *noun*
antonym, *noun*
apostrophe, *noun*
appendix, *noun*
Arabic, *noun*
article, *noun*
asterisk, *noun*
autobiography, *noun*
bilingual, *adjective*
biography, *noun*
book, *noun*
capital, *noun*
chapter, *noun*
character, *noun*
Chinese, *noun*
classic, *noun*
clause, *noun*
cliché, *noun*
coherent, *adjective*
colon, *noun*
comma, *noun*
comparative, *noun*
compound, *noun*
concise, *adjective*
conclusion, *noun*
conjugate, *verb*
conjunction, *noun*
consonant, *noun*
context, *noun*
contraction, *noun*
contrast, *verb*
Danish, *noun*
dash, *noun*
debate, *noun*
define, *verb*
definite article, *noun*
definition, *noun*
describe, *verb*
description, *noun*
dialect, *noun*
dictation, *noun*
dictionary, *noun*
double negative, *noun*
edition, *noun*
EFL, *noun*
ELT, *noun*
emphasis, *noun*
English, *noun*
entry, *noun*
epic, *adjective*
epic, *noun*
ESL, *noun*
essay, *noun*
exclamation point, *noun*
express, *verb*
expression, *noun*
fable, *noun*
fairy tale, *noun*
fantasy, *noun*

fiction, *noun*
figurative, *adjective*
figuratively, *adverb*
fluency, noun
fluent, *adjective*
fluently, *adverb*
formal, *adjective*
future, *noun*
future tense, *noun*
gender, *noun*
German, *noun*
glossary, *noun*
grammar, *noun*
grammatical, *adjective*
Greek, *adjective*
hardback, *noun*
hero, *noun*
heroine, *noun*
hyphen, *noun*
idiom, *noun*
idiomatic, *adjective*
imperative, *noun*
indefinite article, *noun*
indefinite pronoun, *noun*
index, *noun*
indirect object, *noun*
infinitive, *noun*
informal, *adjective*
initial, *noun*
interjection, *noun*
interpret, *verb*
interpreter, *noun*
intransitive, *noun*
introduction, *noun*
IPA, *noun*
ironic, *adjective*
irony, *noun*
irregular, *adjective*
Japanese, *noun*
language, *noun*
Latin, *noun*
legend, *noun*
letter, *noun*
line, *noun*
linguistics, *noun*
literal, *adjective*
literary, *adjective*
lowercase, *noun*
main clause, *noun*
masculine, *adjective*
mean, *verb*
meaning, *noun*
metaphor, *noun*
metaphorical, *adjective*
modal auxiliary, *noun*
modifier, *noun*
modify, *verb*
monolingual, *adjective*
narrate, *verb*
narration, *noun*
narrative, *noun*
narrator, *noun*
negative, *adjective*
negative, *noun*
nonfiction, *adjective*
noun, *noun*
novel, *noun*
object, *noun*
oral, *adjective*
paperback, *noun*
paragraph, *noun*
paraphrase, *noun*
parentheses, *plural noun*
parody, *verb*
part of speech, *noun*
participle, *noun*
passive, *adjective*
past participle, *noun*
past tense, *noun*
pen name, *noun*
period, *noun*
personal pronoun, *noun*
phonetic, *adjective*
phonetics, *noun*
phrasal verb, *noun*
phrase, *noun*
plagiarism, *noun*
plot, *noun*
plural, *adjective*
poem, *noun*
poet, *noun*
poetic, *adjective*
poetry, *noun*
point, *noun*
Polish, *noun*
Portuguese, *noun*
possessive, *noun*
predicate, *noun*
preface, *noun*
prefix, *noun*
preposition, *noun*
present participle, *noun*
present perfect, *noun*
present tense, *noun*
pronoun, *noun*
pronounce, *verb*
pronunciation, *noun*
proper noun, *noun*
prose, *noun*
proverb, *noun*
publication, *noun*
punctuation, *noun*
punctuation mark, *noun*
put, *verb*
qualifier, *noun*
question mark, *noun*
quotation, *noun*
quotation marks, *plural noun*
quote, *verb*
quote, *noun*
refer to, *phrasal verb*
reference, *noun*
reference book, *noun*
regular, *adjective*
relative clause, *noun*
relative pronoun, *noun*
reported speech, *noun*
rewrite, *noun*
rhyme, *verb*
rhyme, *noun*
romance, *noun*
Russian, *noun*
saga, *noun*
sarcasm, *noun*
satire, *noun*
saying, *noun*
second person, *noun*
semantics, *noun*
semicolon, *noun*
sense, *noun*
sentence, *noun*
sequel, *noun*
short story, *noun*
simile, *noun*
singular, *noun*
slang, *noun*
slogan, *noun*
sonnet, *noun*
Spanish, *noun*
speech, *noun*
spell, *verb*
spelling, *noun*
statement, *noun*
stereotype, *verb*
story, *noun*
stress, *noun*
stress, *verb*
subject, *noun*
subject matter, *noun*
suffix, *noun*
sum up, *phrasal verb*
summarize, *verb*
summary, *noun*
superlative, *noun*
syllable, *noun*
synonym, *noun*
syntax, *noun*
tale, *noun*
tense, *noun*
term, *noun*
term, *verb*
text, *noun*
theme, *noun*
thesaurus, *noun*
third person, *noun*
thriller, *noun*
tongue twister, *noun*
topic, *noun*
topic sentence, *noun*
transitive, *adjective*
translate, *verb*
translation, *noun*
trilogy, *noun*
underline, *verb*
understatement, *noun*
uppercase, *adjective*
usage, *noun*
verb, *noun*
verbal, *adjective*
verse, *noun*
villain, *noun*
vocabulary, *noun*
vowel, *noun*
Welsh, *noun*
word, *noun*
write, *verb*
writer, *noun*
writing, *noun*

11 Math

add, *verb*
add up, *phrasal verb*
addition, *noun*
algebra, *noun*
angle, *noun*
arc, *noun*
area, *noun*
arithmetic, *noun*
average, *adjective*
average, *noun*
axis, *noun*
billion, *number*
bisect, *verb*
by, *preposition*
calculate, *verb*
calculation, *noun*
calculator, *noun*
chart, *noun*
circle, *noun*
circular, *adjective*
circumference, *noun*
cone, *noun*
converse, *noun*
crescent, *noun*
cube, *noun*
cube, *verb*
cubic, *adjective*
cylinder, *noun*
cylindrical, *adjective*
decimal, *noun*
decimal, *adjective*
decimal point, *noun*
deduct, *verb*
degree, *noun*
denominator, *noun*
diagonal, *adjective*
diagonally, *adverb*
diameter, *noun*
digit, *noun*
dimension, *noun*
distance, *noun*
divide, *verb*
division, *noun*
equal, *adjective*
equal, *verb*
equal sign, *noun*
equation, *noun*
equilateral triangle, *noun*
even, *adjective*
factor, *noun*
figure, *noun*
foot, *noun*
fraction, *noun*
geometric, *adjective*
geometry, *noun*
gram, *noun*
graph, *noun*
height, *noun*
high, *adjective*
horizontal, *adjective*
integer, *noun*
length, *noun*
long, *adjective*
make, *verb*
mathematical, *adjective*
mathematics, *noun*
measure, *verb*
measurement, *noun*
meter, *noun*
million, *number*
minus, *preposition*
minus, *noun*
minus sign, *noun*
multiplication, *noun*
multiply, *verb*
number, *noun*
numerator, *adjective*
oblong, *adjective*
odd, *adjective*
oval, *adjective*
parallel, *noun*
percent, *noun*
percentage, *noun*
perimeter, *preposition*
plus, *noun*
plus sign, *noun*
point, *noun*
power number, *noun*
probability, *noun*
problem, *noun*
product, *noun*
proportion, *noun*
pyramid, *noun*
quantify, *verb*
radius, *noun*
ratio, *noun*
rectangle, *noun*
rectangular, *adjective*
right angle, *noun*
round, *adjective*
scale, *noun*
semicircle, *noun*
side, *noun*
size, *noun*
sphere, *noun*
square, *adjective*
square, *noun*
square, *verb*
square root, *noun*
statistic, *noun*
straight, *adjective*
subtotal, *noun*
subtract, *verb*
subtraction, *noun*
sum, *noun*
table, *noun*
take, *verb*
tall, *adjective*
thick, *adjective*
thickness, *noun*
three-dimensional, *adjective*
times, *preposition*
total, *adjective*
total, *noun*
trapezoid, *noun*
triangle, *noun*
trigonometry, *noun*
unit, *noun*
wide, *adjective*
width, *noun*

12 Music

accompany, *verb*
acoustic, *adjective*
band, *noun*
banjo, *noun*
bass, *noun*
bassoon, *noun*
beat, *noun*
blues, *noun*
brass, *noun*
cello, *noun*
choir, *noun*
chord, *noun*
chorus, *noun*
clarinet, *noun*
classical, *adjective*
classical music, *noun*
compose, *verb*
composer, *noun*
concert, *noun*
conduct, *verb*
conductor, *noun*
country music, *noun*
cymbal, *noun*
double bass, *noun*
duet, *noun*
fiddle, *noun*
flat, *adjective*
flat, *adverb*
flute, *noun*
group, *noun*
harmonica, *noun*
harmony, *noun*
harp, *noun*
headphones, *plural noun*
instrument, *noun*
instrumental, *adjective*
jazz, *noun*
key, *noun*
keyboard, *noun*
lyrics, *plural noun*
march, *noun*
major, *adjective*
melodic, *adjective*
melody, *noun*
minor, *adjective*
note, *noun*
oboe, *noun*
orchestra, *noun*
organ, *noun*
percussion, *noun*
pianist, *noun*
piano, *noun*
pitch, *noun*
play, *verb*

pop, *noun*
quartet, *noun*
R & B, *noun*
rap, *noun*
record, *noun*
record, *verb*
reggae, *noun*
rhythm, *noun*
rhythm and blues, *noun*
rock, *noun*
rock 'n' roll, *noun*
salsa, *noun*
saxophone, *noun*
scale, *noun*
sharp, *adjective*
sing, *verb*
singer, *noun*
single, *noun*
solo, *noun*
sonata, *noun*
song, *noun*
soprano, *noun*
soundtrack, *noun*
string, *noun*
symphony, *noun*
tambourine, *noun*
tempo, *noun*
tenor, *noun*
tone-deaf, *adjective*
tour, *noun*
trio, *noun*
trombone, *noun*
trumpet, *noun*
tuba, *noun*
tune, *noun*
tune, *verb*
video, *noun*
viola, *noun*
violin, *noun*
vocalist, *noun*
vocals, *plural noun*
wind instrument, *noun*
woodwinds, *plural noun*
xylophone, *noun*

13 Physics

AC, *noun*
acoustic, *adjective*
amp, *noun*
astronomy, *noun*
atom, *noun*
atomic, *adjective*
atomic energy, *noun*
battery, *noun*
beam, *noun*
beam, *verb*
boil, *verb*
boiling point, *noun*
bubble, *noun*
bubble, *verb*
bulb, *noun*
cable, *noun*
capacity, *noun*
Celsius, *noun*
Centigrade, *noun*
charge, *noun*
charge, *verb*
circuit, *noun*
comet, *noun*
communication, *noun*
condensation, *noun*
condense, *verb*
constellation, *noun*
consume, *verb*
consumption, *noun*
contract, *verb*
current, *noun*
cylinder, *noun*
DC, *noun*
degree, *noun*
density, *noun*
distort, *verb*
distortion, *noun*
echo, *noun*
echo, *verb*
eclipse, *noun*
elastic, *adjective*
electric, *adjective*
electrical, *adjective*
electricity, *noun*
electron, *noun*
electronic, *adjective*
electronics, *noun*
energy, *noun*
engine, *noun*
evaporate, *verb*
expand, *verb*
expansion, *noun*
Fahrenheit, *noun*
flexible, *adjective*
float, *verb*
fluid, *adjective*
force, *noun*
form, *noun*
freeze, *verb*
freezing, *noun*
frequency, *noun*
friction, *noun*
full moon, *noun*
fundamental, *adjective*
fuse, *noun*
fusion, *noun*
galactic, *adjective*
galaxy, *noun*
gaseous, *adjective*
generator, *noun*
gravity, *noun*
harness, *verb*
heat, *noun*
heat, *verb*
hydroelectric, *adjective*
image, *noun*
inaudible, *adjective*
infinite, *adjective*
infinity, *noun*
insulate, *verb*
kilowatt, *noun*
laser, *noun*
lens, *noun*
lever, *noun*
light, *noun*
light year, *noun*
line, *noun*
liquid, *adjective*
lunar, *adjective*
magnet, *noun*
magnetic, *adjective*
magnetism, *noun*
magnetize, *verb*
magnification, *noun*
magnify, *verb*
magnifying glass, *noun*
mass, *noun*
matter, *noun*
melt, *verb*
meteor, *noun*
meteorite, *noun*
Milky Way, *noun*
momentum, *noun*
moon, *noun*
motion, *noun*
movement, *noun*
nuclear, *adjective*
nuclear energy, *noun*
nuclear weapon, *noun*
nucleus, *noun*
ohm, *noun*
optical, *adjective*
orbit, *noun*
orbit, *verb*
outer space, *noun*
outlet, *noun*
planet, *noun*
power, *noun*
pressure, *verb*
radiation, *noun*
radio, *noun*
ray, *noun*
reflect, *verb*
reflection, *noun*
solar, *adjective*
solar system, *noun*
solid, *noun*
space, *noun*
spectrum, *noun*
speed, *noun*
star, *noun*
static, *noun*
stress, *noun*
sun, *noun*
supersonic, *adjective*
temperature, *noun*
terminal, *noun*
thermal, *adjective*
thermometer, *noun*
ultraviolet, *adjective*
vacuum, *noun*
vapour, *noun*
velocity, *noun*
vibration, *noun*
volt, *noun*
watt, *noun*
wire, *noun*
X-ray, *noun*

14 Sports

athlete, *noun*
athletic, *adjective*
backstroke, *noun*
ball, *noun*
ballpark, *noun*
base, *noun*
baseball, *noun*
basketball, *noun*
bat, *noun*
bat, *verb*
batter, *noun*
beat, *verb*
body building, *noun*
breaststroke, *noun*
canoe, *noun*
canoeing, *noun*
captain, *noun*
catch, *noun*
center, *noun*
center field, *noun*
champion, *noun*
championship, *noun*
cheerleader, *noun*
compete, *verb*
competition, *noun*
court, *noun*
dash, *noun*
defeat, *verb*
defeat, *noun*
defense, *noun*
diamond, *noun*
dribble, *verb*
dunk, *verb*
exercise, *noun*
field, *noun*
football, *noun*
foul, *verb*
foul, *noun*
game, *noun*
goal, *noun*
goalie, *noun*
goalkeeper, *noun*
golf, *noun*
gym, *noun*
gymnasium, *noun*
gymnastics, *noun*
half time, *noun*
high jump, *noun*
hockey, *noun*
infield, *noun*
inning, *noun*
intercept, *verb*
javelin, *noun*
jog, *noun*
judo, *noun*
karate, *noun*
kayak, *noun*
kick, *verb*
kick, *noun*
kickoff, *noun*
kung fu, *noun*
lead, *noun*
lead, *verb*
leader, *noun*
long jump, *noun*
lose, *verb*
loser, *noun*
loss, *noun*
marathon, *noun*
martial arts, *plural noun*
match, *noun*
miss, *noun*
mound, *noun*
offense, *noun*
opponent, *noun*
outfield, *noun*
overtime, *noun*
pass, *verb*
pass, *noun*
penalize, *verb*
penalty, *noun*
period, *noun*
pin, *noun*
ping-pong, *noun*
pitch, *verb*
pitch, *noun*
pitcher, *noun*
place, *noun*
play, *verb*
play, *noun*
point, *noun*
pole vault, *noun*
qualifier, *noun*
quarter, *noun*
quarterback, *noun*
race, *noun*
race, *verb*
racehorse, *noun*
racetrack, *noun*
racket, *noun*
racketball, *noun*
relay, *noun*
round, *noun*
run, *noun*
runner, *noun*
running, *noun*
score, *noun*
score, *verb*
semifinal, *noun*
series, *noun*
set, *noun*
shoot, *verb*
shot, *noun*
skiing, *noun*
skydiving, *noun*
soccer, *noun*
softball, *noun*
spectator, *noun*
sport, *noun*
sprint, *noun*
stadium, *noun*
surf, *verb*
tackle, *verb*
tackle, *noun*
team, *noun*
teammate, *noun*
tennis, *noun*
tie, *verb*
tie, *noun*
time out, *noun*
touchdown, *noun*
tournament, *noun*
track, *noun*
train, *verb*
trampoline, *noun*
triathlon, *noun*
trophy, *noun*
umpire, *noun*
versus, *preposition*
volleyball, *noun*
warm-up, *adjective*
water skiing, *noun*
weightlifting, *noun*
windsurfing, *noun*
work out, *phrasal verb*
work out, *phrasal verb*
world record, *noun*
World Series, *noun*
wrestle, *verb*
wrestler, *noun*
wrestling, *noun*
yoga, *noun*

WEIGHTS AND MEASURES

U.S. Customary System

Units of Length

1 inch		= 2.54 cm
12 inches	= 1 foot	= 0.3048m
3 feet	= 1 yard	= 0.9144m
1,760 yards (5,280 feet)	= 1 mile	= 1.609km
2,025 yards (6,076 feet)	= 1 nautical mile	= 1.852km

Units of Weight

1 ounce		= 28.35g
16 ounces	= 1 pound	= 0.4536kg
2,000 pounds	= 1 ton	= 907.18kg
2,240 pounds	= 1 long ton	= 1,016.0kg

Units of Volume (Liquid)

1 fluid ounce		= 29.574ml
8 fluid ounces	= 1 cup	= 0.2366l
16 fluid ounces	= 1 pint	= 0.4732l
2 pints	= 1 quart	= 0.9463l
4 quarts	= 1 gallon	= 3.7853l

Units of Volume (Dry Measure)

1 peck		= 8,809.5cm^3
4 pecks	= 1 bushel	= 35,239cm^3

Units of Area

1 square inch		= 645.16mm^2
144 square inches	= 1 square foot	= 0.0929m^2
9 square feet	= 1 square yard	= 0.8361m^2
4840 square yards	= 1 acre	= 4047m^2
640 acres	= 1 square mile	= 259ha

Temperature

degrees Fahrenheit = (°C × 9/5) + 32
degrees Celsius = (°F − 32) × 5/9

Metric System

Units of Length

1 millimeter		= 0.03937 inch
10mm	= 1 centimeter	= 0.3937 inch
100cm	= 1 meter	= 39.37 inches
1,000m	= 1 kilometer	= 0.6214 mile

Units of Weight

1 milligram		= 0.000035 ounce
1,000mg	= 1 gram	= 0.035 ounce
1,000g	= 1 kilogram	= 2.205 pounds
1,000kg	= 1 metric ton	= 2,205 pounds

Units of Volume

1 milliliter		= 0.03 fluid ounce
1,000ml	= 1 liter	= 1.06 quarts

Units of Area

1 square centimeter		= 0.1550 square inch
10,000cm^2	= 1 square meter	= 1.196 square yards
10,000m^2	= 1 hectare	= 2.471 acres

GEOGRAPHICAL NAMES

Name	Adjective
Afghanistan	Afghan *or* Afghanistani
Africa	African
Albania	Albanian
Algeria	Algerian
America (=the U.S.)	American
North America	North American
South America	South American
Andorra	Andorran
Angola	Angolan
Antarctic	*adj:* Antarctic
Antigua and Barbuda	Antiguan *or* Barbudan
Arctic	*adj:* Arctic
Argentina	*adj:* Argentinian *person:* Argentinian *or* Argentine
Armenia	Armenian
Asia	Asian
Atlantic	*adj:* Atlantic
Australia	Australian
Austria	Austrian
Azerbaijan	Azerbaijani
Bahamas, the	Bahamian
Bahrain	Bahraini
Baltic	*adj:* Baltic
Bangladesh	Bangladeshi
Barbados	Barbadian
Belarus (Belorussia)	Belorussian
Belgium	Belgian
Belize	Belizean
Benin	Beninese
Bermuda	Bermudan
Bhutan	Bhutanese
Bolivia	Bolivian
Bosnia and Herzegovina	Bosnian Herzegovinian
Botswana	*adj:* Botswanan *person:* Motswana *people:* the Batswana
Brazil	Brazilian
Brunei	Bruneian
Bulgaria	Bulgarian
Burkina Faso	Burkina *or* Burkinabe
Burma (*former name of* Myanmar)	Burmese
Burundi	Burundian
Cambodia	Cambodian
Cameroon	Cameroonian
Canada	Canadian
Cape Verde	Cape Verdean
Caribbean	*adj:* Caribbean
Cayman Islands	*adj:* Cayman Island *person:* Cayman Islander
Central African Republic	Central African
Chad	Chadian
Chile	Chilean
China	Chinese
Colombia	Colombian
Comoro Islands, the	Comoran
Congo, the Democratic Republic of	Congolese
Congo, Republic of	Congolese
Costa Rica	Costa Rican
Croatia	Croatian
Cuba	Cuban
Cyprus	Cypriot
Czech Republic, the	Czech
Denmark	*adj:* Danish *person:* Dane
Djibouti	Djiboutian
Dominica	Dominican
Dominican Republic, the	Dominican
East Timor	Timorese
Ecuador	Ecuadorian
Egypt	Egyptian
El Salvador	Salvadorian
England	*adj:* English *person:* Englishman, Englishwoman *people:* the English
Equatorial Guinea	Equatorial Guinean
Eritrea	Eritrean
Estonia	Estonian
Ethiopia	Ethiopian
Europe	European
Fiji	Fijian
Finland	*adj:* Finnish *person:* Finn
France	*adj:* French *person:* Frenchman, Frenchwoman *people:* the French
Gabon	Gabonese
Gambia, the	Gambian
Georgia	Georgian
Germany	German
Ghana	Ghanaian
Gibraltar	Gibraltarian
Great Britain	*adj:* British *person:* Briton *people:* the British
Greece	Greek
Greenland	*adj:* Greenlandic *person:* Greenlander
Grenada	Grenadian
Guatemala	Guatemalan
Guiana *also* French Guiana	Guianese
Guinea	Guinean
Guinea-Bissau	Guinea-Bissauan

Name	Adjective
Guyana *also* British Guyan	Guyanese *or* Guyanan
Haiti	Haitian
Holland (*another name for* The Netherlands)	*adj:* Dutch *person:* Dutchman, Dutchwoman *people:* the Dutch
Honduras	Honduran
Hong Kong	Hong Kong
Hungary	Hungarian
Iceland	*adj:* Icelandic *person:* Icelander
India	Indian
Indonesia	Indonesian
Iran	Iranian
Iraq	Iraqi
Ireland, Republic of, the	*adj:* Irish *person:* Irishman, Irishwoman *people:* the Irish
Israel	Israeli
Italy	Italian
Ivory Coast (*former name of* Cote d'Ivoire)	Ivorian
Jamaica	Jamaican
Japan	Japanese
Jordan	Jordanian
Kazakhstan	Kazakh
Kenya	Kenyan
Kirabati	Kirabati
Korea, North	North Korean
Korea, South	South Korean
Kuwait	Kuwaiti
Kyrgyzstan	Kyrgyz
Laos	Laotian *or* Lao
Latvia	Latvian
Lebanon	Lebanese
Lesotho	*adj:* Sotho *person:* Mosotho *people:* the Basotho
Liberia	Liberian
Libya	Libyan
Liechtenstein	*adj:* Liechtenstein *person:* Liechtensteiner
Lithuania	Lithuanian
Luxemburg	*adj:* Luxemburg *person:* Luxemburger
Macedonia	Macedonian
Madagascar	Malagasy
Malawi	Malawian
Malaysia	Malaysian
Maldives, the	Maldivian
Mali	Malian
Malta	Maltese

Name	Adjective
Marshall Islands, the	*adj:* Marshallese *person:* Marshall Islander
Mauritania	Mauritanian
Mauritius	Mauritian
Mediterranean	*adj:* Mediterranean
Melanesia	Melanesian
Mexico	Mexican
Micronesia	Micronesian
Moldova	Moldovan
Monaco	Monegasque *or* Monacan
Mongolia	Mongolian *or* Mongol
Montserrat	Montserratian
Morocco	Moroccan
Mozambique	Mozambican
Myanmar	Burmese
Namibia	Namibian
Nauru	Nauruan
Nepal	*adj:* Nepalese *person:* Nepali *or* Nepalese
Netherlands, The	*adj:* Dutch *person:* Dutchman, Dutchwoman *pl. people:* the Dutch
New Zealand	*adj:* New Zealand *person:* New Zealander
Nicaragua	Nicaraguan
Niger	Nigerien
Nigeria	Nigerian
Norway	Norwegian
Oman	Omani
Pacific	*adj:* Pacific
Pakistan	Pakistani
Palestine	Palestinian
Panama	Panamanian
Papua New Guinea	Papuan *or* Papua New Guinean
Paraguay	Paraguayan
Persia (*former name of* Iran)	Persian
Peru	Peruvian
Philippines	*adj:* Philippine *person:* Filipino
Poland	*adj:* Polish *person:* Pole
Polynesia	Polynesian
Portugal	Portuguese
Puerto Rico	Puerto Rican
Qatar	Qatari
Romania	Romanian
Russia (Russian Federation, the)	Russian
Rwanda	Rwandan
Saint Kitts & Nevis	Kittitian, Nevisian
Saint Lucia	Saint Lucian

Name	Adjective
Saint Vincent and the Grenadines	Vincentian
Samoa	Samoan
San Marino	Sammarinese San Marinese
São Tomé & Principe	São Tomean
Saudi Arabia	*adj:* Saudi Arabian
person: Saudi	
Scotland	*adj:* Scottish
person: Scot	Senegal
Senegalese	
Seychelles, the	Seychellois
Sierra Leone	Sierra Leonean
Singapore	Singaporean
Slovakia	Slovakian
Slovenia	Slovenian *or* Slovene
Solomon Islands, the	*adj:* Soloman Island *person:* Solomon Islander
Somalia	Somali
South Africa	South African
Spain	*adj:* Spanish *person:* Spaniard *people:* the Spanish
Sri Lanka	Sri Lankan
Sudan	Sudanese
Surinam, Suriname	*adj:* Surinamese *person:* Surinamer
Swaziland	Swazi
Sweden	*adj:* Swedish *person:* Swede
Switzerland	Swiss
Syria	Syrian
Tahiti	Tahitian
Taiwan	Taiwanese

Name	Adjective
Tajikistan	Tajik
Tanzania	Tanzanian
Thailand	Thai
Tibet	Tibetan
Togo	Togolese
Tonga	Tongan
Trinidad and Tobago	Trinidadian *or* Tobagonian
Tunisia	Tunisian
Turkey	*adj:* Turkish *person:* Turk
Turkmenistan	Turkmen
Tuvalu	Tuvaluan
Uganda	Ugandan
Ukraine	Ukrainian
United Arab Emirates	Emirati
United Kingdom of Great Britain and Northern Ireland, the	*adj:* British *person:* Briton *people:* the British
United States, the	*adj:* American
Uruguay	Uruguayan
Uzbekistan	Uzbek
Vanuatu	Vanuatuan
Venezuela	Venezuelan
Vietnam	Vietnamese
Wales	*adj:* Welsh *person:* Welshman, Welshwoman *people:* the Welsh
Yemen	Yemeni
Yugoslavia	Yugoslavian *or* Yugolslav
Zambia	Zambian
Zimbabwe	Zimbabwean

WORKBOOK ANSWER KEY

LESSON 1

Exercise 1

Group 1: bag *2*, desk *4*, apple *1*, electric *5*, clock *3*
Group 2: hospital *2*, kiss *5*, jump *4*, ID *3*, guest *1*
Group 3: cell phone *2*, circle *4*, Christmas *3*, carry *1*, company *5*
Group 4: king *4*, king-size *5*, key *2*, keep *1*, kind *3*
Group 5: Labor Day *4*, labor *3*, label *2*, labor union *5*, lab *1*

Exercise 2

1 c **2** b **3** c **4** a **5** c **6** b

Exercise 3

1 excellent **2** fix **3** necessary
4 judge **5** huge

LESSON 2

Exercise 1

1 addition **2** baseball **3** beautiful
4 communicate **5** difference
6 fascinating **7** interesting
8 restaurant

Exercise 2

1 happiest **2** putting **3** knives
4 bigger **5** worried **6** frantically

Exercise 3

1 photo **2** excitement **3** always
4 honesty **5** schedule **6** character
7 psychological **8** guard

LESSON 3

Exercise 1

1 c (*celebrate* → verb)
2 a (*president* → noun)
3 d (*between* → preposition)
4 b (*them* → pronoun)
5 h (*and* → conjunction)
6 f (*sometimes* → adverb)
7 g (*should* → modal verb)
8 e (*terrible* → adjective)

Exercise 2

1 beside: preposition,
2 ✔ box: noun, verb
3 ✔ color: noun, verb
4 ✔ direct: adjective, verb
5 habit: noun **6** friction: noun
7 explode: verb
8 ✔ guarantee: verb, noun

Exercise 3

1 ladle: noun, verb
2 maroon: noun, adjective
3 tow: verb, noun
4 giggle: verb, noun
5 crimson: noun, adjective
6 litter: noun, verb
7 shame: noun, verb
8 camouflage: noun, verb

Exercise 4

1 noun **2** verb **3** verb **4** noun
5 noun **6** verb **7** adjective
8 adverb **9** verb **10** noun

Exercise 5

Answers will vary.

LESSON 4

Exercise 1

1 generate **2** method **3** legislate
4 similar **5** hypothesis **6** context

Exercise 2

1 consume: 2 **2** area: 3 **3** source: 2
4 lose: 10 **5** lookout: 2 **6** major: 4
7 environment: 2 **8** long: 11

Exercise 3

1 major^2: 2 **2** generation: 1
3 structure^1: 1 **4** core^1: 2 **5** target: 3
6 contact^1: 3

Exercise 4

1 b **2** b **3** b **4** a **5** b **6** b

LESSON 5

Exercise 1

1 children **2** deer **3** feet **4** fish
5 mice **6** people **7** teeth **8** women

Exercise 2

1 (a) bit, (b) bitten **2** (a) did, (b) done
3 (a) ate, (b) eaten **4** (a) fell, (b) fallen
5 (a) chose, (b) chosen
6 (a) wrote, (b) written

Exercise 3

1 grouchy **2** lug **3** end **4** stuff
5 find **6** polite **7** can't stand
8 tired
Responses to questions will vary.

Exercise 4

1 construct **2** sector **3** occurred
4 indicates **5** estimate **6** conduct
7 respond **8** created

LESSON 6

Exercise 1

1 get **2** move **3** come **4** give
5 go **6** make

Exercise 2

1 go on **2** come down with
3 move in **4** get up **5** give up
6 make up

Exercise 3

1 up **2** out **3** down **4** on **5** up
6 down **7** out **8** in
Responses to questions will vary.

Exercise 4

1 b, for good **2** e, a close call
3 d, a slap on the wrist
4 a, be a piece of cake
5 f, off the top of my head
6 c, give it a shot

Exercise 5

1 know something by heart, True
2 lose your head, True
3 Cut it out, False
4 make the most of something, False
5 keep your word, True
6 play games with someone, False

LESSON 7

Exercise 1

1 white **2** medicine **3** leather
4 greedy **5** simple **6** tyranny

Exercise 2

1 hike **2** homesickness
3 miraculous **4** modestly
5 snobbery (noun), snobbish (adjective), snobby (adjective)
6 transformation

Exercise 3

(n = noun, v = verb, adj = adjective, adv = adverb)
1 correction, correct, correct
2 glory, glorification (n), glorify (v), glorious (adj), gloriously (adv)
3 magic, magician (n), magic (adj), magical (adj)
4 sadness (n), sadden (v), sad, sadly (adv)
5 temptation (n), tempt, tempting (adj)

Exercise 4

1 b creative c creativity,
2 b machinery c mechanical
3 b satisfactory c satisfied
4 b generally c generalize

LESSON 8

Exercise 1

1 babysitter **2** neat **3** seat belt
4 tip **5** pants **6** goodbye
7 science fiction **8** refrigerator

Exercise 2

1 help **2** safety **3** tape **4** think
5 behavior **6** scary **7** rarely
8 following

Exercise 3

1 different meanings
2 the same meaning
3 different meanings
4 the same meaning
5 different meanings
6 the same meaning
7 different meanings
8 different meanings

Exercise 4

1 a glad b delighted c cheerful
2 a decide b pick c opt
3 a change b cash c currency

Exercise 5

List 1: 1 taxi **2** really **3** *X* **4** *X*
5 used **6** fatally **7** *X* **8** briefly
List 2: 1 excellent **2** honest **3** *X*
4 *X* **5** barely, hardly **6** reason
7 *X* **8** *X*

LESSON 9

Exercise 1

1 banana **2** bad **3** book **4** cry
5 came **6** thing **7** ship **8** church

Exercise 2

1 feet, field, seat **2** meant, red, said
3 bought, saw, taught **4** do, food, true

Exercise 3

1 ceiling, circle, cycle, psychology
2 category, chorus, contrast, kilo
3 gnaw, kneel, know, pneumonia

Exercise 4

1 the same **2** different **3** the same
4 different **5** the same **6** the same
7 the same **8** the same

Exercise 5

1 available **2** luxury **3** economy
4 levee **5** income **6** invest
7 enemy **8** engagement

LESSON 10

Exercise 1

1 page vi **2** page A1 **3** page 783
4 page 802 **5** page 786 **6** page A32
7 page 803

Exercise 2

1 general science **2** math **3** history
4 music **5** English

Exercise 3

1 paid, page 784 **2** Dutch, page 803
3 Peru, page 803 **4** a pint, page 802
5 a square mile, page 802
6 an ounce, page 802
7 Mississippi, page A32
8 Possible answers: Dallas, Odessa, Austin, San Antonio, Houston, page A32